D0883180

THE ARCTIC
THE COMPLETE STORY

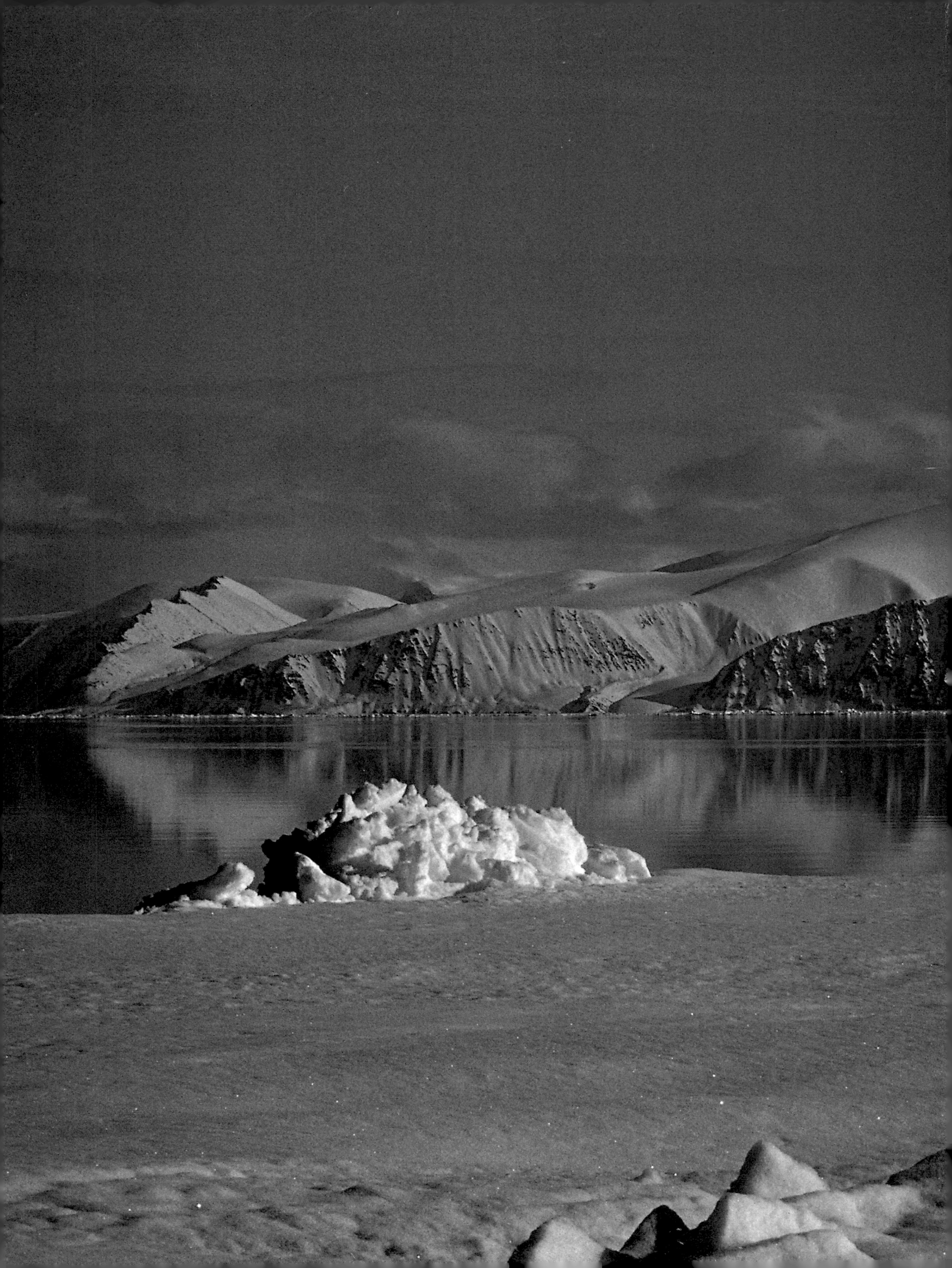

THE ARCTIC

THE COMPLETE STORY

RICHARD SALE

Photographs by Per Michelsen and Richard Sale

FRANCES LINCOLN LIMITED
PUBLISHERS

Frances Lincoln Limited
4 Torriano Mews
Torriano Avenue
London NW5 2RZ
www.franceslincoln.com

British Library Cataloguing in Publication Data. A catalogue record for this book is available from the British Library.

Richard Sale would like to thank Susan Barr, Pétur Björnsson, Jens Bocher, Tom Critchley, Jan van Engel, Maria Gavrilo, Timo Halonen, Chris Hamm, Anatoli Kochnev, Yevgeni Lobkov, Martha Madsen, Per Michelsen, Alexei Mironov, Tony Oliver, Eugene Potapov, Dave Reid, Nathan Sale, Bob Shade and James Wyatt for their companionship on trips, and help and assistance associated with the production of this book. Particular thanks are due to my wife Susan without whose support and encouragement the project would not have flourished.

Per Michelsen would like to thank Sigurdur Adalsteinsson, Harriet Backer, Mike Dunn, Geir Helland, Brian Kahler, Mamarut Kristiansen, Ray LeCotey, Aka Lynge, Arnfinn Nielsen, Lassi Rautiainen, Bengt Rodin, Richard Sale, Arild Thorsen, Kjell Tysdal and Boyd Warner for their help and companionship. He also thanks Stavanger Foto for assistance with equipment. Finally he thanks his wife May Brit and son Mats for their patience when he has been away, and their interest in his experiences when he returns.

Captions for images in the preliminary and section opening pages

Page 1	Northern Sweden on the outskirts of the Padjelanta National Park
Page 2-3	Northern Baffin Island from the sea ice of Baffin Bay
Page 4-5	Bylot Island
Page 6-7	Midnight, Lundquistfjella, Isfjorden, Spitsbergen
Page 8-9	Magdalenefjorden, Spitsbergen
Page12-13	Seyðisfjordur and Drangajökull, Iceland
Page 92-93	Mattsutsiak Eipe in his kayak at Thule, north-west Greenland
Page 246/7	Migrating Caribou, Barren Lands, NWT, Canada
Page 306/7	Migrating Snow Geese, Barren Lands, Nunavut, Canada
Page 434/5	Musk Oxen, Nunavut, Canada
Page 514/5	Ilulissat, west Greenland
Page 576/7	Bowhead Whale rib, Hornsund, Spitsbergen

First published by Frances Lincoln Limited 2008

ISBN 13: 978-0-7112-2707-1

9 8 7 6 5 4 3 2 1

Designed by Carreg Limited, Ross-on-Wye, Herefordshire.

Printed in Singapore.

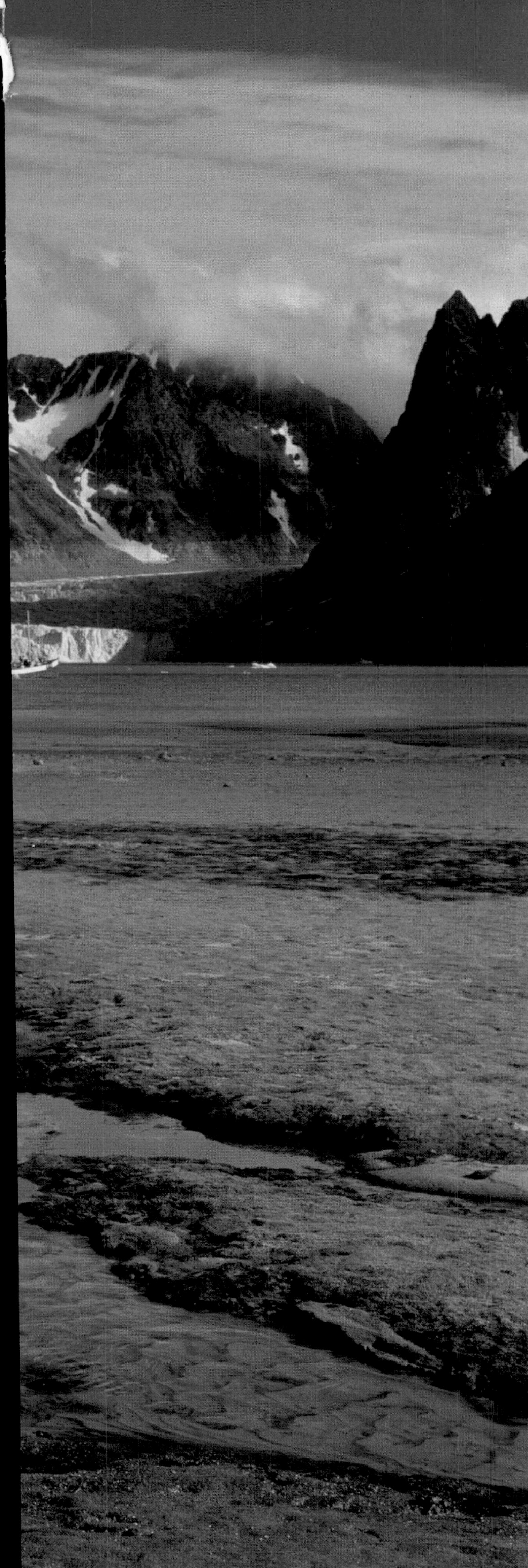

Introduction

In 1829 John Ross sailed to the Arctic. He had been before, commanding one of the first attempts by the British Royal Navy to find a North-West Passage. For Ross the expedition had not been a success. Vilified for his apparent lack of gumption, he had been ignored as a succession of further expeditions had looked for, and failed to find, a passage. In 1829 Ross was given command of a private expedition and asked to search again for the elusive route. He overwintered in the ice, something he had avoided on his first trip. It must have been a traumatic experience as, writing in the spring of 1830, he noted that it was 'for philosophers to interest themselves in speculating on a horde so small, and so secluded, occupying so apparently hopeless a country, so barren, so wild, and so repulsive; and yet enjoying the most perfect vigour, the most well-fed health, and all else that here constitutes, not merely wealth, but the opulence of luxury; since they were as amply furnished with provisions, as with every other thing that could be necessary to their wants'.

In that one sentence Ross encapsulated the lure of the Arctic for travellers from temperate regions to the south. Here was a wilderness populated by a people and animals that not only survived its harshness but seemed to thrive. This fascinated scientists and laymen. The country was, as Ross contended, wild, but its wildness was also its beauty. Travellers discovered a land that could not only be harsh and unforgiving, but a land of crystal, of silent cold, at times filled by the ghostly pale, trembling light of the aurora. Where the summer light was of breathtaking purity but illuminated monochromatic scenery, white geese and swans on a black tundra, white ice on a dark sea. A land where the Sun, when it appeared after the Arctic night, could be cold and red and dishevelled, not the Sun they knew. A land that seemed empty, with the people and animals being thinly spread so the loneliness could be awesome.

Early travellers brought back tales of amazing creatures and of the endurance required of visitors, the Arctic becoming a land of inspiration and imagination. When Mary Shelley wrote her tale of Dr Frankenstein and the creature he created, she ended with the creature heading towards the North Pole.

The Arctic still inspires. Adventurers test themselves against it. Its wildlife still amazes – when film and television show Earth's natural wonders it is always the polar regions that draw the biggest audiences.

But today the Arctic is in retreat. Humanity's relentless exploitation of the Earth's resources in the pursuit of progress has, it seems, altered the climate and threatens the ice and ice-living organisms. It is a cliché that the loss of a species diminishes us, but it is true nonetheless. Even to people who have never seen a Polar Bear its loss will be immeasurable as the bear is iconic, both defining and reflecting the Arctic.

This book celebrates the Arctic, exploring the nature and scenery, the history and the natural history that has so inspired generations. It ends with an assessment of the Arctic's future: it is bleak, but while there is a chance to save this wonderful place we should strive to do so.

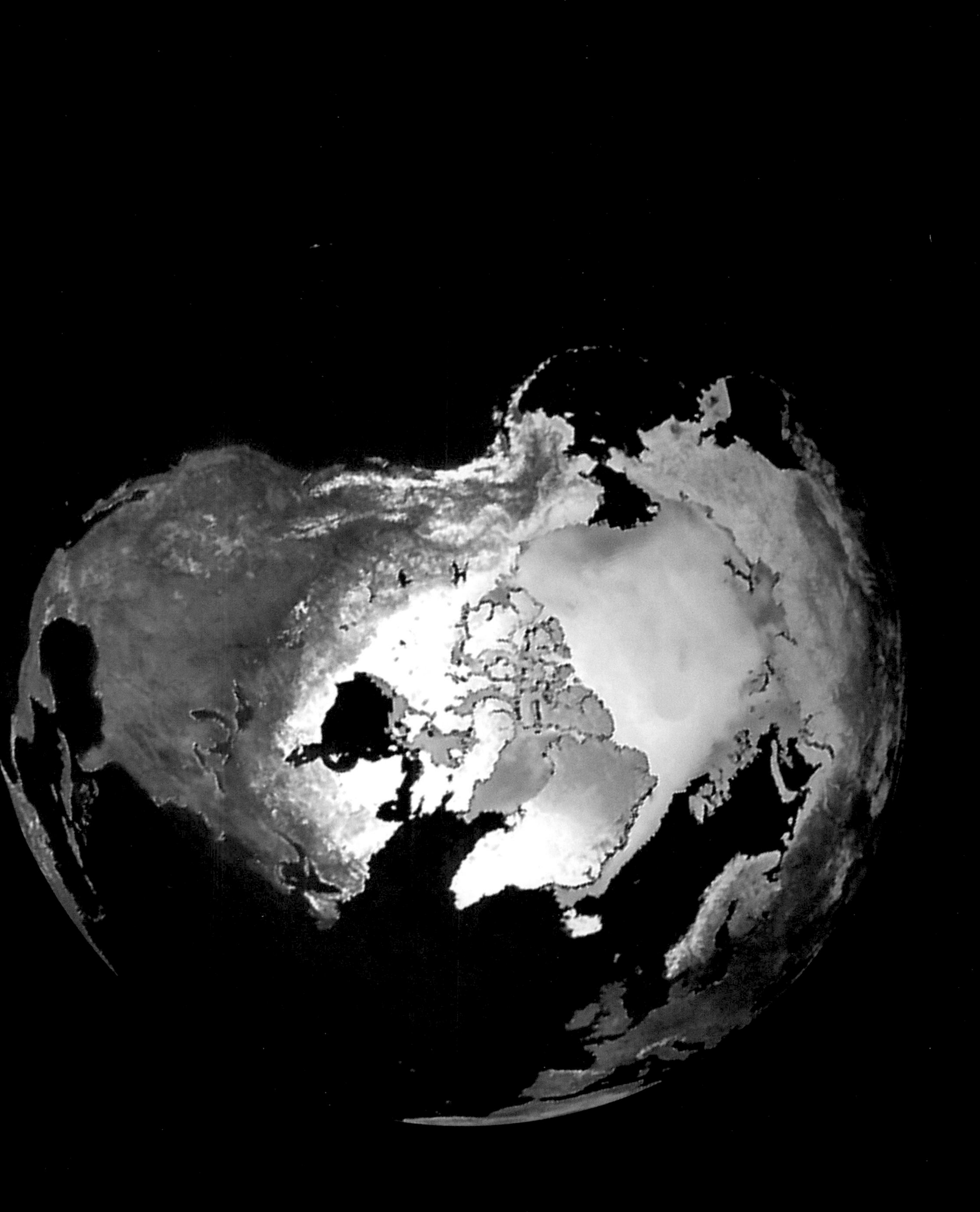

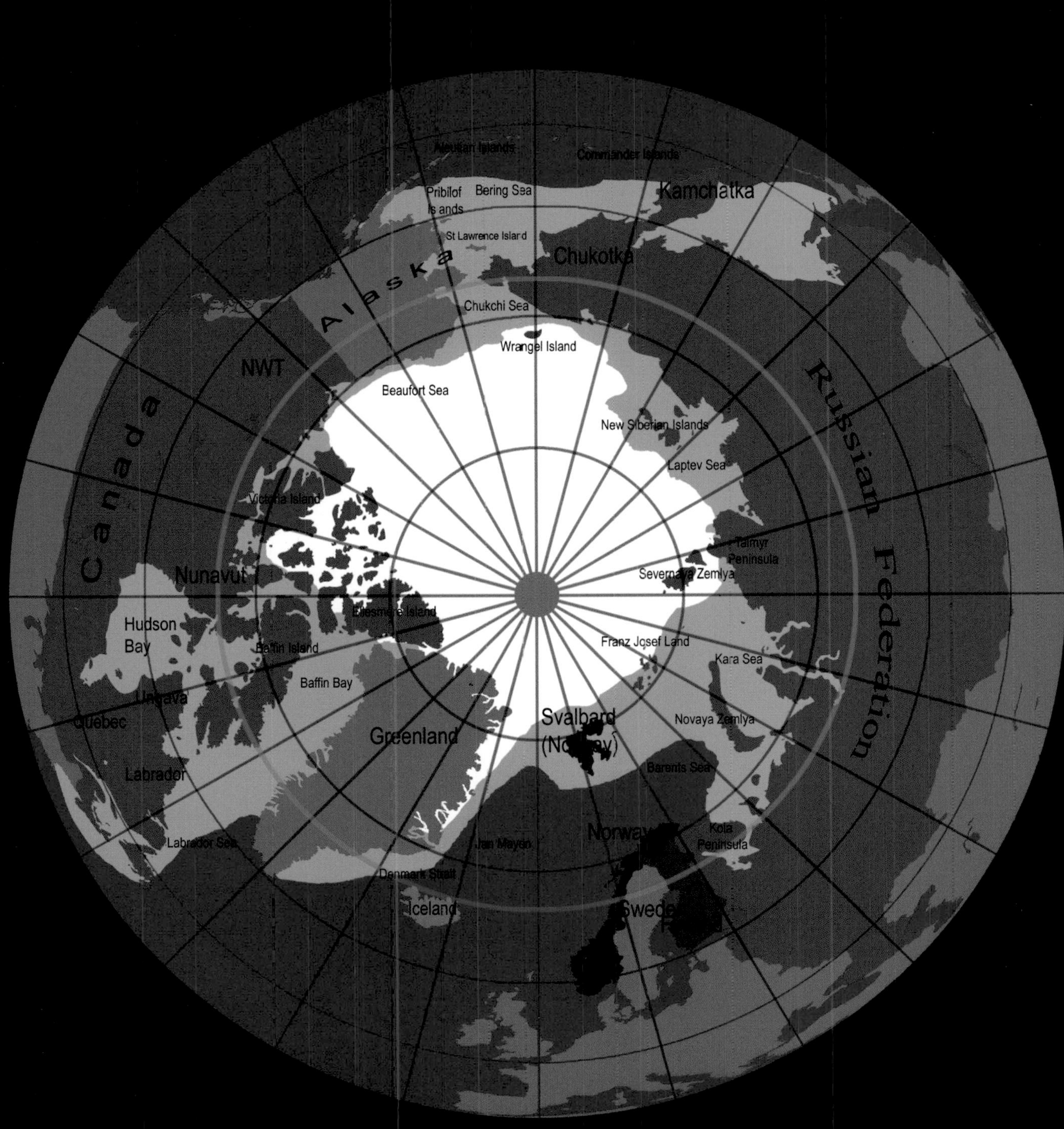

Aleutian Islands
Commander Islands
Pribilof Islands
Bering Sea
Kamchatka
St Lawrence Island
Chukotka
Alaska
Chukchi Sea
Wrangel Island
NWT
Canada
Beaufort Sea
Russian Federation
New Siberian Islands
Laptev Sea
Victoria Island
Taimyr Peninsula
Nunavut
Severnaya Zemlya
Hudson Bay
Ellesmere Island
Franz Josef Land
Baffin Island
Kara Sea
Baffin Bay
Ungava
Quebec
Svalbard
Novaya Zemlya
Greenland
Labrador
Barents Sea
Norway
Kola Peninsula
Labrador Sea
Jan Mayen
Denmark Strait
Iceland

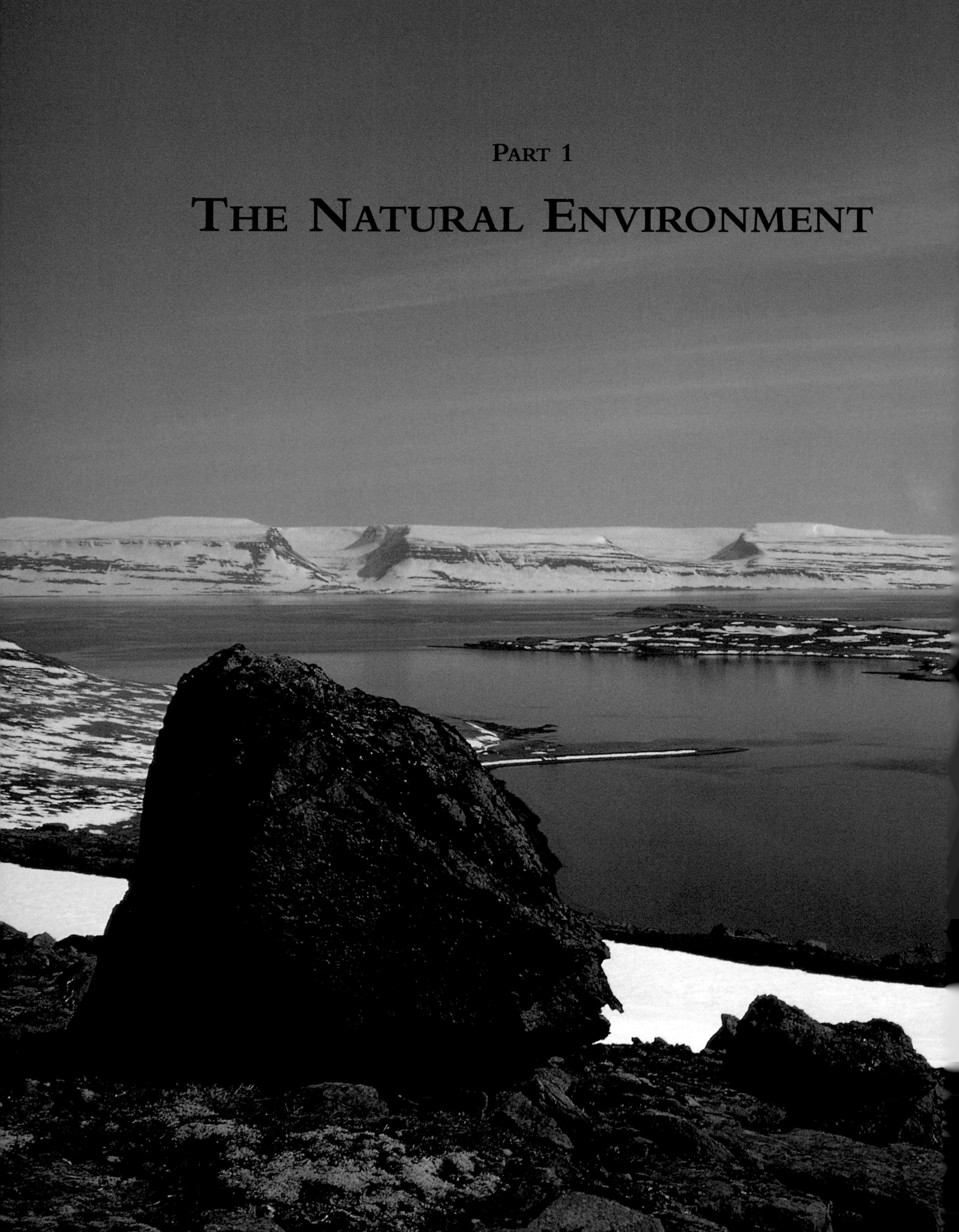

Part 1

The Natural Environment

1. Defining the Arctic

At first glance a definition seems straightforward – the Arctic is the area surrounding the North Pole, an area of ice and snow where polar bears are hunted by native peoples who live in igloos. While this is true (though the last suggestion is an exaggeration in this era of snow scooters and Inuit settlements), the statement does not help us to define 'The Arctic'. The geographic North Pole is a good definition of the Arctic's northern limit, but it is no help in defining a southern border. Before we can begin any discussion of the geology and geography, ecology and wildlife of the Arctic, we need to define exactly which part of the Earth we are describing.

People have no doubt studied the heavens from the first appearance of an enquiring mind. Those first observers would have noted that some stars were always visible throughout the night, but that others rose and set at different times throughout the year. The Chaldeans, living in what is now southern Iraq, were the first to set this knowledge down in writing more than 5,000 years ago. The Greeks were the first to systematise the knowledge, naming individual star patterns and noting how they moved (though zodiac figures are found on tablets from Mesopotamia dating back to at least 3,000 years ago).

The Greeks also realised that if it was assumed that the stars of the night sky were set on the inner face of a sphere, the celestial sphere, then lines could be drawn upon it. If the Earth was then projected on to it, a celestial Equator, equivalent to the Earth's Equator, could be drawn. The Greeks also knew that at noon on any day of the year the Sun would be directly overhead at a given latitude on Earth. This latitude varied over the year, but always lay within 24° of the Equator. Drawing circles around the Earth at these latitudes and projecting them onto the celestial sphere the Greeks found the lines went through the constellations of Cancer, in the north, and Capricorn, in the south. On the Earth these circles are the Tropics of Cancer and Capricorn. The Greeks realised the Earth was spherical, not flat or cylindrical, and would have known that 24° was the inclination of the Earth's axis to the plane of the ecliptic (the plane which defines the Earth's orbit around the Sun). Although they never travelled to latitude 66° the Greeks knew that those who travelled north found that the midsummer day was longer than it was in Greece. They were also good enough mathematicians to realise that at this latitude 66°, i.e. at (90–24)°, the Sun would be visible all day at midsummer, and absent all day at midwinter. They also knew that if the Pole could be reached then the day would be six months long in summer. When they projected the 66° circle on to the celestial sphere they saw that it grazed the particular constellation they called *Arktikos*, the Great Bear. They therefore called it the Bear's Circle – the Arctic Circle. Astronomers still use the names of stars and constellations set down by Ptolemy in the 2nd century AD, and so have retained the Greek name for the Great Bear, though it has been converted to its Latin form – Ursa Major. To casual observers it is known as the Plough, the stellar pattern that allows Polaris, the Pole Star (and therefore north) to be located. Earth and the other planets of the Solar System orbit the Sun on, or close to, a plane known as the plane of the ecliptic. As well as orbiting along this plane, the planets also rotate, the Earth's rotation being about an axis through the North and South Poles.

Although it might be expected that the axis about which the planets rotate would be normal (i.e. at right angles) to the plane of the ecliptic, this is not the case. Though for most planets this is approximately the case (and for Mercury almost exactly correct), for Venus the angle is 177° and for Uranus 98°. For the Earth the angle, known as the equatorial inclination, between the axis of rotation and the plane of the ecliptic is 23.44°. If equatorial inclination was zero then for all points at the same latitude, both north and south of the Equator, the lengths of night and day would be the same throughout the year. But the angle means that night and day are not equal and

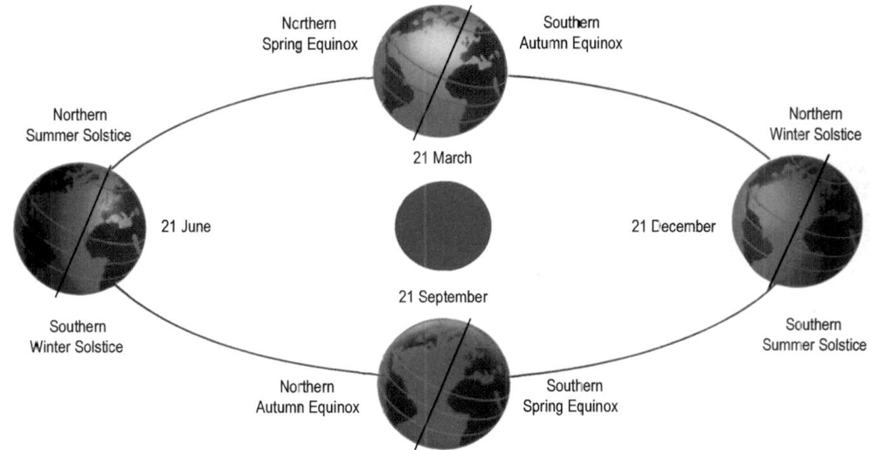

Figure 1.1
The Earth's orbit around the sun.

vary through the year for all points on the Earth, except at the Equator (see Figure 1.1). At the summer solstice (a solstice is either of twice annual times when the Sun is furthest from the Earth, these corresponding to the longest and shortest days) the Sun is visible throughout the day at a latitude of 66°34'N, and at all points north. This is the Arctic Circle.

Because of equatorial inclination the Sun is visible at all times for six months each year at the North Pole. For the other six months the Sun does not rise above the horizon. In Antarctica and the South Pole the reverse is true, the long northern winter coinciding with the austral (southern) summer.

If we stood at the North Pole during the northern summer we would see the Sun circling the sky. On any given day the elevation of the Sun is (more or less) constant, but the elevation changes each day. The elevation reaches a maximum (of 23°26') at Midsummer's Day, then falls until the autumnal equinox when the Sun skims the horizon. On that day the Sun appears at the South Pole, heralding the beginning of the austral summer. For an observer at the South Pole the Sun now rises each day, reaching a maximum elevation (again of 23°26') at the southern summer solstice, which corresponds to the northern winter solstice. This is illustrated in Figure 1.2. Figure 1.3 shows the variation of the hours of daylight with time of the year for places north of 60°.

The neat idea that our North Pole observer sees the Sun continuously for six months and then not at all for the next six

Opposite page
Midnight, 21 June. Looking west from the sea ice of Baffin Bay. To the left is Baffin Island, to the right Bylot Island.

Author's Note

For reasons of clarity I have capitalised Earth, Sun and species names throughout the book.

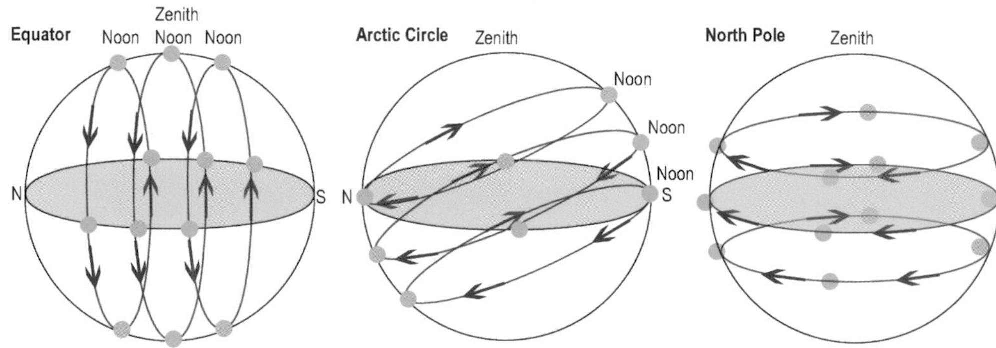

Figure 1.2
The Sun's path at solstice and equinox. For the Equator the three paths are, from the left, June solstice, Equinox and December solstice; for the Arctic Circle and North Pole the paths are, top to bottom, June solstice, Equinox and December solstice.

months is debunked by the phenomenon of atmospheric refraction (the deflection of light by the atmosphere), which causes the Sun's image to appear above its true position by about 2½ times its diameter. The Midnight Sun – the romantic name given to the phenomenon of the continuously visible Sun – is therefore visible at sea level for about 150km south of the Arctic Circle. The phenomenon also means that the Arctic summer lasts longer than the Arctic winter, by an amount that increases with distance north: at the North Pole the summer is about 16 days longer than the winter. Refraction can also cause the Sun to rise after it has set for the Arctic winter, or to rise early for the Arctic summer. One of the most extreme examples of the latter occurred during the 1596–97 overwintering of the Dutch expedition of Willem Barents on Novaya Zemlya when the Sun appeared almost two weeks before it was actually due to rise. Such images are usually distorted or broken.

As a definition of the Arctic, the Arctic Circle would seem ideal. But though it has its attractions, chiefly the delineation of that part of the Earth which experiences the cold, dark northern winter, the Circle has very limited climatic significance and, therefore, limited significance for either people or Arctic wildlife. In the western Arctic the influx of cold air and cold water chills North America, while to the east the North Atlantic Drift moves vast quantities of warm water to northwest Europe. This warm water, and the warm, damp air above it, has a huge influence on the climate of the region, particularly on the British Isles and Norway. North of the Arctic Circle in Norway there are large towns, and both industry and agriculture are possible. The effect of the Drift is less pronounced in Sweden and Finland, though both benefit to an extent, and it is eventually lost altogether in western Russia. The effect is most clearly seen in Svalbard, the Arctic archipelago that lies to the north of Norway. The capital of the archipelago, Longyearbyen on Spitsbergen, the largest island, lies at 78°N. Longyearbyen is a town with hotels and shops, and it is served by an airport with scheduled flights from Norway that arrive and depart throughout the year. At the same latitude in North America the land is essentially uninhabitable (for people), as, indeed, are places on the same latitude in those parts of Eurasia that do not receive any warming effect from the North Atlantic Drift.

Noon, 21 December. The Arctic Circle lies a few kilometres north of Rovaniemi in northern Finland. At the Circle a collection of buildings is devoted to Christmas, visitors arriving from across the world to post cards and letters bearing a Santa Claus postmark.

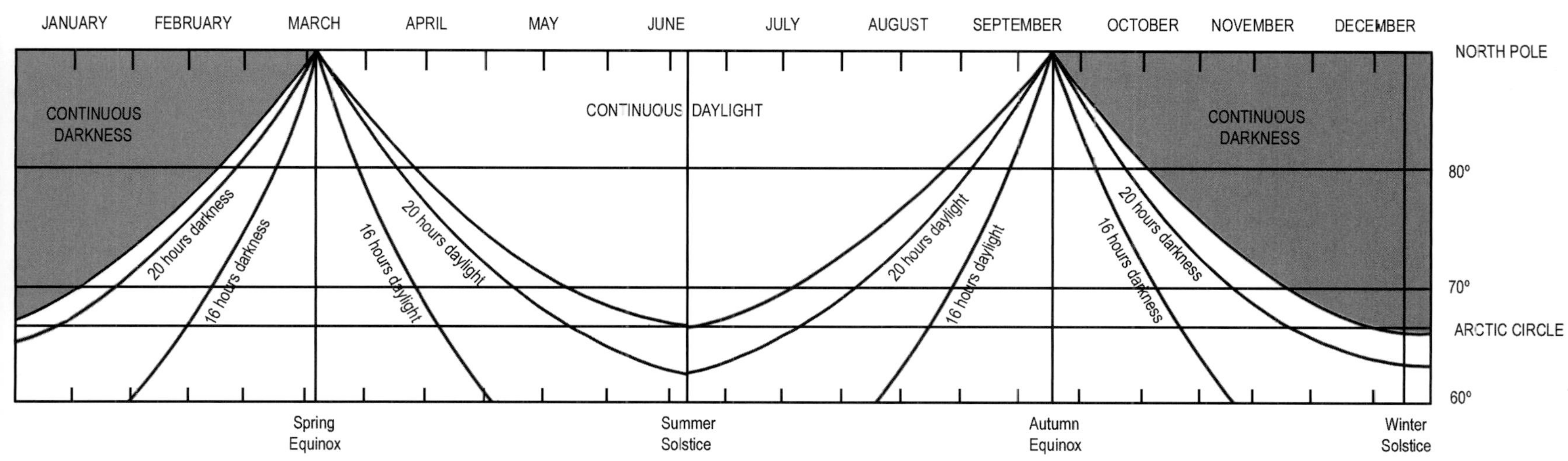

Figure 1.3
Variation of daylight hours with latitude throughout the year.

After discarding the Arctic Circle in our search for a definition of the Arctic, it is instructive to ask how the Antarctic is defined. The Antarctic Convergence, where cold polar waters meet warmer waters from further north, provides a neat way of defining the southern polar region, but in the north a search for an Arctic Convergence is defeated by geography: convergence exists, but is discontinuous and much less clearly defined. Another sea-based suggestion is the use of the southern limit of pack ice. This too has problems: the limit is seasonal and there are also unpredictable annual variations. It would also be extremely difficult to interpolate the position of the pack ice edge across land masses, and the Arctic Ocean is virtually surrounded by land.

One suggested definition avoids the problems created by climate and geography and considers only the incident solar energy on the Earth. In the Arctic the Sun is always at a low angle in the sky and, as a consequence, light from it must traverse more of the atmosphere to reach the ground, and so loses more energy to absorption and scattering. Because of this low angle the Sun also illuminates a larger area of the Earth than it does at the Equator, for example. This reduces the energy input per unit surface area. A proposal from the 1960s defined the Arctic as covering an area where the incident energy was less than 15kcal/cm^2/year. This definition, though scientifically sound, has the disadvantage of not being an easily recognisable unit or feature in the way that, say, temperature or the treeline (the northern limit of trees) are. The search for a definition was therefore transferred to these options.

Use of a definition based on a land feature has one distinct advantage: the large land masses surrounding the Arctic mean

Defining Antarctica

The Earth's polar regions are very different. While the Antarctic consists of land surrounded by ocean, the Arctic is an ocean surrounded by land. The table below indicates the contrast between the two regions. The fact that Antarctica is surrounded by water means that defining it is much simpler than defining the northern polar region. Antarctica, the continent itself, is, of course, reasonably straightforward to define (though the formation and break-up of sea ice means the 'edge' of the continent moves throughout the year). Defining the Antarctic is trickier. The most usual definition is that it lies south of the Antarctic Convergence, the junction of southern, colder Antarctic waters and northern sub-tropical waters. The Convergence (sometimes called the Antarctic Polar Front) forms a boundary about 30–50km wide that zig-zags around Antarctica, lying between 48°S and 61°S. It is sometimes visible, and always detectable as a change from relatively warm, salty northern waters to the cold, less salty southern sea. The Antarctic Treaty, signed initially by the 12 countries with an active interest in the continent on 1 December 1959 (and later signed by other countries), which protects Antarctica from exploitation, defines the Antarctic as lying south of 60°S.

Antarctica	Arctic
South Pole: 2,836m above sea level. The closest open ocean is at least 1,400km away.	North Pole: 2–3m of sea ice above an ocean approximately 4,000m deep. Nearest land is Oodaq Island off the northern Greenland coast, some 700km away.
Mean annual temperature at South Pole: -50°C.	Mean annual temperature at North Pole: -15°C.
Sea ice mainly annual with high salinity.	Sea ice mainly multi-year with low salinity.
No terrestrial mammals.	Many terrestrial mammals.
Few bird species south of 70°S.	Many bird species north of 70°N.
Limited plant life south of 80°S.	Abundant plant life north of 80°N

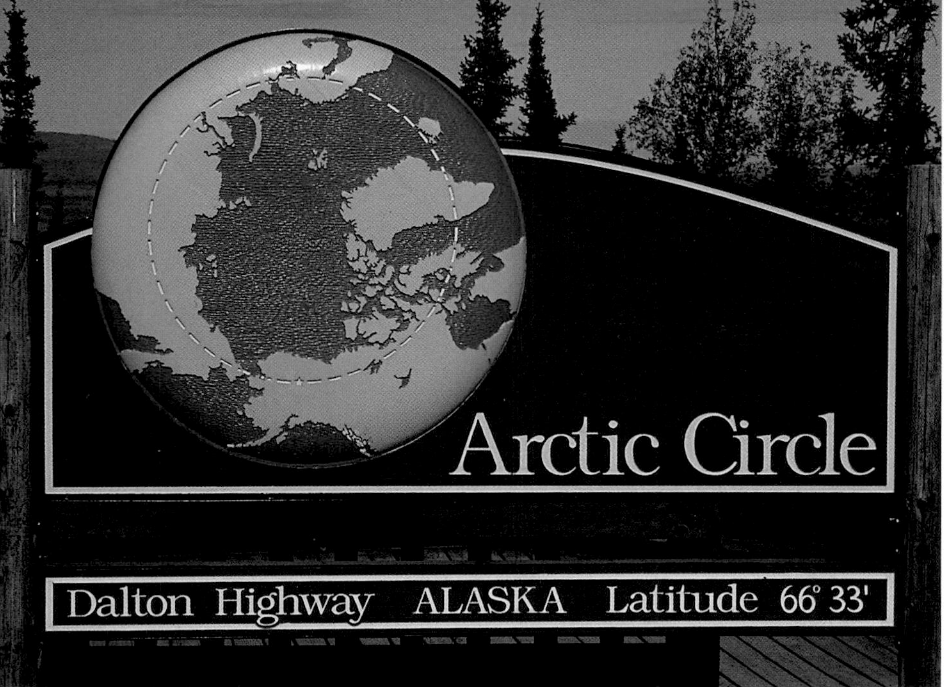

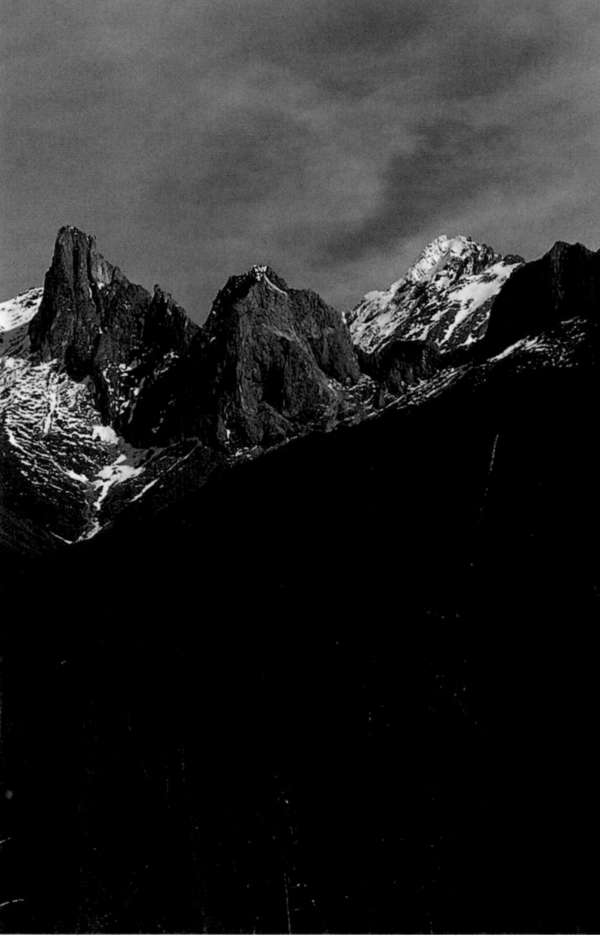

Though they are trophies for the traveller, neither the Arctic Circle or the treeline is a useful definition of the Arctic.

Above
Arctic Circle indicator board on the Dalton Highway, Alaska.

Right
The treeline on the southern slope of the Brooks Range, northern Alaska.

that the extrapolation required across water is much more limited than that required by a sea-based definition. Use of the treeline is therefore attractive, but brings its own problems. First, a tree must be defined. Such a need raises a smile, but it is not, in fact, trivial. Arctic Willow (*Salix polaris*) is a tree by all the usual definitions, even changing the colour of its leaves in autumn as do more southerly deciduous trees. Yet in places where it has to contend with severe winds and extreme cold, factors that limit the height to which any tree will grow, Arctic Willow occasionally grows to a height of only 10cm: travellers from temperate places are used to walking beneath a forest canopy, but in the Arctic they are effectively walking on the canopy.

Use of the tree limit to define the Arctic smooths out climatic differences. In Europe, the influence of the North Atlantic Drift allows tree growth well north of the Arctic Circle, while in North America trees have generally faded away before 60°N is reached. However, the treeline is not as precise and easily identified boundary as might be expected. Local geology and geography, as well as local climatic effects, play a role in defining the habitability of an area. Ground elevation and aspect, drainage and soil composition all influence plant growth so that occasionally patches of forest exist, to the south of which there are areas, sometimes significant areas, of tree-free tundra. On paper the tree-line is a solid, immutable line, but on the ground it is rather more insubstantial, forming a band over which the transition from true boreal forest to true tundra occurs. In Siberia this transitional band can be as much as 300km wide. A further complication is that there are places where local conditions (e.g. shelter from wind) allow trees to grow north of the latitude at which those species can propagate by seed formation, because the summer is now neither warm enough nor long enough for this process to occur. Though the ancestors of these trees all germinated from seeds, climatic changes mean their seeds cannot do the same. They instead propagate by a form of 'suckering' in which branches that touch the ground produce roots from which new trunks grow. The branch dies off but a new tree grows in its place. In some places whole stands of trees can grow, each a clone of the original parent tree.

To overcome the difficulties of tree-line definition, scientists turned to a temperature-based definition. The initial proposal was use of the 10°C summer isotherm, a line that links points on the Earth's surface at which the mean temperature of the warmest month of the year is 10°C. The isotherm has the advantage of being closely aligned to the tree-line. It is usually assumed that the factor limiting the northerly spread of trees is the cold: that is correct, but not in the sense that is usually inferred. It is not winter cold that is the limiting factor – in Siberia trees grow at a latitude that experiences the lowest winter temperatures recorded in the northern hemisphere. The limit is summer cold. In the Arctic summer there is abundant light, but the tree can only utilise this energy source if its cell temperatures are sufficiently high for the chemical reactions of photosynthesis to occur. Thus it is summer temperature – which must be high enough for a long enough period – that is critical to tree growth. As temperature is both easily measured and understood, the required extrapolation over water is limited, and the 10°C summer isotherm is closely aligned with the tree-line, a more-or-less tangible feature of the landscape, the use of this isotherm as a definition of the Arctic would seem ideal.

But again there are drawbacks. The isotherm is poorly (often very poorly) defined across the intercontinental waters

Plants and temperature

The treeline aligns closely to the 10°C isotherm. Not surprisingly, further north the vegetation continues to vary with temperature. To the north of the 5°C isotherm vegetation cover is thinner, with shrubs growing only to about 20cm in height, while north of the 2°C isotherm there are only lichens and mosses, with small flowering plants occasionally seen in sheltered hollows.

of the Arctic fringe, and it makes no allowance for winter cold. The former is not too much of a problem since the isotherm is a less valuable measure in the oceans, but the latter means that the place where the lowest-ever temperature in the northern hemisphere was recorded (at Oymyakon in Siberia) actually lies south of the 10°C isotherm.

Despite these drawbacks, the isotherm has been adopted as a useful measure of the border between the Arctic and the sub-Arctic by many specialists since it was first suggested in the late 19th century, though there have been attempts to address the problem of winter cold. The first was by Danish scientist Morten Vahl, who suggested that 10°C should be replaced by the temperature V, where V < 9.5°-(K/30), with V and K the mean temperatures of the warmest and coldest months of the year. For the Siberian forest, where the mean temperature of the coldest month might be -40°C, the mean temperature of the warmest month would then be 10.8°C. The Swedish scientist Otto Nordenskjöld – nephew of the first man to sail the North-East Passage, and himself a noted Antarctic explorer – considered that the Vahl formula did not adequately allow for the effect of winter cold and suggested a refinement, with V < 9°-(K/10). Now for the Siberian forest the mean temperature of the warmest month becomes 13°C. On the Nordenskjöld formula the 10°C isotherm is applicable for sites where the mean temperature of the coldest month is -10°C. The Nordenskjöld modified formula pushes the Arctic boundary south in Asian Russia and North America, but still excludes some areas that would be considered Arctic by the layman – Iceland, much of Alaska and northern Fennoscandia (Fennoscandia being the combination of Norway, Sweden, Finland and the Kola Peninsula, and land immediately south of the White Sea in Russia). These exclusions seem anomalous for reasons other than common perception. For instance, although Iceland lies almost entirely south of the Arctic Circle it is north of the treeline (though whether the island's present tree-less state is a manmade rather than natural phenomenon is a matter of debate). This issue, and others, were addressed by the Arctic Council – a joint initiative of the Scandinavian countries (including Iceland), Russia and Canada – which defined a boundary for CAFF, the programme for the Conservation of Arctic Flora and Fauna, which pushed the Arctic boundary well south, including not only Iceland, but extensive areas of Fennoscandia as well as the hinterlands of Russia and Canada, and much of south-western Alaska. However, the CAFF definition excludes Russia's Kamchatka Peninsula and Commander Islands, while including the Aleutian chain, a decision that is surprising.

In this book I have taken a pragmatic approach, the southern boundary of the Arctic being essentially defined by the Nordenskjöld modified 10°C isotherm, but being pushed south to take in areas whose exclusion seems incorrect. In North America James Bay is included. It would be excluded by the modified 10°C isotherm line, but its importance to Polar Bears requires its inclusion. Alaska's Denali National Park is also included. A specific problem exists in the Bering Sea where the use of the modified 10°C isotherm omits much of what is usually considered Arctic. Here it is assumed that the Pribilof Islands, the Aleutian Island chain, the Commander

Lapporten in northern Sweden. This curious mountain feature, photographed here one winter evening, lies close to the Abisko National Park. The name means 'Gateway to Lapland', which could be interpreted as an entrance to the Arctic.

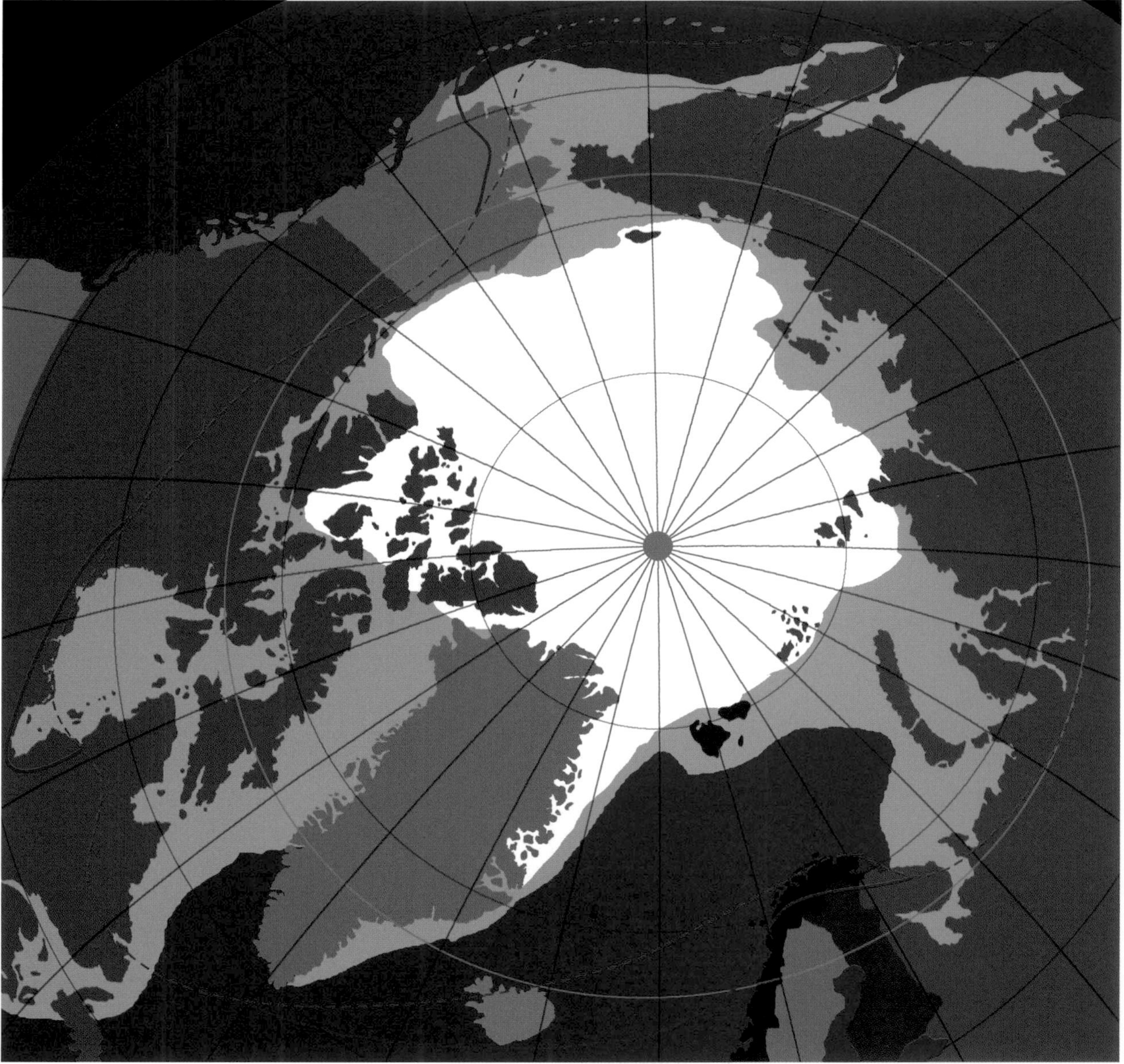

Figure 1.4
The definition of the Arctic used in this book. The green line is the Arctic Circle. The red, dotted line is the modified 10°C isotherm. The purple line is where the definition departs from the isotherm line.

Islands, the Kamchatka Peninsula, and the north-eastern coast of the Sea of Okhotsk lie within the Arctic. In Eurasia northern Fennoscandia and the northern coast of Russia are included. The modified 10°C isotherm and boundary of the Arctic assumed in this book are shown in Figure 1.4. The treeline is shown in Figure 14.1.

One other definition must be addressed before continuing. Many books and reports dealing with Arctic species use the terms 'High' and 'Low' Arctic without necessarily defining what is meant by them. This is partly because such definitions are largely arbitrary. In this book High Arctic refers to polar desert, while Low Arctic refers to the more southerly tundra (see Figure 1.5). The High Arctic has an average summer temperature of about 4°C and a plant growing period of about 8–10 weeks; it is drier and has fewer species (about half the number) of plants, insects, birds and mammals, though rather more bryophytes (mosses and liverworts: though fewer wet area species, e.g. sphagnums). By contrast, the average summer temperature of the Low Arctic is 7°C with a growing period of 3–4 months. However, it has to be accepted that the transition from one to the other is often gradual – polar desert becoming semi-desert becoming tundra – a fact that can make the use of the terms occasionally unhelpful.

Figure 1.5
Polar desert is marked in red, while the purple line marks the southern limit of the tundra.

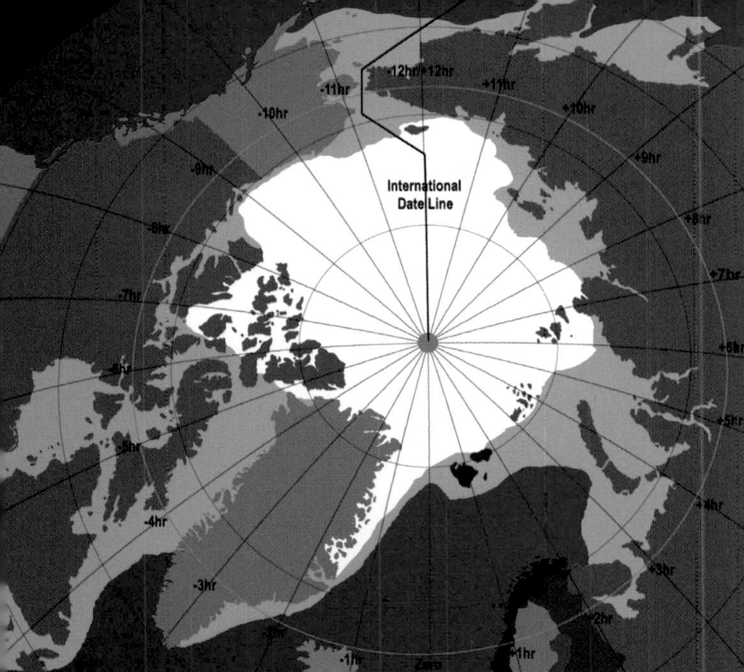

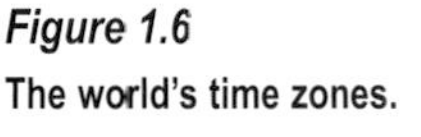
Figure 1.6
The world's time zones.

Time at the pole

Before 1884, towns and cities throughout the world had their own times based on local Sunrise, so it was possible for clocks in places that were relatively close to show different times. When travel between them was measured in hours that hardly mattered, but once the telegraph and telephones had been invented these minor differences in time became a nuisance. In October 1884 it was agreed that time would be standardised throughout the world. Since Greenwich, England was already recognised as sitting on the Prime Meridian (0° longitude), standard time was referred to as Greenwich Mean Time (GMT), with all other clocks being set relative to it. Because the day is 24 hours long and there are 360° of longitude, a traveller following the Equator finds local time changing by one hour for every 15° of longitude (though time zones are not always so rigorously applied). But if that same traveller is intent on reaching the North Pole this time change becomes increasingly meaningless. The traveller will head out towards the pole from one of the surrounding land masses with a watch set to local time. As our traveller moves north, the crowding together of the lines of longitude means that although the time differences between them remains the same, the distance that needs to be travelled between them reduces fast. At the Equator the circumference of the Earth is about 40,000km, so the difference that needs to be travelled there for a time difference of 1 hour is around 1,670km. At the Arctic Circle this distance reduces to about 663km. At 85° it is down to 145km and by the time the traveller is within 1° of the pole it is a mere 29km. At the pole itself of course the distance has shrunk to zero and the heavily booted traveller can circle the Earth as fast as he can turn circles and for as long as he can repel giddiness. At the pole the time is all times – it is the time the traveller is facing right now, but also the time faced with a turn of the head. This seemingly strange state of affairs is illustrated in Figure 1.6.

A line also had to be agreed at which the day changes – head west across it and today becomes tomorrow, head east and it becomes yesterday. The agreed line, the International Date Line, was chosen to run away from occupied lands, and takes a more-or-less north–south course from the North to the South Pole through the Bering Strait and across the Bering Sea, deviating to ensure that the Aleutian Islands, part of the United States, all lie to its east, while Russia's Commander Islands lie to the west. Western Alaska does not accommodate the full 12 hour time difference from London, but eastern Russia does. Arctic travellers in, for instance, Kamchatka can therefore be a full half-day distant from friends in the UK. As Kamchatka is 9 hours different from Moscow, and the flight time from Petropavlosk to Moscow is about 9 hours, travellers can also enjoy the slightly surreal experience of leaving Kamchatka as the Sun is going down in the evening and arriving in Moscow to see the same phenomenon. If the flight has made good time, arrival can even be a few minutes before departure. Take an onward flight to London and arrival can be on the same day – although that day has lasted 36 hours.

For all travellers the International Date Line has comic potential, but because of the effect of decreasing distance for 15° of longitude travelled as one heads north, the Arctic traveller has the better deal. Here the cliffs of Chukotka, about 100km away, are seen through morning haze. In the foreground a Vega Herring Gull and Glaucous Gull stand at the water's edge on the western tip of St Lawrence Island. Over there in Chukotka it is already tomorrow.

2. The Geology of the Arctic

The similarity of the outlines of the east and west coasts of the Atlantic had been noticed by scholars such as Francis Bacon as early as the 1620s. Over the succeeding centuries the similarity of species on different continents raised issues that scientists found hard to explain. Why was it that fossil plants of the genus *Glossopteris* were found in coal measures, apparently of the same age, in southern South America, southern Africa, southern India and across Australia? The distances between these areas were so vast and the seeds of the plants so large (relatively speaking) that wind could be discounted as a dispersal mechanism. Instead it was suggested that at one time the continents had been connected by land bridges. The name Gondwanaland was coined for the huge, hypothetical southern continent across which *Glossopteris* flourished, the existence of which also explained other apparently anomalous fossil organism distributions. But while Gondwanaland solved one mystery, it created others. Since *Glossopteris* was a deciduous plant with a ringed trunk, implying a seasonal climate, why were its fossils found in tropical areas? Why was the fauna of Madagascar, an island on which *Glossopteris* had grown, so different from that of nearby Africa? And there were other questions; why, for instance, were there coal seams on Svalbard, a cold, inhospitable archipelago on which plants could barely grow at all, let alone produce the growth necessary for laying down such deposits?

Alfred Wegener and the theory of continental drift

In 1906 the German meteorologist and geophysicist Alfred Wegener took part in a Danish expedition to Greenland, which was intended to complete the exploration of the north–eastern part of that huge island. The expedition, aboard the *Danmark*, was marred by tragedy, three men dying during their return from an attempt to confirm Robert Peary's claim that a channel – the Peary Channel – split Greenland in the far north-east. Wegener returned to Greenland in 1912, taking part in an expedition that made a 1,100km crossing of the Inland Ice (Greenland's ice sheet), a crossing that was twice as long as that of Nansen on the first-ever traverse. In 1915 he published a book entitled *Die Entstehung der Kontinente und Ozeane* (first published in English as *The Origin of Continents and Oceans* in 1924) in which he presented his theory of continental drift, a theory he had developed as a result of watching the movement of ice floes during his time in the Arctic. Wegener's theory was that the continents had once been joined together in a single supercontinent that he called Pangaea, from the Greek for 'all land'. Wegener's Pangaea was surrounded by a single ocean, Panthalassa ('all water'), and had broken up, the land masses drifting apart to form the world we see today. Wegener's theory helped explain the distribution of *Glossopteris* and other fossils across the continents, and also made the similarities of geology at continental edges more readily explainable.

But despite the explanation it offered for observable distributions, the theory of continental drift was rejected by most scientists, partly because it was based on flawed data. Wegener compared survey data from his 1906 expedition with data collected in 1870. This led him to deduce that Greenland and Scotland had moved apart by several hundred meters over that

Glossopteris fossil. The curious distribution of this fossil plant across the world puzzled scientists until the theory of plate tectonics was accepted.

36 year period (Wegener's data suggested that the two land masses were separating at between 18m and 36m annually; the presently accepted drift is closer to 4cm/year, about the same rate as fingernail growth). Wegener's calculated separation speed led him to propose that Pangaea had not broken up until the start of the Tertiary period (about 65 million years ago). Evidence for a rapid evolution of the biotas of the continents following Pangaea's break-up did not exist.

Furthermore, Wegener's theory required that the continents drift apart, a suggestion dismissed by geologists who could not conceive of a method whereby a continent could move through the Earth's crust. The structure of the Earth, though not at that time well understood, was known to consist of a very dense core surrounded by a rocky mantle, with the crust laying on top. The discontinuity between the rocks of the crust and the mantle below was first identified by Croatian seismologist Andrija Mohorovičić (not surprisingly the discontinuity is now known as a Moho). Studies of the Moho showed that the Earth's crust was continuous everywhere – how could the movements required by Wegener's continental drift possibly occur?

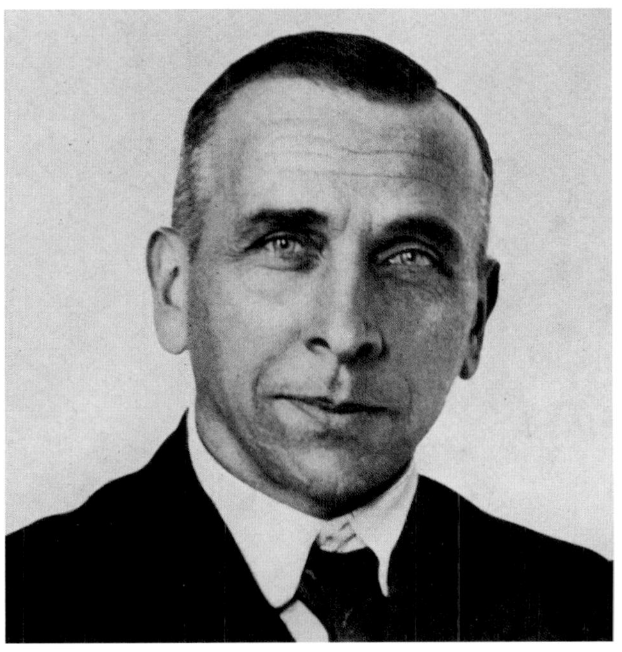

Alfred Wegener. His theory of continental drift was initially dismissed, but is now accepted by mainstream science.

One geologist who did not dismiss Wegener's theory despite this apparently overwhelming difficulty was the South African Alexander Du Toit. Du Toit found further fossil forms that fitted with the theory of continental drift, but most telling was the evidence of striations left by Palaeozoic glaciers. These scourings indicate the direction of flow of the glacier that created them. What Du Toit, and others, found was that in southern Australia and southern South America striations indicated glaciers flowing from an area that was now only ocean; in southern Africa and southern India the scourings indicated similar anomalous directions. There were also new data that

Opposite page
Close to Iceland's Skaftafell National Park Svartifoss, the Black Waterfall, drops over a cliff of black basalt columns.

showed that Wegener's rate of separation of the northern land masses was wrong, the measured movement being slower. From all this new information Du Toit concluded that Wegener had been correct, but that his timescale had been wrong: Pangaea had broken up not at the start of the Tertiary, but at the end of the Palaeozoic era, about 250 million years ago. But by then Wegener was dead; he died of exposure in 1930 during another expedition to Greenland.

The new evidence solved the biogeographical riddle of the drift theory, but left the problem of how continents could move through a continuous crust, a problem so apparently intractable that scepticism remained. Not until the 1960s was the solution discovered. It came from evidence amassed by the American geophysicist Harry Hess, in part from data obtained from ship-borne echo sounders while Hess, at that time a rear-admiral, commanded a vessel during World War II. Hess realised that the depth of sediment on the oceanic floors was insufficient to account for the accumulation that must have taken place throughout the life of the Earth (the sedimentation rate was known to be about 1cm per millennium, but that implied that the sediment depth should be some 30 times deeper than that observed). Hess also noted, as others had, that ridges rising from the beds of the ocean were often positioned mid-ocean (the Mid-Atlantic Ridge being the prime example; the ridge was discovered in the 1870s by a British naval research vessel commanded by Captain George Nares, but its significance had not been understood at the time), and that there was a trench at the peak of these ridges. His echo soundings also identified curious flat-topped sea-mounts (which he called *guyots* after a similarly shaped campus building at Princeton, which was itself named after the American geologist Arnold Guyot). The uniformity and comparative youth of the oceanic beds, and the position of the guyots, led Hess to suggest that the ridges were the driving force behind continental drift.

Plate tectonics

Hess's theory now forms the basis of the study of plate tectonics. The plates in question are a series of rigid structures that together make up the Earth's crust (geologists generally consider there to be seven major plates, together with some smaller ones and a number of microplates – Figure 2.1) that float on the mantle, which is known to be predominantly solid (despite being much hotter than the melting point of the rocks of which it is comprised – they remain solid due to the enormous pressure) but with zones that are demarcated by the elasticity of the material. The crustal plates are of two basic forms, continental and oceanic, the latter being denser and therefore floating lower on the mantle. The difference in density reflects a difference in composition; oceanic plates are made of mafic, mainly basaltic rocks of high iron and magnesium content (the name mafic deriving from Mg and Fe), while continental plates consist mainly of felsic, a mainly granitic rock with a higher aluminium content and less iron. The name felsic derives from feldspar, the most common mineral in continental plates – feldspar is high in silicon and aluminium. The two crustal plate forms make up the lithosphere, a 100km–thick layer that floats on the upper, plastic portion of the mantle (known as the asthenosphere). The world's oceans lie above the oceanic plates, lapping the edges of the continental plates.

Convection currents occur in the mantle, as a consequence of the temperature gradient between the Earth's hot core and the cold crustal plates. In a fluid such currents result in motions familiar to everyone who has watched water boil, hot liquid rising from the base, cooling at the surface and falling back down again, leading to a circular motion of water and bubbles. The mantle is not fluid but similar currents arise, the material of the mantle moving by crystalline creep, a movement analogous to (but much slower than) that of the hot water. The currents (Figure 2.2) circulate the material of the asthenosphere, moving the plates lying directly above. It was

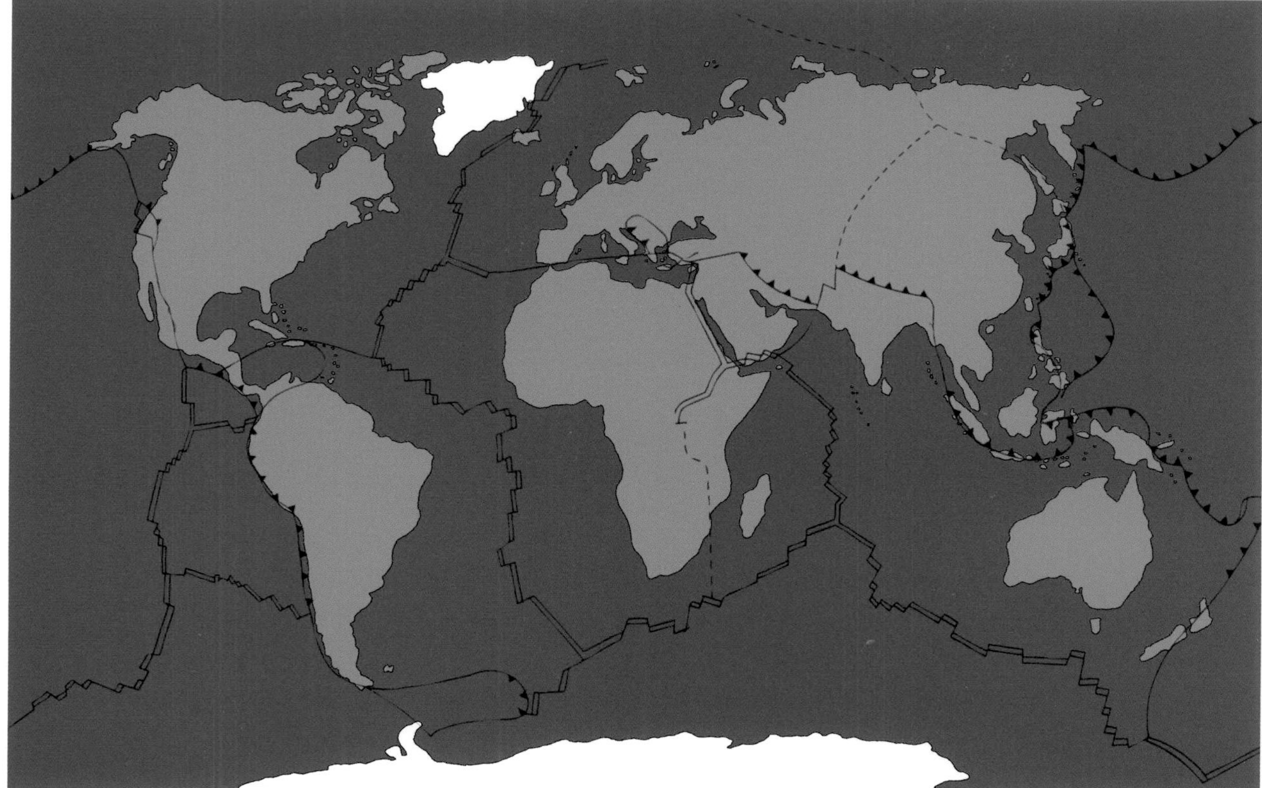

Figure 2.1
Parallel lines represent spreading ridges. Single and dashed lines represent transform boundaries. Single lines with arrowheads are subduction boundaries, the arrow indicating the direction of subduction.

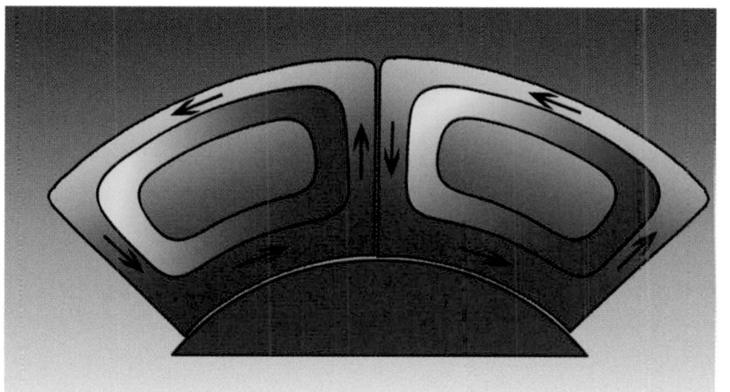

Figure 2.2
The present understanding of plate tectonics is illustrated here. Convective currents within the mantle give rise to mid-ocean ridges where upward flows are adjacent.

thought that the movement of the plates was due to viscous drag (essentially that the plate was embedded in the asthenosphere), but this is now thought to be just one of several components of the movement. For example, there is a gravitational effect; hot, rising mantle material driven by a convection current creates a dome in the crustal plate above it. The plate then slides away from the dome under gravity.

Where two rising currents lie in parallel a ridge, topped by a trench-like rift, is formed. The guyot sea-mounts are created where pillow lavas (lava flowing beneath the sea and cooled by it to form solid rock) from the ridge break the ocean surface. Weathering produces a flat-topped mount, which then moves below the sea as the oceanic floor moves away from the ridge. Once below the surface weathering is effectively eliminated, explaining why Hess was able to see the mounts and why they were further below the surface the further away they were from the ridge. Although the existence of young, uniform oceanic beds and the number and distribution of guyots convinced most scientists, further observations led to the theory of continental drift receiving general assent. One was the curious discovery that the Earth's North Magnetic Pole moves (as does the South Magnetic Pole). When the North Magnetic Pole was first reached by James Clark Ross in 1831 it was on the western coast of Canada's Boothia Peninsula. When rediscovered in 1903 it had moved north. Cooling rock is magnetised by the Earth's magnetic field, the precise orientation of the magnetism being dependent on the position of the two Magnetic Poles. Studies of the declination (the direction of magnetism) of rocks in Europe showed that the North Magnetic Pole did indeed wander over considerable distances with time, but when the studies were repeated in North America, although the wander was observed, the path was different. There was no mechanism by which different continents could have different poles. It was then found that the wander paths of the pole for each continent could be made the same – but only if the continents were assumed to be much closer together millions of years ago; they must have drifted apart.

A second discovery was the magnetic 'striping' of the ocean beds. Over time the polarity of the Earth's magnetic field has reversed many times. As molten rock emerging from the mid-ocean ridges crystallises, it acquires a magnetic polarisation consistent with the current orientation of the Earth's field. Studies showed that the changes in polarisation formed a series of magnetic 'stripes' (of reversed polarity) and that the pattern of these stripes on each side of the ridge was identical. Clearly the sea floor had spread from the mid-ocean ridge and this spread had pushed the continental plates apart. The mid-ocean ridges explained the youth of the ocean beds and the separation of continents, but since the surface area of the Earth had clearly remained constant over time, if oceanic bed was being created, somewhere plate material had to be lost. The creation of material at the spreading ridges and the loss of material elsewhere leads to geological processes that are evident in many places in the Arctic.

Formation of the Arctic

CONTINENTAL MOVEMENTS AND LAND BRIDGES

Pangaea formed about 350 million years ago and began to break up about 100 million years later. To the south Antarctica and Australia separated from the other continents, with Australia later breaking away as Antarctica drifted across the South Pole. The northern movement of Africa began to close the Mediterranean, while the northern movement of India against Eurasia has created, and is still raising, the Himalayas. The mid-Atlantic Ridge began to rotate the Americas away from Eurasia and Africa, forming the Atlantic Ocean. Other

At Þingvellir, close to Iceland's capital Reykjavik, the mid-Atlantic Ridge is visible. At one point a path has been laid through a rift in the ridge allowing visitors to walk with the North American plate to their left and the Eurasian plate to their right.

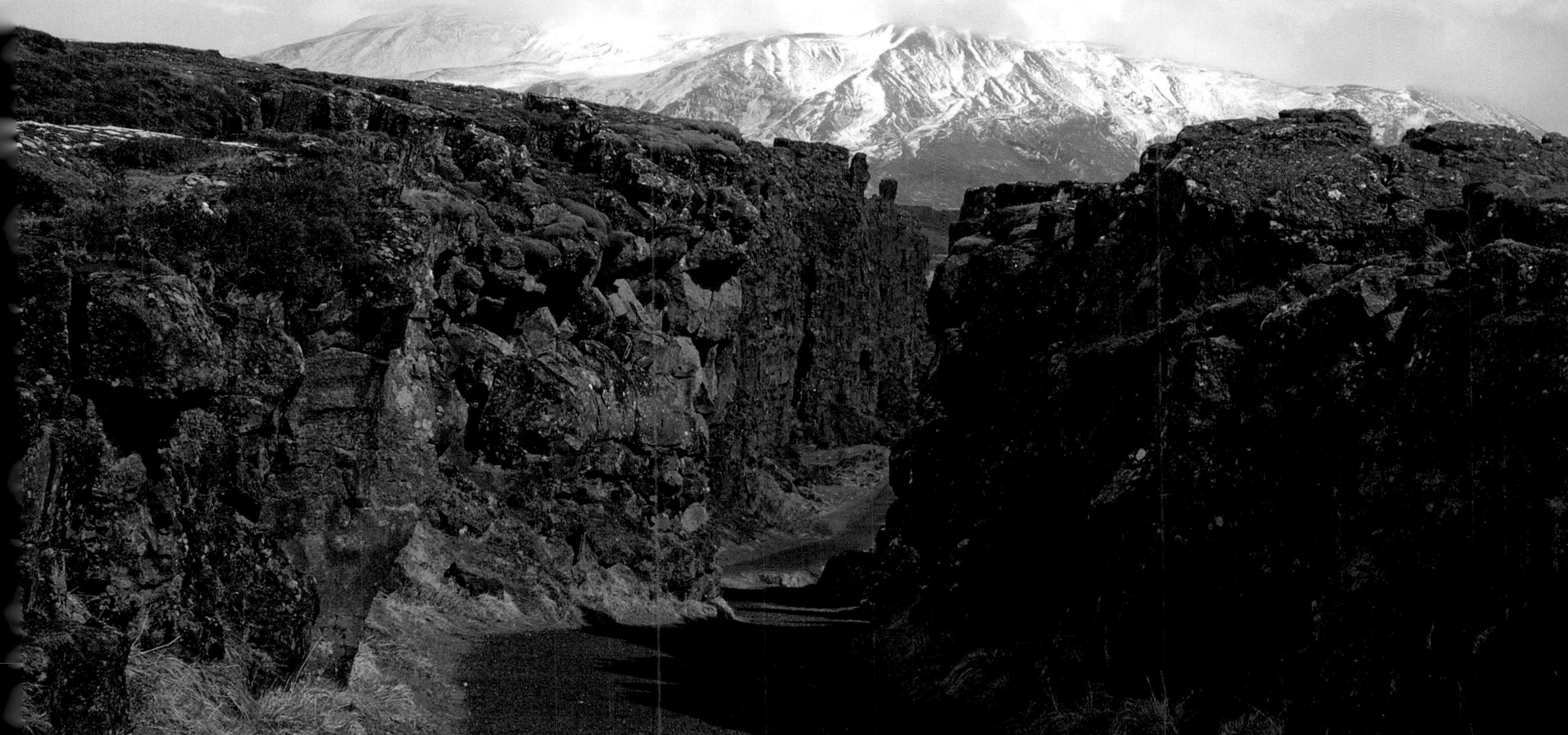

spreading ridges have formed, but unlike the mid-Atlantic ridge they have failed to produce oceans. Spreading ridges formed the Labrador Sea and also Lancaster Sound/Baffin Bay, but the land mass that was to become North America, Greenland and Eurasia resisted the spreading, perhaps because they formed a circumpolar continental mass capable of doing so, the Atlantic spreading leading to a rotation of the continental landmasses so that Eurasia was brought into contact with North America. The Arctic Ocean formed within this pole-circling landmass.

About 55 million years ago the Arctic Ocean was essentially landlocked, with Beringia, the Bering Sea land bridge, connecting Alaska and Siberia. Greenland and the Canadian High Arctic archipelago were connected to the north by the Thulean land bridge. To the south of this Baffin Bay represented a failed spreading ridge. South again the Davis Strait land bridge connected what would become Baffin Island to Greenland. The exact nature of the separation of Greenland from North America is still not resolved. The Nares Channel, a seaway some 500km long but only 25km wide at its narrowest point, separates north-west Greenland from Ellesmere Island. One suggestion is that Greenland detached itself from North America (Ellesmere Island) and started to slide northward, moving as much as 300km. However, some scientists believe that the rock formations on the opposite sides of the Strait are too similar for such a large movement to have occurred and favour a smaller slippage, coupled with an expansion of the Strait due to large-scale movements of the high Canadian Arctic.

On the north-eastern side of ancestral Greenland the De Geer land bridge connected it to Fennoscandia, the land bridge including what is now the Svalbard archipelago. Further south Greenland was attached to Scotland. South of the De Geer land bridge was an embryonic sea that would become the Norwegian Sea. It was connected to the proto-North Sea,

Beringia

The name Beringia was coined by the Swedish botanist Eric Hultén, who mapped the occurrence of plants in Kamchatka, Chukotka and Alaska and noted that the range of many was an oval, elongated east–west. The ovals could be centred on either side of the Bering Sea or, apparently, in the sea itself, suggesting that at one time land had connected the two continents.

Whaler's grave, Magdalenefjord, Spitsbergen, Svalbard. The mountains that form the backdrop to one of the most beautiful fjords of Svalbard are remnants of the Caledonides, a range which stretched for 10,000km across central Pangaea.

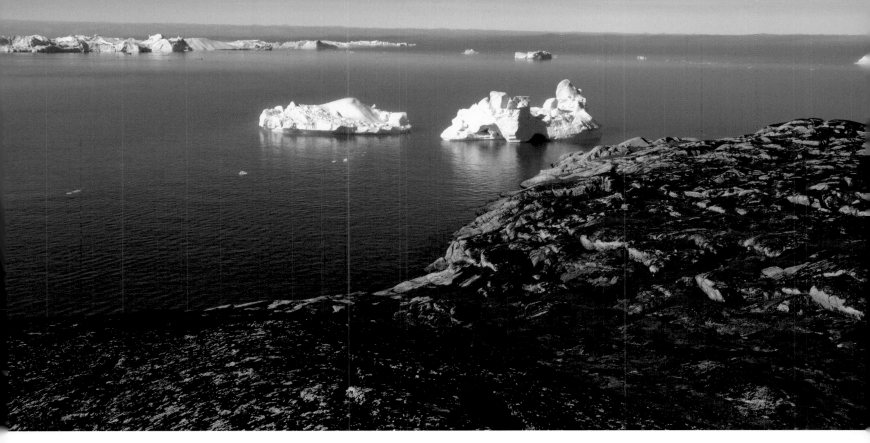

but that, too, was landlocked by the land bridge that connected what would become the countryside around Dover and Calais.

Greenland separated from Europe around 35 million years ago, as an extension of the mid-Atlantic Ridge forced the two land masses apart. The Greenland-Scotland land bridge was severed as the ocean bed spread, but to the north the De Geer land bridge (named for the Swedish geologist Gerhard De Geer) was severed by transform faulting. Transform faulting is a shear motion, the Spitsbergen Fracture Zone opening as Greenland slid past Svalbard. The fracture zone connected the Arctic and Atlantic oceans, the mixed waters forming what is now called the Fram Strait. But this mixing was of surface waters only, deep currents of cooler water being prevented from flowing into or out of the Arctic Ocean as the spreading ridge between Greenland and Scotland presented a deep sea barrier. Bathed in relatively warm water, the Arctic at this time bore little resemblance to the region today.

But at about this time the global climate started to deteriorate; this became more marked when Antarctica, by then stationed over the South Pole, became detached from South America as the latter drifted north. Now completely surrounded by cool water – the Southern Ocean – which could circulate unimpeded around it, Antarctica grew colder. Glaciers formed on its high mountains and sea ice became a feature of its coastline. The cold southern waters sank and were replaced by warmer waters flowing in from the north. The interaction of the two caused clouds to form and snow to fall on the continent. The Antarctic ice sheet began to grow; since ice reflects up to 90% of incident radiation, the growing ice sheet led to a cooling of the Earth. However, the Arctic remained relatively warm for several million years more, though tectonic activity eventually allowed colder deep waters to flow. Seasonal sea ice may have begun to form in the Arctic by about 3½ million years ago, but permanent ice probably did not appear until global temperatures fell – according to an analysis of ice cores – about 2½ million years ago. Only then did the Arctic as we now know it appear.

Formation of the Arctic

ROCKS, SEAS AND MOUNTAINS

The central areas of the tectonic plates that enclose the Arctic Ocean have shields of exposed PreCambrian bedrock, surrounded by further cratonic areas (i.e. regions that isolate them from the geologically active areas at the continental margins). In Eurasia the Baltic Shield covers much of eastern Fennoscandia, while the Anabar Shield of central Asian Russia (south of the Laptev Sea) is surrounded by the extensive Lena-Yenisey Plate – an area occasionally split into the eastern Siberian Craton and the western West Siberian Basin. In North America, the Canadian Shield surrounds Hudson Bay, extending as far west as the Great Bear Lake, east as far as the Atlantic coast and northwards across Baffin Island. The Greenland Shield, which underlies all but the eastern part of the island, is separated from the Canadian Shield by Baffin Bay and the Davis Strait, this separation having occurred about 60–65 million years ago. The Canadian Shield is surrounded by an extensive Palaeozoic platform that covers virtually all of the High Arctic islands (though there are shield rocks on some, particularly on Baffin Island where only the Brodeaur Peninsula is of platform rocks). The shields comprise metamorphosed rocks (gneisses and crystalline schists).

Rocks of the Greenland Shield exposed above Disko Bay on the western side of the island.

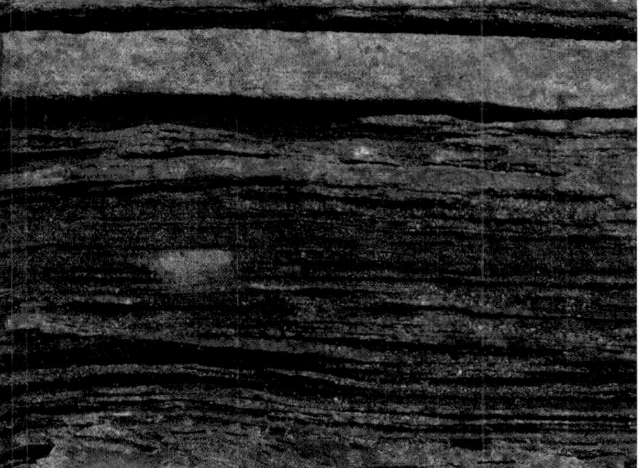

Although it measures only 175km² Bear Island exhibits rocks from the PreCambrian to the Triassic with many areas showing transition in sedimentary layers.

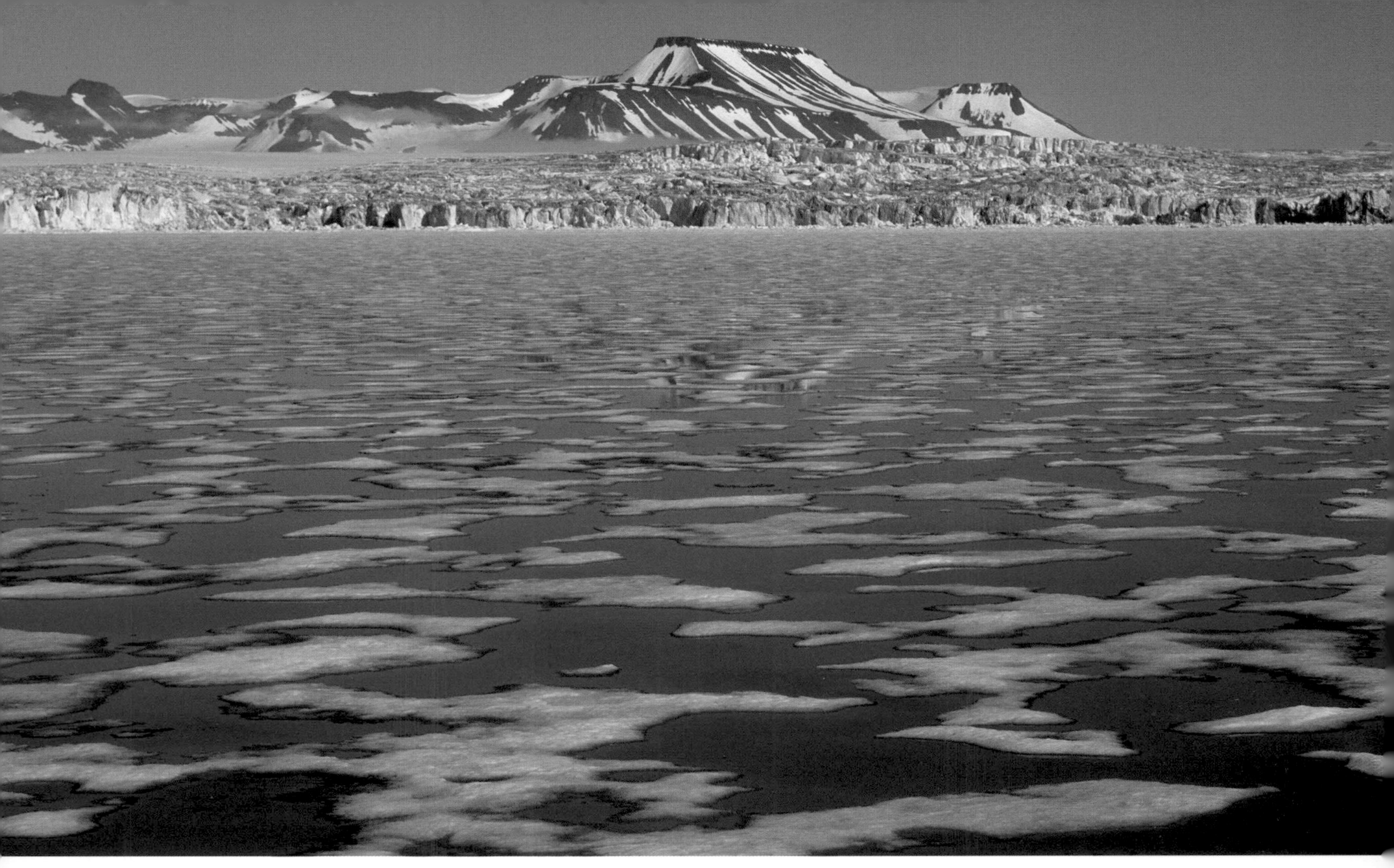

Winter at Brepollen, Hornsund in southern Spitsbergen. Across the sea ice are flat topped peaks indicative of the existence of a relatively hard rock band which has escaped erosion.

Some of these PreCambrian rocks are among the oldest on Earth. Close to the Acasta River, in Canada's North West Territories, rocks have been dated through the examination of zircon crystals that formed as volcanic rocks cooled. This analysis gave an age of just over 4,000 million years. In the Isua upland close to Nuuk, the Greenlandic capital in the south-west of the country, pillow lavas and fine-grained sedimentary rocks laid down in deep waters have been dated to 3,750 million years ago. Most of the shield rocks date from 2,500–3,500 million years ago. During the period from about 1,000 million years, sedimentary rocks were laid down below a shallow sea. Later, tillites – a mix of material from clay to boulders – were deposited. Tillites can be seen in north-east Greenland; they are good supporting evidence for the 'snowball Earth' hypothesis. This suggests that the Earth was wholly, or largely, ice-covered around 650 million years ago, with the tillites a product of glacial activity.

Surrounding the ancient continental cores of essentially stable bedrock are areas of massive folding, with these orogenies associated with tectonic activity. One orogeny was responsible for the Urals, a range that continues across Novaya Zemlya. The Caledonian Orogeny created a mountain range against the stable Baltic shield that extended from what is now western Scandinavia to the Appalachians by way of Scotland and east Greenland. In the Nearctic, further folding created the mountains of Ellesmere and Axel Heiberg islands. These orogenies all date from the Palaeozoic, though the folding that led to the great ranges of Alaska took place later in the Mesozoic.

Mountain building was accompanied by metamorphosis and igneous intrusions. Newtontoppen, the highest peak in Svalbard (at 1,717m) is a granite intrusion from this period, as are some of the granite formations in east Greenland. By far the most spectacular intrusions are the huge granite faces of the peaks of the Auyuittuq National Park on Baffin Island. The faces on Mounts Thor and Asgard are among the tallest in the world and are a constant attraction to trekkers and climbers (and others – Auyuittuq was used for a famous parachute jump scene in a James Bond movie).

From the Carboniferous and on through the Mesozoic, fossil-rich sedimentary rocks were laid down in extensive basins that covered much of the Canadian Arctic, Greenland and Svalbard. The basalt intrusions of Franz Josef Land date from this long period of continent-building. In the subsequent Palaeocene epoch at the start of the Tertiary, the mid-Atlantic Ridge began the process of forming the Atlantic Ocean and moving the Old and New Worlds apart, laying the foundation for the present structure of the Arctic. The break-up of Pangaea, of which the creation of the Atlantic was a part, was also accompanied by the accretion of various terranes (well-defined pieces of land whose geology differs markedly). Terranes are a particular feature of Alaska and the far east of Russia, the geology of those areas showing that over time disparate pieces of land were 'glued on' to the existing shorelines.

In conclusion, although the general form of the landmasses that surround the Arctic Ocean can be said to derive from tectonic activity, primarily the sea-floor spreading of the mid-Atlantic Ridge and the subduction zone of the 'Ring of Fire' (see below), that is a simplification. The Arctic land masses exhibit a full range of igneous, sedimentary and metamorphic rocks, while the accretion of terranes, igneous intrusions and local geological history has created highly complex areas at the edges of the otherwise stable continental masses, these areas unfortunately not exhibiting simple geological boundaries.

Evidence in support of plate tectonics include the rocks of the mountain range folded by the Caledonian Orogeny in north-east Greenland (*above*, where they have been exposed at Badlanddalen after glaciation) and (*left*) at Hastein in northern Norway.

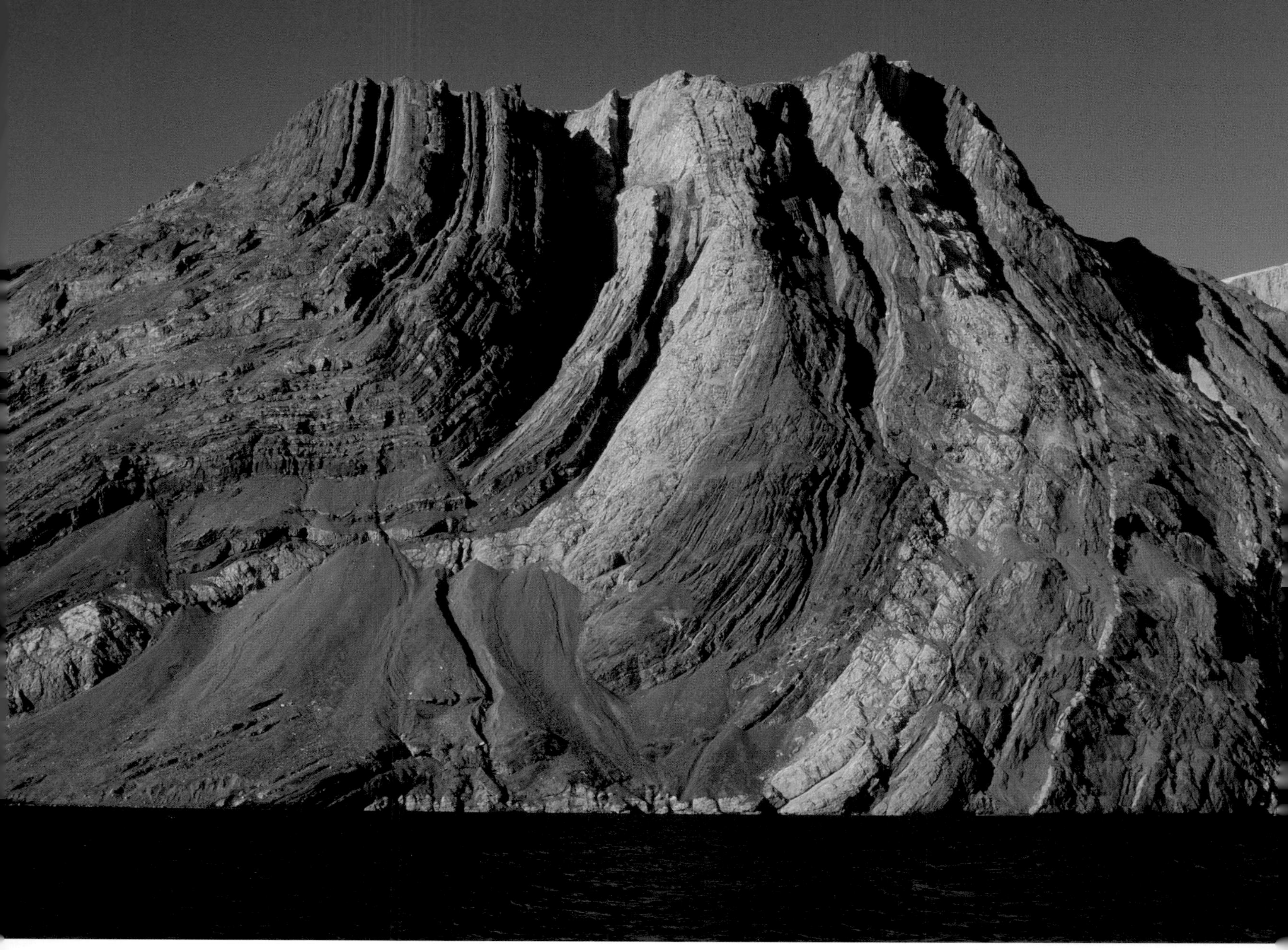

Contorted rock strata in Antarcticsund, north-east Greenland, illustrate the power of the forces which have shaped the Arctic.

Formation of the Arctic

VOLCANICITY AND SEISMICITY

The interaction of the crustal plates that make up the ocean beds and continents can take one of several forms. At spreading zones new ocean floor is created. If two spreading zones meet – the meeting point of three plates – then a ridge junction can form; an example occurs close to the Azores where the North American, African and Eurasian plates are being forced apart. Where two continental plates collide an intervening sea can be squeezed out of existence (e.g. the Mediterranean Sea, which is being lost as Africa moves into Eurasia) or mountains can be formed (e.g. the Himalayas, where the Indian and Eurasian plates meet). Where an oceanic plate collides with a continental plate, the lower, heavier oceanic plate dives beneath the continental, disappearing into the mantle where its material is recycled. Where plates slide relative to each other fault lines are created, giving rise to earthquake zones. California's San Andreas Fault and the Fairweather Fault in south-east Alaska occur where the Pacific plate slides past the North American plate. The tectonic activity of these plate interactions is manifested as volcanoes and earthquakes; both these phenomena have contributed to the physical form of the Arctic we see today and continue to be a feature of the area, both in the Nearctic (in Alaska and Kamchatka) and in the Palearctic (in Iceland and Jan Mayen).

Iceland's volcanic activity is well known. The activity – indeed, Iceland's very existence – arises because of its position above a hot plume in the mantle. The cause of such plumes is not well understood, but it is thought that they arise when hotter rock, perhaps of different chemical properties, rises from low in the mantle, leading to increased heating of the crustal layer and forming a larger dome than at, for instance, a spreading ridge. Many such plumes have now been identified around the world. Though they are chiefly associated with spreading ridges, they are not exclusive to these regions; the Hawaiian Islands, for example, have formed above a hot spot that lies virtually at the centre of the Pacific Plate. A hot spot has pushed the mid-Atlantic Ridge up to 2½km higher beneath Iceland than elsewhere, high enough to break the water's surface and so create an island. The plume has stayed stationary as North America and Eurasia have been pushed apart, with areas of cooled magma contributing to the geology of eastern Greenland and creating the famous features of the Giant's Causeway in northern Ireland and Fingal's Cave off the north-western coast of Scotland. The position of these features indicates the direction of the ocean-floor spreading that has separated Greenland from Europe. It is extraordinary that because of Iceland's position it is both volcanically active and home to four large ice caps, including one, Vatnajökull, which extends over 8,000km^2. The juxtaposition of volcanoes and ice is such

Evidence of volcanic activity abounds on Iceland. *Far left* is a bubbling mudpit at Krisuvik, close to the international airport at Keflavik, while *left* is a steaming hot water vent at Hveragerði, east of Reykjavik.

a feature of the island that it often leads to the well-worn, but reasonable, guide book description of 'land of ice and fire'.

The most famous of Iceland's volcanoes is Hekla, which dominates the country east of Reykjavik. Hekla's cone, now 1,491m high, has built up over the last 6,500 years, the last significant eruption being in 2000. After a devastating eruption in 1104, when ash destroyed many local settlements, the Icelanders believed that Hekla was an entrance to Hell; this may have influenced Jules Verne, who sent the heroes of his book *Journey to the Centre of the Earth* into the crater of Snæfellsjökull, a volcano north-west of Reykjavik across Faxaflói. But if these two volcanoes are the most famous on the island, another Icelandic eruption, at Laki, dwarfed anything they have mustered. The 1783–85 Laki eruption, emanating from a 32km fissure, produced a lava flow that covered more than 560km^2, the largest in historical times (and the largest ever witnessed by human eyes). It is estimated that 12km^3 of rock, chiefly basaltic lava (about 2½ times that produced by the 1955 Mauna Loa eruption), was ejected by the Laki eruption. The eruption also produced some pyroclasts (unconsolidated material fragmented by the explosion), chiefly tephra. The flow engulfed many settlements, but the direct loss of life was nothing in comparison to that which occurred subsequently. It is estimated that 70 million tons of acid were belched out by Laki, this falling as a toxic blanket that poisoned the Icelandic soil. Millions of tons of dust blotted out the Sun, causing crop failure in areas far from the poisoned soil and leading to the 'haze of hunger', a famine in which a significant proportion of the Icelandic population died. Some historians believe that the poor harvests in northern Europe resulting from the Laki eruption were a contributory cause of the French Revolution.

The 1996 *jökulhlaup*

On 5 November 1996 an estimated 4km^3 of water and one million tons of ice engulfed Iceland's southern coast. At the height of the release 50,000m^3 of water per second flowed from Grímsvötn's caldera. Because of the nature of the flooded land, damage was chiefly limited to power lines and the coastal road – the latter was re-opened within two weeks. Because of the volcanic nature of Iceland such an event, which might at first glance appear unique or, at the least, very infrequent, is actually familiar enough to Icelanders to have been given a name – *jökulhlaup* (glacier flood). Such events are not restricted to Iceland or even to volcanic areas, as there are other processes that may give rise to ice-dammed reservoirs.

Another well-known volcanic event in Iceland took place in November 1963. A plume of steam rose from the sea to the south of Vestmannaeyjar (the Westmann Islands), which lie off Iceland's southern coast. The eruption would continue for three years, and it gave birth to the Earth's newest land, the island of Surtsey. Surtsey is a shield volcano, one created by relatively short-term lava flows – of the order of months or years – which therefore have relatively shallow flanks (2–8°) that fall away symmetrically from a central crater. A commoner volcano form is the strato or composite, a volcano that comprises layers of lava and tephra built up over thousands or millions of years, and which are therefore of increasing thickness as the cone is approached. Mainland Iceland has many examples of both forms. Ten years after the creation of Surtsey, in January 1973 on the nearby island of Heimaey, a new mountain, Eldfell was created when lava flowed from a 1½km fissure. The island's inhabitants were evacuated, some of their houses being saved by the pumping of seawater on to the lava's front edge to create a rock dam.

In September 1996, on the Icelandic mainland, the volcano Grímsvötn erupted through a 4km fissure beneath the Vatnajökull ice cap. Vatnajökull is Europe's largest ice sheet, but it sits astride the mid-Atlantic Ridge. The ice melted by the volcanic eruption created a vast water-filled chamber within the ice cap, which threatened to create a tidal wave of water when it escaped. Fortunately the *jökulhlaup* at Grímsvötn did not occur until November, by which time those at risk had been relocated and no lives were lost.

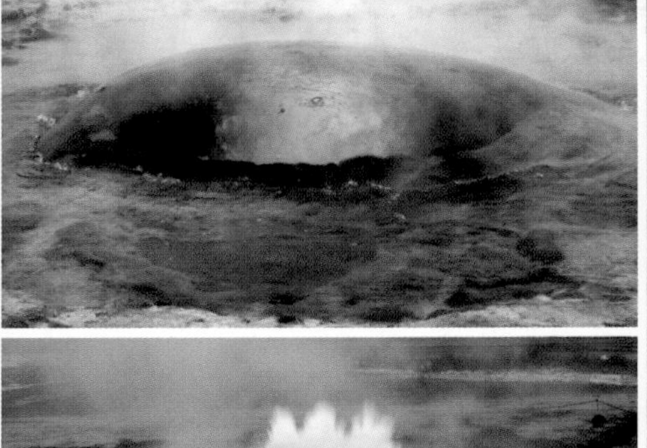

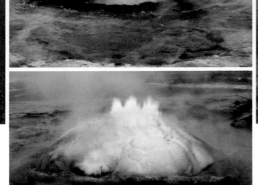

Individual geysers have different, sometimes highly complex, mechanisms, but they are all variations on a theme. The geyser has a main pipe, which reaches the surface, connected to a myriad of feeder pipes at depth. Water flowing into the base of the main pipe from the feeders is pressurised, and heated by the geothermal energy. It is superheated, i.e. above the normal boiling point of water, and maintained liquid by its pressure. As it reaches the main pipe the pressure falls and the inflowing water flashes to steam. The water already in the main pipe is heated when this steam condenses, but eventually reaches boiling point itself. Now the steam bubbles produced by the feed water cannot condense and so rise through the water column. Eventually the accumulation of bubbles is such that they coalesce and act as a piston, forcing the water above them out of the pipe explosively. After the eruption, which vents the system, the cycle begins again.

In addition to these intermittent, but highly explosive, indications of the hot plume that gave birth to Iceland, there are other volcanic phenomena that make the island popular with tourists. Sulphur-rich hot water has been harnessed for home heating and swimming pools – the latter most famously at the Blue Lagoon – as well as for geothermal power plants; bubbling mud pools are a highlight of trips to Krisuvik and Hveragerði; and the original *geyser*, the one that gave its name to the form, can be seen at Geysir, to the east of Reykjavik. To the north of Iceland, Jan Mayen lies above another hot spot of the mid-Atlantic Ridge, though in this case the activity is much more limited, being essentially limited to a single volcano.

Subduction

When an oceanic plate converges with a continental plate, the denser oceanic plate dives beneath the lighter continental. The movement, known as subduction, results from the same processes that drive the separation of plates at a spreading zone (i.e. currents in the mantle), but the subducting plate is also dragged by the disappearing slab as it drops into the asthenosphere. If the slab breaks away from the parent plate the drag ceases, but the slab can continue to exert an influence by suction. Where the subducting plate disappears it pulls the over-lying continental plate down, creating a deep trench. The existence of such trenches had been known before study of plate tectonics provided a mechanism for their creation.

Subduction creates a zone where both earthquakes and volcanoes can occur. A subducted plate bends as it disappears, with the distortion creating fault lines, movement of which may result in earthquakes. These earthquakes may occur at substantial distances below the Earth's surface, as deep as several hundred kilometres. Earthquakes also occur as a consequence of the dragging of the overlying plate by the subducting plate. Volcanoes result from partial melting of the subducted plate as it reaches a critical depth, with lighter fractions melting and rising as 'blobs' of magma which, if they reach the surface, result in volcanoes. Water may assist the process; trapped water dragged down from the ocean becomes superheated. As it rises through the mantle it causes local melting, with the rising pools of molten rock in which the water is trapped erupting if they reach the Earth's surface.

Volcanic events in the region

The Aleutian Islands lay along a line where the Pacific Plate is subducted beneath North America, as is Russia's Kamchatka Peninsula, formed where the Pacific Plate is subducted beneath the Eurasian; up to 7cm of the Pacific Plate is subducted annually. The arc of volcanoes and seismically active landmasses around the Pacific Ocean caused by subduction of the Pacific plate is given the somewhat fanciful (but not entirely inappropriate) name of the 'Ring of Fire'.

Alaska

In June 1912 the volcanoes of Katmai and Novarupta, on the Alaska Peninsula, south-west of Anchorage, ejected 20km^3 of pyroclasts – chiefly rhyolitic-andesitic tephra – in one of the most productive eruptions of historic times. Before the eruption Katmai was a 2,285m glaciated, cratered peak; after the event the peak's height had been reduced by around 800m and a caldera 4km across and up to 1,000m deep had been created. On Novarupta the eruptions were from fissures as well as from the summit crater. It is said that for several days after the eruption people on nearby Kodiak Island could not see more than a metre ahead, so thick was the air-borne debris. The debris cloaked virtually the entire northern hemisphere, lowering mean monthly temperatures by several degrees and effectively eliminating the summer. The area around the peaks now forms the Katmai National Park. One feature is the evocatively named Valley of 10,000 Smokes, named by Robert Grigg, leader of a National Geographic Society expedition to the area in 1916. Grigg named the valley after observing the numerous steam vents from the Katmai Pass.

The 1964 Alaskan earthquake raised or lowered more than 250,000km^2 of land. It was caused by slippage of the North American Plate over the Pacific Plate, but the reasons for local subsidence and expansion, or of uplift, were not clear on any geological models of the time. It was subsequently discovered that the Earth's crust is not rigid but elastic, and so capable of being both stretched and compressed. Following a major earthquake in the Anchorage area, the North American Plate becomes locked in a new position along its slip plane with the Pacific Plate. Subduction of the latter causes a compression of the former, the compression causing local doming and, hence, an uplift. Eventually a breaking point is reached, with the North American Plate unlocking and slipping – and another major earthquake results. The overriding slab causes a local uplift while the compressed, domed area rebounds, causing a subsidence. Investigation on Middleton Island after the 1964 quake showed a succession of uplift terraces, proving that there had been a number of earlier earthquakes along the same fault line. Carbon dating of driftwood from these terraces indicated that major earthquakes such as the 1964 event occur on average every 800 years.

Although the tsunamis initiated by the 1964 quake were significant, they cannot compare with another earthquake-generated wave that occurred just a few years earlier. In 1958 a quake released an estimated 40 million cubic metres of rock

into Lituya Bay (part of the Glacier Bay National Park). Following the slump a wave crossed the bay at around 200km/h and left a 'tidemark' some 500m up the opposite cliff. The wave destroyed 10km^2 of forest and killed two fishermen, whose boats it swamped.

As well as these headline-grabbing events Alaska also exhibits less well-known evidence of volcanic activity, most particularly the *maars* that form the Devil Mountain Lakes at the northern end of the Seward Peninsula (a short distance south of Cape Espenberg and the Arctic Circle). A maar occurs where rising magma reaches an area of porous rock saturated with ground water. The steam produced causes a rise in internal pressure, and eventually the ground above fails, rather in the way that a cork 'erupts' from a champagne bottle. The maar results in an essentially circular crater surrounded by the plug material, and it often fills with water to produce a lake. Most maars are about 700m in diameter, but the Seward Peninsula lakes are several kilometres across; they are the largest maars to have been discovered to date. They have also been extremely important in recreating the vegetation of Beringia as the ejected material was a plug of permafrost which included the surface material.

These shots are of Strokkur at Geysir, Iceland. At the left of the photographs on p32 is the start of a new cycle, the water level in the eruption pipe being well below the surface. In the upper of the two central photographs on p32 the bubble of water being driven by the steam in the lower pipe can be seen. In the lower of the two central photographs the steam driving the water bubble becomes apparent; surface tension is holding the steam in place, but only just. In the right-hand photograph on p32 the steam has erupted through the water bubble, though surface tension is still holding the bubble edge intact. The photographs on this page show the final stages of the eruption.

The 1964 Alaska Earthquake

On 27 March 1964 (which happened to be Good Friday) an earthquake struck Alaska. The now-accepted magnitude of the earthquake is 8.6 on the Richter Scale, but seismographs actually registered readings varying from 8.2 to 9.2. The quake's epicentre was at the northern end of Prince William Sound, to the east of Anchorage, roughly midway between Valdez and Portage. Earth movements and landslips were accompanied by significant tsunamis, some waves reaching 50m which engulfed and destroyed parts of Kodiak, Valdez and Seward. At Portage the ground subsided by 2m and was swamped by seawater from the Turnagain Arm. When it became clear that Portage would be flooded at all subsequent high tides the settlement was abandoned. Pine forests were killed by the inundation of salt water. After the quake, survey teams discovered that the local area had not only subsided, it had also expanded horizontally. However, at Cordova, some 100km east of Portage, the local area had been raised by 2m; high tides no longer filled the harbour, leaving some fishing boats above the new high-tide mark. Even more dramatically, on the island of Middleton, 150km south of Cordova, a wrecked Liberty ship that could not be reached without a boat, even at the lowest tide, was lifted 9m, clear of the water. Large areas of the continental shelf close to Cordova and Seward were also raised permanently above the high-tide mark. The earthquake claimed the lives of 107 people in Alaska.

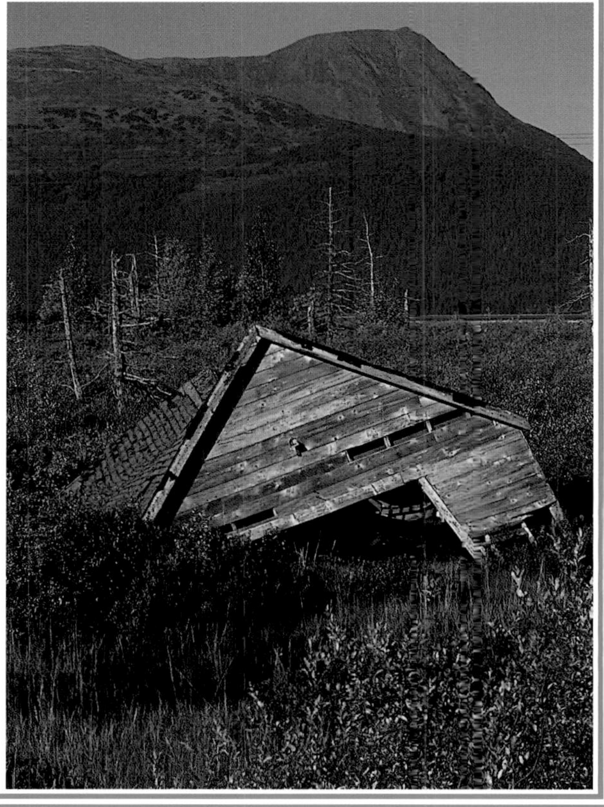

The 1964 Alaska Earthquake

Right
Looking east along Fourth Avenue, Anchorage.

Below right
A startling illustration of the power of seismic events. At Whittier a 6 by 2inch (15 x 5cm) plank of wood was driven right through a 10-ply tyre.

Below left
A contemporary photograph of dead trees at Girdwood. The trees were inundated and killed by salt water.

Kamchatka

On the Russian side of the Bering Strait, subduction of the Pacific Plate beneath the Eurasian Plate has created the arc of volcanoes along the Kamchatka Peninsula. The arc has about 60 active or potentially active volcanoes, and many more that are now extinct. The Kamchatka arc is more than 700km long and responsible for about 20% of the total material ejected each year by the Earth's volcanic activity.

Of recent Kamchatka events, the most spectacular was the 1956 eruption of the Bezymianny volcano in the northern peninsula. Best-estimate calculations suggest that the volcano ejected a stream of incandescent tephra at more than 500m/s

Above
Alaska's evocatively named Valley of 10,000 Smokes.

Below
Avachinsky volcano in southern Kamchatka.

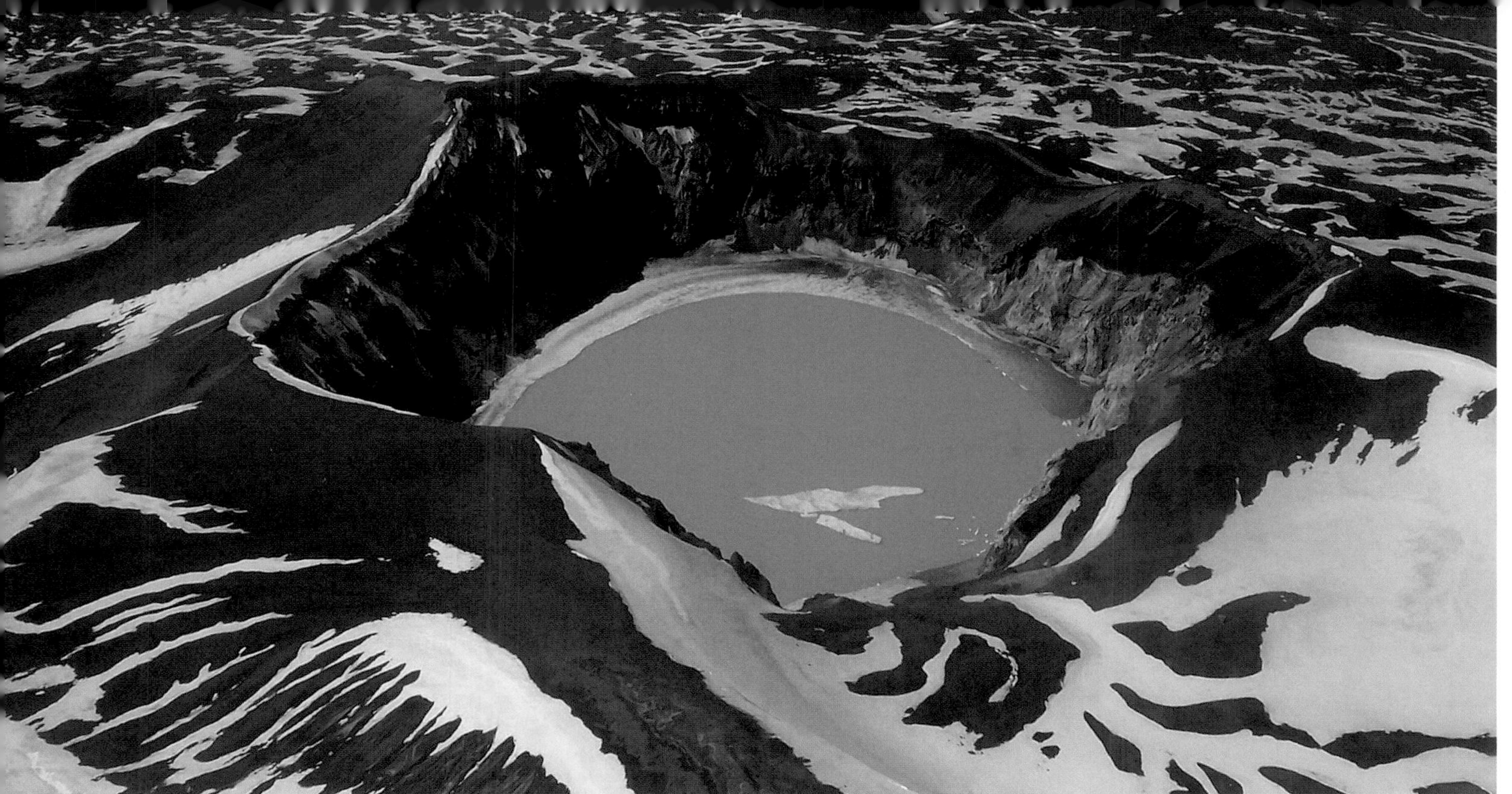

The most impressive of the volcanic scenery of Kamchatka, including the Uzon Caldera and the Valley of the Geysers, lies within the Kronotsky National Park. A massive mudslide in 2007 seemed to have destroyed the Valley, but it is now thought that it will recover.

(i.e. about twice the speed of sound), which reached an altitude of 45km. Volcanic dust reached the UK – almost exactly halfway around the Earth – in just 72 hours. Before the eruption Bezymianny had been a 3,085m volcano. The eruption reduced its height by 200m; a huge caldera had also been created. Another Kamchatka eruption, of the peninsula's highest volcano, the 4,750m Klyuchevskoy in October 1994, ejected so much ash that international flights between North America and Asia were disrupted for many days. Between these two events the eruption of Plosky Tolbachik over a 17-month period in 1975–76 produced in excess of 2km^3 of basaltic lava.

In addition to its volcanoes, many of which are textbook cones, Kamchatka has an array of huge geysers in the appropriately named Valley of the Geysers, and the Uzon Caldera, which exhibits mud volcanoes, hot mud pots and crater lakes, sulphur-rich hot streams and associated thermophilic micro-organisms.

Figure 2.3

The Arctic Basin. The depth contours are labelled in metres.

The Arctic Basin

North of Iceland, the mid-Atlantic Ridge continues towards the North Pole, separating Svalbard and north-eastern Greenland, then continuing as the 1,500km Nansen-Gakkel Ridge, which rises 2,000m above the sea bed. The seismically active area of Siberia's Verkhoyanskiy Mountains are on a continuation of this ridge (though the mountains also lie between tectonic areas of the Siberian platform and the micro-continents of far eastern Siberia). The Nansen-Gakkel is one of several ridges making up the geologically complex Arctic Basin (Figure 2.3). Running parallel to it are the Lomonosov Ridge, which lies beneath the pole itself, and the Alpha Cordillera/Mendeleyev Ridge, which forms an arc extending from northern Ellesmere Island to Wrangel Island. The Lomonosov Ridge is even larger than the Nansen-Gakkel, extending for 1,800km and rising 3,000m above the sea bed, but its formation is not well understood, current opinion suggesting it is made of felsic (i.e. continental) rock. The Basin's ridges define deep oceanic basins: the Nansen Basin, between the Barents Sea and the Nansen-Gakkel Ridge; the Fram (or, occasionally, Amundsen) Basin between the Nansen-Gakkel and Lomonosov ridges; the Makarov Basin between the Lomonosov and Alpha/Mendeleyev ridges; and the Canadian Basin between the Alpha Cordillera and Alaska/Canada. Sampling of the basins suggests they are from 60–135 million years old and that they were indeed formed by sea-floor spreading. These young but deep basins – at its deepest the Fram Basin is almost 4,500m in depth and the Makarov exceeds 4,000m, while the other basins are all at least 3,000m deep – are ringed by shallower seas, which lie above the continental shelves.

The continental shelves of Eurasia are extensive, reaching to and beyond Svalbard and the islands of Arctic Russia. The shelves occupy 35% of the area of the Arctic Ocean, yet account for only 2% of the water volume. The Siberian shelf, which forms part of the Eurasian shelf, is the world's widest, being up to 900km wide. The seas that overlie the Eurasian shelves are defined by the islands bordering them the Barents Sea between Svalbard, Franz Josef Land and Novaya Zemlya; the Kara Sea from Novaya Zemlya to Severnaya Zemlya (though many would define the Kara's eastern edge as the Taimyr Peninsula); the Laptev Sea between Severnaya Zemlya and the islands of Novosibirskiye Ostrova (the New Siberian Islands); the East Siberian Sea as far east as Wrangel Island; and the Chukchi Sea at the northern end of the Bering Strait, between the Chukchi Peninsula, Wrangel Island and northern Alaska. These seas are shallow, being only 10–20m deep in the west; the East Siberian and Chukchi Seas are 30–40m deep. Though similar in terms of depth and the width of the underlying shelves, the seas differ markedly. The Barents Sea has the mildest climate because of the influence of the North Atlantic Drift. The White Sea, in western Russia, is an almost completely enclosed shallow sea, connected by the narrow Gorlo Strait to the Barents Sea. Its climate is more continental than the Barents, with warmer summers but colder winters – sea ice occasionally persists for more than six months of the year.

The islands of Novaya Zemlya act as a barrier to the eastern transfer of the Drift's warm waters, so the climate of the Kara Sea is much colder. While the mean January temperature of air above the Barents Sea is -10°C, the mean temperature above the western Kara is -15°C, falling to -30°C at the eastern side. The climate of the Laptev Sea is much more benign. The warm-water outflow from the huge rivers that discharge into the sea cause the sea ice to melt, the enhanced heat pick-up of the dark open water creating positive feedback, so in summer the sea can be ice-free to 77°N. Some areas also remain ice-free throughout the winter. For this reason, the Laptev population of Walrus is the most northerly in the world. Further east, the minimal river flow into the East Siberian Sea means it experiences a harsher climate. The Chukchi Sea is colder in winter, but warm water passing through the Bering Straits promotes significant summer melting of ice.

To the west of the Barents Sea the deeper Greenland Sea (more than 2,000m deep) separates Greenland and Svalbard. The sea represents the widest breach in the continental landmasses surrounding the Arctic Basin. The Greenland Sea merges into the Norwegian Sea (which is just as deep), the name given to the body of water that washes the western coast of Norway. Conventionally, the Norwegian Sea extends west as far as Jan Mayen and south as far as the Faroe Islands.

The North American continental shelf is generally considered to be less extensive than that of Asia (though as the shelf underlies the Canadian Arctic islands the contention is arguable). Baffin Bay, between Greenland and Baffin Island, is deeper (over 1,000m), as is the Beaufort Sea (over 3,000m at its northern extreme), which washes the northern coast of Alaska (east of Point Barrow) and Canada's Yukon and North West Territories. The shelf beneath the Beaufort Sea is certainly less extensive than that beneath the Chukchi Sea bordering it.

Ancient life in the Arctic

As well as some of the Earth's oldest rocks, evidence of some of the Earth's oldest life forms has been found in the Arctic, in the banded ironstone formations of western Greenland. The existence of these organisms was inferred by measuring the ratio of carbon isotopes, though organisms with the appearance of grains of rice – but a thousand times smaller – have been detected in rocks similar in both age and geology at Barberton, South Africa. This early life, dating to 3,800 million years ago, probably existed only near thermal springs. By about 3,500 million years ago life forms capable of harnessing the energy of the Sun by photosynthesis had evolved. These were cyanobacteria; they created stromatolites, layered calcareous structures formed from mats of cyanobacteria. Stromatolites are found in many places within the Arctic. At the Arctic fringe, on the shore of the eastern arm of Canada's Great Slave Lake, a superb fossil reef chamfered by the ice of the last ice age has been dated to about 2,000 million years ago.

Fossils from more recent geological periods can be found all over the Arctic. Perhaps the best destination for Arctic fossil hunters is Spitsbergen. Spitsbergen is a geologist's dream; the lack of overlying vegetation allows the rock to be readily examined, while strata from PreCambrian times to the Tertiary are exposed across the island, and they are often rich in fossils. Cambrian and Ordovician rocks yield marine invertebrates – trilobites, brachiopods and graptolites, while from the Silurian and Devonian come armoured fish – pteraspids and cephalaspids. Early 'true' (bony) fish have been found in rocks of late Devonian age. At that time the land that was to become Spitsbergen lay much closer to the Equator. In the Carboniferous and Permian, Spitsbergen was an area of shallow seas and swamps, with luxuriant vegetation that became the island's coal measures. From Spitsbergen's Triassic and Jurassic rocks there are ammonites and fossils of marine reptiles, such as pliosaurs, while Cretaceous rocks sometimes contain the fossilised bones and footprints of dinosaurs. During the Tertiary Spitsbergen was again cloaked in forests, these producing further coal measures, the coal occasionally yielding beautiful leaf fossils.

Below left
Fossilised corals, Nordaustlandet, Svalbard.

Below right
Stromatolites on the eastern arm of the Great Slave Lake, North West Territories, Canada.

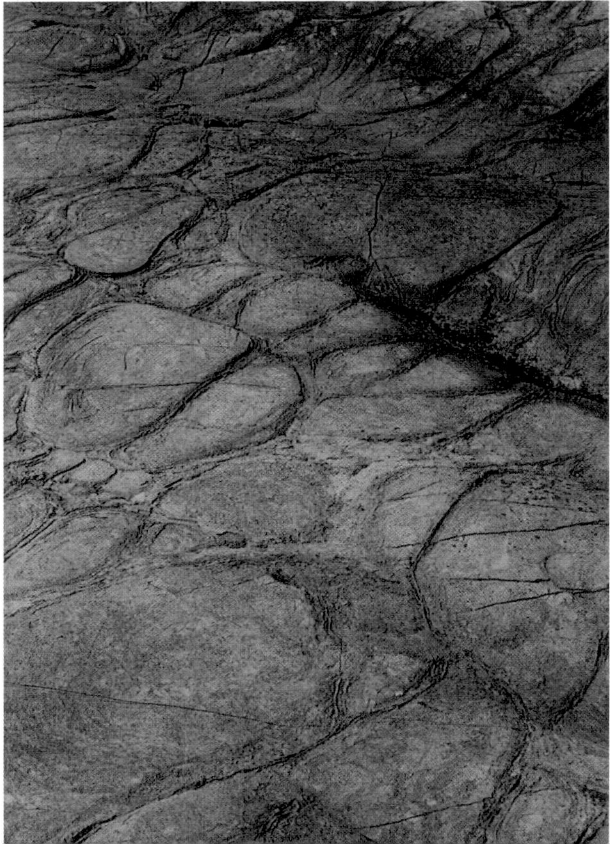

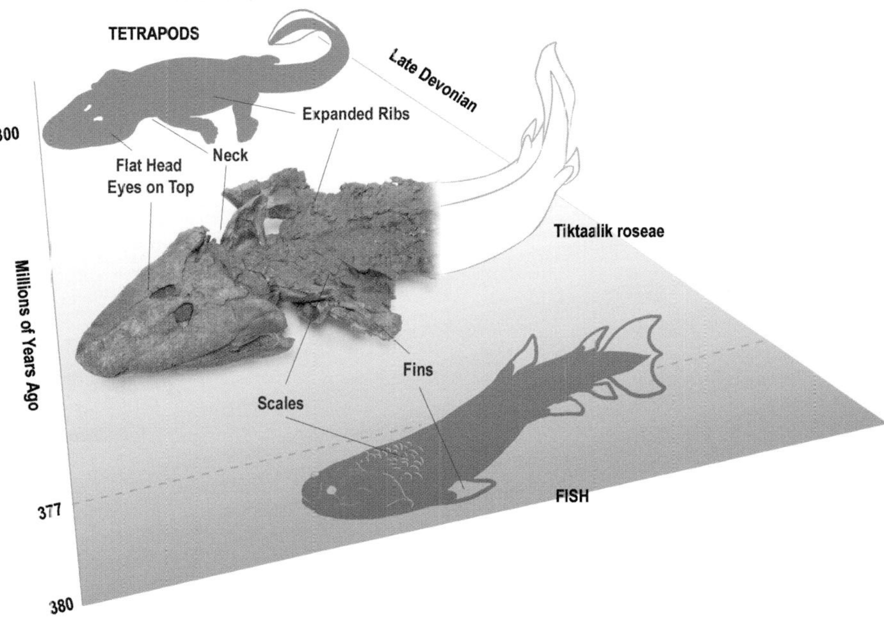

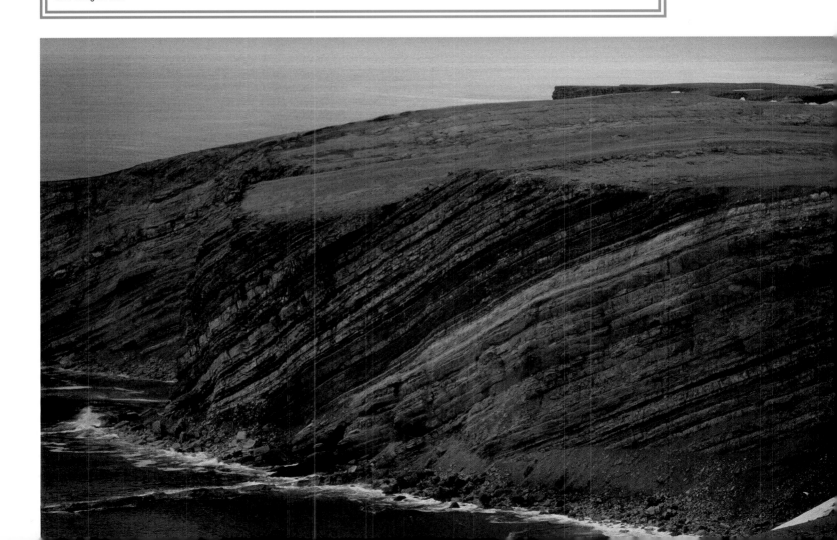

Transitional tetrapods in the Arctic

Although Spitsbergen is rich in fossils, without doubt the most important Arctic finds have come from eastern Greenland and Ellesmere Island. Late Devonian deposits there have yielded a stunning array of primitive tetrapods, intermediate between fish and the first terrestrial vertebrates, the amphibians. The first such find was made in 1931 by a Danish team. They found the fossils of *Ichthyostega*, a 1.5m long animal that paddled through the swamps of Greenland 365 million years ago. While mainly aquatic, it had a range of adaptations to deal with the lack of buoyancy on land, such as a well-developed shoulder and hip girdle, and sturdy ribs. Each of its feet bore seven fingers, but another animal from east Greenlandic deposits of a similar age had an amazing eight toes on each foot. This animal, *Acanthostega*, was more fish-like than *Icthyostega*; it lacked a functional wrist, and was poorly adapted for terrestrial movement, but instead was probably a paddler in weedy swamps. It is possible that both these species hauled themselves on to land, perhaps to bask in the manner of modern Marine Iguanas.

However, perhaps the most remarkable of all fossils from this early period in tetrapod evolution was found in 2006 on Ellesmere. Named *Tiktaalik roseae*, this animal was some 10 million years older than *Ichthyostega* and represents a true transitional form; similar in many respects to a lobe-finned fish, with fish-like fins instead of toes, *Tiktaalik* had front skeletal elements more like those of a crocodile, with a functional shoulder and wrist that may have been able to support the animal on land. It also had a mobile 'neck', giving it freedom to hunt in shallow water, and had both lungs and gills. Palaeontologists believe that *Tiktaalik* was specialised for life in shallow stream systems, perhaps in swamps, and it may have been able to move overland using its fins.

Above left
***Tiktaalik roseae*, the important fossil discovered on Ellesmere Island in 2006.**

Above right
***Tiktaalik*'s assumed position on the evolutionary scale from fish to land-living creatures.**

Below
Layered strata at Landnordingsvika, Bear Island.

Rock formations at Bellsund on Spitsbergen, Svalbard.

The Formation of Antarctica

Long ago, Antarctica formed part of Gondwanaland, a southerly landmass that also included Australia, South America and the Indian subcontinent. Initially Gondwanaland was part of Pangaea, but about 250 million years ago it broke away. At around the same time the Indian subcontinent broke away from the rest of Gondwanaland and began to move north, eventually colliding with Eurasia to begin the process that would see the world's highest mountains form on the border between the two plates. To the south, about 44 million years ago, Australia split from South America/Antarctica. Antarctica began to move over the South Pole. The link between South America and Antarctica was slender, so when the latter came to a halt over the pole, South America broke free, the rift filling to form the last section of the Southern Ocean some 35 million years ago. The Falkland Islands, South Georgia and the South American continent were left north of the rift, while the South Orkneys and Antarctica remained to the south. Spreading zone activity in the Southern Ocean is evident in the volcanic islands of the South Shetlands and in Bouvet Island, which owes its existence to its position above a hot plume. Deception Island is one of the most visited of the South Shetland Islands. There is a huge colony of Chinstrap Penguins close to rocky Bailey Head, and the flooded caldera offers one of Antarctica's more unusual spectacles. The caldera is entered through Neptune's Bellows, a 400m gap in the volcanic wall – a gap which is actually made much narrower by a huge rock just a few metres below the surface approximately halfway along its length, which forces ships to follow a route close to the northern wall. Once inside the caldera, visitors can wander among the gaunt ruins of old whaling and research stations, or swim in waters warmed by volcanic activity; Deception Island is by no means dormant, with major eruptions in the 1960s forcing the British to abandon their station.

Evidence for continuing tectonic activity in Antarctica exists in the active volcanoes of Erebus, Terror and Melbourne, which are chemically similar to the rocks of the spreading zone of the African Rift Valley. This suggests that in time the continent will separate into a western section, which will include the Antarctic Peninsula, Ellsworth Land and the area around the Ross Sea, and an eastern section. Geologically, east Antarctica comprises PreCambrian shield rocks, which are common to other parts of ancient Gondwanaland including western Australia, southern Africa, southern South America and India. These shield rocks are extremely ancient, dating back almost 4,000 million years. As in the Arctic, geological research in Antarctica was important in developing theories of plate tectonics. Geologists on the Scott and Shackleton expeditions of the early 20th century discovered Palaeozoic fossils beneath the Beardmore Glacier and, later, *Glossopteris* fossils. Alexander Du Toit predicted that if Gondwanaland really had existed as a supercontinent, then rocks similar to the folded strata of the Cape Fold Belt near Cape Town must appear in western Antarctica. Although mountains had been seen in the right area by Lincoln Ellsworth during his 1935 transcontinental flight, it was not until 1958 that the area was explored and examined geologically. Twenty years after Du Toit's prediction, the Ellsworth Mountains (as the range is called) were confirmed as a continuation of the Cape Fold Belt. The exact nature of this orogeny, dated to the early Mesozoic, which formed the Ellsworth Mountains and was responsible for not only the Cape Fold Belt in South Africa but the folded strata of central Argentina, is not well understood as it appears to have occurred within Gondwanaland, i.e. within a plate rather than at a plate boundary.

Between the strata of this orogeny and the East Antarctic Shield lie the Transantarctic Mountains, which date from a much earlier period of mountain building – the Ross Orogeny of the early Palaeozoic era, which is assumed to have resulted from the subduction of the Pacific Plate beneath the continental shield rocks. The Ellsworth Orogeny might then have been created after the accretion of further material from a similar, later subduction. On the side of the Ellsworth Orogeny strata, the rocks of Antarctic Peninsula and the western coast of the Ross Sea were formed during the Andean Orogeny of the late Mesozoic/early Tertiary, when subduction of the Pacific Plate again accreted material on to Antarctica. The same subduction also saw the formation of the Andes mountains in South America.

Antarctica represents the harshest climate on Earth, the coldest temperature ever recorded being -89.2°C at Russia's Vostock base. The base is set at 3,488m above sea level and almost 1,400km from the sea; this position means that the highest temperature ever recorded there is -22°C. Antarctica is cold, very cold. However, the assumption that this cold derives from the continent's position above the South Pole, and that the lack of plant and animal life is a direct result, is not entirely correct. The mean annual temperature at the South Pole is -50°C (compared to the mean at the North Pole of about -18°C). The profound difference between the two is due to the absence of any substantial heat flux from the oceans to Antarctica. In the north, warm Atlantic and Pacific waters moderate the climate of the Arctic. In the south the currents of the Southern Ocean, continuously circulating Antarctica while absorbing little energy from the Sun, prevent the warmer waters of the north from influencing the continent's climate.

Only after South America broke free of Antarctica was the Southern Ocean able to circulate the Earth uninterrupted, and it is since then that the continent's climate has cooled. Prior to this break-up, as fossils indicate, there were large areas of forest on the continent. Even five million years ago, flowering plants covered significant areas of inland Antarctica. Today there are mosses and lichens on the continental mainland, but only two species of flowering plant. Fossils of dinosaurs have been found on Antarctica; later, the ancestors of the marsupials that now inhabit South America and Australia occurred there, the continent forming a bridge between the two ends of Gondwanaland. Today there are no terrestrial mammals: indeed, mainland Antarctica has no resident tetrapods at all. Those that occur there, birds and seals, visit only to breed, spending the winter further north.

Paradise Bay, Antarctic Peninsula.

3. Snow and Ice

Although plate tectonics organised the landmasses that surround the Arctic Ocean, it is snow and ice that have shaped the landscape. Here we explore these two substances, each of which is more complex and fascinating than might at first be apparent.

Frost and snow

Add heat to most solids and they melt into liquid. With further heating, the liquid boils to form a gas. Water is different, for although it usually follows this standard 'three phase' model – changing from ice to liquid water to steam – it can also transfer from the gaseous phase to the solid phase, and *vice versa*, directly. The transformation from ice to water vapour is called sublimation: the product of vapour transforming directly to solid is known as hoar-frost. Although hoar-frost differs from true frost, the two forms are occasionally difficult to distinguish. It is not necessary to travel to the Arctic to see hoar-frost formation; it can occur in temperate areas, though this may also be frozen dew. Dew is formed close to the ground when water droplets condense from vapour-saturated air. (The highest temperature of a surface at which this can occur is known as the 'dew point'.) If the dew freezes – which usually happens only if the temperature falls below about -3°C – it forms 'silver frost', so called to differentiate it from hoar-frost: to further complicate matters, plants may also produce guttation drops, water droplets exuded from leaf tips during nights with cool air but warm soil temperatures. The frosting of window panes is a more definite sign of hoar-frost, with the spidery webs of frost forming on a dry pane.

One of the most familiar demonstrations of hoar-frost for the Arctic traveller is 'diamond dust', the gentle, glittering fall of thousands of minute ice crystals (typically less than 0.2mm across), which occurs from cloud-free skies in very low temperatures (usually below -30°C). Rarer, but even more awe-inspiring and breathtakingly beautiful, is the diamond dust that sparkles in the light of the moon. Diamond dust is often the basis of parhelia.

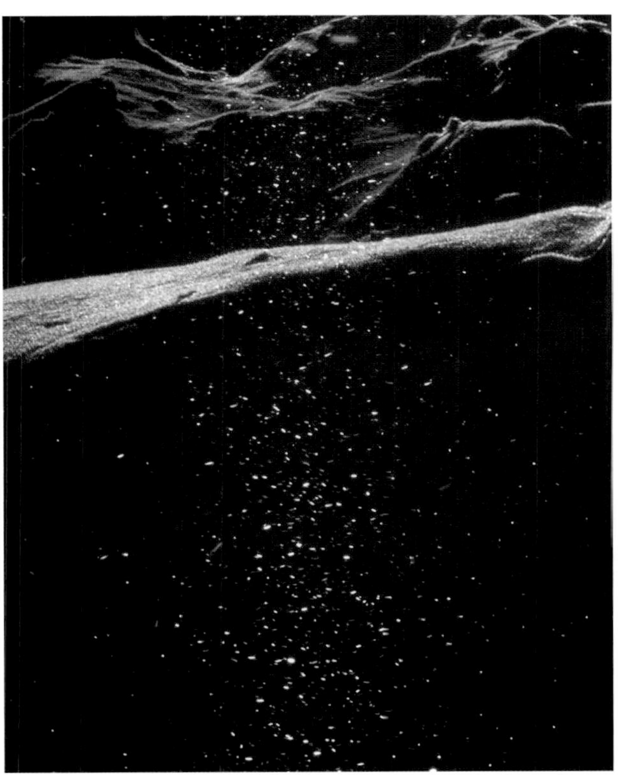

Diamond dust is difficult to photograph, especially with a digital camera which has a restricted latitude compared to film, resulting in the delicate shimmering light tending to be reproduced as larger blobs.

The forms of precipitation

The droplets of water rising through a cloud may freeze, but they may also remain as water. Small droplets collide and coalesce and eventually fall. If the droplets remain large they fall as rain. Rain falls if the droplets have diameters greater than 0.5mm. If the droplets have diameters of 0.2–0.5mm the precipitation is technically 'drizzle'. Droplets of diameter below 0.2mm form a mist. Meteorologists also differentiate between forms of rain based on the rate of precipitation; if the rate is below 0.5mm/hour the rain is 'slight'. For rates of 0.5–4mm/hour the rainfall is 'moderate', while if the rate is above 4mm/hour the rainfall is termed 'heavy'.

People often think that snow is frozen rain, but this is not the case. Frozen rain drops, usually mixed with melting snow, fall as sleet. This is a British term: in the United States the normal term for frozen rain is 'ice pellets'. However, this is not an entirely useful term as there is another form of precipitation that perhaps fits this description better – hail. Hail is produced by the collision and coalescing of supercooled water droplets, or by snowflakes accumulating water. Hail is generally assumed to consist of ice droplets with diameters greater than 5mm, with sleet or ice pellets being smaller.

Snowflakes

Within clouds, small water droplets are swept upwards by rising air. As air temperature falls with height the water droplets may become supercooled; that is, they reach a temperature below the freezing point of water. The supercooled droplets may be triggered to freeze into ice crystals by the presence of minute dust particles, which act as nucleation centres. The accumulation of many such crystals as they collide and coalesce forms a snowflake.

Snowflakes are usually about 1–2mm across. Their amazing beauty was first described following naked-eye observations in the early 17th century by French philosopher René Descartes and German astronomer Johannes Kepler, both of whom described the hexagonal (six-fold) shape that is such a feature of the flakes. However, the complex nature of the symmetry of individual flakes was not unravelled until the invention of the microscope; in 1665 the English scientist Robert Hooke published drawings of snowflakes from microscope observations. Over 150 years later William Scoresby made a series of superb drawings of snowflakes he observed during whaling voyages to north-east Greenland. Scoresby noted that Arctic snowflakes were much more symmetric than those he had observed in his native Britain.

The symmetry of snowflakes results from the crystalline structure of ice, which derives from the way that the hydrogen and oxygen atoms that make up a water molecule interact. Ice crystals can actually take several forms but the commonest – and the only form that can exist outside conditions of extreme pressure and very low temperatures – is a hexagonal lattice, given the prosaic name 1h by snow scientists. The hexagonal lattice of the 1h crystal gives the snowflake its six-fold symmetry. 1h also forms the basis of the rarer 12-sided and triangular

Opposite page **Iceberg frozen into Storfjorden, Svalbard in mid-winter.**

Are all snowflakes different?

An oft-heard tale is that no two snowflakes are identical. This is, of course, not provable, but is very likely to be true. The 'standard' form of the hydrogen atom comprises a single electron orbiting a nucleus that consists of a single proton. But in a small percentage of hydrogen atoms the nucleus comprises a proton and a neutron. This form (or isotope) is known as deuterium. As there are also several isotopes of oxygen, there are a number of different forms of water molecule. Each snowflake is composed of millions upon millions of molecules, the different forms of which vary the crystal structure in a minuscule but cumulatively significant way. The isotopic make-up of the molecules forming the crystal is random, so even though humidity and temperature can be considered constant across every flake, the minute differences are sufficient to create different shapes. The chances of two snowflakes being the same are, therefore, infinitesimally small.

snowflakes, with the former created by the coalescing of two six-sided flakes. The latter are more difficult to explain; larger triangles are probably produced by the splitting of a six-sided flake, but the smaller ones are more puzzling. The drawings of Scoresby show the variety of shapes that hexagonal symmetry offers; though many are stars, there are also columnar forms – cubes, six-sided prisms and strange dumb-bells, with hexagonal 'weights' at the ends (and sometimes also in the middle) of six-sided 'bars'. Formation of snowflakes under laboratory conditions has shown that the different shapes relate to differences in the temperature and saturation level of the cloud. In general, columnar flakes form in relatively low saturation atmospheres, with plate-like flakes being produced at high or very low saturations.

Although it is often assumed that all snowflakes are symmetrical, this is actually not the case; indeed most snowflakes are asymmetric by the time they reach the ground, since many interactions and changes in atmospheric conditions can affect the flake on its journey earthwards (almost all photographs of snowflakes show perfect symmetry, but that is only because they are the most beautiful ones and so are chosen for immortality). However, most, if not all, snowflakes do start out symmetrical. Because the flakes are very small the conditions of humidity and temperature are effectively identical across the entire surface. Therefore when growth of the flake occurs as a result of further condensation, the rate and conditions are the same at every point across the arms or faces.

William Scoreby's drawings of snowflakes. From his book *An Account of the Arctic Regions...* published in 1820.

Falling snow

Snowfall accounts for about 5% of the total precipitation that falls on the earth annually. That does not sound like a great deal, but it amounts to more than 30 million million tonnes per annum. The bulk (about 90%) of this snow is seasonal – or rather more temporary in temperate areas – with the rest contributing to the earth's ice sheets. There are different forms of snow depending on its density.

There are several things that affect the density of snow when it is first deposited, but in general it has a specific gravity of about 0.1 (which means that 10cm of snow is the equivalent in terms of water volume of 1cm of rain). Once deposited, snow is compacted: as individual snowflakes break up, the pieces pack closer together. Compaction can therefore occur entirely due to the snow's own weight if the snowfall is heavy, but it is also aided by the action of wind. Melt water from the surface also percolates down into the spaces between the snow crystals. As a result of these processes the snow's specific gravity increases and its characteristics change. When the specific gravity reaches about 0.5, the snow is well compacted and granular, a form well known enough to skiers and mountaineers to have been given a specific name: *firn* in German or *névé* in French, though in each case the name can apply to snow with a range of specific gravities. The wind may affect the surface of such snow; it can create a crust fashioned into wave-like ridges, comparable in appearance to the waves the wind induces on the surface of a lake. This ridged surface is known as *sastrugi* and can produce an uncomfortable ride for a traveller on a snow scooter: sastrugi can be too hard to break through, making the ride a bone-shaking experience. The wind can also create a more level surface crust called wind slab, which can be very dangerous on slopes (and so is carefully watched for by mountaineers) as it can slide on the relatively unconsolidated base below it, causing an avalanche.

As compaction increases, either due to additional snowfall or through an increase in local temperature that causes further surface-melting, the specific gravity rises further. Another process is also at work deep within the snow. Known as sintering, it involves the transfer of water molecules by sublimation: a complex, lattice-like structure is formed, with the air that formed a major constituent of firn being squeezed upwards, out of the lattice. When the specific gravity reaches about 0.8 the remaining air within the lattice becomes trapped in bubbles as escape routes to the surface are closed off. The snow has now turned to ice.

As compaction continues and specific gravity increases further, the air within the trapped bubbles becomes compressed. Glacial ice usually has a specific gravity of 0.9. The specific gravity can increase still further, but not by much: the value for pure ice is 0.917, but glacial ice always has some trapped air.

Sastrugi on sea ice, Barents Sea.

The trapped air in glacial ice has two interesting side effects. One is that glacial ice fizzes when added to a drink, giving a moment's pleasure to passengers on a polar cruise who collect ice from a passing iceberg to add to an evening aperitif. The other side effect is the phenomenon of blue ice. Air and other impurities in the ice scatter light at all frequencies, and as 'normal' ice is impure this means that it appears white. But the water molecule preferentially absorbs light with wavelengths at the red end of the spectrum. Pure ice, free of impurities, allows light to travel a relatively long distance, increasing the absorption of red wavelengths while allowing transmission of wavelengths at the blue end of the spectrum. The ice therefore appears blue, and the purer (and more compacted) the ice the bluer it appears. Blue icebergs, one of the

Blue glacial ice. Tracy Arm, Alaska.

Right
Latent heat is the heat absorbed or released by any substance as it changes phase (from solid to liquid, for example, or from liquid to gas). There are two forms, usually termed the latent heat of fusion (for water this is ice to liquid water or *vice versa*) and the latent heat of vapourisation (water to vapour or *vice versa*; this is sometimes called the latent heat of evaporation). When latent heat is absorbed or released, the temperature of the substance does not change – only the phase changes. Changes of temperature without a change of phase require the absorption or release of what is termed 'sensible' heat.

In lakes close to freezing, and leads in sea ice on the verge of freezing, convection currents release latent heat into the cooler air above, with the water vapour condensing to form frost smoke, an ethereal, strangely beautiful phenomenon.

Below
Galbraith Lake, close to the base of the Brooks Range on Alaska's North Slope, still frozen in mid-summer.

most breathtakingly beautiful of all polar visions, are most frequently seen in the Antarctic, where they are calved from ice sheets with ice that has travelled for many hundreds of years and become highly compacted. In the Arctic, icebergs are calved from glacier fronts and, in general, these are much less ancient. Blue ice is therefore rarer in the north, though it does occur and is an equally thrilling sight. Icebergs may also be blue-green, but this has less to do with the physics of ice, the colour coming from organic material trapped during the formation process. Travellers on pack-ice may also occasionally see patches in shades of brown; this is caused by the defecation of hauled-out seals or walruses.

Snow is extremely important for Arctic rodents. Unlike birds, most Arctic mammals cannot migrate away from the harsh northern winter (reindeer being a notable exception, though even these move only to the Arctic fringe). Rodents use the snow as a blanket to protect them from the extreme cold of winter. This unlikely scenario arises from the low thermal conductivity of snow – it acts as an insulator. The thermal conductivity of snow varies with its density, but it can be as low as that of some cavity-wall insulating materials. So good is it as an insulator that a metre of snow is capable of maintaining a soil temperature of around 0°C in air temperatures of -40°C. The warmth of the soil stimulates sublimation in the basal snow layer. The water molecules rise through the snow, to be replaced by cooler, denser air which is warmed by the ground, encouraging further sublimation. The net effect is to create a basal snow layer composed of needle-like crystals, a layer with a specific gravity of 0.2–0.3. This layer is exploited by rodents, which are able to continue searching for food while benefiting from the insulating properties of the snow blanket. Mountaineers are less enamoured of this since, on slopes, basal layer weakening by sublimation can result in avalanches.

Freshwater ice

There are two main forms of ice that the Arctic traveller will meet. Sea ice is frozen sea water, and so is salty; glaciers are formed of freshwater ice, i.e. they originate from water in the atmosphere that falls as precipitation on land. Two other forms of freshwater ice may also be encountered, on lakes and rivers.

As freshwater cools its density increases, as might be expected. But the density reaches a maximum at 4°C (the maximum occurs at 3.98°C for pure water) and then decreases. There is further reduction in density of about 8.5% when water freezes. As a consequence ice is less dense than water, and so it floats. As the surface layer of a lake cools the water therefore becomes denser and sinks, drawing warmer water to the surface. This process continues until the temperature of the entire water column reaches 4°C and the maximum density is achieved. Once this point is reached, further cooling of the surface water causes it to becomes less dense, and this cooler, less dense water can form a stable layer on top of the denser water column. If the air temperature above the lake is lower than 0°C ice can therefore form in a layer on the surface. Freezing starts at some point: needle-like ribbons of ice may occasionally advance rapidly from this point, an interesting feature of these being that they are eventually curtailed by their own success – as the water freezes it gives up its latent heat, warming the water ahead of the needle and so bringing further freezing to a halt. As will be familiar to anyone who has stepped on the sheet of ice formed on a puddle after a frosty night, this first skin of ice on still water can be extremely thin, perhaps only 0.2mm thick: it is essentially two-dimensional. Because the surface skin acts as an insulator, the process of

Despite the flow of water, rivers freeze.

Above left

On this river in northern Finland, freezing has begun from the banks, the bank in the foreground being littered with ice sheets broken up by a sudden thaw. In the main body of the river, ice is advancing from both banks towards the centre.

Above right

Even waterfalls are not immune to freezing, though complete freezing depends on water volume and may not always be complete before the spring thaw commences. Here at Gullfoss, Iceland, river water is freezing across the top of the falls.

increasing the thickness of lake ice is slow, with further layers forming beneath the original. There is little downward (i.e. three-dimensional) growth, the junction between the water and the ice being very smooth. Again, anyone who has ever extracted a sheet of ice from a frozen lake will know that it is glass-like, a smooth-sided pane of ice. Usually the ice will also be as clear as glass; freshwater ice forms relatively slowly, and impurities are expelled from the crystals as it grows. If the ice forms very quickly these impurities remain trapped in the lattice and the ice is opaque, but this is rare. The purity of most freshwater ice means that the water below it can usually be seen. On road surfaces this results in the occurrence of 'black ice', where the dark road surface beneath the ice is visible; as black ice is essentially invisible it can be a major hazard to drivers.

Fish survive in lakes as they can swim in the water below the ice cover. Oxygen in the water is replenished by inflowing streams, though in many ponds this is not the case: if the freezing is deep enough, or if the ice coverage prevents oxygen absorption for long enough, the oxygen dissolved in the water may be exhausted, and fish and other aquatic organisms may die.

River ice

Although the flow of rivers involves the transfer of potential to kinetic energy and acts against freezing, the tumbling action of the water takes cooler water to depth and so promotes a chilling that extends across the entire water column. Ice can therefore form throughout the column. This ice is carried by the flow, but is extremely 'sticky' and will plate out on any cold surface. It therefore accumulates at the river edge where rocks are exposed to cold air. In slow-moving sections of a river ice also migrates to the surface where it can form sheets that extend across the river. Ice sheets can also grow from each bank to meet in the middle. In both cases, river ice is unusual in that, not being continuous, water may flow both above and below it. Because, as a general rule, ice forms in slower moving water, the freezing 'front' advances upstream from the river mouth. During melting, ice-jams occur as large chunks of ice are driven downstream by the flow.

Frozen lakes and rivers are a hazard for the Arctic traveller, and extreme caution must always be exercised. A good general rule is to cross a river at its widest point. This seems counter-intuitive, but it minimises the risk that the ice thickness has been eroded by sub-ice river flow. On lakes, do not walk one behind the other: if the first walker causes the ice to crack it may not break until the second man arrives. In general, 5cm of freshwater ice will support a man, but as with all general figures there are parameters that can affect the strength of the ice and this figure should not be taken as anything other than a guide.

Sea ice

Although glacial ice has carved the landmasses of the Arctic, it is the sea ice which, in both the popular imagination and in terms of extent, defines the region. The central Arctic Ocean is covered in perennial sea ice, at the fringe of which is further seasonally varying ice cover. Due to its salinity, sea ice forms in a very different way to freshwater ice.

The salinity of sea-water is usually quoted as a single number that gives the weight, in grams, of salt in one kilogram of water. The average salinity of the Arctic Ocean is about 33. This is less than the average for the planet's oceans for two reasons: first, the huge continental rivers that run into the Arctic Ocean dilute it (although the Arctic Ocean has only about 1% of the earth's volume of sea-water, it receives around 11% of the total freshwater input); second, the rate of evaporation is much lower than in temperate and tropical seas – where there is sea ice evaporation is eliminated, and at the sea-ice edge the rate of evaporation from cold water to a cold atmosphere is lower than in warmer oceans. These effects also mean that the salinity of Arctic waters is highly depth dependent, varying from 28–30 close to the surface to a 'standard' oceanic value of 35 at depths of 200–300m.

The presence of salt (chiefly sodium chloride, which constitutes 78% of the salt burden, with magnesium chloride (*c.*11%) and other salts at lower concentrations) lowers the temperature at which water freezes to between -1.8°C and -2.0°C. It also changes the *way* in which water freezes. By contrast to freshwater, sea-water does not exhibit a maximum density at 4°C, with the density continuing to rise as temperature falls. So as the surface layer cools it sinks, a situation never being reached where cool water floats on a layer of slightly warmer water. Therefore the whole water column has to cool to its freezing point before ice can form. However, this does not mean that the entire Arctic Ocean must freeze solid to the bottom at once: the depth of a water column is dependent on

The forms of sea ice

Top
A band of grease ice between open water, at the top, and pancake ice, at the bottom.

Centre
Sheets of nilas ice form on a calm sea.

Bottom
Pancake ice.

salinity, and there are sharp discontinuities in salinity in the ocean that effectively demarcate the water columns. Discontinuities occur at depths of 10–40m (though this does mean that in shallow seas the water column must be at freezing point all the way to the sea bed before freezing can occur). There is also a further effect of salts being lost from the surface layer of water as the temperature falls; this leaching leads to a surface layer of lower salinity (and therefore a higher freezing point) that aids the freezing process.

In the first stage of sea-ice formation, crystals (usually plates or needles 3–4mm across) grow. This is called frazil ice. The crystals multiply to form a greyish surface layer that behaves something like a thick, syrupy liquid. This is known as grease ice. The crystals in this thick soup now coalesce, forming plates that initially remain flexible enough to bend and move with the action of waves and winds. If there is little wind and a calm sea, the plates may form extensive sheets known as nilas ice, but in more turbulent seas the plates thicken and collide, forming pancake ice. Pancake usually consists of roughly circular plates, each with a raised edge as a result of rubbing against other plates. Eventually the plates coalesce to form a continuous sheet that thickens as it ages. The thickening process is again dependent on sea conditions; in turbulent seas ice usually thickens through the accumulation of frazil ice crystals on the lower surface, but in calmer seas long, columnar crystals may form. Because the Southern Ocean is, in general, much more turbulent than the seas of the Arctic, columnar ice crystals are much less common in the south, forming only 20–40% of sea ice, while they form 60–80% of Arctic sea ice.

Whether the thickening of the ice is by frazil or columnar crystals, it is, of course, temperature-dependent. If the air temperature is very cold the ice may thicken by up to 20cm daily, though this rate inevitably declines because the thicker the ice becomes the more it acts as an insulator. As a consequence, thickening rates are rarely more than 40cm in a week or more than 2m in a year. Seasonal ice is therefore usually about this thick, though 'old ice' (the name given to ice more than one year old; it is also often called multiyear ice) can be up to 8m thick (though 4–5m is more usual). This thickness derives not only from freezing of sea-water on the lower ice surface, but the accumulation of snow on the upper surface, which compacts to form new (freshwater) ice. In general, sea ice of about 20cm thickness will take the weight of a human (compare with *c*.5cm for freshwater ice) – but again this should not be taken as a golden rule, as there are many factors that can potentially weaken the ice sheet. Since much of the salt is leached from the surface layer of sea ice, one wonders why there is such a substantial difference in ice strength. The answer is entrained brine pockets (which, due to their high salinity, do not freeze). A sheet of freshwater ice only 5–6mm thick can be handled as if it were a pane of glass. To handle sea ice in the same way requires a thickness of about 6cm (around ten times the thickness). The nature of the different ices is clear if the two 'panes' are dropped. The freshwater ice will shatter into myriad shards, but the sea ice will splash, rather as a ball of treacle or ice-cream would.

Comparing ice

Much of the central Arctic Ocean is covered by perennial ice, i.e. ice that does not melt from season to season and is, in general, more than two years old. The existence of this perennial ice is an important difference between the Arctic and the Antarctic; in the latter the majority of sea ice (about 85% – there is some perennial sea ice in both the Weddell and Ross seas) forms annually. The perennial ice coverage of the Arctic is about half the winter maximum cover. Because the winters at the two poles are out of phase, the Earth's sea-ice cover is approximately the same throughout the year (although about 20% less in January–March) and averages about 25,000,000km². This is about 7% of the surface area of the Earth's oceans, an area roughly equal to that of North America. Although this area represents almost two-thirds of the Earth's total ice coverage, sea ice is relatively thin, so it represents less than 0.1% of the Earth's ice volume. In terms of land area covered, the Antarctic ice sheet provides more than 80% of the Earth's ice coverage, with the Greenland ice sheet accounting for about 12%, and glaciers the rest.

Sea ice on the Beaufort Sea.

Another rule of sea ice that is helpful for a traveller (but again not absolute) is that grey sea ice is thin and should be treated with caution (the colour being due to the dark sea visible through the ice), while white ice is thick and therefore likely to be stronger. However, snow falling on grey ice can turn it white.

Sea ice has a much lower salinity than the water from which it formed, as salts leach out of the ice lattice into pockets of brine during the freezing process. The brine pockets then migrate downwards, either under the influence of gravity or because melting snow on the surface percolates down and flushes out the brine. If the surface layer of sea ice freezes very quickly the salinity can remain high, but in general freezing is slower and the salinity drops to about 5 (i.e. about 85% of the salts have gone). Further salt leaching can mean that old ice has a salinity as low as 2, meaning it can be used as a source of freshwater. The leached salts increase the salinity of the water beneath the ice, helping, in part, to drive the Atlantic conveyor.

Fast ice and pack ice

Sea ice can be anchored to the shore, forming what is called fast ice. Away from the shore sea ice is usually known as pack ice (to complete the picture, ice scientists define three forms of Arctic sea ice – pack, fast and polar cap ice, the latter being the permanent ice around the North Pole: polar cap ice, though a permanent feature, varies in thickness between summer and winter). Unbroken pack is the term for complete sea-ice cover. However, heavy swells, the wind and currents can break up a continuous ice sheet, particularly during the Arctic summer when the ice thins due to melting. When the ice covers about 75–80% of the water surface it is called close pack ice. Open pack ice refers to a coverage of 50–75%. There is no accepted term for coverage below 50%, the term ice floe being used to describe large sections of broken sea ice littering the water. As the floes are broken up by wave and wind erosion, or by collision with other chunks of ice, a mass of small ice pieces is created; this is termed brash ice. Occasionally a vast expanse of sea ice will be eroded at its edge, so that rather than forming an area of closed or open pack, sections break free and are quickly smashed into brash. This abrupt edge, which can look as clean cut as the division between land and sea at a temperate shore line, is often called (a little confusingly) the floe edge.

The attachment of sea ice to the shore – the fast ice – is often so tenacious that movement of the pack causes a fracture between the pack mass and a section of fast ice. The fracture line often runs more or less parallel to the shore, the pack retreating to leave a lead of open water. Leads may also form where the pack fractures due to currents or wind erosion. Leads are a nuisance to travellers on the sea ice; they often require long detours to a point where the lead narrows sufficiently to allow a crossing. An alternative is to wait until the lead freezes over. Leads can be hazardous to boats, even to ships, and to Arctic cetaceans. They can form relatively quickly and close just as swiftly, trapping and crushing boats or

Right
After a short thaw spell the sea ice refreezes at Forlandsundet, Svalbard.

Below
Natural sea ice scupture at Storfjorden, Svalbard.

marooning whales far from open water. Whales have often been seen desperately keeping a breathing hole open in a closing lead, in the hope that an escape route will open. Polar Bears may 'fish' for Beluga in such situations. Each time a whale surfaces to breathe, the bear inflicts damage with teeth and claws until the exhausted Beluga is incapable of further dives and can be hauled on to the ice.

The fracturing of pack ice can also result in the formation of pressure ridges, as currents and waves force one section of pack to ride over another as a lead closes. Pressure ridges can also form in open or close pack ice if floes are driven against each other, a general freezing then creating unbroken pack with ridges *in situ*. Such ridges can reach 15m in height and, as with leads, are a considerable challenge for sea-ice travellers. As well as a ridge on the pack surface there is also a downward-pointing ridge below the ice, where the over-ridden flow has been pushed down. In shallow water this ridge can be driven into the sea-bed. Such downward ridges (occasionally given the tongue-in-cheek name of 'bummocks' – the opposite of 'hummocks') can be a hazard to drilling rigs or underwater pipes and cables.

Much more dangerous is the *ivu*, an Inuit word that describes a potentially lethal event in which a jumble of floes are pushed – by what process is still not absolutely clear, though it must involve strong onshore winds or currents – at speed on to land, rather like a frozen tsunami. Ivu can kill, but are thankfully very rare. Scientists were initially sceptical of ivus, but their existence has now been verified, and several have been observed and studied. The best known of these studies followed the excavation in 1982 of an ancient site at Utqiagvik, near Barrow, Alaska, where the bodies of a family of five were discovered. It is thought the family was overwhelmed by an ivu some 400 years ago. An ivu was reported in January 2006, again at Barrow, when a wall of ice up to 12m high was pushed almost 100m on to the shore, overriding a large protective berm and partially destroying a road.

Above
Sea ice in Pond Inlet. In the foreground is fast ice attached to the shore of northern Baffin Island. A lead of open water separates the fast ice from the main sea ice mass. The mass is split by a lead stretching back towards distant Bylot Island.

Left
One way of crossing narrow leads on a snow scooter is to open the throttle and skip across like a stone skimmed across a lake. The technique requires strong nerves; any last minute deceleration can result in loss of the machine and a cold bath. Pond Inlet, with Bylot Island in the background.

Figure 3.1
Arctic ice drift.

Ice drift

As well as the local movements of sea ice that may break up the pack and create leads, there are also macro-movements (Figure 3.1). Of these, the most famous is the Transpolar Drift, which flows from Russia's New Siberian Islands across the Pole to Svalbard and the Denmark Strait. It was this drift that carried relics of the *Jeanette* from the eastern side of the Laptev Sea to the coast of Greenland, where their discovery prompted Fridtjof Nansen to undertake the *Fram* expedition. The Drift has two well-defined branches, the Siberian ice current taking ice towards Franz Josef Land and Severnaya Zemlya, creating a small gyre (circular current) in the Laptev Sea, while the Polar ice current hauls ice towards Ellesmere Island and western Greenland. The rate at which ice drifts is dependent on wind as well as the ocean currents. The *Fram* took three years to move from where it became ice-locked close to the New Siberian Islands to its point of release west of Spitsbergen. That time is actually less than the average, which is closer to five years (an average drift rate of about 0.1km/hour). The rate is not linear, however, since the ice accelerates from the North Pole to the Fram Strait, that part of the journey taking about one year (at an average drift rate of about 0.5km/hour). For comparison, drift rates of up to 2km/hour have been measured in storms.

Nansen's journey has made the Transpolar Drift the most famous of Arctic ice currents; the most infamous is the Beaufort Gyre, a mass of circulating ice some 1,200km across, centred on the frozen ocean to the north of Alaska (see photograph on p49). The gyre often caused problems for the American whaling fleet based at Herschel Island; it trapped the *Karluk* and still makes journeys difficult, even for powerful ice breakers. Ice in the Beaufort Gyre takes 7–10 years to complete a circuit, the strength of the Gyre being variable; in the 1980s it was very strong, but it weakened in the 1990s.

Glaciers

As we have seen, once snow has been sufficiently compacted it forms ice. Though ice usually appears as a very hard but brittle substance, glacial ice is actually a plastic material that will flow downhill under the influence of gravity (though the actual method by which glaciers move is complex, as we shall see below). Because of the effect of gravity, an ice cap or sheet formed on flat land will be higher at the centre than at the edges, forming an ice dome. Ice radiates outward from the dome, forming glaciers (known as outlet glaciers) that move the ice to the sea or to a point where ablation (as the reduction in ice volume is termed) causes the glacier to disappear.

In general glaciers gain mass in their upper region as the average annual temperature in that area tends to be below freezing, so that the mass accumulated from snowfall exceeds that lost through surface melting. In the glacier's lower region, mass loss exceeds accumulation; this is known as the ablation zone. Mass accumulation occurs solely as a result of precipitation, but ablation can result from melting for one of several reasons, or by direct mass loss. Melting can be from solar or geothermal energy input, or from friction due to sliding (though that is by far the least effective in terms of energy input). Direct mass loss occurs in tidewater glaciers where the collapse of the glacier front (or calving) creates icebergs. If the mass balance of a glacier is positive, i.e. accumulation exceeds ablation, the glacier grows. If the mass balance is negative the glacier retreats. The theoretical line across a glacier where accumulation and ablation are equal is known as the equilibrium or firn line (Figure 3.2).

Having accepted that although ice can occasionally seem as hard and unyielding as steel it is actually influenced by gravity,

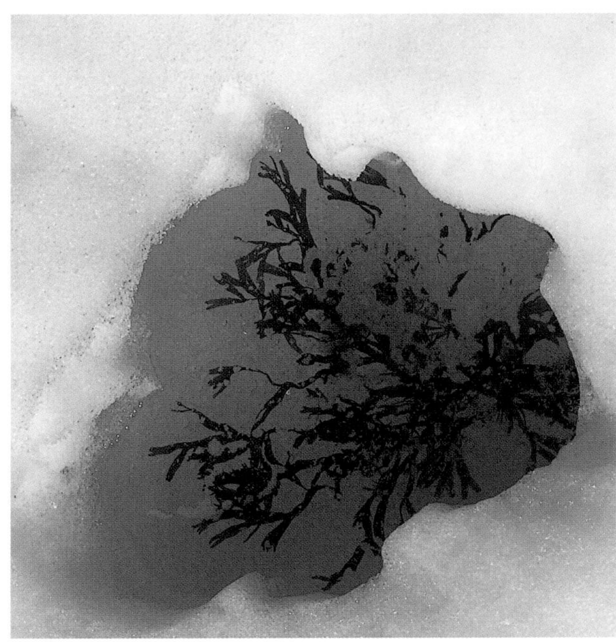

Seaweed trapped in sea ice. Because the seaweed is dark it absorbs heat, melting the local ice.

This extraordinary photograph shows 20,000–30,000 King Eider congregated in a polynya off the west coast of Greenland.

Open waters

The summer thaw of Arctic sea ice is chiefly due to rain and sun, assisted by wave effects at the floe edge. Melting can start away from the floe edge, particularly if seaweed has become trapped in the ice. Dark matter absorbs sunlight more rapidly than the ice surface (where the albedo – see below – is high) and local melting begins. This forms a meltwater pool on the ice surface, the darker water absorbing more heat so the pool spreads and melting accelerates. However, in some places open water surrounded by sea ice can occur throughout the year, with some of these in summer sea ice recurring annually. These are called polynyas, the name deriving from a Russian word for a forest clearing. North Water in Smith Sound at the northern end of Baffin Bay and the Great Siberian Polynya in the Laptev Sea are classic examples. Annual polynyas result from reliable currents such as those between islands, or from reliable weather patterns, such as off-shore winds. However, some polynyas exist away from such sources and are thought to be caused by upwellings of warm water, though the precise reasons for this are not fully understood. Polynyas are important ecologically, with the annual ones being critical for some species. The open water allows oxygenation, light penetration and the surface water to warm. The salinity of open water differs from adjacent waters beneath the ice. Gradients in salinity and temperature set up in the water create currents that take oxygen to the depths and bring nutrients to the surface, allowing organisms to thrive. The importance of North Water is reflected by the fact that the seabird population nesting within flying distance of it is measured in tens of millions. The abundance of food also attracted Bowhead Whales to North Water where they overwintered, a fact that was rapidly understood by 19th-century whalers.

glacial flow would seem to be a straightforward process, but this is far from the case. The natural assumption would be that ice, which after all is well known for being slippery, slides over the rock at the glacier's base. For this to take place, the basal ice of the glacier must not be frozen to the substrate. This may be the case if geothermal heat raises the temperature of the substrate, or if the basal ice layer's melting point is lowered due to the pressure of the overlying ice. Even if the substrate temperature is sub-zero, it may still be higher than this lowered melt temperature. In such 'warm-based' glaciers the basal layer of ice melts and the glacier slides, with the meltwater acting as a lubricant.

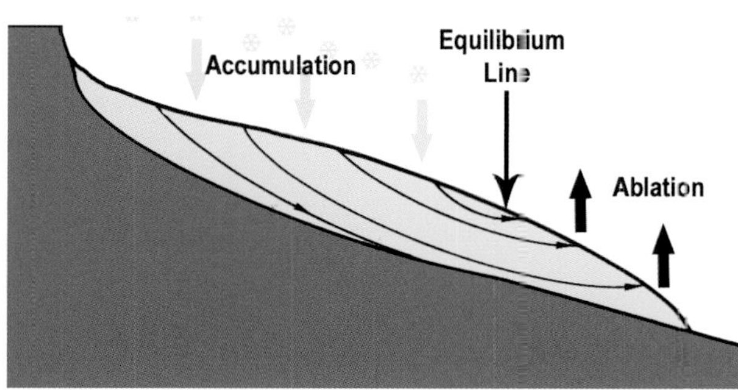

Figure 3.2
Equilibrium line on a glacier.

However, such glaciers are rare in the Arctic, most of the region's glaciers being 'cold-based', with the substrate being colder than the basal ice layer's melting point: in other words, the glacier is frozen to the substrate and basal sliding cannot occur. The advance of glaciers like this is by a process called ice creep. This differs from the flow of a liquid, as it is caused by the elongation and displacement of individual ice crystals. If a bar of ice is suspended in a room at a temperature below freezing point it will slowly elongate; that is ice creep. Under certain circumstances the bedrock may itself deform, contributing to glacial flow.

In many Arctic glaciers the situation is even more complex, as the glacier may be cold-based in its upper regions and warm-based at lower altitudes. Recent measurements of the speed of some Arctic glaciers have shown that they are speeding up due to climate change: increased surface melting causes a downward trickle of water to the glacier's base where, if it remains unfrozen, it acts as a lubricant, turning a previously cold-based glacier into a warm-based one. The measurements indicate that this rise in glacial speed occurs primarily in glaciers south of 60°N, but more recently the phenomenon has been observed in glaciers to 70°N. In particular, Greenland's Kangerlussuaq Glacier (north of the Arctic Circle

Crevasses

Ice creep is a slow process, so if the glacier's bed changes slope it cannot react fast enough to adjust to the change. Fractures then develop in the ice as ice masses on differing slope angles split from each other. Where these faults reach the surface they form a series of parallel crevasses. Crevasses are usually transverse, i.e. they form at right angles to the ice movement. However, chevron crevasses also occur; these are angled across the glacier and result from the effect of drag on the ice by the walls of a containing valley. A third form, splaying crevasses, are a combination of the other two.

A particular form of crevasse, a single, wide crevasse called a bergschrund, can often be seen where a glacier separates from the valley headwall. However, despite this often being claimed as the sole position of bergschrunds, they can also form where fast-moving ice separates from slower-moving sections of a glacier.

Icefalls occur where the slope of the substrate underlying a glacier is steep, causing the ice to break up: the numerous crevasses result in the isolation of large, unstable blocks of ice, called séracs. Icefalls are rare in polar glaciers; the most famous example is the Khumbu Icefall on the approach to the Western Cwm, on the southern (Nepalese) side of Everest, where falling séracs have resulted in the deaths of several climbers.

The heavily crevassed glacier pictured here is Blomstrandbreen, Svalbard.

on the west coast – the local village has the alternative Danish name of Søndre Strømfjord) doubled in speed in the period 2000–2005. Faster glacial movement means that a greater volume of Greenland's ice sheet is now being discharged into the sea by this tidewater glacier; it is estimated that the ice discharge has increased by as much as 700%.

Although glaciers flow downhill, the ice will also pass over large impediments to its movement, such as large bodies of rock that form part of the substrate. The flow of the ice in such situations is complex, involving an enhancement of ice creep, but also regelation. Regelation is the melting of ice due to pressure and its subsequent refreezing when the pressure is released. The clearest example of this process can be seen in a cold room, if a wire with a weight attached is looped around a suspended block of ice. In time the wire will cut through the block and fall away, but the block will remain intact, with little trace of the wire's passage. Where the wire touches the ice, the pressure from the weight lowers the melt temperature. The ice melts, the wire descends through the thin water layer, and the water refreezes above it. The same process occurs in a glacier; pressure from the ice mass upstream causes the ice at an obstacle to melt. The water flows around the obstacle and refreezes on the downstream side.

Types of glaciers

There are a number of types of glacier, but most of these are confined to mountainous areas; the tortured landscapes of mountain ranges produce a range of different glaciers. In the Arctic, though, there are essentially two types: valley (often called alpine) and piedmont glaciers. Valley glaciers are those confined to the valleys that the glacier itself has carved. Such glaciers terminate in a convex ice snout, which either gives birth to a river or, if the glacier reaches the sea, calves icebergs. Those that reach the sea are often called tidewater glaciers. Tidewater glaciers often carve their base to below sea level, and the sea fills the subsequent trench if the glacier retreats. This process is the origin of fjords; the most famous fjords indent Norway's coast. These are now essentially free of the glaciers that carved them, but in the Arctic some fjords still retain their glaciers.

Piedmont glaciers are those in which the ice has reached a plain at the base of the mountains from which they form: the name means 'mountain foot' (and is shared by an Italian region, named after its position below an alpine mountain chain). Having escaped from the confines of its valley walls, the ice spreads on the plain to form a characteristic lobe. Piedmont glaciers are rare, and global glacial retreat is making them even rarer. The oft-quoted 'classic example' is the Malaspint Glacier on the southern edge of Alaska's St Elias Mountains near Yakutar. The Malaspint lies outside the Arctic as defined in this book, but there are several, lesser-known examples within the Arctic.

Icebergs and ice islands

Though icebergs are an oceanic feature, they form from terrestrially derived (i.e. freshwater) ice, the bergs being calved

Left

In winter glaciers freeze, movement slowing dramatically or ceasing at the glacier front. The observer here, at Paulabreen, Svalbard, is standing on sea ice. In summer this would be a dangerous place to be as the rising temperature releases the glacier and iceberg calving begins again.

Below

The longest glacier front in the Arctic, the 200km long tidewater edge on Nordaustlandet's eastern coast, Svalbard.

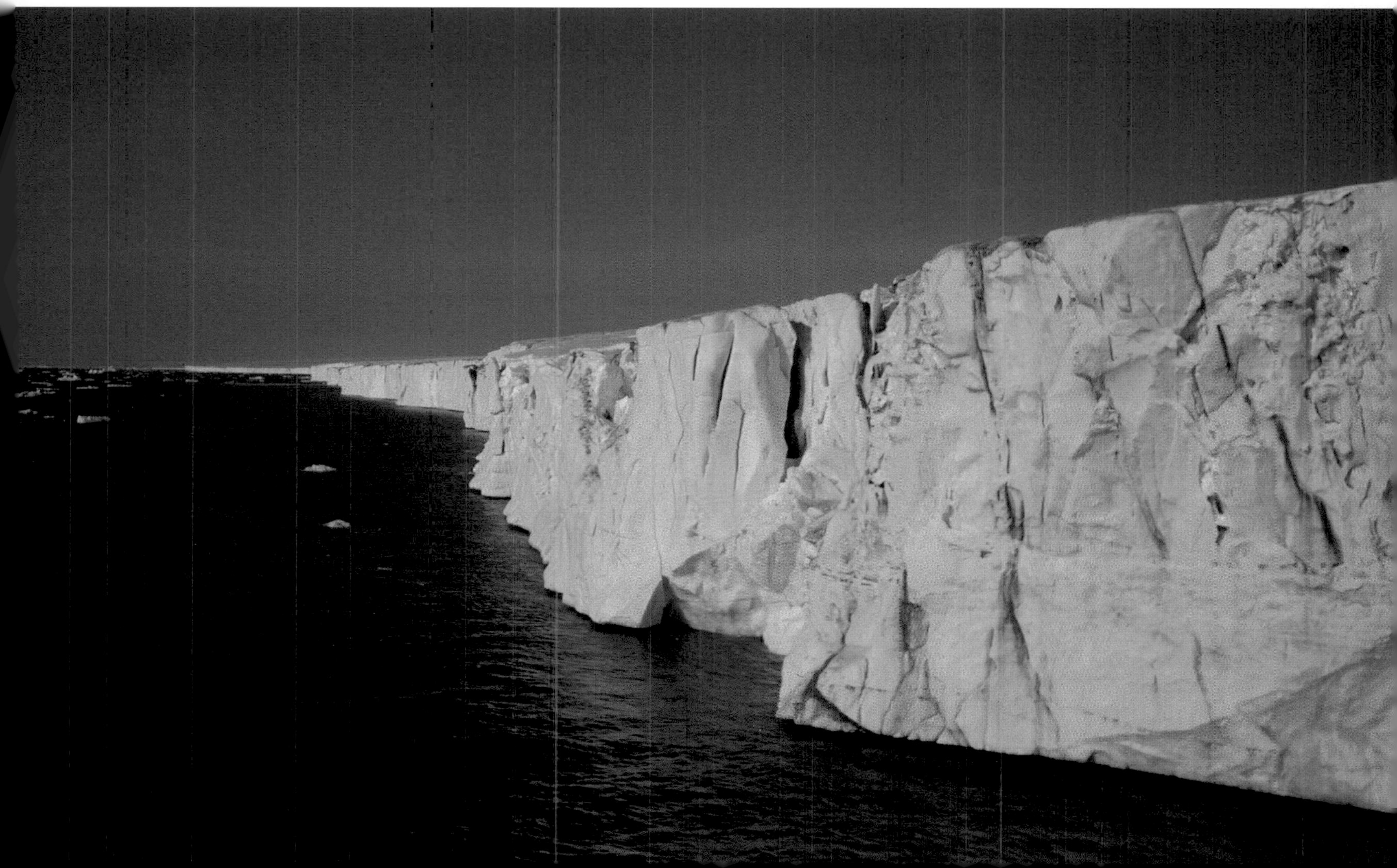

through the fracturing of the fronts of tidewater glaciers. Most Arctic icebergs therefore differ from the majority of Antarctic icebergs, which form when the ice sheets flowing above the waters of the Southern Ocean fracture. Such fracturing creates tabular bergs, which are often vast. But the Arctic has fewer, and much smaller, ice shelves and so produces fewer tabular bergs. This key difference is related to temperature; Antarctica's ice is much colder than the majority of Arctic ice masses, and cold ice has a much higher tensile strength than 'warmer' ice. Thus while the tides acting on Arctic glaciers that reach the sea cause the ice to flex and, ultimately, fracture, the tides of the Southern Ocean do not impart sufficient energy to overcome the strength of the ice. Only in certain limited areas of the Arctic is the ice sufficiently cold to resist tidal forces: in most places the temperature does not drop low enough for long enough to allow ice sheets to form.

The Arctic's glacially derived icebergs are smaller than the tabular bergs of Antarctica. Calving also produces much less angular shapes, Arctic bergs often being misshapen in an aesthetically pleasing way. But smaller does not mean trivial, as the *Titanic* found out with terrible consequences when it collided with the underwater section of an iceberg on 15 April 1912. The collision opened a huge rift below the ship's water line, and resulted in the deaths of 1,503 people. The *Titanic* did not, of course, have radar, but radar has its limitations as a tool for detecting icebergs; ice is only about 2% as reflective as metal (i.e. another ship) and to make matters worse a misshapen berg scatters a radar beam in many directions. Today the International Iceberg Patrol (IIP) uses aircraft to spot bergs in the North Atlantic, the white berg being readily visible by eye, even on overcast days or when there is some fog (though dense fog obviously makes spotting impossible). There is no equivalent of the IIP in the North Pacific as icebergs are only calved in south-eastern Alaska; these are few in number and rarely escape the Gulf of Alaska.

Ice on Earth

Though in the popular imagination ice is the dominant feature of the Arctic over much of the land surrounding the frozen Arctic Ocean, there is actually little or no permanent ice (with the notable exception of Greenland and, to a lesser extent, some islands of Arctic Canada and Russia). For the Earth as a whole, ice holds some 33 million cubic kilometres of freshwater. This is a vast amount; if all this ice were to melt, sea levels would rise by some 70m. Yet this volume represents only about 2% of the water on Earth. The oceans account for 93.5% of the total, rivers and lakes the other 4.5%. Of the ice, about 90% forms the Antarctic ice sheet. Greenland's ice sheet accounts for a further 8%, the smaller ice caps on the Arctic islands (the largest of which is on Ellesmere Island, that being twice the size of the next biggest, on west Spitsbergen) and the world's glaciers making up the remaining 2%.

The largest Arctic iceberg on record was 13km long and 6km wide. Icebergs more than 150m high have been observed but they are comparatively rare. It is estimated that 30,000–40,000 icebergs calve annually from Arctic glaciers, though perhaps only 300–500 reach the open sea, as most are too small to survive for long periods. Of this total, about 3% emanate from a single glacier, the Jakobshavn Glacier on Greenland's west coast. This, one of earth's fastest moving and most productive glaciers, moves at over 20m daily and calves about 25km^2 of ice annually from an 8km-wide front. The bergs are calved into Jakobshavn Isfjord (south of Ilulissat, a settlement whose name means 'iceberg'), the mouth of which (leading to Disko Bay) is restricted by a morainic bar, from a time when the glacier reached as far as the bay itself. This bar

Heavily crevassed tidewater glacier flowing down from the Beerenberg volcano on Jan Mayen.

Piedmont glacier in west Greenland.

Tabular iceberg, Southern Ocean. Such bergs have exceeded 100km in length. In 2000 a section of the Ross Ice Shelf fractured, creating a tabular berg almost 300km long and up to 25km wide, with a total area of about 11,000km². In the same year two vast sections of the Ronne Ice Shelf also fractured free. As the Earth's temperature rises it is likely that more of these huge tabular bergs will form (in 2002, for example, a 3,250km² section of the Larsen B shelf broke away), though ultimately, of course, the ice shelves that produce them will cease to exist.

acts as a barrier to larger bergs, and such is the volume of ice produced that the fjord can be filled with stalled bergs, to the point where open water can be difficult to find.

As ice is less dense than water, icebergs float with the larger fraction of their bulk (about 85% as a general rule) below the surface. This mass distribution represents a crucial difference between icebergs and sea ice. Although both ice forms are affected by ocean currents, icebergs are much less affected by the wind than is sea ice (though if the above-water section of a berg is sail-like they will catch the wind). This difference can occasionally result in the bizarre vision of a berg and sea ice moving in opposite directions, the berg ploughing a course through the ice. Historically this curiosity has been used on more than one occasion by an icebound ship as a means of escaping its entrapment. Icebergs can also plough the sediments on the sea bottom, or the sea bed itself. Examples are known of trenches up to 20m deep and many tens of metres wide being ploughed, sometimes over distances of several kilometres; such ploughing would seriously endanger oil pipelines and underwater cables.

Icebergs are eroded by a combination of sunlight, wind and wave action above the surface, and water temperature and wave action below. In time they disintegrate, often rolling over when differential erosion makes them unstable. Rolling bergs are extremely dangerous; people on them would be thrown into the sea and sucked under to almost certain death by induced currents, and boats beside them can be overwhelmed.

Collapsing front of a tidewater glacier, Tracy Arm, Alaska.

Iceberg in Baffin Bay, off Baffin Island's northern coast.

As a consequence few scientists now ever land on large Arctic bergs and the rule for all travellers is stay well away.

Overturned bergs can usually be spotted by the surface pattern created by underwater wave action. Some bergs actually disintegrate explosively, though most die more quietly. The fragments of a disintegrating berg have been given the rather banal name of bergy bits. Bergy bits are classified as being in the size range 2–5m across. As with broken pack ice, smaller chunks of iceberg are known as brash ice. The expressive name 'growler' is given to a specific class of berg debris; growlers, which can also be produced by the collapse of a glacier front, are flat-topped masses that float low in the water, rather as sea ice does. Large growlers can be a problem for ships as they can be easily missed by radar. Smaller growlers can be a problem for boats such as zodiacs, as if unseen they can be steered over, causing damage to propellers.

As noted above, the ice shelves of the Arctic are smaller and far fewer in number than their counterparts in Antarctica. Arctic ice shelves also form in a different way. While some are created by the flow of glacial ice across the ocean (e.g. the Milne ice shelf off Ellesmere Island's northern coast), others form when fast ice develops over many years. The most famous of the Arctic's ice shelves, that at Ward Hunt Island off the northern coast of Ellesmere Island (the starting point for many adventurers heading for the North Pole), was formed from such an accumulation of fast ice. The Alfred Ernest ice shelf (also off Ellesmere Island's northern coast) was created by a combination of the glacial and fast ice mechanisms. Once an ice shelf has been created, snow accumulating on the upper surface and sea ice accumulating on the lower surface tend to thicken the shelf, while the accretion of sea ice on the ocean edge tends to elongate it. The seaward edge of the shelf may also break off, though the calved ice is not known as a tabular berg, but rather as an ice island, a specifically Arctic name. Arctic ice islands comprise both freshwater and sea ice, whereas the tabular bergs of Antarctica are almost entirely freshwater ice. Arctic ice shelves are limited to Ellesmere Island's northern coast (where there are five, the Markham and Ayles, together with the Milne, Ward Hunt and Alfred Ernest ice sheets mentioned above), some fjords of northern Greenland, and the Russian archipelagos of Franz Josef Land and Severnaya Zemlya. The shelves of northern Ellesmere Island are by far

Jökullsarlon in southern Iceland, where a glacier calves into a tidal lagoon.

At the firft fight of this great and monftruous peece of yce, it appeared in this waye

In comming near unto it, it fhewed after this fhape

In approaching right againft it, it opened in fhape like unto this, fhewing hollow within

In departing from it, it appeared in this fhape

¶ Thefe foure being but one Ifland of yce, and as we came neere vnto it, and departed from it, in fo many fhapes it appeared.

Above left
The first depiction of an iceberg, from Thomas Ellis' book ***A true report of the third and last voyage into Meta Incognita acheived by the worthie Capteine Martine Frobisher Esquire, Anno 1578.***

Above right
Iceberg in Kaiser Franz Josef's Fjord, north-east Greenland. The smooth lower surface and etched wavelines indicate that the berg has tipped.

the biggest, though as with their Antarctic counterparts they are shrinking. It is estimated that at the end of the 19th century the Ellesmere ice shelves covered 7,500km²; today the total area is around 15% of that figure.

All Arctic ice shelves and ice islands are recognisable by the undulations or rolls on their surface. These rolls are a few metres high and separated by valleys up to several hundred metres wide. The rolls are parallel, and parallel to the coast on which they formed. It is believed that the roll-valley structure is caused by summer melting.

Ellesmere's ice islands are normally captured by, and contained within, the Beaufort Gyre, but they have been known to escape and reach the Fram Strait, where they join those originating in the Russian Arctic and some from northern Greenland. Ice islands from northern Greenland and Canada may also reach Baffin Bay. Ice islands are stable, and have been used as floating platforms for research projects. Indeed, the possible use of Arctic ice islands as airfields resulted in their discovery – by the Americans and Russians independently, and at virtually the same time – being kept secret for many years.

Glacial landforms

Although Arctic icebergs are perhaps the best-known product of glaciation, glaciers are also renowned for their influence on the landscape over which they flow. In general, this shaping of the land is more obvious in mountain areas, as cold-based glaciers (which predominate in the Arctic) are much less abrasive than those that slide – rock debris caught up in basal layers of warm-based glaciers acting as a very effective sandpaper, particularly as glacial flow is relentless. The sheer power of glaciers to transform a landscape is illustrated in the carving of U-shaped valleys, and for the alpine scenery of arêtes (thin ridges between U-shaped valleys) and cirques (circular glacier-cut basins).

Glacial erosion also creates moraine, the often very fine debris of rock abraded from the valley sides and the glacier base by the ice. This debris accumulates within, and at the edges of, the glacier. At the edges it forms narrow lines of lateral moraine. Sometimes these lines can be seen on the glacier's surface away from the edges. Termed medial moraine, this usually forms from the lines of lateral moraine where two glaciers have met, but it may be derived from entrained debris reaching the surface. Debris is also deposited at the glacial snout – terminal moraine. Terminal moraine may pile so high that it dams the valley created by a retreating glacier, with a lake forming behind the dam. Behind the terminal moraine there is often an area of hummocks where rock debris covers mounds of unmelted ice, the debris having slowed the ablation processes.

Glaciers may leave behind other evidence of their existence when they retreat. Perhaps the most obvious is the rock over which the glacier once flowed, chamfered smooth or with striations caused by rock fragments embedded in the ice. *Roches moutonnées* are isolated, asymmetric rock masses over which glaciers have passed, with one side (the glacier upstream side) shallow-angled and abraded smooth, the other (downstream)

Meltwater cascades off the ice of Nordaustlandet's eastern glacier, Svalbard. This glacier front is the longest in the Arctic and includes, at its southern tip, Bråsvellbreen. The name derives from *brå svell breen* – rapid-swell-glacier. In the early 20th century, and particularly in 1938, the glacier surged, sending the ice front across the sea to form an ice shelf. Since then the glacier front has retreated. The present position is a little unclear as radar investigations suggest that there is still some 'floating' ice at the front; Bråsvellbreen could therefore be an ice shelf, though that suggestion is open to debate and it is not listed as such by most authorities.

lee side high-angled and roughened by ice plucking and frost erosion.

Although *roches moutonnées* are usually relatively small (a few metres across), they can be much larger, 100m or more in height and a kilometre or so long. In Sweden *flyggbergs*, vast asymmetric hills, sometimes more than 300m high and 3km long, are *roches* and may even have smaller *roches* studded across their surfaces. *Roches* that lack the clear-plucked lee side are known as rock drumlins. A further example of glacial activity is the erratic, a boulder of specific rock type carried by the glacier and then deposited in an area of dissimilar rock. Such erratics caused much head-scratching among geologists before glacial retreat and advance was understood.

Rock drumlins are named after a more common form of glacial landform, the drumlin. Glacial debris is known generically as till, and retreating glaciers can leave behind mounds of this. These mounds are called drumlins, from the Gaelic *druim*, a rounded hill. Though the exact development process of drumlins is still debated (it has been said that there are as many theories of drumlin formation as there are drumlins – and there are a great many drumlins), the form is more or less constant, a drumlin being an elongated mass of till, the long axis giving the direction of ice flow, with an upstream, high-angled, blunt end, the shallow, tapering downstream side ending in a point. The form is, therefore, somewhat similar to an egg; drumlins normally occur in groups known as swarms, the swarm sometimes referred to as forming a 'basket of eggs' topography.

Cirques, corries and cwms

The various names for this bowl-like feature of mountain scenery reflect the country of origin: *cirque* is French, *corrie* – or *coire* – is Gaelic, *cwm* is Welsh. The Welsh form has given its name to one of the most famous examples, the Western Cwm on Everest's southern side.

Glaciofluvial effects

The features discussed above are all caused by direct glacial erosion and deposition, but the landscape can also be transformed by meltwater flowing beneath or away from the glacier, by processes known collectively as glaciofluvial effects. The most conspicuous of these is the outwash fan, a lobe of till formed by numerous meltwater streams flowing over a plain. Such plains are often called *sandar* and are a feature of southern Iceland (hence the name – *sandar* is the plural of *sandur*). In Iceland *sandar* extend for many kilometres not only along the south coast, but also from the base of the glaciers of Mýrdalsjökull and Vatnajökull to the sea. Individual meltwater streams flowing beneath the ice can cut channels in the

Roches moutonnées

The name of this feature, which means 'rock sheep' in French, is usually said to derive from the sheep-like appearance of such rocks studding alpine meadows. However, it is more likely to be from the resemblance of the rocks to the sheepskin wigs worn by judges and advocates of the French court in the 18th century; the wigs were waved, with the waves cemented in place with mutton fat, giving further credence to the name.

bedrock. Such channels, usually narrow (up to a few tens of metres) but surprisingly deep, and sharp-edged if the glacier retreat was recent so that there has been limited weathering, are called Nye channels (or N channels) after John Nye, the British glaciologist who first defined them. Nye channels can be very long, up to several kilometres (very much larger forms – up to 100km – are termed tunnel valleys).

Under-ice streams may also form eskers (from the Irish *eiscir*, a ridge; they are also occasionally called by their Scandinavian name, *osar*). Eskers are long, sinuous ridges of debris formed by the silting of ice-walled stream channels. A broken form of esker is termed a kame (the name is Celtic in origin, from *cam*, crooked or winding). Kames are often steep cones, though at the edges of the glacier the streams can form extended kame terraces. They differ from drumlins in being produced beyond the glacial snout rather than being exposed by a retreating glacier, but can be difficult to distinguish from eskers by non-experts. Kames are usually associated with 'kame and kettle-hole topography', a landscape in which the kames are mounds of glaciofluvial deposit, the kettle holes being intervening hollows that are often water-filled. The kettle holes form where large chunks of ice embedded in the till melt. Kettle lakes are water-filled kettle holes.

The main landforms of glacial and glaciofluvial effects are illustrated in Figure 3.3.

Permafrost

Periglacial is the term applied to cold but non-glacial landscapes (the fact that the term includes 'glacial' is unfortunate as it can cause confusion). Periglacial regions are often taken to include any area affected by freezing and thawing, as this erosional process modifies the landscape, but strictly the definition applies only to areas adjacent to ice sheets (or close to the margins of the ice sheets of the last ice age), where intense cold penetrates deep into the ground. This cold penetration often results in the development of permafrost, a major periglacial feature. Although often assumed to be ice-based, permafrost is actually frozen ground (though that does mean there is no ice present), and it is technically defined as rock and soil in which temperatures do not rise above 0°C during two consecutive years. Permafrost requires groundwater – in rock crevices, soil cavities or as lenses of water (which can be formed by the migration of groundwater towards a pocket of

The ice-choked Jakobshavn Isfjord, west Greenland.

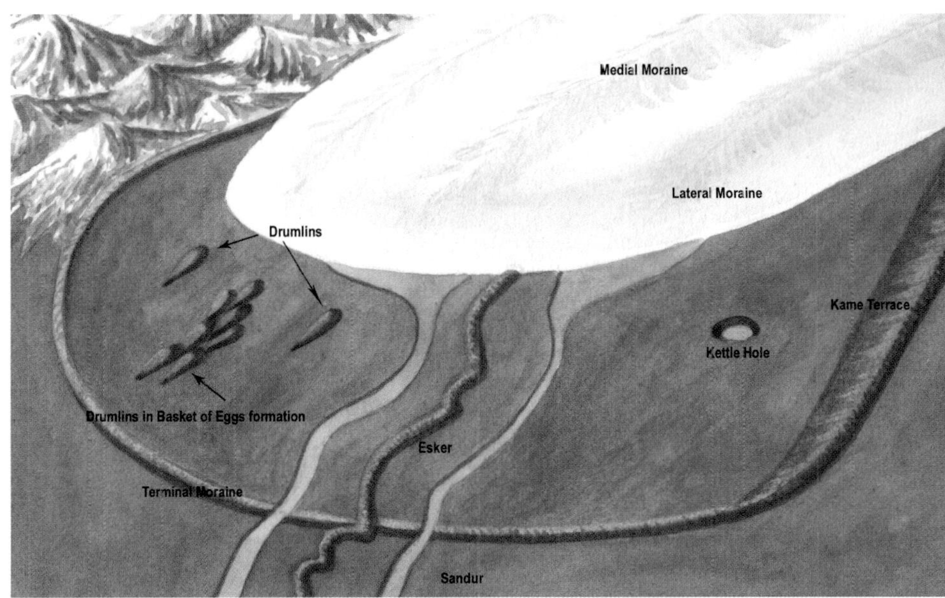

Figure 3.3
Glacial and glaciofluvial landforms.

Above
Polychrome, Denali National Park, Alaska. In the foreground is a kettle lake. Beyond, and to the right of it, is a large glacial erratic.

Below left
Photographer Per Michelsen on a kame mound, Suldal, Norway.

Below right
Esker near the Wright River in Nunavut, Canada.

already frozen water, or can be formed around buried remnant glacial ice) – to be frozen. However, the leaching of salts into the pockets from the soil can increase their salinity, so they can therefore remain liquid even if the ground temperature remains permanently below 0°C.

If the annual air temperature of a locality is below about -6°C (there is actually a range of temperatures depending on locality, but the variation is small, perhaps -5°C to -8°C) then continuous permafrost will be found. At higher ambient air temperatures, between -6°C and -1°C, the permafrost is thinner and may be fragmented; in such an area the permafrost is said to be discontinuous.

Despite a popular assumption that permafrost is a polar phenomenon, it actually occurs a considerable distance south of the present treeline, e.g. far to the south in Asian Russia and in China (see Figure 3.4). In fact around 25% of the Earth's landmass is underlain by permafrost. Permafrost in Asia results from the intensely cold winters of the continental climate of those areas. In Europe the influence of the North Atlantic Drift largely prevented the creation of permafrost, so Europeans only became aware of its existence when Arctic explorers attempted to bury their dead and encountered the unyielding, frozen ground beneath the shallow, seasonally thawed layer. Even after the discovery little interest was taken in the phenomenon in North America until the gold rush of the late 19th century began the economic development of the area, and the need to erect permanent structures. By contrast, the Russians knew of the existence of permafrost by the early 16th century, and writings from the 18th century include references to the remains of mammoths being found in the permanently frozen ground of Siberia.

The depth of the permafrost depends largely on the geothermal heat flux into the ground below the frozen layer and the net energy balance at the surface. In parts of Siberia, the permafrost layer is almost 1,500m thick; in North America it reaches depths of about 1,000m on Baffin Island and 600m on Alaska's North Slope. Such depths are almost certainly relics of the extreme cold of the Earth's recent geological history rather than a result of the present Arctic climate. One interesting feature of the distribution of permafrost beneath northern North America is that it is much more northerly to the east of Hudson Bay than to the west. The prevailing westerly winds in northern Canada blow across Hudson Bay; as the bay remains ice-free during the early winter, these winds pick up moisture, which is deposited as snow in northern Quebec and Labrador. Consequently snowfall in those provinces is much higher than in provinces west of Hudson Bay. The layer of snow acts as an insulating blanket, preventing cold penetration into the ground.

Strangely, ice itself, the 'progenitor' of the permafrost, also occasionally acts as an insulator, and it is thought that in some cases ice shielded the ground from extreme cold during the ice

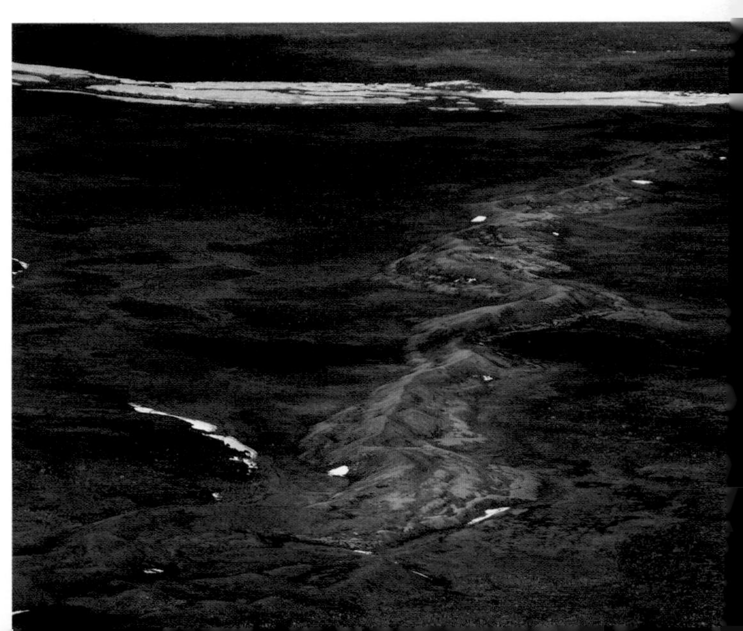

ages. As a consequence, the permafrost beneath most High Arctic glaciers is much thinner than in those areas of Alaska and Siberia that were not ice-covered during the last glaciation. The same is true under the sea, where unfrozen water insulated the sea-bed from extreme cold; permafrost occurs below the sea-bed only in areas where the shallow seas above the continental shelf froze solid, i.e. beneath the seas of eastern Russia and the Beaufort Sea.

In general, seasonal variations in the temperature of the permafrost do not occur at depths below about 20m. In summer the surface layer, known as the active layer, thaws. The depth of the active layer depends on the local energy balance; it may be as little as a few millimetres or more than several metres deep. Because the still-frozen permafrost beneath the active layer inhibits drainage, sections of the active layer may become saturated, forming an adhesive porridge (which rapidly accumulates in the tread of walking boots). Such areas are often called *taliks*. For the Arctic traveller in winter, taliks can be the cause of serious inconvenience as they may form hidden pockets that, if they lie beneath a thin surface crust, can overtop the boot of anyone unlucky enough to break through.

Above
Glacial outwash fan, near Pituffik, Thule, north-west Greenland.

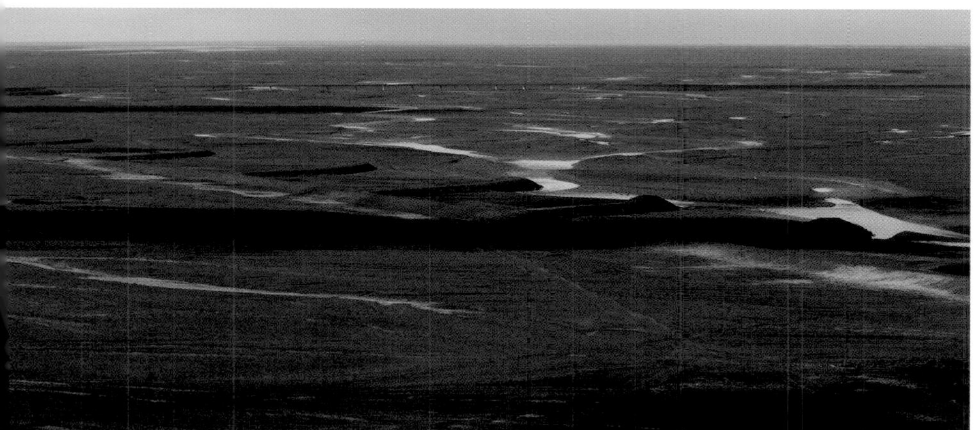

Left
***Sandur*, south Iceland. This extensive outwash fan is associated with several glaciers flowing from the Vatnajökull ice cap. The sandur was inundated by the 1996 *jökulhlaup*. The road crossing the sandur was repaired and re-opened after only two weeks, despite the vast rush of water.**

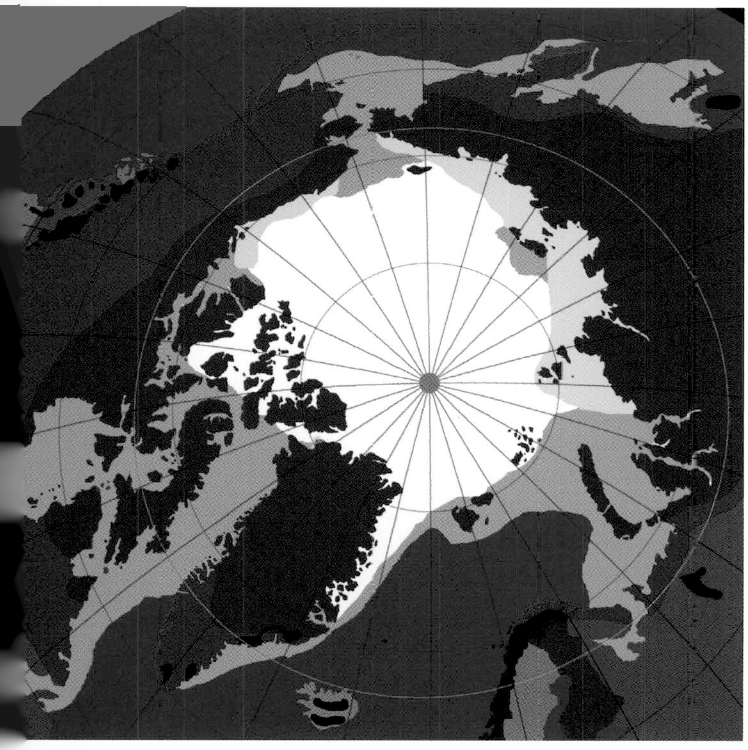

Figure 3.4
The distribution of permafrost in the Arctic and sub-Arctic. Dark red is the region of continuous permafrost. Pale red is the region of discontinuous permafrost. Yellow indicates sub-sea permafrost, while black indicates areas of alpine permafrost.

Nivation

In periglacial areas cold also sculpts the landscape directly by the process of nivation, the frost erosion of rock, which, over time, causes it to break down. During summer, rain or melted snow seeps into cracks in the rock. As ice is less dense than water, the water expands on freezing. The pressure exerted is considerable, and over time levers chunks of rock from cliffs or bedrock (this is the same process that causes household pipes to fracture; the damage is done when the water freezes, pushing joints in the pipe apart or, sometimes, causing the pipe

Building on permafrost

One of the problems associated with the construction of buildings in areas of permafrost is the escape of heat downwards from the structure. If placed directly on the frozen layer the inevitable heat production in buildings – particularly living accommodation – warms the permafrost. Melting of the top layer causes subsidence of the building, this problem increasing with time.

The top left photograph is of Third Avenue, Dawson City, Yukon Territory, Canada, built at the time of the Klondike gold rush and preserved as one of the best examples of subsidence due to permafrost melting.

The second photograph is of Inuvik in Canada's North West Territories. To minimise heating of the permafrost that underlies the town, water, heating and sewage pipes are not buried but are instead run in aluminium enclosures supported on wooden piles. Buildings are also raised on piles to minimise downward heat flow. Such a technique requires significant underfloor insulation as a chilling wind blows beneath the structure.

A particular problem was the construction of the Trans-Alaska oil pipeline from Prudhoe Bay to Valdez. Ignoring any discussion on the merits or otherwise of the decision to exploit the Bay's oil reserves, the transport of the oil presented engineers with several difficulties. The oil at the well heads is at about 70°C, cooling to about 33°C at Valdez. Assuming that leaks could be avoided, burying the pipeline would have been environmentally worthwhile, but insulating the hot oil from the permafrost would have been difficult and expensive. The pipeline is therefore buried only in the permafrost-free areas of southern Alaska, in areas of particular sensitivity for local wildlife, and on mountain passes where ground erosion would have compromised an overground structure. Elsewhere the 1.2m diameter pipe is surrounded by 10cm of fibreglass and encased in galvanised steel. The pipe sits on the cross-beam of a total of 78,000 H-section structures known as a Vertical Support Member, or VSM for short (see the third photograph), the legs of which are deeply piled into the permafrost. To further reduce heat flow to the permafrost the legs of the VSMs are filled with ammonia and topped by aluminium heat sinks, comprising radiating fins. Residual heat from the pipeline heats the ammonia. Ammonia boils at a lower temperature than the permafrost temperature, the vapour rising and releasing its heat through the heat sinks. As it loses heat, the ammonia condenses, falling back to the base of the support for the process to start again. So efficient are these thermal siphons that the local permafrost temperature is actually reduced, which adds further stability to the VSMs. For further information on the pipeline see A Vulnerable Ecosystem (p596).

For natural gas pipelines, which may become a feature of certain areas as exploitation of the Arctic's natural resources increases, the situation is different. As it is more efficient to pump the gas as a liquid, burying the line in the permafrost is advantageous since the medium both insulates and chills the pipe.

Thawing permafrost affects not only buildings but also trees; tilted trees (final photograph) are a sign of a deepening active layer leading to a lack of root support.

The author using a muskox rib to clear talik from his boot treads, Ellesmere Island, Canada.

itself to rupture, but this does not become apparent until a thaw sets in).

Frost erosion occurs in both glacial and periglacial landscapes. In periglacial areas it is responsible for such distinctive features as scree slopes, created by the frost erosion of a cliff, the rock debris (or scree – the debris also has the more formal name 'talus', so scree slopes and talus slopes refer to the same feature) formed littering the slope below the cliff. If there is a snowfield on the slope, rocks can slide down it, piling up at the base. If the snowfield then disappears the rocks form a distinctive rampart – called a protalus rampart – beneath the cliff from which they have been prised.

Frost shattering of rock. Mackenzie delta, North West Territories, Canada.

Pingos are among the most impressive landforms of the periglacial zone. The name is a Mackenzie Delta Inuit word for a conical hill; use of the name is reasonable as it is estimated that about 25% of all the world's pingos are to be found on the Tuktoyaktuk Peninsula to the north-east of the delta. Pingos are mounds of ice covered with a layer of sediment, usually circular in form and occasionally of extraordinary size, up to 75m high and over 500m in diameter.

Pingos form in one of two ways. 'Open system' pingos are produced by artesian (underground) water feeding an expanding ice dome, and they are usually found in discontinuous permafrost where groundwater movement is feasible. 'Closed system' pingos form beneath a surface lake. The lake insulates the ground beneath it so it does not freeze, creating a volume of talik. If the lake drains, the talik freezes and the ice expands into the characteristic mound. Because closed pingos form from talik they have a sediment cap, the active layer of which can support considerable growth as the domed nature of the pingo allows good drainage and, if the pingo is sizeable, there will also be a sheltered side. In areas beyond, though not far beyond, the treeline, pingos occasionally have trees growing on their southern slope. Other plants also benefit, pingos having a more diverse and luxuriant growth than the neighbouring tundra. The plant life brings animal life, and the pingo becomes a small oasis of life. People, too, occupied pingos, though only on a temporary basis, the local Inuit using them as look-outs for spotting caribou herds.

If a pingo's ice core is exposed it may thaw, the tops of some pingos having collapsed craters reminiscent of volcanoes. If, rather than draining away, the meltwater forms a lake this insulates the remaining ice of the core, extending the pingo's life.

One aspect of pingo creation that may be critical to human endeavours, if warming of the Arctic opens the North-East and North-West Passages to regular commercial traffic, is that, as permafrost underlies the sea-bed in some areas of the passages, underwater pingos may form. If conditions allow the passages to be used by deep draught vessels, large oil tankers, for example, these could collide with submarine pingos. Submarine permafrost will also make any attempt at drilling for oil or gas in these areas difficult.

Palsas and patterns

Similar in appearance to pingos are palsas, mounds or ridges of frozen peat. Palsas are found in areas of discontinuous permafrost, usually in the damper areas of marshland. They are thought to be created by frost-heaving processes, or the expansion of a perennially frozen ice lens. Palsas can reach 6–8m in height in southern regions of the Arctic, though they rarely attain heights above 1m in the High Arctic. Palsa mounds are usually 10–30m across, while ridges can be up to 150m long, though lengths of 15–50m are more common. In the High Arctic the peat forming the palsa may be 5,000 or 10,000 years old.

If pingos are the most physically impressive periglacial landform, patterned ground is the most exotic. In some soils winter temperatures can cause shrinkage of the soil and cracks to appear. Linking of these crack lines then creates a pattern of polygons or circles. In summer, water seeps into the cracks

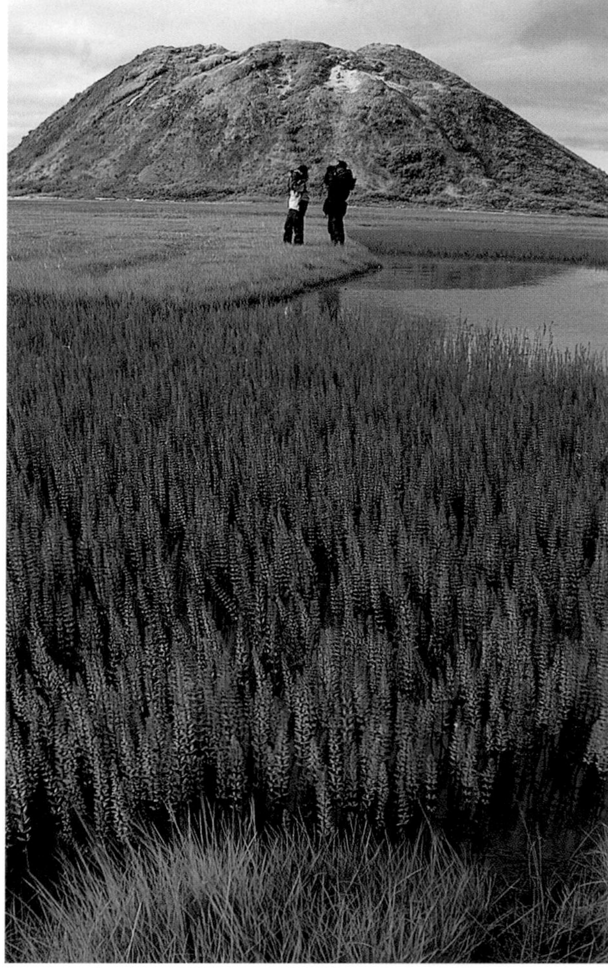

Above
Scree slope, south Iceland.

Above right
Ibyuk pingo, Tuktoyaktuk. The Tuktoyaktuk Peninsula is the world capital of pingos, with Ibyuk the largest of them.

Right
A more 'normal' pingo near Kongsfjorden, Spitsbergen, Svalbard.

from the active layer. The water freezes in the following winter, forming wedges of ice. The annual cycle of freeze and thaw causes the wedges to expand as layers of ice are added. Wedge expansion pushes the ridge of soil at the rim (i.e. at the surface) upwards so that raised polygons are formed (see Figure 3.5). The polygons range in size from a metre or so across to around 100m, the ice wedge itself being as much as 2m wide. The widest wedges can take decades to form.

The polygons are one of several forms of patterned ground, a feature that puzzled early Arctic travellers. Most curious of them is the sorting of the ground material by size, larger stones forming the sides of some polygons, with finer material in the centre. The sorting appears man-made, but it is actually a natural process – frost-heaving. Frost-heaving is a consequence of the different thermal inertia of stones and finer material. Stones have a lower specific heat and so cool quicker. As the ground cools the upper surface of the stone sticks to overlying frozen material and is pulled upwards as this expands (this is termed frost-pull). As the freezing front moves downward it moves faster through the stone, reaching the material beneath which expands and pushes the stone upwards (frost-push). The net effect is to force the stone to the surface.

When the thaw occurs the finer material sinks below the stone, leaving it on the surface. Doming of the ground as a consequence of frost-heave cycles now causes the stones to move outwards from the dome centre (frost-thrust). Over many freeze-thaw cycles circles of stones form, these eventually interacting to form polygons.

Stone stripes may form on sloping ground, where the polygons extend downhill (Figure 3.6) and gravity completes the sorting process. In all cases, the lines of stones are narrower

than the intervening areas of finer material. The more homogeneous the ground material, and the more uniform the freezing and heaving process, the more regular the polygons and patterns produced.

One form of patterned ground that can be useful to nesting birds, but may be a nuisance to the traveller, is the hummock field. Earth hummocks are essentially non-sorted circles, though their exact creation method is poorly understood (currently popular is the idea that they form in areas where frost-heaving is irregular and concentrated in discrete areas, though why this should be so is not clear). The raised hummocks, which are often hemispherical and vary in height from a few centimetres to several metres (though smaller mounds are more common), usually support various plant colonies. The hummocks offer a convenient nesting place for birds, but make traversing an area difficult, particularly if the hummocks are around knee-high.

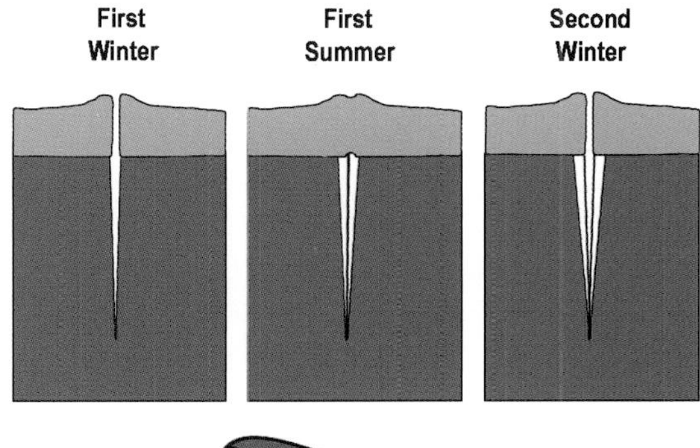

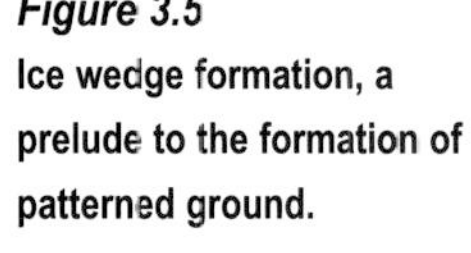

Figure 3.5
Ice wedge formation, a prelude to the formation of patterned ground.

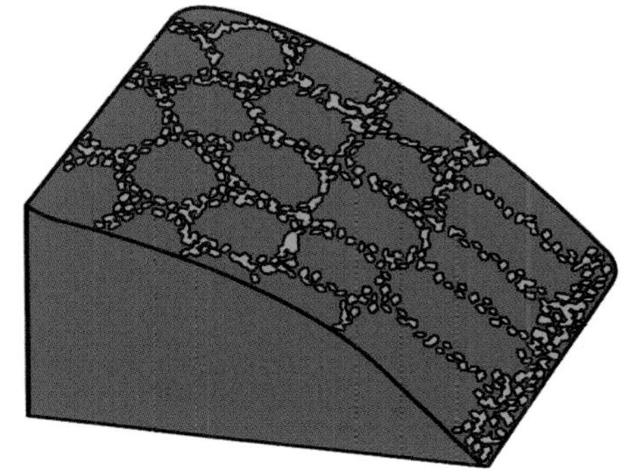

Figure 3.6
Polygons are formed on level ground, but where the ground slopes, the polygons extend to form stripes.

Other periglacial landforms

Three final periglacial landforms are worth noting. Thermokarst is the periglacial equivalent of a karst landscape in temperate zones, but in periglacial areas water is lost by melting rather than by the dissolving of bedrock and subsequent sub-surface flow. Thermokarst landscapes occur where drainage is poor because of a permafrost layer beneath essentially flat country. Ground-ice thawing creates a series of waterlogged hollows dotted across an area of hummocky ground, the hollows occasionally coalescing to form thaw lakes. If sections of the area slope gently, beaded drainage may occur, with a linear series of lakes linked by small streams.

A second interesting periglacial landform is the gradual downhill drift of soil. This can occur as a consequence of frost-heaving on sloping ground, stones brought to the surface being moved downhill by each freeze-thaw cycle in a process often called frost creep. Soil drift also results from gelifluction, the periglacial equivalent of solifluction, the downhill slumping of saturated material. When the active layer of the permafrost freezes it expands perpendicular to the frozen layer beneath, even if the ground is sloping. However, when the active layer thaws it moves with gravity (i.e. downhill), rather than back towards the layer below. Successive freeze-thaw episodes then cause distinctive gelifluction lobes to form.

The final landform is one of the most enigmatic, the rock glacier. In cold, relatively dry, high-relief landscapes in which

Patterned ground, near Kongsfjorden, Spitsbergen, Svalbard.

Right
Rock glacier, Snæfell, Iceland.

there is a good supply of scree, this debris may flow downhill. The exact structure and creep method of rock glaciers is not understood. Some are believed to have an ice core, perhaps having begun as a debris-covered glacier (in which case the rock glacier would be a glacial, rather than a periglacial, landform). However, a rock glacier may consist of an upper layer of larger scree (which may be aggregated using ice as a 'cement') covering a layer of frozen rock sitting on a layer of smaller scree, which acts in a similar way to ball-bearings. Most rock glaciers are mid-latitude alpine landforms, there being around a thousand examples in Switzerland. But they also occur in the Arctic, an example in Greenland being 5.5km long, the longest rock glacier known. In general rock glaciers are smaller than this, less than 800m long and 100m wide, and they travel slowly, usually at speeds of less than 1m annually.

Right
Hummocky ground on Ellesmere Island, Canada.

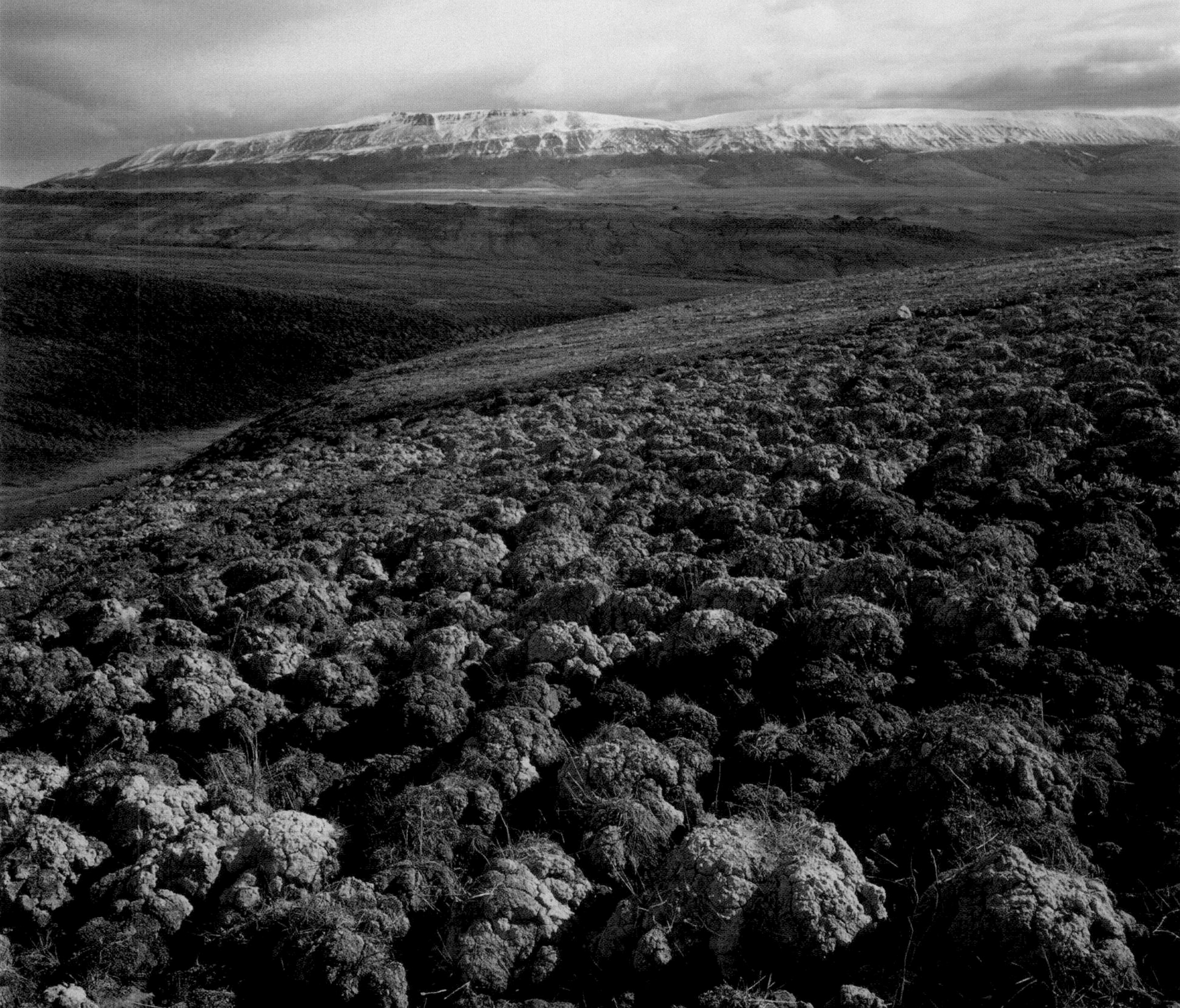

Opposite page
The midnight Sun over thawing sea ice, Kvaduhuken, Svalbard.

Right
Thermokarst scenery, near Coldfoot, Alaska.

Below
Valley glacier, Trygghavna, Svalbard.

Above
Drifting sea ice, south-west Spitsbergen, Svalbard.

Left
Iceberg detail, Jakobshavn Isfjord, west Greenland.

4. The Climate of the Arctic

The Arctic is cold. A factually accurate statement of the obvious – the cold is one of the defining features of the region, particularly in the popular imagination. But the reasons *why* it is cold are not at all clear: 'the Arctic is cold' is one of those statements which, like 'the sky is blue', is both self-evident, yet, when considered in detail, perplexing.

When the search for the North-West Passage began, one idea was to sail north directly over the North Pole. It was reasoned that since the sun was visible throughout the summer close to the Pole, sunlight should melt the sea ice. Only further south where there were significant periods of darkness could the sea ice persist. All a captain needed to do was to find a gap in the ring of sea ice and sail through; beyond would be the open polar sea and (apart from the need to find another gap on the other side) the journey to the east would be straightforward. But it was eventually discovered that the long Arctic summer did not melt the sea ice; the extra sunlight did not compensate for the long Arctic winter.

There are several reasons why not. The first is that in the Arctic the sun is always at a low angle in the sky, so the sunlight illuminates a greater area of the Earth's surface than it does at more southerly latitudes (and especially at the Equator), and therefore there is a significantly smaller energetic input per unit area. Despite the polar summers, the North and South Poles receive only 60% of the insolation (incident solar radiation) of a point on the Equator. Because of this low angle, radiation from the sun (i.e. light) must also pass through more of the Earth's atmosphere before reaching the surface. Some of the sunlight is absorbed or scattered by the molecules that make up the atmosphere (carbon dioxide and water vapour absorb and re-radiate some of the incident radiation, and dust particles scatter it).

Radiation that reaches the Earth is absorbed, warming the surface. But not all of it is absorbed – some of it is reflected. This effect, termed albedo, varies with the make-up of the surface. Darker surfaces absorb more of the incident radiation than lighter ones. Dark soils absorb 90% of incident radiation and reflect only 10%, but for the ice of the Greenland ice sheet these figures are reversed. Clouds may also have a high albedo, reflecting as much as 80% of the incident radiation, so that much of the insolation does not even reach the Earth. As summer cloud cover in the Arctic tends to be high this can have a significant effect; the low-level stratus cloud that dominates the Arctic sky during the summer has an albedo of 60–70% (though direct absorption by the cloud cover is minimal). High surface albedo then reflects much of what insolation actually reaches the Arctic surface, though some of this can be reflected back by the cloud base. Multiple reflections by the Earth's surface and the cloud base creates a 'flat' light in which people can find travel difficult; on occasions, this flat light can even produce white-out conditions.

The radiation absorbed by the Earth is partially re-radiated, but at longer wavelengths than the incident radiation. Incident radiation is a spectrum, with all but about 0.1% in the wavelength band 0.15–4μm (the peak intensity is at 0.5μm (500nm): visible light, in the wavelength band 400–700nm, accounts for about 50% of the total). The re-radiated energy is at wavelengths of 4–300μm with a peak intensity at about 10μm. While the Earth's atmosphere is essentially transparent to the incident radiation (though there is, as noted above, some absorption and scattering), it is only semi-transparent to the longer wavelength, re-radiated radiation, which is absorbed by water vapour and some atmospheric gases and warms the atmosphere. Cold air holds up to ten times less water vapour than warm air, one reason that the atmosphere of the Arctic is often amazingly clear. That means that less of the re-radiated energy is absorbed by the atmosphere above the Arctic; the energy escapes into space.

The Arctic is cold. Winter night, Kapp Dufferin, Svalbard.

By contrast to the Arctic, at the Equator the Earth receives more energy from the sun than is radiated back. There is, therefore, an energy surplus at the Equator, just as there is a deficit at the North Pole. In fact, there is a surplus of received over radiated energy at all latitudes below about 38°N. The laws of thermodynamics require the redistribution of that energy, and air and ocean currents transfer heat from lower latitudes to the Arctic. Latent heat is also gained each time water vapour is converted to snow. However, although the air and ocean currents go some way to redistribute the extra solar energy reaching the tropics to the polar regions, their effect is not large enough to entirely compensate for reduced energy input from insolation. The Arctic is cold as a result.

General weather patterns

The rising of warm, buoyant air at the Equator and the sinking of cold, dense air at the Poles, together with the deflection of resulting air streams by the Coriolis force due to the rotation of the Earth from west to east would, in an ideal world, create a stable, easily understood wind pattern. However, an idealised view such as this quickly breaks down when macroscopic and local effects are imposed on the simple pattern. But there are some permanent and semi-permanent features of the Arctic atmosphere that consistently influence the region's weather patterns, so some general comments on the weather the traveller might experience can be made. One such feature is the polar vortex, a stable, low-pressure system in the middle

Opposite page
Wind disturbs the trees and cloud blankets the mountains as an autumn storm crosses southern Alaska.

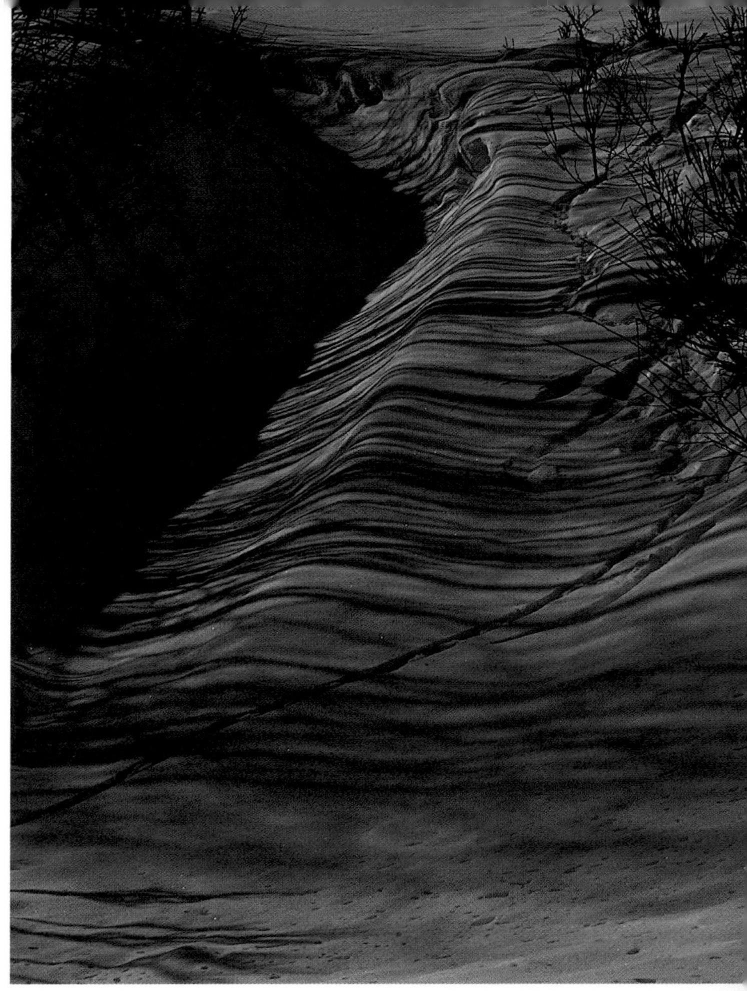

The low-angled Sun of the Arctic winter creates long shadows. Near Abisko National Park, Sweden.

A general overview of the Arctic climate

The effects of the circumpolar distribution of land masses in the Arctic on prevailing winds, together with the influence of ocean currents, mean that the climate of specific places is influenced by local conditions much more than in, say, Antarctica. However, some general comments can be made. The Greenland ice sheet is cold and dry, both in summer and winter, though the coastal regions of the island are, of course, influenced by the adjacent seas. The Atlantic Arctic is dominated by the North Atlantic Drift, which gives rise to cool winters and warm summers (even in Svalbard and Franz Josef Land), with wind speeds higher in summer than in winter. In Siberia, the wind speeds are reversed and increase in winter. The continental climate of Siberia means cold winters and cool summers. The northern Pacific is warmer than the adjacent landmasses (but colder than the Atlantic). The area is cloudier and has higher wind speeds and precipitation. Arctic North America is generally cold in winter and warm in summer (often surprisingly so). Summers tend to be cloudy with higher precipitation. Eastern Canada is influenced by the extent of Baffin Bay (as is western Greenland); the Bay is climatically similar to the Atlantic but cooler. The Arctic interior is cold, and cloudier in summer than in winter.

upper atmosphere (at altitudes between 15km and 80km) around which westerly circumpolar air flows. The vortex, which usually sits above the Pole (though it can move hundreds of kilometres from it), steers both the cyclonic and anticyclonic systems that affect the Arctic traveller. More local features are the winter low-pressure systems that form over the Aleutians and between Iceland and south Greenland, the winter high-pressure system above eastern Siberia, and the persistent highs above the Beaufort Sea and the Greenlandic ice sheet.

The polar vortex and the Icelandic and Aleutian lows are associated with climatic oscillations; these are well-documented but poorly understood. The wind speed of the polar vortex influences the Arctic Oscillation (AO), which affects the entire Arctic area. When the winds are high there is lower pressure near the pole and cold temperatures in Arctic Canada, though warmer temperatures in Eurasia (and in Alaska) and more winter ice in the Bering Sea. The AO is very closely linked to the North Atlantic Oscillation (NAO) – some experts claim the NAO is one of the components of the AO – which depends on the pressure difference between the winter low over Iceland and winter high over the Azores. This influences the flow of westerlies over the Gulf Stream and, therefore, how much heat is picked up and carried to northern Europe and Siberia. When the pressure difference is high, European winters are warmer and wetter and there is less ice in the Barents Sea. However, eastern Canada is colder and there is more ice in Baffin and Hudson Bays, and in the Labrador Sea. When the pressure difference is low, the reverse is true. The oscillation between the two states takes about ten years. A third oscillation is the Pacific Decadal Oscillation (PDO), which is associated with the Aleutian low (though it is less well correlated with air pressure than the NAO). When the PDO is in a positive phase the surface temperature of the North Pacific rises (and, interestingly, the Alaskan salmon catch is higher). Both the NAO and the PDO are associated with the AO, though the nature of the correlation, as with the oscillations themselves, is poorly understood. Like the AO and NAO, the PDO exhibits a ten-year periodicity.

Deep depression off southwest Iceland.

Ocean currents

Since the North Atlantic Oscillation is associated with heat pick-up from the Gulf Stream, it is worth considering what drives ocean currents around the Arctic, and the effect they have on climate. The most important of the currents is undoubtedly the North Atlantic Drift, the warm water current that drives the Arctic boundary northward in Europe relative to North America.

The rotation of the Earth induces a prevailing west–east wind in the northern hemisphere, which induces surface currents in the Atlantic and Pacific Oceans of similar direction. In each case, this results in sea levels being higher on the eastern side of the oceans: in the Panama Canal, for example, the Pacific side is several metres higher than the Atlantic side. This difference is less marked in the Arctic, but sea level on the Pacific side of the Arctic basin is still about 45cm higher than the Atlantic side. This height difference generates the trans-Arctic drift, with water flowing into the Arctic basin through the Bering Strait. The northern Pacific Ocean is less salty than the North Atlantic. The Bering Sea is less salty again as a consequence of the inflow of freshwater, chiefly from the Yukon River, to a relatively small, shallow sea. With the massive freshwater run-off of the rivers of Asian Russia, and of the Mackenzie River in Canada, the salinity of the Arctic Ocean on the Bering Sea side falls further, creating a surface layer of cold, low-salinity water on the Pacific side, the leaching of salt during sea ice formation not compensating for the inflow of freshwater. This surface layer is 10–60m thick; below it lies a layer of water in which temperature remains relatively constant but salinity increases with depth.

In the North Atlantic the Gulf Stream – 100km wide and 1,000m deep, flowing at 100km per day – carries warm water north-eastwards, the salinity of this water being high as a result of evaporation. Close to the Azores, at about 47°W, the Gulf Stream bifurcates, one arm (the Azores Current) turning south, while the North Atlantic Drift heads towards northern Europe. It is the heat flux of the drift (which is about 5°C above the average temperature for its latitude and adds an extra 35% to the heat input from the sun), and its associated winds, which pushes the Arctic northwards in Europe. As the drift heads north it cools. At the temperatures of sea-water in the Arctic, water density is dependent more on salinity than temperature; the salty waters of the drift therefore dive below the layer of increasingly salty water (known as the cold halocline), which itself lies beneath the less salty surface waters. The cold halocline prevents the warm Atlantic waters from melting the sea ice. The Atlantic waters circulate in the Arctic Basin, cooling further and sinking as they do. This deep, cold, salty water forms the Arctic Ocean deep water current, which flows south at depth to balance the northward flow of the North Atlantic Drift. This exchange is known as a thermohaline circulation, so called because it depends on both temperature and salinity.

The exchange of warm surface water from the western mid-Atlantic to the Arctic Ocean and the reverse flow of deep, cold water is occasionally called the Atlantic conveyor. It is known that historically the conveyor has been halted, and it is thought that a weakening of it caused Europe's 'Little Ice Age' in the late 17th and early 18th centuries (though what would have caused such a weakening is unclear). One effect of global warming might be the switching off of the conveyor again, as freshwater from the melting Greenland ice sheet dilutes the salty waters of the halocline. Such a stoppage would be of limited duration as there is a finite volume of water in the ice sheet, and the Earth's rotation would always push warm waters west–east, but it would have a very significant effect on the climate of northern Europe, producing winter temperatures more comparable with those of similar latitudes in North America. It is worth bearing in mind that 'limited duration' in this context is relative to geological timescales, not to those of the human lifespan.

There is no similar thermohaline circulation in the Pacific, though why this should be is not completely understood. Clearly the net flow of water into the Arctic basin is an influence, though another effect seems to be that the waters of the North Pacific have a more stable stratification pattern than those of the Atlantic. Consequently, the North Atlantic Drift is the major ocean current affecting the Arctic climate. Away from the drift, in Asian Russia and North America, ocean currents have less effect on local temperature than do air masses moving from close to the Pole. However, the Labrador Current brings cold water and air through the Davis Strait, chilling eastern Canada and western Greenland.

Borgefell, Norway (above), and Canada's Barren Lands near the Mackaye Lake (below), at 63°N. The difference in vegetation indicates the effect of the Gulf Stream on northern Europe.

Temperature

Temperatures in the Arctic are not as low as those of Antarctica, the Arctic climate being moderated by the Atlantic and Pacific Oceans, while Antarctica is insulated from the effect of warmer water masses by the Southern Ocean circulating around the continent. At Russia's Vostok research station in Antarctica a temperature of -89.2°C has been recorded, making it the coldest place on Earth. In the Arctic, the lowest temperatures are recorded at points away from the

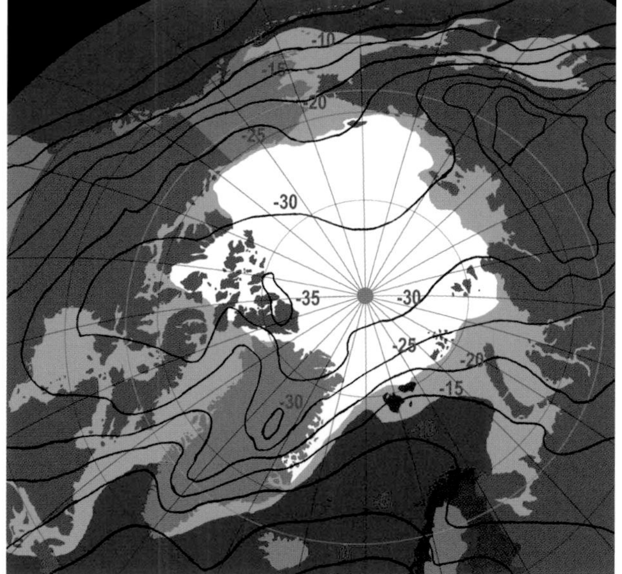

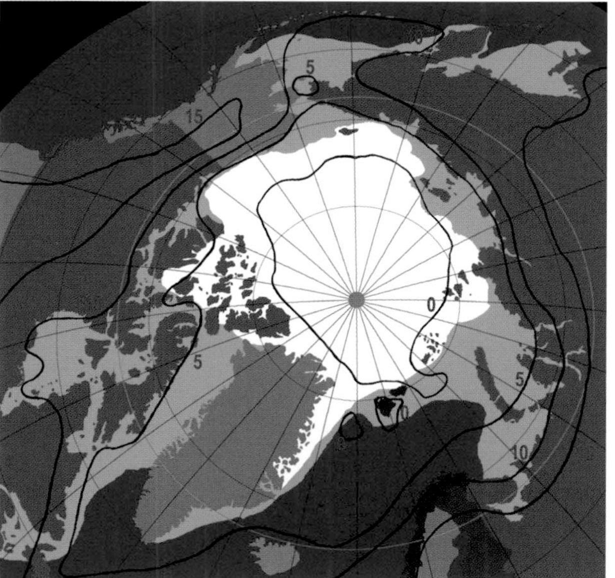

Figure 4.1
Temperature contours (°C) for January (above) and July.

seas, at the North Ice station in Greenland (-66.1°C) and at Oymyakon in the Verkhoyanskiy region of north-east Siberia (-77.8°C). Surprisingly, Oymyakon lies to the south of the boundary used to define 'the Arctic' in this book, its extreme temperature arising, in part, from its continental (as opposed to maritime) climate. Climatologists occasionally divide landmasses into zones of approximately equivalent temperature. On that basis, the islands of Arctic Russia are classified as 'cold'. The northern coast of Russia from the White Sea to the Chukotka border is classified as 'moderately cold', though Chukotka itself is 'cold'. However, inland Siberia east of the Yenisey river is classified as 'very cold'. To this classification must be added the effect of temperature inversion. Normally, temperature decreases with increasing height above the Earth's surface, but within continental landmasses 'cold air lakes' can arise, layers of cold air being trapped below a layer of warmer air created when sinking air heats adiabatically (as a result of compression) as it descends. Such inversions are both more intense and longer-lived where the cold air is trapped within a valley, particularly one remote from the sea. Cold air lakes occur both in North America, particularly in the area to the west and south-west of Canada's Great Bear Lake, and in Siberia. The combination of a 'very cold' zone and a cold air lake give Oymyakon its record-breaking temperatures.

One other effect of temperature inversion with which Arctic travellers soon become familiar is ice fog. This is produced when water vapour is released into air at very low temperatures (in general around -30°C), the water vapour freezing to form ice crystals (usually about 30μm in diameter, but even smaller in some very dense fogs) to form the fog. Because of the requirement for water vapour such fogs are usually associated with areas of settled population, the vapour derived from vehicle exhausts and industrial sites. Famously, Fairbanks, Alaska suffers from such fogs, with visibility reduced to a few metres within the fog bank, though the bank itself may only be 10–15m thick. Fairbanks' ice fogs have been known to cover an area of around 200km^2 and to persist for up to 15 days.

Summer temperatures in parts of the Arctic can be surprisingly warm, a sharp contrast to winter temperatures. Gullfoss, Iceland.

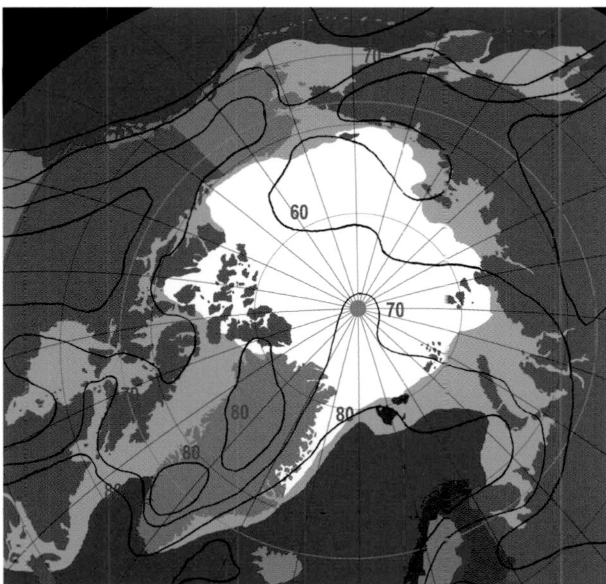

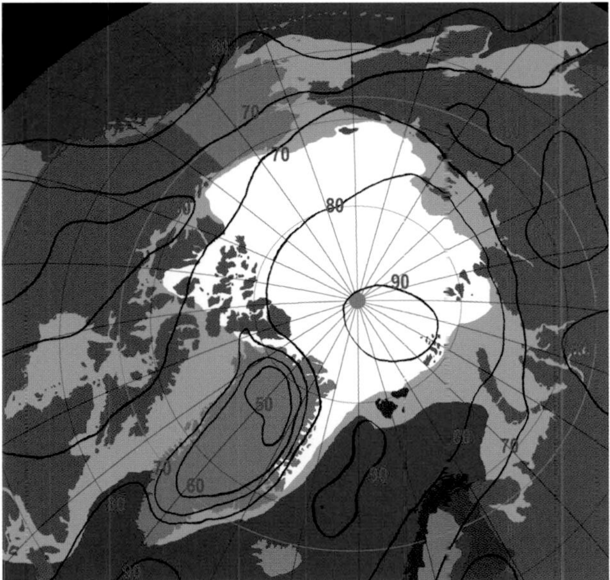

Figure 4.2
Cloud cover contours (% of month) for January (above) and July.

Over such a large area and with macroscopic effects such as the North Atlantic Drift to be taken into consideration, together with more local effects, it is difficult to generalise about the variation of temperature through the Arctic year. The effect of the drift on northern temperatures can be seen in the temperature difference between Oymyakon and the Norwegian coast at the same latitude. In January the difference in mean temperature is about 50°C, about the same as the difference between the North Pole and the Equator. The warming effect of the open sea alone can be seen when considering the difference between inland and coastal Greenland. Though less dramatic than the difference between Oymyakon and Norway it is, at about 30°C, still very pronounced.

Figure 4.1 shows the mean surface air temperature of the Arctic in January and July. It is interesting to note the change in the difference between mean summer and mean winter temperatures across the region. As well as the descriptive definitions given above for dividing the Arctic into regions of similar winter temperature, three climatic regions are also defined and these can be inferred from Figure 4.1. In maritime areas, a classic example of which is Jan Mayen, the summer–winter variation is of the order of 10°C. In general the maximum summer temperature in such areas occurs in August, with the minimum in March. In continental areas, such as inland Siberia, this variation is 40°C, perhaps even more. In these areas the maximum and minimum temperatures are seen in July and January respectively. Between the two lie continental coastal areas in which the variation is transitional, usually about 20°C. In these areas maximum temperatures are observed in July or early August, and minimum temperatures in January or early February.

These seasonal differences are not matched by daily differences such as those familiar in temperate regions; these are ironed out by the continuous daylight of the Arctic summer and the long sunless winter. Usually the difference between maximum and minimum daily temperatures is only 3–5°C.

Though the data of Figure 4.1 are of use for a traveller who wonders what temperatures might be encountered at a particular time of the year, local conditions play a significant role in how cold it will actually be. Air temperature is only one factor in this equation. Wind speed is a dominating factor, leading to wind chill that can be considered as an effective reduction in ambient temperature (see Table below). Wind chill can, of course, be mitigated by reducing or eliminating skin exposure. Cloud cover is also important. On clear days in summer the sun can enhance effective temperature by many degrees, turning otherwise cool Arctic days into idyllic, warm ones. However, clear skies in winter permit increased heat loss from the Earth and, if the sun is below the horizon so there is no corresponding heat input, can lead to intense cold.

Cloud cover

The Arctic is a cloudy region, particularly during the summer when grey, low-level stratus dominates (Figure 4.2). The cloudiest area is the Atlantic Arctic, which averages 80% cover almost constantly throughout the year. By contrast, cloud cover in the Eurasian, central and Canadian Arctic is highly seasonal. For these regions the summer average is 80%, reducing to 60% in winter. The coverage is relatively stable for each season, with the change from summer to winter coverage and *vice versa* being remarkably sudden, and occurring over the space of a month (May and October). Further analysis of the data on cloud types indicates that the variation in cover is largely the result of changes in low cloud cover, low cloud constituting the 'normal' Arctic cloud cover of stratus plus cumulus, cumulonimbus and stratocumulus. Low cloud cover varies from about 25% in winter to 70% in summer. Medium (altocumulus, altostratus and nimbostratus) cloud is relatively constant throughout the year (at around 35%), but does show an autumnal peak. High cloud (cirrus, cirrocumulus and cirrostratus) also shows an autumnal peak, but otherwise reverses the low-level variation by reducing during the summer months. Observations during the latter years of the 20th century indicate that the seasonal variation in cloud cover seen over most of the Arctic is accentuating, with an increase in summer and a reduction in winter.

As cloud cover obscures the sun, on average the Arctic traveller sees the sun for only about 20–25% of the time when it might be visible. Accumulated data suggests that the sunniest place in the Arctic is the inland ice of Greenland, followed by central Canada and east central Siberia (with about 80% of the inland ice sunlight total). Next come Alaska and Canada's Arctic islands (about 67%). Coastal Greenland, Iceland, western Siberia and eastern Canada have about 50% of the inland

Windswept ground free of snow, Van Mijenfjorden, Svalbard.

ice sunlight, while Svalbard, the Bering Sea coast of Siberia and the Atlantic coast of Canada reach only about 40%. The cloud cover above Svalbard associated with this minimal sunshine means that southern Spitsbergen receives the lowest insolation of any place in the Arctic. That said, one of the most idyllic days I ever spent in the Arctic was in southern Spitsbergen on a calm, sunny day with a temperature of about 20°C; as elsewhere, Arctic weather can confound both a traveller's plans and expectations.

Precipitation

The central Arctic basin is an arid area, with precipitation comparable to Antarctica, which is frequently referred to as a polar desert. Areas of the Arctic are similarly defined. In strictly scientific terms polar desert refers to an area where the annual precipitation does not exceed 130mm annually. As we have already seen (Figure 1.5), the polar desert area of the Arctic covers virtually the entire Canadian Arctic archipelago, together with coastal areas of northern Greenland, Svalbard, the Russian Arctic islands and a section of the Russian mainland. Although the Canadian archipelago does indeed receive less than 130mm of precipitation annually (indeed, the northern islands receive less than 100mm), the other areas are considered polar deserts in terms of plant growth, with the precipitation being somewhat higher. The central Arctic receives 100–200mm of precipitation annually, as do Svalbard, the Russian Arctic archipelagos and islands, much of the Russian northern mainland and the northern mainland of Canada. Annual precipitation is higher on the eastern side of Canada (up to 700mm in Labrador) and on the Pacific coast of eastern Siberia (up to 600mm); Kamchatka receives as much as 900–1,000mm annually. This is exceeded by southern Greenland, where the south-eastern tip of the island receives 1,500–2,500mm (though the south-western tip sees 900–1,000mm). The higher figures relate, as would be expected, to the proximity of the sea, and to wind direction, the aridity of the central Arctic deriving from the reduction in insolation of the area relative to the Equator; at the Equator the solar energy causes hot air to rise, while cold air sinks in the Arctic. The sinking air inhibits precipitation.

Though the closeness of an area to the sea creates local distortions in precipitation rates, some general comments can be made. Precipitation tends to decrease as one moves north. It is lowest in spring, since the frozen sea limits moisture take-up. That said, the seasonal variation of precipitation is rather muted. As an example, on average there are the same number of days (12) with precipitation greater than 0.1mm in Svalbard in both January and July. Something similar is observed in virtually all parts of the Arctic (though the number of days varies). Those looking for dry days in January should head for inland Greenland or, since that is not an entirely practical suggestion, for Nunavut or northern Asian Russia. Those looking for dry days in July should head for the same areas, but to their surprise will find that the monthly average of days with more than 0.1mm of precipitation has risen from 9 to 12.

One obvious Arctic precipitate is snowfall, and it is instructive to look at the persistence of snow cover across the region. However, it must be remembered that there is no correlation between days of snow cover and days of precipitation, as the extent of cover also depends on temperature; given a low temperature and limited sublimation, snowfall can persist for a long time. Persistence of snow cover peaks close to the North Pole, where there is snow cover for about 350 days annually. Heading south this persistence inevitably falls. In Severnaya Zemlya it averages around 300 days, with about 240 days on the other islands of Russia's western Arctic and 250 days in Svalbard. The northern coast of Russia sees 260 days of snow cover. In the New World the northern areas of Canada's Arctic islands see 300 days, while Alaska's northern coast and the southern Canadian Arctic archipelago see 260 days. However, these figures relate to data averaged over the last half of the 20th century. With temperatures increasing in the Arctic the day rates are likely to change, perhaps significantly, in the decades ahead.

Wind

The cold, dense air of the Arctic draws warmer air northward, the Earth's rotation combining with this airstream to create an anticlockwise vortex over the pole. Superimposed on this global pattern are the effects of topography of the landmasses and local climatic conditions (e.g. proximity of the sea). Though these effects mean that it is very difficult to be specific about winds in particular areas, some generalisations are possible. As with precipitation, the Arctic wind pattern does not exhibit a pronounced seasonal variation. Winds tend to blow from the central Arctic towards Arctic Canada, sweeping east across Hudson Bay (the effect of which is to reduce the extent of permafrost on the eastern side of the Bay). Winds are also funnelled through the Denmark Strait, though in summer the wind heads towards the pole from northern Greenland. The prevailing wind is also northward from the Russian Arctic. The Barents and Norwegian Seas are infamous for the winter 'polar easterlies' that sweep across them. In general, the Nearctic is less windy than the Palearctic; during the last half of the 20th century, Canadian Arctic weather stations reported calms on about 120 days annually.

In winter, the average wind speed over much of the Arctic is 4–6m/s, with higher average speeds experienced between Svalbard and Fennoscandia (8–10m/s) and in the North Atlantic, particularly on the western side. In summer, there is little difference in average wind speed over much of the Arctic, though it tends to be lower between Svalbard and Fennoscandia (4–6m/s) and in the North Atlantic. Summer winds are only 50% as strong as winter winds in the western North Atlantic. In the central Arctic wind speeds above 25m/s (90kph) are rare; for comparison, speeds of up to 50m/s (180kph) have been measured in the North Atlantic Arctic, which is generally the windiest part of the region.

As well as katabatic winds (see Box), the upland areas of the Arctic can also experience *föhn* winds.

Katabatic and anabatic winds

One type of wind that is a feature of the polar regions is the katabatic. Katabatics, named after the Greek for 'going downhill', develop where cold, dense air descends from an upland area into a valley under the influence of gravity. A famous example is the wind created when cold air masses fall from the high Antarctic plateau and accelerate towards the coast. These winds reach phenomenal speeds of more than 300kph, and was the reason behind Douglas Mawson's book on the Australasian Expedition of 1912–13. Mawson was unfortunate enough to have placed his base in the path of regular katabatics – his book is called *The Home of the Blizzard*. Mawson's book helped make the Antarctic katabatics famous, but what is less well known is that Nansen's team used katabatics – known in Greenland as piteraqs – to sail their sleds down the western edge of the Greenland ice sheet during the first traverse of the island (though their first attempts – see above – were far from successful; the illustration is from Nansen's book on the crossing).

Anabatic winds – the opposite of a katabatic, with the airstream moving uphill when the air in a valley is heated by the Sun – also occur. As might be expected, they are much weaker than katabatics.

The changing weather of the Arctic occasionally produces beautiful light patterns. Beaufort Sea, Canada.

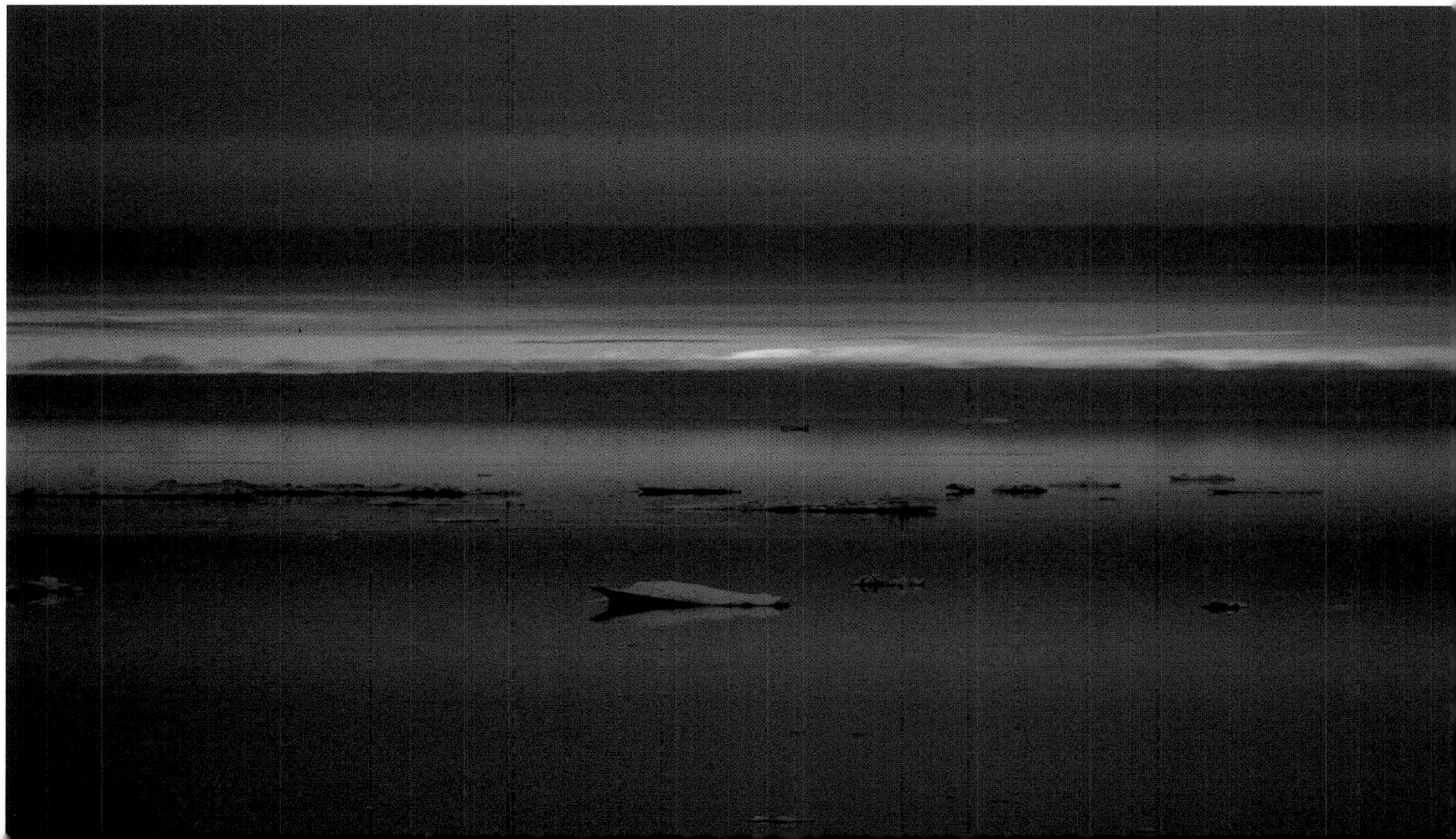

Orographic cloud, Helgeland, Norway.

Descending air in the lee of a mountain is compressed and so warms adiabatically, causing a sudden rise in temperature at the mountain base. Such winds are relatively common in Greenland where they are called *neqqajaaqs*. They can be disastrous for ungulate herds in winter as the local increase in temperature can melt snow, which then subsequently refreezes as an ice-coating of the vegetation that the animals cannot break through.

Although wind may be the bane of the Arctic traveller's life it does have advantages. For one, it makes life difficult for mosquitoes – always a positive – and it is also responsible for one of the Arctic's most beautiful phenomena, orographic clouds. Water vapour in Arctic air is usually close to saturation point. As a result, when the air is forced to rise over a mountain the resultant cooling creates a cloud of condensed water droplets. The cloud produced has remarkably clean-cut edges

Wind chill

The table below has been compiled from an equation relating wind speed at 1.5m above the ground and ambient temperature to effective temperature. The original equivalent temperatures were derived in Antarctica by observing the freezing rate of water. These rates were then converted into an empirical formula. A revised equation has now been adopted by the US and Canadian weather services, and it is that equation that has been used to derive the data below. Note, however, that other tables also exist and there may not be complete correlation between those and the data presented here. The red 'danger area' is also open to various interpretations. The US and Canadian weather services note only that frostbite may occur within 30 minutes if conditions are within the red zone. Other tables are more specific, noting, for instance, that exposed flesh can freeze in less than 30 seconds at temperatures of -40°C and below in wind speeds greater than 25kph. The table should, therefore, be taken as indicative, and is really useful only for pointing out the dangers of exposed flesh in cold, windy conditions. In the table the apparent (wind chill) temperature is given for a range of air temperatures (°C) and wind speeds in kph.

	10	**5**	**0**	**-5**	**-10**	**-15**	**-20**	**-25**	**-30**	**-35**	**-40**
Still	10	5	0	-5	-10	-15	-20	-25	-30	-35	-40
5	9	3	-3	-8	-14	-20	-26	-32	-38	-43	-49
10	8	2	-4	-11	-17	-23	-29	-35	-41	-48	-54
15	7	1	-6	-12	-18	-25	-31	-37	-44	-50	-57
20	7	0	-6	-13	-20	-26	-33	-39	-46	-52	-59
25	6	-1	-7	-14	-20	-27	-34	-40	-47	-54	-60
30	6	-1	-8	-15	-21	-28	-35	-42	-48	-55	-62
35	5	-1	-8	-15	-22	-29	-36	-43	-49	-56	-63
40	5	-2	-9	-16	-23	-30	-36	-43	-50	-57	-64
45	5	-2	-9	-16	-23	-30	-37	-44	-51	-58	-65
50	5	-3	-10	-17	-24	-31	-38	-45	-52	-59	-66
55	4	-3	-10	-17	-24	-31	-38	-46	-53	-60	-67
60	4	-3	-10	-17	-25	-32	-39	-46	-53	-61	-68

and is a shape-replica of the underlying land. As wind moves the air across the mountain, the droplets at the leading edge revaporise as the air mass falls on the lee side. Since the vapour of the new air in the trailing edge is condensing, the cloud shape remains stationary, irrespective of the wind speed.

Wind speed is directly related to wind chill, the name given to the enhanced cooling of exposed flesh caused by the wind. In still air, hot objects lose heat primarily by conduction (although radiation and convection do contribute). Convection is a more effective method of heat transfer than conduction, and convective heat loss dominates in moving air: warm-blooded animals therefore lose heat more rapidly if skin is exposed to the wind. One way of considering this extra cooling is to evaluate the still air temperature which produces equal cooling by, chiefly, conductive losses. This, much lower, temperature is the one which is now often quoted in winter weather forecasts.

One further effect of wind is the creation of blizzard conditions. Generally blizzards occur as a result of wind and falling snow, but this is not always the case. In wind speeds above about 10m/s, lying snow that has not been completely compacted will be picked up and sent scudding across the landscape. As wind speed increases, the height to which the snow is lifted also increases; above about 15m/s the snow layer created is deep enough to overtop a man – a blizzard has been created in the absence of falling snow. Even in the absence of falling snow, the whirling snow lifted from the surface can make travel impossible.

The climate of Antarctica

Antarctica is colder than the Arctic as it lacks the moderating influence of a warming ocean; the Southern Ocean is cold, its circum-Antarctic flow little influenced by warmer waters to the north. Most of Antarctica is also a high plateau, very different from the sea ice at the heart of the Arctic. Together, these effects make the southern continent about 10°C cooler on average than the Arctic. The coldest place in Antarctica, as recorded by a thermometer, is Russia's Vostok station where -89.2°C was recorded on 21 July 1983. The warmest place is the Antarctic Peninsula, where summer temperatures as high as 15°C have been registered. By contrast, inland summer highs can be as low as -25°C. As well as being the coldest, Antarctica is also the windiest place on Earth with winds sweeping the plateau, funnelling between islands and the coast, and katabatic winds dropping off the plateau to batter coastal regions High pressure sits constantly above the continent, a contrast to the endless succession of low pressure systems that form above the encircling ocean. Because the air above the continent is too cold to hold much water vapour there is little precipitation. Indeed, precipitation adds up to no more than the equivalent of 50mm of rain annually, making Antarctica the world's driest desert. But since the precipitation falls as snow it is retained by the continent – only the wind moves it, and that is just a redistribution rather than the creation of a river-like flow to the sea. As a result, the precipitation of eons lies locked on Antarctica, the ice holding almost 70% of the Earth's freshwater.

Sunrise through sea mist, Starichkov Island, southern Kamchatka.

5. Atmospheric Phenomena

For people living below the Arctic Circle – and that means almost the entire population of the Earth – the Arctic is a place where for six months of the year the Sun shines all day, and then for the next six months the darkness of the Arctic winter is alleviated only by the flickering light of the aurora. Though broadly speaking these statements are true, the play of light on the Arctic landscape is actually far more subtle.

The Arctic day

Arctic travellers arriving from temperate regions bring with them the assumption that the Sun rises in the east and sets in the west, and can be disorientated when they discover that this 'law of nature' no longer applies. A traveller at the North Pole on Midsummer's Day sees the Sun move across the sky along a flat circle at a constant angle of 23.5°. On that same day, a traveller standing at the Arctic Circle will see the Sun higher in the southern sky at noon and touching the northern horizon at midnight. A short distance south of the Circle the Sun rises and sets in almost the same place, rising a little east of north and setting a little west of north. Only much further south does the familiar eastern rise, western set become established. One further difference for the temperate traveller is that the effect of the Sun rising and setting in the north but being southerly at noon means that it appears to go across the sky rather than around it; although the Sun is actually following a curved path, to the human eye it seems to follow a straight line from Sunrise to noon, then reverses along the same line to set. One other interesting aspect of the Sun's motion at the North Pole is that because of its constant elevation, the shadow cast by a stick is always the same length, the shadow tip tracing a circle over the course of 24 hours.

At the Arctic Circle on Midwinter's Day the reverse occurs, with the Sun touching the southern horizon at noon. Now a short distance to the south the rising and setting Sun appears in the southern sky.

An issue related to the Sun's movement across the Arctic sky is whether, with 24 hours of daylight, the day can be divided into periods of 'day' and 'night'. In practice the answer is yes, as it is only at the Pole (and there only for a relatively short time) that the Sun is at a constant elevation in the sky. Over much of the Arctic – and all the area in which wildlife is normally found – the Sun's passage across the sky includes a dip towards, and a rise away from, the Earth. Because of this, and a small but discernible temperature variation as a consequence, most Arctic animals maintain a recognisable day-night activity pattern.

The Arctic night

While it is true that all places above the Arctic Circle do not see the Sun for a period varying from one day at the Circle to half the year at the Pole, the idea that this means that there is total darkness at all times is incorrect as there are extended periods of twilight. Twilight is divided into three types, the difference depending on the position of the Sun below the horizon. If the Sun is less than 6° below the horizon there is 'civil twilight'. At this time many activities that generally require daylight can still be carried out. This is not usually the case during the next type of twilight – 'nautical twilight', which occurs when the Sun lies between 6° and 12° below the horizon. The name derives from the fact that during this period the brighter stars are visible, allowing celestial navigation; this type of twilight was therefore of benefit to sailors. When the Sun lies between 12° and 18° below the horizon there is 'astronomical twilight', when the fainter stars are visible and astronomers can begin their observations of the night sky. Most travellers would consider both nautical and astronomical twilight to be total darkness, but technically the latter does not occur until the Sun is more than 18° below the horizon.

At the North Pole at the winter solstice (a time of total darkness) the stars do not rise and set. A time exposure photograph of the night sky would reveal a series of parallel rings, the radius of each diminishing until Polaris, the North Star, was reached. Polaris does not actually sit above the North Pole: it too would create a ring, but one only 2° across. The blackness within that circle is the region of the sky that truly sits above the North Pole.

The behaviour of the moon during the long Arctic summer and winter is rarely mentioned, but that too can surprise the traveller. The moon's orbit around the Earth lies about 5° from the plane of the ecliptic (the plane of the Earth's orbit around the Sun). As a consequence, at places to the north of 72°N there are periods each month when the moon does not set, and other periods when it does not rise. During the winter the moon does not set during the full moon (and periods close to it), with moonlight enhancing the otherwise bleak winter darkness. In summer the moon does not set when it is new (and in periods close to the new moon). As these are periods of continuous Sun the moon is rarely seen, so the fact that these are also periods of minimal moonlight is of little consequence.

Above
The first stage of twilight, Adventdalen, Spitsbergen, Svalbard.

Opposite page
Aurora, northern Scandinavia.

Below
A 'blood moon', northern Sweden. The name is given to the reddish moon observed during a lunar eclipse.

James Clark Ross at the North Magnetic Pole, an illustration from Robert Huish's book *The Last Voyage of Capt. John Ross* pubiished in 1836. Despite the delightful idea behind the engraving almost every relevant feature is incorrect: the aurora borealis is shown, but Ross travelled during the continuous daylight of the Arctic summer when it would not have been visible; a telescope is used to spot the pole, but the pole is not visible, being detected by the use of a dip circle, essentially a magnetised pointer suspended by a fine thread which points vertically downwards when it is positioned above the pole; and a party climbs to the top of the 'pole peak' implying a mountain to be conquered, whereas the pole can sit beneath any feature, including the sea – Ross actually found the pole more or less at sea level.

Magnetic fields

Planet Earth has a magnetic field, and as with all such fields there are north and south magnetic poles, these being aligned, more or less, with the geographical poles. The alignment is not perfect, with Earth's North Magnetic Pole, to which compasses point, wandering about the Canadian Arctic. The pole was first reached in 1831 by a team under the leadership of James Clark Ross who accompanied his uncle, John Ross, in the *Victory* in an effort to discover a North-West Passage. The discovery was heralded as a triumph for British exploration and featured as a delightful, but entirely incorrect illustration in a popular book.

At the time it was first reached, the pole was on the western coast of the Boothia Peninsula. In the 200 years prior to its discovery the pole had migrated south across Prince Patrick and Melville Islands and along the McClintock Channel. By a curious coincidence, Ross's discovery was at the southernmost point of the pole's wander; since that time it has migrated north across Bathurst Island and the Ellef Ringnes islands into

The Earth's poles

Looking at an atlas it seems that the Earth has two poles, a north and a south. But there are several more, some fixed, some moving, and all have their uses.

Geographical poles: *These are fixed. They are the North and South Poles in the atlas, with the Equator lying equidistant from them. In 1793, a few months after the execution of Louis XVI, the French Revolutionary Council appointed the scientist Joseph Lagrange – Italian born but of French ancestry – to head a commission whose task was the creation of a new system of weights and measures. The Council hoped that this new system would be adopted world-wide; their hope was eventually realised as the metric system is now used almost everywhere. The new unit of length was to be defined as one ten-millionth of the distance between the North Pole and the Equator, measured along the line of longitude that passed through France's most northerly town, Dunkerque. But measuring that distance was not easy and an approximation had to be made. Because of this it was decided to create a length standard; it would be the distance between two marks scratched on a bar of platinum-iridium alloy in Paris. The name chosen for the new unit of length was the metre, and not surprisingly the distance between the North Pole and the Equator is about 10,000km.*

Rotation poles: *These are movable. They are the poles around which the Earth rotates. They lie within 20m of the geographical poles, around which they precess with a period of 435 days.*

Magnetic poles: *These are movable. These are the ones at which a dip circle measuring the Earth's magnetic field points straight down, i.e. the magnetic field at that point is at right angles to the Earth's surface. Compasses point to the North Magnetic Pole.*

Geomagnetic poles: *These are movable. On what might be termed an astronomical scale, that is, considering the Earth's magnetic field from space (ignoring the 'microscopic' effect of rock asymmetries in favour of a 'macroscopic' view), the Earth behaves as a simple bar magnet, with north and south poles that align themselves through the planet's centre, but do not, of course, align with the magnetic poles. As with the magnetic poles these drift, but on much longer timescales. At present the North Geomagnetic Pole lies in the southern part of the Kane Basin between north-west Greenland and the eastern coast of Ellesmere Island.*

Poles of inaccessibility: *These are fixed. These are the points that are furthest from land (in the case of the Arctic) or the sea (in the case of Antarctica). The term is contrived as the points are not really any more inaccessible than others, and in the case of Antarctica they depend on the extent of the sea ice. The Arctic pole of inaccessibility is at 84°03'N, 174°51'W. The southern pole is, on average, at 85°50'S, 65°47'E.*

Far left
For walkers on Canada's Ellesmere Island the magnetic deviation which must be catered for to ensure correct map bearings is very large as the island lies almost due north of the North Magnetic Pole.

Left
Some experts believe that serpentine rock drawings – such as those on the walls of the La Pileta Macaronis cave in Spain, which date from about 20,000BP – may represent the aurora, though that is a somewhat controversial view.

the Arctic Ocean north-west of Axel Heiberg Island. In recent times the pole's wander has become more rapid; it is now moving at about 40km/year. The wander is thought to be caused by changes in electric currents in the Earth's metallic core (the same differential movements responsible for the planet's magnetic field). Short-term changes in these electric currents also cause the magnetic pole to oscillate with a period of hours, the oscillation being along an essentially oval path which, over a 24-hour period, may have a long axis of *c.*100km. The magnetic and geographical poles do not align perfectly because of the distribution of magnetic rocks in the continents. The asymmetric nature of this distribution worldwide also explains why a line drawn between the North and South Magnetic Poles does not pass through the centre of the Earth.

The aurora borealis

The Earth's magnetic field is responsible, in part, for the aurora borealis or northern lights, the most spectacular of all Arctic phenomena. The first documented observation of the aurora is found in a Chinese text from about 2600BC, which tells the story of Fu-Pao who witnessed strange lightning at night high in the northern sky and soon after became pregnant. The tale is an early indication of the mystical properties with which early observers imbued the aurora. Chinese texts include a list of auroral observations dating from 687BC, but by then – indeed, long before Fu-Pao's witnessing of the lights – the aurora would have been well known to northern peoples (and those of the south, too, though they were much less likely to see it as the southern auroral oval is entirely encompassed by Antarctica). The lack of extraneous light at night – which tends to obscure the aurora in northern cities today, as auroral light is very faint and easily overwhelmed by, for instance, street lighting – allowed the lights to dominate the night sky.

It is no surprise that these curious, moving lights became entangled with myth and legend. In New Zealand, the southern aurora was believed to be the reflection in the sky of fires lit by ancestors of the Maori, who had paddled their canoes south and become trapped in a land of snow and ice. For the Inuit of North America the lights lit the path of the recently dead to the heavens, emanating from torches held aloft by ravens. The Inuit (among others) claim to occasionally hear the lights, the faint crackle they describe being identified as the feet of the dead walking across the crisp snows of heaven. Greenland Inuit saw the lights as the souls of babies who had died soon after childbirth, peering down at a world they never knew and offering comfort to their parents. The Sámi peoples spoke of a 'fire fox' that raced across the sky each night, his coat sparking each time he clipped a mountain. They also wondered if, far away and out of sight, huge whales were spouting, with the jets of exhaled breath scattering the light of the stars. For the Chukchi of north-eastern Siberia the lights were the spirits of those who had died a violent death, perhaps from murder, suicide or childbirth. In the sky these wounded spirits played a suitably violent game, kicking and hurling a

A depiction of the aurora seen over Bamberg, Germany in 1560. Rarely seen so far south, the aurora terrified the locals who believed they were witnessing a battle between celestial armies, the light flashing from their armour and swords.

Figure 5.1
Auroras are generated when particles of the solar wind interact with the Earth's magnetosphere and atoms of the upper atmosphere.

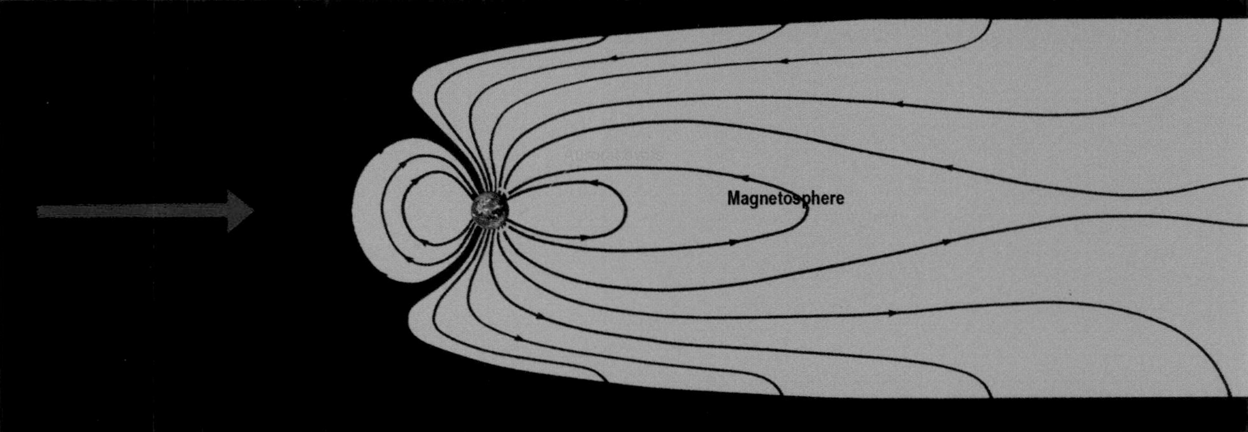

walrus skull around the sky. Later, people saw the lights as heralding great events or foretelling disasters, while the medieval Christian church saw the occasional red light mixed with the more usual green as being an indication of the blood of martyrs.

Early scientific theories on the aurora concentrated on the burning of gases; not until the work of the Norwegian scientist Kristian Birkeland did it become clear that the phenomenon was linked with electricity and magnetism and, therefore, the Earth's magnetic field. Even today, although the basis of the aurora is well understood, there are many aspects of it that remain perplexing.

Most of the Earth's atmosphere (about 75% of it) is confined in the troposphere, which extends to about 12km above the surface. Above this is the stratosphere, which extends to about 50km and includes, towards its top edge, the ozone layer that protects life on Earth from harmful ultraviolet radiation (see A Vulnerable Ecosystem p603). Further up are the mesosphere and the thermosphere, extending to about 1,000km. At that height the Earth's magnetic field creates an envelope called the magnetosphere. This is the lower edge of the Van Allen belts, shells of solar particles trapped by the magnetosphere. During the second half of the 20th century in the early days of space travel, rockets carried Geiger counters into the upper atmosphere; they stopped transmitting at a height of about 1,000km. Most scientists assumed that the counters had failed, but US physicist James Van Allen suggested that the counters had been so overloaded with incident particles that they were unable to function. He was correct and the belts were named after him.

Each year the Sun discharges about 50 million million tonnes of material into space as a 'wind' of charged atomic and subatomic particles. When the solar wind, which is travelling at many thousands of kilometres per second, encounters the magnetosphere it distorts it, compressing the Sunward side and drawing the opposite side into an extended tail (Figure 5.1). The charged particles of the solar wind spiral along the field lines of the Earth's magnetic field, reaching their lowest altitude in the polar regions where the magnetic field lines are almost perpendicular to the Earth's surface. As the particles penetrate towards the Earth they are accelerated in the magnetic field and collide with atoms of gases of the high atmosphere (chiefly in the lower thermosphere, but also in the mesosphere). The collisions excite (energise) the atoms (strictly the electrons of the atoms). As they return to their unexcited ground state, these emit energy in the form of light. This light is the aurora.

The electrons have fixed 'excitation states' between which they move, and emit light at different wavelengths accordingly. Light emitted by electrons in oxygen atoms moving from a

The northern and southern auroras occur in oval belts. The oval remains constant with respect to the position of the Sun, the Earth rotating beneath it. The satellite photograph to the right shows the northern aurora oval.

Because the solar wind bathes the Earth symmetrically, auroras occur at the north and south polar regions at the same time. The photograph to the far right shows such conjugate auroras.

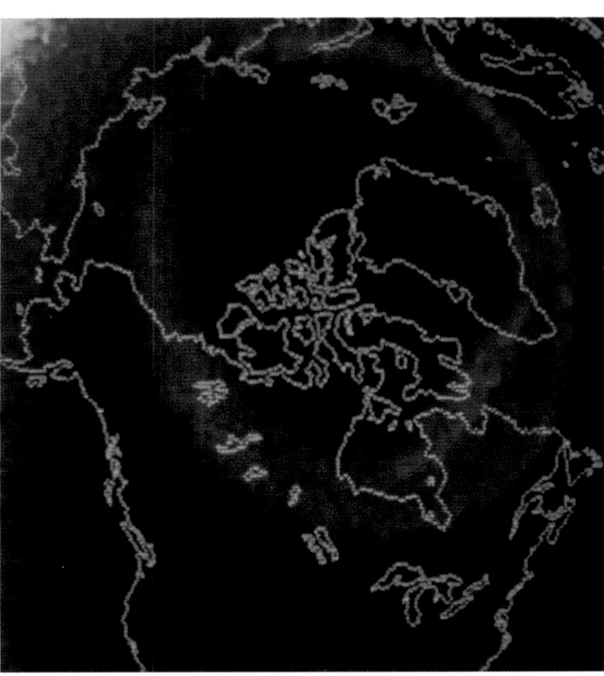

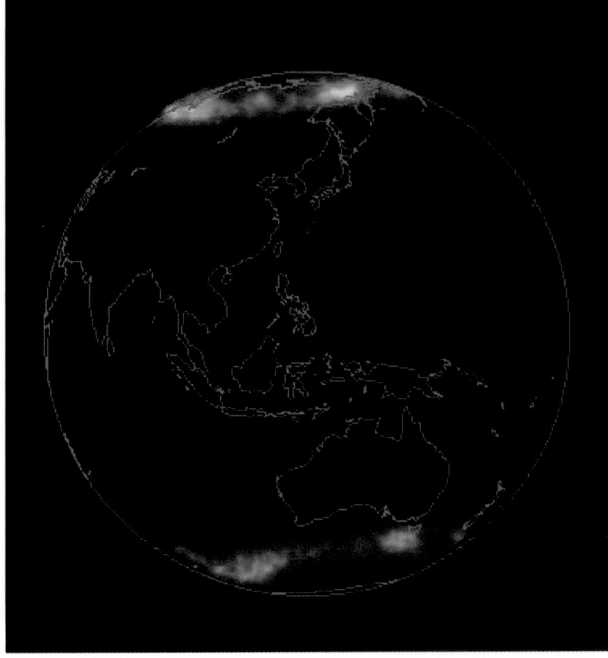

second excitation state to a first excitation state is at a wavelength of 557.5nm – yellow-green, the general colour of the aurora. Movement of electrons in oxygen atoms from the first excitation state back to the unexcited state leads to the emission of red light at 630.0nm or 636.4nm. However, this transition is delayed if the atom has already emitted green light and it is likely that the oxygen atom interacts with other atoms in the atmosphere before the red light is emitted. Red light is therefore rarer than green. The upper sections of some auroras can be red, but auroras that are overall red are very rare.

Excited electrons in nitrogen atoms emit a pale blue or violet light (at wavelengths of 391.4nm and 427.8nm), this light usually being overwhelmed by oxygen's green. However nitrogen also emits red light (at wavelengths between 661.1nm and 686.1nm), this occurring mostly at low altitudes, so green auroras sometimes have a red basal fringe.

Types of aurora

Auroras are classified into six colour forms (of which type C – overall green – is the most common) and four light intensities, with around 33 shapes also having been identified, though these are essentially combinations of a small number of basic shapes. The arc is an even crescent of light stretching across the sky. If the arc is folded, usually towards its base, it is known as a band. Veils are arcs without defined edges that appear to fill the sky, fading away at the top and bottom. Rays are beams of brighter light that may be seen within arcs and veils, or may occur independently. Coronas are the most spectacular; they are arcs or bands seen from directly below so the light seems to erupt from a central, bright, linear area. Auroras move, the light appearing to shimmer in the way that rustled curtains might. These effects are caused by variation in the flux of solar wind particles.

Although auroras can, like rainbows, sometimes appear to touch the Earth, the lower edge is rarely less than 60–80km from the surface. At lower heights the density of the atmosphere is such that oxygen atoms have no time to emit light before they collide with other atoms. However, nitrogen's red light is emitted very quickly, so at the lowest heights, if the incident particles get that far, it is this red light that may be seen. Auroras extend to about 400km above the Earth's surface, the brightest light usually occurring at a height of about 110km.

Because the solar wind 'blows' constantly, the conditions for the development of auroras are, in principle, present at all times. But certain factors affect visibility. The intensity of the wind is not constant, so displays are sometimes too faint to observe. Auroral light is faint and so is not visible during the day, and is affected by background light during the night; a bright moon can make the aurora invisible. Visibility is also, of course, affected by the weather.

Auroras primarily occur in a flattened oval belt. The shape is akin to that of a guillemot's egg and is caused by the distortion of the Earth's magnetic field: the flattened section of the oval faces the Sun, the elongated part is away from it. The Earth rotates beneath the oval. The aurora oval has a 'diameter' of about 5,000km, lies at about 60–65°N, and is centred on the North Geomagnetic Pole. At latitudes above and below the oval the aurora is less likely to be observed. At the Geographical North Pole the probability is about 20% (assuming 90–100% visibility in the oval). In London the probability is less than 5%, about the same as it is in New York. In September 1909 an aurora was visible at Singapore and Jakarta, which lie close to, but on opposite sides of, the Equator. An equivalent auroral oval exists in the southern hemisphere, centred on the South Geomagnetic Pole. As would be expected, auroras occur symmetrically in the Arctic and Antarctic as the solar wind is equivalent at all points of the Earth's magnetosphere.

Though symmetrical at the magnetosphere, the particle flux of the solar wind is not constant, varying with the 11-year Sunspot cycle. At the peak of solar activity auroras are more intense and may then be visible a long way south. There are also shorter cycles: if there was a good aurora last night, there will probably be a good one tonight as well, as the solar wind rises and falls in intensity gradually rather than being switched on and off. As the solar wind is also dependent on solar activity, if there was a good aurora last night, there will probably be another good one in 27 days, the rotation time of the Sun.

Although auroras are now reasonably well understood (though the exact production mechanisms for the various identified forms of aurora are unclear), there is still much to intrigue scientists. For example, there is debate about whether the lights can be 'heard'. Native Arctic peoples claim to be able to occasionally hear the lights, a claim that was echoed by some European explorers, and is still contended by 'southerners' who have moved to the Arctic and by the occasional modern-day Arctic traveller. One of the earliest descriptions of the noise associated with the aurora was that of Samuel Hearne, an 18th-century Hudson's Bay Company employee who made several important exploratory journeys. Hearne heard 'a whistling and cracking noise, like the waving of a flag in a fresh gale', a description with which most who have claimed to hear the lights concur. However, there is no known

Coloured auroras are rare. This one, which includes the full spectrum, was photographed in northern Scandinavia.

Although auroras are now reasonably well understood, some aspects are still puzzling. The photographs to the right show a northern aurora oval with a distinct gap which persists over time. The photograph to the far right shows a 'theta' or 'cap' aurora in which a thin band of auroral light links the oval across the pole (in this case the South Pole).

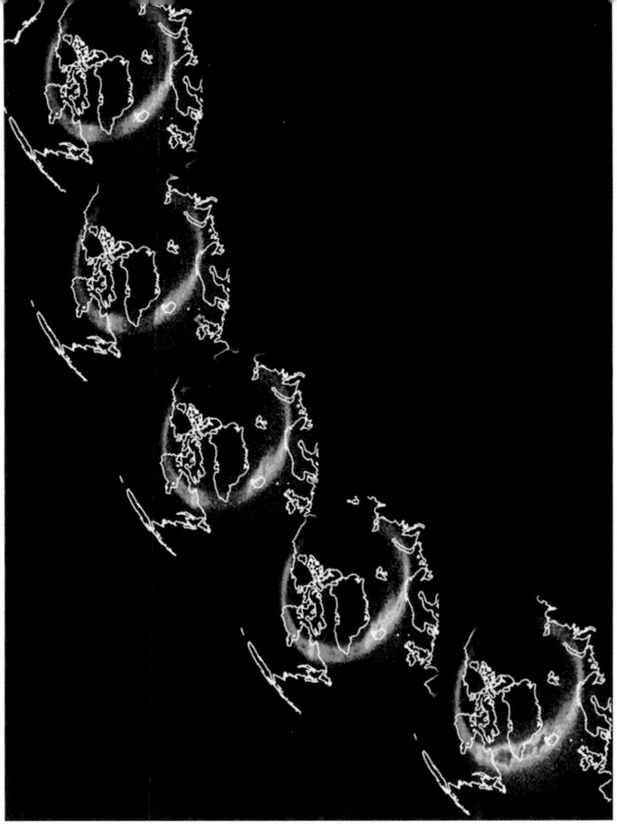

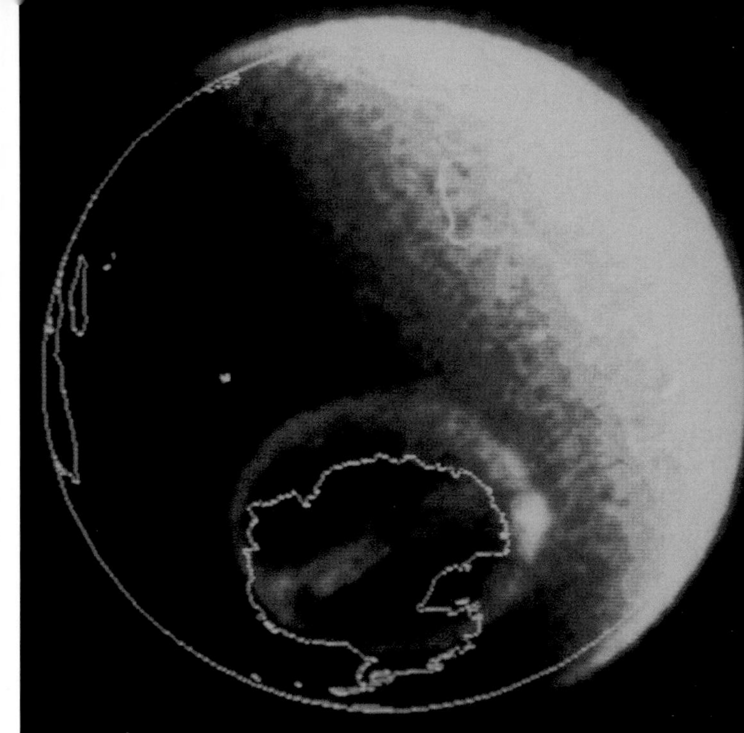

reason for the light production mechanism to produce sound. Indeed, there are good reasons to believe that auroras cannot generate sound waves. The light is too high for any sound from it to reach the Earth, as the density of the air at the altitude of auroras is too low for the efficient transmission of sound waves. The light is also too high for the suggested synchronicity of changes in light intensity or pattern with sound; even from the lowest level of the auroral base, sound would take several minutes to reach the observer while the light arrives virtually instantaneously.

Many explanations have been suggested for the noise. One of the most popular is coronal discharge – the ionisation of the air close to the observer. As this would be strongest at sharp points it has been suggested that discharge from the observer's hair might be the cause. Piezoelectricity in nearby rocks has also been proposed, as has a mechanism that again depends on the observer. In this, leakage of electrical impulses from nerves within the eye would be 'heard' by the brain. Obviously such leakages would occur all the time in an observer, the reason they would only be picked up by the brain in aurora watchers being that the aurora is usually viewed in a quiet, wilderness area. In support of this, many observers claiming to have heard the aurora notice that the noise stops if they cover their eyes. As the sound has yet to be definitely recorded, most of these mechanisms – indeed, for many scientists the whole idea of auroral sound – have been dismissed as fanciful. However, there are other aspects of auroras that were also once decried but are now supported by scientific observations. Auroral light should be contained within the oval, the centre of the oval – known as the polar cap – being light-free. But in the early 20th century Australian scientists in Antarctica gathered evidence of what appeared to be auroras crossing the oval. This work was either dismissed or ignored, but in the 1980s photographs taken from satellites clearly showed a thin, linear aurora crossing the polar cap, linking with the oval on both sides. This so-called cap aurora was aligned with the Sun, apparently sweeping across the sky as the Earth rotated below it.

Equally perplexing are the gaps that occasionally occur in the aurora's oval. Some gaps mean that the oval is not complete, others that, though complete, the oval has a curious notch in its otherwise smooth outline. The gaps are assumed to occur because of discontinuities in the magnetosphere, but what these are, and what mechanism drives them, is not understood.

Parhelia

Parhelia is the general term given to the range of solar and lunar haloes, arcs and Sun dogs that occasionally surround the Sun, the effects being created by light refraction in ice crystals suspended in the troposphere. Most tropospheric ice crystals are either hexagonal flat plates or hexagonal columns. Light traversing these crystals is refracted at angles varying from about 22° to about 50°. As smaller angles are the most probable, the most frequently seen parhelion is a 22° halo surrounding the Sun. The minimum angle is 21.7° for red light, so the inner edge of the halo often appears red, with the remaining spectral colours becoming fainter (or being absent) as the halo fades away.

One of the most famous examples of parhelia is that sketched by William Parry at the Melville Island winter quarters (1819–20) of the *Hecla* and *Griper* during Parry's first voyage in search of the North-West Passage (see Box). Some of Parry's parhelia were prismatic, the rainbow colours adding to the beauty and wonder of the sighting.

Parry's example includes most of the frequently seen parhelia phenomena (though 'frequently' here is, of course, a relative term). As well as the phenomena that Parry drew so assiduously, further, very rare, parhelia have also been observed and given names – Hastings, Tricker and Wegener arcs among others. All these phenomena are produced by subtle variations of the path of light through ice crystals.

One other related phenomenon may also be seen, the Sun pillar, a form of Sun dog, produced when the plate-like crystals that produce Sun dogs are aligned vertically. Sun pillars usually form directly below or above the Sun.

In the Arctic, good viewing days (i.e. with a low Sun and plenty of ice crystals) are much more common than at southern latitudes, and a 22° halo and associated Sun dogs will be seen as often as on one day in four. Tangential arcs occur on about one quarter of the days when the halo/Sun dogs are

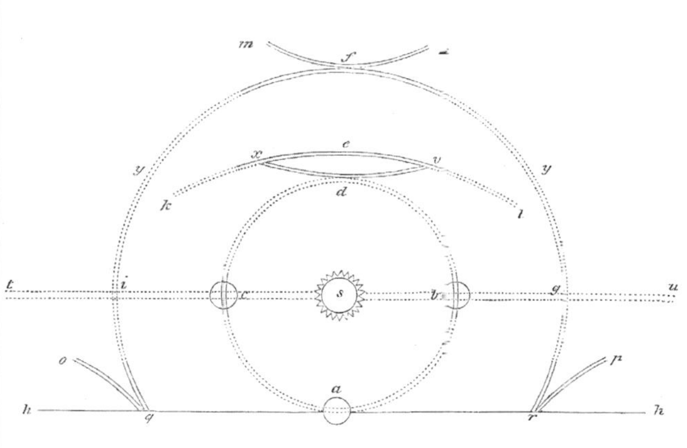

a, b, c, d is the 22° halo. Outside it is a 46° halo. This is formed by light passing through the side and end faces of ice crystals.

t–u is a parhelic circle, produced when light is reflected from near-vertical faces of the ice crystals. Usually the light is reflected from an outer crystal face, but it may be due to one or more reflections from internal faces. Parhelic circles may encircle the whole sky.

k, e, l is an upper tangential arc, formed by light entering a crystal through a side face and leaving through another inclined at 60° to the first. When the Sun is close to the horizon, the upper arc forms a tight V, but as the Sun climbs, the arc opens to form 'gull wings'.

x, e, v was a previously unknown arc lying above the V notch of the upper tangential arc. It is now known to be caused by light interacting with crystals of a specific orientation. Known as the Parry arc, this feature is strongly prismatic (i.e. features all the colours of the spectrum).

a which Parry drew as a circle and probably thought was a Sun dog (see b and c) is actually a lower tangential arc. This also forms a tight but inverted V, of which Parry only observed the apex.

m, f, n is a circumzenithal arc, created by light refracting in horizontal, plate crystals. The light enters the crystal through the horizontal upper face and leaves through a side face. Circumzenithal arcs are always prismatic, the inverted arc appearing as a 'smile' in the upper sky.

o–q and r–p were long assumed to be a mis-drawing by Parry, but it is now known that he was absolutely correct and had depicted 'subhelical arcs'. Two forms, supralateral and infralateral arcs, appear infrequently and are caused by light passing through a side and the base of hexagonal ice columns. The arcs are prismatic.

b and c are Sun dogs or mock Suns. Together with the 22° halo these are the most frequently seen parhelia. They are formed by horizontal plate crystals (those that form the circumzenithal arc) and are strongly prismatic.

The Box to the left includes Parry's sketch of the parhelia he saw during the winter at Melville Island on his 1819–20 voyage in search of the North-West Passage, together with an explanation of the various arcs.
The photograph below is of an equivalent parhelion. The photograph was actually taken in Antarctica.

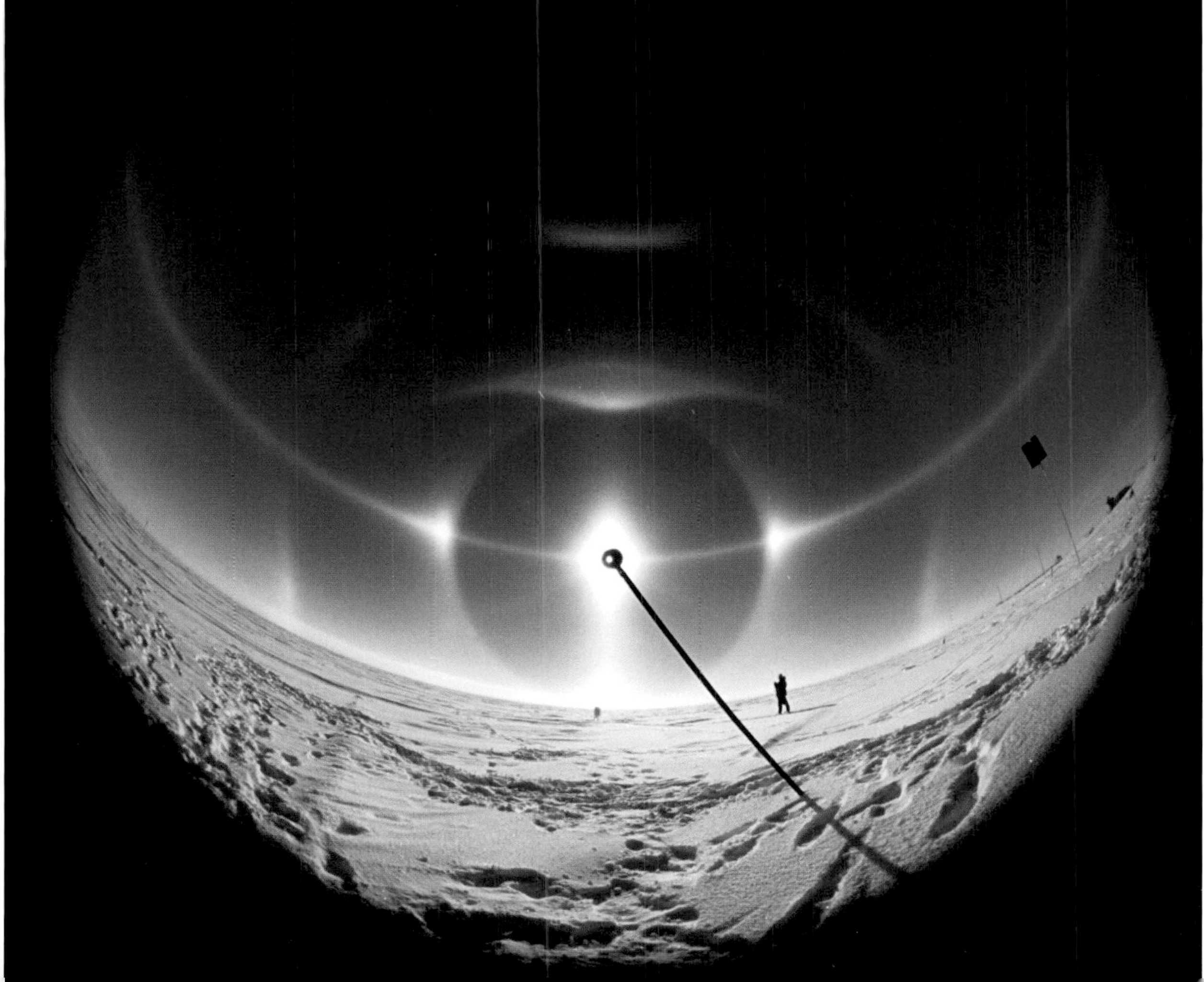

Painting of parhelia in Stockholm's Storkyrkan. The painting dates from the early 15th century and is interesting for being both the earliest depiction of the phenomenon, and also the first depiction of the city of Stockholm. However, a recent dendrochronology study of the wood substrate suggests the painting is actually a mid-17th century copy.

seen, 46° haloes on about one occasion in 25, Parry arcs about 1 in 100, and the rarer arcs on perhaps one occasion in 300.

Mirages

Mirages are caused by the refraction of light from distant objects to the observer as a result of the light travelling through layers of air at different densities, the differences resulting from changes in humidity and temperature. The refraction results in the light being bent into a curved path, but the observer assumes it is following a straight path, as is usual, and is fooled into seeing distorted images of objects. It is refraction that allows the Sun to be seen when it is actually below the horizon. It also gives rise to two forms of mirage.

If the temperature falls from a warm surface then 'inferior' mirages occur, the image appearing below its 'true' position. Desert mirages, and the 'water pools' frequently observed by drivers above hot metalled roads in summer are examples of 'inferior mirages'; such mirages are rarely encountered in the Arctic. If the temperature change is an increase from a cold surface, then the mirage is said to be a 'superior mirage', as the image appears above its 'true' position. The more usual name for this form is *fata morgana* (from Morgana le Fay, sister of King Arthur, who was said to be able to conjure such images). *Fata morgana* are relatively common in the Arctic, where warm air above ice sheets and the cold sea set up the right conditions. In superior mirages, the light follows a convex path so the observer sees a much taller object than is actually present. This explains the range of mountains that was seen by John Ross during his first attempt to discover the North-West Passage, and the non-existent lands, such as Crocker Land, famously 'discovered' by Robert Peary. The shimmering quality of most mirages results from turbulence in the atmosphere.

The purity of Arctic air and the clarity of the light, together with the often flat terrain, also allow objects that are far away to be observed, a phenomenon that can occasionally lead to misidentification due to the difficulties of depth perception. In one of his books the experienced Canadian Arctic traveller Vilhjalmur Stefansson wrote that he once spent an hour trying to get close to a Brown Bear only to finally discover that it was a Marmot.

Ice blink, water sky and white-out

When sunlight is reflected from sea ice or an ice sheet it brightens the base of overlying clouds. For the observer, too far away to see the ice in question (which may be below the horizon), this brightening is an indication of the existence of the ice and is termed ice blink. Ice blink can add a delightful

As parhelia are produced by the refraction of light by ice crystals they can occur at night as well as during the day. Full moons are best as they provide more light. A full moon behind thin cirrus cloud will often produce a 22° halo and moon-dogs may also be seen. However, as moonlight is so faint relative to sunlight, the more exotic haloes are much rarer at night, although many have been observed. The one shown here is from an illustration in Francis M'Clintock's book *The Voyage of the* Fox *in the Arctic Seas - the Fate of Franklin* and was observed during a funeral of Leading Stoker Robert Scott following his death as a result of a fall in December 1857.

Left
Water sky above Forlandsundet, Svalbard.

Below
White-out on east Spitsbergen.

element to sunsets viewed from eastern Greenland when out of sight, sunlit sections of the inland ice act as a mirror for the setting Sun, which may also be out of sight.

The opposite of ice blink is the darkening of sections of cloud when it overlies the dark ocean between areas of pack ice. These dark streaks are called water sky. Early polar explorers, who spent relatively long periods exploring the pack ice because their sailing ships were slow and vulnerable, became experts at reading the base of the clouds, looking for the dark lines in the silver glare that indicated worthwhile leads that could be utilised to continue their journey.

A final atmospheric condition that can assail the traveller, one that is actually more climatic than atmospheric but represents a very real hazard, is the white-out. Though often assumed to be associated with blizzards, white-outs can occur in more benign conditions. If a traveller is journeying across snow under complete cloud cover that diffuses the light, then the conditions for a white-out are almost in place; adding snowfall and a light wind enhances the effect. In a white-out, there is a loss of orientation because of the diffuse light and the lack of a discernible difference between the colour of the ground and the sky. The falling snow reduces visibility so that estimation of distance, already difficult, becomes even more so. A light wind enhances the problem – a strong wind would aid orientation (while adding different hazards of its own). Loss of orientation can be so pronounced that nausea can result as it becomes difficult to register up from down. In such events it is best to stop and wait, as the chances of blundering over a cliff increase dramatically.

PART 2

A HUMAN HISTORY OF THE ARCTIC

6. Native Peoples of the Arctic

In about 330BC, when Aristotle was teaching at his school in Athens and his former pupil Alexander the Great was campaigning in India, a Greek named Pytheas set sail from Massalia, a trading port on the Mediterranean coast to the west of Italy, now the site of Marseille. Pytheas was a gifted astronomer who had worked out how to calculate latitude by measuring the shadow cast by a vertical pillar at a solstice. He probably wanted to travel north to confirm his method, perhaps even to reach the North Pole, which would have given him an exact fix. He may also have been an adventurer who wanted to visit Ultima Thule, the land where the sun did not set in summer or rise in winter, word of which had reached Greece through traders. But it is likely that those who financed Pytheas' voyage were merchants who wanted more direct access to the tin and amber of northern Europe, goods which then reached the Mediterranean by land and river, and whose trade was controlled by, and profit largely made by, others.

Pytheas sailed through the Pillars of Hercules (the Strait of Gibraltar) and turned north. As far as Brittany he was probably following a known, if not well-known, route; it is thought that the Carthaginian explorer Himilco reached the area around Quiberon in around 500BC, while there is evidence that Phoenician vessels had made regular voyages to the Cornish coast, perhaps for centuries, to trade for locally mined tin. But beyond this region Pytheas was crossing waters unknown to the Greeks. He was away for six years and exactly where he went has been the subject of debate ever since. Later Greeks and Romans who had access to the account he wrote dismissed Pytheas as a fraud, but modern scholars are more sympathetic. It is likely that Pytheas followed the coast to the western tip of Brittany then crossed to Britain, with Cornwall, due north of Brittany and another tin-producing area, being a regular trading outpost for merchants from the Mediterranean. Pytheas continued north, sailing around Britain to reach Orcas (probably the Orkneys, but some have suggested the Shetlands), then continued north again, sailing for six days to reach 'Thule' where the summer day was 21 or 22 hours long (too long for the Shetlands, which some have suggested as the location of Thule). In Thule, Pytheas heard that further north the sea stiffened or congealed. Some have suggested that Pytheas reached Iceland, but his Thule was inhabited and Iceland was certainly not at that time: Iceland is also more than six days' sail from Scotland. It is likely that Pytheas had actually reached Norway, a remarkable achievement, but one that so outpaced the understanding of the day that it was dismissed, its wonders lost for almost 1,000 years.

Assuming Pytheas' journey was real, and regardless of whether his Thule was Norway or the Shetlands, it was a voyage to a world that was already inhabited. Northern Eurasia was populated with tribes of reindeer hunters, while on the north-eastern coast of Chukotka people hunted the sea mammals of the Bering Sea. When Europeans crossed the Atlantic they found that Greenland and northern North America already had settled populations. These various peoples almost certainly shared a common ancestry and their descendants still inhabit the Arctic and Arctic fringe. In Eurasia there is little land in the High Arctic, and what exists is difficult to access and limited in extent. These factors kept the early Arctic settlers on the mainland. By contrast, in North America there is the vast archipelago of Arctic Canada extending from Alaska to Greenland, which offered limitless possibilities for a people willing to endure the rigours of an inhospitable climate. In the High Arctic of Canada and Greenland the names of the people who took up this challenge – both the first one ascribed to them by Europeans and the one they now give themselves – have become synonymous with the Arctic. Those names are Eskimo and Inuit.

Rock art, Altafjord, northern Norway. This image of a hunter with reindeer and elk is believed to date from 6,000BP, though exact dating is very difficult.

Native peoples of the High Arctic

In 1947, while inspecting a mammoth graveyard at 71°N near the headwaters of the Berelekh River (on the Siberian mainland due south of the New Siberian Islands), Russian scientists found evidence of human habitation dating to perhaps 12,000 years BP, the oldest authenticated remains so far discovered that far north (though recently Russian archaeologists have identified tools near the Yana River at about 70°N that may be up to 30,000 years old). Stone artefacts of contemporary age to the Berelekh finds have also been unearthed in Alaska's Tanana River valley and near the tree-line in Canada's northern Yukon Territory close to the Bluefish River. The Bluefish finds may even be older, as may be worked ivory uncovered in river sandbars at nearby Old Crow. These finds indicate that people were exploring areas close to the southern limit of the great ice sheets of the last ice age, and also crossing Beringia to settle in North America. It is even possible (some experts would say likely) that the folk who crossed Beringia 12,000 years ago were only the latest in several waves of settlers. However, the origins of the native peoples of North America are still debated. An ice-free land bridge between Asia and America probably existed for much of the period from 50,000 to 10,000BP, offering a route for migration. Some authorities claim that this extended period is consistent with archaeological finds that indicate three waves of migration, the first being of ancestral Amerindians. The second wave was of ancestral Na-Dene peoples, whose descendants are the Algonquian tribes of eastern Canada and the Athabaskan tribes of western Canada and interior Alaska. In south-eastern Alaska were the Tlingit and Haida tribes, famous for their totem poles, who appear more closely related to the peoples of the Pacific north-

Opposite page
Wearing traditional costume of embroidered sealskin, including sealskin kamiks, and carrying a posy of wildflowers, a Greenland bride-to-be enters the church. Her husband-to-be also wore traditional sealskin clothing. As a sharp contrast to the ancient costume, the organist played 'Here comes the Bride'.

Right

This ivory mask, apparently displaying tattooing, is at least 3,500 years old and is the oldest known representation of a Paleo-Eskimo.

Below

At Sermiut, an area close to the sea near Ilulissat on west Greenland, excavations have revealed the evidence of occupation from about 4,500BP. The earliest dwellers would have been Saqqaq people, contemporaries of the Independence I people of the High Arctic who occupied the area for about 1,500 years. The Saqqaq hunted terrestrial mammals and, perhaps, seals. They had dogs, but there is no evidence of sledges. The disturbed ground and rocks in the foreground are the remains of a winter residence. It is close to the sea, implying that the mouth of the ice fjord, just off shore, differed then. Today, if an iceberg were to roll, the settlement would likely be inundated by the subsequent tsunami.

west than to those of the rest of Alaska. The third wave was of ancestral Aleut-Eskimo, these arriving about 4,000 years ago. However, the fact that the oldest remains of Amerindians have been found in southern South America, when it would be expected that this area would have been occupied last, creates a real problem for this simple three-wave migration theory.

Despite the debate, what is clear is that the settlement of the Arctic occurred later than that of the southern American continent, finds from Cape Denbigh on Alaska's Bering Sea coast indicating that flint workers producing microblades for the killing and working of caribou had camped there perhaps 5,000 years ago. The worked flints suggested these peoples originated in Siberia, where similar microblades had been recovered near Lake Baikal at sites within the great Siberian forest. At that time Beringia no longer offered an easy traverse between Asia and America, but hunters in Chukotka would have been aware of Alaska – visible across the narrow Bering Sea – and could have made a crossing by way of the annual sea-ice connection, even if they did not have adequate boats.

From around the same time, excavations of camp sites near Independence Fjord in northern Greenland revealed further evidence that peoples of what is now commonly called the Arctic small tool culture had spread right across the Arctic. These people hunted Musk Ox and Caribou with bows and arrows. They also caught fish. They presumably cached food taken at times of plenty during the long hours of summer daylight for use during the winter; Independence Fjord lies beyond 80°N, where the Arctic winter brings months of sunless days. They lived in tents year round, these being of skins draped over driftwood frames, with a central fire for warmth and cooking. What is intriguing is that the design of the tent interior, with a central 'passage' of edge-on stones around a central hearth, and with living areas being on both sides of the passage, are virtually identical to those used by the Sámi within the last 300 years. With driftwood rare and valuable, the fires would have been of dried mosses and twigs, the time

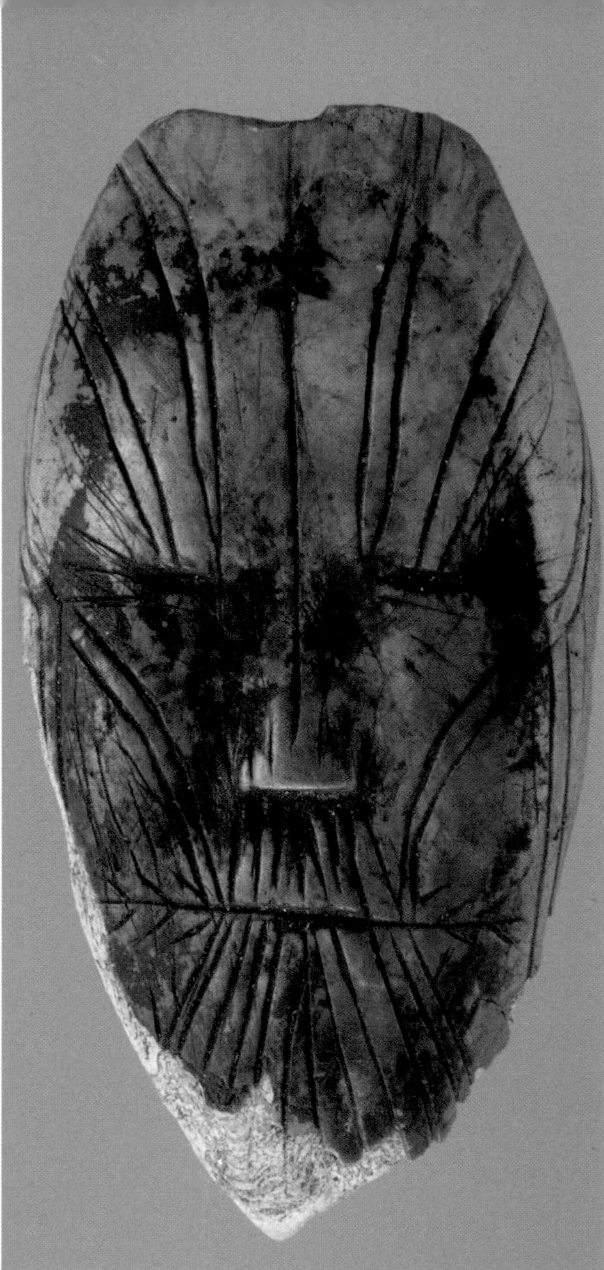

taken to accumulate fuel and its scarcity probably making life very difficult in winter.

Finds of bone needles imply that these people wore skin clothing. It is assumed that they lived in small extended family groups, moving often as prey became scarce. Estimates of population are subject to wide errors because northern Greenland is not an easy place for extensive archaeology, but most suggestions are of a few hundred people, these perhaps meeting casually or more deliberately so that marriages could be arranged and stories told. It was a precarious existence; a winter storm that stopped a cache being reached or lost, an injury to a hunter or a shortage of fuel could all result in the death of an entire group. Such disasters might account for the fact that occupation of the excavated sites does not seem to have been continuous, but involved extended periods with no apparent human presence, so that some experts differentiate between Independence I and Independence II cultures, with hundreds of years between occupations.

The small tool culture people were hunters of terrestrial animals. They do not seem to have had sledges, but probably used dogs to force Musk Oxen to form their standard defensive circle – an adaptation to fight off Wolf attack – for ease of killing, and created drive roads with upright rock slabs that herded Caribou into spaces where they could be more efficiently dispatched. They would have spread east across the

What's in a name?

Collectively, the pre-Dorset and Dorset peoples are known as Paleo-Eskimo; it is worth exploring the derivation of the name 'eskimo' and why it is now occasionally objected to by native Arctic dwellers. Eskimo was the name Europeans gave the Arctic peoples of North America when they first encountered them, having heard the name from the 'indians' of southern Canada when they arrived. The derivation is usually said to be from the Athabaskan or Algonquin for 'eater of raw meat' and so was later viewed as derogatory. But there is no consensus on this derivation, some considering that the origin of the name was from the Ungava for 'snow-shore hunter'. Whatever the origin, it is thought that the word 'eskimo' became corrupted by western native Americans, who had a history of conflict with the people of the north and so chose to use the name contemptuously. Today the Arctic peoples of eastern Canada refer to themselves as Inuit, which means simply 'the people'. Inuit is plural, a single person being an Inuk. In Greenland, where the people share a common ancestry with the Inuit, the preferred name is Kalaallit. In western Canada the native people are the Inuvialuit; they too share a common ancestry with the Inuit.

However, the peoples of the Bering Sea are less bothered by the name, and often refer to themselves as Eskimos, though they usually attach a prefix to acknowledge their specific tribe – for instance Yuppiat (sometimes rendered as Inupiat; the singular of the name is Yupik or, occasionally Yu'pik, the Siberian form). The Yuppiat live in north-western and northern Alaska and across the water in Chukotka. The Yuit live in south-west Alaska, while the Alutiiq live on the Alaska Peninsula east to Kodiak Island; this can cause some confusion with the Aleuts, who live to the west. In most cases, these names actually mean 'the people'.

In Eurasia, too, there has been a trend away from received names to ones based on a common heritage. Lapps now prefer the term Sámi, which means 'ourselves' or 'the people', and is probably the basis of the Finnish word for their own country, Suomi. It may also be the basis of Samoyed, the collective word given by early explorers to the Nenet, Enet and Nganasan, peoples living in European Russia from the eastern shore of the White Sea to the edge of the Taimyr Peninsula. It was widely assumed that these peoples practised cannibalism, and the term Samoyed, given to the northern tribes by their southern neighbours, is thought to have derived from that practice. Consequently the Nenets and other peoples have rejected it in favour of their own words. Both Nenet and Enet mean 'man' in the local language, while Nganasan means 'people', the older tribal terms again having a basis in isolation. The Nenets also occasionally refer to themselves as the Khasava, 'the people'.

Arctic in search of game, the spread assisted by the warmer climate that followed the retreat of the ice of the last Ice Age. They would have crossed the narrow, ice-filled straits from the Canadian mainland to the southern islands of the Arctic archipelago, moving up the Boothia Peninsula and crossing Somerset and Devon islands to reach Ellesmere Island, from where Greenland is just a short distance away. From Baffin Island they would have headed south to Ungava and Labrador.

However, about 2,000 years ago the Arctic cooled. This change may have been disastrous for the Independence people; later springs and earlier winters would have required bigger winter food caches, and these might not have been available, particularly if climatic change altered the migration routes of Caribou and reduced the population of Musk Ox. But elsewhere in the Arctic the change benefited one group of people. Known as the Dorset culture from finds initially made near Cape Dorset on Baffin Island, these folk were culturally very different. They hunted sea mammals, the change to a cooler climate being to their advantage as they were used to hunting on the sea ice. Perhaps they originally lived in areas such as the Foxe Basin – there are finds on Igloolik – where there are few Caribou, but an abundance of Walrus and seals. The Dorset people used harpoons to catch this prey, a device with a barbed head that detached from the throwing handle but remained attached by a rope (usually made of Walrus leather, whose strength amazed early Europeans by being greater than that of their ropes) to a float made from an inflated seal bladder or skin. Once harpooned, the animal grew tired attempting to drag the float under, and each time it surfaced it could be struck again until finally it could be speared to death.

Dorset people had more substantial winter quarters than the Independence folk. These were partially sub-surface, dug into the ground to provide extra insulation, with walls of stones and turf over which skins would have been erected on driftwood frames, though the interior was similar to that of the earlier peoples. The houses were heated with blubber oil burning in soapstone lamps. Yet for all their clear advantages for survival in a colder Arctic that they possessed, the Dorset folk had lost some things that made life for their predecessors more tolerable. They did not have dogs and, therefore, dog-sledges, nor did they have boats. They did not have the bow and arrow, nor did they have drills, making the manufacture of needles a much more difficult task, a long groove being scratched and worn through instead. Yet despite these limitations the Dorset people spread across the central and eastern Arctic and were the dominant culture for about 2,000 years; then the Arctic warmed again, and their sea-ice hunting techniques became less well suited to the new climate.

As the climate warmed around 2,000 years ago, a new people arrived in the eastern Arctic. Contemporary with the Dorset culture of the eastern Arctic was the Old Bering Sea culture of western Alaska, the Bering Sea islands and eastern Siberia. The origins of this people are unclear; perhaps they arose from the Arctic small tool folk, or they may have had an entirely different heritage, spreading north from an ancestral Aleutian Island race. About 1,000 years ago the people of the northern Bering Sea had become efficient hunters of Bowheads and other large whales, animals much bigger than those taken by the Dorset people (who occasionally took Narwhal and Beluga, but do not seem to have ever taken the larger whales). The Bowhead is a huge animal one provides enough

The images below are of the head of a Thule man and Dorset woman. The Thule head forms the top of a skin scraper and dates from the early 11th century. The woman's figure is older, probably from about 900AD. Both figures are of walrus ivory and were found in west Greenland.

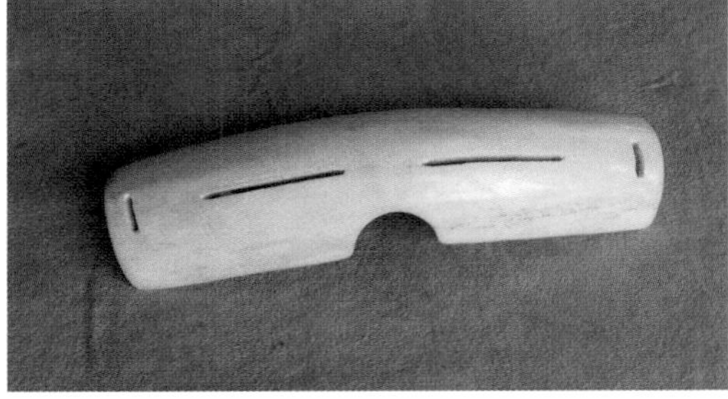

Inuit tools. From the left are snow goggles made of whalebone. They would have been attached to the head using thongs of walrus skin. Next are ulus, scrapers used to remove meat from animal skins so that the skins could be made into clothing. The first example is of driftwood and slate, the second a more modern version in walrus ivory and iron.

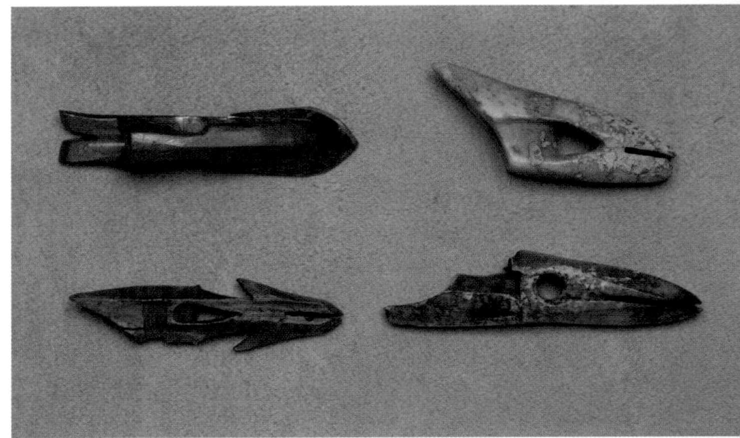

The final photograph is of harpoon heads from north-west Greenland (top left) and St Lawrence Island, Alaska. The Yuppiat of the island and the Polar Eskimo of north-west Greenland hunt sea mammals. The three St Lawrence heads were discovered in the island's midden. The earliest (top right) dates from the 6th century. The other two are perhaps 400–500 years newer. The Greenland head is contemporary and made of brass.

food for a community to comfortably survive the winter. This allowed for the creation of semi-permanent settlements. A settled, rather than nomadic, existence and a full stomach are great drivers of cultural development, and the Bering Sea is an extremely rich environment.

The Bering Sea hunters used kayaks (from the Inuit *qajaq*), made by stretching animal skins over a simple wooden framework, a vessel light enough to carry and that could be rolled if it capsized. The kayak is an amazing craft; a huge technological step forward was the development of a drawstring around the paddler's waist, allowing the kayak to be watertight and so offering much greater security to a hunter than an open boat. The Bering Sea people used tents made of animal skins stretched over driftwood or bone frames – the skins held down by a circle of stones – in summer, those tents being capable of rapid erection and packing to allow a swift change of location. They also used stone and turf winter houses. To let light in, windows were made of seal gut. The people wore skin clothing and slept under skin bedding. The skins for their clothes and *kamiks* (waterproof boots that were ideal for use in kayaks) were prepared by scraping off the blubber. The skin was then soaked in old urine until it became pliable enough to be stretched. This preparation, and the manufacture of clothes and kamiks, was women's work. On land sledges were used, drawn by dogs to hunt Polar Bears and other animals with bows and arrows. In addition to kayaks, the people also had the *umiak* or women's boat, a flat-bottomed boat rowed by 2–6 oars depending on size. This was used to move the family between hunting grounds. Most importantly, these people had iron tools, the metal presumably originating from the Chinese, Japanese and Korean civilisations of the Pacific rim. As the Old Bering Sea folk also had armour – plates made of bone and ivory – it is fair to assume that they were a more warlike people than the Dorset folk of the eastern Arctic.

The Thule people

Perhaps encouraged by the warming of the climate that allowed the Bowheads to penetrate deeper towards the Canadian Arctic, or, perhaps, driven by internal conflicts, the Bering Sea hunters moved east around 1,200 years ago. Today they are called the Thule people as the earliest study of their culture centred on the settlement of Thule in north-west Greenland (named, for its history and isolation, by Knud Rasmussen), and they are considered the ancestors of the modern Inuit. They displaced the Dorset people, though it is not clear whether this was a hostile takeover. Given the plate armour of the Bering Sea finds there probably were skirmishes, but it could just as easily have been diseases introduced by the Thule that caused the demise of the Dorset people. They had been isolated for almost 3,000 years and would have had little resistance to new diseases. And with the climate turning against the Dorset, the hunting techniques of the Thule allowed them to make better use of available game.

It seems that within about 300 years, the Thule had occupied the whole of Arctic North America, though pockets of Dorset people may have survived until the early 16th century (it is possible that when the Norse reached Greenland they met both Thule and Dorset peoples). Even more remarkable is the suggestion that Dorset people survived until the early 20th century on Southampton Island. A people called the Sagdlermiut lived there; they spoke a different language to the Inuit and lacked kayaks, going to sea on inflatable sealskins. They were wiped out by an unknown disease, apparently brought ashore by a sickly sailor from a whaling ship. An examination of DNA from skeletal remains suggests a mixed ancestry, both Dorset and Thule, which makes the Sagdlermiut even more intriguing.

Though the origins and advance of the Thule seem straightforward and well understood, there remain many mysteries. The Inuit tell stories of the people who occupied the Arctic when their Thule ancestors arrived, a people they

The largest of the Cape York meteorites being loaded for transport to the USA. The metal of the meteorites had a high nickel content making them very hard, but difficult to work. But fragments could be produced by pounding the boulder with a stone. The fragment could then be beaten to produce a sharp, long-lasting edge.

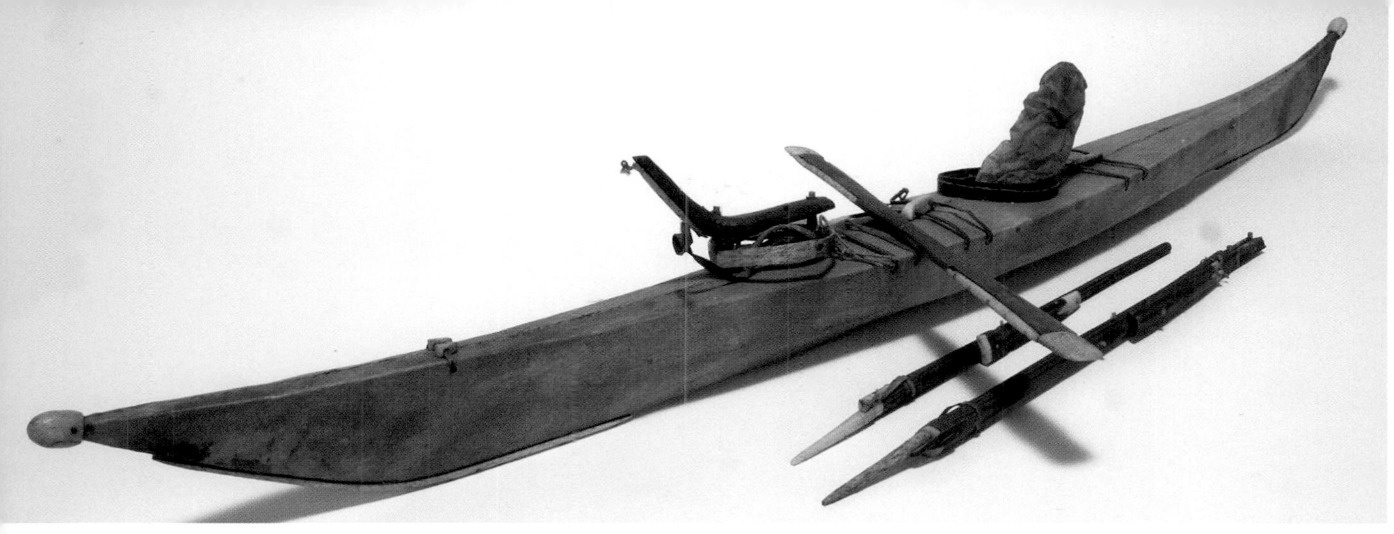

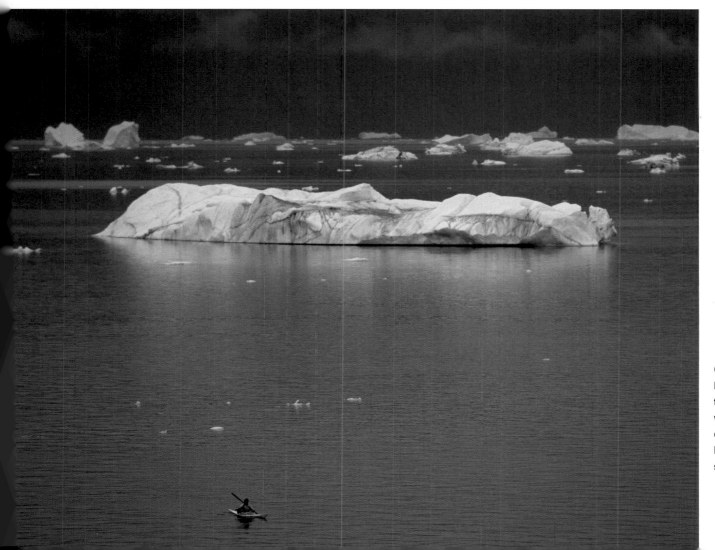

Left
A scale-model kayak faithfully made with driftwood spars covered in fish skin. The paddle and harpoons are tipped with whalebone and walrus ivory. Even the seal bladder - filled with air and attached to the prey to stop it sinking - is reproduced. The model dates from the early 19th century and was made in Greenland. The care and work which went into it indicates the importance of the kayak to the Inuit life.

Centre
A drawing probably made by John White who is thought to have been on Martin Frobisher's second voyage, is the first of a kayak. The Inuk is hunting wildfowl with a spear armed with a triple barb.

Contemporary image of a kayak. The photograph was taken near Qannaq in north-west Greenland where the descendants of the Polar Eskimo still live by hunting seals and Narwhal.

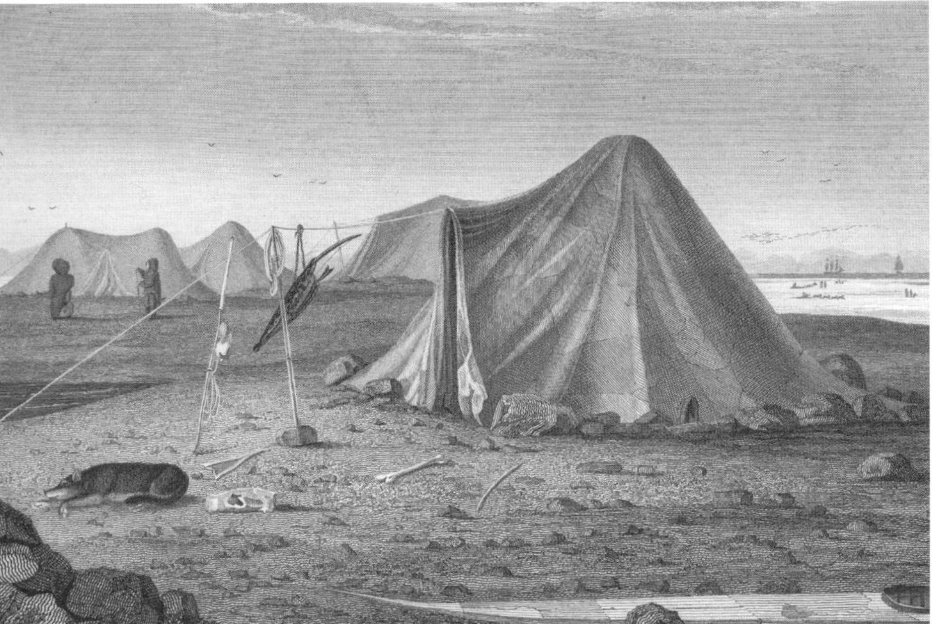

Early Arctic dwellings

The Dorset people lived in tents throughout the year. These were made by hauling walrus skins over a framework of whale bones, the skins then being held down by stones. The Thule people, and their descendants, the modern Inuit, used similar tents during the summer, as depcited in William Parry's book on his second voyage in search of the North-West Passage (centre). Such rings of stones – tent rings – are found throughout the Canadian High Arctic. The example left was photographed on Ellesmere Island.

In winter the Thule people and modern Inuit used houses which were partially underground. The remains of such a winter site (bottom left), were found at Mackenziebukta, north-east Greenland. The photograph below is of a reconstructed winter house on Canada's Cornwallis Island. The roof was made by throwing walrus skins over the whale-bone frame. It would then have been covered in turf or snow for insulation. The entrance passageway was below the level of the living space, acting as a cold air trap. People slept on the raised rock-slab platforms, their meagre possessions stowed beneath the platforms. Given the low entrance crawl, cramped conditions, and the constant threat of hunger or accident, it is no surprise that life expectancy was limited.

Left
The similarity between the reconstructed house and the one photographed at Nutat in north-west Greenland is striking. The house in the photograph was occupied until the 1950s.

call Tunit. These people were big and immensely strong, and were skilled at such things as building fish weirs in rivers. But despite their physical characteristics, the Tunit were a peaceful people and easily displaced as the Thule moved east. Are the Tunit and the Dorset people one and the same?

Most experts believe the answer is yes, but some wonder whether the legendary Tunit were actually a mixed race of Norse and Dorset, some words of the present Inuit language – Inuktitut – seemingly having a Norse origin. The Thule's use of iron is also mysterious. There is little iron ore in the Arctic and no realistic means of smelting it, but the Norse had brought iron to Greenland in the 11th century and it is known to have been taken, or traded, at least as far as Baffin and Ellesmere islands within a century or so. There were also the famous meteorites of Cape York in Greenland, from which the Dorset people had smashed fragments. Was it the iron of the eastern Arctic which drew the Thule eastwards, a journey across the High Arctic being seen as preferable to trading with the peoples to the south of the Aleutians? It would seem a long way to travel, but if the promise was of significant quantities of metal controlled by an easily defeated people, and therefore essentially free, rather than limited amounts of metal available only at high prices from a belligerent seller, it might have been worth the journey.

Below left
Although the common perception of Inuit living is of the snow-built igloo, these were only used during extended hunting trips. In this drawing from William Parry's book on his second voyage in search of the North-West Passage, Inuit are constructing igloos from snow blocks.

Other native peoples of North America

Because of their association with the High Arctic, and their ancestry being common to 'eskimo' peoples of the whole of North America, the Inuit are the native folk most commonly associated with both the Arctic and the continent. But they were not the only native people. Indeed, the 'eskimo' peoples were not even the only group living on the coast. In north-eastern Alaska, in the neighbouring Yukon Territory and in the north-western North West Territories the peoples of the Gwich'in Nation lived an essentially settled life, in a number of villages spread across the migratory range of the Porcupine Caribou herd. Gwich'in life was based almost entirely on the Caribou; they hunted the animals as they passed twice each year, caching the meat to last through the periods when the Caribou were absent and supplementing the otherwise monotonous diet with some fish.

To the south of the Alaskan coastal region occupied by the Bering Sea Eskimo peoples lived the Unangan. They occupied the chain of islands that heads west from the Alaska Peninsula towards Kamchatka, as well as the Peninsula itself and islands off its southern coast. As a consequence of Russian fur trapping (see A Vulnerable Ecosystem), descendants of the Unangan now also inhabit the Russian Commander Islands. When the Russians occupied these islands they gave the native people the name Aleut, which is believed to derive from the Koryak word for 'island'. Although it is possible that the Inuit and the Aleut share a common ancestry, the Aleuts – and the related Alutiiq from the eastern end of the Alaska Peninsula and nearby islands – were culturally quite different. They were generally settled rather than nomadic, having seasonal camps but often living year-round in distinctive houses, now called *barabaras,* a Russian name. The houses were rectangular, up to 12m long and 9m wide, and partially below ground. They

The painting above is of 'Oulak, the chief village of Unalaska' by Louis Choris in *c.*1825. The Aleuts in the double kayak are wearing their famous 'baseball cap' hats. Few of these now survive – there are several fine examples in the Museum of Ethnography of the Peoples of Russia in St Petersburg – and the method of construction was lost until a local artist painstakingly researched and rediscovered it. One of his examples is shown here. It is of painted wood, decorated with feathers, ivory figures and Bowhead baleen.

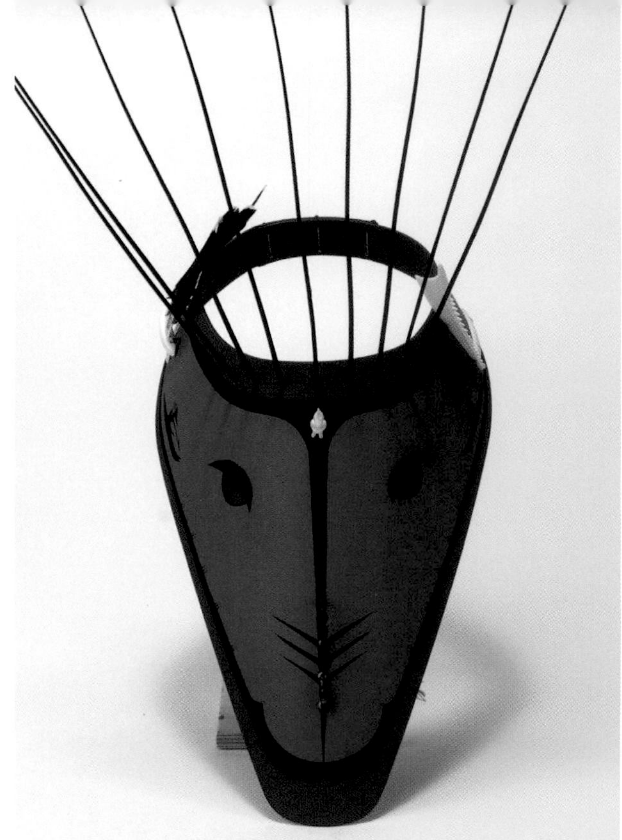

were roofed with sods over a framework of wood or whalebone, and invariably entered through a hole in the roof and down a pole ladder.

Island Aleuts hunted sea mammals, chiefly Steller's Sea Lion, but also Sea Otters, seals and small whales, from a *baidarka*, a craft very similar to the Inuit kayak, made of sea lion skin over a wooden framework. They also had a larger boat, the *baidar*, similar to the Inuit umiak, which was used for transporting families and for trade. The paddler of a baidarka wore a parka of bird skins, usually auks, with the feathers inside so that it was both warm and waterproof, and a highly distinctive peaked hat. Apparently a forerunner of the modern baseball cap, the peak served a similar purpose, keeping rain (a frequent feature of the Aleutian chain) and sun out of the paddler's face and helping to ease glare from the sea. The hats were often decorated with sea-lion whiskers, baleen or beadwork, and their size and shape was an indication of the wearer's social status. It is believed that some Aleut that specialised in hunting whales tipped their harpoons with poison derived from Kamchatka Aconite (*Aconitum maximum*): though a harpooned animal would not die immediately, it could be watched over hours or days as it sickened and eventually either died or became too weak to resist further attacks. Though most of the Aleut were sea-mammal hunters, there were some on the Alaska Peninsula that hunted Caribou, and probably all Aleut groups fished for salmon. Hunters wore waterproof jackets made from stitched strips of sea-lion intestine and boots of Sea Otter rear flippers. There were also highly elaborate ceremonial cloaks made of bird feathers. Among the more notable of Aleut and Alutiiq goods are their baskets, made from woven grasses and the roots of shrubs.

Alutiiq basket. The Alutiiq peoples of Kodiak Island were famed for their weaving of fine tree roots, bark and wild grasses, making sleeping mats, fishing nets, clothing (caps, gloves and socks), 'papooses' for infants and containers for dried foods. Of these objects the most highly prized were those from fine grasses, especially Lyme Grass, the weaving of which was extremely skilled.
This Lyme Grass basket, which measures about 10cm across, is tensioned with Bowhead baleen. It would have taken the lady who constructed it a total of about 300 hours. The baskets are among the most beautiful of all the artwork of the northern peoples.

People of the Eurasian Arctic

While the native peoples of northern North America were to remain isolated from Europeans for centuries, the northern native folk of Europe were in contact with southern peoples from earliest times. In around 500AD, as the Roman empire was in decline, Southern Scandinavia was settled by Germanic tribes moving north, tribes who would eventually become the Norsemen of early medieval Europe. But these ancestral Norse were moving into a land which was already occupied. Stone Age finds in the area still often called Lapland indicate settlement from at least 8,000 years ago. Further finds indicate a continuous occupation of the area throughout the Bronze and Iron Ages. Particularly interesting are the examples of rock art – carvings and paintings – which have been discovered across northern Scandinavia into western Russia (and also in Chukotka). The oldest of these petroglyphs are dated to about 8,000 years ago, the art being produced until as recently as 2,000 years ago, from the Neolithic to the Iron Age, and covering the period of change from a hunter-gatherer lifestyle to a more settled agricultural society. This is reflected in the carved and painted forms, with hunting scenes and depictions of prey species being replaced by more stylised and abstract forms from about 3,500 years ago. Interestingly, the forms – human, animal and more abstract shapes – are highly reminiscent of those on shaman drums from the same areas.

The northern people the ancestral Norse met were the Sámi, the folk – formerly called Lapps – who have become synonymous with the Arctic for many Europeans. For most European children, Father Christmas has an Arctic home – perhaps the North Pole itself, certainly Scandinavia. The tourist industries of the Scandinavian countries exploit that association, offering abundant reindeer and Sámi herders in colourful traditional costumes. But despite being the most visible of the native Eurasian Arctic peoples, the Sámi are

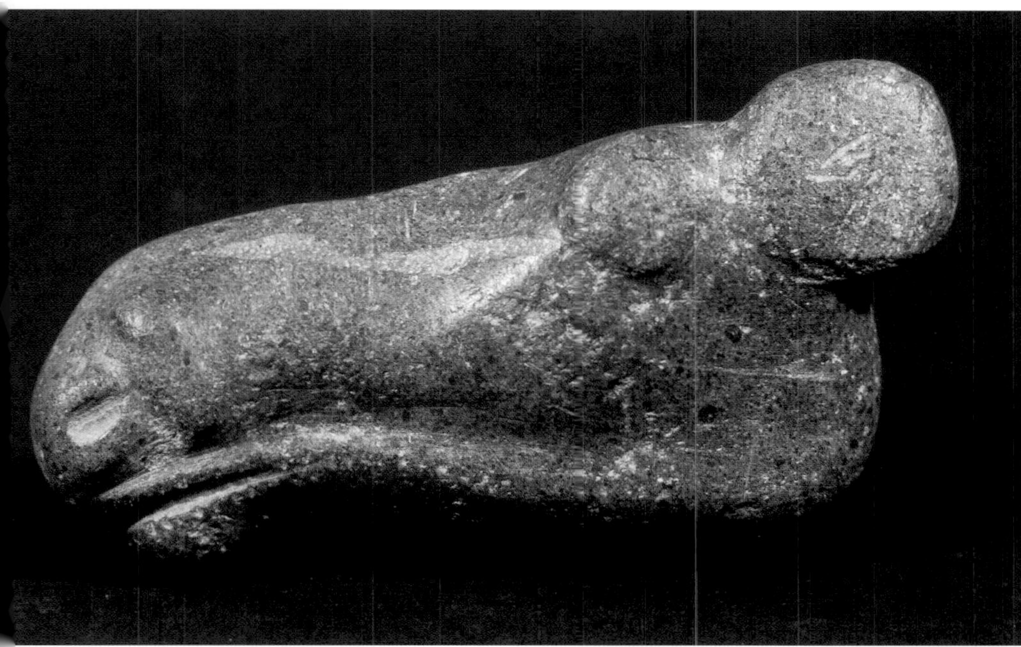

Stone elk head. The head was carved by early Stone Age dwellers of northern Sweden, people who occupied the area before the arrival of the ancestors of the Sámi.

actually the least 'original' of the numerous groups, both in terms of date of arrival and lifestyle.

Like the Finns, the Sámi originated beyond the Urals, in the steppes of central Asia, their language being Finno-Ugric in origin and so sharing a similar ancestry to Finnish and Estonian. Indeed, it is likely that the Sámi and the Finns share a common origin, the Finns settling the southern part of what is now Finland and so being in contact with Europeans who shaped (or, at least influenced) their way of life, while the Sámi remained in the north, escaping the brunt of this southern influence. As the ice retreated at the end of the last glaciation, the ancestral Sámi moved north, following the Reindeer herds. As well as hunting Reindeer, for which they used an early form of skis, the ancestral Sámi fished and probably hunted seals along the northern coast, the diverse scenery of their homeland enabling separate peoples to develop with a degree of isolation so it is possible to differentiate between forest, tundra and coastal Sámi. Different dialects also developed, so that today there is no single Sámi language.

Sámi now occupy the northern parts of Norway, Sweden and Finland, and Russia's Kola Peninsula and eastern Karelia; blood testing of the population suggests that the western Sámi are more closely related to Europeans than their eastern cousins, a result that supports the view that over time there was a greater level of contact between the western peoples and those to the south than there was for the people of northern Finland and western Russia. In support of this, it is certain that the Greeks and Romans knew of the Sámi (see, for instance, Tacitus' *Germania*, where he describes the Fenni, who were clothed in skins and slept on the ground), placing the time of their first contact with southern Europeans several centuries before the arrival of the ancestral Norse.

To the east of the Sámi homeland a string of peoples occupied northern Russia, from the White Sea across to the Bering Sea. The collective name 'Palaeo-Siberians' has been applied to these groups, and it is generally acknowledged that they share a common central Asian ancestry. Across northern Russia, prehistoric sites have been found, often of houses constructed of meshed Reindeer antlers to hold up a roof, which was probably of Reindeer skins, and a floor of rock slabs. The suggestion is that the peoples were essentially

Sámi grave site on Varangerfjord, Norway. The site dates from the turn of the 11th/12th centuries.

A summer camp of Evenki people. The photograph was taken in the early 19th century. The design of the tent is common to the peoples of the western Eurasian Arctic.

Reindeer hunters, living a semi-nomadic life as a consequence of the annual migrations of the herds, probably supplementing their diet with fish, other game and, perhaps, seals.

The native peoples that now inhabit northern Russia occupy specific, occasionally overlapping, regions. Moving east the first group is the Nenets, the most numerous of these peoples. They occupied the coast from the White Sea to the Yenisey, together with the southern island of Novaya Zemlya and the Yamal Peninsula, the word *Yamal* deriving from 'final land' in their language, an interesting echo of the name *Ultima Thule*. Next east are the Nganasan, the most northerly of all Russia's indigenous peoples, whose range extended on to the Taimyr Peninsula. The Nganasan, together with the Enet and Selkup peoples, riverside dwellers that have now almost disappeared as distinct ethnic groups, comprised the Samoyed.

East again are the Yakut (though as with all these groups they were originally a more southerly people, their name deriving from 'horse people', an indication of their origins on the steppes; this southern origin meant they were skilled in the production and use of iron, for which they were renowned) and Evenki, though among these major peoples are smaller groups such as the Dolgan and Yukaghir. Finally, in north-east Siberia, live the Chukchis and Yuppiat Eskimo. To the south of them in northern Kamchatka live the Koryak and Eveni, with Itelmen (sometimes called Kamchadal) occupying the south of the peninsula. When they were first encountered the Itelmen impressed the Russians by hunting and fishing naked (apart from a loin cloth) in summer, though the temperature averaged only 14°C and the mosquitoes were ferocious.

In general all these people were, and remain, Reindeer hunters and herders, though the Bering Sea communities of Chukotka hunted sea mammals, the Yuppiat being hunters of the Bowhead, as can be seen at the ritual site at Whale Alley (see Box below). Despite the assumption that Reindeer herding is a tradition of exceptionally long standing, herding is actually a relatively recent innovation. Such evidence as exists suggests that reindeer were originally domesticated not for milk or meat, but merely as a means of transporting the possessions of nomadic tribes, who followed the herds of wild

One of the earliest depictions of reindeer herding. From Knud Leem's book *Beskrivelse Over Finmarkens Lapper* published in 1767.

Above
Sámi herder with his animals. The costume (in this case of the Inari Sámi of Finland) is now only worn for ceremonies – or for tourists.

Left
Nenet reindeer herder on Russia's Yamal Peninsula. The tents in the background are almost identical to those of the Evenki in the photograph on the previous page, and to the Sámi lavvu.

Nenet herder on the tundra east of Naryan Mar. The Nenet have never used the wheel, shunning the ATV (or Quad bike), though they do use snow scooters and are rarely seen without the thigh-length rubber boots which all visitors to Russia soon purchase. The reindeer are castrated males, fattened for long hard days of pulling the sledge. Unlike their cousins bred for the table, these animals are broad and immensely powerful.

Below
A Chukchi *yarang* or *choom*. Unlike the tents of the Sámi and Nenets, the choom is constructed using long poles which extend from a series of tripods.

Below left
Inside a choom. On a wood fire a large pot of reindeer meat bubbles, the smoke aiding preservation of the hung, jointed deer.

Reindeer and hunted for food and skins. The use of Reindeer as beasts of burden probably dates from the 10th century AD (though recent excavations on Russia's Yamal Peninsula suggest that this may have to be revised back to the sixth century), and is believed to have been introduced by the Evenki and Eveni peoples of central Russia. Both these peoples were later displaced by the Yakuts, the Evenki to the area around the Lena river, the Eveni to north-east Siberia, where they shared the land of the Chukchi and, on the Kamchatka Peninsula, the Koryak, taking their methods with them.

Once established, Reindeer herding spread among the peoples of the Eurasian Arctic, though a true domesticated Reindeer economy was not fully in place until as late as the 16th century. Why Reindeer domestication took place so much later than that of other animals is still debated. Clearly the agricultural revolution of more southerly regions led to better conditions for animal domestication than the hunting lifestyle of the Arctic dwellers, but the explosion of both herding and herd sizes in the late medieval period is a social phenomenon that requires examination. The most likely explanation may have something to do with Reindeer biology. In summer, Reindeer need to put on weight to counteract the rigours of the forthcoming winter, when not only is it cold but food is in short supply, with vegetation being both sparse and hidden beneath snow and ice. Reindeer therefore need to feed well during the short summer. But at temperatures above about 10°C Reindeer become distressed, and if the tempera-

Far left
Winter Reindeer round-up, northern Finland.

Left
Siberian Yupik woman in traditional costume.

Below
Siberian Yupik child. A Bowhead Whale had just been landed and the locals were feasting on *muktuk*, the whale's skin, which is considered a delicacy. The boy decided he preferred a bread roll.

ture rises further they may stop feeding. This is also the time when the animals are under attack from biting insects. A combination of high temperature and high infestation (and the two are invariably linked) means the Reindeer put on less weight and winter mortality increases. Prior to the 16th century the Earth's climate was in a warm (if somewhat erratic) phase, meaning that winter mortality was relatively high. After that time the climate cooled and became more stable, allowing more Reindeer to survive the winter and herding to become viable. Another factor that may have influenced the spread of herding was the control of Siberia by the Tsar of Russia, which began around this time. The somewhat controversial suggestion is that centralised control meant a reduction in inter-tribal conflict, allowing the more stable lifestyle that was a necessary factor in the growth of herding.

A family, or groups of families, could exist by the keeping of a few tens or hundreds of Reindeer, following them on an annual migration along ancestral routes of anything from 50km to several hundred kilometres, depending on the quality of the local pasturage. The people's dependence on their reindeer was almost absolute; not only did the animals provide food, but clothing (reindeer hide being supplemented by the hides of the fur-bearing animals of the tundra and forest) and shelter, hides being used to construct characteristic 'wigwam'-like tents. Though the names of these structures varies from Lapland to Chukotka, being variously *lavvu*, *kota*, *choom* (or *chum*) or *yarang*, the form was essentially the same throughout, a conical or hemispherical framework of poles covered with hides, smoke from a central fire escaping through the hole at the apex. The herders still hunted and fished, but their lifestyle became increasingly dependent on the reindeer herds for food and clothing. The blood of freshly slaughtered animals would be drunk, and some meat would be smoked for later consumption. Bone marrow was a treat, the leading herder taking first share.

With such descriptions (and when viewed photographically), Reindeer herding can seem an idyllic life-style, but it was (and remains) a hard occupation, keeping the animals alive in winter and the Wolves away from new-born calves in spring requiring considerable physical effort. Although the herders supplemented their diet with fish, birds and tundra berries, theirs was subsistence living, a fact reflected in the population density of the various groups. For the Nenets, before the Soviet era. this was about 0.03 people/km^2, that figure declining to the east; for Chukchi reindeer herders it was about 0.01/km^2. By contrast, the Yuppiat of the Chukotka

coast had average population densities as high at 1.3/km^2. Today, Reindeer herding remains a staple of many northern Eurasian groups, though it is much more an established lifestyle in eastern Russia than it is for the Sámi, despite popular assumption; in reality, herding is practised by a minority in Norway, Sweden and Finland, and is only possible at all because of state subsidies.

Right
A Kamchatka shaman illustrated in *Mouers et costumes de la Russie*, a 19th-century French book.

Shamanism

Early peoples around the world were hunter-gatherers, an often insecure and demanding lifestyle. For early Arctic dwellers it led, as elsewhere, to the development of polytheistic religions. If there was bad weather or if animals did not appear in the right place at the right time, then the effect on peoples' lives could be catastrophic, and in these religions such natural events were considered to have god-like qualities over which humanity could have no direct control. From such beliefs evolved a creation mythology and a view of man's place in the world. Collectively, such religions are now termed shamanism, a word derived from *saman* – wise one – in the Tungusic language of the peoples of eastern Siberia. The shaman was the tribe's spiritual helper, a priest. To the Sámi he was the *noaidi*; in Inuktitut, the language of the Inuit, he was the *angakok*.

The earliest polytheistic religions occurred throughout the inhabited continents. Though there were many versions of shamanism among the northern peoples of Eurasia and the Americas, several features were common to all forms. There was a spirit world, usually with several planes. On the upper plane lived the gods, while the shaman himself could travel to a lower plane in order to negotiate on behalf of his people. There was also a belief that it was not only man that had a spirit (the soul); the religion was animistic – all living things had a spirit. Each entity might have its own characteristics, but in the world of the spirits, the spirit of each commanded equal respect. The spirit world was therefore critical; after entering it, one could talk with, placate, appease, or admonish spirits whose co-operation was needed for people to live a tranquil life.

The shamans inherited their status from a supernatural ancestor and were approved by the people at a special ceremony. Knowledge was passed from one generation to the next by the shamans, and also by the shaman's drum, a sacred object, often adorned with pictographs that held the people's cosmogony (or creation beliefs). The shaman's duty was to intercede with the gods on the tribe's behalf, to protect his people from bad spirits, to heal diseases (healing being seen as the defeat of evil spirits) and to explain the structure of the universe and position of various gods and spirits within it. During their ceremonies, shamans often posed as different animals and/or spirits (often a falcon because it might fly to heaven, or a bear because it was feared and admired for its

Below left
A Koryak shaman depicted in the guise of his familiar, a Brown Bear. The head is a bear's claw, the body and clothing of reindeer skin and fur. The shaman drum is reindeer antler. Usually Koryak drums are undecorated.

Below right
Few truly ancient Sámi shaman drums now exist, many having been destroyed by Christian missionaries. Others were collected and later lost (for instance a large collection was destroyed in the Copenhagen fires of 1728 and 1793). The one illustrated here was made and decorated in traditional style, using reindeer hide stretched over a wooden frame, in Finnish Sápmi. The symbols on the drum mirror those on originals, and show a direct link with the petroglyphs of northern Scandinavia and Russian Karelia.

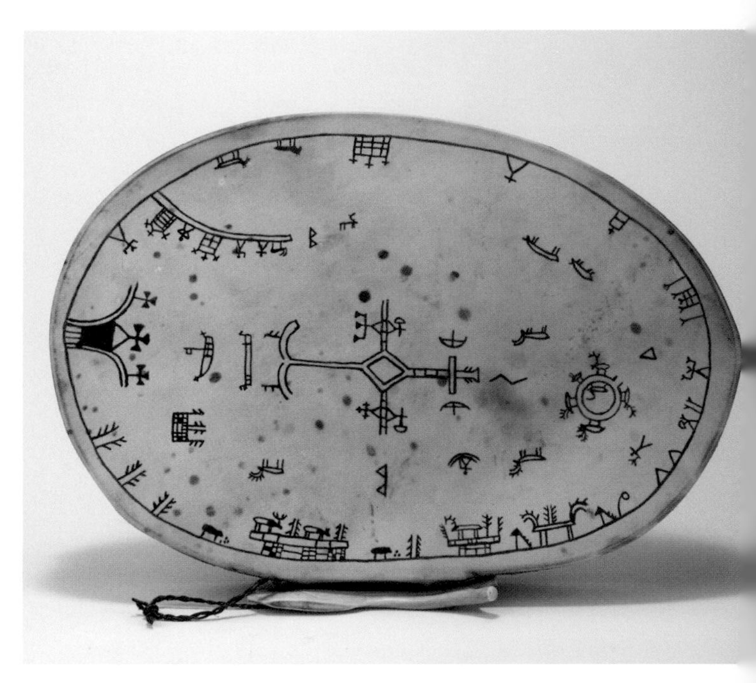

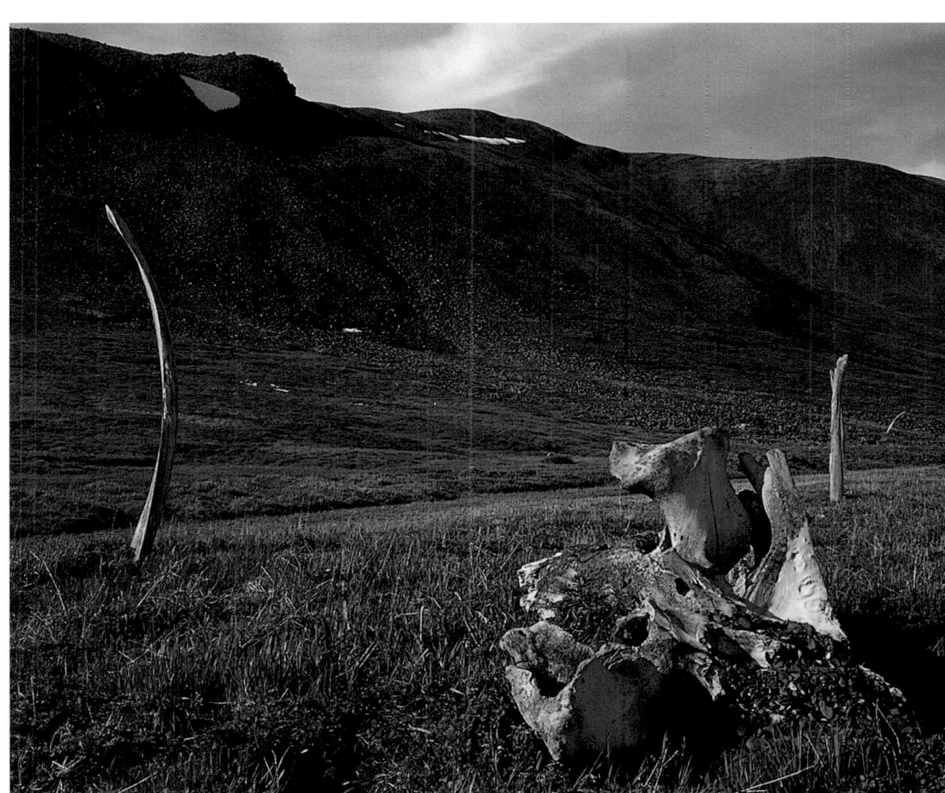

Above left and right
Whale Alley, Yttygran Island, Russia.

Whale Alley

Shamanism fitted well with the nomadic or semi-permanent lifestyle of the northern peoples as it did not require fixed temples or shrines; small ritual sites are known in the lands of the Reindeer-herding peoples of Eurasia, but these are much scarcer for the truly nomadic Inuit. However, a remarkable find was made in 1976 on Yttygran Island off Siberia's Chukotka Peninsula. There, about 60 juvenile Bowhead skulls had been arranged at regular intervals in groups of two or four along a 600m stretch of shore. Many of the skulls have now fallen, but were originally set upright 'nose down'. There are also rib bones, set upright to enhance what appears to be a processional route. Excavation has revealed hearths where, it is assumed, meat was ceremonially burned, and many stone-lined pits in which mummified whale and walrus meat had been placed. The skulls weigh about two tonnes each; bringing these large bones here would have been a major undertaking, indicating the importance of the site to its builders. Bowheads annually migrated past the island and, it is assumed, sacrifices and other rituals were carried out in order to ensure a continuation of the migration and the annual harvest of the whales. Whale Alley, as it is now called, is thought to be at least 700 years old. It is a wonderfully impressive site, and the labour required for its construction places it on a par with the megalithic sites of Europe, particularly as subsistence hunting implies a smaller population than the agrarian-based societies that constructed those structures.

Other ritual sites have also been discovered close to the Bering Sea. Only there, it seems, were the ancient Inuit sufficiently well-fed as to be able to afford the time and effort of shrine construction.

strength and hunting skills), dressing up in special costumes and using their drums to beat a hypnotic rhythm. While his earthly body entered a trance-like state, the shaman's spirit could travel to the lower reaches of the heavens.

Little is known of the belief system of the Dorset folk. It is assumed that after a person died the body was laid outside where it decomposed or was consumed by scavengers. The retrieved bones would be burnt. There may also have been committal to the sea. Each of these practices was also used by the Thule people, though they also had more ritualistic burials, bodies being dressed (and occasionally wrapped) and placed below boulders. Although the Arctic cold preserved bodies – for instance those of men who died on the Franklin expedition – bodies lain on the surface would rapidly have disappeared, even if protected by boulders. Consequently, in most cases only the skull and the larger bones remain of such burials. Notable exceptions are the mummies preserved by the cold ground and dry atmosphere of Qilakitsoq in western Greenland, near Disko Bay. Here the well-preserved bodies of

This ritual site on the island of Vaygach, between the Russian mainland and the southern island of Novaya Zemlya, was discovered by the English explorer Frederick Jackson in 1893. Nothing of the site, which comprised one large and several small carved wooden effigies together with a heap of Reindeer antlers and Polar Bear skulls, now remains.

Ritual Sámi site at Saltfjellet, Norway. It is believed that the site was in use by the 17th century at the latest. Beside each of the three stones a hearth was built. On the fires lit in these hearths meat, blood or antlers from Reindeer would be sacrificed. The animals were not sacrificed, the offerings being taken from deer slaughtered for food.

six women and two children, one a baby of about six months, were discovered in October 1972 in a shallow grave capped with a large flat stone. The bodies were carbon-dated to the late 15th century. The bodies were heavily tattooed and dressed in skins with hooded parkas, trousers and kamiks, a remarkably similar style to that worn by Inuit in the 20th century. The skins were of Ringed, Harp and Hooded Seals. There were also underparkas of bird skins (including divers, geese, cormorants and ducks), with some feathers intact.

The mummification of the Greenland bodies was a chance event, but the Aleut deliberately mummified their dead – or, at least, some of their dead. They removed the inner organs and stuffed the body cavity with dried grasses, drying the body for many weeks before placing it in a dry cave. The volcanic activity of the Aleutian Islands meant that some of these caves were warm, the warm, dry air being as good a preservative as the cold, dry air in western Greenland. In the Aleutians, it appears that mummification was carried out to allow the descendants of the corpses to enter the caves and commune with the spirits of the dead in times of crisis.

The peoples of western Russia laid the bodies of their dead in the open, sometimes in a wooden coffin that occasionally also contained objects (the Yuppiat of St Lawrence Island followed much the same procedure). Some native practices were seen as appalling by outsiders; the Itelmen of Kamchatka were said to feed bodies to their dogs in the hope that the spirit of the dead would help create a better dog team, and the Chukchi were known to kill old people who had become a burden to themselves and their families. This practice was ritualised, the old person seemingly welcoming death rather than a period of hopeless infirmity. But despite the often-told story that the Inuit abandoned old people on an ice floe to die, this was not a common practice. It does seem that occasionally the infirm were left behind, but only in times of food shortage, and if the person made his way back to the group they would be welcomed. The few ancient Inuit graves discovered suggest open-air or ice-floe burial was common, perhaps lending credence to the tale.

Shamanism was viewed with suspicion by Christian missionaries to the region in the years following contact between the people of the Arctic and Europeans. In Scandinavia the Swedish Crown (which in the 16th century extended across Norway and Finland) outlawed trespass on to, or the settlement of, Sámi lands by southerners, maintaining a strict border between their kingdom and Lapland. But by the mid-17th century Lapland had been absorbed into Sweden. In the wake of traders and settlers came missionaries who set about destroying shamanism with a zeal that allowed no place for the fundamental tenets of Christianity. One of the most important of the early missionaries, Gabriel Tuderus, summed up this work by declaring that the Sámi were 'flesh-coveting swine and curs incited by Satan to resist the true, pure and solemn

Despite the advance of the modern world, shamanistic beliefs are still apparent in the Arctic. In north-west Greenland hunters still sit on polar bear skins in their kayaks, believing that this will add to their hunting skills.

sacraments'. Violence against shamans and those who resisted conversion was frequent. The situation of the Sámi improved in the 18th century when most had (nominally at least) converted to the predominant Lutheran faith of the south, and Swedish scientists were travelling north in response to the 'enlightenment' gathering pace throughout Europe. One of those scientists was Carl von Linné, better known today as Linnaeus, whose work included the development of the system of biological nomenclature for plants and animals that remains in use today. However, there were further problems in the early 19th century. War between Sweden and Russia eventually led to the incorporation of Finland into the victorious Russian empire, but in Finnish Lapland the Sámi population was decimated by starvation and disease as the remnants of the Swedish army retreated. Later, there was a general attempt at forced integration of the northern dwellers with the peoples of the south. The Sámi language was banned in schools and Sámi culture was ignored. Not until after the 1939–45 War did this situation change, with an acceptance of the value of Sámi culture, history and language.

The maltreatment of shamanism and Sámi culture was echoed among the Canadian Inuit, but even worse was the

Inukshuk, northern Baffin Island. Examples of these stone cairns are seen across the Nearctic, with various explanations offered for their presence. It is possible some were erected to act as signposts, or to aid the hunting of Caribou – the stones appearing to be men – but others mark sites of particular shamanistic significance. Beyond the stones are Pond Inlet and, across it, Bylot Island.

Mummified child from west Greenland. The child – it is believed to be a boy because of the mode of dress – would have been about 6 months old. He was dressed entirely in sealskin.

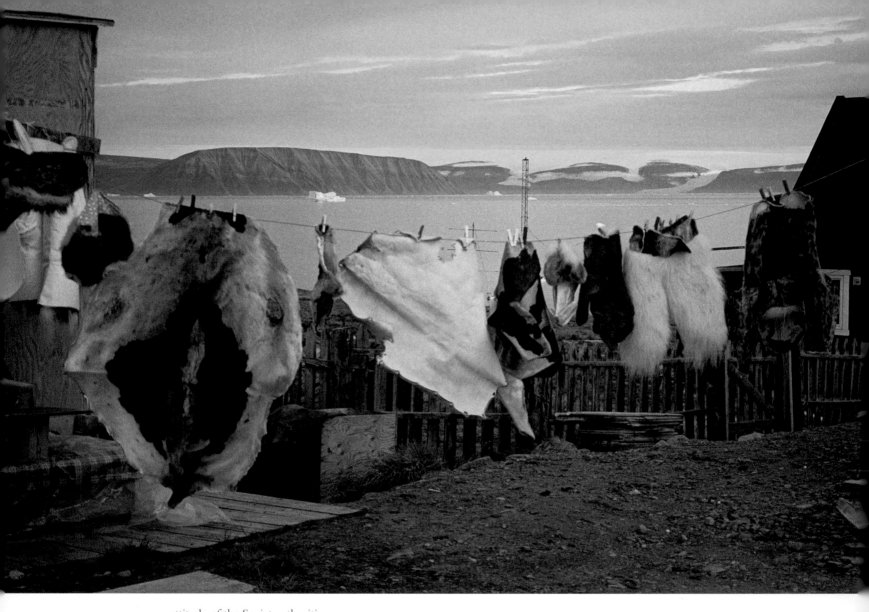

attitude of the Soviet authorities. Shamans were frequently executed, as they represented a belief system alien to Communist doctrine and were considered parasites. The story is often told that shamans were taken up in helicopters and thrown out, with the instruction that since they claimed to be able to fly, now was the chance to prove it. This may be something of a myth (most attacks on shamanism pre-dated the invention of the helicopter), though there is no doubt that Soviet doctrine led to the deaths of hundreds of shamans.

Nowadays, shamanism is viewed more sympathetically, particularly as the West has seen an increase in what might be generalised as 'Mother Earth' beliefs; although across much of the Arctic shamanic practices have been replaced by organised (invariably Christian) religion, elements can still be found, most particularly in the art of the northern peoples, which draws heavily on animistic myths.

Although the Greenland mummies were partially clad in bird skins, and these were also noted by William Parry during his second voyage in search of the North-West Passage (and illustrated in his book of the journey), they are now rarely seen, animal skins and furs being the preferred clothing. The photograph above shows a washing line in Qannaq, north-west Greenland with the skins of various seals and that of a polar bear hung out to dry. To the right a young Inuk girl snuggles into her fur hood at Ungava, Canada.

Above left
Transformation by Qiatsu Shaa. A shaman becomes an eagle in order to hunt a Musk Ox. The sculpture, in serpentine, is typical of the animalistic subjects favoured by Canadian Inuit artists.

Above top
Tupilaks from Greenland. The upper ones are of Caribou antler, the lower one of whale-bone.

Above bottom
A horn doll. Young Inuit girls were given these dolls. The body and head were carved from Caribou antlers. The clothing, of sealskin in this case, could be removed during play.

Art of the northern peoples

The art of the northern native peoples was closely aligned to their belief systems. Most men and women wore amulets to ward off evil spirits, young girls occasionally being weighed down with them, as not only did they need protection themselves, they also had to look out for their as-yet unborn children. Excavations of Dorset culture sites show that as the weather warmed and the Thule people arrived from the west, the number of amulets increased, with the Dorset folk attempting to deter the twin perils that faced them. Dorset art tended to work with the natural shape of the bone or antler from which they were carved. The pieces were powerful in their depiction of animals and birds, or mysterious in their depiction of human faces or shamanic figures. Dorset people often carved their harpoons, usually with a flying Polar Bear or falcon. These two beasts were clearly considered to represent the apogee of hunting technique, and so were held in high esteem; presumably the carvings were made in an attempt to capture the spirits of these great hunters.

Thule art tended to be more graceful, though retaining much of the mystery. Today's Inuit art reflects Thule traditional beliefs and styles. Carved in soapstone, bone, antler and ivory, Inuit themes would almost certainly be familiar to long-dead ancestors. As with both Dorset and Thule art, the pieces often maintain the natural shape and features of the medium. There are depictions of animals, in part a supplication to the spirit of the animal so as to allow a successful hunt, but also a homage to the spirit so that in its anger at the taking of its earthly body, it did not turn on the human who had killed it. There are also studies of shamans, and particularly of the transformation of shamans into other creatures, a change that allows travel to the realms of the spirits.

One interesting form of sculpture are the tupilaqs of the Greenlandic Inuit. These, often grotesque, spirit-form carvings were protective objects, but they could also occasionally be used in the same way as voodoo dolls. Place your tupilaq in an enemy's sleeping bag, and if he did not find it your curse would soon bring him bad luck. But if the carving was discovered and returned the bad luck would also bounce back, multiplied in power.

7. The Exploration of Arctic Russia

It is unclear whether the myth of the unicorn pre- or post-dated the discovery of the first narwhal tusk. There are references in the Bible and early writings in India that may refer to unicorns, but at some stage a real narwhal tusk must have given credence to the existence of an animal no one had ever seen. Consequently, when a tusk was found on the shore of the Kara Sea some time in the 16th century its appearance reinforced the legend. Then, as now, there was money to be made from the gullibility of others. The tusk caused a great deal of excitement among Europeans 'knowing that Unycorns are bredde in the landes of Cathaye, Chynayne and other Oriental Regions'. The discovery added extra impetus to the search for a northern passage to the Orient; the merchants of northern Europe were anxious to find an alternative to the dangerous and heavily taxed land routes that brought silk and spices from the East, or to the long and hazardous sea journey around the Cape of Good Hope.

In medieval Europe the decree of the Catholic Church that only 'cold' food could be eaten on Fridays had made fishermen wealthy, fish being considered cold as they lived in the cold sea. Cod, which, when salted, had a long shelf-life, was particularly prized and the Basques of the northern border country of Spain and France, together with the fishermen of Bristol, England, grew wealthy from catching this fish. At first the Bristolians fished close to Iceland; the Basques' fishing grounds were unknown, and they were too shrewd to reveal their secret. But eventually the Bristolians too found a new cod fishery. There is a legend in Bristol that before his westward journey, Christopher Columbus visited the city and spoke to fishermen who, unlike the Basques, were more open about their finds, and it is known that Bristolian merchants wrote to Columbus after his voyage complaining that he was taking credit for discovering something that was already known. The Basques and the Bristolians were fishing the Grand Banks off Newfoundland and Labrador, but were they also using land bases on the American mainland? Despite the fact that the fishermen were returning with cod that had been dried, a procedure that most authorities claim required a land base, no evidence of such a base has been found.

Following Columbus's discovery of the New World, Pope Alexander VI granted the Spanish the western hemisphere and Portugal the eastern, under the terms of the Treaty of Tordesillas in 1494. This made things difficult for the English, French and Dutch. Shortly after the signing of the Treaty a man arrived in Bristol offering to lead an expedition to Cathay. This man was Giovanni Caboto. It seems unlikely to be a coincidence that Caboto, who, like Columbus, was born in Genoa and at about the same time, chose to approach Bristol with his idea.

The excited English made Caboto an honorary Englishman, and, with a name change to John Cabot, he set sail from Bristol on 20 May 1497 in the *Mathew* (a ship more likely to have been named for his wife, Mathye, than the Disciple despite the assertions of some later historians), with a crew of 18. Cabot carried letters patent from Henry VII to explore for new lands and a passage to Cathay, his licence stipulating that he was to give 20% of all profits from the voyage to the King and that no one was to disembark on any newly discovered land without the permission of the Crown. On 24 June Cabot landed in Newfoundland, just a short distance from L'Anse aux Meadows. Finding evidence of inhabitants and fearful of confrontation because of his limited numbers, Cabot took on water and left, exploring the local coast before returning to Bristol. (As an aside, the chief sponsor of Cabot's voyage, Richard Amerycke, one-time Bristol High Sheriff – his surname derived from *ap Meryck* as he had Welsh ancestry – is a more likely candidate for the origin of the new continent's name than the oft-quoted Amerigo Vespucci.) On his next voyage Cabot (now Grand Admiral Cabot, England's answer to Admiral of the Ocean Columbus) sailed with five ships, one of which soon returned after being damaged in a gale. The fate of the rest is a mystery. Sebastian Cabot, John's son, claimed to have been on this trip and gave a plausible account of crossing the Arctic Circle, where the expedition encountered 'monstrous heaps of ice swimming in the sea', days 18 hours long and the entrance to a gulf heading west where many men died of cold. Kind-minded historians wonder if Cabot had sailed into Davis Strait and found Hudson Strait. Less generous folk claim that as Sebastian was a known storyteller he may not even have been on the expedition. Certainly he sheds no light on the fate of his father.

The British head east

That first attempt at a northern route to the East had been made by heading west, but after its failure attention turned eastwards. In the ninth century Ottar the Norseman is said to have sailed as far as the White Sea. Then, in the 12th century migrants from central Russia arrived in the area close to the White Sea, displacing the native peoples. The newcomers hunted seals, walrus and bears in Arctic waters and used the river systems that feed the White Sea to trade. By the 15th century the area was being called Pomor'ye (from *po mor* – by the sea) and its inhabitants (the Pomores) were famous for their hunting skills. There is a tradition that the Starostin family hunted in Svalbard prior to the founding of the Solovetsk monastery (on an island in the White Sea) in 1425, and documents note that the Russian Tsar had taken possession of Grumant in the mid-16th century. The name means Greenland, but as it was then thought that Svalbard was part of Greenland Russian scholars believe that there was Pomore activity in Svalbard prior to the Barents expedition, and have even claimed dendrochronological evidence dating from the mid-16th century to support this. Western sources are more sceptical, pointing out that wood could have been carried to Svalbard by currents rather than hunters. The debate has political overtones, Norway being consistently nervous about the strength of its sovereignty claim over Svalbard, especially with a Russian presence on the islands.

The Pomores used the *koch*, a superbly adapted vessel for exploring Arctic waters. Kochs were small with curved sides and a flat bottom. They had a single mast and sail, but were light enough to be rowed. This, and their shallow draft, made them highly manoeuvrable in icy waters, the flat bottom allowing them to be readily freed if pack ice threatened entrapment. There was a double hull, an inner layer of boards sewed together with juniper roots, the outer layer nailed; the same basic design, now called a *karbas*, is still in use on the White Sea today. Interestingly, the koch looked somewhat like

Opposite page
The distinctive onion domes of Russian churches are seen throughout Alaska. This one is on Kodiak Island.

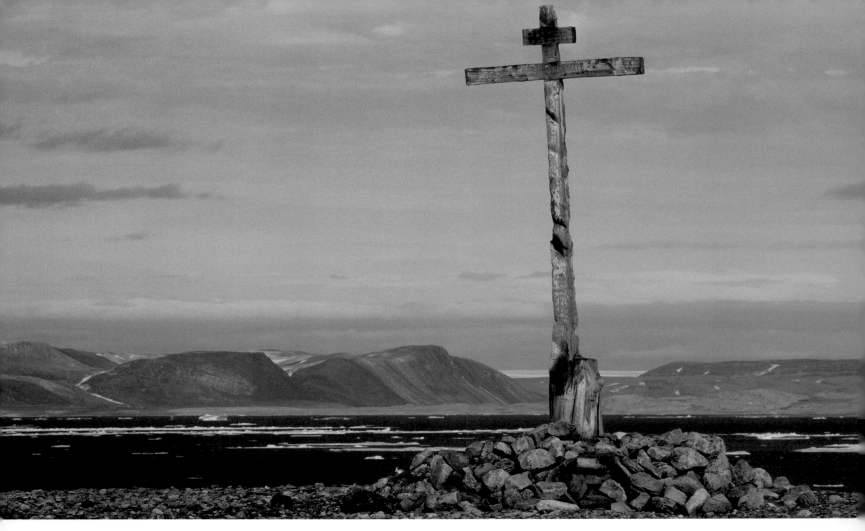

There is clear evidence of Pomore journeys as far as Svalbard, but the earliest date of such voyages is disputed. The photograph above shows a Russian cross at Murchisonfjorden, while that to the right shows a Pomore grave site at Trygghavna Isfjorden. These sites can only be accurately dated to the late 17th/early 18th centuries, but Russian scholars claim earlier dates on the basis of disputed dendrochronology. Such claims are considered to be politically motivated by a nervous Norwegian government.

Gjøa, Amundsen's North-West Passage ship built three centuries later.

The Pomores could survive for several weeks in the boats and almost indefinitely off the land. In 1743 four men were accidentally marooned on Edgeøya (off Spitsbergen's eastern coast) when the ice-bound ship they had left for a night ashore had disappeared next morning. For six years they survived by hunting, drinking blood to ward off scurvy (the one man who objected to drinking blood died), and were in good health when rescued in 1749. Though this was at least 200 years after the supposed first Svalbard journeys, survival technology had altered little over that time, implying integration with the environment to Inuit standards.

Some knowledge of the seas west of Novaya Zemlya almost certainly trickled down to the sea-faring nations of northern Europe, and in 1553 Sebastian Cabot proposed a trip to discover a North-East Passage to Cathay. Despite being able to offer no opinion on the fate of his father, Sebastian's hints that he knew the secret of the North-West Passage kept him comfortable for life, firstly in the pay of the Spanish (despite a disastrous trip to South America when his backers had financed him to head north) and then of the English. The latter made him Grand Pilot of England, and gave him other equally pretentious titles and a fat salary. Trading on his title, Cabot, by now an old man and not fit to travel himself, persuaded London merchants to back his venture, though why he chose the North-East Passage when his claim was to know the whereabouts of the north-western route is not clear.

The three ships were separated by a storm off northern Norway; only the *Edward Bonaventure* under Richard Chancellor (who carried, as did the other captains, a letter signed by Edward VI beginning 'Kings, Princes and Potentates inhabiting the North-east partes of the worlde...') continued east to reach a place where there was 'no night at all, but a continual light'. The ship eventually arrived at Kholmogori – which later became Arkhangelsk (Archangel). There Chancellor discovered to his amazement that he was not in Cathay but Muscovy (Russia). He was enthusiastically welcomed by officials of Tsar Ivan IV (the Terrible) and taken the 2,400km to Moscow by sledge. At the capital he was equally warmly received and negotiated an Anglo-Russian trade treaty that made his London backers (who subsequently formed the Muscovy Company) rich. Sadly on the return trip to England, his ship, now carrying a Russian ambassador

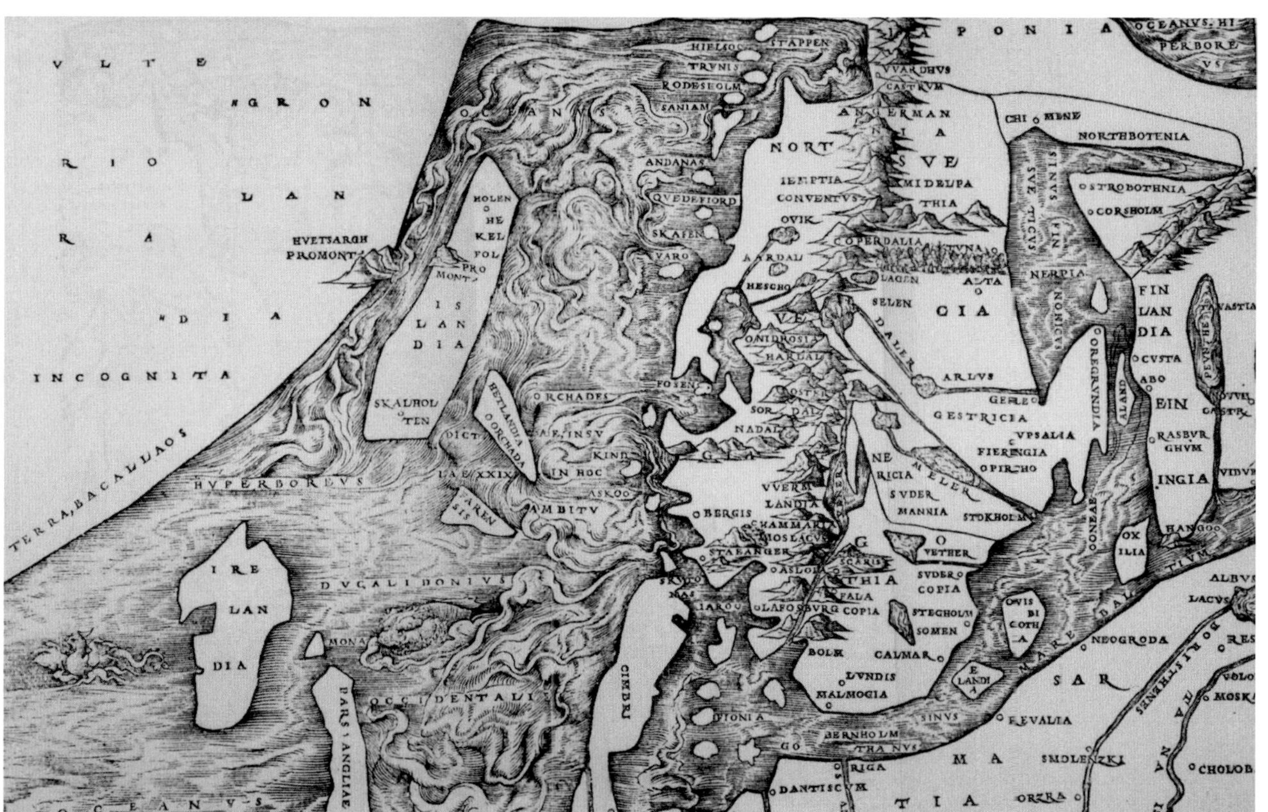

Before the journeys of Barents and Russian explorers the maps of north-eastern Europe were chaotic, as this one, published in Strasbourg in 1532 by Jacob Ziegler, illustrates.

(Ossip Nepeja, the first such ambassador to England) was wrecked off Scotland. Chancellor died saving Nepeja's life.

In 1556 the Muscovy Company, emboldened by their trade agreement, put the miseries of 1553 behind them and tried again, Stephen Burrough sailing the *Searchthrift* to the Kara Sea where his progress was blocked by ice. Burrough overwintered at Kholmogori and returned safely, his gloomy pronouncements stopping further attempts until 1580 when, shortly after Frobisher's attempt to go west, the Company tried one more time, this time with two ships, Arthur Pet commanding the *George* and Charles Jackman the *William*. The ships carried a vast inventory of tradable goods and 'a large Mappe of London to make show of your Citie' in order to impress the natives of Cathay. The expedition reached the Kara Sea where Pet, faced with a dispiriting mix of ice and fog, turned back; the *William* was never seen again.

Frozen sailors and the birth of a legend

The other two ships of Chancellor's expedition (the *Bona Esperanza* and *Bona Confidentia*) reached the Kola Peninsula, where they decided to overwinter. Ill-prepared for the Arctic winter and with scout parties failing to find locals to help, all 66 men of the two crews died, probably of a combination of cold and scurvy; their bodies were found by Russian fishermen the following spring. A legend soon sprang up that the English sailors had been frozen to death as they worked, the commander at his desk, pen in hand, others carrying plates or cups, or in the act of eating. This seems absurd now, but the Arctic was an unknown, fearful land in the early 16th century and such terrors seemed all too likely; this version of the death of the crews formed the basis of the tale of *The Flying Dutchman*. The two ships were subsequently sailed back to England; to complete the disaster, both wrecked en route.

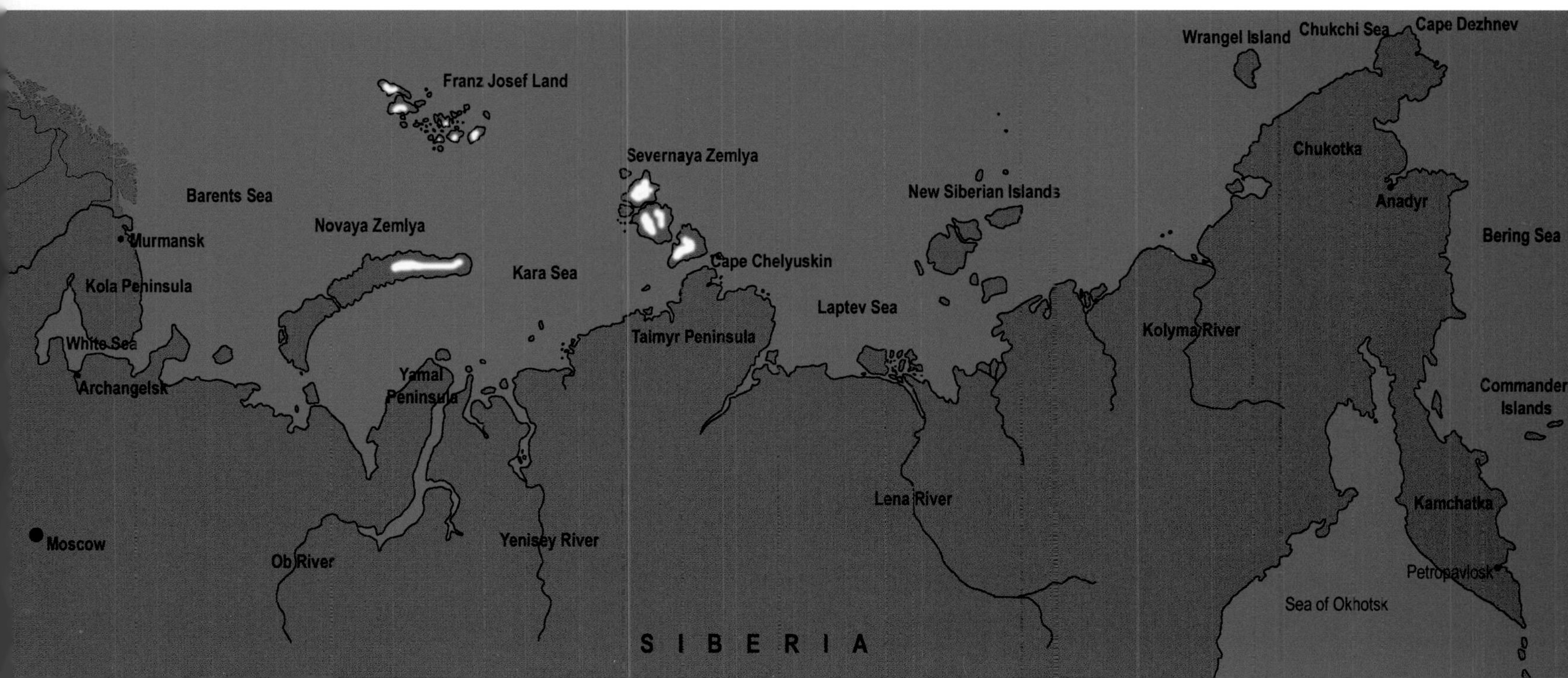

The Dutch head east

When Europeans next headed north-east in an attempt to reach Cathay they were Dutch rather than English. Having recently thrown out the Spanish from the Netherlands, the Dutch were keen to establish themselves on the world stage and, ignoring the English failures along the Russian coast (and that of Oliver Brunel, financed by a Belgian merchant, in 1584), sent three ships to the region in May 1594. Willem Barents, born on the North Sea island of Terschelling, commanded the *Mercurius* while Cornelius Nai commanded *De Swane* and, confusingly, another *Mercurius*. The plan was for Barents to attempt to round the northern tip of Novaya Zemlya, while Nai attempted to penetrate the Kara Sea, either by sailing between Novaya Zemlya and Vaygach Island, or between the latter and the mainland. Barents pushed to about 77°N – probably a record northing at the time, though in the absence of accounts of Norse and Pomore northern voyages the claim cannot be justified – at the northern end of Novaya Zemlya, but from there all that could be seen was ice, with no glimpse or hope of open water. For several weeks Barents probed the ice, but eventually had to admit defeat. When he rendezvoused with Nai he found him jubilant. After sailing through the Yugorski Shar Strait (between Vaygach Island and the Yugorski Peninsula) Nai had negotiated the ice of the Kara Sea and found open water. Deciding that 'there is absolutely no further doubt that the passage to China is free and open' he turned around.

Back in Holland the delighted House of Orange sent a fleet of seven merchant ships in 1595. Barents went again, but was not the leader of the expedition, merely master of the *Greyhound*. But 1595 was a very different year, with the Yugorski Shar Strait, reached in late August, being blocked with ice. After several weeks of trying to break through, during which time two men were killed by a bear, the fleet sailed home. Disappointed, the Dutch royal family declined to

Two drawings by Levinus Hulsius which illustrated Gerrit de Veer's book *The Three Voyages of Willem Barents*. The upper one includes a parhelia below which the crew attack a bear. The drawing was titled 'A wonder in the heavens and how we caught a bear'. The capture would appear to have been by sheer weight of numbers and ferocity. The lower drawing is of the hut on Novaya Zemlya. Every attempt appears to have been made to make the overwintering look idyllic. The reality was very different. As the photograph below indicates, northern Novaya Zemlya is a hostile environment.

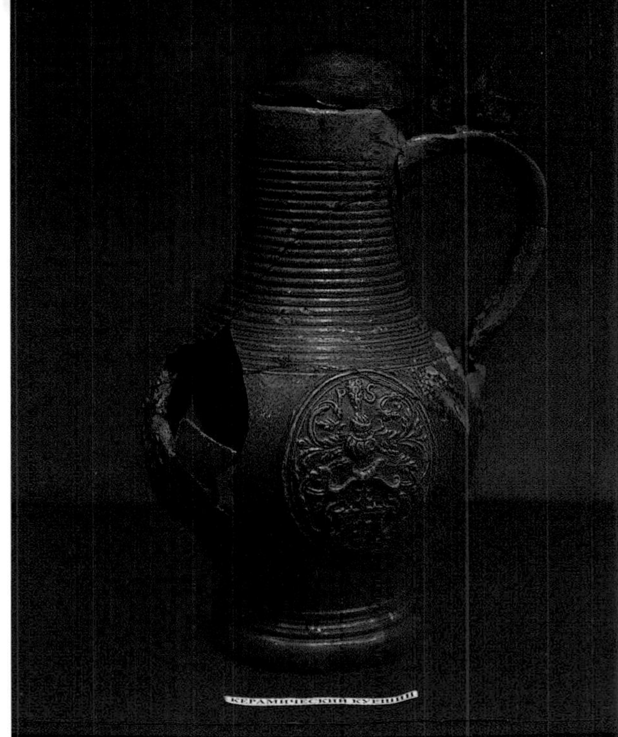

Today all that remains at Barents's wintering site is a memorial cross. The artefacts recovered from the site are in museums: in the photograph to the left is a drinking pot in the museum of the Arctic and Antarctic Institute, St Petersburg.

organise another official expedition, but offered a substantial return to anyone discovering the passage. A group of Amsterdam merchants took up the challenge, financing two ships which sailed in May 1596. The ships were commanded by Jacob van Heemskerk and Jan Cornelius Riip, much to Barents's aggravation. He was, however, offered a place on a ship and chose to go with Heemskerk. In what is now called the Barents Sea the Dutch chased a Polar Bear in a rowing boat, slaughtering it with muskets and an axe.

Sailing north from Bear Island the Dutch passed icebergs (which, delightfully, a sailor new to the Arctic thought were huge swans when he first saw them) and a dead whale that 'stank monstrously', before reaching another island with an array of pointed mountains. These gave the island its name – Spitsbergen (though on their charts they called their discovery *Het Nieuwe Land* – The New Land). The Dutch had discovered – or, perhaps, rediscovered – the Svalbard archipelago. Exploring the island's west coast the Dutch named Amsterdam Island and wondered at the plant life, birds and warm days so far north. When the Sun allowed a latitude calculation the Dutch had reached 79°49'N, the north-western tip of Spitsbergen.

Ice now blocked further progress and the Dutch returned to Bear Island where, after an argument with Barents, Riip decided to head home. Barents persuaded Heemskerk to head east and, dodging icebergs and floes, was able to go around the northern tip of Novaya Zemlya. They reached a sheltered bay, but it was now early September and the sea ice soon blocked the bay's entrance. The Dutch had called the bay Ice Haven: it was an optimistic and entirely inappropriate name, with ice soon tumbling in to trap the ship. The crew of 17 were 'forced, in great poverty, misery and grief, to stay all that winter', while the noise of the ice 'made all the hair of our heads to rise upright with fear'. The men built a hut of driftwood; when they put nails in their mouths before use they noticed that icicles formed on them before they could begin hammering. Inside the hut were bunks and a bath, and a huge central fire over which they cooked food from the ship, supplemented by the meat of local wildlife, of which Polar Bears were particularly abundant. When the weather permitted they played a form of golf on a course between the hut and the ship, about 3km away.

The cold of the Arctic winter was so intense that all cracks in the hut were sealed, almost poisoning the men with fumes from the unventilated fire. To escape the crushing cold the men huddled close to the fire, but often found that they smelled burning socks before their cold feet had registered they were too close to the flames. They also suffered from scurvy, despite the fresh meat they ate. In all, five of the 17 were to die from the disease, one being Barents who died on the journey home. That journey was an epic. The ship had been so battered by the ice it was unseaworthy, so two rowing boats were converted to sailing skiffs allowing the men to sail south along the Novaya Zemlya coast as soon as the summer Sun of 1597 had cleared the ice. Barents died on 20 June; five weeks later Heemskerk and the other survivors met a group of Russian fishermen at Novaya Zemlya's southern tip. Almost dead from scurvy, their gums so deteriorated that their teeth were falling out and they were unable to take solid food, the Dutch were nursed back to health and taken to the mainland, where they were met by Riip, who had come in search of them.

On arriving home the Dutchmen, still wearing caps of Arctic Fox fur complete with a tail, were greeted as heroes. In Heemskerk's case it was a true reflection of the man; years later, during a battle between the Dutch and Spanish, he lost a leg to cannon shot, but holding on to his sword he urged his men forward until he bled to death. His monument in Amsterdam notes that he 'steered his way through ice and iron'. But Heemskerk returned from the ice empty-handed, while another expedition, which had gone around the Cape of Good Hope, was laden with cargo. The Dutch stared wide-eyed at these riches and forgot about the North-East Passage. Somewhat half-heartedly, the English did try again – sending Henry Hudson, more famous for his exploits in Arctic Canada – before exploration of the region passed largely into the hands of the Russians.

Siberia

Across the Urals, traditionally the boundary between Europe and Asia, lay Siberia, named after the Mongolian word *siber*, meaning beautiful or pure, or, perhaps, from the Tartar sibir, which translates as 'sleeping land'. The sheer scale of Siberia is breathtaking. Trains on the Trans-Siberian Railway take eight days to chug their way from Moscow to Vladivostok, six of those spent east of the Urals. East of the obelisk which traditionally marks the 'boundary' between Europe and Asia the train crosses five time zones, while east of Vladivostok, a traveller would cross three more while edging around the Sea of Okhotsk and on to the Bering Sea. Siberia stretches from the Arctic Ocean to the Mongolian steppe; it covers almost 8% of the world's land area. The whole of the United States, including Alaska, together with all the countries of Europe (excluding European Russia) could fit comfortably into Siberia. Lake Baikal, Siberia's largest lake, is, by volume, the largest freshwater lake on Earth, holding 20% of the world's fresh water. Each of Siberia's three great rivers, the Ob, the Yenisey and the Lena, drains a basin bigger than western Europe. Of the vast Siberian forest – the taiga – Chekhov wrote that that only migrating birds knew where it ended.

It is difficult to capture the sheer size and beauty of Siberia, but the photographs below go some way. To the left is an aerial view of the Sinyaya River, a tributary of the Lena, snaking its way through the taiga. To thr right is a small section of the taiga.

The conquest of Siberia

In 1533 the three-year-old Ivan IV inherited the title of Grand Prince of Muscovy from his father. Ivan's grandfather, Ivan III, had freed Muscovy from the rule of the Mongol Golden Horde and had expanded the principality as far as the Urals. In 1547 Ivan was crowned Tsar, the first Russian to hold the title. Six years later he established a relationship with western Europe by signing his trade agreement with Richard Chancellor. Ivan IV is known to history as Ivan the Terrible, the cruelties of his reign being gross even for a period of history not noted for benign treatment of those considered enemies of the state. Ivan's reign of terror, aided by disease, ill-considered military campaigns and, in particular, a decline in the supply of furs, had brought Russia to the edge of disaster. The sable, a member of the weasel family with a much-prized thick coat, had been all but exterminated in northern Muscovy; without new sources Ivan faced economic ruin. He therefore encouraged (or, at least, failed to discourage – Ivan's support was vague and ambiguous) the Stroganovs, one of Muscovy's most powerful mercantile families, to probe eastwards beyond the Urals.

It is usually claimed that the Stroganovs sent Vasily Timofeyevich, a notorious bandit and Volga pirate known as Yermak, to explore Siberia. In reality Yermak crossed the

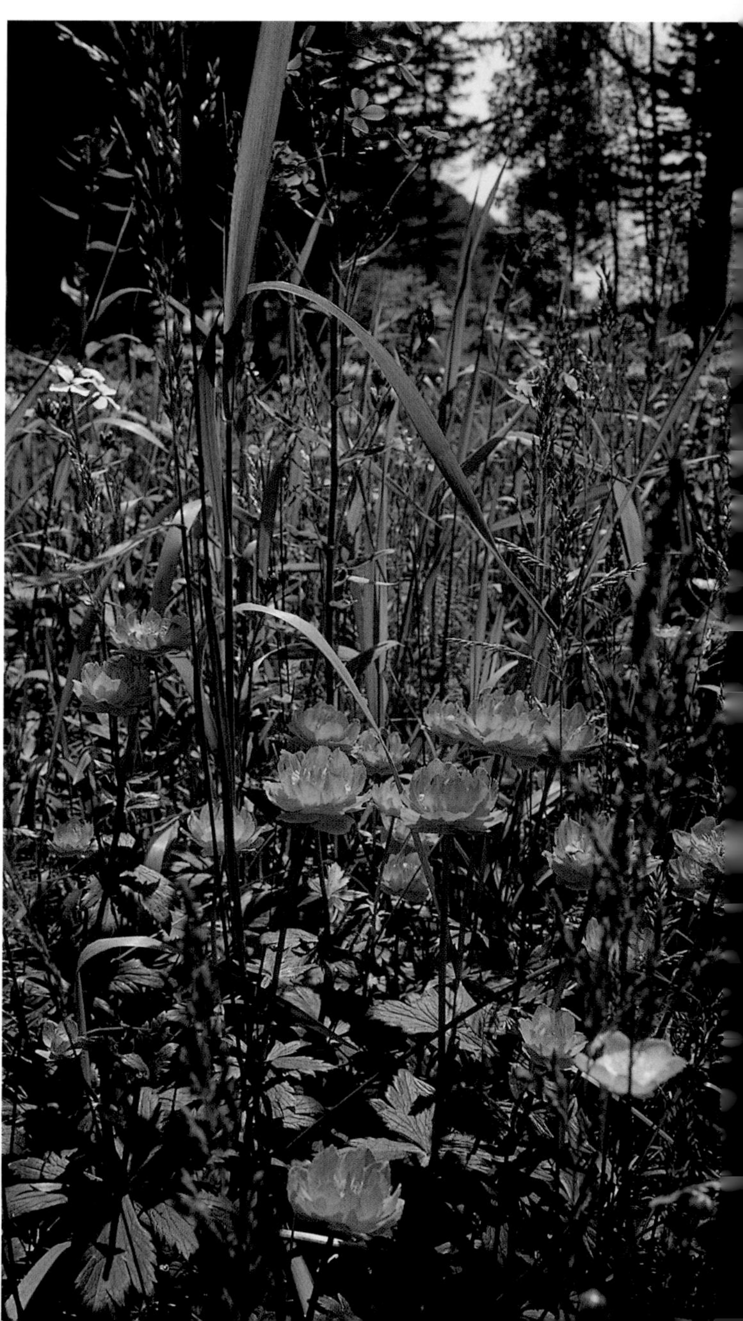

Urals – hauling boats over the mountains so he could make use of the rivers beyond – to attack the Mongolian khanate, which comprised what is now the south-western corner of modern Siberia. Yermak was a leader in the Ivan the Terrible style, with anyone foolish enough to question his authority dying horrifically; people were often hung upside down by one foot, a slow, agonising death. On more compassionate days Yermak had his enemies tied in a sack with a bag of sand and dumped in the nearest river. Yermak seems to have been driven by the prospect of plunder rather than any expansionist zeal, but the vast wealth in furs he discovered led to a massive Russian expansion eastwards. In that sense Yermak can be seen as having led the Russians into Siberia. Ironically, in view of one method he used to dispose of his enemies, Yermak died by drowning. Natives attacked a group of men he was leading, killing them all; Yermak broke free and attempted to reach a boat to escape, but the boat slipped from his grasp and, weighed down by his massive armour, he sank below the water.

At first, despite his tacit support for the Stroganov initiative, Ivan was appalled by the reprisal raids Yermak's incursions generated on Russia's southern border. His mood soon changed when the first batch of furs, thousands of sable, arrived. Within a century the Russians had reached Kamchatka, leaving only the extremities of Taimyr and Chukchi beyond the Tsar's grasp. In Moscow the arm of government that administered Yermak's first conquest was called the Siberia Department; as Russia expanded eastwards the department took over the administration of all the land east of the Urals, but the name remained the same and so modern Siberia came into being.

The fur trappers and, to a lesser extent, the religious dissidents who followed them explored Siberia by water rather than land. In this they were not only applying common sense in so vast a region, but following the centuries-old Pomore tradition. Over the years that followed, Pomore skills at navigating rivers and the icy seas off the northern Siberian shore were critical. The term 'cossack' originally meant a frontiersman, the tough breed who were Russia's first line of defence against Mongol and Tartar incursions, and who led the settlement of Siberia. Yermak was a cossack, and it was cossacks who led the groups of *promyshlenniki* (technically the word means 'hunt' or 'hunting', but in the West has tended to mean hunters and trappers) that pushed ever-eastwards. In 1602 the port of Mangazeya had been established at the mouth of the Ob to export Siberian furs. Russian merchants to the west, envious of the port's success which was destroying their overland trade, forced its closure and even falsified maps so that Novaya Zemlya appeared to be a peninsula of the mainland rather than an island to give the impression that a northern sea route was not possible. Yet despite this, the Russians had reached Taimyr by 1620, rounding Cape Chelyuskin, the northernmost point on the Eurasian mainland (in 1940 a survey team working on the eastern side of the Taimyr Peninsula discovered the skeletons of several people, including a woman and a boy, together with various pieces of equipment; the material was dated to 1618).

By 1630 the Russians had reached the Lena. In 1633 the cossack Ivan Rebrov sailed down the Lena to the sea, turned east and reached the Yana River and, later, the Indigirka. In 1642 Mikhail Stadukhin reached the Kolyma River, though by then another cossack, Dimitri Kopylov, had already seen an arm of the Pacific. In 1639 Kopylov had led a band of *promyshlenniki* along the Okhota (hunter) River; at its mouth was a foggy bay crammed with driftwood. Kopylov had reached the Sea of Okhotsk, naming it after the river.

Dezhnev sails east

In 1648, one of the most significant of all expeditions to the Arctic took place. Despite the vast wealth of Siberia, new sources of sable and other fur-bearing animals were always being sought. It is estimated that during the last half of the 17th century more than 100,000 sable were trapped annually. By 1648 rumours were spreading that the country of the Anadyr River, which reaches the Bering Sea in southern Chukotka, was rich in furs. That way, too, lay mammoth and walrus ivory, and an expedition set sail to discover a sea-route to these treasures. The nominal leader of the expedition was a trader, Fedor Alekseyev, an agent for a wealthy Moscow merchant. To protect Alekseyev and his *promyshlenniki* Moscow appointed the cossack Semen Ivanovich Dezhnev. Little is known of Dezhnev. He was probably a Pomore, born in about 1605, and had seen service with Stadukhin. The expedition that now bears his name consisted of seven kochs, his own, those of Alekseyev, and others filled with unattached but eager *promyshlenniki*, a total of 90 men.

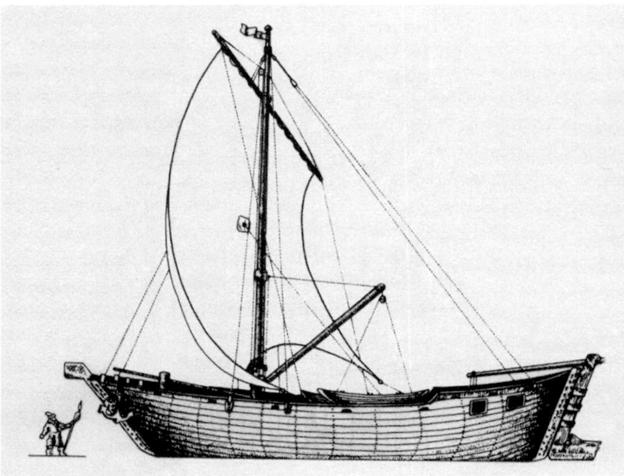

Below left
A koch, the ship used by the Pomores. It was in such a ship that Semen Dezhnev became the first man to sail through the Bering Strait.

Below right
The memorial to Semen Dezhnev which stands at Cape Dezhnev, the most easterly point of Eurasia.

In ice conditions that must have been remarkably favourable but weather that was not, the expedition lost four ships before Chukotka was reached; another was later wrecked on the northern Chukotka coast. The remaining two, commanded by Alekseyev and Dezhnev, rounded Cape Dezhnev, Eurasia's north-eastern tip, and sighted the Diomede Islands. The men landed and there was a skirmish with the native Chukchis; back at sea the two ships were separated in a storm. Alekseyev and his men were never seen again, though Alekseyev's Yakut mistress did survive. Dezhnev's koch was driven south of the Anadyr River and then ashore. The ship had travelled over 3,000km in 100 days and had passed through the Bering Strait.

Dezhnev still had 25 men with him, his own crew and survivors from the various wrecks. They crossed the mountains to reach the Anadyr but discovered that, despite the rumours, its valley had neither sable nor game animals. A group of 12 men therefore went upriver looking for food, but found none, nine men disappearing as they trekked back to the river mouth. The survivors overwintered, then built boats of driftwood and went upriver again. They overwintered again and then, amazingly, met a group of men from a team commanded by Mikhail Stadukhin who, unaware of the sea expedition, had walked to the Anadyr. Several men were now killed in fights with the locals, but Dezhnev, emboldened by the relative ease with which Stadukhin had reached the Anadyr overland, was determined to explore the area. At the river's mouth he found a huge walrus colony, and he collected a load of ivory. He also met Alekseyev's mistress. She told him that Alekseyev's koch had been driven ashore, that all but a handful of the men had been killed in a battle with the natives and that the survivors had died (there was a persistent rumour that they had reached Kamchatka and lived there for several years, but no firm evidence has ever been discovered to substantiate this). Finally, Dezhnev returned home. Over subsequent years he returned to the Anadyr, collecting more than two tons of walrus ivory. Later he successfully petitioned for a reward for his discoveries and eventually retired to Moscow.

Bering and Russian America

Strangely, despite both its significance and its value as an epic tale of adventure and survival, Dezhnev's journey was forgotten for almost a century. Before its rediscovery Peter the Great had sponsored an expedition which, though achieving much less than Dezhnev's, has become much better known. Tsar Peter was an enthusiastic amateur geographer interested in mapping Russia's coast, though it is also clear that he understood that if a shipping route existed along Russia's northern coast he could tax the ships that used it. For much of his life these interests had to take second place to foreign wars and feuding at court. But eventually a good excuse for the Tsar to exercise his interests in the region arose. Peter needed to subdue the Chukchis and Koryaks of far-eastern Siberia and the Kamchatka Peninsula. As with the other native peoples of

Southern Kamchatka. It was across this landscape that Bering's expedition had to make their way twice before setting out on their voyage. The volcano in the background is Dzenzursky.

Are Asia and America joined?

The order given by Peter the Great to Vitus Bering suggests that he had seen, or knew of, a map that indicated 'a passage through the Arctic Sea', implying that a misty memory of Dezhnev's journey existed. There was also other knowledge that the two continents were close but perhaps not joined, and several maps known to have been drawn before Bering's journey imply that there was no link. The Russians certainly knew of the existence of the Diomede Islands before Bering sailed, and they also knew that the Chukchi had occasionally crossed a frozen sea to trade with people of another land. The Chukchi had taken furs and had returned with pelts of an unknown animal, one whose tail was ringed red and black – these must have been racoon skins and, if they were, had presumably been traded from well to the south as the racoon is not (now) an Alaskan animal. Bering's journey left the answer on the continental link ambiguous, though he certainly proved that if a link existed it was well to the north, but before his discovery of Alaska, North America was seen by another Russian. In 1732 Mikhail Gvozdev took Bering's ship, the *St Gabriel*, north from the Anadyr River. He visited the Diomede Islands, then sailed east until he sighted land – probably Cape Prince of Wales. Gvozdev could see that this land turned east, but he failed to make a landing; it would be another ten years before a non-native foot stepped on Alaska.

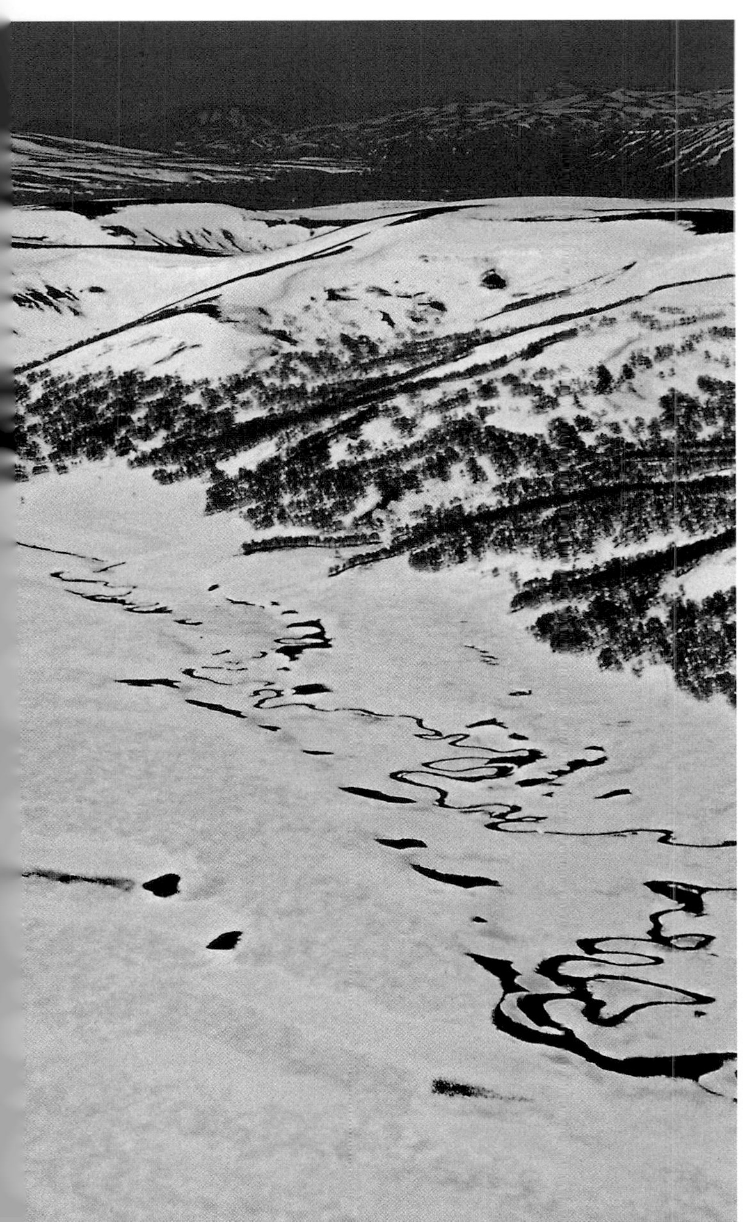

the north, the Tsar extracted *yasak*, tribute, from both groups (see below), but lately the tribute – in furs whose sale was a mainstay of the Russian economy – had not been paid and the natives were also killing Russian trappers, meaning there was also less 'private' fur to tax. The situation needed remedying, and an expedition to map the area was an essential prelude to the establishment of a local police force.

On 5 November 1724 Peter helped to rescue sailors from a capsized boat in the Gulf of Finland, wading waist deep into the sea. The icy waters chilled him and he developed pneumonia. As he lay dying he gave orders for an expedition to explore Siberia's eastern coast. The expedition would also see if Asia and America were joined at the Chukchi Peninsula and if there were further lands Russia could exploit for their furs. On 26 January 1725 Peter signed the papers that finalised the expedition. Two days later he died. The man appointed to lead the expedition was Vitus Jonassen Bering, a 44-year-old Dane recently retired from Russia's Imperial Navy. Peter's directions were commendably brief, though the first seems somewhat obvious, requiring Bering to 'build one or two boats with decks' in 'Kamchatka or some other place'; Bering was also instructed to discover whether Asia and America were joined, and to explore America far enough east to find a town occupied by Europeans.

To make the voyage the Russians decided to take the expedition overland to the Sea of Okhotsk, then to cross it in ships built there. They would then cross Kamchatka overland and build ships for the northern journey on the peninsula's eastern shore. This epic preparation took 3½ years. On the journey across Siberia one section of the expedition, separated from the forward party, had to eat their horses, then their leather harnesses and finally their clothing and boots to fend off starvation. Ill-clad and bootless they survived the winter in holes dug in the snow. At the Sea of Okhotsk the expedition discovered that the local timber was so poor that nails were useless, so they built a craft (the *Fortuna*, probably named in hope rather than expectation) that was held together with leather straps, more raft than ship. In this they successfully crossed to Kamchatka twice (a crossing of 1,000km each way, a remarkable achievement), ferrying all their supplies and men.

On Kamchatka, Bering had to cross the rugged volcanic mountain chain that runs down the peninsula's spine, an epic journey through blizzards that 'rolled like a dark smoke over moors' with the nights spent in snow holes. Living off the land after his supplies dwindled away, Bering built one ship, the *Svyatoy Gavriil* (St Gabriel) and on 14 July 1728 sailed from the Kamchatka River. Bering had spent 3½ years getting to this point; his ship was stacked with enough food for another year, but his voyage lasted just 51 days. Sailing north-east, Bering hit the southern Chukotka coast, where local Chukchis told him that the coast headed north-east but beyond an island turned west. Bering saw the island, calling it St Lawrence Island as it was spotted on 10 August, the saint's feast day. He then sailed north, bad weather preventing him from seeing the Alaskan coast to the east. On 15 August Bering was no longer able to see the coast of Asia (but could not see America either) and he stopped to discuss options with his two deputy commanders. Alexei Chirikov, a Russian, felt they should press on to the Kolyma River and so prove the absence of a land bridge. Martin Spanberg, a Dane like Bering, disagreed, believing that the Chukchi suggestion that the Asian coast fell

A memorial to Bering's men has been erected at their grave site on Bering Island. In 1991 a Russo-Danish expedition exhumed the bodies on the island. The skeleton of Bering himself was identified from the description of the way he had died, in a pit of sand which had collapsed over him. The sand had been warm and Bering refused to be moved. When his head was reconstructed from the exhumed skull it bore resemblance to the assumed portraits of him.

away westward meant that their mission was accomplished. Bering sided with Spanberg and after reaching 67°19'N, the ship turned south again.

History has not been kind when considering Bering's decision to give up the search for a land connection between Asia and America, but that may not be entirely fair. When he returned to St Petersburg Bering reported that the Chukchis had told him that many years earlier a ship had arrived in their area from the Lena – that ship can only have been Dezhnev's, so Bering did have information to back his decision and he could hardly have acted out of cowardice, given the rigours he had already endured in getting as far as he did.

In St Petersburg, Bering's cautious, uninspiring performance was greeted with muted enthusiasm. Not only had he failed to explore the coast of America (and had not even sighted it), but he had not explored Chukotka either. He had not proven beyond doubt that there was no land bridge between Asia and America, and he had returned along his outward route when an eastern deviation might (and almost certainly would) have brought new discoveries. But the leadership he had shown during the crossing of Siberia was undeniable and so when Bering submitted plans for a second expedition they were approved. During this second Kamchatka Expedition (1741–42) Bering, in the *St Peter*, discovered Kayak Island and some of the Aleutian Islands, while his deputy – Alexei Chirikov again, now commanding the *St Paul* – discovered Prince of Wales Island. Chirikov's attempted landing in southern Alaska was disastrous; he sent his first mate, Abraham Dementiev, ashore with ten armed men, but they did not return, forcing Chirikov to depart. A local legend maintains that the natives killed the Russians, but some experts believe it is more likely they were drowned when their boats were caught in the now-notorious rip tides of the Lisyansky Strait.

As well as the discovery of 'Russian America', Bering's expedition also made other important finds. One member of it was Georg W. Steller, a German naturalist (who became the first European to land on Alaska when, sensing history in the moment, he leapt ashore first at Kayak Island). Steller's name is associated with several Alaskan species, most notably Steller's (or Northern) Sea Lion and Steller's Sea Cow, and he also 'discovered' the Sea Otter. These animals kept some of the members of the expedition alive when Bering's ship was wrecked on one of the Commander Islands. Steller's Sea Cow, a huge manatee, was quickly hunted to extinction. Steller's Sea Lion and the Sea Otter have fared better, though that owed more to good luck than any attempt at conservation. The rush to slaughter the animals for their fur that followed Bering's expedition was such that it was actually believed at one time that the Sea Otter had indeed become extinct, and the number of sea lions was drastically reduced.

Bering and many other members of his crew died of scurvy on what is now called Bering Island. Close to death, he was taken ashore and placed in a shallow pit inside a tent. The pit and tent offered him some protection against marauding Arctic Foxes, which regularly attacked dying members of his crew as well as the corpses of the dead. When the sand of the pit collapsed Bering declined to be dug free as the sand was warm, so before he could be buried he had to be partially exhumed. It was a sad end for an under-rated explorer. James Cook, who surveyed the area 50 years later, named both Strait and Sea after Bering.

The Great Northern Expedition

Bering's second Kamchatka Expedition was one detachment of what became known as the Great Northern Expedition, an enterprise that surveyed the entire north coast of Russia from the White Sea to Chukotka (and also the east coast as far as Japan), a monumental exercise. In part, the work was carried out to explore the feasibility of a sea route to China, a search for the North-East Passage that had eluded the English and Dutch. The Arctic coast work was completed by five separate teams, their timescales indicating the capricious nature of the Arctic ice. The team charged with surveying from the White

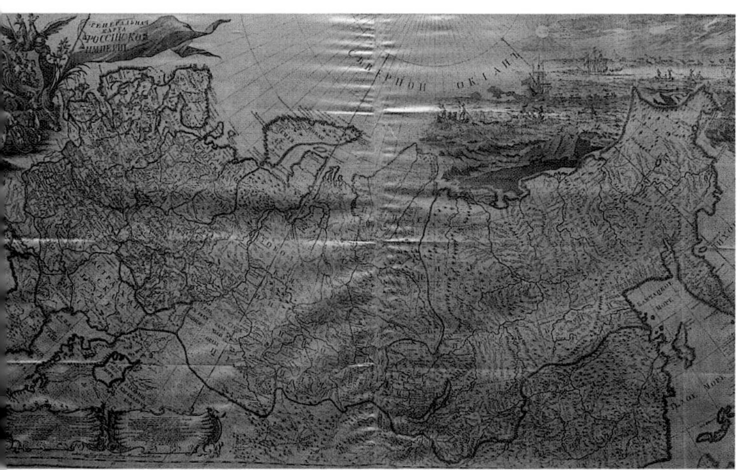

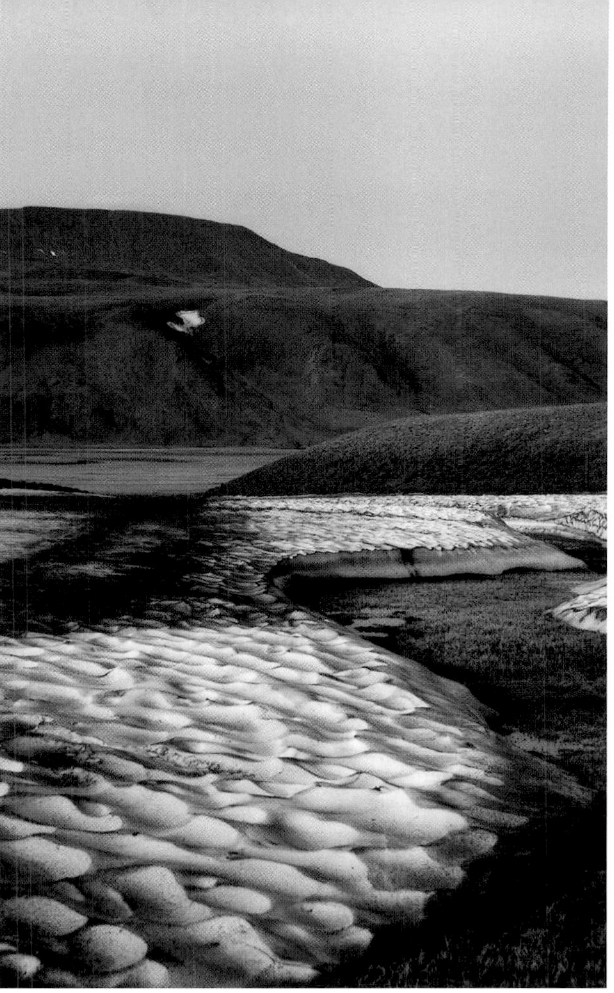

Far left
In 1745 an embroidered silk map of Russia detailing the findings of the Great Northern Expedition was finally completed and presented to the Tsaritsa Elisabeth. The achievements of the expedition cannot be overstated – it was another 100 years before the surveying of the northern Canadian coast was completed. Today the silk map, somewhat forlorn and neglected, is stored in the attic of a St Petersburg museum.

Left
Probably the hardest part of the Great Northern Expedition was the surveying of the Taimyr Peninsula, a beautiful but rugged area which extends to Cape Chelyuskin, the northernmost point of mainland Eurasia.

Sea to the Ob River failed to complete the task in 1735, driven back by ice and scurvy. The team leaders were court-martialled for failing to carry out their orders, the harshness of that official view being shown when the new leaders did no better in 1736, being forced to overwinter and finally reaching the Ob Gulf in 1737. The return journey proved no easier, the team finally arriving back in Arkhangelsk in 1739. It had taken six summers to complete the survey.

The team surveying between the Ob and the Yenisey fared even worse. In the three years 1734–36 they failed to exit the Ob Gulf. Only in 1737, after a sledge party (using reindeer rather than dogs) had been sent out in desperation to complete the task, were ships finally able to make the journey. The teams surveying from the Yenisey to the Khatanga River had by far the hardest task, having to round the vast Taimyr Peninsula, Siberia's northernmost landmass. Consequently, two teams were used, travelling east from the Yenisey and west from the Lena. The Yenisey team used a ship (the *Ob Pochtalyon* – Ob Postman!), which had reached the Yenisey in 1737. Its commander was Fedor Minin; in five summers he failed to travel more than 450km, was court-martialled and reduced in rank to the lowest grade of seaman. Heading westward was a team under Vasily Pronchishchev which included his wife, who could not bear to be separated from him, and Semen Chelyuskin. In 1736 the team, in the *Yakutsk*, reached Cape Chelyuskin (then North-east Cape, but subsequently renamed) but were forced to turn back by ice and scurvy; Pronchishchev died of the disease and, within a week, his heartbroken wife had died too. Not until 1739 did the *Yakutsk*, now under Khariton Laptev, try again. Laptev reached Cape Faddeya but was forced to overwinter. In 1740, trying again to reach Cape Chelyuskin, the ship became trapped in the ice and sank, with the scurvy-riddled crew only just reaching safety in time. At this point Laptev gave up on the idea of a sea survey, sending out sledging teams that explored all but the northernmost reaches of Taimyr in 1741. In 1742 Semen Chelyuskin completed the survey, journeying 4,000km by sledge, mostly on sea ice. While admiring the tenacity of the Russian surveyors, it is worth recalling that Cape Chelyuskin had been rounded over a century earlier.

The final section of coast, from the Lena to Chukotka and on to Kamchatka, occupied the years 1735–41. In 1735 Peter Lasinius in the *Irkutsk* managed no more than ten days' sailing from the Lena before the ice trapped him. During the subsequent winter Lasinius and many of his crew died of scurvy. In 1736 Dimitri Laptev, a cousin of Khariton Laptev, took the *Irkutsk* as far as Cape Svyatoy Nos. Not until 1740 was the Indigirka River reached. From there a sledge party set out for the Anadyr, leaving one small section of the Chukotka coast poorly surveyed. Not until 1820 was the area resurveyed, though the imperative then was less the need to improve the mapping than persistent rumours that there was undiscovered land to the north of Chukotka's northern coast, land which might even provide a link to North America.

The commander of the 1820 expedition was Ferdinand Petrovich von Wrangell. Though only 23 years old, Wrangell had already distinguished himself on a circumnavigation of the world in 1817–19. The Chukotka expedition lasted four years (1820–23) but though the coastal survey was completed no sight of land to the north was seen. However, von Wrangell did meet Chukchis who confirmed its existence, claiming that some of their ancestors had once been forced to flee to it when conflict broke out with Eskimos, who pursued them north. The Chukchis said that on clear days the mountains of this northern land were visible from Cape Jakan. Though Wrangell did not see the land (now called Wrangel Island) he was convinced of its existence.

The North-East Passage

Following the success of the Great Northern Expedition, the idea of searching for a North-East Passage was revived by Mikhail Lomonosov. He suggested that while a coastal passage had been found to be impracticable, a more northerly route might exist. Lomonosov died just before his expedition to explore this possibility set out, with Vasili Chichagov taking command. The expedition travelled beyond 80°N between Svalbard and Greenland, aiming for the Bering Strait, but was then stopped by ice. Exploration stalled too; it was a hundred years before another effort was made, and then not by a Russian, but a Swede.

Adolf Erik Nordenskiöld was born in Finland of Swedish parents and studied geology at university. Moving to Sweden at the age of 25, Nordenskiöld took part in a number of Arctic expeditions, primarily to Spitsbergen, but also to the Russian Arctic, particularly the Kara Sea and as far east as the Yenisey River. These latter journeys taught him a great deal about the area and its ice conditions, and by 1878 he was convinced that with appropriate timing a transit of the North-East Passage was possible.

In 1878 Nordenskiöld acquired the *Vega*, a 300-ton, three-masted whaler with a steam engine and, with a crew totalling 30 (including Louis Palander, the ship's captain), set out from Karlskrona in southern Sweden on 22 June. On the first stage of the journey the *Vega* was accompanied by the *Lena*, a much smaller ship with a crew of nine. By early August the ships had reached the Kara Sea, finding it ice-free – Nordenskiöld's earlier voyages had shown him that in late summer the sea had much less ice, though it was frequently ice-filled in early summer.

Nordenskiöld crossed the Kara Sea without incident, reaching Dickson Island (named after Baron Oscar Dickson, patron of many early Arctic voyages) at the northern end of the Yenisey estuary on 6 August. The *Vega* and *Lena* took on fuel from two supply ships that had accompanied them, then headed east again; the *Lena* often led since she drew less water, the coastal waters off Taimyr being shallow. On 19 August the two ships reached Cape Chelyuskin, Nordenskiöld noting that 'the landscape was the dullest and most desolate I have seen in the high north', a sad picture of Eurasia's most northerly point.

Nordenskiöld now attempted to head directly for the New Siberian Islands, but ice forced him south, back to the coast. The Lena delta was reached on 27 August, the *Lena* then leaving to follow the river to Yakutsk. The *Vega* continued through open water, detouring to the southernmost of the New Siberian Islands, but being unable to land because of shallow water. By 5 September Nordenskiöld had reached the huge bay of Chaunskaya Guba, where the crew met their first Chukchis. Interestingly, the Chukchis could speak no Russian but they did have a smattering of English, presumably picked up from American whalers. Continuing along the coast Nordenskiöld met the first serious ice of the voyage at Cape

Two illustrations from Nordenskiöld's book on the North-East Passage voyage, *Vegas färd kring Asien och Europa*. The upper drawing shows the Vega and Lena at Cape Chelyuskin being watched by a curious Polar Bear. The lower drawing depicts living conditions during the winter frozen into the ice of the Chukchi Sea. It seems that the winter was far more tolerable than Barents and his fellow crewmen had endured on Novaya Zemlya.

Amundsen and the *Maud*

The second west-to-east transit of the North-East Passage, and the third overall, was made by Roald Amundsen in the *Maud*. Amundsen's plan was to repeat Nansen's drift in the *Fram* (Nansen's ship - see p197) itself, but the ship was in too poor a condition. Amundsen therefore had Maud (named after the Norwegian Queen) built, modelling it on *Fram*. At her launch, Amundsen smashed a block of ice rather than the customary bottle of champagne across her bow saying 'You are for ice. You shall spend your best years in ice and you shall do your work in ice.' Maud left Oslo in June 1918 with a crew that included Helmer Hanssen, veteran of *Gjøa* and the South Pole, and Oscar Wisting who had also been on the South Pole team. Amundsen went north, passing Cape Chelyuskin the first summer, but he was forced to overwinter soon after. During the winter Amundsen fell, breaking his shoulder, was mauled by a polar bear and almost died of carbon monoxide poisoning. Two sailors (Tessem and Knutsen) left the ship and headed for Dickson on skis. Both died on the way. Later authors have suggested that Amundsen's well-known lack of sympathy for sick crew members was the reason that Tessem left the ship, and that Amundsen must therefore bear responsibility for his death. The evidence is not persuasive; Tessem was certainly suffering from headaches, but there does not seem to have been undue pressure on him to go. Knutsen volunteered to accompany him; although the journey to Dickson was straightforward it was obviously foolhardy to go alone. What exactly happened is a mystery, but Russian historians who have studied the trip believe Knutsen probably died in an accident, though his body has never been discovered. A body believed to be that of Tessem was found; it is thought that as he was crossing a frozen river close to Dickson he slipped, hit his head and died. A memorial to him has been raised above his grave at Dickson.

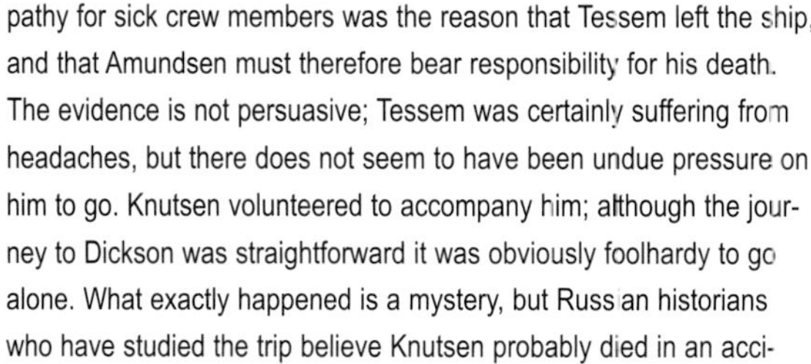

Maud was not released from the ice until September 1919, but she could only sail for 11 days before being frozen in again near Ayon Island. In 1920 *Maud* was released in early July and rounded Cape Dezhnev. By now Amundsen had given up the idea of immediately repeating the *Fram* drift and headed for Nome, Alaska where he arrived on 27 July. After resupplying the ship he went north again. Only three of the original crew were willing to sail this time – one was Oscar Wisting, who had been a member of Amundsen's team to the South Pole and was also on the *Norge* when it made its historic North Pole flight – and Amundsen intended to recruit Chukchis for the voyage. Maud was forced to overwinter at Cape Sverdzekamen (Cape Stoneheart). During the winter her propeller was damaged and in July 1921 she sailed back to Nome and then on to Seattle. By now Amundsen had lost interest in the expedition, his enthusiasm fired by the thought of instead flying to the North Pole. Oscar Wisting tried to take *Maud* north once more, but failed to reach 77° at the New Siberian Islands. *Maud* returned to Seattle where she was seized by Amundsen's creditors. She was bought by the Hudson's Bay Company, renamed *Baymaud* and intended for use as a supply vessel. She was unsuitable since she drew too much water and was abandoned at Cambridge Bay, where she sank at her mooring in August 1930. Today the sad remnants of the ship, just breaking the surface, are a curiosity for visitors.

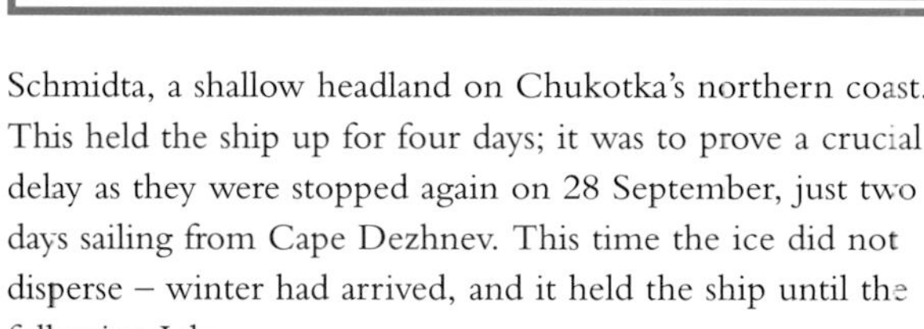

Schmidta, a shallow headland on Chukotka's northern coast. This held the ship up for four days; it was to prove a crucial delay as they were stopped again on 28 September, just two days sailing from Cape Dezhnev. This time the ice did not disperse – winter had arrived, and it held the ship until the following July.

The winter was spent comfortably, a credit to Nordenskiöld's thorough preparation. Scurvy was eliminated by stocks of cloudberries and cranberry juice, and good clothing, together with four cast iron stoves, kept the crew warm in temperatures as low as -46°C. The ship's food was good and plentiful, and often traded with the Chukchis for fresh meat. A hole was kept open in the ice in case water was needed to douse a fire, and to measure the tides, one of a series of scientific studies that included the building of a geomagnetic observatory from snow blocks.

On 18 July 1879 the *Vega* was released from the ice. Two days later she passed Cape Dezhnev and reached the Bering Strait. The completion of the North-East Passage had been a masterpiece of good organisation and seamanship, and is one of the greatest of polar voyages. But Nordenskiöld had not yet finished. The *Vega* sailed on to Japan, then around China to the Indian Ocean and across it to reach the Suez Canal. She sailed across the Mediterranean to the Straits of Gibraltar, then around Portugal, Spain and France to the English Channel and the North Sea, finally reaching Sweden in April 1880. At every stop on the way Nordenskiöld was feted. On 24 April (still Vega Day in Sweden) the ship reached Stockholm. As the ship sailed into the city the Sun broke through the clouds and a double rainbow formed above her, entrancing the thousands who had turned out to see the explorers return. Nordenskiöld was made a Baron and continued his travels to the Arctic, making important journeys to the Greenland ice sheet. He died in 1901 aged 68.

Russia closes its borders

During the winter of 1893–94 Frederick George Jackson, later to become famous for meeting Nansen on Franz Josef Land, made a remarkable sledge journey across the tundra of north-western Russia, travelling from Norway's Varanger Fjord, across the Kola Peninsula, along the southern edge of the White Sea, then north-east to reach Vaygach Island. Along the way he visited Sámi camps, as well as those of the Nenets (Samoyeds as he called them). It is to Jackson that we owe the fine drawing of the Nenet ritual site on Vaygach. But such journeys were soon to become impossible. Although Jackson later visited Franz Josef, and several expeditions used the archipelago as the starting point for expeditions aimed at reaching the North Pole, the Russian revolution of 1917 effectively put an end to foreign exploration of the Russian Arctic. During the Soviet era expeditions were aimed at surveying the Arctic islands and investigating the possibilities of a Northern Sea

Above left
This extraordinary rock formation, looking strangely similar to the Easter Island statues, is on Bolshoy Lyackovskiy, one of the New Siberian Islands.

Above right
Vilkitskiy, another of the New Siberian Islands.

Route (as the Soviets preferred to call the North-East Passage; the Russians still use this phrase).

Russia's Arctic islands

The achievements of the Great Northern Expedition in surveying Russia's northern coast were commemorated in a silk map of Russia that was presented in 1745 to the Empress Elisabeth, the last surviving child of Peter the Great. The map (see p125) shows Novaya Zemlya, which had been known from very early times, but none of the other islands and archipelagos of Arctic Russia.

Of the others, Novosibirskiye Ostrova (the New Siberian Islands) were first recorded in 1770 when Ivan Lyakhov, a fur trapper at work near Cape Svyatoy Nos, noticed a herd of reindeer heading south towards him across the sea ice. Lyakhov reasoned that the herd must be coming from land and, following their tracks northwards, he discovered two islands, and reindeer tracks coming from even further north. In 1773 Lyakhov took a boat and discovered a larger island to the north. On this he found a copper kettle, indicating that more discreet trappers or hunters had come this way before; the island is still called Kettle Island. Those earlier discoverers would perhaps have been distraught when Empress Catherine II gave Lyakhov the sole rights to Arctic Fox trapping on the islands.

In 1848 Henry Kellett, captain of the *Herald*, sailed through the Bering Strait as part of a Franklin search expedition and discovered Herald Island, naming it after his ship. He climbed to the top and saw land to the west; this was called Kellett's Land on early British maps. Though it is likely that this was the first time Wrangel Island had been seen by non-native eyes, it may have been sighted previously by whalers; the American Thomas Roys in the *Superior* made the first whaling trip through the Bering Strait in the same year (1848) and he was soon followed by others. By 1852 there were more than 200 whalers working the waters near the Strait. The whalers were by then already searching for new grounds, so reduced was the Bowhead population. By 1858 the Strait was effectively devoid of whales so the whalers transferred to the Sea of Okhotsk, exhausting that by 1860. The whalers then turned to the Chukchi Sea, and also stepped up walrus hunting.

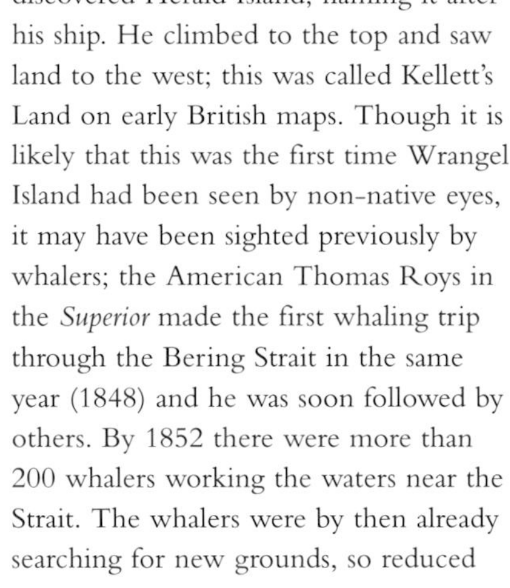

In 1867 Thomas Long in the whaler *Nile* saw the island west of Herald again, naming it after Baron von Wrangell. Wrangel – Long's name, but, by convention, with a single 'l' – rather than Kellett's. Although people certainly lived on the island when Mammoths also roamed it, Wrangel had long been uninhabited. After Long's 'discovery' it was rarely visited and was largely ignored. Vilhjalmur Stefansson's abortive attempt at settlement in 1921 (see the *Karluk* story below) seems to have stirred the Soviets into action, and in 1924 the armed vessel *Krasny Oktyabr* (Red October; the ship was an icebreaker and had previously been named the *Nadezhny*, but it was renamed when it took up a more military role) reached Wrangel. Although the expedition formally claimed sovereignty of the island for the USSR, few observations were taken and no people were left behind, with formal Soviet occupation waiting a further two years until George Ushakov, one of the greatest of all Russian Arctic explorers, led a team that stayed from 1926–29.

Franz Josef Land was the next island group to be discovered, though its formal discovery of 1873 was almost certainly preceded by a sighting in 1865 by the Norwegian Nils Fredrik Rønnbeck in the sealer *Spidsbergen*. Rønnbeck sighted what he modestly called Rønnbeck Land while sailing

Snow Geese on Wrangel Island. The island and nearby mainland are the only places in the Palearctic where the geese breed.

north-east from Svalbard; there are no candidates other than Franz Josef. The now-official name of the islands derives from the undisputed discovery by an Austro-Hungarian expedition. The 24-man team left Bremerhaven in June 1872 in the *Tegetthoff*, under the joint command of Karl Weyprecht and Julius van Payer. Weyprecht, a naval lieutenant commanded at sea, while Payer, an army lieutenant, was in charge on land. The object of the expedition was to reach Asia, but to do so by way of the open polar sea rather than the North-East Passage, with belief in the existence of this sea yet to finally die off. The *Tegetthoff* met the *Isbjørn*, which had made a preparatory journey as far as 79°N the previous year, on 12 August. The two crews celebrated the birthday of Emperor Franz Josef on the 18th before going their separate ways.

On 21 August, at 76°22'N the *Tegetthoff* was trapped in the ice. All winter the ship drifted, but the hoped-for release in 1873 failed to materialise. By 30 August 1873, now fogbound as well as trapped, the ship had drifted to 79°43'N. When the fog lifted the crew was astonished to see land – Cape Tegetthoff on Hall Island. Not until November had the ice around the ship consolidated sufficiently for the Austrians to walk across the 40km or so and set foot on the new land. They headed east, reaching an island named Wilczek (after the *Isbjørn*'s commander) where they formally claimed all the land of the archipelago for Austro-Hungary, naming it Franz Josef Land after the Emperor.

With the ship sealed in for another winter, and it becoming clear that she might not survive a second period of intense ice pressure, the decision was made to abandon her in the summer of 1874. But before heading home, Payer decided to explore Franz Josef. He made three trips, on the second of which, lasting 28 days, he sledged north to Cape Fligely on Rudolf Island (named after the Emperor's son), the most northerly point of the archipelago. There Payer erected a cairn and left a note (found in 1899 by the Duke of the Abruzzi). With summer now approaching, Payer's team made a nervous journey back to Wilczek Island, wondering if the *Tegetthoff* would still be there. She was, and the entire crew – now of 23 as one man had died of tuberculosis – took what they could and began hauling the ship's boats south. Their journey, begun on 20 May, rapidly became a fight for survival against cold, hunger and scurvy. Then on 15 July the men were appalled to see the *Tegetthoff* in the distance. Despite eight weeks of body- and mind-shattering effort, the northward drift of the ice had returned them to within 14km of the ship. Many wanted to re-board, but Weyprecht and Payer persuaded them that the ship was doomed and that their only chance of survival lay in heading south again. With the wind shifting in their favour they now made real progress and in mid-August finally reached open water. They had hauled their boats more than 550km, but they were still only 240km from the *Tegetthoff*.

The ordeal was not yet over. They were running very short of food, and when they finally reached Novaya Zemlya they were unable to land near supply depots that the *Isbjørn* had laid

Cape Tegetthoff, Franz Josef Land. The Austrians named the headland, with its distinctive rock towers, after their ship. The drawing of the towers (left) illustrated Julius Payer's book on the expedition (*New Lands within the Arctic Circle*). The photograph below shows that the towers have changed little over the century since the Austrians made landfall.

down because of rough seas. With the boats being driven away from the coast and things looking distinctly bleak, the men were fortunately spotted and rescued by the Russian ship *Nikolai*.

The sovereignty of Franz Josef Land was, as in the case of Wrangel Island, an anomaly until 1926, when the Soviet Union formally declared its sovereignty over all the Arctic lands within its sector of the Arctic (following the principle established earlier by Canada). The Soviet decision seems in part to have been forced by the use of the archipelago for a half-hearted, and soon abortive, British expedition to the North Pole in 1925. However, the Soviet Union did not formally announce its decision, even allowing the publication of an atlas of the country in 1928 that did not include the archipelago, and Norwegians continued to hunt in the area. Only in 1930 did the Soviets turn Norwegian ships away and, after establishing a weather station, formally raise the flag of the USSR above Hooker Island. The Norwegians, nervous over the position of Svalbard, were appalled, but with virtually no interest from any other international government they were powerless to act; Franz Josef Land had become part of the Soviet Union.

The final Russian Arctic archipelago, Severnaya Zemlya, was not discovered until the Arctic Ocean Hydrographic Expedition of 1910–15, though its existence had been predicted by Mikhail Lomonosov through study of sea currents. Anxious to establish an easily navigated Northern Sea Route in the wake of its defeat by Japan in the war of 1904–05, Russia built two ice-breaking steamers, *Taimyr* and *Vaygach*, to more thoroughly explore the Siberian coast. The series of voyages by the two ships culminated in the first transit of the Passage from east to west, and during the 1913 voyage the eastern coast of the Severnaya Zemlya archipelago – initially called Nicholas II Land, but changed to Northern Land after the Revolution – was explored.

The leaders of these historically important expeditions were Boris Vilkitski and Alexander Kolchak, both of whom were anti-Bolsheviks. Vilkitski escaped to London after the transit, but Kolchak went on to lead the White Russian forces in Siberia in the civil war that followed the Russian Revolution. He was captured and executed by firing squad in 1920.

The archipelago was thoroughly explored by George Ushakov (who had led the Wrangel team in 1926–29). Ushakov was made leader of the Northern Land expedition in 1930 and, accompanied by Sergei Zhuravlev, a hunter and trapper, and Nikolai Urvantsev, set out by dog-sledge on a journey of 3,000km that took two years. Ushakov was a proud communist – names he gave to features on the archipelago include Mount Hammer and Sickle, and the islands of October Revolution and Bolshevik – but Urvantsev was not. Following the expedition Ushakov was awarded the Order of Lenin while Urvantsev, an Arctic explorer with a pedigree almost the equal of Ushakov's, was ignored, even being written out of the first edition of the official book on the expedition. In fact Urvantsev, exiled to one of Stalin's gulags, was influential in the development of mining at Noril'sk and

Severnaya Zemlya. The upper photograph is from the first full exploration of the archipelago by Ushakov and Urvantsev. The lower photograph shows the west coast of October Revolution Island.

today, thankfully, has been rehabilitated with his contribution to Russian history recognised. One other landmark named by Ushakov was the archipelago's northern cape, which he names after the communist politician Vyacheslav Molotov; now called Cape Arktichevsky (Cape Arctic), it is the starting point for many expeditions to the North Pole.

In 1947 the skeletal remains of a human, together with traces of a camp, were discovered on Severnaya Zemlya. Though never formally identified they are believed to be of a member of a team lead by Russian geologist V. A. Rusanov. Rusanov, accompanied by his French fiancée Juliette Jean and a small crew, disappeared in 1912 during an attempt to take a ship west–east through the North-East Passage. This sad discovery suggests that Rusanov had perhaps made it to the archipelago before the official discovery, but the evidence is by no means conclusive. Other items from Rusanov's expedition were found hundreds of kilometres to the west, suggesting that the expedition failed to escape the Kara Sea. The skeletal remains are, therefore, another enduring Arctic mystery.

Voyages in the eastern Arctic

Russian interest in a Northern Sea Route was rekindled by Nordenskiöld's voyage. In the 1890s Vice-Admiral Makarov had the *Yermak* built, the world's first ice-breaker. Although Makarov did not officially attempt to reach the North Pole with the ship, instead embarking on cruises to test *Yermak*'s capabilities, in 1899 he reached 81°28'N close to Svalbard. His voyages laid the groundwork for the voyages of the *Taimyr* and *Vaygach* which, as noted earlier, completed the second transit of the North-East Passage. Continuing enthusiasm for a Northern Sea Route led to a near disaster in 1933 (see Box on the *Chelyuskin* Rescue below), but before that, in 1914, a Russian ship was involved in a trip every bit as harrowing as the more famous voyages of the *Jeanette* and the *Karluk*.

The *Saint Anna*, with Georgi Brusilov in command, left Arkhangelsk on 4 September 1912 – much too late in the year for Arctic travel. Brusilov had been delayed in Alexandrovsk (now Murmansk) and had also failed to sign on the crew he needed. His second-in-command had not arrived and he could find only five experienced sailors. As he left the White Sea, Brusilov had an unknown deputy, Valerian Albanov, and his crew of 23 included a woman, Yerminiya Zhdenko, who was to act as nurse. The objective of the trip was to discover new whaling and sealing grounds, and to make a second transit of the North-East Passage.

Brusilov may have been seduced by Nordenskiöld's (correct) suggestion that the Kara Sea was ice-free in the late summer; if so he was abruptly brought back to reality when, after traversing the Yugorski Shar Strait, the *Saint Anna* became ice-bound close to the Yamal Peninsula on 15 October. The crew walked to the peninsula and saw the tracks of local reindeer herders. These locals offered salvation, but the crew decided to stay with the ship. It was an understandable but incorrect decision – during the next 17 months the *Saint Anna* drifted slowly north, finally reaching 82°58'N off the northern tip of Franz Josef Land. There a simmering conflict between Brusilov and Albanov finally boiled over. Albanov demanded to be relieved of his duties and requested permission to leave the ship. The problem seems to have been Albanov's exasperation with Brusilov's incompetent leadership. Food and fuel were running low, (the samovar, that ubiquitous Russian feature, was by now fuelled only by bear fat and seal blubber), but Brusilov had no plan other than to hope the ship would break free. Brusilov gave his permission for Albanov to leave. To his surprise, and delight, 13 men decided to go as well.

Albanov supervised the construction of sledges and kayaks and loaded them with supplies that Brusilov itemised and made him sign for, increasing Albanov's antagonism. For a map Albanov had only the one in his copy of Nansen's book *Furthest North*. Using this he hoped to reach the base camp of the Russian Georgiy Sedov, who was using Franz Josef as the starting point for his expedition to the North Pole (though he did not know which island Sedov had decided to use), or Frederick Jackson's Elmwood Camp.

Albanov seems glad to have been away from the ship. It was only 120km to land and the second winter had been appalling, the bear grease lamps creating an evil smoke and condensation that caused mildew to form on all surfaces; everyone on board was soon covered in a layer of greasy residue. Yet the ice turned out to be little better. The 14 men left on 10 April and dragged their sledges just 5km. They were then kept in their tents for three days by a blizzard, an inauspicious start. In the absence of sleeping bags the men slept in *malitsas* – smocks of reindeer hide with fur on the inside – two men huddling together, their legs inside one malitsa, their heads and torsos in another. After the blizzard, Albanov sent one ailing man back to the ship; another man volunteered to take his place, a remarkably brave gesture given that those on the *Saint Anna* thought the ice party were, at the very least, misguided.

Albanov calculated their position as the weather improved – they had walked 5km south but drifted 35km north. Despite this discouraging news the men pressed on. By 16 April the daily visits they had received from their shipmates stopped; they had finally travelled too far from, and also now lost sight of, the ship. By day 11 of the trek their fuel was exhausted and they were forced to suck icicles or drink small quantities of seawater to survive. On that day three men gave up and returned to the ship.

The trek of the remaining 11 men became a nightmare. If they arrived at a polynya (an area of open water; such pools are often found in the frozen ocean, kept open by currents or consistent winds) they could shoot seals and so obtain blubber to heat water, but if they did not the hunger, cold and thirst were almost overwhelming. On 3 May one man went off in search of flat ice he claimed to have seen and disappeared – was he brave or had he gone mad? The rate of progress was only about 3km each day, despite the use of the kayaks in leads, and this slowness, and the monotony, began to sap the men's mental strength. To Albanov's horror they became listless and child-like – one fell into the sea when he attempted to climb an iceberg from his kayak, just for the fun of it. To add to Albanov's worries the symptoms of scurvy began to appear and the south-westerly drift of the ice (the wind had changed) meant he was now unsure in which direction Franz Josef Land lay. Even when they shot a polar bear the men's health did not improve; they ate the liver and so overdosed on vitamin A. Without knowing the true reason, Albanov realised that the liver was the cause of their subsequent illness and forbade its future appearance on the menu, probably saving them from the fate of Andrée's balloon team (see To the Pole p201).

Albanov was now becoming increasingly frustrated by the men's attitude. Some had become fed up with hauling the

Champ Island, Franz Josef Land.

kayaks and wanted to abandon them, despite the fact that when the pack ice broke up they would be crucial for their survival. Their failure to realise this, coupled with their lack of interest in where they were, a problem that exercised their leader constantly, exasperated him. Albanov was aware that they had drifted west, but if they were now drifting south they would miss Franz Josef altogether and reach the Barents Sea, meaning almost certain death. Finally on 9 June he spotted land to the east, though it was another 17 days of exhausting trekking over unruly ice before they reached it. During that time two men made off with the best of the equipment, clearly intent on saving themselves at the expense of their comrades. Albanov swore that if he ever saw them again he would kill them. Ironically he did see them, catching up with them when they finally made landfall at Cape Mary Harmsworth on Alexandra Land. Mellowed by the flowers blooming on the island, by the thought of feasting on eider duck eggs and by their remorse, Albanov relented.

Albanov was able to fix his position. He found a note left by Frederick Jackson and so decided to head east for Cape Flora. Again he was frustrated by his men who seemed willing only to sleep. One man declined to move at all and was left behind. When, overcome by conscience, the men returned for him he was dead. The apathy of the men is strange given the imperative of reaching Cape Flora, one possible explanation being that the periods of malnutrition had led to vitamin deficiencies, which can create such a condition. Whatever the cause, another man soon died, leaving eight to struggle on. During the crossing of Prince George Land four men, including Albanov, had used the remaining two kayaks (the other kayaks having been abandoned at various times when exhaustion was overwhelming) to take all the equipment by sea while four men skied cross-country. The expected rendezvous failed and the four kayakers (which included Albanov) pushed on alone. These survivors reached Bell Island, a base used by Englishman Benjamin Leigh Smith during his expeditions of 1880–82. Leigh Smith's trips were for exploration, scientific study and hunting, and he built a substantial hut at a place he named Eira Harbour after his ship; it is still there and in remarkably good condition. The *Eira* suffered the same fate as her predecessor the *Tegetthoff*, being holed and sunk by ice pressure. As a result Leigh Smith and his crew were marooned on Cape Flora, unable to reach the Eira Harbour hut. The misery of their enforced winter was doubtless relieved by the fact that they managed to offload 320 litres of rum and a huge quantity of champagne, whisky, gin, sherry and beer before the ship went down.

Had Albanov found Leigh Smith's hut he might have been able to rest and eat well, and to make use of a rowing boat Leigh Smith had left behind. But despite walking within 100m of the hut (as he later discovered) he missed it, and so decided to press on for Cape Flora. On the sea crossing between Bell and Northbrook Islands a violent storm forced Albanov and his companion Alexander Konrad on to an ice floe. To escape the savagery of the weather the two got into their malitsas. When the floe broke up in the violent seas they fell into the water 'like two unwanted kittens thrown together in a sack to be drowned'. But they survived, and managed to reach Cape Flora on 9 July, 90 days after leaving the *Saint Anna*. Of the second kayak there was no sign. At Cape Flora Albanov and Konrad found huts and supplies in plenty, remnants not only of Jackson's expedition, but those of Abruzzi, Ziegler and Sedov. Exhausted, filthy and dressed in lice-infested rags, the two men were finally able to relax. They expected to overwinter, but were discovered just 11 days later by the *Saint Foka*, a supply ship looking for Sedov.

Albanov and Konrad were the only survivors of the *Saint Anna*. No trace was ever found of the four skiers, the other two kayakers, or the *Saint Anna* and those who remained with her.

The *Chelyuskin* rescue

Despite the obvious difficulties involved in transits of the North-East Passage, Soviet enthusiasm for their Northern Sea Route was undiminished. In July 1932 Vladimir Voronin took the ice-breaking steamer *Aledsandr Sibiryakov* (a converted sealer, formerly called the *Bellaventure*) eastwards, going around the northern tip of Severnaya Zemlya, the first vessel to make that trip. Heavy ice off Chukotka smashed the ship's propeller, but using a makeshift sail the *Sibiryakov* reached the Bering Strait, the first one-season transit. Encouraged, the Soviets sent other ships east. One was the 4,000t *Chelyuskin*, which had no ice-breaking capacity but was considered large enough to nose through significant ice. Entering a narrow lead off Chukotka in 1933 the *Chelyuskin* became ice-bound, eventually drifting north-west towards Wrangel Island. After wintering in the ice, on 13 February 1934 the ship was crushed and sank. The quartermaster, who had stayed on board until the end, was knocked over by a shifting barrel as he attempted to jump to safety and was drowned. The 104 survivors – including a baby girl born on 31 August 1932 in the Kara Sea and named, of course, Karina – set up camp on the ice, the expedition leader Professor Otto Schmidt citing Albanov's journey as the reason for not attempting a crossing of the ice to Chukotka or Wrangel.

Ample supplies were removed from the *Chelyuskin* before she sank and the campers had a relatively comfortable time awaiting rescue by air, their stay enlivened (or perhaps not) by a non-stop series of lectures by Schmidt, a devout communist. Starting on 5 March and continuing until 13 April, seven pilots made repeated flights to a makeshift ice runway and safely rescued all the survivors. The pilots (Lyapidevski, Levanevski, Molokov, Kamanin, Slepnev, Vodopyanov and Doronin) were the first to receive the award of Hero of the Soviet Union, with Anatoli Lyapidevski being the very first recipient.

The photographs here show the camp on the ice and the trapped ship (above) and the first plane to land (below). To the right, Stalin is given a souvenir of the rescue at the investiture of the first Heroes of the Soviet Union.

8. Canada and the North-West Passage

After the unrewarding trips north-east, the English decided in 1576 to follow Cabot's original plan of reaching the Orient by heading north-west. The expedition's leader was Sir Martin Frobisher, a Yorkshire-born pirate and slave-trader who had won his knighthood (as had his contemporary Sir Francis Drake) by presenting Queen Elizabeth I with the looted treasure of Spanish galleons. Unfortunately, Frobisher had followed up the raid that won him his knighthood with one on a French ship carrying wine for an English merchant. Had it been a Frenchman's wine the capture would almost certainly have brought him loud applause, but as it was an Englishman's he was thrown in jail and lost all his money. Needing to restore his fortunes, Frobisher persuaded Michael Lok (brother of a slaving captain he had previously sailed with) to finance a trip to Cathay. Frobisher left London in June 1576 with the Queen's blessing with three tiny ships, on a journey 'for finding of the passage to Cataya (beyng a matter in oure age above all other, noteable', as George Best, Frobisher's lieutenant, noted in his book on the trip). One ship, so small it was manned by just four sailors, sank off Greenland's southern tip, and a second turned for home (where the captain reported the loss of Frobisher and his ship the *Gabriel*, a premature obituary). Frobisher continued, finding Baffin Island and entering the bay that now bears his name. He sailed along it, convinced that to his right was Asia, to his left America.

In the bay Frobisher recorded two firsts – an encounter with the Inuit (the first since the Norsemen, at least), and the first account of that merciless tyrant of the Arctic, the mosquito. Frobisher's meetings with the Inuit were, at first, the less aggravating of the two, with an exchange of gifts and attempts at an exchange of language, but then five of his men went missing. This reduced him to a crew of just 13, and he had also lost his only boat. Frobisher was enraged and concerned – had the men mutinied or been captured? And if it was the latter, would they be eaten by these natives, who had earlier been seen eating raw fish and raw seal? The men had been ordered not to go out of sight of the ship; historians have wondered whether the five had gone ashore to do some trading of their own and, having disobeyed direct orders and being fearful of returning, stayed too long. Almost 300 years later, the local Inuit told the American explorer Charles Francis Hall that the men had stayed in the village for some time before departing in a boat they had built, never to be seen again. Frobisher, resigned to loss of the men and the boat, took a hostage (and his kayak) as evidence of the success of his voyage, and sailed for home. There, in damp, chilly and autumnal London, the Inuk died, probably of pneumonia.

Frobisher also brought back a lump of black rock, so like coal that Michael Lok's wife threw it on her fire. To her amazement it glistened. Retrieved and tested it was, said Lok, gold ore of astonishing concentration. Three official assayers dismissed it as pyrite – fool's gold – but a glib-tongued Venetian alchemist resident in London convinced Lok's business associates that it was the real thing. In 1577, carrying the hopes of the 'Company of Cathay' which was framed to exploit the source, Frobisher was back in Frobisher Bay. This time the meeting with the Inuit was less cordial. Frobisher found some items of clothing from the five missing men of the first expedition in an Inuit tent, rekindling his fears of abduction. In trying to grab a hostage he was shot in the backside with an arrow, the incident precipitating a battle in which five Inuit were killed and one sailor badly wounded. Ironically in view of Frobisher's fear of Inuit cannibalism, wounded Inuit in this battle threw themselves into the sea as they were convinced the English sailors would eat them. Frobisher captured a man, woman and child, loaded 200 tons of ore into his ship and sailed for home. Back in London the male Inuk entertained the Queen by killing swans from his kayak, but all three Inuit soon died of pneumonia.

Despite expert misgivings over the gold ore, Queen Elizabeth was convinced and underwrote a huge expedition of 15 ships that sailed, again under Frobisher, in May 1578. She even allowed Frobisher to kiss her hand before he departed. By error, the fleet reached Hudson Strait, where ice destroyed

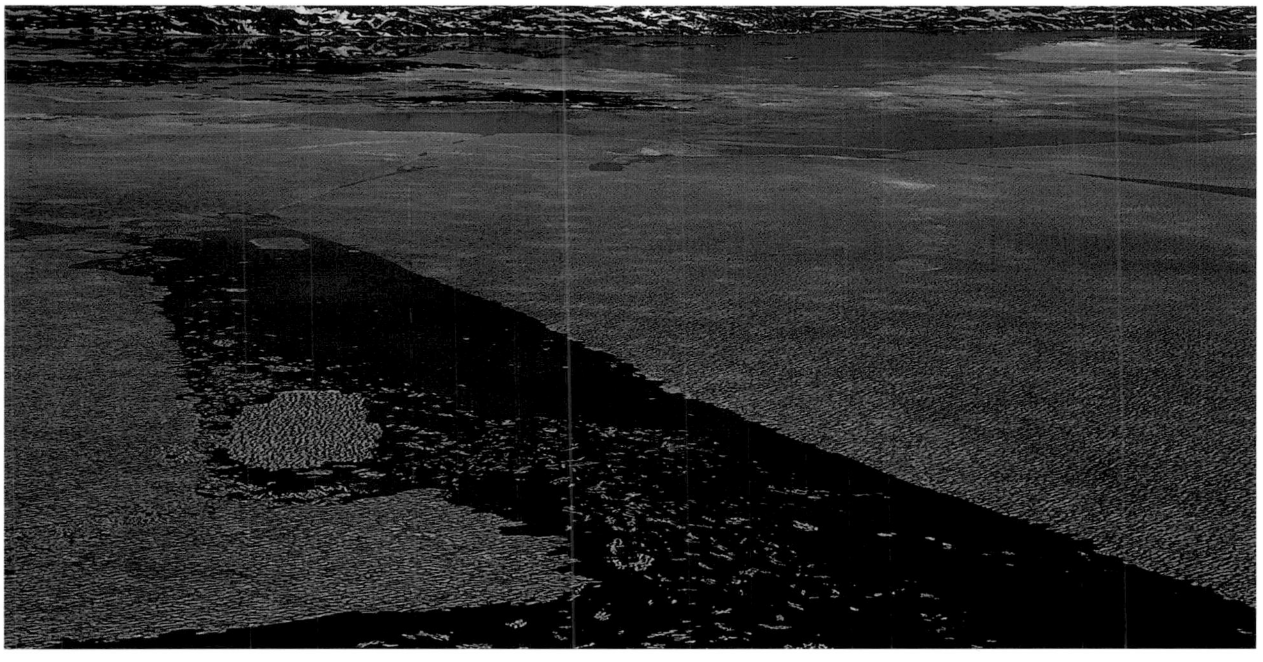

The southern coast of Meta Incognita Peninsula, Baffin Island. It is spring, and in the foreground the sea ice of Hudson Strait is breaking up. Martin Frobisher reached the bay which bears his name, on the northern side of the Peninsula.

Opposite page
The graves of William Braine, John Hartnell and John Torrington on Beechey Island. The headstones are replicas, the originals having been removed to the museum in Yellowstone to preserve them. Beechey is not really an island, being linked by a narrow causeway to Devon Island which is seen in the background.

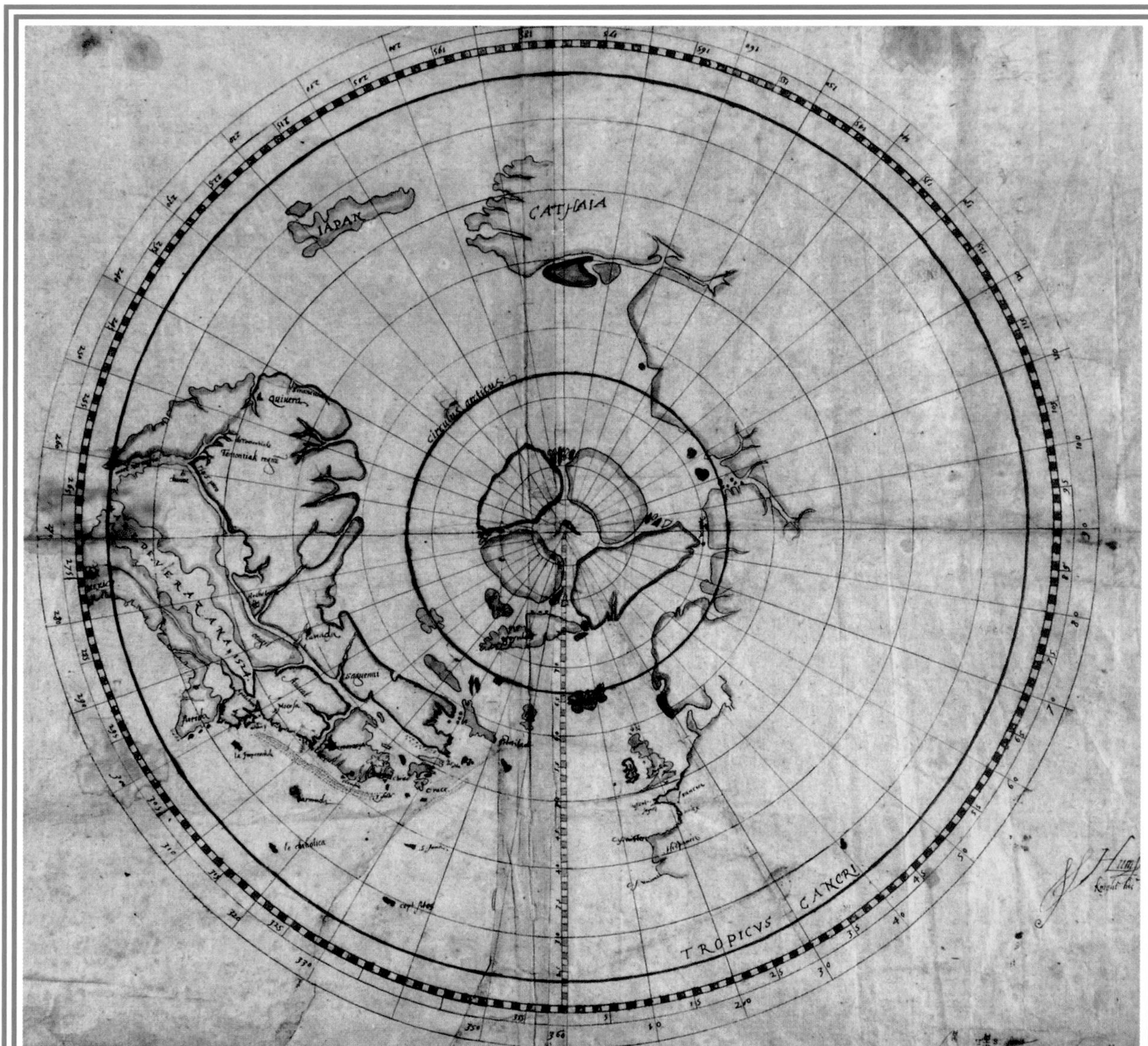

It could be argued that John Davis's ship *Moonshine* was aptly named, as the Elizabethan mathematician and alchemist John Dee had been involved in the early discussions on the voyage. John Dee was the anglicised name of the Welshman Ieuan Ddu, born in Beguildy, Radnorshire, in 1527, whose brilliance as a scholar took him to Cambridge University and made him tutor to the future Elizabeth I. His fame as an astrologer and necromancer are said to have made him the model for Shakespeare's Prospero. Dee's spirit world contacts had told him of a river that split America and led directly to Cathay; this had been one of the principal reasons for a disastrous attempt by Sir Humphrey Gilbert to create a settlement in Newfoundland. The spirits also guided Dee to form an alliance with John Davis and Adrian Gilbert, Humphrey's brother, but Davis, a shrewd, sea-hardened man may have seen through Dee's occult posturing, because the astrologer seems to have departed the scene before the expedition set out. Perhaps he foresaw failure.

Dee was responsible for the map above, drawn in 1583 for Sir Humphrey Gilbert. Frobisher's discoveries in the New World are included as the double-pronged land at 330°.

one ship (and another fled home), but it eventually worked its way back to Frobisher Bay. There, on an island still called Kodlunarn (White Man's Island), Frobisher built a stone hut and began mining the 'gold' ore. He took back over 1,000 tons, but all attempts by the London alchemists failed to turn it into anything valuable (analysis of the rock in the 20th century showed high iron, aluminium, chromium and nickel content, but no trace of gold). Michael Lok's backers turned on him and he ended up in a debtors' jail, while Frobisher joined his old colleague Drake in raids on the Spanish West Indies. He would eventually die in 1594 from wounds received in the taking of the Spanish fort at Brest in France.

The next to try his luck heading north-west was John Davis, who sailed in June 1585 with the *Sunshine* and the *Moonshine*. Davis reached the east coast of Greenland, then rounded Kapp Farvel (Cape Farewell) and the less desolate fjords the Norsemen had settled. Here he met Inuit, the meeting being a joy of trade and mutual kindness. Pushing on, Davis explored the Strait that now bears his name as far north as the Arctic Circle, then explored Baffin Island's eastern coast, discovering Cumberland Sound. He returned home convinced that a North-West Passage was a reality – it was just a question of locating the right channel. Davis returned in May 1586, this time with four ships, two of which explored Greenland's east coast while Davis took the other pair to the west coast, where the sailors took on the locals at long jump (victory for England, but only because of persistent foul play). Relations turned sour when the Inuit began to steal anything of iron they could lay their hands on, including the ship's anchor. Davis took a hostage against the return of the anchor, but

The open polar sea

Today, the idea of sailing over the North Pole seems foolish, but Henry Hudson believed that near the Pole the Sun was 'a manufacturer of salt rather than ice' and the sea should be clear. He was not alone in this idea, contemporary scientists believing that the perpetual sunlight of the Arctic summer would melt the sea ice of the extreme north, the ocean currents this would inevitably produce pushing a ring of frozen sea southwards to encircle it. The myth of the 'open polar sea' would be a recurring theme over the many years of failure that were to follow.

The drawing above was by John Shelden in 1869 who claimed to have reached the Pole by way of the open polar sea. The Pole, he said, was a huge cone of diamond or topaz.

when good weather arrived he sailed with the Inuk still aboard – the man died before England was reached. Davis again explored the coast of Baffin Island, finding, as Frobisher had, that the 'muskyto … sting grievously' before heading home.

Davis sailed again in 1587 in the *Ellen*, a 20-tonne ship that leaked so badly the crew almost lost heart. Yet despite the leak the *Ellen* reached 73°N on the west Greenland coast, a new northing record, then crossed Baffin Bay before being forced south by sea ice. Davis explored more of Baffin Island's east coast, then headed into Cumberland Sound again, reaching Pangnirtung where, in hot July sunshine, the crew went ashore and organised a foxhunt with the dogs they had taken with them as company. Further south Davis also reached the eastern end of Hudson Strait, but he did not explore it.

Henry Hudson

The danger of Spanish invasion kept the English at home for several years, but in 1602 George Weymouth sailed north-west again, reaching 69°N. He was followed by John Knight in 1606, but he only got as far as Labrador before vile weather damaged his ship and forced him home. These failures dulled enthusiasm for a north-westerly route, while the way north-east seemed perpetually at risk from ice. But in 1607 the English headed north again, Henry Hudson and his crew (of 11, one being John, Hudson's 14-year-old son) sailing the *Hopewell* out of Gravesend on 1 May. The Muscovy Company was losing profits on its Russian trade to Dutch companies and had decided to try for Cathay again. Hudson's plan was simple; as attempts to go north-east and north-west had failed, in part because of the ice, he would instead sail over the pole.

Hudson reached the east coast of Greenland and headed north as far as Hold-with-Hope (73°N). From there he headed north-west, eventually reaching Barents' New Land (Svalbard) and sailing north, to a point where it became clear that the theory of salt rather than ice was wrong. Hudson had reached 80°23'N, a northing that would not be bettered for more than 150 years. Heading south, Hudson was pushed west. He spotted a volcanic island to the north of Iceland; he had sighted Jan Mayen, calling it Hudson's Touches. Back in London, Hudson was able to tell his merchant paymasters that while the route to Cathay had eluded him, the bays of Svalbard were home to great numbers of whales of vast size.

The Muscovy Company were impressed enough with Hudson's journey to back him again, this time to try for the North-East Passage. The journey, again in the *Hopewell*, was unsuccessful, the ship being stopped by the ice of the Kara Sea, but was significant for two reasons. First, the crew spotted a mermaid – 'from the navel upwards her back and breasts were like a woman's … her body was as big as one of us, her skin very white … long hair hanging down behind, of colour black. In her going down they saw her tail which was like the tail of a porpoise and speckled like a mackerel'. Was this an illusion created by a Harp Seal and months at sea in all-male

Spring on the southern coast of Hudson Bay. A storm has pushed the last of the sea ice to shore.

company? Secondly, Hudson made a curious entry in his log to the effect that the return of the *Hopewell* was 'my free and willing return, without persuasion or force of any one of (my company)'. Many have speculated that this entry implies problems between Hudson and Robert Juet, his first mate. Hudson was an old man, already a grandfather. He was moody and capricious, his indecisiveness a burden to his crew. Juet was also well past his prime, an irritable troublemaker who many captains would have rid themselves of, but Hudson took him on each of his journeys. They appear to have behaved like a grumpy married couple.

The Muscovy Company was less pleased with Hudson this time, and declined to finance a third voyage. So Hudson approached the Dutch East India Company who, in 1609, financed another trip to the Kara Sea, this time in *De Halve Maan* (*The Half Moon*), a decision very much at odds with the prevailing Dutch lack of enthusiasm for the area. At the ice edge there was a mutiny (perhaps instigated by Robert Juet), as a result of which Hudson turned around and sailed across the Atlantic, discovering the Hudson River, Coney Island and Manhattan (the future site of New Amsterdam, later New York). The crew shot half a dozen native Americans for fun and fed alcohol to many more for the amusement of getting them drunk, behaviour which reflects badly on both Juet, who seems to have been the ringleader, and Hudson, who not only allowed but assisted the folly.

Back in England, Hudson's discoveries lit up the faces of London's merchants (while the activities of his crew barely raised an eyebrow), and in April 1610 Hudson sailed the *Discovery* back to America with a crew of 22. One of the crew was Henry Greene, who seems to have usurped Robert Juet's place as Hudson's favourite (and may also have been acting as a paid informant, spying on the rest of the crew). Juet's response was to become drunk and belligerent. Hudson calmed him, but the mood of the whole crew was further depressed by the journey through the violent waters of the Hudson Strait. Hugging the northern Quebec shore, Hudson sailed between it and Digges Island to reach the vast, calm waters of what he was convinced was the Pacific Ocean. Turning south, Hudson watched the shore, waiting for the cities of Japan that would soon hove into view. Instead, the bleak Arctic tundra held his eye, all the way to the entrance to James Bay. There, at about 51°N, in Rupert Bay, the *Discovery* was frozen in as a distinctly un-Cathaylike winter took hold. In dismay at not finding Java (where Hudson had told his crew they would spend Candlemas), Hudson replaced Juet, now openly sneering at his captain's hopes, with Robert Bylot. Juet nursed his grievances during a hard winter that saw several men succumb to scurvy, one dying of it. As the winter toyed with the men's minds, Hudson picked a fight with Greene, his one-time favourite, then demoted Bylot. The pair joined Juet and others in plotting the takeover of the ship, reasoning that with so little food and so many men sick with scurvy no one would escape alive without positive action.

After the ship was freed from the ice in June 1611, Hudson was seized. He, his son, four sick men and three others were

A section of a large map of the North Atlantic drawn by Hessel Gerritz in 1628 and published in France. It includes the Davis Strait (*Fretum Davis*), Baffins Bay, Sir Thomas Smith's Sound (almost illegible at the the top of Baffin Bay), Alderman Jones Sound and Sir James Lancaster's Sound. The map suggests that Baffin's discoveries had not been entirely overlooked, though they did not influence British explorations for almost two centuries.

placed in an open boat. The ship's carpenter, who the mutineers wanted to stay, chose to go with Hudson. The nine in the boat had only the clothing they wore, no water or food, no means of making fire and just one gun. They stood little chance of surviving – and were never heard of again.

The thirteen mutineers sailed to Digges Island, which they knew was rich in wildfowl. There, in a fight with the local Inuit, four men, including Henry Greene, were killed. Later, Robert Juet died of scurvy, leaving Robert Bylot to steer the boat into Berehaven in Ireland's Bantry Bay. Back in London the eight survivors might have expected to be tried and hanged, their 'excuse' for mutiny hardly holding water as in addition to the sick men they had also cast adrift healthy ones and the captain for no better reason than that they did not like them. But Bylot's claim to have found the North-West Passage allowed economics to triumph over both the law of the land and justice. By 1612 Bylot, Prickett (whose account of the mutiny is the fullest and, hardly surprisingly, exonerates him completely) and Edward Wilson, the ship's surgeon, were heading back to Hudson Bay, and when four of the mutineers were eventually tried for mutiny they were found not guilty.

Button and Baffin

The expedition of 1612 was commanded by Sir Thomas Button. Not only did it include some of the Hudson mutineers, but it also featured Hudson's ship *Discovery*. Bylot navigated it to Hudson Bay, which Button crossed, wintering at the mouth of the Nelson River (named after Francis Nelson who died there, as did several others, of scurvy; an additional five men were killed by Inuit), then heading north to reach Southampton Island and Roes Welcome Sound (though the sound was not actually given that name until Foxe's expedition of 1631). Button thought the sound was the channel that would finally lead to the Pacific, but he returned to England having done little more than nose the *Discovery* into it.

In 1615 Bylot sailed again, now as master of the *Discovery*, with William Baffin as pilot. This time the northern coast of Southampton Island was reached, but Bylot and Baffin concluded that the Roes Welcome Sound was not the way to Cathay. On this journey Baffin calculated the longitude of the *Discovery* by taking a complete lunar observation on 21 June, a feat that earned him the admiration of all that followed him and is one reason why many consider him the greatest of the early Arctic explorers. It was the lunar observation that led Sir William Parry to name Baffin Island (close to which the observation was made) in his honour.

Munk, James and Foxe

In the 17th century Denmark controlled what is now Norway, giving them not only an Arctic seaboard but a perceived right to the legacy of the Vikings. In 1610 a Norwegian-born Dane, Jens Munk, was dispatched to look for a North-East Passage, that voyage failing in the Kara Sea ice as had so many others before it. In May 1619 Munk set out again, this time heading north-west with two ships, the *Enhorningen* (*Unicorn*) and *Lamprenen* (*Lamprey*). Munk reached and crossed Hudson Bay, wintering at the mouth of the Churchill River, now famous for its annual congregation of bears and bear-watchers. Sixty-five men overwintered, the illustration in Munk's book on the expedition – the first for a general readership, and one of the more charming examples – suggesting that conditions were really not too bad. In reality things were grim; by early June all but three men were dead from scurvy and Munk, one of the last three, wrote in his journal 'Herewith, goodnight to all the world and my soul into the hand of God'. In fact he survived, and with his two companions sailed the *Lamprey* back to Denmark, where King Christian IV ordered him to go back and retrieve the *Unicorn*. Not surprisingly Munk failed to raise a crew, and the second trip was abandoned.

The next attempt to find the North-West Passage was in 1631, when two ships left London and Bristol, the most celebrated ports of 17th-century England. Each ship was 70 tons, square-rigged and manned by a crew of 22. They were named after King Charles I and his Queen, Henrietta Maria. Master of the *Charles* was Yorkshireman Luke Foxe. A career seaman with an arrogant (but largely justified) opinion of his worth who called himself 'North-West' Foxe, he had been trying for years to gain sponsorship for a voyage to discover the Passage. Finally he had persuaded London merchants to fund the trip. Sir Thomas Roe, an ambassador of the King, agreed to act as patron, and a renamed ex-Royal Navy ship was made available. Foxe boasted that his was the best ship in the world though in reality it was a pensioned-off tub, barely seaworthy.

When the merchants of Bristol heard about Foxe's voyage they hastily gathered the money to mount a rival search. Whichever port controlled the trade with Cathay, with its priceless merchandise of silk and spices, would be the richest in England and Bristol was not prepared to come second in that particular race. The Bristolians chose Thomas James to captain their ship, a Welsh-born barrister and a gentleman with only limited experience of the sea and sailing, though he had once taken charge of a small fleet to tackle piracy in the English Channel.

On the afternoon of 3 May 1631, James took the *Henrietta Maria* out of Bristol's harbour, to be followed two days later by Foxe and the *Charles* from London. Foxe caught and passed his rival at Resolution Island at the entrance to the Hudson Strait. In late August the two ships met by chance in Hudson Bay,

William Baffin

Baffin, poor-born in about 1584 and self-taught, had been on an expedition to east Greenland and on two whaling trips to Svalbard before accompanying Bylot. He was clearly a superior seaman, and though Bylot was still nominally master when the *Discovery* sailed again in 1616, Baffin was the real commander. Baffin was convinced that Hudson Bay was not the way to go (in this he was correct; the vast bay drew explorers for more than a century but it was a waste of time as far as the North-West Passage was concerned) so he headed north through Davis Strait, discovering Baffin Bay, then Lancaster Sound, Jones Sound and Smith Sound, each named after an expedition backer. It was a masterful journey, one of the greatest of all in terms of discoveries, but, ironically, Baffin's maps were not published (the man charged with publishing Baffin's data decided that the maps and some tables, were too expensive to produce and so left them out), and the details were soon forgotten. Baffin subsequently joined the East India Company; he died fighting for the Company against the Portuguese, shot in the stomach in the Persian Gulf in January 1622. With the first phase of exploration of the Canadian Arctic coming to an end, it was 200 years before Baffin Bay was entered again – at that time it was thought to be a new discovery.

Jens Munk's winter camp, as illustrated in *Navigatio Septentrionalis*, the book of the expedition. As with the similarly idyllic scenes of Barents' overwintering on Novaya Zemlya, reality did not match the artist's view.

with the captains and their officers sharing a meal on the *Henrietta Maria*. It was not a happy occasion, Foxe writing that the time spent with James was 'the worst spent of any time of my discovery'. James, he noted, was a gentleman who 'could discourse of Art, but he was no seaman', recalling Macaulay's famous suggestion that the navy of King Charles comprised gentlemen and seamen, but the gentlemen were not seamen and the seamen were gentlemen. James was no more impressed with Foxe, but he did try to persuade him to winter together. Foxe declined and sailed north, exploring the western coast of Hudson Bay as far as Southampton Island, and then exploring the vast basin that now bears his name between Southampton and Baffin islands, naming 'Sir Thomas Roes Welcome', now Roes Welcome Sound, in the process. But before winter could

Johannes Jansson's *Nova et Accurata Poli Arctici et terrarium Circum lacentium*, a copper-engraved and hand-painted map from *c.*1645. Baffin's discoveries are again included. The European figure at the top of the map is likely to be Henry Hudson, though the bay which now bears his name is called after Thomas Button.

take hold of his ship he turned east and sailed home to be greeted not by the congratulations of his sponsors as he had imagined, but some communal spleen-venting instead. James was overwintering and might discover the Passage in the spring – where was the glory in returning empty-handed?

For his part James headed south, discovering James Bay and building huts on Charlton Island – which he named in honour of the King – for overwintering. On nearby Danby Island he found a row of stakes driven into the shore, presumed to be the only evidence ever discovered of the fate of Henry Hudson after the mutiny on the *Discovery* in 1610. James's crew spent an appalling winter. It was so cold that frost formed on their beds, adding to the misery of scurvy. Finally spring arrived, but so did the mosquitoes, which plagued the men further. James, anxious to contact (hopefully friendly) natives on the shore, climbed a tree to watch for a signal as his men set fire to brushwood. The fire spread rapidly across the tinder-dry island woodland, James being lucky to escape from his look-out and his long-suffering men escaping death only by fleeing to the ship. After months during which they had all but frozen to death, the possibility of death by burning must have seemed an ironic twist of fate. The survivors then sailed home.

Both Foxe and James wrote books. Foxe's is less polished but probably more honest. It begins with a plea (and a side-swipe at James's effort) 'Gentle Reader, expect not heere any flourishing Phrases or Eloquent termes, for this Child of mine begot in the North-West cold Clime, (where they breed no Schollers), is not able to digest the sweet milke of Rethorick, that's food for them …', and goes on to note that Foxe had done his best 'with such Tackling, Cordage and Raftage as I had, to Rigge and Tackle this ship myself' which, if stretching the nautical simile to breaking point, at least leaves the reader in no doubt about Foxe's view of himself as a master mariner. It must have been a great disappointment to Foxe that James's *The Strange and Dangerous Voyage of Captain Thomas James* became a classic; it is said to have inspired Coleridge to write the *Rime of the Ancient Mariner*.

A letter to the Emperor

To avoid a charge of favouring either Luke Foxe or Thomas James (above), King Charles gave each man an identical letter. The winner of the race for the Passage was to deliver it to the Emperor of Japan. The letters were in English as it was reasoned that the Emperor, being both a king and a cultured man, would obviously speak the language.

Hearne and Mackenzie

In England, the failure of the Foxe and James expeditions ended any immediate prospect of further attempts to find a North-West Passage, while the upheaval of the Civil War and the execution of Charles I meant little thought would be given to the New World at all for some two decades. With the Restoration the country turned its eyes outwards again, only to see North America occupied by the French. Fishermen from Brittany's St Malo had followed the Basques and Bristolians to the great cod-fishing grounds off Newfoundland, so it is no surprise that a Malouin also followed in the wake of Cabot's ship. Jacques Cartier made three journeys (1534, 1535 and 1541), discovering the St Lawrence River and naming the country Canada (it is said that he got the name from a Huron Indian, asking him what the place was called and not realising the Huron had given him the name of his village; it is a plausible tale. Samuel de Champlain, who followed Cartier, named Quebec after the Huron *kebek*, 'a narrowing of the waters'). French enthusiasm for their new colony was based on cod-fishing and the trapping of Beavers on the rivers that threaded the forests of Quebec. Ultimately the fur-bearing animals of the northern Canadian forests were exploited by the Hudson's Bay Company (see A Vulnerable Ecosystem p583), the Company charged with not only trapping furs but also with exploring for a North-West Passage. But the Company was much less committed to the Passage than it was to profit – if a Passage were found then the area might open up to competition – and this lack of initiative was criticised in Britain. Eventually, in 1719 the Company provisioned an expedition of

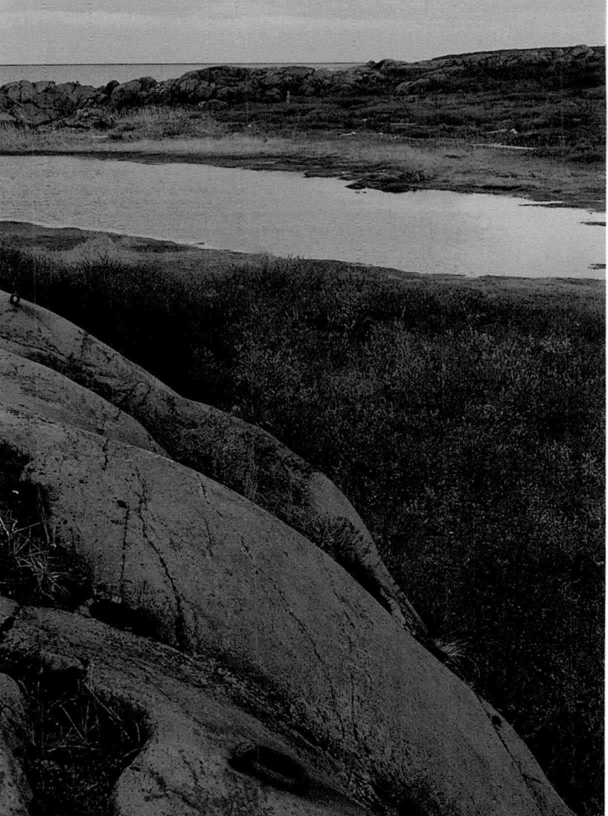

Close to the mouth of the Churchill River, and therefore close to Prince of Wales Fort, a 'bite' is taken out of the river bank, forming a natural harbour. Named Sloop Cove, this inlet empties each low tide. It was used as a natural dry dock for repairing ships prior to Atlantic crossings. The iron rings set into the rocky cove bank are still visible, as is the graffiti carved by bored sailors on a nearby smooth rock face. The inscriptions include references to Middleton's ships, and a 'signature' of Samuel Hearne (overleaf).

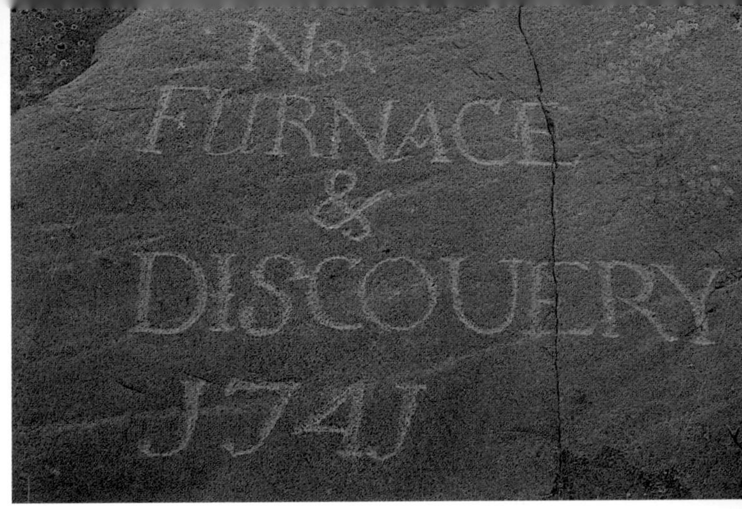

The Hearne signature and Middleton ship names inscribed at Sloop Cove.

two ships commanded by John Knight to explore the inlets of western Hudson Bay. The expedition of 40 men disappeared. Later explorers found their wintering quarters on Marble Island, near Rankin Inlet, and there were Inuit stories that men had survived until at least 1721 before succumbing to hunger and disease. Excavations on Marble Island in 1989 and 1991 revealed many artefacts from the expedition, but no human remains. Astonishingly, it also discovered both of the expedition's ships, which had been stripped of much valuable material and then deliberately sunk. This is not as crazy as it sounds; Thomas James had also deliberately sunk his ship, the idea being that the ship was more likely to survive the winter intact below the ice, from where it could be refloated when the thaw came, than remaining afloat and being crushed by the ice. No clues were found on Marble Island as to the fate of Knight's men.

In 1741 the Company, responding reluctantly to further suggestions that it was deliberately avoiding finding (and perhaps even covering up the existence of) the Passage, allowed one of its captains, Christopher Middleton, to lead another expedition. Middleton commanded the *Furnace*, with William Moor in charge of a second ship, the *Discovery*. The

Right
Samuel Hearne made this drawing of Prince of Wales Fort, at the mouth of the Churchill River, himself.

Below
Prince of Wales Fort seen across the ice-strewn shore of Hudson Bay as the Sun sets.

expedition discovered Wager Bay but was accused of having actually discovered a channel not an inlet, an accusation that ruined Middleton and resulted in a second expedition, in 1746, this time with Moor in command. Moor confirmed Middleton's findings – which was hardly surprising as he merely sailed along a route he had already followed a few years earlier – and also discovered Chesterfield Inlet.

Although they had been involved in these sea-borne expeditions, it wasn't until 1769 that a Hudson's Bay Company man set out to explore the wilderness that lay west of Hudson Bay. The man was Samuel Hearne, and though the Company's main aim in sending him west was to see if there was any truth in the rumour that a river flowed between banks of solid copper, Hearne also travelled for its own sake. He was a keen naturalist, a good artist and loved to camp out in the wilds beyond the walls of Prince of Wales Fort, built at the mouth of the Churchill River, where the London-born Hearne was employed. Hearne's first two attempts to find and follow the legendary river failed due to incompetent guides and poor equipment, but when he set out for a third time in December 1770 he was guided by a group of Chippewyan Indians, led by a brilliantly resourceful man named Matonabbee.

Despite occasional severe hardship – the men lived off the land, and on one occasion, when hunting failed to provide food for the seventh day in succession, an old pair of boots was boiled and eaten – the group eventually reached and followed the Coppermine River to its mouth. There, to Hearne's horror, the Chippewyans massacred a group of Inuit. One badly wounded Inuit girl clung to Hearne's knees begging for help, but when Hearne pleaded for her life the Chippewyans ignored him and speared her to death as she lay at his feet.

Hearne found one piece of copper ore and visited an Indian mine from which limited metal was extracted. At the mouth of the river, the imaginatively named Coppermine, Hearne erected a cairn and claimed all the local land for the Hudson's Bay Company. It was July 1771 and Hearne was the first European to have seen the ocean between Hudson Bay and Siberia, though there are still some who doubt that he actually reached the coast, believing much of his account was concocted from Indian tales; Hearne's woefully incorrect latitude and longitude of the river mouth certainly reinforces the doubters' claims.

After his trip Hearne became governor of Prince of Wales Fort, but he was forced to surrender it to a French gunboat. Hearne was captured and the fort destroyed, and tragically Matonabbee, believing that Hearne and the other Englishmen had been killed, hanged himself as his own position among the Chippewyan had depended on the Company's existence. In fact Hearne survived captivity, was released and regained the governorship. Eventually he went back to England where he died, virtually penniless, in 1792, while awaiting receipt of £200 from a publisher for his classic book *A Voyage from Prince of Wales' Fort … to the Northern Ocean … for the Discovery of Copper Mines, a North West Passage …* Although £200 does not seem such a large sum today, it is worth recalling that 20 or so years later, Jane Austen was being offered £10 for her first novels.

Three years before Hearne's death, another explorer set out westward. Alexander Mackenzie was born on the Hebridean island of Lewis, his burning ambition to succeed perhaps stemming from the poverty of his childhood. Orphaned by the age of 16, Mackenzie joined the North-West Fur Trading Company (a rival to the Hudson's Bay Company, though later the two merged) and rapidly rose through its ranks. In Canada, Mackenzie met Peter Pond, a tough Connecticut-born American who had explored west of Hudson Bay and discovered Lake Athabasca. Pond told Mackenzie of native stories of a river that flowed west from the Great Slave Lake to the sea. Hoping that the river might be navigable and the sea was the Pacific Ocean, Mackenzie left Fort Chippewyan on the southern shore of Lake Athabasca on 3 June 1789. With him were four French-Canadian *voyageurs* (expert paddlers), an Indian guide called English Chief (named because he was a chief and spoke English!), a German and a number of other Indians. The group travelled in three canoes, which were paddled and portaged north to the Great Slave Lake. There ice

Turnagain Arm, near Anchorage, Alaska. James Cook named this inlet of the sea in exasperation at discovering that it was another blind alley as he searched Alaska's western shore for an exit from the North-West Passage.

Midnight, Lancaster Sound. A storm is moving in, a band of sunlight illuminating the sea ice and Cornwallis Island.

made progress difficult and mosquitoes made life virtually intolerable, but the team pressed on, reaching and journeying down the legendary river. Travelling at a remarkable rate (covering, on average, 40km daily) the party headed west, then north-west.

Mackenzie's account of the journey is a curious mix of styles. He is sometimes eloquent about the sheer beauty of the landscape through which they passed. He is also interesting when talking about the native peoples they met (though often disapproving of their habits and life-style). But on his companions he is almost silent. Mackenzie was clearly driven by his ambition to reach the Pacific, his men merely the means of achieving that end – hardly worth mentioning except to occasionally complain about them. As the expedition moved further north, the Indians' fear of Inuit (a strange, and mutual, loathing; the two peoples seem to have regarded each other as enemies just because they existed) meant that local guides were difficult to obtain. Mackenzie got around this by kidnapping – nothing was allowed to prejudice his great exercise.

Eventually Mackenzie reached the river's huge delta, a complex of narrow channels, swamp, taiga islands and pingos. He resolutely tried to force a way through the chaos and on 12 July he camped on what most experts now believe to have been Garry Island (at 69°29'N, 135°35'W). That night the team had to move because the water lapping the shore rose into their camp. Mackenzie thought this was due to the wind but two days later he realised it was a tide – he had reached the sea. Mackenzie hurriedly climbed to the high point of the island and looked north. All he could see was ice. This was not the Pacific Ocean.

Mackenzie called the river he had explored Disappointment. He returned along it, arriving back at Fort Chippewyan on 12 September. Today the river is called the Mackenzie. It is North America's second longest (after the Mississippi/Missouri complex, though it is longer than either, draining 20% of Canada). Mackenzie's employers were unimpressed – he had returned with neither furs nor a route to the Pacific – but his journey is now seen as one of the greatest in Canadian history. It was not his last. Sharing his employer's frustration he headed west again in 1793, following the Peace and Parsnip rivers, then the Bella Coola. On 19 July Mackenzie noted, 'I could perceive the termination of the river and its discharge into a narrow arm of the sea'. He had reached the Pacific Ocean. He was the first European to gaze at the ocean from the American shore, the first to have crossed the continent.

The northern Pacific had already been explored by sea, of course, with one of the most significant journeys being that of James Cook in the *Discovery* and *Resolution*, when, in 1776–80, he sailed to investigate the western end of the North-West Passage. Cook arrived late in the year and was unable to travel very far north because of the ice of the Beaufort Sea. It was on this journey that Cook named the Bering Strait, and after sailing through it he satisfied himself that Asia and America were not joined by turning east and following the Alaskan shore as far as Icy Cape. He also found a safe anchorage on the southern Alaskan shore at the end of an inlet he explored; the place is now called Anchorage, and the inlet is the Cook Inlet. Cook also sailed along a nearby arm of the sea that headed eastward, thinking, optimistically, that it might be the start of a passage. But as before, it turned out to be just another blind alley. His weariness with this discovery is almost tangible in the name he gave it – Turnagain Arm. Cook then turned south, landing in Hawaii in December 1778. Two months later he was murdered in a confrontation with the locals over a stolen boat. It was a sad end for one of the greatest explorers of any age.

The Royal Navy heads north-west

By the close of the Napoleonic Wars in the early 19th century, Britain was the major world power, its pre-eminence based on naval might. Such status brought fears as well as benefits, and these were, in part, exploited to persuade the British Admiralty to use naval ships to search for an Arctic seaway. Russia, a competitor on the world stage, lay at the other end of such a passage and seemed intent on expanding into America. The Russians had taken the Aleutian Islands and Alaska and one reason for the Antarctic journey of Faddey Faddeyevich Bellingshauzen (Estonian born and with a Cyrillic name that roughly translates as suggested, though it is more usually given in its Germanic form, Thaddens von Bellinghausen) had been to look for naval bases, a point hardly likely to have been lost on the British.

But the maintenance of British superpower status was not the only reason for the search. John Barrow, Second Secretary to the Admiralty (and the senior civil servant, as opposed to politician or naval officer, there), was the major influence on the decision to use naval ships. Though he undoubtedly understood the need to maintain an active navy and a complement of experienced officers, Barrow was also a geographer and historian with a number of published articles behind him.

He was interested in exploration for its own sake, and the naval expeditions of which he was the architect went not only to the Arctic but also to Africa and Antarctica.

Barrow's enthusiasm for exploration coincided with a sudden break-up of the Arctic ice, icebergs spilling down into the Atlantic and cooling Europe. This change was noted by William Scoresby, a Whitby-based whaler. Whitby, on the Yorkshire coast of England, had a fleet of Arctic whalers that made a good living during the late 18th and early 19th centuries, and Scoresby was one of its most successful captains. But he was much more than a sea captain; he was also a scientist and surveyor and, later, a social worker and clergyman. His observational science in the Arctic has led many to call him the 'father of Arctic science', and his book *An Account of the Arctic Regions* is still considered one of the great books on the area.

Noting the lack of ice in Arctic waters, Scoresby sailed beyond 82°N (probably a record northing at the time). When he returned he wrote to Sir Joseph Banks, president of the Royal Society, suggesting that conditions made it an ideal time for a renewal of the quest for a northern sea route to the east. Scoresby hoped that he might lead a British expedition, but when Barrow heard of the idea he chose naval men. Barrow organised two expeditions in 1818; John Ross and William Edward Parry were to search for the North-West Passage, David Buchan and John Franklin were to sail over the North Pole (the notion of an open polar sea still had many advocates, and Scoresby's findings were consistent with a 'ring' of ice breaking up). The two expeditions were then to meet off the Siberian Coast.

Ross and Parry by sea

Buchan (in the *Dorothea*) and Franklin (in the *Trent*) fared badly. A violent storm forced them to shelter in Spitsbergen's Magdalenafjord, then pack ice, probably pushed south by the storm, imprisoned them and threatened to crush the ships. Once extricated (by a subsequent storm that broke up the ice) the expedition sailed home. Ross and Parry, in the *Isabella* and *Alexander* respectively, had a more interesting time. They were heading north-west: Samuel Hearne had found the sea at the mouth of the Coppermine River to still be frozen in July and, if the science was correct, the sea to the north should have been open. The expedition included John Ross' nephew James Clark Ross, Edward Sabine, a Royal Artillery officer, and a south Greenlander called John Sacheuse; Sacheuse, who had reached Britain as a stowaway on a whaler, would act as interpreter during any encounters with the Inuit.

The first meeting with native Arctic peoples was in Greenland's Prince Regent Bay. It is often claimed that the Inuit of north-west Greenland had been isolated from their fellow Inuit to the south for generations by a minor ice age (ironic in view of the ice-melting that had brought Ross to the spot), and had come to believe they were the only people on Earth. That is a disputed interpretation, but even if it was not the case the sight of vast ships manned by people who were clearly not Inuit would have been enough to terrify the locals. What Ross considered the calls of the Inuit from the shore to be friendly greetings, but Sacheuse was able to interpret them as shouts for the expedition to go away.

As interesting as the reaction of the Inuit was the reaction of the British. They measured the Inuit, collected examples of their sledges and other equipment, all the things they might have been expected to do, yet they completely failed to understand the significance of what they were seeing. The image which most clearly exposes this is the depiction of the first meeting in Ross' book of the expedition (below).

Apart from making contact with the Inuit, Ross discovered red snow, a phenomenon caused by growth of the algae *Protococcus nivalis*. He also rediscovered Baffin Bay (which at the time was believed mythical) and the entrance to Smith, Jones and Lancaster Sounds. He ignored the first two, but sailed a short distance into Lancaster Sound. Then he stopped, sighting a mountain range which, he said, clearly showed the sound was a bay. Parry could not see these mountains (though as he was several kilometres behind Ross this is not surprising) and urged him to continue, but Ross declined and returned to Britain, where he was damned for his timidity, both privately and publicly. That red snow was the only discovery of the expedition formed the basis of cartoons in the newspapers, a pompous Ross leading a motley collection of sailors who carried a polar bear and a barrel of red snow, the men without noses, these rubbed away from vigorous repetition of the reported Inuit method of greeting. The cartoons did nothing to endear Ross to an already furious Barrow. When Ross

The British meet the Inuit of north-west Greenland, an illustration from Ross' book on his first Arctic voyage. On the right are skin-clad Inuit with a dog-sledge, on the left British naval officers in dress uniform – tailed coats, buckled shoes and cocked hats. The British dress can be excused by the good weather on the day, but there is something more on display here: it is a show of British might, hardly surprising since Britain was in its imperial phase and had just become (in its own eyes at least) the master of Europe. But the innate feeling of superiority that Britain's position engendered in its naval officers prevented them from seeing what was really in front of them. The Inuit were superbly adapted to the local environment in terms not only of clothing and equipment, but also in terms of the size of their group. The British missed that and consistently sent ill-clad men in parties too large to feed themselves off the land. When trips went reasonably well these things became annoyances, but when they went badly, they were disastrous, as the British were later to discover at appalling cost.

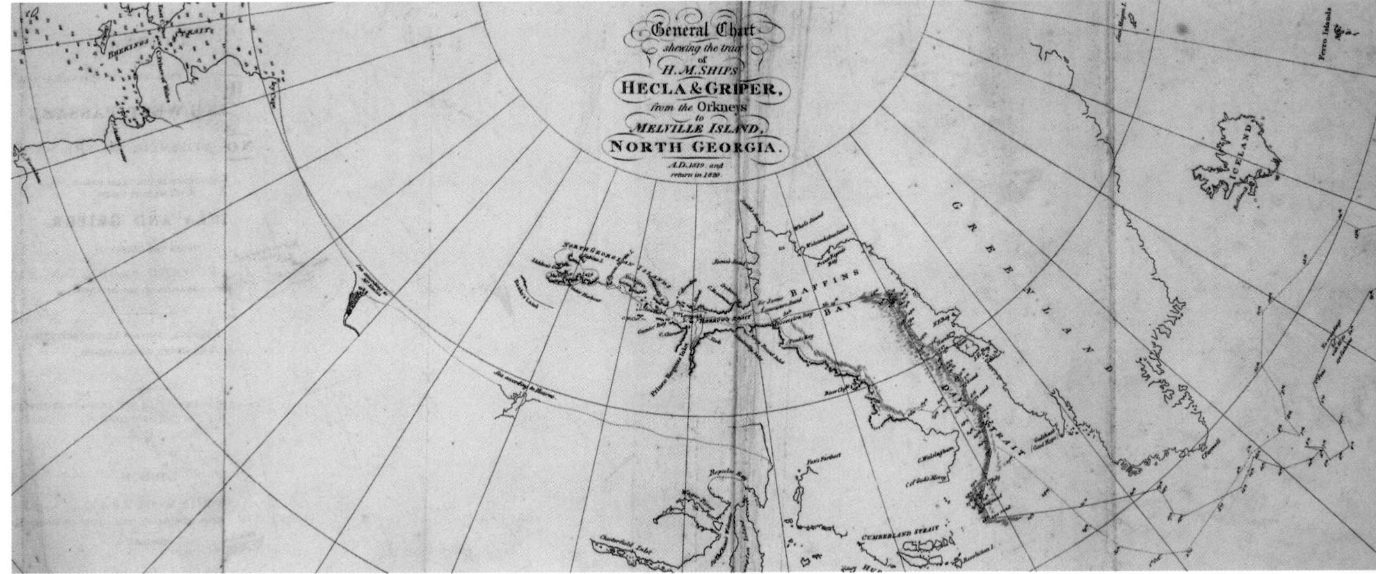

Map from William Parry's book of his voyage of 1819–20. It indicates the sparse understanding of the northern shore of North America at that time.

offered his services for future expeditions, Barrow declined, though Ross' naval superiors obviously did not share the view of the civil service as they promoted him, perhaps to show their independence by thumbing their own noses at the criticism.

When Barrow tried again in 1819 it was Parry who commanded the expedition in the *Hecla*, accompanied by Matthew Liddon in the *Griper*. Parry had been unmerciful in his condemnation of Ross' decision to turn back in Lancaster Sound. Parry was 29, and most of his crew, which included Sabine, were younger. This young, energetic team were intent on pushing forward; it is said that the crew cheered when Parry decided to enter Lancaster Sound despite heavy pack ice and numerous icebergs. Parry pushed west through what is now called the Parry Channel (comprising Barrow Strait and Melville Sound), discovering and naming Devon, Somerset, Cornwallis, Bathurst and Prince of Wales Islands. As they sailed, Sabine noted that the compass needle appeared to be pointing north. It was not of course, it was still pointing towards the North Magnetic Pole, but the expedition were now north of that pole.

Parry headed south into Prince Regent Inlet but was stopped by ice, then continued west to Melville Island. From there he could see (and name) Victoria and Banks Islands, but further progress into what is now called McClure Sound (but was then Banks Strait) was impossible because of ice. Parry had reached 110°W (and was therefore able to claim a prize of £5,000 offered to anyone who could reach that longitude north of the Arctic Circle; Parry shared the reward among his crew). He may have guessed that beyond the McClure Sound was open sea; if so he was correct: he was within 160km of open water and had found the northern North-West Passage

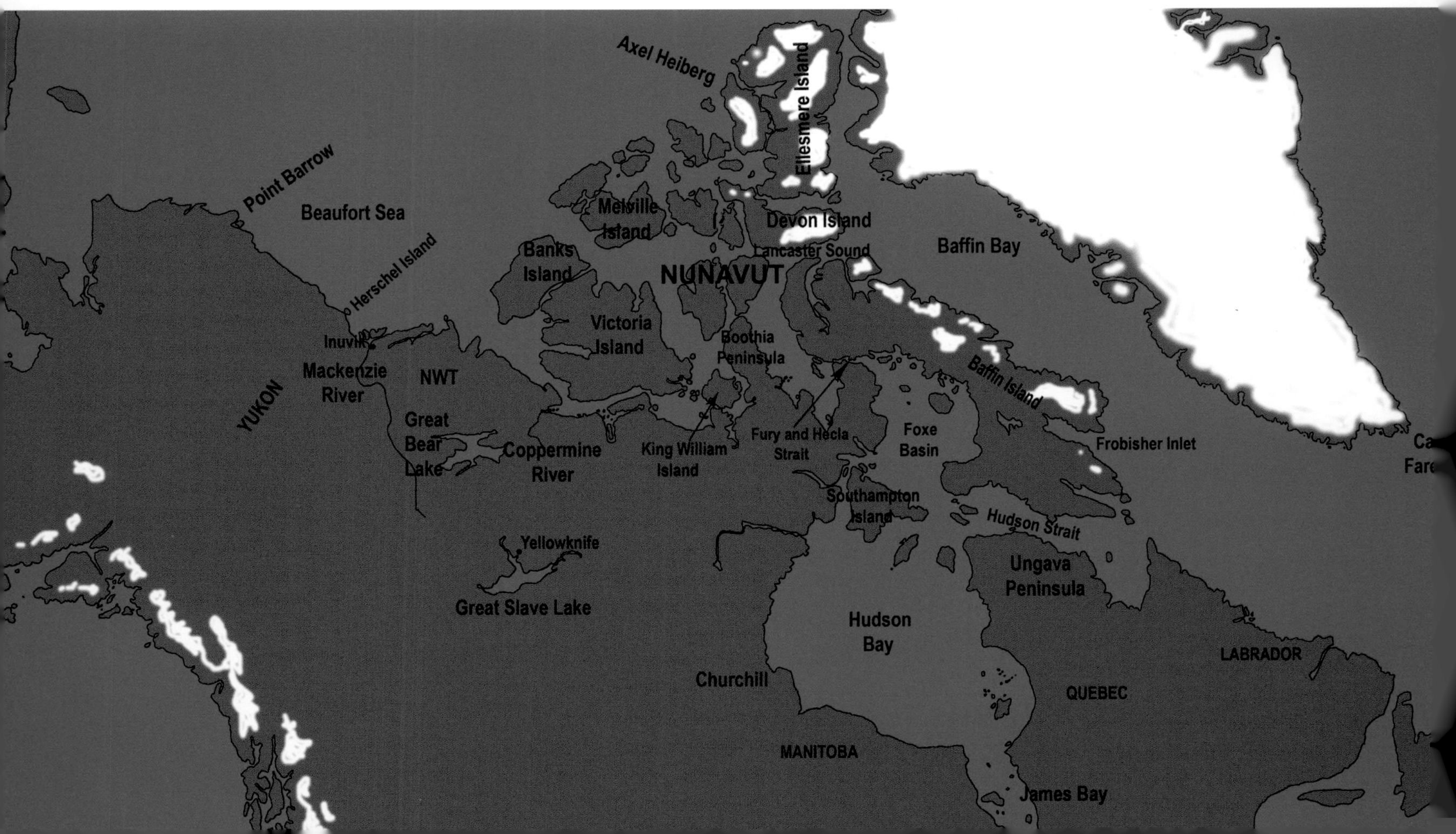

Two illustrations from William Parry's book on his 1819–20 voyage. At the top sailors are cutting a lead through the ice so that the ships can enter Winter Harbour, Melville Island. The illustrator has drawn the lead as a sinuous British river; in reality cutting the path was very hard work and a straight line – as short a path as possible – would almost certainly have been made.
The lower illustration shows the *Hecla* and *Griper* in Winter Harbour. The snug-looking ships, clear night, scampering dog and camp fire are likely to be at odds with the hardships the crews actually faced.

(not that traversed later by Amundsen), though it would be many years before that would be proven.

On Melville Island Parry sought shelter in Winter Harbour. There he overwintered, his ships de-rigged and covered with wagon cloth to form an exercise yard. Bread was baked, beer brewed and a reasonable, scurvy-free winter was passed. In June 1820 Parry explored Melville Island while waiting for the ice to free his ships, adding Musk Oxen, Caribou, hares and birds to the ship's menu. In August the ships were finally freed and the expedition returned to Britain, where Parry became extremely famous. His expedition had been an undoubted success. John Barrow thought that the finding of the passage was now just one journey away, a view endorsed publicly by Parry, though in private he was much less certain.

Franklin by land

Parry's sea-borne journey had been supported by a land expedition led by John Franklin, which was intended to survey the North American coast east and west of the river mouths reached by Hearne and Mackenzie. Franklin had no experience that fitted him to command such an expedition, but then neither did any of the other candidates available to Barrow. With Franklin were John Richardson, surgeon and naturalist, George Back, Robert Hood and John Hepburn. Late in the expedition Franklin was forced to separate Back and Hood when they fell out over the attentions of a beautiful native girl they named Greenstockings (after a particularly striking aspect of her attire).

Accompanied by four Orkney Islanders collected on the way to Canada, Franklin headed west in late August. The expedition landed at the Hudson's Bay Company's York Factory on the south-western shore of the Hudson Bay, then moved inland to Cumberland House, a Company outpost, where the Orcadians turned back. Richardson and Hood overwintered at Cumberland House, but Franklin, Back and Hepburn continued to Fort Chippewyan on Lake Athabasca. The cold was intense, with temperatures so low that their tea, left to brew in the finest English tradition, froze before they could drink it. At Fort Chippewyan, Franklin found that he had walked into a bloody feud between the rival Hudson's Bay and North-West Fur Trading companies. He managed to avoid getting caught up in the conflict, but it prevented him from buying the supplies he had been banking on. So when his team, accompanied by guides, *voyageurs* (European fur traders, experts in the use of canoes) and assorted camp-followers, headed north in 1820, it was poorly provisioned. It was also too big to service easily by hunting. Starting in July and going by way of Fort Providence on the Great Slave Lake, Franklin was forced to overwinter in 'Fort Enterprise', which he built close to the source of the Coppermine River. From this log-built camp, Franklin's team had no alternative but to shuttle supplies from Providence and Chippewyan through the winter.

In June 1821, Franklin finally started down the Coppermine River, but there were more problems; at Bloody Falls (named after the massacre of the Inuit on Hearne's journey; skulls and other bones were still visible when Franklin arrived) the Indian guides and hunters deserted, fearful of reprisals. The *voyageurs* expressed fears about using their fragile, birch-bark canoes on the sea, but Franklin persevered, becoming the first European to reach the river's mouth since Hearne. From the mouth and with a depleted party, he set out

Greenstockings and her father, an illustration from Franklin's book on his first land expedition. Back and Hood fought a duel over the girl, one of Franklin's other men wisely removing the powder from their pistols. Franklin was seriously concerned that murder would eventually result if the two men were left together. His decision to send Back away on a trip allowed Hood to gain Greenstockings' affections, and she later bore him a child.

Another illustration from John Franklin's book – *Narrative of a Journey to the Shores of the Polar Sea* – on his first land expedition. It illustrates the view north across the Arctic Ocean from the mouth of the Coppermine River at midnight.

east along the coast. The plan had been to reach Repulse Bay, but by late August, with both supplies and men almost exhausted, Franklin was forced to admit defeat. He named the furthest point he reached Point Turnagain, then, after wasting time wondering whether to overwinter, he headed back towards the river. The weather was atrocious, with the sea threatening to destroy the canoes (just as the *voyageurs* had feared), and in desperation the team landed and started to trek across the tundra. The country was devoid of animal life and almost barren of vegetation, and as their food ran out progress slowed to a crawl, despite the abandonment of the canoes. Surviving on *tripe de roche*, a lichen scraped from rocks, and the leather of their boots and jackets, they finally reached the Coppermine River. There Richardson almost died trying to swim across with a line, and precious days were lost in building a canoe to replace those they had abandoned.

Once across the river George Back and the three strongest *voyageurs* headed for Fort Enterprise; one man died before it was reached. The Indians who had fled from Bloody Falls were supposed to have stocked the fort with food and to have waited for Franklin, but they had done neither. Finding Enterprise empty, Back started out after the Indians. In the main party Franklin was forced to abandon Hood, who was too weak to move; Richardson and Hepburn stayed with him while Franklin continued slowly behind Back. Two men died and four tried to return to the river camp. Only one arrived, a half-Iroquois, half-European called Michel Teroahauté. He brought meat he claimed to have cut from the body of a wolf, but his curiously healthy appearance and odd behaviour convinced Richardson the meat was human flesh. His fears that Teroahauté had killed the other three men were, he felt, confirmed when Hood died of a single gunshot wound. Teroahauté, the only one present at the time, claimed it had been suicide – but the wound was in the back of Hood's head. When the three men set off for Fort Enterprise, Richardson and Hepburn feared for their own lives when Teroahauté claimed to have stopped to gather *tripe de roche*, but returned without any. To Richardson it was clear that he 'had halted for the purpose of putting his gun in order with the intention of attacking us'. To forestall this Richardson shot the heavily armed Teroahauté.

At the fort Franklin and his team were in the last stages of starvation. More men died, and the rest were only days from death when the Indians found by George Back arrived with food. The hint of cannibalism (by the foreigners of course, not the English), the murders and the general horror of the trip made Franklin a hero in Britain when the team finally made it

Right above
The grave of one of Parry's men on Igloolik Island.

Right
The *Hecla* and *Fury* in winter quarters at Igloolik. The line across the bollards between the two ships aided men to find their way between them when the weather was poor. To keep morale high, a game of cricket has been organised, a somewhat incongruous idea given the conditions.

home. Franklin became known as the 'man who ate his boots' and his book on the trip rapidly sold out. It is no surprise; the book is a fine one, the copy at the British Library being inscribed, in an unknown hand, 'this is one of the most affecting narratives ever written'.

Parry by sea, again

Despite his misgivings about undertaking another Arctic voyage, Parry agreed to lead another expedition in 1821, the *Fury* replacing the worn-out *Griper*. This time Parry went to Hudson Bay, a decision that seems curious in the light of the string of early failures there, but reasonable when considered against his opinion that the ice at the western end of the Parry Channel would prove a consistent bar to progress. Parry hoped that the ice would be less severe in the south and hoped to find a westerly route out of the bay to the north of Southampton Island.

Parry confirmed Middleton's discovery that Repulse Bay was not the way west. The expedition overwintered on Winter Island at the mouth of Lyon Inlet. (Parry's choice of name here is consistent with those on all his expeditions and indicates a distinct lack of romance – if he was not honouring an aristocrat who might return the favour at a later date he was stating the obvious; on Melville Island he had wintered at Winter Harbour, this time it was on Winter Island. Had Parry made many more journeys the map of the Canadian Arctic might have become a source of great confusion). On Winter Island the British made friends with a group of local Inuit, one of whom, a woman called Iligliuk, drew a map that led Parry to a strait he named Fury and Hecla after his ships (Iligliuk's son had been given a pencil and paper and became the first Inuk to draw using these amazing new materials; the boy's drawings still survive.)

During the summer of 1822 Parry navigated the eastern end of the strait, but was unable to break through the ice choking it. He therefore crossed the ice to the northern side and trekked along it until he could see the western end, and what he called the Polar Sea (but was later renamed the Gulf of Boothia) beyond. Parry then wintered on Igloolik, an island close to the mouth of the strait. He tried to get through the strait again in 1823, but failed, and returned to Britain. Parry's failure to negotiate the strait was, with hindsight, not surprising; not until 1948 was the Fury and Hecla Strait navigated from the Gulf to Foxe Basin, and not until 1956 in the other direction – the way Parry attempted it – with both journeys requiring an ice-breaker.

Parry went north again in 1824, this time trying to find a route by way of Lancaster Sound and Prince Regent Inlet, avoiding both Fury and Hecla Strait and the exit from Parry Channel. This time he hoped to forge a route from the western end of the strait. The attempt was doomed; the British had not discovered just how far north the Boothia Peninsula reached. That year there was also heavy ice in Baffin Bay and it took Parry all summer to reach Lancaster Sound, much of the time spent hauling the ships (*Fury* and *Hecla* again) through the thick ice by the back-breaking work of anchoring a hawser to a floe far ahead and heaving on it. The sound itself was almost free of ice, allowing Parry to reach Port Bowen on the eastern shore of Prince Regent Inlet, where he wintered. In July 1825, when ice freed the ships, Parry went south along the Inlet's western coast (Somerset Island), but a sudden storm pushed ice against the ships, pinning them against the shore. *Fury* was repeatedly smashed against the shore; damaged beyond repair she was abandoned (at Fury Beach), and Parry retreated for home with everyone on board the *Hecla*.

Northern Foxe Basin, en route to Fury and Hecla Strait. Until the beginning of this century the Strait and its approaches were invariably choked with ice making a transit impossible, but now there is usually much less sea ice.

This illustration from William Parry's book on his third expedition in search of the North-West Passage shows the position of the *Fury* and *Hecla* on 1 August 1825. After the furious battering the two ships took, the *Fury* was not repairable. Fortunately the *Hecla* was, the entire expedition returning home safely in it.

Franklin's second land trip

There had been other voyages in 1824 and 1825 linked to Parry's third voyage, and also a second land expedition led by John Franklin, the British committing a great deal of effort not only to the discovery of the passage, but also to the mapping of Canada. In 1824 George Lyon sailed the *Griper* northwards with the intention of reaching Repulse Bay and then sledging across the narrow peninsula (the Rae Isthmus) at its back, which Iligliuk had shown on her map, to reach the sea beyond (Committee Bay), perhaps linking up with Parry. It was a good plan, but heavy ice and appalling weather in Roes Welcome Sound so badly damaged the *Griper* that Lyon did well to get the ship back to Britain at all: he had not even reached Repulse Bay. In 1825 Frederick Beechey took the *Blossom* to the Bering Strait, in the expectation of meeting Parry when he exited the passage or Franklin when he reached the strait overland. Beechey waited in vain; Franklin reached Foggy Island, just 250km away, but Parry was half a continent away, battling the ice of Prince Regent Inlet.

Given the horror of his earlier land journey, one wonders why Franklin was willing to lead another in 1825, and why Richardson and Back were willing to go with him. But go they did, with Franklin's resilience seeming even more astonishing when it is considered that he learned of the death of his wife in Canada before setting out on the expedition. This expedition was better equipped, supplies being easier to obtain now the fur-trade war between the rival companies was over. The men followed the Mackenzie River, which was much easier to navigate than the Coppermine, and with fur-trade forts now spaced at intervals along its length the journey can hardly be compared to that of Alexander Mackenzie. The expedition was remarkably successful. At the river's delta Franklin led one team west in two boats, *Lion* and *Reliance*, passing Herschel Island – which he named after the Herschels, father and son, and famous astronomers. Had his team not been halted by thick fog, they would almost certainly have reached Point Barrow and met Beechey's expedition there. At the same time, Richardson led a team eastwards in two ships, *Union* and *Dolphin*, naming Franklin Bay after the expedition leader as a mark of the 'respect and regard' he had for him, and becoming the first European to see the Smoking Hills, whose fires, from bituminous shale, are thought to have been ignited by a lightning strike and have perhaps smouldered for several thousand years. Richardson also named the strait between the mainland and Victoria Island after his two boats on his way to the Coppermine River. When Franklin's team returned to England in 1827, the coast of North America had been mapped all the way from near Point Barrow to Point Turnagain, a distance of more than 2,200km – an outstanding achievement.

The North Magnetic Pole

Despite the success of Franklin's expedition, the overall failure of the concerted efforts of 1824–27 drained the Admiralty's resolve, and with the public's enthusiasm turning to apathy there was no incentive for further government investment, particularly as it had been clear for some time that even if a passage existed it would not be useful as a trade or military route. The early attempts had at least provided good horror yarns to entertain the people back home, but now the failures were merely banal. What was needed to revitalise public interest was a major success or a major tragedy. The North-West Passage was to supply the latter, but first there were more failures.

An illustration from Franklin's book on his second land expedition. It would be interesting to know if the illustrator put the men in British upper class dress because he felt that was what the reader expected or because it was the truth. Did the man sketching really take a top hat and frock coat on an Arctic expedition?

First to fail was an expedition financed by Felix Booth, Sheriff of London and gin bottler. As his commander, Booth chose John Ross, ignored since 1818 for his timidity but a man with an interest in steam navigation who had tried, unsuccessfully, to persuade the Admiralty to let him take a steamship to the Arctic. Ross was so keen on the idea that he part-financed the trip from his own pocket. Ross' ship was the paddle steamer *Victory*, the first steam-driven ship to head north-west, his crew including his nephew James Clark Ross, who had been on all Parry's voyages as well as his uncle's first.

The *Victory's* engine and fuel stores were so vast that another ship was needed to carry the expedition's supplies. There were other problems too; the steam engine provided a speed barely above walking pace, the boilers leaked (despite dung and potatoes being put in them, on the manufacturer's instructions!), and the boiler room was so hot the stokers could only work for short periods before becoming exhausted and fainting. Fortunately, when the paddles were lifted out of the water the *Victory* sailed well and Prince Regent Inlet – which Booth had decided would be the first objective, as he thought the passage might open from its western shore – was eventually reached.

Ross now sailed south of Parry's Fury Beach – the beached *Fury* had disappeared, either drifted away or sunk – naming the Gulf of Boothia and Boothia Felix (now the Boothia Peninsula) after his patron. Ross overwintered in Felix Harbour in Lord Mayor's Bay (again named in Booth's honour; Booth was also remembered in Sheriff Harbour, to round off a fine bag of dedications), the steam engine that had so enthralled him being dismantled and manhandled on to the shore as so much rubbish. During the winter of 1829–30 *Victory* was visited by local Inuit, who told Ross that there was no westward channel to the south. This influenced Ross' later explorations, though it was not finally confirmed that Boothia Felix was a peninsula until Rae's trip of 1846.

The spring of 1830 did not release the *Victory* and James Ross decided to

During Franklin's second land expedition, John Richardson led a team eastwards along Canada's northern coast, reaching and naming Franklin Bay in which the Smoking Cliffs (*above left*) are of bituminous shale, probably ignited by a lightning strike several thousand years ago. The cliffs were illustrated (*above*) in Robert McClure book of his expedition.

Left
Point Barrow, reached by Frederick Beechey's 1825-28 expedition which went to the Bering Sea to meet Franklin and Parry. The Point is where the Chukchi Sea (shown here) meets the Beaufort Sea.
Below
The Franklin Bluffs, exquisitely coloured layers of sandstone and shale near Prudhoe Bay. The Bluffs were reached by Franklin. The two locations are just 250km apart.

An illustration from John Ross' book on his second expedition. It shows Somerset House during the summer.

trek – with dog- and man-hauled sledges, and Inuit guides – across Boothia Felix to see what lay to the west. He discovered King William's Land (now King William Island), reaching its northern tip, which he naturally called Cape Felix. At the cape, James Ross noted 'the pack ice … had … been pressed against that shore, consisted of the heaviest masses that I had ever seen in such a situation … the lighter floes had been thrown up, on some parts of the coast … having travelled as much as half a mile beyond the limits of the highest tide-mark'.

Ross now turned south-west and continued to Cape Victory on King William's western coast; he was only about 350km from Point Turnagain, but he was out of food and had to return to Felix Harbour. It had been an epic journey, but the most significant discovery was missed: Ross did not explore southwards on the west side of King William. Had he done so he would have found that King William was an island rather than a peninsula. During the summer of 1830 the *Victory* could be moved only 6½km to Sheriff Harbour, where the winter of 1830–31 was spent. When summer 1831 came the ship remained entombed and James Ross set out on another sledge trip. He re-crossed Boothia Felix and headed north along the coast. At 8am on 1 June at 70°5'17"N, 96°46'45"N, magnetic measurements showed that Ross had reached the North Magnetic Pole. His team raised a cairn and a jackstaff, since 'nature had erected no monument', from which fluttered the Union Flag as Ross solemnly claimed the territory for the British Crown.

The *Victory* was finally freed from the ice in late summer, but managed to gain just a few kilometres northward before being entombed again. During the winter of 1831–32 the crew began to show signs of scurvy, despite John Ross' intelligent use of fresh meat to keep it at bay. Ross therefore decided to abandon the ship, hauling boats and supplies north to Fury Beach where there were still supplies available from Parry's last voyage. Fury Beach was reached in July and a hut (Somerset House) built. But winter set in again before the boats could be rigged for a voyage to Lancaster Sound. During this fourth winter one man died of scurvy. With most of the crew now ill, many weeks in 1833 were spent transporting supplies to the ice edge. Finally, on 15 August, the boats were launched. To the men's joy Lancaster Sound offered open water. And on 25 August, a sail was sighted. The ship lowered a boat and rowed towards the expedition. When Ross asked what ship it was he was told it was 'the *Isabella* of Hull, once commanded by Captain Ross'. The ship had been John Ross' first Arctic

Another illustration from John Ross' second expedition book. This one shows the saving of the expedition by the *Isabella*.

This drawing is from George Back's book of his land expedition. The expedition camped on Montreal Island in Chantry Bay at the mouth of the Great Fish River, an island which was probably visited by survivors of Franklin's last expedition. No clue is given as to why the man in a top hat is carrying a suitcase up the beach.

command in 1818 and was now a whaler. Ross noted that when he told the *Isabella*'s mate (who had brought the boat across to them) that he was the same Captain Ross, 'with the usual blunderheadedness of men on such occasions, he assured me I had been dead two years'.

Back in Britain, John Ross was knighted and James Ross promoted. The only sour note was Sir John Barrow's unfair review of John Ross' book – he had still not forgiven what he saw as the cowardice of 1818. But just as with his earlier attack on Ross, Barrow's article was published anonymously. Not that there was much need for secrecy, since John Ross was at war with just about everyone. There was even a feud between John and nephew James. Ludicrously, John was claiming to have discovered the North Magnetic Pole, while James was claiming to have commanded the *Victory*.

Searching for Ross

In 1832, nothing having been heard from John Ross for nearly three years, people in Britain began to clamour for a search expedition. With the expedition having been a private venture, the government and Admiralty were not keen to finance a search, but eventually some private money was raised and George Back, veteran of the two Franklin overland expeditions, returned to Canada with instructions to follow the Great Fish (now Back) River to the sea and then to head north to Fury Beach where, it was assumed, Ross would head if he ran low on food. The assumption was correct, though the search was far too late, few having much hope that Ross could have survived four winters. That he had is likely to have influenced the Admiralty when, later, there was an equal clamour to search for the missing Franklin expedition in the late 1840s and early 1850s.

Back established a base on the shores of the Great Slave Lake and overwintered. During the winter he met Greenstockings again, immediately recognising her because she had retained her beauty. She now had a number of children, one of whom, presumably, was that born after her relationship with Robert Hood; not surprisingly, Back makes no such comment in his book of the trip. In April 1834 news arrived that Ross had returned safely to England, but Back continued with his trip, though on a reduced scale, following the Great Fish River to Chantry Inlet. Ice and lack of time prevented more than a survey of part of the bay's shoreline, but that did add to the map of the mainland.

Despite the failure of John Ross to find the passage, the success in terms of mapping more of the Canadian north and the journey to the North Magnetic Pole, coupled with Back's exploration, persuaded the Admiralty to send George Back northwards again in 1836, with instructions to survey the last section of uncharted coast, southwards from the Fury and Hecla Strait to Point Turnagain. To do this Back sailed the *Terror* to Repulse Bay with the intention of crossing the Melville Peninsula on foot. But the *Terror* was trapped in the ice, squeezed and battered for ten months. When she was eventually released she was almost unseaworthy and Back sailed for home immediately. He just made it to Ireland's west coast, beaching the ship to prevent her sinking.

Dease and Simpson

Following Back's unsuccessful attempt to complete the mapping of the missing eastern section of the North American coast, it was left to staff of the Hudson's Bay Company to fill the gaps. Between 1836 and 1839 Peter Dease, a senior Company official, and Thomas Simpson, cousin of Company Governor George Simpson, made a series of journeys. Though Dease was nominally in charge it was Simpson, a young man of burning ambition and amazing stamina, who was the driving force. Simpson's abilities were remarkable: he could travel up to 80km daily on foot, sometimes in winter, for days on end, and shrug off conditions that would have repelled lesser mortals. On the pair's first expedition, to fill in the gap between Franklin's Foggy Island and Point Barrow, Simpson and five others left Dease and the rest of the team behind and pushed west across dreadful country, wading rivers up to their waists in freezing water and being cold day and night. Borrowing an Inuit umiak for the last stage of the trek they finally reached Point Barrow.

Next, Dease and Simpson made for the coast east of Point Turnagain. In 1838 Simpson descended the Coppermine River and pushed east over ice, passing Turnagain and discovering an island he named after the young Queen – Victoria Island. Halted by the conditions, he returned in 1839 and sailed two boats, *Castor* and *Pollux*, all the way to Back's Chantry Inlet, discovering, *en route*, that King William was an island not a peninsula of the mainland; the channel separating King William Island and the Adelaide Peninsula is now called Simpson Strait.

Simpson's ambition then seems to have overcome him. He wrote 'Fame I must have, but it must be alone'. Fed up with Dease, nominally his senior, Simpson walked to the Red River settlement (Fort Garry, now the site of Winnipeg), a journey of almost 3,200km, which he completed in 61 days, on foot, in winter. He was hoping there would be a message at the fort telling him to continue his explorations by linking Chantry Inlet to Fury and Hecla Strait. There was no message. Disillusioned and probably furious, Simpson headed south, intending to reach a US port and a ship for Britain. Soon after he left, the instructions he craved arrived – but it was too late as Simpson was dead. He had started his journey with four other men. The survivors told how Simpson, enraged by the injustices of life, shot dead two of them, the other two fleeing in terror. When they returned to camp Simpson had shot himself. Perhaps that tale is true – but why go back to a camp occupied by a murderous companion? The events surrounding Simpson's death may never be known. What is clear is that, at only 31 years of age, a great explorer had died without fulfilling his potential.

The last big piece of the jigsaw was finally fitted in 1847 when Dr John Rae, a Hudson's Bay Company surgeon, who was later to discover Sir John Franklin's fate, crossed the isthmus from Repulse Bay to Committee Bay (which he had already crossed in 1846) and headed north along the bay's western shore. Rounding what is now called the Simpson Peninsula, Rae headed north, looking for the channel that separated Ross' Boothia Felix from the mainland. When he reached Lord Mayor's Bay he realised there wasn't one. Boothia Felix was the Boothia Peninsula; the northern coast of mainland North America had now been mapped, though the search for the North-West Passage would continue.

Franklin's last expedition

In 1845 Sir John Barrow was in his 81st year. Despite that he continued to occupy the same post he had held for 41 years, though he felt the time had come to retire. James, now Sir James, Ross had returned from Antarctica with the news that there was little to encourage the British to go there again, a fact that may have persuaded Barrow to remember unfinished business in the north. He wrote to the Admiralty pointing out Britain would be a laughing stock if, having expended so much effort and having found both the eastern and western ends of the North-West Passage, she did not explore the last remaining section in the middle. The Admiralty agreed, making *Erebus* and *Terror*, Ross' Antarctic ships, available.

But who should command? James Clark Ross declined: he was, he said, too old at 44. John Ross was, of course, still beyond the pale as far as Barrow was concerned. Parry could not be tempted out of retirement and Back's health had not recovered from the excesses of 1836–37, while Sir John Franklin was not only old, but had just been dismissed from his position as Governor of Van Diemen's Land (Tasmania). Nominally, the dismissal followed an unseemly row with a junior, though it was actually engineered by vested interests on the island that feared Franklin's humanitarian view of prisoner treatment might affect the profits they made from prison labour.

Franklin had had a distinguished service career. He had fought at the Battle of Copenhagen when he was just 15. He had been a signal officer at Trafalgar on the *Bellerophon*, which had been among the most heavily engaged British ships in the battle. Franklin emerged unscathed, but was later wounded at the Battle of New Orleans during the US-British War of 1812, where Sir Edward Pakenham's army was routed by Andrew Jackson's forces. But despite all this he was not promoted. He was, it seems amiable and competent, but dull, and the governorship of a prison colony was his only reward. After his dismissal Franklin returned to Britain looking both

Victoria Island, named by Dease and Simpson for the young British Queen.

A painting by W. H. Browne who accompanied James Clark Ross's Franklin search expedition. The work shows Port Leopold at noon in midwinter.

for justice and a job. He was almost 60 and overweight, clearly not suited to what might be an exhausting command. But his second wife, Lady Jane Franklin, campaigned relentlessly on his behalf, seeing the expedition as a way of allowing her husband to regain the prestige cruelly robbed by his unfair dismissal from Tasmania. Eventually the Admiralty succumbed to her pressure.

Erebus and *Terror* were strengthened to withstand pressure from the ice and fitted with railway locomotive steam engines that turned screw propellers, a radically new idea. Sir John Barrow reasoned that the ships, reinforced at the bow and powered from the stern, would plough through the Arctic ice. John Ross had his doubts and was also worried about the size of the crew. The complement was 133 men and Ross noted how hard it had been to feed one-sixth that number when the *Victory* had been lost. But Barrow was hardly likely to listen to John Ross, and anyway the food problem had been solved, the ships being stocked with tinned food, a revolutionary new idea that promised to eliminate both hunger and scurvy. The canned meat and vegetables were supplied by Stephen Goldner, the man with the lowest tender and a production line that left much to be desired in terms of the quality of the food in the cans and the cleanliness of his production methods. It was said that the only part of the pigs that did not go into Goldner's can was the squeal; with the slaughter of pigs, sheep and cows being carried out on the premises and within sight of other animals, the filth that reached the cans was indescribable. Goldner's cans arrived only hours before the ships sailed, too late for samples to be taken to check on the quality of the contents or the adequacy of the can seals.

On 19 May 1845 the *Erebus* and *Terror* were made ready to depart the River Thames. Just before sailing a dove flew down and perched on a mast. The commander and crew were cheered by this obviously happy omen. On 26 July the two ships were seen, by a whaler, moored to an iceberg close to the entrance to Lancaster Sound. After an exchange of greetings the whaler sailed away. It was the last time either ship or any of the crew – reduced to 129 after four men had been sent home from Greenland – were seen by European eyes.

Searching for Franklin

History had told the British not to be too concerned if nothing was heard of Arctic expeditions for several years, but by 1848 James Clark Ross was demanding a rescue mission. That year Ross took two ships to Somerset Island, where he was forced to overwinter before retreating in the face of heavy ice. At the same time two more ships were dispatched to the Bering Strait. Despite sledge journeys eastwards (ironically following one of Franklin's land routes) no trace of the expedition was found. During his trip Ross tried the ingenious idea of trapping Arctic foxes and fitting them with collars that carried a message of hope to Franklin before releasing them again. It was the first of many ideas for getting messages to the beleaguered crew, one of the more entertaining being that of releasing thousands of message-bearing balloons.

During the decade that followed the first rescue attempts, more than three dozen expeditions set out in search of Franklin or for clues to his disappearance. Many of these were official expeditions from Britain, but some were private. Of the latter, most were at the instigation of Lady Jane Franklin. Jane Griffin had met Franklin when he married her friend Eleanor Porden, marrying him after Eleanor's death and after several chaste dalliances of her own, most notably with Peter Roget, author of the famous thesaurus. Lady Jane was a formidable woman who campaigned relentlessly on behalf of her lost husband, badgering the Admiralty into further searches and spending a fortune on her own. She also wrote to Zachary Taylor, President of the United States, asking for help. That request failed to elicit an official response, being defeated by procrastination in the government, but it did result in a semi-official one when Congress backed and part-funded an expedition by Henry Grinnell, a New York shipping magnate. The 'First Grinnell Expedition' was also the first American expedition to the Arctic, igniting a public enthusiasm which was to lead, ultimately, to the tragedies and successes of Greely, Cook and Peary.

Charles Francis Hall, another American, also went north on a Franklin search. Hall was a curious man whose death remains one of the Arctic's most enduring mysteries. Hall believed he had been chosen by God to lead Franklin

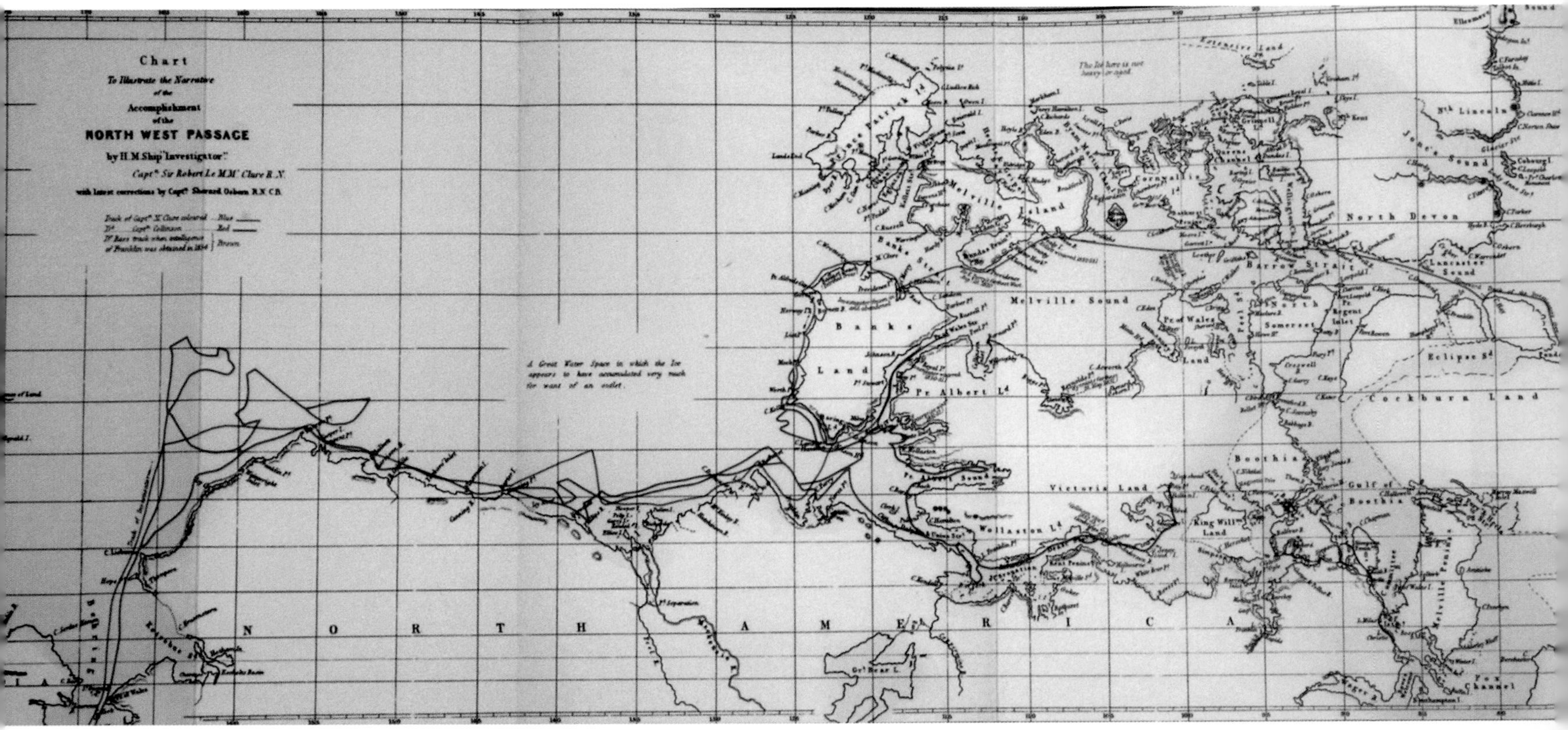

McClure's map of the North-West Passage. His route through the Passage is shown in blue. The red line shows Collinson's voyage.

survivors who had sought refuge with the Inuit back to civilisation. Hall actually murdered one travelling companion who he thought was inciting mutiny, so intent was he on his crusade and so deep was his paranoia that mankind was seeking to stop him. Yet Hall's notes of his interviews with the many Inuit he met form the basis of a coherent story that gives a good impression of what actually happened to Franklin's men. Hall also retrieved the skeleton of one of them, and took it back to the United States; the skeleton, believed to be that of Henry Le Vesconte, an officer on the *Erebus*, was eventually taken to Britain and buried at Greenwich. Another skeleton, believed to be that of John Irving, an officer on the *Terror*, was also repatriated, being buried in Edinburgh.

The search for Franklin helped fill in almost all the gaps in the map of Canada's southern Arctic islands. The numerous expeditions also gathered such evidence as existed on the fate of Franklin and his men. In 1850 Richard Collinson was given command of an expedition of two ships, Collinson himself commanding the *Enterprise*, with Robert McClure commanding the *Investigator*. The pair sailed to the Bering Strait to search eastwards. Probably by design, the ambitious McClure found himself ahead of his commander, and instead of waiting headed east. He reached the mouth of the Mackenzie River and sailed eastward towards the Coppermine. There, hearing from local Inuit that they had not seen a ship like his before, he reasoned that Franklin had not followed the mainland coast, and headed north-east. McClure entered a waterway (which he named after the Prince of Wales) between Victoria and Banks islands and, to his growing excitement, realised that he was heading directly for Parry's Barrow Strait

This watercolour was painted by Lt S. Gurney Cresswell, an officer on McClure's Franklin search expedition. Cresswell was in command of the sledge party which he has illustrated setting out from HMS *Investigator*.

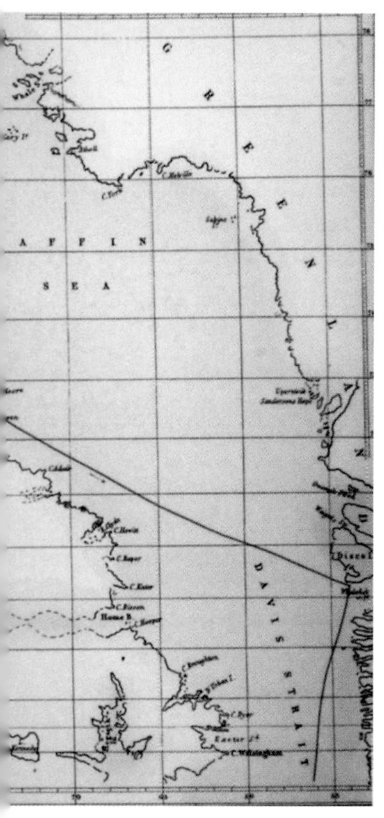

and Winter Harbour. When he was finally stopped by heavy ice McClure was only 50km from Barrow Strait; he sent out a sledge party, which found that Prince of Wales was a strait not a sound; McClure had discovered the North-West Passage, a fact which he promptly marked by building a cairn. *Investigator* spent the winter in the ice of Prince of Wales Strait, then sailed south around Banks Island, McClure intending to reach Barrow Strait by going north along the island's west coast. He rounded the northern tip of Banks, but was forced by heavy ice to overwinter in Mercy Bay, so-called because the finding of such a comfortable harbour seemed an act of providence. But though it offered a safe winter quarters, the bay was a trap which *Investigator* was never to escape.

McClure sledged to Winter Harbour, proving that a passage existed north of Banks Island as well, then waited for the ice to free his ship or for rescue to arrive. When neither happened, and with his crew now dying of scurvy and starvation, he decided that, in the spring of 1853, two parties would set out by sledge, one east towards Port Leopold on the north-eastern tip of Somerset Island where James Ross had left supplies in 1848, the other south-west to (and up) the Mackenzie River. These teams were to comprise the sickest men and carry few supplies. McClure and the fitter men would overwinter again in the hope that *Investigator* would be freed and could sail east to complete the passage. That McClure was intending to send men to their deaths is obvious from the comment of Johann Miertsching, a Moravian missionary who accompanied the ship as interpreter. Miertsching, who was to go with the Mackenzie team noted, 'How many of us will in this way see Europe? The answer is "No One".'

But before McClure could carry out his ridiculous plan a man arrived at the ship, a Lt. Pim of the *Resolute*, one of the ships of Belcher's 'Arctic Squadron', which had sailed west along Lancaster Sound looking for both Franklin and McClure. The *Resolute* had wintered on Dealy Island (off Melville Island), finding a note McClure had left at Winter Harbour giving the position of Mercy Bay. McClure returned with Pim to the *Resolute* where its commander, Henry Kellett, a senior officer, effectively ordered him to abandon his plan and the *Investigator*, and to bring his men to the *Resolute*. In doing so McClure's crew completed a transit of the passage from west to east, but in two ships and by sledge between them. Back in Britain, McClure received a knighthood and claimed – and was given – the government reward for discovering the North-West Passage; technically he had actually found two passages, completing both by sledge. McClure declined to share the reward with Kellett on the grounds that he had ordered the abandonment of the *Investigator* which, McClure complained, could have been freed and so completed the journey. Kellett, presumably amazed and appalled, gave money for the relief of McClure's still sick crew, who also got nothing from McClure, receiving only the Arctic pay that was due to them.

Trailing his second-in-command, Collinson in the *Enterprise* unwittingly followed him up Prince of Wales Strait, finding his note on the discovery of the passage, and then up the west coast of Banks Island, though ice prevented him from reaching Mercy Bay. Collinson then sailed south again before turning east. He sailed between Victoria Island and the mainland, overwintering in Cambridge Bay. Had it not been for his timidity it is possible that Collinson would have reached Victoria Strait and perhaps discovered the remains of Franklin's expedition, perhaps even sailing north to reach Lancaster Sound. But Collinson did not push too hard into doubtful country, so much so that one of his officers noted, 'Poor Sir John. God help you – you'll get none from us.' However, sledge parties from the *Enterprise* explored the east coast of Victoria Island, proving that there was another North-West

In the past Bellot Strait was very rarely traversed except by ice-breaker, though the predicted decrease in sea ice coverage and thickness will allow easier future access. This photograph was taken during a west–east transit. To the right is the northern end of the Boothia Peninsula. Ahead is Zenith Point, the actual northern extremity of the North American continent.

Passage to the south of McClure's. Collinson then returned to Britain. Interestingly, during this sledge journey along the Victoria coast Collinson's men found a cairn erected by John Rae and, beyond it, three further cairns. Exactly who built these has never been satisfactorily explained, but Collinson chose to ignore them. They also found a piece of washed-up doorframe, which almost certainly came from one of Franklin's ships. Again the find was ignored. It is true that his expedition's only interpreter was with McClure and so he could not properly question the local Inuit, who may well have had information on the fate of Franklin (they actually drew a picture of a ship trapped in ice, but Collinson did not realise the significance of it). Collinson did attempt to sledge across the ice of Victoria Strait to King William Island – had he succeeded he would probably have discovered the bodies of some of Franklin's crew – but did not complete the journey. Collinson's journey to Cambridge Bay was a masterpiece of navigation in such a large ship, but his decision not to follow up clues relating to the main objective of his trip delayed the discovery of the fate of Franklin for several years.

The *Resolute* and the White House desk

In a curious sequel to Belcher's decision to abandon his ships, in 1855 an American whaler discovered the *Resolute* in Davis Strait the ship having drifted undamaged 1,600km eastwards through the Parry Channel. It is claimed that, when they boarded, the Americans found full wine glasses still on the mess room table, though as successive freezing and thawing had destroyed, or at least badly damaged, everything else that is likely to have been an exaggeration. The ship was towed back to the United States where it was refitted (even pictures and books being carefully restored or replaced) and returned to Britain as a gift to Queen Victoria. It was a fine gesture, but the Admiralty failed to live up to it; in 1880 the *Resolute* was broken up. From her timbers a writing table was made and presented to the American President. The table later languished in the White House basement for many years until it was rescued and used by John F. Kennedy.

Later still the desk achieved notoriety when it was used as an impromptu prop in a meeting between President Bill Clinton and Monica Lewinsky.

The fate of Franklin

The first trace of where Franklin had gone after the whalers had left the expedition team in Baffin Bay was found in 1850 when a whole fleet of ships had gathered at Beechey Island – Beechey is not strictly an island, being attached by a long, narrow causeway to Devon Island – prior to searching from the Arctic's eastern end. The Americans De Haven and Kane from Grinnell's first expedition were there, as were several Royal Navy ships, and John Ross on a private search mission. While many of the commanders were conferring on the island, men from the *Assistance*, a Royal Navy ship commanded by Horatio Austin, who had already found some naval stores and meat cans at Cape Riley on nearby Devon Island, found three graves. They were of William Braine and John Hartnell of the *Erebus*, and John Torrington of the *Terror*. All three had died in early 1846, Torrington the first to die on 1 January. Clearly Franklin had spent the winter of 1845–46 on Beechey Island. But though the discovery was welcomed, it offered no clues as to what had happened to the other 126 men and the two ships.

In Britain Lady Jane Franklin, dismayed at the lack of positive news, continued to finance her own expeditions. One of these, in 1851 in the *Prince Albert*, led by William Kennedy, included Joseph René Bellot, a handsome Frenchman who captured the hearts of every lady in England, not least by offering to work for nothing in such a noble cause. The trip discovered nothing about the fate of Franklin, but did find the narrow strait separating the Boothia Peninsula from Somerset Island. This – Bellot Strait – was sledged, but at its far side the party crossed Peel Sound rather than exploring southwards. On a later expedition Bellot disappeared when a crack opened in an ice floe.

An illustration from Edward Belcher's book, *The Last of the Arctic Voyages*. It is entitled *The Departure of the South-West Division*. The sledge party was one of many sent out by Belcher, none of which found anything of note. Belcher also abandoned five ships, an offence for which he was court-martialled by a furious Admiralty. Though his reputation, both with the public and the Navy, was shredded, Belcher was found not guilty, because he was able to show that his orders were vague enough to allow the interpretation he had chosen to find in them.

The *Resolute*, which rescued McClure and his crew, was part of the 'Arctic Squadron' of five ships commanded by Sir Edward Belcher, which sailed in 1852 to search from Lancaster Sound. Belcher was a tyrannical man, intensely disliked by his junior officers, and with dissension causing his expedition to disintegrate he ordered all the ships that were sealed in ice to be abandoned, transferring all the crews to the one free ship (and two supply ships which had fortuitously arrived). To comply with the order to desert the *Resolute* Kellett, though appalled by the decision, closed up his ship, with his and McClure's men sledging to Beechey Island.

The next news of Franklin's fate came from Dr John Rae, the Hudson's Bay Company surgeon who had earlier filled in the last missing section of the map of mainland North America. Rae was an Orkney islander who rapidly learned that the adoption of Inuit methods made survival much easier than it was for naval officers who insisted on maintaining naval methods in an environment for which they were entirely unsuited. This idea – 'going native' as the British Establishment contemptuously called it – almost certainly added to the venom with which Rae's news was greeted. In 1853, on a second overland journey in search of Franklin (and with a secondary purpose of surveying small sections of unexplored coast – specifically to absolutely confirm that Boothia was a peninsula, as not everyone was convinced by his earlier survey), Rae met Inuit who told him of their meeting with a large group (of perhaps 40) white men, who were dragging a boat along the western shore of King William Island. By signs and pidgeon-Inuit they learned that the white men had abandoned ships crushed in the ice and were looking for Caribou and birds to hunt. Later, the Inuit found the remains of many men closer to the Great Fish River. Some were in a tent, others under an upturned ship's boat and, as Rae reported, 'from the mutilated state of many of the bodies, and the contents of the kettles, it is evident that our wretched countrymen had been driven to the last dread alternative – cannibalism – as a means of sustaining life'.

Rae brought back relics traded from the Inuit. These proved beyond doubt that the men were Franklin's (though given the size of the party they could not really have been anyone else). But these positive finds were all but washed away by the wave of public indignation that followed the publication of Rae's suggestion of cannibalism, particularly as the account was based exclusively on Inuit testimony, as Rae had not himself visited the campsite and seen the kettles. *The Times* thundered that no one could take the testimony seriously as the Inuit 'like all savages are liars'. The author Charles Dickens was equally outraged. Egged on by Jane Franklin, who orchestrated a campaign against Rae and his account, Dickens published articles in *Household Words*, a magazine of his own. Speaking for much of the country he claimed that the story was bound to be false as it was based on the word of 'the savage' and 'we believe every savage to be in his heart covetous, treacherous and cruel'. Dickens went on to hint that it was more likely that the Inuit had murdered Franklin's men, and that if there was indeed human flesh to be found in kettles it was an offering by the Inuit 'to their barbarous, wide-mouthed, goggle-eyed gods'. Having demolished the Inuit testimony to his own satisfaction Dickens went on to note that 'it is in the highest degree improbable that such men, i.e. Franklin's, would, or could, in any extremity of hunger, alleviate the pains of starvation by this horrible means'. In another sneer at the Inuit, Dickens noted that as Franklin's men had no fuel and so could not light fires they could not have practised cannibalism, not being able to cook the meat; the Inuit ate raw meat, but they were savages of course, not civilised Englishmen.

The reaction to Rae's news is a lesson in Victorian values. The belief in the innate superiority of the Briton to any native is manifest (though the reality is that the upper classes in Britain put the working class in much the same category as the 'savages' they so despised). The logical extension of this xenophobia was that the British officer class had nothing to learn from natives and everything to teach them. It was an attitude that had sent men in dress uniforms to the Arctic and would, in a few years, send others equally unprepared to Antarctica.

The controversy hurt Rae immensely. He felt humiliated, a feeling heightened when the government did not honour him with the knighthood they had bestowed on much less deserving individuals, and quibbled over the payment of the reward for finding the fate of Franklin, with Lady Jane Franklin consistently lobbying against him. She chose not to believe his story and pressed for another search expedition. The Admiralty and government were reluctant; too many ships and lives had been lost already, it was now 10 years since Franklin had sailed away, and there were more pressing concerns in the Crimea to deal with. The Admiralty's publication of Rae's story – it was they, not he, that had told *The Times* – was an effort to call a halt to further expeditions. Despite public pressure and Lady Franklin's moral blackmail they stood firm, forcing Lady Franklin to finance the final search herself.

In 1857 Francis McClintock, already a veteran of several search missions and a sledging expert, took command of the *Fox*, a small but highly manoeuvrable ship, and headed north. The *Fox* almost failed to make a search at all, with heavy ice sealing it in. It drifted south for eight months before being released, and did not make Lancaster Sound until July 1858. McClintock found Peel Sound closed by ice, and in desperation went down Prince Regent Inlet in the hope that Bellot Strait was navigable. McClintock pushed through the strait but was unable to exit its western end, and retreated to overwinter close to the eastern end, spending the dark months laying down supply depots for sledge journeys in the spring.

In April 1859 three teams set out. One headed north-west, while McClintock and Lt William Hobson headed south to explore King William Island. McClintock almost reached Starvation Cove on the Adelaide Peninsula before turning north along King William Island's west coast. Along the shore he found remnants of the expedition including an almost intact skeleton. Ahead of him Hobson was finding the only notes ever discovered from the Franklin expedition as well as a boat (pointing north) holding two skeletons and many other items, and a vast pile of supplies at Victory Point. The fate of the Franklin expedition had been discovered, though the manner in which that fate came about was, and still is, a matter of conjecture.

Despite their brevity the notes reveal a great deal. The two ships had left Beechey in summer 1846 and headed south, presumably through Peel Sound, becoming beset off King William Island in September and abandoned two years later. Lt. Gore, who left the first note, was dead, as were 23 others (three on Beechey, 20 later, including Franklin himself). That

H. M. S. hips Erebus and Terror

28 of May 1847 } Wintered in the Ice in **Lat.** 70°5' N **Long.** 98°23' W

Having wintered in 1846–7 at Beechey Island in Lat 74°43'28" N. Long 91°39'15" W. After having ascended Wellington Channel to Lat 77° and returned by the West side of Cornwallis Island.

~~Commander.~~

Sir John Franklin commanding the Expedition.

All well

Whoever finds this paper is requested to forward it to the Secretary of the Admiralty, London, *with a note of the time and place at which it was found:* or, if more convenient, to deliver it for that purpose to the British Consul at the nearest Port.

Quinconque trouvera ce papier est prié d'y marquer le tems et lieu ou il l'aura trouvé, et de le faire parvenir au plutot au Secretaire de l'Amirauté Britannique à Londres.

Cualquiera que hallare este Papel, se le suplica de enviarlo al Secretaric del Almirantazgo, en Londrés, con una nota del tiempo y del lugar en donde so halló.

Een ieder die dit Papier mogt vinden, wordt hiermede versogt, om het zelve, ten spoedigste, te willen zenden aan den Heer Minister van de Marine der Nederlanden in 's Gravenhage, of wel aan den Secretaris den Britsche Admiraliteit, te London, en daar by te voegen eene Nota, inhoudende de tyd en de plaats alwaar dit Papier is gevonden geworden.

Finderen af dette Papiir ombedes, naar Leilighed gives, at sende samme til Admiralitets-Secretairen i London, ellér nærmeste Embedsmand i Danmark, Norge, eller Sverrig. Tiden og Stedet hvor dette er fundet önskes venskabeligt paategnet.

Wer diesen Zettel findet, wird hierdurch ersucht denselben an den Secretair des Admiralitets in London einzusenden, mit gefälliger Angabe an welchen Ort und zu welcher Zeit er gefunden worden ist.

Party consisting of 2 Officers and 6 Men left the Ships on Monday 24th May 1847

Gm. Gore Lieut.

Chas. F. Des Voeux [illegible]

25th April 1848. HMShips Terror and Erebus were deserted on the 22nd April. 5 leagues NNW of this having been beset since 12th Sept 1846. The officers & crews consisting of 105 souls – under the command of Captain F. R. M. Crozier landed here – in Lat 69°37'42" Long 98°41' This paper was found by Lt. Irving under the cairn supposed to have been built by Sir James Ross in 1831 – 4 miles to the Northward – where it had been deposited by the late Commander Gore in June 1847. Sir James Ross' pillar has not however been found and the paper has been transferred to this position which is that in which Sir J. Ross' pillar was erected – Sir John Franklin died on the 11th June 1847 and the total loss by deaths in the Expedition has been to this date 9 officers & 15 men.

F. R. M. Crozier Captain & Senior Offr.

James Fitzjames Captain HMS Erebus

and start on tomorrow 26th for Back's Fish River

A message from beyond the grave

The 'McClintock note' is actually two notes, written one year apart, on an official form that requested, in six languages, its return to the Admiralty or the local British Consul. The first note, signed by Lt. Graham Gore and Charles Frederick Des Voeux, Mate was written in May 1847. It reads:

HMS Ships Erebus and Terror 28 May 1847 wintered in the ice in Lat 70°05'N, Long 98°23'W. Having wintered in 1846–7 at Beechey Island in Lat 74°43'28"N Long 91 39'15"W after having ascended Wellington Channel to Lat 77° and returned by the west side of Cornwallis Island. Sir John Franklin commanding the Expedition. All well. Party consisting of 2 officers and 6 men left ship on Monday 24th May 1847.

The date of the wintering on Beechey is wrong – it was 1845–46 – but the remarkable information is that Franklin had sailed around Cornwallis Island, finding open water in Wellington Channel but presumably being stopped by ice at about 77°N. What was the condition of the ice in the Parry Channel? Could he have sailed west from Cornwallis and gone beyond Melville and Banks islands towards Alaska?

The second note reads:

[25th April 1]848 HM Ships Terror and Erebus were deserted on the 22nd April 5 leagues NNW of this [hav]ing been beset since 12th Sept 1846. The officers and crews consisting of 105 souls under the command [of Cap]tain FRM Crozier landed here – in Lat 69°37'42" Long 98°41' [This] paper was found by Lt Irving under the cairn supposed to have been built by Sir James Ross in 1831 – where it had been deposited (4 miles to the northward) – by the late commander Gore in June 1847. Sir James Ross' pillar has not however been found and the paper has been transferred to this position which is that in which Sir J Ross pillar was erected – Sir John Franklin died on the 11th June 1847 and the total loss by deaths to this date 9 officers and 15 men.

This note was signed by *James Fitzjames, Captain HMS Erebus*. It was also signed *FRM Crozier, Captain and Senior Officer*, Crozier adding a postscript *'and start on tomorrow, 26th, for Backs Fish River'*.

is a much higher death rate than on any previous expedition. A later discovery of the likely grave of Lt. Irving at Victory Point suggests that if he was the man who went to Ross' cairn he was fit enough to have survived for some time after the suggested journey south towards the Great Fish (Back's) River.

The conventional scenario established within 30–40 years of the expedition is that with *Erebus* and *Terror* entombed in ice, and food and fuel running low, the men abandoned the ships and started south, intending to use boats to follow the Great Fish (Back) River to a Hudson's Bay Company outpost. Then, overcome by hunger and (perhaps) scurvy they died one by one, the last groups dying at Starvation Cove, on the Adelaide Peninsula, and Montreal Island in Chantry Inlet. This story is now challenged, in part by analysis carried out on bones from King William Island and autopsies on the three corpses (almost perfectly preserved by the permafrost) at Beechey Island in 1984, and also by close examination of Inuit testimony gathered by Charles Francis Hall. The bone analysis shows high levels of lead as well as distinct signs of scurvy. High lead levels are also present in the Beechey corpses, though their deaths were from natural causes.

The finding of significant levels of lead has led Owen Beattie, the leader of the teams that carried out the analyses, to suggest that lead poisoning from the solder used to seal the food tins carried by the expedition was a factor in the deaths of the crew. Canning was a new technique in the 1840s and the poisonous potential of lead was not understood. Another suggestion is that the food within the cans was itself contaminated because of poor hygiene at Goldner's canning factory; one writer has even suggested botulism as a cause of death. Certainly the death rate was very high and the preponderance of officer deaths also suggests a can-based mechanism; as a rule officers ate better than crew, and the canned food might have been considered superior fare. Roald Amundsen also related a story told to him by Inuit he met at Gjøahaven during his journey through the passage, which maintained that Inuit retrieving cans of food from the Franklin trip died after eating the contents. However, hundreds of empty cans were left on Beechey Island, more than could have been consumed in a single winter: the toxin produced by the bacteria that causes botulism is staggeringly toxic, and the cans were large and would have fed many men at once. If the cans were really infected with botulism then hundreds of cans could not possibly have been opened as the expedition would have been swiftly wiped out.

An alternative scenario, one supported by Inuit stories and now gaining credibility, suggests that with men dying, perhaps from a combination of lead poisoning, contaminated food (but not botulism) and scurvy, Crozier (in command after Franklin's death) decided to abandon the ships. He brought as much as possible ashore, then set out south. At first his crew managed to shoot a lot of game (after the Franklin expedition the Inuit abandoned King William Island because its animal life had been exterminated), but eventually the food ran out. One group of men now tried to regain the ships, some dying along the way – this scenario would explain why the boat found by Hobson was pointing north not south – while others continued south, driven eventually to cannibalism. One ship appears to have broken free of the ice and was probably sailed to Kirkwall Island off Adelaide Peninsula's western coast, where it was beset again. This ship sank when Inuit cut into it to plunder its contents and let in the sea.

This account seems much more plausible. But there are certainly some mysteries in the Franklin story; why did Crozier go south when Fury Beach, where there were still supplies, was closer? Why were so many luxury items hauled by a sick, starving crew? Who was the giant with long teeth the Inuit claimed to have found on the ship near Kirkwall Island? And why did the survivors, if they were heading for the Great Fish River, choose to cross Simpson Strait at its widest point rather than at its narrowest? The latter offers the intriguing possibility that the very last survivors may have been heading for Repulse Bay, and there are tantalising Inuit tales of white men surviving for many years, and even that some almost made it to Hudson's Bay Company forts.

When McClintock returned, Lady Jane Franklin used her formidable powers of persuasion on his behalf, using him as a

Right
A stormy day on Beechey Island. In the foreground are the ruins of Northumberland House, a timber-built depot erected during the Belcher expedition. Belcher was also responsible for the monument to Franklin which can be seen above and right of the ruin. The monument also once served as a Post Office. It now has a plaque to Bellot and other inscriptions.

final weapon against Rae. She lobbied for McClintock to receive a knighthood, which he did, and for his name to be placed on her husband's memorial in London's Westminster Abbey, which it was. She also ensured that the Abbey memorial, and another in Waterloo Place, London, bore inscriptions stating that Sir John Franklin was the discoverer of the North-West Passage. If the discovery requires only the identification of a waterway then it was John Rae who made that discovery in 1846, though if a Franklin ship really was sailed to Kirkwall Island then his expedition may have found a waterway, even if they did not realise it. McClure's discovery of the northern passage post-dated both. But if the requirement is to have completed a navigable route rather than merely identifying it, then Norwegian Roald Amundsen wins the race.

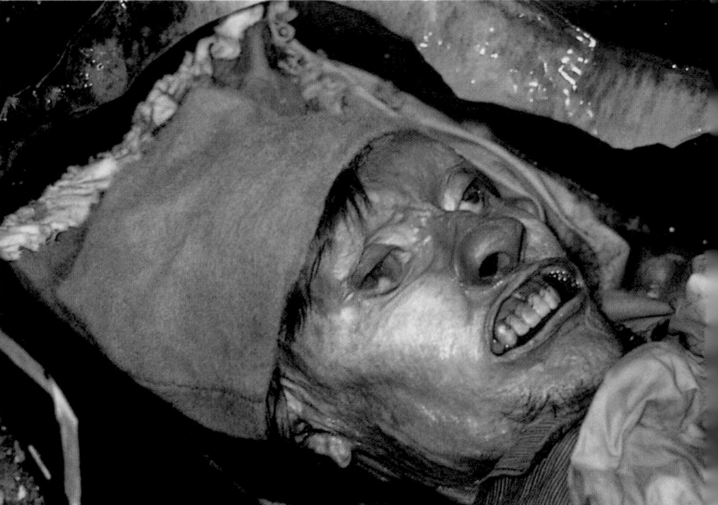

The corpses of John Torrington (*right*) and John Hartnell (*far right below*) almost perfectly preserved in the permafrost of Beechey Island. The autopsies carried out on the Beechey bodies have offered new ideas on the fate of Franklin's expedition. One theory involves lead from the solder used to seal the cans of preserved food used on the expedition. The photograph (*far right above*) shows Goldner cans on Beechey Island.

Amundsen and the completion of the passage

After the disastrous loss of the Franklin expedition and the costly and exhausting searches, the British gave up the idea of a North-West Passage; it was clearly of no commercial value, the need to keep naval officers and ships occupied had slackened, and given a choice between national honour and the national exchequer pragmatism won. Not until 1902 did an expedition return to the Canadian Arctic, when Otto Sverdrup sailed in the second *Fram* expedition. A few years later the North-West Passage was finally completed by ship, under the leadership of Roald Amundsen, a man who had long cherished the idea of making the first transit.

Amundsen had learned well from the early accounts of the British in the Arctic. He realised that safety lay in small ships that were highly manoeuvrable and had shallow drafts; that it lay in fewer, not more, men as the land could only support a limited number; and that it lay in adopting Inuit methods of dress. In 1901 he bought *Gjøa* (pronounced *you-ah*), a tiny (47-tonne) fishing boat. The ship was refitted, with the hull sheathed against ice and a small engine installed. At midnight on 16 June 1903, Amundsen and his crew of six (including Adolf Lindström, who had been with Sverdrup on *Fram*'s second voyage and Helmer Hanssen, who would later accompany Amundsen to the South Pole) took *Gjøa* out of Oslo Fjord. On 25 July Amundsen stopped at Nuuk in west Greenland to add 10 dogs to those he had. In Greenland Amundsen met the Danes Rasmussen and Mylius-Erichsen, men whose names are prominent in the history of Greenland exploration.

Leaving Greenland, *Gjøa* made good progress, going through Lancaster Sound to reach Beechey Island on 22 August. Faced with a choice of routes, Amundsen headed south-west, then south through Peel Strait. This choice, rather than west towards Banks Island, was probably due to Amundsen's wish to reach the North Magnetic Pole (or at least to study magnetic variations close to it), as he had been concerned that without some scientific purpose his trip would be dismissed as a mere adventure. Making amazing progress through open water, *Gjøa* reached the entrance to Sir James Ross Strait (between the Boothia Peninsula and King William Island) on 30 August.

Amundsen soon found – as Franklin had, perhaps, already found – that Sir James Ross Strait was shallow and shoal-filled. *Gjøa*, despite her limited draft, ran aground early on 31 August, damaging her keel. After getting the ship afloat again, another near-disaster occurred when fire broke out in the engine room and threatened to engulf the fuel tanks. The fire was put out quickly, but Amundsen was left in no doubt about the 'inevitable sequel' had the fuel ignited. Soon after, *Gjøa* grounded again, this time much more seriously as it happened at high tide. The next high tide failed to refloat the ship, which was then battered by a storm that threatened to haul her along the reef on which she was stuck, tearing her bottom out. Amundsen decided to abandon ship, but Anton Lund, ship's mate, suggested jettisoning cargo to reduce the draft. This worked and the ship floated free – *Gjøa* and the expedition were saved.

Continuing south, *Gjøa* rounded the southern tip of King William Island. Amundsen could see that Simpson Strait was ice-free, but it was now mid-September and he preferred to overwinter in a natural harbour where the ship would be protected and could be anchored just metres from shore. There was, too, the need to stay close to the North Magnetic Pole – the passage could wait a little. The chosen anchorage was named Gjøahavn; it is now Gjøahaven, a Canadian Historic Park.

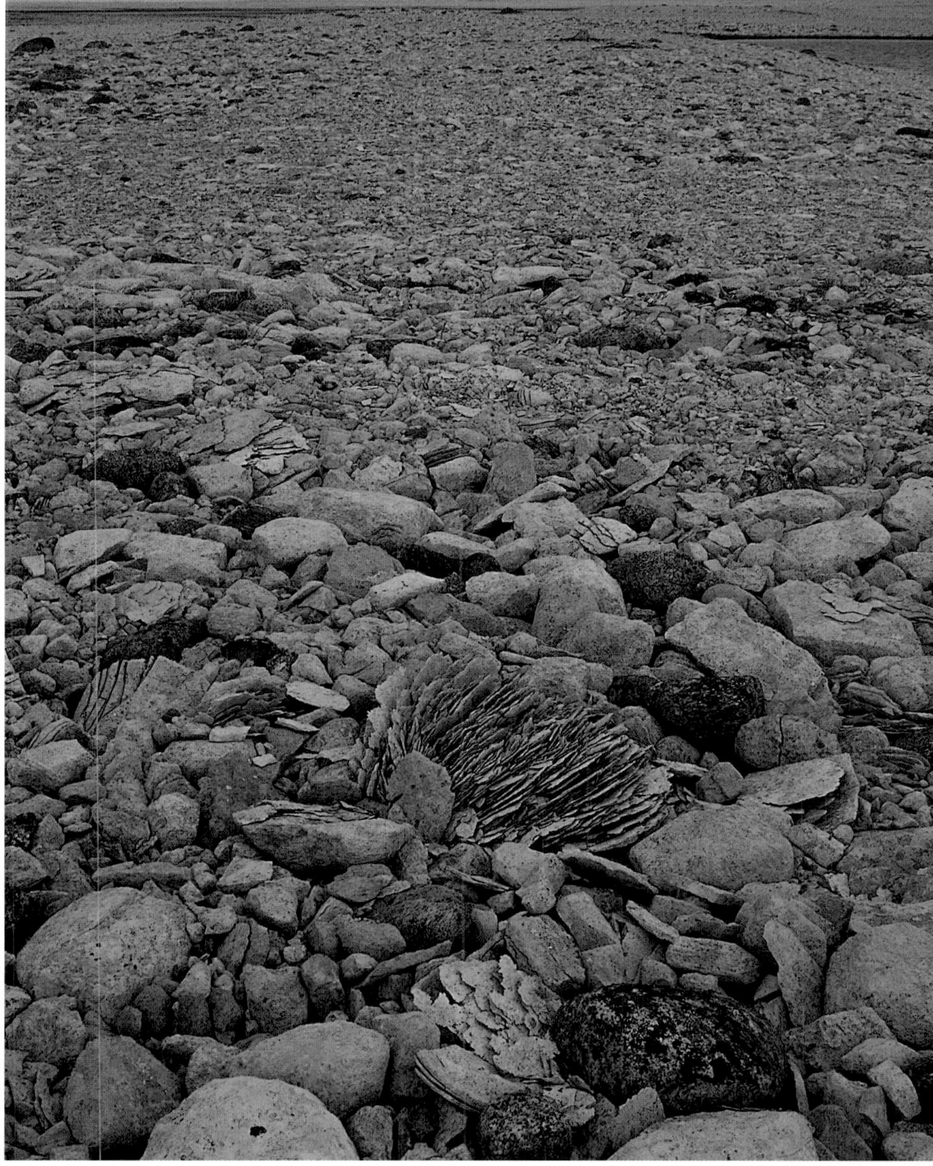

King William Island. It is probable that Franklin's expedition landed on the northern coast of this frost-shattered and lifeless island and faced a bleak, and ultimately tragic, trek south.

At Gjøahavn the crew were visited by the local Inuit, and Amundsen learned all he could from them, on dog-driving, sledging (particularly how to coat sledge runners with ice so they slid more easily), clothing, igloo-building, and survival techniques, lessons that proved invaluable later in Antarctica. On 1 March he set out on a sledge journey to find the North Magnetic Pole, but it was too cold for both men and dogs. Forced to retreat, the men had to help haul the sledges. From this Amundsen learned that man-hauling was 'futile toil' (a lesson that the Royal Navy had failed to learn despite dozens of lessons). Amundsen had started out too early; he made the same mistake in Antarctica, a mistake that almost cost him the South Pole.

When Amundsen set out again he took just one companion, Peder Ristvedt. The two reached Sir James Clark Ross' cairn and found that the magnetic pole had moved, the first proof that it migrated. The two men circled the area, but though in his book on the passage journey Amundsen claims to have passed over the 'new' pole, he did not actually approach closer than 50km of the new site. It is not clear why Amundsen did not reach the pole, and the miss rankled with him for the rest of his life.

Above left
The *Gjøa* frozen in at Gjøahavn.

Above right
The crew of the *Gjøa*. Amundsen is in the centre, with Helmer Hansen at top right.

Both the above illustrations are from Amundsen's book on the transit of the Passage.

Below right
The *Gjøa* today. It is now out of the water, outside the Fram Museum at Bygdøy across the water from Oslo.

The sledging took most of the summer; winter came early and the expedition stayed at Gjøahavn. The next summer Ristvedt and Helmer Hanssen explored the east coast of Victoria Island by sledge. Then, on 13 August 1905 *Gjøa* left its harbour and became the first ship to navigate Simpson Strait. After four days the ship had reached Collinson's most easterly point; a North-West Passage had now been fully explored. On 26 August *Gjøa* met the US whaler *Charles Hansson* off Nelson Head, the southernmost point of Banks Island. Further east, at King Point near Herschel Island (west of the mouth of the Mackenzie River), ice stopped *Gjøa*, forcing the crew to overwinter for a third time. In October, using dog-sledges Amundsen, two Inuit and William Moys, captain of a shipwrecked US whaler, travelled south to Eagle City, where Amundsen formally announced his completion of the passage. Technically, of course, that was not completed until 1906 when, with Amundsen back on board but one crewman, Gustav Wiik, having died, *Gjøa* was sailed around Point Barrow and through the Bering Straits. The ship reached San Francisco on 19 October 1906 where it stayed until 1972; it was then returned to Norway to stand close to *Fram* on Oslo's Bygdøy museum's site.

Not until 1940 was Amundsen's traverse repeated, and then in the opposite direction, the Canadian Henry Larsen skippering the *St Roch* from west to east, overwintering at Cambridge Bay and Sir James Ross Strait. In 1942 St Roch went through Bellot Strait to reach Lancaster Sound rather than following

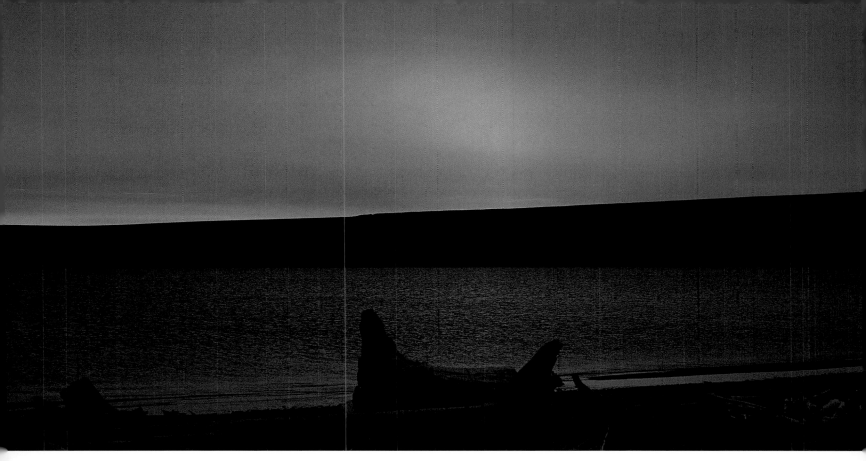

Gjøa's route. In 1944, Larsen took the *St Roch* west again, following the Northern Passage – west from Lancaster Sound, then south-west along the Prince of Wales Strait. The journey was completed in 86 days, *St Roch* becoming the first vessel to complete the passage in both directions, and the first to complete it in one season. In 1962 the USS *Skate* made the first submarine transit, travelling east-west. Then in 1969, the 155,000t US tanker *Manhattan* made the first commercial transit, using the northern route, escorted by the Canadian icebreaker *John A. Macdonald*. Eight years later in 1977, Dutchman Willy de Roos piloted the 13m ketch *Williwaw* east–west, the first singled-handed transit.

In 1984 and 1985 the first commercial passenger transits were made east–west, then west–east. Today there are regular passenger trips and, with the possibility of the Arctic ice reducing due to global warming, there are again whispers that a commercial route might become a reality.

The northern Canadian Arctic islands

In 1880 the British ceded their rights to the islands discovered by its North-West Passage expeditions to Canada. The move formally ended British interest in the route and would also, it was hoped, encourage the recently established Canadian Confederation to take control of the area, which was by then being seen as 'open land' by whalers and explorers. But the young Canada had more pressing problems – expanding and consolidating its confederacy south of the treeline.

In 1902, Otto Sverdrup, captain of the *Fram* on Nansen's expedition, led his own expedition, the second in *Fram*. The expedition was a masterpiece of organisation and execution. During 1898–1902 Sverdrup and his 15-man crew (one of whom was Sverre Hassel, later to go with Amundsen to the South Pole) charted over $250,000km^2$ of the Arctic, using *Fram* and sledges. Ellesmere Island's west coast was explored,

Summer sunrise at 1am on Herschel Island, where Amundsen landed to break the news of his successful North-West Passage transit.

In the 19th century German expeditions completed the mapping of Baffin Island. Two men who died were buried at a site overlooking Pond Inlet and Bylot Island. The site was carefully laid out: the men were a long way from home, but it is no bad place to spend eternity.

Memorial cross on the Fosheim Peninsula, Ellesmere Island. The cross is obviously ancient but exactly who or what does it commemorate? The obvious choice would be the Sverdrup expedition on which two men died. But both were supposed to have been buried at sea. However, scurvy grass is growing at the base of the cairn and after Sverdrup's expedition teams would have used more advanced anti-scorbutants. Seeds of the plant could have fallen from the clothing of a man making the cairn or erecting the cross – or have been in the clothing of someone beneath the cairn. The site remains a mystery. Behind the cross is ice-bound Slidr Fjord leading to Eureka Sound, across which is Axel Heiberg Island.

and Axel Heiberg and the Ringnes islands were discovered. The 'new' lands were named after the expedition's sponsors (Heiberg was a Norwegian consul, while the Ringnes brothers owned an Oslo brewery) and claimed for Norway. This claim eventually awakened concerns in Canada over the ownership of all the Arctic islands off the mainland. With the United States making noises that suggested it might dispute ownership with both Canada and Norway, and disturbing news from Herschel Island that whalers were 'debauching' the local Inuit, Canada eventually claimed all lands north to the pole, and compensated Sverdrup for taking possession of his charts as a means of substantiating the claim. The amount owed was argued over and eventually settled at $67,000, which was duly paid on 11 November 1930. Sverdrup died on 26 November aged 76. He had worked until he was 72, when the Norwegian government belatedly awarded him a pension; he was grateful for the Canadian cash as it offered his family security.

The *Karluk* disaster

In 1904 the Canadian government bought the *Gauss* (which had taken Drygalski's German expedition to Antarctica), renamed it *Arctic* and placed it under the command of the Quebecois Joseph-Elzéar Bernier. In a series of expeditions from 1904 to 1911, Bernier visited many of the islands of Arctic Canada, retrieving historically important documents left by the British, rebuilding cairns, and adding his own cairns and plaques to reinforce Canadian sovereignty. He also made several attempts to navigate the North-West Passage, but was thwarted each time.

Following Bernier's expeditions, Canada underwrote the Canadian Arctic Expedition of Vilhjalmur Stefansson, which sailed in 1913. The voyage, in the *Karluk*, was an Arctic contemporary of Shackleton's *Endurance* and followed the same pattern – ship is beset in the ice, ship sinks, crew faces difficult journey to land. However, there was to be no joyful ending, the *Karluk* crew's retreat being a harrowing tale of death and misery. Nor was their journey made under the guiding light of a great leader, the tale – largely ignored for decades, but recently revived – adding another chapter to the story of a controversial explorer.

Stefansson was Canadian-born of Icelandic parents. He attracted early attention with his claims that British failure in the Arctic had been the result of a mind-set that it was a hostile, barren wasteland where man could not survive unless he took civilisation with him. In reality, Stefansson claimed, the Arctic was a friendly place, its tundra a vegetation-rich prairie, its sea a wildlife paradise, its abundance able to support any party willing to exploit it. His argument was compelling, but failed to acknowledge that the Inuit rarely travelled in groups of more than ten or so and, despite his description of them as 'fat and healthy', were frequently the victims of hunger. However, his view that Franklin's men had died through ignorance made the valid point (also made by others) that had they split into smaller groups and gone in different directions they might have survived. Stefansson's pseudo-science convinced the Canadian government and the Hudson's Bay Company, who funded the introduction of Reindeer (for herding) to south Baffin. Despite Stefansson's claims of an 'Arctic prairie', the project failed.

Stefansson had some training as an ethnologist and, based on the flimsiest of evidence, suggested that there was a race of blond Inuit on Victoria Island who were the descendants of settlers from Norse Greenland. The tribe proved to be a myth. Knud Rasmussen savaged Stefansson for his poor ethnography, while Roald Amundsen criticised his claims as an explorer – though some have suggested that Amundsen's criticisms derived as much from self-interest as fact ('why do you need more funding for your expedition, Mr Amundsen? – Mr Stefansson says it is possible to live off the land'). But despite the critics, Stefansson's gift for self-publicity and the apparent plausibility of his arguments to a government willing to be convinced led to his appointment as leader of the Canadian Arctic Expedition. Stefansson's aim was to search for new land in the Beaufort Sea. Some scientists claimed that currents and ice drift rates meant that there must be land there, perhaps even a vast amount, and Stefansson relished the prospect of being its discoverer. He had talked several organisations into funding a search, but when the Canadian government offered to provide more money he immediately switched allegiances.

To captain the *Karluk*, his chosen vessel, Stefansson employed Bob Bartlett, the captain of Peary's North Pole ship and arguably the finest ice captain on the planet. Bartlett had serious reservations about the ship and about the lack of organisation of the expedition, but nevertheless took *Karluk* northwards from British Columbia in June 1913, heading for the Bering Strait, Point Barrow and Herschel Island, the expedition's winter base.

Karluk's limited speed made for a long trip. Stefansson told Bartlett to hug the Alaska/Yukon coast so that the expedition could go ashore and continue by sledge if need be, but as they neared Herschel Bartlett chose to head north, following open water leads which, he hoped, would eventually allow him to travel east again. But by September the ship was stuck in the ice. The ship was carrying a curious band of travellers. There were, as would be expected, scientists and sailors, but there were also Inuit hunters Stefansson had recruited in Alaska, one of whom had brought his wife and two children, girls aged three and eight. On 19 September Stefansson announced that he was heading for the shore to hunt Caribou and would be gone for 10 days. It was a surprising decision as he had already told the party that Caribou were virtually extinct on this section of coast. The team he took – his personal assistant, the expedition photographer (Hubert, later Sir Hubert, Wilkins,

An aerial photograph of Glacierfjorden, Axel Heiberg Island.

the pioneering polar aviator), the ship's anthropologist and two Inuit hunters – looked more suited to finding blond Inuit or new lands than game. Stefansson also took the best dogs. Certainly the men left behind on the ship were not convinced by Stefansson's feeble excuse, one man writing 'They [the team] pass over the first ridge and out of sight. Goodbye Stefansson.' It is difficult to know if this comment was prophetic or ironic.

Soon after Stefansson's departure a violent storm battered the area and pushed the *Karluk* west. Stefansson claimed to have seen the ship, stuck fast in its ice floe, being driven westwards by the wind, and that open water between his team and the ship prevented him from returning to her. It is probable that he did – he can hardly have fortuitously invented the correct story. He then claimed to have headed west to see if *Karluk* had reached shore. What is certain is that he linked up with two ships which had also headed for Herschel carrying other scientists and supplies for the expedition. He reported the situation to Ottawa, noting that the ship might, or might not, sink and that those on board would probably survive. Then he headed north to seek his new continent.

The *Karluk* and its 25 passengers and crew drifted west to the Bering Strait, then on towards Siberia. Bartlett knew that the ship's design meant she would probably be crushed and sink, rather than surviving the ice pressure, and organised his inexperienced team – Alastair Mackay had been the doctor on Shackleton's *Nimrod* expedition to Antarctica (indeed, he had reached the South Magnetic Pole with Douglas Mawson and Edgworth David), and James Murray had also been on *Nimrod*, but the remainder were mostly polar newcomers – to build igloos and transfer supplies onto the ice. He also built sledges for the evacuation he knew would be necessary. On 10 January 1914 the ice pressure that had threatened the ship finally succeeded in rupturing the hull. Bartlett was the last to leave, hoisting the ship's flag and putting Chopin's *Funeral March* on his gramophone. It was still playing when the ship sank.

Bartlett now organised the setting up of supply dumps south along a route to Wrangel Island. He also sent a party of six to try to reach Herald Island, a small island north-east of Wrangel. Two of this team returned, reporting that the other four had reached open water short of the island and were searching for a route to it. Mackay and Murray, together with Henri Beauchat, another anthropologist, and Stanley Morris, a sailor, now decided to strike out on their own. Bartlett tried to dissuade them, but when he failed he gave them the supplies they asked for in exchange for a letter absolving him of responsibility for their future welfare, and wished them well. Several days later a returning supply party told Bartlett that there was no sign of the men sent to Herald Island, or any apparent hope of reaching it, and that Mackay's party had been spotted, utterly exhausted. Bartlett swore them to secrecy so as to avoid alarming the rest of the group; so well did they obey that writing years later, one survivor was still unaware of the conversation.

Finally Bartlett felt ready to leave 'Shipwreck Camp'. Harnessing all of the dogs and man-hauling as well, the survivors moved between supply dumps, at each of which an igloo had been built. The team was eventually stopped by perpendicular ice ridges almost 20m high, stretching away in both directions. Here Bartlett proved a brilliant leader, encouraging his team to carve through the ridges, using the debris they created to fill in the troughs between them, rather than trying to find a way around and, perhaps, failing. Ignoring Herald Island, Bartlett pushed for Wrangel, which was finally reached on 12 March after a gruelling 20-day trek.

But land brought only relative safety. Wrangel was (and is) uninhabited and relatively barren, a home to Walrus and Polar Bear. It was still 320km to the Siberian coast, and with spring fast approaching the sea ice bridge to the mainland would soon be gone, so on 18 March Bartlett and one of the Inuit crossed the island and headed south. Their journey took 45 days through some of the most dangerous ice Bartlett could remember. Finally they reached Siberia and a Chukchi village. With replenished supplies they travelled 650km to the shore of the Bering Strait and found a ship bound for Alaska. On 28 May they landed and raised the alarm.

Back on Wrangel three of the remaining members of the *Karluk* team tried to reach Herald Island and the four-man team that had headed there. Slowed by breaking ice they failed, then in a blizzard on the return route they became lost and were stopped by open water. They used a small ice floe as a raft but it capsized, dumping the three into the water. Sodden and freezing they camped, but the ice broke up again, separating them. One man, Ernest (Charlie) Chafe, frostbitten and exhausted but still with the last of the dogs, tied himself to one and released the rest. He reasoned the loose dogs would find the Wrangel camp and that his would follow them, dragging his stumbling body. He was right and, to his joy, he

Stefansson leaving the *Karluk*. Of his departure, one man left on the ship wrote, 'They pass over the first ridge and out of sight. Goodbye Stefansson.' a highly prophetic comment.

discovered the other two men had also made it. Chafe had six minor operations to stop the spread of gangrene, carried out with a pocket knife; one of the other two had a frostbitten toe amputated with a hacksaw blade.

To comply with Bartlett's instructions, three men walked to Rodger's Harbour on Wrangel's southern shore, Bartlett believing it was the easiest place a relief ship could reach. Two of them died there, possibly from poor diet exacerbated by frostbite and exhaustion. Later, another member of the team, back at the main camp, died of a bullet wound to the head. It is not clear whether the death was murder, suicide or an accident as the man was cleaning a gun.

In Alaska Bartlett hired the *Bear* to rescue his team. On 20 August 1914, five months after he had left, he brought the ship to within 30km of Wrangel, but was stopped by heavy ice. Forced to return to Alaska for more coal he returned in September to discover that a schooner, the *King and Winge*, alerted by a Russian trader he had met in Siberia, had rescued the survivors on 7 September.

Three men had died on Wrangel. Mackay's team of four were never seen again. In September 1924 an American ship intending to claim Herald Island for the USA found a tent and the bodies of four men; the team Bartlett had sent had reached the island after all, and had died there. The survivors included all four members of the Inuit family.

While war raged in Europe nothing was heard of Stefansson and it was assumed that he, too, had died. Then in 1918, after five years out of contact, living off the land as he claimed men could, he returned. He had found the last three islands of Canada's Arctic archipelago – Borden, Brock and Mackenzie – but had not discovered the continent he craved. By then the *Karluk* disaster had faded from the public eye and Stefansson was greeted as a hero. He wrote a book called *The Friendly Arctic* – an ironic title in view of the death toll on his expedition – in which he gave a biased account of the disaster, blaming Bob Bartlett. Bartlett, who along with other members of *Karluk* believed Stefansson had abandoned the ship rather than going hunting, and had already published his own book on the trip, maintained a dignified silence.

In 1921 Stefansson organised an expedition to colonise Wrangel Island, an astonishing decision, but not as astonishing as the decision of one of the *Karluk* survivors, Fred Maurer, to join it: perhaps Maurer was trying to exorcise ghosts. Strangely (or perhaps not), Stefansson did not accompany his team of four men and an Inuk woman; one man died and Maurer and the other two men tried to escape by following Bob Bartlett's route to Siberia; they were never seen again. The Inuk was the lone survivor.

William Laird McKinlay, a 25-year-old Scot, survived the *Karluk* disaster then, after a period in hospital, added the horrors of the Western Front to those of Wrangel Island. McKinley was wounded and discharged in 1917. For decades he brooded over the injustice of Stefansson's claims about Bartlett. Finally, 60 years later, he published his own account because, he said, he wanted 'to destroy the Stefansson myth, for the man was a consummate liar and cheat'. He also wanted people to understand that despite Stefansson's claims it was Bob Bartlett who was the true hero. The latter wish was granted, Bartlett now being seen as a great explorer in the Shackleton mould, but the book was probably too late to secure the former. Stefansson was long dead, his last years spent in honour – though the Canadian government turned down all his subsequent requests for the funding of another expedition.

Below left
William Laird McKinlay using goose down to clean his mug after a meal of blood soup. McKinlay and the other Wrangel survivors lived on a diet of eggs, the roots of the island's sparse vegetation and the occasional seal. But these meagre items were often in very short supply and they endured long periods of near starvation.

Below right
The forbidding cliffs of Herald Island. It is amazing that the four men from the *Karluk* managed to reach the interior of the island, but less surprising that they died there, probably of starvation.

9. Greenland

The first Europeans to encounter the Inuit were Norsemen from Iceland. The Norse reached, and settled, Iceland in about 860, the pioneers apparently fleeing the tyranny of King Harald Finehair, who would go on to unify Norway. But the Iceland they settled was already inhabited, the southern coast being home to Irish monks who had arrived in *curachs* (boats of cowhide stretched over a wooden frame) via the Faeroes, perhaps as early as the middle of the eighth century, and there may have been more permanent Celtic settlement, though this is controversial (the recent discovery that modern Icelanders bear some Celtic genetic sequences was explained away as the influence of Norse slaves from Ireland or Britain, but this could also be the genetic heritage of a small pre-Norse Celtic community). These Irish monks have never been given the credit they deserve and are usually ignored by scholars, with many books on Iceland failing to note their pre-Norse arrival on the island, and other books on Arctic history ignoring such early journeys to the north. The early 6th-century saint Brendan the Voyager is said to have journeyed north of Iceland, meeting a floating crystal column – presumably an iceberg – and seeing a smoking mountain rising from the sea – Beerenberg on Jan Mayen? If he really did see Jan Mayen then not only did he discover it 750 years before Henry Hudson, but he had also travelled at least 500km to the north of Iceland. On another journey north of Iceland a monk reached a place where the sea was frozen and, at midnight in summer, there was enough light 'to pick the lice off one's shirt'. The idea that Irish monks could have made such journeys seems, at first, absurd – why would they risk such perilous journeys when they did not know that there was land in that direction? But such questions ignore the world in which the monks (and, later, the Norse) lived. In Ireland the annual migration of geese would have been observed: to a people utterly in tune with their world these movements would have confirmed that land existed and the direction of it, while an understanding of the capabilities of birds would have given a reasonable idea of how far away land was. More importantly, the monks had a mission to spread God's word, journeys to unknown, pagan lands across the sea being an act of faith.

From Iceland, the Norsemen made journeys both north and west. To the north they discovered Svalbard – 'cold edge'. For political reasons the Norwegians have claimed that this was the Svalbard archipelago, but most experts believe it is much more likely to have been north-east Greenland. To the west of Iceland Norse sailors certainly saw the east coast of Greenland, one ship being blown off route towards the end of the 9th century and seeing a land of mountains. The first landing on Greenland was by Eirik the Red in 982, following his banishment from Iceland for the murder of a neighbour, who had declined to return to Eirik a set of ornamental seat posts he had borrowed. Eirik spent three years in exile in the land to the west, having been unable to return to Norway from where he (and his father) had already been banished for another murder. He returned with tales of a lush, green land. This was actually true; even today, the coastal plain of Greenland is vegetated, and it was likely to have been even more so in Eirik's time, as his trip coincided with the warming of the Arctic climate (which at the same time aided the rise of the Thule people and the decline of the Dorset).

Above

At Brattahlíð the ruins of Eirik the Red's farm can be seen. It is usually claimed to be the first settlement in Greenland, though in recent years that claim has been challenged. There is also a reconstruction of what is believed to have been the first Christian church built in the Nearctic. The church was named after Eirik's wife Þjóðhildur. Legend has it that Þjóðhildur was a devout Christian and that she withdrew Eirik's conjugal rights, stating that they would only be restored when he was baptised. Eirik was a committed pagan and resolutely declined. In time the position became unsatisfactory for both parties and a compromise was reached, Eirik building his wife a church in exchange for a return to the marriage bed. His only stipulation was that the church should be built out of sight of the farm.

On his return to Iceland, Eirik persuaded many Norse to return with him. In 986, 35 ships set out, and although 21 turned back or were wrecked, 14 reached the safety of the fjords near Qaqortoq (later called Julianhåb in Danish, though the name has reverted to the Greenlandic version). More Icelanders arrived in 987, and two settlements were established, Østerbygd, or East Settlement, at Qaqortoq, and Vesterbygd, West Settlement, at Nuuk (formerly Godthåb). The ruins of Eirik's own settlement of Brattahlíð, close to the shore of Tunulliarfik (Eiriksfjord) across from Narsarsuaq, can still be seen. At the height of Norse occupation the East Settlement had 190 farms, the West Settlement about 90, with a combined total of perhaps 4,000 people. The farmers reared cattle, sheep and goats, and following the establishment of Christianity their spiritual well-being was looked after by 16 churches, two monasteries and a cathedral (in the East Settlement).

Journeys to Vinland

In 986 Bjarni Herjolfsson was blown west when he set off to sail from Greenland to Iceland and saw land. Despite the Norse enthusiasm for exploration, it was 15 years before Liefur Eiriksson, son of Eirik the Red and reputedly the man who introduced Christianity to Greenland, set out to find this new land. This was the first of at least three (and perhaps as many as six) voyages to Vinland. The Icelandic sagas suggest that the Norse explored southern Baffin Island, the Labrador coast and Newfoundland (where the ruins of a winter camp at L'Anse aux Meadows are the only indisputable site so far discovered), and perhaps even the Cape Cod area of New England if the vines of Vinland were really vines and not just berries. In the winter of 1002–03, Snorri Thorfinnsson was born in a Vinland winter camp, the first non-native American to be born in the New World.

In Greenland the Norse certainly reached 73°N on the west coast, where three cairns were discovered on the island of Kingigtorssuaq, north of Upernavik. Inside one a stone had been hidden; inscribed with runes, it recorded that the cairns had been built by Erling Sigvatssón, Bjarne Thordssön and

Opposite page

The statue of Leifur Eiriksson outside the Hallgrimskirkja, Reykjavik, Iceland.

The rune stone discovered in north-west Greenland.

Erinride Oddssön on the Saturday before Rogation Day. As this is in April it is likely that the three men had overwintered near the site. The rest of the inscription is illegible, so the exact year is unknown (even the approximate age is debated, with experts able only to say some time in the late 13th or early 14th century). In addition to the cairns there have been finds of Norse origin at sites on Baffin and Ellesmere islands, though some of these are more likely to have been taken there by Inuit rather than by Norse sailors. The Norse certainly had contact with native people on Greenland. They called them *skrœllinger*, a word that might derive from *skral*, small or weak, or from Karelia, a district of northern Finland/Russia whose native inhabitants were short, stocky and dark. A small horde of Norse material was found during excavations in 1978 on Skraelling Island, off Ellesmere's east coast. The items seem too haphazard a collection to have been the result of trade, and it is thought they are more likely to have been the result of a Norse shipwreck or, perhaps, from an enforced overwintering when a Norse ship was trapped in the ice. Sadly, the island's name does not have a history stretching back as far as the remains; it dates only from 1898, when Otto Sverdrup visited. Other finds on Ellesmere's west coast seem to reinforce the view that the Norse reached this far north.

If the Norse name *skrœllinger* does indeed derive from Karelia it would be appropriate, as the description of the native people of that area fits the Inuit, and so would have fitted Thule people if the Norse met both them and Dorset folk on Greenland. But, of course, the Norse might not have meant the term to accurately describe the people they met, but merely as a term of abuse, applied to all foreigners they came across.

There was probably trade between the Dorset (and later the Thule) and the Norse settlers – the former wanted iron, the latter ivory. But there was probably conflict too. One Norse account notes that when *skrœllinger* were wounded their wounds turned white and bled little, but that fatal wounds bled copiously. Such information can hardly have been discovered entirely by witnessing accidents, and other Norse writings suggest that Greenlanders attacked both the Norse settlements towards the end of the 14th century, killing several settlers. Again it was likely to have been iron that the attackers sought. Yet despite these attacks it is unlikely that the Greenlanders killed off the Norse even though the dates of the attacks (probably 1360 and 1379) are close to the last known dates that the settlements were occupied; the last Bishop of Greenland died in 1378, while the last recorded ship to have sailed from there left in 1410.

What happened to Greenland's Norse settlers is a mystery, but it is likely that a combination of factors led to their demise. A change to a colder climate probably made farming more difficult and animal husbandry marginal because of the lack of hay for winter fodder. The cold would also have increased local sea ice, making travel to Iceland and Scandinavia more difficult. The Greenlandic Norse also supported a relatively large number of churches and two monastic houses, presumably with tithes. As agriculture failed life became untenable. Probably those who could leave, the far-sighted and the relatively prosperous, went back to Iceland, perhaps even to Scandinavia. Some settlers almost certainly would have stayed – the optimistic and, perhaps, those who waited in vain for a returning ship. Of these there may have been a few who integrated into Inuit society. The majority probably died of starvation. In 1448, Pope Nicholas V asked Icelandic bishops to send priests to Greenland to aid the settlers, though no trip seems to have been made. Then in 1472

The ruins of the Norse church at Hvalsø, close to Qaqortoq in south-west Greenland.

In the mid-19th century the Danish scientist Hinrich Rink travelled to Greenland to study the island's geology. While there he became fascinated by the traditions and folklore of the Greenlanders and collected a host of tales which he eventually published (*Grølandske Folkesagn....* 1859). The book was illustrated with woodcuts by Aron, a Greenlander artist. Of the tales four dealt with the interaction of the native islanders and Viking settlers. The oral tradition of the Inuit, as with other peoples with no written language, is known to be very accurate – Franklin searchers were astonished to be told tales of Frobisher's voyages, stories which proved accurate despite being over 300 years after the event – so the four tales, of trading and co-existence mired by murder and revenge, are likely to be based on truth. One story tells of an Inuit who kills a settler. The settlers retaliate by slaughtering the Inuit village. Only the killer's brother escapes, the settler's chieftain cutting the arm of the killer and waving it at the fleeing brother. Eventually the brother returns, kills the chieftain, cuts off an arm and waves it. One of Arno's woodcuts shows this act of revenge.

or 1473 King Christian I of Denmark sent an expedition to see if the settlers were still alive. The expedition, which included a Portuguese who was interested in discovering a northern route to the Orient, reached east Greenland, where they were attacked by Greenlanders 'in small boats without keels'. The settlements in south-west Greenland were not reached, but by then there would almost certainly have been nobody left to find.

With the departure of the Norse, the western Arctic was forgotten for a century or so, though a trade in prized white Gyrfalcons continued (mainly from Iceland, with white birds from Greenland reaching Iceland during the winter).

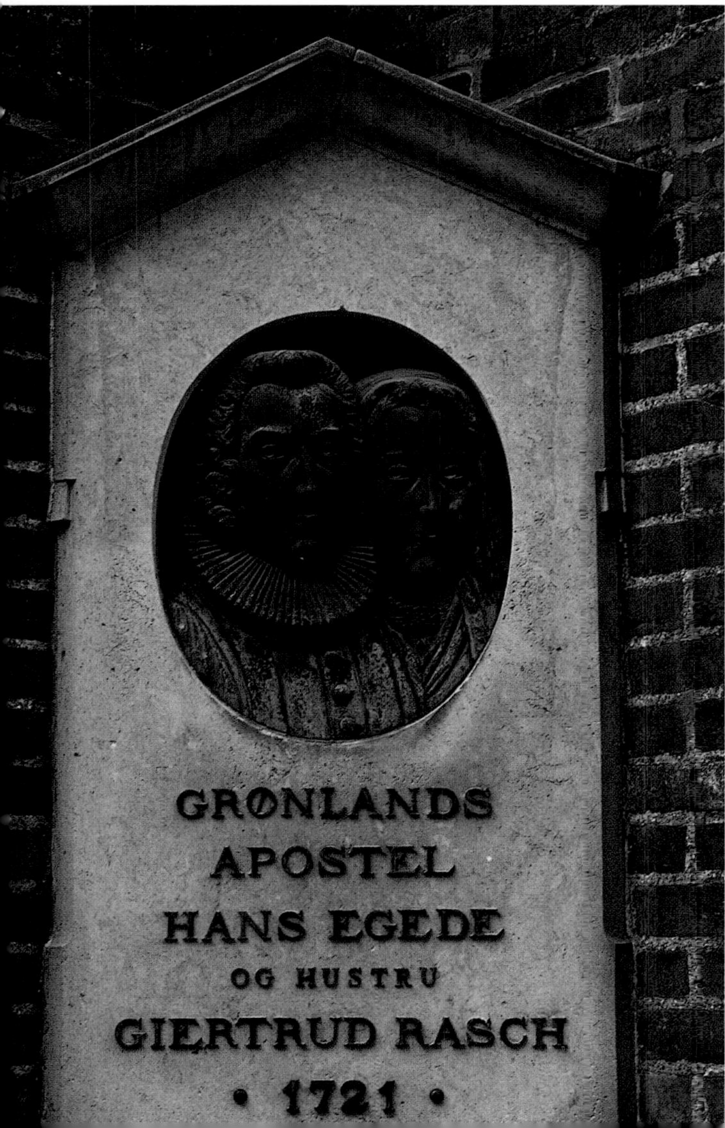

Memorial to Hans Egede and his wife, Giertrud Rasch, who accompanied him to Greenland, in Copenhagen. Revisionist history has been less kind to Egede than was 18th century Denmark.

Rediscovering Greenland

After the failure of the Norse settlements in Greenland there was no contact between Europeans and the Greenland Inuit for more than 50 years. The expedition sponsored by King Christian I of Denmark in 1472 or 1473 made contact with east coast Greenlanders, but it was a hostile one. The Englishman John Davis met Inuit in 1585 during his voyage, and there was spasmodic contact and bartered trade during the 17th century, with several Greenlanders being abducted and taken to Denmark and Norway. None of these sad folk survived for long, succumbing to disease, climate and the hopelessness of their situation. The oral tradition of the Greenland Inuit was such that when Hans Povelsen Egede arrived in 1721 the native people he met could tell him the names of the abductees. Hans Egede was a young pastor from near Bergen, Norway who wished to find the Norse settlements, or to minister to the 'savages' on the island as he believed they might be the living descendants of the original Norse. He petitioned the Danish King (whose territories then included Iceland and Norway, and, he could claim, Greenland) for permission to mount a search expedition. It was a persuasive suggestion, for not only did the Danish Crown have responsibilities to any remaining Norse settlers, however unlikely that might be, but such an expedition would reinforce Denmark's claim to the island.

Egede's search for Norsemen was sadly but inevitably unsuccessful, but he was charmed by the Inuit and stayed for almost 15 years, though his attempt to create a new Danish colony failed. During Egede's stay an Inuit child who had been taken to Copenhagen returned carrying smallpox. Around 25% of the Greenland Inuit population died of the disease, Egede distinguishing himself by his work with the sick and with orphaned children. The pastor also converted the islanders to Christianity. Egede had to change the Lord's Prayer to accommodate the fact that the Greenlanders had no idea what 'bread' was, and so were taught 'Give us this day our daily meat', and in the absence of sheep the 'Lamb of God' was transformed to the 'Seal of God'. Despite these charming touches there was a disturbing undercurrent in Egede's evangelism; an inability to comprehend how the Inuit could be so (relatively) good and peaceful, coupled with an apparent belief that Christian behaviour in a pagan community was itself shameful. Egede called the shamans liars and swindlers, intent only on relieving poor, gullible people of their money, an opinion at odds with the views of other observers. He was no less scathing about the ordinary Greenlander, considering them all to be stupid, appallingly dirty and with an array of disgusting habits. Those who wore amulets despite his directives or who grew tired of his endless Bible stories and threats of eternal damnation he beat across the back with a rope. It seems impossible to justify such behaviour, and later scholars (for instance Nansen) have also questioned the wisdom of Egede's enforced replacement of shamanism with Christianity, and the consequent loss of social cohesion.

Egede had hoped that Greenland would be settled by worthy Christians from Denmark, but the Bergen company that had supported his visit (for potential profit rather than to spread Christianity) lost several ships on the journey to Greenland, and decided they had had enough. Egede's sorrow at this was amplified by the decision of the Danish King to ensure his sovereignty by creating his own settlements –

Above
Scoresbysund, named for the British whaling father and son. The fjord is the longest in the world, and among the most beautiful places in Greenland.

populated not with worthy Danes but with convicts. The convicts, and the 'women of easy virtue' who accompanied them, settled Godthåb (Nuuk), their behaviour in the new settlement being so appalling that Egede had to be protected from the Greenlanders, who held him responsible for the newcomers. Sadly for the women and convicts, but less so for Egede and the development of Greenland, scurvy decimated Godthåb, and subsequent settlers were traders and other, less disreputable persons; a Danish governor was appointed and a group of Moravian missionaries arrived, the combination meaning that the problems of Godthåb were not repeated. Also, Greenland's climate and limited agricultural land meant that it could sustain far fewer people than, say, Australia, so the native Greenlanders were never overwhelmed and marginalised (though the trading nature of the Danish settlers resulted, as is inevitable, in both winners and losers, and for Greenlanders the growth of settlements resulted in poverty and misery), and have maintained a large measure of control over their country to this day.

During his time in Greenland, Egede searched for a mythical channel that was said to link the west and east coasts. Greenland's west coast was always the more accessible of its vast coastlines; it had the larger number of Inuit settlements (the east coast settlements were not only fewer in number, but much poorer than those on the west, with their inhabitants constantly on the verge of starvation) and remained (relatively) ice-free, so that North-West Passage seekers and Franklin-searchers had sailed almost its entire length by the 1860s. The east coast was more forbidding. Whalers who headed north along its deeply indented shore risked confrontation with ice that seemed almost malevolent in its relentless pursuit of their ships. In 1777 a dozen ships were trapped there, then smashed and sunk in turn, their crews transferring to those that remained beset but above water. When the last went down over 300 men died. Later the Scoresbys, father and son, mapped sections of the east coast while carrying out one of the most successful whaling operations. William Scoresby senior explored Scoresby Sound (now Scoresbysund), which he believed, wrongly, was the elusive channel that Egede had

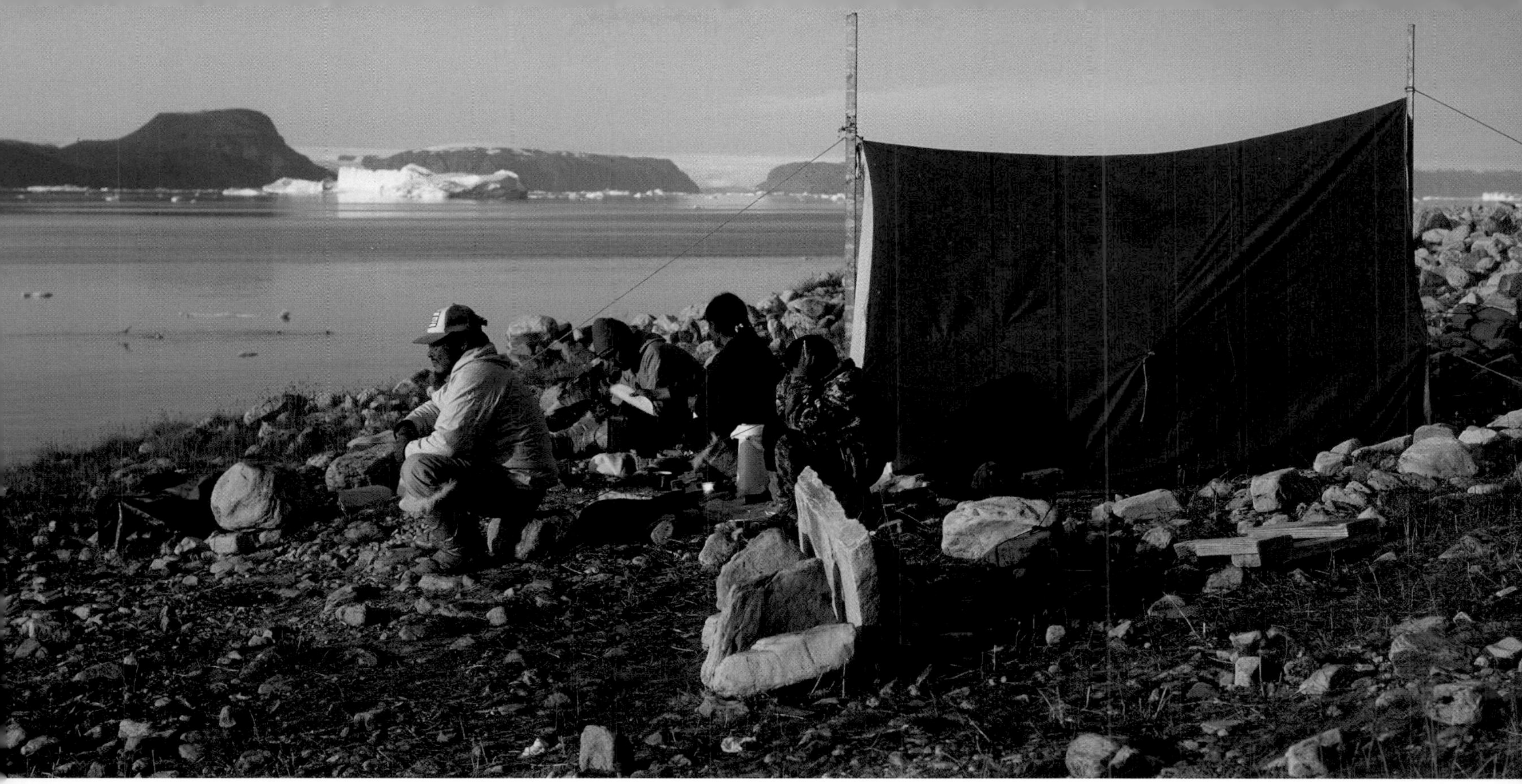

sought, while William junior sailed to 72°N, noting the reduction in ice that led him to call for renewed attempts to find the North-West Passage.

Following the younger Scoresby's voyage, the British naval officers Clavering and Sabine went even further north along the coast, while to the south of Scoresbysund the German Ludwig Giesecke (reputedly the librettist of Mozart's *The Magic Flute*) and Danish naval officer Wilhelm Graah filled in the gaps on the map to Cape Farewell (Kapp Farvel), though it was not until 1883 that two other Danish naval officers, Holm and Garde, discovered Ammassalik, the main Inuit settlement on the east coast. Also active was the German Polar Expedition of 1869–70 under Karl Koldeway and Julius von Payer (later the co-discoverer of Franz Josef Land). The expedition comprised two ships, the steam-driven *Germania* and the sailing ship *Hansa,* and was intended to reach the North Pole. When the pack-ice threatened, the *Germania* steamed away, an apparently misunderstood message not warning her that the *Hansa* was trapped. The *Hansa*'s 14-man crew built a house of coal on the ice as they watched the ship sink, 'groups of feeble rats struggling with death and trembling with cold', and the weather batter their floe almost out of existence. With death seemingly inevitable the crew finally escaped the ice and reached southern Greenland. Meanwhile the *Germania*, all hopes of the North Pole gone, surveyed the east coast.

Nordenskiöld, Peary and Nansen

With surveys of those sections of the Greenlandic coast amenable to exploration by ship completed, attention naturally turned to the vast interior, an icefield covering almost 2,000,000km².

After the early, tentative, steps on the ice sheet, journeys were made by the three giants of late-19th-century polar exploration – Nansen, Nordenskiöld and Peary.

First was Nordenskiöld. In 1870 he made an expedition with a Swedish colleague and two Inuit from a base camp in Auleitsivik Fjord, south of Disco Bay, reaching about 57km inland. He did not return until 1883. By then he was over 50 and his great journeys were behind him. Starting from the same place, his team this time penetrated about 116km. From a camp there the expedition's two Sámi members, Pava Lars Tuorda and Anders Rossa, skied on, returning 2½days later. They claimed to have reached 42°51'W, a distance of 230km, though as they had no means of measuring distances modern opinion favours a turning point at about 46°W (some 100km from Nordenskiöld's camp). The two men reported seeing no exposed land during their whole journey, surprising Nordenskiöld, who believed that Greenland had an ice-free, perhaps even wooded, heart.

The next of the three to visit the ice was Robert Peary. In 1886 Peary was an engineer in the US Navy. That year he requested, and was granted, three months' leave and with the Dane Christian Maigaard (assistant governor of the now-defunct settlement of Ritenbank) set off for the inland ice. He claimed to have pushed 160km inland, though both at the time and subsequently this claim was greeted with some scepticism. Two years after Peary's first expedition, Nansen arrived on Greenland's east coast.

Nansen had dreamed of crossing Greenland by ski since the early 1880s, Peary's 1886 trip giving him the incentive to try immediately. Peary's plan was to return and complete the crossing in 1887, but his navy work took him to Nicaragua where, after a survey expedition, he advocated a canal across that country rather than across Panama; many thought his idea had the greater merit, but Panama was the eventual choice. Peary's absence gave Nansen his chance. His preparations were meticulous. Many of the teams searching for Franklin had used dogs, particularly the Americans Kane and Hall, but Nansen had no experience with them. The Sámi used Reindeer, but they were vegetarian and there might be no vegetation. Nansen therefore decided to use skis and to man-haul his sledges, though he did take a pony.

Until Nansen's journey no one considered man-hauling practical – the sledges were either too heavy, or the runners were too thin and so sank into the snow. But Nansen constructed sledges based on the wide-runner type favoured by

The photographs *above* and *opposite page below* were taken at Qannaq, north-west Greenland. The Greenlanders of this small community remained isolated until the arrival of Ross's expedition in 1818. They still maintain a traditional way of life, the last Greenlanders truly to do so.

Greenland's Inland Ice is the Arctic's largest expanse of freshwater ice. The first steps on it (apart from possible short excursions by the Greenlanders) were made in 1751 when Lars Dalager, a Danish trader, and five Greenlanders penetrated about 15km from near Paamiut (then called Frederikshåb, named in honour of Danish King Frederick IV). Dalager did as well as other early attempts and rather better than the English mountaineer Edward Whymper, conqueror of the Matterhorn, who in two attempts in the 1860s barely got out of sight of the ice edge near Ilulissat (then called Jakobshavn). The upper photograph here shows the Hart glacier running down from the Inland Ice near Thule in north-west Greenland. The lower photograph shows a storm over the Inland Ice on the west coast not far from where Whymper took his tentative steps.

Norwegian farmers. He made the first skis with metal edges, and created sleeping bags and clothing of new designs. He went to Sweden and questioned Nordenskiöld, then the world's foremost polar expert, who was amazed that the Norwegian was planning to ski east-to-west, the opposite way to all previous expeditions. The logical reason for Nansen's choice might have been that Greenland's west coast had more settlements and so it would be easier to reach a satisfactory end point. But that was not Nansen's stated view – he saw a start from the east as a cutting off of the possibility of retreat. It would be, as he later sensationally remarked, 'death or the west coast'.

For his trip Nansen chose five companions, all of them expert skiers; Otto Sverdrup (later captain of the *Fram*), surgeon Olaf Dietrichsen, Kristian Kristiansen Trana, and two Sámi, Ole Nielsen Ravna and Samuel Johannesen Balto. Nansen had arranged for the sealer *Jason* to take the men to Greenland's east coast, but the deal was that their drop-off should not interfere with sealing. So despite sailing from Iceland in mid-May it was not until 17 July that the ship was close enough to the coast – off Sermilik Fjord – for Nansen to feel able to leave her. The team still had 20km to go – the *Jason* did not dare risk the coastal ice – and this soon proved to be a very long way indeed. The scattered pack coalesced and the expedition's two boats were trapped. They were now at the mercy of the drifting ice, with attempts to reach the shore being defeated by violent storms. With pony-feed dwindling and their own rations depleted, the pony soon took its place on the menu. That improved the meals, but not the spirit of the party; all the men feared a possible drift into the Atlantic, with the Sámi, no seafarers, fearing it most. Then a visiting bear so terrified Balto that he swore that if he survived he would never drink again. When questioned about this strange remark he confessed that he had only volunteered for the trip because he had been drunk at the time!

The team finally reached the coast on 29 July, but were by then almost 400km south of Sermilik. Determined to approach, if not to regain, the fjord, Nansen rowed north,

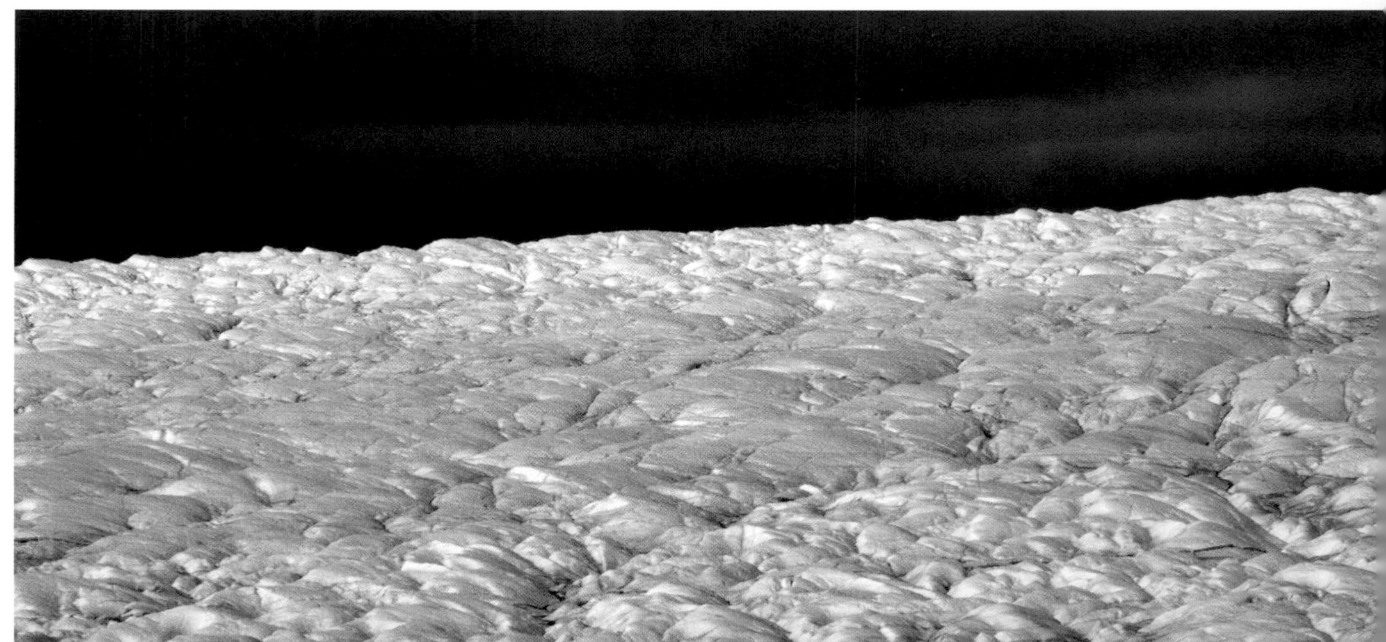

keeping the boats close to the shore. On the journey they met an Inuit group who acted as guides, and by 10 August the team had reached Umivik, an excellent harbour. Nansen decided that, though still 160km short of Sermilik, Umivik would have to do as a start point. For five days the weather kept them in camp, then, on 15 August, after safe-guarding the boats and leaving some supplies (in case 'death or the west coast' proved a questionable slogan – sensation is one thing stupidity quite another) they set off. The steep climb on to the ice sheet was hard going – on the first day they managed just 5km and a climb of 200m, all of it in *finnesko* (Reindeer skin boots) as the gradient was too much for skis. Two more days of hard labour were followed by a storm that kept them pinned in their tents, in which they slept three to a reindeer-skin sleeping bag to share warmth.

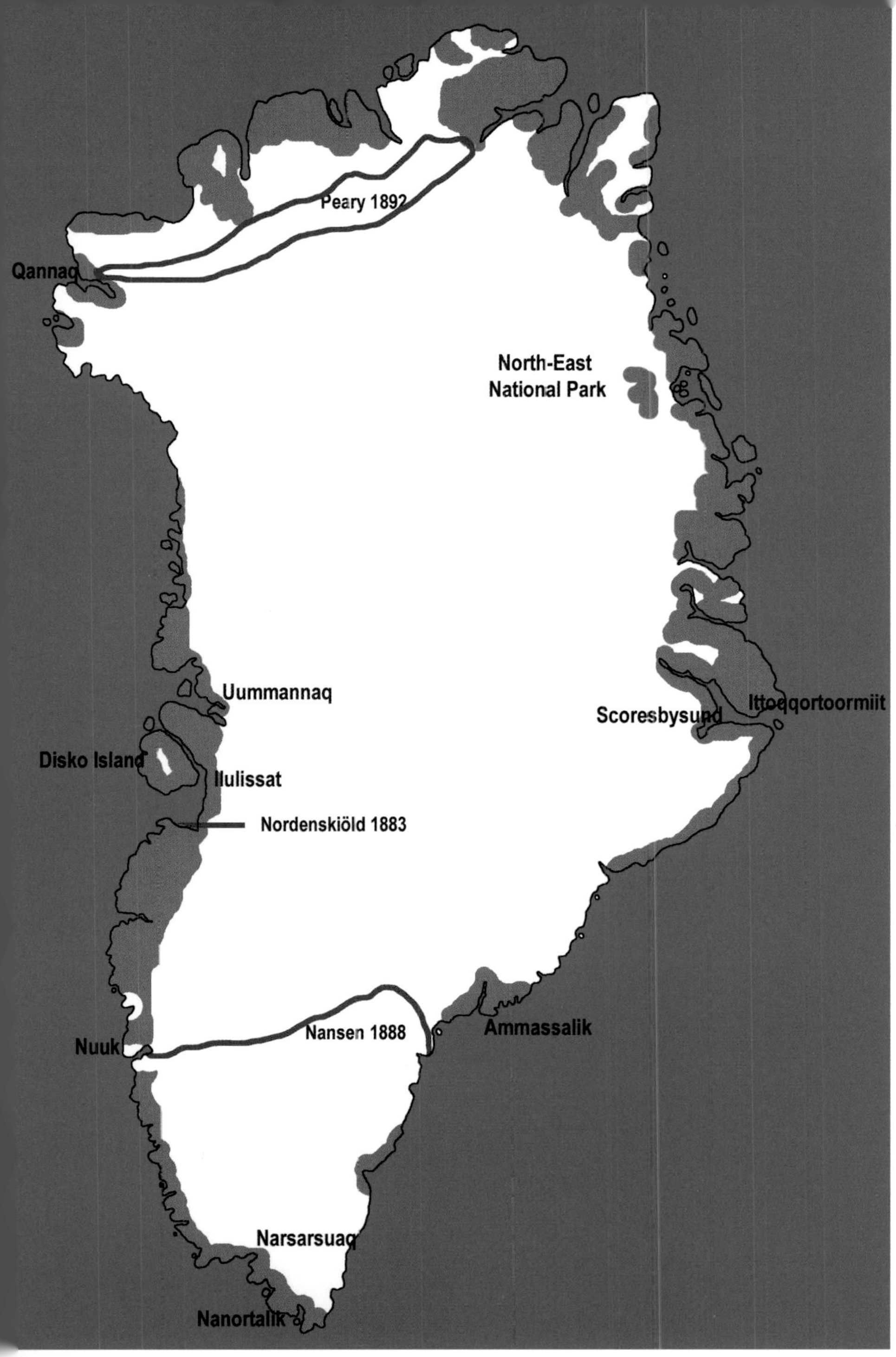

The relentlessly hard climb caused Trana to ask 'How can people wish so much suffering on themselves that they do this?', but still they continued. By 27 August they were more than 2,000m above sea level, but progress was so slow that Nansen was forced to change objectives. He had planned to cross from Sermilik to Qasigiannquit (Christianshåb). The change of start point had been forced by the ice drift, the time lost now forcing a change to the finish point. The team would, he decided, head for Nuuk, which was 150km closer. On 29 August they reached ice which sloped gently upwards and could be crossed in showshoes, but not until 2 September at more than 2,500m above sea level were they finally able to use skis.

Even with skis the effort was considerable, and the men were hungry and thirsty almost every day. They were also skiing across a polar desert, with nothing to break the white monotony; as the first people to do this the psychological burden must have been considerable. The weather was also trying, with temperatures falling to -40°C and occasional gale force winds creating white-outs and forcing snow through every tiny opening in the tents. On the move, the chill factor of the wind was appalling. On 4 September Nansen noticed that his nose hardened and had to be massaged, then that his throat went numb and stiff and he had to wrap 'some mittens and other things' around it. Then, worst of all, 'the wind found its way in through my clothes to the region of my stomach and gave rise to horrid pains'. That

Two drawings from Nordenskiöld's book *Den svenska expeditionen till Grönland 1883.* The one on the left shows Anders Rossa and Pava Tourda, the two Sámi team members, skiing away from the camp. In Scandinavia at the time it was common to use a single, long stick while skiing, but both the Sámi are using double sticks. They are still long, however, and have no baskets at the end to spread the thrust. Nansen's men usually used similar double, long sticks on their journey (see drawings on p178). The drawing to the right shows the preparation of a meal. Given the method of cooking, the transport of fuel was a limitation on how far the team could penetrate the ice sheet.

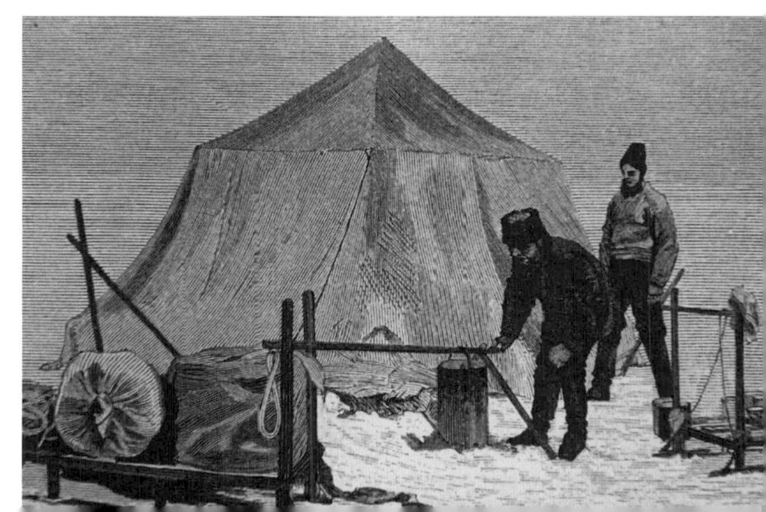

Fridtjof Nansen

One of the greatest of all polar explorers, Nansen was born on 10 October 1861 at Christiania (now Oslo) to middle-aged parents, whose previous marriages had already provided them with six children. He was very bright and a good sportsman, excelling at skiing (where he was brave enough to compete in ski jumping, then an infant and extremely dangerous sport). He spent a season on a sealer in Arctic waters while at university, then took the curatorship of the Zoology Department at Bergen Museum. His zoological research earned him a doctorate: later in his life after his years of exploration were behind him, his work as a statesman with the League of Nations, and specifically for aiding the relief of victims of the Russian famine of 1920, earned him the Nobel Peace Prize in 1922. Nansen was a handsome man, attractive to women, and he was happy to play on this. One of his many lovers was Kathleen Scott, Robert Scott's wife. They had conducted the affair while Scott was returning from the South Pole (and dying in the process).

As a man Nansen was vain and arrogant, and by contrast to his success with women made few male friends. But as a scientist and statesman he was a man of immense accomplishments, and as an Arctic explorer he was a genius, his arrogance being transformed into a single-mindedness that carried all before it. He died on 13 May 1930.

quote is from his book. His diary is more explicit, noting 'p[enis] was in the process of freezing'. He solved the problem by stuffing a felt hat down his trousers.

On 19 September the wind blew from behind (katabatic winds were accelerating as the team dropped off the high inland ice) and the men rigged sails on their sledges. After several unsuccessful attempts, a steering system was developed and the team was soon speeding along. So much ground was being covered – 70km during the day – that Nansen decided to keep going as night fell. This was almost a fatal decision, as a huge crevasse was only spotted at the last second. As the ice dropped sharply Nansen was able to see that below them was a fjord that ran inland from Nuuk. By 24 September they were off the ice, for the first time in 40 days; they had crossed 560km of ice. By 26 September they had almost reached the head of the fjord. The men built a boat, stretching tarpaulin over a scrub-wood frame. In this Nansen and Sverdrup, after a trying time following a river to the fjord, set off for Nuuk. They arrived on 3 October, though it was the 12th before the rest of the team were returned for and brought in.

Though Nansen managed to get mail on to the last ship leaving for Denmark that summer, he and his men spent the winter in Nuuk. When the team returned to Norway an estimated one-third of the population of Oslo was there to greet them and they were feted for ten days. Nansen in particular was greeted as a hero, not only in Norway but all over Europe.

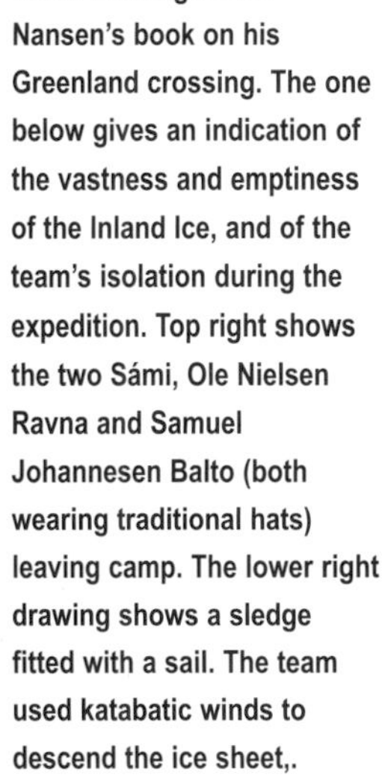

Three drawings from Nansen's book on his Greenland crossing. The one below gives an indication of the vastness and emptiness of the Inland Ice, and of the team's isolation during the expedition. Top right shows the two Sámi, Ole Nielsen Ravna and Samuel Johannesen Balto (both wearing traditional hats) leaving camp. The lower right drawing shows a sledge fitted with a sail. The team used katabatic winds to descend the ice sheet,.

His reputation as a polar traveller was made; the *Fram* expedition would further it and it would never diminish. In that respect, the difference between Nansen and Amundsen, whose polar achievements were greater, deserves a book in itself.

Peary's response

Nansen's crossing was a bitter blow to Peary. A desire for fame had become the focus of his life; Peary believed that his reconnaissance of 1886 had given him proprietorial rights over the ice sheet (much as he later felt about the North Pole), and he therefore resented Nansen's intrusion, which he saw as cheating. But Peary was determined to make his own journey, choosing a part of Greenland that was still unexplored so that his trek would be both dangerous and one of real discovery – an altogether better effort than Nansen's. Peary's team for this trek was a curious one, comprising his wife Jo; Matthew Henson, his valet from Nicaragua; the Norwegian Eivind Astrup, an expert skier; Langdon Gibson, a hunter; the meteorologist John Verhoeff; and Dr Frederick Cook, 'surgeon and ethnologist'. Cook was ten years younger than Peary and had no previous experience of exploration. After the expedition Peary was to note that he felt 'much confidence' in Cook, but later he would fear and despise him as a rival, and loathe him as the attempted usurper of a prize he felt was rightfully (if not, perhaps, actually) his own.

The expedition also included nine fare-paying passengers sent by the Philadelphia Academy of Natural Sciences, who were to conduct experiments while the ship was in Greenland. The team sailed from New York in June 1891 in the *Kite*. On 11 July in the pack-ice of Melville Bay, north-west Greenland, the ship's rudder struck ice; the tiller swung violently and broke the bones of Peary's right leg, just above the ankle. He had Cook to thank for setting the leg expertly so his recovery time was minimised and the leg healed completely; Cook also placated the fee-paying passengers when it looked as if the expedition might be called off.

The team established a winter camp in Red Cliff House, McCormick Bay. There Peary and Cook took the first of the series of photographs, many of which appear in Peary's books. Some images of naked Inuit women would grace the pages of *Playboy*, but most are formal poses, and include men as well. That Peary's interest was not entirely anthropological is supported by his fathering children by an Inuit woman, as did Matthew Henson. Their part-American, part-Inuit descendants still live in north-west Greenland.

On 3 May 1892 the fit-again Peary, with Astrup, Cook and Gibson, each with a four-dog team, set off on the 'white march' on the inland ice. In using dogs, Peary logically extended Nansen's advances in polar equipment, adding Inuit lore – Peary also built snow igloos for camps – to Nansen's Sámi-based ideas. The route to the ice was difficult; Peary's leg was hurting, and once on the ice two dogs died and another escaped. Peary sent Cook and Gibson, with two dogs, back, continuing with Astrup and the remaining dogs (one of which soon died). Both men and dogs ate pemmican (a solid cake of meat and fat), the dogs supplementing this later in the trip when the weakest remaining dog was fed to the rest.

On 5 June Peary and Astrup crossed the high point of the ice (at 1,740m) and sledged on, the days merging in monotonous similarity until finally, on 1 July, they reached ice-free land again. In bright, warm sunshine, Snow Buntings twittered above purple, white and yellow flowers. As well as the buntings there were Musk Oxen, a fortuitous find as Peary's food rations were wholly inadequate; without the meat from the oxen the two men would probably have died.

What Peary believed he saw to the east was the Arctic Ocean running through a channel – Peary Channel – separating Greenland from a neighbouring island. To the south he saw only frozen sea (Astrup was much less sure, but he was in awe of Peary and kept his doubts largely to himself). Seeing land where there was only ocean, and (more rarely) ocean where there was land were mistakes others had and would

The east coast of Greenland, close to where Nansen's team landed. The east coast is more rugged, and consequently more sparsely populated, than the island's west coast.

An illustration from Peary's book *Northward over the Great Ice* about his Greenland journeys of 1886 and the 1890s. Peary quickly learned some good ideas on polar travel. Here he is using the Scandinavian single, long stick for his skiing, but allowing gravity to do the real work in a drawing labelled 'Coasting'.

make, but Peary's mistaken identification of the Peary Channel would have serious implications for future explorers, as we shall see.

After three idyllic days – warm and sunny, with bees buzzing, butterflies flitting between the flowers, delightful birdlife (including a Gyrfalcon) and Musk Ox steaks – the two men set off for the return to Red Cliff House. Taking a more southerly route that rose to 2,440m, they arrived on 6 August. It had been a remarkable journey even if its successful outcome had owed more to good fortune (i.e. finding the Musk Oxen) than did the meticulously planned expedition of Nansen.

In the time they had before the *Kite* sailed, the team explored Inglefield Gulf. Verhoeff and Peary had developed a mutual dislike early in the expedition – one reason why Verhoeff did not go on the Inland Ice. This may have been the reason why Verhoeff decided, after one exploratory trip, that he would prefer to walk back to Red Cliff House than return by boat. The next day, Verhoeff went off on his own again. He was never seen again, and despite searches no trace of him was ever found.

Back in the United States, Peary's journey – he had sledged some 2,200km – was well-received; he even had a congratulatory letter from Nansen signed 'Your Admirer'. Peary lectured extensively, with Matthew Henson bringing the five dogs that had survived the Inland Ice trip on stage at the start of each talk: the dogs lay at Peary's feet as he spoke and, so it is said, stood and howled, in unison and on cue, when he finished. The lecture usually brought the house down. Peary enjoyed the adulation, but knew that he must keep travelling to ensure a constant supply of applause.

In 1893, with the approval of the President (but most definitely not of his over-ruled naval superiors), Peary went north again. Astrup and Henson ('my coloured man' as Peary ungraciously called him) were with him, but Cook was not. Cook had asked permission to publish a short report in a medical journal and had been refused; Peary would tolerate no competition. The refusal annoyed Cook and undoubtedly contributed to his decision not to join the expedition, though he and Peary remained on cordial terms and exchanged several letters.

A new winter hut, Anniversary Lodge, was built at Inglefield Gulf and there, on 12 September 1893, Jo Peary gave birth to a daughter, the Pearys' first child. Apart from the birth the expedition achieved little, an attempt on the inland ice failing in bad weather. Eivind Astrup surveyed Melville Bay while Peary was away on the attempt – a significant survey, much to Peary's great annoyance – and most of the team went home in 1894. Peary, Henson and Hugh Lee stayed on, and in 1895 Peary repeated his sledge journey to the north-east coast. He took a different route, but again survived only because of the Musk Oxen found there. He then journeyed to the three meteorites that were a major source of Inuit iron, taking two back to the United States. The meteorites helped turn an indifferent expedition into an apparent success, in the view of the public. As a consequence Peary's powerful Washington friends persuaded a reluctant navy to allow him to return in 1896 to collect the third, and largest, meteorite. The weather intervened and Peary failed to retrieve it.

In 1897 the navy, exasperated with the trips, posted Peary to the west coast, far away from the Arctic, but Peary's friends again intervened, and against official desires he was granted five years' leave of absence. That year he brought home the largest meteorite and six Inuit. Though the acquisition of both the meteorites and Inuit was seen positively at the time, it is now viewed with suspicion. Peary often spoke of 'my Eskimo' and seems to have occasionally believed that he owned the Inuit around his Greenland bases, just as he later felt that he owned the North Pole. He once asked of the Inuit 'Of what use are they?' and answered himself by suggesting that they existed only to help him discover the pole. Peary felt that taking the meteorites, which had supplied the Inuit with iron for generations, was acceptable, since he now gave them all the iron goods they required. He also apparently felt justified in

Two photographs illustrating Peary's Greenland journeys from pamphlets printed for his sponsors.

Above right
Fort Conger, the destination which cost Peary his toes and, almost, his later career as a polar traveller.

Right
The cairn erected at Cape Morris K. Jesup, the most northerly point of mainland Greenland. It was named by Peary for his main expedition sponsor who was the President of the American Museum of Natural History, when Peary reached the cape in 1900.

Tukemeq Peary, Robert Peary's great grand-daughter, photographed at her village of Querqertat on Inglefield Bredning, north-west Greenland. The man beside her is wearing traditional Polar Bear fur trousers.

surrendering six of their number to the cause of science as he was their 'saviour'. In reality the Inuit did not have the unreserved adoration of Peary that many (including, of course, Peary himself) have claimed. They were impressed by the size of his ships and by his gifts, but much less so by him.

Peary returned to Greenland in 1898 intending both further exploration and an attempt to reach the North Pole. Henson was with him again, but not Astrup who had died in January 1896. Frederick Cook later accused Peary of responsibility for the death, claiming Peary's rage at Astrup over the Melville Bay survey had unhinged the young Norwegian, and that he had committed suicide as a result. Cook extended the argument to include Verhoeff, who he also maintained had committed suicide as a result of Peary's dreadful behaviour. These were shocking accusations, without even the merit of being categorically correct; the true cause of Astrup's death is still unknown, while Verhoeff's death also remains a mystery. The accusations are, however, an indication of the animosity which Cook felt towards Peary, an animosity which, not surprisingly, was reciprocated. The mutual ill-feeling probably goes a long way towards explaining the later behaviour of both men.

Consistently paranoid, Peary was now concerned that Otto Sverdrup, who was at this time exploring northern Canada in the *Fram*, would steal his ideas, just as Nansen had So he decided to push to Adolphus Greely's Fort Conger base on Ellesmere Island with Henson, the Inuk Ahngmalokto, 16 dogs and three sledges in mid-winter, to ensure that Sverdrup could not use it the following spring. Peary and Sverdrup

Minik and the other Peary Inuit

The fate of the six Inuit Peary brought back to the United States sums up neatly Western attitudes to Arctic peoples prevalent at the time. They were displayed as circus freaks, and four died quickly in an unfamiliar New York climate among unfamiliar American illnesses. One of the two young survivors, Minik, an eight-year-old boy, lived on for another 20 years. It was hardly a happy life – as a boy he had not only watched his father and relatives die, but he attended a fake burial for his father (a log had been placed in the coffin to give it weight), eventually discovering that his father's skeleton was being exhibited in a museum glass case. Later he demanded a return to Greenland, accused the Americans of being 'a race of scientific criminals' and said he wished he could shoot Peary. But Minik could not speak the language of his homeland or hunt, and grew increasingly ill. He eventually returned to the United States, where he was finally to gain two years of peace and happiness before dying of bronchial pneumonia (following a bout of influenza). Minik fought hard to take his father's bones back to Greenland. Ironically, after his death the bones, and those of the other three adult Inuit, were returned, but Minik lies in a New Hampshire cemetery.

The story of the six Inuit is an unpleasant tale of racist abuse; Peary's involvement, and his silence regarding it, does him no credit. The same is true of his sale of Inuit corpses to the American Museum of Natural History for study. Peary's technique for the retrieval of the bodies – he simply dug up fresh graves – makes the activity even more sordid.

Northern Greenland. This is a section of the map in Peary's book *The North Pole* showing the Peary Channel which he believed he had seen on his Greenland journeys.

actually met in August 1898 – Sverdrup invited Peary for a coffee, but Peary snootily declined; Henson later claimed that it was this meeting that made Peary decide on the winter trip to Fort Conger, so convinced was he that Sverdrup had designs on the pole. In fact, Sverdrup had no interest in either the pole or Fort Conger, and this hasty decision was to cost Peary his toes. Though his report of the incident to Morris K. Jesup, sponsor of the trip, is laconic and dispassionate ('I found, to my annoyance, that both feet were frosted', 'it was evident I should lose parts or all of several toes', and 'the final amputation was performed'), the reality was horrific. When Peary removed his boots frostbitten skin fell from his toes, leaving bones emerging from festering flesh. Yet Peary, after

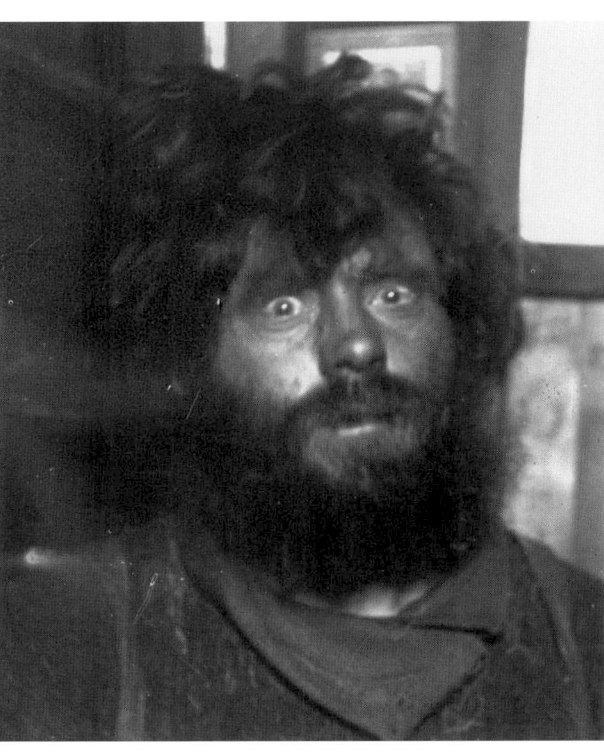

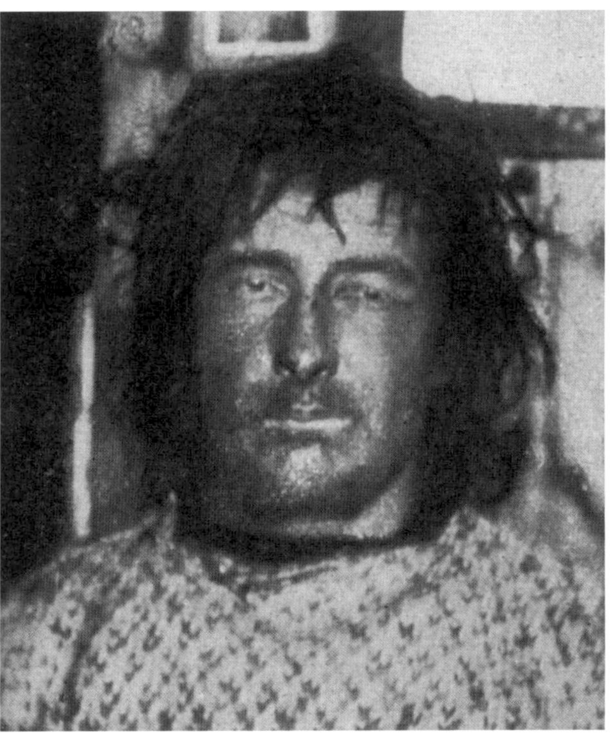

The photograph (*top right*) shows Ejnar Mikkelsen and Iver Iversen before their epic journey. In the lower photographs the wide, staring eyes of Mikkelsen, to the left, and the vacant, expressionless face of Iversen show the extent of their suffering.

losing the toes by 15 March 1899, was back on the ice by 19 April. No matter how dubious his treatment of the Inuit and his team members (particularly of Henson, who undoubtedly saved his life at Conger), Peary could be eye-wideningly brave.

In 1900, after a winter on north-west Greenland, Peary followed Lockwood's route along the north coast (see To the Pole), then pushed on, reaching and naming Cape Morris K. Jesup (mainland Greenland's most northerly point, at 83°39'N). The team continued past Cape Bridgman until their supplies finally ran out at Cape Wyckoff on Clarence Wyckoff Island, off the eastern tip of Peary Land, the island that lay beyond the 'Peary Channel'. This trip was the most significant of all Peary's expeditions on Greenland, though Peary spent two more winters in Greenland. In both 1901 and 1902 he tentatively pushed towards the pole from Ellesmere Island, reaching 84°17'N in April 1902.

The Danes complete the coastal map

Peary's exploration left only the north-eastern coast of Greenland unexplored. A Danish expedition to fill the gap set sail in the *Danmark* in 1906. Led by Ludvig Mylius-Erichsen, the expedition included Alfred Wegener among its number. The Danes established a base at Danmarkshavn at about 75°N.

After overwintering, a series of supply depots was established northwards, including one in a cave near Lambert Land, an area north of Peary's supposed coastline. Eventually two teams set off north. At North-east Foreland (well to the east of Peary's supposed coastline) the teams separated. Mylius-Erichsen, with Höeg Hagen and the Greenlander Jorgen Brönlund, headed west to find the Peary Channel, while Johan Peter Koch, Tobias Gabrielson and Aage Bertelsen headed north to find the cairn Peary had erected at Cape Bridgman. Koch successfully found the cairn and, during the journey, peered into Independence Fjord. On his return he met Mylius-Erichsen, whose team had spent a wearying time exploring Danmark Fjord; Peary's Channel had not been found. Koch was convinced it did not exist at the end of Independence Fjord either, but Mylius-Erichsen felt duty-bound to check. The two teams parted, Koch returning to the ship after 84 days sledging; his team had covered almost 2,000km.

When Mylius-Erichsen had not returned by September search parties went out, but found nothing. After another winter the search was resumed in spring 1908. At the cave on Lambert Land they found the huddled body of Brönlund and a note he had written explaining that Hagen had died on 15 November and Mylius-Erichsen on the 25th, after they had tried to return to the ship over the Inland Ice. In an act of selfless bravery, Brönlund had struggled on, with frostbitten feet, carrying the notes of the trip to a place where he knew his body would be found. His own poignant last message began 'Succumbed at 79 Fjord after attempting return across inland ice in November. I arrived here in fading moonlight and could go no further because of frost-bitten feet and the dark ...' The three had followed Independence Fjord to Peary's viewpoint. Forced on to the Inland Ice by open water as the sea ice melted in late summer, their dogs had died and, as winter folded its cold, dark arms around them so had they.

Koch's search for the bodies of Mylius-Erichsen and Hagen failed. In 1910 the Danes tried again to find them, sending Ejnar Mikkelsen and six others in the 40-ton *Alabama*. One of the crew was Iver Iversen, a mechanic collected in Iceland from another ship when the *Alabama*'s mechanic turned out to be incompetent. Landing near Cape Bismarck, Mikkelsen relocated Brönlund's body and erected a cairn over it, though the journey, in autumn, was at the cost of five toes from one man's foot, amputated without a doctor or antiseptic, and with half a bottle of whisky as anaesthetic.

After wintering on the ship, two teams set out in the spring of 1911. Mikkelsen and Iversen went north hoping to find the bodies of Mylius-Erichsen and Hagen, and to follow the Peary Channel to the west coast. There should have been three men, but Jørgenson, who had survived the amputation of his toes, was not fit to travel. A second team of three men went inland to explore a nunatak (a rocky 'island' protruding from the ice) discovered by Alfred Wegener during the *Danmark* expedition.

Two men were left on the ship. When the sea ice near the *Alabama* melted she sank, but the men escaped in time and, together with the returned nunatak team, built a hut and erected a series of cairns to the north as a warning to Mikkelsen should he be forced to return that way. One of these cairns was found by a sealer who sailed to their rescue. Far to the north and, of course, unaware of the *Alabama*'s fate, Mikkelsen and Iversen had crossed the inland ice and descended, with difficulty, to the head of Danmark Fjord. They found no bodies, but did locate a note in a cairn built by Mylius-Erichsen. It said that the Peary Channel did not exist, and that Peary Land was not an island, but part of the mainland. A second note detailed the desperate journey in the heavy snow of late summer, with the dogs dying of exhaustion, a prelude to the terrible journey across the inland ice and Brönlund's heroic struggle. That struggle was about to be repeated by Mikkelsen and Iversen.

By the time the two men had reached Lambert Land, struggling through the same wet snow that had done for the earlier expedition and unable to find any wildlife, with all but two of their dogs dead from exhaustion and starvation, Mikkelsen was so debilitated by scurvy that he could no longer walk. Had they not found depots laid down by Koch for Mylius-Erichsen, the two Danes would have died. As it was, their journey was a struggle against appalling weather and starvation, punctuated by short periods of eating at the depots. They also ate their last two dogs, even consuming the livers though they knew they were poisonous. Iversen was so desperate for food that at one point he asked Mikkelsen to carry their rifle, as he feared he might shoot and eat him. Interestingly, during a discussion the pair had on cannibalism (and whether one could eat the other if he died) Iversen said that first he would have to cut off the hands, as they are what make a person human – several of the skeletons found by the Franklin search teams had had their hands removed.

Eventually, 30km from Danmarkshavn and its hut, the two Danes had to leave everything behind as they no longer had the strength to carry anything except their own weight – and barely that. As they approached the hut they had to have a rest less than 50m from it as they were too exhausted to walk those last few steps. After resting at the hut they tried to go back to recover their records, but could make no progress through vile weather. In desperation they turned towards the *Alabama*. Utterly exhausted, they reached the site; the ship was gone, and a note in the hut they found there said their colleagues had gone too.

The two men survived the winter by hunting, and by eating the supplies left at the hut. During one hunting trip Iversen claimed that he saw his grandfather sitting on a rock

Koch and Wegener used horses to cross the Inland Ice in 1912, believing that the advantages of food-on-the-hoof outweighed the disadvantages of carrying fodder. In fact they found that the animals worked well on the frozen surface of the ice, rarely falling through the crust, though stables cut into the ice were required to give the horses protection from the worst of the elements.

North-east Greenland, a magnificent, but unforgiving land.

wearing his familiar red cap; when he returned to Denmark he found that the old man had died at precisely the time he had the vision. In the spring the two returned for their records, recovering everything except Mikkelsen's diary, which had been eaten by a bear. Too weak to attempt the journey south to the Inuit settlement at Scoresbysund, they waited all summer for rescue. It did not come. After another winter things were looking grim; they were short of food, suffering from scurvy, and Mikkelsen had a threatening, boil-like tumour on his neck. Using the knife he ate and skinned carcasses with and a pool of water as a mirror as Iversen could not bear to do it, Mikkelsen lanced the tumour; the pain caused him to faint. Soon after this operation the two fell out for the first time in the two years they had spent together – a mutual silence over an ill-chosen song by Iversen. They had just made up when a rescue ship arrived.

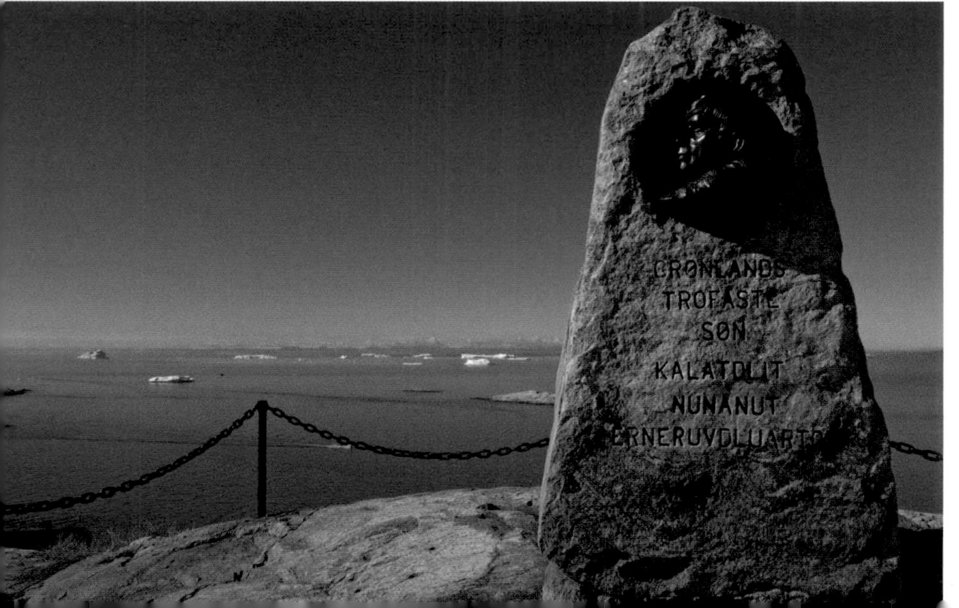

The memorial to Knud Rasmussen at Ilulissat where he spent his childhood. From the site there is a marvellous view across Disko Bay.

Mikkelsen and Iversen's survival against almost overwhelming odds is arguably the greatest in the history of polar exploration. Others have endured similar, perhaps worse, conditions, but never for as long; the pair also managed to hang on to the records that completed the mapping of Greenland.

Mylius-Erichsen's discovery of Peary's errors were confirmed in 1912 by the first expedition in a series that would become legendary – the Thule expeditions. It was led by Knud Rasmussen, born in Greenland of Danish parents (his father was the vicar at Ilulissat) and raised to speak the local language and to appreciate its culture. Rasmussen was accompanied by Peter Freuchen who had been on the *Danmark* expedition. In part the journey was a search for Mikkelsen, but as it started from the west coast it linked the journeys of Peary and Mylius-Erichsen. Rasmussen, a brilliant anthropologist, went on to lead most of the seven Thule expeditions, which did much to bring the culture of the Inuit to the western world. On the fifth expedition of 1923–24, Rasmussen sledged all the way to the Bering Strait, becoming the first man to traverse the North-West Passage by land (though land in this case equals ice). During the journey, Rasmussen heard Inuit stories about British sailors dating back to John Ross (in 1818), showing that the oral tradition of the

Left
An old Norwegian fur trapper's hut at Moskoksfjorden, north-east Greenland.

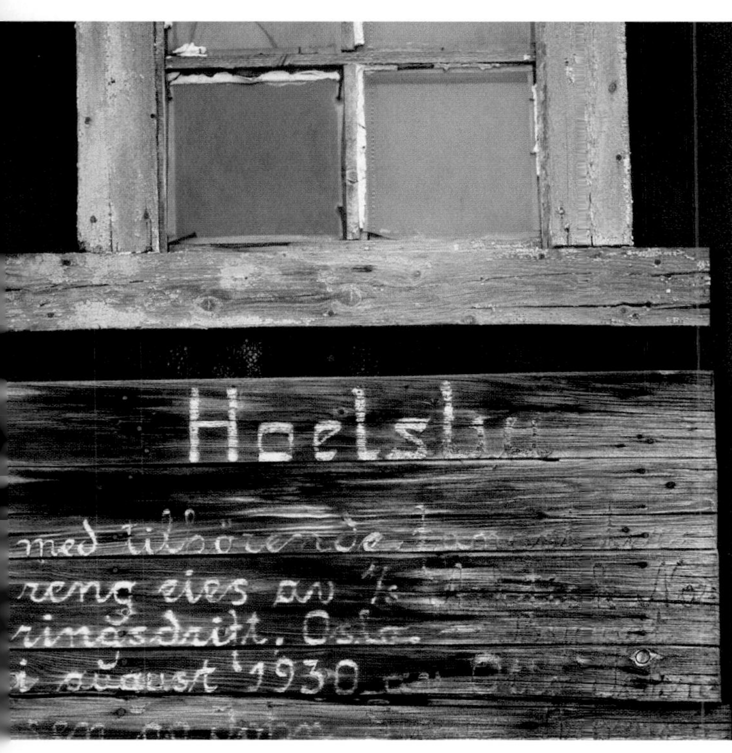

Below
A declaration of Norwegian land rule painted on to the hut.

Inuit was almost as good as the written word. Rasmussen also discovered further relics of Franklin's last expedition.

After the delineation of Greenland's coast, the island became a scientific study area. In 1912 J.P. Koch and Alfred Wegener (both of whom had been on the *Danmark*) and two others crossed the inland ice westwards from Danmarkshavn to Laxefjord, a distance of 1,100km, about twice as far as Nansen's transit and 300km more than either Peary and Rasmussen. They also overwintered on the ice before starting out, the first men to do so. The team used horses rather than dogs, eating them in turn as they became exhausted; they had taken 16 animals, but six died in a stampede when they first went ashore.

Wegener was later to die in another overwintering (1930–31) on the ice, exhaustion overtaking him as he struggled to get off the plateau. At the same time the British Arctic Air-Route Expedition set up a base on the inland ice to study weather conditions and so determine if trans-Atlantic flights across Greenland were feasible. The expedition, led by the 23-year-old Henry George (Gino) Watkins, established their base in August 1930. On 3 December, Augustine Courtauld was left alone at the base when it was realised there were insufficient supplies for the planned two-man team. Not until 5 May 1931 was he relieved, a total of 153 days of solitude. A search party on 18 April failed to find the buried station and Courtauld was feared dead, but he survived with none of the mental scars that might have been expected given that he had lived in fear of his tent collapsing under the weight of snow or his air becoming exhausted. He had not changed his clothes for five months, had run out of lighting oil and so lived in darkness, had taken no exercise, had little food, and had been forced to suck snow for water to conserve fuel. His pressure cooker failed on the morning of his rescue.

Eirik Raudes Land

At about the same time as these first winterings on the Inland Ice, Greenland was at the centre of an international court case. Norwegian fur-trappers had been overwintering on Greenland's east coast since the early years of the 20th century, their presence fuelling a dispute that had rumbled on since Norway had transferred from the Danish to the Swedish

The headquarters of the Sirius Patrol, Daneborg, north-east Greenland.

crown in 1814. Eirik the Red was born in Norway, and in 1261 the Norse population of Greenland had petitioned the Norwegian King Håkon Håkonsson to be incorporated into his realm. Denmark and Norway were united by royal marriage in the following century, but when Denmark – by now the stronger partner in the union – was forced to cede Norway to Sweden in the 19th century, it retained Greenland (and the former Norwegian colonies of Iceland and the Faroes). Norway protested about the continuing Danish possession of west Greenland after gaining its independence from Sweden in 1905, but the upheavals in Europe over the next two decades meant that Norway did not make moves to acquire a share of Greenland until 1931. On 27 June 1931 four men raised the Norwegian flag at the Myggbukta trapping station on east Greenland and Norway claimed Eirik Raudes (Eirik the Red's) Land, encompassing east Greenland north of the Inuit settlement of Illoqqortoormiut (Scoresbysund), a settlement established only in 1924–25 when the Danes moved a number of Inuit from Ammassalik. The ownership of Eirik Raudes Land was contested at the International Court in The Hague in 1933. The Danish claim was supported by Greenland (a campaign led by Knud Rasmussen) and by the United States, whose foreign policy was still dominated by the Monroe doctrine which sought to minimise European influence in the Americas: the US had no wish to add a third country to Canada and Denmark in the American Arctic sector. The court found in favour of Denmark. Today, though Greenland has been granted Home Rule, the Danes still maintain a military presence at Daneborg on the north-east coast and annually patrol the east and north coasts by dog sledge (the Sirius Patrol) in order to reinforce its sovereignty.

Recent journeys on Greenland

Greenland's vast ice sheet has been a magnet for adventurers ever since the first traverse by Nansen. Today, crossings of the inland ice are virtually a rite of passage for polar explorers and mountaineers, with east–west or west–east traverses being completed regularly, but some of the more significant journeys are worth noting. In 1978 Naomi Uemura, the first Japanese to climb Everest, used a dog sledge to travel to the North Pole (5 March–28 April), the first solo journey there. Evacuated by air because of poor weather, Uemura began a second journey on 10 May from Cape Morris K. Jesup. Resupplied during his trip, he sledged the length of the inland ice, completing his journey on 22 August, the first 'long axis' crossing of the ice sheet. In 1996 two 25-year-old Norwegians, Rune Gjeldnes and Torry Larsen, parachuted on to the southern Inland Ice on 19 March, determined to make the first complete south-north traverse of Greenland. Abseiling down the ice front, they used kayaks in an attempt to paddle to, and around, Kapp Farvel (Cape Farewell), Greenland's southernmost point. This was defeated by the weather, which made the crossing

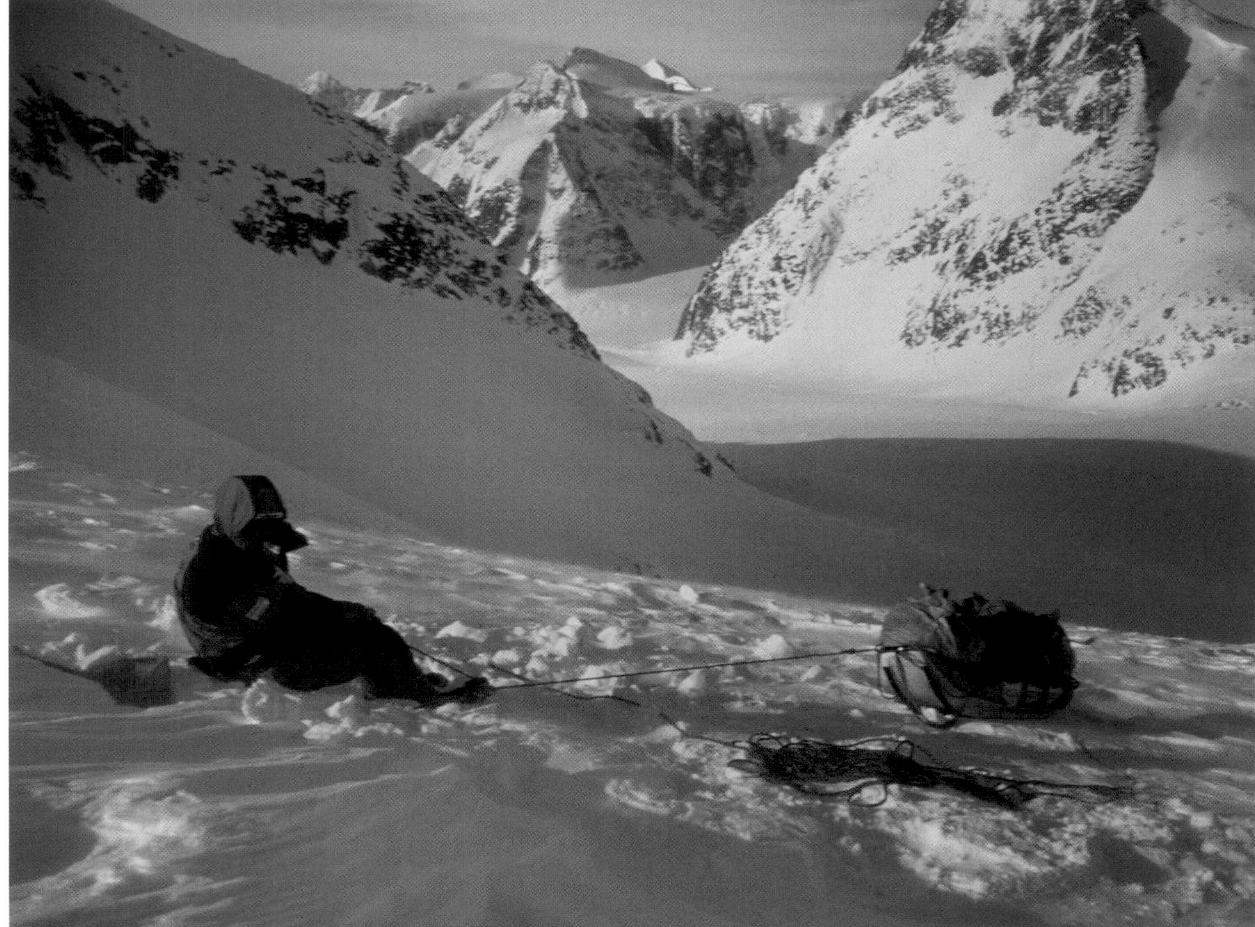

Pulk-hauling during the 1996 south–north traverse of Greenland by Rune Gjeldnes and Torry Larsen.

dangerous, though the two did come within sight of the cape. Having paddled back to the mainland they regained the ice sheet, and using sails to aid the towing of 175kg pulks, they skied north, reaching Cape Morris K. Jesup where they were collected by air on 13 June. Their trek of 2,928km was the longest unsupported ski journey at the time, though it has since been bettered by others in Antarctica.

In 1997, American Lonnie Dupre (who in 1991 had completed the first west-to-east dog sledge transit of the North-West Passage) and Australian John Hoelscher planned an 18-month clockwise circumnavigation of Greenland by kayak and dog sledge. Their plan called for a 2,400km kayak trip along the west coast from Paamiut to Qaanaaq during the summer of 1997, then a 4,160km dog sledge trip from Qaanaaq around the northern tip of the island and along the east coast to Ammassalik during the spring of 1998. Finally, there would be a 190km kayak journey around Greenland's southern tip to complete the venture. The men's kayaks could be tied together to form a catamaran, a safer option on the open sea, and one which also allowed the possibility of a sail to aid progress. The trip did not go according to plan. Fierce headwinds made the first leg much more difficult than had been imagined and it was not completed in full before the men had to move to Qaanaaq in late August. After training runs during the winter Dupre and Hoelscher set out on 14 February, but were forced to abandon the trek in late March by relentless bad weather and appalling ice conditions. They had reached Cape Jefferson at the northern end of the Kane Basin. The pair then transferred to Ammassalik and kayaked 1,200km to Qaqortoq. They were forced to stop there by the fast-approaching winter. Next, from February to May 2000 Dupre and Hoelscher sledged 2,900km between Constable Point near Scoresbysund, and Qaanaaq. The trip, rivalling Uemura's as one of the longest ever undertaken by dog-sledge, involved both pressure-ridged sea ice and travel on glaciers, the latter at one point requiring the dog-sledges to be roped and belayed because of crevasse danger. One night their camp was invaded by a pack of hungry wolves, and the weather was also unkind; on one occasion the two were tent-bound for five days during a storm. During the trek, Dupre and Hoelscher rediscovered Oodaaq, an island with a strong claim to being the world's northernmost piece of land. The island is elusive and often hidden by ice; Dupre and Hoelscher were able to fix its position accurately using GPS.

Returning in 2001, the pair kayaked the short stretches of the west coast that they had not been able to complete in 1997 (Paamiut to Qaqortoq and a section south of Savissivik), then completed the journey from Constable Point to Ammassalik, a distance of 1,100km between late July and early September. This part of the east Greenland coast is among the most inhospitable on the island, with mountains rising up directly from the sea; the kayak trip was extremely hazardous as it involved long sections of open sea. In all, Dupre and Hoelscher travelled more than 8,000km around Greenland, and also added an extra 2,300km of 'cultural' journeys around the Kane Basin, Nares Strait and various Inuit settlements, a truly remarkable journey and one unlikely to be repeated in the foreseeable future.

The scenery of southern Greenland is very dramatic, with huge, sheer walls, which attract rock climbers, enclosing tight fjords. This photograph, taken from the summit of Titan 1, looks south along Kangikitsoqfjord.

10. To the Pole

It is debatable which expedition has the right to be termed the first to attempt to reach the North Pole, as many of the early travellers, Henry Hudson, for example, assumed that to reach Cathay it was necessary merely to sail north over the pole, the pole itself being incidental. Arguably, the first to sail north with the specific intention of reaching the pole was the Englishman Constantine Phipps who, in 1773, sailed the *Racehorse* and the *Carcass* (the latter commanded by the gloriously named Skeffington Lutwidge) past Svalbard. He failed, of course, but the trip was a valuable experience for a 14-year-old midshipman called Horatio Nelson. It was also almost Nelson's last trip, as he only narrowly avoided being killed by a Polar Bear. It is said that only the firing of a gun from the ship, which frightened the bear away, saved Nelson's life. The young man's excuse for the encounter was that he wished to take a bear skin back for his father.

Next came William Parry, hero of several attempts at the North-West Passage. In 1827 Parry took the *Hecla* (and his newly married wife's pet dog Fido) to Spitsbergen's north coast. Having pocketed the £5,000 prize for reaching 110°W he was now intent, at the very least, on collecting another £1,000 for reaching 83°N. It was not to be; Parry had realised that his best hope lay in dragging sledges across the ice, but hedged his bets on finding open water by fixing steel runners to the two boats he took on the trek. This allowed his men to use the boats to cross leads, but the boats were heavy and exhausting to drag. The expedition set out with Parry in charge of one boat and James Clark Ross the other. The weather was awful, almost constant rain making the snow soft, increasing the friction on the runners. The men were soaked, often falling into pools on the ice surface to add to the misery of the downpours, and so were perpetually cold. Parry also discovered, as others were to find later, sometimes with disastrous consequences, that as his team went north – painfully slowly, often covering less than 250m per hour – the ice was drifting south at almost the same speed. Finally, he was forced to admit defeat. He had established a record northing (82°45'N), but had not won the prize; he was 220km north of the *Hecla*, but had walked several times that distance to get there.

After Parry's attempt, British naval expeditions returned to the quest for the North-West Passage, but during the search for Franklin further voyages were made northward. The graves on Beechey Island opened the possibility that Franklin had headed north, and in 1852 Edward Belcher explored Wellington Channel, his men sledging across northern Cornwallis, Bathurst and Melville islands. In the same year Lady Jane Franklin provided a ship, the *Isabel*, and the Admiralty a crew under Edward Inglefield, to try another route northward. Inglefield followed Baffin's route, passing Cape Isabella and naming Cape Sabine (soon to become infamous: see Adolphus Greely below) as he traversed Smith Sound and looked into what he thought was the Polar Sea. Inglefield also named Ellesmere Island, which forms the west side of Kane Basin and Smith Sound.

The Americans head north

Inglefield's route north attracted the attention of the Americans, who were keen not only to help find Franklin but to pursue their own polar ambitions. American exploration of the north was soon to prove that the British did not have a monopoly on disaster in the Canadian Arctic. The first American to follow Inglefield was Elisha Kent Kane, a man whose courage and perseverance outweighed poor health (he suffered from rheumatism and a bad heart, and died of a stroke when only 37). Kane had already been on one search expedition, the first to have been sponsored by the New York businessman Henry Grinnell as a response to Lady Franklin's request to the United States. Kane had been surgeon on the first Grinnell expedition (two ships, the *Advance* and the *Rescue*, commanded by Edwin De Haven), which had been one of several at Beechey Island when the first traces of Franklin's men had been found. Now, three years later, Kane was commanding his own expedition. In the *Advance* – which was little bigger than the ship Frobisher had used in 1576 – with a crew of 17, Kane sailed beyond Inglefield's northernmost point, reaching the Kane Basin. His hope that this was the open Polar Sea – which was still claimed to exist by some scientists and whalers – were now dashed; the ice advanced and Kane was forced to overwinter at Rensselaer harbour on the Greenland coast. He had come equipped with dogs and sledges to pursue the journey north, but the dogs died of a mysterious illness.

Despite this setback, much was achieved. Isaac Israel Hayes, Kane's surgeon, sledged along Ellesmere Island as far as Cape Frazer, and another team reached the Humboldt Glacier on Greenland ('a plastic, moving, semi-solid mass, obliterating life, swallowing rocks and islands and ploughing its way with irresistible march [to] … the sea' as Kane noted in his book of the expedition). The *Advance* failed to escape the ice when summer came, forcing a second overwintering. With little fuel or fresh food, and scurvy beginning to take its toll, Hayes took half the men and headed south, hoping to reach a Danish settlement. They managed 480km, but were forced to retreat after spending three months held captive by the savage winter. The return trip was an epic, involving the rounding of Cape Alexander on a ledge that narrowed to 40cm above a drop into the sea and certain death. On the *Advance* Kane and the others survived only because local Inuit gave them food.

The *Racehorse* and *Carcass* on 31 July 1773. Leapfrog seems a curious game for ice-bound sailors, but is rather safer than the Polar Bear molesting which almost cost the life of the future Admiral Lord Nelson.

Opposite page
The *Norge* airship mast at Ny Ålesund, Spitsbergen, Svalbard.

An illustration from Parry's book on his North Pole expedition. It is entitled *The boats drawn up for the night* which, together with the composition, was perhaps an attempt to impose a pleasant domesticity on to what was in reality an unpleasant experience for the team.

Finally, in the summer of 1855 with the *Advance* still locked into the ice, all the men headed south. Using sledges and boats they made it to Upernavik in August.

Isaac Hayes returned with his own expedition in 1860. Sailing in the *United States* with a young astronomer, August Sonntag, Hayes overwintered near the entrance to Smith Sound. He and Sonntag made trips on to glaciers flowing from Greenland's Inland Ice, but on one Sonntag fell through the sea ice. Though he was quickly dragged clear he died during the night and Hayes abandoned the trip.

As he neared the United States on his return journey Hayes passed the *Rescue,* which was taking Charles Francis Hall north for the first time. Hall was on another Franklin search expedition, one which was to form the basis of most subsequent attempts to piece together Franklin's fate from Inuit testimony. Hall's was the last American expedition for a decade, the Civil War calling a halt to such frivolous adventures. But when peace returned, so did Hall, heading north again in 1871, this time in the *Polaris* and intent on reaching the North Pole.

Hall believed that he 'was born to discover the North Pole. That is my purpose. Once I have set my right foot on the pole, I shall be perfectly willing to die.' It was a partially prophetic comment. Hall had with him Sidney Budington as captain, the German Emil Bessels – a surgeon with previous Arctic experience – and two Inuit families (including several children). Hall had befriended one of these families on his Franklin searches; the other was that of Suersaq, also known as Hans Hendrik, who had already proved invaluable to Kane and Hayes and would later accompany Nares. The *Polaris* sailed to 82°11'N, the furthest north reached so far in the Kane Basin, then overwintered on Greenland's coast at 81°37'N, the furthest north anyone had done so. Though Hall called the winter base Thank God Harbour it was not really a harbour, the ship lying in the lee of a vast iceberg called Providence Berg, clearly a heartfelt name.

On 8 November 1871, Hall died at the base; the expedition now broke up in confusion. Budington and Bessels were the senior expedition members, but Budington thought Bessels arrogant, and Bessels though Budington an ignoramus. When summer came Budington tried to take the ship south, but it was soon beset again. The ice was drifted south and had soon cleared Smith Sound, so there might have been optimism among the crew. If so, it was shattered when, on 15 October, gale-driven ice threatened to sink the ship. Anxious to save what they could the team began to unload boats and stores on to an ice floe. This job had not been completed before the gale separated floe and ship; the two drifted apart and were soon lost to each other's view. As the ship drifted away, above the screaming wind a voice could be heard calling forlornly from the ice floe – 'Goodbye *Polaris'*.

Those on the ship were driven north to the Greenland coast near the Inuit settlement of Etah, whose hunters had earlier kept Kane's team alive. The crew of 14 built a house with wood from the *Polaris*, survived a reasonably comfortable winter and then, in boats made from more *Polaris* timber, went south in June 1873 and were soon picked up by a whaler.

On the ice floe, the other 19 members of Hall's team – one a baby born on 12 August 1872 to Hans Hendrik and his wife, an addition to the three children they already had – had a more dramatic winter. All the Inuit were on the floe; they could build snow igloos and hunt seals from the kayaks that had been off-loaded. That kept the party alive when the stores from the ship ran out. The men, women and children spent the winter on the floe, which was roughly 150m square; they were often hungry and, when the Sun returned, they feared

Emile Bessel's sketch of Hall's funeral. In the background is Hall's observatory where a coal-burning stove kept the team warm as they studied astronomy, meteorology etc.

Murder on the ice?

Hall's expedition had been an official US venture, sanctioned by President Grant and underwritten by the navy, and so there was a board of inquiry into its conduct and the death of the leader. It heard that the expedition had been far from a happy one. Budington had been a secret (and not-so-secret) drinker, which brought him into conflict with the god-fearing Hall; Hall and Bessels had disagreed repeatedly, Bessels once threatening to leave the ship and take the German crewmen, of whom there were several, with him. Some members of the crew were upset with Hall's strange and occasionally autocratic methods, and fearful of continuing the northern journey. The inquiry also learned that Hall had experienced strange symptoms for two weeks before his death, bouts of violent sickness interspersed with periods of recovery. The problems had started with what Dr Bessels called an 'apoplectical insult' – a stroke – which he verified by noting paralysis, testing it with a needle. The inquiry decided that Hall had, indeed, died of apoplexy.

Suspicious of the inquiry's finding, Chauncey Loomis, a Dartmouth professor who was writing a biography of Hall, persuaded the Danes to allow an autopsy in 1968. This proved difficult, for although Hall's body was preserved in the permafrost, the internal organs had fused with (and become indistinguishable from) his flesh. However, hair and fingernail samples showed large amounts of arsenic, almost certainly administered during the last two weeks of his life. Hall had exhibited classic symptoms of arsenic poisoning and had also been convinced he was being poisoned by Budington or Bessels, but, as Loomis noted, nothing definite could be determined this long after the event. Perhaps Hall did indeed have a stroke. He noted on one sledge trip that he could no longer run in front of the dogs; clearly he was unwell and, perhaps fearful of Bessels, had self-administered patent medicines. In the 1860s many of these contained arsenic. Yet Bessels' treatment of Hall – when it was allowed – was curious. He declined, when requested, to administer an emetic which would have cleared Hall's stomach of any poison and continued to inject him (nominally with quinine, but quinine crystals and arsenic powder would have been indistinguishable to those crew members who saw the injections prepared) long after the 'fever' he said he was treating had subsided. When Bessels was not allowed to treat Hall his condition improved. Yet what, if he was guilty, was Bessels' motive for murder? He was clearly at odds with Hall, but could that really have led a civilised man to murder? Of course, the harshness of the Arctic and the fear this induces has done strange things to people's minds. Hall's death was suspicious, but it remains a mystery.

Hall's body, exhumed in 1968 for autopsy. The US flag in which Hall had been wrapped had stained his body. Though humour has little place in a possible murder, it is difficult to avoid a smile when hearing that Hall was laid to rest in a structure created by the ship's carpenter, Nathaniel Coffin.

that the ice floe would suddenly break up and hurl them into the sea. Eventually, on 1 April 1873, they crowded into the two salvaged boats – built to accommodate a maximum of 12 men – and prayed for a ship to spot them swiftly, as they had to abandon a lot of food and clothing. Two ships passed without seeing them, but on 30 April, close to the Labrador coast after having drifted about 2,400km, they were taken on board the *Tigress*. Two days after their rescue there was a violent storm – it would almost certainly have overwhelmed the two boats.

The British try again

Having stayed away from the Arctic since Belcher's near-farcical expedition, the British navy, inspired by Hall's voyage, decided to try once more for the North Pole. In 1875, with the blessing of Queen Victoria and Prime Minister Disraeli (just as Hall had received a blessing from President Grant), George Nares set out with the *Alert* and the *Discovery*. Despite the lessons of the Franklin disaster and the myriad search expeditions, the British Admiralty appeared to have learnt nothing. Both ships were huge, rather than small and manoeuvrable; the crew numbered 120, too many to live off the land; the sledges, which had already proved too heavy and cumbersome, were again taken; and the food was much the same as that which had probably contributed to Franklin's downfall.

Yet despite their size, Nares brilliantly took his ships through the Kane Basin ice. The *Discovery* wintered in Lady Franklin Bay, the *Alert* continued and finally wintered near

Cape Sheridan (where the Alert meteorologist station is now placed). It was a new record northing, both for a ship and for a wintering station. In 1876, Albert Markham took a sledge team north from the *Alert,* establishing a new furthest north record of 83°20'26"N on 12 May. By then all hope of reaching the Pole was gone and survival was in the balance, the men exhausted by boat-hauling. The two sledges carrying the boats (taken in case open water was reached) were heavy, weighing around 800kg each: so heavy that in soft snow the haul was only a metre at a time, with the sledge barely moving before it came to a halt again. To aid the men, the officers in charge ordered morale-boosting messages to be pinned to the backs of the front men in the team so that they would inspire the men behind: it is difficult to imagine anything less likely to work. As well as being exhausted, the men were also wet for much of the time, and many suffered frostbite as a result. When they gave up, the team had reached a point only 117km from the ship, but they had walked over 800km, having had to return for the second sledge each time as they could only haul one at a time. The men were also crippled by scurvy. Finally, the one reasonably fit man was sent alone to cover the last 50km to get help. Nares, concerned by the state of Markham's men – one of whom died – immediately sent a rescue party out for his second land party which had set out to map Ellesmere's north coast at the same time that Markham had left. This team had successfully traced the coast as far as Alert Point, but would have died of scurvy without the rescue party.

Two sledge parties were also sent out from the *Discovery*. The crew of this ship had enjoyed better health, due largely to Hans Hendrik (Suersaq) supplying them with fresh meat. One sledge party surveyed the Ellesmere coast south of the ship and returned in reasonable health, but the other, under Lewis Beaumont, which had surveyed Greenland's north coast, found itself returning in deep, soft snow. Exhausted and with two men dead from scurvy, Beaumont found open water between him and the *Discovery*. At that stage a rescue party arrived and the remaining men were saved. Nares now had less than one-fifth of his men free of scurvy: he wisely decided to abandon a second overwintering and to head for home.

Adolphus Greely

In 1875, Karl Weyprecht, co-leader of the expedition that discovered Franz Josef Land, proposed that rather than the piecemeal approach to Arctic exploration that had so far been carried out, a co-ordinated international effort should be made to undertake scientific studies in the area. This was agreed, and during the International Polar Year of 1882–83 a dozen stations were set up and manned through the winter. A Dutch expedition in the *Varna* was trapped by ice in the Kara Sea before reaching the proposed station, but the crew and scientists escaped to the mainland unharmed. All except one of the other stations were manned successfully and uneventfully. The exception was the US expedition under the command of Adolphus Washington Greely; its story is one of the most horrific for which there are the first-hand accounts of survivors.

Greely took his expedition of 25 men (including two Inuit hunters) north in the *Proteus* in the early summer of 1881, eventually reaching the point where Nares' *Discovery* had over-

After the early attempts to reach the Pole via Svalbard, interest turned to Smith Sound between eastern Ellesmere Island and north-west Greenland where ships could also penetrate a long way north. This photograph shows the scenery close to the southern entrance to the Sound.

Scurvy

Although the Egyptians noted the symptoms 4,000 years ago and 13th-century crusaders suffered from it, scurvy was relatively unknown in Europe until the voyages of exploration of the late medieval period; Vasco de Gama lost two-thirds of his crew to scurvy while sailing to India in 1497–99. The condition was first described as a disease in 1541 by a Dutch physician, though he assumed it was infectious rather than dietary. A year earlier, the French explorer Jacques Cartier had been given a remedy for scurvy by Canadian native peoples, who boiled pine needles in water. In the early 17th century the British physician John Woodall published a book, *The Surgeon's Mate*, in which he suggested that scurvy resulted from a dietary deficiency and could be treated with citrus fruits. Woodall persuaded the managers of the East India Company, of which he was Surgeon General, to issue their sailors with lemon juice. Yet more than a hundred years later another Briton, naval officer James Lind, was still having trouble convincing his superiors that the prevalence of scurvy in navy crews could be eliminated by following the same regime.

Scurvy results from a lack of vitamin C (ascorbic acid) in the diet, the known cures for the disease actually pre-dating an understanding of vitamins and their role in human health by centuries. The body needs about 60 milligrams per day, though as little as one-tenth of that will prevent scurvy. Without this minimum dose people become anaemic, suffer a general lassitude and weakness, joint pain, gum diseases and, eventually, spongy gums and tooth loss. Ultimately, sufferers die. It was clear to Arctic explorers that the Inuit did not suffer from scurvy, but the reason was misunderstood. The Inuit ate meat so the travellers did too, but they cooked the meat, destroying the vitamin C. This was particularly problematic when Musk Ox was on the menu, as the foul taste of male ox was hidden by overcooking. There were other problems too. Although fresh vegetables, and plants such as 'scurvy grass' (*Cochlearia* species), are rich in vitamin C, cooking again removes the vitamin; though much of the vitamin remains in the water, the vegetables were strained and the water thrown away. Copper also seriously depletes vitamin C, so scurvy returned when that metal replaced iron for cooking utensils (as it was lighter and had better thermal properties). Another problem was the British decision to exchange Mediterranean lemons for West Indian limes, the latter having less vitamin C.

In the inquiry following the Nares expedition, the evidence of two doctors that the sledge party's scurvy had been caused by a lack of lime juice was rejected. The view that fresh meat, fish and vegetables were effective anti-scorbutants, and evidence that lime juice aged significantly – a problem exacerbated by fixing the juice with spirits, with alcohol breaking down vitamin C, so it became less effective with time – were quietly ignored. The fact that the consumption of lime juice was a naval order (most of the men hated it and so it was not taken when the men were on land, was also not considered. The good work of Lind was compromised, with other quack remedies being suggested as the 'real' cure. Even Nansen became convinced that food past its sell-by date was the actual cause.

As if all of this were not bad enough, one of the Nares inquiry committee who decided that everything possible had been done and nothing could be improved was Clements Markham, cousin of Albert Markham who had almost died returning from the furthest north, and the man instrumental in appointing Robert Falcon Scott to lead the expeditions to Antarctica. It is now believed that one of several factors in the tragedy that overtook Scott's party on its return from the South Pole was scurvy.

wintered. Here a base – Fort Conger, named after a US senator who had been a principal supporter of the expedition – was built, and scientific studies began. But Greely's trip had a dual purpose – he had also been told to try to reach the Pole or, at least, to better Nares' record. To that end James Lockwood, one of Greely's two officers, laid down depots along a route towards the north Greenland coast.

The summer of 1882 seems to have been idyllic, with butterflies flitting among flowers and Musk Oxen providing a ready source of fresh meat, but there was dissension within the team, as Greely had alienated his other officer, Frederick Kislingbury, the team doctor Octave Pavy, and some of his men, with his stubbornness and poor decision-making. Pavy said of him, 'If he could read my thoughts, he certainly must have read all the contempt I have for his person.' Greely's view of Pavy was no better – 'if he was anything but a doctor, I would deal with him summarily.' But dreadful though interpersonal relationships had become, they were not to have an instrumental effect on the course of the expedition. In early April Lockwood headed north with one dog-sledge and three man-hauled sledges. After four weeks of travelling most of the party was sent back, Lockwood continuing with Sgt David Brainard, the Inuk Frederick (Thorlip Frederick Christiansen) and the dogs. Finding and using depots left by Beaumont's party from the Nares expedition, Lockwood pushed on, eventually reaching the northern end of Lockwood Island at 83°24'N. They had extended Beaumont's survey by 240km and Markham's northernmost point by 6.5km. After 60 days they were back at Fort Conger. It had not, strictly been an attempt at the pole, but it was a notable achievement and established a new northing record.

During that summer Greely explored Ellesmere Island, surveying a good deal of country and discovering Lake Hazen (named after General William Hazen, Chief Signal Officer of the United States and Greely's Commanding Officer). The expected supply ship did not arrive, but with supplies and game still (relatively) abundant there was no need for concern. Another winter passed and in the summer of 1883 Lockwood tried to go north from Ellesmere. Unfortunately, open water stopped him (though it is doubtful if he would have managed to break his own record by more than 1° or so). Instead Lockwood headed west, discovering and tracing Greely Fjord.

Back at Fort Conger, the long period of separation from civilisation and continuing uncertainty over the arrival of a relief ship was by now taking its toll. As Greely's dispute with Pavy intensified, the commander tried to have the doctor arrested for insubordination. With the situation at Fort Conger spiralling out of control, Greely decided to head south, to find the supply dumps that should have been laid down since the relief ships had been unable to reach the expedition. There were two possible destinations, Cape Sabine on Ellesmere or Littleton Island on the Greenland coast. He chose Cape Sabine; this has been debated ever since. Should he have stayed at Fort Conger where game was plentiful? Should he have gone to the Greenland side, where the Inuit of Etah had a history of helping expeditions?

The *Proteus* sinking.

spending related to the expedition. Eventually a ship, the *Neptune*, sailed. Despite several attempts to get through the ice it got no further than the mouth of Kane Basin. Minimal supplies were left at Cape Sabine and Littleton Island and the ship retreated. The next year the command of the relief operation was given to Ernest Garlington. He was a cavalry officer, promoted when many of the officers on his unit, the 7th Cavalry, were killed with Custer at Little Big Horn. As an army man he was an odd choice for a naval expedition, but Hazen was from the army too, as were Greely and his expedition.

The relief party had two ships, the *Proteus* (which had taken Greely north) and the *Yantic,* a much slower ship, which soon lost contact with the faster vessel. The *Proteus* reached Cape Sabine on 22 July, but Garlington did not unload any supplies, preferring to head north. The ship's captain, Richard Pike, favoured waiting one or two days as there was considerable ice in the Kane Basin, but he eventually agreed to steam north again. Soon, in sight of clear water, the *Proteus* was caught by ice floes and very quickly began to sink. Garlington threw as much material overboard as possible, but the majority of the supplies for Greely were lost, and much of what he did salvage drifted away on the ice. Garlington left enough at Cape Sabine to last Greely three weeks, then took the rest and headed south. He left a note on Littleton Island, which was picked up by the *Yantic* when she arrived. Faced with deciding whether to go north towards Greely or south after Garlington, Frank Wildes, the *Yantic*'s captain, headed south, leaving no supplies at Littleton. The *Yantic* and Garlington's men were eventually united at Upernavik. There it was decided that it was too late in the year to go north again, and the *Yantic* sailed back to St John's on Newfoundland. A flurry of telegrams now sought advice. But though pressed by General Hazen and, especially, by Greely's wife, Robert Lincoln vetoed a further attempt to go north. Greely had been abandoned.

Loading everything into two boats, the team headed south through difficult ice and bad weather. It took 16 days to cover the 320km to Cape Sabine, but just as they approached it the wind dropped, the pack-ice came together and the boats were trapped. It was, said Dr Pavy, 'like a nightmare in one of Edgar Allen Poe's stories'. It took a further 19 days for the men to cross the last 21km of ice to Ellesmere, and for most of that time they were buffeted by blizzards. They reached land on Ellesmere to the south of Pym Island. It took two men a further eight days to reach Cape Sabine on Pym Island and return. They returned with a note that told Greely he and his men were in for a long, hungry winter. General Hazen had attempted to get a relief ship north in the first summer, but had at first been thwarted by Robert Lincoln, son of Abraham Lincoln and now US Secretary of War. Lincoln responded to requests for a ship with queries on the

Greely's team collecting ice at Fort Conger. From left to right are the Inuk Jens, Greely, Cross and Kislingbury.

Winter on Cape Sabine

Despite the note retrieved by his men from the Cape, telling him about the sinking of the *Proteus,* Greely decided to move his men there as it was the most likely landfall of a further rescue attempt. At Camp Clay, a little way north-west of the Cape, his men built a rough hut of stone around an upturned boat. They collected what Garlington had left and, as there was so little of it, Greely sent a team of four to collect such supplies as Nares had left at Cape Isabella, 65km away. It took five days to get there, but the cache contained only about 65kg of meat. On the way back one man, Joseph Elison, became so cold that two others had to stay with him, attempting to warm him in a four-man sleeping bag, while the last man went for help; all four were saved, but a greater nightmare was to come. The two Inuit hunters tried desperately to find game, but apart from the odd seal there was nothing; Pym Island was no Fort Conger. Eventually one Inuk died of scurvy aggravated by exhaustion, the other drowning when his kayak was ripped by ice.

The death of the Inuit and the coming of winter meant an end to fresh food. With supplies dwindling, Greely cut the daily food ration to about 160g. This consisted of mouldy bread and soup heated by burning rope and bootsoles. Eventually, even the buffalo-hide or sheepskin sleeping bags were boiled and eaten; by May men were dying daily. One day Charles Henry was discovered to be stealing food. Greely convened a court martial and Henry was sentenced to death in his absence. Too weak to carry out the sentence himself, Greely allowed three NCOs to organise it. The facts of the execution were never published, but it seems that fearful of Henry's strength – he was bigger than most in the crew, and now better fed – the men lured him away on a pretext and shot him in the head without warning. On the day of the execution the doctor died, his end perhaps aided by self-administered drugs.

When spring came the diet of old leather and tallow was supplemented by seaweed, lichen, flowers, sand fleas and shrimps. These 'supplements' became the only 'food' when everything else edible ran out on 12 May. It took all the energy the survivors had to bury their dead comrades in the shallow graves of a makeshift cemetery. More energy was lost when the survivors were forced to move from the hut to a tent because melting water was making the hut unbearable. Many of the men could now hardly stand and death seemed to be both inevitable and welcome. Greely wrote what he thought might be his last note, a curious mixture of pathos and bathos that prefigured Scott – 'Seven of us left – here we are – dying, like men. Did what I came to do – beat the old record.'

In Washington, the government had finally realised that Greely might be in trouble, though funding was stalled while a Relief Bill was debated (at length) and passed. Finally the *Thetis* and *Bear* sailed north. To his considerable aggravation Garlington was not given command, that going to Winfield Schley. After following notes left by Greely's men at Cape Isabella and Cape Sabine, the ships reached the horrors of the camp on 22 June. Only seven of the 25 men were still alive. Joseph Elison was in a particularly pitiful state; frostbitten on the trip to Cape Isabella, he had seen all the flesh rot from one foot, leaving the bones exposed. Dr Pavy had amputated both feet and some of his fingers: his comrades had tied a spoon to what remained of his hand so he could eat. On the *Thetis* Elison lost his remaining fingers, then half his legs. His condition worsened and his leg stumps were amputated: it was all to no avail, Elison dying two weeks after rescue.

Schley not only brought back the survivors, but those bodies he could retrieve. The cemetery was a gruesome sight, the heads and feet of bodies sticking out of the Earth, a testimony to the exhaustion of the burial parties. The exhumed bodies also showed unmistakable signs of cannibalism, flesh having been cut from the bones, but the survivors denied all knowledge of this and an official inquiry decided that any flesh that had been removed had been 'with a view no doubt to use as shrimp bait'.

The aftermath of the expedition was sordid. Some of the survivors exhibited themselves in a freak show for $1,000 per week until ordered to desist. Hazen accused Garlington and Wildes of cowardice, and Lincoln of incompetence. The government closed ranks to defend Lincoln, and Hazen was tried for 'conduct prejudicial to good order'. He was found guilty but merely censured and allowed to retire quietly; he died two years later. Garlington's career suffered, but having been party to one infamous act he was later involved in another, the massacre of Native Americans at Wounded Knee. For that he received the Congressional Medal of Honour, the United States of America's highest award. Greely did well on the lecture circuit and wrote a book on the expedition that blasted Lincoln, Garlington and Wildes. It sold in large numbers, especially to the British. Some details of the terrible winter on Pym Island were, not surprisingly, left out of Greely's book, but are now available in print; it makes harrowing reading.

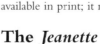

The tent at Cape Sabine, photographed by the team which arrived to rescue the remnants of Greely's expedition.

The *Jeanette*

Two years before Greely set out, another American expedition had set out with the aim of reaching the Pole. It too was a disaster – though that was not known to Greely when he left for Fort Conger – but it led to one of the most audacious attempts ever on the North Pole. The purpose of the US Navy expedition led by George Washington De Long in the *Jeanette* – the renamed *Pandora* bought from Sir Allen Young, a veteran of the British Navy's Franklin searches – was to discover if Wrangel Island was part of a continent that reached as far as Greenland and to explore its coastline northward. De Long hoped to find the open polar sea and so be able to reach the North Pole. In case ice intervened, his team of 33 had sledges and dogs. The *Jeanette* sailed in July 1879, reaching pack-ice close to Herald Island where she was soon beset. De Long hoped he might now drift north to open water, but instead he went north-west, passing close enough to Wrangel to realise it was an island rather than part of a larger land mass.

For two years the *Jeanette* drifted. In May 1881 the De Long Islands (Jeanette and Henrietta) were discovered. Soon after, the ice squeezed the ship and she began to take on water. Boats, equipment and food was off-loaded on to the ice and tents were erected, but in the middle of the night the ice beneath the camp split. The men moved the tents, and as they did the *Jeanette* sank into the lead the crack created. De Long now started for the New Siberian Islands, a difficult journey that involved hauling three heavy boats. It took 47 days to reach Bennett Island from where, after a ten-day rest, the men set out for mainland Russia. They were now rowing their boats, picking a route through the New Siberian Islands and drifting pack-ice. Though De Long was anxious to keep the boats together, a storm blew up, separating the three; no trace of the smallest boat or its crew of eight was ever found.

The other two boats reached the coast near the Lena delta. One of them, with 11 men led by George Melville and John Danenhower, had the good fortune to land at the delta's south-eastern corner and so rapidly found the main stream. They soon met local people, who provided food and shelter and took them to a village. Melville decided he needed to reach Bulun, the largest local settlement, where he might find Russian officials who would help organise a search for the other boats, and also help his own men reach Yakutsk and safety. But first he rested his men, an understandable decision, but one that would later be criticised.

De Long's boat, with 13 men aboard together with Snoozer, *Jeanette*'s mascot dog (all the other dogs had been killed as they took up room and ate precious food), landed in the maze of streams that make up the delta. Forced to wade ashore through new-forming ice to reach marshy ground, the men were soon chilled and exhausted. On 6 October the first men died from the effects of frostbite. The remainder struggled on, occasionally finding huts erected by local hunters – tantalising glimpses of security. With their food running out, De Long made the painful decision to kill Snoozer for his meat. Then, when the dog meat ran out, he decided to send the two strongest men ahead while he remained with the others. Soon after they departed, a native hunter Alexei, who had joined the *Jeanette* in Alaska, died of exhaustion after hunting every day without luck. On 17 October the men ate the last of their leather: four days later two men died. On 29 October the ship's doctor James Ambler wrote a poignant last letter to his brother. By then only he, De Long and the Chinese steward Ah Sam remained alive. De Long made a last diary entry on 30 October, the 140th day since leaving the *Jeanette*. It is thought that Ambler was the last to die; he was found holding a gun, presumably to ward off scavengers that had been attracted by the corpses.

Nindemann and Noros, the two men sent forward by De Long, survived at first by eating discarded fish heads they found in a hut. Then, near starvation, they finally met some locals, but they were unable to make them understand that

The *Jeanette* sinking. This and the illustration on p197 are from woodcuts engraved at the request of the US Navy. The *Jeanette* voyage was an official Navy expedition and many woodcuts were made to illustrate its fate.

George Melville discovers the bodies of De Long and his team.

men were dying nearby. Instead the two were taken south, though a message they wrote quickly found its way to Melville. He immediately joined them in Bulun, discovered where De Long and the others were and set out to find them. But it was now 5 November and Melville was suffering from frostbite. By 11 November he was in the vicinity of De Long's camp, but was running short of food. Certain that De Long was dead (he was probably correct) he spent his last day searching for, and finding, the expedition records, then abandoned his rescue attempt. The following spring (March 1882) Melville again set out. After a two-week search, the bodies of the first to die were uncovered from the snow. As he walked nearby Melville tripped over something – it was the frozen hand of De Long protruding from the snow.

Twenty men had died, eight in the lost boat with little to show for the loss except the discovery of two small islands. Of the survivors, Danenhower later shot himself, while another went insane. Melville, who took the brunt of the criticism for his delay in reaching Bulun, was in the *Thetis* when the remnants of Greely's expedition were found at Cape Sabine.

Nansen and the *Fram*

Professor Mohn's lecture on the *Jeanette* relics was read by the 23-year-old Fridtjof Nansen. He realised that such a current might take a trapped ship over, or very close to, the North Pole. If the ship could survive entrapment it would be released near the coast of Greenland. What was needed was a ship strong enough to resist ice pressure and a team of men willing to spend perhaps five years on board.

For the ship, Nansen turned to Colin Archer, son of a Scottish immigrant to Norway and a genius in the field of boat design. The ship Nansen and Archer built was the *Fram* (*Forward*) her cost borne by the Norwegian government as an expression of national pride (Norway was in a loose union with Sweden at the time, but had its own constitution and government: the union was peacefully dissolved in 1905). *Fram*'s hull was a half-egg in cross-section with a minimal keel (on some ships the keel had been gripped by ice and then pulled downwards) and a removable rudder (for similar reasons). The cross-beams and stern were huge and of well-seasoned oak to withstand ice pressure. The ship had both a steam engine and sails. She also had a wind turbine, which generated electricity for lighting. *Fram* was large, 34.5m long on the waterline and grossing more than 400 tons. Visitors to Oslo who take a trip to the Fram Museum at Bygdøy, across the harbour from the city, can compare *Fram* and *Gjøa*, which are both preserved there. The latter is tiny by comparison, but *Fram* did not need the manoeuvrability of *Gjøa*; her task was merely to be imprisoned in, resist the pressure of, and drift with, the ice.

Besides Nansen, *Fram* had a crew of 12. This included Otto Sverdrup, who had crossed Greenland with Nansen, as captain, and Hjalmar Johansen, the son of a town hall caretaker. Johansen had gained a place at University to study law but had to leave when his father died as he could no longer afford to stay. So keen was he to go with Nansen that he not only applied in writing, but visited Nansen unannounced. Johansen agreed to do any job and was taken on as a stoker.

When the ship arrived in Vardø, the last Norwegian port before departing for Siberia, the crew celebrated their final night ashore in the time-honoured way – by getting drunk. To

Driftwood and the *Jeanette*

In the late 18th century Olav Olavius made an inventory of the driftwood found on Iceland's beaches. The aim was economic – driftwood was an important resource in treeless Iceland – but Olavius was also interested in where the wood came from. He concluded it was Siberian, brought to Iceland by North Atlantic currents. Olavius was partially correct, but it was a further 100 years before Professor Henrik Mohn suggested that a current flowed across the Arctic Ocean from Siberia. The trigger for Mohn's idea was the discovery of relics of the *Jeanette* on an ice floe off Qaqortoq on the south-west coast of Greenland. In a lecture in 1894 Mohn suggested that the only realistic way in which these relics could have made the journey was across the Arctic Basin.

their shock Nansen berated them, telling them that if it were not for the fact they were leaving that day he would dismiss them all. It was the first hint of the occasionally difficult times to come. Nansen was a strange leader; he was domineering and arrogant, his undoubted intelligence producing, as one man noted, 'a mania for interfering in everything'. Nansen believed he was an authority on all subjects and could do everyone's allotted job better than they could themselves. Yet he was often cheerful and humorous, and good company.

Fram in the ice. The ship had both a steam engine and sails for motive power, and a wind turbine to provide electrical power.

The *Fram* sailed through the Kara Sea, around Cape Chelyuskin and north past the New Siberian Islands to enter the pack. On 5 October 1893 the rudder was raised: *Fram* was frozen in. At first, to Nansen's confusion, the ship drifted south, but soon began his expected steady drift north. Though the ship was cramped, life was tolerable. By luck Nansen had loaded food – canned vegetables and preserved cloudberries, a Norwegian delicacy – that kept the crew free of scurvy. The winter was brutally cold at first as Nansen, fearful of fire and wishing to preserve fuel, refused to allow any heating; he was persuaded to relent when the temperature inside the vessel dropped to -30°C. There were excursions on the ice enlivened by occasional Polar Bear visits, and regular feast days. And the *Fram* behaved just as Nansen and Archer thought she would; on the open sea she rolled and pitched dreadfully, but when the ice closed around her she rose on to it and drifted serenely.

Fram drifted through the winter, the summer of 1894 and into a second winter. By now it was clear that her direction was north-west rather than north. On 12 December 1894 she passed the record northing for a ship (set by Nares's *Alert*), but Nansen had realised she would never reach the Pole and announced his intention of heading north with one companion and all the dogs. His chosen partner was Hjalmar Johansen. During the winter, sledges and kayaks were built, ready for the trip. On 6 January 1895 *Fram* broke the record for northward travel (held by Lockwood), but almost succumbed to ice pressure, the most frightening time of the whole journey. Neither the new record nor the careful preparations for the voyage on foot curbed Nansen's mood swings. When he and Johansen finally departed on 26 February 1895 almost everyone left behind on the *Fram* was glad to see the back of him. But those who cheered did so too soon. Only 500m from the ship a sledge broke. It had to be repaired, and not until 28 February did Nansen head off again: that day the *Fram* was at 83°50'N and still heading north-west.

Nansen and Johansen had six sledges, 28 dogs and 1,100kg of equipment. Accompanied by other members of the crew, they covered just 6km despite shedding some load. After two further days of agonising progress Nansen had to admit that they had started too early (the Sun only reappeared on 3 March) and with too much weight. He returned to *Fram* leaving Johansen on the ice (though two men skied out to join him). *Fram* was now beyond 84°N. Again the loads were reorganised and on 14 March they set off again, now with just three sledges and 760kg of equipment.

Nansen had secretly thought that with just 6° of latitude to cross, the North Pole would

Nansen (second from the left) and Johansen (fourth from the right) about to set off from *Fram*.

An exquisite drawing from *Farthest North*, Nansen's book on the *Fram* expedition. With the men's hats, the dogs, and the rolls of equipment at the back, the illustration looks rather better suited to a child's book than one dealing with a life-and-death struggle in the Arctic. The harsh reality was, of course, that the dogs, here taking it easy as the kayaks (converted to a catamaran) took the strain, were all slaughtered and eaten.

be easily reached. But the pressure ridges of the ice soon proved him wrong. Progress was slow and it was bitingly cold, with daytime temperatures down to -40°C and reaching -47°C at night. For days neither man had any respite; even in their double reindeer-skin sleeping bags they were cold. Fixing latitude from the Sun, Nansen found that they were travelling much more slowly than he anticipated. At their rate of progress they would not arrive at the Pole until at least two weeks after his calculated date; unless progress improved they would have to turn back before reaching it.

Progress did not improve. Their clothes, the sweat of effort freezing them into suits of armour, chafed their bodies to cause sores, Johansen fell through the ice and almost froze, and now the dogs had to be killed one by one. On 4 April Nansen calculated they were at 86°2.8'N when he had hoped they would be much further north. They continued for three more days, then Nansen went ahead on skis. Before him lay a sea of hummocky ice. Later he wrote of his thoughts at the time: 'There seems little sense in carrying on any longer; we are sacrificing valuable time and doing little.' And so, at 86°14'N, a new record by almost 3°, they turned for Franz Josef Land.

At first the going was comparatively easy, a fact which led them to travel for too long without camping. That in turn led them to forget to wind their watches. The watches stopped, but as they had little idea how long they had stopped they could now no longer be sure of their longitude. To compensate they steered an easterly course as, like Albanov before them, the pair could not afford to miss Franz Josef on its west side and finish in open ocean. The weather continued to hold, though the routine killing of dogs darkened their mood, and latitude checks showed they were still a long way from Franz Josef.

Then the weather changed; the wind shifted, bringing blizzards and, worse, altering the ice drift unfavourably. Johansen was becoming tired, the strain of managing two sledges to Nansen's one wearing him down. When the third sledge was finally abandoned on 13 May Johansen was joyful. With summer having arrived the temperature rose, but against this positive was the negative of more open water slowing their progress. Nansen was also increasingly concerned about their position. Julius von Payer had claimed to have seen 'Petermann Land' lying north of Cape Fligely: he had been fooled by ice and atmospherics, but Nansen did not know that Petermann Land did not exist.

As May progressed the melting ice proved more difficult, and food was also running low and had to be rationed. June

Below left
An illustration of the winter quarters of Nansen and Johansen which appears in Nansen's book.

Below right
A contemporary photograph of the same scene. The log which the pair used to support the walrus hide roof of their 'hut' (hidden by the snow in the scene to the left) is still in place. The skyline is also as Nansen and Johansen saw it.

brought the first sightings of seals and gulls; Nansen shot two gulls, giving the men their first fresh meat for months. But the temperature also rose above freezing, making the going, through slush, even worse. Despite the gulls, both dogs and men were now starving. Slaughtered dogs provided blood soup for Nansen and Johansen but meagre meat for the remaining dogs. When the slush would no longer support a man on skis the two kayaks were bound into a catamaran and paddled. It was almost as hard as walking. On 21 June, 100 days after leaving the *Fram*, Johansen shot a seal, the first of several. It was the first sign that things were improving, and they improved further when a Polar Bear and her two cubs were shot.

No longer hungry, Nansen and Johansen waited in the camp they had established on 21 June until 19 July. By then rain and high temperatures meant that kayaking was easy. Four days later they recognised that the cloud bank they had been staring at for a month was actually a glacier. Currents and wind made sure that reaching land was not easy, and Johansen was lucky to survive an attack by a bear (he shouted for Nansen to get the gun and then told him 'you must look sharp', remembering to use the formal Norwegian form of 'you', the two men maintaining that formality despite four months together on the ice; not until New Year's Day 1896 did they agree to exchange the formal *de* for the familiar *du*). On 7 August they reached the ice edge. It was a joyous moment, but meant the end for the last two of the 28 dogs that started out from *Fram*.

What the two men had seen was Eva-Liv Island (named later by Nansen after his wife and daughter) in north-eastern Franz Josef. They landed on Adelaide's Island, a little way south, on 10 August. Thinking he was on the west side of the archipelago Nansen decided to kayak west to Gilles Land and then on to Svalbard. Gilles Land had been seen by Dutchman Cornelius Gilles in 1707, but it was not where he claimed it was; he had actually seen Kvitøya. Had Nansen been where he thought he was and headed west he and Johansen would have found 400km of open sea. It is doubtful whether the men would have survived.

As it was, when they headed west, the two kayaks strapped together as a catamaran again, the two men had to endure a Walrus attack before finally landing at Helland's Point on north-west Jackson Island (as Nansen later named it). Now, in late August, it was clear that winter was coming. Desperate to avoid another winter, but trapped by ice and weather, the pair eventually landed on the southern coast of Jackson Island. There they built a hut with low walls of stones, the gaps plugged with moss, strips of walrus and hide and, later, snow. They dug out the floor and draped Walrus skins over a huge log laid between the end walls. Inside, the 3m by 2m hut was remarkably snug. With plenty of fresh bear and Walrus meat cooked over a blubber fire, a comfortable enough winter was passed. Nansen actually gained weight, though he also had a bout of chronic lumbago and had to be nursed by Johansen.

On 19 May 1896 the two Norwegians refloated their catamaran and headed west again, still unsure of their exact whereabouts. Disaster almost struck in June when the poorly-moored catamaran floated away. Nansen took off his top clothes and dived into the chilling water to retrieve it. With all his limbs becoming numb Nansen barely reached the shore again. A few days later a Walrus almost sank them. They beat the Walrus off, but one kayak was holed and by the time they

Left
The meeting between Nansen and Jackson. The photograph was staged the day after the meeting, Nansen having had a wash, shave and change of clothes. But the photograph is close enough to reality to represent one of the most significant handshakes in Arctic history.

got ashore much of their equipment was wet. For two days they stayed in their camp to dry things out. On the second day Nansen thought he heard a dog barking and, leaving Johansen behind, set out on skis to investigate.

On 17 June, at his Elmwood base near Cape Flora on Northbrook Island, Frederick Jackson was told that there was a man approaching and wandered out to meet him. Jackson recalls in his book on his own trip, 'I saw a tall man on ski with roughly made clothes, and an old felt hat on his head. He was covered with oil and grease, and black from head to foot ... His hair was very long and dirty, his complexion appeared to be fair, but dirt prevented me from being sure on this point, and his beard was straggly and dirty also ... I inquired if he had a ship. "No" he replied "my ship is not here" – rather sadly I thought.'

Jackson thought he recognised a man he had met when he lectured in London in 1892. As recorded by Jackson, after discovering he was right he said 'I am damned glad to see you'. The relief Nansen and Johansen must have felt can only be imagined, yet within days Johansen was noting that his once sociable, agreeable companion had returned to his normal arrogant self. The change was probably not helped by Jackson's attitude; Jackson admitted to having been overwhelmed to meet Nansen, but of Johansen he stated only that he 'seems a splendid little fellow'. The two Norwegians sailed in Jackson's ship *Windward* on 7 August and were in Vardø on the 13th. On the 20th they heard that *Fram* was also safely home. The ship had reached 85°56'N in November 1895, but had then drifted south again. She was released from the ice in August 1896. After calling at Svalbard to see if there was any news Sverdrup took the ship on to Norway, arriving on 20 August just a week after Nansen and Johansen.

Nansen returned to Oslo a hero, the raptures his courageous trek engendered echoing not only across the country, but the world. The dissenting voices – those who thought that for a leader to abandon his expedition was a monstrous act and could never be justified; those who felt the trek had been foolhardy (even Jackson thought 'that great luck has attended [the] daring trip'); Peary, who commented acerbically that Nansen should at least have tried to return to the *Fram* ('he could certainly have followed his own trail back ... [the ship] would drift very little in five or six weeks ... was he ashamed to go back after so short an absence') – were drowned out by the acclaim. *Fram* was the second and last great expedition of Nansen's life, but such was the success of it and his Greenland crossing, and the manner of the accomplishment of both, that they were to maintain his reputation as an explorer for the rest of his life.

Andrée and the *Eagle*

Otto Sverdrup had two reasons for stopping at Svalbard on his way home with the *Fram*. The prime reason was, of course, to hear of any news of Nansen and Johansen. The other was to check on the progress of the Swede Salomon August Andrée, who was planning a balloon flight to the North Pole. Andrée had become interested in balloons in 1876 at the age of 22, but it was not until 1893 that his interest had developed into a passion with practical applications. From 1893 to 1895 he undertook nine flights in his balloon *Svea*, including one of 400km that took 16½ hours, and one of 284km that crossed

Opposite page
The memorial erected at the wintering site of Nansen and Johansen on Franz Josef Land.

Jackson's Ponies

Frederick Jackson, whose team Nansen and Johansen had the good fortune to meet, was himself making a (rather unconvincing) attempt on the North Pole. Jackson took both dogs and ponies on his expedition, noting that the latter suffered from the cold and frequently fell belly-deep in snow because of their small hooves. Nevertheless he concluded that the ponies were 'an unqualified success', a summary thought to have influenced both Robert Scott and Ernest Shackleton.

the Baltic Sea from Stockholm to Eskörn Island. The latter was particularly interesting, since Andrée used a guide rope trailing on the sea to slow the balloon, and sails on it to alter the direction of travel. Andrée found he could vary the direction by up to 27° from the wind. By 1894 Andrée was considering the use of a balloon in the Arctic. He believed that he had one that was gas-tight for 30 days, more than enough time judging from his earlier flights, and thought he had solved the potential problem of icing on the fabric – the guide ropes, three of them, each 350m long and made of coconut fibre, would not only allow manoeuvrability but keep the balloon low enough for ice not to form. The endpoint of the flight could not, of course, be fixed; Andrée assumed that given enough time in the air the balloon was bound to reach land somewhere.

In June 1896 the *Virgo* took Andrée's balloon, the *Örnen* (*Eagle*), to Danskøya, an island off Spitsbergen's north-western corner. The site is now called Virgohamna, Virgo harbour. The crew of three – Andrée, Nils Ekholm and Nils Strindberg – waited until 21 August (Sverdrup visiting them on the 14th) but the wind was consistently wrong. On that day the *Virgo* had to leave for Sweden and the three men went with her. Andrée returned in 1897. Nils Ekholm, concerned with the hydrogen leakage rate he had measured in 1896, had pulled out, and his place had been taken by Knut Frœnkel. The *Eagle* was launched on 11 July, but there was an immediate problem. Andrée had changed his guide ropes, attaching the coconut-fibre ropes to hemp ropes with a simple screw, the idea being that if the lower section of the rope hooked firmly on to any projection on the ice the screw could be used to detach it. But the wind rotated the balloon and the coconut ropes unscrewed themselves. Without their ballast the *Eagle* rose to 600m. Within seconds of launch Andrée had lost not only his steering potential but his perceived protection against icing. The balloon headed north-east and, an hour later, disappeared from view.

In those days before radio, Andrée's only available means of communication were carrier pigeons (fast, but not too reliable) and buoys, which, rather like messages in bottles, were unpredictable. Five buoys were eventually picked up, but by then all hope of finding the team alive had gone. Only one pigeon was recovered when it was shot four days after release; its message read 'July 13 at 12.30pm. Lat 82°02'N, Long 15°E, good speed towards east 10° south. All well. This is the third pigeon post. Andrée'. Despite many searches, which continued until 1899, nothing else was heard of, or from, the balloon.

On 6 August 1930 the Norwegian sealer *Bratvaag* anchored off the south-western tip of Kvitøya, the rarely visited island to the north-east of Svalbard's Nordaustlandet. The scientists brought by the ship disembarked and, 200m inland, discovered a snow-covered camp and the remains of the three balloonists. A more extensive search in September revealed the diaries of the crew and, most remarkably, about 20 photographic negatives that could still be printed. The images that appeared when the photographs were developed must have given the darkroom staff a start, reaching across 30 years to record the sad end of the *Eagle*.

The flight had been uneventful at first, *Eagle* heading north-east to about 82°30'N. Then, at about 2am on 12 July, the wind backed to east. The balloon headed west, then north-east again. Rain now caused the balloon to descend and the gondola struck the ice. It banged across the ice for several hours, then one of the shortened guide ropes became trapped. For 13 hours it stayed trapped, then broke free. Ice now began to form on the balloon and soon it was dragging the gondola across the ice again. By 7am on 14 July the flight was over.

The balloon had travelled 830km in 65½ hours and had landed at 82°56'N.

The three men were now forced to head south across the ice, hauling three sledges, on one of which was a boat. At first they decided to head for Cape Flora on Franz Josef Land but soon revised the plan when they realised how slowly they were moving. By early September the three were sick with stomach cramps and severe diarrhoea. They were also exhausted and set up camp on an ice floe, allowing its drift to carry them south. On 5 October they reached Kvitøya, but now, inevitably, faced an Arctic winter with little chance of relief and none of escape. The diary entries became shorter, more fragmented and enigmatic, and finally stopped in mid-October.

From the position of the bodies it was clear that Strindberg had died first as his body was buried beneath rocks in a gap between two boulders. Strindberg's death must have occurred after the diaries of Andrée and Frænkel stopped as it is not mentioned in either. The cause of death of the men has been the subject of speculation ever since the discovery. From the photos and diaries it is clear that Polar Bears were shot for food. Analysis of meat samples discovered at the camp showed the presence of parasitic nematodes called *Trichinella*. If the meat had been eaten raw or poorly cooked the men could have developed trichinosis (which would explain the severe diarrhoea), a condition that can be fatal without treatment. That remains the opinion of many experts, though cold, exhaustion and even suicide induced by their hopeless position cannot be ruled out.

Attempts on the Pole from Franz Josef

After the geography of Franz Josef Land had been established, many explorers with designs on being the first to reach the North Pole believed it would make an ideal starting point for expeditions. The first of these was Walter Wellman, an American journalist, who arrived in 1898. Wellman had already tried once from Svalbard, reaching 81°N in 1894. Accompanied by three other Americans (one of whom was Evelyn Baldwin – see below) and five Norwegians, Wellman (in the *Frithjof*) took one of Jackson's huts and many supplies from Elmwood and, prevented by ice from heading far north, set up a base at Cape Tegetthoff on Hall Island and a northern camp on Wilczek Land. The main expedition spent a comfortable winter at Cape Tegetthoff, but two Norwegians, Bjørvik and Bentsen, had a rougher time at the northern camp. Bentsen sickened and eventually died, leaving Bjørvik

A marvellous cartoon – surely the best ever produced. Swedish in origin (of course!) it shows Andrée's balloon being reeled down to the North Pole by a friendly Inuk while Nansen, in *Fram*, looks on in dismay. The men's respective countrymen are suitably appalled (the Norwegians) or delighted (the Swedes). Exactly where the Inuk and his cog wheels were going to appear from or indeed, how Andrée was actually going to get down to the Pole, or back if he succeeded in doing so, has been ignored.

The Andrée expedition

In the upper photograph the three men are in the basket and the balloon is ready for launch.

The lower photograph was taken just after launch. The trailing ropes, meant to restrict altitude and to give a measure of steering, can be seen. Their loss may have precipitated the immediate crisis with the balloon, but in truth the chances of success were minimal, as were the chances of survival of the crew.

Two of the most poignant photographs in Arctic history. Each is from the exposed negatives found on Kvitøya. The photograph above was taken immediately after the *Eagle* had landed on 14 July. That to the left shows Strindberg (on the right) and Frœnkel inspecting a bear they had shot.

The only Andrée pigeon recovered was stuffed and presented to Anna Charlier, the inconsolable fiancée of Nils Strindberg. In the aftermath of the discovery in 1930, the bodies of the three men were taken back to Sweden, where they were given a state funeral attended by the King. But the most remarkable gesture was that of Gilbert Hawtrey, an English schoolmaster. After more than a decade, with all hope of Strindberg's return gone, Anna Charlier had married Hawtrey and moved with him to New Hampshire in the United States. There she taught piano at his school, the stuffed pigeon 'flying' above the instrument. Anna died before the Kvitøya discovery, but Hawtrey did not. He had her body exhumed and the heart removed, sending it to Sweden to be buried beside her first love.

alone and miserable. In February Bjørvik was relieved by Wellman as he moved north. Already disheartened by the death, Wellman and his team of four and 42 dogs were enveloped in a storm that disrupted the ice, causing the loss of most of their equipment and eight dogs; the attempt was abandoned short of 82°N, with the expedition sailing for home on the *Capella*, a Norwegian sealer.

The next to try his luck from Franz Josef was Luigi Amedeo, Duke of the Abruzzi, who arrived in 1899 with a large team of Italians and Norwegians. The Duke's plan was to sail his ship, the *Stella Polare*, north until ice prevented further progress, then to sledge on. On 6 August the Italians were visited by Wellman and the *Capella*'s captain; Captain Støkken's son was engineer on the Duke's ship. The *Stella Polare* sailed

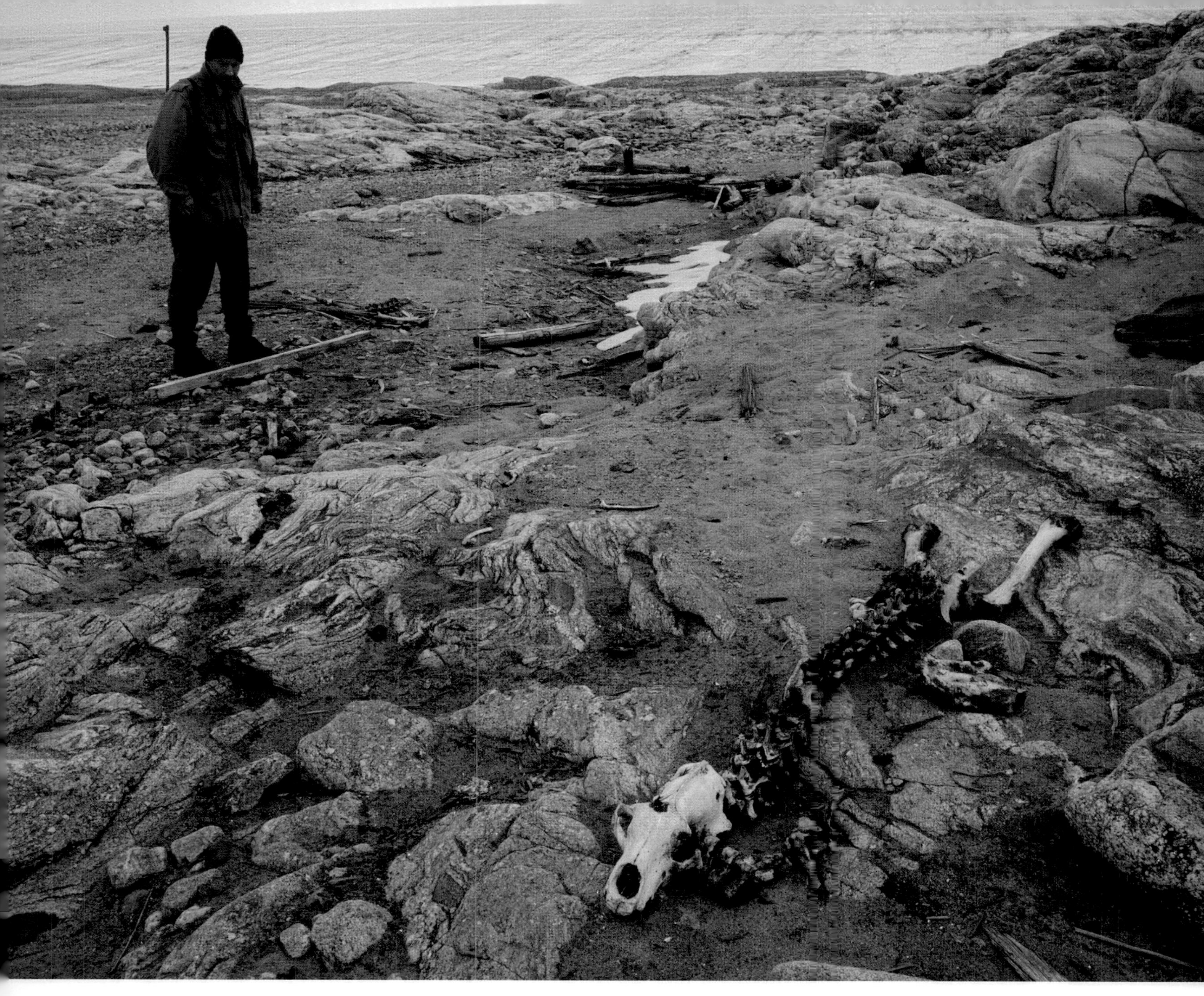

north of Rudolf Island. The Duke hoped that Petermann Island did exist, despite Nansen's claim, but he was disappointed, and as wintering in the open sea was a recipe for disaster the ship returned to Teplitz Bay on the west coast of Rudolf. The journey to the pole started in the spring of 1900. In charge was the Duke's deputy, Umberto Cagni, who led a team of four (himself, Simone Canepa, Alessio Fenoillet and Giuseppe Petigax), supported by three teams who returned at intervals after carrying supplies. All the teams used dog sledges. Sadly, the second support team failed to reach Teplitz Bay; one of the three men lost was Henrik Støkken, son of the *Capella's* captain – the meeting of father and son on the *Stella Polare* had been their last. In 1901 Captain Støkken returned to look for his son; he failed to find any trace of him or his two Italian colleagues and erected a memorial to them at Cape Flora.

Cagni's team spent 104 days on the ice, travelling 1,200km and reaching 86°34'N, a new record. On his return, Cagni claimed that the journey over the sea-ice was too difficult and that future attempts should be made from Greenland. But another expedition, the first of two financed by New Yorker William Zeigler, arrived in Franz Josef in 1901, intent on disproving Cagni's pessimistic assertion. It was led by Evelyn Baldwin, who had been with Wellman in 1898–99 and also with Peary in Greenland in 1893. With 15 Siberian ponies (as a result of which the expedition's ship, the *America*, was elegantly described by one observer as being like a floating haystack), more than 400 dogs and a total of 42 men, the enterprise was massive. Baldwin set up base (Camp Ziegler) on Alger Island, well south of the location he had hoped for, when ice prevented the *America* going further north. In the summer of 1902 Baldwin started laying depots to the north. His teams worked under a considerable handicap as the leader refused to allow them to take sleeping bags, as these took up space which could be better used. Despite the misery this involved, by June a series of depots had been laid to Rudolf Island. At that point, and for no very good reason, Baldwin took the expedition home. It had been a complete waste of time and effort.

In 1903 Zeigler financed a new attempt. Not surprisingly he did not appoint Baldwin as leader, preferring Anthony Fiala, who had been with (and was unimpressed by) Baldwin in 1901–02. Again the expedition was large (though only half

Because of its position and local sea ice conditions Kvitøya is rarely visited.

Above
Photographer Per Michelsen, one of the first to visit the site in modern times, inspects the Andrée crew's camp site.

Opposite page
The site of Strindberg's grave.

The farthest north camp. From Amedeo's book *On the Polar Star in the Arctic Sea*.

the size of Baldwin's). Its base was in Teplitz Bay, where supplies from the Abruzzi expedition were found to be usable. The *America*, which again transported the team, was frozen in, but ice pressure in December wrecked her and she disappeared in a storm in January 1904. Fiala's first attempt at the Pole was thwarted by bad weather and equipment failures after just two days. Faced with a lack of enthusiasm for continuing, Fiala returned to Cape Flora with most of the team. Jackson's Elmwood was occupied and coal was found locally, securing fuel in case of a second winter. A supply ship (Wellman's *Frithjof*) failed to reach the base and a second overwinter was indeed required. In March 1905 Fiala finally attempted to reach the Pole again. His team got as far as 82°N, but open water then stopped progress. Again the expedition lost heart and a retreat was ordered. This time a relief ship managed to reach Cape Flora. It was the *Terra Nova* which, five years later, would take Scott to Antarctica.

As Fiala's team was being evacuated from Franz Josef, Robert Peary was heading north again. During the long expedition of 1898–1902 Peary had twice attempted to reach the North Pole from Ellesmere Island, his northernmost point in 1902 (84°17'N) being a record in the western Arctic, though more than 2° less than Cagni's attempt from Franz Josef Land. The attempts seem curiously tentative, at odds with his obsession with fame and the pole; though ice conditions and the cold in 1902 had contributed to the limited achievement, the attempt had lasted only 16 days. Arguably the most experienced polar traveller of the time, with an enviable record of exploration in northern Greenland, he had actually achieved little in his quest for the pole. His 1901 journey seems lacking in conviction, an opinion apparently shared by his backers who sent a Dr Frederick Cook to examine him. Cook later claimed to have diagnosed suspected pernicious anaemia and recommended eating liver, to which Peary replied 'I would rather die'. Cook also looked at his feet and told him 'you are through as a traveller on snow on foot'. Peary was then 46. The news would have been unwelcome, the messenger, a rival and a younger one at that, unpopular. A relationship which had started with mutual respect was turning sour. However, there are doubts whether the examination actually took place as no record, other than Cook's own writings set down many years later, have ever been discovered. Cook's diagnosis and suggested cure were both two decades ahead of their time, and his account seems to have benefited from his knowledge of recent discoveries. It would not be the last time that Cook and Peary would clash.

Since 1902 Peary had recharged his mental batteries, refilled his expedition coffers (despite Cook's verdict and the lack of enthusiasm of some of his backers, Peary had not lost his touch for keeping real power on his side) and by 1905 was

Rudolf Island, Franz Josef Land.

Looking a little like the cavalry arriving in the nick of time, Fiala's expedition sets out across the ice in 1905.

ready for another try. He was approaching 50 years old and probably knew it might be his last attempt. He had a new ship, the *Roosevelt*, named after the new, young American President (a shrewd piece of PR by Peary) and built with money supplied by his backers. The ship was designed along similar lines to Nansen's *Fram*, but with the prow engineered to cut through the ice. *Roosevelt* could be described as the world's first icebreaker, the intention being to go as far north as possible and so avoid days of sledging. In fact Peary only managed to get the ship to a little way past the point reached by the *Alert*; it was only 3km further north, but it satisfied Peary's lust for records. Early the following year supply depots were established ready for the pole attempt, which began on 6 March. Progress was hampered by a huge lead, ice drift and bad weather, and by early April it was clear the pole was unattainable. Even a new record northing was doubtful. But Peary decided on a last dash and, achieving daily travel rates which were, if true, remarkable, reached 87°06'N on 21 April. He had bettered Cagni's record by 32'. There are many who doubt Peary's claim (particularly as he was still troubled by his amputated toe stubs and also had a hernia), though most experts believe he probably got very close to Cagni's latitude, perhaps even going a little further. But the doubts generated by his unlikely account of the last dash colour judgements over his later claims.

At his northernmost point, whatever it was, Peary turned and headed, not for his ship, but for the Greenland coast, which, because of ice drift, was now due south. Feeding some of his dogs to the rest and burning sledges for fuel, the team made it – but only just. Then on the route west to the ship Peary's team overtook one of their supply teams. It was fortunate they did; though Peary was almost out of food and fuel,

Robert Peary

Robert Edwin Peary was born on 6 May 1856 at Cresson, Pennsylvania. When he was three Peary's father died and his mother moved back to Maine, her home state. Peary grew up as an only child, his mother treating him as the girl she wished he had been, so he often had to fight against other boys who ridiculed him. That and a lisp that bothered him (and would continue to do so into adulthood) made him a silent, strangely preoccupied boy. Peary was a good scholar, graduating in civil engineering, and good at sport. He worked as a draughtsman in the US Coast and Geodesic Survey, then joined the US Navy as a lieutenant.

Early in his career he went to Nicaragua to survey a possible canal linking the Pacific and Atlantic. Later, while on leave of absence from the navy, he made his first expedition to Greenland, his report of the trek resulting in his election to the American Society for the Advancement of Science. Shortly after he wrote to his mother, following it with another to her after Nansen's successful crossing of Greenland's Inland Ice. In these letters he clearly sets down feelings that were to influence the course of his life as a polar explorer. In the first he notes 'I <u>must</u> have fame', while in the second he writes 'Fame, money, and revenge goad me forward till sometimes I can hardly sleep with anxiety lest something happen to interfere with my plans'. Peary's Arctic journeys and his claim to have reached the pole, and his rivalries, particularly the vicious attacks on Frederick Cook, are an amplification of these written desires.

Peary achieved the fame he sought, though whether it was truly his due is debatable, but it came at a price because the veracity of his claim was questioned. This affected him badly, despite the many honours he received and his promotion to Rear Admiral. The doubts soured the fame he craved and made him bitter; the stress may have affected his health. He contracted pernicious anaemia in 1917 and died on 20 February 1920, and was buried in Arlington National Cemetery.

Frederick Cook

Frederick Albert Cook was born on 10 June 1865, the fourth child of a German doctor who had moved to New York in 1855 and changed his name from Koch. Cook's father died when he was five – early parental death seems to be a recurring theme in great polar explorers – giving the young boy an independence that was to serve him well in later life. Cook was shrewd and had started printing and milk delivery businesses while still at school. He also found time to train as a physician. Cook married while still at college, but his wife died shortly after giving birth to their first child. The baby, a girl, also died within a few hours of the birth. Cook opened his first surgery in 1890 but failed to be an instant success, and fired by Kane's book of his Arctic journey he joined Peary's 1891 Greenland expedition. After his return Cook tried to organise his own expedition to Antarctica. He failed, and joined the 1898 expedition of the Belgian Adrian de Gerlache instead (De Gerlache's team also included Roald Amundsen). The expedition, aboard the *Belgica*, was the first to overwinter in Antarctica, its success due in no small way to Cook's insistence on the men eating seal and penguin to stave off scurvy, in ensuring that the men had prolonged exposure to the heat and light of a fire each day, and in suggesting hacking through the sea ice to free the ship when spring arrived. Amundsen claimed that Cook was the mainstay of the expedition; he became a friend and admirer. To Cook's list of innovations on the *Belgica* can be added new clothing, sleeping bag and tent design; the tent Amundsen used on his South Pole journey was of Cook's design.

In 1906 Cook claimed to have climbed Mount McKinley, the highest mountain in the United States. His claim was accepted at first, but eventually questioned when the photographs of the climb were analysed. After his North Pole claim of 1908, Cook's companion on McKinley wrote an affidavit stating that the climb had not taken place. Cook's McKinley and North Pole claims have been picked over carefully over the years. As with Peary's North Pole claim, the consensus is that Cook's climb and pole journey were both fictitious, yet each still has its firm adherents.

Following the rejection of both the McKinley and pole claims, Cook suffered further humiliation in the 1920s when he was convicted of fraud over an oil company with which he had become involved; he was accused of selling land as oil-bearing when it was not. He was sentenced to 14 years imprisonment, serving seven in Fort Leavenworth, where he rapidly became the most popular inmate with both other prisoners and the staff. He was visited by Amundsen, powerful evidence of the Norwegian's admiration for the man. After the visit, Amundsen told reporters that from his reading of Cook's and Peary's accounts of their journeys there was little to choose between them. The Americans were outraged; how could this great explorer be siding with a liar and fraudster? Invitations to talks were rescinded; Amundsen cut short his US visit and went home. In the end it was shown that the land at the centre of the fraud case was oil-bearing, just as Cook had claimed. He was released from prison in 1930. On 5 May 1940 he suffered a cerebral haemorrhage. He was given an unconditional pardon by President Roosevelt on 16 May but died on 5 August.

the supply team was in a far more desperate position and would probably have died had he not arrived. The last miles to the ship were difficult. Had Peary not known the coast so well and been so experienced it would have ended in tragedy. As it was he brought 12 men (his eight and the supply team's four) to safety.

Cook and Peary

In September 1909 an astonished world was informed that the North Pole had finally been reached – not once, but twice. On 2 September Dr Frederick Cook, the man who in 1902 had told Peary he was through as a polar explorer, announced by a way of a telegram office in the Shetland Islands (where the Danish supply ship taking him from Greenland to Denmark stopped briefly) that he had stood at the pole on 21 April 1908. Then, on 6 September Robert Peary used a similar office in Indian Harbour, Labrador to say that he had reached the pole on 6 April 1909. Each had friends in high places, and within days the *New York Herald*, which had backed Cook, and the *New York Times* and National Geographic Society, Peary's backers, had declared war. It was a dirty war, one in which the reputations of both men were tarnished beyond redemption, and one which, a century on, shows no signs – nor has much chance – of ending in a truce, honourable or otherwise.

Returning from his claimed furthest north in 1906, Peary found that his ship, the *Roosevelt*, needed a refit. The work was not completed in time to sail in 1907, so not until 1908 did Peary head north again. If he had not believed that his 1905 attempt would be his last, Peary, now aged 52, must have known that if he failed this time he would not come this way again. Such considerations may explain why his expedition was huge. In addition to the 22 who started out on the *Roosevelt* there were 49 Inuit from Etah and 246 dogs. The *Roosevelt*'s captain, Bob Bartlett (who had also been captain in 1905, and was later captain of the *Karluk* and a great Arctic explorer in his own right) again took the ship to Cape Sheridan on Ellesmere's north coast. From there a wintering base was established at Cape Colombia. From it, on 28 February 1909, 24 men, 19 sledges and 133 dogs set out north.

Dog-sledging on sea-ice. The photograph (*left*), taken off Spitsbergen's coast, shows that on calm, sunny days when the ice is relatively flat, the experience can be both a tranquil and beautiful one. But, as the two photographs below (from Peary's final Pole expedition) indicate, moving on sea-ice can also be difficult, exhausting and time-consuming, which has led experts to doubt Peary's claimed rate of progress.

At one stage Peary's team were held up by a huge open lead for six days (of good weather). When the lead closed the caravan moved on. One by one the support teams departed south. During the return of one of these support teams Ross Marvin, Peary's 'secretary', drowned in a lead. Finally, on 1 April Peary sent Bartlett and the last support team back. Bartlett had wanted to go all the way, and had certainly wanted to reach 88°; he took one last latitude observation at 87°46'49"N. Peary and his team were 246km from the Pole. With him Peary now had Matthew Henson, the Inuit Egingwah, Ooqueah, Ootah and Seegloo, five sledges and 40 dogs. This team reached the pole at about 1pm on 6 April. On those last five days they had averaged almost 50km/day (straight line distance). On the first 31 days they had averaged

The Pole photographs of Peary (*above*) and Cook (*below*). As with the shot of sledge-hauling (p211 *centre*) the Peary photograph was hand-tinted after his arrival back in the US rather than being colour shots.

about 17km/day (straight line distance again). Peary remained at the Pole for about 30 hours, then raced back to the *Roosevelt,* arriving on 27 April. He arrived just three days after Bartlett, who had travelled at least 490km less. At Etah on 17 August Peary heard that Cook was claiming to have beaten him to the North Pole, but on Labrador went ahead with his announcement.

Cook's claim was even more remarkable than Peary's as the latter had retraced his own earlier journeys, while Cook had pioneered a new route. Cook was sponsored by John R. Bradley, gambling club owner and big game hunter, and sailed, in 1907, in a ship bought by and renamed after him. The *John R. Bradley* was captained by Moses Bartlett, cousin of the *Roosevelt's* Bob, and dropped Cook and Rudolph Francke at the Inuit village of Annoatok, close to Etah. Francke had been employed by Bradley as a cook, and was somewhat taken aback to discover he was now to accompany Cook on a journey towards the North Pole. After overwintering at Annoatok the two set out in February 1908 with nine Inuit. Instead of going north, along the 'normal' (and Peary's), route they headed west, crossing to Cape Sabine, then traversing Ellesmere Island to reach Cape Thomas Hubbard at the northern tip of Axel Heiberg Island, a journey of more than 800km. At the Cape, Cook left a large supply dump, then on 18 March headed north across the sea ice with just two Inuit companions, Ahwelah and Etukishook, two sledges and 26 dogs. He reached the North Pole on 21 April, having travelled about 800km in 34 days.

On the return journey, ice drift pushed them west and persistent fog and poor weather prevented them from calculating their position. With food running very short they at last had clear weather and were able to pinpoint their position. They were in the Prince Gustav Adolf Sea, with land to the south and west, and Axel Heiberg off to the east. Cook now continued to head south, taking Hassel Sound between the Ringnes Islands, and reaching the Grinnell Peninsula on the north-western tip of Devon Island. They had by now run out of ammunition and had to fashion harpoons, and bows and arrows from Musk Ox horn and whalebone in order to hunt. The three men headed east along Jones Sound, then overwintered in an old Inuit winter house, continuing towards Greenland in February 1909. Once more low on food, they existed for a short time on candles and hot water until a bear was killed. By the time they reached Annoatok they were hungry again, so much so that they were barely able to stand and had eaten all their leather straps. They had been away for 14 months, having taken food for just 2 months.

Cook was feted on his arrival in Copenhagen, but things rapidly turned sour for him. On his journey south Peary spoke with the two Inuit who had accompanied Cook and claimed they told him they had never been out of sight of land. But in the United States Peary's vitriolic attacks on Cook, in telegrams and to the press, had the opposite effect to that intended, rapidly drawing sympathy for Cook. In several polls public opinion was 80% in Cook's favour, often higher. Outside the States the less heated atmosphere allowed more sober judgements, and these tended to favour Peary. Cook's position was made much worse by his Mount McKinley claim being declared a fraud. In the end Peary won over the majority, often grudgingly as Cook was a much more amiable man, a complete contrast to the blustering Peary who lacked Cook's

social skills. After his imprisonment, Cook's reputation as a liar and fraud remained, despite his pardon. But to the end he maintained the validity of his claim to have been the first to the Pole, recording a tape for posterity. Its final words were 'I state emphatically that I, Frederick A. Cook, discovered the North Pole.'

By contrast to Cook, who suffered public humiliation with forbearance and good grace, Robert Peary railed against the injustice of not being given full credit for his discovery for the rest of his life. He had sacrificed his best years to the search for fame and the pursuit of the pole. He had been away for most of his eldest daughter's formative years and had never seen a second daughter who had died aged seven months. The honours he received could not assuage his bitterness, a bitterness which, his wife claimed, hastened his death (ironically of the disease that Cook had diagnosed all those years before). It is of course possible thatPeary's bitterness was not solely due to what he felt was his just reward for his life's work – the Pole – had become soured by dispute. If he had not actually reached the Pole and had known he had not, then the bitter taste could have been that of defeat. Peary managed to convince most of the world of the validity of his claim. A dishonest man might convince himself that he deserves a prize, but unless he is especially deluded he will not be able to convince himself that he has actually secured it.

Summarising the evidence

Millions of words have been written on Cook and Peary. At the time the dispute was simple – which of the two was first to reach the North Pole? Now the question is different – did either of them? Peary's claim is based on extraordinary rates of travel during the days after Bartlett was sent back (ironically, Peary's supporters used Cook's claimed rate of travel of 25km/day as evidence of his fraud when compared to rates achieved by earlier travellers, an argument they hastily dropped when Peary's account, with claimed rates of 50km/day, was published). Most of those who have sledged to the Pole consider Peary's rates are unfeasibly (even ludicrously) high. In a carefully considered book Wally Herbert judged that Peary did not reach the Pole, his claim being immediately rebuffed by a 'scientific study' commissioned by the National Geographic Society, Peary's staunchest supporter. There is also the fact that Peary took only Henson (his coloured valet) and the Inuit to the Pole. Was this because he wanted to be the only white man there, or was it to hedge his bets as nobody would take the word of a black man or a native against his own? Amundsen, initially at least, accepted Peary's claim – indeed, he changed his own plans and headed south as a result – but noted that Peary's word had to be taken as he was alone; 'of course, the Negro Henson was too ignorant to know whether they reached it or not'. This now-shocking view accords with Peary's own view of Henson; despite occasional admissions that Henson was his right-hand man and an essential part of the team, Peary famously upbraided Henson for not calling him 'sir' at all times – 'you will pay attention when I am talking to you and show that you hear directions I give you by saying yes sir, or all right sir' – a clear indication of how Peary saw their relationship.

But much more important was the fact that by his own admission, Peary made no measurements of his longitude, took no measurements of magnetic variation and made no allowance for ice drift. This gave even his staunchest supporters pause for thought, particularly those who had experience on ice. Peary's claim to have gone north along the 70°W meridian is at odds with all experience of ice movements and, unsupported by longitude readings, stretches credibility. If he really did travel by dead reckoning as he claims, then at his final camp he had no idea where he was. This would explain his poor humour when approached by Henson: his Sun shot might have told him that he was still some way from the pole. The strange omissions from his diary are certainly consistent with that view.

But if Peary's claim lacks credibility the situation is no less problematic for Cook's supporters. There is the curiosity of cropped photographs that appear to show land where none should be. There is the contradictory testimony of his Inuit companions; when interviewed by others, Cook's Inuit companions at first backed-up his claim to have reached the 'Great Navel' as the Inuit call the Pole (the Inuit name is usually given as 'Great Nail', the explanation being that the place the white explorers sought must be something tangible or why else go there, and iron was the most valuable commodity to an Inuk, but the true translation of the Inuit is *navel* not *nail*), but they are later said to have stated that they had never been out of sight of land. Cook's supporters make much of the earlier statements, claiming that the later ones were made under duress – the Inuit were often accused of telling the white man what he wanted to hear. This charge was made at the time of Rae's discovery of Franklin's fate, and there was some truth in it. Cook claimed to have told the two Inuit that they were never far from land to calm them as they feared being far out on the sea ice, and Knud Rasmussen, who met Cook on his return to Greenland and later interviewed many Inuit who had spoken to his companions, believed that the pole had been reached. Yet it seems that Cook's two Inuit told a consistent tale throughout the rest of their lives, a tale that, though ambiguous, did suggest that they believed they really had not gone far from land.

There is also the issue of whether enough supplies could be carried by the three men to last the trip as described, since Cook made no mention of hunting (but then, as noted above, Cook had set out with food for eight weeks and survived for 14 months, so his team were clearly well capable of looking after themselves). There is the fact that Hassel Sound, 'narrow' according to Cook, is 24km wide at its narrowest point. In claiming it to be narrow Cook was following Sverdrup, who also stated it was narrow (but from observation only). Cook was a remarkably good observer of natural phenomena and would not have been expected to get the width wrong, yet it has to be said that it is occasionally very difficult to be sure where sea ice ends and a low coast begins, and Cook did accurately place a small island at Hassel Sound's northern end. His supporters note that whether or not he traversed the Sound has no bearing on the validity of his Pole claim, but it does, of course; if he was not telling the truth about that, relatively trivial, aspect of his trip, why should we believe him when he said he went to the Pole? All the doubts raised by the sceptics about Cook's journey are rebutted by Cook's supporters, usually by cogent argument though occasionally the logic of the rebuttals is clamorous and suspect. But then Cook's opponents are often equally hysterical.

One interesting consideration is the fact that Cook, a humane man, was appalled by Peary's treatment of members of his expeditions and the Inuit. Cook claimed that both Verhoeff and Astrup had been driven to suicide by Peary, and felt that Peary's constant reference to 'my Eskimo', implying ownership, was distasteful. He also disliked Peary's assumed 'ownership' of the Pole. Did Cook conspire to teach Peary a lesson for his arrogance?

Finally, there is the mystery of the phantom and actual land of Cook's journey. On his 1905–06 expedition Peary claimed to have seen land to the north-west of Axel Heiberg. He named it Crocker Land after George Crocker, railway magnate and part-sponsor of the expedition. It is usually said that Peary had been deceived by a mirage, just as Ross had been all those years ago, though as Peary claimed to have seen Crocker Land from an altitude of around 600m (a very unlikely, though not impossible, vision) some have claimed that the sighting and naming was a deliberate act to extract more money from the

Wellman's airship being moved out of its hangar at Virgohavn, Spitsbergen, Svalbard.

flattered railwayman. On his trip Cook claimed to have seen Bradley Land (as he called it, naming it after his main sponsor) to the north of Peary's. It has been suggested that Cook's Bradley was based on Peary's Crocker and is evidence of his fraud. When Donald McMillan, once a member of a Peary team, went to explore Crocker Land in 1913–17 he too saw it from Ellesmere Island. When he reached it, it had disappeared – it did not exist. Yet when he returned to Ellesmere McMillan saw it clearly again and would have sworn to its existence had he not known with certainty there was nothing there – Crocker/Bradley was a phantom. But there are those who believe that Cook may have seen ice islands now known to exist at about the same position as he claimed for Bradley Land. And if he did see those ice islands then he must have been in a position to do so.

Meighen Island, to the west of Axel Heiberg, *does* exist. When Cook had his first clear day after fog on his return from the pole he claimed to have seen land to the west and south, and Axel Heiberg to the east. As has been pointed out, from where he was at that time Meighen Island would have been clearly visible – it rises to about 150m (500ft). Some of the anti-Cook faction claim it would have obscured his view of Axel Heiberg, but that is not so if his position was calculated accurately. However, he said there was land to the west, which is only possible if he was further south than he thought. In that case Meighen would have been even further north. But these are minor issues in comparison to a real mystery. Cook's Inuit companions plotted the journey they said they had actually made on a map based on Sverdrup's discoveries. On that map they accurately plotted the position and size of an island they claimed to have seen to the north-west of Axel Heiberg. It was clearly Meighen Island, at that time undiscovered (it was not officially located until 1916, when Stefansson came this way). Why then, if Cook had discovered Meighen, did he not mention it to lend greater credence to his supposed fraudulent story?

At this remove in time the truth of the two claims can no longer be ascertained. While in general the polar environment does a remarkable job of preserving objects left either deliberately or casually, the nature of the Arctic Ocean precludes such survivals. No new evidence is likely either from the north or from the diaries and logs of the two men and their expeditions. No one will ever know for certain which, if either, was telling the truth. Overall it is probable that Peary got close to

Below
The remains of Wellman's airship hangar, Virgohavn.

Below right
Iron for the making of hydrogen at Virgohavn.

the Pole (probably within 150km), but did not reach it, defeated by his own navigational naiveté and incompetence. It is likely, too, that Peary knew he had failed. Cook's claim is more intriguing. There are seemingly compelling reasons for discounting it, not least the fact that by his own admission Cook was a novice navigator – how could someone incapable of plotting longitude and having difficulty with latitude possibly know where he was on the shifting ice of the Arctic Ocean? Yet equally compelling is the evidence that suggests he did indeed travel a long way out across the ocean towards the Pole and so, perhaps, might have reached it. Intriguingly, in their early retelling of the journey before Peary's supporters interviewed them, Cook's two Inuit companions gave a very accurate description of how the Sun moved at the Pole, something they had never seen before. That curious movement only occurs at (or very close to) the Pole. Either way, Cook's was a remarkable journey, and both more interesting and tougher than Peary's.

Airships and aeroplanes

Throughout the period 1906–09, voyagers continued to attempt to reach the pole by air. Andrée's flight had failed, but that had always been a risky, hit-and-miss venture. Balloon technology was at its limit and Andrée's steering method was, at best, haphazard. Ten years later airships had replaced balloons, offering acceptable steering in all but the worst weather. Gas leakage had also been reduced, and with a higher speed and better steering, flight times were also lower so gas losses were less of a constraint. The first to try the new technology in the Arctic was Walter Wellman, the man who had already tried his luck with a dog-sledge.

This time Wellman chose Spitsbergen for his base. In 1906 he brought the first airship to Danskøya (from where Andrée had launched), but he abandoned the attempt when it became apparent that his engines were useless. He returned in June of the following year. It took until August to reconstruct the 1906 hangar, but in that month the weather was continuously awful. Only on 2 September could the airship (the *America*) finally be pulled from the hangar. Initially towed by a small steamer, the airship flew 24km northwards, but was then hit by a storm. As Wellman noted, 'there ensued a hard fight between the storm and the motor. The latter triumphed.' It was just as well, since the storm threatened to crash the *America* into jagged mountains.

Wellman was back on Danskøya in 1909, the *America* being launched on 15 August. This time, Wellman had fitted two guide ropes, just as Andrée had. But in a re-run of Andrée's launch, one of the guide ropes fell off and the *America* climbed rapidly. Fortunately this incident was observed by the Norwegian coastal steamer *Farm* (not to be confused with *Fram*) which, sensing trouble, gave chase and was able to rescue the *America*'s four-man team.

After Wellman, interest in reaching the Pole by air died off, despite the debate over the validity of Cook and Peary's Pole claims. The 1914–18 war halted further efforts altogether; not until the 1920s was another attempt made to reach the North Pole. The technology of air travel, both airships and aeroplanes, had moved on and, as always, people were eager to apply the latest technology to the problems of remoteness and climatic hostility. The main enthusiast was Roald Amundsen, whose *Maud* expedition had completed the North-East Passage but entirely failed to emulate *Fram*'s ice drift. Amundsen left *Maud* in 1921 to buy an aircraft, but his first attempted flight from Alaska to Spitsbergen failed due to bad weather. He tried again in 1923. This time he used a plane with insufficient fuel capacity, his idea being to carry a sledge and kayak, completing the journey with these after he had made a forced landing. He was perhaps fortunate that his plane crashed on its first trial flight.

In 1925 Amundsen tried again, this time with the help and finance of Lincoln Ellsworth. Ellsworth was the son of a wealthy American financier who agreed, after some soul-searching, to underwrite an expedition of two seaplanes, seaplanes being used as they could land on both ice and water. The two Dornier-Wal planes (numbered *N-24* and *N-25*) were to take off from King's Bay (Ny Ålesund) on Spitsbergen, each carrying three men and food for three weeks. The plan was to land at the Pole, transferring all fuel and men into one plane for a continuing flight to Alaska. The planes took off on 21 May 1925 and flew for eight hours. Then, assuming they were close to the Pole, they landed. Once down they discovered that a head wind had reduced their speed; they were only at 88°N. *N-25*, piloted by Hjalmar Riiser-Larsen, with German mechanic Ludwig Feucht and Amundsen on board, had engine trouble on the descent. Riiser-Larsen was forced to land on a narrow lead and came to rest against an iceberg. *N-24*, piloted by Leif Dietrichsen, with mechanic Oskar Omsdal and Ellsworth, landed in a large pool of open water, but collided with an ice floe, filling the cabin with water. The two crews could not at first see each other, but after 24 hours they had made visual contact and exchanged messages by semaphore: they were 5km apart. Over the next few days ice drift took *N-24*'s crew closer to *N-25*. Eventually the entire team was back together again, but only after Omsdal had fallen into the sea, knocking out seven teeth on the ice edge as he did so.

The six men managed to get *N-25* safely on to the ice floe. Then Amundsen spelled out the reality of their situation. They could try and build a runway for *N-25*. Going on half-rations gave them until 15 June to do so. At that time each man could choose to try to get to Greenland (across several hundred kilometres of sea ice) or to stay with the plane, trying to get it off the ice until food ran out. The stark choice galvanised the men, but several attempts to construct a runway failed. Finally, and desperately, *N-25* was hauled on to another floe and a channel was cut in a pressure ridge, allowing access to an area of level snow. This was stamped down, the nightly drop in temperature freezing it. On the morning of 15 June Riiser-Larsen fired the engines. The plane lifted off just metres from the runway's end, missed an iceberg by centimetres and flew on. Using dead reckoning they reached Hinloppen Strait, off northern Spitsbergen, where they were forced to land as fuel was running out. The next day a sealing ship was spotted and, using the remaining fuel, *N-25* was driven towards it. They had been away for 26 days; the sealer's captain looked at them as though they were ghosts. The team were taken back to King's Bay on Spitsbergen.

The following year, 1926, saw Amundsen and Ellsworth back at King's Bay ready to try for the Pole again, but this time in an airship, a dirigible designed by the Italian Umberto Nobile, who was to accompany the expedition. Despite Amundsen's attempts to reduce his role, Nobile was intent on maximising his share of the glory of the trip; Italian dictator

One of the Dorniers in the ice. A photograph from the Amundsen/Ellsworth book *Our Polar Flight*.

Roald Amundsen

The Norwegian Roald Engebreth Gravning Amundsen was born on 16 July 1872 and grew up, a pugnacious boy, on the outskirts of Oslo (then Christiania), acquiring early the skills of skiing and seamanship. Having obtained his master's certificate, chiefly by working on sealing boats, Amundsen served his polar apprenticeship on the *Belgica* which carried the first expedition to overwinter in Antarctica, the team also including Frederick Cook. By 1901 Amundsen felt ready to take command of his first expedition, the first ship transit of the North-West Passage. This was followed by his expedition to the South Pole. Amundsen had originally intended to tackle the North Pole, but he turned south when news of Peary's claim broke. After winning the race for the South Pole, Amundsen continued his polar journeys, taking *Maud* through the North-East Passage, then making his North Pole flights. As the first man to reach the South Pole, perhaps the first to see the North Pole, the first to complete the North-West Passage, and the third to transit the North-East Passage, Amundsen has a strong claim to the title of the greatest of all polar explorers.

The photograph above is of a bust of him at Nome, Alaska, commissioned to commemorate the *Norge* flight.

Benito Mussolini was equally intent on maximising the propaganda benefits for his own ends. Amundsen and Ellsworth arrived on Spitsbergen in early April and were joined on 29 April by Richard Byrd of the US Navy, his plane a Fokker trimotor named the *Josephine Ford*, and his pilot Floyd Bennett. Byrd had asked permission to use King's Bay for a proposed flight to Greenland but now announced that he intended to fly to the Pole. Amundsen, perhaps conscious of his own switch from North to South Pole and the subsequent furore did not object. Perhaps, too, Amundsen reasoned that the main prize was already lost since the Pole had already been reached. Amundsen offered Byrd every assistance, including a stack of survival gear, none of which, despite his plan, Byrd possessed.

On 7 May Amundsen's airship, the *Norge* (originally designated the *N-1* or *Nobile 1*, its name changed by Amundsen), arrived, having been flown from Italy. During the flight the Norwegian pilot, Riiser-Larsen again, had been horrified by the poverty of Nobile's piloting efforts. Nobile was equally horrified by Amundsen's refusal to race Byrd for the privilege of the first flight to the North Pole; the loss of this chance for glory must have been a hard blow for the Italian.

Unaware of any problems with Byrd's claim (see Box on p217), at 1am on 11 May Amundsen's crew of 16 – including Ellsworth, Nobile, Riiser-Larsen, the Swede Finn Malmgren and Oscar Wisting, who had been with Amundsen at the South Pole and on the *Maud* – lifted the *Norge* off from Ny Ålesund. At 1.30am on 12 May the *Norge* circled over the Pole, dropping the flags of Italy, Norway and the United States on to the ice; they were attached to sharpened aluminium stakes so they stood upright and flapped in the wind. Nobile defied Amundsen and Ellsworth by making the Italian flag much bigger than the others, so large it fouled on the airship and momentarily threatened a propeller. Amundsen and Wisting, the first men to see both poles (and, perhaps, in the teams that were first to reach each) shook hands.

So far the flight had been uneventful, but beyond the Pole the *Norge* ran into fog and began to ice up. Icing on the radio aerials made communication impossible and chunks of ice thrown from the propellers threatened the gas bag. By adjusting altitude the icing was minimised, allowing the airship to continue. At 7.30am on 13 May the Alaskan coast near Point Barrow was seen, but low cloud forced the *Norge* to fly high, the airship having to go along the coast to reach the Bering Strait so as to avoid Alaska's inland mountains. Now one of

First flight to the North Pole?

At 00.37 GMT on 10 May 1926, Bennett and Byrd took off in the *Josephine Ford*. At 16.07 they returned, claiming to have reached the pole. Byrd said that just as they began their return trip from the pole he had dropped and broken his sextant, with the flight back to King's Bay involving navigation by dead reckoning – a fantastic feat. Byrd was welcomed as a hero at King's Bay, his and Bennett's achievement soon being heralded across the world. Then, in 1960, the Swedish meteorologist Gösta Liljequist analysed the capabilities of the plane, its flight timings and local weather charts, and concluded that Byrd was unlikely to have flown beyond 88°N. By then Byrd, who went on to an illustrious naval and polar career, had died. It was assumed that he was unaware of his failure, but more recently it has been noted that his charts were altered after the flight, with many computed positions being added. There was also the curiosity that Byrd had taken a huge number of small flags to drop at the Pole, and not one of them was seen from the *Norge* two days later. It has also emerged subsequently that Floyd Bennett confided in a friend that he and Byrd had made no attempt at the Pole; the Josephine Ford developed an oil leak early in the flight, and they had merely flown about for the requisite number of hours beyond the view of King's Bay before returning. The idea that Richard Byrd died unaware that he had not reached the Pole and that he had performed a near-miraculous feat of navigation on the return route must therefore be re-evaluated.

The photograph above shows Amundsen, left, and Ellsworth, right, congratulating Byrd and Bennett.

the two engines began to fail and the spare would not start. After a flight of more than 50 hours the crew were exhausted (not least because there were only two seats, so many had been standing for almost the entire flight). The intended landing at Nome was abandoned and at 8am on 14 May the *Norge* touched down at Teller, 90km to the north-west.

The flight had been a major success, but its aftermath was ugly. To their annoyance, Amundsen and Ellsworth discovered that Nobile had, in secret, persuaded the Norwegian backers of the expedition to add his name as co-leader. In Italy Mussolini promoted Nobile to general and ordered him to lecture to the 'Italian colonies' in the United States. A large crowd of Italian-Americans gathered at Seattle when the expedition team arrived; Nobile, in military uniform, made the fascist salute and was feted, while Amundsen and Ellsworth were virtually ignored. Nobile's lecture tour – in which he claimed to have both masterminded the expedition and piloted the airship, neither of which was correct – creamed off much of the available audience (and their entrance money), leaving both Amundsen and Ellsworth short of cash. Ironically, Nobile eventually believed his own propaganda about being a major explorer, a delusion that would lead to tragedy.

The *Italia*

Buoyed by the adulation, Nobile organised an expedition of his own in 1928, in which he intended to make a series of three flights, exploring Severnaya Zemlya, the area north of Greenland, and a trip back to the Pole. He decided to use an airship similar to the *Norge*, but called *Italia* to reinforce the national identity of the expedition. The flight to the Pole was to include the setting down of a party of six scientists during an extended stay. Despite Nobile's attempts to drum up enthusiasm for the venture, even Mussolini seems to have been lukewarm, as nothing very new was being proposed.

After one aborted attempt, a 60-hour flight from King's Bay to Franz Josef Land, Severnaya Zemlya and Novaya Zemlya was reached in mid-May. Then, on 23 May, the *Italia* with a crew of 16 (14 Italians, Finn Malmgren, who had been

Above
The *Norge* at King's Bay (Ny Ålesund).

Right
Nobile (top), Wisting, Amundsen (with his back turned) and Riiser-Larsen in the *Norge*.

on the *Norge* flight, and a Czech) took off for the pole, flying via Cape Bridgman on Greenland's north coast. On the journey north the wind was favourable, boosting the average speed to 105kph, and the Pole was reached just after midnight (00.20) on 24 May after a flight of only 20 hours. But the same wind slowed the return, while cloud hamperednaviga-tion. Although the airship was in radio contact with the *Citta di Milano*, her support ship, the fixing of position by radio was a young science. Cloud caused heavy icing of the *Italia* and at 10.33 on 25 May, after 55 hours of flying, she began to descend rapidly. The gondola smashed into the ice, ripping it from the ship which, freed of the load, rose rapidly, taking six men to their doom. No sign of the ship or the men was ever found, though the survivors later reported seeing a column of smoke, suggesting that the airship's hydrogen had caught fire.

Of the ten men who lay on the ice, one was dead, Nobile had a broken arm and leg, and Natal Cecioni (another who had also been on *Norge*) had a compound fracture of the leg. The survivors had little equipment and their radio did not, at first, work. With little polar experience between them there was fear and dissension, and eventually three men, Adalberto Mariano, Filippo Zappi and Finn Malmgren, set off in an attempt to reach Spitsbergen and get help. With the gondola on the ice north of Nordaustlandet this was probably a forlorn hope, but with no radio and few supplies, waiting for rescue was far from enticing either.

The radio operator, Giuseppe Biaggi, repaired the radio and began to transmit their position, but all that was heard from *Citta di Milano* was an endless string of telegrams and press statements. In fact a radio operator on the ship had picked up the SOS, but his superior, convinced everyone was

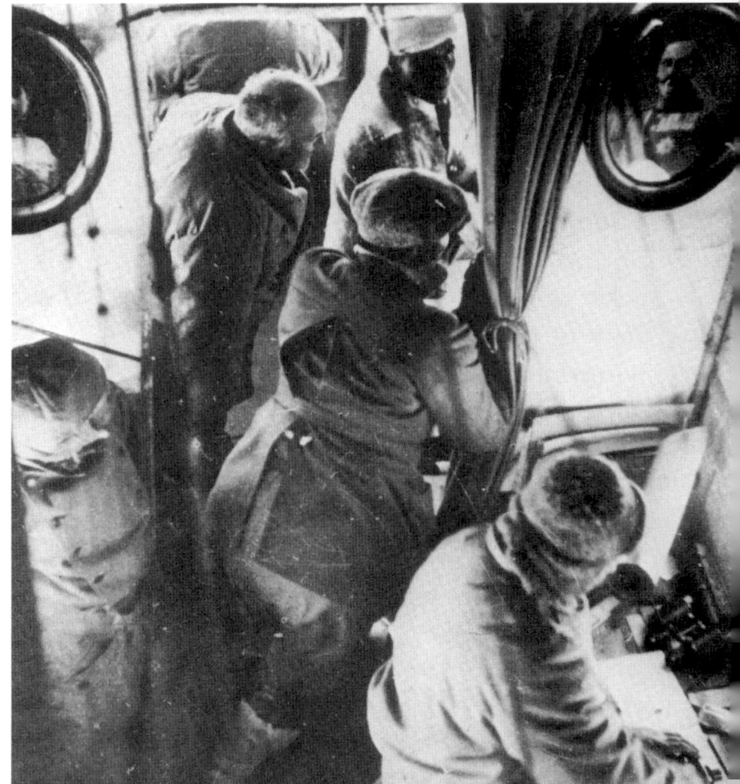

dead, dismissed the report. Only when a radio ham near Arkhangelsk in the Soviet Union heard the SOS and informed Moscow was the position of the survivors fixed.

The loss of the *Italia* was a blow to Italian pride, especially when of the 18 ships, 22 planes and 1,500 men of six nations deployed to search for survivors, only one seaplane was Italian. After the position of the survivor's camp – which included a red tent, soon to become famous as the symbol of a failed expedition – was fixed it was overflown on 18 June, 23 days after the crash. On 23 June the Swedes Einar Lundborg and Birger Schyberg landed at the camp. The plan was to evacuate one man (as the Swedes' Fokker CVD could accommodate only three), then to return with a single pilot to rescue two men at a time. Nobile wanted Cecioni taken as he was the most seriously injured, but Lundborg thought Nobile himself should go to co-ordinate rescue operations. That was a strange, wrong-headed idea, but Nobile agreed and, accompanied by his dog, Titina, his constant companion (it had been on *Norge*), flew out. The news spread around the world rapidly – a fascist general had saved himself and his dog before his companions. A furious Mussolini demoted Nobile, and the expedition leader's attempts to influence the rescue were quietly ignored. In his own version of the *Italia* disaster, Nobile claimed that it took more courage for him to go than to stay as he understood the possible consequences. He did not, perhaps, understand them clearly enough.

On 24 June Lundborg returned alone, but his plane's skis dug in on landing, turning it over. Lundborg now became a reluctant member of the Red Tent camp. Further flights were cancelled due to fog until 6 July, when Schyberg flew in to pick up Lundborg. Before further flights could be made the Russian ice-breaker *Krassin*, the world's most powerful, developing 10,500hp, crashed through ice up to 3m thick and reached the Red Tent on 12 July. Two days earlier a look-out plane from the ice-breaker had spotted men on the ice. This turned out to be Mariano and Zappi. Mariano was exhausted and frostbitten, but Zappi was in much better shape and told a remarkable story. The three-man team had made slow progress, then Malmgren (who had been in pain since the crash) had collapsed and asked to be left to die. Not only had the Italians done this, but they had also taken his food portion. Zappi, who claimed not to have eaten for 12 days, was wearing some of Malmgren's clothes when he was found. The Russians, appalled by Zappi's demeanour, were also suspicious of his healthy appearance – this was not a man who had gone 12 days without eating. Zappi later contradicted himself and claimed Malmgren had died before they left him, and even admitted cannibalism, though this was officially denied. The suspicion that Malmgren might have been murdered further tainted the expedition. By contrast to Zappi, Mariano's condition was wretched; he lost a foot to amputation and died a few months later. The crew of three of the only Italian rescue plane also died when their plane crashed on the way back to Italy.

Most tragically of all, the *Italia* disaster resulted in Roald Amundsen's death. Amundsen was nearing his 56th birthday, but looked much older. He had been at a celebration dinner for Hubert Wilkins and Carl Eielson, who had flown a Lockheed Vega plane from Point Barrow to Spitsbergen via the Pole, when news of the *Italia* came through. He immediately offered his services, claiming past disagreements meant nothing when lives were at stake. It has been suggested that in addition to his burden of guilt over Johansen and Scott, Amundsen felt guilty that his feud with Nobile had forced the Italian into an expedition to prove himself, and that spurred his offer. But Mussolini told the Norwegian government their help was not required. Sensing a bitterness over the Amundsen-Nobile feud, the government declined Amundsen's offer, but then put Hjalmar Riiser-Larsen in command of official Norwegian efforts.

The government's decisions embittered Amundsen. He felt his honour was at stake – Amundsen had said he would go and so he had to. So when the French offered him a Latham 47 seaplane for a private mission he immediately accepted. He met pilot René Guilbaud and his crew of three in Bergen, together with his own chosen companion, Lief Dietrichson. By the time they reached Tromsø it was clear that the Latham was unsuitable. But Amundsen had given his word, so the six men took off on 18 June. When they were overdue in Spitsbergen the rescue effort was so directed towards *Italia* that nothing was done. Amundsen was, after all, the great survivor. Searches were made some days later, but not until 31 August

Above
The Red Tent from the air. The structure of the plane from which the photograph was taken seems to have been superimposed, suggesting the photograph has been manipulated.

Below
Lundborg's plane after the crash of 24 June. Amazingly Lundborg escaped serious injury.

The bitterness of Amundsen

The brooding Amundsen never received the respect afforded Nansen, his fellow countryman, in Norway, and only grudging admiration throughout the rest of the world. His autobiography (*My Life as an Explorer*) stunned everyone, including his friends, with its paranoia and bitterness. In common with many great achievers Amundsen was a demonically driven man, perpetually striving to the limit, yet lonely and fearful. One-third of his book was taken up by his feud with Nobile over the aftermath of the *Norge* expedition. He was relentless, just as he had been relentless in his feud with Hjalmar Johansen after the South Pole expedition. Johansen, who had been with Nansen on his Pole attempt on *Fram*, had been a member of Amundsen's South Pole team. Amundsen, whose Antarctic base camp was further from the Pole than Scott's, had started south too early, fearful of losing the 'race', and had been forced to retreat in the face of devastating cold. Johansen had advised against the start and when the retreat turned into a rout had stayed behind to rescue the last man. Johansen saved the man's life and, probably, the expedition, but when he told Amundsen exactly what he thought of his leadership he was excluded from the team and, eventually, sent home in disgrace. Back in Norway Johansen drank heavily, became depressed and committed suicide in 1913.

The chapter of Amundsen's book on the South Pole expedition is short, but includes the incident at the Royal Geographical Society's dinner in London, where Lord Curzon had proposed 'three cheers for the dogs' after Amundsen's speech. Curzon's toast was a clear insult, suggesting that Scott had reached the Pole 'properly', not towed by dogs, and he made the situation worse by urging the Norwegian to stay calm and not respond. There was also the aftermath of his visit to Frederick Cook during his United States lecture tour after the *Norge* expedition. Amundsen had made a kind gesture to an old friend fallen on hard times, but his remarks after the visit were seen as support for Cook against Peary. The Curzon incident probably betrayed a guilt Amundsen felt over Scott's death, while the Cook incident merely heightened his bitterness and alienation.

The autobiography further clouded his reputation at home. Norway had always been ambivalent about him, especially in comparison to Nansen. Nansen had a wife and children, and was a lady's man. Amundsen had a reputation for pursuing married women by letter with pleadings of overwhelming love that disappeared the moment they left, or were tempted to leave, their husbands. These strangely platonic relationships contrasted with rumours of sordid deeds in seedy brothels. The curious incident of Kakonita and Camilla also did not help. These two young girls had been rescued from poverty in Chukchi during the *Maud* expedition – Kakonita was motherless, dirty and lice-infested, Camilla an unwanted 'half-breed'. They had been taken to Oslo as foster children, to be given a home, security and an education. It was a laudable act until Amundsen, apparently tiring of them and the responsibility they demanded, packed them off to Seattle for a return to Chukchi. The two settled in America and lived contented lives there, but it was no thanks to Amundsen.

was anything found, when fisherman hauled in a float and fuel tank from the plane. It seemed they had been removed in an attempt to construct a raft. It is hard to know if the idea of the indomitable explorer striving to the last and dying a lingering death is more, or less, painful than a tired old man's life ending quickly in a plunge into the sea.

Drift stations and submarines

The general acceptance of Peary's claim to have reached the North Pole not only forestalled Amundsen's attempt, and persuaded him to head south, but also all ground-based attempts for almost 60 years, with the exception of that by the Russian Georgi Sedov, who made an attempt from Franz Josef Land in 1912. After two winters and summers largely involving science and survey, Sedov set off with two others. Scurvy had already killed one man and Sedov was himself sick; it was mid-February, the polar night, and the trio had insufficient equipment and supplies for the proposed six-month trek to the Pole and back (or on to Canada). Other expedition members tried to stop the men, but they continued. Sedov died on Rudolf Island in early March: the other two managed to return safely. It was during the retreat of the remainder of Sedov's expedition that Albanov and Konrad (the survivors of the *Saint Anna*) were met. It was on Sedov's expedition that the first flight by an aeroplane (as opposed to a balloon or dirigible) was made in 1914 by the Russian pilot Jan Nagursky. He flew a French-built Maurice Farman seaplane from Krestovaya Bay, Novaya Zemlya. The plane had been shipped there in pieces and assembled by Nagursky and his mechanic Kuznetsov, in the open and in appalling weather. The two then made a total of five flights across the Barents Sea, but they failed to find any trace of Sedov.

In the Soviet Union the *Chelyuskin* affair had shown that camping for long periods on sea ice was feasible, even comfortable if supplies were adequate. It could be argued that Nansen, Cook, Peary and others had already shown this, but *Chelyuskin* showed the viability of a fixed camp and team. The logical extension was a deliberate floe camp, the Arctic drift allowing science to be pursued across the Arctic Ocean. Specifically, such drift stations would help scientists understand

The last photograph of Roald Amundsen, taken as he was about to board the *Latham* on 18 June 1928.

the drift itself, and would contribute to the opening of a sea route along Russia's northern coast. The first drift station was set up in June 1937. In charge was Ivan Papanin. He was accompanied by two scientists, Yevgeni Fedorov and Petr Shirshov, and radio operator Ernst Krenkel. Shirshov and Krenkel were veterans of the *Chelyuskin* camp. There was also a dog (*Vesydy* – Happy), the Polar Bear guard. The team were landed about 25km from the pole, and they drifted until February 1938, when they were rescued from a melting floe close to Scoresbysund in east Greenland.

The 1939–45 war halted the Soviet drift station programme, but it began again in 1950, a series of stations being set up and manned through to the 1980s. As a prelude to the 1950 stations the Soviets also landed an aircraft at the Pole on 23 April 1948. The team comprised scientists led by Mikhail Somov – the others were Pavel Sen'ko, Mikhail Ostrekin and Pavel Gordienko – and they became the first men to be confirmed as having stood there; it seems that Gordienko was actually the first man out of the plane. On 4 August 1958 the US Navy submarine USS *Nautilus*, commanded by William R. Anderson, reached the Pole on a sub-surface crossing of the Arctic Ocean. The submarine's name recalled that of Sir Hubert Wilkins' craft, in which he had also tried to reach the Pole underwater as far back as 1931. He failed to do more than descend beneath a single ice floe; it is believed his *Nautilus* had been damaged by sabotage, perhaps understandably since the technology of the time made the projected trip dangerous if not foolhardy. On 12 August 1958 James Calvert, commander of the submarine USS *Skate*, surfaced at the Pole. Not until 1977 did a surface ship reach the Pole, the nuclear-powered Russian ice-breaker *Arktika* arriving on 18 August.

Over the ice to the Pole

The first overground expedition to indisputably reach the Pole was in April 1968, when a Canadian/US team led by Ralph Plaisted used snowmobiles to travel from Ward Hunt Island, off Ellesmere Island's northern coast. Four men reached the Pole on 19 April, and were then taken out by aircraft. That same year a team of four set out to cross the Arctic by way of the Pole. The British TransArctic Expedition, comprising leader Wally Herbert, Allan Gill, Kenneth Hedges and Fritz Koerner, set out from Barrow on Alaska's north coast on 21 February 1968 with 40 dogs and four sledges. They were forced to retreat early in the trip when a pressure ridge of ice heading south threatened to overwhelm them. Sustained by air drops of supplies the team pushed on, sometimes making lengthy detours because of leads. By the time Plaisted reached the Pole Herbert's team were about 500km from Barrow. By the beginning of July, Herbert noted, they had sledged 1,900km, but were still only at 81°33'N.

On 14 July the four established a summer camp and waited for autumn to bring easier sledging conditions. Polar Bear and seal meat were added to the menu during their summer 'holiday' – by which time ice drift had moved them 1°30' closer to the Pole. They set off again on 4 September, but on the 8th Allan Gill stumbled and injured his back. They returned to their summer camp intending to have Gill evacuated, but the weather and ice conditions would not allow an aircraft to approach or land. They therefore had to remain at the camp throughout the winter, though the statements that

Above
Papanin's tent on the ice.

Left
Inside Papanin's tent. Today the tent, complete with its original contents, is in the Arctic and Antarctic Institute, St Petersburg.

Papanin and the pistol

Papanin's team lived well in an insulated, but cramped, tent, with electricity for the radio generated by an 'exercise cycle' that powered a generator. The drift station was a success, the men remaining healthy throughout and obtaining excellent data. It is also a memorable trip for one incident (based on truth, but probably apocryphal) that has gone down in the annals of Russian polar science. Papanin was a devoted communist. The two scientists were also party members, but Krenkel was not. Regular party broadcasts were received, but Krenkel, who took them down, was not allowed to either hear them read by Papanin or to discuss them. He was therefore required to walk around the tent while the party members held their meeting. Papanin was not a scientist and therefore had no allotted task (other than as leader, which was hardly taxing as there were few decisions to be made). He apparently spent most of his time dismantling and re-assembling his pistol. Krenkel, aggravated by his enforced retirements to the cold outside the tent and driven to distraction by Papanin's constant activity with the pistol (Papanin would work blindfolded and with the gun behind his back to vary the work) took revenge on the ship home. After Papanin had again dismantled his gun, Krenkel inserted a likely looking item into the disassembled bits and retired. It is said that two days later Papanin had to be rescued from his cabin after he was heard beating his head on the wall in frustration at not being able to re-assemble the gun.

local ice conditions precluded a landing – made by Herbert – caused dissension with the expedition's organising committee in London, who wanted the injured man taken off the ice as soon as possible. Gill remaining with the team was seen as Herbert's preferred option, and a not altogether sensible one.

Gill eventually recovered and was able to start out with the team on 24 February 1969. Winter drift had taken them north, but also east, and it was still a long way to the Pole. The winter cold was intense (below -50°C), but progress was steady and the North Pole was reached on 5 April, 407 days after leaving Barrow. The remainder of the journey was rather less fraught, though one of their two-man tents caught fire on the first day south of the Pole; a new tent dropped to them had a 'No Smoking' sign fixed inside it. On 23 May the team sighted land. They reached it ('Little Blackboard Island' off Nordaustlandet, Svalbard) on 29 May and after a further 13 days of difficult travel over broken ice they were picked up by a relief ship.

Later trips to the Pole filled in some of the gaps in these tales of human endeavour. On 5 March 1978 the Japanese Naomi Uemura set off alone (apart from a dog team) from Ellesmere Island, reaching the Pole on 29 April. He was then taken by air to Cape Morris K. Jesup on Greenland's north coast, and sledged the island's length between 10 May and 22 August. In 1986 the Frenchman Jean-Louis Etienne made a solo ski journey to the Pole, with air resupply every 10 days. The first unsupported journey was made in 1986 when a team of eight (one of whom was evacuated when his ribs were broken by a sledge), led by Will Steger and Paul Schurke, used dog teams hauling three tons of equipment. Steger's team included Anne Bancroft, the first woman to reach the Pole. On Day 32 of the 47-day journey, the team met Etienne on his solo ski trek. It was this chance meeting that led to Steger and Etienne (and others) organising the TransAntarctic Expedition of 1989.

In 1990 the Norwegians Erling Kagge and Børge Ousland made an unsupported ski trek from Ward Hunt Island. They had started out as a threesome, but on the ninth day Geir Randby injured his back and had to be evacuated. Despite all his equipment and food being taken out with him, the purists maintained this invalidated the journey. The discussion was rendered academic when Børge Ousland made a solo, unsupported journey from Cape Arktichesky at the northern end of Severnaya Zemlya in 1994. Ousland had chosen a Russian start because although it was 200km further to the Pole the ice was usually less disrupted. Ousland pulled a sledge constructed of inner and outer shells that could be locked together with skis to form a catamaran, which he used to cross leads. Starting on 2 March 1994 he covered an area of very broken ice, but then maintained a steady average of 15km daily. This increased as he neared the Pole, which he reached on 22 April.

When he set out in 1986, Will Steger's intention was to journey to the Pole and back unsupported, but he had been unable to complete the return trip. The out-and-back, unsupported journey was not completed until 1995, when it was achieved by Canadian Richard Weber, who had been part of Steger's team in 1986, and the Russian Mikhail Malakhov. Weber rightly noted that the early pioneers had not had the advantage of air evacuation from the Pole, and that the pair's journey would therefore be closer in spirit to them. The two had already tried the trip once before in 1992, when they started from Ward Hunt with a team of three on 13 March. But on 22 April (day 39) Bob Mantell realised he would not complete the trip and returned to Ward Hunt alone, reaching it on 7 May. Weber and Malakhov were eventually forced to accept defeat in June at 89°38'N. During the trek they saw whales at 89°N, the furthest north they have ever been seen. In 1995 Weber and Malakhov started on 14 February, hauling one sledge at a time because of their weight (each man had two sledges, each weighing more than 50kg, as well as a heavy backpack) and so covering double distances. On 28 February they established a depot at 83°50'N, returning to Ward Hunt for more supplies. Starting out again they experienced temperatures down to -58°C. They reached their depot on 17 March and, now with sledges weighing 140kg and 20kg backpacks, they started for the Pole. They reached it on 12 May and, with lightened loads, they returned to Ward Hunt, reaching it on 14 June, 107 days after setting out. They had covered 1,500km.

The next landmark was the unsupported crossing of the Arctic Ocean. This was achieved by the Norwegians Rune Gjeldnes and Torry Larsen, who had already completed an unsupported south–north traverse of Greenland. The pair set out from Cape Arktichesky on 16 February 2000, starting in the Arctic twilight as the Sun did not appear until the 29th. They crossed ice so thin that they had to keep moving, as to stop might mean a fall through it; a survival time measured in minutes and no chance of rescue by their team-mate concentrated the skiers' minds powerfully. They reached the Pole on 29 April after 74 days of travel. Progress towards Canada was slow and on 13 May, at 88°N with 550km to go, they made the bold decision to leave their pulks behind, continuing on ski with everything in backpacks. Their packs weighed 45kg, so heavy that a fall meant waiting for assistance

USS *Skate* surfaced at the North Pole on 1 April 1959. This return trip for the submarine was carried out to bring the ashes of Sir Hubert Wilkins so they could be scattered. Wilkins had been the first man to attempt a sub-ice crossing of the Arctic Ocean as well as being a pioneer polar aviator.

to rise and the possibility of a broken leg. With time, food and fuel running out, their crossings of leads became increasingly audacious. Inevitably one (Gjeldnes) fell through the ice of a lead and was lucky to be wedged by his pack rather than pulled down. He was rescued by Larsen after several minutes of partial immersion. The pair ran out of food and fuel 45km from Ellesmere Island's Cape Discovery and were then stopped by an open lead. Had this been continuous around the coast it would have been disastrous, but they forced a way across, landing on 3 June after a trek of 109 days.

Gjeldnes's fall through the ice clearly showed the hazards of any solo trek, but Børge Ousland was back on the ice in 2001, intent on repeating the Gjeldnes/Larsen crossing of 2000 but solo and unsupported. He also started from Cape Arktichesky, on 3 March. After one week his sledge cracked. Despite efforts to repair it a new sledge had to be brought to him by helicopter. Continuing against a head wind and across extremely broken ice Ousland reached the Pole on 23 April. There was a collection of people there, including Weber and Malakhov who were on a commercial Pole trip and with whom Ousland enjoyed a meal. He then continued alone; the wind was occasionally favourable and he was able to use a sail to assist him, on one day covering a record 72km, and several times covering more than 50km. Ousland also used a dry suit to swim across leads and so reduce the time taken to bypass them, towing his sledge behind him. In all he used the suit 23 times. Ousland reached Ward Hunt Island on 23 May after covering 1,996km in 82 days. Purists will argue that the replacement sledge and a meal at the Pole invalidates Ousland's claim of a first solo, unsupported traverse of the Arctic Ocean, but the fabled man-in-the-street has little sympathy for such arguments and generally the journey is seen as a great success. Ousland followed his solo traverse with an even more audacious trip in 2006 when, with the South African Mike Horn, he made an unsupported trip to the North Pole during the Arctic winter. The pair left Cape Arktichesky on 22 January, travelling first in darkness, but then with the aid of the moon. The moon was soon replaced by a glow on the horizon as the Sun hauled its way upwards, appearing on day 58 of the trek. Three days later, on 23 March, the pair reached the Pole.

Today the North Pole is regularly reached by commercial trips on Russian ice-breakers. Each year the Russians construct ice runways at 89°N, flying in adventure seekers who ski the 'last degree' and are then taken back to the 89° base by smaller planes. The Pole has been reached by motorcycle, hot air balloon and relay teams, a number of 'firsts' of varying degrees of importance being established. Yet despite this commercialism, journeys to the Pole from Canada or Siberia (or any other starting point) remain extremely hazardous. The broken nature of the ice, the open water (a Japanese explorer drowned in a lead while Ousland was completing his solo crossing) and the risk from Polar Bears (surprisingly stealthy hunters whose approach can go unnoticed, and which represent a particular hazard to the tent-bound, sleeping trekker) add to the problems of cold and bad weather, making the Arctic a more daunting challenge than Antarctica. The substantial thinning of the sea ice noted by Ousland in 2001 – he carried out thickness measurements as he had in 1994 – makes matters worse. Yet the lure of the North Pole will no doubt continue to encourage the brave and the reckless northwards.

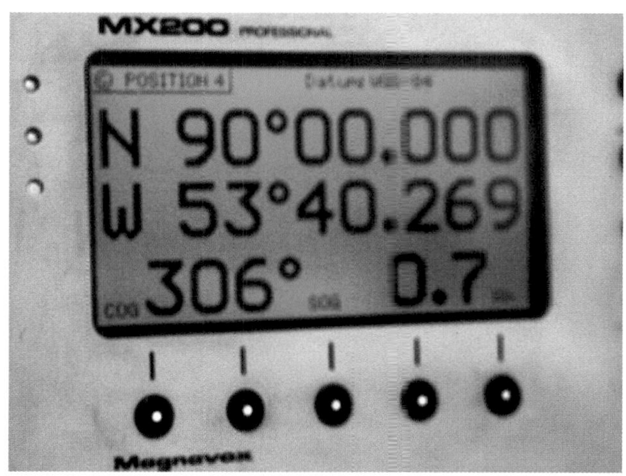

The lure of the Pole. GPS read-out on the *Yamal* (shown in the photograph on p221).

Børge Ousland self-portrait on his solo Arctic crossing.

Opposite page

Above
The Russian nuclear ice-breaker nearing the North Pole on a commercial trip

Below
On 16 January 1913 Roald Amundsen (to the right) lectured to the Geographical Society of Philadelphia on his South Pole expedition. He was introduced by Robert Peary (centre), with a tribute to him being given by Ernest Shackleton (left).

11. Indigenous Peoples in the Modern World

The interaction of Europeans and the peoples of the Arctic followed the same general pattern of all such meetings between a group that was technologically advanced and saw itself as civilised and one that it considered 'primitive'. In North America the British were suspicious of the Inuit whom they considered little more than savages and, after the Franklin expedition, lying, potentially dangerous savages. In Siberia the Russian authorities saw the native people only in terms of their usefulness in obtaining furs; the tundra dwellers were largely ignored. When the native peoples showed signs of restlessness they were treated brutally, a treatment that had its echoes in North America (though in general the treatment there was less harsh). In the Aleutians Russian fur trappers angered the native Aleut not only by invading their lands but also by the way that they slaughtered the animals of one island then moved on to the next, carving a relentless path of destruction across the island chain. When Aleuts killed the hunters, the Russians retaliated by killing Aleut men and raping their women. It was hardly a real contest as the Russians possessed guns while the Aleut had much more limited weaponry.

The Russians soon effectively enslaved the Aleuts, committing, in the process, acts of cruelty that almost defy belief; Aleut men were lined up in single file while a Russian fired a gun at the first man and others bet on how many the bullet would pass through; men were castrated or blinded in front of their families; groups were transported to remote islands to act as fur hunters, these people dying of hunger or disease. Many lost the will to live and committed suicide Some estimates suggest that the Aleut population was reduced by as much as 80% as a result of a combination of disease, malnutrition, suicide and punishments.

The treatment of the Aleuts was arguably the worst meted out to any Arctic native population, and the change of ownership of Alaska did not put an end to the suffering, in part because the Americans made them 'wards' of the government rather than citizens of the United States, a status that was not corrected until 1971 despite Alaska becoming the 49th State of the Union in 1959. During the 1939–45 war the Japanese bombed Dutch Harbour and occupied the western islands of Attu and Kiska. Fearing an attack on mainland USA by way of the island chain, the Americans evacuated the remaining Aleuts to inadequate housing on the Alaska Peninsula while they fortified the islands. The Aleuts in south-east Alaska had a miserable time, with as many as 10% dying of malnutrition and disease. Some never returned to their island homes, but those that did found their houses had been looted and burned by the occupying American troops. Churches and houses had also been used for artillery target practice. The final settlement for these abuses was not paid until 1988; by that time there were only some 400 living survivors of the evacuation. Despite this tragic history the Aleut population as identified in US census returns is now 24,000: estimates of the population before the Russian discovery of the islands is 10,000–20,000 implying either a remarkable rise in such a short time, or a number of unjustified claims.

The Church of the Holy Ascension at Dutch Harbour, Unalaska Island in the Aleutian. The church was built in 1825 and is the oldest Russian church still extant in Alaska. The church survived the bombing of 1942 and is now a US National Historic Landmark. The photograph was taken on a typical Aleutian day: set where warm Pacific air meets cold northern air, the islands are often cloud-covered. Perched on the cross of the highest onion dome is a Bald Eagle: there is an abundance of the eagles locally.

Ownership

Although the position of the Aleuts is an extreme example, in general the meeting of Europeans and native Arctic dwellers inevitably favoured the former at the expense of the latter. The Europeans brought diseases against which the native folk had little resistance (and whose lifestyle, with often malnourished families living in cramped conditions, favoured the spread of disease), and an interpretation of how the world was organised that was totally alien. After James Clark Ross had reached the North Magnetic Pole he claimed 'the Pole and its adjoining territory' for Great Britain. Later back at the *Victory* this act of possession took on a surreal aspect when the British attempted to explain to the Inuit that the local area no longer belonged to them. Since the essentially nomadic Inuit did not understand the concept of land ownership their baffled response dealt with the lack of seals that year and the need to acquire more fish-hooks. It would have made just as much sense to them if Ross had told them that Britain owned the sky.

Because ownership was not understood, the Inuit, and other northern peoples, were later to be equally baffled when they discovered that one consequence of it was citizenship, which meant that people you had never seen, who knew nothing of your land and lived far away could exercise authority over you and how you lived. Most dramatically, this ownership meant that those far-off people could grant the rights to exploit your land to others without consulting you. At the time this seemed no more than fair; as John Quincy Adams, the sixth President of the United States once said, 'What is the right of a huntsman to the forest of a thousand miles over which he has accidentally ranged in quest of prey?' To modern eyes this seems a monstrous injustice, but it was a common idea then and, it has to be said, variations of the theme are still current. When nickel was discovered on the

Opposite page
Gedion Kristiansen preparing his lance prior to a Narwhal hunt, Qioqit, north-west Greenland.

Above
Thule Air Base, north-west Greenland. When the American air base expanded in 1953, the Greenlanders of Pitffik, the local village, were moved 250km north to Qannaq to make way.

Right
Providenya, eastern Chukotka, Russia. When it was a centre for military activity just across the Bering Sea from Alaska, the town had a population of some 30,000 soldiers and almost 10,000 support staff. Now the population is less than 3,000, an air of decay hanging over the town.

Taimyr Peninsula, and gold and oil in north-west North America, outsiders arrived to dispossess confused and angry locals. In Scandinavia farmers moved north, appropriating Sámi lands, clearing forests and shooting Reindeer, either for food or if they strayed on to the newly planted fields. During the 1939–45 war, areas of the northern lands were annexed to aid the war effort, the Soviets developing Murmansk and militarising the Kola Peninsula, the Americans building bases in Labrador, southern Greenland and Iceland. The Germans built weather stations on north-east Greenland: a little known fact is that the Germans also clandestinely built a station on Labrador in 1943. Jan Mayen and Svalbard were drawn into the conflict, though in these cases there was no indigenous population. The Cold War reinforced the value of the north, the Americans building the Thule airbase in north-west Greenland, while the Soviets built bases (as many as 250, some of them massive) in the Russian far east, just across the water from Alaska. One tragic consequence of the proximity of the USA and USSR in the Bering Sea was the forcible relocation of native people from Big Diomede Island. The peoples of the northern Bering Sea were related, the familial lines independent of the (to them arbitrary) decision that the international border between the USA and the USSR ran between the Diomede islands, which are just 4km apart. Soviet perception that espionage between family members was a threat to their security resulted in separation for some families that lasted throughout the Cold War.

Hunting traditions in the modern world

The Reindeer herders of northern Russia evolved an essentially self-sustaining lifestyle, but Inuit society was based on hunting. Because of shamanism and the uncontrollable occurrence of prey, Inuit society was characterised by two factors that have inevitably transferred poorly to the modern world. To cater for the lack of dependability of prey the Inuit had large families, the population increasing when prey was abundant, with people dying in times of prey shortage. One aspect of shamanism was the relationship between man and the animals on which he preyed. It was believed that the prey willingly sacrificed itself to a hunter, but this willingness depended on the prey recognising that the hunter deserved the kill because he would kill properly, observing rituals and limiting suffering, and would treat the body with respect. The other side of such an understanding of the relationship between hunter and hunted is that if the hunter fails to find prey it is because the prey is declining to make the sacrifice, punishing the hunter for his incompetence or lack of respect. As a consequence of this

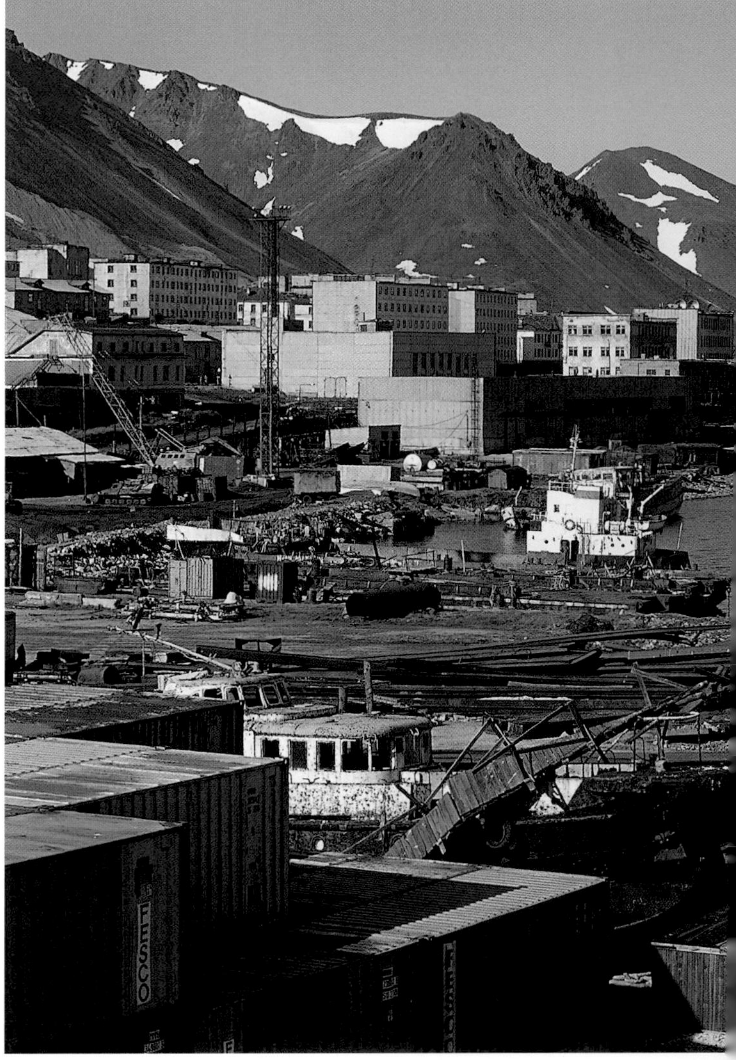

view the Inuit killed as many animals as they could find – each animal had, after all, sought the hunter. Such killing led to prey shortages, but these were interpreted according to the understanding of the relationship rather than as a consequence of overhunting, and the starvation and deaths that resulted were accepted as part of the scheme of things. The possibility of prey extinctions just did not occur to the Inuit; the Inuit did not live in true harmony with the rest of nature.

A problem arises when Inuit families continue to have traditionally large families, but modern medicines and social welfare prevent the deaths in times of famine that once limited numbers. A continuation of the hunting tradition, particularly if the overkill tradition is also maintained, now rapidly results

Southern justice vs Northern justice

Nothing illustrates the problem of integrating the Inuit into southern ways better than two celebrated murder trials in northern Canada in the early 20th century. In each case Inuit killed southerners and were then subjected to a process beyond their comprehension. In the most important case the application of the law was aimed specifically at ensuring that Inuit lands could be safely appropriated.

In 1913 two Roman Catholic missionaries, Father Jean-Baptiste Rouvière and Father Guillaume LeRoux, left Fort Norman on the Mackenzie River with the intention of converting the Inuit of the area near the mouth of the Coppermine River. They were never seen again and when rumours of Inuit wearing cassocks reached Fort Norman, three policemen under Charles ('Denny') LaNauze were sent to investigate. They discovered that the two priests had been murdered by two Inuit, Sinnisiak and Uluksuk. The two were arrested and taken to Edmonton to stand trial. According to the two men they had overtaken the two priests during their journey and walked with them. They were, however, afraid of them, particularly LeRoux, who was known to have a temper. When the Inuit spoke to each other about their concerns LeRoux put his hand over Sinnisiak's mouth to silence him. Now in fear of their lives the Inuit decided to leave the two priests, but LeRoux objected. The priest might well have, rightly, considered that the two southerners were safer with the Inuit around, but his objection seems to imply that he felt able to order the Inuit to do as he wished. Despite LeRoux's order the Inuit attempted to leave. There was a skirmish and a fearful Sinnisiak stabbed LeRoux. Rouvière ran and, fearing he was going to get a gun, Sinnisiak shot him. Uluksuk completed the killing of each man. The two Inuit then each ate a piece of LeRoux's liver.

At the trial in Edmonton in 1917 only Sinnisiak was tried, and only for the murder of Rouvière. The Crown Counsel, Charles Cursolles McCaul, made it clear in his speech that this was not just a trial about a killing, but one intended to make it clear that Canadian law applied throughout the north, and that white men could go safely anywhere they chose for whatever purpose. At one point he spelled this out – 'If we are to believe the reports of the copper deposits near the mouth of the Coppermine River, many white men more may go to investigate and to work the mines. The Eskimo must be made to understand that the lives of others are sacred, and that they are not justified in killing on account of any mere trifle that may ruffle or annoy them.' The two Inuit, not understanding a word of what was going on, fell asleep during McCaul's address. Sinnisiak's defence team maintained that the killing had been self-defence and that it was unreasonable to apply a law to a man who knew nothing of it. In his summing up the judge, Chief Justice Harvey, told the jury of six local men not to acquit, but to his horror they did.

The authorities were outraged. A second trial was ordered, this time both Inuit being tried for the murder of LeRoux. The trial was moved from Edmonton amid suggestions of anti-Catholic bias, with a new, more compliant jury being found in Calgary. With the same judge presiding, the two men were found guilty and sentenced to death. The sentence was commuted to life imprisonment. The two were model prisoners and acted as odd job men in prison rather than being confined. They were quietly released in 1919 and eventually found their way home. There Uluksuk became a nuisance, the locals claiming his notoriety made him arrogant; he was killed in a fight in 1924. Sinnisiak died in 1930.

The second case concerned the killing of a southern trader, Robert Janes, at Pond Inlet in 1920. Janes had been a crewman on some of Bernier's early sovereignty trips and had arrived in the village in 1916, setting himself up as a fur trader. The ship that he clearly expected to return each year to bring supplies and take his stock did not arrive in each of the next three years, and by 1920 Janes had become a desperate and, by all accounts, violent man. The local Inuit were afraid of him and were concerned about how he would behave towards their women when they left for the hunting season. In line with Inuit custom they therefore decided to kill him. After the killing the trial of an Inuk called Nuqallaq was held locally. Nuqallaq was found guilty of murder and transported to Winnipeg to serve a life sentence. There he very rapidly contracted tuberculosis and was freed on compassionate grounds to return to Pond Inlet where he soon died. (Robert Janes' grave at Pond Inlet is shown in the photograph below.)

Whether there were any benefits to the native populations from contact with southerners depends on an individual's opinion of what constitutes a benefit. Inuit found work in the whaling industry, acquiring more dependable access to food, and to southern material goods. Many developed a taste for southern things. But the destruction of the whales meant that with the collapse of the industry those Inuit who had chosen to work rather than maintain their traditional way of life rapidly found what was already apparent to the poor of the south – that capitalism could be a callous master.

The Arctic dwellers' embrace of the technology of the south is itself a moot point: to what extent does a tradition stay a tradition in the face of the development of technology? If the tradition is for the killing of a seal with a lance from a kayak, is the tradition maintained when a boat with an outboard motor replaces the kayak and a rifle the lance? It is no surprise that the hunters of the north were keen to accept the benefits of technology, and equally no surprise that their arrival led to a decay of traditional skills. Some have claimed that the enthusiasm for the acceptance of Christianity when the first missionaries arrived in the north had more to do with smoothing the path for the influx of goods than any genuine conversion, pointing to the fact that for many native peoples the old shamanistic rituals still strongly underpin the way of life of those who have not entirely assimilated to the southern lifestyle.

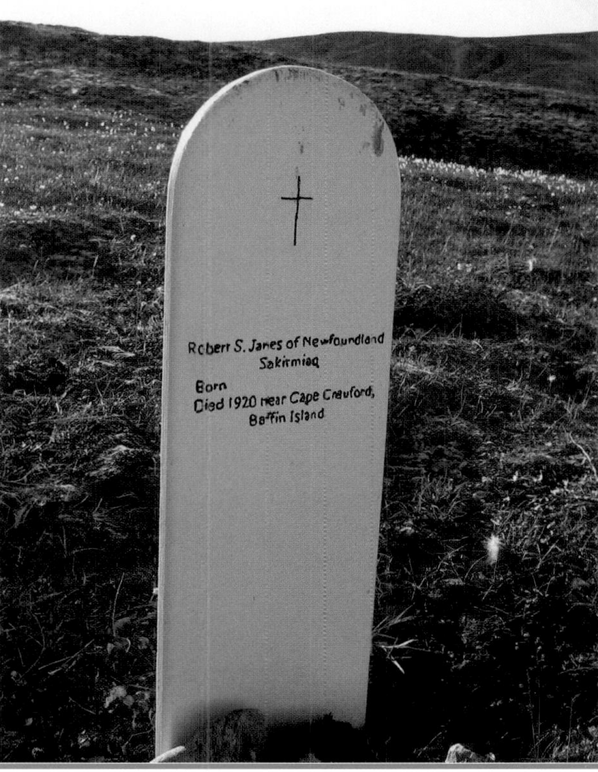

Inuit hunting camp on the sea ice of Baffin Bay. The Inuit were hunting Narwhal at the floe edge. In the background are the mountains of northern Baffin Island.

Seal hunter, Ungava Peninsula, Quebec, Canada.

in local prey extinctions, while attempts by environmentalists to limit hunting are met by fierce local opposition by native peoples, who see such concerns only as a threat to their way of life. Examples of the problems caused by the tradition of overkill can be seen on Greenland where the populations of bird species nesting close to settlements have been brought to the edge of extinction; one study concluded that in west Greenland the population of Brünnich's Guillemot had been reduced by 98% in the second half of the 20th century.

Modern weapons assist modern medicine in tipping an age-old balance between native hunters and prey. Humans and the Polar Bear were the top predators of the Arctic and their numbers were comparable for centuries. The arrival of increased numbers of hunters and the gun means that the balance has gone: bear numbers are declining while the population of native hunters rises. Guns have also eroded traditional values. Having myself witnessed boys using double-barrelled shotguns to shoot dawn-returning auks into the sea, and youths firing at Narwhal neither knowing nor caring whether the animal was hit, it is hard to stomach the indignant response of village elders that these are young men learning to hunt.

Canadian native peoples

For the purposes of understanding how the treatment of northern native peoples developed it is convenient to consider five nation groups – Canada, Denmark (Greenland), Russia, Scandinavia (Norway, Sweden and Finland) and the USA (Alaska). Each of these addressed the problem in a different way: perhaps this is not surprising as there were regional differences that required a different approach, but it is also the case that as with so many other walks of life, the number of excellent solutions to a social problem is roughly equal to the number of the people in a room.

In Canada, decisions over the Inuit population were complicated by the issue of sovereignty over the northern Arctic islands and the lifestyle of many Inuit families. The journeys of Bernier and the sending of police officers to northern islands allowed Canada to establish sovereignty, but the case for it was seen as being challenged by such events as the *Manhattan*'s transit of the North-West Passage. International law recognises the existence of settlements as 'effective occupation' and such occupation as grounds for sovereignty, so in the 1950s, in an attempt to further reinforce its claims, Canada moved Inuit groups from around Hudson Bay to new settlements such as Resolute on Cornwallis Island and Grise Fjord on Ellesmere Island. The moves were an indication of the casual attitude of the southern authorities to northern peoples. It was assumed that one bit of barren Arctic was much as the rest, and that an Inuit was an Inuit, the authorities not understanding that the skills required to live in the (comparatively) animal-rich Low Arctic were far different from those required for life in the darker, colder, more barren High Arctic. The moves actually went surprisingly well, though even now there are negotiations in progress on the payment of reparations for forcible removal.

A second problem was that the Canadian Inuit were still, in part at least, nomadic. In both Alaska and Canada, responsibility for the northern peoples had been accepted reluctantly, and only when it became clear that a watching world would be unimpressed if famines or epidemics were ignored. But accepting the need to distribute the welfare offered to southerners was one thing, actually doing so to a semi-nomadic people was another. This problem was particularly Canadian as the Canadian Arctic is vast, the population small. The only realistic solution was to concentrate the people in settlements where welfare can be administered. But that solution brought its own problems; local wildlife was hunted to virtual extinction and the desire for the accumulation of southern material goods – TVs, cars, etc. – without the work to support payment created dependency.

Nunavut

Since the end of the 1939–45 war, with the greater access that improved communications offered the Inuit, successive Canadian governments have also had to contend with an increasing desire by the Inuit to control their own destinies

The SS *Manhattan* nearing Point Barrow during the first commercial transit of the North-West Passage in 1969. Though the ship was escorted for part of its journey by a Canadian icebreaker, the transit was not authorised and aroused concerns in Ottawa over the USA's long-term intentions.

Left
Air North plane at Old Crow, Yukon, Canada. The native population of Yukon has invested grant money in setting up and maintaining its own airline.

and to have a greater say in the administration of their ancestral lands. In 1993 the Nunavut Land Claim transferred a vast area of land and substantial funds to an Inuit corporation. This was followed in 1999 by the creation of Nunavut. This is an essentially self-governing region covering more than 2,000,000km² and constituting about 20% of Canada's land area. The population is about 80% Inuit, the now smaller North West Territories being about 50% Inuit. Canada's total Inuit population is 30,000–35,000, the bulk living within Nunavut and North West Territories, though there are also populations in northern Quebec and in Labrador.

Greenland

In Greenland the Danish government faced a similar sovereignty problem when Norwegian fur trappers claimed Eirik Raudes Land in the 1920s. Although the issue was settled by an immediate appeal to international law, the Danes also felt the need to establish 'effective occupation'. In 1925 the Danes therefore resettled some residents of Ammassalik to Illoqqortoormiut (Scoresbysund). Ammassalik had itself been created by the Danes in 1894 in order to save the east Greenlanders, whose situation had become desperate as a result of overhunting. During the 1939–45 War Danes, assisted by Americans, patrolled the north-east Greenland coast searching for German weather stations. After peace returned permanent military presence was established at Daneborg in north-east Greenland, the Sirius patrol that operates from there continuing the wartime journeys, though these now police the borders of Danish Greenland annually (rather in the way that animals mark the boundaries of their territories to dissuade usurpers, though it is not advisable to suggest this similarity too strongly to the Danish authorities). Following the agreement on Home Rule Greenland has effectively become an independent nation with a population of some 50,000.

Scandinavia

In Scandinavia the relationship between the Sámi population and the people of the south was different, contact having been established centuries earlier and trade (or, at least, the collection of tribute and trade) continuing over that entire period. The encroachment of southern farmers on Sámi land had been ignored, and then accepted as a method of assimilating the northerners into the southern way of life. Though sounding rather more benign, this approach included enforced conversion to Christianity, the banning of Sámi languages and the execution of 'rebels' who resisted, much as happened among other northern native populations. The idea of assimilation of the Sámi was not really questioned until the late 1960s and remained government policy until a decade or so later. The issue that brought the subject of the Sámi as a distinct people and culture rather than a group of curious northern folk resisting a move to the real world to a head was the proposal to dam the Kautakeino/Alta River in 1978. Sámi opposition to the proposal shocked the Norwegian government into accepting that the Sámi had legitimate rights over their homeland. It took another nine years for this acceptance to evolve into the creation of the Sámediggi, a parliament with control over many aspects of governance of Sámi land. Similar parliaments were formed in Sweden in 1993 and in Finland in 1996. In 2000 a Sámi Parliamentary Council, with representatives from the three parliaments, was formed. It will be interesting to see how the situation develops as pressure for forestry, hydro-electric production and mining in Sámi areas increases, particularly as the formation of the Parliamentary Council has led to fears from central government that the long-term aim is the creation of a single Sámi nation. This country (known as Sápmi), though notional, is often referred to in Sámi literature and politics.

Below
School sign in Pond Inlet, Nunavut, Canada. The school is named in Inuktitut, the sign incorporating Narwhals, which are regularly hunted nearby.

The Rasmussen Museum, Ilulissat, Greenland. The juxtaposition of the old vicarage in which Knud Rasmussen grew up (his father was the town's pastor) and the modern flats says much about modern Greenland where tradition and modernity live side by side, sometimes uneasily.

Russia

Unfortunately the position for the 2,000 Sámi who live on Russia's Kola Peninsula is not so healthy. The exploitation of the area's mineral wealth has had some disastrous environmental consequences; one example is the waste land of dead trees and poisoned soil downwind of the nickel smelter at Nikel. During the communist era Reindeer herding was collectivised, sales allowed only through the *sovchose*, the state office, which also sold life's essentials so the herders were effectively tied to the system. With communism's collapse the Sámi were offered the opportunity to buy their herds, but with limited capital, few outlets for the meat and land rights open to dispute this offer was less substantial than it seemed. Since the Soviet era ended, the widespread privatisation of resources has made matters worse for the impoverished Sámi. One example is the acquisition of the Ponoy River, the Kola's primary salmon river. Now leased to a US outfitter, the salmon have been 'privatised', the Sámi being forbidden to fish a river that historically was theirs.

In the rest of northern Russia, the communist hierarchy was seen as just another group of outsiders intent on making life miserable for the native peoples. Under the Tsar peoples whose primary means of life was Reindeer hunting were required to spend time hunting fur-bearing animals, the time lost causing hardship that was added to the abuses perpetrated by the incomers. A Nenet chief writing to Tsar Alexis Romanov noted that 'for five years ... they have been robbing and abusing us ... taking from us ... with violence and all manner of threats our sable and beaver furs, our deerskin bedding and clothing, our ropes and all kinds of footwear, our geese, ducks and reindeer'. But the abuses did not stop. When the Koryaks and Chukchis offered sterner resistance than usual, punitive forces were sent with the intention of subduing or killing them. The Koryak eventually capitulated, but by then the population had been reduced by 60%. The Chukchis did not falter: in one campaign in the early 18th century a Russian armed band of some 500 men killed over 800 Chukchi men, enslaved their wives and children and destroyed every camp they found. Such numbers are not large in terms of later ethnic cleansing campaigns, but at the time the Chukchi population numbered 6,000–8,000, so the slaughter represented 10–12% of the population in just a few months. Yet the Chukchis were not cowed and 100 years later a treaty acknowledged that they were 'peoples not completely subdued' with rights to their homeland.

The years of abuse and exploitation meant that by the end of the 19th century it seemed some of the native communities might become extinct. Ironically it was tsarism that became extinct, communism initially aiding the northerners by offering tax concessions and exemptions from military service. But although initially helpful (if the treatment of shamans is set aside for a moment), collectivisation and the accompanying education programmes, each of which was aimed at the imposition of a Soviet-style ideology, meant cultural upheaval. The Koryak resisted the collectivisation of their Reindeer, killing the animals rather than allowing them to become state property. But the gesture did not halt the imposition of the collective. Formerly nomadic peoples were forced into settlements as the new ideology abhorred nomadic and semi-nomadic lifestyles. Children were often removed from their parents and sent away to be educated. At distant schools they were forbidden to speak their own languages and taught an ideology intended to result in their integration into mainstream Soviet life. The Yuppiat Eskimos of the Chukchi coast suffered even more as the Russians took over the sea mammal hunts and over-exploited the animals. Yuppiat villages were forcibly abandoned, the people moved to Chukchi villages (causing friction between the two peoples) or to large settlements where their skills were useless, forcing them to take jobs that no one else wanted and resulting in abject poverty.

Later in the communist era the wholesale exile of 'dissidents' and criminals to Siberia made matters worse for the native peoples. The incomers often arrived stripped of all possessions; they felled trees to build cabins and grow crops. As an example of the effect of this movement, in the lands of the Selkup about 4,000 natives were eventually overwhelmed by 120,000 settlers. When the gulag era was over there was further inward migration as Russians arrived to exploit Siberia's mineral wealth. Overall, by the end of the 20th century the native peoples of Siberia constituted less than 5% of the population of their previous homelands, though this

The Sápmi flag flying in northern Sweden.

figure is an average; in the far east and extreme north the percentage was higher, though even there the effect of Russian military install-ations meant it was only perhaps 10% when military activity was at its height.

During the late 1980s the USSR was in a state of near collapse. The external debt had become enormous, gold funds had dropped by 90% and there were severe food shortages. The problems led to a rise in nationalism among the various republics and ethnic groups of the Union, each seeing its future as best served by breaking away. The peoples of Siberia, far removed from Moscow, were often left to fend for themselves as the country went into economic decline. But now, 70 years or more from their traditional way of life and without the safety net that socialism had offered, the people were often unable to adjust. Some of those who had moved to the north to aid the expanding communities, such as doctors and other professionals, moved out, making matters worse. The poverty and hopelessness was appalling, the cultural vacuum left too often filled by vodka. Life expectancy dropped dramatically, as did the birth rate as the northern societies disintegrated. To add to these woes the unregulated development of Siberia in Russia's new market economy created further problems.

In 1990, just a few months before the break-up of the USSR, the Russian Association of Minority Peoples of the North (RAIPON) was founded with the aim of addressing these problems. In that same year a census suggested that the total population of the 26 indigenous native groups represented by RAIPON north was 180,000. Today the organisation has expanded to cover 41 indigenous groups, a total of about 250,000 people occupying some 65% of Russia's land area. Of the Arctic dwellers the most numerous are the Nenet and Evenki, with populations of around 35,000, followed by the Eveni and Chukchi which number about 15,000. Some groups are numbered only in hundreds, while the Kereks of southern Chukotka number less than 100 individuals.

Alaska

Following the purchase of Alaska from the Russians, the US government all but ignored the state, selling fur-trading rights to outsiders and then, during the Gold Rush, allowing a general lawlessness that further aggravated the condition of the native peoples. Eventually, faced with demands from indigenous folk for restitution of their lands or significant compensation for the loss, and also from settlers for the right to continue to exploit lands for the benefit of the state and the country as a whole, the US Government passed the Alaska Native Claims Settlement Act in 1971. This rejected all claims to original ownership of land by the indigenous population in exchange for a sum that totalled almost one billion dollars, and packages of land that amounted to 200,000km². No future claims on land ownership would be allowed. For completeness, it would be useful to give a population figure for the native peoples of Alaska, but this is complicated by the influx of southerners and true status of some who claim indigenous descent. US census returns suggest a figure of 60,000 'Eskimos' in Alaska, but it is likely that the number of truly native peoples is much lower than the official figure.

The village of Illoqqortoormiut (more usually called Scoresbysund) is the most remote in Greenland, so remote it has its own time (two hours ahead of the rest of east Greenland). The village was created in the 1920s when Greenlanders were moved north from Ammassalik to aid Danish resistance to Norwegian claims over Eirik Raudes Land.

12. A Brief History of Antarctica

From around 1500BC, sea-faring peoples of south-east Asia began a slow advance eastwards across the islands of Melanesia. They settled Vanuatu, Fiji, Tonga and Samoa, then crossed the vast and empty Pacific, reaching the Marquesas Islands by about 300AD. From there settlers headed north and south across the islands of Polynesia, reaching Hawaii in about 400AD, New Zealand around 500 years or so later. A stepping-stone to New Zealand were the Cook Islands. In about 650 AD, Ui-Te-Rangiora pointed his canoe *Te-Ivi-O-Atea* southwards from Rarotonga, one of the more southerly islands of the group. After days at sea Ui-Te-Rangiora and his crew discovered either sea ice or an island covered in ice. Though often dismissed as a legend the remarkable feats of seamanship required by the colonisation of Polynesia make such a journey feasible, at least theoretically. We cannot know for sure exactly what Ui-Te-Rangiora discovered; as with the story of Pytheas' journey to the Arctic, Ui-Te-Rangiora's voyage implies achievements by early travellers at odds with the accepted wisdom that exploration of the polar wildernesses awaited the rise of western civilisation.

By the early years of the 16th century the assumed southern continent was taking shape, as discoveries by Portuguese and Spanish sailors extended the frontiers of the known world. It had been assumed that *Terra Australis*, as it had become known, might be an extension of Africa, but Bartolomeo Diaz and Vasco da Gama showed that it was not. Ferdinand Magellan and Sebastian del Cano negotiated the straits between the South American mainland and Tierra del Fuego, then crossed the Pacific to reveal that the land of the south was not connected – as had also been considered likely – to Asia. Magellan believed Tierra del Fuego was an island, though back in Europe most believed it to be the tip of the southern continent. Not for another century would the Dutch explorers Willem Schouten and Jacob Le Maire in the ships *Hoorn* and *Eendracht* show that Tierra del Fuego was indeed an island, though Drake's observations of the passage that bears his name had hinted as much 40 years before. In 1642 Abel Tasman sailed around Australia, proving it was not part of a southern continent, and in the years that followed expeditions beyond latitude 50°S showed that the Southern Ocean was an empty place, pushing back the possible shores of the expected landmass.

Voyages from Sir Francis Drake onwards established records for man's 'furthest south'. In 1578, during his circumnavigation of the world, Drake sailed through the Magellan Strait and headed north-west across the Pacific. On 9 September a strong north-easterly wind pushed Drake's flotilla of three ships southwards to about 57°S.

The Antarctic Circle (the southern equivalent of the Arctic Circle, defining the position at which the midsummer Sun never sets and the midwinter Sun does not rise) was crossed in 1773 during the second great voyage of James Cook, the Yorkshireman who has a claim to being the greatest seaborne explorer of all time. Cook's ships *Resolution* and *Adventure* crossed the Circle twice, reaching 67°31'S on 22 December. The *Resolution* then reached 71°10'S in early 1774. Cook also landed on South Georgia, naming it after King George III and claiming it for Britain. Cook sailed all the way around Antarctica. He had not proved conclusively that the southern continent existed (though he conjectured, correctly, that the presence of icebergs implied land), but he had established that if it did exist it was unlikely to be either inhabited or habitable.

Not until 1820 was the continent actually sighted, when the Estonian-born Faddey Faddeyevich Bellingshauzen saw the Fimbul Ice Shelf on 27 January. Three days later the Englishman William Smith, master of the *Williams*, and Edward Bransfield, a Royal Navy officer, saw what they called Trinity Land. Today this is the Trinity Peninsula, the northernmost part of Graham Land on the Antarctic Peninsula. Finally the southern continent had been discovered, though its shores had still to be mapped, an exercise that would occupy whalers, sealers and scientists for decades.

Despite the sightings, it was more than 70 years before there was an official landing on Antarctica, though there are many stories of earlier landings by whaling and sealing captains

The existence of Antarctica

From observing that the stars of the Great Bear were visible in Greece but sank into the sands of Egypt, the ancient Greeks deduced that the earth was curved in some way; by the time of Plato the Greeks realised it was a sphere, and in the second century BC Eratosthenes measured the diameter by noting the difference in shadow length of a stick in two places in Egypt. Eratosthenes, who died in 194BC, was head of the great library of Alexandria. He observed the stick's shadow there at noon on the summer solstice, and compared it to the shadow at Aswan at the same time. At Aswan there was no shadow, while at Alexandria the shadow was estimated to be 7°12'. The latter is 1/50th of the circumference of a circle. Eratosthenes reasoned that, if Alexandria was due north of Aswan (which he thought, more or less correctly, that it was) then the distance between the two sites was 1/50th the circumference of the Earth. The distance between the two was obtained by pacing, allowing Eratosthenes to calculate the Earth's circumference; he came up with a diameter (of a spherical Earth) of 12,560km (converted to modern units). The Earth is not, of course, a true sphere, but the accepted mean diameter is *c.*12,675km – Eratosthenes had underestimated by less than 1%. This level of accuracy has led many to question the claim – how could Eratosthenes have been so accurate given the inaccuracy of measuring the shadow angle, the inaccuracy of pacing and the fact that Alexandria is not exactly due north of Aswan? But it is now generally agreed that the experiment, though low-tech, was probably well-executed and the Greek scholar really was that accurate. The idea of a spherical Earth, along with much of Greek science, was later lost, and it had to be rediscovered after centuries of flat Earth-type philosophies. But the idea had one important outcome that did survive. The Greeks, much taken by the idea of symmetry and harmony in nature, knew of the existence of the lands to the north of their homeland and reasoned that to harmonise the spherical Earth there must also be lands to the south, a symmetric Antarktos to balance Arktos.

The idea of an Antarctic land mass was so ingrained that maps showing the position and extent of this yet-to-be-discovered southern continent were drawn throughout the medieval period. In that sense, while the Arctic was mapped by sometimes tragic voyages of discovery, Antarctica was 'undiscovered', with southern voyages that were anticipated to reach the continent merely identifying where it was not.

Opposite page
Sunset, Paradise Bay, Antarctic Peninsula.

Antarctic stats

Whoever was the first man ashore on Antarctica, the land he had reached was impressive. In summer it is the fifth largest continent (and is much larger than Europe), covering 14 million km² (about 5.5 million square miles). Under winter ice this area doubles and Antarctica becomes the third largest continent. If the ice melted the continent would consist of East Antarctica and an island archipelago, the area would halve and Antarctica would be the smallest continent. At its deepest (the East Antarctic Dome) the ice is 4,800m (15,750ft) thick. The South Pole is at 2,836m (9,304ft), the highest point on the continent being Vinson, at 4,897m (16,066ft), in the Ellsworth Mountains.

The first ship beyond 60°S

The first undisputed claim of reaching 60°S was by George Shelvocke, a British Royal Navy captain turned privateer who reached 61°30'S in the *Speedwell* during the austral summer of 1719–20. Shelvocke's expedition was also notable for two other events. Firstly, on 1 October 1719, William Camell fell overboard and drowned. Camell was probably the first man to drown south of 60°S, a fact that was doubtless of no comfort as the chilly waters of the Southern Ocean closed over his head. Secondly, after passing through the Le Maire Strait (between Tierra del Fuego's eastern tip and Staten Island) the *Speedwell* was followed for several days by a solitary black albatross, 'hovering above us as if he had lost himself'. Thinking this a sinister omen, Simon Hatley, Shelvocke's second captain, killed the bird with a shotgun (after several attempts), in the hope that its death would bring an end to the 'contrary tempestuous winds, which had oppressed us ever since we got into this sea'. In 1728 Shelvocke published *A Voyage round the World by way of the Great South Sea*. In 1797 the book was read by William Wordsworth who, it is said, suggested use of the incident to his friend Samuel Taylor Coleridge for the epic poem he was writing. Coleridge substituted a more romantic crossbow for the shotgun and used the killing as the central theme of *The Rime of the Ancient Mariner*, allowing the Antarctic an equal claim to the Arctic voyage of Thomas James as inspiration for the poem.

who kept quiet about them because they had no wish to hand details of their finds (particularly if it involved large colonies of animals) to rivals. Officially, the first landing was on 24 January 1895. In keeping with the mystery of that first step, exactly whose foot was first is disputed. The landing was by rowed boat from the Norwegian ship *Antarctic*, the voyage financed by Sven Foyn, inventor of the steam-powered whaling ship and the explosive harpoon (a combination that had made him extraordinarily rich). As the boat reached the shore the *Antarctic*'s captain, Leonard Kristensen, stepped out at the prow; a young New Zealand sailor, Alexander Van Tunzelman, leapt out to hold the boat steady for the captain; and Carsten Borchgrevink (an Anglo-Norwegian who had been a childhood friend of Roald Amundsen) jumped into the water from the stern and rushed ashore. Each of the three was later to claim the first step.

After the official landing the pace of exploration increased rapidly. The *Belgica* became the first ship to overwinter in Antarctic waters in 1898. On board were Roald Amundsen, on his first polar expedition, Dr Frederick Cook, and a cat called Nansen. Cook was instrumental in maintaining the health of the ship's company during the winter. He also modified equipment to make life easier. Amundsen was extremely impressed, the voyage sealing a life-long friendship.

The following year an expedition under Carsten Borchgrevink overwintered on Antarctica itself, building a hut at Cape Adare. The expedition was not entirely a happy one, mostly as a consequence of Borchgrevink's poor leadership – he was short-tempered and made arbitrary decisions – but it did record a number of firsts. One of these was a new record southing of 78°50'S (though many experts believe this to be debatable; it was reached by two parties travelling two days apart, which seems suspicious). Another record was tragic, the Norwegian Nicolai Hanson becoming the first man to die, and be buried, on Antarctica. Hanson had wanted to see Adelie Penguins coming ashore to breed; two days after his death 250,000 birds arrived.

Left to right are Henryk Arctowski, Dr Frederick Cook and Roald Amundsen photographed in a studio in Patagonia before setting out in the *Belgica*. The reason for striking these poses can only be guessed at. Did the photographer suggest he was after as natural a look as possible?

Scott visits the Antarctic

The British establishment had been trying to raise funds for a national expedition to Antarctica when Borchgrevink's team had departed, with the fact that his trip had been financed by a British businessman really hurting their pride. Efforts to obtain finance were redoubled, as the establishment believed that not only should Antarctica be explored by the British, but that only the British really knew how to do it. By 1901 the money had been raised and the *Discovery* had left for the south. The leader was Robert Falcon Scott. He was a naval officer, the choice of the highly influential President of the Royal Geographical Society (which organised the finance) who, being a naval man himself, preferred an officer to a scientist. Scott met Nansen, who recommended the use of dogs and skis, but although the British took both they did so reluctantly and without bothering to learn how to use either. This led to a trek involving men struggling to manhaul a heavy sledge (just as the British had on Nares' North Pole expedition), their skis on the sledge and the dogs trotting beside it. Scott took the *Discovery* to McMurdo Sound where a hut was constructed for the winter.

The expedition included the first-ever balloon flight on the continent and a record southing when, in December 1901, Scott, Ernest Shackleton and Edward Wilson reached 82°15'S. From a camp there Scott and Wilson continued to 82°17'S.

The Southern Ocean is notorious for mountainous seas. On his journey south in *Nimrod* Shackleton lost two ponies which had to be destroyed due to injuries received during a period of bad weather. The photograph to the left was taken on a journey from South Georgia to the South Orkneys.

Scott and Shackleton had fallen out on the trek; Scott's decision to order Shackleton to remain at camp while he and Wilson added this extra distance to the record seems to have been a deliberate slight. The return from the record position was terrible, the weather appalling and food constantly short. The men grew weak and Shackleton sickened to such an extent that Wilson thought he would die, but all three men survived.

Despite the British view that Antarctica belonged to them, other nations now mounted their own expeditions south. A German expedition under Erich von Drygalski made important scientific studies, particularly of southern wildlife (though whether the discovery that penguins were so rich in oil that, skinned, they could be used to feed the ship's boilers over winter can be added to the list is debatable). Then the Swede Otto Nordenskjöld (nephew of the first man to sail the North-East Passage) led an expedition that made important discoveries on Antarctica's plant life, oceanography and geology. The Frenchman Jean-Baptiste Charcot wintered on Booth Island, which forms the western side of the famous Lemaire Channel. The expedition seems to have been a happy one, though its discoveries were limited. There were problems, however; Charcot's pet pig, Toby, ate fish still attached to fish-hooks and died a miserable death, and when the expedition returned to France Charcot discovered he had been divorced by his wife on the grounds of desertion. William Bruce led a Scottish expedition which made major discoveries in the Weddell Sea area, but is now chiefly remembered for a photograph (eventually made into a postcard) showing an Emperor Penguin apparently enraptured by a kilt-clad, pipe-playing Scotsman. Only later was the truth discovered – the penguin was held in position by a cord tied around one foot and anchored to the ice.

Back in Britain after his return from the *Discovery,* Ernest Shackleton nursed a burning desire to return. Although he was to write that he had been invalided home, he must have known – or been suspicious at the very least – that his health had not been the only reason for his departure. He had already said when still on the *Discovery* that one day he would come back and show himself a better man that Scott. This resentment was sharpened by the heroic reception Scott received on his return, and by the account of the southern journey in Scott's *Voyage of the Discovery* in which he referred to Shackleton as 'our invalid' and implied that the trek south had failed because of Shackleton's 'sudden break-down'. Aware that there was little chance of his being invited on another Scott expedition, Shackleton decided to launch his own, working quickly to ensure a return south before any second Scott trip could be organised. He obtained finance from William Beardmore, a rich industrialist and shipbuilder based in Glasgow, and bought a sealing ship called the *Nimrod.* He attempted to sign up several members of the *Discovery*'s crew, but many turned down the invitation. Of these the one that caused Shackleton the greatest pain was Edward Wilson; Wilson had taken on work and would not give it up. Worse was to follow when Wilson took Scott's side after a row broke out over the use of the Discovery base. Scott had decided to return to Antarctica – but not yet – and claimed rights on the site. Indeed, he tried to claim rights to the whole Ross Sea. Shackleton was aghast, but under pressure from Wilson, who saw the dispute as a morality issue, agreed to stay east of 170°W.

Shackleton visited Nansen, who was now the ambassador in London for newly independent Norway. Nansen was amazed that Shackleton had learned so little from the *Discovery* trip. He was intending to walk, not ski, and instead of taking dogs he was taking ponies. If the former, given Shackleton's own experience of skis on his journey with Scott and Wilson (when they had arguably saved his life on the return trip), was beyond comprehension, the latter was beyond reason. How could anyone contemplate taking a vegetarian animal to a continent essentially devoid of plant life? Ironically, after Nansen had met Frederick Jackson on Franz Josef Land following the *Fram* expedition, they had discussed the use of horses in Antarctica. The incredulous Nansen had advised against it; now here, despite all the evidence in support of dogs, was another Briton with the same idea. An even greater irony is that Shackleton got his idea from Jackson. History does not record Nansen's view, if any, of Shackleton's decision to take a motor car as well.

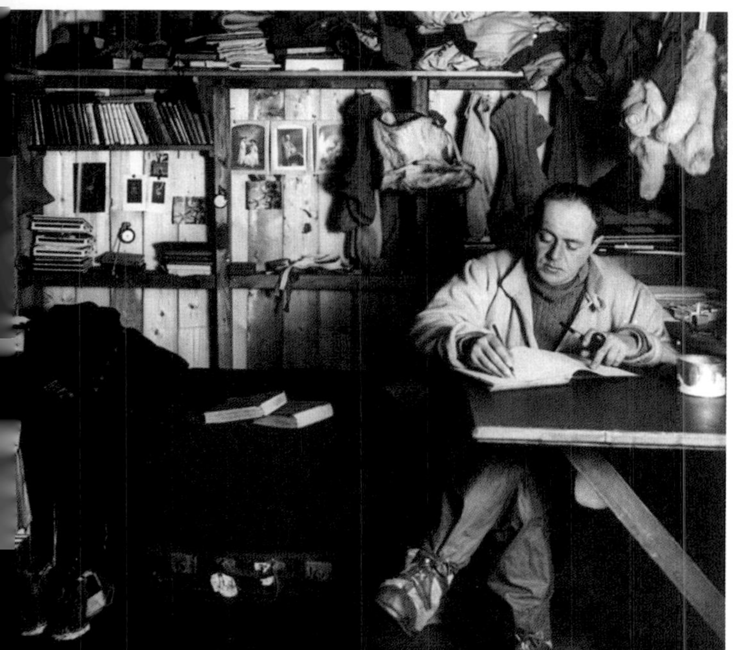

Shackleton sets off

The *Nimrod* left London in July 1907, but bad weather and the need for the ship to be towed because of a shortage of fuel forced Shackleton to break his promise to Scott and cross the 'forbidden' 170°W line for McMurdo Sound, something that caused him great distress. Shackleton built a new hut near Cape Royds, about 35km to the north of Scott's hut, and settled down for the winter. Shackleton's team made the first ascent of Mount Erebus, drove their motor car a few kilometres (a first for Antarctic mechanised transport, but of

Robert Falcon Scott in the hut at Cape Evans. This photograph was taken in 1911 shortly before he set out for the South Pole.

Shackleton's *Nimrod* expedition claimed two notable firsts. Adams, Wild and Shackleton himself (*above*) reached a new furthest south, just 155km from the Pole, while Mackay, David and Mawson (*right*) reached the South Magnetic Pole.

extremely limited practical use) and made ready for two trips in the austral summer; Edgworth David, Douglas Mawson and Alistair Mackay would attempt to reach the South Magnetic Pole, while Shackleton, Jameson Adams, Eric Marshall and Frank Wild would head for the true pole. The magnetic pole team were successful, reaching it on 16 January 1908 after a journey which had started by motor car, but rapidly became a man-haul when the vehicle became embedded in a snow drift.

Shackleton's team set out with four ponies, the remainder of those originally taken having died or been destroyed when they were injured in the appalling weather on the way to Antarctica. It was soon clear that the animals were not suited to the environment; they sank belly-deep into soft snow, they became chilled and had to have blankets draped over them when they stopped and snow walls built to protect them from the wind, and their food required thawing. The only positive was that they provided a large quantity of 'food on the hoof', early supply dumps being organised around a pony carcass with the animals being shot in turn as they weakened.

The team passed Scott's furthest south mark and, man-hauling parallel to the coast, aimed for an apparent pass in the mountains (now called the Transantarctic Mountains) ahead. It turned out to be only the entrance to a glacier (named Beardmore by Shackleton after the expedition's sponsor). The glacier was a nightmare – the men had no crampons and Socks, the only remaining pony, disappeared into a crevasse. As they climbed higher the thinning air also became a problem (the pole lies at the centre of a plateau at a height of about 3,000m). As time was lost rations were reduced to maintain the possibility of reaching the pole, so the four were constantly hungry. Eventually Shackleton realised that reaching the pole would require an all-or-nothing dash. The four dumped what they could, but it was soon apparent that they were still going too slowly. By 3 January 1909 they were at 87°22'S, still 250km from the pole. They were exhausted, cold, hungry and dehydrated, and the weather, fine early on, had turned foul. It was clear they had come to the end, yet Shackleton would not give in. He was determined to get within 100 miles (160km) of the pole so the men dumped half of what little they had and continued. On 9 January 1908 the team reached 88°23'S. They were 155km (97 miles) from the pole. His target reached, Shackleton bowed to inevitable defeat and turned around. The return journey was a nightmare, the four on the edge of starvation for almost the whole 1,170km. Several times they ran out of food altogether and only luck with the weather allowed them to reach the next of their supply dumps – bad weather would have meant certain death.

Though Shackleton felt the loss of the South Pole keenly, the expedition had been a major success. It was only 14 years since people had first (officially) stepped on Antarctica, only nine since the first overwintering, barely six since the first attempt to journey inland. Now his expedition had journeyed within 100 miles of the pole and stood on the South Magnetic Pole. And they had all returned safely. The comparison with Arctic exploration, which had taken centuries and resulted in the loss of hundreds of lives, was extreme. Shackleton was knighted and produced a book that won excellent reviews. But the praise was not universal. Though civil in public, Scott and other members of the British 'Antarctic establishment' were bitter in private. They even spread rumours that Shackleton had not gone as far south as he claimed and were almost certainly happy that he had not reached the South Pole. So too was Nansen (probably relieved rather than happy – Nansen was an honourable man) who had decided on one last expedition; he intended to take *Fram* south, though the ship's next journey would be north with Amundsen, who was attempting the North Pole.

Amundsen heads south

For his proposed North Pole expedition Amundsen chose his men wisely, taking excellent skiers and dog-drivers, one of whom was Hjalmar Johansen, Nansen's companion on the epic attempt to reach the North Pole from *Fram*. The preparations for the northern trip were well-advanced when word came that both Cook and Peary were claiming to have reached the pole. Although Amundsen does not seem to have been entirely convinced by either claim, he changed his plans and decided to head south. He did not tell his team until after they had sailed, and told Nansen by telegram. He also telegrammed Scott who had left for his own attempt on the South Pole two months earlier. The British were appalled, considering Amundsen's decision an act of betrayal. Interestingly, Shackleton's view was that Amundsen stood little chance of reaching the pole as he was taking dogs rather than ponies, and dogs 'are not very reliable'.

Amundsen set up a base in the Bay of Whales, which was at least 100km closer to the pole than the hut Scott was occupying for his own bid. In what remained of the austral autumn Amundsen laid out supply dumps southward, reaching 82°S. Although he had started later than Scott and so had arrived later in Antarctica, by setting up these dumps Amundsen was now effectively ahead of the British. The description of the Norwegian base during the winter makes impressive reading. It was a hive of activity as the sledges, traces, skis, clothing and supplies were modified and perfected. The Norwegians were clearly in tune with their environment and with the job at hand in a way in which the British, who had brought England to Antarctica, were not. This can most readily be seen in one detail: Greenland dogs will, if given the chance, eat human excrement, a disgusting habit. The Norwegians made use of this as a means of keeping their base cleaner: the British stopped any dog that tried.

But despite Amundsen's meticulous preparations he was fearful of one thing – Scott's motor sledges, which had the potential to be faster than dogs, if they were reliable. Perhaps because of this Amundsen set out too early, leaving on 8 September and encountering temperatures down to -57°C, which caused him to retreat. The retreat turned into a near-disastrous rout, and caused a split between Amundsen and the experienced Johansen. This resulted in Amundsen throwing Johansen off the team; Johansen left as soon as they reached civilisation and travelled back to Norway independently. There is some evidence that Amundsen engineered this, and also telegrammed ahead to ensure that Johansen did not receive a hero's welcome.

Amundsen left again on 20 October, with 52 dogs pulling four sledges. There were five men – Amundsen, Bjaaland, Hanssen, Hassel and Wisting. Usually Bjaaland, the best skier, moved ahead of the convoy, giving the dogs something to chase. At the 80°S dump four dogs were released to make their way back to base. When the team set out again on 24 October they were 240km ahead of Scott; his attempt set out that same day from his McMurdo base. Despite occasional requests from his men to go faster Amundsen set and maintained a daily distance target of 24km so as not to wear out the dogs. By 4 November they were at 82°S, their last dump. Here it was decided to create dumps every 1° south to progressively reduce the weight carried. To help in finding the dumps on their return journey cairns were raised along the route. As the load reduced, so did the number of dogs, the weakest being shot to feed the rest.

Ahead now lay a range of mountains Amundsen named after the Norwegian queen (the Queen Maud Mountains are part of the Transantarctic range). Amundsen had hoped that the ice shelf rose gently to the polar plateau, but now he, like Shackleton and Scott, would have to find a way through the mountains. His route took him to a glacier named after Axel Heiberg, steeper, but shorter, than the Beardmore; its ascent took four hard days. At the top, in a camp at the plateau, all but 18 dogs were shot, both men and the remaining dogs eating the carcasses. One sledge was left behind and the party moved on again. Shackleton's mark was passed on 8 December. The next day the last dump was made and marked. In fine weather on 14 December 1911 Amundsen was pushed to the front for the last few kilometres. At 3pm they reached what they thought was the pole. There was no sign of Scott – the snow was virginal, the Norwegians had won. For three days the Norwegians stayed at Polheim, their polar camp, boxing the area with flags as they took readings from the Sun to confirm their position. It is estimated that on 17 December Bjaaland and Hanssen passed within a few tens of metres of the actual pole – Polheim was probably 2km from it. At Polheim Amundsen left a tent, a pole from which flew the Norwegian flag, and a letter for the Norwegian king with a covering letter asking Scott to deliver it.

On 17 December the Norwegians left for their base. Sometime around 31 December the Norwegians and British

Morning mist in the Lemaire Channel.

Sverre Hansen, one of Amundsen's team of five, at the South Pole, 14 December 1911.

were at the same latitude and probably less than 100km apart. Though they were well out of sight of each other it is interesting to speculate what would have happened had they met. Would Scott have turned around? The Norwegians had a comfortable journey back, reaching their base on 26 January 1912. On 30 January the men boarded the *Fram* and sailed for Hobart where, on 7 March, the world was told of the success.

Scott's team

On 7 March the four survivors of Scott's five-man team were struggling towards what they hoped would be a supply dump laid down for them by the other members of the expedition at McMurdo. Scott's second expedition included two from Shackleton's *Nimrod* team, Edward Wilson and the pick of several thousand volunteers. One was Captain Lawrence Edward Grace Oates, a cavalry officer serving in India. Oates was a sports enthusiast and fancied the adventure. He appears to have had little idea about Antarctica – when he heard he was likely to be accepted he wrote to his mother that 'the climate is healthy, but inclined to be cold'. As Shackleton had taken ponies and had passed 88°S, Scott decided to take them as well. He also took motor sledges and, after another meeting with Nansen, a few token dogs. He took skis, and also a young Norwegian ski expert, Tryggve Gran, who was mortified when the news of Amundsen's race south came in a telegram on 13 October. McMurdo was reached on 2 January 1911; during unloading one motor sledge was lost when it fell through thin sea ice. In the remainder of the austral summer Scott began to organise southern supply dumps, but was only able to establish the One Ton Depot at 78°28.5'S because the ponies found the going hard. On the return from the dump seven of the eight ponies used were lost attempting to cross unstable sea ice, and at his base Scott discovered that Amundsen was in the Bay of Whales.

During the winter that followed Lt Henry Bowers, Apsley Cherry-Garrard and Wilson made a trip to Cape Crozier, on the east side of Ross Sea, to obtain the eggs of Emperor Penguins, a round trip of some 240km that was the central theme of Cherry-Garrard's book *The Worst Journey in the World*, which many have claimed to be the finest ever written on an Antarctic expedition. Scott called the journey 'one of the most gallant stories in polar history'. Considering that its objective was merely to retrieve penguin eggs it could also be termed one of the most ridiculous. Cherry-Garrard wrote that 'the horror of the nineteen days it took us to travel ... to Cape Crozier would have to be re-experienced to be appreciated ... it is not possible to describe it'. The men averaged just 2½km each day; their clothes froze so solid that it took two men to bend them into shape. Their balaclavas froze to their heads; once, Cherry-Garrard raised his head as he stepped from the tent and his clothes froze so quickly he could not look down for four hours. The temperature fell to -61°C, Cherry-Garrard noting that temperatures of about -48°C seemed luxurious. They were so cold that the agonies of warming extremities became a daily occurrence. In the perpetual darkness they could not see the crevasses. Walking was like playing blind-man's bluff as they fell in often, held by their sledge harnesses, an event that frayed the nerves.

Finally they arrived at Cape Crozier, becoming the first men to see incubating Emperor Penguins. They collected the eggs they had come for but had a terrible journey back to camp, Cherry-Garrard noting that by now the three were beginning to think of death as a friend. They were struck by a storm so ferocious it was 'as though the world was having a fit of hysterics'. They had built an igloo beside their tent; the tent blew away and the roof blew off the igloo. They survived by staying in their sleeping bags for 36 hours and allowing snow to drift over them. Cherry-Garrard thought of peaches and syrup, and then, knowing that without the tent they were unlikely to survive the return journey, hoped for death. All three survived and then, miraculously, found the tent. At night – there was twilight now at midday, so they could differentiate night and day – they were so cold in their sleeping bags they could not sleep, and often fell asleep as they walked. Finally they arrived back at base and 'thus ended the worst journey in the world'.

On 24 October 1911 Scott's remaining motor sledges started from Cape Evans as an advance party. On the same day the Norwegians were leaving their dump at 80°S. The motor sledges lasted just five days before failing. Two days later, on 1 November, Scott and the main party set off, following the route he and Shackleton had pioneered. The ponies sank into the snow (as they had every time previously), and by 9 December at the bottom of the Beardmore Glacier the animals were finished and were shot. Two days later Scott's limited dog teams turned north, leaving him with 11 men. These, some on skis, man-hauled up the glacier. At the top four men turned and headed north, their job of hauling supplies for intermediate depots completed. The eight who continued were organised in two teams of four, but when it was time to choose the final South Pole party Scott added Bowers to his own team of four. This curious decision (which, it has been speculated, was because Bowers was a better navigator than anyone in his team) meant that the pole party had to sleep five in a four-man tent, and share rations for four. More seriously, it meant that Bowers had to haul on foot, while the other four were on skis because Scott had earlier ordered the second team to leave their skis behind. That had also been a strange choice, the speculation being that he had wished to slow the second team so that his decision to take his own would be justified.

The South Pole team managed 14km a day with hours of exhausting effort (in contrast to Amundsen restricting his travel to 24km daily so as not to tire his dogs). On 16 January the men detected something ahead; it was one of Amundsen's black flags, the surrounding snow etched with ski marks, sledge marks and paw prints. The British had lost the race Scott's diary is matter-of-fact. 'The Norwegians have forestalled us and are first at the pole. It is a terrible disappointment, and I am very sorry for my loyal companions' but the next day's entry when the British actually reached the South Pole is a more telling description. 'The Pole, Yes, but under very different circumstances from those expected ... none of us having slept much after the shock of our discovery ... Great God! this is an awful place and terrible enough for us to have laboured to it without reward of priority.' Scott's words are as chilling a statement of defeat and failure as could be imagined.

On 18 January, close to what they believed was the actual pole, Scott's team found Polheim and the letter for King Haakon. Other cairns and flags led Scot to note 'There is no doubt that our predecessors have made thoroughly sure of their mark' – there was not even the satisfaction of knowing that the British were the first to mark the exact spot, even if they had come second in the race. After the obligatory photograph there was nothing left but to turn north for home. Scott noted, prophetically, in his diary, 'Now for the run home and a desperate struggle. I wonder if we can do it.'

The journey back

The homeward journey was indeed a desperate struggle. Food, fuel and time were all short, yet a gloriously fine half-day on the Beardmore Glacier was spent collecting 16kg of rock samples which were then towed for the rest of the journey. The lost time equates to perhaps 8km, the extra load perhaps as much again in terms of energy spent. And the last camp was 17½km from One Ton Depot. Edgar Evans' condition was also worsening; he had injured his hand badly and also seemed to be fragmenting mentally. On 17 February he collapsed in the snow and was, at first, left behind. That night he died.

Oates was next. He had frostbitten feet, the pain making walking agony and survival unlikely. His condition made hauling near impossible and probably slowed the rest. On 16 March he asked to be left behind. The request was turned down and next morning Scott records that Oates famously said 'I am just going outside and may be some time', before struggling into a blizzard. Wilson, writing to Oates' mother, does not mention these iconic words. The last three struggled on until 21 March when they set up camp. Scott was finished, his right foot probably gangrenous. The other two tried to get to

Gold Harbour, South Georgia.

the depot on 22nd and 23rd, but they could not because of a blizzard. The tent with the three still inside their sleeping bags was discovered in November 1912 by a British search party. They were buried where they lay.

Shackleton and the *Endurance*

As remarkable a story of survival against the odds as Mawson's, though less tragic, was Shackleton's expedition of 1914 in the *Endurance*. The idea was to trek across Antarctica from the Weddell Sea to the Ross Sea, Shackleton sending another team to the Ross Sea to lay down dumps for use after he passed the pole.

The *Endurance* became trapped in the ice of the Weddell Sea and eventually had to be abandoned. The crew then hauled two boats across the frozen sea, launched them and sailed to Elephant Island. From there Shackleton made what is now considered to be one of the great sea voyages of all time, taking the small *James Caird* across the Southern Ocean to South Georgia. The epic voyage, a masterpiece of navigation and seamanship, was followed by an equally epic trek across South Georgia's glaciated heart to the whaling station at Stromness. From there Shackleton launched a rescue mission, bringing all the Elephant Island men safely home.

In the wake of the 1914–18 war – in which one of the six-man crew of *James Caird* died – trips to Antarctica were carried out in order to fill the gaps on the map, many of these involving aeroplanes. The first flight over the continent was made in 1928 by planes taking off from Deception Island. Early the following year came the first flight from the continent. The same plane, a Ford Tri-Motor, piloted by Bernt Balchen and carrying Richard Byrd, who had already claimed the first flight to the North Pole, reached the South Pole on 28 November 1929 after both the team and the plane had overwintered on the continent.

Setting up base

Next, as part of the International Geographical Year (IGY), the Americans set up a base at the South Pole, tactfully naming it Amundsen-Scott. On 31 October 1956 a DC3 (called the *Que Sera Sera*) piloted by Gus Shinn landed at the pole and Admiral George Dufek became the 11th man, and the first American, to stand there – and the first to have arrived there without weeks of cold, relentless effort. The following month Lt Richard Bowers – the second Lt Bowers to stand at the pole, but the first to arrive safely back at McMurdo – arrived to supervise construction of the base. As part of the IGY the British decided to realise Shackleton's

The home of the blizzard

While Amundsen and Scott were striving for the pole, a third expedition was also at work on the continent. The Australasian Antarctic Expedition was led by Douglas Mawson, who had declined Scott's offer of a place on *Terra Nova* in favour of leading his own trip. Mawson was hoping to fill in gaps on the map of Antarctica, but chose one of the windiest places on Earth for his base, with his team subjected to a constant battering by katabatic winds; Mawson titled his book of the expedition *The Home of the Blizzard*. Mawson survived one of the most harrowing retreats in polar history when one of his three men team fell into a crevasse, taking almost all the supplies with him. Mawson and Dr Xavier Hertz, a Swiss lawyer, had to trek 500km back to base eating what remained of their food, and then their dogs. Both men suffered from Vitamin A poisoning from the dogs' livers, Mertz eventually dying of it while Mawson lost skin from his legs and the entire soles of his feet. So bad was his condition that when he finally reached base, his team members' first question was 'Which one are you?'

Scott's team at the South Pole, 18 January 1912. Standing are, left to right, Bowers, Scott and Wilson. Evans is seated to the left, with Oates beside him.

dream of crossing Antarctica from the Weddell Sea to the Ross Sea. In charge of the project was Vivian Fuchs, the plan being for his team to start from the Weddell and, after reaching the pole, to use supply depots laid down by a New Zealand team working from McMurdo to continue to the Ross Sea. The New Zealanders were to be led by Sir Edmund Hillary who, three years earlier, had, with Tenzing Norgay, been first to the summit of Mount Everest. Before leaving for Antarctica, Fuchs visited Olav Bjaaland, the last surviving member of Amundsen's South Pole team. Bjaaland was told of the intended trip, but was unimpressed, claiming that it was unlikely that much had changed there.

Using a combination of dog teams and tracked vehicles Fuchs reached the pole on 20 January 1958, but he had been beaten to it by Hillary's team, which had travelled by way of the Skelton Glacier. The fact that Hillary had actually reached the pole, which had not been part of the plan, and had done so first, caused a diplomatic incident between the British and the New Zealanders. Hillary's had become the third team to reach the pole overland; later Fuchs' team became the first to complete the traverse.

Following the IGY the South Pole became, as with the North Pole, a target for adventurers, with expeditions making impressive journeys and establishing equally impressive firsts. Scott's journey was repeated, the traverse was repeated on foot (though using parawings), and an international team using dogs completed the longest possible traverse. The first solo, unsupported journey to the pole was made in 1993–94 by the Norwegian Erling Kagge, and another Norwegian, Børge Ousland, completed the first unsupported traverse. Today, with plane travel to a blue-ice runway at Patriot Hill near the south-western edge of the Ronne Ice Shelf, commercial ski and mountaineering trips have become relatively commonplace (though hardly inexpensive), though as with the Arctic, Antarctica will always attract those seeking a rite of passage as a polar adventurer.

Above left
Shackleton's grave at Grytviken, South Georgia.

Above
The *Endurance* trapped in the ice. As well as the famous series of black and white photographs taken by Frank Hurley, the expedition's photographer, he also took a small number of colour shots using an, at the time, state of the art system known as Paget plates. These used dyed screens to produce the image, A true-coloured print from the resulting plate was difficult to obtain and the system soon fell into disuse.

Ed Hillary's Antarctic team used standard Ferguson tractors with tracks fitted between the wheels. This photograph shows Hillary trying out one of the (trackless) tractors. His team, all arrayed in their Antarctic clothing, look suitably bemused.

Part 3

Habitats and Wildlife

13. After the Ice

During the early years of the 20th century, details of past climates began to become available to scientists. Serbian mathematician Milutin Milankovich noticed an apparent periodicity in the climate of the Earth. Based on his analysis of the periodicity, Milankovich developed a theory based on the cyclical nature of the planet's orbital movements. There are three such variations (Figure 13.1), each of which affects the Earth's position relative to the Sun and so has the potential to effect insolation (the solar energy reaching the Earth) and, hence, climate. The first concerns the Earth's path around the Sun, which varies over time so that it is alternately closer to, then further from the Sun, the changes resulting in a variation of incident solar energy, with a period of approximately 96,000 years. The second cycle is in the obliquity of the Earth's axis of spin (i.e. the angle between the spin axis and the plane of the ecliptic). This varies from about 21.4° to 24.4°, with a period of approximately 41,000 years. This change moves the poles closer to, and further from, the Sun (relative to the present angle of 23.5°). The third cycle, with a periodicity of about 20,000 years, results from the Earth's precession (wobble) around its spin axis. This precession also moves the poles towards and away from the Sun.

Milankovich's work led scientists to assume that these cycles, together with differences in atmospheric gas make-up, explained the gross changes in the Earth's climate, but more recently doubts have been expressed. Although the changes in obliquity and precession make differences between the northern and southern hemisphere more marked, as they affect the tilt of the Earth, both they and the eccentricity of the Earth's orbit have a more limited effect on the total input of solar radiation than was first assumed. The periodicity of the obliquity and precession can be observed in the climatic record, but obtaining evidence for any marked effect due to orbital eccentricity has been more problematic. There seems, for instance, to be a periodicity of about 100,000 years over the last million years or so, in agreement with the orbital eccentricity period, but no such periodicity prior to that time, which is curious. What is equally strange is that orbital eccentricity should, climatically, be the weakest of the three Milankovich effects, but its periodicity produces the strongest signal during the Quaternary era. Overall, the actual climate record does not readily accord with any of the Milankovich effects. While it was once considered that Milankovich's theory might explain most of the observed cyclical variation in the Earth's climate, it now seems that these effects are only part of the story, and other mechanisms have been proposed to account for cyclical climatic variations.

About 1,000 million years ago the appearance and evolution of photosynthesising organisms caused a dramatic decrease in atmospheric carboc dioxide (CO_2) and a massive rise in oxygen (O_2) which killed off competing organisms. As CO_2 is a major contributor to the trapping of heat within the atmosphere (without the present concentration of CO_2 in the atmosphere the Earth's average temperature would fall from a balmy +15°C to a much more chilling -20°C: this is the 'greenhouse' effect, which is the subject of much current debate on climate change), this reduction caused a major cooling of the Earth. Eons later, a period of intense tectonic activity led to the emission of vast quantities of CO_2 and a rise in the planet's temperature. This cycle of increasing and decreasing levels of CO_2 in the atmosphere has repeated throughout the Earth's history. These cycles combine with the Milankovich effects to create variations in the Earth's climate. When other effects are also included – chemical processes during mountain building and erosion, thermohaline ocean currents and the distribution of land across the Earth's surface – it is easy to see why no fully comprehensive theory of Ice Age periodicity has yet been established. However, whether the mechanisms that initiate Ice Ages are fully understood or not, their existence is beyond doubt. Just as carbon exists in different isotopic forms, aiding radiocarbon dating, oxygen also has different isotopes. Two of these, O16 and O18 – the most abundant forms – are of great value for measuring past climate. The ratio of the two isotopes depends on the volume of terrestrial ice. Water molecules in which the oxygen atom is O16, being fractionally lighter, evaporate more easily from the oceans. In interglacial periods the evaporated water falls as rain or as snow, returning the lighter oxygen isotope to the oceans. However, in glacial periods the volume of ice on land increases and the amount of O16 locked in the ice rises: at the same time, since the O16 is not being returned to the sea, the concentration of the lighter oxygen isotope in the ocean falls (Figure 13.2). Measurement of the ratio of the two isotopes of oxygen in ice cores from the Greenlandic and Antarctic ice sheets, and of the ratio in alkenones (chemicals produced by marine phytoplankton) in ocean sediments, indicate that the temperature of the Earth began to fall some 2½ million years ago.

Ice cores indicate a sustained period of cold from about 250,000 years BP, with interglacial periods when temperature

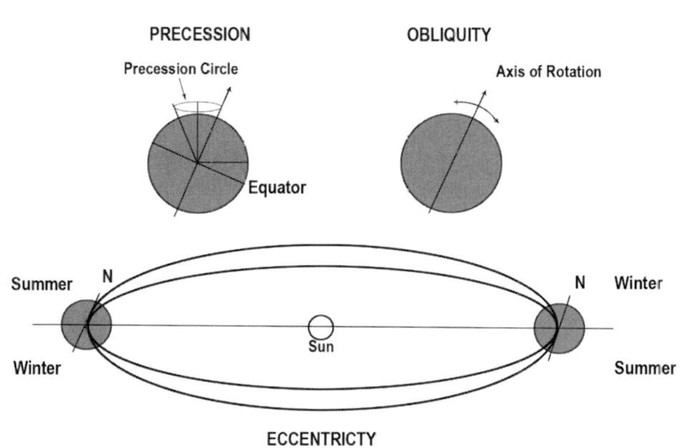

Figure 13.1
Variations in the Earth's orbit.

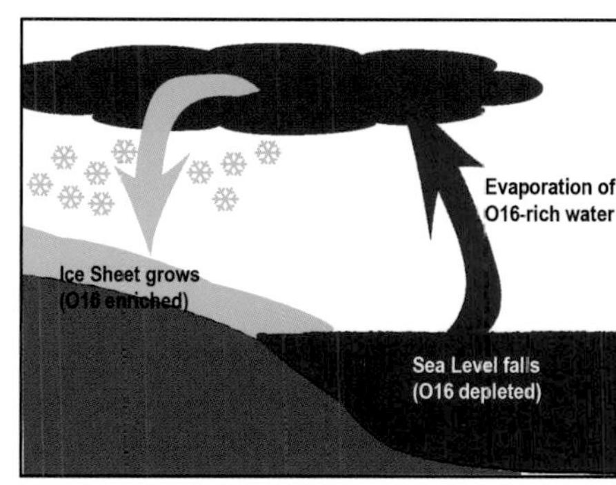

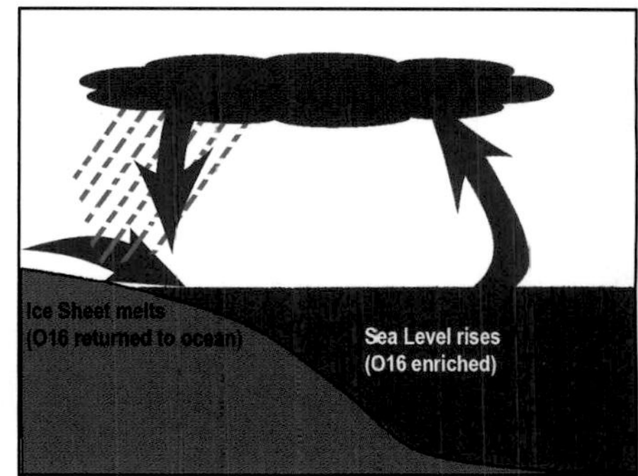

Figure 13.2
Oxygen isotopes and sea level changes.

Opposite page
Returning Sun. Winter in Sassenfjord, Spitsbergen, Svalbard.

rose. There was a significant glacial maximum about 150,000 years ago, and another that ended about 18,000 years ago. Since that last maximum, the Earth's mean temperature has been more or less stable, with temperature fluctuations within a range of about 4°C. A rise in temperature led to a warmer period in the 9th and 10th centuries, when the Vikings settled Iceland and Greenland, and discovered and attempted to settle North America, while a cooling caused the 'Little Ice Age' of the 17th–early 19th centuries when, in Britain, the River Thames froze in almost all winters; the ice was thick enough for Frost Fairs to be held on it each year, attended by thousands of Londoners.

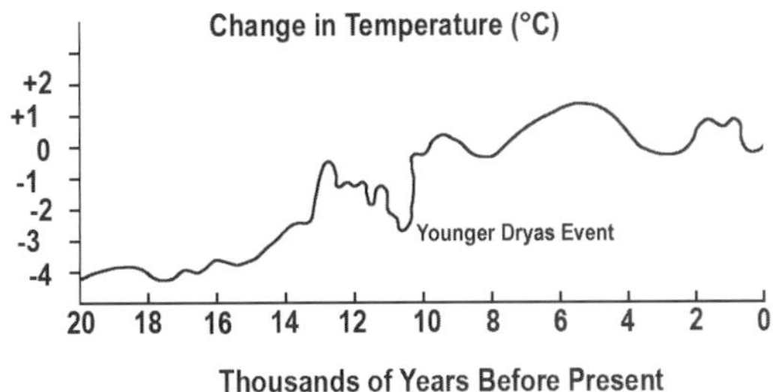

Figure 13.3
The change in the Earth's temperature over the last 20,000 years, as derived from ice cores. The mean temperature (i.e. the 0 point) is that for the first half of the 20th century.

Ice core samples also reveal two events that may indicate what the future holds for northern Europe if the present increase in the Earth's temperature continues. The samples indicate that about 13,000 years BP the climate warmed, but then abruptly cooled again (Figure 13.3). Then, about 11,500 years BP the climate warmed dramatically, the temperature in the Arctic rising by about 7°C in only 50 years (implying a mean temperature rise across the Earth of 4°C; temperature fluctuations are more pronounced in the polar regions, as we shall see later). This cooling and rapid warming is known as the Younger Dryas event (named after the spread of Mountain Avens – *Dryas octopetala*) and is thought to have resulted from a switching off and on of the Atlantic conveyor, which drives the North Atlantic Drift.

The initial warming phase induced copious glacial meltwater, which diluted the Arctic Ocean's surface water. This led to an interruption of thermohaline circulation. The North Atlantic Drift shut down (though the Gulf Stream would have remained as an Atlantic gyre) and the northern hemisphere cooled. The cooling reduced the meltwater flow and, eventually, the conveyor switched on again, causing a rapid temperature rise. Then the warmer climate resulted in an increase of precipitation and a thickening of the Greenlandic ice sheet. It would seem that the warming would again increase melting, but if local temperatures remained close to freezing then melting might not have been appreciable, preventing another switch-off of the conveyor. Following the Younger Dryas event, further cold troughs occurred about 8,000 years and 3,000 years BP, suggesting that switching off of, or reductions in, the Atlantic conveyor is not as difficult a process as might be hoped. These cold troughs could imply that if the present increase in the Earth's temperature continues, then the conveyor might again be reduced or switched-off, with disastrous climatic effects for northern Europe.

***Dryas octopetala* in the Barren Lands of Nunavut, Canada, near the Hood River.**

Northern King William Island, Canada. The land here has risen above the sea due to isostatic rebound since the last Ice Age.

The last Ice Age

The last glacial maximum occurred about 18,000 years ago. At that time ice covered about 30% of the Earth's land surface, but it was not distributed evenly across the northern hemisphere, differing in extent between North America and Eurasia, and also within those continental landmasses.

The Ice Age in North America

In North America there are currently large ice caps on Axel Heiberg, Devon and Ellesmere islands as well as smaller caps elsewhere, and glacier ice in both Canada and Alaska. At the glacial maximum, ice sheets covered most of the continent south to latitude 39°N, a combination of the enormous Laurentide ice sheet, the smaller Cordilleran sheet on the Pacific coast, and the much smaller Innuitian sheet on Ellesmere and Axel Heiberg. The three ice sheets coalesced at their borders, effectively giving continuous ice coverage over virtually the whole of Canada and the northern United States. The Innuitian ice sheet also coalesced with the ice sheet on Greenland. However, although there was an ice cap on Alaska's Brooks Range, much of central, western and the extreme north of Alaska was ice-free.

The ice sheet was up to 4,000m thick near Hudson Bay. So heavy was the ice that it compressed the land beneath it, creating corresponding bulges in land at the periphery of the sheet. When the ice later retreated, the compressed land rebounded, the process – known as isostatic rebound – having raised King William Island above the sea and lifted the land beneath Hudson Bay, to the north of James Bay, by 120m in the subsequent 7,000 years. The shorelines of Hudson Bay have risen by about 80m: rebound can now be measured with great accuracy using GPS systems so the continuation of the uplift can be confirmed. By the time the rebound has been concluded, the shape of Hudson Bay will be very different from that of today. James Bay will cease to exist, Southampton Island will become part of the mainland, and the Bay's area will have been reduced to some 35% of its present extent. The long-term history of Hudson Bay is a fascinating insight into the way the maximum glaciation of the last Ice Age affected, and continues to affect, modern geography.

As well as isostasy – the rise and fall of the land relative to the sea – there is eustasy, the rise and fall of the sea relative to the land. In the area now occupied by Hudson Bay a much larger sea – the Tyrrell Sea – formed as the Laurentide ice sheet retreated. The size of the sea was governed by the opposing processes of isostasy and eustasy. At first the eustatic rise of the sea dominated because the melting of ice was faster than isostatic rebound, and the Tyrrell Sea grew. Ultimately, as the volume of ice shrank, the situation reversed and the Tyrrell Sea began to shrink: it became today's Hudson Bay and will eventually become a much smaller sea.

In addition to the rebound seen around Hudson Bay, there has also been a lowering of the peripheral bulges by up to 13m south of the Great Lakes. One of the effects of such isostatic rebound is the creation of raised beaches as the shoreline is uplifted. Such beaches provide valuable information about glaciation and sea level changes: the raised beach is an indicator of both, of course, because the shoreline is uplifted as the ice retreats, but the sea level also rises as the ice volume returns to the ocean, though, as in the case of Hudson Bay, the response of the land is much slower than the response of the ocean.

The ice retreated because of a warming of the Earth. Initially this warming would have chiefly affected the thickness of the ice sheets, as the calving of glaciers into the northern oceans would have maintained low water temperatures. Only as the ice sheets retreated from the sea would this calving have ceased: the oceans then warmed and on-shore winds would have enhanced melting. The major effect of melting was to produce proglacial lakes, water masses formed at glacial snouts, the lakes dammed on one side by naturally higher ground or by land undergoing isostatic uplift and on the other by the ice sheet. The waters of proglacial lakes aided ice retreat, with wave action gnawing away at the sheet and calving icebergs, which drifted south to melt in water warmed by winds blowing north across the continental landmasses. Among the proglacial lakes formed by the retreat of the Laurentide ice sheet in North America were precursors of the Great Lakes, which sit on the border between Canada and the United States. Large though the Great Lakes are, they would have been dwarfed by Lake Agassiz, which formed south of the present south-western corner of Hudson Bay. The lake is named in honour of the Swiss-born glaciologist Jean Louis Agassiz, who first suggested the existence of the Ice Ages after studying the movement of Alpine glaciers. Lake Agassiz existed for about 2.000 years and reached a maximum size of more

Old sea bed at Badlanddalen, north-east Greenland. The bed is now 10km from the sea.

than 350,000km². The vast lake drained into Hudson Bay, an event (around 8,000 years ago) that lasted perhaps only two days – the greatest of all *jökulhlaups* – and involved the discharge of as much as 150,000km³ of fresh water. It is estimated that such a discharge would have raised the global sea level by 20–40cm over the same two-day period. The discharge would also have radically affected the surface salinity of the North Atlantic, and it is speculated that the cooling of the Arctic that occurred at the time of the discharge was caused by a corresponding change in the North Atlantic Drift. Today Lake Winnipeg is set at the heart of what was Lake Agassiz, the remainder of the old lake having become prairie. To the north, the proglacial Lake McConnell, another enormous body of water, was the precursor of the Great Bear Lake, Great Slave Lake and Lake Athabasca.

The Ice Age in Eurasia

In the Palearctic during the last glacial maximum, much of Britain, Scandinavia and Denmark, together with parts of Germany, Poland and Russia, were ice-covered. But, as with the Nearctic, the coverage was not complete, with ice coverage in northern Asian Russia being surprisingly limited. There were ice caps on Franz Josef Land, the northern island of Noyava Zemlya and Severnaya Zemlya (much of which is still glaciated), but there was little ice on the mainland, and Wrangel Island was ice-free. As in North America there were several ice sheets, these again coalescing at their borders. The principal sheets were those covering the British Isles, Scandinavia and Eurasia, the latter often referred to as the Barents Ice Sheet; an ice sheet would also have covered much, probably all, of Iceland, with the ice coverage increasing the number of *jökulhlaups* that would have occurred. It is also probable that Jan Mayen was completely ice-covered. The ice sheet reached a depth of 3,000m at the head of the Gulf of Bothnia, where the isostatic rebound has been approximately 100m to date, with peripheral lowering of about 10m in northern Germany.

Finally, on Greenland it is probable that the entire island was covered with ice, either as a continuation of the present ice sheet, or by glaciers. The weight of the present ice sheet has complicated the isostatic rebound of the island, but considerable uplift has been detected under the sea off the east coast near Scoresbysund, off the west coast south of Disco Bay and off the north-east coast north of Qannaq. The present isostatic depression of Greenland by the overtopping ice sheet has

created a saucer-shaped landmass beneath the ice. On its eastern edge Greenland rises to an average of more than 2,000m above sea level. On the west the average is lower, closer to 1,000m above sea level. However, over most of central Greenland the land beneath the ice is at, or below, sea level. Occasionally, elevated parts of the landmass protrude through the overlying ice: such protrusions are known as nunataks. Nunataks (which may occur or formerly have existed in other Arctic areas as well as Greenland) can either have been formed as a consequence of ice retreat or ice depth reduction, or they could always have existed because they were never inundated by the ice. The latter may have acted as small refugia for plant life and so aided the recolonisation of the Arctic fringe when the ice receded.

Though conditions on most nunataks were so harsh that most plants could not survive, the plant life of today's Arctic includes species whose habitat suggests that they could indeed have survived (if not flourished) during the glacial maximum in such refugia. In particular, the Woolly Lousewort *Pedicularis lanata* has been discovered in well-separated places – northern Greenland, north-east Siberia and some northern Canadian islands – suggesting they survived on nunataks when a formerly more extensive circumpolar distribution was largely inundated by ice. However, caution is necessary when making such suggestions. Grasses have been discovered growing on Canada's Arctic islands well to the north of the rest of their range; these are assumed to have been brought there in the kamiks of Inuit, who are known to have used grass as an insulator in their boots. Similarly, some plant species in south-eastern Greenland are believed to have arrived with Norse settlers (they also brought insect species that have survived in the areas the Norse settled), and scattered outcrops of Ross's Avens *Geum rossii* in the Canadian and Greenland High Arctic seem best explained by their having been transported as seeds on the feet or plumage of geese.

However, it is worth noting that plant refugia were not absolutely necessary for the rapid recolonisation of the land as the ice retreated. Seeds from winter caches have been found in lemming burrows dating back some 10,000 years – the subfossil skeletons of the lemmings that collected them were also found. When given ideal growing conditions the seeds germinated rapidly and grew into healthy flowering plants. In places where the soil was not entirely scraped away by the ice, seeds may therefore have survived the glacial maximum and flourished as soon as more equable conditions returned.

Jan Mayen Island. It is likely that the island was completely ice-covered during the last Ice Age. Recolonisation has therefore occurred in about the last 20,000 years. Colonising plants have had to contend with the island's volcanic evolution.

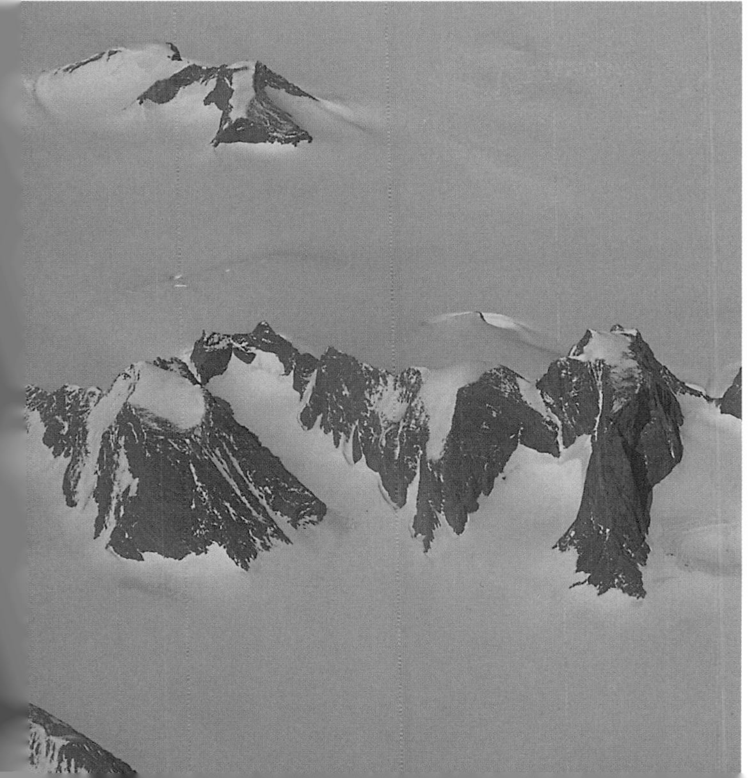

Nunataks in southern Greenland.

The development of Arctic habitats

As the ice of the last glacial maximum retreated it left behind bare ground. Not until plants had colonised this bare ground could birds and animals thrive. The position in freshwater lakes was analogous, with the establishment of photosynthetic organisms such as diatoms required to form the base of any potential food chain. Freshwater systems do differ however, for although some aquatic organisms can become established by means other than direct inflow from streams or rivers, larger aquatic organisms such as fish cannot. For lakes to acquire fish there must have been inflowing rivers, implying either the existence of freshwater refugia in ice-free areas or changes in local hydrology caused by the retreating ice. But freshwater systems represent a special case: elsewhere it is the return of plants that establishes habitats.

The retreating ice left behind areas of bare rock, but also areas of glacial till, much of it in the form of a silt of ground-up rock debris. The thickness of the ice sheet coverage (even during the retreat of the ice) probably generated fierce katabatic winds, which would have redistributed the silt to form extensive deposits of loess (as the silt from such wind-driven processes is known), which would have also included soil blown in from unglaciated areas to the south by the persistent anticyclonic winds that swept the ice. These winds would have brought seeds and spores, while the large proglacial lakes formed at the ice sheet front would have induced a local 'maritime' climate. Rain therefore added to the fertile loess to create an excellent medium for the growth of plants. Analysis of pollen from lake and pond sediments allows such colonisation to be studied. Although the results of pollen capture must be treated with caution because several factors affect the precipitation of pollen, analysis allows not only the date of colonisation to be established, but also the rate of progress northwards of some individual plant species to be estimated. Not surprisingly, the rate of travel depended not only on the speed of retreat of the ice, but on wind speed for seed transfer, and on local conditions as the colonisation of ground exposed by retreating ice was not straightforward. For a range of plants – flowering plants, conifers and shrubs – to establish, factors beyond available soil and retreating ice were involved. One was the depth below the surface of the permafrost, with a shallow active layer restricting root growth. Another was that nitrogen-fixing plants had to become established before other plants could flourish; the decomposition of nitrogen-fixers acts as an effective nitrogen fertilizer. Yet another was the presence in the soil of mycorrhizal fungi, which form relationships with many plants, invading their roots. The fungi benefit by obtaining carbon (in sugars) from the plant, in exchange for providing the tree a greater area for absorption of minerals from their hyphae (the fungal filaments). This association, termed a mutualism, is particularly beneficial for trees attempting to establish themselves in soils that are poor in nutrients or poorly drained, precisely the conditions encountered by trees moving north in the wake of the retreating ice. Although deciduous trees form such relationships conifers are, not surprisingly, particularly rich with them. For trees and many other plants to become well-established, the spores of mycorrhizal fungi (e.g. basidiomycetes) must therefore be present in the soil.

The rate of colonisation of newly uncovered ground was initially dependent on the speed at which seeds arrived, plants with winged seeds preceding those which required dispersal by birds, with seeds with large wing areas relative to weight arriving before those with smaller wing-to-weight ratios. Later, the rate became dependent on the extent of available bare soil after the first plants had taken root. It is easy to assume that the plant cover we see today has existed throughout the time since the ice retreat. In fact, the coverage has changed due to fluctuations in climate. Pollen analysis shows that towards the northern limit of the forest there were once oaks and elms among the spruce; there are none now, indicating that the winter temperature (the limiting factor for these groups) has become colder.

Plants are subject not only to snowfall, but to the effects of icing due to wind. In this photograph wind has blown water from a lake at Orre, Norway on to plant stems, the water then freezing. Hoar frost can also build up directly on trees and plants from moist, wind-driven air. In each case the plant has to contend not only with the effects of freezing, but with the weight of the ice. Hoar frost build-up on trees has been known to become so heavy that branches break.

Avoiding freezing

In general, the effect of temperature on biological function is straightforward. Organisms depend on enzymes to allow the chemical reactions that drive life processes to occur, and these proteins have optimal temperatures at which they work best. As the temperature of an organism increases the function rate of the enzyme increases until this optimum temperature is reached. At high temperatures enzymes denature (i.e. undergo structural change) and stop working. At low temperatures the enzymes do not denature but they do cease to function. Both extremes lead to death of the organism. At high temperatures damage to the cell structure may also occur, so the organism dies even though the enzyme function may not have actually ceased. In the absence of systems to combat changes in temperature the organism therefore has a limited temperature range over which it can survive (ignoring spectacular survivals such as those of nematodes, water bears and the eggs of some insects that can survive, in an inactive state, after a bath of liquid helium at just a few degrees above absolute zero).

In the Arctic it is, of course, low temperature that presents a threat to the survival of an organism. It might seem that the problem of reduced function rate would apply solely to ectotherms (those organisms whose temperature depends largely on the ambient temperature – fish, insects and amphibians), since endotherms (those organisms that can regulate their own temperatures – birds and mammals) can in principle increase their body insulation by adding blubber, fur or feathers, or increase their metabolic rate, assuming sufficient food is available. It is worth noting that while the distinction between ectotherms and endotherms appears straightforward, organisms of each group can utilise some of the techniques of the other to their advantage. Small birds and rodents often reduce their metabolic rates – this may be seasonal or at night – while mammals and birds 'sunbathe', the heat absorbed reducing the level of internal heat generation required. Bumblebees rapidly vibrate their wing muscles to generate body heat in order to raise their flight muscles to working temperature, and also have insulatory body hair. Some other insects also use this shivering technique. However, despite this minor blurring of the distinction between cold- and warm-blooded organisms, it is the ectotherms that require very specific techniques to avoid death as ambient temperature falls.

If the temperature of individual cells in an organism falls enough that cellular water freezes, the ice crystals created can grow rapidly and damage membranes and other cell structures. In order to survive at low temperatures ectotherms have therefore had to evolve strategies to combat these damaging and fatal effects. There are two strategies, freeze-tolerance and freeze-avoidance. These strategies are not mutually exclusive: some species may use both (some beetle larvae actually switch strategies). Neither are they foolproof: each has a lower temperature limit below which cold injury or death will occur regardless, and within a species there is variation in effectiveness, so some individuals survive while others succumb.

Freeze-tolerance utilises the fact that ice crystals must have a nucleus around which they can form. Such particles inevitably exist, but hydrophilic proteins are pumped out of the cells into the extracellular fluid. There they act as ice-nucleators, so the freezing occurs outside the cell. The proteins also order the water molecules so that crystal formation is slow, limiting local damage. The cellular fluids remain ice-free: it is within the cell that ice crystals do the damage that causes injury or death of the organism. Solutes concentrated in the cell lower the freezing point of the cell fluids; glycerol is the most frequently found, and sugars are added to aid the prevention of damage to membranes and to maintain cell function. Freeze-tolerance is found in many invertebrates, including many marine species and some insects. It is rare in vertebrates, but does occur in some amphibians. Freeze-tolerance is effective in some species to temperatures as low as -70°C, though temperatures of -25°C to -40°C are more common.

Freeze-avoidance utilises the fact that very pure fluids, ones from which nuclei for crystal formation have been excluded, can be supercooled, that is cooled well below the normal freezing temperature. In this way water can be supercooled to about -40°C without ice formation. If solutes are added to the fluid so that the freezing temperature is further reduced, the strategy becomes even more effective. The added solutes are known, not surprisingly, as antifreeze compounds: glycerol and related compounds are again the most commonly found (and are also the basis of the antifreeze compounds which drivers routinely add to their car cooling systems). In some Arctic insects, antifreeze compounds can amount to 25% of body weight. To reduce the amounts of particles that can aid ice crystal formation, organisms have efficient cleansing methods so that, for instance, they can empty their gut of food as residual particles can act as nuclei. Freeze-avoidance is practised by insects and many spiders, and by more vertebrates – particularly polar fish – than practise freeze-tolerance. Though more energy-costly, as it requires the manufacture of antifreeze compounds, freeze-avoidance has the advantage of being more rapid in terms of switching from an inactive to an active state, and reduces the water loss that can arise through using freeze-tolerance. However, in general the lowest tolerable temperature is higher (usually in the range -5°C to -20°C) and the strategy is riskier: if intracellular freezing occurs it is very rapid and results in the swift death of the organism.

Moss Campion on an esker in the Barren Lands of Nunavut, Canada. The plant grows in the extreme north, the cushion-like form allowing it to create a healthy microclimate.

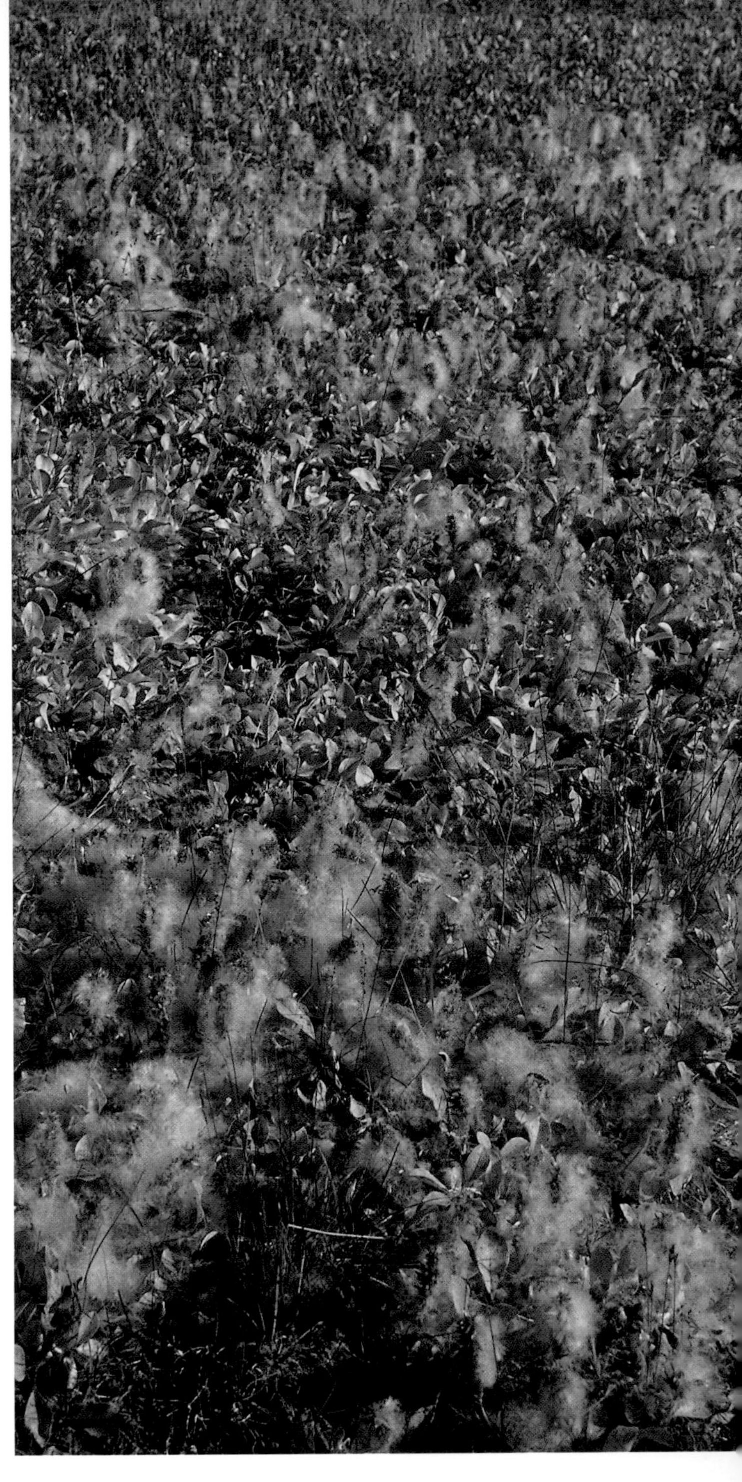

Above
Purple Saxifrage, another extreme northern species. This also forms low cushions.

Right
An Arctic forest. An expanse of Arctic Willow, the 'trees' never more than a few centimetres high.

Both photographs were taken on Igloolik, Canada.

Plant adaptations

Plants exhibit a combination of freeze-tolerance and freeze-avoidance as well as a variety of insulation adaptations in order to survive low Arctic temperatures. These adaptations allow broad-leaved evergreen trees to survive at temperatures of about -15°C. Broad-leaved deciduous trees push this survival temperature down towards -40°C, but at lower temperatures only conifers can survive.

Though low temperatures are, of course, a problem, one aspect of the temperate climate that young, tender Arctic plant parts have to deal with less frequently is frost. In temperate regions the cooling of the soil at night, particularly if the sky is clear, causes the temperature at ground level to fall rapidly, cold air becoming trapped below the air slightly removed from the ground. This temperature inversion allows ground frosts even on nights when the ambient temperature is above freezing. The 24-hour Arctic day reduces – indeed, may eliminate – frosts so that plant growth is not retarded as it often is in temperate areas.

Arctic plants grow close to the ground, but this low form can be either a genetically inherited morphology or one fashioned by the local environment. A classic example of the former is Arctic Willow *Salix arctica*, a dwarf willow species that grows as such even if transplanted to an environment which is less hostile. In species where form is determined by the environment a dwarf will grow taller. The low form of Arctic plants offers protection from the wind as well as allowing a more hospitable microclimate to be created. Wind desiccates the plant, a particular problem in winter when the frozen ground prevents water uptake. Because of friction, wind speeds are lower closer to the ground than they are higher up. Lower wind speeds also mean that abrasion from dust particles and snow is reduced. The depth of the active layer of permafrost also affects plant height; if the active layer is shallow (and so uniformly cold) and root growth is restricted, plant growth is slowed. Arctic travellers will notice that plants prefer to grow in sheltered places, but they may also be surprised to come across plants in isolated and exposed positions. The tenacity of life, here as elsewhere, is remarkable.

Air temperature is higher closer to the ground, and the matted or cushion form of most High Arctic plants allows air to be trapped. Held close to the (relatively) warm ground, the warmer air helps to create a local microclimate of higher temperature. Many species show this convergent evolution, the most notable examples being Moss Campion *Silene acaulis* and Purple Saxifrage *Saxifraga oppositifolia*, both of which are often claimed to be the most northerly flowering plant in the world (a claim that is difficult to prove, but these species must be strong contenders). Moss Campion in particular can, in certain circumstances, be easily confused with a true moss, so tightly packed are the stems and leaves. Studies in the field have shown that in some cushion plants the internal temperature of the cushion can be as much as 15°C above ambient.

In winter the low form of Arctic plants also allows a covering of snow, which insulates the plant against plunging

The Arctic Poppy, photographed here at Hold-with-Hope, north-east Greenland, has parabolic flowers to concentrate sunlight. The plant is also phototropic.

ambient temperatures. This is of particular value for species that are evergreen. Evergreen plants have the advantage of being able to photosynthesise in winter if there are bright days, and of being able to gain time at the start of spring by not having to wait until new leaves have grown. The new year's leaf growth is also protected during the early stages by the overtopping older leaves. While dead leaves at the top of the plant add insulation, those at the base are trapped close to the plant and ultimately add nutrients to the soil. Arctic soil is poor, and plants need to take advantage of any available nutrient resource: Arctic travellers will often see relatively luxuriant plant growth beneath the breeding sites of birds where the ground is fertilised by droppings, or near an animal carcass. Some species also overwinter with well-developed flower buds to save development time in the short Arctic spring and summer.

Other adaptations

There are many other adaptations. Leaves and stems, and the branches of woodier forms, are darker for greater heat absorption. Many species have hairs on stems, leaves and even flowers. The hairs on willow catkins not only trap air for insulation purposes, but the still air also reduces water loss. The parabolic shape of many flowers mimics that of solar furnaces directing sunlight towards the plant's reproductive structures to aid speedy development. The 'Sun trap' that this induces within the flower proves a warm, welcoming microhabitat that attracts pollinating insects. One adaptive characteristic of the trees at the edge of the boreal forest will be very obvious to the traveller: while the trees of temperate forests take the traditional cone shape, the lower branches extending beyond those above to collect maximum light, the low angle of the Sun at the Arctic fringe negates this form, so the trees instead have branches of approximately equal length along the trunk. This shape also helps reduce the weight of accumulated snow, which might otherwise cause branches to break. Boreal forest trees are usually evergreen, to allow photosynthesis to begin as soon as the Sun returns. But the needles are thin and wax-coated, with the stomata (pores through which gas exchange takes place) set deep to reduce desiccation.

Arctic flowering plants exhibit other adaptations in addition to these physical characteristics. Most are perennials; annuals are few in number, because even with overwintering buds and evergreen leaves, the Arctic summer is often too short for the plant to go through its entire life-cycle, particularly in the High Arctic. However, some species are annual/biennial, being annuals if the polar summer is long enough, but taking two years for the life-cycle if not.

Many Arctic flowers are highly phototropic, tracking the Sun throughout the 24 hours of the polar summer day. The flower does not follow the Sun by rotating – a recipe for disaster as following the midnight Sun for day after day would

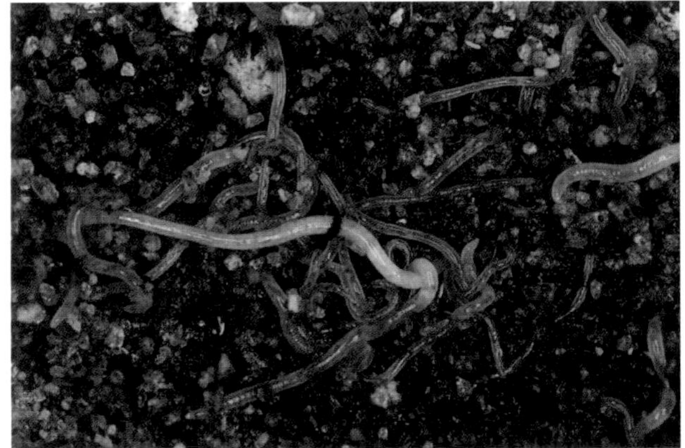

Oligochaetes (*Enchytraeides*) and dark blue Springtails beneath a stone in south Greenland.

twist the flower stem. The movement is created by the stem growing continuously, but always at a slower rate on the side towards the Sun so the flower head tilts. Though the polar day is long, Arctic plants are able to photosynthesise at low light levels in order to take full advantage of available light.

Just as in more southerly plants, Arctic species disperse seeds using the wind, birds and mammals. Many Arctic plants are berry-producers, the berries being an especially rich food source for animal life. However, not all Arctic species are seed-producers. Some spread by producing rhizomes (horizontal, underground stems that take root at intervals), some by growing stolons (above-surface stems that produce new plants at their tips), while others produce bulbils (or bulblets), buds that form in the place of some, or all, flowers. Rhizomes and stolons have the advantage that the new plant will grow in a suitable habitat. Bulbils, as with seeds, are at the mercy of the wind, and root only if they land in a suitable spot. Bulbil production has the advantage over seed formation of being asexual: the plant requires neither a pollinator nor another plant, each of which may be scarce. However, there is a disadvantage: unlike seeds, bulbils, being much more fragile, cannot survive for long periods if they do not implant.

The adaptations of terrestrial invertebrates

Though most Arctic invertebrates are aquatic (and chiefly marine), a surprising number inhabit both the tundra and the taiga edge. In terms of abundance the most numerous are worms (particularly nematodes and oligochaetes) and rotifers, with planarian worms being important within the taiga. There is also a diverse collection of freshwater copepods, and many insect species. Spiders are also important within the taiga. Almost all insect orders are represented in the Arctic (though there are very few beetles) and most are important as food sources for birds or as plant pollinators. Those species that are parasitic on Caribou have an extremely deleterious effect on an infected animal, while mosquitoes can be a great nuisance to Arctic travellers, the resultant blood loss from them even being life-threatening to Caribou and other species.

In general, insects found in the Arctic are smaller, darker and hairier than their southern cousins. All three characteristics are adaptations to the northern environment. The smaller size is almost certainly because the insects are constrained by food resources (a smaller size also enables the insect to warm faster – but, of course, it also cools quicker). Arctic individuals also tend to be stockier, reducing their surface area-to-volume ratio, resulting in a relative reduction in both heat and moisture loss. The darker colour seems at first a contradiction of 'Gloger's Rule', which suggests that individuals tend to be white in the Arctic to aid camouflage. But that rule was formulated for vertebrates, and does not allow for the fact that in ectotherms the increased heat absorption (both direct radiation from the Sun and reflected heat from the ground) of dark colours is generally more important than camouflage: a warmer insect can fly faster. The hairiness has arisen for similar reasons to the hairs of Arctic plants – the hairs trap air, reducing convective heat losses and providing insulation. Experiments have shown that if the hair is shaved from a caterpillar, the insect will lose heat by convection much faster than its unshaven siblings. It is difficult to know whether to marvel most at the ingenuity of the experiment or to pity the poor caterpillar.

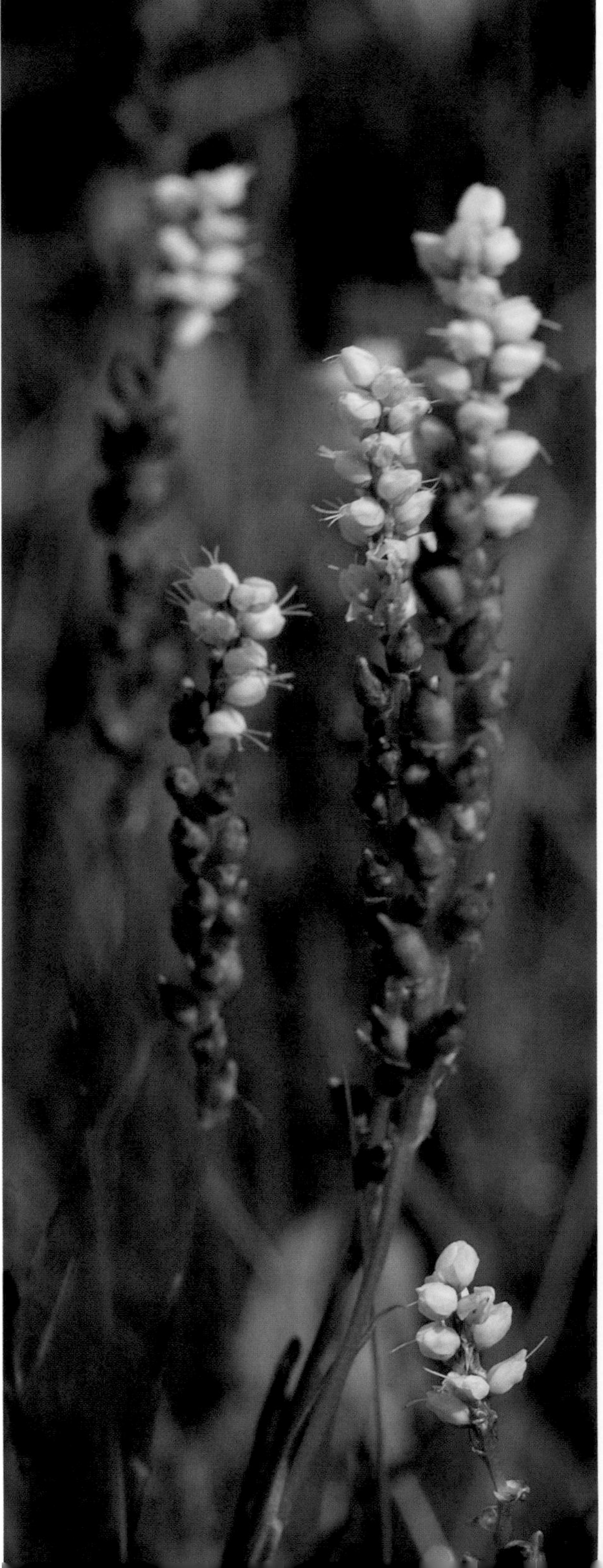

Viviparous Knotweed, which reproduces by bulbil production, central west Greenland.

Mosquito Avoidance
Caribou have two mosquito avoidance strategies that the traveller will also find beneficial. The animals seek out windy ridges, as the insects cannot compete with even moderate winds – if mosquitoes cannot fly, they walk towards their food source – and patches of snow, as these lower the local air temperature and so reduce insect activity.

Wings and basking

Antennae and wing sizes are, in general, smaller than in southern species, to reduce heat loss. This is particularly noticeable in stoneflies, crane flies and some moths. In some species wings are entirely absent. Those insects that do have wings fly close to the ground where the air is warmer and wind speed lower. However, the wings of Arctic butterflies are not significantly smaller and are utilised as solar 'catchers'. Indeed, the basking strategies of butterflies are often useful in helping to identify species. Butterflies use one of three strategies – though individuals may not always limit themselves to just one. Dorsal basking involves flattening the wings so that the back and the upper wings are exposed to the Sun. The butterfly leans towards the Sun. This strategy is favoured by members of the *Pieridae*, the white butterflies (chiefly *Colias* spp. in the Arctic). In lateral basking the wings are raised so that the upper surfaces touch: the body is then turned sideways to the Sun so the flanks and lower wing surfaces are exposed to it. Most fritillaries use this strategy. The wings may also be held in a V-shape, sunlight now being trapped between them, the wings acting as both collector and reflector. Members of the *Lycaenidae*, the blue butterflies, often adopt this strategy.

Basking is not, of course, limited to butterflies, and travellers looking for insects should seek out sheltered areas that favour both the insects and the plants on which they feed. An alternative for camping travellers is to look at the sunny side of the tent. In order to maximise solar heat input all insects bask, and there are few better places than a tent panel, the fabric warming quickly and so offering not only a conveniently flat platform, but also the advantage of heat on both sides. In the absence of a convenient tent, insects bask on bare ground, which offers similar 'all-round-heat'.

Insect flight muscles must achieve a minimum temperature before they can function, and those species that do not generate muscle temperature by shivering must bask. However, flying produces a lot of heat, particularly as wingbeat frequency can be incredibly high (up to 200Hz). So insects, even Arctic insects, have mechanisms to prevent overheating, as flight muscles must be maintained below a critical temperature to function efficiently. Normally this is accomplished by having an uninsulated section of the abdomen – usually the ventral side.

The search for extra energy from the Sun is also seen in insect larvae. Basking is practised by some; the Woolly Bear caterpillar spends 60% of its active time basking, with just 20% spent eating. Mosquito larvae will move around a pool to track the movements of the Sun, while the larvae of blow flies hatched from eggs laid on a carcass will be found in greater abundance and at a more advanced state of development on the southern side of the corpse.

Though these Sun-seeking strategies are clearly effective, Arctic insects nonetheless have to complete their life-cycles in ambient temperatures that are lower than those enjoyed by their southern cousins. They are therefore more active at lower temperatures. High Arctic mosquitoes go through their egg and larval stages in temperatures that may exceed 1°C only rarely, and Arctic travellers will note that mosquitoes continue to fly and feed at temperatures close to freezing, though they become much more active as the temperature increases.

Extended life-cycles

Yet despite being able to remain active at lower temperatures, many Arctic insects take much longer to go through their life-cycle than do related southern species. Some insects that range across both the temperate and Arctic zones have different life spans in different places. The springtail *Hypogastrura tullbergi*, for instance, has a life span as short as eight weeks in southern areas of its range, but in the High Arctic these insects can live for as long as five years. Though this difference may be

Arctic Woolly Bear caterpillars, which display an extraordinarily extended life-cycle.

extreme, there are many High Arctic insects with life spans of three or four years, and some High Arctic midges may take seven years to pupate. The most extreme case of such an extended span is the Arctic Woolly Bear caterpillar (of the moth species *Gynaephora groenlandica*), which takes at least seven, and as many as 14, years to develop to the pupal stage. In sharp contrast, the adult moth completes the life-cycle within a few days. The male dies after mating, the female after egg-laying: neither adult feeds. The caterpillar is parasitised by wasps and bristle flies, which each take three or four years to develop. However, some Arctic insect species have life spans that are the same as those of southern counterparts. In almost all cases of extended spans, the insect may take advantage of favourable conditions by shortening the life-cycle.

Such life-cycle extensions result from extended periods in the larval stage. Few species overwinter as adults (although it is not unknown, with the adults seeking shelter beneath a stone or detritus and trusting to their freeze-avoidance or freeze-tolerance strategies). Most insects, however, overwinter as larvae or pupae: for some species this has clear advantages, young flies, for instance, being able to overwinter within the carcass or dungheap in which they hatched. However, mosquitoes overwinter as eggs. Female mosquitoes lay their eggs close to the water surface of the southern edge of the chosen pond. Small ponds are usually selected as these thaw and warm more rapidly. Snow coverage insulates the eggs during the winter. In the spring the Arctic Sun, rising in the south, melts the snow, this both triggering the eggs to hatch and providing a pathway to the pond as the water level rises. Eggs that undergo a prolonged period of freezing probably survive, but their development will be delayed. Larval mosquitoes can develop in four weeks in water temperatures down to 1°C. On first emerging as adults, mosquitoes feed on nectar and are important plant pollinators before the females become the misery that afflicts all Arctic animals and travellers.

The reproduction of Arctic insects is, in general, as for southern species, but there are notable exceptions. In some species males are rare and females reproduce parthenogenetically (for example, some stoneflies, midges, black flies and caddisflies). Asexual reproduction allows spectacular and rapid population increases and so is favoured as it reduces the time for courtship, but it reduces genetic diversity. In the extreme case of the High Arctic black fly *Simulium arcticum*, the insects do not even go through the full life-cycle of egg, larva, pupa and adult, eggs developing inside the pupa and being released when the pupa dies, without an adult stage occurring at all.

The adaptations of aquatic organisms

As fresh-water freezes at 0°C and sea-water at about -1.8°C, aquatic organisms – which are ectotherms apart from the

It is not only insects which bask. Here a Grey Jay is enjoying both the day's sunlight and reflected heat from a carpet of pale, high albedo, Reindeer moss lichen.

marine mammals and birds, and some large fish such as tuna – need in principle employ only freeze-resistance techniques adequate for a range of temperatures close to those figures. However, this logic only holds if the organism is in liquid water; for both fresh-water and marine organisms situations may occur whereby they experience much lower temperatures, low enough to require more sophisticated freeze-resistance methods in order to avoid certain death.

Survival in freezing fresh-water

Large lakes and most rivers do not freeze entirely (surface ice acts as an insulator), with fish and aquatic invertebrates surviving by employing freeze-resistance techniques and avoiding contact with the surface ice. Some river species may migrate to large lakes to reduce the risk of freezing. Invertebrates move to the depths to escape the advancing ice and may burrow into the lake bottom, though some insect larvae actually freeze into gravel beds close to the pond edges, using freeze-avoidance or tolerance to overwinter without ill effect. It is not, however, only the cold that has to be endured. With ice coverage preventing the absorption of oxygen at the surface, and the halting of photosynthesis, decomposition may cause an oxygen deficiency. Some species can actually switch from aerobic to anaerobic respiration (metabolising without the need for oxygen) to survive, but for many – both plants and animals – oxygen starvation results in death.

Survival in freezing sea-water

Though tuna and other large, fast-swimming fish exhibit what is termed regional endothermy, in which metabolic output allows certain muscles to operate at temperatures above that of the remainder of the body, all marine creatures, with the exceptions of the cetaceans, pinnipeds and sirenians (together with penguins and certain other marine creatures, such as the largest turtles), are ectotherms, with body temperatures only marginally above that of the water. They are also stenothermic, i.e. they can tolerate only minor deviations from normal body temperature. Most marine ectotherms use freeze-tolerance or freeze-avoidance techniques, but also rely, to a lesser or greater extent, on the fact that the freezing point of sea-water declines as depth increases, so that migration to greater depth is an effective precaution against freezing.

For intertidal animals (e.g. shellfish that graze algae at the tide level) the situation is very different as they may be exposed to ambient temperatures that are much lower than the freezing point of sea-water. Such animals are invariably freeze-tolerant, able to survive if as much as 90% of their body water freezes. However, even for these remarkable survivors there is a problem if they remain above the sea ice, as prolonged exposure to the low ambient temperatures of the Arctic winter would almost certainly result in death. These animals must also avoid being caught where the sea is actually freezing, as during this time the ice is still in motion: moving ice is highly abrasive, with fast ice destroying most local life-forms during its formation. Being entombed within the sea ice as it forms would be equally deadly. Intertidal animals therefore migrate downwards as winter approaches. In rock pools sea ice formation results in salt leaching into the underlying water, raising its salinity and hence depressing its freezing point. Animals within these pools can therefore safely remain below the ice, often buried in the bottom sediment.

Arctic amphibians and reptiles

There are no truly Arctic amphibians or reptiles, but several species are found north of the Arctic Circle in the Palearctic. Only one species has been recorded north of the Circle in the Nearctic. In Fennoscandia and Russia as far east as the Urals, the Common Frog *Rana temporeria* is found to the northern coast and remains active to +2°C. The frog's range then becomes more southerly. The Moor Frog *R. arvalis* is even more cold-resistant. It is found in northern Sweden and Finland, on the Kola Peninsula and east to the Urals. In eastern Russia the Siberian Wood Frog *R. amurensis* breeds to the Arctic Circle around the Lena River and around the northern shores of the Sea of Okhotsk. The Marsh Frog *R. ridibunda* has also been found in Kamchatka, though its status there is not clear. In the Nearctic, the Wood Frog *R. sylvatica* breeds in Alaska as far north as Bettles, and in north-west Canada, where it has been found in the Mackenzie delta. This frog is capable of surviving short periods (up to about two weeks) at temperatures to -4°C.

The Common Toad *Bufo bufo* has been found north of the Arctic Circle in Scandinavia. The Great Crested Newt *Triturus cristatus* occurs north of the Circle in Sweden. However, the most astonishing of all these amphibians is the Siberian Newt *Salamandrella keyserlingii*. This dark-spotted, brown or olive newt is 120–160mm long and is the most widespread of all 'Arctic' amphibians. Its range includes the southern Taimyr Peninsula and central Chukotka (to Anadyr). Adult newts are able to survive freezing to -40°C for extended periods and are active (though obviously sluggish) to +1°C. Most remarkable of all, newts excavated from depths of 14m in the permafrost have revived without apparent trauma. The species is very long-lived (probably up to 100 years); this may be a response to periods of prolonged freezing. The eggs of the species are known to survive short periods of freezing within an ice matrix.

All these amphibians hibernate during the winter, choosing burrows or piles of rotting vegetation where they stay either singly or in groups. The Siberian Newt may hibernate for up to 8 months.

Two species of terrestrial reptile, the Adder *Vipera berus* and Common Lizard *Lacerta vivipara*, have been regularly recorded north of the Arctic Circle in Fennoscandia and western Russia. The Common Lizard is the more northerly of the two species, having been recorded to the northern coast. There are also records of the Grass Snake *Natrix natrix* above the Circle, though these are fewer and from more southerly latitudes. At sea, the Loggerhead Turtle *Carette caretta* has been recorded in the Barents Sea, and the Leatherback Turtle *Dermochelys coriacea* in the Bering, Chukchi and Labrador seas, and in waters around Iceland.

Shellfish of the intertidal zone, Disko Bay, west Greenland.

14. Arctic habitats

The Arctic Ocean can paradoxically be described as among both the least and the most productive seas on Earth. The central ocean, where the thick multi-year ice restricts sunlight transmission to the open water beneath, is an area of very low productivity, but the shallow seas above the extensive continental shelves that surround the ocean are, seasonally, highly productive. The reduced sunlight of winter, coupled with seasonal sea ice, restricts the growth of the photosynthetic organisms that are at the base of the Arctic Ocean food web, but with the annual thaw the increased sunlight of the Arctic summer, coupled with the nutrients that flow in from the huge rivers of Asia and North America, increases productivity dramatically.

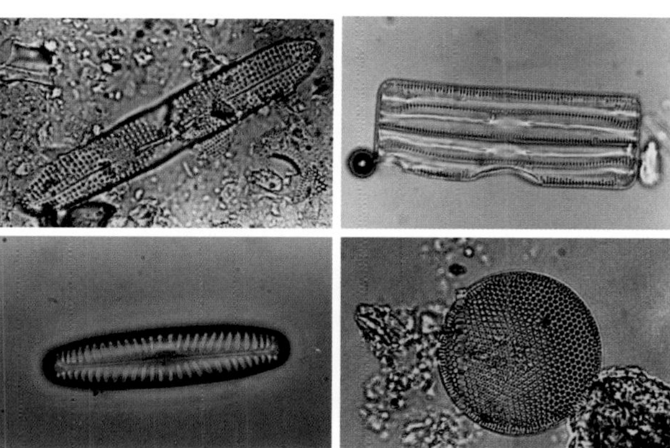

Left
Typical diatoms of Arctic waters.

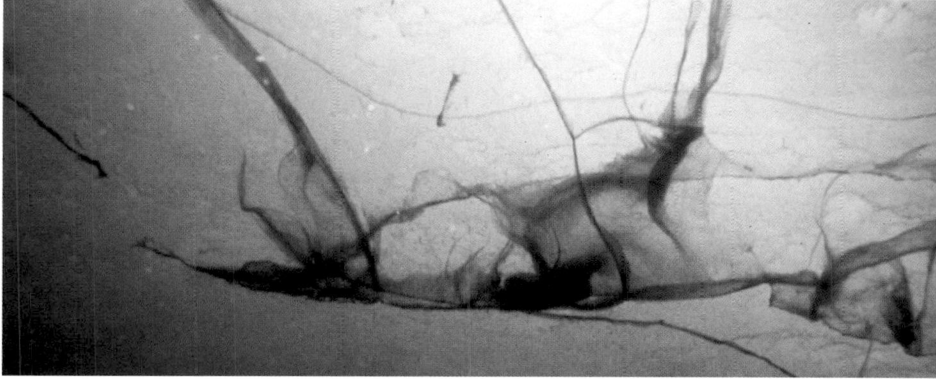

Below
Diatom strands hanging below an Arctic ice floe. The strands wave in any passing current.

Life under the ice

Even though the sea ice restricts light transmission and so limits sub-ice productivity, it should not be assumed that either the seas below the ice or, indeed, the ice itself is devoid of life. On the surface of the ice there may be meltwater pools, particularly during the summer thaw. Within these pools micro-organisms deposited either by overtopping waves, by the inflow of river water or from the feet of seabirds can flourish. As sea-ice forms it traps organisms. Many of these will die, but some survive, living within the ice matrix, while other organisms live on the lower surface of the ice. Within the ice phytoplankton occur – diatoms and other types of algae, such as flagellates. Diatoms are single-celled organisms that reproduce by dividing into two: more than 200 species have been identified so far living within Arctic ice. They live in the brine channels of the ice matrix, a home that demands not only an ability to withstand very low temperatures, but one that also requires adaptations to cope with the osmotic pressures created by high salinity. The reproduction of the diatoms depends on local temperature. Although they can survive at low temperatures their growth rate is slow; a diatom that might divide every day at 0°C, would perhaps take three days at -4°C, and 50 days or more at -8°C.

Diatoms stain the ice brown; as this darker colour absorbs more heat, the local temperature within the ice increases. This causes local melting, and the multiplying diatoms spread into the honeycomb structure this creates. Larger organisms feed on the diatoms and other phytoplankton (these also live within the ice matrix – the juvenile stages of many crustaceans are found within or on the underside of the ice). These amphipods, copepods and euphausiids are themselves part of a food chain that includes fish, marine mammals and seabirds at higher trophic levels.

Phytoplankton also live on the underside of the ice; one diatom, *Melosira arctica,* forms filaments and even sheets that can grow up to 15m long. These filamentary structures act as nets, trapping nutrients from the water. Under-surface phytoplankton is grazed directly by some fishes.

It is now believed that in some Arctic waters bacteria and viruses may also be a significant biomass, though the exact role of both in the production processes of all the Earth's oceans is still debated. It seems possible that they are a major source of organic material, caused by cell breakdown, on which zooplankton, the lowest trophic level of the marine ecosystem, feed. Phytoplankton, and some bacteria, photosynthesise.

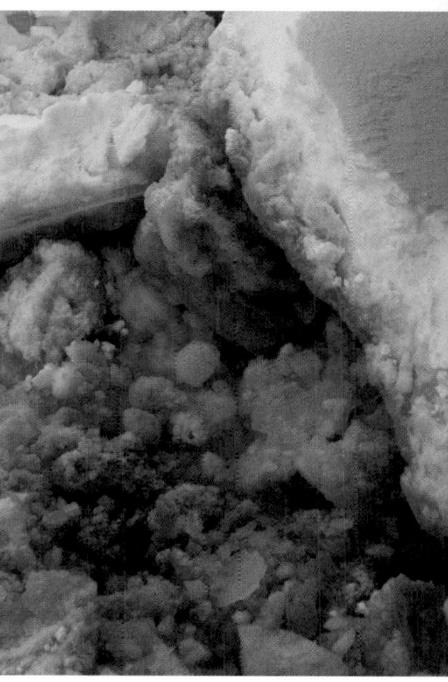

Above
Pack ice stained brown by diatom growth in brine channels.

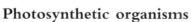

Living in the ice

Although the earliest travellers to both polar regions noticed that sea ice, which would have been expected to be white or shades of grey, was often brown or yellow-brown, the reason for this was not discovered until the 1840s, when German naturalist Christian Gottfried Ehrenberg realised that diatom growth was responsible for the coloration. Ehrenberg was the pioneer of microscopic study of sea-water, and was also the first to recognise that luminescence in the sea was caused by micro-organisms. Ehrenberg's work was quickly confirmed by the work of others, both in the Arctic and the Antarctic. At the time, diatoms were considered to be animals, but they are now classified as algae.

One interesting difference between Antarctica and the Arctic is the lack of ice-living organisms in the southern polar region. Antarctic sea ice is mainly annual, so its fauna tends to be visiting species rather than true inhabitants. The permanence of sea ice in the north explains the greater animal diversity in this habitat than in Antarctica.

Photosynthetic organisms

Where the sea ice has melted, photosynthesis occurs at all depths to which light penetrates. As light is transmitted through water, the red wavelengths are preferentially absorbed. In clear oceanic water, the energy input from red light at a depth of 10m is only about 1% of that falling on the surface. By contrast, blue light penetrates much further, only reaching 1% of the surface at *c.*150m. These percentages change in turbid waters. The net effect of this differential absorption is, of course, to make the water appear blue. But the fact that

Opposite page
Fertilised by droppings from the seabird nesting cliffs, the plant growth below Alkhornet, Isfjorden, Svalbard, is luxuriant.

Phytoplankton bloom off south-west Iceland.

light can be transmitted to 150m creates a euphotic zone – a zone in which photosynthesis is possible – of corresponding depth. The euphotic zone is the habitat of the photosynthetic phytoplankton, the organisms varying their light-sensitive pigmentation to allow for changes in light wavelength. During the winter months beneath the ice, photosynthesising phytoplankton enter a state that can be compared to hibernation, with cell metabolism depressed to a level merely capable of sustaining life.

The most regularly encountered marine photosynthetic organisms are the seaweeds. Seaweeds grow surprisingly far north, and some intertidal species can survive temperatures as low as -60°C. Equally surprising is the fact that some species can actually begin to grow during the late stages of the Arctic winter, i.e. in darkness, using starches stored during the previous summer. As elsewhere, kelp 'forests' are an important marine habitat for invertebrates and fish, which feed on and hide among the swaying blades. The most important Arctic species are the brown seaweeds *Laminaria saccharina* and *L. solidunula*.

Seaweeds form part of the diet of Snow Geese during the late summer (a dietary change from tundra vegetation that makes the geese unattractive to local Inuit: they claim that seaweed spoils the taste). Eelgrass *Zostera marina*, a flowering plant that thrives in the shallow water of estuaries and tidal lagoons, also provides a rich microhabitat. Crustaceans and small fish live on and within the plants, while geese and other wildfowl feed on it. When it dies, the decomposing plant is home to myriad crustaceans, which are taken by shorebirds and even by foxes and bears.

The smell of the seaside

As organisms trapped in sea ice – either marine organisms, or freshwater organisms brought to the Arctic Ocean by the huge rivers of Russia and North America – decay, they produce the gas dimethylsulphide, one of the main contributors to the 'smell' of the seaside. The smell is an occasional feature of travelling by ice-breaker as the gas is released when the sea ice is broken up.

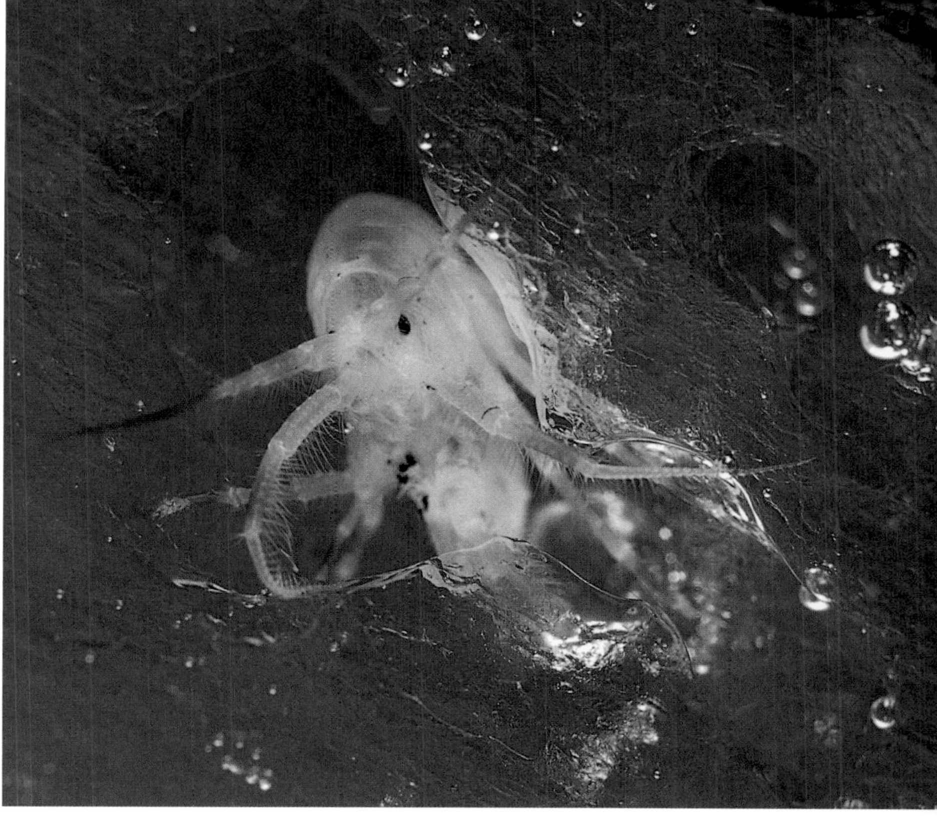

Marine invertebrates

When the ice melts and sunlight increases, the phytoplankton blooms as do the herbivorous zooplankton that feed on them. The most abundant of these are the *Calanus* copepods (particularly *Calanus glacialis* and *C. finmarchicus*) and amphipods (particularly *Apherusa glacialis* and *Gammarus wilkitzkii*). These creatures are the Arctic equivalent of the Southern Ocean's Krill *Euphausia superba*: Krill is a euphausiid, a group not found in significant numbers in the Arctic. In certain circumstances the dominant grazers on the phytoplankton are nematode worms, which are common in Arctic waters but virtually absent in the Antarctic. The reason for this (and the fact that this imbalance also occurs in rotifers) is not known.

Most adult crustaceans do not penetrate the ice matrix, due in part to their inability to squeeze into the brine channels,

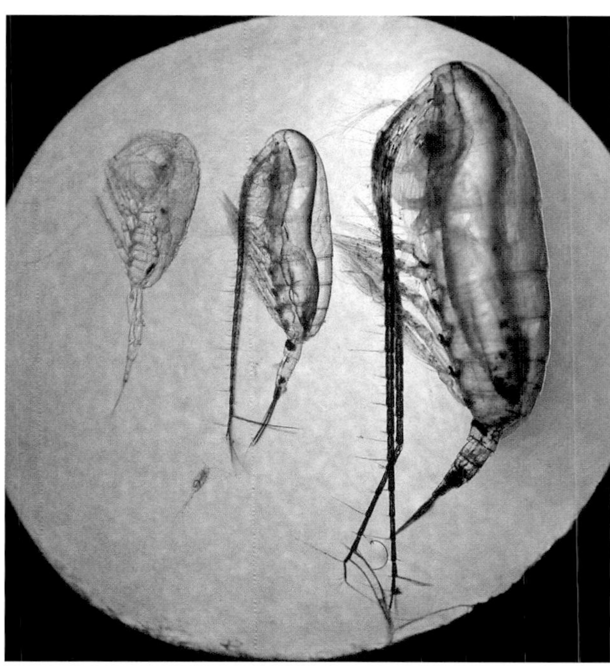

but also because they are unable to cope with the high salinity. Copepods (particularly *Halectinosoma*, *Harpacticus* and *Cycolpina*) are the crustaceans most likely to be found within the ice. Those that do not enter the ice feed on diatoms that fall from the matrix. Many of the smaller crustaceans are essentially planktonic; they have cilia or flagella for local locomotion, but generally drift with ocean currents. Larger copepods are less at the mercy of ocean currents and migrate to depths below about 300m during the winter. When the phytoplankton blooms they rise to begin feeding. They tend to rise during the night in order to reduce their chances of being eaten.

Marine fish

The herbivorous zooplankton sustains the nekton, the generic name given to marine organisms capable of moving independently of currents. Nektonic organisms comprise small fish, the larger fish that feed on them and other marine animals up through the food chain. A little over 100 species of fish have been identified to date in Arctic waters. Of these two of the most important are the Arctic Cod *Boreogadus saida* and Glacial Cod *Arctogadus glacialis*, smaller cousins of the Atlantic Cod *Gadus morhua* and Pacific Cod *G. macrocephalus*. Cod is an important prey species of pinnipeds and whales. The Arctic Cod (which can occur in huge shoals; one studied in Canada was believed to comprise almost 1,000 million fish) has an unusual mouth morphology, with the lower jaw being elongated beyond the upper so the fish can graze on the underside of sea ice. These fish have been known to use cracks within the sea ice as feeding, resting and hiding places, implying an ability to survive across a range of salinities. In more southerly waters halibut (the Greenland Halibut *Reinhardtius hippoglossoides* and the Pacific Halibut *Hippoglossus stenolepis*) are commercially important. Halibut have an extraordinary life story, starting out as 'conventional' fish. The left eye then migrates across the top of the head until it is close to the right eye. The fish turns on its left side, which becomes white, while the right (now upper) side becomes mottled, an excellent camouflage for the bottom-feeding habits of this voracious species. Other southerly species include the Capelin *Mallotis villosus* (which has two subspecies, one in the north Atlantic and the other in the north Pacific), herring (*Clupea* spp.) and pollock (particularly the Alaskan or Walleye Pollock *Theragra chalcogramma*). Neither the Arctic cod species nor capelin have been extensively fished commercially, though the Atlantic Cod has been fished to the point where extinction of the species has become a possibility. The range of the Atlantic Cod included the formerly rich fishing grounds close to Canada's Labrador coast, which lay within the 10°C isotherm. The increase in fishing for Walleye Pollock in the Bering Sea is raising fears of over-exploitation of another species important to the Arctic food chain.

Top left

Eelgrass in Izembek Lagoon, Alaska Peninsula. The lagoon's eelgrass beds are the largest in the world and visited by migrating and wintering wildfowl.

Top right

The amphipod *Gammarus wilkitzkii* (2–3cm). It is a predator, sitting head down in a brine channel on the underside of the ice waiting for prey. Typical prey are calanoid copepods, as illustrated to the left.

Left

The four major copepod species of the Beaufort Sea. From the left *Metridia longa* (c.2.5mm), *Calanus glacialis* (c.4mm) and *Calanus hyperboreus* (c. 7mm). The smallest is *Oithona similis* which is below left of *C. glacialis*. It is only 0.5mm in length.

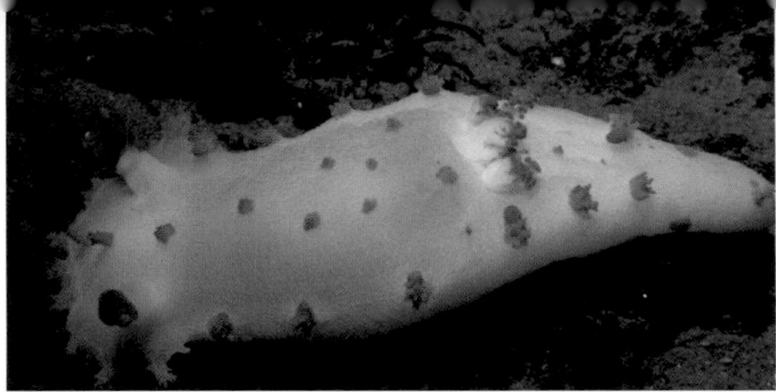

Marine organisms

Top
To the left is the Clown nudibranch *Triopha catalinae*. To the right is the sea slug *Coryphella fusca*. Both from the Bering Sea.

Middle
To the left is a *Branchiomma* polychaetes. To the right are two specimens of the sea anenome *Urticina eques* with a *Hyas* 'toad crab' between them. The crab is an occasional prey of the anenomes. Below right is the sea lily *Heliometra glacialis* whose arms grow to 20cm. All these species are from waters around Svalbard.

Right
Arctic Cod *Boreogadus saida*.

As well as cod, capelin and pollock, and several eel species (particularly ammodytids or sandeels – sandlances in North America – which are the regular prey of auks), a major food resource for Arctic marine mammals are members of the *Salmonidae* family. The salmonids are chiefly anadromous. Adult fish are pelagic, but migrate to freshwater streams in order to mate and lay eggs, young salmonids reversing their parental swim to reach the ocean. However, certain subspecies may be resident in rivers or estuaries. The spawning journey of the salmon is one of the most remarkable in the natural world: some King Salmon *Oncorhychus tshawytscha* travel almost 2,000km to reach their spawning grounds in the Yukon River. A young salmon is still attached to a large yolk sac when it hatches. It remains in or close to the redd (nest) prepared by its mother (the adult female salmon makes a shallow depression in the gravel of the stream bed with its tail). Once the yolk sac has been absorbed the young fish, or fry, feed on copepods and larval insects. The amount of time they spend in freshwater before heading downstream to the ocean depends on the species, and varies from weeks to several years.

The salmon runs of spawning adult salmon are a famous feature of the Pacific Arctic fringe and are an important food resource, particularly for Brown Bears; the bears that feed on the annual salmon run are the largest of their

species. There are seven salmon species that spawn in the rivers of Alaska and north-eastern Russia within the Arctic. Of these seven, five are widely distributed – Pink Salmon *Oncorhychus gorbuscha* (the smallest species), Chum or Dog Salmon *O. keta*, Coho or Silver Salmon *O. kisutch*, Sockeye Salmon *O. nerka* and King or Chinook Salmon, the largest, with specimens reaching more than 50kg. A further species, Steelhead Salmon *O. mykiss*, breeds in the rivers of the Alaska Peninsula, in south-east Alaska and in western Kamchatka, while a seventh species, Masu Salmon *O. masou* breeds in the rivers of western Kamchatka, plus Japan and the adjacent Asian mainland. Steelheads and Masu are the least Arctic of the seven species, and also have resident (i.e. non-anadromous) subspecies (though the taxonomy of the Masu is still debated, with some experts considering the resident fish to be a different species, *O. rhodurus*, the Amago Salmon).

All Pacific salmon undergo remarkable changes in their appearance prior to spawning (after which they die). Sockeyes change from the normal silver-blue colour to bright red, while the male Pink Salmon develops a humped back, hooked jaw and enlarged teeth. The purpose of these strange changes is not understood, and nothing similar is seen in the Atlantic Salmon *Salmo salar*. Atlantic salmon also differ in frequently surviving spawning to return to the sea. All salmon are fished commercially, over-fishing having eliminated some populations. Concerns have been expressed over the effect of over-fishing on the Atlantic Salmon, and also on the effect salmon farming might have on wild stocks if diseases and genetically modified fish were able to escape.

The Arctic Char is another salmonid; strictly the char is *Salvelinus alpinus*, but there are many closely related fish, the taxonomy of which has kept experts busy for years and now includes around 20 recognised subspecies. The char complex has a circumpolar distribution, breeding throughout North America including the Aleutians and islands of the Canadian Arctic, in Greenland, Iceland, mainland Scandinavia and across Russia to Kamchatka, including the more southerly Russian Arctic islands. Some char subspecies are anadromous, but others are purely freshwater fish, some populations having presumably been isolated in lakes by the effects of glaciation.

One particularly diverse family of fish found in the Arctic are the *Cottidae* or sculpins, some species of which are circumpolar. These benthic fish inhabit the shallow seas above the continental shelves, often being found close to the shore and even in less salty parts of coastal estuaries. Sculpins are known to the Inuit as sea scorpions, and were sought beneath stones in the shallows.

The shallow Arctic seas above the continental shelves are, because of their silt burden, home to rich benthic communities – jellyfish, sea anemones, sea urchins, sponges, starfish and worms. The largest of the world's jellyfish, *Cyanea arctica* (a lion's mane jelly), which has tentacles up to 25m long, lives in Arctic waters, while some of the Arctic sea's unsegmented worms can reach 10m in length. To the surprise of many, corals are also found; Coral Harbour on Southampton Island is named after the fossil corals found there, and although these undoubtedly lived in much warmer waters, cold-water corals are found, in small numbers, in the seas close to the Aleutian Islands and southern Alaska. Significant numbers of molluscs, such as clams, mussels, oysters and scallops, occur in Arctic waters. Scallops are fished commercially in the Barents Sea and near Iceland, as are whelks in the Sea of Okhotsk.

In the north Pacific king crabs are fished commercially. The largest of these, the Red King Crab *Paralithodes camtschaticus*, has a leg span of up to 2m, though the carapace is rarely more than 25cm across. King crabs are interesting creatures, migrating annually to and from shallow waters, where they breed, and deeper waters down to 100m, where they feed, often travelling more than 150km between the two. The life-cycle of the crab is complex, with an egg stage (the number of eggs per female can be as high as 500,000, an astonishing number given that she incubates them between her abdomen and cephalothorax), and four larval stages before tiny crabs with carapaces little more than 2mm across emerge. Travellers to Alaska will often see king crab on restaurant menus, along with locally caught salmon and halibut. As well as the Red King Crab, Blue King Crabs *P. platypus*, which are smaller, and Golden (or Brown) King Crabs

Above left
Sockeye Salmon and Dolly Varden Char (one of the sub-species of Arctic Char), Alaska.

Above right
Sockeye Salmon, Alaska.

Unfortunately this salmon probably died before successfully spawning. Kodiak Island, Alaska.

Arctic Salmonids

Atlantic Salmon

Chum Salmon

Coho Salmon

King Salmon

The fish are shown in both breeding and oceanic colours and forms.

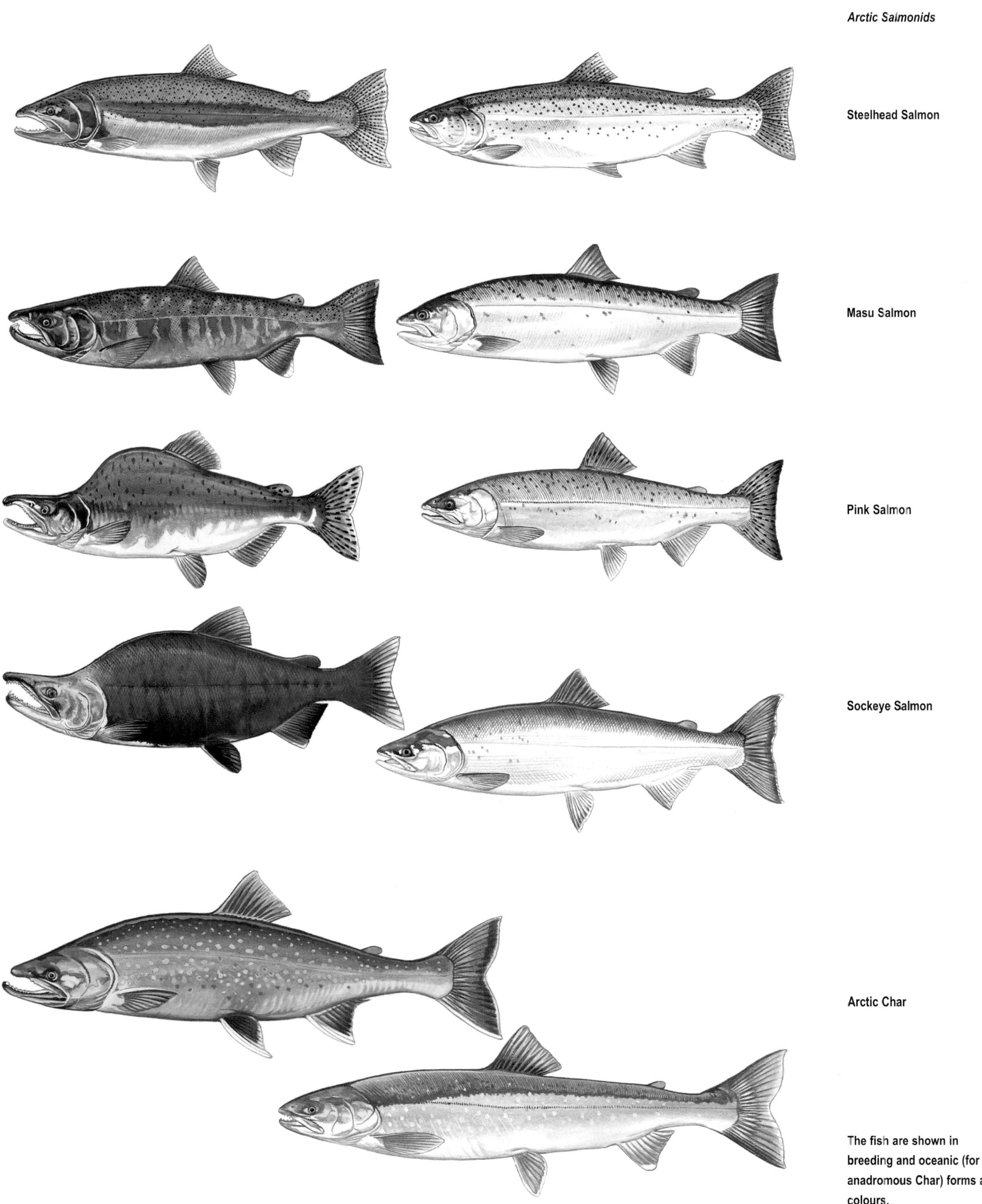

Arctic Salmonids

Steelhead Salmon

Masu Salmon

Pink Salmon

Sockeye Salmon

Arctic Char

The fish are shown in breeding and oceanic (for anadromous Char) forms and colours.

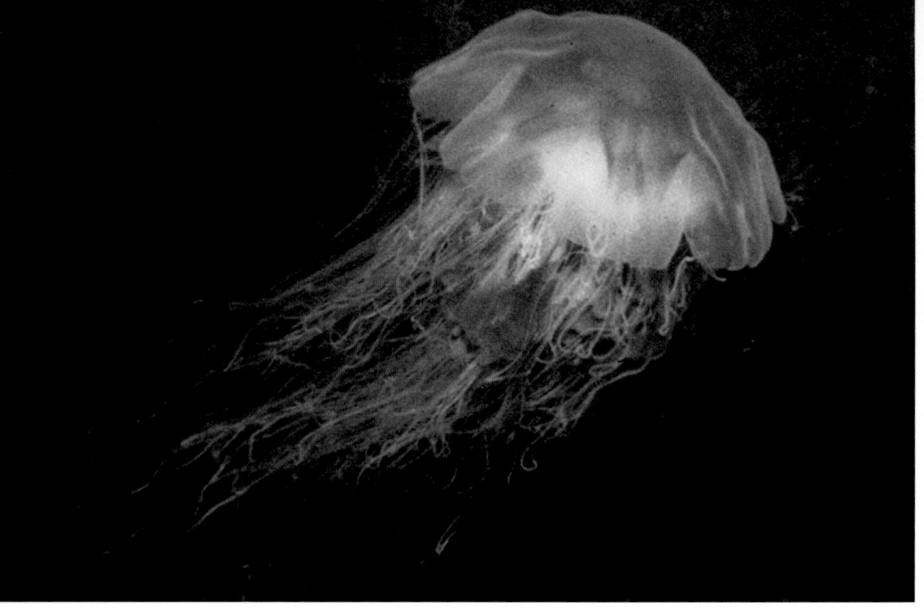

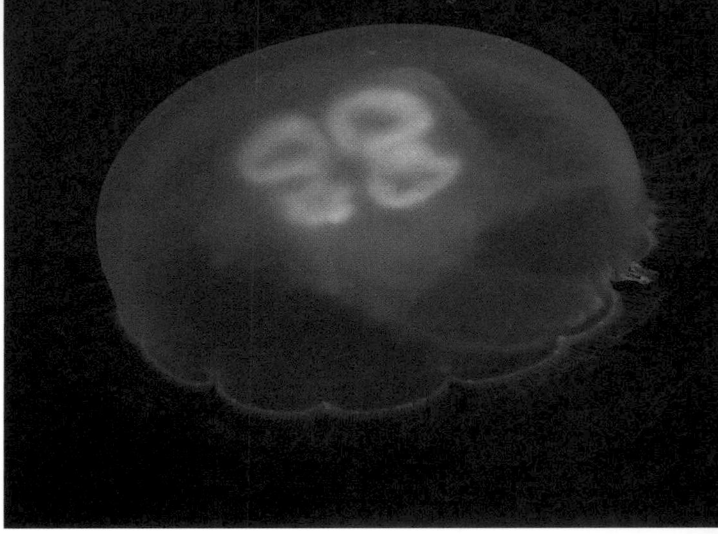

Left
The giant Lion's Mane jellyfish, North Atlantic.

Right
The Moon Jelly (*Aurelia aurita*) is a commoner jellyfish. Resurrection Bay, Alaska.

Lithodes aequispina, which are smaller again, are also fished. Blues are chiefly found around the Bering Sea islands, while the Golden Kings are fished close to the Aleutians. Tanner Crabs *Chionoecetes bairdii* and Snow (or Queen) Crabs *C. opilio*, which are smaller than the king crabs, are also caught for the table in the Bering Sea.

The northern deepwater shrimps of the Atlantic and Pacific are also fished commercially. *Pandalus borealis* is found in Atlantic waters from eastern Canada to the Barents Sea and is fished in Canada, Greenland (where it is a major export), Iceland, Norway and Russia (and by other, non-Arctic nations). In the northern Pacific *P. goniurus* is found in the Bering and Chuckchi seas where it is fished by the Canadians, Americans and Russians. The sand shrimp *Crangon crangon* is fished commercially in Russia's White and Barents seas.

Fresh-water rivers and lakes

Fresh-water in the form of rivers, lakes and ponds is a very important habitat on the landmasses that surround the Arctic Ocean. In Canada close to the Great Slave Lake and southern Hudson Bay, in European Russia and in parts of Siberia, land coverage of fresh water exceeds 30%, and over much of the rest of mainland Arctic Canada and Siberia it exceeds 15%. At Canada's Arctic fringe there are two huge lakes, with the area of Great Bear Lake exceeding 30,000km^2 and that of Great Slave Lake more than 28,000km^2. Each is more than 400m deep. No other Arctic lakes can compare to these, though Baffin Island's Lake Netilling and Russia's Lake Taimyr are close to 5,000km^2. To these statistics must be added those of the rivers that discharge into the Arctic Ocean. These rivers are among the biggest in the world and form important habitats at their coastal boundaries. The Yenisey and Ob river systems of northern Russia are the fifth and sixth longest in the world at more than 5,000km. The catchment areas of both rivers are in excess of 2,500,000km^2. The annual discharge of the Yenisey (whose name derives from the Evenki *Ioanessi*, meaning 'great river') exceeds 600km^3, while that of the Ob exceeds 400km^3. The Lena, which also drains continental Russia into the Arctic Ocean, is more than 4,000km long, as is Canada's Mackenzie River. The annual discharge of the Lena is about 525km^3 while that of the Mackenzie is about 320km^3. But though these numbers are enormous, they must be viewed in context; the total annual inflow of river water into the Arctic is estimated to be about 2,800km^3, which is a little over 1% of the annual water transfer (i.e. warm water in, cold water out) of the Fram Strait, between Greenland and Svalbard.

Bering Sea Crabs

Top - Red King
Middle - Snow
Bottom Left - Golden (Brown)
Bottom right - Tanner

An Arctic shark

The Greenland Shark (*Somniosus microcephalus*) is the only shark, and the largest fish, found in Arctic waters. It is also one of the world's largest sharks, reaching a length of up to 7m, exceeded only by Whale Rhincodori typus, Basking (*Cetorhinus maximus*) and Great White (*Carcharodon carcharias*) Sharks, and one of the largest deep-water fish known. It has been recorded at depths of more than 2,000m, but is frequently seen close to the surface. The shark, the skin of which is uniformly covered in tooth-like denticles, has a varied diet, feeding on fish and other marine creatures (such as crabs and jellyfish), but it will also take birds and seals, and is claimed to have taken swimming Reindeer. Mammalian prey must be ambushed as the shark is a slow, somewhat ponderous fish that would be unlikely to catch a seal by pursuit. Greenland Sharks are most numerous in the waters of the eastern Canadian Arctic and west Greenland, being found as far north as Ellesmere Island, but they are also seen off Iceland and Svalbard and in Russia's White Sea.

One curiosity of the shark is the presence on almost all females of a parasitic copepod, *Ommatokoita elongata*, which attaches itself to the fish's cornea. These parasites, which can grow to 3cm in length and hang like pale pink worms from the eyes, feed on cells of the corneal surface and ultimately cause lesions that cloud the fish's eyesight. Some scientists have suggested that the parasite and the shark are an example of a mutualism, the copepod being highly visible and perhaps even luminescent and so attracting prey to the fish. As the shark is thought to hunt mainly by smell in the murky waters of the deep Arctic seas, the partial loss of vision may be a relatively minor handicap.

The illustration above left is from William Scoresby's *An Account of the Arctic Regions* (1820) which included both the shark and the cornea parasite. The photograph to the right is of a dead shark washed up on a beach in north-west Greenland.

These huge inflowing rivers, together with other smaller but still sizeable rivers – the Yukon (annual discharge 200km^3), Pechora (140km^3), Kolyma (130km^3) and Nelson (75km^3) – form large deltas. The deltas result from sedimentation build-up (the Lena River, for example, deposits more than 11 million tonnes of sediment into the Laptev Sea annually, the silt creating a dark plume that extends for up to 100km offshore). The Lena's delta covers about 30,000km^2 and comprises more than 6,000 channels and a collection of about 30,000 lakes. The delta of the Mackenzie River begins just north of Tsigehtchik, the river dividing into three main channels and hundreds of lesser watercourses that wind through a vast maze of islands, ponds and lakes to the ocean, some 200km away. The entire delta covers about 10,000km^2. Ice damming of these great rivers results in a seasonal back-up of water as the spring thaw begins in the higher reaches of the river before it occurs at the coast. Periodic flooding by water and ice as these ice dams break drastically changes the deltas, forming networks of channels interspersed with flooded plains. It was the nightmare maze of the Lena delta that doomed one group of sailors, who had escaped the sinking *Jeanette* in 1881.

Deltas are a good habitat for wildfowl and shorebirds, but the shifting nature of the channels, ice abrasion of the channel banks and the new layer of silt the flooding leaves behind makes much of the area too unstable for plant growth. Silt and sand

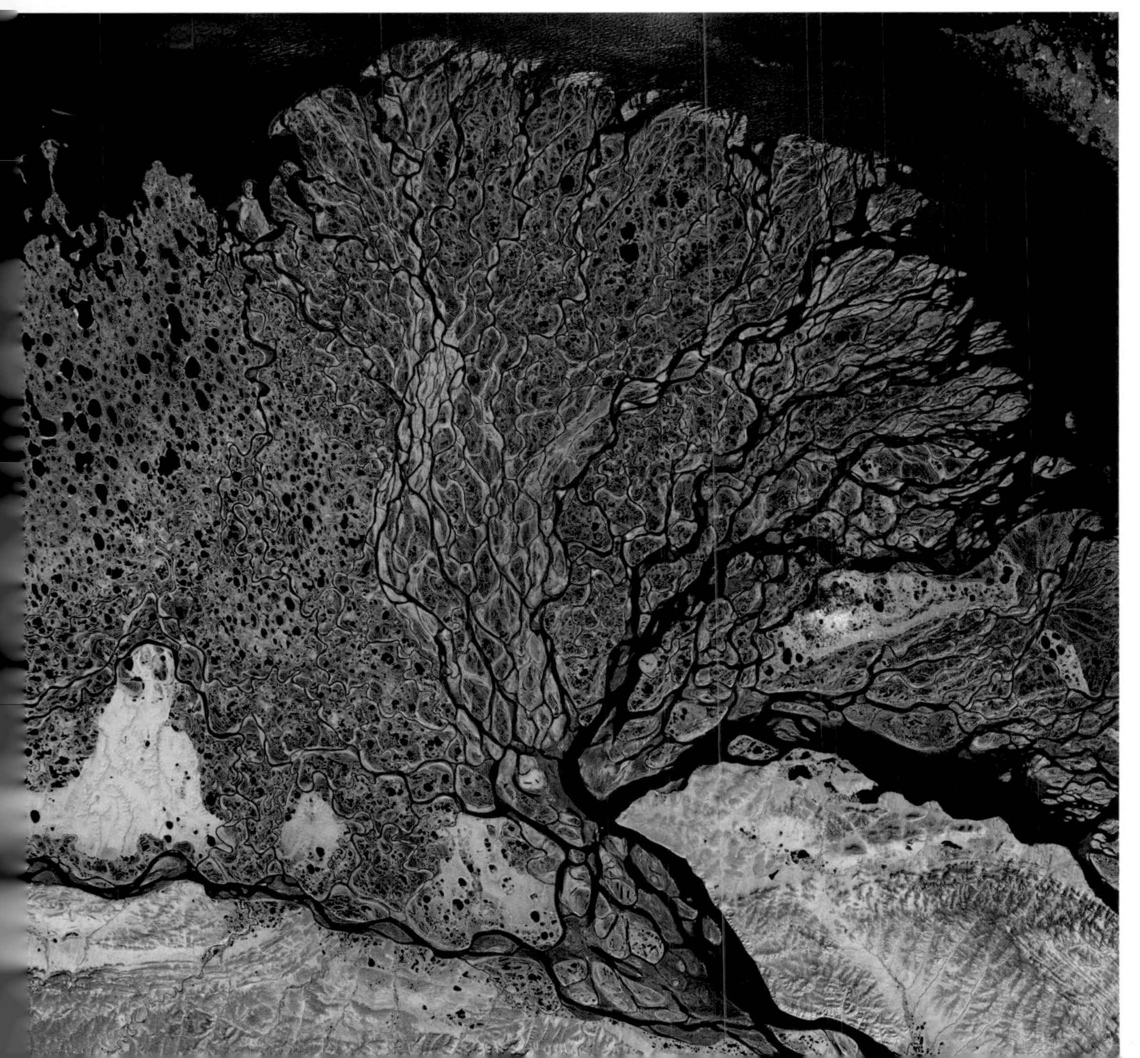

Colour-enhanced satellite image of the Lena delta. The myriad of channels is well illustrated.

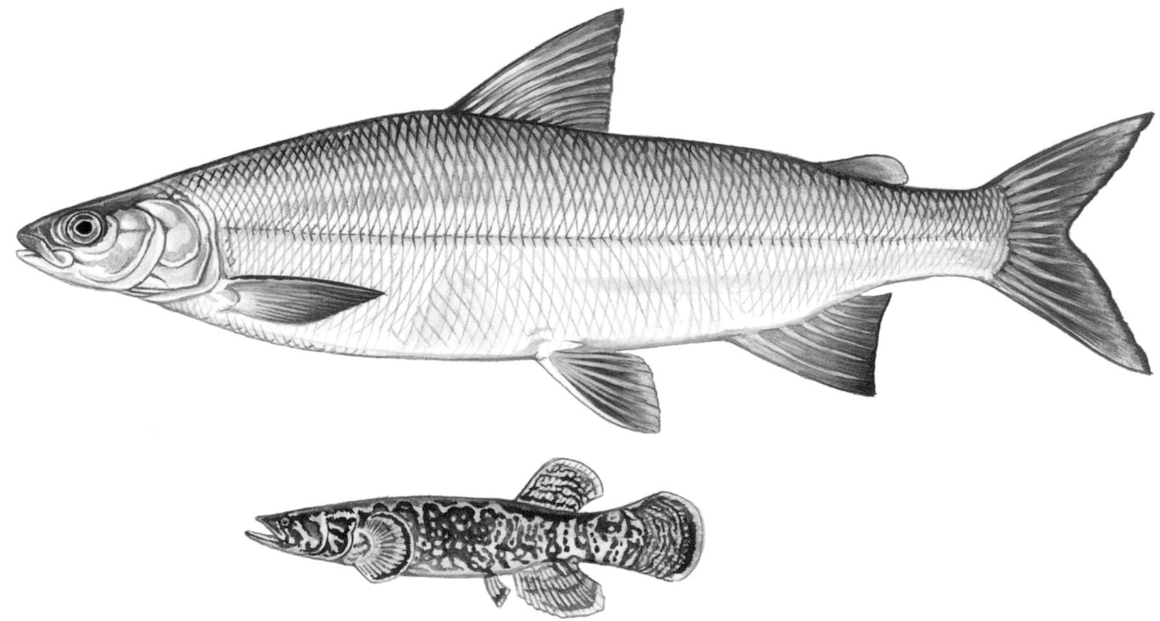

Above
Lake Whitefish *Coregonis clupeaformis*.

Below
Blackfish *Dallia pectoralis*.

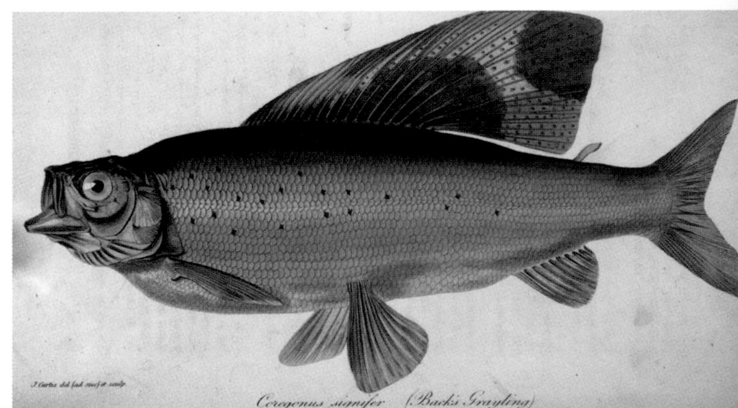

Right
Arctic Grayling
This illustration from John Franklin's book on his first Arctic land journey shows Back's Grayling *Coregonus signifier* which is now known as the Arctic Grayling *Thymallus arcticus*.

bars at the river's edge shift too often for anything to grow successfully, though horsetails and sedges can take hold a little further back, with trees on higher ground where flooding is less frequent.

Arctic lakes and ponds are usually limited in vegetation – with horsetails *Equisetum* spp. and pondweeds dominating – because of the unpredictability of ice depth and duration. Some aquatic invertebrates can arrive as eggs, carried on the wind or on the feet of birds, as can the seeds of aquatic plants, both eggs and seeds being unharmed by periods of drying. Many adult aquatic insects are poor fliers (dragonflies are an obvious exception), and the distribution of these, and particularly that of fish, which may use a water route to become established in a new area, aids an understanding of the Earth's periods of glaciation. The present distribution of mayflies and stoneflies in central Canada confirms the existence of Lake Agassiz, in which their aquatic larvae would have matured, while the distribution of fish in the Alaska/Yukon area helps unravel the sequence of events as the Laurentide ice sheet retreated and the Bering land bridge became submerged. The Lake Whitefish *Coregonis clupeaformis* is found in both the Mackenzie and Yukon rivers, despite the fact that the two are separated by a substantial mass of high land. In this case it seems that two proglacial lakes formed as the ice sheet retreated north-eastwards. The lakes were connected by a channel that allowed the fish free passage. As the water levels in the lakes fell (when iceberg calving ceased), the lake populations were isolated. The linked lakes had drained into the Yukon River, and the western lake continued to do so. But as the ice retreated across the valley through which the Mackenzie now runs, the more easterly lake drained that way, taking the fish with it.

Other freshwater fish

The Blackfish *Dallia pectoralis*, a form of mud-minnow, has an even more curious distribution, being found in the rivers of Chukotka, western Alaska and on islands of the northern Bering Sea (such as St Lawrence Island). These islands were once hills rising above the plateau of Beringia, a plateau that included both Chukotka and Alaska. The plateau became the seabed as the ice melted, but by then the fish had populated all Beringia's rivers.

Of the fish identified in Arctic freshwaters the most northerly is the Arctic Char, a population of which lives in Ellesmere Island's Lake Hazen at 82.5°N. In the cold waters of that lake, and other Arctic lakes and rivers, the Char grows slowly, a fact that has given rise to concerns over the survival of some populations as it is also a popular sport fish. Another sport fish is the brilliantly coloured Arctic Grayling *Thymallus arcticus*. The Grayling is circumpolar in distribution, as are Burbot *Lota lota* and Northern Pike *Esox lucius*, though in all cases the inevitable isolation of discrete rivers and lakes means that subspecies with marked differences have arisen. Other lake and river fish include trout, minnow, carp and perch species. During the Arctic winter river fish can migrate towards the sea, ensuring that they reach a section of river that remains unfrozen. Fish in large lakes survive below the ice, though those in smaller bodies of water or in small streams that freeze entirely cannot survive. It is often claimed that Blackfish can survive freezing, but this is not so. They can survive very low temperatures and short periods of freezing, during which they may be partially frozen, but a complete freezing is fatal.

There are numerous species of zooplankton, as well as molluscs (including gastropods and bivalves) in Arctic freshwaters. There are also some freshwater mites. There are few Arctic aquatic insects, though many insects with terrestrial

Red algae staining the snow of the Trygghavna Glacier, Spitsbergen, Svalbard.

adult forms have aquatic young – e.g. caddisflies, black flies, mayflies, stoneflies, midges and mosquitoes. The larval stages of these are important food resources for fish and birds, and are present in astonishing numbers; mosquito larvae have been recorded at densities of more than 2000/m^2. The curious 'spinning' of swimming phalaropes is a way of stirring up insect larvae, which are then pecked from the water surface.

The Greenland ice sheet

Perhaps the most astonishing of all Arctic habitats are cryoconite holes, the 'oases' of micro-organisms found on the Greenlandic ice sheet. Dust finds its way on to the ice sheet, both wind-blown towards its edge and, remarkably, cosmic dust collected by the Earth as it sweeps through space. In each case the dust is dark and so absorbs heat, forming water-filled holes in which the temperature can be up to 5°C higher than the surrounding ice. Within these miniature ponds, which can vary between a few millimetres to several centimetres in diameter and can be as much as a metre deep, bacteria and algae find a home and are grazed by nematodes, rotifers and water bears.

Lichens and Bearberry (***Arctostaphylos uva-ursi***), near the Mackenzie delta, Canada.

Terrestrial habitats

The total number of vascular plants identified within the Arctic is around 1,000. When subspecies are taken into consideration that number rises to 1,600–2,000. There are also many hundreds of embryophites (mosses and liverworts), more than 1,000 lichens and a surprising number of fungi. Most Arctic vascular plants are tundra-specific, though some are also found in the taiga and to the south. Many species are circumpolar, though with subspecies, while others show the influence of Beringia by having a trans-Beringian distribution. Yet others show a distinct trans-Atlantic distribution. The Hairy Lousewort *Pedicularis hirsuta*, which is familiar to visitors to Svalbard, Greenland and Baffin Island, is a good example of a trans-Atlantic species.

Given the number of tundra plants and the complexity of the relationship between the various species and subspecies, no detailed description is possible here. Instead, only a general introduction to the species likely to be seen in terrestrial Arctic habitats is given, together with details of some of the more common species. About 60% of tundra vascular plants are circumpolar (with subspecies), this number rising to about 90% for the polar desert. Non-vascular plants show similar percentages, but with a greater number of species.

The importance of lichens

Lichens are particularly important in the Arctic, providing a valuable winter food source for Musk Oxen, rodents, hares and, especially, Reindeer. The Rock Tripes *Umbilicara* spp. helped save the first of Franklin's overland expeditions from starvation. Lichens also add splashes of colour in otherwise uniform landscapes, something which all travellers to the area appreciate. Lichens are dual organisms, a combination of fungus and alga, the algae lying a little way below the surface of the fungal thallus. Lichens are an example of a facultative

Right
Northern forest carpeted with Reindeer Moss, Sweden. Reindeer Moss is actually several species of *Cladonia* lichen.

Below
***Cladonia milis* (*upper*) and *Cladonia stellaris* (*lower*) are illustrated below.**

Below right
A specimen of *Rhizocarpon geographicum*, north Norway.

mutualism, the fungus providing water and minerals to the algae in exchange for the products of photosynthesis; free forms of lichen fungi exist, but they grow more slowly. Most lichen reproduction is vegetative, but some associated fungi produce spores, these only forming lichens if they are able to capture algae cells.

Lichens are of three forms – crustose (crusty), foliose (leaf-like) and fruticose (shrub-like), and they will grow on virtually any substrate – soil, rocks or tree bark. In the High Arctic grey and orange crustose forms that colonise rocks are frequently seen, sometimes in places where no other vegetation is visible. One of these, *Rhizocarpon geographicum* (occasionally called Map Lichen because of its irregularly shaped black patches) grows slowly but at a defined rate, and it can be used to measure the time since the retreat of ice from an area; it is estimated that some specimens of the lichen are at least 9,000 years old. Of the fruticose forms the most famous is the inaccurately named Reindeer Moss (*Cladonia* spp. but particularly *Cladonia stellaris* and *C. rangiferina*), which occasionally forms extensive and dense patches in open areas at the edge of the treeline. These lichens represent as much as 90% of

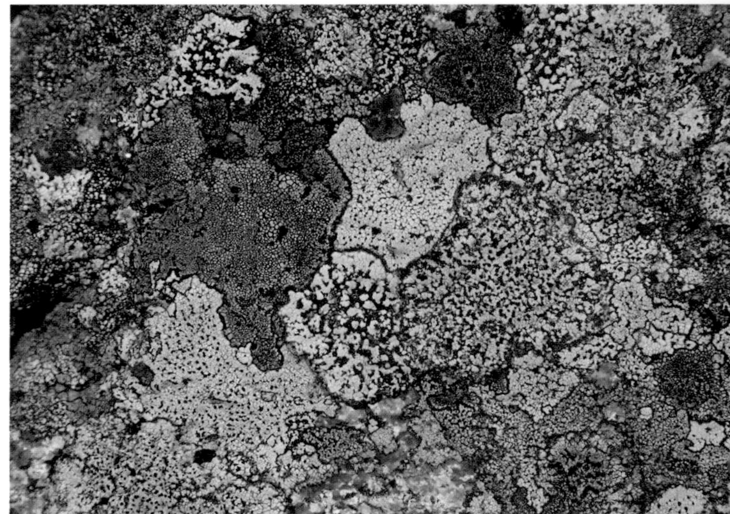

Reindeer winter diet and a good fraction of the summer diet as well.

Lichens derive much of their nutrient uptake from the air and so accumulate pollutants and, as they are long-lived, represent a long-term indicator of local pollution. Lichens were used to check radioactive fall-out levels during early nuclear weapon testing, and following the Chernobyl accident. A significant amount of the fall-out from Chernobyl came to ground in Fennoscandia, where the Reindeer consuming lichens became contaminated, as did the Sámi and other Reindeer-herding groups who ate the meat.

Barren Lands

In North America, the northern section of the Canadian mainland between the Smoking Hills and Hudson Bay is often called the Barren Lands or Barren Grounds. This was the last section of the Canadian Shield to emerge from the ice after the last Ice Age, its lack of vegetation reflecting that limited ice-free history. The name is used to describe forms of Caribou and Brown Bear, and will occasionally be heard across North America to describe the northern lands, though in general 'tundra' is now the accepted label worldwide.

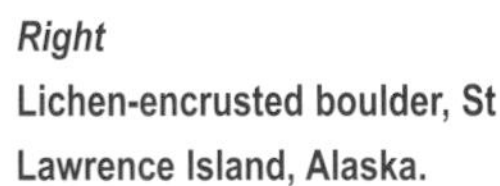

Right
Lichen-encrusted boulder, St Lawrence Island, Alaska.

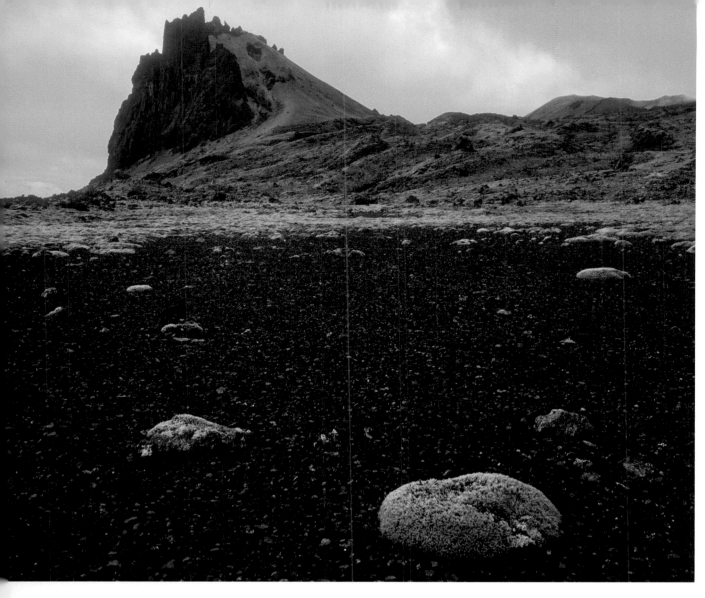

The tenacity of life is illustrated in these photographs of the greening of Jan Mayen Island (*left*) and the Laki lava flow, Eldhraun, Iceland (*below*).

On Jan Mayen the mosses, liverworts etc. grow in any crack in the lava which has gathered enough wind-blown soil to support them.

At Eldhraun the *Racomitrium* mosses have grown to a thickness which overtops the boot of a walker.

The photograph (*lower left*) illustrates that not only bird droppings can offer valuable nutrients (see p262). Here, on Igloolik Island, Canada, a skull has leached minerals into the soil allowing red moss and lichens to flourish.

The importance of mycorrhizal fungi in aiding plant growth and, therefore, the development of Arctic habitats has already been discussed (see After the Ice); other fungi are much more conspicuous. Indeed, the number of fungi in the Arctic is very high, probably greater than the number of vascular plants, though there are many more Low-Arctic than High-Arctic species. With the invertebrates that are the primary decomposers of the temperate world relatively scarce, fungi are the major agents of decomposition in the Arctic, and many of the fungal families familiar in more southerly latitudes have representatives north of the treeline.

The tundra

The Finnish word *tunturia*, describing a treeless plain, has evolved into the word *tundra*, which describes the circumpolar treeless belt that lies between the Arctic Ocean and the tree-line.

Tundra is characterised by low temperature (in general the temperature is below 0°C for at least half the year), low precipitation (particularly to the north) and a short growing season. But despite these characteristics applying in large part to the entire land belt between the treeline and the ocean, the tundra is not homogeneous: it has sub-divisions based on latitude and the characteristics of the landscape, each sub-division having its own vegetation.

Beneath the tundra lies permafrost, the annual thaw of which provides water to compensate for the area's low

precipitation. The active layer created by the annual thaw allows plants to become established. But though it provides a growing medium, the active layer is a harsh environment. It may have a negative thermocline, i.e. the temperature decreases through the layer, and it may also be waterlogged, as the underlying permafrost inhibits drainage. The depth of the active layer also defines the depth of the root structure of plants, as permafrost is as impenetrable to roots as it is to water. The summer thaw of the active layer is slowed by plant growth, leaf coverage preventing soil heating; in areas where vegetation is absent, the active layer may be two or three times deeper than that beneath local vegetation cover.

Attempts have been made to divide the tundra into zones of vegetation, and while this has been reasonably successful, the boundaries between zones are flexible since local conditions – shelter from the wind, differences in snow accumulation, presence or absence of streams, etc. – can mean that oases of plant life occur in otherwise unsuitable locations. I attempt here to define the differing types of tundra. In the main these are also latitude-based, but they do allow for the influence of microclimates.

Polar desert

In the most northerly region of the tundra, covering the Arctic islands of Eurasia (but see below regarding Wrangel Island) and most of those of Canada (though the southern parts of the southerly islands have more extensive plant coverage), and also the shield area of the Canadian mainland (the Barren Lands), the polar desert is dark, cold, arid and windswept. A number of factors reduce vegetation cover: the long polar night and low sun angle of the polar summer shorten the growing season and reduce the sunlight available for photosynthesis; low temperatures and lack of water inhibit plant growth; and the wind scours exposed places, and piles snow into depressions where long melt times mean that the advantages of insulation are outweighed by a further shortening of the growing season for emerging plants. Consequently there are only scattered patches of vascular plants, the ground cover often being less than 5%. This lack of ground cover indicates a further problem – a form of 'negative feedback'; fewer plants means that an individual plant is offered less protection against the elements by its neighbours and so finds it increasingly difficult to survive.

The polar desert is a place for only the hardiest of plants, such as *Saxifraga*, *Papaver*, *Cerastium*, *Dryas* and *Draba*. 'Saxifrage' derives from the Latin 'stone-breaker', which has led to the occasional suggestion that the plants aid the production of soil in the often stony alpine terrain or tundra they prefer; this is not correct, since the name actually refers to the similarity of its reproductive buds to kidney stones, a similarity that once led to the use of the plant as a remedy for dispersing the stones. The saxifrages include Purple Saxifrage *S. oppositifolia*, which grows to 83°N in northern Greenland, making it probably the most northerly flowering plant. Competition for this title comes from Moss Campion *Silene acaulis* and perhaps from Mountain Avens *Dryas integrifolia/D. octopetala*. The

Fungi are also a feature of southerly Arctic habitats.

Above from top
Puffball (*Leccinum* spp.), Victoria Island, Canada.
***Russula nana* and *Russula citrinichlora*, central west Greenland.**

Right from top
Alpine Arnica *Arnica alpina*, Hold With Hope, north-east Greenland.
Arctic Poppy *Papaver* spp., Fosheim Peninsula, Ellesmere Island, Canada.
Marsh Saxifrage *Saxifraga hirculus*, Myggbukta, north-east Greenland.

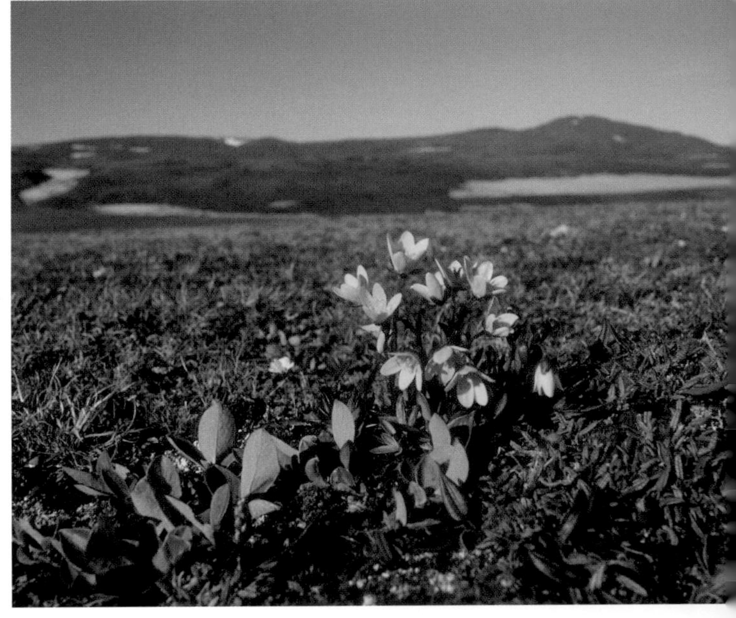

hesitation over the scientific name for this species arises from there being two closely-related species whose ranges overlap in eastern Siberia and western North America, and also in eastern Greenland. In North America the two plants are both called Mountain Avens, with the two differentiated by being given a second name (White Dryas and Eight-petalled Dryas). In limited areas of North America and in north-west and north-east Greenland hybrids of the two species have been identified. Just to add further confusion, the Eight-petalled Dryas occasionally has seven or nine petals.

The *Papaver* poppies are among the most delightful of the northern flowers, the long stems making them look particularly fragile. Arctic Poppy *P. radicatum* can be sulphur-yellow, but also white or even pale pink. As with other northern species, although the plant is essential circumpolar, closely related species are recognised in certain areas (for instance the Svalbard Poppy *P. dahlianum*). Many of the other polar desert plants are also circumpolar, but with subspecies. *Draba*, the white and yellow Whitlow-grasses, and *Cerastium* (mouse-ears and the related chickweeds) are particularly difficult to differentiate for the non-expert. Other plant genera represented in the tundra of the extreme north include *Ranunculus*, which includes the Snow Buttercup *R. nivalis*, Lapland Buttercup *R. lapponicus* and Arctic Buttercup *R. hyperboreus*, each of which is circumpolar. As with the northern poppies, the long-stemmed, fragile appearance of the buttercups is in sharp contrast to their actual hardiness. *Potentilla* (cinquefoils) and *Minuartia* (sandworts) may also be seen.

In sheltered spots the northern dwarf willows occur – Arctic Willow *Salix arctica*, a Chukotka and North American shrub, and Polar Willow *S. polaris*, which is found in the European Arctic. The difference between the two is marginal and they may well be subspecies. Arctic Bell-Heather *Cassiope tetragona* may also be found in these places. In more exposed areas the willow is more of a creeping woody plant, often barely more than 2 or 3cm high. Yet it is a true tree, its leaves changing to a beautiful red in autumn. Arctic Bell-Heather, a circumpolar species called Arctic White Heather in North America, is common on Svalbard and Greenland; in the latter it was important as a fuel for the local Inuit.

Miniature grasses occur both inland (*Poa* spp. and *Festuca* spp.) and close to the coast (*Puccinellia* spp.), and despite the region's aridity there are also sedges, particularly the drought-tolerant Cushion Sedge *Carex nardina* and Rock Sedge *C. rupestris*. In wetter areas such as stream valleys there may be Arctic Sedge *C. stans*.

Occasionally within the polar desert there are areas of exceptional plant vitality, akin to the oases in the more familiar hot deserts. These exist where local topography allows a good, well-drained soil to develop in a spot where those plants that manage to take root are protected from the wind. Such an area is the valley of Ellesmere Island's Lake Hazen, at about 82.5°N, where more than 100 flowering plant species have been identified. Similar oases may also be discovered on a micro-scale; small areas where there is protection from the wind, where an animal has died and so fertilised the soil, or beneath a look-out perch frequently used by a raptor, will all show greater productivity, either in terms of species diversity or an abundance of growth.

The southern tundra

To the south of the polar desert, tundra vegetation covers a greater percentage of the land, though initially the list of species is much the same. Ultimately more species appear – close to the treeline there are about four times the number of vascular plants as seen in the High Arctic. Some of these are shrubby plants, a fact that has led to the suggestion that in addition to a treeline there is also a shrubline. The height of the shrubs, and of some other plants, also increases as the climate becomes, relatively, more benign. But within this graded approach to the treeline there are specific forms of tundra in which differing species dominate.

Left from top
Moss Campion *Silene acaulis*, south Iceland.
Arctic Thrift *Armeria maritima*, west Greenland.
Bistort *Polygonum bistorta* eastern Chukotka, Russia.
Wild Iris *Iris setosa*, Kamchatka, Russia.

Above from top
Pasque-flower *Pulsailla ludoviciana* near Inuvik, NWT, Canada.
Tufted Saxifrage *Saxifraga cespitosa*, Spitsbergen, Svalbard.
Northern Jacob's Ladder *Polemonium boreale*, Spitsbergen, Svalbard.

Dry tundra or fell fields

Both names are frequently used for this tundra type, the latter deriving from the Scandinavian *fjell*, mountain. Dry tundra is an area of poor soil, a rocky or stony habitat, often exposed and so with a limited number of vascular plants, most of which maintain a low form to avoid desiccation. Dry tundra is common in the southern areas of Canada's southerly Arctic islands, Russia's Taimyr Peninsula, and other upland Arctic areas. Because dry tundra tends to be windswept and so has limited snow cover, it is an important winter feeding area for Musk Oxen. The plant species are similar to those of the polar deserts – *Dryas*, *Potentilla*, *Draba*, *Salix* – but sometimes with a more extensive coverage. There are often species of *Oxytropis* (the oxytropes and crazyweeds of North America, and the milk-vetches of Eurasia). In more southerly areas of dry tundra, patches of the matted Alpine Azalea *Loiseleurisa procumbens* add a splash of colour, the gentle pink-and-white bell-shaped flowers contrasting with the deep green of the leaf mat, while the Black Bearberry *Arctostaphylos alpina* adds a valuable berry to the diet of Arctic wildlife. Lapland Diapensia *Diapensia lapponica*, another species that forms low cushions, also occurs here.

Dry tundra also occurs in more southerly locations, particularly those with limited snowfall. In such locations the number of berry-producing heath species increases – *Vaccinium* spp. such as Northern Bilberry or Blueberry – *V. uliginosum*, Cranberry *V. oxycoccos* and Rock Cranberry *V. vitis-idaea*, of which there are subspecies throughout the Arctic, and Crowberry *Empetrum nigrum*, a circumpolar species, while other heath species such as Labrador Tea *Ledum palustre* and some heathers flourish.

Mesic tundra

Mesic tundra is an intermediate form between dry tundra and the wetter sedge and tussock forms. Watered by streams of melting snow yet adequately drained, mesic tundra is home to many varieties of grasses and other flowering plants. Mesic tundra is found across eastern Canada and through the European Arctic to the Taimyr Peninsula, though east across the Asian Russian Arctic and in Alaska and Yukon it is largely replaced by tussock tundra. On mesic tundra Dwarf Birch *Betula nana* occurs among several varieties of willow – e.g. Woolly *Salix lanata* or Downy *S. lapponum* Willows. On southern mesic areas alders (e.g. *Alnus crispa* and *A. fruticosa*) occur. Berry-producing plants and heaths also thrive, with additional circumpolar species such as Arctic Bramble or Dwarf Raspberry *Rubus arcticus* and Cloudberry *R. chamaemorus*; the latter is particularly common in northern Fennoscandia where it is much sought after. In damper areas of mesic tundra a wide range of mosses and sedges occur.

Some authorities recognise another form of tundra, dwarf-shrub tundra, as being intermediate between dry tundra and mesic tundra. They place this form on well-drained soils, usually close to rivers or in areas with limited snow fall. However, the vegetation species list for such areas is largely as that listed above – birch and willows, berry-producing plants and species such as Labrador Tea, Arctic Rhododendron *Rhododendron lapponicum* and Lapland Diapensia (with Matted Cassiope *Cassiope hypnoides* more common in eastern Canada, Greenland and Fennoscandia). Dwarf-shrub tundra is considered to be prevalent in western Alaska, Fennoscandia and eastern Chukotka. In those areas it is an important feeding ground for Reindeer and for Snow Sheep in Chukotka, particularly as fruticose lichens often thrive among the shrubs.

Above
Roseroot _Rhodiola rosea_, Iceland.
Northern Bilberry _Vacciunium uliginosum_ west Greenland.
Crowberry _Emperium nigrum_, west Greenland.

Above centre
Autumn colours, Muskusoksfjorden, north-east Greenland.

Right
Labrador Tea _Ledum palustre_, Victoria Island, Canada.

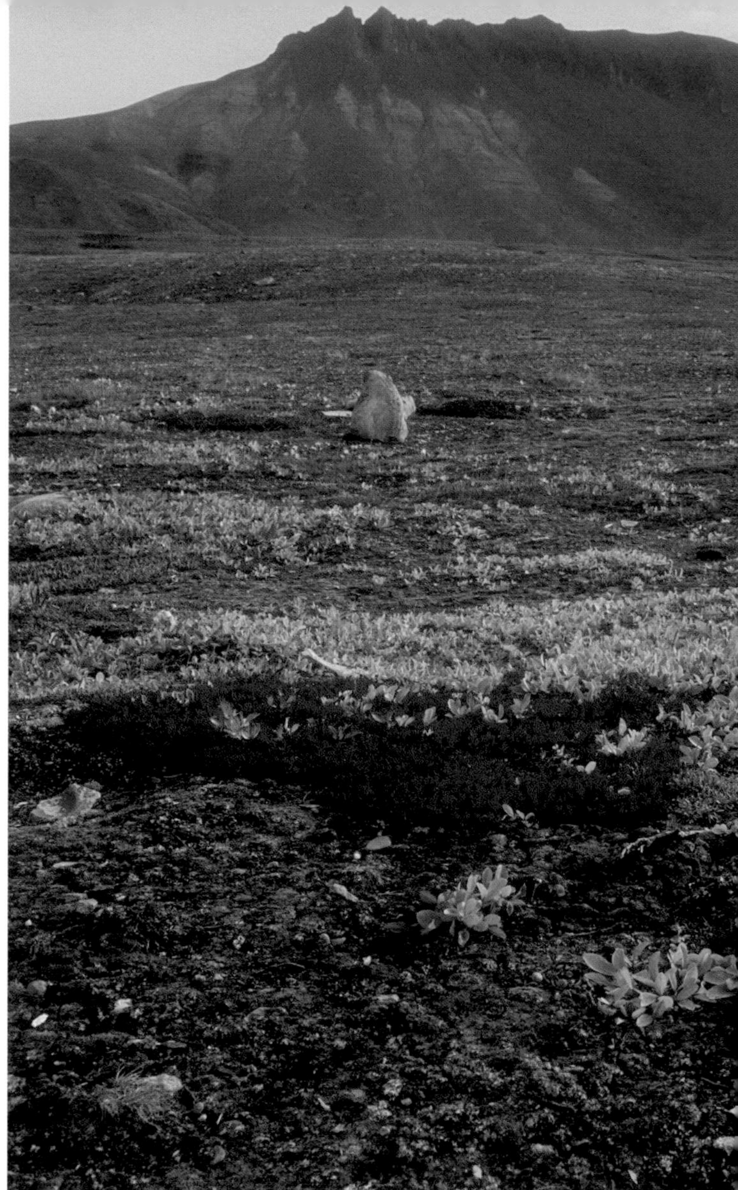

Although it is one of Russia's Arctic islands, the dominant habitat on Wrangel Island is mesic tundra, with a remarkable collection of around 400 species of plant. The island was not covered by an ice sheet during the last Ice Age, and it is thought that this variety has developed as a consequence not only of this lack of glaciation, which allowed an existing flora to flourish, but from occasional periods of attachment to Beringia that would have allowed the spread of southern species. Periods of isolation from Beringia allowed the development of endemics, of which the island has many.

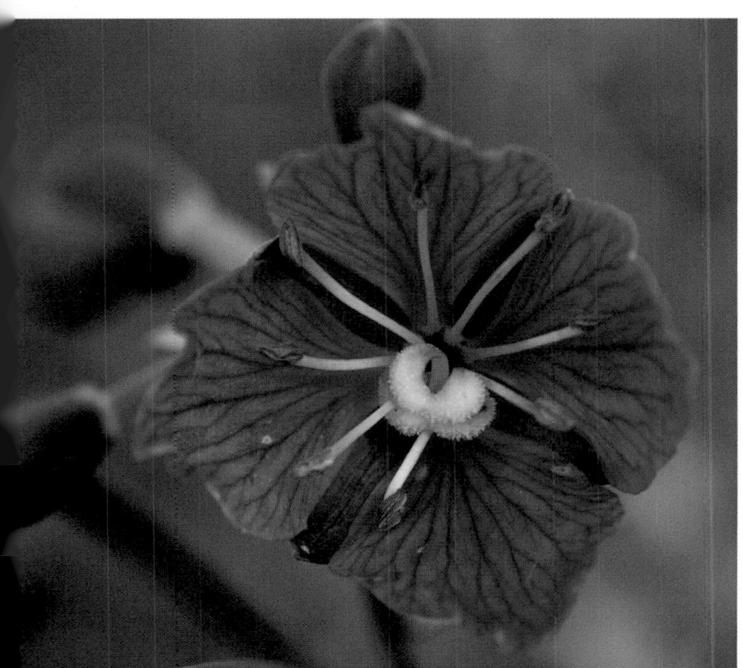

Wet tundra

Wet tundra covers around half of northern Siberia, large areas of the central Canadian mainland, much of northern Alaska and areas of Greenland. In many places in the southern tundra it is the predominant form, and though an excellent habitat for waders and waterfowl is rather less welcomed by the Arctic traveller. In wet tundra the dominant plant species are the Common Cottongrass *Eriophorum angustifolium*, a circumpolar species, together with the Harestail Cottongrass *E. vaginatum* and White Cottongrass *E. scheuchzeri*, and Arctic Sedge *Carex stans*, Mountain Bog Sedge *C. rariflora* and Water Sedge *C. aquatilis*. In western Siberia the dominant sedge is a particular subspecies, *C. ensifolia arctisibirica,* the absence of which signifies the transition to east Siberia for Russian scientists. As well as this broad switch there are also more local changes. For example, on the southern island of Novaya Zemlya and on adjacent Vaygach Island, Shortleaf Hairgrass *Deschampsia brevifolia* dominates.

In general, either the cottongrasses or the sedges dominate in any one particular area of wet tundra. Where cottongrass dominates the white, fluffy seed heads create one of the Arctic's most aesthetically pleasing sights. Mixed with the cottongrasses and sedges are grasses such as Arctic Marsh Grass *Arctophila fulva* and mosses. Where the ground is continuously waterlogged there are sphagnum mosses, while on drier ridges dwarf birch, heathland vegetation and berry-producing shrubs occur.

A particular form of wet tundra is tussock tundra. This has a circumpolar distribution, but is most frequent in areas where the active layer of the permafrost is about 50cm deep. It is a feature of the Russian Arctic east of the Kolyma delta, particularly in Chukotka, and of the western North American Arctic from Alaska to the Mackenzie. Tussocks are formed when the dead leaves of cottongrass and sedges take time to decompose in the cool and acidic waterlogged ground at the base of the plants. Dead material therefore builds up at the plant base. Eventually this material is converted to soil, and as more is added it breaks the water surface. It is then exploited by other plants, dead leaves from these being added to the base so the tussock height increases. As a micro-habitat tussocks are superb for microtines, wading birds and insects. But for the Arctic traveller they are a nightmare. An individual tussock wobbles and is unstable, making tussock-hopping a risky means of travel. However, the ground between the tussocks is waterlogged, the water often overtopping a walker's boot. The combination makes for slow, hazardous travel, the

Above
Arctic Harebell *Campanula uniflora*, west Greenland. Broad-leaved Fireweed *Chamaenerion latifolium* - individual flower photographed to the left - is the National Flower of Greenland. It grows in some improbable places.

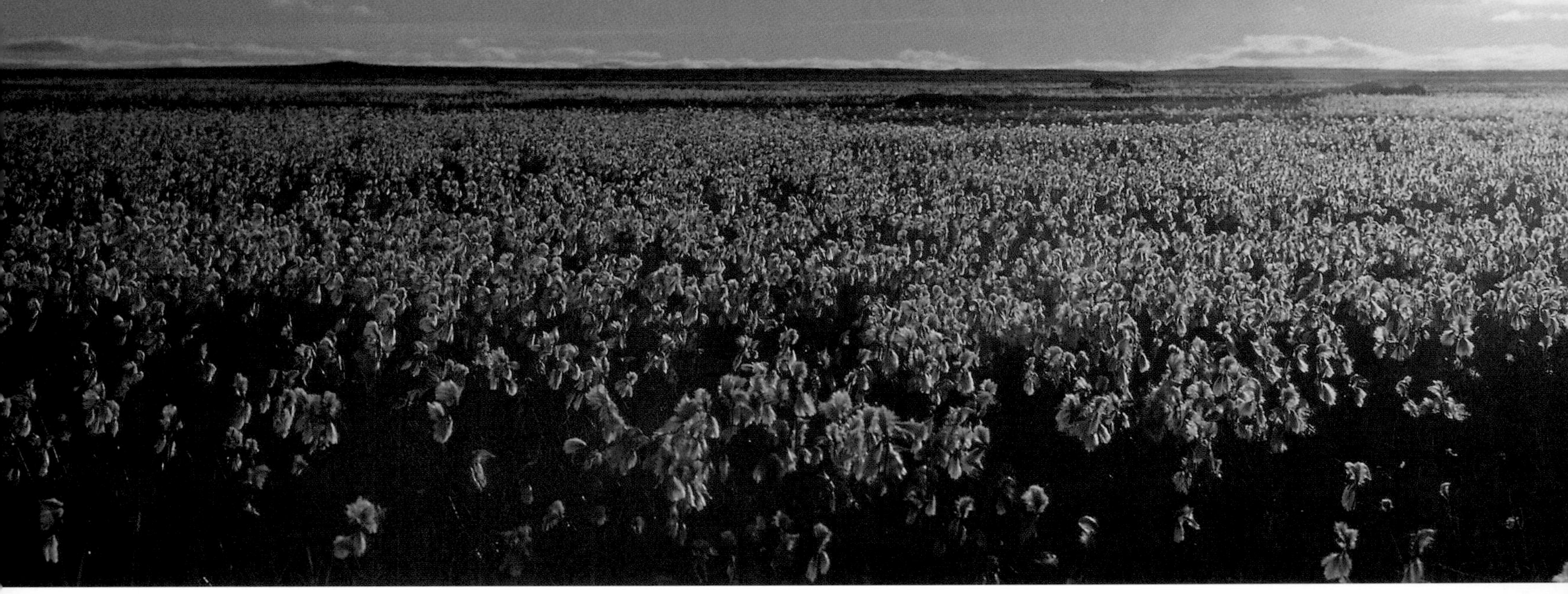

Common Cottongrass *Eriophorum angustifolium* is seen across the Arctic.

Above
Evening light illuminates a vast area of the plant on Igloolik Island, Canada.

Right
Cottongrass on west Greenland.

misery compounded by the fact that tussock tundra is the ideal breeding place for mosquitoes. Tussocks can burn, the dead, dry leaves at the tussock base making good tinder, but as the new buds of the cottongrasses and other plants are often buried deep inside the tussock they survive, so that the flames become a useful regenerator.

Forest or shrub tundra

Close to the treeline the shrubs, particularly the birch, willow and alder species, grow taller and further species – *Populus* spp., i.e. aspens and poplars – become established, creating an area of forest tundra. Interestingly, forest tundra often has fewer species than either the tundra to the north or the boreal forest to the south. In forest tundra berry-producing shrubs tend to grow taller and set more fruit, making the area particularly

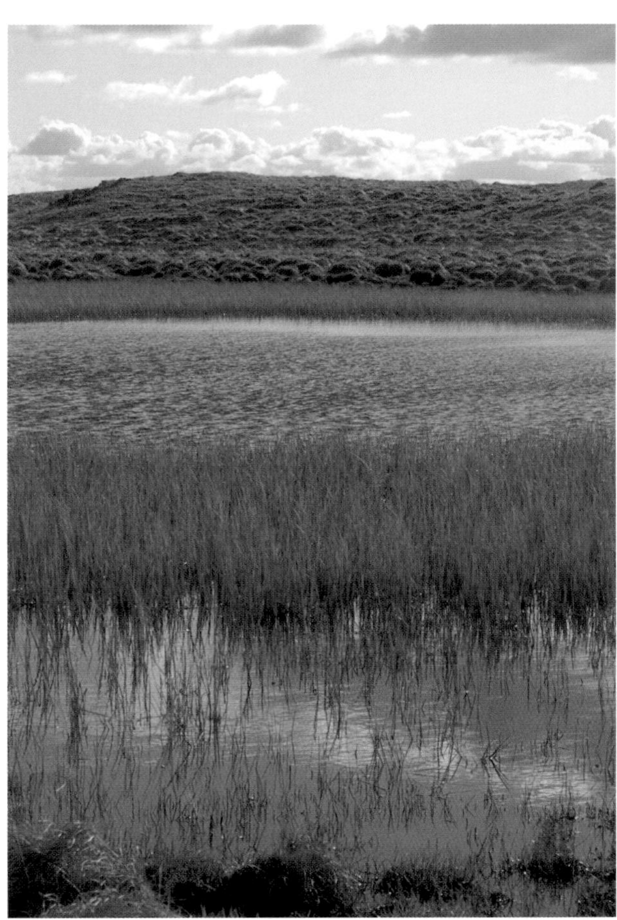

Arcitc pools are often surrounded by horsetails and sedges, south Iceland.

attractive to Reindeer. Rushes are found in the wetter areas. Forest tundra is a particular feature of eastern Russia, where there are large expanses between the tundra of the Taimyr Peninsula and the taiga, and significant expanses to the east of Taimyr, extending as far as the border with Chukotka.

Some Arctic flowers are genuinely impressive. Of the lily family, the Chocolate Lily *Fritillaria camschatcensis* of Kamchatka and the Aleutians, a magnificent chocolate brown flower, is perhaps the finest example. Among the orchids Calypso *Calypso bulbosa* has a flower reminiscent of a masked carnival figure. It grows in northern Fennoscandia, across northern Russia and in north-western North America. Spotted (or Pink) Lady's Slipper *Cypripedium guttatum* has a distribution that includes the Mackenzie delta and the Aleutians, and Eurasia (though in the latter it is usually confined to areas south of 60°N). The purple-spotted white flowers are distinctive. Also in Fennoscandia and across Russia are the various marsh orchids, while Kamchatka and the Aleutians are home to several local species. One of these, the Bering Bog Orchid *Platanthera tipuloides*, which grows on Attu and more rarely on islands east to Unalaska, is considered to be the

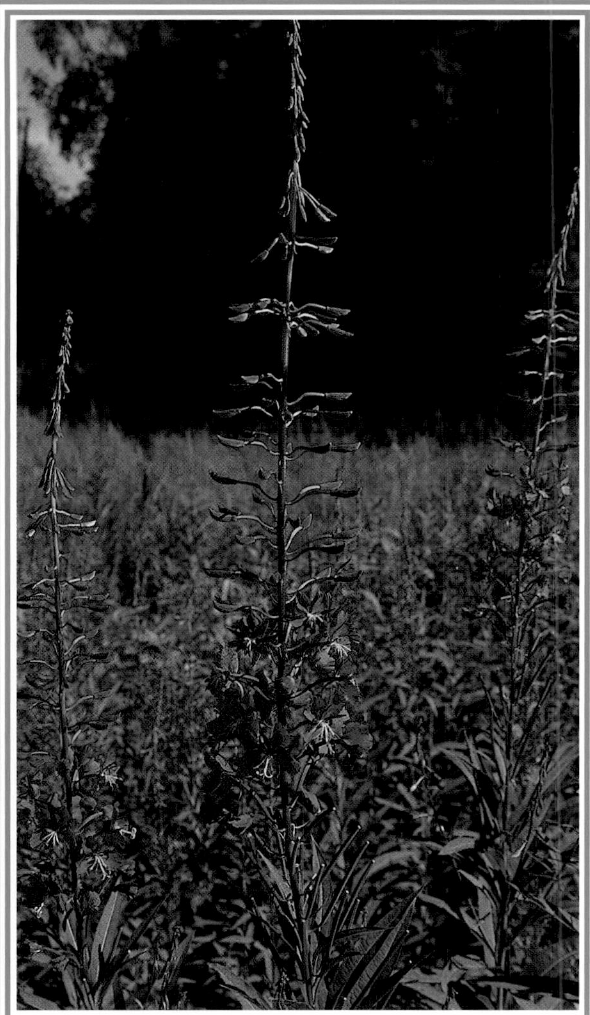

A natural calendar

Fireweed *Epilobium angustifolium*, a coloniser of burned or otherwise disturbed areas, acts as a makeshift calendar for the inhabitants of Alaska and Canada's Yukon Territory. The flowers open progressively up the tall stem; when the last flowers, at the stem tip, open, then winter is just around the corner. In reality this progressive opening is a reproductive strategy, as bees visiting a plant always start collecting at the bottom and work their way upwards. The official flower of Yukon Territory, Fireweed is related to the willowherbs of Eurasia.

rarest North American orchid. It is tall (*c.*20cm) and has up to 20 tiny, golden-yellow flowers on a single stalk. The Pasque flowers are a collection of related species of circumpolar distribution. Species include *Pulsatilla ludoviciana* of north-western North America and *P. pratensis* of Fennoscandia. Wrangel Island has its own endemic species *Pulsatilla nuttaliona*. Visitors to Alaska and the Yukon will see the Nootka Lupine *Lupinus nootkatensis*, which thrives on the Aleutians, the Pribilofs and in southern Alaska, and the Arctic Lupine *L. arcticus,* which occurs in northern areas of Alaska and nearby Canada. Finally there are the gentians – the Alpine Gentian *Gentiana nivalis* of northern Eurasia and the Northern Gentian *G. acuta* of North America and the Aleutians. On the Aleutians the Aleutian Gentian *G. aleutica* is an endemic species.

There is a wide range of flowering plants on the Aleutians, with the climate of the islands, set where cold northern air meets warm Pacific air, creating frequent cloud cover that aids growth. One strange species on the islands is Cow Parsnip *Heracleum lanatum*, a member of the hogweed family, which grows up to two metres tall in sheltered stream valleys.

Boreal forest or taiga

Boreal forest and taiga are names given to the northern reaches of the forest belt that crosses North America and Eurasia, characterised by a climate of long, dark, cold winters and short, cool summers. In general precipitation is low. There are, of course, variations; the Pacific coast of North America is warmer in winter and wetter overall, while inland Siberia has winters that are ferociously cold. The two words are interchangeable; *boreal* derives from *Boreas*, the North Wind of Greek mythology. *Taiga* has a much less definite origin. Some authorities suggest a Turkic word meaning a dense coniferous forest area rich in wildlife, while others see origins in the indigenous peoples of what is now Russia, these deriving from phrases for 'swamp-forest' or 'stick forest', a reference to the short, stunted form of trees at the northern forest edge. Another possible origin is the word *tiy*, the Russian native peoples' name for the Reindeer.

Although the treeline is a useful construct it is not a clear-cut limit (see Figure 14.1). There are no trees north of Alaska's Brooks Range, while across the border in Canada, near the Mackenzie delta, trees grow to the shore of the Beaufort Sea. From there the treeline heads south to the southern shore of Hudson Bay, then north again into Quebec and Labrador. In Eurasia, the treeline is no better behaved, being well above the Arctic Circle in Fennoscandia (because of the influence of the North Atlantic Drift), then heading south to the Circle, before turning north yet again. In the far east of Russia the treeline is almost a north-south line, with minimal encroachment on to the tundra of Chukotka. In mountain areas, where elevation adds extra complexity, the treeline is even more difficult to draw.

At the northern edge of the taiga, trees become more widely spaced, creating an area of forest tundra as noted above. This zone is of variable extent, depending upon local topography. On Russia's Taimyr Peninsula and inland Labrador in Canada it is occasionally several hundred kilometres wide, but it is only a few kilometres wide in eastern Labrador and on mainland Scandinavia. Yet frequently there are stands of trees

Above

Chocolate Lily *Fritillaria camschatcensis*, Kamchatka, Russia.

Kamchatka Rhododendron *Rhododendron camschaticum*, Chukotka, Russia.

Chukchi Primrose *Primula tschuktschorum*, St Paul Island, Pribilofs, Alaska.

The Nootka Lupin *Lupinus nootkatensis*, formerly a western Nearctic species, but now also found in other, more remote areas, including Iceland.

even further north. These indicate where the treeline used to be when the climate warmed after the retreat of the ice at the end of the last Ice Age; today's treeline is now several hundred kilometres south of its position during that period. These stands often survive by suckering. In North America Black Spruce *Picea mariana* sucker relatively easily, while White Spruce *P. glauca* and Tamarack (or American Larch) *Larix laricina* sucker less often. Suckering means that a whole stand of trees can be clones of an original tree or trees on a site and so could be viewed as being perhaps 5,000 years old. If fire destroys them they would not be replaced, but if climate improves then it is possible they will revert to sexual reproduction. In exposed places close to the edge of the taiga, trees can be deformed and twisted. Such expanses of misshapen trees are known as *krummholz* (from the German 'twisted wood') and they can occasionally form areas that are almost impossible to penetrate.

Despite many species of birds and mammals having circumpolar distributions, the trees of the taiga differ in the Nearctic and Palearctic, though in each case the dominant species are coniferous; these, as we have seen, are better adapted to withstand the Arctic climate. As most of the taiga grows on permafrost, the distribution of both trees and species depends on the thickness of the annual active layer. Spruces and larch dominate where the active layer is thinnest, as they produce only shallow root systems. Larches shed their leaves in winter as a protection against the intense cold: they are the only deciduous conifers. The ground cover of larch forests is dominated by lichens, while that of spruce forests is mainly green mosses, though there are clear exceptions to these general rules.

The North American taiga is dominated by spruce, though Alder, a nitrogen-fixer that is intolerant of shade and so prefers open ground, probably preceded the first spruces. White Spruce favours well-drained land, but it can grow on inorganic soils and so was among the first to colonise ground uncovered by the retreating ice. Black Spruce prefers a damper environment and requires a soil richer in organic material, and so would have moved in later. Other prominent species are the Jack Pine *Pinus banksiana* and Tamarack. Other species include the broad-leaves Balsam Poplar or Cottonwood *Populus balsamifera* and Trembling Aspen *P. tremuloides*. Firs *Abies* spp. are almost entirely absent except in northern parts of coastal Labrador, where the Balsam Fir *A. balsamea* is a dominant species right up to the treeline.

The Palearctic taiga is vast, particularly the section that extends across Russia. This Siberian forest covers over 500 million hectares – about 20% of the Earth's entire forested areas, and more than 50% of the total coniferous forest. This taiga covers a huge longitudinal range (from Scandinavia to the borders of Chukotka) and it has the form of a closed, often dense forest across most of that great range, except in eastern Siberia where the dense forest gives way to open larch forests in the north (but with the southern taiga maintaining its denser form). South of the Taimyr Peninsula, in the valley of

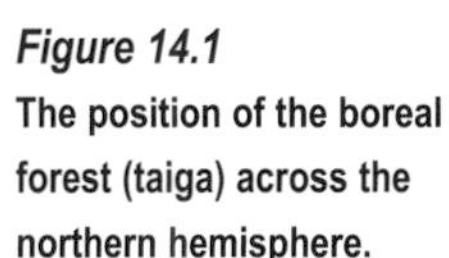

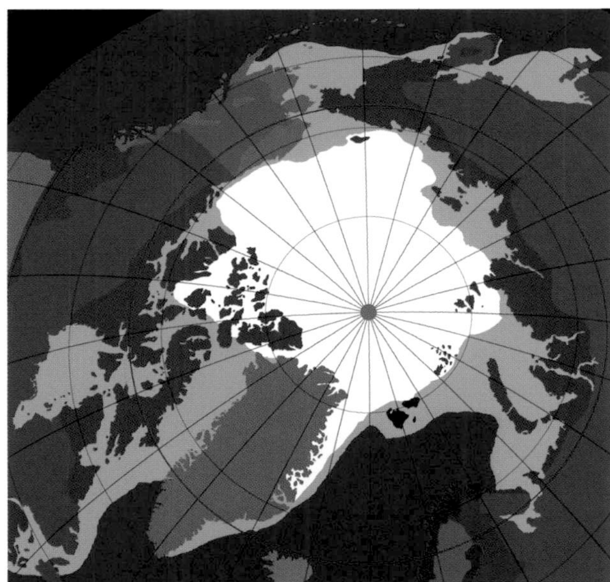

Figure 14.1
The position of the boreal forest (taiga) across the northern hemisphere.

Centre
Birch trees in winter, near Yellowknife, NWT, Canada.

Far left
The treeline, Churchill, Manitoba, Canada.

Left
As with Arctic Willow, dwarf Birch also changes colour in autumn, south Greenland.

the Novaya River, are the world's most northerly stands of trees, with 'forest islands' of Daurian Larch *Larix gmelinii* at 72°30'N. One of these, Ary-Mas, is actually the world's northernmost forest, separated by more than 30km from the taiga. Ary-Mas extends to almost 60km^2 and is home to several species – plants, birds and rodents – which are not found on the surrounding tundra, only in the taiga to the south.

Though the form of the Eurasian forest remains more or less constant, the tree species change as the traveller heads east. In mainland Scandinavia, the forest is chiefly of Norway Spruce *Picea abies* and Scots Pine *Pinus sylvestris*. In European Russia, Norway Spruce and Siberian Spruce *Picea obovata* dominate. Further east, the great forests of western Siberia are predominantly Siberian Spruce, Siberian Fir *Abies sibirica* and Siberian Stone Pine *Pinus sibirica*. Western Siberia also has swathes of wetlands (the largest wetland area in the world) because of its poor drainage.

In central Siberia, larch species dominate, particularly Siberian Larch *Larix sibirica*. To the east, Daurian Larch is the main species, together with *L. cajenderi*. To the south of the larch forests Siberian Spruce and Siberian Pine grow, and Scots Pine is found at the edge of the steppes. One characteristic of the central Siberian taiga is the presence of alases, treeless areas with a meadow-like vegetation. Alases form when thawing permafrost creates a lake. The soil near the lake collapses, halting tree growth so that the area surrounding the lake changes to meadow. Alases may vary from a hundred metres or so across to about 10km, and can form as much as 50% of the taiga in some areas.

East again, the severe Siberian climate limits the spread (and size) of *Larix* spp., the forests of Daurian Larch becoming more open with the shrubby Dwarf Siberian Stone Pine *Pinus pumila* often dominating. Ayan Spruce *Picea ajanensis*, White-barked Fir *Abies nephrolepis* and Sakhalin Fir *A. sachalinensis* also occur. *Larix ochotensis* is endemic to the coast of the Sea of Okhotsk.

In western Eurasia alders, birches and willows are the main broad-leaved trees. In western and central Siberia broad-leaved species, particularly aspen and birch, form a narrow band at the southern edge of the conifer forest, separating the conifers from the wooded steppe to the south. In eastern Siberia this narrow band disappears, the conifers extending to the edge of the steppe, though there are scattered stands of broad-leaves, principally the alder *Alnus fruticosa* and the birch *Betula middendorffii*. In Fennoscandia, in sheltered spots, a zone of Mountain

Muskeg, Admiralty Island, south-eastern Alaska.

Sundew *Drosera rotundifolia*, Kamchatka, Russia.

Birch *Betula pubescens* is often found between the conifer forest and the tundra. The birch is not drought resistant and so requires shelter to avoid desiccation. The species can withstand winter temperatures to at least -30°C, low for a broadleaf, though the Stone Birch *B. erminii* of north-eastern Eurasia can apparently withstand temperatures even lower (to -45°C). Stone Birch is a feature of the coastal plains and river valleys of Kamchatka, Stone Pine and the alder *Alnus maximowiczii* being found on the mountain slopes.

Within the taiga a surprisingly high number of vascular plants flourish. Much less of a surprise is that shade- and cold-tolerant species dominate. In the Nearctic the main species are members of the *Asteraceae* (aster), *Onagraceae* (willowherb), *Ranunculaceae* (buttercup) and *Rosaceae* (rose) families, as well as berry-producing shrubs. In the Palearctic taiga the main species are similar, with the addition of the *Brassicaceae* (crucifers).

There are also areas of bog on the taiga, some of which are extremely large. The bogs of the Palearctic are known by a variety of names, most of them local in origin and with little standardisation, while in North America the most usual term is muskeg. To the specialist the use of muskeg to describe all northern bogs is wrong, though the difference between the various forms is academic to the casual traveller. Muskeg refers to the wetter bogs, created where meltwater saturates the ground, and is, technically, not a true bog. True bogs form by the infilling of lakes and ponds so that the bottom layer of peat is formed of pondweeds and other water plants, while muskeg forms in areas of poor drainage. Bogs are also formed by the process of paludification. Here tree litter such as leaves falls to the forest floor and decomposes slowly because of the low temperature. Mosses flourish on the litter, retaining moisture and adding to the insulating properties of the litter itself. The underlying soil cools, the combination of wet litter and cold soil inhibiting the growth of seedlings. Over time a bog forms. In principle all northern forests would give rise to bogs in this way, but fire can eradicate the sodden ground cover, giving seedlings a chance to establish. The northern bogs are home to fine marshland plants, including the insectivorous Sundew *Drosera rotundifolia* and Pitcher Plant *Sarracenia purpurea*. But as with tussock tundra to the north, they are breeding grounds for mosquitoes and other biting insects, and a misery to cross.

Within the taiga fire is a hazard. Detritus on the forest floor builds up, acting as tinder when a lightning strike starts a blaze. The fire spreads rapidly, and consequently temperatures do not become sufficiently high for long enough to damage the soil. Taiga trees have evolved to deal with regular fires; their seeds are stimulated to mature and release by fire, with the mineral-rich ash soil being an ideal growing medium, while the open areas created by fire allow seedlings to develop without competition for light. Fire may also aid the introduction of species that specialise in colonising 'disturbed' ground. However, if the natural cycle is interfered with, particularly if fires are suppressed so that detritus builds up, then blazes can be catastrophic as local temperatures are elevated, allowing real damage to occur to both the soil and the trees. Regular fires are both useful and important to the forest and its well-being. In general Moose benefit from the new growth, though Reindeer and Caribou do not as the flames destroy the lichens on the forest floor.

Fire has recently swept through this area of Alaska to the south of the Brooks Range. Already, new growth has sprung up to regenerate the landscape.

Invertebrates of tundra and taiga

Although most Arctic invertebrates are aquatic (mainly marine), a surprising number of terrestrial species inhabit both the taiga edge and the tundra. In terms of abundance the most numerous are worms (particularly nematodes and oligochaetes) and rotifers, with planarian worms being important in the taiga. There is also a diverse collection of freshwater copepods and many insects. Though there are marine and freshwater molluscs, there are no Arctic slugs or snails.

Spiders occur as far north as northern Ellesmere Island. Indeed, several species from that area are endemic, suggesting the presence of an ice age refuge that allowed speciation to occur. Many of these spiders are very small, but on the tundra the traps of funnel web spiders can occasionally be seen, while the larger wolf spiders are among the more likely specimens to be encountered. Spiders are also important on the taiga.

Arctic insects

Insects are the most numerous of Arctic animals (yet the number of species represents only about 0.3% of known insect species on Earth), with densities sometimes reaching staggering proportions. On dry tundra in Svalbard the density of springtails was found to be almost 40,000/m^2; on damp tundra this density rose to more than 240,000/m^2. Similar densities have been measured on the tundra close to Barrow in Alaska. For larger insects the densities decline sharply, but even for dipteran (fly) larvae a density of 50/m^2 has been measured on Svalbard tundra.

Almost all insect orders have Arctic representatives, though there are relatively few beetles. Of the insects the most successful are the non-biting midges or chironomids, which account for as much as 25% of the total insect population in areas of the High Arctic. Many insect species are circumpolar – as many as 80% of mosquitoes and nymphalid butterflies – while many of the others show distinct trans-Atlantic or trans-Beringian ranges.

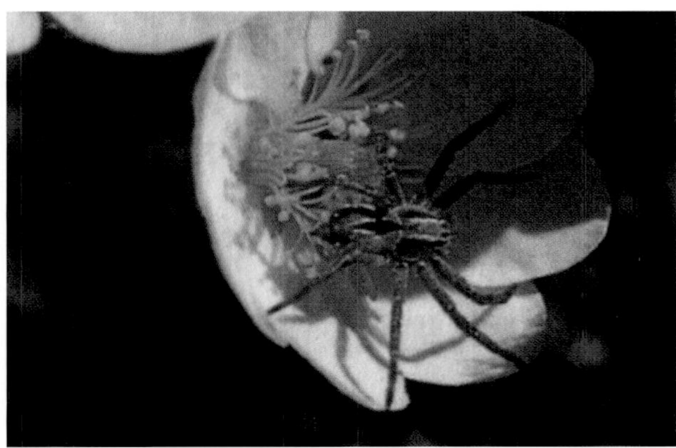

Taiga Bluet Damselfly ***Coenagrion resolutum*****, Potter Marsh, Alaska.**

Many insects are nectar and/or pollen feeders, these species being important as pollinators and food for birds. They can, however, also have a negative effect. Because sections of taiga can effectively be a monoculture, any outbreak of insects that feed on the trees can swiftly reach epidemic proportions. Trees may then be killed off by the insect horde (or by micro-organisms that they introduce). As well as herbivorous insects there are also species that feed on carcasses, dung feeders, and a number of predatory species. There are also significant numbers of parasitoid wasps and flies. The hosts of these insects are often home to the larvae of two or more parasitoid species.

The High Arctic has no mayflies, stoneflies or dragonflies, though these occur in the low Arctic, as do grasshoppers, though these are few in number and found only at the Arctic fringe. As noted earlier, there are few beetles in the Arctic – they represent only some 10% of the total number of species (this figure reaches about 35% in temperate areas) There are two Arctic diving beetles (*Hydroporus polaris* and *H. morio*), some rove beetles and a single ground beetle, *Amara alpina*. Interestingly, subfossil *A. alpina* have been found in Greenland though the beetle is no longer extant there, it having failed to survive the last glaciation. In the low Arctic there are representatives of other coleopteran families, including ladybirds and leaf beetles.

There are about 15 species of caddisfly in the Low Arctic, but of these only *Apatana zonella* can be termed a High Arctic species as well. The aquatic larvae of these species share the same unusual habit as their southerly cousins; they construct protective tubes of twigs and small stones.

Of the hymenopterans, there are stingless ants on the tundra, and some Arctic bees, although there are only two

Above left
A *Thanatus arcticus* spider on a Mountain Avens flower, east Greenland.

Below left
This spider on Victoria Island, Canada, was rather too rapid for definite identification. Probably a *Pardosa* spp. wolf spider.

Queen of the Bumblebee *Bombus polaris*, west Greenland.

species in the high Arctic. Each is large and uses shivering to raise body temperature. The muscle mass required for this process, together with dense insulating hair, explains their large size, which usually comes as a surprise to the first-time Arctic traveller. The queen of *Bombus polaris* overwinters, having been fertilised during the summer. In spring she founds a new colony, laying two batches of eggs. The first may contain workers, but sometimes does not, but both the first and second batches contain fertile young – new queens and male drones. In some colonies the absence of workers means that the queen herself must forage in order to feed the colony in its early stages. The second, larger, bumblebee species, *B. hyperboreus*, is a social parasite. A queen of this species overwinters as in *B. polaris*, but on emergence in spring seeks out a *B. polaris* nest site. She bypasses any workers (perhaps using chemical secretions), then finds and kills the *B. polaris* queen. She lays her own eggs, which are coated with chemicals that trick the *B. polaris* workers into treating them and the larvae that hatch from them as their own siblings. All the *B. hyperboreus* larvae are queens or drones, with the queens ready for overwintering and a new year of cuckoo-like social parasitism with a twist.

Mosquitoes

The Inuit have an expression for the curse of the Arctic summer, the swarms of mosquito – they call them *sordlo pujok*, 'like smoke'. And the countless number of the insects can occasionally look just like that. Although the normal density of the insects is 1/m² this can rise to over 1,000/m². Given that the presence of a potential meal also makes them congregate, swarms of legendary size can envelop the traveller. One of the first descriptions of the annual swarms is from Frobisher's account of his journey to Baffin Island in 1576, where he met insects that were like 'a small fly or gnat that stingeth and offendeth so fiercely that the place where they bite shortly after swelleth and itcheth very sore'. It is a description that can hardly be bettered.

The photograph above was taken on the southern edge of the Brooks Range, Alaska. The hand is that of the author, sacrificing blood in the cause of science reporting.

The flies

Dipterans represent about half of all insect species, and there are representatives of the order in the high Arctic wherever their 'normal' larval habitats of dung, carrion and other detritus are available. Of particular interest to the Arctic traveller are mosquitoes and black flies, the females of which are facultative bloodsuckers, i.e. they will feed on blood if the opportunity presents itself. Male mosquitoes feed exclusively on nectar. Females feed on nectar to obtain the energy required to fly, but seek a blood meal to provide the nutrients for producing abundant, healthy eggs. Females who do not obtain a blood meal may also lay eggs, but these will be far fewer in number, and they may also produce eggs autogenously, using food reserves accumulated while they were larvae.

Female mosquitoes that find a host may consume up to five times their own body weight in a single blood meal. The insect injects saliva into the host's blood to prevent clotting: it is this that causes the swelling and irritation. Female

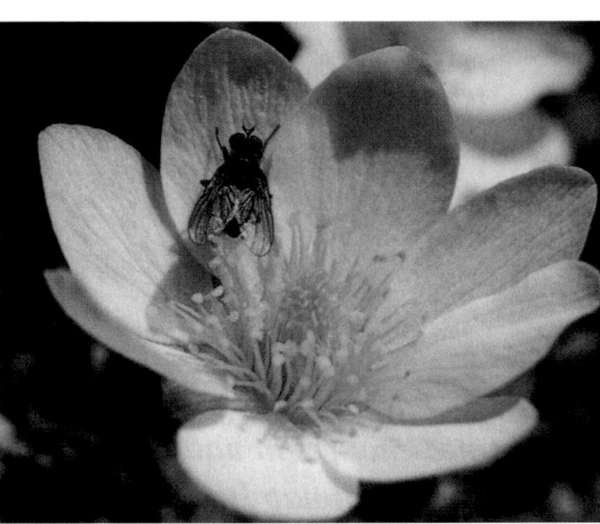

Right
The fly *Spiligona sanctipauli.*

Far right
The dung fly *Scatophaga furcata.*

Both flies are sunbathing on flowers of Entire-leaved Avens *Dryas integrifolia.* which is particularly heliotropic. The much larger dung fly is having much less success in getting a good position. Both photographs in west Greenland.

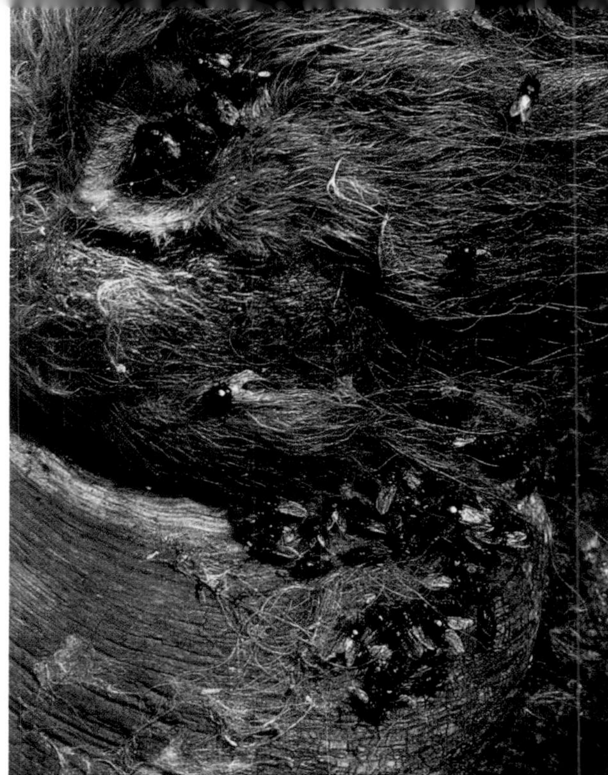

The Arctic is no different from any habitat in needing insects to aid the decomposition of corpses. Here blowflies are laying eggs on a dead Musk Ox. The maggots will play a major role in disposing of the corpse, and may also overwinter in it.

mosquitoes will feed on any warm-blooded animal – bird or mammal. The great herds of Caribou in the Nearctic are driven, it sometimes seems, to the point of madness by their attention. Although it is rare, cases are known of Caribou dying from blood loss due to mosquito bites. Birds have also been known to succumb; a team researching a Brünnich's Guillemot colony during a particularly warm spring noted the deaths of many birds resulting from blood loss, mosquitoes attacking the feet of the birds, which had blood vessels close to the surface to aid heat loss. It has been calculated that a naked human making no effort to protect himself from the attentions of mosquitoes would die from blood loss within a day. The main mosquito species in the region are *Aedes impiger* and *A. nigripes*, which are widespread with ranges that extend into the High Arctic. There are, however, about a dozen species of Arctic mosquito in total.

Mosquitoes are drawn to sources of carbon dioxide, and, when close to a victim, to body heat. The ability of the insects to sniff out victims is both amazing and infuriating. On one canoe trip to the Canadian Arctic I deliberately camped on an island situated over 1km from the bank; while it is not possible to state with certainty that there were no mosquitoes on the island when my canoe landed, none were seen for about 40 minutes, at which point they appeared in a swarm. It is often claimed by some people that they are more prone to biting than their companions, and some experiments with (non-Arctic) species, using a Y-shaped tube so that the insects could travel in one of two directions, showed that they often preferentially chose one person rather than another. This has yet to be explained, but one plausible theory suggests that 'healthier' people are more likely to be bitten; 'unhealthy' people would have relatively fewer nutrients in their blood and therefore represent a poorer investment for the insect, though exactly how a mosquito decides on fitness by smell alone is difficult to understand. It is also known that mosquitoes preferentially bite pregnant women.

Black flies are numerous and particularly ferocious in the taiga and at the taiga edge, where their blood-sucking habits produce a more damaging wound than that of a mosquito. Black flies are thankfully less common and less damaging in the High Arctic, as there the females do not suck blood; their mouthparts (and those of their mates) do not fully form. Instead the eggs are produced solely using reserves built up during the larval stages. In the Nearctic taiga the famed no-see-ums, ceratopogonid biting midges, are another dipteran scourge, particularly as they seem able to penetrate the tightest mosquito netting.

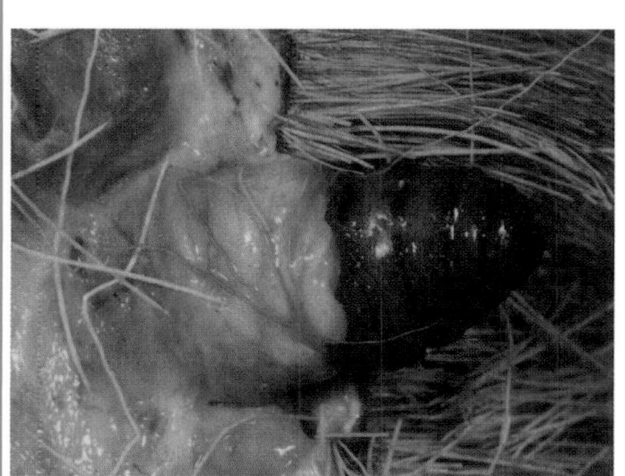

Parasitic insects of Caribou

Not only do Reindeer and Caribou suffer blood loss from the swarms of mosquitoes that fill the summer skies – they also have infestations of two highly specialised fly parasites to contend with. The Caribou Warble Fly *Hypoderma tarandi* lays a sticky egg on the legs or underside of the animal. When the larvae hatch they burrow into the animal, then migrate subcutaneously to the back, close to the spine. There they excavate a breathing hole and begin to feed on the tissues of their host. Most Caribou are infested; some carry up to 2,000 larvae, their skins becoming useless to native hunters. The larvae overwinter in the animal then emerge through their breathing holes in spring, falling to the ground to pupate. Occasionally the breathing holes become infected, adding to the suffering of the host animal.

The Caribou Nose Bot Fly *Cephenomyia trompe* deposits live larvae (that hatch inside their mother) at the entrance to the host's nostrils. The larvae then migrate to the opening of the throat, where they cluster. The larval mass can be so large that it interferes with the host's breathing; the coughing often heard in groups of Caribou is usually caused by animals attempting to dislodge the mass of parasites. The Caribou eventually succeeds in expelling the mass, but only when the larvae are ready to pupate.

Both warble and bot flies are stronger fliers than mosquitoes and so are more difficult for the host animals to evade. The animals lower and shake their heads when a Caribou Nose Bot Fly is seen, and the apparently random jump and run of an individual animal is usually a sign that one or other fly has been spotted.

The photographs left are of an adult and larva Warble Fly, northern Norway.

Arctic butterflies

Butterflies are one of the surprises and joys of the Arctic summer. They can be seen as far north as flowers bloom – the Greely expedition famously spent an idyllic summer at Fort Conger at the northern end of Ellesmere Island (at almost 82°N), with butterflies flitting among the flowers before the horrific series of incidents that led to most of the expedition being lost. Despite their apparent fragility, butterflies are adept at using their wings as sun-collectors to raise their body temperature.

Although there are more moths than butterflies in the Arctic they represent a smaller fraction of the resident lepidopterans than is usual in more temperate areas. Of the 90 or so moth species so far identified, most are micro-moths from the families *Tortricidae*, *Noctuidae*, *Geometridae* and *Lymantriidae*. As noted earlier, the caterpillar of the Arctic Woolly Bear *Gynaephora groenlandica* may develop for up to 14 years before pupating.

Of the families of butterflies, the nymphalids (*Nymphalidae*) and whites (*Pieridae*) include the true Arctic dwellers, with blues (*Lycaenidae*) at lower latitudes, and skippers (*Hesperiidae*) and Swallowtails (*Papilionidae*) prominent in the Low Arctic. High Arctic species are invariably darker than their southern cousins, an adaptation to allow greater absorption of heat from solar radiation. All Arctic butterflies overwinter as larvae or pupae, with some species requiring several years for the larvae to develop sufficiently to pupate.

Circumpolar species

The most northerly of the butterflies are circumpolar. Of the nymphalids the Polar Fritillary *Boloria polaris* is found on the tundra of the Arctic islands to northern Ellesmere Island, on north-west Greenland and across northern Eurasia. The larvae feed primarily on Mountain Avens. The Arctic Fritillary *B. chariclea* has a similar distribution, though it is not found as far north on Canada's islands and is uncommon in Fennoscandia. The larvae feed on Arctic Willow. The taxonomy of some of the High Arctic butterflies is still debated, as some species and areas are poorly studied. Consequently there are species recognised by Russian lepidopterists that are not generally recognised elsewhere. In Chukotka and on Wrangel Island *B. butleri* is recognised and is also considered to be a west Alaska species, but it may well be conspecific with *B. chariclea*. Other *Boloria* species also occur in both Chukotka and Alaska (though problems occasionally occur with the nomenclature due to inconsistencies between Russian and American authorities).

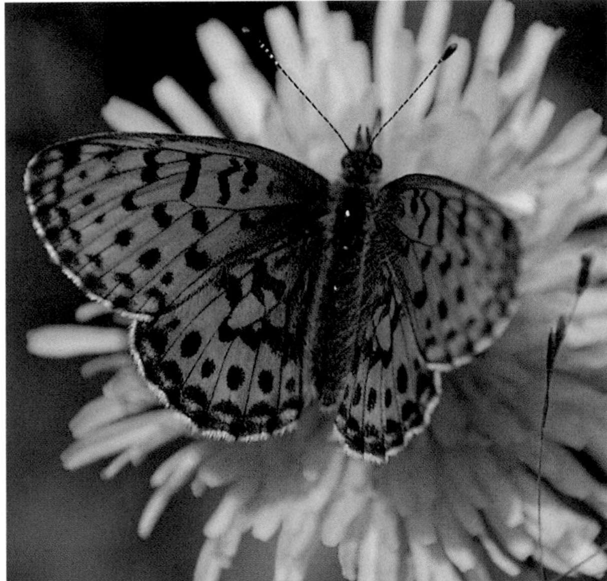

Pearl-bordered Fritillary (*Clossiana titiana*), east Siberian taiga, Russia.

Mating Polar Fritillaries (*Boloria polaris*), Victoria Island, Canada.

Of other nymphalids, the Dusky-winged Fritillary *Boloria improba* breeds on Novaya Zemlya and Canada's southern Arctic islands. Frejya's Fritillary *B. freija* has a similar distribution. Of larger butterflies the Camberwell Beauty *Nymphalis antiopa* (Mourning Cloak in North America) is rare everywhere, but may be seen at the treeline throughout the Arctic. The Red Admiral *Vanessa atalanta* and Painted Lady *V. cardui* may be seen, but are uncommon, north of the Arctic Circle in Eurasia, and they also occur on the southern shores of Hudson Bay and in southern Quebec and Labrador.

Of the pierids the Northern Clouded Yellow *Colias hecla* (known as the Hecla Sulphur in North America) is found to northern Ellesmere Island and in north-western Greenland as well as across Arctic Eurasia. The Pale Arctic Clouded Yellow *C. nastes* (Labrador Sulphur in North America) has a more southerly distribution on Canada's Arctic islands, but a similar range in Eurasia. Booth's Sulphur *C. tyche* has a similar distribution; some authorities consider this to be a hybrid of *C. nastes* and *C. hecla*.

Of the skippers the Northern Grizzled Skipper *Pyrgus centaureae* is found in bogs and damp heathland in more southerly areas of Fennoscandia, Siberia and Kamchatka, Alaska and the Yukon, while the Chequered Skipper *Carterocephalus palaemon* (Arctic Skipper) and Silver-spotted Skipper *Hesperia comma* (Common Branded Skipper) have similar ranges. The papilionid *Papilio machaon*, the Swallowtail, may be seen to, but rarely beyond, the treeline.

Trans-Beringian species

Species common to the far east of Siberia and western North America include some that are found to the coast. Nymphalids include the Eskimo Alpine *Erebia occulta*, which is found on gravelly areas of rocky tundra, and Young's Alpine *E. dabanensis*. The latter is the subject of debate as there are several butterflies in Chukotka considered by some to be full species but which may be subspecies of *E. dabanensis*. Similar taxonomic confusion surrounds other alpines. Although in general the swallowtails of the region are restricted to the Low

Arctic, Eversmann's Parnassian *Parnassius eversmanni* is seen on the open tundra of northern Alaska and the Yukon. In Siberia its range extends west to the Altai Mountains. The Phoebus Parnassian *P. phoebus* ranges from the Urals to central Alaska, but is more southerly, being seen on rocky areas of open woodland and at the forest edge.

Eurasian Arctic butterflies

Apart from the circumpolar species noted above, most Eurasian species are from southern Arctic areas. Nymphalids include fritillaries, ringlets and browns. The Small Tortoiseshell *Aglais urticae* has a wide Low Arctic range, while the Indian Red Admiral *Vanessa indica* breeds in Kamchatka. There are several whites of the family *Pieridae*, together with the lycaenids such as Green Hairstreak *Callophrys rubi* and a small number of other blues and coppers. The only skipper is the Alpine Grizzled Skipper *Pyrgus andromedae*, which may be seen on open moors, heathland and alpine grass of western Fennoscandia and the Urals. There are no Parnassus in the European Arctic, but *Parnassius tenedius* may be seen on the forest-tundra of Siberia from east of the Altai Mountains to western Chukotka.

The resident butterflies of Iceland, and many of the moths, are introduced species, arriving with imported garden plants etc. It is not known if the island has any 'indigenous' species as some moth species that appear to predate the recent introductions may themselves have arrived with the crop plants imported by Viking settlers. Vagrant butterflies – Monarch *Danaus plexippus*, Painted Lady and Red Admiral – and moths – both macro- and micro-moths, and including the Death's Head Hawk Moth *Acherontia atropos* – are seen fairly regularly on the island. Eastern Greenland exhibits a similar lack of resident butterflies, and those on the west coast are limited to the north-west where just a few kilometres of water separates Greenland from Ellesmere Island.

North American butterflies

North American Arctic nymphalids include fritillaries, commas, alpines and arctics. Some of these may be seen as far north as the Mackenzie delta (being essentially treeline rather than tundra species), though the Polixenes Arctic *Oeneis polixenes* breeds not only throughout Alaska and on the northern Canadian mainland, but also on the southern Canadian Arctic islands, including Baffin Island. Pierids include whites, sulphurs and marbles. Lycaenids are few in number, while of the skippers only the Persius Duskywing *Erynnis persius*, which breeds in central and east central Alaska, the Yukon and North West Territories, can be considered Arctic. It breeds to the coast at, and to the immediate east of, the Mackenzie delta. Travellers arriving in Anchorage prior to exploring northern Alaska should make their way to Potter Marsh for a chance to see the only truly Arctic papilionid, the exquisite Canadian Tiger Swallowtail *Papilio canadensis*. This fine butterfly also breeds near the Mackenzie delta.

Canadian Tiger Swallowtail *Papilio canadensis*, Potter Marsh, Alaska.

15. The Adaptations and Biogeography of Birds and Mammals

The survival strategies against the cold used by Arctic endotherms, or warm-blooded animals, are very different from those exhibited by the region's ectotherms. The simplest of these is adopted by the vast majority of Arctic breeding birds – they fly south, escaping the cold and reaching places where food is abundant. Several seabirds stay within the Arctic, feeding at the ice edge or in polynyas, but few terrestrial species remain. The Snowy Owl *Bubo scandiacus*, the *Lagopus* species – (Rock) Ptarmigan and Willow Grouse (known as Willow Ptarmigan in North America) – Gyrfalcon *Falco rusticolus*, Common and Arctic Redpolls *Carduelis flammea* and *C. hornemanni* and the Raven are often said to be resident throughout the winter. In practice all will move south if local food supplies fail; individuals that remain on their breeding grounds throughout the winter tend to be at the Arctic fringe and so do not contend with the full rigours of the Arctic winter. Nevertheless, these species must have adaptations to allow them to survive periods of intense cold.

Avian adaptations

All Arctic birds have an increased feather density, while the *Lagopus* species and the Snowy Owl have feathered feet. The Snowy Owl also has modified foot pads to reduce heat loss, a characteristic it shares with the Raven. The owl's insulation is superior to that of the *Lagopus* species, but the gamebirds can reduce their metabolic rate, and also dig holes in the snow to gain shelter and the benefits of an insulating snow layer, something the owl does not do. The redpolls also excavate snow holes, the ability of these much smaller birds to increase their feather density being limited, as there is always a trade off between insulation and efficient function.

As well as having a greater density, the feathers of Arctic birds form a particularly smooth outer surface, shedding the wind so that ruffling, with a consequent breakdown of the insulatory layer and increased heat loss, are reduced. Arctic species also have down feathers below their contour feathers, the down having a modified structure, being 'fluffier' so as to trap air and enhance insulation properties. The down of the Common Eider became synonymous with warmth in the second half of the 20th century, when the 'eiderdown' became the standard word for the down-filled covering on British beds in the days before widespread central heating. The down of the Common Eider *Somateria mollissima* has the best insulating properties of any natural substance; weight for weight and thickness for thickness, no synthetic material can better it. So good is the down at repelling winter's chills that it has been commercially harvested for centuries. The mammalian strategy of adding insulation in the form of subcutaneous fat, or blubber, is not readily available to birds. Penguins do this, but flight is compromised by increasing weight relative to wing area; birds able to add sufficient blubber to survive an Arctic winter would be unable to fly.

In very cold conditions birds seek shelter from the wind and stand motionless, occasionally with one foot tucked into the body to reduce heat loss, or sitting so that both feet are covered. Foraging for food requires energy and if food is scarce and local conditions hostile, doing nothing may be the most energy-efficient strategy (though if the temperature is low enough so that the bird has to shiver to maintain warmth then the strategy may fail, more energy being required to shiver than to forage). As in marine mammals, the arteries of Arctic birds are enveloped by veins in the legs and feet so that venal blood is warmed by arterial blood, allowing heat to 'bypass' the feet, reducing heat loss. The temperature of the feet of some Arctic species may be 30°C lower than the body temperature. Systems like this are known as counter-current heat exchanges, and are common in Arctic animals.

Birds can, of course, migrate south to avoid the Arctic winter. For the terrestrial mammals of the Arctic migration is, at best, a limited option. For almost all, the gaining and holding of a territory is critical to breeding success and so cannot be lightly rejected. The energetic requirements of long journeys, and the physical impossibility of such journeys for small animals such as rodents, also preclude migration. However, both Reindeer *Rangifer tarandus* and Musk Ox *Ovibos moschatus* move south in search of richer herbage. In

Both the Snowy Owl (*above top*) and Ptarmigan (*above*) have feathered feet.

The owl was photographed in northern Norway, the ptarmigan near the Hood River, Nunavut, Canada.

Opposite page
Polar Bear tracks beside the sea ice at Kvalvaagen, Svalbard.

A male of the subspecies of the Ptarmigan *Lagopus mutus hyperborea*, which breeds on Svalbard and Franz Josef Land, crosses frozen tundra at Forlandsundet, Svalbard. Ptarmigan are one of the few bird species that overwinter in the Arctic.

neither case are the animals territorial; reproductive success in these species is decided by harem possession (won by trials of strength) rather than territory possession.

Torpor

One common strategy in terrestrial mammals that overwinter in the Arctic is torpor, the state in which an endotherm reduces its body temperature to a new, lower norm, with metabolic processes slowing as a result, usually to about 5% of the rate at normal body temperature. Just as the normal body temperature is critical in maintaining body functions (meaning the animal must increase metabolic rate and take positive steps to avoid hypothermia, or suffer potentially lethal effects), the new, lower temperature is also critical, so that if the body temperature falls below it then the same response is observed. It is, therefore, not true to say that mammals that pass the winter in a state of profound torpor are independent of their surroundings – if they do not respond to a significant fall in temperature they become hypothermic and die, just as any non-hibernating mammal would.

True torpor is confined to small mammals (primarily rodents, insectivores and bats; Arctic marmots seem to be at the upper weight limit for true torpor, with body weights of about 8kg) and a limited number of birds (some hummingbirds, poorwills and swifts, none of which are Arctic species), and is often practised not only during the winter but also at

Common Eider nest, northern Iceland. Weight for weight, eider down is the best natural insulator in the world, and superior to man-made synthetics.

night, so as to reduce the call on fat reserves. Before entering winter torpor fat reserves are laid down, but these may not be sufficient to survive the long Arctic winter and Arctic rodents prepare food caches, waking at intervals to feed. Once torpid, heart and breathing rates decline and the carbon dioxide level in the blood increases, reducing the metabolic rate. The animal falls into torpor relatively slowly, but arouses from it much more quickly. During early arousal the body temperature is raised without shivering, but eventually shivering does occur, this causing a rapid increase in body temperature. Field Voles *Microtus agrestis*, from the fringe of the European Arctic, huddle together during winter, a strategy that may also be used by less well-studied Arctic species. Huddling as a survival strategy is also practised by reptiles whose range extends to the Arctic fringe. The European Adder *Vipera berus* in Scandinavia overwinters in aggregations of up to 100, while the Red-sided Garter Snake *Couleuvre rayée* of Canada, which winters in places where temperatures may reach -40°C, has been known to form aggregations of thousands.

The winter state of Arctic Brown and Black Bears *Ursus arctos* and *U. americanus* differs from true torpor, and might more correctly be termed a state of winter sleep or dormancy. In these bears (and other large mammals such as beavers and skunks) the fall in body temperature is limited to perhaps only 2–4°C. However, the heart rate falls significantly (by about 80%) and the metabolic rate falls to about half that of the waking state. This would not be a sufficient fall to prevent hypothermia unless the animal accumulated very large fat reserves prior to dormancy. Prior to the onset of winter the bears gorge on a high-calorie diet. During the winter they lose some 25% of their body weight. The animals avoid dehydration during dormancy by neither urinating nor defecating.

Female Polar *Ursus maritimus*, Brown and Black Bears also give birth during winter dormancy. The cubs are very small at birth. As a proportion of the weight of the mother, bear cubs, at 0.4%, are the smallest of any mammal; by comparison, a human baby is around 5% the weight of its mother. Even when they emerge from the birthing den, the bear cub usually weighs much less than 5% of its mother. Although female Polar Bears sleep the winter away, the males do not, though they may excavate a den in the snow in order to shelter during periods of bad weather.

Not all Arctic rodents enter a state of winter torpor. Lemmings, for instance, excavate burrow systems beneath the snow which, when lined with grass, allow communal living (with huddling augmenting the insulating value of the snow cover) while they remain active, feeding on sub-snow vegetation. This system is not without its drawbacks. Owls can hear the rodents even when they are moving below a substantial thickness of snow and will dive through to catch them (lemmings also have to contend with a summer hazard from raptors, which can detect rodents by looking for their urine, since this is visible at ultraviolet (UV) frequencies; in an attempt to overcome this, the lemmings have latrine chambers in their summer burrows).

Other mammalian adaptations

Beside torpor, the other principal mammalian strategy is to increase insulation, either internally by using layers of fat (called blubber), or externally through having a dense pelt. Blubber is the preferred option of most marine mammals, with fur being used mainly by terrestrial mammals. The Polar Bear, which spends significant parts of the year both on land or sea ice and in the sea, uses a combination of blubber and fur, while beavers and otters use fur only. Beavers and otters have a dense underfur that traps air as an insulator, and a coarser outer fur. This outer fur becomes wet and must be shaken to remove water when the animal emerges. Wet fur is only about 2% as efficient an insulator as dry fur, but these animals spend only relatively short times in water and so are able to maintain a dry underfur. The Sea Otter *Enhydra lutris*, which spends virtually its entire life in sea water, also uses fur as an insulator. Sea Otters have the densest fur of any mammal, with the hairs of the underfur reaching *c.*125,000/cm^2, giving a total of *c.*800 million on the entire body. This density allows the animals to survive in cold waters, but requires a great deal of grooming to remove the salt crystals that form within the pelt and to keep the fur in good condition. Sea Otters spend about 20% of their time grooming. Mother otters also frequently groom their young, the cub lying across the mother's chest, clear of the water. The Sea Otter has to maintain a very high metabolic rate to stay warm, and must eat up to a third of its body weight each day. Sea Otters also blow into their fur or create water bubbles in order to enhance the air layer at the base of the pelt. This creates a layer of still air close to the skin. Still air is a marvellous insulator (about seven times better than the rubber of a wet suit) and the best furs can create insulating layers that are about 60% as good.

The reduced efficiency of wet fur and the need for grooming mean that fur is not a comfortable option for pinnipeds and is out of the question for cetaceans. Nevertheless, pinnipeds do employ a combination of fur and blubber, though for most species the fur is sparse. Only for pups and the fur

Brown Bear, Karelia, Finland.

Female Polar Bear and cubs, sea ice off east Spitsbergen, Svalbard. The family has only recently emerged from the maternity den.

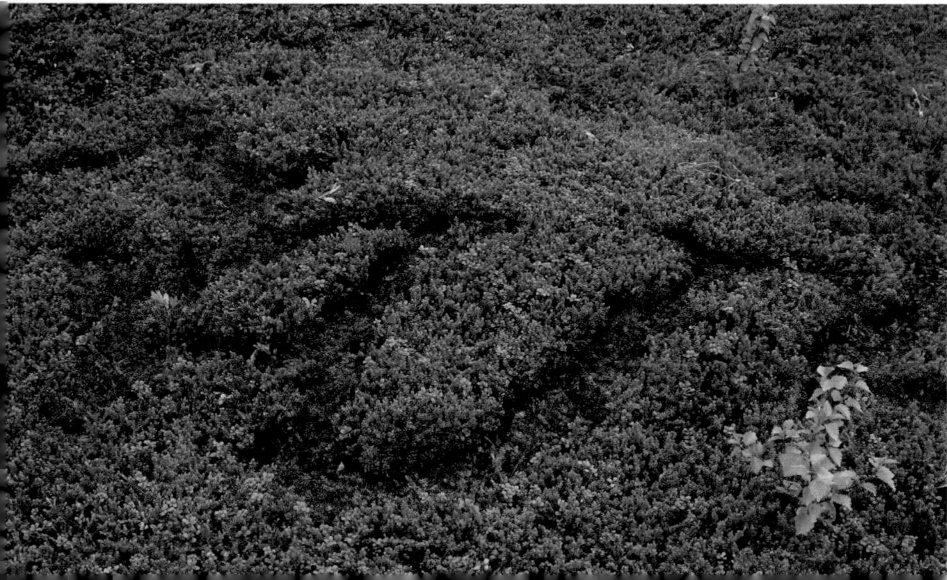

'Rodent roads', the name given by Norwegians to the paths made through vegetation by lemming and other rodents which are revealed by the spring snow melt. These roads were photographed beside Varangerfjord in north Norway.

seals is fur a significant aid to insulation. The pelt of the Northern Fur Seal *Callorhinus ursinus* was so prized for its luxurious fur that the species was hunted ruthlessly. An adult has a hair density of 40,000–60,000 hairs/cm^2, about 35–50% of the density of the Sea Otter. Seal pups are born with a coat known as lanugo, this coat being shed when the pup has accumulated a blubber layer by feeding on milk that is super-rich in fat. Lanugo is thick as the pups rely upon it for insulation, and usually white for camouflage as most Arctic seal pups are born on ice. Interestingly, the fur seals and seal pups do not curl as an aid to staying warm (by reducing exposed surface area) in the way that terrestrial mammals do (the Arctic Fox *Alopex lagopus* gains a further advantage by wrapping itself in its luxurious tail). Seals need to be relatively inflexible to allow efficient use of their hind flippers, while their body shape, optimised for hydrodynamic efficiency, also acts against curling. Their blubber insulation is also so efficient that overheating is the more usual problem for a hauled-out seal.

In principle, making fur thicker also increases its insulation properties. The insulation properties of fur are so good that Arctic species can maintain their metabolic rate over a wide range of ambient temperatures. This range, known as the thermoneutral zone (TNZ), is a measure of the adaptation of Arctic animals. The TNZ is narrow for tropical species, as they have evolved in an environment with a limited range of ambient temperatures. It widens for temperate species, and is massively enhanced for Arctic species. For example, a tropical mammal might have a TNZ of no more than 3 or 4°C, centred around 30°C. If the temperature falls below about 26°C the mammal must increase its metabolic rate to avoid hypothermia. For the Arctic Fox, the TNZ is very wide, about 60°C, extending to -40°C when it is clothed in its thicker winter fur, which extends over the paws, both top and bottom. When the temperature falls below -40°C, the fox's metabolic rate increases, but much more slowly than that of a tropical mammal as its fur continues to provide good insulation.

However, there is a limit to how thick fur can be. The Polar Bear can grow fur up to 6cm thick, a length that would not be feasible on a small rodent. Because of the limit on fur thickness, smaller animals must compensate by increasing their metabolic rate and burrowing beneath the snow in order to take advantage of its insulating properties. It is not winter but autumn that presents the greatest danger to small animals, as it brings low temperatures without snow cover. For larger animals that remain active, snow is a very real hazard. Deep snow makes movement difficult and energy-intensive, and blankets food. Moose *Alces alces* and woodland Reindeer create 'yards', relatively small areas of significant resources where they maintain tracks in the snow to minimise the problem.

Blubber

Subcutaneous blubber is important for insulation in marine mammals, including the Polar Bear (though not, as noted above, by the essentially marine Sea Otter). It has advantages

The pelts of the Sea Otter (*above*, sleeping in Resurrection Bay, Alaska) and the Northern Fur Seal (*left*, sleeping on St Paul, Pribilofs, Alaska) are so luxurious that hunting once almost drove both species towards extinction.

for marine mammals as weight is much less of an issue for these species, and not an issue at all for cetaceans. Indeed, for marine mammals bulk is an aid to keeping warm. Water is cold relative to body temperature, and it is highly conductive in comparison to air. Heat loss is proportional to body surface area, but thermal inertia (i.e. heat capacity) is proportional to body volume. Animals with small surface area-to-volume ratios can therefore maintain body temperature more easily. A straightforward example of this is the cooling time of dead animals; a dead shrew will cool to ambient temperature in a matter of minutes, while a dead whale cools much more slowly. The body temperature of a large, dead Blue Whale *Balaenoptera musculus* reduces by just 1–2°C over a 24-hour period.

Blubber comprises lipids (fatty substances), collagen fibres and other connective tissues, and water. Cetacean blubber is rich in collagen fibres; they prevent the non-rigid mass from hanging, bag-like, from the animal, which would influence streamlining. The lipid content of blubber varies from about 60% to 80%. It varies both from species to species and within an individual animal depending on age, position on the body and the time of year. In general, marine mammals have more blubber than is necessary purely for insulation purposes, the excess being an energy reserve. The insulating properties of blubber are dependent on thickness, lipid content and blood flow. Centimetre for centimetre it is a poorer insulator than fur, but it has the advantage of being essentially maintenance-free. But though not as effective as fur, blubber is so efficient in keeping pinnipeds and cetaceans warm in water that the animals need a method of keeping cool. This is particularly true for pinnipeds, which haul out of the water into an environment in which heat loss is usually much reduced (since water is a far better conductor of heat than air). To allow for this their flippers have a blood supply system in which a central artery is surrounded by a network of veins, another example of a counter-current heat exchange. When in the water the venal blood acts as an insulator for the inflowing arterial blood, absorbing heat in the process and so reducing overall heat loss. Then, when the animal is hauled out, venal blood flow can be increased, so increasing heat loss and helping the animal keep cool. As we have seen, similar systems are widespread in Arctic animals; for example, in the legs of Arctic birds and mammals, in the flippers of cetaceans, in the tails of rodents (such as beavers) and in the horns of ungulates. A particularly efficient counter-current system allows the tongues of baleen whales (particularly the Grey Whale *Eschrichtius robustus* and the right whales), which are large and uninsulated and therefore represent a potentially huge heat-loss surface, to remain cool even though they are richly supplied with blood.

Counter-current heat exchange systems result in the extremities being kept constantly cold relative to the core body temperature; the feet of an Arctic seabird may be below 5°C when the bird's core temperature is around 40°C. Similarly, the paws of an Arctic wolf might be only just above freezing and its nose at about 5°C, with a core temperature of 38°C. Counter-current exchangers may be used in conjunction with vasodilation of extremities, with the restriction of blood flow helping to reduce temperature. However, an animal must guard against frostbite; an occasional pulse of warm blood can be sent to the extremity if the ambient temperature is below 0°C.

Polar Bear fur

In common with other species, Polar Bears have guard hairs, longer and thicker hairs that add little to the insulation properties of the fur. The hairs of the underfur are wavy, which allows them to interlock when overlapped, trapping air, with the guard hairs protecting the integrity of the system when the animal is underwater. When the bear emerges from the water, the springiness of the guard hairs allows the fur to 'bounce' back and so encourages air entrapment. As the skin of Polar Bears is black, it was thought that these guard hairs 'piped' sunlight to the skin where its heat was absorbed. While the conditions that would have made this feasible certainly exist, further research has shown that it is, at best, a minor effect.

The adaptation of humans

Though the Inuit have lived in the Arctic for millennia and have developed a remarkable culture, their survival has depended on the use of specialised clothing derived from Arctic species. Humans evolved in the tropics and are essentially a tropical species. Although the Inuit, and other northern dwellers, have a greater ability to resist cold than their southern cousins, humans, in general, have a limited TNZ; if the temperature falls below about 27°C human metabolism must increase to maintain a core temperature of 37°C. If the temperature decreases further, clothing must be added to prevent hypothermia.

The colour of fur and feathers

The winter pelage of the Arctic Fox is not only thicker than its summer coat, but it is also white. This appears to be counter-productive as white is highly reflective, while a black pelage would absorb more of the Sun's radiation, allowing the animal to gain 'free' energy. But white camouflages the animal against winter's snow, a fact that has led to the assumption that all white coloration serves the same purpose. Animals that change colour tend to be prey species (even if, as in the case of the Arctic Fox, for example, the species is also a hunter) and so camouflage is beneficial. But this simple theory does not stand close scrutiny. Some Arctic species are white all the time – Polar Bears, the Snowy Owl and Gyrfalcon. A case could be made for this being to camouflage the animal against detection by its prey, the bears against the snow, the birds against the cloudy sky, but again there are contradictions. High-Arctic Wolves *Canis lupus* are white throughout the year and so are highly visible against snow-free tundra. Their main prey, the Arctic Hare, is also white throughout the year in the High Arctic. In these cases it seems that because the High Arctic summer is short, and moulting to a cryptic summer pelage is energetically costly (since it requires pigment production and hair growth), it makes more sense for these High Arctic species to forego the effort of moulting into a summer coat altogether. To further complicate matters, the Raven, a truly Arctic bird, is black at all times. In this case it seems that camouflage is not required – the bird is big enough to look after itself – and, as it is an omnivorous, opportunistic feeder, camouflage is of much less value.

Overall, several notes of caution must be sounded when considering colour. The UV vision of many animals has not been studied, but in those cases where it has, particularly in birds, UV sensitivity has often been found. It is, therefore, dangerous to make too many assumptions about animal coloration based solely on what we see as humans.

Counter-current heat exchangers must also work in reverse in cetaceans. Because the testes of male cetaceans are held within the body cavity to improve streamlining, the temperature of the organs would be too high for successful sperm production. Consequently, cold blood from the flippers and fins is diverted to cool the spermatic arteries to maintain a cooler environment. A similar system is employed to cool the uterus of female cetaceans, as the metabolism of the foetus is about double that of its mother and so overheating would otherwise be a problem.

One significant adaptation of Arctic mammals, both seals and terrestrial species, concerns the newborn. They experience a large temperature differential at birth, with as much as an 80°C change from the uterus to the outside world. Despite insulation this could lead to thermal shock. The youngster will shiver to generate heat – shivering as a means of heat production is also used by almost all adult endotherms – but it will also employ 'non-shivering thermogenesis', a process unique to young mammals. Heat is produced by the metabolism of brown adipose tissue (BAT or brown fat), which is found in

Most Arctic Foxes moult to a white pelage in winter, though the so-called Blue Foxes do not. The large and very luxurious tail is wrapped around the animal when it sleeps. The photograph was taken at Kongsfjorden, Spitsbergen, Svalbard.

Staying white in summer makes the Arctic Hares of Ellesmere Island, Canada very conspicuous (*above* and *left*), but the Wolves which prey on them also stay white and so are equally conspicuous.

Because of the high maintenance required for effective insulation from fur, blubber is the preferred option of most marine mammals such as these Walrus, photographed here at Fosterbukta, Hold With Hope, north-east Greenland.

body cavities and around major organs. The colour of this tissue type derives from the mass of capillaries within it. Heat production by brown fat metabolism is about ten times higher than that of normal shivering. As the young animal develops, its brown fat deposits diminish, though a small amount is maintained in the adults of some species, the Musk Ox, for example.

Size and shape

In addition to these specific adaptive strategies, the body shapes of northern species conform, in general, to a couple of 'rules', each of which was first propounded in the mid-19th century. Bergmann's Rule states that within a particular species, as latitude increases or ambient temperature decreases, there is a tendency for a larger body size in order to reduce the surface area-to-volume ratio, and so reduce relative heat loss. A large body size is helpful if periods of torpor are a winter strategy, allowing the storage of the fat necessary to survive periods of starvation. A larger body size also helps females to give birth to higher numbers of young, a useful investment as the Arctic summer is unpredictable: periods of harsh weather can spell disaster for small litters. The latter argument is supported by birds, which (again only generally) obey the Clutch-size Rule. This states that more northerly species tend to have larger clutch sizes. In general, northern species of birds also hatch after shorter incubation periods and fledge faster than their more southerly counterparts, each a response to the short Arctic summer.

Allen's Rule states that endotherms such as mammals tend to have smaller appendages in cold regions, to reduce heat loss. A good example of this would be the ears of the Arctic Fox compared to those of, for instance, the African Bat-eared Fox *Otocyon megalotis*, which has large ears through which heat can be lost. However, this rule would imply smaller feet and this is certainly not the case in many terrestrial Arctic mammals, as large feet allow easier travel over soft snow. The Arctic Hare *Lepus arcticus* has much larger feet than its southern cousins (the Snowshoe Hare *Lepus americanus* is actually named after this feature) and Wolves not only have large feet but long legs, the better to move over soft snow.

The biogeography of Arctic mammals

The current distribution, or biogeography, of birds and mammals in the Arctic depends not only on adaptation, but also on the distributions that preceded the last Ice Age. In general, northern species moved south as the ice advanced, then moved back north once the ice had retreated and acceptable habitats had been recreated. A good example of this is the Reindeer; subfossil evidence shows that this tundra species occurred periodically in England (and as far south as northern Spain and Italy) throughout the Pleistocene; the latest subfossils found so far date from 10,000BP, while the species clung on in Scotland until as recently as 8,000BP.

Indeed, the effect of the ice retreat can be seen by observing the distribution of more localised species. One good example is a bird of the Arctic fringe, the Ring Ouzel *Turdus torquatus*. This is a bird of cold climates. At the height of the last Ice Age its range probably extended across Europe and western Asia. When the ice retreated and the climate warmed, Ring Ouzels sought out the remaining colder areas for breeding (while spending the winter further south); today they are found in the uplands of southern Europe, on the Caucasus, on the uplands of Britain and Norway, and in northern Fennoscandia.

Refugia

In addition to the general northward movement of species after the last Ice Age, there were ice-free areas in which species would have been able to survive the glaciation. Nunataks have already been mentioned as potential 'micro-refugia'. Much larger refugia also existed; these formed in north-west Siberia (the Angaron refuge), in north-east Greenland (the Peary Land refuge) and on some Arctic Canadian islands (e.g. the Banksian refuge). The most important refuge was Beringia, an area that included ice-free areas in Alaska, Yukon and north-east Siberia, and the negotiable land bridge between the two continents that now lies beneath the waters of the Bering Strait. These refugia are the basis of the three most important tundra areas of today's Arctic in terms of species numbers, emphasising their importance to Arctic biogeography: Russia's Taimyr Peninsula (with 43 species of bird), Canada's Arctic islands (42 species) and the Beringia region of east Siberia and west Alaska (47 species). Each of these areas has endemic species, Beringia having the greatest number. For bird species the Bering land bridge may have been useful, but even today the narrow Bering Strait is little impediment to birds, and several have extended their ranges across it since the last time Beringia was above the sea. The Arctic Warbler *Phylloscopus borealis* has spread east from Siberia to Alaska, while the Grey-cheeked Thrush *Catharus minimus* and Yellow-rumped Warbler *Dendroica coronata* have travelled the other way.

Beringia was important not only as a refuge but also because it offered a bridge to mammal species, including humans, between Asia and the Americas. However, the exact role Beringia played in the movement of mammals is debatable, in large part because there is no consensus on the land bridge's vegetation, evidence from the pollen analysis of lake sediments in Alaska being at odds with that from the study of surface remains of the permafrost near the Seward Peninsula maar lakes. The pollen analysis suggests that Beringia was a polar desert (it is the density of pollen rather than the number of species that implies this), unable to sustain herds of ungulates spreading east. However, ejected material from maar explosions, a plug of permafrost topped with the actual surface vegetation of Beringia, suggests a richer vegetation, one capable of supporting herds.

Further work is required to resolve the paradox, though what is clear is that Beringia did indeed represent a corridor for mammalian migration and a range of large-mammal groups of Eurasian origins were established in northern North America by the end of the last Ice Age. The species included mammoths and mastodons, horses (a group that actually evolved in North America, expanded into Eurasia and then re-invaded following extinction in the Americas), several species of bison, Stag-moose *Cervalces*, Giant Beaver *Castoroides* (the size of a Black Bear, with huge incisors), and carnivores such as sabre-toothed cats, American Lion *Panthera atrox*, Dire Wolf *Canis dirus* (a larger, more formidable version of the Timber Wolf), and the massive Short-faced Bear *Arctodus* (moose-sized, but apparently a fast-moving animal). Many of these large mammals, some 40 in total, became extinct in a very short period (3,000 years or less) from about 12,000BP, an extinction that raises the question – why? Particularly as a similar level of species extinction did not occur in Eurasia. There are several possible explanations. One suggests over-hunting by humans, the logic being that people with sophisticated hunting techniques crossed the Beringia land bridge and came into contact with species that had never been hunted (by humans) and so had not evolved to become wary and elusive as they had in Africa and Eurasia. The theory suggests that humans would have concentrated on large herbivores and that some carnivores and scavengers would have become extinct as a result of loss of prey. But though humans are a ferocious and relentless predator, could people really have killed off entire species, reducing numbers below the limit of biological survival continent-wide?

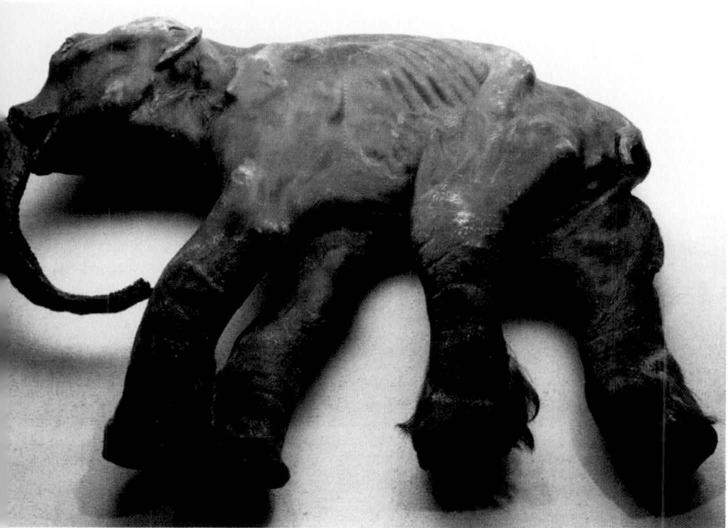

Another theory is that the change of climate was responsible for the extinctions. But a changing climate affects all species, so why should North American species fare worse than those of Eurasia, particularly as the continent is vast, allowing species to move to more equable areas? And besides, such groups had survived the transition from glacial to interglacial period (and *vice versa*) many times before. Perhaps it was disease that accounted for the extinctions, pathogens brought from Asia – perhaps by humans or their commensals – killing off local animals, which had no time to develop immunity. Probably it was a combination of all these factors, perhaps with the addition of others yet to be identified.

Refugia and speciation

As well as the major refugia formed by the uneven distribution of ice during the last glacial maximum, refugia would also have been formed during the glacial and interglacial periods of the entire 250,000 years of the late Quaternary ice ages. Evidence from studies of mitochondrial (mt) DNA support this, indicating that in some species identifiable changes occurred each time populations were separated by glaciation events, with genetic divergence resulting in the formation of distinct subspecies. A good example is the Dunlin *Calidris alpina*, a wader with a circumpolar distribution. The Dunlin is polytypic, with subspecies distinguished only by subtle differences in plumage colour and pattern. mtDNA studies indicate that the oldest form of the bird is the subspecies that breeds in central Canada, and that this split from an ancestral form about 225,000 years ago, a time that coincides with the Holstein interglacial. The studies indicate that further splits occurred during the Emian interglacial (120,000 years ago), and during a glacial period about 75,000 years ago. These data suggest that during interglacial periods the Dunlin was able to expand its range, populations then being isolated by further glaciation. Splits during a glacial period would arise if significant ice tongues developed, isolating populations on ice-free tundra to either side.

Such subspecific differentiation is possible only if the ancestral form of the species had a significant distribution. If that was not the case then glaciation might isolate an entire population, the species only being able to expand its range when the ice retreated. mtDNA studies indicate that this has also occurred, some northern species being monotypic, while in others the differences between subspecies indicate that splits have occurred only in relatively recent times. The Ruddy Turnstone *Arenaria interpres* is a good example of this phenomenon, having few (and virtually identical) subspecies.

Dima, the baby Mammoth in St Petersburg's Zoological Museum. The complete body was found on 23 June 1977 on the bank of the Dima river near Magadan. Dima is believed to have been about 6 months old when she became lost and died, some 40,000 years ago. She weighed about 90kg and stood about 1m tall.

In the case of the Dunlin, glaciation has driven speciation – the development of new species or subspecies – east–west, as might be expected by an ice front that developed southwards, with ice tongues separating populations to either side. However, the ice could also work north–south, pushing one population of a species southwards while another remained in a northern refuge. For example, this process may have allowed the evolution of the two forms of diver seen in North America. The Great Northern Diver *Gavia immer* and the White-billed Diver *G. adamsii* are so similar that some authorities consider them subspecies of a single species. In general, in North America the Great Northern Diver breeds to the south of the White-billed, suggesting that an ancestral form remained in a northern refuge, from where it spread west to Siberia, while another population moved south and evolved subtle differences. A similar separation appears to have occurred with an ancestral form of sheep. During one of the Ice Ages a population became isolated in a forerunner of Beringia, while another moved south ahead of the ice and occupied the mountains of the western United States. The northern species is Dall's Sheep *Ovis dalli*, the southern one the Bighorn Sheep *O. Canadensis*.

An equally interesting example of north-south speciation is seen in the Gyrfalcon and Saker Falcon *Falco cherrug*. The former is one of the Arctic's most magnificent and emblematic birds; it is the world's largest falcon, and some individuals are almost entirely white. The Saker is a more southerly bird, breeding on the steppes of southern Russia and Mongolia. The birds look very similar and interbreeding by falconers has shown that cross-bred chicks are fertile, indicating that the two species are very closely related. In this case, it seems that the separation of two populations of an ancestral form occurred when, after the ice had pushed one population south, the development of the taiga across Asia separated the two completely; the falcons, being birds of open country, did not cross the forest belt. A similar process is assumed to have given rise to the Polar Bear, when a population of Brown Bears was isolated to the north of the ice. A study of mtDNA of these two species suggests a divergence within the last few hundred thousand years, perhaps even fewer. As with the Gyr and Saker, Polar and Brown Bears can mate and produce fertile offspring.

Although the differences between Dunlin subspecies are minor, as are the differences between the two divers, there are more pronounced variations between the two falcon species (though the casual observer might be confused if a pale Saker and darker Gyr were seen together), and Polar and Brown Bears are very different. Adaptations required for survival in the harshest of environments have clearly hastened the evolution of the Polar Bear.

Merging populations

With the retreat of the ice, populations could expand their ranges, perhaps contacting populations from which they had been long isolated. When contact occurred hybridisation might have taken place (the populations being subspecies and so able to interbreed), or the two populations might overlap without interbreeding (the populations then being considered species). A third outcome is also possible, the two populations occupying slightly different ecological niches so that they appear in adjacent habitats or geographical areas. The gull

Dunlin (*above*, photographed on Southampton Island, Canada) and Dall's Sheep (*right*, photographed above the Turnagain Arm, southern Alaska) provide clear evidence of speciation.

A small flock of mixed blue and white Snow Geese, Southampton Island, Canada.

species (or subspecies) of the Arctic – for example Iceland *Larus glaucoides*, Thayer's *L. thayeri* and Kumlien's Gulls *L. g. kumlieni* – provide a good example of this. Many authorities consider Iceland and Thayer's to have derived from a single ancestral gull, populations of which were glacially separated. With the retreat of the ice the two populations met again, with Kumlien's being the hybrid form.

One of the most interesting examples of contact between populations is the merging of two forms of the Snow Goose *Anser caerulescens*. Until the early years of the 20th century there were two distinct populations of geese, white geese in western North America and 'blue' geese to the east. So distinct is the colour of the two that it was long assumed that they were two different species, the Snow Goose and the Blue Goose, a view reinforced by the fact that the two geese did not share either breeding or wintering ranges. Changes in agricultural practices then allowed the geese to expand their populations and ranges. When the two forms met they interbred, the young being fertile so population merging could occur. Not until the 1960s was it finally confirmed that the geese are colour morphs of a single species – the Snow Goose. As the blue morph is genetically dominant, the population is tending to become blue, though this is a slow process as the birds prefer mating with geese of their own colour. Almost all flocks of Snow Geese now comprise some birds that are white, some that are blue and some that are intermediate between the two.

To add further interest to the Snow Goose story and its value in understanding the way in which the Ice Ages have isolated populations, and what happens when the ice retreats, there are also two other goose types to be considered. Blue and white Snow Geese make up about 80% of the total population of the species. The other 20% comprises a larger form of the goose, sometimes called the Greater Snow Goose, which breeds on the eastern coast of North America and on Greenland. These birds are larger and heavier, and mostly white, but there is also a blue form – though it is very rare. In the central Canadian Arctic there is another goose species, Ross's Goose (*Anser rossii*), which is almost identical to the white Snow Goose but about half the size. Blue forms of Ross's are also known, but these, too, are very rare. The rare blue morphs of Greater Snow and Ross's Geese might have resulted from hybridisation with blue Snow Geese. There is also the possibility of 'egg dumping', as it is known that some female Snow Geese occasionally lay eggs in the nests of other birds if their own clutch is already as large as they can manage. Blue Snow goslings imprinting on Ross's Goose parents might then hybridise with Ross's Geese when they mature.

When the ice retreated, populations could expand their ranges northwards. Another broad biological rule, Rapoport's Rule, states that, in general, northern species have larger ranges than their southern cousins because of the relative lack of food in northern habitats. Combined with the shrinkage of the circumference of the Earth towards the North Pole and the fact that the Arctic is surrounded by a near-continuous continental chain, an expansion of population and, therefore, range, means that the occurrence of circumpolar species increases with latitude. Many Arctic species are circumpolar, and while the majority of these are birds, some are mammals – Polar and Brown Bears, Reindeer, Arctic Fox, Musk Ox. There are, of course, exceptions to Rapoport's Rule (indeed, it really applies only to resident terrestrial vertebrates). One of the most pronounced exceptions is an Arctic breeding species, the Bristle-thighed Curlew *Numenius tahitiensis*. The species breeding range in Alaska is much smaller than the available habitat. In this case population size is capped by the extent of the species' wintering quarters, small Pacific islands that are not capable of accommodating the population that might be expected from the size of the potential breeding range.

The seas between Greenland, Iceland and Eurasia were never crossed by land bridges, so mammalian traffic between Eurasia and North America during the Pleistocene must have been via Beringia. For birds these gaps were less important; on Greenland about 70% of the breeding bird species are circumpolar. As the island is thought to have been completely covered by ice until about 6,000 years ago, all breeding land birds

Interestingly, although the Beringia land bridge assisted in the expansion of Eurasian species into North America, it may also have assisted speciation by preventing the Pacific and Atlantic populations of ancestral species from interbreeding. The distribution of northern auks is highly asymmetric, with far more species in the north Pacific than in the north Atlantic. It is assumed that the few which are circumpolar – three species of guillemot – and the one that shows similarities – the Atlantic Puffin *Fratercula arctica*, which is very similar to the two Pacific puffins – crossed from one ocean to the other via the Arctic Ocean (probably some time in the early Pleistocene), a route that was then closed to them by the presence of Beringia and the frozen sea to the north. The evolution of the numerous

have arrived during that period. Immigration of species has occurred in both directions; Nearctic species breed on the west coast, and Palearctic species on the east coast. Although Eurasian species could reach North America most easily across Beringia, it was also possible for them to head for the Americas westwards, with Iceland and Greenland stepping stones *en route* to the eastern coast of Canada. One species, the Northern Wheatear *Oenanthe oenanthe*, actually spread to North America in both directions; it now breeds in eastern Canada and in Alaska and the Yukon Territory, but not in the huge expanse of the Arctic that lies between. The winter migration of some populations continues to indicate their origins; some species that breed in North America migrate to Eurasia, using wintering grounds that have been visited for millennia, since long before the expansion of the breeding range. A classic example of this is seen in the Light-bellied Brent Goose population *Branta bernicla hrota* of eastern Canada, which winters in Ireland, crossing Greenland and Iceland on a journey that forms the longest migration flight of any Arctic goose.

Above
Atlantic Puffin, Kjorholmane, Norway.

Right
Horned Puffin.

Far right
Tufted Puffins.

The two Pacific puffins were photographed on St Paul Island, Pribilofs.

species of auklets and murrelets in the Pacific and why there is only one corresponding form in the Atlantic (the Little Auk *Alle alle*) is one of the puzzles of Arctic biogeography. The asymmetry in the number of auk species is mirrored in the distribution of pinnipeds that have a similar diet; again the reasons for this are not clearly understood. Much less of a puzzle is the fact that in both the Atlantic and the Pacific there are more species (in general, rather than just of auks) on the eastern sides than on the western sides because of the direction of cold, productive currents.

A related issue concerns the distribution of penguins – why are there no penguins in the Arctic? The Arctic birds that most closely resemble the penguins in terms of diving ability are the larger auks, the smaller auklets and murrelets more closely resembling the diving petrels. Penguins are essentially confined to the southern polar region, but do extend northwards where cold water currents allow. It is thought that there are several reasons why penguins have not reached the northern hemisphere. Firstly, warmer waters are less productive. As the hunting method of penguins requires a large energy input, tropical seas are therefore unlikely to be able to support the birds. Secondly, the number of breeding sites free from terrestrial predators declines in equatorial areas, particularly in the Atlantic. Auks probably did not cross the equator southwards for similar reasons. While foot-swimmers such as grebes have colonised both hemispheres, wing-swimmers have not.

Wing-swimming is a high-energy technique, as is the flight of auks, which all have short, rapidly beating wings. Auks need to be volant because there are terrestrial predators in the north and the birds need to nest on cliffs the better to avoid them (though the flightless Great Auk *Pinguinus impennis* survived until people with the capacity to reach its limited breeding sites arrived). Northern auks also breed preferentially on islands, a good strategy for avoiding terrestrial predators, except in the High Arctic where annual sea ice allows predators to reach them. Of the auks only the Atlantic Puffin is a truly ground-nesting bird (their nests being set at the ends of excavated burrows), the other auks being ledge nesters. However, Atlantic Puffins nest primarily on islands south of the sea ice limit. Where rats, cats or pigs have been introduced, Atlantic Puffin colonies have been rapidly depopulated, usually to the point where the island has been completely abandoned. The introduction of Arctic Foxes to some Aleutian Islands (for fur farming) led to similar destruction of those auks that nested in vulnerable positions.

Human influences on biogeography

As noted above, the spread of the Snow Goose may have been as a result of human changes to the environment. People have also aided other species, the population increase and range expansion of both the Northern Fulmar *Fulmarus glacialis* and Great Skua *Stercorarius skua* being attributed to the growth of the fishing industry, since fish processing on ships produces a great deal of waste. However, human influence has only rarely been beneficial. Humans may have caused or hastened the extinction of the mammoths and other megafauna. Arctic cetaceans have suffered from overhunting, fur-bearing mammals have been threatened and, in some cases, almost extirpated, and some bird species have been drastically reduced by egg-collection and hunting. The Great Auk was driven to extinction by the mid-19th century (the last recorded birds were killed in 1844, the final phase of extirpation being by specimen collectors), and the once-abundant Eskimo Curlew *Numenius borealis* was relentlessly hunted during its migration across the southern United States. This, together with loss of habitat and a consequent loss of essential food resources when the prairies were converted to agricultural land means that this species is now very probably extinct; there has been no confirmed sighting of the bird since 1963, though apparently reliable sightings were made as recently as the mid-1980s. The flightless Spectacled Cormorant *Phalocrocorax perspicillatus* was first described by Steller during the Bering expedition of 1741–42; it was extinct by the 1850s. Even more dramatic and appalling was the fate of Steller's Sea Cow *Hydrodamalis gigas*), which was described by Steller on the same voyage. It was hunted to extinction within 27 years, its fate sealed by a lethal combination of docility, slowness and being good eating (see also p488).

Evidence now suggests that humans are altering the earth's climate. The warming of the Arctic will have a direct, and disastrous, effect on many Arctic species. But there will also be a more subtle effect. Iceland has gained ten bird species since the early 20th century, probably in large part due to climatic changes as there has been little change in land usage on the island, since Iceland's geology negates significant increases or changes in agriculture. Climatic changes and this northern movement of bird species has pushed other Arctic species further north – but there is a limit to how far north they can go, as birds need land sites for nesting. The same effect is also seen in the sea; as fish species move north, traditional hunting grounds for birds disappear. Nest sites are chosen to be close to those traditional sites, so chicks starve; population decreases add to the problems of a shrinking range. If global warming continues this double-edged effect will, ultimately, result in a dramatic reduction in the number of Arctic species.

Great Auk, illustrated in Audubon's *Birds of America*.

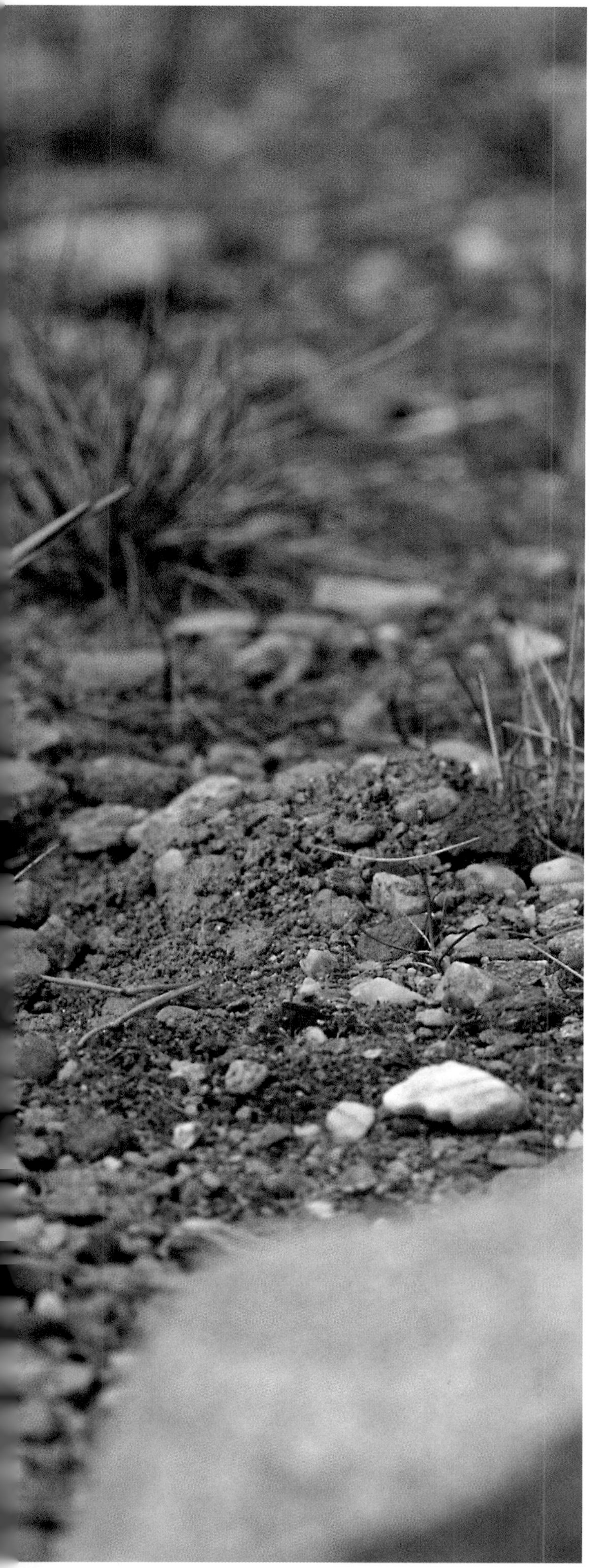

16. Arctic Wildlife

In the following sections wildlife that breeds beyond, or may be seen beyond, the Arctic boundary as defined in this book is explored. For some species with ranges whose northern extent barely overlaps the Arctic, only brief notes are given. For some areas – Fennoscandia, Kamchatka and southern Alaska – a more pragmatic approach has been required as many non-Arctic species may be seen in those areas; some may also occasionally be found breeding. For those areas, therefore, the species lists that could be developed from the following sections are not complete, species that are essentially non-Arctic having been omitted.

For each species with an IUCN and/or CITES classification, the classification is given.

IUCN and CITES

In 1963 Sir Peter Scott (son of Robert Falcon Scott and the driving force behind the founding of the UK's Wildfowl and Wetlands Trust) suggested the setting up of 'a register of threatened wildlife that includes definitions of degrees of threat'. That register is now maintained by the International Union for the Conservation of Nature and Natural Resources (IUCN) and it is periodically published as 'Red Lists' or 'Red Data Books'. A series of threat categories are defined and allocated to species on the lists. Of the species evaluated some have insufficient data for an assessment of the risk to their survival. These are classified as **Data Deficient**. For those with adequate data, the category of **Threatened** species is subdivided. The most extreme sub-category is **Extinct** where there is no reasonable doubt that the species has disappeared. **Extinct in the Wild** means the species exists only in cultivation, captivity or naturalised away from its former range. **Critically Endangered** means the species has an extremely high risk of extinction in the wild in the immediate future. **Endangered** means a very high risk of extinction in the near future. **Vulnerable** means a high risk of extinction in the near future. **Near-threatened** species are at lower risk of extinction and are of less immediate concern. A further sub-category of Threatened species, **Least Concern**, covers species with a lower risk again. In the species accounts below the relevant categories are noted for all Arctic birds and mammals.

The international trade in at-risk species is controlled by the Convention on International Trade in Endangered Species of Wild Fauna and Flora (CITES). The species covered by CITES are listed in three Appendices. **Appendix I** species are those threatened by extinction. Trade in these is permitted only in exceptional circumstances. **Appendix II** species are less vulnerable, but unregulated trade is incompatible with long-term survival. **Appendix III** species are protected in at least one country, that country having requested others to control trade. In the species accounts below the relevant CITES Appendix is noted. Appendix III species are not listed for non-Arctic countries.

Far left
Arctic Tern, Seward Peninsula, Alaska.

Left
Stoat (Long-tailed Weasel) Kodiak Island, Alaska.

Arctic Birds

Throughout the species accounts, measurements are given. These are L (length), WS (wingspan) and W (weight). Taxonomy and taxonomic order broadly follow the *Clements Checklist of the Birds of the World* (6th edition, 2007); nomenclature generally follows Gill and Wright's *Birds of the World: Recommended English Names* (2007).

DIVERS

With their delicately patterned plumage – seemingly the work of a talented painter rather than comprising individual feathers – the divers are among the most attractive of all Arctic birds. For many, the haunting wailing or yodelling call of the Great Northern Diver is also redolent of the wilderness. It is no surprise to discover that these birds have become entwined in the myths of northern dwellers. In North America the call was thought to be the anguished cry of the dead calling for a lost love. This evocation led to the belief that the birds guided the dead to the spirit world, and sometimes the skull of a diver would accompany grave goods, carved ivory eyes replacing the originals, the better for it to find the correct pathway. The bird's diving abilities also led to the belief that it could see in the dark and, therefore, could restore sight to blind people, the bird diving with the blind person on its back. It was claimed that the prominent white markings on the backs of the Great Northern and White-billed Divers were necklaces presented to the birds in thanks. In Siberia, native people incorporated the birds into creation myths, claiming that mud dredged from the bottom of the sea and brought to the surface on a diver's webbed foot began the process of building the land. Several Inuit dances included diver masks. Today, the Canadians have the Great Northern Diver (or Common Loon) on their one-dollar coin, as a reminder of the wilderness that holds such a special place in the country's heart. Its appearance on the coin explains why, to the puzzlement of first-time visitors from Europe, the coin is frequently called a 'loonie'.

Yet despite the reverence, the birds were killed for both meat and clothing. The dense feathers allowed a diver carcass to fit snugly on the head: the clothing of the Greenland mummies included an inner parka, the hood of which was made from the skins of two Red-throated Divers. The waterproof skins were also useful for carrying the means to prepare fire, with the bird being gutted to produce a bag. These are still occasionally seen in Nunavut (where it is called a loonie bag).

Diver is the British name for the five species of the genus *Gavia*, birds so highly specialised for swimming that they have considerable difficulty walking. It is this inability that is believed to be the basis of the North American name – loon – for the birds, the word deriving from the Old Norse word *lømr*, lame or clumsy. The feet are webbed between the three front toes, with the legs positioned far back on the body, allowing the thrust from the feet to be developed behind the body for maximum efficiency when diving. The birds are superb divers, reaching depths of up to 75m, though much shallower dives are more normal. Immersion is usually for about 45s, though longer dives have been recorded. The effi-ciency of the bird underwater is clear to the observer; they are shy birds, and an approach invariably results in the bird submerging, its reappearance usually being startlingly far away. Underwater, the bird draws a transparent nictitating membrane across its eye as a form of 'contact lens' so as to retain excellent vision. During the paddle stroke, just prior to the recovery of the feet, there is a brief moment when the head remains stationary relative to the bird's surroundings so that it can reassess the position of prey. The wings are held close to

With a lot of frantic scampering and wing-beating a Red-throated Diver becomes airborne in southern Kamchatka, Russia. The larger divers must work even harder over a long length of water for the same result.

> **Wing loading**
>
> Wing loading expresses the weight of a bird relative to the size (i.e. surface area) of its wing and is usually measured in N/m^2. Birds with low wing loadings (such as swifts and swallows with loadings of 15–20 N/m^2) are agile fliers and can feed on the wing. The wing loadings of divers (more than $100N/m^2$) are among the highest of any bird.

Centre
Pacific Divers at dawn, Mackenzie delta, Canada.

Great Northern Diver (Common Loon) in the Barren Lands of North West Territories, Canada.

the body to improve streamlining, though they are occasionally used to assist in turning, which gives the birds excellent manoeuvrability, allowing them to pursue and catch fish. The dagger-like bill is a highly efficient fishing tool. Other adaptations to a life spent largely on water include dense plumage as insulation against the chill, a counter-current heat exchanger to reduce heat loss from the feet and heavy bones that reduce buoyancy; divers sit noticeably lower in the water than most other aquatic birds.

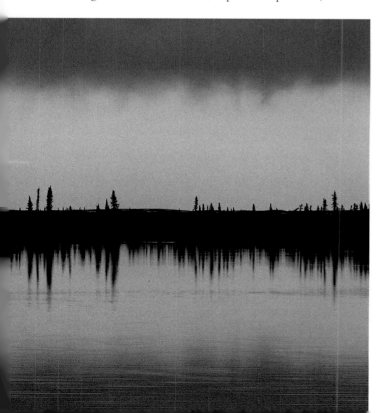

On land the position of the legs makes walking difficult and divers rarely travel far from water. The larger species move by a series of inelegant hops or an equally inelegant shuffle, with the body held at an angle. Only the smallest species, the Red-throated Diver, is capable of a more upright stance. Divers have very low wing loadings. Because of the difficulty of locomotion on land, the birds take off from water. On water the birds scurry across the surface to obtain speed before lifting off. They then gain height slowly. As a consequence divers look for large lakes that offer long stretches of water. If the lake is smaller and tree-surrounded, it is not unusual for the birds to have to circle, gaining height, until they are high enough to clear the trees. Yet despite these problems, divers are strong fliers, often travelling considerable distances to feed when they are rearing chicks. The position of the legs also prevents the birds from landing feet first as other water birds (e.g. swans) do. In landing the diver resembles a seaplane, landing undercarriage-free, on its underside. In flight the feet extend beyond the tail, a diagnostic characteristic.

Divers eat a variety of fish species, though they will make do with just one kind if that is all their lake provides. They also eat amphibians and shellfish. The preferred nest site is an islet or floating mass of vegetation, but a marshy part of the lake shore will be used if these are not available. The nest, a pile of aquatic vegetation, is always close to the water because of the birds' poor walking abilities. There are usually two eggs, though one is not uncommon. The chicks are downy and precocial, able to swim within 1 or 2 days, though they often rest on their parents' backs where they snuggle beneath the wings for warmth. Divers breed at two or three years of age. The birds are migratory, but do not travel far from the breeding territories.

Great Northern Diver (Common Loon)

Gavia immer

L: 70–90cm. WS: 120–150cm. W: 3.8–4.4kg, exceptionally to 6kg.

A magnificent bird, with black head and prominent red eye. The throat is black, ringed by a black-and-white striped collar, with broader areas of striping on the sides of the neck. The upperparts are checked black-and-white, the underparts white. Sexes similar. In winter the red eye is lost, as is the chequerboard back and throat collar. Requires a large area for breeding, either a sizeable lake or a good area of a larger one.

Great Northern Divers breeds across northern North America, including southern Baffin Island, on Greenland, Iceland, Jan Mayen and Bear Island. In winter they may be seen off both coasts of the USA, and off the coasts of the British Isles and Norway.

White-billed Diver (Yellow-billed Loon)

Gavia adamsii

L: 80–90cm. WS: 135–150cm. W: 4.5–5.5kg, exceptionally to 6.5kg.

The largest of the divers. The bill of the adults varies in colour from pale yellow to ivory (which allows both European and

Above top
Red-throated Diver, southern Kamchatka, Russia.

Above lower
All divers nest either on floating vegetation or at the water's edge because of their difficulty with walking. This nest is of Red-throated Divers in southern Kamchatka, Russia.

American names to be correct). The bird is similar to the Great Northern Diver, but the chequerboard pattern of the upperparts has fewer, but larger, white spots. The white areas of the throat stripes are also larger. Sexes similar. Winter birds as Great Northern, but duller overall. The two species evolved from a single ancestral species with populations isolated during the Ice Ages; some authorities consider the two conspecific. In habits and calls the two species are similar.

Threat ceremonies of the Red-throated Diver

In a paper in 1923 the British biologist Sir Julian Huxley – grandson of T. H. Huxley, who famously took on Bishop Wilberforce as part of his defence of Charles Darwin – noted the ceremonies that a pair of Red-throated Divers undertake when another diver invades their territory. They might perform what Huxley called the Snake Ceremony, the pair swimming slowly side by side with necks outstretched. They then call in duet as they point their bills downwards. The ceremony often develops into Huxley's 'Plesiosaur Race', a silent dance in which the two birds dip their tails and rear-up, extending their necks and bills upwards and running across the water. The whole 'dance' is highly synchronised and, curiously, the intruder will occasionally join in before beating a retreat. Other divers have territorial displays, but none are so elaborate.

White-billed Divers breed along the northern coast of Russia to the east of the Urals, and on the southern island of Novaya Zemlya. In North America breeds in northern Alaska and the central Canadian Arctic, including Banks and Victoria islands. In winter they are seen off the north Norway coast, in the Bering Sea and the Great Slave Lake.

Black-throated Diver (Arctic Loon)

Gavia arctica

L: 60–75cm. WS: 110–130cm. W 1.8–2.5kg with some birds to 3.4kg.

Similar in appearance to the Great Northern Diver, though the striped patches on the neck are much larger and the head and nape are pale grey. Sexes similar. In winter the birds lose the marvellous patterning. As with the larger bird this species holds a lake or large area of a lake, seeing off intruders with loud calls and a menacing show of throat-showing and bill-dipping. Nest on islets, at the lake shore and even occasionally in sheltered bays if the tidal reach is low. Incubation and chick rearing as the Great Northern Diver.

Black-throated Divers breed in Fennoscandia, across Arctic Russia and in Kamchatka, with a few pairs also breeding in western Alaska. In winter birds are seen off the Japanese coast, and in the North Sea and North Atlantic.

Pacific Diver (Pacific Loon)

Gavia pacifica

L: 57–70cm. WS: 105–120cm. W: 1.8–2.2kg.

Very similar to Black-throated Diver in breeding and winter plumages, though the latter has a white flank patch, which is diagnostic. The two birds share habitats, habits and calls and for many years it was assumed that the Pacific Diver was a subspecies of Black-throated. However, it was then discovered that the two birds bred sympatrically in both Alaska and Chukotka.

Pacific Divers breed across North America and on the southern Canadian Arctic islands, and also in north-eastern Chukotka. In winter Pacific Divers are seen in the Bering Sea off Kamchatka and along the western US coast.

Red-throated Diver (Red-throated Loon)

Gavia stellata

L: 55–70cm. WS: 105–115cm. W: 1.1–1.8kg.

The smallest of the divers and, with a red throat that develops for the breeding season, one of the most attractive. The head and remainder of the neck are pale grey. The upperparts lack the chequerboarding of the larger divers, being grey-brown with white speckling. Sexes similar. In winter the grey neck and red throat are lost The call of the Red-throated Diver is also distinct from the voices of the other divers, being more duck- or goose-like. Being smaller, Red-throated Divers can nest on smaller lakes. This often means that the local food supply is inadequate for chick-rearing, the birds having to fly to gather food.

Red-throated Divers are circumpolar, breeding on the northern Canadian islands, Greenland, Iceland, Svalbard, Fennoscandia and Russia's Arctic coast and islands. In winter they are seen in the North Atlantic, North Sea, Bering Sea and North Pacific.

GREBES

Though superficially similar to divers, grebes have some distinctly different characteristics, suggesting a very different evolutionary path. The feet are not webbed, the toes being lobed to provide the paddles necessary for pursuit of prey underwater. The paddle stroke is also different from that of divers, a surface paddling grebe using the feet one at a time, and twisting them so that they move parallel to the surface. Both the ankle and toe joints are very flexible, giving the bird great manoeuvrability underwater, the feet operating both as paddles and rudder. As with the divers, the feet are placed far back on the body, making walking difficult. Grebes seem to have even more problems than divers on land, often falling over during their short journeys. The birds do not share the divers' heavy bone structure; grebes reduce their buoyancy by forcing air out from between their feathers to dive.

Apart from the flight feathers, grebes shed and replace their feathers continuously throughout the year, and have the curious habit of ingesting moulted feathers. The birds also drink more than would be expected for their size, the water and feathers creating a paste-like mass that can amount to half the stomach volume. At intervals paste is regurgitated, leading to the suggestion that it allows the bird to rid itself of fish bones that might otherwise damage the lining of the digestive tract. However, other fish-eaters do not share the habit. The paste may also help the birds rid themselves of intestinal parasites.

Red-necked Grebe, Great Slave Lake, North West Territories, Canada.

Grebes have conspicuous courtship ceremonies, which caught the eye of Sir Julian Huxley before he had published his observations on divers. A pair of birds will stand upright on the water, breast-to-breast, with the heads turning from side to side. They may then swim side by side, or even rush across the water side by side while remaining upright. In the 'weed ceremony' the birds dive together, each surfacing with its bill filled with weeds. They then stand facing each other, their heads moving sideways to display the weeds. The weeds may be used to build the nest, which comprises a heap of weed floating in the chosen pond or lake. The nest is anchored to aquatic vegetation and 3–5 eggs are usually laid. The chicks are downy, leave the nest soon after hatching and often ride on their parents' backs. They are fed the same diet as the parent birds – fish and aquatic invertebrates. The prey is collected in short dives, usually less than 30s in duration, at moderate depths of up to 20m.

Grebes are poor fliers in comparison to divers, the wings beating so fast the birds appear panic-stricken. As a consequence they are rarely seen in flight at their breeding

Slavonian Grebe pair, Great Slave Lake, North West Territories Canada.

Nesting Slavonian Grebe, Churchill, Manitoba, Canada.

territories. Nevertheless, the two Arctic breeding grebes are migra-tory, moving to southern coastal waters in winter. On migration they frequently fly at night. This has led to instances where in the early morning light exhausted birds have mistaken wet roads for streams and landed. They are then stranded, being unable to take off from land.

The luxurious nature of grebe plumage led to a European fashion fad for 'grebe fur', which was used to trim lady's clothing. This led to severe reductions in grebe numbers in Europe, though numbers have now increased. Some grebe species are endangered by habitat destruction.

Red-necked Grebe

Podiceps grisegena

L: 24–30cm. WS: 75–85cm. W: 700–900g, with North American birds to 1.1kg.

Handsome birds with black crowns, white or pale grey faces and a red neck in breeding plumage. The upperparts are grey-brown, the underparts paler. Sexes similar. In winter the birds lose the bright coloration, being dull brown and white. Highly territorial and very aggressive during the breeding season, Red-necked Grebes have been known to kill intruding ducks. If several chicks hatch the parents may split the brood when carrying them around.

Red-necked Grebes are circumpolar, but absent from Greenland and Iceland, and the High Arctic. Wintering birds are found off both coasts of America, and in the North and Baltic seas.

Slavonian Grebe (Horned Grebe)

Podiceps auritus

L: 18–25cm. WS: 45–60cm. W: 350–450g.

Even more handsome than the Red-necked Grebe when in its breeding plumage of yellow 'horns', these being highly conspicuous between the black crown and black throat. The throat and flanks are chestnut, the back pale grey. In winter the horns and bright colours are lost, the birds being muddy brown and white. Sexes similar. Slavonians are smaller than Red-necked Grebes and cannot compete for larger prey; this probably explains why the smaller birds are found in a wider range of habitats. However, both birds may have been forced northwards by competition from larger southern species such as the Great Crested Grebe.

Slavonian Grebes are circumpolar, breeding throughout both the Nearctic and Palearctic. However, absent from Greenland, though does breed in Iceland. In winter the birds are seen around the British Isles, in the North and Baltic seas, and off both American coasts.

ALBATROSSES

Albatrosses are essentially birds of the southern oceans, the majority of species being confined between 45°S and 70°S. There are exceptions, four species breeding in the equatorial and northern Pacific. There are no species in the North Atlantic; one wonders why, especially since individuals brought to the area by freak weather have survived, sometimes for many years (there have been a few individual Black-browed Albatross living off British coasts, for example). It is also known that until the Pleistocene there were Atlantic albatrosses. It is assumed that the climatic changes of the Pleistocene caused northern species to head south, or to become extinct, and that recolonisation has not occurred in the last 10,000 years or so. Presumably if chance brought several birds to the North Atlantic a breeding colony could become established. That said, the winds above the Southern Ocean, blowing right around the world without the hindrance of landmasses, are ideally suited for birds that evolved to take advantage of just such conditions.

The bird's name is believed to derive from the Arabic *al-cadous*, apparently used for the pelican, but probably substituted for any unusual large white seabird. The name was picked up by the Portuguese who subtly changed the sound to *alcatraz* and applied it to all large, stiff-winged seabirds. The stiff wings characterise the albatrosses and other large procellariiformes. In the albatrosses, the stiff wings result from tendons that lock the extended wing into position for maximum lift. The wings allow the coverage of huge distances at sea with minimal energy output. It is, however, a fallacy that the larger albatrosses never land on the sea; seeing a Wandering Albatross *Diomedea exulans* take off from the sea may be unusual, but it is also inspiring.

Albatross wings are not only stiff, they are also long and thin, the high aspect ratio this produces allowing a high gliding speed and a low rate of descent. The combination allows the characteristic wave-riding seen by the birds. Wind speed decreases towards the ocean – just as it does towards the ground – as a result of friction, the birds accelerating down the speed gradient, then turning into the wind in order to be pushed back up by its increasing speed. In windy weather the birds also take advantage of the updraught of air on the windward side of waves to gain lift.

For the Arctic traveller, whose glimpses of albatrosses will be confined to lucky observations in the north Pacific and southern Bering Sea, the Northern Fulmar will be the only bird of the family demonstrating this flight pattern. The Fulmar also follows ships, riding the air streams a moving ship creates just as albatrosses do, this allowing a close-up view of its effortless flight. On occasions the Fulmar will approach a ship so closely that it is a matter of metres away, the bird apparently as intent on observing the passenger as *vice versa*.

Of the four northern albatrosses the Waved Albatross *Phoebastria irrorata*, which breeds on the Galápagos Islands, is a very rare visitor to the Arctic fringe. The other three species are more likely to be seen. Of these, two are listed as Vulnerable by the IUCN. Several other albatross species are also listed. Albatrosses are long-lived, but slow breeders, often not breeding until they are at least five years old (and sometimes up to 15 years old) and producing a single chick. The Wandering Albatross produces one chick every two years. Historically, some species were harvested for their feathers (these including the Short-tailed Albatross) and are now threatened by long-line fishing. If populations crash, it takes many years for them to regain their numbers, making them especially vulnerable to long-term threats. Ironically, it was the fact that albatrosses are late breeders that contributed to the survival of the Short-tailed Albatross. Japanese plume gatherers exterminated the last birds on the last known breeding island (Torishima), but immature birds, which spend the first few years of their lives at sea without making landfall, eventually returned to recolonise the island.

Laysan Albatross

Phoebastria immutabilis

L: 70–80cm. WS: 1.9–2.1m. W: 2.8–3.2kg.

The most numerous of the northern species. White head and body apart from dark brown back. The upperwings are dark brown, the underwing white with dark brown edging and patches. Dark brown terminal bar on tail. Sexes similar.

Laysan Albatrosses breed on the Hawaiian islands. Seen as far as 55°N, but uncommon. May be seen throughout the year, though rare in winter.

Black-footed Albatross

Phoebastria nigripes

L: 65–75cm. WS: 1.9–2.1m. W: 2.8–3.2kg.

Status: IUCN: Vulnerable.

Overall sooty brown, but with prominent white circle at base of bill and pale eye patch. Sexes similar. Breeds on Hawaiian islands. Relatively common off the southern shores of Alaska, but much rarer off the western (Arctic) shore.

Short-tailed Albatross

Phoebastria albatrus

L: 85–95cm. WS: 2.0–2.2m. W: 3.0–3.4kg.

Status: IUCN: Vulnerable.

Very rare, with a population of perhaps no more than 1,500. Breeds only on two islands off Japan's southern coast. White head and body (though often with pale yellow nape-patch) and black wings. Sexes similar. Very rare sightings off Alaska's south-western coast.

SHEARWATERS AND PETRELS

The shearwaters and petrels share important characteristics of the albatrosses. In particular they have the long, stiffened wings, tilted downward at the tips. In soaring birds, such as vultures and other raptors, the wing-tip is upturned, this configuration giving greater stability but less manoeuvrability. The downturned wing-tip reverses this, allowing the bird to make quicker adjustments in the occasionally frenetic air streams close to the waves, but requiring greater control. All things are relative, however, and those who have watched Fulmars landing on nesting cliffs will know that the birds – much more

Dark phase Northern Fulmar, Hornsund, Spitsbergen, Svalbard.

impressive fliers when viewed from a ship – are nowhere near as comfortable as gulls when landing on the same nesting cliff.

These species have a lower body temperature relative to other birds, and a layer of subdermal fat (which adds insulation, but increases weight: the Procellariiformes are heavy birds). Most significantly, they have a highly distinctive bill form, with the nostrils housed in tubular channels set on top, structures which have led to the birds often being called tubenoses. The reason for the tubenose is still debated, though most authorities believe it is either an enhanced olfactory system, or acts as a pitot tube, measuring air pressure. In support of the former is the fact that the birds feed equally well during the day or night. Night feeding has advantages because although the birds can dive for food, they more normally feed by plucking food from the surface, and many prey species come close to the surface during the night. In support of the idea that the structure measures wind speed is the birds' requirement to be able to 'read' the wind accurately because of their pelagic habitat. The characteristic flight pattern of the birds, gliding down with the wind and rising against it, is known as 'shearwatering', from which one group derive their common name. Shearwaters and petrels feed on fish, crustaceans and cephalopods.

Short-tailed Shearwater

Puffinus tenuirostris

L: 40–45cm. WS: 95–105cm. W: 500–800g.

Sooty-brown bird with a paler, greyish panel at the centre of the underwing. Sexes similar. Breeds on Tasmania, but winters in the north Pacific and Bering Sea where huge flocks form. Flocks of more than 100,000 birds (or significantly more, perhaps to 500,000) have been reported as far north as St Lawrence Island.

Northern Fulmar. The 'tube nose' of tubular channels housing the nostrils are seen clearly in this close-up shot.

Muttonbirds

The young of Short-tailed and Sooty Shearwaters were once harvested for food by sailors. They were known as 'muttonbirds' because of their sweet-tasting flesh. Although this practice died out when refrigeration and better welfare improved the diet of sailors, chicks are still taken on the island of Tasmania and sold as Tasmanian Squab. The population of both species is thought to exceed 20 million, so the annual harvest has little effect on population dynamics.

Sooty Shearwater

Puffinus griseus

L: 40–50cm. WS: 100–110cm. W: 650–950g.

Very similar to Short-tailed Shearwater but larger, with paler underparts and a more pronounced pale panel on the underwing. Sexes similar.

Sooty Shearwaters breed on New Zealand and Tasmania, and some small southern islands. In winter may be seen in the Atlantic as far north as the Denmark Straits and Norwegian Sea.

Great Shearwater

Puffinus gravis

L: 40–50cm. WS: 100–110cm. W: 750–950g.

Adult is large, with a diagnostic black cap as far as the eye. Grey-brown upperparts and upperwing, with white collar and rump-band. White underparts. Underwing white, but with grey tips to flight feathers and dark leading edge on wing. Male, female and winter plumages similar.

Great Shearwaters breed on Falkland Islands, Tristan da Cunha and Gough Island. Wintering birds seen in the Atlantic as far north as the Denmark Strait and Norwegian Sea.

Manx Shearwater

Puffinus puffinus

L: 30–40cm. WS: 75–90cm. W: 375–450g.

Black upperparts, including back and wings, white underparts, including underwing. Male, female and winter plumages similar.

Manx Shearwaters breed on Iceland, but otherwise essentially non-Arctic. The birds nest in burrows and, being vulnerable on land, they leave and return to their nests only at night. Wintering birds seen as far north as northern Norway.

Northern Fulmar

Fulmarus glacialis

L: 45–50cm. WS: 100–115cm. W: 600–850g. ♂>♀.

Superficially similar to gulls in its lighter morph, the Fulmar is distinguished at close quarters by the prominent tubenose and the fact that the suture lines of the bill plates are visible, and at a distance by the stiff-winged flight, the wings remaining stiff even during bouts of vigorous flapping. The bird comes in two basic morphs, dark and light. Light morphs have pearly-grey heads and upperparts, with whiter underparts. There is also a so-called 'double-light' (or L2), which is even paler. Dark-morphs are darker grey above, though often with a paler head and tail, and pale grey underparts. There is also a darker form (the double-dark or D2) which is much darker overall above, though still with paler underparts. Intermediate forms are also seen. Male, female and winter plumages similar.

The foul gull

The Dutch name for the Fulmar was 'mollymauk', meaning 'strange gull', once a general word used by sailors to describe all petrels and the smaller albatrosses. The name Fulmar is Icelandic, meaning 'foul gull'. This almost certainly derives from the way the birds regurgitate fish oil when approached at a nest site. Both adults and young do this. The oil is viscous and evil-smelling, and it is renowned among rock climbers and birdwatchers who have been hit for being almost impossible to fully remove from clothing. Fortunately the bird's aim does not match its enthusiasm for regurgitation, and most oil jets miss their target. An alternative suggestion for the name is that the high oil content of the birds meant they could be rendered down and used as lamp oil. As the oil would have had much the same smell as the defensive jet, the name again seems appropriate.

The distribution of the forms implies that the dark morph evolved in the North Pacific, the paler birds in the North Atlantic, when ice isolated an ancestral population. However, there are anomalies; there are many dark birds on Svalbard, and pale morphs in Chukotka. In general the number of dark morphs increases as the traveller heads north, which is also anomalous if the distribution hypothesis is strictly true.

Fulmars are circumpolar, breeding on sea cliffs. Pelagic in winter, moving ahead of the ice. In recent years there has been a marked increase in the population, probably as a result of the bird's habit of following trawlers to feed on fish offal. This has resulted in breeding sites becoming saturated and the species extending its range southwards. Northern expansion has been impossible as the range already extends to the ice edge. Fulmars feed as far as the ice edge, either by surface feeding or making shallow dives. A single chick is raised (two chicks are rare), this being fed by regurgitation, the adult's bill placed inside that of the young.

STORM-PETRELS

It is difficult to imagine a stronger contrast in flight characteristics between the shearwaters and their cousins the storm-petrels. While the former have low wing loadings and glide above the waves, the wing loadings of storm-petrels are very high (about 6cm^2/g), which allows them to flutter just above the water surface pecking at small fish and planktonic crustaceans. The birds also follow trawlers in the hope of discharged offal. Storm-petrels are rarely seen on shore, being truly pelagic. At breeding sites the birds nest in natural rock crevices, well-sheltered sites among boulders or the unused burrows of other species. As with shearwaters, they arrive at and depart from the nest site after dark. A single egg is laid. Incubation is long, about 40 days. The chick is fed by regurgitation, but may not be fed for several days at a time.

In the southern hemisphere several storm-petrels have polar distributions, with Wilson's Storm-petrel (*Oceanites oceanicus*) actually breeding at several sites on the Antarctic mainland. In the northern hemisphere there are no true Arctic species, but

Northern Fulmars, Hornsun, Spitsbergen, Svalbard.

Northern Gannet, Runde, Norway.

one nests on north-eastern Atlantic shores, one is circumpolar, and another breeds on the Kuril islands, the Aleutians and mainland southern Alaska.

European Storm-petrel

Hydrobates pelagicus

L: 18–22cm. WS: 35–40cm. W: 22–30g.

Dark brown head and upperparts, slightly paler underparts. There is a distinct white band along the length of the underwing and a white rump patch. Male, female and winter plumages similar. European Storm-petrels breed on Iceland's Westmann islands and the Norwegian coast. The birds winter in the North Atlantic from Iceland to north Norway.

Leach's Storm-petrel

Oceanodroma leucorhoa

L: 18–21cm. WS: 44–48cm. W: 40–50g.

Dark brown head with much paler face. The upperparts are also dark brown, but the upperwing-coverts are paler, creating a noticeable pale patch. White, V-shaped rump patch, though a dark morph without this patch is found in the south Pacific. The underparts are uniformly dark brown. Tail deeply forked. Male, female and winter plumages similar.

Leach's Storm-petrels breed on southern Iceland, Newfoundland and across the island arc from southern Kamchatka to southern Alaska. The birds winter in the North Atlantic to central Norway, northern Pacific and central Bering Sea.

Fork-tailed Storm-petrel

Oceanodroma furcata

L: 20–23cm. WS: 42–46cm. W: 50–55g.

The only pale storm-petrel in the region. Pale grey, with a paler carpal bar on the upperwing and darker leading edge. There is a distinct black eye patch. The rump is very pale. The tail is deeply forked. Male, female and winter plumages similar.

Fork-tailed Storm-petrels breed across the island arc from southern Kamchatka to southern Alaska, and winter in the northern Pacific and central Bering Sea.

Sheltering water walkers and Mother Carey's chickens

It is thought that the origin of the name storm-petrel is the species' habit of sheltering in the lee of ships during storms, and the fluttering flight above the water of the feeding birds. This often involves them pattering across the surface with their feet, giving the impression that they are walking on the water. 'Petrel' could then derive from St Peter. An alternative name popular with sailors was Mother Carey's chickens. That name almost certainly derives from Mater Cara (Latin for 'Dear Mother' a synonym for the Virgin Mary) who was considered the protector of sailors. Although the names might suggest a reverence for the birds, this was not shared by everyone. It is said that storm-petrels were occasionally used as lamps, the oil content of their bodies being so high that a wick pushed down the bird's throat and then lit would give a light that lasted for several hours.

GANNETS AND BOOBIES

Members of the *Sulidae* are plunge-diving birds that occur in a broad band across the Earth's oceans, primarily concentrated towards the Equator. There are no northern Pacific sulids, but the Northern Gannet breeds to the Arctic fringe.

Northern Gannet

Morus bassanus

L: 85–100cm. WS: 170–195cm. W: 2.4–3.6kg.

Magnificent birds with white plumage apart from black wingtips, a darker trailing edge on the wings, and a pale yellow head. Sexes similar. In winter the head is paler. Long, dagger-like bill is used to grab fish after a plunge, which can be from heights of up to 40m. The nostrils open inside the bill to prevent water ingress when hitting the water. The eyes are well forward, giving excellent stereoscopic vision.

The sight of a Gannet plummeting into the sea, wings closed, is thrilling. The dive's momentum takes the bird down a few metres to its prey.

Nests colonially, laying a single egg on a heap of seaweed and other vegetation, largely held together by excrement. The birds have no brood patch and so incubate by standing on the egg, using the blood vessels of the foot webs for warmth. Hatched chick stands on the adults' feet during brooding. Chick is fed to greater than adult weight, then abandoned. It spends several weeks swimming before being able to fly.

Gannets breed on Iceland, northern Fennoscandia and Newfoundland/southern Labrador. Partially migratory to southern waters.

CORMORANTS

The cormorants are a successful group of diving, fish-eating birds. They are well-adapted to the aquatic environment; with pelicans and the sulids they are the only birds with webs between all four toes, which gives them a strong paddle stroke. They have a long, flexible neck which aids the capture of prey. The bill is long and hooked at the end, while the tongue is rough, both adaptations to deal with slippery prey; the neck is pouch-like and can distend to allow fish to be swallowed whole (as they are after the bird has juggled them to ensure a head-first descent). Features to assist diving include an eye lens that can be modified to assist underwater vision and dense, buoyancy-limiting bones.

A consequence of the lack of waterproofing of the feathers (see Box) is that most cormorants are tropical species but there are exceptions. One species, the Imperial Shag *Phalacrocorax atriceps* breeds on the Antarctic Peninsula, while in the north the Pelagic Cormorant breeds on Wrangel Island, and everal other species breed at the Arctic fringe. These species have the additional problem that hanging the wings out to dry results in the body being exposed to chilling temperatures, as the birds have little body fat. Such polar distributions are, therefore, remarkable.

Despite the adaptations of the feet for an underwater life cormorants are much better on land than, for instance, divers. They can stand upright, and some species even perch and nest in trees. Cormorants are strong fliers, usually skimming low over the water, but because of the need to dry the feathers they are not pelagic, usually fishing close to the shore. They are gregarious, both at fishing and nest sites, the latter usually on cliffs. During the breeding season the adults often acquire a white thigh patch and prominent crests and head plumes, together with coloured throat pouches. These are used in mating displays, the wings being flicked to reveal and cover the thigh patches, the head being thrown back to reveal the throat patch and to give prominence to the crest. Nests are masses of seaweed held together with excrement. Up to 6 eggs are laid, the chicks feeding by reaching into the parental throat for regurgitated prey of fish and aquatic invertebrates. Young cormorants form crèches, returning to the nest site for feeding.

European Shag

Phalacrocorax aristotelis

L: 65–80cm. WS: 95–110cm. W: 1.3–2.3kg. ♂>♀.
Plumage is black with green sheen. Breeding crest is black and forward curve. No thigh spot or prominent throat pouch. Sexes similar. In winter the birds lose the crests.

European Shags are resident in western Iceland and on the Norwegian coast to the Kola Peninsula.

Great Cormorants, Randaberg, Norway.

> **Waterproofing feathers**
>
> Despite all the adaptations cormorants have for a diving lifestyle, one that would seem essential is missing – the cormorant's contour feathers are not completely waterproof, only the inner down layer preventing the skin from wetting. Most birds, and all wildfowl and other water birds, have waterproof feathers, the proofing assisted by oil from the preen gland above the tail. The wetting of the cormorant's outer feathers may help reduce buoyancy, though that does seem a rather drastic solution. But even if that is correct, there is a price to be paid for the lack of waterproofing; the feathers must be dried after dives. This results in the bird's characteristic pose with its wings 'hung out' to dry.

Great Cormorant

Phalacrocorax carbo

L: 75–95cm. WS: 120–150cm. W: 1.9–2.5kg. ♂>♀.
Plumage black with blue sheen. Prominent white cheeks and throat. White breeding thigh patch and short black crest. Sexes similar. In winter the birds lose the thigh patches.

Great Cormorants breed on south-west and south-east Greenland, Iceland, northern Norway and the Kola Peninsula. In North America breeds on Newfoundland and adjacent coasts. Some birds are resident, but some move south along the coast. All Greenlandic birds move to the south-west coast, but Icelandic birds are resident.

Red-faced and Pelagic Cormorants, Unalaska, Aleutian Islands, Alaska.

Above left
Pelagic Cormorant showing its white breeding thigh, Starichkov Island, southern Kamchatka, Russia,

Above right and below
European Shags, Kjorholmane, Norway.

Double-crested Cormorant

Phalacrocorax auritus

L: 80–90cm. WS: 140–150cm. W: 1.5–1.7kg. ♂>♀.
Plumage black with subdued green sheen. Throat pouch orange. Breeding plumes are the twin ear tufts of the name. These are black or grey, tending to be paler in northern birds. Double-crested is the largest of the North Pacific cormorants. Sexes similar. In winter the birds lose the crests.

Double-crested Cormorants breed on both coasts of North America, as far north as Newfoundland to the east and to southern Alaska and the Aleutians to the west. Alaskan birds are resident, or may move short distances along the coast. Eastern birds move south.

Pelagic Cormorant

Phalacrocorax pelagicus

L: 60–70cm. WS: 90–100cm. W: 1.6–1.8kg.
The smallest of the North Pacific cormorants. Plumage is black with distinct metallic green sheen. At close quarters the neck sheen may be seen to have a bluish tinge. Breeding birds have one or two short crests on top of the head and small red throat patch. They also have prominent white thigh patches and may have white flecking on the neck. Sexes similar. In winter the birds lose the crests and thigh patches. Pelagic Cormorants feed closer to the shore than the other Bering Sea cormorants, but in much deeper water, up to 100m, suggesting that they dive much deeper than related species.

Pelagic Cormorants breed on both sides of the Bering Sea, but much further north on the western side, reaching Chukotka and Wrangel Island; birds on Wrangel are the most northerly of all breeding cormorants. Also breeds along the Aleutian chain. Birds in the southern part of the range are resident. Northern birds migrate as far south as Baja California and Taiwan.

Red-faced Cormorant

Phalacrocorax urile

L: 65–75cm. WS: 110–120cm. W: 1.9–2.2kg.
Plumage black with purple-green sheen. The red face of the name is prominent and much more extensive than the breeding red of the Pelagic Cormorant. Breeding birds have one or two short crests on the head and a white thigh patch. In winter the birds lose the crests and thigh patches.

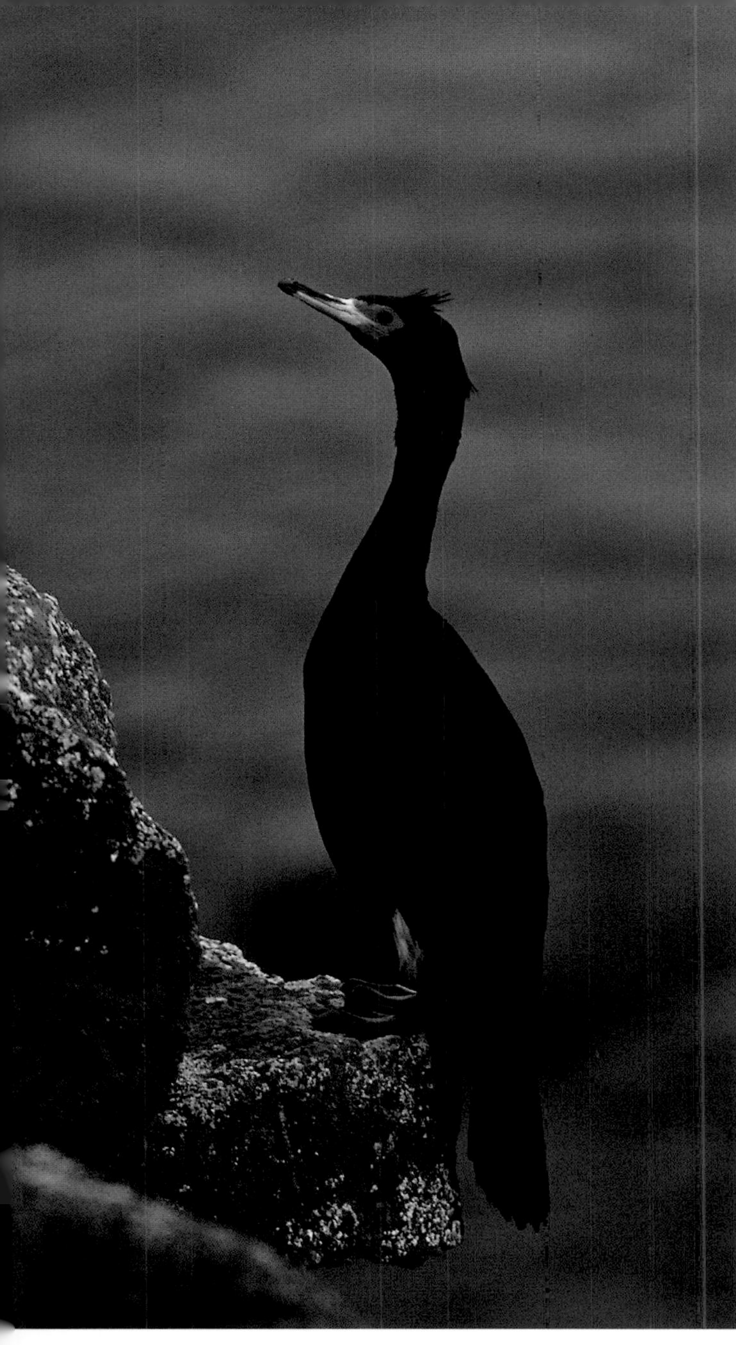

WILDFOWL

For the Arctic traveller, there are few sights that herald the arrival of spring more evocatively than skeins of geese arriving from the south. And there are few that announce the coming of the Arctic winter more than those same geese departing south again. The skein will have the V-formation for which flying wildfowl are renowned. This pattern allows birds to take advantage of the updraught of air created by the wingbeat of the bird ahead, using it to reduce its own energy output. The bird at the head of the formation works hardest and is regularly replaced by a bird further back in the pattern. Geese can fly at astonishing heights, formations having been reported from over 10,000m. At such a height a human could not survive, let alone work hard, because of reduced oxygen levels. It seems that for the geese the reduction in oxygen level is compensated by the speed of the jet stream. However, in general geese fly at much lower altitudes, probably because flying at altitude risks wing-icing, which would be catastrophic.

Wildfowl – swans, geese and ducks – are a successful group with more than 150 species spread across every continent except Antarctica. Their absence from the southern continent can be explained by the species' being chiefly herbivorous although there are also piscivorous ducks.

Wildfowl share some general characteristics. They are broad-bodied, long- (or very long-) necked aquatic birds. They have flattened bills with a horny 'nail' at the end, the edges of the mandibles having comb-like lamellae for straining food from water, and rasp-like tongues for manipulating food. In a few species, the sawbills, the lamellae are replaced by 'teeth'. Vegetarian wildfowl do not have bacteria in their gut to break down cellulose, so they gain nutrients only from cellular juices. The plant structure is broken down in the bird's gizzard, grit being ingested to aid the process. One consequence of this is that the birds have to eat a great deal, spending virtually the entire day feeding. They take the most nutritious parts of plants, the new growth, which has not had time to build up structural fibres.

The name cormorant derives from the Latin *corvus marinus*, sea raven. The black plumage is raven-like and the birds have a similar inquisitive, opportunistic way of feeding.

Left
Red-faced Cormorant, St Paul, Pribilofs, Alaska.

Red-faced Cormorants breed across the island arc of the southern Bering Sea (including the Pribilofs) and on eastern Kamchatka and southern Alaska. Alaskan birds tend to be resident or move only a short distance, but Russian birds may move as far as Taiwan.

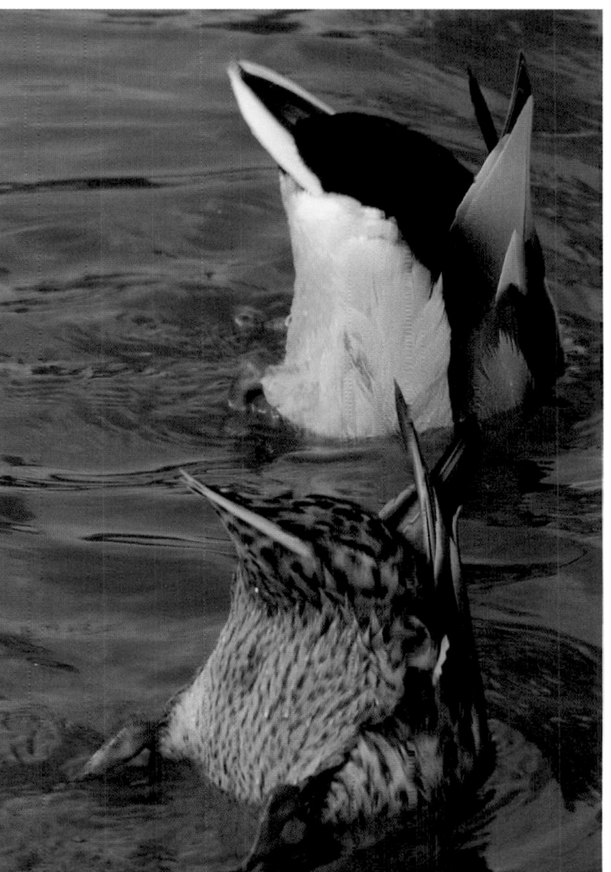

Upending Mallards. This inelegant, though amusing, feeding method is favoured by many wildfowl, including swans, the largest Anseriformes.

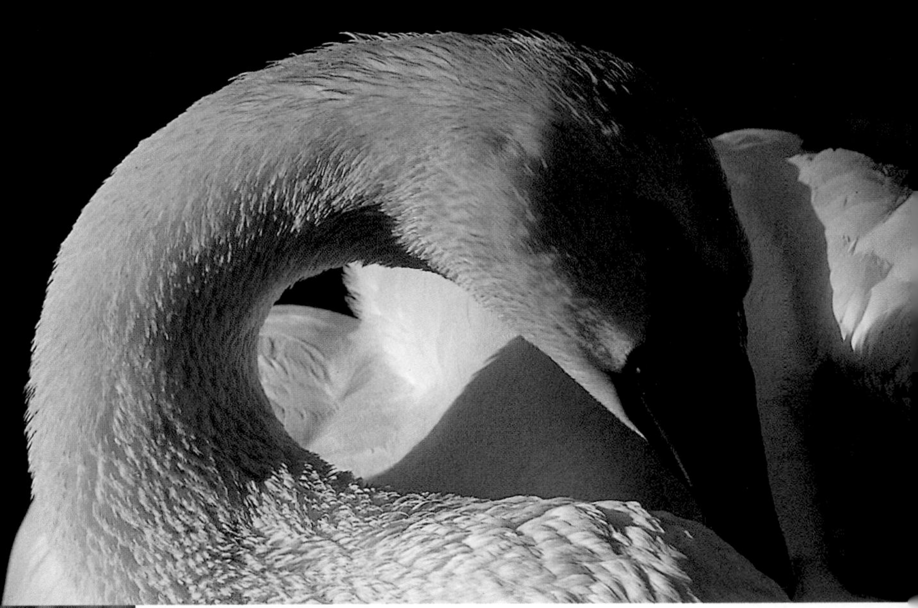

Wildfowl have webbed feet (though in a very small number there are either no webs or the feet are semipalmated). The legs are set far back on the body, making walking difficult. This is especially true of the swans, whose legs are also short; though swans are more terrestrial than, say, divers, they are essentially aquatic birds. This is also true of the ducks, which have similarly short legs. In geese the legs are longer and set more centrally on the body. These birds are therefore more mobile, in keeping with their more terrestrial habits. Though geese can occasionally look awkward on land, they are surprisingly quick, as a traveller who blunders close to a goose nest will rapidly discover. The cryptic incubating bird can show a remarkable burst of speed which, allied to a very aggressive nature, can lead to a worrying few seconds.

Swans and geese usually mate for life, but ducks do not, taking mates seasonally. These different mating systems account for the plumage differences between swans, geese and ducks. In the swans and geese the sexes are alike. In ducks most males are brightly coloured, with the female cryptic brown.

Wildfowl moult their flight feathers simultaneously and so undergo a flightless period, which varies in length from about three weeks for small ducks to six weeks for swans and large geese. During this flightless phase the male ducks of most Arctic species moult to an 'eclipse' plumage which closely resembles that of the female. In general eclipse plumage is seen in the autumn, the males then moulting to their breeding plumage. It is unusual for a bird to show its breeding plumage

Above and above right **Trumpeter Swans, Kenai Peninsula, Alaska.**

Wildfowl and people

The predictability of wildfowl migrations, the large size of migrating flocks, the size of the birds, and the good eating of their meat means that wildfowl have always been important to people. Even today, when hunting is a 'sport' rather than a necessity for virtually all hunters, the effect of the hunt has been to dramatically shorten the life expectancy of the birds. It is estimated that without hunting the average life expectancy of a large goose would be about 20 years. Because of hunting this has been reduced to about 10 years. It is as well that numbers are healthily large for the most vulnerable species, as the late maturing of swans (3–4 years) and geese (2–3 years), combined with the reduction in average life, might otherwise lead to a sharp fall in population.

Swans in legend and history

The grace and beauty of swans has inspired people for thousands of years. The Greek legends of Leda and the Swan, and of Phaeton and Cygnus (the latter story giving its name to the genus – Cygnus, and has given us 'cygnet' as the name of a young swan) are early examples, while a later Scandinavian tale was the basis for the ballet *Swan Lake*. For sheer elegance, a swimming swan is hard to beat. The bird is occasionally mocked, the suggestion being that the above surface elegance is belied by frantically paddling feet below the water. In reality, the paddle stoke is usually leisurely and every bit as elegant.

The grace that excited poets did not always stretch to the more pragmatic human; swans are large birds and make good eating. Northern native peoples have always prized the swan for food, and also for the luxury of its feathers; the preferred bed of the Inupiat of northern Alaska was swan skin. In medieval England swans were owned by the sovereign who was the only person allowed to harvest the birds. The penalty for poaching a swan was severe. Even today the British monarch owns the majority of swans on the River Thames; the remainder are owned by one of two ancient Companies the Dyers and the Vintners. The annual catching and marking, by nicks on the bill, of this year's cygnets – a ceremony called *swan-upping* – is typically British and would thoroughly confuse an Inuk.

in winter, but waterfowl bonds tend to be formed at that time (often during migration in non-resident species). Drake courtship displays are limited to simple movements such as tail wagging and water flicking. For swans and geese the displays are even more limited (as pair bonds are lifelong). There is, however, a triumph ceremony, performed by the pair when a real (but sometimes imaginary) intruder is expelled from the nesting territory. The male usually chases the intruder, or engages in the mock chase of a non-existent intruder to illustrate his aggressive, protective intent for the sake of the pair bond. He returns to the female and they stand facing each other, extending their necks and calling loudly 'in triumph'.

Wildfowl habitually nest close to freshwater – even the sea ducks. Female wildfowl lay large clutches. In swans and geese the female incubates the eggs while the male stands guard. In the ducks the males usually abandon the females once incubation has begun. Goslings and ducklings are downy, and can swim, dive and feed themselves as soon as they are hatched. They are, however, brooded and cared for by their parents, in the case of swans and geese, and the female alone in the case of the ducks. In some duck species, the chicks of many females form crèches under the care of a small number of females. Swans and geese tend to migrate in family units after the young have fledged, and even stay together as a unit during the winter. Young swans and geese breed at three or four years, but depart from the family unit when the breeding site is reached after the spring migration.

Most wildfowl are gregarious in winter, rather more solitary at their breeding grounds, though geese in particular are more colonial nesters.

SWANS

Swans are the largest and heaviest of the wildfowl. There are seven species, of which three are Arctic birds. The distribution of the species is curious; apart from the northern swans there are two in southern South America and one in Australia and New Zealand. The northern species are predominantly white and have very long necks. Male, female and winter plumages are similar. Swans are strong fliers once they have taken off. Take-off follows an energetic (and awesome) race across the water. Landing swans are a great sight, feet splayed out as brakes and landing carriage, with a good touchdown seemingly as much of a surprise to the swan as to the onlooker. Landings on ice are hilarious, though presumably traumatic for the bird, and a great deal more traumatic for birds already on the surface as they are skittled by the on-rushing swan.

Swans are wholly or primarily vegetarian, grazing aquatic vegetation and dabbling in shallow water. They also up-end to feed. Dabbling takes in aquatic invertebrates as well as vegetation, and some swans paddle with their feet in order to bring larvae to the surface. They are, however, opportunistic and have been seen to swallow sizeable fish. Wintering birds feed in cereal fields and on waste grain, and will grub for tubers and potatoes, the latter a relatively recent addition to the diet.

All northern species are migratory, some travelling great distances, though these are usually accomplished in relatively short flights between 'refuelling' stops. Swans have been seen at heights of more than 8,000m, but chiefly fly at 2,000–3,000m.

Trumpeter Swan

Cygnus buccinator

L: 1.5–1.7m. WS: 2.1–2.5m. W: 9.0–13.0kg. ♂>♀.

Plumage white overall, occasionally rust-stained on head and upper neck from iron deposits in feeding lake. Bill is black, with no basal yellow. The scientific name of the species derives from the Latin for a military trumpet. As a family the swans are a noisy bunch (though the Mute Swan *Cygnus olor* though definitely not mute is less noisy), the name 'swan' apparently deriving from the Saxon for noise. The Trumpeter has a long, twisted windpipe and its deep, resonant bugling is the loudest of all wildfowl and ranks with the loudest of all birds.

Trumpeter Swans are not truly Arctic, breeding in south-eastern Alaska, though occasionally seen in western and central Alaska.

Centre
Whooper Swans, Orre, Norway.

Whooper Swan family, Dalarne, Sweden.

Whooper Swans and the Vikings

Each year the Norse settlers of Iceland watched as the highly visible, huge white Whooper Swans disappeared south across the sea. The settlers held the birds in awe, believing they were imbued with supernatural powers. They did not know that some Icelandic birds migrated to northern Britain for the winter, and would not have believed that so big a bird was capable of crossing such hazardous waters. Myths grew that the swans headed to Valhalla or the Moon, returning each spring.

The Norse view is understandable, as the journey the swans actually undertake is incredible – more than 800km across hostile seas. Today the tracking of individual birds has shown that the journey can take as little as 13 hours, but if the weather is poor birds may take several days, sometimes resting on the sea to recover. In particularly bad weather, many birds will not make it.

Whooper Swan

Cygnus cygnus

L: 1.4–1.6m. WS: 2.1–2.5m. W: 7.5–10.0kg. ♂>♀.

Plumage white, occasionally with a pale yellow wash to the head and neck. Head and neck also sometimes tinged red from iron deposits in feeding lake. The bill is black with a yellow base. The yellow coloration is variable, but usually extends to and beyond the nostril. As a diagnostic, Whoopers have the most extensive yellow on the bill of any of the northern swans. Whoopers are the most accomplished walkers of the northern swans, a point worth recalling if tempted to approach too closely – Whoopers are intolerant of, and aggressive towards, intruders.

Whooper Swans breed in Iceland and across Arctic Eurasia to Kamchatka (though uncommonly in Norway); has also bred in western Alaska. In general a bird of the taiga, but nests on tundra in both Iceland and Russia. Some wintering birds are resident, but most move to southern rivers and coasts.

Tundra Swan

Cygnus columbianus

Two distinct subspecies of this swan, that have in the past been considered full species.

Whistling Swan *C. c. columbianus*

L: 1.2–1.35m. W: 1.6–1.9m. W: 6.0–7.0kg.

Plumage white, the bill black with minimal yellow at the base. The yellow base is diagnostic in those areas of Alaska where Whistling and Trumpeter swans overlap, but to confuse the issue there are instances of Whistling Swans having all black bills. The northern habitat of the birds, which nest beside tundra pools but occasionally some distance from water, has led to the birds frequently being called Tundra Swans.

Whistling Swans breed on the Aleutian islands, western Alaska and across northern North America to the western Ungava Peninsula, including the southern Canadian Arctic islands. Absent from north-eastern Canada, but breeds in places on the southern shores of Hudson Bay; also breeds in eastern Chukotka.

Bewick's Swan *C. c. bewickii*

L: 1.15–1.25m. WS: 1.8–2.15m. W: 4.5–6.5kg, exceptionally to 7.5kg.

Plumage white, the bill black with a yellow base. Similar to Whistling Swan but with more yellow on the bill, though generally smaller. Interbreeding is known to occur where the two swans overlap in eastern Chukotka.

Bewick's Swans breed across Arctic Russia from the Kanin Peninsula to western Chukotka. Swans breeding west of the Urals migrate to the British Isles, while those to the east head for Japan, Korea and south-east China.

Whistling Swan pair, Southampton Island, Canada.

The two Tundra Swans.

Above
Whistling Swan, Southampton Island, Canada.

Below
The bill pattern of Bewick's Swans is so distinctive that individuals can be readily identified when they return to their wintering grounds in Britain.

GEESE

The 'true' geese – birds of the genera *Anser* (the grey geese) and *Branta* (the black geese) – are all found in the northern hemisphere. The colour groupings are not exact, as we shall see, and are not the primary reason for the separation of the genera. The sexes of all northern geese are alike.

Of the fifteen species, twelve are Arctic dwellers. These are essentially terrestrial, though they do feed in water and may even be seen upending in search of food. On land they consume vegetation, while the larger species also grub for roots and tubers. In winter they feed on agricultural land, taking waste grain, but also more substantial foods such as beets and potatoes. Geese migrate considerable distances; they cannot afford the weight of a large digestive system that would maximise the nutrient extraction from their poor diet. They therefore take fresh green shoots, which are more easily digested and are rich in protein and carbohydrate. Migrations are timed so the geese move north into continuous spring, with green shoots in abundance. They will also occasionally move to higher ground to gain advantage of an 'altitudinal' spring. Though it was long assumed that females laid as soon as they reached their nest sites, it is now known that many geese actually spend the first few days feeding continuously to replenish bodily reserves lost during the long flight north. Egg-laying cannot be delayed for long, however, as the best strategy for raising young to the point where they are able to migrate is to have them hatch early. The need to be in good condition for laying while laying early represents a dilemma for the female goose. The female grows many ovarian follicles, but will choose how many eggs she will produce. In bad years, when poor weather means the migration flight has been poorly timed and food resources are limited, the female may resorb the follicles and lay no eggs. Some females lay too many eggs. If the female cannot find enough food to continue incubation she has two choices, and both are known to be taken: some females desert the eggs, saving herself in order to breed the following year, but some have been known to die of starvation on the nest.

Even if incubation is successful, chick-rearing is stressful and fraught with danger. There are foxes, skuas, Ravens and other predators, both avian and mammalian, to whom goslings are an easy and welcome meal. The climate, too, plays a part – a spell of bad weather may kill off the vulnerable chicks, or a poor growing season for plants may not allow some chicks to fatten sufficiently to make it to winter quarters. Life for northern geese is harsh, and that is without the extra problems caused by human hunters.

The male, female and winter plumages of geese are similar.

GREY GEESE

Grey geese differ from their black cousins not only in colour, but also in having serrated mandibles and vertical furrowing of the neck feathers. The latter is prominent, particularly when the feathers are vibrated, a sign of aggression.

GREYLAG GOOSE

Anser anser

L: 75–90cm. WS: 150–175cm. W: 3.0–4.5kg. ♂>♀.

The largest grey goose. Overall grey-brown, the chest and belly paler, sometimes with darker striping. The vent and undertail are white. The bill is pink. The legs and feet are dull

Greylag Geese at Orre, Norway.

pink. The neck furrowing of Greylags is very pronounced, particularly when a bird charges a real or imaginary intruder prior to a 'triumph' display.

Greylag Geese breed in Iceland and northern Norway, otherwise only in more southerly areas of Eurasia. The species is not, therefore, a true Arctic dweller. Wintering birds fly as far as northern India and southern China.

The Greylag – saviour of Rome

The Greylag is the ancestor of farmyard geese; it was a domesticated Greylag (or the descendant of one) that famously saved Rome from a Gaulish horde in 390BC. The geese made such a noise that the city was awakened to the danger (literally as well as figuratively – Greylags and their farmyard cousins are well known for the racket they make when disturbed, a formidable combination of honks and hisses).

(Greater) White-fronted Goose

Anser albifrons

L: 65–80cm. WS: 130–160cm. W: 1.7–3.2kg. ♂>♀.

Plumage similar to Greylag Goose, but brown rather than grey-brown, the head and neck distinctly brown. The underparts are pale brown, darker on the flanks, with dark brown/black horizontal stripes. The vent and undertail are white. The bill is pink, with a large white basal ring. The legs and feet are orange.

White-fronted Geese breed in Russia eastwards from the White Sea, including the southern island of Novaya Zemlya, in west Greenland around Disko Bay, Alaska and in isolated areas of northern Canada. In North America migrating birds head south to California and Mexico. Birds from Asian Russia winter in China and Japan, European Russian birds head for the British Isles and Low Countries. Greenland White-fronts fly to Iceland, but this is only a staging post on the way to Ireland and Scotland.

Lesser White-fronted Goose

Anser erythropus

L: 55–65cm. WS: 115–135cm. W: 1.6–2.3kg. ♂>♀.

Status: IUCN: Vulnerable.

Similar to Greater White-fronted Goose but smaller with a shorter neck. The bill is pink with a white nail. The basal ring is white and extends to the crown, and there is a distinct yellow orbital ring. These features are important where Lesser and Greater White-fronted Geese overlap in Russia.

Lesser White-fronted Geese breed in northern Fennoscandia, where it has been reintroduced following severe depletion due to overhunting. However, hunting is still a problem, as is habitat loss at wintering sites. The population is probably no more than 30,000 and decreasing. Wintering birds are seen across northern Europe from east England (where it is a very rare vagrant) to eastern Germany, in the Balkans and near the Caspian Sea, and in parts of China.

Pink-footed Goose

Anser brachyrhynchus

L: 60–75cm. WS: 135–165cm. W: 1.9–3.2kg. ♂>♀.

The head and neck are brown, the rest of the bird grey or grey-brown, the underparts paler except on the flanks. The vent and undertail are white. The legs and feet are, as might be expected, pink. The colour of the feet is a useful diagnostic – the feet of Greylags are also pink, but they breed much further south. The bill is the best diagnostic characteristic when confronted with swimming birds; it is short and brown,

A family of Greylag Geese head for the sea on Norway's Lofoten Islands.

with a pink band behind the brown nail.

Pink-footed Geese breed in east Greenland, on Iceland and Svalbard. In winter western birds head to northern England and Scotland, while Svalbard birds fly to Norway, Denmark and Holland.

Bean Goose

Anser fabalis

L: 60–85cm. WS: 130–175cm. W: 2.0–4.0kg. ♂>♀.

Very similar to White-fronted Goose but lacking the dark striping on the underparts, and the upperparts are greyer. The bill is yellowish orange, usually with a dark grey base and dark grey tip or nail. Some birds show a narrow basal white ring There are two distinct forms, which have occasionally been considered separate species. The 'Tundra' Bean Goose *A. f. rossicus* is as described. The 'Taiga' Bean Goose *A. f. fabalis*, the larger of the two, has a shorter, thicker bill which is black, with a yellow band close to the nail.

Taiga Bean Geese breed in Scandinavia east to the Urals. Tundra Bean Geese breed on the northern Russian tundra east of the Urals and on the southern island of Novaya Zemlya.

Snow Goose

Anser caerulescens

L: 65–80cm. WS: 130–160cm. W: 2.2–3.4kg ♂>♀.

Unmistakable. Two morphs, white and blue. The white morph is entirely white apart from black primary feathers and pale grey coverts. The head and upper neck are occasionally tinged pale yellow and may also be stained red by iron in feeding ponds. The bill is red with a white nail and has prominent dark edges, giving the bird a pronounced 'grin' that cannot be mistaken. The second morph, the 'blue goose', has blue-grey lower neck, breast, belly, flanks and mantle. Intermediate forms between the two morphs are also seen, with most flocks including a range of birds. The taxonomy of the two morphs is considered in more detail in The Adaptations and Biogeography of Birds and Mammals. Greenlandic birds are considered a subspecies, as is the Greater Snow Goose of Baffin, Bylot and Ellesmere islands.

Snow Geese are essentially a Nearctic species, breeding across North America and in north-west Greenland. However, a small population also breeds in north-east Russia, and a more significant population on Wrangel Island. In winter, North American birds fly south to the southern states, from California to Florida, and also in Mexico. Greenland birds join them, as do many Russian birds, though some of the latter head south to China and Japan.

Above right
The Lesser White-fronted Goose is virtually identical to its larger cousin apart from being about 25% smaller. It also has a prominent yellow eye-ring. Some Greater White-fronts also show such a ring, particularly the so-called Tule Goose (*Anser albifrons elgasi*) which breeds in southern Alaska. Tule Geese are named for tules (bullrushes) which they eat at their Californian wintering grounds. The eye-ring of the Lesser goose is more prominent, and the ranges of it and the Tule do not overlap.

Above
White-fronted Geese in flight over Alaska's North Slope.

Left
Pink-footed Goose and nest in southern Iceland.

Three Greylag Geese and a single Bean Goose in flight at Orre, Norway.

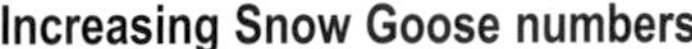

Increasing Snow Goose numbers

In recent years the number of Snow Geese has been increasing, probably, it is thought, as a result of changes in agricultural practices that have benefited the birds. While this is obviously good news for this most charismatic goose, it does come with a downside. The birds' droppings were once a fertilizer, but increased numbers of birds means a greater weight of droppings and these have altered water chemistry in places where the birds congregate, the change resulting in reduced plant growth.

ROSS'S GOOSE

Anser rossii

L: 50–60cm. WS: 110–120cm. W: 1.0–1.5kg. ♂>♀.
Plumage as the Snow Goose, though blue morphs are much rarer. Some authorities believe that blue morphs result from hybridisation between Ross's Goose and blue-morph Snow Goose (perhaps following egg-dumping by a blue goose into a Ross's nest, with the chicks imprinting on its foster parent). The bill of Ross's Goose differs from that of its larger cousin, having no, or minimal, 'grin' and blue-grey protuberances (called caruncles) around the base.

Ross's Geese breed in just a few places in Arctic Canada – Banks and Southampton islands and the mainland near Bathurst Inlet, and the western shores of Hudson Bay. Wintering birds are seen in Mexico and California.

EMPEROR GOOSE

Anser conagica

L: 60–70cm. WS: 115–125cm. W: 2.4–2.8kg. ♂>♀.
Small and exquisitely marked, the only grey goose to show an exotic plumage. The head and back of the neck are white, the front of the neck dark grey. The rest of the bird is silver-grey, flecked and barred with dark grey and white. The tail is white. The short bill is dull pink. Emperors (which were named for the Russian Tsar) are the most musical of the grey geese, with a trisyllabic call. They are also the most maritime, though rarely seen far from the coast.

Emperor Geese breed on the west Alaskan coast and, in small numbers, on the east coast of Chukotka. Many birds are resident, but some move to the Aleutians and Kodiak Island and, occasionally, further south along the western seaboard of the United States.

BLACK GEESE

While the black geese are generally darker than the grey, the distinguishing features of the five northern species are the bold patterning – only the Emperor Goose breaks the rather dull monotony of the greys – and the lack of prominent mandible serrations. Of the five only one, the Hawaiian Goose (or Nene, *Branta sandvicensis,* a non-Arctic breeder), shows any furrowing of the neck feathers.

Bathing Blue Snow Goose, Southampton Island, Canada.

Comparison of the heads of a Snow Goose (*far left*) and Ross's Goose (*left*). The distinctive 'grin' of the former, and carbuncles of the latter are diagnostic.

Left
Each year the majority of the world's population of Emperor Geese move to the Izembek Lagoon, near Cold Bay, Alaska Peninsula, to feed on eelgrass.

Brent Geese (Brant)

Branta bernicla

L: 55–60cm. WS: 105–120cm. W: 1.2–1.6kg. ♂>♀.
Black head and neck with a triangular black-and-white striped patch on each side of the neck. The rest of the plumage is dark grey, the underparts paler (though often not much paler). The vent and undertail are white.

Brent Geese breed in northern Greenland, Svalbard, Franz Josef Land, across Arctic Russia east from the Taimyr Peninsula, including Severnaya Zemlya, the New Siberian Islands and Wrangel Island, and across northern North America from Alaska to western Hudson Bay and all Canada's Arctic islands. The nominate race *bernicla* (described above), often called the Dark-bellied Brent, breeds in Arctic Russia apart from Franz Josef Land. There, and on Svalbard, Greenland and eastern Canada, the Light-bellied Brent *hrota* breeds. It has paler underparts with darker flecking on the flanks. The Black Brant *nigricans* breeds in western North America. It has a much larger black-and-white neck patch and is usually much darker overall. However, this tidy organisation is confounded by some Black Brants having underparts as pale as the nominate, by the fact that some authorities claim that in Russia, apart from on the Taimyr Peninsula and Franz Josef land, all breeding birds are Black Brants, by the existence of intermediate forms, and by the general distribution of colouring in all forms.

In winter birds, from Greenland, Svalbard, Franz Josef and western Russia fly to the Low Countries and British Isles. Those from eastern Russia move to Japan, while American birds winter on the east and west coasts of the United States.

Canada Goose

The taxonomic status of the Canada geese has recently changed with Greater Canada Goose *Branta canadensis* (with seven subspecies) and Lesser Canada Goose *B. hutchinsii* (with four) now being recognised. A fifth subspecies of Lesser Canada Goose, *B. h. asiatica*, which bred on the Kuril and Commander islands, is now thought to be extinct as no specimen has been verifiably sighted since 19[illegible].

Greater Canada Goose

Branta canadensis

Length: 85–110cm. Wing span: 145–185cm. Weight 2.5–5.0kg. ♂>♀.
The largest black goose (the largest subspecies is the Giant Canada Goose *B. c. maxima*, which breeds in south-west Canada). Head and neck black apart from a prominent white band which extends from the throat to the ear. The upperparts are pale grey-brown, the underparts paler, but with darker flecking on the flanks. The vent is white, the tail black.

Greater Canada Geese breed across North America, including southern areas of the central Canadian Arctic islands. Has recently begun to breed on west Greenland. However, as they are attractive birds they have been introduced into, or escaped captivity in, other countries, including the British Isles, Scandinavia and other areas of northern Europe. This has led to the position that travellers wishing to see these geese need not visit Canada's Victoria Island, but merely visit London's Hyde Park. The Lesser Canada has not been recorded in the UK.

Below
Brent Geese at Randeberg, Norway.

Lesser Canada Goose
Branta hutchinsii
Length: 55–90cm. Wing span: 120–150cm. Weight 1.3–2.3kg. ♂>♀.
Status: CITES: Aleutian Canada Goose B. h. leucopareia is Appendix I.
Identical in pattern to the Greater Canada Goose, the differences between the two being related to size alone. The smallest of the subspecies is *B. h. minima* of northern Canada. The Aleutian Canada Goose has a conspicuous white neck ring.

Lesser Canada Geese breed in Alaska, including the Aleutian islands, and north-east Canada. There is a small population in west Greenland.

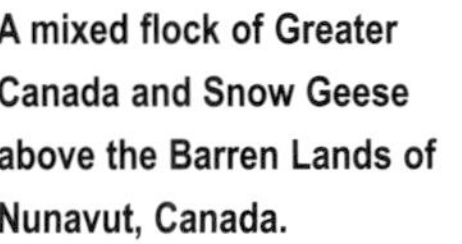

A mixed flock of Greater Canada and Snow Geese above the Barren Lands of Nunavut, Canada.

The Aleutian Canada Goose

The Aleutian Canada Goose *B. h. leucopareia* once bred on all the islands of the Aleutian chain. To increase fur production, Russian settlers introduced Arctic Foxes to all the readily accessible islands. The effect on the geese, and other ground-nesting birds, was catastrophic, and it was feared they had become extinct. But they were found breeding on inaccessible islands, and a programme of fox elimination and goose reintroductions has ensured the survival of the subspecies

Lesser Canada Goose pair, Kenai Peninsula, Alaska.

Barnacle Goose
Branta leucopsis
L: 55–70cm. WS: 130–145cm. W: 1.4–2.2kg. ♂>♀.
A beautiful small goose. The face is white, apart from a black stripe from bill to eye. The rest of the head and neck is black. The upperparts are white and pale grey, with black barring. The underparts are white with pale grey barring. The vent and rump are white, the tail black.

Barnacle Geese have the most restricted range of the Arctic black geese, breeding only in north-east Greenland, Svalbard, the southern island of Novaya Zemlya and nearby parts of Russia's northern coast. In recent years Barnacle Goose has also bred on Iceland. The Greenland and Svalbard birds winter in Scotland and Ireland, the Russian birds in Denmark, Germany and the Low Countries.

Red-breasted Goose
Branta ruficollis
L: 50–55cm. WS: 110–130cm. W: 1.0–1.3kg. ♂>♀.
Status: IUCN: Vulnerable. CITES: Appendix II.
Perhaps the most attractive of the black geese. The head and neck are patterned black, white and red-brown, the red-brown of the neck extending to the breast. The upperparts are black with white stripes on the coverts, the underparts black with distinctive white barring on the flanks.

Red-breasted Geese formerly bred only on Russia's Taimyr Peninsula, but in recent years seem to have extended their range both east and west. Despite this good news, the position of the goose remains vulnerable. Wintering birds are concentrated in a small number of places on the Black Sea where changes to local agricultural methods represent a threat. The birds are also hunted as they migrate.

On tussock tundra, incubating Canada Geese can occasionally be difficult to spot, but the goose soon leaves the visitor in no doubt that their presence is not welcomed. Churchill, Manitoba, Canada.

Geese and barnacles

Each winter little black-and-white geese appeared in northern Europe and the people who observed them were puzzled by their origin – so much so that a belief arose that they hatched from the barnacles, attached to flotsam wood, that occasionally washed ashore. Writing in the early 17th century, the herbalist Gerard noted an extension of the legend – 'There are found in the North parts of Scotland and the Islands adjacent, called Orchades, certain trees whereon do grow certaine shells of a white colour tending to russet, wherein are contained little living creatures: which shells in time of maturitie do open, and out of them grow those little living things, which falling into the water do become fowles, which we call Barnacle Geese ... and in Lancashire, tree Geese: but the other that fall upon the land perish and come to nothing.' So the myth had extended, the fact that barnacles washed ashore were invariably attached to wood meaning that there must, somewhere, be a tree with very strange fruit. Eventually, of course, the truth was discovered, but the name (Barnacle Goose rather than Tree Goose) stuck, in part because barnacles, being 'fish' could be eaten on Fridays by Christians (especially Catholics) and the goose, being a 'fish goose had meat that could also be eaten as fish.

SHELDUCKS

Shelducks are southern hemisphere, warm climate birds – apart, that is, from the Common Shelduck.

Common Shelduck

Tadorna tadorna

L: 55–65cm. WS: 100–120cm. W: 0.8–[illegible]kg. ♂>♀.
Male has a black head and upper neck with a green sheen, and red bill with a prominent fleshy knob at the base when breeding. The rest of the plumage is black, white and chestnut. Eclipse male is overall duller and lacks the bill knob. Female is as male, but the bill is pink and lacks the fleshy knob, and the breast band is narrower. Though the size of a small goose, Common Shelducks have many duck-like characteristics, such as the ability to perch in trees. They also nest in burrows.

Common Shelducks breed in north Norway, and a small number breed in northern and western Iceland. In Iceland the bird was a rare vagrant until 1990, when it first bred. Numbers have since increased and continue to rise. Almost all northern birds winter on Heligoland Bight off northern Germany.

Barnacle Geese at Badlanddalen, north-east Greenland.

Red-breasted Geese are the most beautiful of the northern geese.

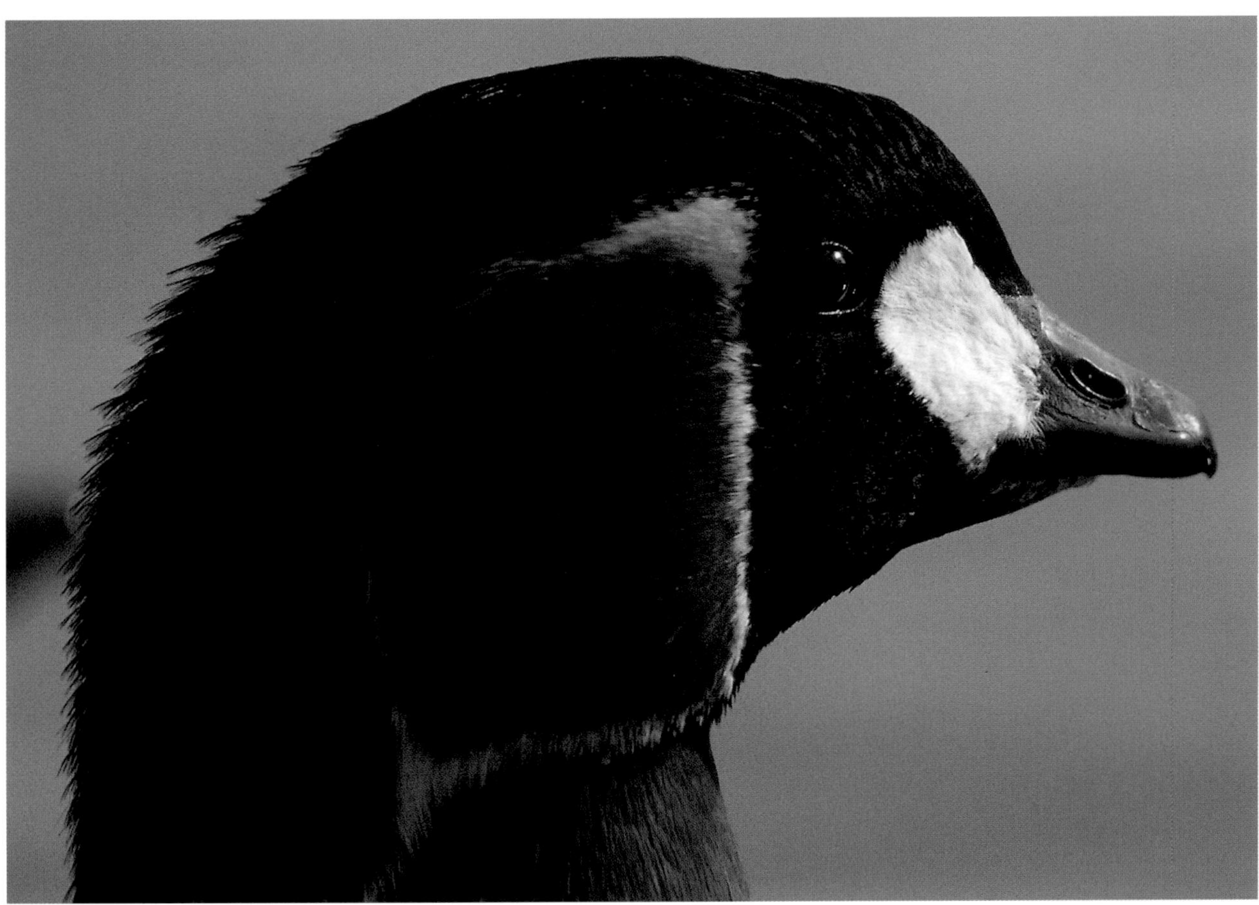

Prey and predator

One interesting aspect of wildfowl nesting is that some species deliberately choose nest sites close to those of a predatory bird. This apparently nonsensical arrangement is actually beneficial to both. Wildfowl nests are frequently plundered by foxes and piratical birds. However, if the nest is close to a raptor or owl nest, the bird of prey will see off gulls and skuas to the advantage of the wildfowl. The raptor gains since geese and ducks are noisy if a potential predator is viewed, so they act as a useful early-warning system. Most famous of these mutual arrangements are those between Red-breasted Geese (one of the smallest, rarest and most beautiful of the northern geese) and Snowy Owls or Peregrine Falcons. The geese occasionally nest within 5m of the bird of prey and occasionally a colony of a dozen or more geese nests will be placed near the same raptor nest. Falcons rarely hunt close to their nests so the geese are afforded a measure of protection. Snowy Owls are much less particular, and once hatched the goslings must run the gauntlet of the owls, though predation is limited if the owl chicks have yet to hatch. The unusually short fledging time for Red-breasted goslings may be a response to this potential predation. The extent to which the geese benefit from the relationship became apparent when Peregrine numbers fell dramatically due to DDT use in the 1960s and 1970s. The crash in falcon numbers was mirrored by that in goose numbers, with the population of Red-breasted Geese climbing as falcon numbers recovered after the ban on DDT was introduced.

Although the Red-breasted Goose is the most obvious example of this arrangement, it is not the only one. Long-tailed Ducks have been observed nesting closer to Red-breasted Goose colonies (and therefore raptor nests) than would normally be expected. King Eiders occasionally nest close to Long-tailed Skuas or Snowy Owls, Steller's Eiders may nest near Pomarine Skuas, and Brent Goose nests have been seen unusually close to those of Snowy Owls.

Shelducks are not strictly an Arctic species, though now increasing in numbers on Iceland. With their distinctive bill 'knob' Sheldrakes are very attractive birds.

DABBLING DUCKS

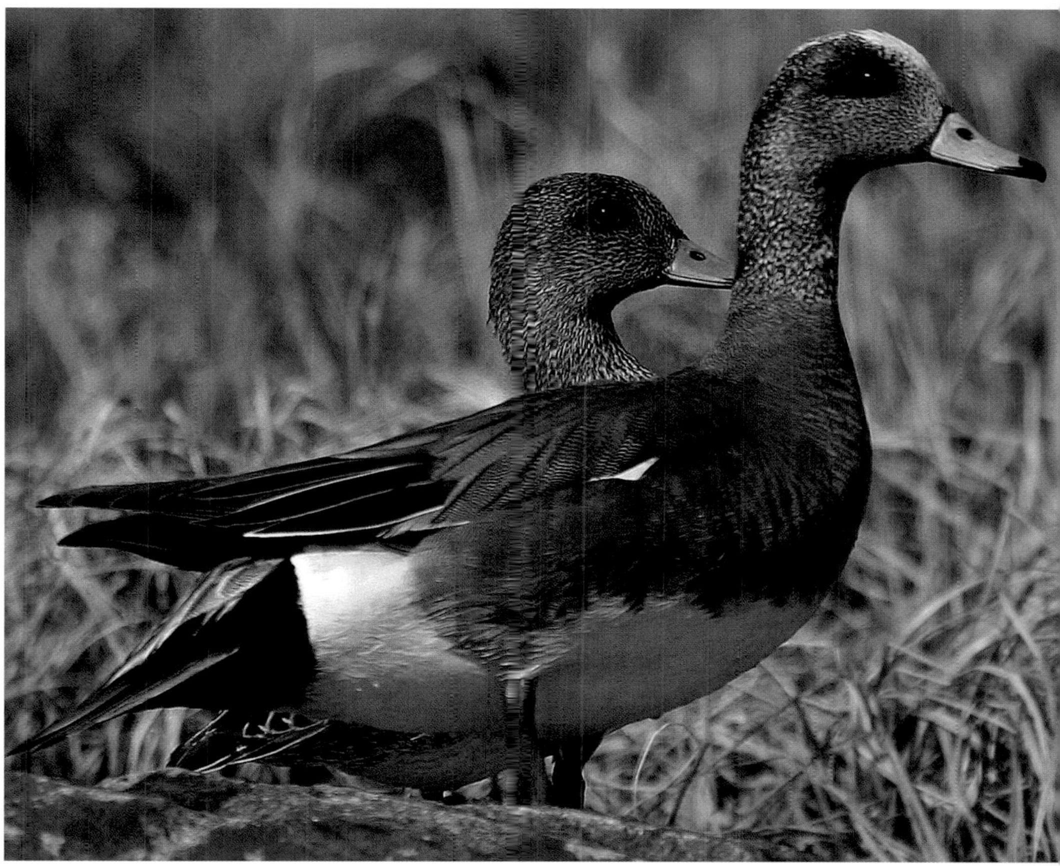

American Wigeon. Great Slave Lake, North West Territories, Canada.

Dabbling ducks are the largest duck group, highly successful, with representatives on all continents except Antarctica (though some species breed on Southern Ocean islands). These ducks are named for their habit of working the surface of the water for food. They feed chiefly in fresh water, though they are not unknown in marine areas. They are primarily pluck aquatic vegetation (but not fish); dabbling ducks also take aquatic invertebrates. Dabbling involves taking in a volume of water that is then squeezed out through lamellae at the edges of the mandibles, seeds and other particles then being swallowed. This feeding method is analogous to that of the large whales (and as such can be considered an example of convergent evolution).

Ducks have long, broad wings. These allow not only a fast flight but also a short take-off, some ducks being able to rise almost vertically from the water if necessary. The ducks are sexually dimorphic, males (drakes) usually being brightly coloured during the breeding season, and the females (ducks) always remaining cryptic brown as camouflage. After the breeding season the males also adopt a more cryptic 'eclipse' plumage. Drakes have a coloured speculum, which is maintained in eclipse. Females usually have a speculum as well, but it may be much smaller or less clear-cut. Pair bonding is seasonal, often occurring during the winter or spring migration. Male ducks have limited displays, the female invariably unmoved by the performance and rarely joining in. The drakes of many species forcibly inseminate available females; in some circumstances several drakes will attempt to forcibly mate with a female (sometimes the female is forced under the water by the relentless activity of squabbling drakes and drowns).

In general, insemination is the only contribution of the drake, with the males deserting the females after laying. Ducklings are precocial, able to swim and feed, but they are brooded at first by the female, and cared for until fledged. Females are diligent in their care of their young.

American Wigeon

Anas americana

L: 45–55cm. WS: 75–90cm. W: 600–850g. ♂>♀.

The drake (breeding) has a black-speckled buff head with a cream forehead and green crescent to the rear of the eye. The upperparts are brown-speckled grey, the underparts salmon pink. The speculum is black with a central band of green. Females are cryptic rufous brown or dark brown with a similar speculum but reduced white patch. Eclipse drakes are as female, but brighter.

American Wigeon breed across northern North America, but only within the Arctic in western Alaska, near the Mackenzie delta and southern Hudson Bay. Wintering birds are seen in the southern United States.

Eurasian Wigeon

Anas penelope

L: 43–50cm. WS: 70–85cm. W: 550–800g. ♂>♀.

As elegant as their North American cousins, with which they will hybridise. Drake (breeding) has a dark brown head with buff forehead. The upperparts are as the American Wigeon, but the breast is pink-buff, the belly white with pale grey flanks. The speculum is dark grey bordered by black bands. Female is as American Wigeon, but darker. Eclipse drake is as female, but with more rufous underparts and brighter overall.

Eurasian Wigeon breed in Iceland and across Eurasia, though not to the northern coast except in Fennoscandia and European Russia. Birds from northern Iceland migrate to the south of the island, though some move to the east coast of North America. Eurasian birds head south to Japan and central Asia.

Eurasian Wigeon, Orre, Norway.

Drake Green-winged Teal, Great Slave Lake, NWT, Canada. Until recently Nearctic and Palearctic birds were considered a single species, but the subtle differences between them have resulted in them now being classified as separate species.

Northern Pintail

Anas acuta

L: 50–65cm (drake's tail 10–15cm extra). WS: 80–95cm. W: 0.7–1.2kg. ♂>♀.

With their elongated tail feathers, drake Pintails are unmistakable. They are also elegantly patterned, with a dark brown head and upper neck. The front of the neck, breast and belly are white, the flanks speckled grey. The upperparts are grey and black. The speculum is metallic dark green bordered by a buff band at the front and a white band at the rear. Female is cryptic brown and cream. Has elongated tail feathers, though not as long as the drake. The speculum is dark brown, bordered front and rear by white bands. Eclipse drake is as female, but paler and with longer tail feathers.

Northern Pintails breed across northern Eurasia, mostly to the coast, but not on any Arctic islands. Breeds in Iceland, but absent from Greenland. Breeds across North America as far east as the Ungava Peninsula, to the north coast except on the Boothia Peninsula, and also on southern Banks Island. Wintering birds are found in central Africa, central Asia, Japan, the southern United States, Mexico and Central America.

(Northern) Shoveler

Anas clypeata

L: 45–55cm. WS: 70–85cm. W: 400–750g. ♂>♀.

The spatulate bill of this species is diagnostic. Drakes are handsome birds, with a dark green sheen on the head and neck, and mottled grey and white upperparts. The breast is white, the belly and flanks chestnut. The speculum is green with a white band at the front. Female is cryptic brown and white, with a duller speculum. Eclipse drake is as female, but brighter and with greyer head and neck.

Shovelers breed in Iceland and across Eurasia, but only to the Arctic fringe. In North America confined to the area west of Hudson Bay, though can be seen on the southern shores of the bay. Breeds to the Mackenzie delta but more southerly in Alaska.

Eurasian Teal (Common Teal)

Anas crecca

L: 35–40cm. WS: 55–65cm. W: 200–450g. ♂>♀.

The smallest of the northern *Anas* ducks. Drake has a chestnut head, the coloration interrupted by an upside-down horizontal 'comma' of dark green from the eye to the nape. The comma is delineated by narrow buffish-yellow bands. The upperparts are grey and grey-brown. The breast is grey-speckled buff, the rest of the underparts grey with darker wavy barring. The speculum is metallic green and black, with white/buff bands at the front and rear. Female is cryptic brown, with a similar speculum enclosed in narrower bands. Eclipse drake as female, but darker.

Eurasian Teal breed in Iceland and across Eurasia, but rarely to the north coast. They fly to Japan, southern Asia and the Middle East for the winter.

Green-winged Teal

Anas carolinensis

L: 35–40cm. WS: 55–65cm. W: 200–450g. ♂>♀.

Until recently considered a subspecies of the Eurasian Teal but now accorded species status. Drake is as Eurasian Teal but lack the delineating bands around the head comma and much less white on the speculum bars. Females and eclipse drake are as Eurasian Teal.

Green-winged Teal breed across North America, including west and north Alaska and northern Yukon/western North-West Territories. Breeds around southern Hudson Bay and near Ungava Bay and in northern Labrador.

Drake Northern Pintail, Churchill, Manitoba, Canada. While females are, as with most other duck species, drab for nesting camouflage, the drake Pintail is among the most attractive of the ducks.

Baikal Teal

Anas formosa

L: 39–45cm. WS: 60–70cm. W: 250–450g. ♂>♀.

Status: IUCN: Vulnerable. CITES: Appendix II.

Arguably the most exquisite of all the northern ducks; drakes have marvellously patterned heads, the crown dark grey, the face buff-yellow, split into two by a narrow black line from the eye to the black chin. The nape is bottle-green, this continuing towards the buff-yellow throat as a thinning curve. The breast is salmon pink merging with a white belly and pale

The Green-winged Teals of the Aleutian islands are considered a subspecies, *nimia*; drakes of these resident birds are larger than their mainland cousins, but otherwise identical. The photograph was taken on Unalaska.

steel-grey flanks. The upperparts are streaked brown, grey and white. The speculum is green with a rufous band at the front and broad white band at the rear. Female is cryptic brown, but with cream underparts and a distinct white loral spot. Eclipse drake as female but more rufous overall.

Baikal Teal breed from Russia's Taimyr Peninsula east to Chukotka, but patchily. Also breeds east from Lake Baikal, around the shores of the Sea of Okhotsk and in Kamchatka. Mainly resident, but northern birds move to Korea and eastern China. Formerly the most numerous of Asian ducks, but decimated by hunting. The habit of feeding on arable fields in winter has led to large-scale killing with poisoned grain.

Mallard

Anas platyrhynchos

L: 50–65cm. WS: 80–100cm. W: 0.85–1.4kg. ♂>♀.

The most widespread and probably most recognisable of the dabbling ducks. Drakes are handsome birds with metallic green sheen on heads and necks. A thin white collar separates the neck from a dark brown breast. The rest of the underparts are speckled pale grey. The upperparts are darker grey. The tail is black, the two central feathers curling upwards. The speculum is blue, bordered by thin black and wider white bands. Female is cryptic brown but with the same speculum. Eclipse drake is as female but darker.

Mallard breed in west and east Greenland, in Iceland, and across Eurasia (though only to the northern coast in Fennoscandia and then increasingly southerly to the east, though occurs in Kamchatka). In North America, Mallard breeds throughout Alaska to the Mackenzie delta, but more southerly across Canada. Greenland and Icelandic birds are resident, but northern birds in Eurasia and the North America move south for the winter.

Greenland's Mallards

Greenlandic birds are considered a separate subspecies, conboschas. They are the most Arctic of all Mallards, breeding on the west coast from northern Disko Bay to the island's southern tip, and around Ammassalik on the east coast. All the island's birds spend the winter in the open water area off the south-east coast, the east coast birds flying across the ice sheet. Greenland Mallards have a precarious existence. Although the open water area can be relied upon, its extent varies and some birds need to search for areas of unfrozen ocean.

(American) Black Duck

Anas rubripes

L: 52–62cm. WS: 85–95cm. W: 1.0–1.3kg. ♂>♀.

Somewhat poorly named as the drake is not black, having a brown head with darker crown and eye stripe. The rest of the bird is dark brown. The speculum is purple bordered by dark brown bands. Female is cryptic brown, with the same speculum. Eclipse drake as breeding but washed grey.

Black Ducks breed around the southern shores of Hudson Bay and northward into Quebec and Labrador, though rarely to the northern coast.

Black Ducks v Mallards

The Black Duck (also known as the Redfoot because of the colour of its feet) has been severely overhunted, this reducing its numbers significantly. The bird now also faces two further threats. One is the loss of its preferred habitat, hardwood wetlands. The other is more serious – the advance of the Mallard. Mallards are expanding their range northward, bringing them within the Black Duck's range. Mallards are highly adaptable and tend to win out in competition with Black Ducks. They also hybridise with them so that pure-bred Black Ducks are becoming rarer. Black Ducks are more cold-resistant than Mallards, but as the Earth warms and Mallards adapt, this is likely to become an increasingly less useful advantage.

Drake Mallards are among the best known of all ducks. Although essentially non-Arctic, Mallards have been expanding their range over recent years and now breed on Greenland and Iceland, and, in the Nearctic, to the northern coast at the Mackenzie Delta.

Gadwall are another non-Arctic species gradually expanding their range north. The ducks now breed in isolated places on the west (as photographed here) and north coasts of Iceland.

GADWALL

Anas strepera

L: 45–55cm. WS: 75–90cm. W: 650–950g. ♂>♀.

Breeds only to the Arctic fringe. Drake is overall grey-brown, the head paler, the tail-coverts black. The speculum is white. Female is cryptic brown, as other *Anas* females, with a similar speculum. Eclipse drake as female but with a paler head.

Gadwall breed in isolated places around Iceland's coast, uncommonly on the Aleutians (though more commonly on the southern Alaskan coast) and on Kamchatka. Elsewhere the species breeds across south-western United States and west central Eurasia. Resident or migratory to the southern states/Mexico and Middle East/central Asia.

POCHARDS

Pochards, the members of the genus *Aythya*, share the same diet as dabbling ducks, but primarily feed with shallow dives, usually to depths of a few metres. Pochards are heavier than dabblers, they have longer necks, and the feet are set further back on the body to act as more efficient paddles; this makes them awkward on land and they are rarely seen away from water. Their heavier weight means pochards have more difficulty becoming airborne, with take-off following a run across the water, a sharp contrast to the often near-vertical lift-off of dabblers. In general, pochards are drabber than dabbling ducks, and lack the colourful speculum. However, they share some behavioural habits; for example, the drakes desert the females after they have begun incubation. They also interbreed as some of the dabbling species do, but do so much more readily, a fact that can cause the observer problems. Why ducks and geese in general, and pochard in particular, are apt to interbreed is not understood.

LESSER SCAUP

Aythya affinis

L: 35–45cm. WS: 60–75cm. W: 750–950g. ♂>♀.

Drake has a black head with a purple gloss (not always easily distinguishable). The neck and breast are black, the upperparts white, vermiculated dark grey and black. The underparts are white with grey flecks on the flanks. Female is overall grey-brown. There is a distinct white basal ring to the bill. Eclipse drake as breeding but much duller, with the upperparts more grey-brown and the underparts flecked grey-brown. The patterning is also much less well-defined.

Lesser Scaup breed across North America, though to the north coast only near the Mackenzie delta. Also breeds on the south-eastern shore of Hudson Bay, but otherwise subarctic. Wintering birds are seen along the east and west coasts of the United States and Mexico.

GREATER SCAUP

Aythya marila

L: 40–50cm. WS: 70–85cm. W: 0.85–1.2kg. ♂>♀.

Very similar to Lesser Scaup, but the head gloss is green rather than purple and the upperparts tend to be lighter. Female and eclipse drake are also similar to Lesser Scaup. In the Nearctic where both species breed there is ample scope for confusion. In general the head gloss is diagnostic, but in some lights the sheen colours can be reversed, which can render the difference useless for identification purposes. Head shape is usually a more reliable characteristic. The Lesser Scaup has a tall, narrow head, whereas the Greater Scaup's head is wider and more oval. Head shape when viewed from the side also differs, the Lesser Scaup's head being squarer, the crown and nape flatter, while the Greater Scaup's head is more rounded and has a peak on the crown. Caution is still required as the head shape

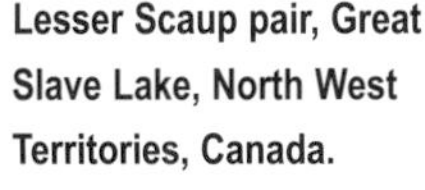

Lesser Scaup pair, Great Slave Lake, North West Territories, Canada.

Great Scaup drake, Churchill, Manitoba, Canada. The green head sheen is usually the best way of distinguishing the two Scaup species.

can change with activity. In the Palearctic, where the Lesser Scaup does not breed, there is confusion with Tufted Duck; the crest of the Tufted drake and the more clearly discernible purple head gloss are diagnostic. In females the crest of the Tufted duck and the white facial ring at the base of the bill of the Scaup female are diagnostic.

Greater Scaup breed in Iceland and across Eurasia, though only to the coast in Fennoscandia and Russia to the Taimyr Peninsula. Also breeds on Kamchatka. Nearctic wintering birds share the same range as the Lesser Scaup. Western Palearctic birds head to the coasts of southern Scandinavia, the British Isles, the Low Countries and France, and the Mediterranean, Black and Caspian seas. Eastern Palearctic birds move to the coasts of Japan, Korea and China.

Tufted Duck

Aythya fuligula

L: 40–50cm. WS: 65–75cm. W: 0.65–1.0kg. ♂>♀.
Drake has a black head with a distinct purple sheen and a long, downcurved crest. The upperparts are black, the underparts white. Female has a dark brown head and upperparts, the breast lighter brown, the belly white. Female shows a smaller crest, but has the same white wing-stripe as the drakes. Eclipse drake is as breeding but much duller on the head and underparts, and the white underparts are heavily flecked brown.

Tufted Ducks breed in Iceland across Eurasia, though only to the northern coast in Fennoscandia. Also breeds on Kamchatka. Wintering birds largely resident but some move to the Mediterranean coasts of southern Europe and north Africa, the coasts of the Black and Caspian seas, across central Asia and the coasts of Japan, Korea and south-east China.

Canvasback

Aythya valisineria

L: 50–60cm. WS: 70–80cm. W: 0.9–1.[illegible]kg. ♂>♀.
Drake has a handsome rufous head and neck and a black breast. The upperparts are whitish grey (this feature giving the bird its name), as are the underparts apart from the undertail-coverts, which are black. Female has the same pattern, but the head, neck and breast are brown with white flecking, and the upper- and underparts are brown, speckled pale grey. Eclipse drake is as breeding but head, neck and breast are dark brown, with the rest of the plumage as the female.

Canvasbacks breed in a band across central Alaska from the west coast, but are scarce throughout much of the range. Breeds to the Mackenzie delta, but then much more southerly to the Ontario border. Absent from eastern Canada. In winter the birds fly to areas of the east and west coasts of the United States, the Gulf of Mexico and the Mississippi delta. In central Alaska the birds may be confused with the Redhead *Aythya americana*. The latter has a redder head, a less heavy (and bluer) bill, and greyer upper- and underparts.

EIDERS

The four eiders are the most maritime of all wildfowl, and are pelagic for much of their lives. The eiders are dive-feeders, making the deepest dives of any duck. Common Eiders are known to dive to 20m at least and it is believed that the Spectacled Eider, reckoned to be the deepest diver of all, reaches depths of 50m. However, eiders usually dive to no more than 5m. During dives the birds use their feet as paddles, with occasional wing strokes. The prey comprises molluscs, which are prised from rocks, crustaceans and other benthic animals. Prey is crushed either by the powerful bill or in the grit-free, muscular gizzard. Steller's Eider, the smallest of the group, feeds extensively on aquatic larvae, especially in freshwater, and its dives rarely exceed depths of 8m.

Below left
Tufted drake, Stavanger, Norway.

Below
A drake Canvasback proving the adage that rain is lovely weather for ducks (if not necessarily for photographers), south central Alaska.

Common Eider, Kjorholmane, Norway.

Eider down

Eider females pluck down from their breasts to insulate their eggs. The value of eider down to humans in keeping the northern winter at bay has been obvious since at least the 7th century when St Cuthbert, the first Bishop of Lindisfarne, set up a sanctuary for Common Eiders on one of the Farne islands off the Northumberland coast; eiders are still known by locals as Cuddy Ducks in his memory. Commercial farming was begun by the Vikings two centuries or so later, and in the early 20th century down remained a major export of Iceland. The down was collected from nests after the chicks had departed. Each nest produces about 15g of raw down, the cleaning process reducing this to about 1.5g of usable material. A kilogram of exported down therefore required the input from 700 nests; at the industry's height, Iceland exported over 4 tonnes of raw down annually, representing the output from almost 300,000 nests. Though now reduced in scale as a consequence of competition from Chinese goose down producers and other sources, Iceland still exports down worth around $2 million annually.

The scientific names of the bird reflect this usage. *Somateria*, the genus name for the three large eiders, derives from the Greek for 'down body', while *mollissima*, the specific name for the Common Eider, derives from the Latin for 'softest'.

The photograph above shows how well camouflaged female Common Eiders are on their nests, north-west Iceland. See also the photograph of a Common Eider nest on p292.

As an adaptation for diving the birds are heavy, take-off requiring a lengthy run across the surface. They are strong fliers but not manoeuvrable, a fact that is particularly noticeable when they land; landings have none of the grace of the smaller ducks, involving more of the crash-landing technique of the swans.

Drake eiders are finely patterned, the females having the familiar cryptic brown plumage required of tight-sitting nesters. The drakes parade their plumage in mating displays while calling their musical three-syllable *coo*. They also coo at sea, the call, when heard through an opaque Arctic sea mist, being ethereal and evocative. Female eiders have an additional protective technique when incubating; if forced to flee they will, just before departing, defecate evil-smelling faeces on their eggs. This may well deter Arctic Foxes but it is of little benefit against gulls and skuas, which have a limited sense of smell. Eider ducklings frequently form large crèches of up to 100 birds (500+ have been seen) in the care of one or more females.

Common Eider

Somateria mollissima

L: 50–70cm. WS: 85–110cm. W: 1.8–2.8kg. ♂>♀.

Drake has a wonderfully patterned head, something it shares with males of the other two *Somateria* eiders. The face is white, the crown black, the nape pale green and divided into three by thin white stripes. The breast is cream, tinged pink, the remaining underparts black apart from a white patch on the rear flank. The upperparts are white. The primary and secondary wing feathers, rump and tail are black. Female is cryptic brown with a brown 'speculum'. Technically only Steller's Eider and Harlequin Duck of the sea ducks have a true speculum, though several other species have colour patches on the secondaries that give a similar appearance. In the drake Common Eider this is black. Eclipse drake has a grey-brown head, the white of breeding replaced by grey-brown.

Common Eiders breed on both coasts of Greenland (though not to the far north), on Iceland, Svalbard, Franz Josef Land, in Fennoscandia and the southern island of Novaya Zemlya. In Arctic Russia breeding is patchy, occurring on the New Siberian Islands and Wrangel Island, with isolated breeding sites on the mainland (more concentrated in Chukotka). In North America the birds breed on the Aleutians, the west and north coasts of Alaska, on the northern Canadian mainland coast (including Hudson Bay), and on the southern Arctic islands.

Greenland birds winter in Iceland, where the ducks are resident. The birds of the Eurasian Arctic islands move to the southern Scandinavian coasts or the Bering Sea. Nearctic birds move to the both coasts of the United States.

King Eider

Somateria spectabilis

L: 50–65cm. WS: 85–100cm. W: 1.4–2.0kg. ♂>♀.

Drakes justify their name with a regal head pattern that includes an orange and black forehead shield (which the Inuit sometimes bite off and eat immediately after killing a bird). The crown and nape are pale blue, while there is a pale green patch below the eye merging to white cheeks. The upper mantle is white, the rest of the upperparts black with two 'shark's fins' arising from the tertials. The breast is cream tinged pink, the rest of the underparts black apart from white patches on the rear flanks. Female is cryptic with a dark brown 'speculum'. Eclipse drake maintains the forehead shield, but the rest of the head is grey-brown, as is the breast. The rest of the plumage is as breeding, but duller.

King Eiders breed in west and north-west Greenland, on the island's east coast (around Scoresbysund) and on the north-east coast. Also breeds on Svalbard, Novaya Zemlya and along the north Russian coast from the White Sea to Chukotka, including the New Siberian Islands. In North America breeds along the north coast from Alaska to Hudson Bay and on all Canada's Arctic islands. Absent from Canada's coast east of Hudson Bay. In winter east Greenland birds join resident Icelandic birds. On western Greenland the birds make for the

Drake Common and King Eiders, Sirevaag, Norway.

King Eider flock, Southampton Island, Canada.

Drake Spectacled Eider, Barrow, Alaska.

open water off the south-west coast. Svalbard and west Russian birds move to the Barents and Kara seas, with east Russian birds heading to the Bering Sea. American birds move to the Bering Sea and Labrador coast.

Spectacled Eider

Somateria fischeri

L: 50–60cm. WS: 85–95cm. W: 1.5–1.9kg. ♂>♀.

The smallest and least known of the three *Somateria* eiders. Drake has spectacular goggles (the spectacles of the name), the 'lens' being white, the 'frame' black. The forehead is pale green, as is the nape. The rest of the neck and upperparts are white. The underparts and tail are dark grey. Female is cryptic brown, but also have 'goggles' with pale brown lenses, the rest of the head darker. Eclipse male is as female but darker. Newly hatched chicks also have 'goggles'.

Spectacled Eiders breed on the Asian Russian coast east of the Lena and on the New Siberian Islands and Wrangel. Also breeds on the western and northern coast of Alaska. The Alaskan population crashed in the 1990s for reasons unknown and has continued to decline ever since; the birds are now rare and much sought-after by Arctic travellers.

Wintering Spectacled Eiders

Until the mid-1990s the wintering range of Spectacled Eiders was completely unknown. Only with the advent of radio-tracking did it become possible to follow tagged birds. This led researchers to the central Bering Sea, where photography revealed perhaps thirty flocks comprising a total of at least 150,000 birds. It is now known that the birds winter in large numbers in areas of open water, chiefly near St Lawrence and St Matthew Islands. Aerial photography suggests that the birds help keep the leads free of ice by their diving and swimming.

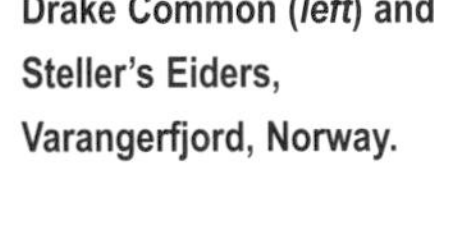

Drake Common (*left*) and Steller's Eiders, Varangerfjord, Norway.

Steller's Eider

Polysticta stelleri

L: 42–50cm. WS: 70–80cm. W: 0.75–1.0kg. ♂>♀.

The smallest of the four eiders, and the drake is the least spectacular. Has a white head with a black eye ring, pale green patches on the lores and forehead, and a curious green tuft on the back of the head. The throat, mantle, rump and tail are black. The wings are white with black primaries and a black speculum, bordered white. The underparts are buff-orange, the belly darker, but the flanks white. Female is cryptic brown with a blue speculum, bordered white. Female also has drooping tertials. Eclipse drake is as female, but with a paler head and white flanks.

Steller's Eiders breed on the Asian Russian coast east from Khatanga Bay, and on the New Siberian Islands. May also breed on other, isolated sections of the Russian coast, perhaps as far west as the Kola Peninsula; birds have been seen off the Fennoscandia coast and in the Baltic Sea in winter. Also winters in the Bering Sea. In North America it breeds in western and northern Alaska.

Georg Steller

Georg Wilhelm Steller (1709–46) was a German naturalist who accompanied Bering's second journey. Steller was the first European to land on Alaska, when he leapt ashore at Kayak Island. Steller's name is associated with several Alaskan species. Steller's Eider is named after him; he took the first specimen of the bird off the coast of Kamchatka. He also named the now-extinct Spectacled Cormorant (*Phalacrocorax perspicillatus*), while Steller's Jay (*Cyanocitta stelleri*), Steller's Sea Eagle, Steller's Sea Lion and another extinct species from the region, the Sea Cow (occasionally called Steller's Sea Cow), are all named after his first descriptions. Steller was also the discoverer of the Sea Otter. See p488 for an illustration of how the Sea Cow is believed to have looked.

SEADUCKS

Seaducks are a group of pelagic waterfowl (which, technically, should include the eiders, though they have been considered separately here as their flamboyant plumage makes them different from the other, essentially black-and-white, birds). Seaducks dive much deeper than the diving ducks and occasionally pursue prey, particularly the sawbills, which take fish and swimming invertebrates, while the rest chiefly feed on benthic animals. As with the eiders, shellfish and crustaceans are often swallowed whole and crushed by the muscular gizzard.

As in the dabbling and diving ducks, drakes abandon incubating females. The precocial chicks have good down coverings and some subcutaneous fat, which allows them to dive in icy waters almost from hatching. Northern seaducks are partially migratory, moving south ahead of the sea ice in winter.

Bufflehead pair, Great Slave Lake, North West Territories, Canada.

Bufflehead

Bucephala albeola

L: 32–40cm. WS: 55–60cm. W: 390–450g. ♂>♀.

The face, crown and neck of the drake are black with a purple, green or bronze sheen. The rest of the bird is black-and-white. Female is much drabber, dark grey-brown above, with a prominent white patch behind the eye and creamy brown below. There is a white speculum. Eclipse drake is as female, but black rather than grey-brown and generally with a larger white eye patch.

Buffleheads are subarctic, breeding in central Alaska but more southerly across Canada, though occasionally seen north of the Arctic boundary as defined here. In winter the birds are seen to the south of the Aleutians, and off the coasts of the Pacific seaboard.

Common Goldeneye

Bucephala clangula

L: 40–50cm. WS: 65–80cm. W: 0.8–1.2kg. ♂>♀.

Drake has a black head with a green sheen. There is a prominent white patch in front of the eye. The rest of the bird is black-and-white. Females have chocolate brown heads without a white patch. The rest of the plumage is grey-brown. There is a white 'speculum'. Eclipse drake is as female, but some retain the white head patch.

Common Goldeneyes breed in Fennoscandia and across Russia, but only to the north coast around the White Sea. Also breeds on Kamchatka. North American birds breed in southern Alaska, at the Mackenzie delta, then south towards Hudson Bay's southern shore and in southern Quebec and Labrador. In winter the birds move south of the breeding range, to both inland and coastal locations.

Barrow's Goldeneye

Bucephala islandica

L: 40–55cm. WS: 65–85cm. W: 0.9–1.3kg. ♂>♀.

Drake has a black head with a purple sheen. There is a crescent-shaped white patch between the eye and bill. The rest of the body is black-and-white. Female has a dark brown head, pale grey-brown body. Eclipse drake as female but shows more white on the upperparts.

Barrow's Goldeneyes breed in Iceland (mostly at Lake Mývatn where the population is declining) but otherwise restricted to the Nearctic (the breeding birds of west Greenland are now thought to be extinct). In North America breeds in central and southern Alaska, southern Yukon and British Columbia. Icelandic birds are resident; Nearctic birds move south in winter to inland and coastal sites.

Long-tailed Duck

Clangula hyemalis

L: 40–50cm (male tail adds 10–15cm). WS: 65–80cm. W: 650–950g. ♂>♀.

Drake is unmistakeable, with long, upcurved tail feathers. The head is white with a black patch on the cheek, the rest of the plumage black-and-white apart from a brown mantle and back. Female has brown-smudged white head and brown upperparts. The breast is paler brown, the underparts white, though some birds have pale brown bellies. Female tail feathers are much shorter. Eclipse male is much whiter, particularly on the breast and upperparts. Male moults again before breeding, making it the only duck with different bonding and breeding plumages. In winter female is much paler.

Long-tailed Ducks breed throughout the Arctic, including most of the Canadian Arctic islands. On Ellesmere Island the ducks vie with King Eiders for the title of most northerly breeding waterfowl. In winter the birds are seen in the Bering Sea, off eastern Canada, southern Greenland, around Iceland, north Norway and in the Baltic and North seas.

Harlequin Duck

Histrionicus histrionicus

L: 38–45cm. WS: 60–70cm. W: 550–750g. ♂>♀.

Drake is the most colourful of the non-eider seaducks, with blue-grey head marked by white spots and crescents, and rufous streaks. The rest of the body is blue-grey, with white streaks and large rufous patches on the flanks. Female much drabber, being mottled brown and white overall, with white patches around and behind the eye. Eclipse drake is as the female but darker.

Hole-nesting ducks

Some ducks nest in tree holes, and will even accept nesting boxes as sites. Given their webbed feet and general awkwardness, this is surprising. For species that nest this way (e.g. Common and Barrow's Goldeneyes, Smew and Bufflehead of the northern ducks), their ability to colonise an area is dependent upon the presence of woodpeckers to excavate holes large enough for them to occupy. It also, of course, means that the birds cannot expand their range north of the treeline. It has been suggested that the reason the Common Goldeneye did not become a nesting species in the British Isles until the 1970s was the absence of the Black Woodpecker *Dryocopus martius*, no British woodpecker making large enough holes to accommodate the ducks. It is assumed that not until the arrival of a female who had been raised in a nesting box were boxes exploited. However, in Iceland, where Barrow's Goldeneye use crevices in ancient lava flows as nest sites, the birds took to using nesting boxes on the sides of houses, despite it being extremely unlikely that any Icelandic bird had ever been so raised. When they leave the hole the chicks drop to the ground, occasionally falling 10m. There were once stories of the chicks riding away on their parents' backs or on their feet, but these are myths.

Below
These Common Goldeneyes are the Nearctic sub-species *B. c. americana*, photographed at Churchill, Manitoba, Canada.

Below right
Barrow's Goldeneye is named after Sir John Barrow, the man behind the British Royal Navy's expeditions in search of the North-West Passage in the 19th century. Where the two Goldeneyes overlap, drakes can be distinguished by the head gloss and the patterning of the upperparts, Barrow's showing less white, with the white forming more discrete patches. The white facial patch of Barrow's drakes is also comma-shaped, rather than blob-like. Where the two species overlap they will hybridise. The ducks were photographed at Mývatn, Iceland.

Long-tailed Ducks, Mackenziebukta, north-east Greenland. An alternative name for Long-tailed Duck is Oldsquaw. This is apparently a reference to the noisy drake of the species, which reminded early travellers of the chatter of elderly Inuit women. In this age of political correctness, the name was considered inappropriate and changed, though it is still often used in North America. The scientific name for the bird translates as 'noisy winter bird'.

The perils of childhood

Some years ago, on Ellesmere Island, the author and Per Michelsen watched as a Glaucous Gull attacked a family of Long-tailed Ducks on a large tundra pond. The female duck had half a dozen newly hatched chicks, which dived below the surface each time the gull swooped. Eventually one chick became so exhausted that it failed to dive quickly enough as the gull approached. It was snatched up, taken to the far shore of the pond and eaten. The gull rested for a short while, then again began to swoop across the pond. As both Sale, Michelsen and the female duck watched helplessly, the gull exhausted and ate each duckling in turn.

Harlequin Ducks breed in south-west and east central Greenland, in Iceland, in Chukotka, Kamchatka and around the northern shore of the Sea of Okhotsk, in southern Alaska, Yukon and North-West Territories and in southern Quebec and Labrador. In winter the ducks are resident or partially migratory.

Common Scoter

Melanitta nigra

L: 45–55cm. WS: 70–85cm. W: 0.85–1.3kg. ♂>♀.

Drake is glossy black overall, though the underparts are paler. The bill has a prominent black knob at the base of the upper mandible, forward of which is a yellow patch, which extends beyond the nostril. Female has a chocolate brown crown and nape, but the rest of the head is light brown. The remaining plumage is grey-brown. There is no eclipse plumage, but first-winter drake is browner with a less prominent bill knob.

Common Scoters breed in Iceland and across Eurasia to the Lena delta, but only to the north coast west of the Urals. Wintering birds move to the North and Baltic seas.

Black Scoter

Melanitta americana

L: 45–55cm. WS: 70–85cm. W: 0.85–1.3kg. ♂>♀.

Formerly considered conspecific with the Common Scoter. Very similar to that species, but the drake's bill is yellow-orange in the breeding season, and smaller.

Black Scoters breed in Asian Russia east of the Lena delta (but not to the north coast) and on Kamchatka. Also breeds in west and south Alaska, and in southern Quebec and Labrador. In winter the birds move to the Bering Sea and coasts of Japan.

Surf Scoter

Melanitta perspicillata

L: 45–55cm. WS: 75–95cm. W: 0.8–1.1kg. ♂>♀.

Drake is dull (rather than glossy) black apart from a white patch on the nape. The bill is a marvel. The upper mandible is swollen both up and out. The culmen is black-feathered to the nostril, the rest of the upper mandible being orange-red, white and black. Female is as Common and Black Scoters but with a pale patch at the base of the bill. First-winter drake is as

Harlequin duck pairs (*above*) on the surging waters of the north Pacific at Starichkov Island, off southern Kamchatka's eastern shore, and (*below*) at Skógafoss, southern Iceland. Formerly Mývatn was the only European breeding ground, but in recent years the ducks have expanded their Icelandic range.

breeding bird but duller, and lacks the white nape patch and glorious colours of the bill.

Surf Scoters breed patchily throughout Alaska (though rare in the north), the Yukon and North-West Territories, and in southern Quebec and Labrador. Wintering birds move to the Aleutians and east and west coasts of North America.

Velvet Scoter (White-winged Scoter)
Melanitta fusca
L: 50–60cm. WS: 90–100cm. W: 1.5–2.0kg. ♂>♀.
Despite the name the drake has a glossy dark chocolate/black plumage apart from a white half-moon eye patch. The bill is black at the base, becoming yellow and with a red tip. There is a small knob at the base of the upper mandible. Female is light brown overall, with a small white patch below and behind the eye. First-winter drake is as female but duller; lacks the white half-moon and has a duller bill.

Velvet Scoters breed across Eurasia, but only to the north coast west of the Urals. Largely absent from Chukotka, but breeds on Kamchatka. Also breeds across North America from Alaska to the western shores of Hudson Bay, but only to the north coast near the Mackenzie delta. The Nearctic and east Asian race, *M. f. deglandi*, is considered a full species, the White-winged Scoter, by some authorities. In winter the birds are seen in the Baltic and North seas, in waters off Japan, off the Aleutian islands and the west coast of the United States.

MERGANSERS

The *Mergus* ducks are commonly known as sawbills because of their elongated, thin bills, which have serrations on the mandibles in order to grasp fish and hooked tips to aid their capture. There are three Arctic and subarctic breeders, though a fourth species, the Hooded Merganser *Lophodytes cucullatus,* while essentially a temperate bird, has recently been increasing its range to the north.

Mergansers are the only ducks capable of catching fish, but they also take other prey opportunistically, including amphibians, molluscs, crustaceans and even small mammals.

Goosander (Common Merganser)
Mergus merganser
L: 55–70cm. WS: 80–100cm. W: 1.1–1.6kg. ♂>♀.
Goosanders are primarily freshwater rather than marine ducks. Drake has a dark green head and neck with a green sheen. The upperparts and tail are dark greyish black, though the inner wings are white. The underparts are white. Female has a brown head and neck, light grey upperparts and grey-smudged white underparts. The 'speculum' is white. Eclipse drake is as female but retains the completely white inner wing.

Goosanders breed in Iceland and across Eurasia, though only to the north coast in Fennoscandia; also breeds on Kamchatka. In North America the birds breed across the continent, but they are essentially subarctic, being rare in west and central Alaska. They do, however, breed on the southern shore of Hudson Bay. Wintering birds are seen in northern France and the Low Countries, central Asia and eastern China, and off both coasts of the United States.

Red-breasted Merganser

Mergus serrator

L: 50–60cm. WS: 70–85cm. W: 0.95–1.2kg. ♂>♀.

Drake is a handsome bird with a dark green, glossy head and neck and a prominent crest on the nape. The upperparts are black and white, the underparts grey and white. Female has a brown head and neck, also with a nape crest. The upperparts are grey, the underparts paler grey. The 'speculum' is white, split by a thin black bar. Eclipse drake as female. When diving, Red-breasted Mergansers use their wings as well as their feet. The birds will also feed cooperatively, an unusual trait, corralling a shoal of fish and driving it into shallow waters.

Red-breasted Mergansers breed on west and east Greenland, on Iceland and across Eurasia, though rarely to the north coast. Breeds on Kamchatka. Also breeds across North America, often to the north coast and including the southern part of Baffin Island. Most birds are resident or partially migratory, though western American birds move along the west coast of the United States.

Smew

Mergus albellus

L: 37–45cm. WS: 55–70cm. W: 550–750g. ♂>♀.

The drake is beautiful, with a white head apart from a large black eye patch and a black V on the nape. There is a small crest on the crown. The upperparts are black and white, though the tail is grey. The underparts are white and pale grey. Female has a chestnut crown, a similar black eye patch, but an otherwise white head. The rest of the plumage is grey, black and white above, white below. Eclipse drake is as female but paler and with a white crest.

Smew breed in southern Fennoscandia and across Russia to the Lena delta but always essentially subarctic. Also breeds in southern Chukotka and northern Kamchatka. Wintering birds are resident or partially migratory.

Top
Goosander pair, Orre, Norway.

Centre
Male Smew, surely the most beautiful of all Arctic seaducks, Orre, Norway.

Left
Evening light illuminates a Red-breasted Merganser pair in southern Hudson Bay.

RAPTORS

Raptors are superbly equipped for the task of locating and catching live prey. They have talons for gripping fast-moving prey keen to make its escape, and hooked beaks for tearing flesh. The wings can be broad and long to allow the birds to soar with minimal effort as they seek relatively slow-moving animals or carrion, or tapered to allow very fast flight, the better to overhaul speedier prey. Raptors are solitary in the breeding season but are sometimes gregarious in winter, when congregations of birds and communal roosting of several of the larger species may occur, though most falcons do not share this behaviour, being solitary or in mated pairs at all times. The mating displays of the Arctic raptors often involve some form of 'sky-dance', in which the male circles the chosen nest site. There may even be mutual dancing, the pair touching or even linking talons. Sky-dancing is less common in falcons, though the 'high circling' flight of males above the nest site is an equivalent. Courtship-feeding is also common. In general the pair bond is monogamous and may be long-lasting, though in some raptors it appears to be seasonal. The nests of raptors are often re-used annually and they can become huge, the sites highlighted by the streaks from years of defecation. The arboreal nests of Steller's Sea Eagles sometimes attain such vastness that they overwhelm the tree, causing major branches (or even the entire tree) to break so that the nest falls. By contrast, the nests of falcons are minimal, often mere scrapes with little or no lining, even at sites that have been used annually over many years. The Gyrfalcon actually makes no nest at all, laying eggs on to a bare cliff ledge or, frequently, usurping the nest of a Raven, Rough-legged Buzzard or even an eagle.

The larger raptor species lay 1–3 eggs, the falcons more. These are incubated by the female, which is fed by the male. The chicks have minimal down and are altricial or semi-altricial. They are fed by the female at first with food brought by the male. The female also broods. Later when the chicks have down and can thermoregulate, both birds will feed the young. The chicks are independent soon after fledging. Raptors take a long time to mature, and often do not breed until they are two or three years old, though the Merlin may breed at one year. Steller's Sea Eagles do not breed until they are at least four or five years old, and perhaps even as late as eight years.

Apart from the harriers, hawks and some falcons, the sexes are similar in plumage. All species except the Osprey are sexually dimorphic and, interestingly, this is the reverse of the norm, with females being larger than males. This trait is shared by other avian predators such as owls, frigatebirds and skuas, though to nothing like the same extent in the latter two groups. It is not entirely clear what the basis for this reversed sexual dimorphism is; the size of prey taken by the two birds (smaller males are more agile and can catch smaller prey) is clearly important since it reduces interspecific competition, but why it should be the females that are larger (rather than the males as in almost all other avian groups) is not understood.

Breeding and winter plumages are similar in all Arctic raptor species.

Opposite page
Ospreys, Sirdalsvannet, Norway.

OSPREY

Pandion haliaetus

L: 50–60cm. WS: 150–170cm. W: 1.2–1.7kg.

Adult has long legs, large feet and long, narrow wings. The head is white with a thick, dark brown stripe from the shoulder through the eye. Ospreys are countershaded, with white underparts that camouflage the bird against the (often cloudy) sky for the fish they are hunting, and darker upperparts as camouflage if viewed from above against the water. Almost exclusively piscivorous – Ospreys are equipped with small spikes on their toes to aid the gripping of their prey.

Ospreys are seen as far north as the treeline and so are marginally Arctic. They breed in southern Fennoscandia, but are more southerly across Russia. In the Nearctic they breed in southern Alaska (but are rare) and at the treeline across Canada, including the southern shores of Hudson Bay. This distribution is the widest of any raptor. In winter the birds move to the southern states of the United States, and to north Africa and south Asia.

This page
Golden Eagles, Bjerkreim, Norway.

White-tailed Eagle, Finnish Karelia, close to the Russian border.

Below
Dispute between adult and juvenile White-tailed Eagles in the Norwegian Lofoten Islands.

Below right
Juvenile White-tailed Eagle, Lofoten Islands, Norway.

Golden Eagle
Aquila chrysaetos
L: 75–90cm. WS: 190–225cm. W: 3.0–5.5kg. ♀>♂.
The only *Aquila* eagle that breeds in the Arctic; magnificent birds with long wings and a large tail. Adult has golden brown head, the rest of the plumage being mottled brown and dark brown, the wings grey-brown. Immature birds show a diminishing white wing-patch. Feeds chiefly on mammals (occasionally very large prey; old and sickly Reindeer have been known to be preyed upon), occasionally hunting co-operatively with mate. Also takes carrion.

Golden Eagles breed in Fennoscandia, though absent from the far north, then more southerly across Russia. In Nearctic breeds in Alaska (though common only in central Alaska) on the Mackenzie delta, then more southerly. Breeds around southern Hudson Bay and across southern Quebec and Labrador. Northern birds move south to join resident southern eagles in winter.

FISH EAGLES

The coastal waters and inland lakes of the Arctic are exploited not only by Ospreys, but also by three of the world's ten species of fish eagles.

White-tailed Eagle, Lofoten Islands, Norway.

Juvenile Bald Eagle, Dutch Harbour, Aleutians, Alaska.

The eagle and the child

Despite the numerous legends and tall tales, there is actually only one documented record of an eagle having picked up a child. On 5 June 1932 a White-tailed Eagle snatched four-year-old Svanhild Hansen, said to have been a particularly small child, at Leka in Norway and carried her for more than a kilometre to a ledge close to its nest site, almost 250m up a mountain. The girl was scratched but otherwise unharmed.

White-tailed (Sea) Eagle

Haliaeetus albicilla

L: 75–90cm. WS: 190–240cm. W: 3.5–5.5kg. ♀>♂.

Status: CITES: Appendix I.

Large, with a long neck and huge bill. Europe's largest raptor, equalling the Lammergeier *Gypaetus barbatus* in weight. Adult is uniformly brown, with white feather tips giving a scaly appearance. The tail is white. Immature birds have brown tails, not achieving the adult white until they are five years old. Chiefly piscivorous but will take waterfowl and carrion.

White-tailed Eagles breed in west Greenland, Iceland and across Eurasia, reaching the north coast in Fennoscandia and Chukotka. Also breed in Kamchatka. Greenlandic and Icelandic birds are resident, west Eurasian birds overwinter around the North and Baltic seas, east Eurasian birds on the coasts of Japan, Korea and China.

Bald Eagle

Haliaeetus leucocephalus

L: 70–95cm. WS: 180–240cm. W: 3.5–5.5kg. ♀>♂.

The Nearctic equivalent of the White-tailed Eagle. Adult has a white head (the origin of the name) and white tail, but is otherwise dark brown, with scalloping from pale feather tips.

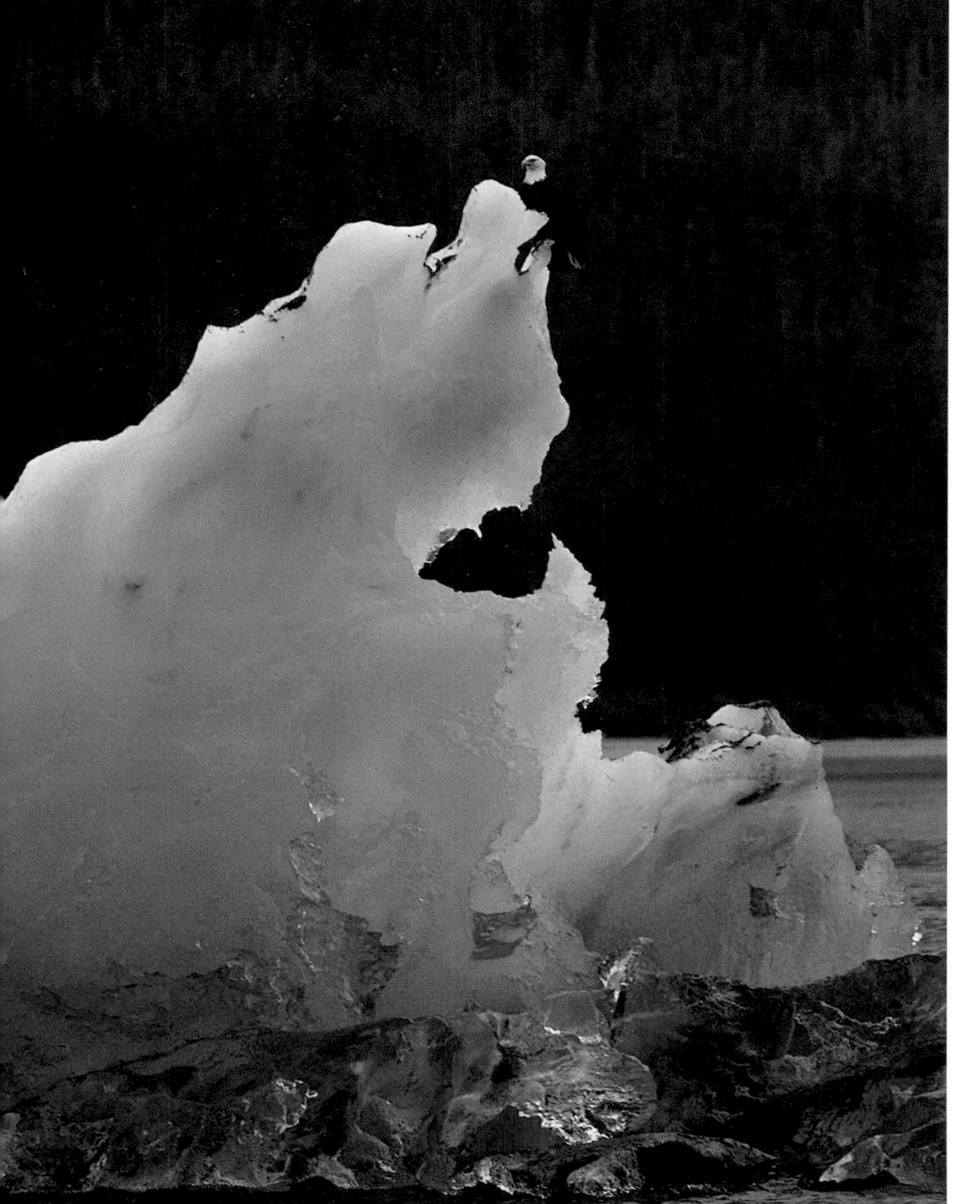

The symbol of the United States

The Bald Eagle is the emblem of the United States, which made it even sadder when numbers declined sharply as a result of subsidised shooting and the widespread use of organochlorides in the continental US. After hunting and DDT were banned, a slow recovery in the population began . In Alaska the use of pesticides was minimal, but a bounty on eagles set in 1917 – the result of lobbying by fishermen and fox trappers – was not lifted until 1953. Although the bounty led to ill-advised slaughter, the state remained a stronghold of the species and continues to do so.

Immature eagles do not acquire the adult colouring until they are five years old. Primarily piscovorous but will also take waterfowl, gulls and small mammals.

Bald Eagles breed in central and southern Alaska, including the Aleutians, and across North America, but rarely north of the treeline, with nests usually built in trees, though nests on cliffs and artificial structures are known. In winter the birds move to the continental United States, though birds in southern Alaska are resident.

Steller's Sea Eagle

Haliaeetus pelagicus

L: 80–100cm. WS: 220–250cm. W: 4.5–6.5kgs, exceptionally females to 9kg. ♀>♂.

The world's largest fish eagle and probably the largest bird of prey; the Steller's huge bill is without doubt the largest of any raptor. Adult has a white tail, legs and forewing, and occasionally a white forehead. The rest of the plumage is mottled dark brown and black. Immature birds do not acquire full adult plumage until they are seven or eight years old. The diet is almost entirely piscivorous which, at most sites, means exclusively salmon for much of the year.

Steller's Sea Eagles breed on Kamchatka, the northern Kuril islands, along the coasts of the Sea of Okhotsk and on Sakhalin Island. The birds are resident or move over short distances in response to local snow and ice conditions.

HARRIERS, ACCIPITERS AND BUZZARDS

Hen Harrier (Northern Harrier)

Circus cyaneus

L: 40–50cm. WS: 95–120cm. W: 350–600g. ♀>♂.

Typical harriers with broad wings and a long tail. Adult male has a blue-grey head and upperparts and paler underparts. Adult female has brown head and upperparts, the latter streaked buff and darker brown. The underparts are cream, streaked brown, the streaking heavier on the breast. The most noticeable feature of the female at close range is the owl-like facial disc. Hen Harriers have the most extreme sky-dance, the pair locking talons and cartwheeling across the sky. They feed on small birds and mammals.

Hen Harriers breed in southern Fennoscandia and then more southerly across Russia; also on Kamchatka. In the Nearctic they breed in eastern Alaska, Yukon and western North West Territories to the north coast, then more southerly to Hudson Bay and into Quebec and Labrador. In winter Nearctic birds move to the continental US, while Eurasian birds head for southern Europe and central Asia.

Rough-legged Buzzard (Rough-legged Hawk)

Buteo lagopus

L: 50–60cm. WS: 120–150cm. W: 700–1300g. ♀>♂.

Large *Buteo* with broad wings and a short fan-shaped tail. Adult has a brown-streaked buff head and mottled buff and brown upperparts. Male underparts are pale buff streaked brown. In the female the pale buff is barred, rather than streaked, brown. Some individuals are very pale, seeming almost white from below. The wing-tips are dark brown. They feed on small mammals and birds but are opportunistic feeders, taking other bird prey and also carrion.

Rough-legged Buzzards breed in Fennoscandia and across Russia, to the north coast except on the Taimyr Peninsula; absent from all Russia's Arctic islands. Also breed in Kamchatka. Nearctic birds breed across the continent and on the southern Canadian Arctic islands. Eurasian, Kamchatka and North American birds are considered separate subspecies. Arctic birds are migratory, moving to southern Eurasia and North America, where there are resident buzzards.

Above left and right

Steller's Sea Eagle adult and week-old chick, southern Kamchatka, Russia. Adult Steller's have the largest bill of any raptor and are arguably the largest of all birds of prey, quoted heavier birds of other species usually being captives and therefore not truly representative.

Opposite page

Top

Adult Bald Eagle at its nest, Great Slave Lake, NWT, Canada.

Bottom

Bald Eagle using an iceberg as an observation point, Tracy Arm, Alaska. The Arm is a breeding ground for Harbour Seals and the eagle is watching for a still-born or unguarded pup, or for afterbirth.

Left

Rough-legged Buzzard above the Barren Grounds of Nunavut, Canada.

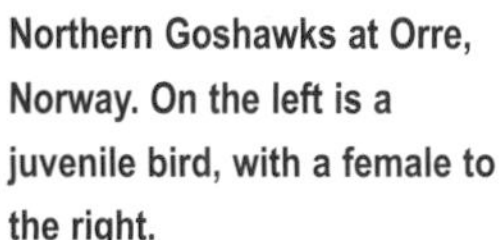

Northern Goshawks at Orre, Norway. On the left is a juvenile bird, with a female to the right.

(Northern) Goshawk

Accipiter gentilis

L: 50–60cm. WS: 95–125cm. W: 650–1250g. ♀>♂.

Adult male has a grey head with a distinct white supercilium. The upperparts are grey, occasionally washed brown. The underparts are white, thinly barred dark grey. Females are generally paler with the supercilium even more pronounced. In far eastern Russia some Goshawks can be almost white and may be confused with Gyrfalcons (until they fly). They feed on birds, taken in awe-inspiringly fast flights through the trees, and small mammals.

Goshawks are boreal and breed to the treeline in both the Palearctic and Nearctic. Most of the population is resident, but some birds move south in winter.

FALCONS

Merlin

Falco columbarius

L: 25–32cm. WS: 55–65cm. W: 150–250g. ♀>♂.

The smallest Arctic falcon. Adult male has a blue-grey head with cream cheek patches, a pale rufous nape and underparts, and blue-grey upperparts, all covered with fine dark streaks. Adult female has a brown head and upperparts and cream underparts, the latter heavily streaked dark brown. They feed on small birds, chased down after being flushed in fast flight.

Merlins breed in Iceland, Fennoscandia, and then more southerly across Russia. Absent from Kamchatka. They breed in central and southern Alaska (but rare throughout) and more southerly across Canada to Hudson Bay and in southern Quebec and Labrador. All northern birds are migratory, flying south to join resident birds.

Peregrine Falcon

Falco peregrinus

L: 35–45cm. WS: 90–110cm. W: 600–1000g. ♀>♂.

Status: CITES: Appendix I.

One of the world's best-known birds, though this has less to do with its beauty and speed than the rapid decline the species underwent in the 1950s and 1960s as a result of the widespread use of organochloride pesticides (specifically DDT), and the reintroduction and conservation programmes that followed, which raised both numbers and public awareness.

Female Merlin, Sirdal, Norway.

Peregrine numbers are now much healthier in Western Europe and North America, though the situation is not as good in all parts of the bird's range.

Peregrines are among the most charismatic of birds. Adult has a dark blue-grey crown and nape, and a cheek patch of the same colour, a feature usually called a moustache, though it does not actually extend below the bill. The upperparts are blue-grey, the underparts pale cream or buff barred with dark brownish black. Female are generally more heavily marked than males. Peregrines chase down birds, usually with a fast stoop from a great height. Stooping falcons rake their prey with their talons, this causing death or serious injury. They often specialise on a single prey species, but across the range Peregrines take diverse prey.

Peregrine Falcons breed on Greenland and across Eurasia, including the southern island of Novaya Zemlya; also on Kamchatka. In North America they breed throughout Alaska and Arctic Canada, including the southern Arctic islands. There are several subspecies across the range, the most significant being the Tundra Peregrine *tundrius*, which is paler than the nominate. Northern birds are migratory, moving south in winter to join resident birds.

Tundra Peregrine Falcons, near the Hood River in the Barren Lands of Nunavut, Canada. The male is above, the incubating female to the left.

Above
Tundra Peregrine, Nunavut Barren Grounds, Canada.

Above right
Gyrfalcon, northern Norway.

Below
White phase Gyrfalcon, Bylot Island, Canada. The bird is a male who was providing food for an incubating female. Gyrs kill by decapitating their prey and the remains of a grouse can still be seen on the bill.

Below right
Grey phase Gyrfalcon feeding chicks, Nunavut Barren Lands, Canada.

The fastest bird?

The Peregrine Falcon is often thought of as the world's fastest bird, with speeds in excess of 300kph often quoted for the stoop speed. In practice the theoretical limit seems to be about 260kph, and the highest measured speed is *c.*180kph. Even worse news for fans of the Peregrine is that higher speeds, of *c.*200kph, have been measured for the Gyrfalcon.

GYRFALCON

Falco rusticolus

L: 50–60cm. WS: 130–160cm. W: 800–1600g. ♀>♂.
Status: CITES: Appendix I.

The world's biggest falcon. Birds of the High Arctic are almost pure white – small wonder that for many travellers the Gyrfalcon is the ultimate tick on the species list. The bird is found in several 'pure' colour phases, and also in intermediate forms. 'White' birds are white, with black barring on the upperparts and lighter barring on the underparts. Some birds really are very white. 'Grey' birds have steel-blue upperparts and white underparts, again with black barring. 'Dark' birds have dark brown upperparts and white underparts, the latter with heavy dark brown barring. Birds of the different forms will mate, often producing broods with chicks of differing colours. They take birds and small mammals, primarily hunting *Lagopus* grouse. The prey is taken after a low quartering flight, or by stooping.

Gyrfalcons breed in Greenland (both west and east coasts), Iceland, across Eurasia, but not on Russia's Arctic islands; they also breed on Kamchatka. They occur across North America, including Canada's Arctic islands as far north as Ellesmere Island. The birds are resident, but move locally in search of prey.

GROUSE

Grouse are a group of northern gamebirds, and a highly successful one, several having wide latitudinal ranges; the (Rock) Ptarmigan resides from about 38°N to 82°N. Grouse are stocky birds, their size a reflection of their diet, particularly the winter diet. Boreal species eat the needles of pine and spruce. Though abundant, the needles have a very low nutritional value so very large quantities have to be ingested to provide the bird's energy requirements. Large crops and long intestinal tracts are therefore necessary.

In winter, tundra birds moult into a dense white plumage offering high insulating qualities and excellent camouflage (both avian and mammalian predators share their winter quarters). The birds have strong claws that allow them not only to dig in the snow for food, but also to excavate shelters to escape the worst of the weather. In spring males moult to a distinctive breeding plumage, while females acquire a cryptic plumage – a necessity for these ground-nesting birds, which provide a high fraction of the vertebrate biomass of the tundra and boreal fringe and are important prey for many species. One such predator, the Gyrfalcon, is, in some places, almost entirely dependent on grouse, taking virtually no other prey throughout the year.

The conspicuous plumage of male grouse would appear risky in situations where some predators rely on grouse meat for survival. But the males must advertise in order to attract females. It seems they also act as decoys for predators, deliberately choosing visible perches. The male is playing a dangerous game, pitting its own ability to outfly a predator against the chances of being chased down. If the male sees a mammalian predator in time, its rapid acceleration will take it clear. In areas with good patches of cover it can usually make it to cover before being overtaken by a pursuing bird; indeed, in areas where the shrub cover is abundant Gyrfalcons often do not breed. It is, however, a different matter on the tundra.

The males of the Arctic species tend to perform solo displays involving tail fanning, dropped wings and exaggerated strutting; the birds perform to intimidate rival males, since the holding of a territory is key for mating success. The males of some southern species take a more communal approach; 'leks' are created, displays grounds in which the males strut their stuff. Females visit the leks, observing the displays before making a final choice.

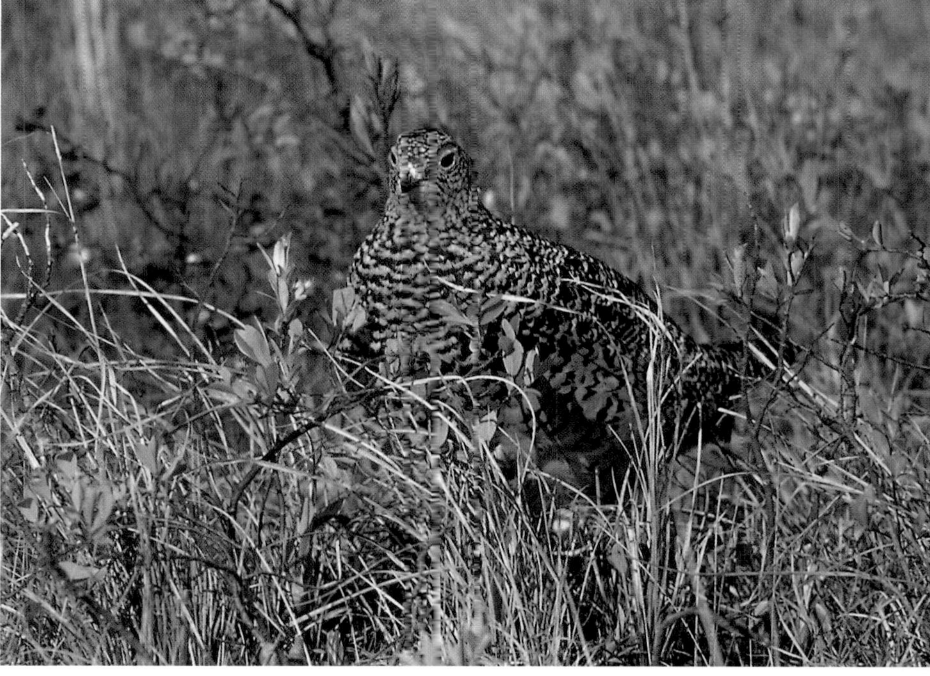

Willow Grouse, Churchill, Manitoba, Canada.
The female (*above*) is superbly camouflaged for security while incubating, in contrast to the male (*left*) emerging from his winter white plumage, who is conspicuous, the better to be seen by rivals for his territory. Males also occasionally take prominent positions, trading their own short-distance speed of flight which often evades an attacker against the extra security for their mates of drawing the predator's attention.

Once mated a female grouse will lay a large clutch of up to a dozen eggs, though 5–8 is a more usual number. The female alone incubates. Grouse chicks are downy and precocial, well capable of feeding themselves. Unlike their parents, the chicks feed chiefly on invertebrates, changing to a more vegetarian diet as they grow. They are fully grown by their first winter, but do not always breed the following spring.

Grouse are resident in many Arctic areas, though they will move if local food sources become too poor or unavailable as a result of bad weather (e.g. rain followed by frost, which seals food beneath an impenetrable coat of ice). Some grouse species do migrate, occasionally travelling considerable distances. In general, though, grouse do not fly often and they are primarily terrestrial birds. This limitation on movement and the wide geographical range of the birds has led to the evolution of many subspecies; as many as 30 have been recognised for the (Rock) Ptarmigan alone.

WILLOW GROUSE (WILLOW PTARMIGAN)

Lagopus lagopus

L: 35–40cm. WS: 55–65cm. W: 500–700g. ♂>♀.

Breeding male has a red-brown head and neck, the mantle and back mottled dark. The breast is red-brown also streaked darker and merging into white belly and vent. The outer wings are white, the inner red-brown. There is a distinctive red comb above the eye. Female is cryptic, mottled dull brown. Some retain a white belly, and some have a red eyebrow. Wings and tail as

Above
Male Rock Ptarmigan in the Barren Lands of Nunavut, Canada. It is spring and the bird is moulting to its breeding plumage.

Above right
Female of the Svalbard subspecies of Rock Ptarmigan (see also p292). It is winter and the bird is in full winter plumage.

male. Winter birds are white but retain the black outer tail feathers, probably for signalling as the birds are gregarious in winter.

Willow Grouse breed across Eurasia to Kamchatka, north to the coast and on the New Siberian Islands. Absent from Greenland, Iceland and Svalbard. They breed across North America including the southern Arctic islands. Resident.

(Rock) Ptarmigan

Lagopus mutus

L: 30–35cm. WS: 50–60cm. W: 300–600g. ♂>♀.
Breeding male has a dark brown head, mantle and back, each streaked darker. The breast is similar, blending to white underparts. The wings are white. There is a red comb above the eye. The tail has black outer feathers. Female is as Willow Grouse. In winter the birds are white, but retain the black outer tail feathers. In summer the colour of the male is diagnostic, though females are extremely difficult to differentiate. The stouter bill of the Willow Grouse is the only distinguishing feature between the two species in winter, though male Ptarmigan have black lores.

Ptarmigan breed on Greenland, Iceland and Svalbard, and across Eurasia to Kamchatka, to the north coast. May breed on Russian Arctic islands. They breed across North America, including all Canadian Arctic islands to northern Ellesmere Island. Resident.

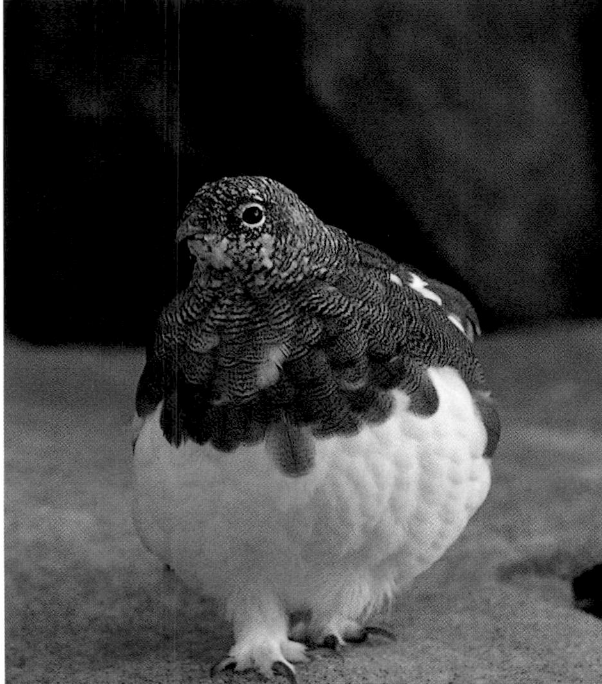

Male Rock Ptarmigan, north-east Greenland. It is autumn and the bird is moulting from breeding to winter plumage.

White-tailed Ptarmigan

Lagopus leucurus

L: 25–30cm. WS: 45–55cm. W: 250–400g. ♂>♀.
An upland tundra species, so not a true Arctic dweller. Breeding male has grey-brown head, mantle and back extensively spotted black. The breast is white, heavily black spotted, the spotting receding on the belly. The wings are white. There is a red comb above the eye. The tail is white. Female is pale yellowish cream, heavily marked black. Winter birds are white.

White-tailed Ptarmigan breed in central and southern Alaska, but are not common. Resident.

Black Grouse

Tetrao tetrix

L: 40–55cm. WS: 55–75cm. W: 1.0–1.5kg. ♂>♀.
Ecologically this species sits between the tundra and forest grouse, and so may be seen by Arctic travellers. Breeding male is a handsome bird; black plumage with a purple sheen, apart from a white undertail and white wing-patches. The tail is lyre-shaped. There is a red comb above the eye. The female is a cryptic brown. Winter plumage is as breeding.

Black Grouse breed in southern Fennoscandia, then more southerly across western Russia. Resident.

Western Capercaillie

Tetrao urogallus

L: 75–100cm. WS: 80–125cm. W: 1.7–2.5kg. ♂>♀.
Boreal species that can be seen to the treeline. Breeding male has shiny blue-black plumage with white spotting on the belly. The wings are brown above, grey below. The tail is blue-black

and fanned into a semi-circle at leks. There is a red comb above the eye. The bill is pale yellow. Female is a cryptic brown. Winter plumage is as breeding. Capercaillies breed in southern Fennoscandia, then more southerly across western Russia. Resident.

Black-billed Capercaillie (Spotted Capercaillie)

Tetrao parvirostris

L: 70–95cm. WS: 75–115cm. W: 1.5–2.2kg. ♂>>♀.
Similar to (but smaller than) the Western Capercaillie, with which it overlaps sympatrically in central Siberia. Adult males are as Western Capercaillie but with white spotting on the upperparts and a black bill. Females are cryptic brown. Winter plumage is as breeding. Habitat is also as Western Capercaillie. Black-billed

Capercaillie breed east of 100°E, but to the treeline; Kamchatka is a stronghold. Resident.

Spruce Grouse

Falcipennis canadensis

L: 38–45cm. WS: 50–60cm. W: 450–650g. ♂>♀.
Boreal species that can be seen to the treeline. Breeding male has a grey-brown head and upperparts, black neck and white-spotted brown underparts. The tail is dark brown with a distinct orange-brown tip, and it is fanned during displays. There

Above
Male Western Capercaillie, Aardal, Norway.

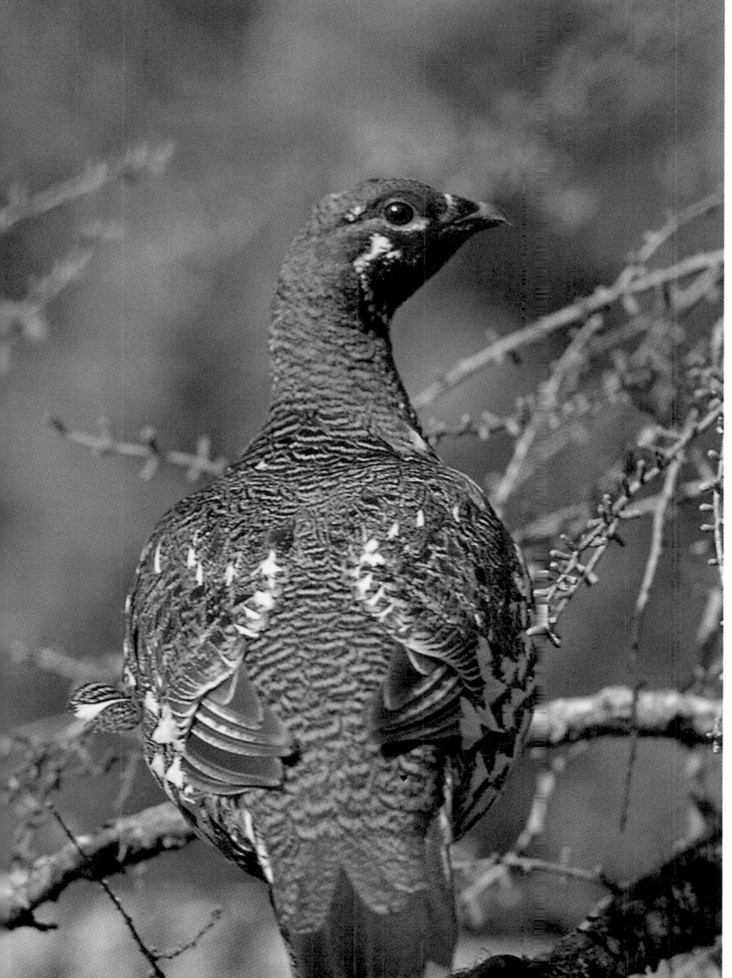

Left
Male Spruce Grouse, Churchill, Manitoba, Canada.

Dancing Sandhill Crane, Churchill, Manitoba, Canada.

is a red comb above the eye. Female is cryptic brown. Winter plumage is as breeding.

Spruce Grouse breed in central and southern Alaska (but are rare in the west), and to the treeline across Canada. Resident.

Ruffed Grouse

Bonasa umbellus

L: 42–50cm. WS: 60–70cm. W: 500–750g. ♂>♀.

Boreal species that prefers deciduous woodland. Not an Arctic species, but may be seen by travellers enjoying Alaska's Denali National Park. Adults have two colour phases, with either red-brown upperparts and white underparts streaked with red-brown or black, or grey-brown upperparts and white underparts with grey-brown or black streaking. There is a crest on the head. The male tail, fanned in display, has a red-brown inner, grey centre and black and pale brown terminal bands. Winter plumage is as breeding.

Ruffed Grouse breed in central Alaska (but not elsewhere in the state) and across North America, though rarely to the treeline. Resident.

Hazel Grouse

Bonasa bonasia

L: 35–40cm. WS: 55–65cm. W: 350–500g. ♂>♀.

Boreal species that may be seen to the treeline. Adult male has grey upperparts and brown wings, each scalloped darker. The underparts are white, heavily marked brown. The throat is black with a white border. The tail is grey with thick black and thin white terminal bands. Female is similar but lacks the black throat. Winter plumage is as breeding.

Hazel Grouse breed in southern Fennoscandia and to the treeline across Russia. Absent from Chukotka and Kamchatka. Resident.

CRANES

Cranes are the tallest of the flying birds, a creature seemingly too delicate to withstand the rigours of the Arctic. Yet two species are found in the north, and each is a true Arctic species. Cranes are omnivorous, opportunistic feeders, taking seeds, berries, invertebrates, amphibians and reptiles, and even small birds. Wintering Sandhill Cranes feed in fields, taking waste grain and potatoes, but the Siberian Crane is less adaptable, feeding only on wetlands. This specialism represents the greatest threat to the species, as wetland drainage along its migration routes and at its wintering sites have reduced feeding sites. The Chinese Three Gorges hydro-electric scheme represents a considerable threat to one of the birds' prime wintering areas, with the hydrology of the lower river being severely affected to the detriment of the cranes. Siberian Cranes are not alone in being threatened, as nine of the fifteen crane species are on the IUCN list and all are either CITES Appendix I or II.

In general cranes are monogamous. Though gregarious on migration and at wintering sites, they tend to be solitary while breeding (though the Sandhill Crane is an exception). Cranes are renowned for their 'dancing' displays, which all species perform (though the Red-crowned Cranes *Grus japonensis* of Japan are justifiably the most famous). The dances consist of wing-stretches, head-tosses and vertical leaps, and calling in unison with extended necks. The calling is also used for territorial claims. Most cranes breed at 3–5 years, but they are long-lived. They make large nests in which, usually, 2 (perhaps 3) eggs are laid. Both birds incubate. Crane chicks are precocial, following their parents into feeding areas at an early age, but they are initially fed by both parents. The chicks do not develop flight feathers until they are 3–4 months old.

Siberian Cranes differ from other species in laying just a single egg. The combination of a single chick and its vulnerability during its long fledging period pose a particular problem for conservationists. Thankfully programmes are now in hand in Russia aimed at stabilising, then raising, the threatened population.

Siberian Crane pair at nest site, northern Yakutia, Russia.

Siberian Crane chick, northern Yakutia, Russia.

Sandhill Crane

Grus canadensis

L: 90–110cm (body 40–50cm). WS: 180–210cm. W: 2.8–3.8kg. ♂>♀.

Status: CITES: All subspecies are Appendix II, though subspecies *nesiotes* and *pulla* are Appendix I.

Adult has a red crown, forehead and lores. The rest of the head is white, the neck grey. The upperparts are a grey-flecked reddish-buff, the underparts pale grey. Sexes similar. Winter birds lose the reddish-buff wash on the upperparts.

Sandhill Cranes breed in coastal Chukotka east of the Kolyma delta and south to the Gulf of Anadyr, and across North America from Alaska to western James Bay. They are uncommon in northern Alaska, yet breed to the north coast along much of the Canadian mainland, and on Victoria and Baffin islands. Migratory, with Russian birds joining those from North America in the southern United States.

Siberian (White) Crane

Grus leucogeranus

L: 120–140cm (body 60–65cm). WS: 230–260cm. W: 4.9–6.9kg. ♂>♀.

Status: IUCN: Critical. CITES: Appendix I.

Adult is pure white apart from red crown, forehead and lores, and black primaries, primary coverts and alula. The black feathering is often visible on the standing bird. Male, female and winter plumages similar.

Siberian Cranes breed in two areas, with a small population near the Ob River and larger one in northern Yakutia. The Ob birds migrate to the Iranian Caspian Sea and northern India, with hunting along the route (especially in Pakistan and Afghanistan) adding to the threats the species faces. The Yakutian birds move to China.

WADERS

Waders (or shorebirds) represent the largest group of Arctic birds. They work the intertidal region of the Arctic coast, and the lakes and marshes created by the summer thaw, feeding on insects, worms, crustaceans and molluscs, together with some plant material, and occasionally other foods such as small fish. There are several wader groups (such as the calidrids) in which plumages are very similar; the birds also generally have distinct breeding, wintering and immature plumages, so the risk of confusion between species is high. In the species accounts that follow some pointers for identification are included, but it must be stressed that these are general; the identification of waders requires patience and perseverance.

Waders generally nest on the ground (though Green, Solitary and Wood Sandpipers use the old nests of other species, often high above the ground; Green Sandpipers do this frequently, sometimes at heights to 10m). The nest is little more than a scrape in the ground or a depression in vegetation, often with minimal lining. Between 3 and 5 eggs are laid. The eggs are large – as they must be to accommodate a chick which is born downy and precocial – and as a consequence represent a large energetic investment for the female; for some of the smaller calidrids (e.g. the stints) the clutch can weigh up to 90% of the female's body weight. Care differs between the species. In most it is shared by the parents. In some it is done by the female alone, and there are species in which the male takes responsibility. In species in which both birds incubate the eggs and care for the young, the female often abandons the chicks before they fledge, with the male continuing with care. Young waders leave the nest within a few days of hatching and are, in general, self-feeding. Waders breed in their second or third year.

OYSTERCATCHERS

Oystercatchers are noisy, gregarious birds (though more solitary at breeding sites). They are also unmistakable with their pied plumage. They use their long bill to probe beneath the surface or to find molluscs attached to rocks. Bivalves are opened by inserting the bill between the two shells and severing the adductor muscle, which holds the shell closed. With limpets, and occasionally with bivalves, the bird may also hammer away with its bill on the shell, excavating a hole through which the flesh is extracted.

Two oystercatcher species breed at the Arctic fringe and so may be seen by travellers to the region.

Eurasian Oystercatcher

Haematopus ostralegus

L: 38–45cm. WS: 70–85cm. W: 475–700g. ♂>♀.

Adult has a black head, black-and-white upperparts and white underparts. The bill is long and red. The legs are red. In winter the birds acquire a white half-collar.

Eurasian Oystercatchers have a discontinuous distribution, breeding on Iceland, on the northern coast of Fennoscandia and around Russia's White Sea coast, and on Kamchatka. Some Icelandic and Norwegian birds are resident, but most northern birds head south, some as far as the Bay of Biscay, but most to coastal Low Countries and northern France. Kamchatka birds move to south-east Asia

Above
Eurasian Oystercatcher, southern Iceland.

Above right
Black Oystercatchers, Unalaska, Aleutian Islands, Alaska.

Black Oystercatcher

Haematopus bachmani

L: 40–50cm. WS: 75–90cm. W: 525–800g. ♂>♀.

Adult is black with a bright red bill and dull pink legs. Winter plumage is similar.

Breeds on the Aleutian Islands and southern and south-east Alaskan coasts. Mainly resident, but some birds move south along the western coast of the United States.

PLOVERS

These are stocky, short-billed birds with large eyes, characterised by their feeding method of 'look–run–peck'. The pecking is of insects on land forays, or of crustaceans and molluscs on the shore. Some plovers also use a foot-paddling technique when feeding; the bird stands on one leg and paddles the water surface with the other, the paddling causing prey to move and betray itself.

In the tundra plovers the pair bond is monogamous and probably lifelong; initial pairing takes place after a display that involves the male running at the female (the 'torpedo run'), which looks far from subtle but seems to work. The ringed plovers have similar displays, though the pair bond, while monogamous, is seasonal. Things are different in the Dotterel. Females take the lead in mating, luring males with raised wing and fanned-tail displays. Though some bonds are monogamous, polyandry is common and males are occasionally polygamous. Usually the female will abandon her eggs soon after laying to seek out another male for a second clutch, leaving the first male to care for eggs and young. Female Dotterel rarely share brood responsibilities.

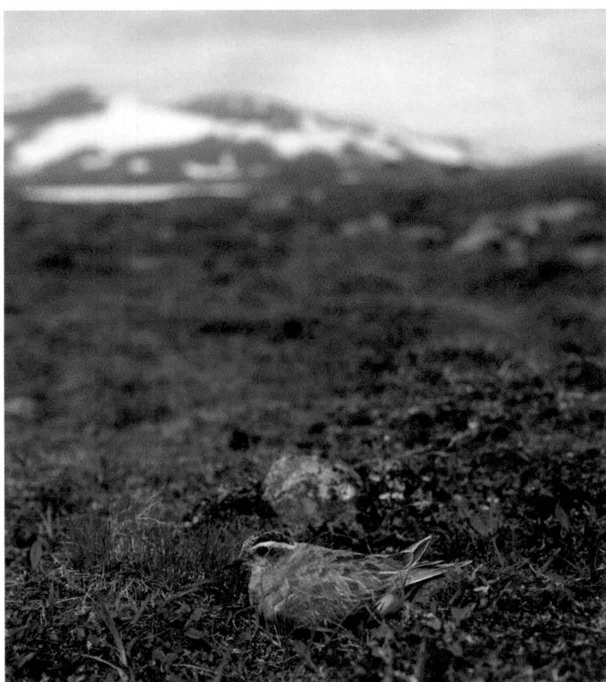

Nesting Dotterel, Jotunheimen, Norway.

(Eurasian) Dotterel

Charadrius marinellus

L: 20–24cm. WS: 55–65cm. W: 85–120g. ♂>♀.

Breeding adult has a black crown above a white face. The upperparts are grey and grey-brown. The upper breast is also grey, separated from the rufous belly by a white band. Females are brighter (and larger) than males. In winter the birds lose the rufous underparts and are duller overall.

Dotterel breed in Fennoscandia and across Russia to Chukotka, to the northern coast and including the southern island of Novaya Zemlya; absent from Greenland, Iceland and Kamchatka. Has bred on the tundras of western Alaska. In winter the birds fly to the Middle East and North Africa as far west as Morocco. East Siberian birds may travel more than 10,000km during migration.

(Common) Ringed Plover

Charadrius hiaticula

L: 18–20cm. WS: 45–55cm. W: 55–75g.

Adult has a black 'highwayman' mask with bands above and below a white forehead. The crown and nape are grey-brown. There is a distinct white crescent by the ear. There is a broad white collar, below which is a broad black chest band. The rest of the underparts are white. The upperparts are grey-brown, the tail black-and-white. Females are less boldly marked than males. In winter the black facial and chest bands are more subdued.

Ringed Plovers breed in Greenland, Iceland, Svalbard, Scandinavia and along the northern coast of Eurasia including the southern island of Novaya Zemlya and the New Siberian Islands; has also bred on St Lawrence Island, northern Ellesmere and western Baffin Island, where it is now thought to be established. In winter European birds move to southern Europe and North Africa, Asian birds to the shores of the Caspian Sea and the Middle East.

Broken-wing displays

Plovers are famous for displays aimed at drawing potential predators away from their nests and eggs. These displays usually involve the bird drooping a wing and calling plaintively as though badly injured as it heads away from the nest. Human invaders seem especially gullible to the performance, following the bird even when they know exactly what is going on. But birders and naturalists are, in general, much less dangerous than other predators, which can rapidly overhaul the faking bird, causing it to take off in a hurry or become a genuine casualty. The bird above illustrating the technique is a Semipalmated Plover, Cold Bay, Alaska. Some Calidrid sandpipers have a similar defensive technique – see Box on p364.

Semipalmated Plover

Charadrius semipalmatus

L: 17–19cm. WS: 43–52cm. W: 45–65g.

Virtually identical to the Ringed Plover in summer and winter, but lacks the prominent white ear patch, having an indistinct crescent (and sometimes no white at all). The name derives from the webs between the inner and middle, and middle and outer toes.

Semipalmated Plovers breed across North America, to the north coast and on Banks, Victoria and Southampton islands, and southern Baffin Island. Wintering birds move to the southern Pacific and Atlantic coasts of the United States, the Caribbean islands and the coasts of Central and South America.

Lesser Sand Plover (Mongolian Plover)

Charadrius mongolus

L: 17–20 cm. WS: 45–55cm. W: 50–75g.

Adult has a 'highwayman' mask similar to Ringed Plover. The crown is grey ringed with pale rufous. The throat is white, sharply delineated from a rufous breast that merges into white underparts. The upperparts are grey-brown, the tail is grey, dark grey and white. In winter the back facial band and rufous colour are lost.

Lesser Sand Plovers breed in Chukotka, on Kamchatka and on the Commander Islands. Has also bred in western Alaska but is not an established species there. In winter the birds move to the Philippines, Indonesia and Australia.

TUNDRA PLOVERS

American Golden Plover

Pluvialis dominica

L: 23–27cm. WS: 60–70cm. W: 125–155g.

Adult has a mottled dark grey and gold crown, nape and upperparts (though the outer wing is dark grey). The face is black, the remaining head and the sides of the neck white. The underparts are black. Females are as males, but with white streaking on the flanks. Winter adults lose the bold patterning and colours and are grey-brown with some gold mottling.

American Golden Plovers breed in western North America from Alaska to Hudson Bay, but also on Banks, Victoria, Southampton, and western Baffin islands. Has also bred on Wrangel Island but is not established. Wintering birds occur primarily in the southern United States and Central America, but they fly as far south as Argentina.

Eurasian Golden Plover

Pluvialis apricaria

L: 26–30cm. WS: 65–75cm. W: 180–240g.

Very similar to American Golden Plover though slightly larger, also has white flanks stretching from the white facial pattern to white undertail-coverts. Winter adults are pale golden brown, quite different from American Golden Plover. Eurasian Golden is more likely to be seen away from the shore than most other plovers. Highly territorial when feeding, chasing other waders away from its chosen patch.

In both summer and winter plumages the Palearctic Ringed Plover and the Nearctic Semipalmated Plover are almost identical, with subtle differences in the 'highwayman's mask'. These photographs show the Ringed Plover in winter plumage (*below left*, Randaberg, Norway) and the Semipalmated Plover in summer plumage (*below right*, Cold Bay, Alaska Peninsula).

Above left
Eurasian Golden Plover, Varangerfjord, Norway.

Above right
American Golden Plover, Barren Lands, North West Territories, Canada.

European Golden Plovers breed in north-east Greenland (in small numbers), Iceland, Scandinavia and northern Russia as far east as the southern Taimyr Peninsula. Absent from Svalbard (though breeding records do exist) and the western Arctic islands of Russia. Greenland and Icelandic birds winter in Iberia, Scandinavian and Russian birds in Iberia and North Africa.

Pacific Golden Plover

Pluvialis fulva

L: 20–25cm. WS: 60–70cm. W: 120–140g.

Very similar to Eurasian Golden Plover, but with longer, darker grey legs, a uniform grey-brown underwing, and less white (and less well-defined white areas) on the flanks. The upperparts are darker overall and less heavily mottled with gold. In winter the birds lose the distinctive pattern on the underparts, being grey, smudged brown.

Pacific Golden Plovers breed in Russia east of the Yamal Peninsula and in western Alaska (though uncommon there). Breeds to the north coast, but not on any Arctic islands. In winter the birds move as far south as Australasia.

Grey Plover (Black-bellied Plover)

Pluvialis squatarola

L: 26–32cm. WS: 70–85cm. W: 200–270g.

Adults are patterned as the European Golden Plover, but with very different coloration, having white/pale grey upperparts which lack any gold mottling, and with the black on the underparts extending to the rear flanks. Females are less boldly marked. In winter the upperparts are more subdued, the underparts white, mottled with brown spotting.

Grey Plovers breed in Greenland (but rare there), in Russia from the White Sea to Chukotka as far north as the coast, and on the New Siberian Islands and Wrangel. Breeds discontinuously in North America, being found on the west and south-west coasts of Alaska but rare in the north, in Yukon and western North West Territories. But also breeds on Banks, Victoria and Southampton Islands and on the nearby mainland, and on western Baffin Island. Eurasian birds winter in south-west Europe, south-east Asia and Australia. North American birds move to the Atlantic and Pacific coasts of the southern United States, and into Central and South America.

Calidris Sandpipers and Related Species

Calidris waders differ from the plovers in having bills adapted for probing rather than pecking. The bills vary enormously in size and shape, with that of the Spoon-billed Sandpiper being among the most remarkable of any bird. The bills have an array of touch sensors (called Herbst's corpuscles) that allow the birds to 'feel' prey beneath the sand or mud (a characteristic shared with the snipes, *Tringa* sandpipers, godwits, curlews and dowitchers).

In general *Calidris* sandpipers have long wings and legs, and relatively short tails. The sexes are similar. Most calidrids are northern breeding species and migrate great distances, reaching Tierra del Fuego and Australia. Indeed, Australia is a major wintering site for wintering northern waders, with close to a million birds of more than 50 species occurring in the north-west.

> **A movable bill**
>
> Some long-billed waders can move the tip independently of the rest of the bill. This ability, termed rhynchokinesis, means that the bird can open the bill tip while the rest of the bill stays closed, and so can grab a worm or insect larva that can then be taken by the tongue and consumed without the bill being withdrawn. Together with the amazing touch sensitivity of the bill, this allows the bird to feed quickly and efficiently.

Dunlin in breeding plumage, Varangerfjord, Norway.

Dunlin

Calidris alpina

L: 16–21cm. WS: 28–45cm. W: 35–55g. ♀=♂.

Breeding adult has a black-streaked brown crown, the rest of the head and breast being white with black streaking. The upperparts are brown and black. There is a distinctive black patch on the belly, the rest of the underparts being white. In winter the belly patch is lost and adults become pale grey above and white below. The black belly patch allows Dunlin in breeding plumage to be easily separated from similar shorebirds. Winter adults lose the distinctive belly patch and are much more subdued overall.

Dunlin breed in east Greenland, Iceland, Jan Mayen, Svalbard, Fennoscandia and across Arctic Russia to Chukotka, including both islands of Novaya Zemlya, the New Siberian Islands and Wrangel Island. In North America Dunlin breed in west and north Alaska and on the northern Canadian mainland west of Hudson Bay, including Southampton Island. Some Icelandic birds stay on the south coast during the winter, but most Palearctic birds move to western Europe, North Africa and southern Asia. Nearctic birds winter on the east and west coasts of North America and in Central America.

Baird's Sandpiper

Calidris bairdii

L: 14–17cm. WS: 40–45cm. W: 35–40g. ♀>♂.

Breeding adult has a buff-scalloped dark brown crown, nape and mantle. The supercilium is buff, the rest of the head is buff and white. The upperparts are distinctively dark brown spotted. The underparts are white, heavily streaked buff on the breast. Winter adults are duller overall and lose the dark spotting of the upperparts. Baird's can be distinguished from other calidrids by the wing-tips, which project beyond the tail and describe an oval as the bird walks and pecks. However, the wings of White-rumped Sandpiper also project beyond the tail. Winter adults are more subdued.

Baird's Sandpipers breed in Chukotka and on Wrangel Island, and across North America from northern Alaska to Baffin Island. On the Canadian mainland breeds only to the west of Hudson Bay; also breeds in north-west Greenland. Wintering birds fly to South America.

White-rumped Sandpiper

Calidris fuscicollis

L: 15–18cm. WS: 40–45cm. W: 35–45g. ♀>♂.

Breeding adult is very similar to Baird's Sandpiper, but the base head colour is white and the streaking is dark brown. The

Many of the Calidrids can be difficult to tell apart (see box overleaf), as the photographs below and on the following pages illustrate.

Below left
A Baird's Sandpiper, Igloolik, Canada,.

Below right
A Semipalmated Sandpiper , Seward Peninsula, Alaska.

Western Sandpiper, St Lawrence Island, Alaska.

Calidrid identification

Differentiating between shorebirds is one of the major problems of Arctic bird identification. Some general rules will help, but there is no substitute for close observation over a period of time. First, try to gain some impression of the bird's size – not easy if it is on its own, but of value if there are other species close by. Shape is also useful, but bear in mind that this can vary with activity. Look at the bill to judge its size relative to the bird and its shape – is it drooping towards the tip? Many calidrids look very similar but have different leg colours – try to be sure that you are seeing the true colour and not the mud from the local habitat. Check the habitat: is it wet or dry, sandy or rocky? This can help, but again is not an absolute. Finally, listen for the call, but be cautious – in North America calidrids are often called 'peeps' because of their voice, and they can sound depressingly similar to first-time observers who have yet to attune themselves to the subtle differences between species.

breast is more heavily streaked, the upperparts more rufous, and streaked (rather than spotted) black. In flight the bird is easily distinguished from Baird's by the highly visible white rump. In winter the birds are dull grey with some brown streaking.

White-rumped Sandpipers breed in Canada from the Yukon to western Hudson Bay and on the southern Arctic islands; rare in Alaska and east of Hudson Bay. In winter the birds head for southern South America, flying as far as Tierra del Fuego and the Falkland Islands.

Semipalmated Sandpiper

Calidris pusilla

L: 13–15cm. WS: 34–38cm. W: 20–30g. ♀>♂.

Very similar to Baird's Sandpiper, but smaller and without the distinctive black spotting. Breeding adults have pale grey-white heads, the crown and nape heavily streaked dark brown and grey. The breast and flanks are white streaked with brown, the remaining underparts white. The upperparts are dark brown scalloped with pale grey and chestnut. In winter pale grey above, white below, retaining a grey-brown streaked breast band.

Semipalmated Sandpipers breed across northern North America, including the southern Arctic islands. In winter seen on Caribbean islands and in South America as far south as Uruguay.

In its breeding plumage the Curlew Sandpiper is one of the more distinctive Calidrids, eastern Chukotka, Russia.

Western Sandpiper

Calidris mauri

L: 14–17cm. WS: 35–38cm. W: 20–35g. ♀>♂.

Very similar to Semipalmated Sandpiper but head and upperparts are distinctly chestnut and there is darker, heavier spotting on the underparts. The spotting is lighter on the belly, but that again differentiates the bird from Semipalmated, on which there is no spotting in that area. In winter adult is pale grey above, white below. Western is almost as pale as Sanderling in winter, but retains a collar of pale grey-brown streaks.

Western Sandpipers breed in Chukotka and western Alaska. In winter Russian birds cross the Bering Sea to join Alaskan birds on flights south to California and the Caribbean islands.

Curlew Sandpiper

Calidris ferruginea

L: 18–21cm. WS: 42–47cm. W: 55–85g. ♀>♂.

Breeding adult is an attractive bird with a black-streaked white crown, the rest of the head, breast and belly being chestnut brown. The upperparts are dappled chestnut, black and white. In winter the colours are lost, the birds being pale grey above and white below. Male Curlew Sandpipers stay on the breeding grounds for just a couple of weeks; they spend their entire time there attempting in copulate with as many females as they can before departing.

Curlew Sandpipers breed from the Taimyr Peninsula to Chukotka, and probably also on the New Siberian Islands. In winter the birds move to Africa, southern Asia, Indonesia and Australia.

Red Knot, Kjorholmane, Norway.

> **Masters of migration**
>
> The Red Knot was once one of the most abundant of all North American waders, but relentless hunting during its annual migration severely reduced their numbers. Thankfully the hunting has now diminished. Red Knot have exceptionally long migration flights; it has been estimated that during its migrations an individual bird may fly up to 30,000km. Some birds cross the Atlantic in one flight, accumulating subcutaneous fat before the flight that can total as much as 80% of the bird's body weight.

Red Knot

Calidris canutus

L: 23–26cm. WS: 57–62cm. W: 115–165g. ♀>♂.

Very similar in pattern and colour to the Curlew Sandpiper, though the underparts of Red Knot vary from red-brown to salmon pink, while the upperparts are dappled red-brown, black and grey, and the patterning is less bold. However, the main diagnostic is the Red Knot's short, straight bill which is very different to the longer, downcurved bill of the Curlew Sandpiper. The legs and feet are also dark olive, whereas those of Curlew Sandpiper are black.

Red Knot breed on Russia's Taimyr Peninsula, the New Siberian Islands and Wrangel, and inland Chukotka. Breeds in northern Alaska (but not consistently), Canada's Melville Peninsula and many Arctic islands; also breeds in north and north-east Greenland. However, this distribution is patchy, the birds often being very local. In winter, Greenland and some east Canadian birds move through Iceland to western Europe. North American birds move to the coasts of the southern United States, to Central America and as far south as Tierra del Fuego. Central Russian birds move to Africa, while east Russian birds fly as far as Australia.

Great Knot

Calidris tenuirostris

L: 25–28cm. WS: 60–67cm. W: 140–210g.

The largest calidrid, with a distinctive long black bill. Breeding adult is heavily streaked black on the white head, mantle and breast. The rest of the underparts are white though there are black arrows on the flanks. The upperparts are chestnut, brown and black. In winter the plumage is more subdued.

Rare, with a very limited range. Great Knot breed in north-east Siberia, but the bird has yet to be closely studied and the range is imprecise. In winter the birds fly to southern Asia and Australasia.

Pectoral Sandpiper

Calidris melanotos

L: 19–23cm. WS: 42–50cm. W: 55–120g. ♀>♂.

Breeding adult has a dark brown crown streaked black and brown, and a vague white supercilium. The throat is white, heavily streaked dark brown, the streaking continuing on the buff neck and breast. However, the coloration ceases abruptly and so forms the pectoral band that gives the species its name. Beyond the band the underparts are white. Upperparts are dark brown, scalloped chestnut and buff. Wintering adults maintain the breeding pattern but are duller and browner overall.

Male Pectoral Sandpiper, Barrow, Alaska. The darker patch on the breast indicates where the air-filled sac is being expanded to make the curious, but deep and far-carrying, mating call.

Above left
Rock Sandpiper, Cold Bay, Alaska.

Above right
Purple Sandpiper, Badlanddalen, north-east Greenland.

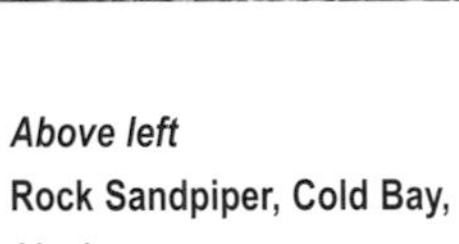

Adult males are larger than females and tend to have darker breasts. Males have a curious hooting call amplified by the expansion of an air-filled sac, which causes the neck/upper breast to puff out. This strange *wow–wow* call carries over large distances; it can be particularly eerie on misty days.

Pectoral Sandpipers breed from the Taimyr Peninsula to Chukotka, to the north coast but absent from all islands except Wrangel. In North America breeds from north-western Alaska along the mainland coast to Hudson Bay and on the southern Arctic islands (as far north as southern Ellesmere Island). In winter both Russian and North American birds move to South America, with small numbers in Japan and Korea.

Sharp-tailed Sandpiper

Calidris acuminata

L: 17–21cm. WS: 42–48cm. W: 55–85g. ♀>♂.

Very similar to the Pectoral Sandpiper; ranges overlap, but Sharp-tailed in breeding plumage has brighter upperparts and much more extensive spotting on the underparts so there is no clear pectoral band. Sharp-tailed has a distinct white eye-ring visible at close quarters. In winter the birds are duller, and virtually indistinguishable from Pectoral Sandpipers.

Sharp-tailed Sandpipers breed in northern Yakutia between the Lena and Kolyma rivers. In winter the birds fly to Australasia.

Purple Sandpiper

Calidris maritima

L: 20–22cm. WS: 38–44cm. W: 60–80g. ♀>♂.

Breeding adult is the darkest of the calidrids. The head is buff streaked dark brown, the underparts pale grey but heavily spotted dark brown, with the spotting thinning towards the vent. The upperparts are chestnut and white, scalloped dark brown. In winter adults are black-scalloped slate grey above, grey-streaked white below. Purple Sandpipers tend to eat more vegetation than other calidrids, particularly algae, which is picked up as the bird searches among seaweed for other morsels. The birds are also more likely to be seen swimming than other sandpipers, this ability probably related to their usual habitat – very close to the waterline – which means they are occasionally collected by tides or waves.

Purple Sandpipers breed on Iceland, Jan Mayen, northern Fennoscandia, Svalbard, Franz Josef Land, Novaya Zemlya, the Taimyr Peninsula and the southern island of Severnaya Zemlya. In North America the bird breeds on Baffin and Southampton Islands and southern Ellesmere island. Also breeds in southern Greenland. In winter many Icelandic birds are resident. Greenland birds move to Iceland and the British Isles, birds from Svalbard and Russia to the Norwegian coast or western Europe. Canadian birds move to coasts of north-east United States.

> **The rodent run**
> Many calidrids have their own version of the distraction display of the plovers (see Box p359). In this case, rather than persuading the potential predator that they are injured, the birds make a crouched run away from the nest while emitting high-pitched squeaks. The effect is of a rodent running across the tundra and most predators will immediately give chase, only to discover that, perplexingly, the 'rodent' can fly.

Rock Sandpiper

Calidris ptilocnemis

L: 20–22cm. WS: 38–44cm. W: 60–80g. ♀>♂.

Very similar to Purple Sandpiper (indeed, so similar that Aleutian birds are almost identical and some authorities consider the two taxa conspecific). Elsewhere the range of the species is the best way of distinguishing the two, though outside the Aleutians Rock Sandpipers tend to be paler and brighter. Rock Sandpipers also occasionally have a black belly

Little Stint, Orre, Norway.

Sanderling, Orre, Norway.

patch (but so do some Purples). Winter adults are as Purple Sandpiper, though non-Aleutian birds tend to be paler.

Rock Sandpipers breed in eastern Chukotka and the Commander and Kuril islands, in western Alaska, the Pribilof and Aleutian islands. In winter the birds move to the east coast of the United States as far south as California.

Sanderling

Calidris alba

L: 20–22cm. WS: 40–45cm. W: 45–65g. ♀≥♂.

Breeding adult has a black-streaked rufous head, neck and breast, the rest of the underparts white. The upperparts are black, white and rufous, dappled grey. In winter the birds are pale grey above, white below. Wintering birds are much paler than other calidrids. In summer confusions are possible, but Sanderlings are more active than other species and tend to be found on drier ground. Feeds at the waterline but never seems to be overwhelmed by the waves as it times its runs forwards and backwards with perfection.

Sanderlings breed in northern Greenland, Svalbard, the Taimyr Peninsula, Severnaya Zemlya and the New Siberian Islands, and on the eastern Canadian Arctic islands north to Ellesmere Island. In winter Greenlandic birds move to west Africa, Asian birds go to Australia and southern Africa, and Canadian birds fly to both coasts of the United States and to Central and South America (as far as south as Tierra del Fuego).

Least Sandpiper

Calidris minutilla

L: 10–12cm. WS: 32–35cm. W: 16–25g.

The smallest calidrid. Breeding adult very similar to Semipalmated Sandpiper but has yellow or yellow-green legs (Semipalmated Sandpiper has black legs). In winter the bird is grey above with significant brown scalloping. The breast is grey-brown, the rest of the underparts white.

Least Sandpipers breed from western Alaska to Labrador but not on the Canadian Arctic islands. In winter the birds fly to the southern US states, Caribbean islands, and Central and northern South America.

Little Stint

Calidris minuta

L: 12–14cm. WS: 33–37cm. W: 20–35g.

The smallest Palearctic calidrid. Breeding adult has a rufous head finely streaked with black. The throat is white blending to a buff breast, speckled with dark brown spots. The rest of the underparts are white. The upperparts are chestnut with black scalloping, though the flight feathers are dark grey-brown. In winter adult is grey or grey-brown above and on the breast, the rest of the underparts are white.

Little Stints breed in northern Fennoscandia and in Russia from Cheshskaya Guba to Chukotka, including the southern island of Novaya Zemlya and the New Siberian Islands. In winter the birds move to North Africa, the Middle East and southern Asia.

Long-toed Stint

Calidris subminuta

L: 13–14cm. WS: 33–35cm. W: 25–35g.

Very similar to both Little Stint (which is brighter and more rufous overall and has black rather than yellow-green legs) and Least Sandpiper (though the ranges do not overlap). The toe of the name is the middle one (though the hind toe is also longer than in other calidrids), but the value of this difference in the field is somewhat limited. Breeding adult has white head and breast, each finely marked with brown and dark brown. The rest of the underparts are white. The upperparts are grey-brown with darker spots and streaks. In flight the long toes project beyond the tail, but this can be difficult to observe in a fast-flying bird. In winter the bird is much duller.

Long-toed Stints are usually found on upland tundra, and are rare. They breed in isolated pockets in central Siberia east of the Ob River, particularly near Magadan, in southern Chukotka, northern Kamchatka and on the Commander Islands. Wintering birds occur in south-east Asia and Australia, where they frequently form flocks with other stints.

Least Sandpiper, Churchill, Manitoba, Canada.

Temminck's Stints at their nest site, Orre, Norway.

RED-NECKED STINT

Calidris ruficollis

L: 13–16cm. WS: 35–38cm. W: 20–35g. ♀>♂.

Breeding adult has an orange-red head and upper breast, the crown streaked darker. The rest of the underparts are white, with some dark brown streaking on the breast below the colour patch. The upperparts are rufous or orange-red with black-and-white scalloping. In winter the bird is grey on the upperparts and breast, with white underparts. In winter the upperparts are pale grey.

Red-necked Stints breed in Russia, patchily from the Taimyr Peninsula to Chukotka. Also breeds sporadically in western Alaska. Migrating birds fly to southern China, Indonesia, Australia and New Zealand.

TEMMINCK'S STINT

Calidris temminckii

L: 13–15cm. WS: 34–38cm. W: 18–30g.

Similar to Little Stint, but much more subdued and with yellow-green legs and feet. Breeding adult has a grey-brown head and breast (apart from a white throat) finely streaked dark brown. The rest of the underparts are white. The upperparts are brown dappled with black spots. In winter the birds have the same colour pattern but are dull grey-brown.

Temminck's Stints breed from Fennoscandia to Chukotka, to the north coast though absent from Russia's Arctic islands (apart from the New Siberian Islands). In winter European birds move to Mediterranean coasts, while Asian birds head for southern Asia and Japan.

OTHER SANDPIPERS

BROAD-BILLED SANDPIPER

Limicola falcinellus

L: 15–18cm (bill 3cm). WS: 36–40cm. W: 30–45g.

Rare and elusive. Recognisable for the bill, which is broad at the base (when viewed from above) and tapers towards the downcurved tip. Breeding adult has a dark brown or black crown delineated by a thin white stripe, which meets the white supercilium in front of the eye. The rest of the head and neck (apart from a white throat) is white with black streaking. The underparts are white, with significant black streaking on the breast, and less heavy streaking on the flanks. The streaking takes the form of arrowheads, these occasionally distinct, but often merging to form long streaks. The upperparts are grey-brown with heavy black markings. Wintering birds lose the

dark crown, the head and upperparts being white or pale grey with black and grey-brown mottling.

Broad-billed Sandpipers breed in northern Fennoscandia and in isolated areas of Asian Russia as far east as the Kolyma river. In winter the birds move to southern Africa, southern parts of Arabia and India, and Indonesia and northern Australia.

Buff-breasted Sandpiper

Tryngites subruficollis

L: 18–20cm. WS: 43–48cm. W: 55–75g. ♀≂♂.

These attractive birds were once numerous, but overhunting in the 19th century caused a dramatic decline from which the species has not recovered, and it remains rare. Breeding adult has a buff head, neck and breast, with paler buff belly and vent. The crown and forehead are streaked brown and there is often some streaking on the flanks. The upperparts are buff, more heavily streaked with black and dark brown. In winter adults retain the buff base colour, but the streaking becomes less heavy and more subdued – brown rather than black. The birds differ from many other shorebirds in being found almost invariably in dry areas, and in pecking rather than probing for their food.

Buff-breasted Sandpipers breed on Wrangel Island and north-eastern Chukotka, in northern Alaska and the Yukon, and on southern Canadian Arctic islands. In winter both Russian and American birds fly south to Argentina and Paraguay.

Ruff

Philomachus pugnax

Male L: 25–30cm. WS: 55–60cm. W: 1[illegible]0–220g.
Female L: 20–25cm. WS: 47–52cm. W: [illegible]0–150g.

Exhibits extreme sexual dimorphism. Breeding male (ruff) has a bare red or orange-red face with many warts, these usually red, but occasionally yellow or green. The prominent ear tufts, which cover the sides of the nape and the circular ruff, which extends to the breast, are highly variable in colour, chiefly being white, black or shades of rufous brown. The ruff may also have complete black rings, incomplete rings or no rings. The underparts are white, the breast heavily streaked black. The upperparts are brown, buff and black. Breeding female (reeve) is much duller, and lacks the bare face, ear coverts and ruff. The head is grey-brown, streaked darker. The upperparts are grey-brown, spotted with black. The underparts are white with heavy buff and black streaking on the breast and flanks.

In winter male birds lose all the showy breeding plumage and become rather anonymous grey-brown birds. Wintering females lose the black feather-centres that give the black spotting, and so are as breeding, but duller.

Ruffs breed in Fennoscandia and across Russia to the border of Chukotka. Breeds to the north coast in places, but absent from all of Russia's Arctic islands. Wintering birds occur in western Europe, along the coast of the Mediterranean, and as far south as the coasts of India and southern Africa.

Male Ruffs, Varangerfjord, Norway.

Stilt Sandpiper, Churchill, Manitoba, Canada.

Spoon-billed Sandpiper
Eurynorhynchus pygmaeus
L: 14–16cm. WS: 36–40cm. W: 20–35g.
Status: IUCN: Vulnerable.
An extraordinary bird, perhaps the most remarkable of all Arctic breeding species. It is, however, also one of the rarest, with a population that might be as low as 2,500 and is declining as a result of habitat loss at the breeding sites, on migration and at wintering quarters. Bill is broad at the base, then tapers before flattening into a diamond shape. Breeding adult has a chestnut head, the forehead, crown and nape being streaked dark brown. The nape, lower neck and underparts are white, the breast smudged chestnut. The upperparts are mottled dark brown, chestnut and white. Winter adult is much paler, the chestnut coloration becoming buff or even white, the streaking grey-brown. The bill is so unusual and so particular a shape that it is diagnostic if it can be clearly seen, but with less-than-perfect views the bird can be confused with Red-necked Stint.

Spoon-billed Sandpipers breed only in far eastern Chukotka and northern Kamchatka. Migrating birds head to south-east Asia.

Breeding Ruffs

Breeding male Ruffs have elaborate lek behaviour, the lek arenas being traditional sites that may have been used over hundreds of years. At these sites the birds form three distinct groups – residents, which hold territories at the arena; migrants, which attempt to obtain territories, and may hold territories at other arenas; and opportunistic satellites. In general the bird that holds the central territory is the dominant male who will have fought off challengers for right of possession; in general, females will head for him, ignoring the displays of other males they pass. Studies show that the colour variations of male ear-coverts and ruff are associated with the groupings. Residents invariably have black ear-coverts, satellites white ear-coverts and ruffs: satellites are tolerated by residents as this coloration is attractive to females. Satellites will hold a territory in the absence of the resident bird, re-assuming a satellite role when the resident returns. Some authorities suggest satellites display a form of behavioural dimorphism and that this and white coloration are heritable.

The displaying ruff flutters his wings and jumps in the air, with the ruff expanded to its full circle and the ear-coverts raised. The ruff will mate with any interested reeve, so polygamy is common. However, some studies show that monogamy is also practised. Display and copulation are the ruff's only contribution to the next generation, the reeve incubating the eggs and caring for the chicks. As if to finally confirm female prejudices regarding the character of males, the testes of the ruff do indeed weigh more than his brain. It is, though, worth noting that reeves frequently mate with several ruffs in the arena, studies suggesting that more than half of the broods contain chicks with different fathers.

Stilt Sandpiper
Micropalama himantopus
L: 18–22cm (bill 4cm). WS: 43–48cm. W: 50–70g. ♀>♂.
Breeding adult has a white head, the crown streaked chestnut. The supercilium is white and very distinct, and the ear-coverts are bright chestnut. The rest of the face and the neck is white, streaked brown. The underparts are white, heavily streaked and barred with dark brown. The upperparts are white, heavily blotched dark brown. Winter adult much as breeding adult but much more subdued, lacking the chestnut patches on the head, and with upperparts that are much duller – a uniform pale grey-brown.

Stilt Sandpipers breed from northern Alaska (where it is rare) to Bathurst Inlet and on southern Victoria Island. Also breeds at the south-west corner of Hudson Bay. In winter the birds move to central South America.

SNIPES AND DOWITCHERS

These shorebirds are all generally stocky birds with long bills that share feeding characteristics. Snipes have identical summer and winter plumages.

Common Snipe
Gallinago gallinago
L: 25–27cm (bill 6.0–7.5cm). WS: 44–48cm. W: 85–125g. ♀>♂.
Adult has a dark brown crown with a thin central buff stripe. The rest of the head is buff with darker stripes through the eye and on the cheek, the buff above the eye appearing as a broad supercilium. The breast is buff, heavily streaked dark brown. The rest of the underparts are white, with dark brown streaking on the flanks. The upperparts are mottled dark and lighter brown. Summer and winter plumages are similar.

Common Snipe breed in Iceland, northern Fennoscandia, and across Russia, though rarely to the north coast and not on any of the Arctic islands. Icelandic birds are resident in winter, but European birds move to Mediterranean coasts and the sub-Saharan belt, while Asian birds fly to India and south-east Asia.

Wilson's Snipe
Gallinago delicata
L: 25–27cm. (bill 6.0–7.5cm). WS: 44–48cm. W: 85–125g. ♀>♂.
Until recently Wilson's Snipe was considered a Nearctic subspecies of Common Snipe. The plumage is essentially identical, though the underwing tends to be darker and there

Common Snipe, Varangerfjord, Norway.

is no, or only a very thin, white trailing edge on the upperwing. However, the Nearctic bird has 16 tail feathers rather than the 14 of the Common Snipe, and the outer feathers are shorter. Summer and winter plumages are similar.

Wilson's Snipe breed across North America from Alaska to Labrador, though only to the north coast near the Mackenzie delta. Absent from islands of the Canadian Arctic. In winter the birds move to southern United States, Central America and northern South America.

Pintail Snipe

Gallinago stenura

L: 25–27cm (bill 5–7cm). WS: 44–48cm. W: 85–125g. ♀>♂.
Very similar to Common Snipe, but with a shorter bill and broader supercilium forward of the eye. The underwing is darker and the tail shorter. The major difference is the tail feathering, the Pintail Snipe having 26 (but sometimes 24 or 28) tail feathers compared to the 14 of the Common Snipe (and 16 of Wilson's Snipe). The outer eight pairs (the usual number, though six, seven and nine have been observed) are only *c.*2mm wide – they are the pins of the name. Because these feathers are so narrow, they are difficult to see in the field. Summer and winter plumages are similar.

Pintail Snipe breed in Russia, from the Ob river to western Chukotka, but not to the north coast. In winter the birds move to south-east Arabia, India, south-east Asia and Indonesia.

> **Drumming snipe**
>
> Snipes are among the few birds that deliberately make a mechanical (i.e. non-vocal) sound. During display flights the birds dive at an angle of *c.*45° while fanning the tail. The two outer feathers of the tail are stiff and have asymmetric vanes, the leading edges being narrow. The bird holds these feathers at right-angles to the body; at speeds of about 60kph or higher they vibrate. The air through the vibrating feathers is modulated, creating a loud drumming noise (also called winnowing), which can be heard over considerable distances. It is often heard before the observer has seen the bird. Although it is male snipe that are chiefly responsible for the drumming, females also make the sound, particularly early in the breeding season.

Jack Snipe

Lymnocryptes minimus

L: 17–20cm (bill 3–5cm). WS: 30–35cm. W: 85–125g.
Very similar to Common Snipe but smaller, and with a shorter bill. The head is paler, and overall the bird has a richer buff base colour. Summer and winter plumages are similar. A bird of the boreal edge so sub-Arctic rather than Arctic, but may be seen by Palearctic travellers.

Jack Snipe breed in southern Fennoscandia, around Russia's White Sea coast, but then increasingly southerly across Siberia as far as the Lena River.

Long-billed Dowitcher

Limnodromus scolopaceus

L: 26–30cm (bill 6–8cm). WS: 48–55cm. W: 90–130g. ♀>♂.
Breeding adult has a chestnut head with a paler supercilium, and a dark brown crown. The underparts are chestnut or pale chestnut, the neck and upper breast finely streaked and barred dark brown. The upperparts are mottled dark brown, chestnut and buff. Winter adult is pale grey-brown above. The breast is mottled grey-brown, the rest of the underparts white. In winter the birds are overall dull grey-brown. When feeding the birds probe with their bills very quickly, an action which is frequently referred to as being 'sewing machine-like'. They also often feed in shallow water, so for the photographer, getting a shot with the long bill exposed rather than half-buried is tricky.

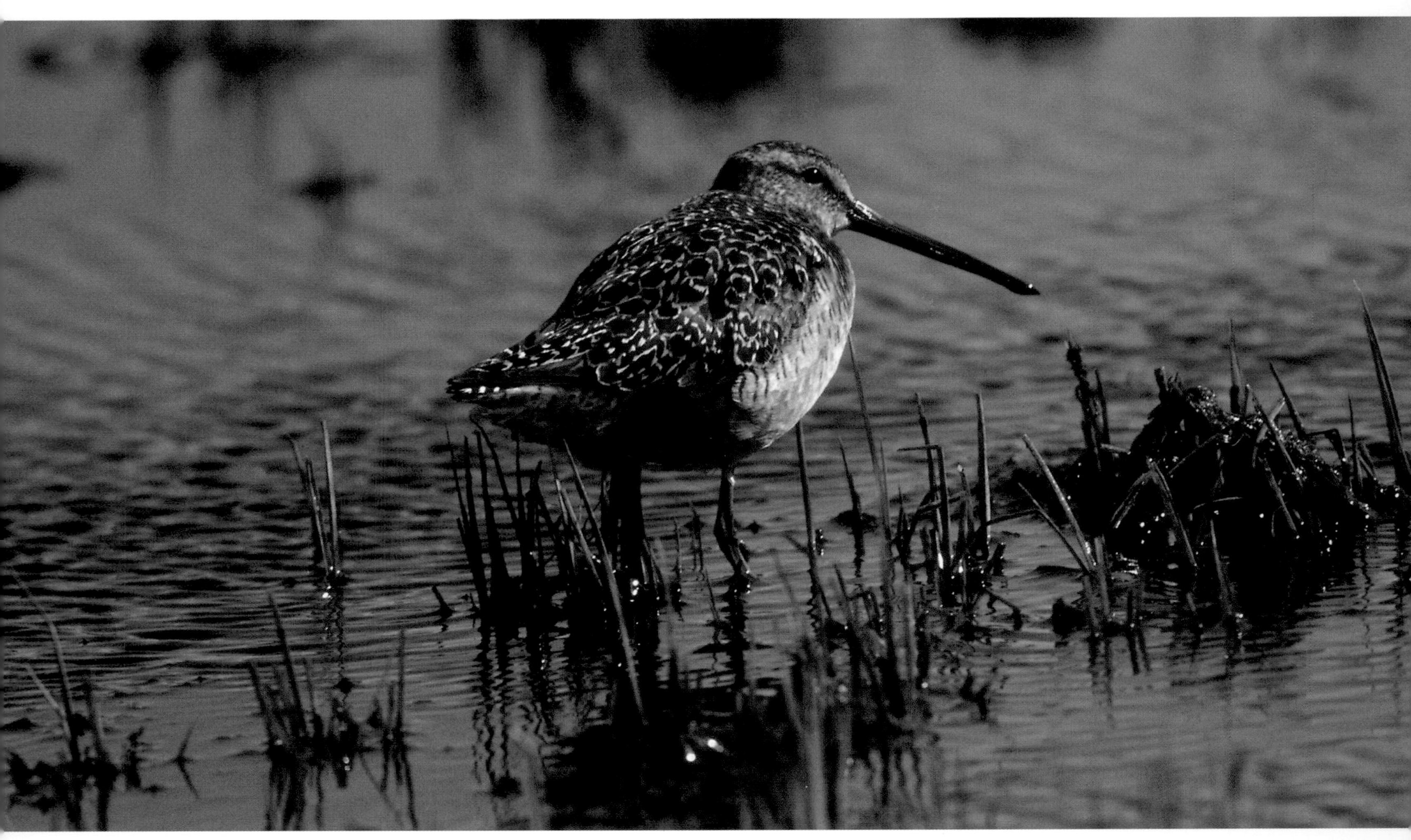

Long-billed Dowitcher, Barrow, Alaska.

Long-billed Dowitcher breeds in Russia east from the Yana River and south to Anadyr, and on Wrangel Island. Breeds patchily in North America eastwards to the western and southern shores of Hudson Bay. Also breeds on southern Victoria Island. Both Russian and American birds winter in the south-west United States and in Mexico.

SHORT-BILLED DOWITCHER

Limnodromus griseus

L: 23–28 (bill 5–6cm). WS: 45–50cm. W: 85–120g.
Until the 1950s the two northern species of dowitchers were considered conspecific, largely because of the similarity of the Short-billed Dowitcher subspecies that overlaps in range with the Long-billed near southern Hudson Bay. The plumage of this race, *L. g. hendersoni*, the 'Prairie' Short-billed Dowitcher, is extremely similar to the Long-billed, though the upperparts are mottled gold and black, and the underparts are orange rather than chestnut. The 'Pacific' Short-billed Dowitcher, *L. g. caurinus*, overlaps with the Long-billed in southern Alaska, but it is usually more easily distinguished, having a white belly and vent with heavy dark brown barring. The longer bill and legs of the Long-billed are diagnostic if the birds are viewed together.

Short-billed Dowitchers breed in three distinct areas of North America – southern Alaska, around the southern shores of Hudson Bay and in southern Quebec and Labrador. In winter the birds move to the east and west coasts of the southern United States, Central America, the Caribbean islands, and the east and west coasts of northern South America.

Black-tailed Godwits, Orre, Norway.

Bar-tailed Godwits, Orre, Norway.

CURLEWS, GODWITS AND *TRINGA* SANDPIPERS

The *Tringinae* shorebird subfamily varies considerably, from the elegant godwits and the curlews with their distinctive bills to the exotic tattlers, encompassing rather more nondescript birds along the way. Some of the species mentioned here are essentially sub-Arctic birds, and only brief details are given.

Bar-tailed Godwit

Limosa lapponica

L: 35–40cm (bill 8–10cm). WS: 70–80cm. W: 250–450g. ♀>♂.

Breeding male is a handsome bird, with rufous brown head and underparts, the crown streaked black-and-white. The bill is long and slightly upcurved. The distal half is dark brown or black, the basal half pinkish-yellow. The upperparts are dark brown, chestnut and white. The tail is barred dark brown and white. Breeding female is similar but paler overall, with a white belly and vent. The female's bill is longer. Non-breeding adults are as female, but pale grey-brown rather than pale chestnut.

Bar-tailed Godwits breed in northern Fennoscandia (chiefly Finland), and patchily across western Russia, though more consistently east of the Taimyr Peninsula to western Chukotka and near Anadyr. Also breeds in western Alaskan. European birds winter in western Europe and west Africa. Asian and American birds move to the Arabian Peninsula, Pakistan and eastern India, Indonesia, Australia and New Zealand.

All the way to New Zealand?

Some Bar-tailed Godwits are believed to fly non-stop from their breeding grounds on the western coast of Alaska to New Zealand. If this is the case then the journey – of about 1[illegible]km – is the longest single flight of any bird. Recently, telemetry has confirmed that one bird flew non-stop from New Zealand to North Korea, a distance of more than 10,000km, at an average speed of [illegible]ph.

Black-tailed Godwit

Limosa limosa

L: 33–40cm (bill 8–12cm). WS: 65–75cm. W: 250–350g. ♀>♂.

Breeding male similar to Bar-tailed Godwit but the breast is (usually pale) rufous, the rest of the underparts white, with heavy black barring on the flanks. The bill tip is dark brown or black, the rest orange-yellow. The tail is black. The sexes are similar. In flight the feet extend well beyond the tail. In winter the upperparts and breast are pale grey-brown.

Black-tailed Godwits breed on Iceland and patchily on the Norwegian coast, but are otherwise more southerly in their Palearctic distribution.

Hudsonian Godwit

Limosa haemastica

L: 37–42cm (bill 7–10cm). WS: 70–80cm. W: 250–450g. ♀>♂.

Breeding male has a pale grey head and neck, finely streaked dark brown. The crown is dark brown, streaked pale chestnut.

Hudsonian Godwit, Churchill, Manitoba, Canada.

The distal third of the bill is dark brown, the rest orange. The underparts are dark chestnut, paler on the vent and undertail, and with dark brown streaking on the breast and flanks. The upperparts are dark brown, chestnut and buff, the rump grey-brown. Breeding female is as the male, but with white underparts heavily barred chestnut. In winter adults are grey above, paler below.

Hudsonian Godwits breed patchily in western North America, at sites on the southern coast of Hudson Bay, near the Mackenzie delta and, rarely, in western and southern Alaska. In winter the birds fly to southern Argentina.

Bristle-thighed Curlew

Numenius tahitiensis

L: 40–44cm (bill 7–9cm). WS: 80–90cm. W: 350–550g.
Status: IUCN: Vulnerable.
Adult has a pale cream or buff head with a darker crown, this split by a buff stripe. The supercilium is pale buff or cream. The bill is long and downcurved. The neck and underparts are buff or pale cinnamon, the neck, breast and flanks heavily streaked brown. The upperparts are dark brown, spotted buff. There is no variation from breeding to non-breeding plumage.

Very similar to Whimbrel, with which range overlaps. The stiff feathering of the upper leg – the bristled thigh of the name – is diagnostic but of no value in the field. The buff, barred tail is diagnostic, as is the white rump of Palearctic Whimbrels. However, Nearctic Whimbrels lack the white rump.

Bristle-thighed Curlews breed in a few places in western Alaska (the Yukon delta and upland Seward Peninsula). In winter the birds move to Polynesia.

Whimbrel

Numenius phaeopus

L: 40–44cm (bill 6–10cm). WS: 75–90cm. W: 300–600g.
Adults, which are identical in breeding and winter plumage, have grey heads, the crown dark brown with a grey central stripe. The bill is long and downcurved. The neck and underparts are grey-buff with heavy brown streaking except on the belly and vent. The upperparts are dark brown, white and pale buff. The tail colour varies; it may be pale with some dark barring, or darker without barring. Winter and summer plumages are similar.

Whimbrels breed on Iceland, in Fennoscandia and western Russia, then more patchily across Siberia. Breeds in North America in western and central Alaska, but more rarely in the north, on the Mackenzie delta and around the south-western

Rare habits for a rare bird

The Bristle-thighed Curlew is rare, probably numbering less than 5,000. This is strange because in Alaska the available habitat could accommodate many more birds. What limits the population is the size of the winter habitat, this being confined to a handful of islands in the south Pacific. To add to the pressure of limited wintering grounds, feral cats and dogs on those islands hunt the birds when they are flightless during moulting. The birds have a strange winter. They take invertebrates and rodents, but also feed on gull eggs, occasionally stealing eggs from beneath incubating birds. The stolen eggs are pierced with the bill or broken by being dropped. A bird will sometimes drop a rock on to an egg – one of the few observations of avian tool-use.

and southern shores of Hudson Bay. In winter Eurasian birds move to sub-Saharan Africa, southern Asia and Australasia Nearctic birds to the southern United States, Central America, the Caribbean islands, and South America as far as southern Chile.

Far left
Whimbrel, southern Iceland.

Far-Eastern Curlew

Numenius madagascariensis

L: 55–65cm (bill 10–15cm). WS: 85–95cm. W: 650–1000g.
The largest of the curlews. Adult has a buff-brown head, neck and breast, each finely streaked with dark brown. The rest of the underparts are paler with less heavy streaking. The upperparts are also buff with dark streaking, the rump paler, but distinctly darker than the white rump of the Eurasian Curlew, which the bird strongly resembles. Winter and summer plumages are similar.

Far-eastern Curlews have a limited range in eastern Russia and north-east China, but some breed around the western and northern shores of the Sea of Okhotsk and on Kamchatka. Wintering birds occur in south-east Asia and Australasia.

Eskimo Curlew

Numenius borealis

L: 30–35cm (bill 3–5cm). WS: 60–80cm. W: 150–250g. ♀>♂.
Status: IUCN: Critical. CITES: Appendix I.
Similar to other curlews; adult has a buff head with dark brown crown stripe and an indistinct dark eye-stripe. The

> **Is the Eskimo Curlew extinct?**
>
> Overhunting and loss of habitat caused a drastic depletion of this once-numerous species. Migrating birds fed primarily on the Rocky Mountain Grasshopper (Melanoplus spretus) that became extinct when the prairies were claimed for agricultural land and fires on the remaining areas were suppressed. The present position of this species is unclear. There has been no confirmed sighting since the early 1980s and most authorities consider the species to be extinct, pointing to the fact that a bird with a migration path that took it across the southern United States and on to southern South America can hardly have escaped detection for 20 years. Even the most optimistic consider the population to be less than 50–100 birds and the long-term survival of the bird to be bleak.

Left
Far-Eastern Curlew, southern Kamchatka, Russia.

underparts are buff, paler on the belly and vent, streaked darker on the breast and flanks. The upper parts are dark brown with buff spotting.

Common Sandpiper

Actitis hypoleucos

L: 18–21cm. WS: 35–40cm. W: 40–50g. ♀>♂.
Adult has a grey-brown head and breast with darker eye stripe. Rest of the underparts white. Upperparts bronze-brown marked by dark arrowheads. In flight a white wing-bar is distinctive. Long tail and persistent bobbing of rear body are diagnostic.

Common Sandpipers are essentially sub-Arctic, but breeds in northern Fennoscandia, more southerly across Russia, and throughout Kamchatka. In winter the birds move to Africa, the Middle East and southern Asia.

Surfbird

Aphriza virgata

L: 22–27cm. WS: 50–55cm. W: 100–150g. ♀>♂.
Breeding adult has a white head and heavily streaked dark grey-brown breast; rest of upperparts white with larger dark spotting. Upperparts are gold with black spotting. Tail is white with terminal black bar. Grey-brown wings show distinctive white bar. In winter adults lose the gold upperpart wash and heavy spotting.

Surfbirds are essentially sub-Arctic; breeds patchily across Alaska, though common only on the south coast. Also breeds in central Yukon, but not common. Winters on west coast of United States.

Common Redshank

Tringa tetanus

L: 25–30cm (bill 3–5cm). WS: 55–65cm. W: 90–150g. ♀>♂.
Breeding adult has a pale olive head and breast, finely streaked darker; rest of underparts white with dark spots. Nape, scapulars and inner wing are olive with darker streaking, rest of upper body white, the tail with dark barring. The bill is black with an orange base. In winter adult loses distinct streaking and is dull mottled grey-brown. The red legs are diagnostic.

Common Redshanks are essentially sub-Arctic but breed on Iceland and western Fennoscandia. Icelandic birds winter in the British Isles and mainland Europe, Norwegian birds in southern Scandinavia or mainland Europe.

Egg protection

The Surfbird – which gets its curious name from its habit of feeding close to the incoming tide and so is occasionally drenched by wind-blown spray – nests in areas where Caribou and Dall's Sheep occur. It has evolved an effective strategy for stopping its eggs from being trampled. The bird sits tight as the ungulate approaches, then suddenly flies up and at the animal's face. Startled, the ungulate will turn and flee or, at least, change direction.

Noisy colonies

Common Redshanks are highly vocal when intruders encroach on their territories, the sharp whistling call bringing adjacent birds quickly to the scene, so the intruder is quickly surrounded by birds and bombarded with noise. The potential predator is soon driven away by the incessant racket. A loose colonial nesting system has resulted from this efficient anti-predator strategy; other species occasionally nest close to Redshanks to take advantage of their protection.

Above
Common Redshank, Varangerfjord, Norway.

SPOTTED REDSHANK

Tringa erythropus

L: 29–32cm (bill 5–6cm). WS: 60–68cm. W: 150–190g. ♀>♂. Adult is distinctive, with black head, neck and underparts. The upperparts are black with white spotting, apart from the back and upper rump, which are white. The legs are black; the bill is black with a red base. Wintering bird is grey above and white or pale grey below, the legs being red; can be difficult to distinguish from Common Redshank.

Females spend a very short time at the breeding grounds. They choose a mate, copulate and lay, and, after a few days of incubation they depart for the wintering grounds, leaving the male to take over incubation and chick care.

Spotted Redshanks breed in northern Fennoscandia, on the eastern shores of the White Sea, and from the Ob east to Chukotka, north towards the coast, except on the Taimyr Peninsula where it breeds only in the south. In winter the birds move to the Mediterranean coast, central Africa, and the coasts of India and south-east Asia.

COMMON GREENSHANK

Tringa nebularia

L: 30–33cm (bill 5–6cm). WS: 65–70cm. W: 135–225g. Breeding birds are similar to Common Redshank but more distinctly marked on the upperparts and less heavily, but more distinctly, marked on the underparts. The bill is longer and slightly upturned, and greyish green, paler at the base. The legs are yellow-green. In winter the plumage is duller, the legs grey-green.

Greenshanks are essentially sub-Arctic but breed in northern Fennoscandia, then more southerly across Russia.

Below
Common Greenshank, Orre, Norway.

LESSER YELLOWLEGS

Tringa flavipes

L: 23–25cm (bill 3–4cm). WS: 58–64cm. W: 60–100g. Long-legged and elegant; breeding adult has white or pale grey head, finely streaked dark brown. The breast is pale grey, heavily marked darker grey, the rest of the underparts are pale greyish white, the marking diminishing towards the vent. The upperparts are dark grey-brown spotted with white. The thin bill is black. The legs are bright yellow. In winter adult is as breeding, but overall more subdued. In areas where they overlap it can be difficult to distinguish Lesser from Greater Yellowlegs, though the calls differ. When seen together the size difference is clear.

Lesser Yellowlegs breed in central and southern Alaska (rare on the west and north coasts), around the Mackenzie delta,

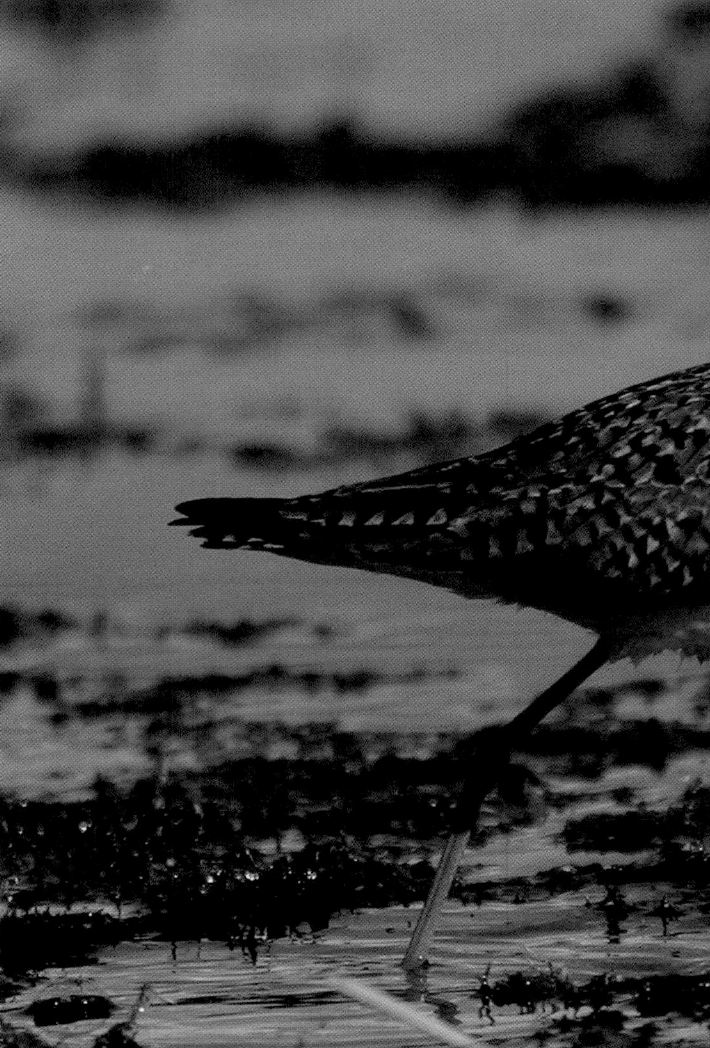

then more southerly to the southern shores of Hudson Bay. In winter the birds move to the coasts of the southern United States, to Central America, the Caribbean islands, and South America as far south as Tierra del Fuego.

Greater Yellowlegs

Tringa melanoleuca

L: 30–33cm (bill 5–6cm). WS: 70–75cm. W: 110–180g.
Similar to Lesser Yellowlegs, size being the best distinguishing feature, though Greater Yellowlegs tends to have more markings on the belly and flanks. As Lesser Yellowlegs in winter.

Greater Yellowlegs are essentially sub-Arctic, but breeds around the southern shores of Hudson Bay, where it overlaps the range of Lesser Yellowlegs. Overlap also occurs in southern Alaska and southern parts of western Canada. In winter the birds migrate to the coasts of the southern United States, to Central America, the Caribbean islands, and South America as far south as Tierra del Fuego.

Solitary Sandpiper

Tringa solitaria

L: 18–21cm. WS: 55–60cm. W: 35–60g.
Breeding adult has an olive-brown head, finely streaked white. There is a white eye-ring. The throat and underparts are pale greyish white, the breast heavily streaked dark brown. The upperparts are dark brownish black with some white or pale buff spotting. In winter adult is patterned as breeding adult, but grey-brown with little streaking. Much less common than Spotted Sandpiper, with which it might be confused. The orange legs and bill of Spotted are diagnostic, with Solitary Sandpiper having a dark grey bill and yellow-green legs.

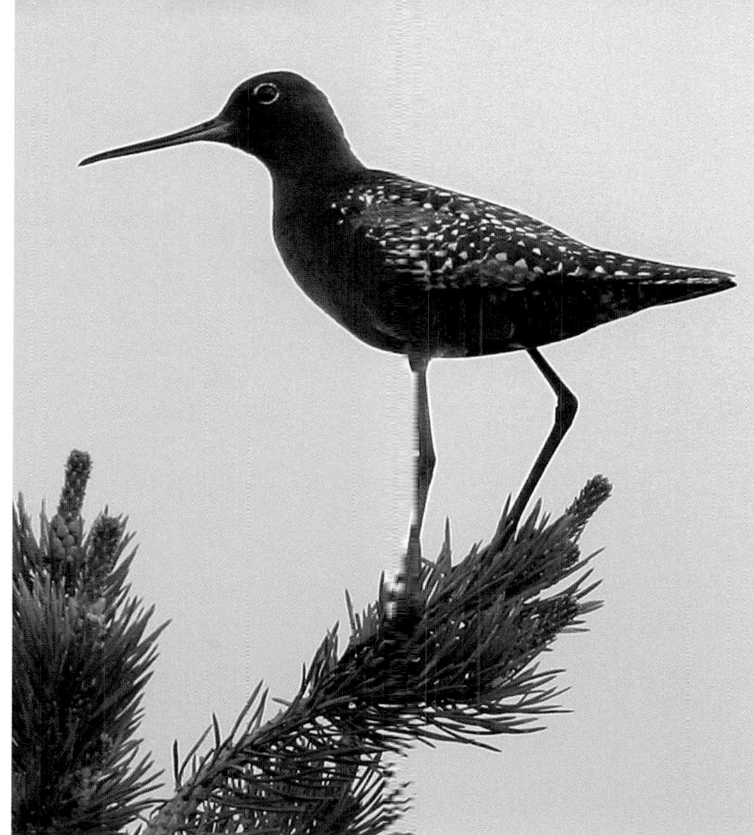

Spotted Redshank, northern Finland.

Solitary Sandpipers breed in central and southern Alaska (where it is uncommon, and rare on the west and north coasts), on the Mackenzie delta, then more southerly to the southern shores of Hudson and James Bays and into southern Quebec and Labrador. In winter the birds are seen in eastern Central America, on Caribbean islands and in northern South America.

Spotted Sandpiper

Actitis macularia

L: 18–20cm. WS: 37–40cm. W: 25–60g.
Breeding adult has a greenish-brown head and nape. The throat, front neck and underparts are white with heavy black spotting as far as the breast, then less heavy spotting on the belly, flanks and vent. The upperparts are greenish-brown. In winter adult loses the heavy spotting on the underparts, and the upperparts are brown. The bill changes from bright orange with a black tip to dark brown in winter.

Spotted Sandpipers breed in central and southern Alaska (but rare on west and north coasts), on the Mackenzie delta, the southern shores of Hudson Bay and James Bay, and in central Quebec and Labrador. In winter the birds fly to southwest coastal United States, to Central America and the Caribbean islands, and to northern South America.

Wood Sandpiper

Tringa glareola

L: 19–21cm. WS: 55–58cm. W: 50–80g.
Breeding adult has a pale grey head with a dark brown crown, streaked pale grey. The neck and underparts are pale grey, heavily streaked dark brown except for the belly and vent. The upperparts are dark brown, heavily barred and spotted pale grey-brown. Winter adult is as breeding but the underparts are more subtly streaked and the upperparts are grey-brown.

Wood Sandpipers are a boreal species, found at the treeline but rarely on the tundra. Breeds in Fennoscandia, across Russia to central Chukotka and throughout Kamchatka. In winter the birds are seen in southern Africa, India and Australasia.

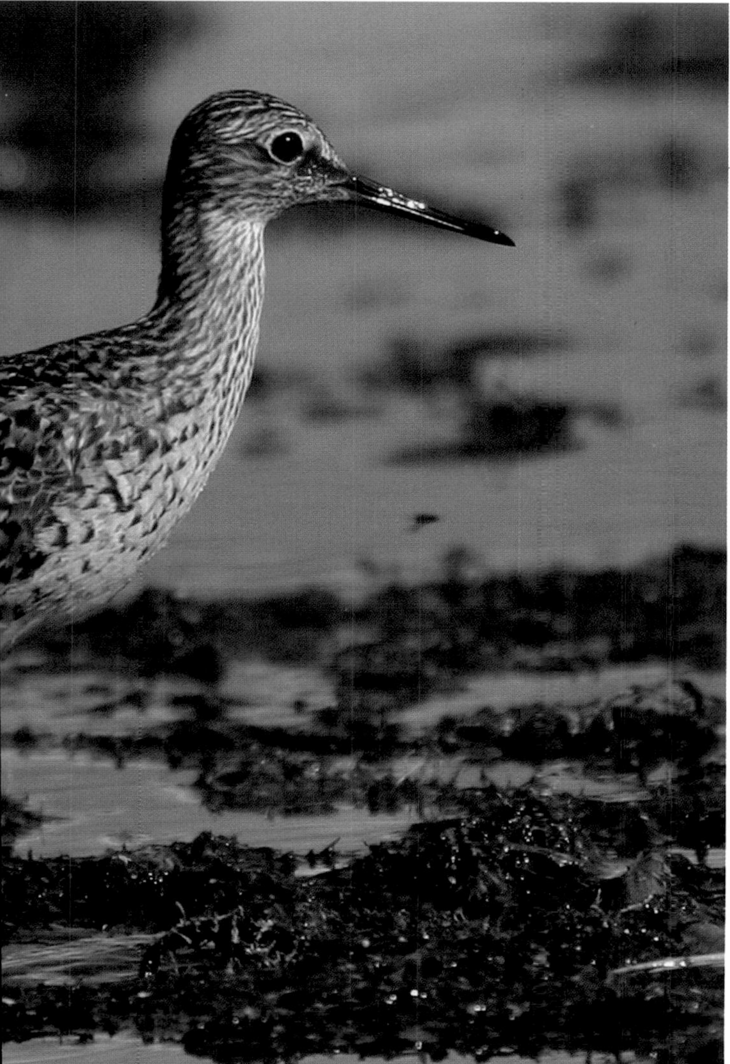

Lesser Yellowlegs, Great Slave Lake, NWT, Canada.

Wood Sandpiper, Vestmanland, Sweden.

Wandering Tattler

Heteroscelus incanus

L: 26–30cm. WS: 55–70cm. W: 90–125g.

The crown, nape and upperparts of breeding adult are a uniform slate grey. The cheeks, throat and underparts are white, heavily barred dark grey. In winter the heavy barring of the underparts is replaced by an overall grey wash.

Wandering Tattlers breed in Alaska and the Yukon, but is uncommon with a patchy range. Rare in north and central Alaska. In winter the birds fly to south-west coastal United States and across the Pacific Ocean to Hawaii and other remote islands.

Grey-tailed Tattler

Heteroscelus brevipes

L: 24–27cm. WS: 50–65cm. W: 85–115g.

Wandering and Grey-tailed Tattlers are very similar, and the two occasionally occur together in Alaska. There are plumage differences between the two: the Grey-tailed has paler upperparts and a thin white bar on the upperwing, and the underparts are less heavily marked. But these differences are very subtle and of limited value even if the two birds happen to be in view at the same time. The calls are also subtly different, the Wandering having a trisyllabic trill, whereas that of the Grey-tailed is disyllabic; unfortunately the alarm calls are identical. The real diagnostic characteristic (which is not as difficult to see as it sounds) is the nasal groove. In the Wandering Tattler this is long, around 75% of bill length, but it is much shorter in Grey-tailed.

Grey-tailed Tattlers breed on the northern Yenisey river, patchily from the Lena to western Chukotka, and throughout Kamchatka. Some Kamchatka birds are resident, staying close to hot springs, but the majority of Russian birds fly to coastal areas of Indonesia and Australasia.

TURNSTONES

The two Arctic-breeding Turnstones have bills similar to those of the plovers, being short for pecking at prey rather than probing for it. The prey is often found beneath stones and other debris, the name giving the search method away – unlike the plovers' 'look–run–peck' foraging, turnstones use powerful neck muscles to overturn objects that look as though they would be good hiding places. Occasionally several birds will team up to overturn a larger object if something that can be shared, such as a dead fish, lies underneath. Stone-turning can reveal all sorts of things, alive or dead, the birds consequently having the most varied diet of any shorebirds, as they will eat just about anything that emerges.

Ruddy Turnstone, Helglandskysten, Norway.

Ruddy Turnstone

Arenaria interpres

L: 22–25cm. WS: 50–58cm. W: 90–140g. ♀=♂.

Breeding male is an attractive little bird with a white head, the crown finely streaked black. There is a variable pattern of black bands on the head and breast. The rest of the underparts are white. The upperparts are chestnut or orange and black, so that the sitting bird has a tortoiseshell appearance. Females have similar patterning but are duller overall. In winter the body and wing pattern remains, but summer colours are replaced by dark grey-brown. The head is also grey-brown, but the black patterning largely remains.

Ruddy Turnstones breed in north-west and north-east Greenland, on Iceland and Svalbard, in Fennoscandia and across Russia, including the southern island of Novaya Zemlya, the New Siberian Islands, and Wrangel Island. In North America, breed in west and north-west Alaska, along the northern coast of western Canada, and on the southern Arctic islands. Icelandic birds and (probably) some from Greenland remain on Iceland's south-west coast in winter. Eurasian birds move to the coasts of western Europe, Africa, the Middle East, India, south-east Asia and Australasia; American birds move to the coasts of the southern United States, Central America, the Caribbean islands and South America to northern Chile and Argentina.

Black Turnstone

Arenaria melanocephala

L: 22–25cm. WS: 50–55cm. W: 100–140g. ♀>♂.

Breeding adult has a black head with delicate white streaking on the crown and nape, and a prominent white spot at the base of the bill. The breast is black, marked with small white spots. The rest of the underparts are white. The upperparts are black, flecked with white. In winter adult is as breeding but dark brown rather than black, and with little white speckling and no white bill-spot.

Black Turnstones breed only in west and southern Alaska. In winter the birds fly to the west coast of the southern United States and to Baja California.

PHALAROPES

Two of the three species of phalaropes (all of which are northern species) are true Arctic breeders and make long migration flights; they are clearly tough little birds, belying their fragile looks. The two Arctic species share many traits, including polyandry. They also share a feeding habit, swimming in tight circles to stir up the water and bring prey to the surface, known as 'spinning'. As well as spinning, phalaropes feed at the shoreline, taking insects found among seaweed and tidal debris. Wintering birds are chiefly pelagic, taking small fish and free-swimming crustaceans, and even picking parasites from the skins of whales.

Red-necked Phalarope

Phalaropus lobatus

L: 18–19cm. WS: 32–40cm. W: 30–40g. ♀>♂.

Breeding female has a dark grey crown and nape, the rest of the neck red-brown. The throat is white. The breast and flanks are grey, the rest of the underparts white. The upperparts are dark grey with buff lines. Breeding male is as female but duller overall. In winter the sexes are similar, the head white with a dark grey hind crown and nape and prominent black eye-stripe, the upperparts pale grey and white, the underparts white with occasional pale grey patching.

Red-necked Phalaropes breed in southern Greenland (but is rare in the north), on Iceland and Svalbard, in Fennoscandia, and across northern Russia to Chukotka and Kamchatka, but not on any Russian Arctic islands. Breeds across North America and on southern Arctic islands. Full details of the species' wintering sites are not known. Asian birds are seen off western South America, in the Arabian Sea and north of Indonesia, but though it is known that the birds congregate in the Bay of Fundy, as many as two million birds being reported, no other Atlantic wintering sites have yet been confirmed.

Grey Phalarope (Red Phalarope)

Phalaropus fulicarius

L: 20–22cm. WS: 40–44cm. W: 40–70g. ♀>♂.

Breeding female is a stunning bird with a black crown and white face (apart from a black and dark grey patch at the bill base). The neck and underparts are bright chestnut-red. The upperparts are dark brown with cinnamon or buff lines. Breeding male is as female, but the crown is streaked buff and dark grey, the face pattern less sharply defined and, like the

Role reversal in practice. Here, on Igloolik Island, Canada, a female Grey Phalarope is frantically signalling to an apparently uninterested male.

Role reversal

In all three phalarope species the females are larger than the males, and have much brighter breeding plumage. The biggest size difference is in the non-Arctic breeding Wilson's Phalarope *Phalaropus tricolor*, in which females are about 35% larger. In the Grey Phalarope the difference is about 20%, and in the Red-necked about 10%. The females court males with aerial and terrestrial displays. After mating and laying a clutch of eggs, the female will abandon the male, leaving him to incubate the eggs and care for the young. The female seeks another male if one is available, laying a second clutch before abandoning him as well. The female stays on the breeding grounds, so if either clutch is lost she can mate and lay again with either male. Such polyandry is uncommon, though not unique, among birds. The chicks are downy and precocial, being self-feeding.

Red-necked Phalaropes, Varangerfjord, Norway. ***Above left***, the more colourful female is closest to the camera. ***Above right***, the pair mating.

Female Grey Phalarope, Igloolik, Canada.

upperparts, much duller. The underparts are paler and heavily streaked white. The sexes are alike in winter, and are similar to Red-necked Phalarope, though pale grey rather than pale greyish white on the upperparts. The Red-necked also has a much thinner bill

Grey Phalarope breeds in north-west Greenland (and also in the north-east, though much rarer), Iceland (where it is among the rarest of breeding birds), Svalbard (where it also very rare) and on the north coast of Asian Russia east of the Yenisey. Also breeds on the New Siberian and Wrangel Islands. Breeds in northern Alaska, around the Mackenzie delta, on Canada's Boothia Peninsula and the north-west shore of Hudson Bay, and on Canada's Arctic islands north to southern Ellesmere Island. The population on Southampton Island has declined drastically in the last few years, for unknown reasons. In winter European birds fly to the Atlantic Ocean off central and southern Africa, while Asian and American birds move to the Pacific Ocean off southern South America.

Phalaropes often employ a feeding method known as spinning, in which the bird describes circles in the water, the swirling action bringing prey to the surface which can then be pecked up. The circular ripples on the water surface in this photograph, from St Lawrence Island, Alaska, indicate the bird's activity.

SKUAS

Of the seven members of the *Stercorariidae* or skuas, four are northern birds. Three of these are true Arctic dwellers, the fourth, the Great Skua, breeding at the Arctic fringe. Skuas have webbed feet and sharp claws that, combined with a powerful hooked bill, make them formidable predators. They take a variety of foods, not only the fish that might be expected but also birds and eggs, small mammals, and even berries and insects. Both Pomarine and Long-tailed Skuas tend to specialise in hunting rodents and are frequently seen far from the coast and in upland areas; in Norway the Long-tailed Skua is actually known as the Mountain Skua.

All northern species are also kleptoparasites, obtaining food by chasing gulls and terns and forcing them to drop or disgorge their recent catches, then retrieving the food, usually in mid-air. This behaviour is characteristic of the Arctic Skua, which obtains most of its food by piracy. This species even tends to migrate with Arctic Terns, so the terns can be kleptoparasitised along the way. Pomarine and Long-tailed Skuas are piratical in winter, but in summer they tend to hunt their own food. Great Skuas are also less frequently piratical.

The northern skuas are sexually dimorphic, females being larger than the males by 10–15%. The three smaller skuas also exhibit plumage dimorphism, having both light and dark morphs (though dark-morph birds are very rare in Long-tailed Skuas).

Skua mating displays are limited, amounting to little more than the male adopting an upright posture in front of the chosen mate, though the bond is reinforced by courtship feeding, this also occurring in long-paired birds. The pair bond is monogamous and life long or, at least, long-lived. Two eggs are laid in a rudimentary nest. These are incubated by both birds (though mainly the female in Great Skuas). The chicks are semi-altricial and are fed by regurgitation. Skuas are long-lived and mature slowly, Great Skuas not breeding until they are seven or eight years old. The parent birds are highly aggressive in defence of their eggs and young, dive-bombing intruders to scare them off. Such attacks are frequently not bluffs; I have been knocked down by a Great Skua and had blood drawn by a Long-tailed Skua, to prove the point. Interestingly, the smaller skuas will also adopt the plover technique of luring a predator away by feigning injury, though this approach is used much less often than a direct attack.

Skuas take long migration flights, these often being overland, hungry birds then incurring the wrath of farmers by attacking chicken or duck flocks. The southern species also migrate over long distances, and vagrants can drift vast distances off course; one South Polar Skua *Catharacta maccormicki*, a species that breeds on the Antarctic continent, was, sadly, shot near Nuuk, Greenland.

Skua or jaeger?

In Britain and some other countries the northern members of the *Stercorariidae* are known as skuas. The origins of the word are unclear but it is likely to derive from the Shetland name *skooi* for the Arctic Skua, though the derivation of *skooi* is obscure. One delightful suggestion is that the word has its roots in s[illegible], the Norse word for what would be best termed 'excrement' in polite company, due to the widely held belief that Arctic Skuas consumed the excrement of other seabirds, with the skuas frightening gulls then cleaning up afterwards. In reality, of course, the skuas were frightening the birds into dropping their fish catch as they are aerial pirates, well deserving their American name of Parasitic Jaeger. The word *jaeger* almost certainly derives from the German for hunter, which also fits the birds rather well.

It is interesting to note that the Shetland islanders gave the Great Skua its own name, bonxie, which probably comes from the Norse *bunski*, an untidy mess, a word usually applied in a very definitely non-PC way, to untidy, wizened old women.

Great Skua (Bonxie)

Stercorarius skua

L: 53–58cm. WS: 132–140cm. W: 1.2–[illegible]kg. ♀>♂.
Breeding adult upperparts are overall cinnamon-brown, the crown, distal section of the flight feathers and tail darker, with buff scalloping on both upper- and underparts. Some adults are paler (though these retain the dark crown) and intermediate forms are seen. Summer and winter plumages are similar.

Great Skua nest, southern Iceland.

Great Skua, southern Iceland.

Great Skuas breed on Iceland, Jan Mayen, Svalbard and Bear Island, and on the northern coast of Norway. In winter the birds are pelagic in the North Atlantic from Ireland to central Africa, with some Icelandic birds flying to the waters off Newfoundland.

Great Skua prey

Great Skuas feed mostly on fish (primarily sandeels *Ammodytes* spp.), but they are opportunistic and will take birds (species as large as geese), mammals (hares have occasionally been seen taken) and even chicks from adjacent skua nests; some Hebridean birds feed nocturnally on returning storm-petrels.

The Great Skua expanded its breeding range in the last half of the 20th century, reaching Svalbard in the mid-1970s. In places the species has ousted the Arctic Skua from breeding sites it once held, with the bigger bird killing both adults and chicks.

Arctic Skua (Parasitic Jaeger)

Stercorarius parasiticus

L: 41–46cm. WS: 110–125cm. W: 300–500g. ♀>♂.

The most piratical of the skuas. Two morphs in breeding adult. Pale morph has a dark brown crown and upper head. The sides of the head and lower nape are yellow, the throat white. The breast has grey-brown sides or a complete collar, the rest of the underparts being white apart from the dark grey-brown undertail. The upperparts are dark slate-grey or grey-brown, apart from the darker flight feathers. Dark-morph adults are overall dark or sooty brown, but with a black crown and paler cheeks. Intermediate forms are also seen. These are as the dark morph but paler, and often tinged yellow on the cheeks and nape. The underparts are occasionally barred darker. In winter the yellow of the head and nape are lost or duller.

The Arctic Skua breeds on the west and north-east coasts of Greenland, on Iceland, Svalbard, Fennoscandia, and across

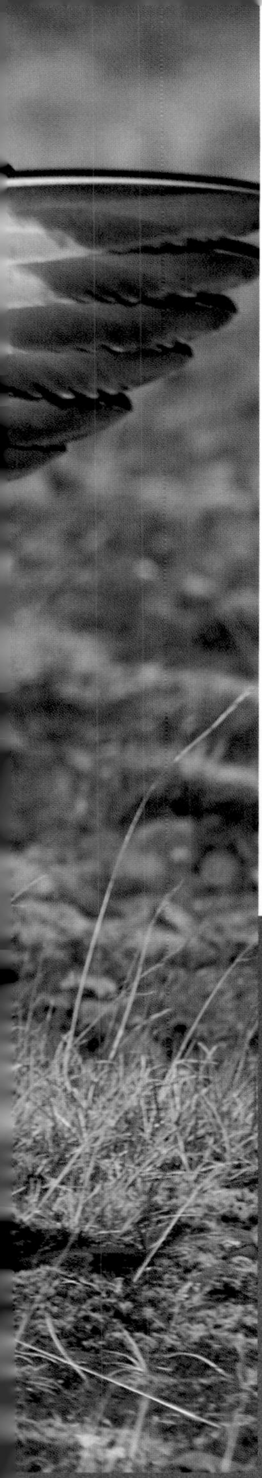

Light and dark morph Arctic Skuas, Runde Island, Norway.

Long-tailed Skua, Fosheim Peninsula, Ellesmere Island.

When Per Michelsen and Richard Sale were on Ellesmere Island they camped close to a nest of Long-tailed Skuas. The birds rapidly learned the meaning of breakfast, and were also partial to using the two men (particularly Per Michelsen as he is taller) as look-out posts, even maintaining their position as the two strode about the island since the perches were more energy-efficient than flying when searching for lemmings. But between the camp site and the nest was an invisible line which the two men dared not cross. If they did, the friendly birds became instantly hostile, defending their territory with vigorous dive-bombing that soon had either man retreating quickly. Once the men had recrossed the boundary line to their own side the birds returned to friendlier ways.

northern Russia to Kamchatka, including Franz Josef Land and Novaya Zemlya. Breeds across northern North America from west Alaska, including Canada's Arctic islands north to southern Ellesmere. In winter the birds move to the coasts of South America, the western and southern coasts of Africa, the Arabian Sea and the coasts of Australasia.

Long-tailed Skua (Long-tailed Jaeger)

Stercorarius longicaudus

L: 48–55cm (tail streamers 18cm). WS: 105–115cm. W: 220–440g. ♀>♂.

The smallest and lightest skua. Dark morphs are very rare and perhaps do not occur at all. Breeding adult has a black upper head and upper nape. The cheeks and lower nape are yellow, the throat white. The breast is white, merging into a pale grey belly, flanks and undertail-coverts. The upperparts are uniformly slate-grey apart from black flight feather and tail. The central tail feathers form long streamers. Although adult birds probably do not show plumage dimorphism, juvenile birds do, with dark-morph juveniles moulting into the 'standard' adult plumage. In winter the yellow of the cheeks and nape are lost or duller.

Long-tailed Skua breeds in west, north-west and north-east Greenland, on Jan Mayen and Svalbard, in mountainous Scandinavia and northern Fennoscandia, and across Russia to Kamchatka, but not on the Taimyr Peninsula. Also breeds on the southern island of Novaya Zemlya and on Wrangel Island. Breeds across Alaska and the northern Canadian mainland to the western shores of Hudson Bay. Absent from eastern Canada apart from a colony on the east-central shore of Hudson Bay. Also breeds on all Canada's Arctic islands to northern Ellesmere. Wintering birds are pelagic off the east and west coasts of southern South America and the west coast of southern Africa.

Pomarine Skua (Pomarine Jaeger)

Stercorarius pomarinus

L: 46–52cm (tail streamers 11cm). WS: 125–140cm. W: 550–830g. ♀>♂.

Two morphs, though dark morphs represent a smaller percentage of the population than in Arctic Skua. Pale-morph adults are patterned as Long-tailed Skuas, but are darker overall and have much darker underwing. Breeding adults has yellow cheeks and nape. The central pair of tail feathers is elongated, twisted at the base and ending in club-like blobs, a diagnostic feature. Dark-morph adults are dark brown, usually even darker than dark-morph Arctic Skuas. In winter the yellow of the cheeks and nape are lost or duller. Pomarine Skuas primarily feed on lemmings and so do not breed where the rodents are absent, or in years of low rodent population.

It has been suggested that Pomarine Skua breeds on west Greenland, but the lack of lemmings there lead many to consider this doubtful. It breeds in Svalbard, and on Russia's northern coast from the White Sea to the Bering Sea. In North America breeds on the west and north coasts of Alaska, on the Canadian mainland around Bathurst Inlet, on north-west and north-east Hudson Bay, on Banks and Victoria islands, and southern Baffin Island. May also breed at remote sites on other islands. In winter the birds fly to the waters of the Caribbean, the Atlantic off northern Africa, the Arabian Sea and the Pacific Ocean off eastern Australia, northern New Zealand, Hawaii and north-western South America.

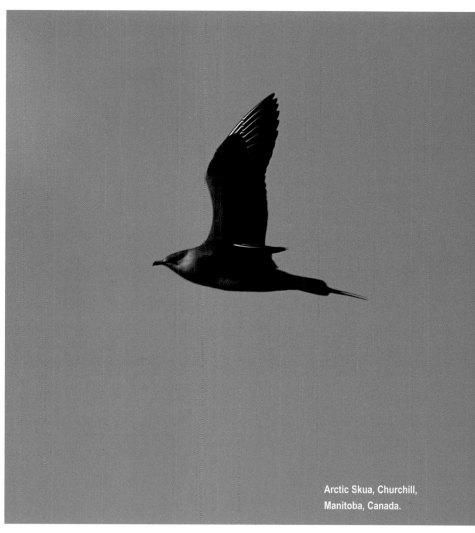

Arctic Skua, Churchill, Manitoba, Canada.

Pomarine Skua, Beaufort Sea.

GULLS

Gulls represent not only one of the most readily identifiable groups of birds for the casual observer (even if the different species are often more difficult to distinguish), but one of the more successful of bird families, in part due to their being supremely opportunistic. People in temperate regions may have seen Black-headed Gulls following ploughs to feed on earthworms; the gulls will also readily visit fields where Northern Lapwings *Vanellus vanellus* are feeding. In the absence of a plough the gulls have little success at finding worms; by contrast Lapwings are excellent at the task, the gulls waiting their opportunity and thieving the Lapwing's meal. Gulls are often seen on rubbish dumps, while in winter they feed on waste grain in cereal fields. Many gulls are also efficient predators, with the larger species feeding on smaller birds and chicks. Some gulls will cannibalise chicks in their own colonies; studies have suggested that in Herring Gull colonies up to 25% of the chicks will be consumed by adult birds each year. Most extraordinary of all, Ivory Gulls feed on the faeces of Polar Bears and cetaceans.

Gulls are voracious feeders. They have large crops that aid courtship feeding and the feeding of chicks, each of which involves regurgitation. Gulls fill their crops during a day's feeding and then digest the food at leisure during the nightly roost. In some species adults have a red gonys spot – the chicks peck at this to stimulate regurgitation.

Aiding the success of gulls is their flying ability. They are excellent at soaring and gliding, and have the high manoeuvrability essential for the cliff nesting that most favour. However, some are ground nesters, while Bonaparte's Gull nests in trees, the sight of tree nesting gulls coming as a surprise when first encountered.

Gulls are chiefly birds of colder waters, and are particularly numerous in the northern hemisphere. Their adaptability is again shown by the fact that some species (such as Little Gull) are birds of inland waters. The majority of gull species are primarily marine, though coastal during the breeding season of course. In winter they are no longer tied to land and some species, such as the kittiwakes, become pelagic.

The northern gulls are divided into two major groups, the 'white-headed' (e.g. Herring and Glaucous Gulls) and the 'hooded' (e.g. Black-headed and Bonaparte's Gulls). In the latter the hood is entirely, or mostly, moulted during the winter. Sabine's Gull is hooded, but is not considered a true member of the hooded group: Sabine's forms one of the trio of much-sought-after Arctic breeders, the others being Ross's Gull and the Ivory Gull. Though head colour may vary all northern gulls (indeed, almost all gulls) are essentially white. It is assumed that this is to camouflage the birds when they are fishing, fish having more problems seeing the birds against the

Gull plumages

Gulls are long-lived and take time to mature, the smaller gulls sometimes breeding in their second year, the larger ones not until they are four or five years old. Juveniles do not acquire their adult plumage for several years, and as the differences in juvenile plumages can be slight, identification of juvenile forms can be tricky. No attempt has been made to identify the changes in juvenile plumages in the descriptions below; whole books have been devoted to these changes. However, the time taken by juveniles to attain adult plumage is given. The species are classified as two-, three- or four-year gulls, the time being the number of winters before a juvenile acquires adult plumage, i.e. a four-year gull shows its adult plumage in the fourth winter of its life and will show full adult breeding plumage in its fourth spring. The sexes are essentially similar in all species.

Black-headed Gull paddling in the waters of the north Pacific on southern Kamchatka's eastern shore.

Above left and right
Bonaparte's Gull is named after the French zoologist Charles Lucien Bonaparte, a nephew of Napoleon Bonaparte. It has the unusual habit, for a gull, of nesting in trees and so is rarely seen north of the treeline. These photographs are from Churchill, Manitoba, Canada, where the nest was located in one of the last stands of trees before the tundra which edges the shore of Hudson Bay.

normally cloudy sky. Unlike auks, gulls are not generally countershaded, presumably because being large they suffer little from predation.

The speciation of gulls is a fertile subject for biogeographers. Herring Gulls and Lesser Black-backed Gulls are sympatric where they overlap, but they do occasionally interbreed successfully. It is suggested that these species arose when two populations of an ancestral gull were separated during one of the Pleistocene ice ages. The ancestral form is thought to have been yellow-legged and confined to central Asia. It evolved into the Lesser Black-backed Gull and spread west towards Europe. In the 1920s it reached Iceland and has now bred in southern Greenland, though it is not yet fully established there. The second population was isolated in north-eastern Asia. It evolved pink legs and spread east, crossing North America. However, this simple story is complicated by the curious distribution of the species in the Palaearctic. As well as breeding in north-east Asian Russia, Herring Gulls also breed around the White Sea and as far east as the Taimyr Peninsula, as well as throughout northern Europe. Herring Gulls also became established in Iceland in the 1920s, just as the Lesser Black-backed Gull did, and have occasionally bred in Greenland (arriving from both Canada and the Atlantic).

Speciation of the two gulls is further enlivened by the existence of subspecies of each, these being classified as full species by some authorities. In the far east of Russia a smaller, paler form of the Herring Gull is occasionally considered a separate species (the Vega Gull *Larus vegae*), while throughout North America the American Herring Gull (in which adults are indistinguishable from the nominate bird, though juveniles are darker) is frequently awarded specific status as *L. smithsonianus*. There are also several Lesser Black-backed Gull subspecies, one of which, a larger bird with paler upperwings (but with black wing-tips) that breeds from the White Sea to the Taimyr Peninsula, is considered by many a full species, Heuglin's Gull *L. heuglini*. To add yet more complication, some authorities consider that not only is Heuglin's Gull a full species, but that it also has subspecies!

Biogeographers also argue about the status of Iceland and Thayer's Gulls. Again it is assumed that an ancestral form was isolated by an ice sheet which separated eastern and western populations which evolved into Iceland and Thayer's gulls respectively. However, some authorities consider the two taxa as sibling subspecies. An extra complication is afforded by Kumlien's Gull *Larus kumlieni*, considered a full species by some and a subspecies of Iceland Gull by others. Add to this mix of species and subspecies the occasional hybrids and the result is a recipe for argument and discussions that will last for years to come.

The displays of gulls are usually territorial, the holding of a territory by males attracting females. Herring Gulls pluck grass from near the nest site as a way of establishing proprietorial rights. Male gulls also have a 'long call', in which the head is thrown back while the bird emits the familiar 'seagull' trumpet-like *kee kee kee*. The position of the head before and during the long call and the exact note are diagnostic of the species. Mated birds engage in head flagging, a sideways flick of the head (which is also used as a threat gesture to intruders, particularly by the hooded gulls, since the movement exposes the full hood), and in courtship feeding. The pair bond is usually monogamous and long-lasting. Nests are made of seaweed or local vegetation, sometimes minimal, occasionally non-existent. Most gulls nest on the ground or on cliffs, but Bonaparte's Gulls nest in trees. In general gulls lay two or three eggs, these being incubated by both birds. The chicks are downy and semi-precocial or precocial. They are fed by regurgitation. The clutch does not hatch simultaneously, with the third chick often being the victim of cannibalistic (or other predatory) attack, or starving to death if there is insufficient food.

Black-headed Gull

Larus ridibundus

L: 33–38cm. WS: 100–110cm. W: 250–350g. ♂>♀.

Two-year gull. Breeding adult has a chocolate-brown hood (extending to rear crown) and white orbital ring. The bill is dark red. Neck and underparts are white. The legs and feet are dark red. Rump and tail are white. The rest of the upperparts are pale grey, but wings are white towards the tip, with black tips. In winter adult loses the hood, though black smudging often remains.

Black-headed Gulls are mainly non-Arctic, but breed in southern Greenland (and increasingly in north-east Greenland), in Iceland, northern Norway and Kamchatka. Some Icelandic birds are resident. Greenlandic, some Icelandic and Norwegian birds winter in western Europe.

Some authorities now consider the American Herring Gull (*above left*, Great Slave Lake, North West Territories, Canada) to be a separate species from the European Herring Gull (*above right*, Olberg, Norway) rather than a subspecies, though the plumage differences are slight.

As with the Herring Gulls above, some authorities also consider the Mew Gull of the Nearctic and the Eurasian Common Gull to be separate species, though again the plumage differences are slight.

Below left
Mew Gull pair, Great Slave Lake, NWT, Canada.

Below right
Common Gull, Ytre Ryfylke, Norway.

Little Gull

Larus minutus

L: 24–28cm. WS: 75–80cm. W: 80–120g.

Three-year gull. Breeding adult has a black hood extending to nape. Bill is dark red. The underparts are white. The legs and feet are red. The upperparts are white and pale grey. The underwing is black with a white trailing edge; this feature is diagnostic. In winter adult loses the hood, though black smudging often remains, and the legs and feet are dull pink. These little birds, the smallest of the Arctic and sub-Arctic gulls, feeds on insects as well as small fish and marine invertebrates.

Little Gulls are mainly non-Arctic but breed patchily on Russia White Sea coast and have recently bred on the southern shores of Hudson Bay. In winter the birds are seen on coasts of Baltic Sea, southern England and northern France, and on the Mediterranean and Black Sea coasts.

Bonaparte's Gull

Larus philadelphia

L: 28–30cm. WS: 90–100cm. W: 180–230g. ♂>♀.

Two-year gull. Breeding adult has a black hood to the rear crown. The bill is black. The underparts are white, as is the tail. The back and inner wing are pale blue-grey, the outer wing white with a black tip. There are also black tips to the outer primaries, creating a black trailing edge. In winter adult loses the hood, though black smudging often remains and the legs and feet are a dull pale pink.

Bonaparte's Gulls breed in southern Alaska, but it is rare on the western and northern coasts. Also breeds in northern Yukon, then southerly to southern shores of Hudson and James bays. In winter the birds move to the east and west coasts of the United States and to the Great Lakes.

Herring Gull

Larus argentatus

L: 55–67cm. WS: 138–155cm. W: 700–1300g. ♂>♀.

Four-year gull. Breeding adult has a white head. The bill is yellow with a red gonys spot. The underparts and tail are white. The upperparts are blue-grey. The wing has a white trailing edge. The outer primaries are black with white tips, giving an overall black-and-white wing-tip. The legs and feet are pink. Winter adults are as breeding, but the head and neck are streaked grey-brown. See The Adaptations and Biogeography of Birds and Mammals p301 for taxonomy.

Herring Gulls breed on Iceland and northern Fennoscandia. In the rest of Russia breeding is patchy, occurring around the White Sea, on the Taimyr Peninsula, and east of the Lena to Chukotka. Also breeds in North America in central Alaska and across Canada, but rare on the north coast, though breeds on Southampton Island and southern Baffin Island. In winter birds move south to wherever food is available.

Lesser Black-backed Gull

Larus fuscus

L: 52–67cm. WS: 135–155cm. W: 450–1100g. ♂>♀.

Four-year gull. Similar to Herring Gull but a more slender bird with a dark grey or black upperwing. The wing has broken white leading and trailing edges. The legs and feet are

Far left
Lesser Black-backed Gull, Kjorholmane, Norway.

Left
Greater Black-backed Gull, Kjorholmane, Norway.

yellow. In winter adult is as breeding, but the head and neck are streaked grey-brown and the legs and feet are duller.

Lesser Black-backed Gulls breed in southern Greenland, on Iceland, in northern Fennoscandia and Russia east to the Taimyr Peninsula. Increasing numbers are now seen in North America, but it is not yet an established breeding species. In winter Greenlandic and Icelandic birds move to Iberia and north-west Africa, while Scandinavian and European Russian birds head for the eastern Mediterranean, the Arabian Sea and east Africa.

Common Gull (Mew Gull)

Larus canus

L: 40–42cm. WS: 110–130cm. W: 300–550g ♂>♀.
Three-year gull. Breeding adult has a white head. The bill is yellow, usually with a brighter tip and greenish tinge to base. The underparts and tail are white. The upperparts and upperwing are grey. There is a white trailing edge and the outer primaries are black with white 'mirrors'. The legs and feet are yellow or greenish-yellow. In winter adult is as breeding, but the head and neck are streaked grey-brown.

Common Gulls breed on Iceland (in limited numbers; the species first bred there in 1936 and the range is expanding). Breeds in northern Fennoscandia and across Russia, but always sub-Arctic. Breeds throughout Kamchatka. In North America breeds throughout Alaska (but rare in the north), in Yukon and North West Territories (again, rare in the north). North American birds are considered by some authorities to be a full species. The plumage is similar, though the wing-tips tend to be whiter, but mtDNA studies show marked differences.

Greater Black-backed Gull

Larus marinus

L: 65–80cm. WS: 150–165cm. W: 1.0–2.2kg. ♂>♀.
Four-year gull. The largest gull. Breeding adult has a white head. The bill is yellow with a red gonys spot. The underparts are white. The back and upperwing are dark grey, with a white trailing edge and black primaries. The outer primaries have white 'mirrors'. The underwing is banded white, pale grey and darker grey, with a white trailing edge. The legs and feet are pale pink. In winter adult is as breeding, but the head and neck are streaked grey-brown. This huge gull often kills auks and other small seabirds in flight, stabbing them with its bill.

Greater Black-backed Gulls breed on Canada's Labrador coast, on the central west coast of Greenland, on Iceland, Jan Mayen and Svalbard (where it became established only in the 1930s), in northern Fennoscandia, on the southern island of Novaya Zemlya, and on the nearby mainland coast of Russia. Partially migratory, but rarely seen beyond the limit of the continental shelf.

Glaucous-winged Gull

Larus glaucescens

L: 58–63cm. WS: 140–160cm. W: 850–1700g. ♂>♀.
Four-year gull. Breeding adult has a white head. The bill is yellow with a red-orange gonys spot. The underparts are white. The legs and feet are pink, sometimes pinkish-purple. The back and mantle are mid-grey, with a blue tinge. The rump and tail are white. The upperwing is mid-grey (again blue-tinged) with a white trailing edge. The outer primaries have mid-grey ends with white tips. In winter adult is as breeding, but the head and neck are streaked grey-brown.

Glaucous-winged Gulls are mainly non-Arctic, but breeds in southern and western Alaska, in southern Chukotka, on Kamchatka and on the Commander Islands. In winter the birds are resident or migratory, some moving as far south as Baja California and Japan.

Glaucous-winged Gull, Resurrection Bay, Alaska.

Glaucous Gull nest, Bylot Island, Canada.

Glaucous Gull

Larus hyperboreus

L: 62–68cm. WS: 150–165cm. W: 1.0–2.2kg. ♂>♀.
Four-year gull. Breeding adult has a white head. The bill is yellow with a red gonys spot. The underparts are white. The upperwing is pale grey with a white trailing edge. The rest of the upperparts are white. In winter adult is as breeding, but the head, neck and upper breast are streaked grey-brown.

Glaucous Gulls are a true Arctic breeder and a formidable predator throughout the region. Breeds on Greenland, Iceland, Jan Mayen and Svalbard, in northern Fennoscandia and across Russia, including all Arctic islands. Breeds across the northern mainland of North America and on all Canadian Arctic islands to northern Ellesmere. In winter the birds move south, but only as required by the sea ice. Wintering birds are both coastal and pelagic.

Iceland Gull

Larus glaucoides

L: 52–60cm. WS: 140–150cm. W: 500–1000g. ♂>♀.
Four-year gull. Breeding adult has a white head. The bill is yellow (often tinged green) with a red gonys spot. The underparts are white, as are the rump and tail. The upper and lower wings are pale grey or blue-grey, with distinct white trailing edge. The legs and feet are pink. In winter adult is as breeding but with some dark streaking on the head (though this is occasionally absent). Kumlien's Gull (often considered a race but regarded as a full species by some authorities) has darker grey wing-tips.

Despite the name, the bird is only seen in Iceland during the winter. Breeds in west and south Greenland and, more rarely, on the south-east coast. Breeds on northern Baffin Island and south-west Ellesmere. Kumlien's Gull breeds on

Glaucous Gull and chicks, Hvalrossbukta, Bear island.

Watching the flight of competitors

Predatory gulls that hold territories on cliffs otherwise occupied by the species whose eggs and chicks, and perhaps adults they take, will watch conspecifics (and other predatory species) closely if they come too close. The taking of eggs and chicks requires a gull to make a slow pass of the cliff, and this, in turn, requires the bird to fly upwind. So if the watching gull sees a competitor moving downwind it will ignore it, knowing the intruder lacks the control needed to seize prey. But those moving upwind will need to be seen off.

southern Baffin Island, western Southampton Island and the extreme northern tip of Quebec. In winter the birds are seen across the North Atlantic from Newfoundland to Iceland, but rarely further east. Wintering birds are both coastal and pelagic.

Thayer's Gull

Larus thayeri

L: 55–63cm. WS: 142–152cm. W: 700–1100g. ♂>♀.

Four-year gull. Breeding adult patterned as Iceland Gull, but in general darker grey on the upperparts (usually the same colour, or a little darker, than Herring Gull). The wing-tips show black areas that are absent from the Iceland Gull, the overall effect being of a streaked black-and-white wing-tip The bill is yellow with a red gonys spot. The legs and feet are pink. In winter adult is as breeding, but the head, neck and upper breast are lightly streaked grey-brown.

Thayer's Gulls breed on the western shore of Hudson Bay and the Canadian Arctic islands from Banks to northern Baffin north to Ellesmere Island, though apparently absent from the Parry Islands.

Slaty-backed Gull

Larus schistisagus

L: 61–66cm. WS: 145–150cm. W: *c.*1.35kg. ♂>♀.

Four-year gull. Breeding adult has a white head. The bill is yellow with a red gonys spot. The underparts, rump and tail are white. The upperwing is slate-grey with a broad white trailing edge. The primaries are dark grey at the base, darkening to black towards the tip, the outer primaries having white crescents that form an often distinct pattern known as the 'string of pearls'. When distinct the 'string' is both diagnostic and delightful. Winter adult is as breeding, but with some grey-brown streaking to the crown, and heavy streaking to the nape and sides of the neck.

Slaty-backed Gulls breed in far eastern Chukotka, on Kamchatka and the northern coast of Sea of Okhotsk. Occasionally seen in Alaska (e.g. Pribilof Islands), but breeding not proven and certainly not established. In winter the gulls are seen off coasts as far south as Japan.

Above left
Iceland Gulls and a Glaucous Gull, west Greenland. The size difference between the two species is very obvious when they are seen together.

Above
An Icelandic Gull coming in to land, west Greenland.

A stand-off between a Glaucous Gull, to the right, and an Ivory Gull over the remains of a Polar Bear seal kill on the sea ice of Baffin Bay. In the background a Thayer's Gull awaits developments.

Black-legged Kittiwake

Rissa tridactyla

L: 38–40cm. WS: 95–120cm. W: 300–535g ♂>♀.

Three-year gull. Breeding adult has a white head. The bill is yellow. The underparts, rump and notched tail are white. The upperparts are grey The upperwing is tricoloured, the inner wing being

Above left
Slaty-backed Gull at the mouth of the Zhupanova River, Kamchatka, Russia.

Above right
Slaty-back Gull nest, Starichkov Island, off southern Kamchatka's eastern coast, Russia.

grey (as the mantle) with a white leading edge, the primaries pale grey and the wing-tip black. The legs and feet are black. In winter adult is as breeding, but with a dark grey crescent from the ear-covert and, often, pale grey on the nape, and the bill is duller, often green-yellow. Juveniles have distinctive black barring on the wings in the form of an M (or W, depending on the direction of flight!). The bird's curious name derives from its call, a trisyllabic *kitt ee wake*.

Black–legged Kittiwakes breed in west, south, east and north-east Greenland, on Iceland, Jan Mayen and Svalbard, in northern Fennoscandia and at a limited number of sites on Russia's northern mainland (though common in Chukotka and Kamchatka). Also breeds on all Russia's Arctic islands. Breeds on all Bering Sea islands, western Alaska (but rare on the north coast) and eastern Canada, including eastern Baffin Island. Pelagic, moving ahead of the sea ice in winter to feed in the North Atlantic and North Pacific.

Red-legged Kittiwake

Rissa brevirostris
L: 35–40cm. WS: 85–92cm. W: 320–470g. ♂>♀.
Status: IUCN: Vulnerable.
Three-year gull. Breeding adult similar to Black–legged Kittiwake, but grey upperparts are darker, with less contrast between the pale inner wing and the darker outer wing. The black wing-tip is broader and less conspicuous against the rest of the dark wing. The white band on the trailing edge of the wing is also broader. The legs and feet are bright red. Winter adult has an ear crescent as in Black–legged Kittiwake, but it is much darker.

Occasionally Slaty-backed Gulls are seen in the USA. Identification is then assured when the gull spreads its wings and reveals the 'string of pearls' as the primary feather mirrors are called. These gulls were photographed at the mouth of the Zhupanova River, Kamchatka, Russia.

Black-legged Kittiwake and chicks, Runde Island, Norway.

Red-legged Kittiwakes have a highly restricted breeding range, breeding only on the Pribilof Islands, Buldir and Bogoslof islands in the Aleutians, and on the Commander Islands. Essentially pelagic, with wintering birds moving to the North Pacific.

Sabine's Gull

Xema sabini

L: 27–32cm. WS: 90–100cm. W: 150–210g. ♂>♀.

Two-year gull. Breeding adult has a dark grey hood extending to the upper nape. On the nape the hood has a thin black rim. The short bill is black with a yellow tip. The underparts are white, occasionally tinged pink. The rump and uppertail are white. The tail has a shallow fork. The upperparts are blue-grey. The upperwing is tricoloured, blue-grey, white and black, each colour forming a triangle. The underwing is white, occasionally with pale grey triangles and black tips on the primaries. The legs and feet are dark grey. In winter adult loses the hood but the nape is extensively smudged black.

Sabine's Gulls breed in northern Greenland, on Svalbard, in northern Chukotka and on Wrangel Island. Also in western and northern Alaska, northern Yukon, Banks, Victoria and Southampton islands, and on western Baffin Island. In winter the birds migrate – the only truly migratory Arctic gull – and are pelagic, feeding in the Benguela Current off south-western Africa, and the Humboldt Current off north-western South America.

Ivory Gull

Pagophila eburnea

L: 40–43cm. WS: 108–120cm. W: 450–[illegible]80g. ♂>♀.

One of the Arctic specialities that all visitors will want to see; the gulls are often viewed above sea ice, occasionally appearing ghost-like from out of the mist, a magical, ethereal sight. A two-year gull. The only pure white gull (all other white gulls will be leucosystic or albino). Adults are white, but the face is

Black-legged Kittiwakes, Ekkeroy, Varangerfjord, Norway.

Above left and right **The rare Red-legged Kittiwake breeds on only a handful of Bering Sea islands. On St Paul Island, Pribilofs, Alaska, it shares nesting cliffs with guillemots and Black-legged Kittiwakes.**

sometimes red after feeding on carrion. The bill is blue-grey with a yellow, orange or red tip. The legs and feet are black. Summer and winter plumages are similar.

Ivory Gulls breed in north-west, north-east and east Greenland, on Jan Mayen, Svalbard, and Russia's Arctic islands (apart from the southern island of Novaya Zemlya). Breeds on all Canada's northern Arctic islands. Moves south with the advancing ice edge.

Ross's Gull

Rhodostethia rosea

L: 29–31cm. WS: 90–100cm. W: 140–250g.

If the Ivory Gull is the most magical of Arctic gulls, Ross's must qualify as the most beautiful. The two are equally elusive, much more so than Sabine's Gull, the third of the Arctic triumvirate. A two-year gull. Breeding adult has a white head with, uniquely, a thin black necklace extending from throat to mid–nape (and wider towards nape). The small, thin bill is black. The underparts are white, usually with a rosy-pink tinge, strongest on the breast and belly. The rump and wedge-shaped tail are white. The upperparts are pale blue-grey, with a broad white trailing edge. The underwing is pale blue-grey. The legs and feet are red. In winter adults lose the rosy-pink tinge, and the black necklace reduces to a black streak on the sides of the neck.

Ross's Gull's breeding range is poorly studied. Known to breed at sites on the southern Taimyr Peninsula, on the Lena and Kolyma deltas and in Chukotka. Has bred in north-east

The trio of sought-after high Arctic gulls.

Below **an Ivory Gull, Svalbard.**
Right **a Sabine's Gull, Igloolik, Canada.**
Below right **a Ross's Gull, Chukotka, Russia.**

Ivory Gulls feeding on the leftovers of a Polar Bear's meal of Ringed Seal, Kongsfjorden, Spitsbergen, Svalbard.

Greenland and on Svalbard but has not become established in either location. Remarkably, the gull has also bred at Churchill on the southern shore of Hudson Bay, but breeding there has been sporadic. It is possible Ross's Gull breeds at remote sites on Canada's High Arctic islands. In winter the birds are seen in the Bering Sea. Flocks were once regularly seen passing Barrow during the autumn, but they are very much less common now.

TERNS

Terns are found on all the continents, though they are mostly tropical birds. The three Arctic breeders belong to the *Sterna* group of black-capped terns. These are slender birds with tapering wings and deeply forked tails. They are fish eaters, catching their prey by plunge diving. They do not swim underwater, with the fish being taken just below the surface. Terns often seek shoals that have been driven close to the surface by the attentions of predatory fish or aquatic mammals.

Tern displays usually involve a 'high flight' in which the male flies fast and high, usually carrying a fish, with an interested female chasing him. Courtship feeding is an important part of pair formation and reinforcement. Terns are monogamous, the pair bond long-lived or life-long. The birds are gregarious at all times, with colonial breeding leading to nests so close together that a pair must defend its small territory. This occasionally means the female stays on the nest site, defending it while the male fishes and feeds her. At the nest two to three eggs are laid, these being incubated by both birds. Chicks are downy and semi-precocial. They are fed by both birds. Terns are long-lived and take up to five years before first breeding.

Two summers each year

Most terns are migratory, with the Arctic Tern making the longest migration flight of any bird, flying 17,500km each way to Antarctica so as to enjoy two summers each year. Recovered birds suggest that although most birds travel over water, which would aid feeding, some travel overland, flying across central Russia at very high altitudes. It has been calculated that including feeding flights at both poles, some birds may fly up to 50,000km annually. They also see more hours of daylight each year than any other animal.

Aleutian Tern

Sterna aleutica

L: 32–34cm. WS: 75–80cm. W: 105–118g.

Breeding adult has a black cap (to the eye) and black upper nape. The rest of the head is white. The bill is black. The throat is white, the rest of the underparts mid-grey. The rump and deeply forked tail are white. The upperparts are mid-grey. The legs and feet are black. In winter the birds lose the black crown.

Above
Arctic Tern, Cook Inlet, Alaska.

Above right
Nesting Aleutian Tern, Seward Peninsula, Alaska.

Left and right
The subspecies of Common Tern on Kamchatka (*S. h. longipennis*), differs in having a black bill and dark red or black legs. The difference in colour is such that the bird was considered a full species in the past. These photographs of an adult and chick were taken in southern Kamchatka, Russia.

Below
Distinguishing Arctic and Common Terns can be difficult, even when the two are seen together. The bill tip of the Common Tern, far left, is black. This photograph was taken on the Arctic Circle, Norway.

Aleutian Terns breed in southern Chukotka, on Kamchatka and the Commander Islands, in western Alaska and on the Aleutians, but it is uncommon throughout the range. Resident, but pelagic outside the breeding season.

Arctic Tern

Sterna paradisaea

L: 33–35cm. WS: 75–85cm. W: 90–120g.

Breeding adult has a black cap (to the eye) and black nape. The rest of the head is white. The bill is bright red. The underparts are pale grey or blue-grey. The rump and tail are white. The upperbody is blue-grey. The legs and feet are red. In winter adult has a smaller, ragged black cap, and the legs and feet are darker, sometimes almost black. Arctic Terns are extremely aggressive to intruders when nesting and will attack, and strike, humans who roam too close.

Arctic Terns breed in Greenland, on Iceland, Jan Mayen and Svalbard, in Fennoscandia and across Russia to the Bering Sea, including Russia's Arctic islands. Breeds across North America from Alaska to Labrador, including the Canadian Arctic islands. In winter the birds move to Antarctica.

Common Tern

Sterna hirundo

L: 31–35cm. WS: 80–95cm. W: 90–140g.

Breeding adult is as Arctic Tern, but the bill is black-tipped, the wing showing a broad, but diffuse, grey band towards the tip but lacking the black trailing edge, and longer legs. The latter are noticeable when the birds are perched, the Arctic Tern looking almost as though it is resting on its belly. In winter Common Tern's black cap becomes duller, and grey-brown towards the bill; the bill becomes black with a red base.

Common Terns are essentially non-Arctic but breed at a small number of sites in northern Norway, on the southern shore of the White Sea, and on Kamchatka. In winter the birds head south to the coasts of southern Africa, India, and to waters around Indonesia.

AUKS

Auks are often referred to as the northern equivalent of the penguins, though the anatomical adaptations of auks are much closer to those of the diving-petrels of the Southern Ocean. However, the auks do share some penguin-like characteristics, adaptations that have resulted from the two bird families having faced similar evolutionary pressures. The legs are set well back on the body, the feet webbed to act as efficient paddles for swimming. Larger auks adopt the same upright stance as the penguins, though some of the smaller auks lie on their bellies on land. The wings are short and used for underwater propulsion; penguins have lost the power of flight, but the auks have had to retain this ability as northern regions have terrestrial predators; the short wings mean high wing loadings, so auks fly with furiously beating wings. The two families share an extraordinary diving ability. Only the larger penguins dive deeper than the larger guillemots; one confirmed dive of a Brünnich's Guillemot reached 210m. Most dives are to shallower depths, but the larger auks regularly dive to 60m and can stay submerged for up to three minutes. Auks can swallow food underwater, an adaptation that allows a longer dive time.

The auks are a northern group. The distribution of species is highly asymmetric, there being many more in the Pacific than in the Atlantic. Although the reasons for this are still debated, it is likely that in part it derives from auks having evolved in the Pacific; the only Atlantic species without a Pacific equivalent is the Razorbill (though there was also no Pacific equivalent of the Great). Auks are birds of the continental shelf, only the puffins being found in deeper waters, particularly in winter, when they are truly pelagic.

Auks show marked specific differences in bill shape, these related to the choice of prey. Fish-eaters tend to have dagger-like bills like other piscivorous birds, while plankton-feeders have shorter, wider bills. The Parakeet Auklet, which feeds on jellyfish (as well as crustaceans), has a curious, rounded bill, rather like a scoop. The bills of the Razorbill and the puffins are laterally compressed and seem, particularly for the puffins, to be important in mating displays, the male often showing it to rivals, laying it across his white breast in territorial disputes. Puffin bills are encased in nine plates that are shed during the autumnal moult, the 'new' bill being much more subdued. Puffins also shed their flight feathers simultaneously, something they share with the other larger auks. This means that the birds are flightless for a period, but the wing loadings of these birds mean that the successive lost of flight feathers would leave them flightless, and therefore more vulnerable to predation, for a longer period.

Some auks have distinctive head plumage that acts in a similar way to the puffin's bill, the plumes being displayed to rivals or potential mates. The Tufted Puffin has both crests and a splendid bill. Apart from the bills and head plumage, auks have other mating displays; these usually involve head-shaking and bowing and, after the pair has formed, bill-nibbling or clacking as bond reinforcement. The murrelets, which find walking difficult, tend to have sea-based displays, often involving parallel swimming. The pair bond is monogamous and long-lived or life-long.

Most auks are colonial breeders, though some colonies are rather loose, and several of the smaller Pacific auks are solitary nesters. Nests vary considerably within the family; some auks

Razorbills, Kjorholmane, Norway.

Common Guillemots, Kjorholmane, Norway.

nest on cliffs, laying eggs directly on to a ledge with little or no nesting material. Some nest in burrows, usually excavating these themselves. Kittlitz's Murrelet occasionally breeds far inland, a curiosity for a bird that finds walking so troublesome; it makes a scrape in bare tundra, sometimes at altitudes to 600m and often amid snowfields. The Marbled Murrelet is exceptional in nesting in trees; its nest sites are extraordinary, the egg being placed on an old, wide branch or where epiphytes create platforms. Even more remarkably, the birds are usually nocturnal at the nest sites, flying through the woodland in darkness.

In most species a single egg is laid (two is more common in a few species). The eggs of the larger guillemots are pyriform i.e. pointed at one end, an adaptation to minimise the chances of the egg rolling off the narrow nesting ledge. The eggs are of highly variable colour, particularly for the Common Guillemot, which has the most variable egg of any bird; the base colour varies from white to a beautiful turquoise, with a

In the two guillemots and the Razorbill there is a narrow channel in the feathers leading away from the eye. This seems to aid the flow of water past the eye when these large auks swim rapidly underwater. Some birds in the North Atlantic Common Guillemot population have this channel picked out in white; these birds also have a white orbital ring. Birds of this form are known as 'bridled' guillemots. The percentage of bridled birds increases as the observer travels north. There are no bridled birds in the south of the species' range (e.g. Iberia), but around 50% of birds are bridled in Iceland, Svalbard and Novaya Zemlya. The photograph above of 'normal' and 'bridled' forms was taken on Runde Island, Norway.

patterning of dark scribbles and splotches. The egg or eggs are incubated by both birds.

The developmental strategies of auk chicks are as varied as the nesting strategies. The chicks of most species are semi-precocial and are fed by the parent birds until they are at, or close to, adult weight, at which point they become independent. The Little Auk differs in one respect, with fledglings joining the adult male on the sea for a short time. The larger guillemots and the Razorbill have a markedly different strategy. The chick is fed until it is about 25–33% of adult weight. At that stage the still-flightless chick is encouraged to leave the nesting ledge by adult calls, and it glides to join its parents at sea. It is assumed that this strategy has developed because the adult birds, which have high wing loadings, can no longer carry the quantities of food required to allow continued development of the chick at the nest site; the chick is therefore fed and continues to grow at sea. The disadvantage of the strategy is the requirement of the chick to reach safety at sea by gliding. If the nesting ledge is on a sea cliff the glide is straightforward, but if it is inland then the glide angle must be low and some chicks land short; they must survive both the landing impact and a hurried scramble to the sea, guided by the calls of anxious parents. At such inland sites the ground below the cliff is patrolled by Arctic Foxes, which eagerly snatch up chicks, while skuas and gulls patrol the skies to pick off the gliders.

A third strategy has evolved among some smaller auks (including Ancient Murrelet). Here the chicks are precocial, with adult-sized feet, so they can swim. They leave the nest soon after hatching (usually within two or three days) and go to sea, where they are fed for several weeks before being abandoned. This strategy has presumably developed to save the adults the energetic cost of flying to the nest, though together with nocturnality, which is a feature of some smaller auks, may also be a defence against avian predators.

Auks are long-lived birds, their chicks taking time to mature, and not breeding until they are two or three years old; this applies even for the smaller auks. The plumages of the sexes are similar. Usually summer and winter plumages differ, but the differences are not always dramatic.

Razorbill

Alca torda

L: 37–39cm. WS: 63–68cm. W: 620–800g.

Breeding adult has a black head with a thin white stripe from bill to eye. The large (and razor-sharp) bill is black with a vertical, curved, white stripe crossing the mandibles in front of the nostril. The upper breast is black, the rest of the underparts white. The upperparts are black, apart from a white trailing edge on the secondaries. Winter adult is as breeding, but the throat, face and sides of the neck are white, occasionally smudged black, and the white facial line is lost.

Razorbills breed on south-west Baffin Island, in northern Quebec and Labrador, west-central and south-west Greenland, on Iceland, Jan Mayen, Bear Island and (in small numbers) Svalbard, and in northern Fennoscandia. There are also breeding colonies on the western White Sea coast, but the bird is absent from the rest of the Russian Arctic. Partially migratory, moving to waters off north-eastern United States and Canada, to the western Atlantic, the North Sea and western Mediterranean.

Common Guillemot (Common Murre)

Uria aalge

L: 38–41cm. WS: 64–70cm. W: 900–1200g.

Breeding adult patterned as Razorbill, but very dark brown rather than black, the flanks showing dark brown smudging. The dagger-like bill is black. The wing shows the same thin white trailing edge as the Razorbill. In winter the birds have white cheeks, throat and upper breast.

Common Guillemots are circumpolar, but the distribution is discontinuous. Breeds in south-west Greenland, on Iceland, Jan Mayen, Svalbard and the southern island of Novaya Zemlya. They breed in northern Fennoscandia, but are absent from the Russian coast except for eastern Chukotka coast and Kamchatka. Breeds on the Aleutians and islands of the Bering Sea, on the west coast of Alaska, but not on the northern

Brünnich's Guillemots, St Paul, Pribilofs, Alaska.

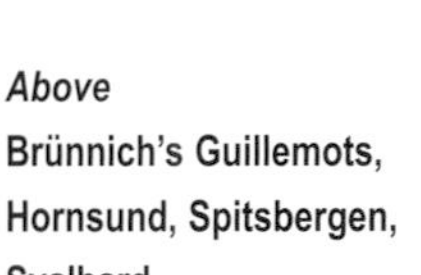

Above
Brünnich's Guillemots, Hornsund, Spitsbergen, Svalbard.

Right
Little Auks, Forkastningsdalen, Van Keulenfjorden, Spitsbergen, Svalbard.

North American mainland (apart from northern Labrador) or on the Canadian Arctic islands. Dispersive rather than migratory, with some birds being resident and others moving to nearby but more southerly waters.

Brünnich's Guillemot (Thick--billed Murre)

Uria lomvia

L: 39–43cm. WS: 65–73cm. W: 800–1100g.

Breeding adult patterned as Common Guillemot, but the upperparts are much darker, essentially black, though paler on the head. No 'bridled' form has been observed. The flanks are unsmudged. The bill is shorter than Common, with a down-curved culmen and a pale streak along the basal edge of the upper mandible. In mixed colonies the difference in colour of the upperparts is striking. In winter there is less white on the head than in Common Guillemot.

Brünnich's Guillemot tends to breed further north than its Common cousin. Brünnich's breeds on west and north Greenland, Iceland, on Jan Mayen, Bear Island and Svalbard, in northern Fennoscandia, on all Russia's Arctic islands. There are also isolated colonies on the northern Russian mainland and on eastern Chukotka and Kamchatka. Breeds on the Aleutians and Bering Sea islands, in west and north-west Alaska, on Baffin and Ellesmere islands, and in northern Quebec and Labrador. Dispersive in winter, to the North Atlantic and North Pacific.

Little Auk (Dovekie)

Alle alle

L: 17–19cm. WS: 40–48cm. W: 145–175g. ♂>♀.

Related to the guillemots and Razorbill despite its similarity to the smaller auks. Breeding adult patterned as the larger auks, with very dark brownish black upperparts. There are white streaks on the upperbody. The short bill is black. In winter, the head and upper breast are white, as in the guillemots.

Little Auks breed in west-central and northern Greenland, on Iceland, Jan Mayen, Svalbard, Franz Josef Land, Novaya Zemlya and Severnaya Zemlya. There is also a small colony on western Baffin Island. Remarkably, in recent years small but expanding colonies have been found on the Diomede Islands and St Lawrence Island in the northern Bering Sea. Partially migratory, moving south to cold currents of the North Atlantic and North Pacific.

Black Guillemot, Helgelandskysten, Norway.

Black Guillemot

Cepphus grylle

L: 30–32cm. WS: 52–58cm. W: 300–450g.

Breeding adult is black overall apart from a white patch on the upperwing. The thin, dagger-like bill is black. The legs and feet (and the mouth) are bright red. In winter adult birds are mottled black-and-white, a complete contrast to the summer plumage.

Black Guillemots breed in west and north Greenland, on Iceland, Jan Mayen, Svalbard, Franz Josef Land, Novaya Zemlya and Severnaya Zemlya, northern Fennoscandia, and the Taimyr Peninsula. Also breeds on the New Siberian Islands and Wrangel Island, and the adjacent Russian coast to eastern Chukotka. Breeds in north-west and north Alaska, on Canada's northern coast from the Yukon to Franklin Bay, on northern Hudson Bay and adjacent islands, western Baffin Island and southern Ellesmere Island. Resident or dispersive, staying as far north as conditions allow.

Pigeon Guillemot

Cepphus columba

L: 32–34cm. WS: 58–65cm. W: 420–540g.

Breeding adult as Black Guillemot but the white wing-patch is partially crossed by a black wedge. The thin, dagger-like bill is black. The legs and feet (and mouth) are bright red. Winter adult is as Black Guillemot.

Pigeon Guillemots breed on eastern Chukotka, eastern Kamchatka and the Kuril and Commander islands, on the Aleutian islands and in west, south and south-east Alaska. Resident, but moves ahead of the sea ice.

Pigeon Guillemot, Cold Bay, Alaska Peninsula.

Least Auklet, St Paul, Pribilofs, Alaska.

Spectacled Guillemot

Cepphus carbo

L: 38–42cm. WS: 65–75cm. W: 620–700g.

Poorly studied and essentially non-Arctic, but may be seen at the Arctic 'boundary'. Breeding adult is as Black and Pigeon Guillemots but larger, dark brown rather than black, and with a prominent white eye patch and two smaller white patches above and below the bill base. There is no white wing-patch. The bill is black. The legs and feet are red. In winter adult is as Black and Pigeon Guillemots.

Spectacled Guillemots breed on coasts of the Sea of Okhotsk and north-west Kamchatka. Resident or with a limited winter movement south.

Kittlitz's Murrelet

Brachyramphus brevirostris

L: 20–24cm. WS: 35–40cm. W: 220–260g.

A rare, small auk with legs set far back so that standing and walking is difficult; the bird rests on its belly on land. Breeding adult has a mottled grey and brown head and upperbody, the underparts mottled grey and golden-brown apart from white undertail-coverts. The wings are dark brown, the tail having a black centre and white outer feathers. The black bill is short and feather-covered above the nostril. Winter adult is grey and white on the head and body and white below, but retains the dark wings.

Kittlitz's Murrelets breed on Wrangel Island, the coasts of eastern Chukotka and north-western Kamchatka, on the Aleutian islands, and in isolated colonies on the west and south Alaskan coasts. The 1989 *Exxon Valdez* spillage is thought to have killed 10% of the world population. Northern birds fly south in winter to join resident southern birds.

Crested Auklet, St Paul, Pribilofs, Alaska.

Marbled Murrelet

Brachyramphus marmoratus

L: 21–25cm. WS: 33–38cm. W: 210–250g.
Status: IUCN: Vulnerable.
Breeding adult almost identical to Kittlitz's Murrelet, but darker overall and with darker undertail-coverts. The bill is also longer. Winter adults have grey crown and nape. The upperparts are grey and white, the underparts white.

An Arctic fringe species. Marbled Murrelets nest in trees. This very particular nesting requirement is best satisfied by old-growth forest, so the birds are vulnerable as much of this has been logged and logging still continues. Breeds in south-western Alaska, on the Alaskan Peninsula, and on the eastern Aleutians. Resident.

Long-billed Murrelet

Brachyramphus perdix

L: 21–25cm. WS: 33–38cm. W: 210–250g.
Status: IUCN: Vulnerable.
Formerly considered a subspecies of the Marbled Murrelet, but now given full species status. Plumage very similar to the Marbled Murrelet, but the throat is paler and the overall colour greyer. Seen together, the longer bill is diagnostic. Winter adults are as Marbled Murrelet, but the grey of the nape extends to the rear cheeks.

Long-billed Murrelets breed on Kamchatka, the coasts of the Sea of Okhotsk and on Sakhalin. In winter the birds move to waters off southern Sakhalin and northern Japan.

Ancient Murrelet

Synthliboramphus antiquus

L: 23–26cm. WS: 35–40cm. W: 190–230g.
Delightful little birds, with their name deriving from the white streaks on the black head that give the look of a grey-haired or balding old man. The throat is black, the rest of the underparts white, heavily streaked grey on the flanks. The underwing is white with slate-grey flight feathers. The upperparts are dark slate-grey. Winter adult loses most of the white head-streaks, but the amount of black on the head reduces.

Ancient Murrelets breed on islands off the south coast of the Alaskan Peninsula, on the Aleutian and Commander Islands, on north-west and south-east Kamchatka, on the north coast of the Sea of Okhotsk, and on Sakhalin and the Kuril Islands. In winter the birds are seen in southern Alaskan waters, and off south-east China, Japan and Korea.

Crested Auklet

Aethia cristatella

L: 24–27cm. WS: 40–45cm. W: 230–330g.
Breeding adult has a very dark grey head and neck, with a forward-curved crest of the same colour and white plumes drooping from behind the eye. The bill is bright orange and has basal tubercles of the same colour. The underparts are mid-grey. The upperparts and tail are dark slate-grey. In winter adult loses the white eye plumes and the bill-base tubercles. The bill is also duller.

Crested Auklets breed on the Aleutians and Bering Sea islands, on Chukotka near Providenya, on both coasts of northern Kamchatka, on the northern coast of the Sea of Okhotsk, and on the Commander Islands and Sakhalin. In winter the birds are seen in a band stretching across the North Pacific from northern Japan to the southern Alaskan Peninsula.

Least Auklet

Aethia pusilla

L: 14–16cm. WS: 28–32cm. W: 70–100g.
Breeding adult has dark and pale morphs, and intermediate forms. However, in all forms the upperparts are the same, with the head dark grey (or grey-brown) with short white forehead plumes and longer white plumes behind the eye. The bill varies from black with a red tip to red with a black base. There is a black knob on the culmen, very prominent in some birds but virtually invisible on others. The throat is white. The upperparts are dark grey with white patches on the wings. The underwing has three colour bands, black towards the leading edge, then mid-grey, and dark grey towards the trailing edge. The underparts distinguish the morphs, being dark grey with white spotting in dark birds and white with dark grey

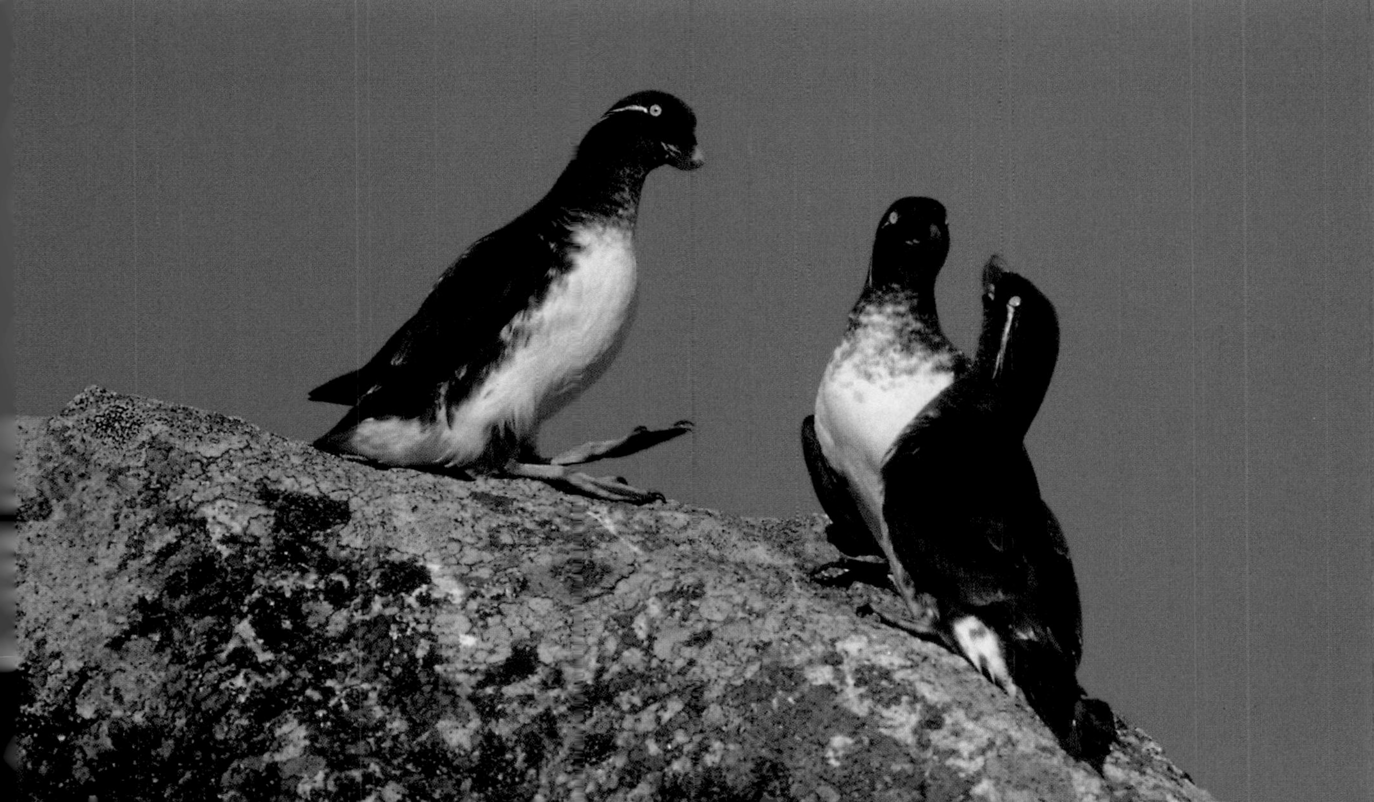

Parakeet Auklets, St Lawrence Island, Alaska.

Opposite page

Top
Horned Puffins gathering nesting material.

Bottom
Tufted Puffin

Both photographs were taken on St Paul, Pribilofs, Alaska.

spotting in pale birds. In winter all forms have white underparts and lose the head plumes.

Least Auklets breed on islands off the southern Alaskan Peninsula, on the Aleutian, Bering Sea and Commander islands, on Chukotka near Providenya, on islands near Kamchatka and in the Sea of Okhotsk. Resident, but moves south ahead of the sea ice.

> **Making least headway**
> Least Auklets are the smallest of the auks and appear far too fragile for their marine environment with its tempestuous weather. On occasions this view is actually borne out when a bird is seen flying very hard into the wind, but actually travelling slowly backwards as its efforts are overwhelmed.

Parakeet Auklet

Aethia psittacula

L: 24–26cm. WS: 42–47cm. W: 250–350g.
Breeding adult has a dark greyish brown head with a long white plume curving down from behind the eye towards the nape. The bill is bright reddish orange. The breast is dark grey, the rest of the underparts white, with grey smudging on the flanks. The upperparts and wings are dark grey. Winter adult has a duller bill but retains the head plumes.

Parakeet Auklets breed on islands off southern Alaska, on the Aleutian, Bering Sea and Commander islands, on eastern and southern Chukotka, and on islands in Sea of Okhotsk and the Kuril Islands. Some southern birds are resident, northern birds move south to join others in a broad band from northern Japan to the west coast of the United States.

Whiskered Auklet

Aethia pygmaea

L: 18–20cm. WS: 33–36cm. W: 100–140g.
Breeding adult very similar to (though much smaller than) the Crested Auklet, with a dark grey head and upperparts and paler grey underparts. The vent is paler again, sometimes even white. The bill is a more 'standard' shape and dull reddish orange. The head plumes are the most ornamented of the auklets, with forward-curving dark grey forehead plumes (as the Crested Auklet, but much more delicate), white plumes from behind the eye towards the nape, and two plumes from the bill base that curve above and below the eye. Winter adult as breeding, but the plumes are vestigial.

Whiskered Auklets are the rarest of the northern auks. They breed on islands in the northern Sea of Okhotsk, on the Kuril and Commander islands, and a few of the Aleutian islands. Essentially resident in winter, but move further offshore in winter.

Cassin's Auklet

Ptychoramphus aleuticus

L: 18–21cm. WS: 32–36cm. W: 140–220g.
Breeding adult has a dark grey head with a small white spot below, and a larger white crescent above, the eye. The long bill is black with a pale grey base to the lower mandible. The underparts are dark grey with a white belly and undertail-

Atlantic Puffins, Runde Island, Norway.

coverts. The upperparts are dark grey. Winter adult as breeding, but slightly paler.

Cassin's Auklets breed on some Aleutian islands, on islands south of the Alaska Peninsula, and on Forrester Island off south-east Alaska. Pelagic. In winter the birds are seen off the south coasts of Aleutian islands and off western United States.

(Atlantic) Puffin

Fratercula arctica

L: 26–29cm. WS: 47–63cm. W: 380–550g.

The three puffins are unmistakeable – the clown princes of the bird world. Breeding adult Atlantic Puffin has a black crown, nape and collar, the rest of the face being white or pale grey. The forward half of the large bill is red, the basal half blue-grey, these colours outlined and separated in yellow. The underparts are white. The upperparts and tail are glossy black. The upperwing is black, the underwing dark grey and silver-grey. The legs and feet are reddish orange. Winter adult loses the bill plates, the distal section becoming dull red, the basal section dull brown. The facial disc becomes grey, and much darker in front of the eye.

Atlantic Puffins breed in Labrador (and, recently, in northern Quebec and south-western Baffin Island where, hopefully, they will become established), in west Greenland, on Iceland, Jan Mayen, Bear Island, Svalbard and Novaya Zemlya, and in northern Fennoscandia. In winter the birds move to a broad band of the North Atlantic from Newfoundland and southern Greenland to the British Isles, and also to the North Sea and the coasts of southern Iberia and North Africa.

Strutting puffins

Having acquired its burrow – either by excavation or by taking ownership of a shearwater burrow (or a rabbit burrow in southern parts of the range) – a male puffin will display ownership with a comical upright walk in which the bill is lowered against the chest and the feet are brought high on each step. The walk has, not surprisingly, been compared to that of a guardsman.

Horned Puffin

Fratercula corniculata

L: 36–40cm. WS: 55–60cm. W: 500–750g. ♂>♀ (but marginally).

Breeding adult very similar to Atlantic Puffin, differing in the bill and facial features. The bill is much larger; the distal third is red, the basal two-thirds yellow. The eye is set in a narrow bare red ring, from the top of which a black horn of skin projects upwards. There are smaller horns below the eye. Winter adult is as breeding, but the facial disc is grey, darker in front of the eye, and the horn is lost or vestigial. The basal upper mandible plate is lost so the base looks very constricted. The distal third is dull red, the basal section dull brown.

Horned Puffins breed on Wrangel Island, in eastern Chukotka, on the shores of the Sea of Okhotsk, on Sakhalin and the Commander and Kuril islands, on the Aleutian Islands and the Alaska Peninsula, Bering Sea islands and the west coast of Alaska. In winter the birds are found in a broad band of the North Pacific from northern Japan to the central United States.

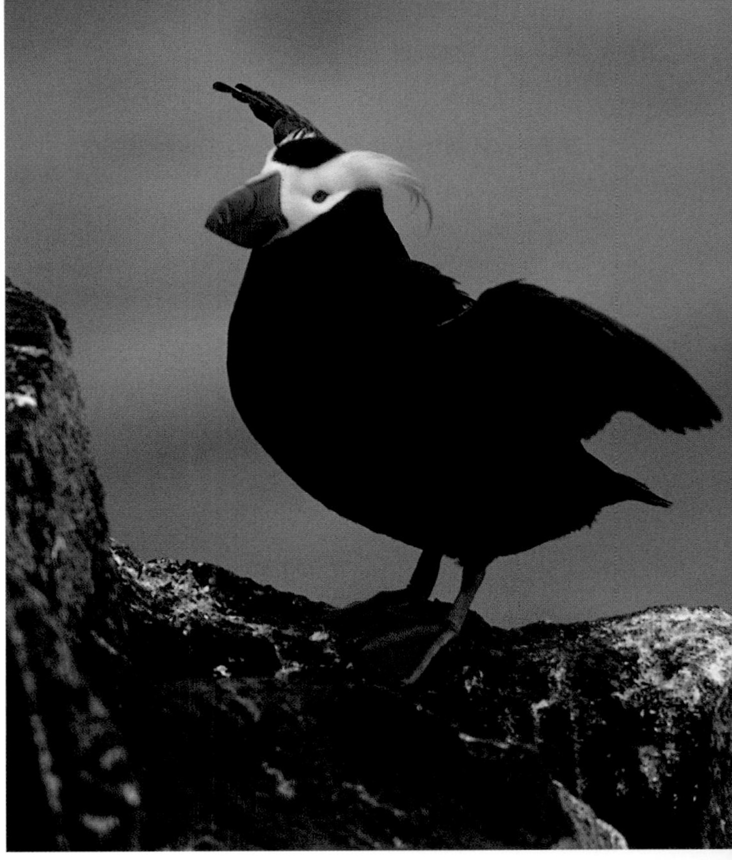
Tufted Puffin, St Paul, Pribilofs.

Tufted Puffin

Fratercula cirrhata

L: 36–40cm. WS: 60–65cm. W: 700–850g.

Breeding adult is very dark brownish black overall, apart from a white facial disc. From above and behind the eyes two long (up to 7cm) sulphur-yellow plumes curve back over the nape. The lower mandible of the large bill is red. The distal two-thirds of the upper mandible is also red, the basal third dull yellow. Winter adult is as breeding but the underparts are paler and often have a few white spots. The facial disc is uniformly dark brown. The exotic plumes are lost, but the feathering behind the eye is yellow-brown. Loss of the basal plate means that the bill is constricted, but much less so than in the Horned Puffin. The distal two-thirds are dull orange-yellow, the basal third dark brown.

Tufted Puffins breed in eastern Chukotka and on Kamchatka, at limited sites in the Sea of Okhotsk and on Sakhalin, the Commander and Aleutian islands, on the Bering Sea islands, western Alaska, the Alaska Peninsula, and on south and south-east Alaska. In winter the birds are seen in a broad band across the North Pacific from northern Japan to the western United States.

OWLS

One of the most recognisable of bird families though, paradoxically, few people have ever seen one because of their nocturnal habits. Although there are diurnal owls most are active at night, when they replace the day-flying raptors as avian predators. The smaller owls take insects, but the larger ones can take mammals to the size of hares and even small deer.

Owls are densely feathered, the feathers having soft fringes so their flight is quiet, the normal hunting technique being a pounce on to the prey from a hovering flight. Tundra species, which hunt by day, have long wings that allow an efficient quartering flight as they visually search for prey. The hooked bill is small and often almost completely hidden in the feathers. The talons are sharp and the outer toe can be reversed, improving both capture area and grip. Owls usually carry their prey in their bills, though occasionally larger prey may be carried in the feet (in the manner of raptors). The prey is ingested whole, with the indigestible portions – fur, bones etc. – being periodically disgorged. The examination of pellets allows a study of the owl's diet. In times of abundant prey owls may cache food. Prey abundance has a dramatic effect on owl numbers, with periodic fluctuations following the rhythm of prey population. In 'lemming years' the number of Snowy Owls increases substantially, though many birds will starve when lemming numbers crash. The owls may also migrate in search of prey, being seen far south of their normal range.

Not surprisingly for essentially nocturnal creatures, plumage colour is generally not so important for owls, with many forest-dwelling species having a cryptic plumage that allows the bird to rest undisturbed during the day. Some species that inhabit a latitudinal range encompassing both deciduous and coniferous forests actually change their plumage base colour from brown in the south to grey in the north. In general plumages are similar for the sexes and for both summer and winter.

Because sight is less important for territorial and mating purposes, sound has replaced it as the primary means of communication in owls. Pair formation is therefore based on the male hooting his territorial claim. For the two true Arctic breeders, visual displays are more appropriate, male Snowy Owls having a flight with the wings raised in a V, and wing-raising ground display. Male Short-eared Owls clap their wings. In general pairs are monogamous and seasonal, though males may be polygamous in good prey years. Owls breed early in the season so that young rodents are plentiful when their chicks are learning to hunt, and when moulting adults are least efficient hunters. The boreal species nest in tree holes, but the two true Arctic owls nest on the ground. The number of eggs is highly dependent on prey numbers and can be as low as 1 or 2 or as high as 10–12. The female incubates while the male feeds her. The owlets are nidicolous and altricial, and are dependent on their parents for a relatively long period. The summer and winter plumages of the owls described here are similar.

Snowy Owl, Orre, Norway.

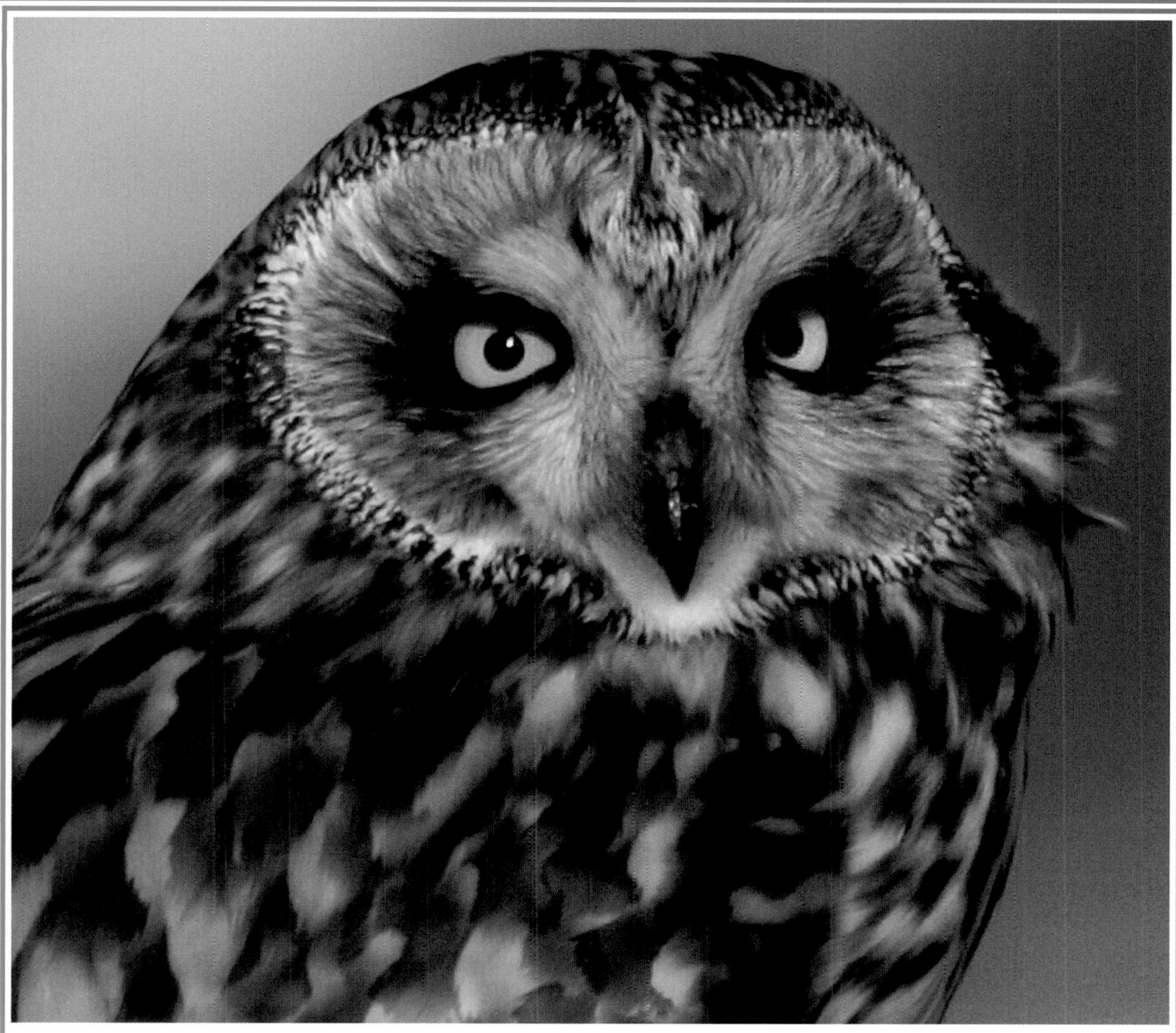

Sight and hearing

Owls are squat birds with wide heads and huge eyes. Head size and shape is an adaptation to help improve the acuity of both sight and hearing. In cross section, the owl's eyes are cylindrical (as opposed to spherical as in mammals such as humans). This allows a larger pupil and lens, and so improved light capture. The eyes are also mounted frontally to improve binocular vision. The disadvantage of these adaptations is that they reduce the field of view (to about 110° compared to 180° in humans). To compensate, owls have highly flexible necks that allow the head to be turned almost 270°. An owl will also bob its head sometimes, allowing it to get a better fix on its target. Owl vision is only about 2–3 times better than that of humans, with this improvement highly significant at night.

The wide head aids hearing. A notable feature of owls is the facial disc, a dish of stiff feathers (much more developed in nocturnal species than in diurnal owls; the day-flying Snowy Owl has a much less pronounced disc than most other owls). The feathers channel sound to the ears, much as parabolic dishes aid sound reception for human observers attempting to catch bird sounds (or for more clandestine reasons). The ears are far apart, allowing the bird to detect small differences in the arrival time of a sound across the head. This gives information on the location of the noise in the horizontal plane. Some owls also have asymmetric ears (usually the right ear set high, the left set lower), providing information in the vertical plane. Those owls that do not have such asymmetric ears can move ear-flaps that alter the size and shape of the ear to obtain the same information. So good are owls at locating sound that in experiments they have been able to catch prey in complete darkness, hunting by sound alone. Indeed, Snowy Owls (and others, such as the Great Grey Owl *Strix nebulosa*) can hunt rodents through several centimetres of snow with no visual clues. One further adaptation is that the ears are particularly sensitive to high frequency sounds, such as the rustling of a rodent making its way through dead leaves.

Despite the name of some owls (such as the Short-eared Owl *above*), the prominent 'ear' tufts of these species have nothing to do with hearing or, indeed, ears. The tufts are for communication between conspecifics.

Snowy Owl

Bubo scandiacus

L: 53–66cm. WS: 142–166cm. W: 1.2–2.9kg. ♀>♂.

Status: CITES: Appendix II.

Magnificent birds that provide one of the great sights of the Arctic. Breeding male is white, occasionally with a few brown spots on the crown and upperparts. Breeding female has a white head, but the rest of the bird is white with dark brown barring, this usually heavy. The eyes are golden-yellow and stare out from an incomplete facial disc. The bill and claws are black.

The Snowy Owl breeds in north Greenland, northern Fennoscandia, northern Russia (including Novaya Zemlya, Severnaya Zemlya and Wrangel Island), west and north

The white plumage of the Snowy Owl makes it highly conspicuous in summer, as these photographs from St Paul, Pribilofs, Alaska (*above*), Orre, Norway (*right*) and the Borgefjell National Park, Norway (*below*) illustrate.

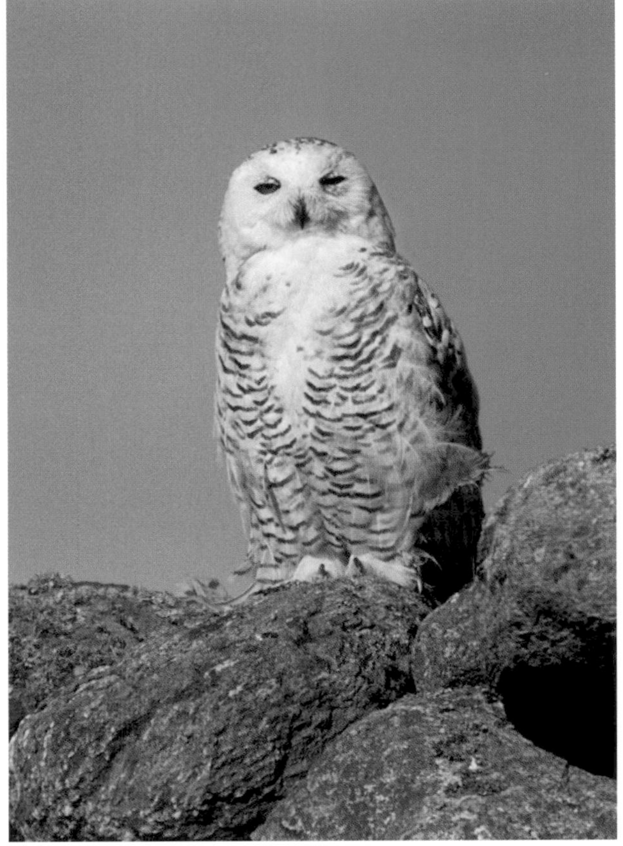

Alaska and northern Canada including the southern Arctic islands. However, the distribution is dependent on prey numbers: Snowy Owls have bred on Iceland and Jan Mayen, probably on Svalbard and the other Russian Arctic islands, and on Canada's Arctic islands north to Ellesmere. The owls are essentially resident, but will move south if prey numbers decline.

SHORT-EARED OWL

Asio flammeus

L: 35–40cm. WS: 95–110cm. W: 280–380g. ♀>♂.

Status: CITES: Appendix II.

Breeding male has a buff and white facial disc, with a black bill and yellow eyes. The underparts are pale buff, paler still on the belly, the whole streaked with dark brown, the streaking heavier on the breast and throat. The upperparts are tawny-buff, heavily streaked dark brown. Breeding females similar but deeper buff and, in general, more heavily marked.

Short-eared Owls breed on Iceland, in northern Fennoscandia and across Russia to Kamchatka, though rarely to the north coast. Breeds in Alaska, the Yukon and North West Territories, around Hudson Bay, in Labrador and on southern Baffin Island. Ranges at all times dependent on prey density, but northern owls do move south to north-west Europe, central Asia and continental United States.

Left
Looking rather more like a Russian doll than a bird, this Short-eared Owl, photographed at Orre, Norway, is showing the flexibility of its neck by turning its head almost completely around.

Above
The same owl in flight.

(Northern) Hawk Owl

Surnia ulula

L: 35–40cm. WS: 75–85cm. W: 250–350g. ♀>♂.

Status: CITES: Appendix II.

Breeding adult has a white facial disc ringed black. The eyes are yellow. The underparts are white finely barred brown (very similar to Goshawk). The upperparts are grey-brown, mottled white. The long tail is dark grey-brown with delicate white barring.

A boreal species, but seen to the treeline, Hawk Owls breed in Fennoscandia and across Russia to Kamchatka. Breeds in central Alaska (but uncommon in west and south) and across Canada to the Atlantic coast. Resident and irruptive, as for other owl species.

Tengmalm's Owl (Boreal Owl)

Aegolius funereus

L: 24–27cm. WS: 55–65cm. W: 100–160g. ♀>♂.

Status: CITES: Appendix II.

Breeding adult has a white facial disc ringed black, similar to Hawk Owl, but usually with a more 'startled' look. The underparts are white heavily smudged dark brown. The upperparts are dark brown spotted white, with the spotting heavier on the head. The tail is dark brown, finely barred lighter brown.

A boreal species, but seen to the treeline, Tengmalm's Owls breed in Fennoscandia and across Russia to Kamchatka. Breeds in central Alaska (but rare in the west and uncommon in the south) and across Canada to the Atlantic coast. In general seen further south than Hawk Owl. Resident and irruptive, as for other owl species.

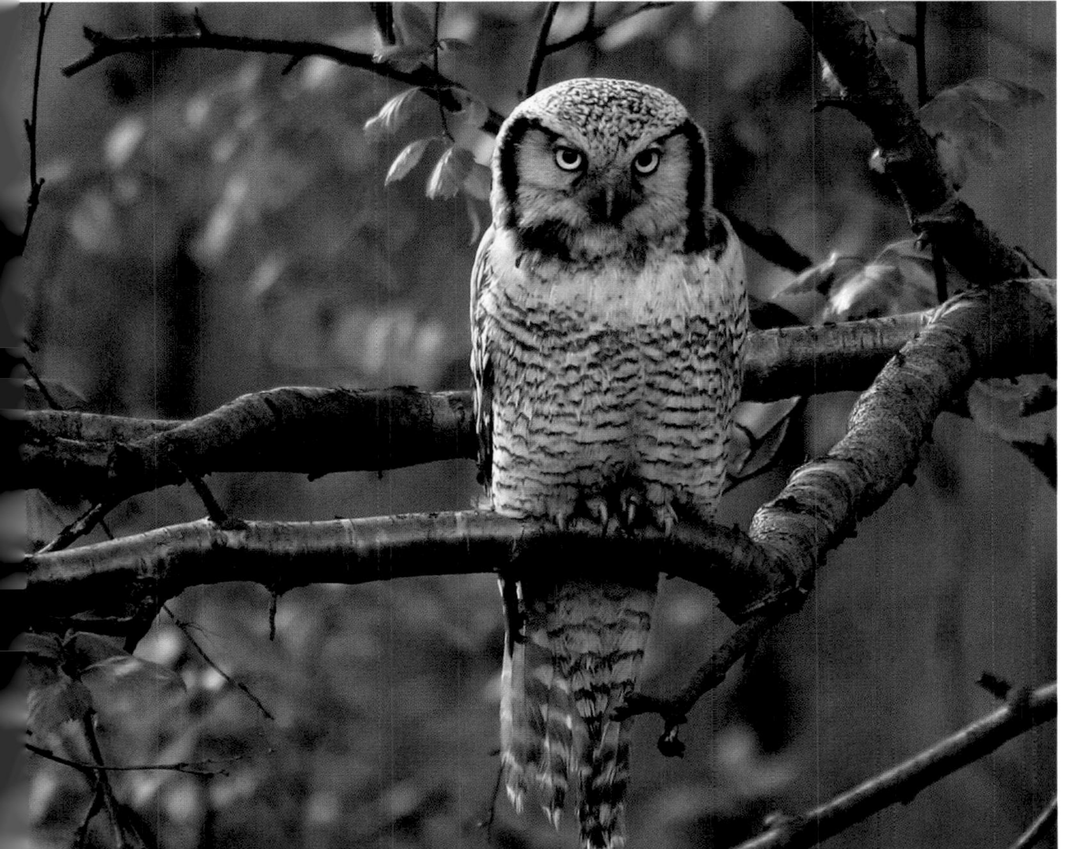

Hawk Owl, Øvre Pasvik National Park, Norway.

Great Horned Owl

Bubo virgnianus

L: 45–65cm. WS: 90–150cm.
W: 1.0–1.5kg. ♀>♂.

Status: CITES: Appendix II.

Breeding adult variable across the range. In central and eastern Canada has a rufous–brown facial disc, ringed black. The underparts are buff, heavily barred dark brown or dark grey-brown. The upperparts are grey-brown mottled dark brown and white. In western Canada the owls are paler, with the facial disc pale

Northern Hawk Owl with prey, Øvre Pasvik National Park, Norway.

grey, the underparts pale grey barred darker, the upperparts mottled grey and white. In Alaska the birds are much darker, with the facial disc brown, the underparts dark buff, sometimes even pale chestnut, with dark brown barring, and the upperparts mottled dark brown, brown and white. Has prominent ear tufts and large yellow eyes.

A boreal species, but seen to the treeline, Great Horned Owls breed in central and southern Alaska (but are uncommon in the west) and across Canada. Resident and irruptive, as for other owl species.

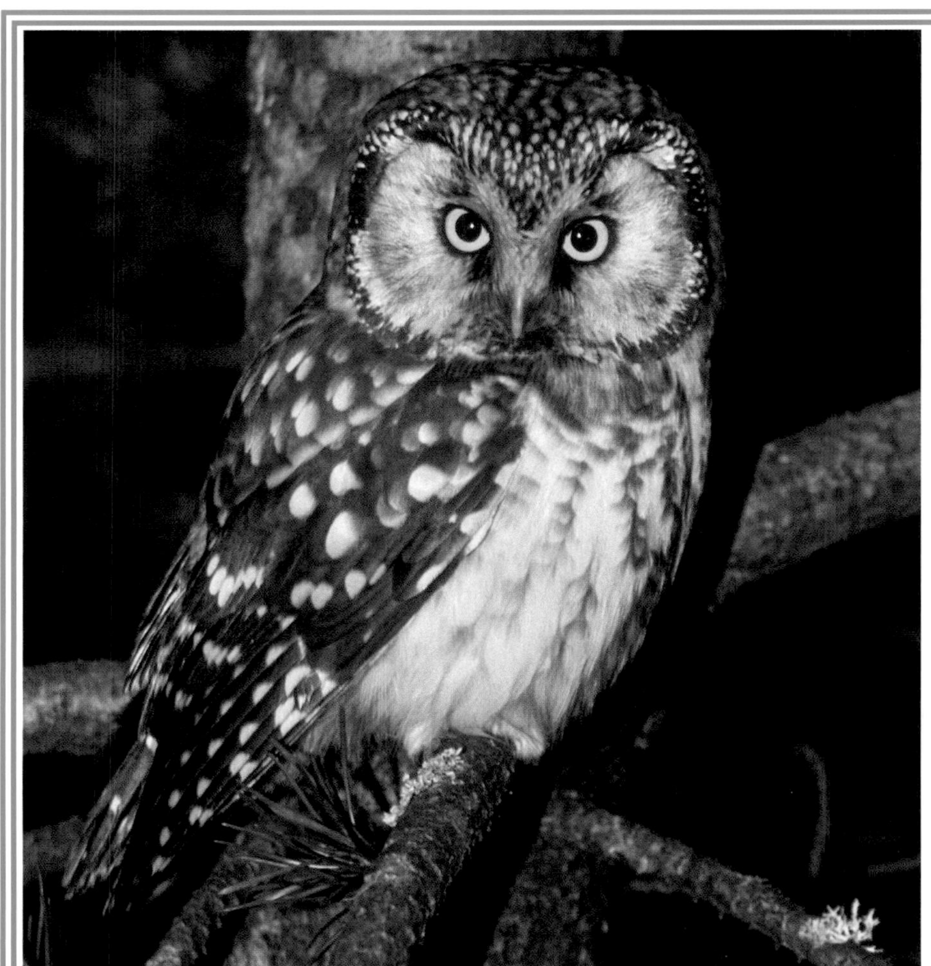

Thawing its food

As with other owls, Tengmalm's Owl will cache prey if it has had a successful day. This is a particularly good strategy in winter as the owl is less able to hunt through the snow. Tengmalm's Owl caches are usually placed in tree holes. In winter the prey freezes, which is useful as a storage method, keeping the food from decomposing, but difficult for the owl when it comes in search of a meal. To overcome the problem the owl will 'brood' the prey item, just as it would its eggs, thawing it to the point where it can be ingested.

The owl to the left was photographed near Stavanger, Norway.

KINGFISHERS

Most kingfishers live in the tropics, with only one bird breeding in the Arctic as defined in this book, and then only at the fringe. As with its more southerly cousins, the Belted Kingfisher of the Nearctic is superbly adapted for its feeding strategy of long periods of patience interrupted by short bursts of activity. Its superb vision allows it to both detect a fish and to pinpoint its position beneath the surface for its plunge-dive. As anyone who has stared into a pond will know, refraction at the water surface gives a false position for sub-surface objects, which needs to be allowed for if dives are to be successful. The Belted Kingfisher has a long, dagger-like bill for taking fish. The male bird holds a territory and entices a female to it, reinforcing the monogamous, seasonal bond by courtship feeding. The nest is in a burrow excavated by the birds. 5–7 eggs are incubated by both birds, the chicks also being cared for and fed by both parents.

Belted Kingfisher

Ceryle alycon

L: 28–35cm (bill 5cm). WS: 47–52cm. W: 140–170g.
Breeding male has a dark slate-blue head with a distinctive crest. Below a white throat collar, there is a slate-blue breast-band, the rest of the underparts being white, with slate-blue smudging on the flanks. The upperparts are dark slate-blue, with white streaking. Breeding female as male but has a second, narrower chestnut breast-band and chestnut striping along the upper flanks. Summer and winter plumages are similar.

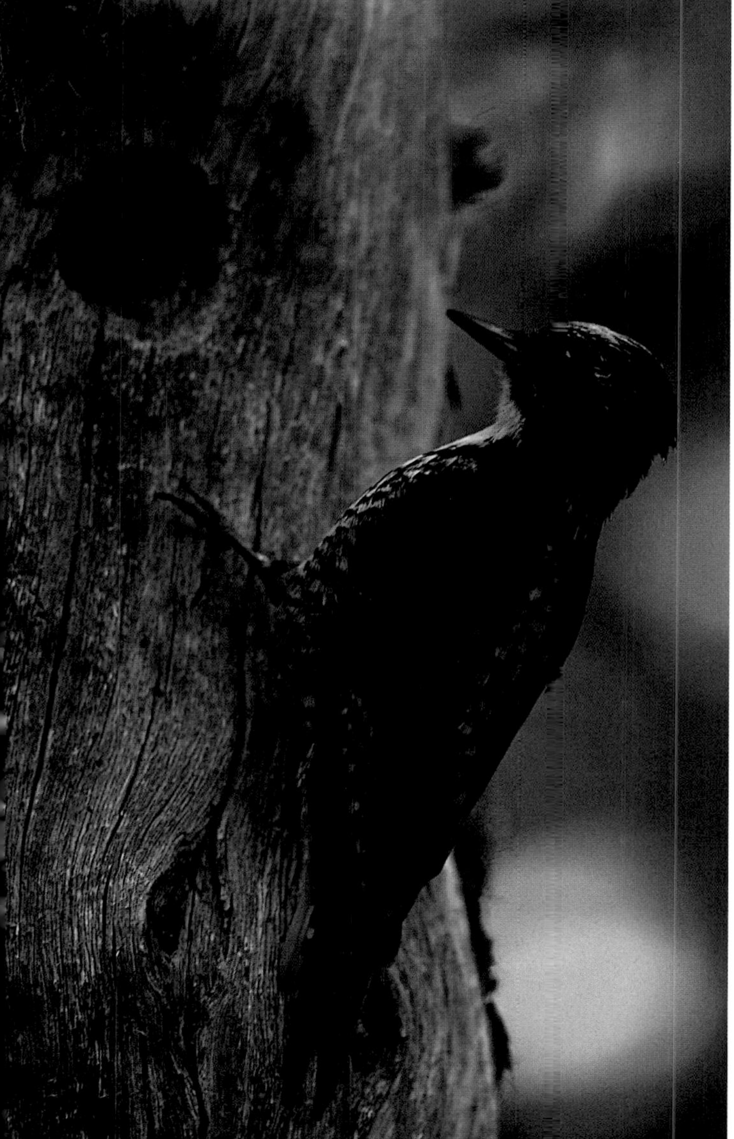

Belted Kingfisher breeds in western Alaska and on the Alaska Peninsula, but uncommon. Also breeds in central Alaska, central Yukon and North West Territories, and on the southern edge of Hudson Bay. In winter the birds move to south-eastern Alaska and the continental United States.

WOODPECKERS

Woodpeckers are boreal species and so technically non-Arctic, but one species is found to the treeline in both the Palearctic and Nearctic.

In most woodpeckers the four toes are arranged as two pairs, one pair pointing forward, the other backward. This allows efficient climbing and provides a solid anchor for pecking. The tail is also stiff, acting as a clamp to further strengthen the position. In some woodpeckers the fourth toe can be moved sideways to allow a rigid position to be maintained whatever the contours of the tree. However, in some species the toe is small, and in the Three-toed Woodpecker it is absent, this accounting for the species name.

The Three-toed Woodpecker exhibits typical woodpecker courtship behaviour, including head-swaying and a great deal of drumming and calling. The pair bond is monogamous and seasonal. The 3–5 eggs are laid in an excavated tree hole and are incubated by both birds. The chicks are cared for and fed by both parents. The bird's diet consists primarily of adult and larval insects.

Avoiding brain damage

The woodpecker's bill is chisel-ended, not pointed as is sometimes assumed: a sharp point might become embedded and stuck in the tree. The bill is also perfectly straight so there is no tendency for it to break. When drumming the bill strikes the tree at *c.*40kph, the bird being able to lock the mandibles at the point of impact to stop them flying apart and being damaged. The brain is protected from damage by the bones and muscles at the base of the bill, which absorb the energy of impact, acting as a shock absorber. Additional protection is also required: the bird's nostrils are feathered to stop wood chips flying into them and the woodpecker closes its eyes as the bill strikes to prevent damage.

Three-toed Woodpecker

Picoides tridactylus

L: 20–23cm. WS: 32–37cm. W: 55–75g.
Breeding adult has an elegant black-and-white head with a yellow crown. The underparts are white with black streaking to the flanks. The upper body is white, the wings black with thin white bars. The underwings are as the upperwings but grey rather than black. The central tail is black, the outer feathers white with black barring. Summer and winter plumages are similar.

Three-toed Woodpeckers breed to the treeline across both the Palearctic and Nearctic. In the western Palearctic and over much of the Nearctic the birds are resident, but in eastern Russia they move south to avoid the harsh Siberian winter. It is likely that some Nearctic birds also move south in winter.

Three-toed Woodpecker at nest hole, southern Alaska.

Shore Lark, Hood River, Barren Lands of Nunavut, Canada.

LARKS

Larks are ground dwelling passerines that walk (rarely running and almost never hopping) in search of seeds and insects. Because of their habitat and lifestyle they are, in general, cryptic brown, and have relatively long legs and a long hind claw to aid standing. Only one species breeds in the Arctic. The Shore (or Horned) Lark is typical of the family. Flocks form for migration and at wintering sites. The male holds a terri-tory and entices a female by calling. The pair bond is monogamous and seasonal. The nest, on the tundra, holds 3–4 eggs, which are incubated by the female. Chicks are, however, fed by both parents.

SHORE LARK (HORNED LARK)

Eremophilia alpestris

L: 14–17cm. WS: 30–35cm. W: 30–45g.

Breeding male is very distinctive. The head is pale yellow, with a black horseshoe through the eyes and bill, a black necklace and a brown crown and nape. At the front of the crown there is a black bar that ends in black tufts (the 'horns'). These are raised as a threat to intruding males. The underparts are white, the flanks smudged pinkish-brown. The upperparts are mottled pink, brown, dark brown and grey. Breeding female does not have horns; the plumage is as the male, but is duller overall and lacks the black horseshoe and necklace, these being pale grey. Female summer and winter plumages are similar. Males lose their horns in winter, and are then similar to the female. Shore Larks have a complex taxonomy, with more than 40 subspecies having been described. In the Palearctic the bird is a northern dweller only, with southern habitats being occupied by the Eurasian Skylark *Alauda arvensis*. Shore larks are the only Nearctic larks, the species breeding in both northern and southern habitats.

Shore Larks breed in Fennoscandia, on the southern island of Novaya Zemlya and across Russia to the Kolyma delta, north to the coast. Breeds throughout Alaska and northern Canada, including Arctic islands north to Devon Island. In winter Palearctic birds are seen in south-eastern Europe and southern Russia, while Nearctic birds fly south to join resident southern birds.

SWALLOWS AND MARTINS

Among the most popular of birds as their arrival in northern Europe heralds the arrival of summer; the birds would be even more popular with the Arctic traveller if only they occurred there in greater numbers, since swallows and martins take insects on the wing and so reduce – but sadly only by a minimal amount – the number of mosquitoes.

These birds are superbly adapted for the task of chasing down insects on the wing, with long, narrow, pointed wings and deeply forked tails. The high aspect-ratio wings make the

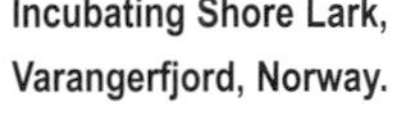

Incubating Shore Lark, Varangerfjord, Norway.

birds fast but with reduced manoeuvrability, the forked tail restoring that so the birds are quick and agile. In general martins have shorter tails than swallows. The specialised diet of winged insects means that northern species are migratory, heading south to where insects can be found during the northern winter.

The birds have limited displays, male Sand Martins holding a burrow that a female might favour. The pair-bond is monogamous and seasonal, but males will attempt to mate other females. Nests are often made of mud pellets, but they may be more conventional if a suitable crevice is found. 4–5 eggs are incubated by the female only, and she also takes responsibility for brooding the chicks, though both parents feed them. The summer and winter plumages of the species described here are similar.

Tree Swallow

Tachycineta bicolor

L: 13–15cm. WS: 34–37cm. W: 18–22g.

Breeding male has a shiny blue crown to eye level. The throat and underparts are white. The upperparts are blue, also with a sheen that can sometimes appear greenish. Adult female is patterned as the male, but the crown and upperparts are a dingy grey-brown. Tree Swallows differ from most other members of the family by feeding on vegetation and berries as well as insects. They take these at all times, but particularly in bad weather.

The Tree Swallows breed throughout Alaska (but are uncommon in the north), in central Yukon and North West Territories, around the southern shores of Hudson Bay, in southern Quebec and eastern Labrador. In winter the birds fly to the southern United States, Mexico, and the east coast of Central America.

Cliff Swallow

Hirundo pyrrhonota

L: 12–15cm. WS: 28–33cm. W: 18–24g.

Breeding adult is an attractive bird with a blue crown, white forehead and red cheeks, a black throat patch and a white nape linking to a white collar on the upper breast. The rest of the underparts are white or pale grey, with pink smudging on the flanks. The mantle and back are blue, the rump pink. The upperwing is blue-grey, the underwing pale grey. The blue-grey tail is notched rather than forked.

The Cliff Swallow is a bird of the Arctic fringe. Breeds in central Alaska but uncommon in the rest of the state; also breeds in northern Yukon and western North West Territories (though not to the northern coast), then southerly across Canada to the southern shore of Hudson Bay. The birds winter in southern South America.

Sand Martin (Bank Swallow)

Riparia riparia

L: 11–13cm. WS: 26–30cm. W: 12–15g.

Breeding adult has mid-brown upperparts, the forehead slightly paler. The brown of the crown extends across the cheeks (usually darker around the eye) and as a broad band around the upper breast. The rest of the underparts are white apart from the brown undertail. The tail is forked, but not deeply.

Sand Martins breed in northern Fennoscandia, around the White Sea and then more southerly across Russia to Kamchatka. Breeds in central and western Alaska (though not common in the west), near the Mackenzie delta, then more southerly to southern shores of Hudson Bay and in southern Quebec and Labrador.

Tree Swallow, Potter Marsh, Alaska.

Sand Martin, Seward Peninsula, Alaska.

Red-throated Pipit, Varangerfjord, Norway.

PIPITS AND WAGTAILS

The members of the *Motacillidae* are seed- and insect-eating passerines, which can be usefully divided into two groups, the wagtails, which are generally boldly coloured with greys, black, white and yellows, and the more cryptic pipits. The wagtails have long tails, the name deriving from the endearing habit of tail-wagging, which the birds do almost continuously while on the ground. The pipits are renowned for the display songs of the males, the birds flying high and delivering territorial claims while apparently hanging motionless (by flying into the wind). Some species fly so high that they are out of sight, reaching over 100m. The flights can also be long-lasting, occasionally taking several hours, though they are often much shorter, and end with the bird 'parachuting' back to Earth, this involving fluttering wings and a near-vertical descent.

A male pipit's song defines its territory and encourages females. Wagtails also have a territorial song, this usually starting from a perch. Male wagtails point their bills upwards to expose the breast patterns, and may also fan their tails. The pair bond is monogamous and seasonal. The nest is a cup of vegetation well hidden on the ground. 2–5 eggs are laid. These are generally incubated by both birds in the wagtails, the female only in the pipits, but there are exceptions. The chicks are nidicolous and altricial and are cared for and fed by both parents.

Red-throated Pipit

Anthus cervinus

L: 14–16cm. WS: 25–27cm. W: 20–24g.

Breeding male has a pale orange-buff head and breast, the crown streaked brown. The rest of the underparts are white with black streaking. The upperparts are mottled tawny brown, black and white – the typical pipit cryptic plumage. Female is as male, but usually with paler head and breast. In winter the head and breast of both male and female are paler.

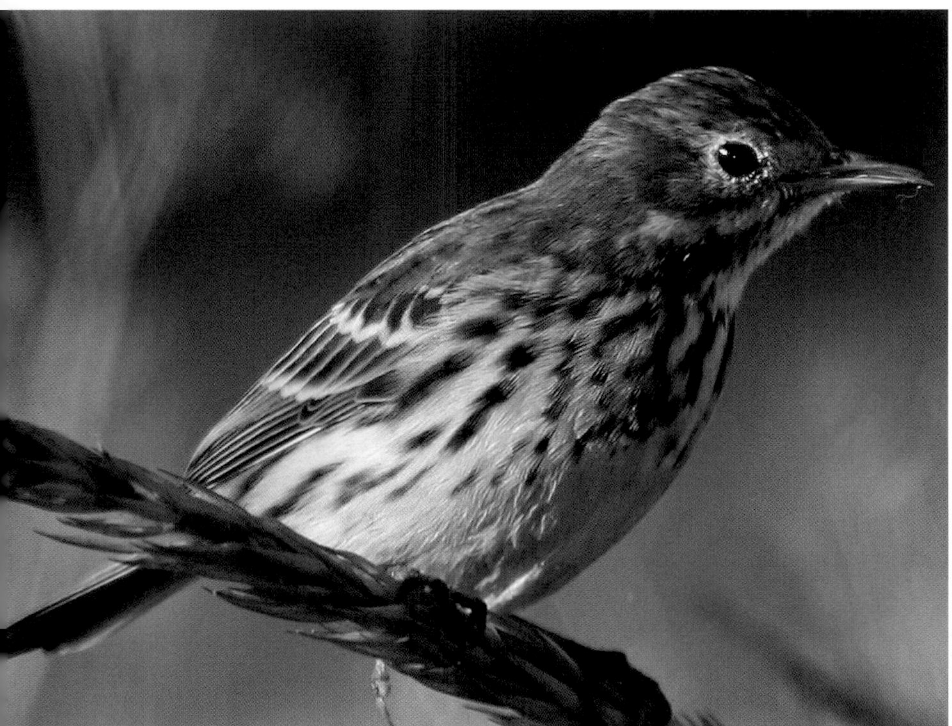

Meadow Pipit, Orre, Norway.

Red-throated Pipits breed in northern Fennoscandia and across Russia to Chukotka and Kamchatka, to the north coast except on the Taimyr Peninsula. Also breeds in small numbers in western Alaska. In winter the birds are seen in central Africa and south-east Asia.

Pechora Pipit

Anthus gustavi

L: 14–15cm. WS: 23–25cm. W: 20–26g.

Breeding adult has a black and buff streaked crown and upper head, the lower head being pale buff or white. The breast and flanks are buff, sometimes yellowish-buff, becoming paler on the rest of the underparts. The breast and flanks are heavily streaked dark brown. The upperparts are typically 'pipit', being mottled black, brown and buff. In winter the birds are duller overall.

Pechora Pipits breed from the Pechora River eastwards to Chukotka, but to the north coast only in Chukotka. Also breeds throughout Kamchatka and on the Commander Islands. In winter the birds fly to Indonesia and the Philippines.

Meadow Pipit

Anthus pratensis

L: 14–16cm. WS: 22–25cm. W: 18–24g.

The archetypal pipit, adults having crown, upper head and upperparts which are mid-, sometimes olive-brown, heavily streaked with dark brown or black. The throat and underparts are cream or buff, often orange-buff on the flanks, with dark brown streaking on the breast and flanks. Summer and winter plumages are similar.

Meadow Pipits breed in south-east Greenland, on Iceland and Jan Mayen, in northern Scandinavia and Russia east to the shores of the White Sea. In winter the birds fly to southern Europe, north Africa, the Middle East and central Asia.

Buff-breasted Pipit (American Pipit)

Anthus rubescens

L: 15–18cm. WS: 24–28cm. W: 18–22g.

Breeding adult has a grey-brown head with a distinct buff supercilium. The throat and underparts are white, buff or yellowish-buff on the flanks. The breast and flanks are heavily

White Wagtail, Skaftafell National Park, Iceland.

streaked dark brownish black. The upperparts are brown or grey-brown, much less heavily streaked than other pipits, the streaking being very fine and only a little darker. In winter the birds are duller overall.

Buff-breasted Pipits breed in Alaska, across mainland Canada to the north coast and on southern Arctic islands from Banks to Baffin. Also breeds in north-west and west central Greenland and in Chukotka and Kamchatka. In winter Nearctic and Greenlandic birds fly to the southern United States and Central America, while Asian birds head for southern Asia.

White Wagtail

Motacilla alba

L: 17–19cm (tail 8–9cm). WS: 25–30cm. W: 20–25g.
Adult male has a white head with a black crown. The throat, lower cheek and upper breast are black. The rest of the underparts are white, heavily smudged dark grey on the lower flanks. The upper body is grey, the tail having a black centre and white outer feathers. Adult female is as male, but the pattern is less striking and smudged, the upperparts darker grey. In winter plumage males and females are similar, and as the summer female.

White Wagtails breed in south-east Greenland, on Iceland and Jan Mayen, in northern Scandinavia, and across Russia to Kamchatka, north to the coast except on the Taimyr Peninsula and on the southern island of Novaya Zemlya and Wrangel Island. Also breeds irregularly in north-west Alaska. In winter the birds are seen in north and central Africa, the Middle East, and south and south-east Asia.

Yellow Wagtail

Motacilla flava

L: 15–17cm (tail 6–7cm). WS: 23–27cm. W: 16–20g.
Breeding male has a slate-grey crown and neck, the rest of the head black. The throat is pale yellow, the rest of the underparts

Yellow Wagtail of the subspecies *M. f. thunbergi*, which breeds in northern Scandinavia and western Arctic Russia, photographed in the Øvre Pasvik National Park, Norway.

yellow with olive smudging on the flanks. The upperbody is olive green, the central tail dark grey, the outer feathers white. Female has a paler head and duller upperparts. In winter plumage males and females are similar, and as the summer female.

Yellow Wagtail breeds in northern Scandinavia and across Russia to Kamchatka, north to the coast except on the Taimyr Peninsula. Also breeds in small numbers on the western and northern coasts of Alaska. In winter the birds head for central and southern Africa, India and south-east Asia.

Citrine Wagtail

Motacilla citreola

L: 15–17cm (tail 6–7cm). WS: 24–27cm. W: 17–22g.
Breeding male has a yellow head and underparts. On the lower nape a dark grey half-collar divides the yellow head from the grey upper body. The tail has a dark grey centre and white outer feathers. The upperwings are grey with delicate white banding, the underwing is pale grey. Breeding female has a grey crown and facial smudging and is duller overall. Citrine Wagtails are usually seen close to water. In winter plumage males and females are similar, and as the summer female.

Citrine Wagtail breeds in Russia from the White Sea to the western Taimyr Peninsula. In winter the birds fly to the Caspian Sea, Iran and northern India.

WAXWINGS

Waxwings are named after the wax-like red 'droplets' found at the tips of the secondary feathers (and, occasionally, the tertials and tail feathers) of two of the three species in the family. The 'droplets' (which are, of course, part of the feather structure) derive their colour from carotenoids in the birds' principal food, fruit. The size and number of the 'droplets' increases with age, and are an indication of mating fitness. The yellow wing feather-tips and tail-band also result from carotenoids and are further fitness indicators.

Irruptive and disorderly Waxwings

Waxwings breed late, a response to the seasonal nature of fruit production. As autumn approaches the birds preferentially seek out the berries of the Rowan (or Mountain Ash *Sorbus aucuparia*). If stocks are poor the birds may be forced to seek alternative foods and this can result in irruptions, large flocks of waxwings being seen well south of their usual range and in areas from which they are usually absent. Irruptions have, for instance, led to large flocks in southern Britain.

Being frugivores (though the birds do take insects), waxwings can find themselves feeding on fermenting fruit as autumn approaches. Studies indicate that the birds have evolved a relatively high capacity to metabolise ethanol, which makes them more alcohol-tolerant than other species. But despite being able to 'hold their drink' waxwings can become a little drunk and disorderly if fermented berries form a high proportion of their diet.

The birds are important seed-dispersers as they are entirely frugivorous, consuming huge quantities daily, up to twice their body weight. The birds are non-territorial even in the breeding season (a consequence of the transitory nature of fruiting). The birds are much more gregarious in winter, a rarity among non-marine species. Pair formation follows male-calling and is monogamous, both birds contributing to the raising of chicks.

(Bohemian) Waxwing

Bombycilla garrulus

L: 17–20cm. WS: 31–35cm. W: 50–75g.
Handsome birds. Breeding adult is overall pinkish buff, paler below than above, with crest at the back of the crown, black mask and throat. The back and rump are grey or grey-buff. The wings are grey with yellow feather-tips forming a trailing edge. The tail is grey with a broad yellow terminal band. Plumages of sexes similar, with summer and winter plumages also similar.

Bohemian Waxwings, Stavanger, Norway.

An Arctic-fringe species. Waxwings breed in southern Fennoscandia, around Russia's White Sea coast, but then more southerly. Breeds in central Alaska, but rare elsewhere in the State, in northern Yukon and north-west North West Territories, but then more southerly to the south-west shores of Hudson Bay. In winter the birds are seen in southern Scandinavia and eastern Europe, southern Canada and northern continental United States.

DIPPERS

Dippers are truly aquatic passerines. Adaptations for this unique lifestyle include thick plumage for insulation, large flight muscles, as the wings are occasionally used to aid walking underwater (each of these adaptations giving the birds a rounded appearance), very large preen gland to ensure that the feathers remain waterproof, a transparent nictitating membrane (acting as goggles to allow the bird to see underwater) and well-developed claws that aid the gripping of subsurface rocks. The claws and strong legs allow movement in fast-flowing streams. Dippers do not dive to submerge, but merely walk into the stream until they are immersed, a remarkable sight. Underwater they seek out invertebrates, particularly aquatic larvae, occasionally turning over pebbles to look for prey. The birds are astonishingly cold-tolerant, surviving in temperatures to -45°C. They can occasionally be seen feeding below ice and may even migrate upstream to find faster flowing, unfrozen water in which to feed. The pair bond is monogamous, the female responsible for all or most of the incubation of the 4–6 eggs, though both birds care for and feed the chicks.

Summer and winter plumages are similar for all three species listed here. None of the three are true Arctic breeders, but may be seen at the Arctic fringe.

White–throated Dipper

Cinclus cinclus

L: 17–20cm. WS: 25–30cm. W: 60–75g.

Breeding adult is dark brown or dark grey-brown overall, apart from a distinctive white patch covering the throat and breast. The eyelids are also white. White-throated Dipper breeds in northern Scandinavia (but not on the north Kola Peninsula), patchily and more southerly across western and central Russia. Resident or partially migratory, moving to southern Scandinavia.

Brown Dipper, Sirdal, Norway.

Displaying Dippers

Dippers derive their name from their habit of dipping the entire body by flexing the legs, a display which has probably evolved because the noise of fast-flowing streams makes the auditory signals of most passerines ineffective. Dippers are also unique in having feathered eyelids. These are white, the blinking eyes being a strong visual signal.

Brown Dipper

Cinclus pallasi

L: 17–20cm. WS: 25–30cm. W: 60–75g.

Breeding adult is paler brown than the White–throated and lack the white throat/breast patch. Brown Dippers breed in far eastern Russia, including Kamchatka. Competes in part of its range with White-throated, but tends to favour wider rivers with less frantic water. Resident or partially migratory.

American Dipper

Cinclus mexicanus

L: 17–20cm. WS: 25–30cm. W: 55–70g.

Breeding adult is dark slate-grey overall, the head usually browner. There is no white throat/breast patch.

American Dippers breed in southern Alaska, but are uncommon in the western and northern state. Also breeds in the Yukon, where again uncommon in the north. Resident, but may move to lower altitudes in winter.

ACCENTORS

The accentors – named from the Latin *cantor* (singer) though the birds actually have a nondescript voice – are a number of drab, sparrow-like high-altitude birds which, apart from the Dunnock, are poorly studied. They feed on insects during the summer, supplementing these with berries during the winter. This diet may explain the odd bill shape, the bill being very pointed at the tip, but broad at the base. The summer and winter plumages of the species described here are similar.

American Dipper, Cold Bay, Alaska Peninsula.

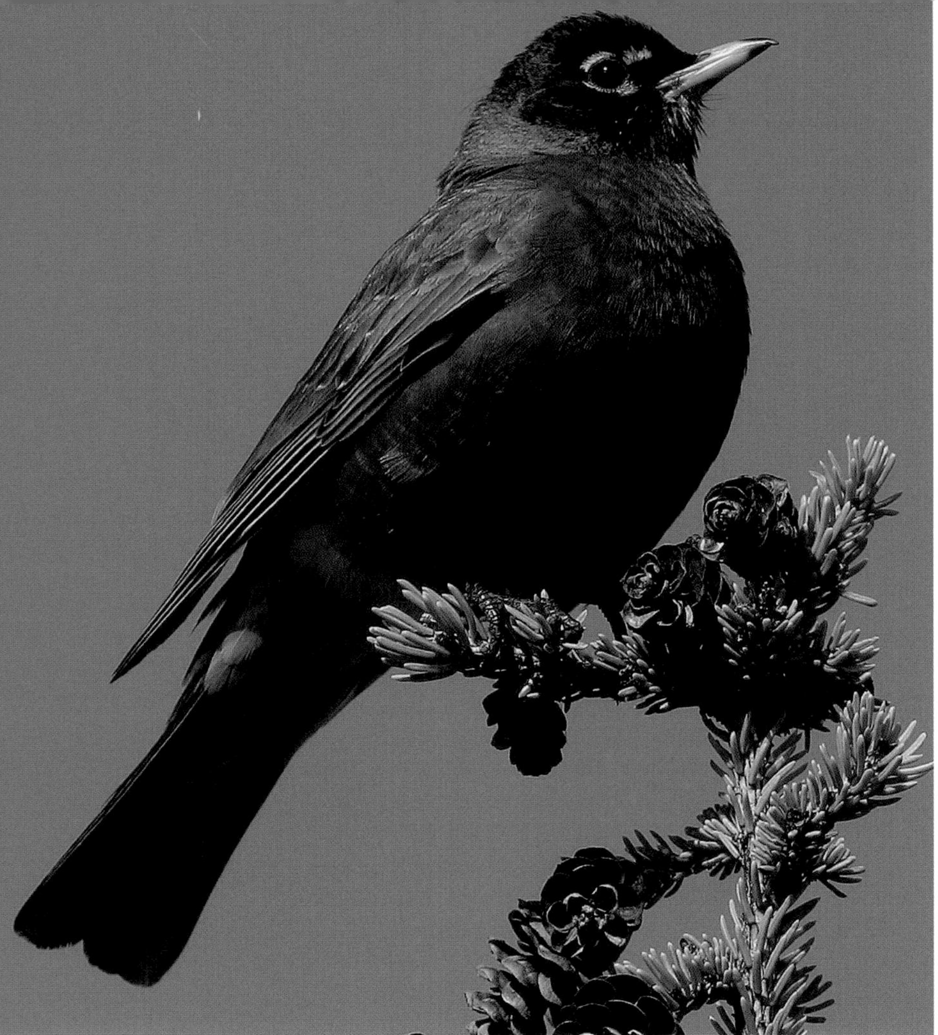

American Robin, Great Slave Lake, North West Territories, Canada.

Strange relationships

The reproductive strategy of the Dunnock is among the oddest of all birds as they exhibit monogamy, polygyny (i.e. one male and two or more females), polyandry (one female and two or more males) and polygynandry (two or more males and two or more females). An individual bird may move from one regime to another during the course of a season if more than one brood is raised. The birds also practise a curious form of sperm competition, a female displaying her cloaca to a male as she quickly wags her raised tail. The male will peck at the cloaca, eventually stimulating the release of a sperm package deposited by a previous male. Copulation then takes place. The process enhances the male's chances of paternity, but also keeps several males interested in providing for the female, who will repeat the behaviour several times during a prolonged (up to ten-day) mating period.

Dunnock

Prunella modularis

L: 13–15cm. WS: 19–22cm. W: 15–25g.

Breeding male has a grey head with brown cheek patches, the latter finely streaked darker. The upperparts are brown, streaked darker, the streaking forming distinct lines. The breast is grey (as the head), the belly paler (even whitish), the flanks buff with darker streaking. Breeding female is as male, but duller.

Dunnocks are birds of the Arctic fringe, but breed in northern Scandinavia (though not on the northern Kola Peninsula) and around the White Sea. In winter the birds move to southern Europe.

Siberian Accentor

Prunella montanella

L: 13–15cm. WS: 20–24cm. W: 20–25g.

Less drab than other accentors; breeding adult has a dark brown crown and cheek patch, the rest of the head being pale rufous or rusty yellow. The throat and breast are also pale rufous or rusty yellow, the belly paler, the flanks streaked orange-brown. The upperparts are brown with darker streaking, similar to the Dunnock.

Siberian Accentors breed across Russia east of the Urals to Kamchatka, but only to the treeline (both latitudinal and altitudinal). In winter the birds move to Korea and eastern China.

THRUSHES AND CHATS

The *Turdidae* are a large and widespread family of birds which includes some of the best-known species to northern peoples – the Eurasian Robin *Erithacus rubecula*, American Robin, Eurasian Blackbird *Turdus merula* and the bluebirds. The family is, however, diverse, the many species having few characteristics in common. The birds are principally invertebrate feeders, supplementing this with fruit. Many species are excellent singers (the Nightingale *Luscinia megarhynchos* being famous for its voice), males calling to establish territories and for pair formation. Pair bonds are usually monogamous and seasonal. There are usually 4–6 eggs, these laid in a well-built nest and normally incubated by the female only, though both birds usually contribute to the care of the chicks. The summer and winter plumages of the species described here are similar.

Redwing

Turdus iliacus

L: 19–23cm. WS: 32–35cm. W: 50–80g.

Breeding adult has a dark brown or grey-brown crown, a white supercilium, dark brown lores and cheeks and a white

Redwing, Varangerfjord, Norway.

throat finely streaked brown. The upperparts are grey-brown, the flight feathers darker. The underparts are white or pale cream, heavily streaked dark brown on the breast and flanks. The undertail is grey-brown. The underwing has rusty coverts, merging with rusty flank patches.

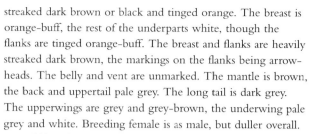

Redwings breed on Iceland, in northern Fennoscandia and across Russia (though not in Chukotka or Kamchatka). Some Icelandic birds are resident, but in general the birds move to northern Europe for the winter.

American Robin

Turdus migratorius

L: 22–26cm. WS: 35–40cm. W: 65–85g.

American Robin is the largest Nearctic thrush. Breeding adult is a striking bird, with a dark grey head and white-streaked throat. The breast, belly and flanks are red, the vent and undertail white. The upperparts are grey, the tail dark grey with white tips to the outer feathers.

American Robins breed throughout North America, including Alaska (though uncommon in the north), the Yukon and much of North West Territories. Range is more southerly in eastern Canada, but includes the southern shore of Hudson Bay and southern Quebec and Labrador. In winter the birds are seen in southern United States and Central America.

Naumann's Thrush

Turdus naumanni

L: 21–24cm. WS: 36–39cm. W: 65–85g.

Breeding male has a buff-speckled dark brown crown and white supercilium. The face is white, with brown cheek patches. There is a dark brown breast-band. The rest of the underparts are white, heavily marked with dark brown arrowheads. The upperparts are chestnut, mottled with black, the wings more evenly chestnut. Breeding females are as males but duller overall. The bird described here is the subspecies *eunomus,* which breeds to the north of nominate *naumanni*; *eunomus* is markedly different from *naumanni* and is often called the Dusky Thrush, particularly in North America where it is a casual visitor.

Naumann's Thrushes breed in Russia from the Yenisey to central Chukotka and throughout Kamchatka. In winter the birds fly to south-east Asia.

Fieldfare

Turdus pilaris

L: 22–27cm. WS: 39–42cm. W: 80–120g.

Breeding males are highly distinctive. The head is blue-grey apart from a white supercilium and throat, the latter heavily streaked dark brown or black and tinged orange. The breast is orange-buff, the rest of the underparts white, though the flanks are tinged orange-buff. The breast and flanks are heavily streaked dark brown, the markings on the flanks being arrowheads. The belly and vent are unmarked. The mantle is brown, the back and uppertail pale grey. The long tail is dark grey. The upperwings are grey and grey-brown, the underwing pale grey and white. Breeding female is as male, but duller overall.

Fieldfares breed in northern Fennoscandia and in western and central Russia, though not to the north coast. Has bred in Iceland, but not established. In winter some Scandinavian birds fly to Iceland (where some may remain to breed), others, and Russian breeders, fly to southern Europe and to southern Russia and central Asia.

Defending the nest

Fieldfares nest colonially, a very unusual habit among thrushes. The reason is a highly coordinated defensive system against predators. When a potential predator is spotted the birds fly towards it. Each in turn then dives at the intruder, letting loose a bomb of excrement. The bird's aim is usually good, with the intruder rapidly becoming peppered with spots of excrement. On a predatory bird such spotting can be dangerous as it affects the aerodynamics of the feathers, and on terrestrial predators it can require a lot of grooming to remove. Not surprisingly the strategy is extremely effective at persuading predators to retreat. It is so effective that other birds choose to nest close to Fieldfares and so benefit from the defence it brings.

Grey-cheeked Thrush

Catharus minimus

L: 17–19cm. WS: 28–32cm. W: 26–34g.

Breeding adult has olive-brown or brown-grey heads with grey-buff cheeks, these occasionally finely streaked paler. The throat is white, separated from the cheeks by a dark stripe. The breast is buff, heavily spotted dark brown. The rest of the underparts are white, smudged brownish-grey on the flanks and belly. The upperparts and tail are uniformly olive-brown, the flight feathers darker.

Grey-cheeked Thrushes breed throughout northern Alaska and the Yukon, then more southerly to the southern shores of Hudson Bay and in most of Quebec and Labrador. Also breeds in small numbers in Chukotka. In winter the birds are seen in northern South America.

Varied Thrush

Ixoreus naevius

L: 23–25cm. WS: 38–42cm. W: 75–85g.

Attractive birds; breeding male has a lilac crown and nape, an orange-brown supercilium, a black forehead and a broad black eye-stripe. The throat and upper breast are orange-brown, becoming paler towards the vent. The flanks are smudged lilac. The upperparts are lilac, the tail dark lilac-black. Breeding female is as male, but duller.

Naumann's Thrush, Kolyma Delta, Russia.

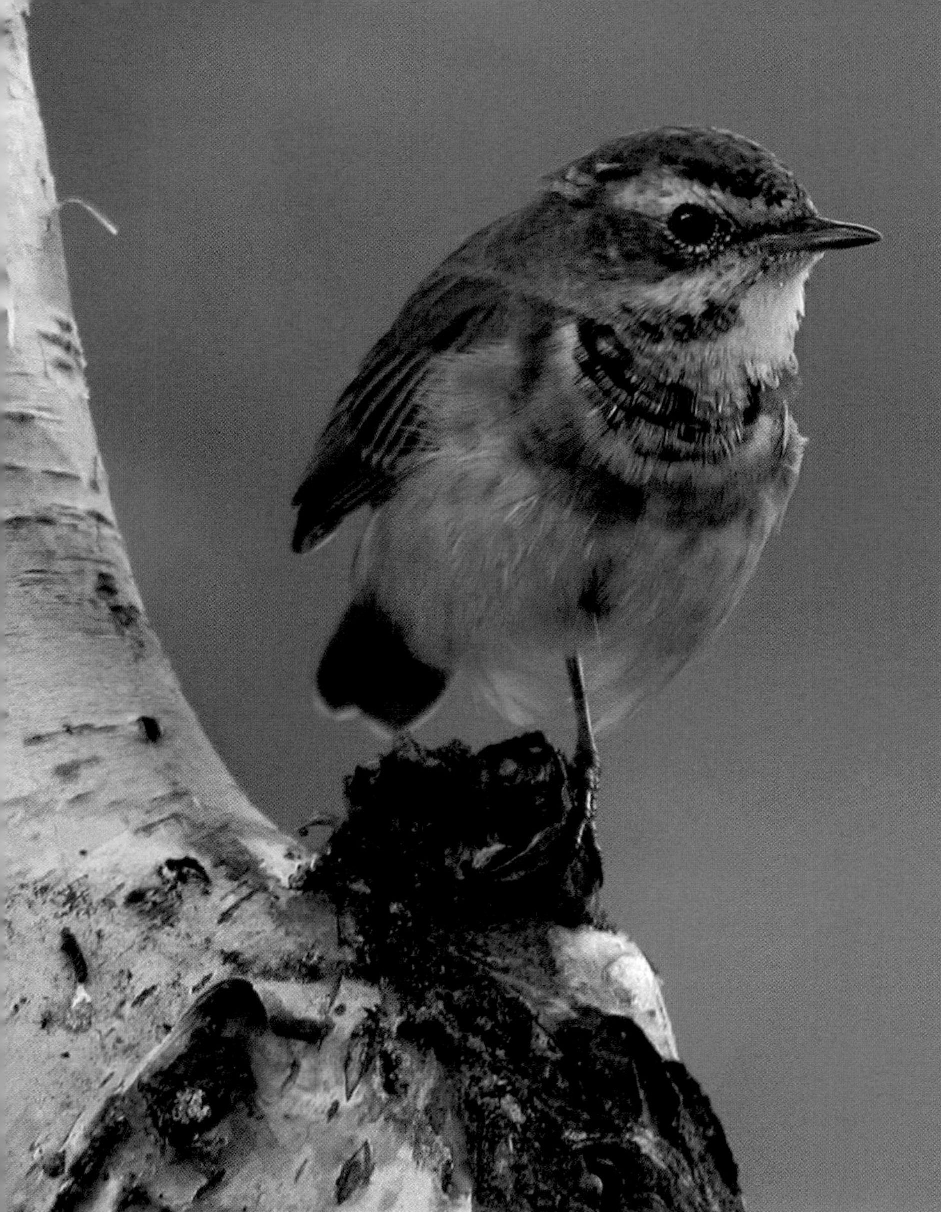

Male Bluethroat, Dovre, Norway.

Varied Thrushes breed throughout Alaska (apart from the extreme north) and in the Yukon and western North West Territories. In winter the birds move to the west coast of the United States.

Bluethroat

Luscinia svevica

L: 12–14cm. WS: 20–23cm. W: 15–23g.

A most beautiful bird, but one that is often elusive. Breeding male has a grey-brown crown, forehead and nape, white supercilium, chestnut upper cheek and pale grey lower cheek, the latter blending into the nape. The throat and upper breast are metallic blue, enclosing an orange-chestnut patch. The breast is bordered by bands of black and orange-chestnut. The rest of the underparts are pale buff or cream. The upperparts are grey-brown. Breeding female is as male, but throat and breast are white with a chestnut breast-band. Some females show two breast-bands, one blue, the other chestnut.

Bluethroats breed in northern Fennoscandia and across Russia to Chukotka, but rarely to the north coast. Also breeds in small numbers in western Alaska. In winter the birds move to the coasts of the Mediterranean and to central Africa.

Northern Wheatear

Oenanthe oenanthe

L: 14–16cm. WS: 26–32. W: 20–28g.

Breeding male has a pale blue-grey crown and nape, a white forehead and narrow white supercilium. The throat is pale orange-buff, the breast paler, the rest of the underparts white. The upperparts are pale blue-grey, the central tail black, the outer feathers white. Adult female has a grey-brown crown, nape and upperparts. The underparts are usually a richer buff but they may be paler than the male. The upperwing is dark brown, the underwing as the male, but washed buff.

Northern Wheatears breed on Greenland and Iceland, irregularly on Svalbard, and from northern Scandinavia to Chukotka, north to the coast in most areas, and on the southern island of Novaya Zemlya. Breeds in western Alaska but rare in the north, and in the eastern Canada High Arctic (Baffin and Bylot islands, southern Ellesmere Island and northern Quebec and Labrador).

Common Redstart

Phoenicurus phoenicurus

L: 13–15cm. WS: 20–25. W: 14–20g.

Breeding adult has a slate-grey crown, nape, back and mantle. The rest of the head is dark grey apart from a white forehead and supercilium. The breast is orange-chestnut, the rest of the underparts paler. The rump and outer tail are orange-chestnut, the central tail dark grey. The upperwings are grey-brown, the underwings pale chestnut. Breeding female has duller underparts, the head and upperparts being brown-buff.

Northern Wheatear, Skaftafell National Park, Iceland.

The Northern Wheatears of Greenland are a subspecies (*O. o. leucorhoa*). The birds are larger than the nominate, their underparts a richer colour. The photograph was taken in west Greenland.

WILLOW WARBLER
Phylloscopus trochilus
L: 10–12cm. WS: 16–21cm. W: 7–11g.
Breeding adult patterned as Arctic Warbler but with grey-brown crown and upperparts, cream or pale yellow-cream supercilium, and grey-brown eye-stripe. The underparts are cream with a pale yellow tinge, particularly on the breast. Unlike the Arctic Warbler, the underparts are unmarked.

Boreal, but seen in forest-tundra. Willow Warblers breed in northern Scandinavia and across Russia to Chukotka. In winter the population flies to sub-Saharan Africa, a very long flight for the birds of eastern Russia.

Migrating Wheatears
Given the circumpolar distribution of the Northern Wheatear it would be thought that in winter the birds would be found equally well spread around the globe. But this is not the case, since the entire population flies to central Africa. This curiously asymmetric winter distribution indicates the original breeding range of the bird – it was a northern European species that has spread east and west. This accounts for the Nearctic distribution, where the bird is absent from a huge central section of the continent.

A boreal, Arctic-fringe species. Common Redstarts breed in northern Fennoscandia and in western Russia to the north coast around the White Sea. In winter the birds move to equatorial Africa, the Black and Caspian seas and Arabia.

WARBLERS

Only two species of warblers are northern breeders in the Palearctic, and only one of these is a true Arctic dweller. In each case both male and female, and summer and winter plumages are similar.

ARCTIC WARBLER
Phylloscopus borealis
L: 11–13cm. WS: 17–22cm. W: 8–11g.
Breeding adult has a dark olive crown, a broad pale greenish-yellow supercilium and a dark olive-brown eye-stripe, each stripe extending to the nape. The cheeks are olive-green. The throat is pale olive, the rest of the underparts cream, the breast and upper belly streaked olive, the flanks smudged olive-brown. The upperparts are uniformly olive-green, the upper wings having two thin, delicate white bars.

Essentially boreal, but seen in forest-tundra, Arctic Warblers breed in northern Scandinavia and across Russia to Chukotka, though infrequently to the north coast. Breeds on Kamchatka and the Commander islands. Has bred on Wrangel Island. Also breeds in western Alaska. In winter the birds are seen in the forests of south-east Asia.

TITS AND CHICKADEES

Tits are small passerines with pale heads beneath dark or coloured crowns. The bill is short and pointed, ideal for catching the birds' main prey of insects, though as any European garden-owner will know the birds also feed on nuts and seeds, particularly in winter when insects are hard to come by. Tit chicks are fed exclusively on insects and insect larvae (requiring upwards of 10,000 individual items before fledging), taking seeds only when they accompany their parents to local gardens. The Nearctic chickadees look very similar and have a similar diet, but are not exclusively tree hole or box nesters. All the birds described here are boreal and, consequently, Arctic-fringe species. The plumages of these species – male and female, and summer and winter – are similar.

GREAT TIT
Parus major
L: 13–15cm. WS: 20–22cm. W: 16–22g.
Breeding adult has a black crown, nape, collar and throat, the rest of the face white. The black of the throat extends as a

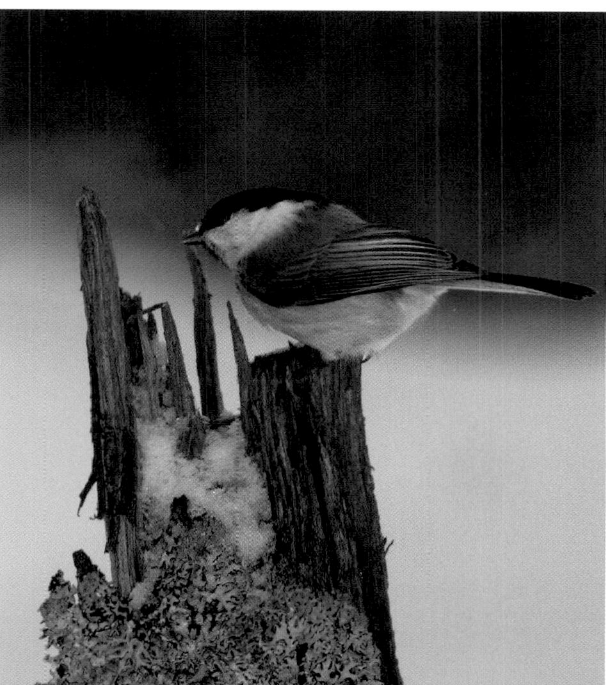

Willow Tit, northern Norway.

diminishing black line across the underside to the vent. The underparts are yellow. The back is greenish-yellow, grading into a blue tail. The wings are blue and dark grey.

Familiar to garden-owners in southern Europe, the Great Tit breeds surprisingly far north, reaching the northern coast of Fennoscandia. Resident in areas well north of the Arctic Circle in Scandinavia.

Willow Tit

Poecile montanus

L: 11–13cm. WS: 18–21cm. W: 10–12g.

Breeding adult has a black crown (which covers the nape, reaching the mantle) and bib, the rest of the head being white. The underparts are white, tinged buff on the flanks and towards the vent. The upperparts are grey-brown. The birds of Kamchatka are a subspecies *kamtschatkensis*; they are very pale, appearing all white apart from the crown and bib.

Willow Tits breed in northern Scandinavia and across Russia to Kamchatka, but only to the treeline.

Siberian Tit (Greyheaded Chickadee)

Poecile cincta

L: 13–14cm. WS: 19–21cm. W: 11–13g.

Breeding adult has a dark brown crown and nape. The rest of the head is white apart from a narrow black line through the eye to the forehead, and a black bib on the throat. The underparts are white, with rusty brown breast sides, flanks, vent sides and undertail coverts. The upperparts are chestnut, the tail dark grey.

Siberian Tits breed in northern Scandinavia and across Russia to Chukotka, but not to the north coast; also in Kamchatka. Breeds in small numbers in western and central Alaska. Resident or nomadic.

The hardy Siberian Tit

Resident Siberian Tits can survive winter temperatures as low as -60°C. At temperatures of about -40°C the birds take shelter in a tree hole, tuck in their heads and feet and fluff out their feathers. The feathers have large numbers of barbs and barbules (up to 100cm³), allowing an insulating layer of still air to form. As the temperature falls the bird drops its body temperature by up to 10°C, entering a state of torpor. In order to maintain normal body temperature and to build the resources necessary to survive periods of torpor, the bird must consume around 7g of food daily (55–65% of its body weight), a quantity that must be foraged in a day as short as 4 hours.

Boreal Chickadee

Poecile hudsonica

L: 13–14cm. WS: 19–21cm. W: 11–13g.

Similar to the Siberian Tit, breeding adult having a paler cap, larger bib and a grey nape. In general the underparts are overall more rusty.

The Boreal Chickadee breeds in central Alaska, but rare in the west. Also in Yukon, then more southerly across Canada to the southern shores of Hudson Bay, and in southern Quebec and Labrador. Resident or nomadic.

Black-capped Chickadee

Poecile atricapillus

L: 11–13cm. WS: 18–20cm. W: 10–12g.

Breeding adult has a black cap and a large black bib. The rest of the face and underparts are white, with rusty smudging to the flanks and vent. The upperparts are mid-grey. The underwing is paler grey.

Black-capped Chickadees breed in northern Alaska, but uncommon except in the central state; more southerly throughout Canada. Resident or nomadic.

SHRIKES

Shrikes are predatory birds, the larger species taking amphibians, small reptiles and birds, and even small mammals as well as insects. They are noted for impaling prey on thorns, a caching technique, the kill being revisited when live prey is scarce. This has occasionally led to the birds being called 'butcher birds'.

Great Grey Shrike (Northern Shrike)

Lanius excubitor

L: 23–26cm. WS: 35–42cm. W: 55–75g.

Breeding male has a grey crown, nape, mantle and back. There is a prominent black mask from the forehead across the eyes. The stout grey bill has a hooked tip. The underparts are white. The long tail is black, the two outer feathers white. The upperwing is black and dark grey, with a prominent white central patch. The underwing is paler. Breeding female as male but the underparts are often faintly streaked. Summer and winter plumages are similar.

A boreal species, though seen to the forest edge. Great Grey Shrike breeds in northern Scandinavia and across Russia to southern Chukotka. Breeds throughout Alaska (though is uncommon everywhere), and in northern Yukon, but then more southerly across Canada to the southern shores of Hudson Bay and southern Quebec and Labrador. In winter Eurasian birds move to southern Europe and Asia. Some southern Alaskan birds are resident; northern birds migrate to the southern United States.

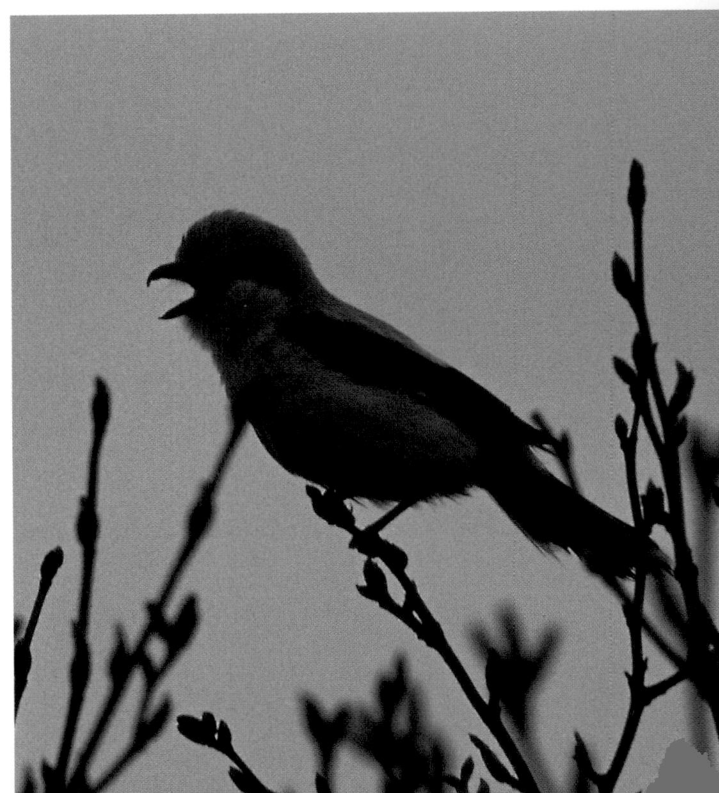

Even in fading light, with colours disappearing, the profile of the Great Grey Shrike is unmistakeable, Alaska Peninsula.

Raven in flight above the Barren Lands of Nunavut, Canada.

CROWS

The crows are among the most familiar of birds: large, noisy and opportunistic, they are well known to people throughout the world. They are also renowned for their intelligence, being good puzzle-solvers and able to use simple tools to obtain food.

The corvids include colonial nesters (e.g. the Rook *Corvus frugilegus*) and co-operative breeders, with last year's young helping to feed this year's brood (several Nearctic jays and crows), but the Arctic and Arctic-fringe breeders are solitary nesters. The pair bond is monogamous (though male Common Magpies are promiscuous) and life-long or long-lived. The (usually 3–6) eggs are incubated by the female only (but both birds in the case of the Spotted Nutcracker), with the chicks cared for and fed by both parents. An old saying maintains that 'a crow lives three times longer than a man, and a raven lives three times longer than a crow', but in reality most crows do not make it past 10 years of age. Yet despite

Intelligent crows

As well as being able to learn, so that once a problem has been solved a bird can apply the solution when faced with the problem again, experiments also indicate that crows have excellent memories, being able to recall the location of thousands of cached food items (and to know which sort of food is in which location), and to show evidence of forward planning based on past events. The latter is fascinating as it implies self-awareness. In one experiment, a crow that watched others cache food and then retrieved it for himself (i.e. stole it) always ensured that no other bird was watching when he cached his own food, changing the location if he thought he had been overlooked. That implies that the crow was capable of understanding the possible actions of others based on his own behaviour. This 'theory of mind' is something that human children do not develop until they are about three years old, and is linked to self-awareness.

Opposite page

Top left
Ravens, Ytre Ryfylke, Norway. The wedge-shaped tail is diagnostic of the species when the birds are in flight.

Top right
Young Carrion Crows in a nest on an old observation tower, Starichkov Island, Russia. The chicks were being fed, in part, on eggs gathered from the Ancient Murrelet and seabird colonies on the western side of the island.

Crows in history

Crows, particularly the Raven, the largest and most powerful of the corvids (and also the largest passerine) have been incorporated into myths and stories from ancient times. They appear in the epic of Gilgamesh, in the Bible, and in the legends of the Romans, Greeks and Celts. One Celtic myth is the likely source of the tale that if the Ravens leave the Tower of London, Britain will fall. In Japanese mythology crows were created to save mankind, seeing off a monster who threatened to swallow the Sun. Crows are common, too, in Chinese myths and stories.

The Vikings associated the Raven with Odin, the main god of their pantheon, who was known as the Lord of Ravens. The Raven could be friendly: in *Flokki's Saga* a released Raven leads Norse settlers to Iceland. But the bird was also associated with death, an association that probably arose from the birds feeding on battlefield dead. Viking chiefs used the standard of a Raven with outstretched wings as a battle emblem, symbolising the future of the enemy as forage for crows.

In medieval Europe the birds also fed on the gibbeted remains of the executed, reinforcing the association with death and encouraging the belief that crows – already sinister because of their black plumage – were birds of ill-omen; in Scandinavia a Raven croaking outside a house foretold a death in the family. This association has endured; in Edgar Allen Poe's famous poem *The Raven* the bird again signifies foreboding.

For the native peoples of the Arctic, crows were invariably seen in a positive light. Ravens are at the heart of the creation myths of the Inuit, Chukchi and Koryak, suggesting a tale inherited from common ancestor. Shamans often took Ravens as their familiars and the birds are frequently seen on the totem poles of the Tlingit and Haida peoples of southern Alaska. The Inuit also believe that the Raven helps them with their hunt; if a raven flies overhead an Inuk will ask it if it has seen Caribou or other prey, and if it has the Raven will dip its wing to point the direction.

this, sexual maturity is not reached until the bird is 6 or 7 in some species, though an age of 2 or 3 is more usual. The plumages of male and female, and in summer and winter, are similar in the species described here.

Of the species listed below only the Raven is a truly Arctic species, the remainder occurring to the treeline, though some are occasionally seen on the tundra.

(Northern) Raven

Corvus corax

L: 54–67cm. WS: 120–150cm. W: 1.0–1.35kg. ♀>♂.
Breeding adults are glossy black with a purple, purplish–blue, or even purplish-green sheen. The Raven's wedge-shaped tail is diagnostic.

The Raven breeds throughout Greenland, on Iceland, in northern Scandinavia and across Russia to Chukotka, north to the coast except on the Taimyr Peninsula. May also breed on Wrangel Island. Breeds throughout Alaska and across Canada, north to the coast and on the Arctic islands north to southern Ellesmere. Resident or dispersive.

The call of the Raven

The Inuit claim that the call of the Raven is *kak*. Their story is that the first Raven was actually a man. Before setting out on a hunting trip with friends, the man, nervous that the blankets (*kak* in Inuktituk) would be forgotten, repeatedly told his companions to look out for them. So fed up did the others become that they deliberately forgot the blankets and then sent him back to fetch them. In his panic the man ran, then flew and then became a Raven, still calling *kak*.

Carrion Crow

Corvus corone

L: 45–50cm. WS: 90–105cm. W: 450–650g. ♀>♂.
Two forms of crow are found in Eurasia. The Carrion Crow is overall black with a purple, blue or green sheen. The Hooded Crow has a black head, neck, wings and tail. The rest of the plumage is grey apart from a black 'splash' on the breast. Although the two birds are usually classified as subspecies, many authorities consider the two are separate species.

Hooded Crows breed in Scandinavia and across Russia to the Yenisey, with black Carrion Crows further east to Kamchatka; hybridisation occurs where the races meet. Resident or dispersive.

Spotted Nutcracker

Nucifraga caryocatactes

L: 32–35cm. WS: 50–55cm. W: 100–180g.
Breeding adult is dark chocolate brown, but the underparts and upperbody are heavily spotted white, the vent is white and there is a white terminal band to the tail.

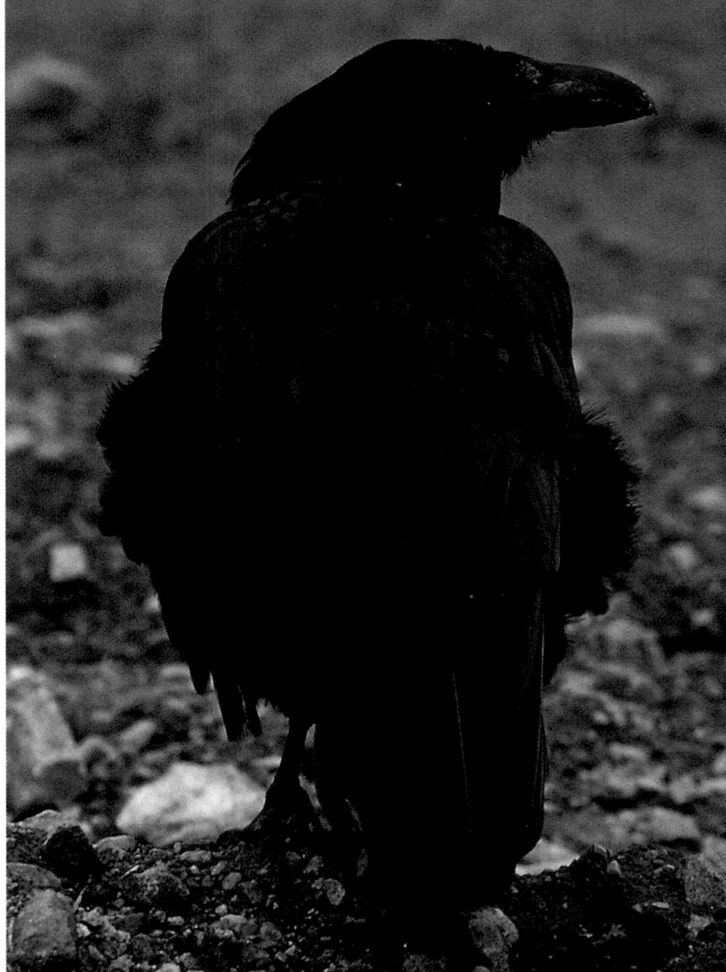

In certain lights the Raven's plumage has a wonderful purple-blue or purple-green sheen. Unalaska, Aleutian Islands, Alaska. North American and Greenlandic Ravens are a subspecies, *C. c. principalis*.

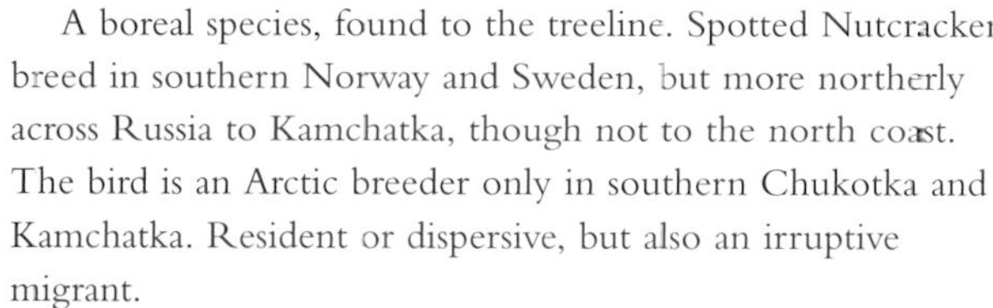

A boreal species, found to the treeline. Spotted Nutcrackers breed in southern Norway and Sweden, but more northerly across Russia to Kamchatka, though not to the north coast. The bird is an Arctic breeder only in southern Chukotka and Kamchatka. Resident or dispersive, but also an irruptive migrant.

(Common) Magpie

Pica pica

Length: 40–50cm (tail 20–30cm). Wingspan: 50–60cm. Weight: 190–250g. ♀>♂.

Breeding adults are black, with blue or green sheen, apart from a white belly and scapulars. The outer wing is black and white. The long tail has a green sheen.

Magpies breed in northern Scandinavia, then more southerly across Russia to the Sea of Okhotsk, and also in southern Chukotka and in Kamchatka. Resident, with limited dispersal.

Black-billed Magpie

Pica hudsonia

Length: 40–50cm (tail 20–30). Wingspan 50–60cm. Weight: 190–250g. ♀>♂.

Breeding adults are as the Common Magpie. Differences between the Nearctic and Palearctic birds are minimal and some authorities consider them conspecific.

Black-billed Magpies breed in central and southern Alaska and in south-western Canada. Resident, with limited dispersal.

Hooded form of the Carrion Crow, Randaberg, Norway.

In the twilight of a winter's day at Kiruna, northern Sweden, a Magpie wrestles with a discarded fast food wrapper to search out a last remaining morsel. The birds are opportunistic feeders which gives them a massive advantage during the long Arctic winter.

Grey Jay
Perisoreus canadensis
L: 27–32cm. W: 40–45cm. W: 65–80g. ♀>♂.
Breeding adult has a dark grey crown apart from a white or pale buff forehead. The rest of the head is pale grey, as are the underparts. The upperparts are dark grey, occasionally grey-brown. The tail feathers have white tips.

Grey Jays breed in central and western Alaska (though are uncommon in the latter), central Yukon and North West Territories, then southerly to the southern shores of Hudson Bay, and in southern Quebec and Labrador. Resident or dispersive.

Siberian Jay
Perisoreus infaustus
L: 26–29cm. WS: 40–45cm. W: 80–100g. ♀>♂.
Breeding adult is an attractive bird with a black crown, with the rest of the head grey. The breast is grey, merging to pale orange-grey belly and vent. The mantle and back are grey, the rump rusty-brown. The tail is rusty-brown, apart from black central feathers. The wings are grey and rusty-brown.

Siberian Jays breed in northern Scandinavia and across Russia to the border of Chukotka. Resident or dispersive.

STARLINGS

Starlings belong to the *Sturnidae* family which also includes the Mynas, famous for their mimicry. Starlings are medium-sized, compact birds with an eclectic diet. They are usually gregarious, breeding in colonies, feeding in flocks and roosting communally. To many urban dwellers used to observing a noisy, often belligerent flock of Common Starlings, the idea that they might also be Arctic dwellers seems ridiculous, yet the birds breed both in Iceland and northern Scandinavia (though more southerly in Russia), and they are increasing their range in North America. In April 1890 some 80 birds were released in New York's Central Park. They had spread into a 400km semi-circle from the coast by about 1910, but then the spread accelerated: by 1970 they had reached the borders of the Arctic throughout North America, with climate rather than population size acting as a limit to the species' expansion. The species now breeds in southern Alaska (though it is rare there), in central Yukon and North West Territories, around Hudson Bay's central and southern shores and in southern Quebec and Labrador. Rising temperatures will inevitably lead to a further northward expansion of the range.

Common Starling
Sturnus vulgaris
L: 19–23cm. WS: 37–42cm. W: 70–95g.
Breeding adult is black with a sheen that varies from purple to green with incident light. Plumage speckled with white spots, these often difficult to see in summer, but prominent in winter. For range see above.

Siberian Jay, Saariselka, Finland.

WOOD (OR NEW WORLD) WARBLERS

The wood warblers of the Nearctic share features with Palearctic warblers, to which they are only distantly related, such as having straight, short, pointed bills ideal for taking insects (though most also take fruit in winter), but they are flamboyant in plumage rather than drab. Indeed, they are the most colourful of the passerines of the Arctic fringe and Low Arctic, and a true delight. Male wood warblers sing to establish a territory and attract a mate, although there are usually some visual displays as well. The pair bond is monogamous and seasonal, but some males with exceptional territories may be polygamous. The 3–6 eggs are incubated by the female. Chicks are brooded by the female, but fed by both parents. Summer and winter plumages are similar for the species described here.

Yellow-rumped Warbler on its way to feeding this year's chicks, Great Slave Lake, Canada.

Orange-crowned Warbler

Vermivora celata

L: 11–13cm. WS: 16–18cm. W: 8–11g.

Breeding adult has the orange crown of the name, but this is often difficult to discern against the olive-green head colour. The underparts are yellow, streaked with olive, the upperparts olive-yellow, the flight feathers grey-olive. However, there is variation in colour across the range, with some birds being overall grey (darker above than below) to the east and some in Alaska being dull brownish-olive.

Orange-crowned Warblers breed in southern Alaska (but uncommon in the west), Yukon, north-west North West Territories, around the southern shores of Hudson Bay and in southern Quebec and Labrador. In winter the birds are seen in the southern United States, in Central America and in northern South America.

Yellow-rumped Warbler

Dendroica coronata

L: 13–15cm. WS: 21–24cm. W: 11–17g.

Breeding male has a yellow skull-cap, the rest of the head black and grey, but with a white throat. The underparts are white, streaked black on the breast and with yellow patches on the flanks. The upperparts are grey with black streaks, and the prominent yellow rump of the name. Breeding female is a little duller overall and lacks the yellow skull-cap. Northern birds of the nominate race *coronata* are known as 'myrtle warblers' because of their exclusive winter diet of *Myrica* spp. fruits (the three southern races are sometimes referred to collectively as 'Audubon's' warbler). The two groups were once regarded as separate species. Arctic birds were once thought to be a separate subspecies, *hooveri*, though this is now considered part of the nominate.

Yellow-rumped Warblers breed in west and central Alaska, central Yukon and North West Territories, around the southern shores of Hudson Bay and in southern Quebec and Labrador. In winter the birds are seen in the southern United States, in Central America and on Caribbean islands.

Yellow Warbler

Dendroica petechia

L: 11–13cm. WS: 17–20cm. W: 8–12g.

Breeding male has a yellow head, the upper head olive-yellow, as are the rest of the upperparts, the wings darker than the body and tail. The underparts are yellow with red streaks. Breeding female as male, but lacks the red streaking of the underparts.

Yellow Warblers breed throughout Alaska (but rare in the north), Yukon and North West Territories, but rare in Nunavut. Breeds on the southern shores of Hudson Bay and in southern Quebec and Labrador. In winter northern birds join resident birds on Caribbean islands and in northern South America.

Blackpoll Warbler

Dendroica striata

L: 13–15cm. WS: 20–23cm. W: 10–16g.

Breeding male has a black crown, the rest of the head white with black streaks except on the cheeks. The underparts are

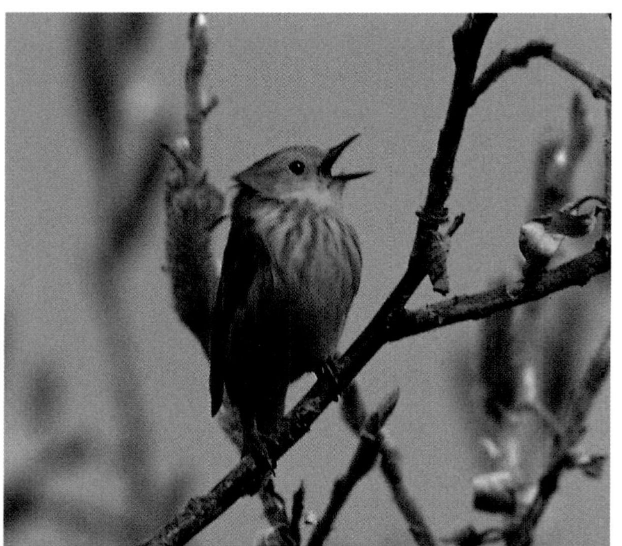

Far left

Yellow Warbler, Churchill, Manitoba, Canada.

Left

Blackpoll Warbler, Churchill, Manitoba, Canada.

It is early in the year and both birds are males, singing to stake a territorial claim.

white, streaked black, except on the vent. The upperparts are grey with black streaks and white barring. Breeding female as male, but lacking the black crown; also, underparts cream with more diffuse streaking.

Blackpoll Warbler breeds throughout Alaska (but rare in the north), across the Yukon and North West Territories (though not to the north coast except at the Mackenzie delta), around south-western and southern Hudson Bay, and in southern Quebec and Labrador. In winter the birds fly to Central and South America, some reaching southern Chile and Argentina.

Northern Waterthrush

Seiurus noveboracensis

L: 12–15cm. WS: 21–25cm. W: 16–20g.

Breeding adult has a dark olive-brown crown and nape, buff supercilium, dark olive-brown eye-stripe and paler cheek patch. The underparts are pale yellow, brighter on the flanks, with dark streaking to the breast and belly. The upperparts are uniformly dark olive-brown.

Northern Waterthrushes breed in southern Alaska, throughout the Yukon, then more southerly to the southern shores of Hudson Bay and in southern Quebec and Labrador. In winter the birds are seen in Central America, on Caribbean islands and in northern South America.

Wilson's Warbler

Wilsonia pusilla

L: 11–13cm. WS: 18–20cm. W: 7–9g.

Breeding male has a black skull-cap. The face and underparts are yellow, the nape and upperparts olive. The tail is olive. Breeding female as male, but lacks the black skull-cap.

Wilson's Warblers breed in southern Alaska (but uncommon in the west), Yukon, north-west North West Territories, around the southern shores of Hudson Bay and in southern Quebec and Labrador. In winter the birds fly to Central America and northern South America.

OLD WORLD SPARROWS

Throughout the world sparrows (members of the family *Passeridae*) are perhaps the best known of all birds because of their association with humans. It is claimed that the House Sparrow has such a close association with humans that some birds have never experienced a 'natural' environment. Due to deliberate introductions the species now breeds on every continent except Antarctica. After the introduction of three birds to a grain elevator in Kamchatka the population had risen to more than 100,000 within 20 years.

House Sparrow

Passer domesticus

L: 14–16cm. WS: 21–25cm. W: 25–40g.

Breeding male has grey crown and cheeks, with a black stripe from bill to eye, this continuing as a chestnut curve linking to the nape. The underparts are grey, with a ragged black bib from throat to upper breast and fine streaking to the belly and flanks. The upperparts are mottled chestnut, dark brown and grey. In both summer and winter females are duller overall and lack the black bib. In winter males are similar to females.

House Sparrows breed in northern Scandinavia, Iceland and Russia wherever there is human habitation. Resident.

NEW WORLD SPARROWS AND BUNTINGS

'Bunting' is an old English word and would have been taken across the Atlantic by early settlers. This resulted in some species being labelled inappropriately as buntings, and a few of these names have stuck. The situation was further confused by the settlers referring to some species that looked similar to birds with which they were familiar by their Old World name. The classic example is the American Robin, named after its similarity to the Old World, red-breasted Robin *Erithacus rubecula*, but many birds were also named 'sparrows'. In fact the New World Sparrows are members of the *Emberizidae* family which also includes the true buntings.

Emberizids evolved in the Nearctic, where most species still reside. They spread to Asia by way of the Bering Straits, and then continued as far as Europe. The birds have the stout bills characteristic of seed eaters. Males sing to establish territories, but usually have an additional repertoire of visual displays. The pair bond is generally monogamous and seasonal, with the notable exception of Smith's Longspur. The 3–5 eggs are incubated by the female. Chicks are usually brooded only by the female, though are fed by both birds.

Little Bunting

Emberiza pusilla

L: 13–15cm. WS: 20–23cm. W: 13–18g.

Breeding adult has a black crown and nape with a distinctive central chestnut streak, the rest of the head and throat chestnut, with some black streaking. The underparts are white with dark brown streaks. The upperparts are brown or grey-brown with dark brownish-black streaking. Summer and winter plumages are similar.

An Arctic-fringe species; Little Buntings breed in northern Finland and across Russia to the borders of Chukotka, but not to the north coast. In winter the birds are seen in a band from northern India to eastern China.

Common Reed Bunting

Emberiza schoeniclus

L: 14–17cm. WS: 24–28cm. W: 16–24g.

Breeding male has a black head with a white collar, and white patch below the bill base. The throat is black and there is a black bib on the upper breast. The rest of the underparts are white with fine brown flecking on the flanks. The upperparts

Male Common Reed Bunting, Zhupanova River, southern Kamchatka, Russia.

are chestnut, streaked with black and buff. Breeding female lacks the head pattern, having a brown crown, finely streaked black, grey-brown supercilium to the nape, and brown cheeks. Breeding female has white patch below the bill base, but the throat is grey. The underparts are more heavily streaked and the upperparts are buff and chestnut, with much less black. In winter males lose the striking black head pattern, looking very similar to females.

An Arctic-fringe species, Common Reed Buntings breed in northern Fennoscandia and across Russia to the Lena River (but not to the north coast), and in Kamchatka. In winter the birds fly to south-east Europe and to southern Asia, including China and Japan.

Lapland Bunting (Lapland Longspur)

Calcarius lapponicus

L: 15–16cm. WS: 25–28cm. W: 20–30g.

Breeding male has a black head with a buff-white supercilium extending to the side of the nape. From the nape side to the breast there is a pale buff or white stripe. The black of the head continues over the throat and breast, though the breast sides are white. The rest of the underparts are white. The nape is bright chestnut. The upperparts are pale chestnut, streaked black. Breeding female lacks the distinctive head colour, having chestnut, white and dark-brown heads. The throat and breast lack the black of the male, though there is occasionally a dark, ragged breast-band. The flanks are yellow-buff streaked with black. The upperparts are brighter, and with more chestnut than the male. In winter males lose the striking black head pattern, looking very similar to females.

Lapland Buntings breed throughout Greenland (though rare in the north-east), in northern Scandinavia and across Russia, including the Arctic islands (apart from the northern island of Novaya Zemlya, and unconfirmed to date on Severnaya Zemlya). Breeds throughout Alaska and on the Bering Sea islands, and across Canada, including Arctic islands north to Ellesmere. In winter the birds are seen in a band across eastern and central Europe and southern Russia, and in the southern United States.

Smith's Longspur

Calcarius pictus

L: 14–16cm. WS: 25–27cm. W: 20–28g.

Very attractive birds; breeding male has a black-and-white head, the nape, throat and underparts a rich buff-ochre. The upperparts are dark chestnut, streaked black and buff. Breeding female has the same head pattern but in shades of brown. The underparts are less rich, and finely streaked darker. The upperparts are brighter. In winter males lose the striking black head pattern, looking very similar to females.

Smith's Longspurs breed in central and northern Alaska (though rare), in northern Yukon and North West Territories,

Above left
Male Lapland Bunting, Varangerfjord, Norway.

Above right
Juvenile Lapland Bunting, Disko Bay, west Greenland.

Below left
Male Snow Bunting, Bylot Island, Canada.

Below right
Female Snow Bunting, northern Baffin Island, Canada.

Female Snow Bunting, south-west Iceland.

and in a narrow band to southern Hudson Bay and James Bay. Does not breed east of James Bay. In winter the birds are seen in a narrow area of the southern United States around Texas.

> **The breeding strategy of Smith's Longspur**
>
> Although male Smith's Longspurs sing from an elevated perch as other buntings do, they do not steadfastly control a territory, with the territories of several males overlapping and even being only loosely defined. The reason is that no pair bond is formed. When a female bird is ready to lay she will mate repeatedly (up to 50 times daily for about a week) with several males. The males also mate with any available female. The result is that a female's brood will be fathered by several males and she can expect help from all of them in raising the young.

Snow Bunting

Plectrophenax nivalis

L: 16–18cm. WS: 32–38cm. W: 30–45g.

Breeding male has a white head and underparts. Upperparts are black or white heavily splattered black. The tail and wings are black-and-white. Breeding female is as male, but the black is replaced with brown, and the head has spots and patches of dark brown. In winter males lose the black-and-white pattern and look very similar to females.

Snow Buntings breed on Greenland, Iceland, Jan Mayen, Bear Island and Svalbard, in northern Scandinavia and across Russia to Kamchatka, including all the Arctic islands. Breeds on the Commander, Bering Sea and Aleutian islands, throughout Alaska and northern Canada including all the Arctic islands. In winter Icelandic and some Bering Sea birds are resident, but most birds fly south to occupy a broad band across central Europe and southern Russia, and a broad band across the northern United States and southern Canada.

McKay's Bunting

Plectrophenax hyperboreus

L: 16–19cm. WS: 34–40cm. W: *c.*45g.

Breeding male white apart from some black on the wings. Breeding female is as male but with some rufous speckling on the crown and forehead, and black streaking on the back. In winter males lose the black pattern and look very similar to females.

Rare and local. McKay's Buntings breed on Hall and St Matthew Islands and, rarely, on the Pribilof Islands. In winter the birds are seen on the west coast of Alaska, from Nome to Cold Bay.

Fox Sparrow

Passerella iliaca

L: 16–19cm. WS: 25–28cm. W: 28–38g.

Breeding adult has a rufous and grey head and upperparts, and white underparts streaked rufous and dark brown. The bird as described is often called the Red Fox Sparrow and some authorities believe it to be a species rather than a subspecies (*Passerella iliaca)* of a bird widely distributed in North America. Another species or subspecies (*Passerella unalaschensis)*, the

Song Sparrow, Unalaska, Aleutian Islands, Alaska.

Juvenile Snow Bunting, Disko Bay, west Greenland.

Sooty Fox Sparrow, is much darker, with uniformly brown (varying from mid- to dark brown) upperparts and white underparts with heavy brown (again mid-brown to dark) streaks and spots. Summer and winter plumages are similar.

Red Fox Sparrows breed in central and western Alaska (but more rarely in the north), the Yukon and North West Territories, on the southern shores of Hudson Bay and in central Quebec and Labrador. Sooty Fox Sparrows breed in the Aleutians and southern Alaska. In winter the birds fly to east and west coasts of the southern United States.

Song Sparrow

Melospiza melodia

L: 15–17cm. WS: 20–22cm. W: 25–35g.

Breeding adult has rufous and grey upperparts, and white underparts heavily streaked with grey and brown so that the flanks look entirely grey and brown. Summer and winter plumages are similar.

Not a true Arctic breeder, Song Sparrows being at the northern extreme of their range in the Aleutian Islands, where they are resident.

Northern passerines

The Snow Bunting is the most northerly breeding passerine on Earth, breeding in the far north of Greenland and on northern Ellesmere Island. A Snow Bunting has been seen at the North Pole, from the deck of a surfaced US Navy submarine.

McKay's Bunting was once thought to be a pale subspecies of Snow Bunting, but is now considered a species. It is very rare, with a population of only a few thousand and is much sought after by bird-watchers, though the breeding grounds are small, uninhabited islands that are difficult to reach. The bird was named after Charles McKay, a US Signal Corps observer and bird collector who drowned in suspicious circumstances in 1883.

Lincoln's Sparrow

Melospiza lincolnii

L: 12–15cm. WS: 17–20cm. W: 15–22g.

Breeding adult has a rufous and grey head. The upperparts are buff and rufous, streaked dark brown. The breast and flanks are buff streaked with dark brown, the rest of the underparts white, either unmarked or with much finer streaking. Summer and winter plumages are similar.

Lincoln's Sparrows breed in southern and central Alaska (uncommon in the west), in central Yukon and North West Territories, around the southern shores of Hudson Bay and in central Quebec and Labrador. In winter the birds fly to the southern States, Mexico and Central America.

Harris's Sparrow

Zonotrichia querula

L: 16–19cm. WS: 23–28cm. W: 35–45g.

Harris's Sparrow is the largest Nearctic sparrow. Breeding adult is a handsome bird with black crown, ear patch and throat, the

Harris's Sparrow, Nunavut Barren Lands, Canada.

rest of the head grey, the bill a contrasting pink. The upperparts are chestnut and grey, streaked dark brown. The underparts are grey, the upper breast bearing a ragged black patch, the flanks buff with dark brown streaks. Summer and winter plumages are similar.

Harris's Sparrows breed in a broad band across Canada from the Mackenzie delta to south-western Hudson Bay. The species is rare in Alaska. In winter the birds are seen in the south-central United States.

White-crowned Sparrow

Zonotrichia leucophrys

L: 15–18cm. WS: 22–25cm. W: 25–35g.

Breeding adult has a distinctive crown of black-and-white stripes, the rest of the head grey. The underparts are unmarked; they are grey apart from brown flanks. The upperparts are chestnut and grey, streaked dark brown. Summer and winter plumages are similar.

White-crowned Sparrows breed throughout Alaska (uncommon in the north and south) and across mainland Canada to the north coast, though absent from the Arctic islands. In winter the birds fly to the southern United States and Mexico.

Golden-crowned Sparrow

Zonotrichia atricapilla

L: 15–18cm. WS: 22–25cm. W: 22–35g.

Breeding adult is as White-crowned Sparrow, but the crown is striped yellow and black. The vent differs in being white. In winter the striped crown is much more subdued.

Golden-crowned Sparrow breeds in the Aleutians (to Unimak Island) and west Alaska, but uncommon in north and central Alaska. Also breeds in southern Yukon and British Columbia. In winter the birds are seen along the west coast of the United States.

A distinctive song

Golden-crowned Sparrows have the most distinctive song of all Nearctic sparrows, a song which, once heard, is never forgotten and allows the observer to find the elusive singer. The song is a descending three syllables, often written as 'Oh Dear Me', but which could as easily be rendered as 'Three Blind Mice'.

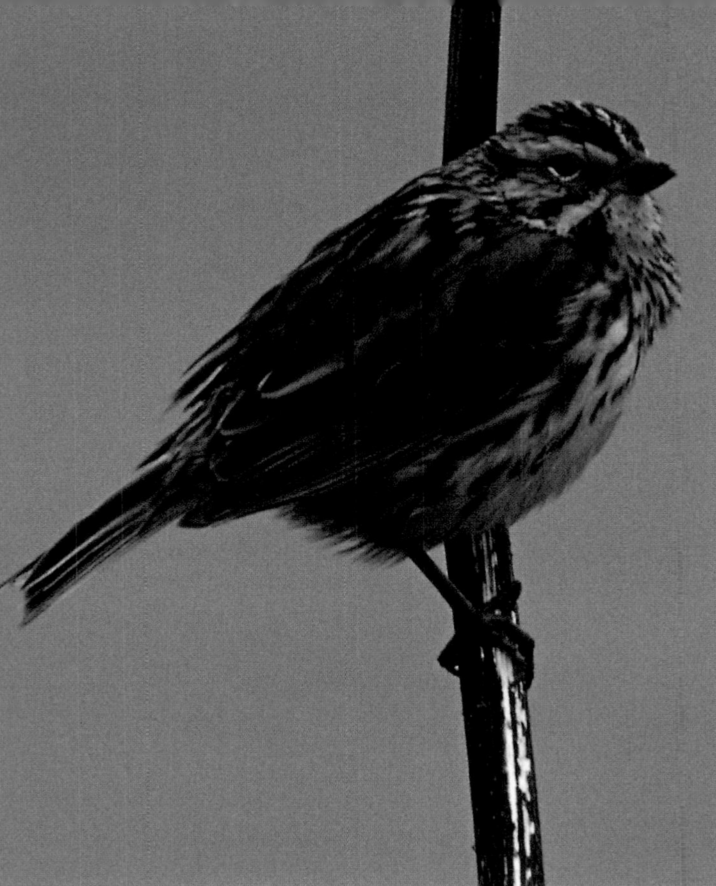

Dark-eyed Junco
Junco hyemalis
L: 13–18cm. WS: 20–25cm. W: 15–25g.
A variable bird with significant plumage differences across the range. The northern (nominate) birds are often referred to as the Slate-coloured Junco. Breeding male has a dark slate-grey head and upperparts, the colour relieved only by pink bill and white outer tail feathers. The breast is also dark slate-grey, the rest of the underparts being white, but smudged dark slate-grey on the lower flanks. Breeding female is brown, sometimes streaked darker on the upperparts and crown, the rest of the head and breast light slate-grey. Summer and winter plumages are similar.

Dark-eyed Juncos breed in south and central Alaska (but rare in the west and the Aleutians), in Yukon to the Mackenzie delta, then southerly to the southern shores of Hudson Bay and in central Quebec and Labrador. In winter the birds move to the southern United States.

Savannah Sparrow
Passerculus sandwichensis
L: 14–16cm. WS: 22–25cm. W: 16–24g.
Breeding adult has a brown head, with upperparts streaked darker, and white or cream underparts streaked dark brown. Summer and winter plumages are similar.

Savannah Sparrows breed throughout Alaska and northern Canada, and on southern Canadian Arctic islands. In winter northern birds move to the southern United States, to Central America and Caribbean islands.

American Tree Sparrow
Spizella arborea
L: 13–15cm. WS: 22–25cm. W: 13–25g.
Breeding adult has a rufous cap and line from behind the eye, the rest of the head grey or grey-buff. The throat and underparts are grey, with rufous smudging on the flanks and a dark brown smudge at the centre of the breast. The upperparts are chestnut with darker streaking. Summer and winter plumages are similar.

American Tree Sparrows breed in western and central Alaska (rare in the north), throughout the Yukon and much of mainland North West Territories, on the shores of Hudson Bay and in northern Quebec and Labrador. In winter the birds are seen in the north and central continental United States.

FINCHES

Finches evolved in the Palearctic, the similarities of the finches to the buntings, which evolved in the Nearctic, arising in response to the evolutionary pressures of seed-eating. As some buntings have crossed to the Palearctic, so some finches have crossed the other way, with several Arctic breeders being circumpolar. Finches have an array of bill shapes, ranging from the massive conical bill of the Hawfinch *Coccothraustes coccothraustes*, evolved for cracking large, hard seeds, to the more delicate bill of the Siskin *Carduelis spinus*, evolved for taking grass seeds. There are also the curious bills of the Pine Grosbeak, designed for extracting conifer seeds, and the even more extreme conifer-seed extractor of the crossbills.

Finches sing to establish territories and also have visual displays. The pair-bond is monogamous and seasonal. The 3–6 eggs are incubated by the female only, but the chicks are usually brooded and fed by both birds. Summer and winter plumages are similar in all the species described here.

Common Redpoll
Carduelis flammea
L: 11–14cm. WS: 20–25cm. W: 11–18g.
Breeding male has a red fore-crown, the rear crown, rest of the head and nape being tawny brown, streaked darker. The breast and upper belly are rose-pink, flecked buff, the rest of the underparts cream or buff, with dark brown streaking on the flanks and undertail. The upperbody is tawny, streaked with dark brown. Breeding female as breeding male but with no, or very little, rose-pink on the underparts.

Opposite page

Left
White-crowned Sparrow, Seward Peninsula, Alaska.

Right
Golden-crowned Sparrow, Cold Bay, Alaska Peninsula.

This page

Above left
Savannah Sparrow, Unalaska, Aleutian Islands, Alaska.

Below
American Tree Sparrow, Barren Lands, North West Territories, Canada

Common Redpoll, Orre, Norway.

An internal food cache

Some Arctic Redpolls are resident through the High Arctic winter, withstanding temperatures down to -60°C. To aid survival the birds have a storage area, called the oesophageal diverticulum, about halfway down the throat, where extra food can be stored. This allows the bird to take in more food than it can digest immediately, storing the rest for later consumption. During the long hours of night the birds fluff their feathers to increase insulation, reduce energy output by resting, and transfer the food from storage to the main digestive tract.

Common Redpolls breed on Greenland (rare in the north-east) and Iceland, in northern Scandinavia and across Russia to Kamchatka, but to the north coast only at the White Sea and in Chukotka. Breeds throughout Alaska (uncommon in the north) and across the north Canadian mainland, but only on western Baffin Island. Some Greenlandic and most Icelandic birds are resident. Other Greenlandic birds move to Iceland or join European birds in northern and central Europe. Asian birds move to Japan and south-east China, North American birds to southern Canada and the northern United States.

Arctic Redpoll (Hoary Redpoll)

Carduelis hornemanni

L: 13–15cm. WS: 21–28cm. W: 11–16g.

Breeding male Arctic Redpoll is very similar to Common Redpoll, but paler overall, the upperparts less brown, the rose-pink of the underparts much paler, the underparts unmarked or minimally streaked. Female is as female Common Redpoll but paler.

Arctic Redpoll breeds on west and north-east Greenland (but is scarce everywhere), in northern Scandinavia and across Russia, but to north coast only at the White Sea and in Chukotka (though also breeds on southern island of Novaya Zemlya and on Wrangel Island). Breeds in west, north and central Alaska and across northern Canada to Hudson Bay, around Ungava Bay and on the eastern Arctic islands (Baffin and Ellesmere). Resident or partial migrant, moving short distance only, to southern Scandinavia, sub-Arctic Russia and southern Canada.

Pine Grosbeak

Pinicola enucleator

L: 18–23cm. WS: 32–37cm. W: 50–60g.

Breeding male has a red head with a pale grey crescent below the eye, and an indistinct dark brown crescent around the ear-coverts. The underparts are red, becoming grey on the lower belly. The upperparts are red-brown, with dark brown chevrons. Breeding female patterned as male, but the head colour varies from russet to golden-yellow, the underparts and upperparts golden-yellow scalloped grey.

Pine Grosbeaks breed in northern Scandinavia and across Russia to the treeline. Breeds throughout Alaska to the treeline (but uncommon everywhere and rare in the north), and to the treeline across Canada, including the southern shores of Hudson Bay and in central Quebec and Labrador. Resident or partially migratory, moving to central Scandinavia, southern Russia, southern Canada and the northern United States.

Male Common Crossbill, Orre, Norway.

Common Crossbill (Red Crossbill)

Loxia curvirostra

L: 15–18cm. WS: 27–32cm. W: 35–50g.

Breeding male has an orange-red head and upperbody, flecked with grey. The breast and belly are similar, merging to a grey vent. Breeding female patterned as male, but the head and back are pale olive, heavily flecked grey. The rump is green, as are the underparts.

An Arctic-fringe species, breeding to the treeline in Fennoscandia and across Russia to the Sea of Okhotsk. Breeds in southern Alaska and across Canada, but rarely to the treeline. Resident and dispersive, and also irruptive.

Two-barred Crossbill (White-winged Crossbill)

Loxia leucoptera

L: 14–16cm. WS: 26–29cm. W: 35–50g.

Breeding male and female are as Common Crossbill, apart from having two distinct white bands on the inner wing. Males are also in general pinkish-red rather than red-orange.

Two-barred Crossbill breeds to the treeline in eastern Finland and across Russia to the Sea of Okhotsk. Breeds to the

Developing a crossed bill

Crossbills do not hatch with crossed bills, as it is not the internal structure of the bill that causes the cross but the external horny layer. The cross begins to develop when the chicks are about 4 weeks old, and is not fully developed until they are 6–7 weeks old. Until that time the chicks cannot feed efficiently and must be fed by their parents.

treeline in Alaska and across Canada, north to the Mackenzie delta and on the southern shores of Hudson Bay.

Grey-crowned Rosy-finch

Leucosticte tephrocotis

L: 14–18cm. WS: 32–37cm. W: 20–25g.

Breeding male has a black forehead, the rest of the head silver-grey. The throat is dark brown, the underparts rufous brown, becoming redder towards the lower belly. The mantle and back are tawny brown, streaked black. Breeding female is as male but duller overall. There are several subspecies in North America, all following the same basic plumage pattern, but with minor differences. The birds of the Pribilof Islands (*L. t. umbrina*, the Pribilof Rosy-finch) is darker and much larger than other races, with length to 22cm and weight of 40–60g.

Grey-crowned Rosy-finches breed in western and central Alaska and throughout the Yukon, and on the Aleutian and Pribilof Islands. In winter the birds head down the west coast of the United States.

Asian Rosy-finch

Leucosticte arctoa

L: 14–18cm. WS: 32–37cm. W: 20–25g.

Breeding adult is as Grey-crowned Rosy-finch but the head is overall dark grey, lacking the dark forehead, the nape is pale grey with a rosy tinge and the underparts are washed silver. The birds of the Commander Islands are larger, with length to 22cm and weight of 40–60g.

Asian Rosy-finches breed from the Lena to the north coast of the Sea of Okhotsk, throughout Kamchatka and on the Commander and Kuril islands. In winter the birds are seen in southern Siberia and in northern Mongolia and China.

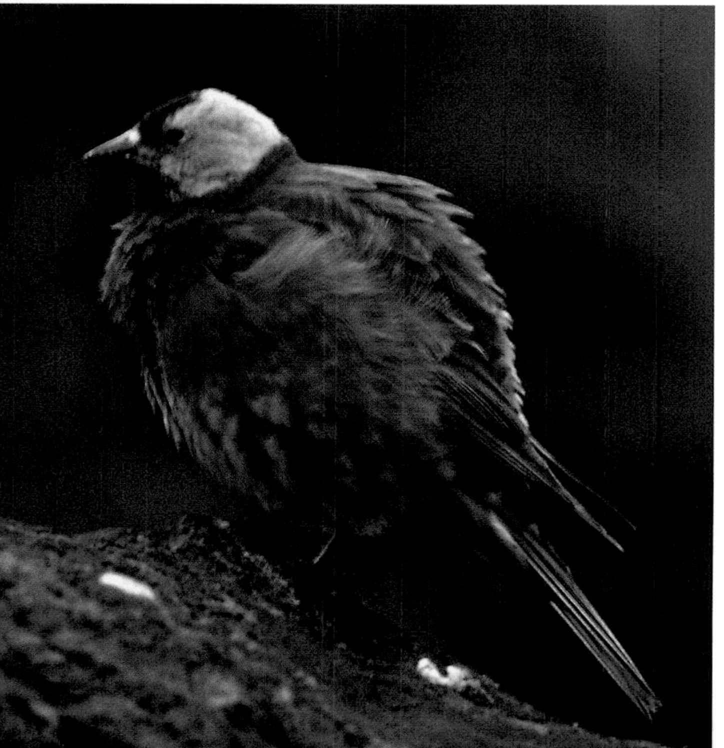

Grey-crowned Rosy-Finch, Unalaska, Aleutian Islands, Alaska.

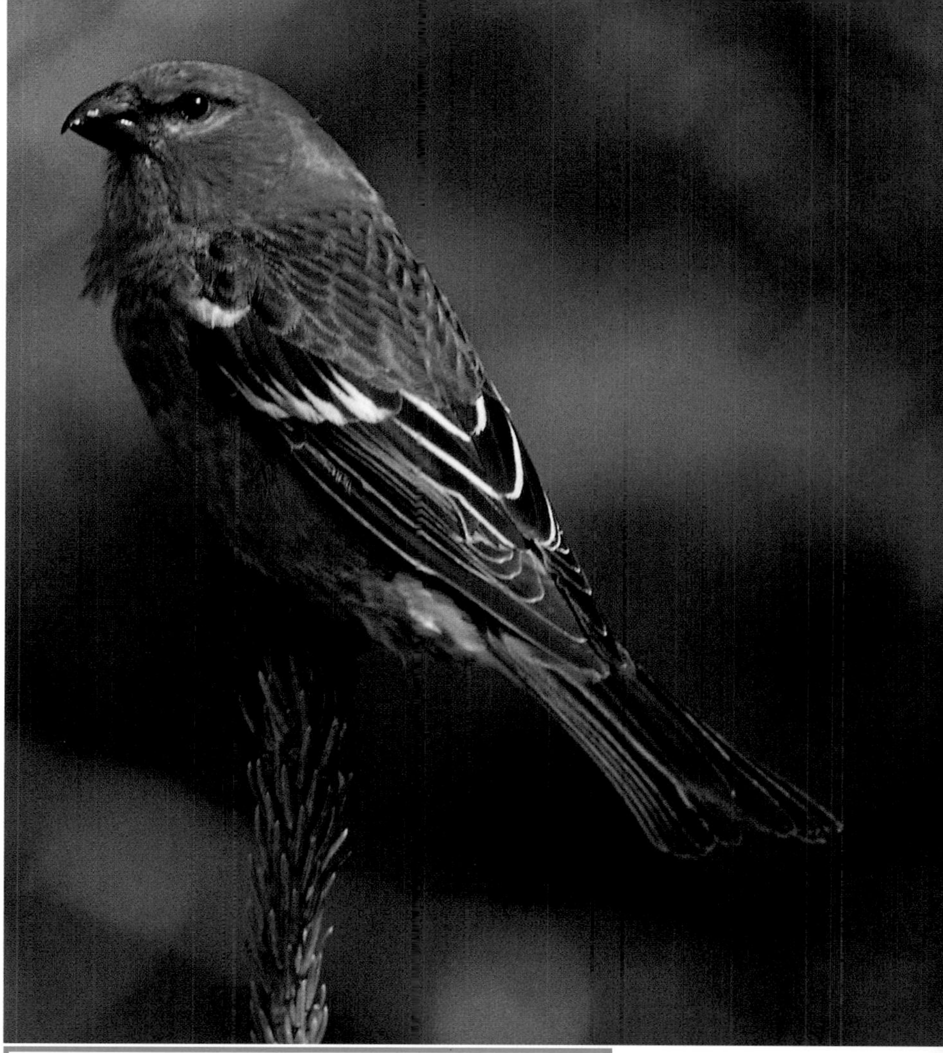

Male Pine Grosbeak, Churchill, Manitoba, Canada.

Difficult rosy-finches

Until the early 1980s the various birds of the Bering Sea were considered to be subspecies of one species, the Arctic Rosy-finch. Then the Russian and American birds were split into two species, but that has not resolved the matter as the taxonomy remains controversial. Are the birds of the Commander Islands a subspecies of the Grey-crowned Rosy-finch or of the Asian Rosy-finch? And if they are a subspecies of the latter, where does that leave the Kamchatka birds?

NEW WORLD BLACKBIRDS

The icterids are a family of more than 100 Nearctic species that includes some of the most abundant birds on Earth (e.g the Red-winged Blackbird *Aegalaius phoeniceus* which has an estimated population of 200 million). One species breeds at the Arctic fringe.

Rusty Blackbird

Euphagus carolinus

L: 21–25cm. WS: 33–40cm. W: 50–70g.

Breeding male is black, the head with a purple sheen. Breeding female brown, darker on the upperparts than the underparts, the latter occasionally with fine barring. In winter males are overall dark brown, often with a discernible rusty wash that gives the bird its name. In winter females are paler than in summer.

Rusty Blackbirds breed throughout Alaska, but uncommon everywhere and very rare in the north. Also breeds in Yukon to the Mackenzie delta, then southerly to the southern shores of Hudson Bay, in central Quebec and northern Labrador. In winter the birds fly to the south-east United States

Terrestrial Mammals

In this section the following measurements are given: TL = total length, T = tail length, HB = head and body length, HS = height at shoulder, WS = wingspan and W = weight.

SHREWS

Shrews are the only members of the *Insectivora* that breed in the Arctic. Apart from the Water Shrew (which breeds at the Arctic fringe) Arctic shrews all belong to the genus *Sorex*, the red-toothed shrews, so called because the tips of their teeth are red, a feature caused by iron compounds in the enamel.

Shrews are small (the Pygmy White-toothed Shrew *Suncus etruscus* is considered the smallest of all adult mammals) and mouse-like, but with long, mobile noses. Their sense of smell is acute, an adaptation for a life spent beneath plant detritus and in subterranean burrows, but as a result their eyesight is poor. Some species use ultrasonic echolocation for both navigation and in the search for prey, though it is not clear how sophisticated these systems are as the shrews are one of the least-studied mammal families, almost all that is known about them deriving from studies of just a handful of species. Some shrews produce a neurotoxin from their salivary glands. This is injected into the prey when the shrew bites; immobilisation of prey is important, as shrews often take relatively large prey. Those species with the most toxic poisons take small vertebrates as well as the invertebrates that make up the 'standard' shrew diet.

Shrews have a cloaca, a single opening for the urinary, digestive and reproductive tracts (as do most birds). They are also plantigrade, i.e. they walk on the soles of their feet (as do bears). Despite these 'primitive' features, the shrew actually first appears in the fossil record during the Tertiary, although many earlier groups of mammals were 'shrew-like' in appearance.

As well as having an unusual anatomy, shrews also practise refection, the re-ingestion of excreted food. To do this, the shrew curls into a ball and licks the cloaca until the rectum is extruded. The rectal contents are then re-ingested. On a second pass through the digestive tract the re-ingested matter is digested further before being excreted as faeces. Refection only occurs when the digestive tract is free of faeces.

Shrews have a very high metabolic rate and must feed very frequently. Indeed, some shrews will actually die of hunger if they are unable to feed every one or two hours. The almost constant need to feed – the shrew's life comprises incessant foraging interrupted by short intervals of rest – is the basis of the many descriptions of shrews as ravenous. The description is aided by the animal's hunting technique – a constant scurrying. Prey is encountered in a haphazard fashion, with the shrew taking anything that crosses its path that can be immobilised and consumed. Yet despite the need for almost continuous feeding, a shrew will cache food if it catches more than it can eat. Cached food is occasionally live, paralysed by the shrew's neurotoxin.

As with metabolic rate, the heart rate of shrews is very high. In some species it can reach more than 1,000 beats per minute, an extraordinary rate that has led to the suggestion that some animals die of fright if captured or handled. In reality it is an unsustainable increase in heart rate (leading to heart failure) that is the actual cause.

The iron-rich red-tipped teeth of the *Sorex* shrews are a necessary adaptation for the genus. In general these species have a higher metabolic rate than other shrews, such as the *Crocidura* white-toothed shrews (interesting, since *Sorex* is a northern group, while *Crocidura* is more tropical; since food abundance is generally higher in the terrestrial tropics, this difference in metabolic rate is difficult to account for). A *Sorex* shrew's first teeth are resorbed before birth, the animal being born with its final set. As shrews do not replace their teeth (the enforced starvation of tooth-loss would result in death), the harder tooth-tips of *Sorex* shrews reflect the higher food intake required. If the shrew lives long enough it will wear its teeth down and die of starvation. Shrew corpses are occasionally found (scent glands on the animal's flanks, which exude an unpleasant secretion, mean that the bodies are often ignored by carrion feeders); invariably, the cause of death is starvation. The dental formula of shrews differs from those of other mammals, the animals having incisors, but then continuous rows of teeth. The length of the dental row is usually an indication of species (tooth shape may also be useful), but the measurement requires the shrew to be immobilised, which in reality means killing it.

Shrews are solitary animals, usually only coming together for mating. Mating is as haphazard as feeding, females in oestrus seemingly copulating with any male that happens along (and males behaving likewise), so any one litter may contain the young of several fathers. The male grips the female by the nape with his teeth during copulation, mated females showing bite marks or patches of white fur in this area. The gestation period is about 20 days, young shrews being naked and

Seventeenth-century opinion

The English naturalist Edward Topsell, writing in the early years of the 17th century, produced one of the first descriptions of the shrew: *It is a ravening beast, feigning itself gentle and tame, but being touched it biteth deep, and poisoneth deadly. It beareth a cruel mind, desiring to hurt anything, neither is their any creature it loveth.*

Topsell was correct in almost all particulars, though he overstated the effect of the shrew's poison on people. In most people a shrew bite will cause local swelling, though some individuals may have a more severe reaction. The shrew's characteristics led to the use of the name as a description of mean, unpleasant people. Shakespeare's *The Taming of the Shrew* is an early indication of the use of shrew for a sharp-tongued, ill-tempered woman, and it is interesting to note that the original meaning of 'shrewd' was cunning, but in the pejorative sense, i.e. a shrewd person was someone to watch as they would likely walk off with your wallet or life's savings. Only with time did the expression take on a more benevolent tone.

Images of Shrews

In about two dozen Arctic expeditions Per Michelsen and I have yet to see an Arctic shrew, and photographs of them by others are extremely rare. As this is not a field guide, no plates have been included of these elusive animals. Those wishing to see images can find them in *A Complete Guide to Arctic Wildlife* by Richard Sale, illustrated with photos by Per Michelsen and Richard Sale.

Opposite page
Arctic Ground Squirrel, Barren Lands of Nunavut, Canada.

Even such apparently hostile areas as Alaska's North Slope (*above:* the Brooks Range from near Galbraith Lake) and Canada's Barren Lands (*opposite page*: the Hood River from the air) are able to support shrew populations.

helpless. The young are weaned after a further 20 days, and even in the Arctic the female may have several litters if resources allow. The process of giving birth and lactation places a huge burden on the females; they may actually have to consume double their own body weight each day (with males and non-breeding females consuming their own body weight on average daily). In northern species, females breed at one year and rarely survive the breeding season. Shrews cannot hibernate, since their metabolic rate cannot be lowered sufficiently to allow survival on fat stores. The Arctic species shrink both their skeletons and internal organs to reduce food requirements, but even so many die of starvation during the winter. Because of the rigours of shrew life, males as well as breeding females usually die in the year following their birth. That means that during the late summer of a given year the entire population is likely to comprise that year's young.

The rapid life-cycle of shrews means that evolution also takes place rapidly; new species are still being discovered regularly, and most species are polytypic across the range. Several very similar shrew species may also be found within a given area; as the animals are omnivorous it is possible for species to co-exist sympatrically by taking different fractions of available prey. Both these factors mean that differentiating shrew species can occasionally be very difficult for experts, and is almost impossible for the non-specialist. As a consequence, only general details of size and range are given below.

Common Shrew

Sorex araneus

TL: 85–140mm. T: 30–55mm. W: 6–12g.

Adult is dark brown (even black) above, paler on the flanks and pale grey below. The feet are white. The tail is brown and ends in a tuft. Breeds in northern Scandinavia, on the Kola Peninsula, around the White Sea, then southerly to central Russia. Essentially boreal.

Eurasian Masked Shrew

Sorex caecutians

TL: 75–115mm. T: 30–45mm. W: 3–8g.

Adult is golden-brown above, silver-white below, the colours strongly delineated. The feet are white with fine silver hairs, the brown tail is long and ends in a tuft. Breeds in northern Sweden and Finland, and across Russia from the Kola Peninsula to Kamchatka, but not to north coast. Occurs on tundra and in the taiga.

American Masked Shrew (Cinereus Shrew)

Sorex cinereus

TL: 75–125mm. T: 30–50mm. W: 2.5–5.5g.

Adult is brown or grey-brown above, paler below, the delineation less precise than in the Eurasian Masked. The feet are brown. The tail is brown above, paler below and tipped black, sometimes with a black tuft. Breeds in Alaska to the west coast and on the Aleutian Islands, and north to the Brooks Range. Breeds near the Mackenzie delta, but otherwise follows the treeline across Canada. Primarily boreal, but also found in tundra shrub.

Large-toothed Shrew

Sorex daphaenadon

TL: 75–125mm. T: 25–45mm. W: 5–8g.

Rare and poorly studied. Adult is brown above, paler below. Tail and feet pale brown. Breeds in central and eastern Siberia,

Caravanning shrews

Young American Masked Shrews sometimes form 'caravans', a chain of animals, the first holding the mother's rump in its teeth, each subsequent youngster taking hold of the one in front in the same way. Such caravans help the female move her young if the natal nest is endangered. The young shrews are extremely tenacious; the whole chain can be lifted clear of the ground if the female is picked up. Some other shrew species also show this behaviour.

Kamchatka shrews

As well as the shrews mentioned specifically here, two other species breed in Kamchatka. The Kamchatka Shrew *Sorex camtchaticus* is confined to the peninsula and the shores of the Sea of Okhotsk. It is small (total length about 80mm, weight about 5g). The Eurasian Dusky or Taiga Shrew *S. isodon* is found across Russia to the treeline and in southern Chukotka as well as Kamchatka. It is larger (total length about 120mm, weight about 23g). Each species is bi-coloured and essentially boreal.

including southern Chukotka and Kamchatka. Boreal, but found on shrub tundra.

Pygmy Shrew

Sorex minitus

TL: 70–120mm. T: 30–45mm. W: 2–7g.

Adult is mid-brown above, pale grey below. The feet are white. The tail is brown, the hair dense so that the end tuft is barely discernible. Breeds in northern Scandinavia, though not to the north coast, on the Kola Peninsula, around the White Sea, then more southerly across Russia to Lake Baikal. Found in taiga clearings and at the forest edge.

Dusky Shrew (Montane Shrew)

Sorex monticolus

TL: 95–140mm. T: 30–60mm. W: 5–10g.

Adult is brown (usually red-brown) above, paler, and often silver-washed, below. There is no clear delineation between the colours. The feet are pale brown. The tail is bi-coloured, brown above, paler below. Breeds in south-west and central Alaska, south and (less commonly) northern Yukon and southern North-West Territories. Found in damp tundra and taiga, often besides streams with thickets of willow or birch.

Flat-skulled Shrew

Sorex roboratus

TL: 90–150mm. T: 30–55mm. W: 8–14g.

Adult is dark brown above, paler below. The feet are pale brown. The tail is bi-coloured, darker above Breeds in eastern Siberia, to the north coast near the Lena and Indigirka deltas. Essentially boreal, but found on damp tundra.

Tundra Shrew

Sorex tundrensis

TL: 80–120mm. T: 20–35mm. W: 5–10g.

Adult is dark brown above, with pale grey-brown flanks and pale grey underparts. The feet are pale brown. The tri-coloured pelage is very distinctive. The tail is bi-coloured, brown above, paler below. Breeds in Siberia east of the Pechora River, north to the northern coast except on the Taimyr Peninsula. Absent from Kamchatka. Also breeds on the Aleutian Islands, in west, central and northern Alaska and, to a limited extent, in northern Yukon. Found on dry tundra and shrub tundra.

Bering Sea shrews

In about 1840 Russian scientists collected two specimens of a shrew from 'Unalaska'. It was assumed this was the Aleutian island of that name, but no shrew has ever been found by American scientists. Some authorities think that the Russians were using the name as a general one for the Bering Sea islands and were probably referring to the Pribilof Islands where a shrew (*Sorex hydrodamus* or *S. pribilofensis*) has been found on St Paul. Related species have also been found on St Lawrence Island (*S. jacksoni*) and in north-east Chukotka (Portenko's Shrew *S. portenkoi*). These shrews are similar in size and colour to the American Masked Shrew, at a time of lower sea levels (i.e. during periods of glaciation), an ancestral shrew spread across the Beringia, with populations then being isolated on certain islands as sea levels rose. Although there no longer seems to be a shrew on Unalaska, it must be remembered that the animals are extremely elusive and so may merely have escaped detection. It is also possible that some island species may have become extinct since Beringia was flooded. Russian scientists claim there are differences between the two 'Unalaska' shrews and those of St Paul, supporting the view that there may once have been shrews on the island.

Barren-ground Shrew

Sorex ugyunak

TL: 75–105mm. T: 22–30mm. W: 3–5.5g.

Adult is brown above, paler below, the two colours strongly delineated. The feet are brown. The tail is brown above, paler below and ends with a brownish buff tuft Breeds in northern Alaska and across northern Canada, including the Boothia Peninsula, to the western shore of Hudson Bay. Absent from the southern shore of Hudson Bay and north-east Canada. Found in damp tundra and shrub tundra.

Treeline shrews of North America

Though most Arctic travellers rarely see a shrew of any species, some lucky visitors to the treeline in North America may see species not mentioned specifically here. The ill-named Arctic Shrew *Sorex arcticus* is actually a boreal species of Canada, breeding to the southern shore of Hudson Bay. This shrew (total length about 115mm, weight about 8g) is very dark above and tri-coloured. The American Pygmy Shrew *S. hoyi* breeds across the continent, but only to the treeline. It has a total length of about 100mm, weight about 5g, and is bi-coloured.

Water Shrew

Neomys fodiens

TL: 75–105mm. T: 22–30mm. W: 3–5.5g.

Adult is very dark brown above, pale grey or white below, the two colours strongly delineated. The feet are pale brown and covered with silver hairs. The tail is dark brown with a double row of paler, stiff hairs to aid swimming. Breeds in northern Fennoscandia, but not to the north coast, around the White Sea, then more southerly across Russia. Found near (usually fast-flowing) streams.

BATS

The ability to fly, together with the possession of sophisticated echolocation systems that allow prey-capture in total darkness, would appear to give microbats an advantage for Arctic living. But the lack of roosting sites, together with the harshness of the Arctic winter and absence of winter prey, mitigate against the group being found in the north. Yet there are hardy species in both the Palearctic and the Nearctic.

Flight in bats has been achieved through the modification of the typical mammalian forelimb and finger bones into a wing, the elongated finger bones bearing a membrane that is attached to the body and to a shortened hindlimb. To accommodate the membrane the hindlimbs of bats project sideways from the body, and the knee joint bends the opposite way to the norm. These adaptations mean that walking is almost impossible, with bats able, at best, to crawl in an ungainly fashion; only a handful of bats (mainly on tropical islands) ever visit the ground. They roost by hanging upside-down, dropping from this position into flight; thrust is not needed from the legs to take off, as in birds. Roosts are often in caves and buildings, though hollow trees can also be used in some species; all these features are largely absent from the Arctic.

Northern Bat

Eptesicus nilssoni

TL: 50–70mm. WS: 250–280mm. W: 8–14g.

The fur on the adult upperparts is dark brown, the hairs buff-tipped to give the animal a 'highlighted' appearance. The underparts are yellow-brown. The nose, ears and wing membranes are dark brownish black.

The Northern Bat breeds in northern Scandinavia (though apparently not on the Kola Peninsula), and across Russia to the treeline. Also breeds in south-eastern Kamchatka (where it may be confused with Brandt's Bat *Myotis brandtii,* an otherwise southern species; Brandt's is much smaller, the dorsal fur more golden and the wing membranes paler). Northern Bats hibernate during the winter.

Little Brown Bat

Myotis lucifugus

TL: 45–70mm. WS: 240–270mm. W: 7–12g.

The fur on the adult upperparts is golden-brown with a glossy sheen. The underparts are paler. The nose and ears are dark brown, the wing membranes dark grey-brown.

The Little Brown Bat breeds across North America to the treeline. Northern dwellers may migrate south in winter, joining more southerly residents to enter a state of torpor in caves or mines.

Hoary Bat

Lasiurus cinereus

TL: 75–90mm. WS: 380–410mm. W: 20–35g. ♀>♂.

The dorsal fur is mottled grey, brown and white, the overall appearance being frosted or hoary (hence the name). The fur of the head and throat is yellow-brown. The underparts are pale grey-brown. The nose is dark brown, the ears have dark brown tips. The wing membranes are dark brown, the dorsal tail membrane being heavily fur-covered.

The most northerly Nearctic bat. Breeds in Canada to the north shores of Hudson Bay on both the west and east sides. Absent from Alaska. It is believed that most migrate south for the winter, but some are resident, entering a state of torpor.

Bats live as far north as the treeline, sometimes hibernating within the taiga rather than migrating south. This photograph is of the thinning taiga near the Great Slave Lake, North West Territories, Canada.

White Wolf pair, Fosheim Peninsula, Ellesmere Island, Canada. Behind the wolves is frozen Slidre Fjord.

CARNIVORES

Carnivores are a large and diverse group of mammals, found from polar regions to deserts. One branch of the carnivore family tree, the pinnipeds, is wholly aquatic (and almost exclusively marine); these animals, the seals, sea-lions and walrus, are considered in detail in the marine mammals section which follows later. The other branch, the fissipeds, includes the familiar terrestrial carnivore groups, such as dogs, cats and bears. The difference in weight between the largest and the smallest terrestrial carnivores – both of which are Arctic species, the Polar Bear and the (Least) Weasel – is astonishing; up to 800kg compared to just 25g, a factor of 32,000.

So different are the forms of carnivores that only a few general comments on physiology can be made. Compared to a human, there are two obvious skeletal differences; there is no large clavicle, and a penis bone is present in almost all species. The function of the clavicle in humans and other primates is to allow sideways movement of the arms. For carnivores, whose main hunting strategy is to run down prey, such a movement would be disadvantageous; they have a smaller clavicle, free at each end, which allows only a forward and backward movement, ideal for fast pursuit. The baculum or *os penis* bone of carnivores prolongs copulation and is assumed to have evolved because in general copulation stimulates ovulation. The 'copulatory tie' seen in mating canids is not thought to play the same role, though it clearly has that effect. The tie, which can last for up to 30 minutes, is almost certainly related to sperm competition; longer mating helps ensure that rival male's sperm will not subsequently fertilise the female.

Carnivores have a unique and diagnostic dentition. In all carnivores (even in the only species that has become secondarily herbivorous, the Giant Panda *Ailuropoda melanoleuca*), the last upper premolar and first lower molar on each side of the jaw have high cusps and sharp tips. These teeth, called carnassials, allow flesh to be sheared.

In addition to the physical attributes for hunting such as powerful limbs and sharp teeth, terrestrial carnivores also have well-developed senses, sight, hearing and smell all being important. These senses are also used in communication, carnivores marking their presence by urinating and defecating at strategic points throughout their territories.

DOGS

Dogs (or canids) are noted for pack formation, the pack normally comprising a monogamous 'alpha' pair which breeds, and a number of family members that help with hunting and pup-rearing. However, although this is the normal society for Wolves and Coyotes, Red and Arctic Foxes are more solitary animals. Family groups have been noted in these foxes, but solitary pairs are more likely to be seen in both species. The number of pups produced is dependent on prey density; Arctic Fox numbers increase rapidly in 'lemming years', but the animals may not breed if rodent numbers are low. Many foxes will starve during their first year if the lemming population crashes.

In general canids kill their prey by grabbing the neck or nose, and shaking their heads violently to break or dislocate the neck or spinal cord.

Wolf

Canis lupus

HB: 90–150cm. T: 30–50cm. HS: 65–80cm. W: 30–80kg. ♂>♀.

Status: IUCN: Least Concern. CITES: Appendix II.

The largest wild dog. The first animal domesticated by humans, perhaps as many as 50,000 years ago, and certainly by 14,000 years ago. However, despite this ancient association, the view of people has undergone a significant change over time. The Wolf was often the familiar of shamans and was revered by early northern dwellers. In legend a female Wolf nurtured

Above left

The male of the wolf pair shown on p441. The year the photograph was taken the pair had two cubs and the male worked hard all day catching hares to feed them, his mate and himself. High Arctic packs are frequently small and, in this case, with just the two adults, was too small to hunt the Musk Oxen which were often seen in the area.

Above right

Male Wolf on the Barren Lands of North West Territories, Canada. Unlike the Ellesmere wolves, the wolves in this area tend to moult to a darker summer pelage. This animal is a little late in choosing a less conspicuous coat.

Romulus and Remus, and was therefore instrumental in the birth of Roman civilisation. The Vikings also revered the animal for its speed, stamina and skills as a hunter, Viking chieftains often taking the name Ulf to indicate their prowess in battle; Ulf is still a common name in Scandinavia. But by the early medieval period things had changed, the Wolf becoming an evil presence, the change reflected in a host of folkloric tales in which the animal is represented as deceitful, greedy, ferocious and, most significantly of all, dangerous. Most terrifying was the werewolf, the man who became a wolf and then carried out deeds of bestial cruelty. Barry Lopez, in his marvellous book *Of Wolves and Men,* conjectures that, in portraying the wolf as evil, man was '[externalising] his bestial nature, finding a scapegoat upon which he could heap his sins and whose sacrificial death would be his atonement. He has put his sins of greed, lust and deception on the wolf and put the wolf to death, in literature, in folklore and in real life.' In many European countries a bounty was placed on Wolves: they were exterminated from England by the early 16th century, from Scotland about 150 years later. In Scandinavia eradication took longer, but the last Wolf was killed in Sweden in 1966, and in Norway in 1973. They were almost exterminated in Finland too, but recolonisation from Russia prevented total extinction. As attitudes changed, the recolonisation of Sweden and Norway from Finland was officially welcomed, though the animals still face illegal killing by farmers convinced that the Wolf represents a serious threat to livestock, and by people who, fearing attacks on children and the vulnerable, feel that such large carnivores should not be allowed to co-exist in a civilised society.

Policemen Wolves

The Inuit were familiar with the hunting techniques of the Wolf, the seeking out of the sick or injured animal so that the kill was less dangerous for the hunter. When policemen were first introduced into Inuit societies by the Canadian government they rapidly acquired the name *amakro* (wolf) because they stood in the background observing, watching for mistakes.

Unfortunately, Europeans settlers to North America took their prejudices with them, and Wolves were persecuted mercilessly. Only relatively recently has the change in public attitude allowed the Wolf reintroduction to the Yellowstone National Park. However, in many places outside National Parks the Wolf is still under threat.

Adult wolves are usually grey, but this can vary (particularly in North American animals) from almost black to white. White Wolves are found in northern Canada and the Canadian Arctic islands, in Greenland and areas of Arctic Russia. Wolves are

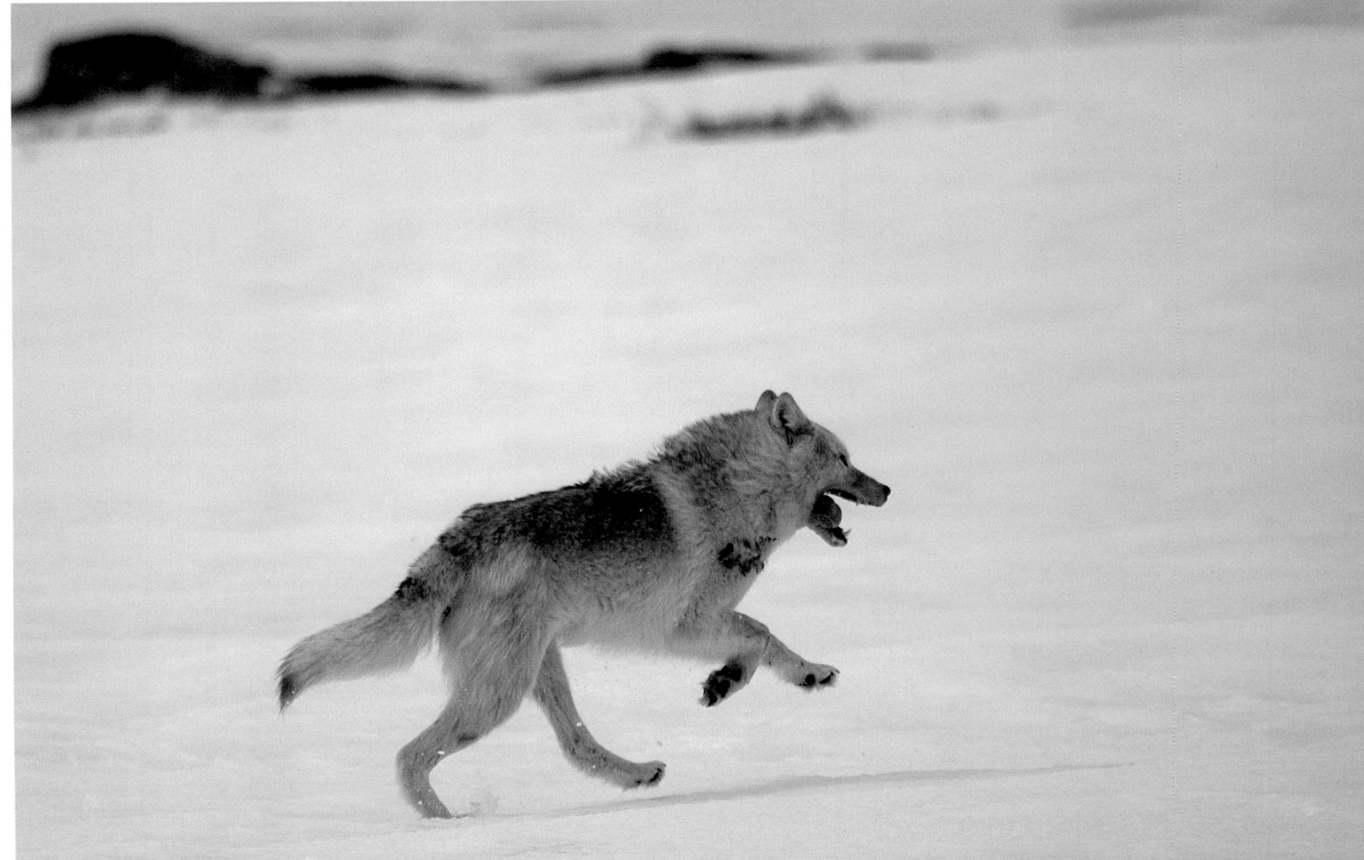

Male Wolf on the Barren Lands of NWT, Canada in winter..

social animals living in packs, which are cohesive, extended family groups. Packs form when a mature male and mature female from two packs meet, form a breeding pair and establish a viable territory. Pack sizes vary with prey size, prey density and Wolf mortality (rabies and other fatal diseases being endemic in Wolf populations). A pack can contain as many as 30 animals (with numbers as high as 60 recorded). Pack sizes in general are much smaller for High Arctic Wolves: on occasions a 'pack' might consist only of a male and female. The pack is dominated by the 'alpha' pair. In general the alpha animals are the only pack members that breed, the non-breeding members being earlier offspring who help with hunting and cub-rearing. The female breeds annually, but in the High Arctic breeding may not occur if resources are inadequate. In those cases the foetuses are resorbed.

The howl of the Wolf is one of the most evocative sounds of the wilderness. Howling helps the pack to reform after a dispersive hunt. In the Arctic the prey is often Reindeer, though animals as large as Elk may be taken. In the High Arctic, Wolves take rodents and hares and, if the pack is large enough or the prey is weak, they may take Musk Ox.

Wolves breed throughout the Arctic, but they are absent from Iceland and Svalbard. Breeding on Russia's Arctic islands is conjectural as the species has not been well-studied in those areas.

Coyote

Canis latrans

HB: 75–100cm: T: 30–40cm. HS: 50–70cm. W: 8–18kg. ♂>♀.

Status: IUCN: Least Concern.

Adults vary from red-brown to grey or even dark grey or black. Coyotes are essentially sub-Arctic, but they are opportunistic feeders and so may venture north if resources allow. They breed across the United States and southern Canada. They have been seen on Alaska's North Slope and around the Mackenzie delta, though the treeline is the more normal limit.

Arctic Fox

Alopex lagopus

HB: 55–75cm: T: 25–45cm. HS: 25–35cm. W: 3–9kg. ♂>♀.

Status: IUCN: Least Concern.

Together with the Polar Bear, the Arctic Fox is the most specialised terrestrial Arctic mammal. Though usually seen on land hunting rodents, the foxes are often seen on sea ice in the winter, where they account for about 25% of the annual kill of seal pups, and follow Polar Bears to feed on the remnants of bear kills (and on bear faeces *in extremis*). The foxes also follow Wolves on land for the same purpose, and regularly patrol bird nesting cliffs to collect eggs and chicks from poorly sited nests, or to take young birds whose first flights (or glides in the case of some auks) end in disaster.

Adults have two colour forms. In one the summer pelage is grey-brown above, paler below and, usually, on the tail. In the winter this form turns white. The second form, the so-called blue fox, is dark chocolate brown or dark blue-grey in summer, with a paler tail, and pale blue-grey in winter. In general white-morph foxes are continental, blue foxes being found on islands, but interbreeding of the forms occurs and litters may comprise both colour forms.

Female Wolf in Finnish Karelia. Wolves have been severely persecuted in Scandinavia, and are now very rare in Norway and Sweden. The Finnish Wolf population is higher because of animals arriving from Russia where they are still relatively plentiful. Finnish animals attempting to establish themselves in Norway and Sweden invariably receive a very hostile reception.

Arctic Fox feeding on the remains of a Polar Bear Ringed Seal catch. In winter the foxes often follow bears to pick up scraps, but need to be careful as they may finish up as prey. The photograph was taken on the sea ice of Kongsfjorden, Spitsbergen, Svalbard.

Above
Arctic Fox on the sea-ice of Kongsfjorden, Spitsbergen, Svalbard.

Right
Arctic Fox in evening light, Bellsund, Spitsbergen, Svalbard.

Below
'Blue' Arctic Fox patrolling a Northern Fur Seal birthing beach on St Paul Island, Pribilofs, Alaska. Foxes have a daily routine during the birthing season of searching out still-born pups and afterbirth.

Winter fox fur

The luxurious winter coat of the Arctic Fox – so thick it makes the animal look much bigger than it actually is – is such a good insulator that the animal's body temperature of 40°C can be maintained without the need for shivering, down to ambient temperatures of about -60°C. Unfortunately, the coat was so prized that the animals were relentlessly hunted both in Russia and Canada. Although staggering numbers of foxes were killed (hunting still continues, but at a lower level) the species has, thankfully, survived.

The Arctic Fox breeds throughout the Arctic, but it has been hunted to extinction on Jan Mayen. It is possible that the island might be recolonised if sea ice allows animals to reach it again. Icelandic animals have been persecuted since human colonisation of the island, with indigenous animals now reinforced by fur-farm escapes.

Red Fox

Vulpus vulpus

HB: 55–90cm. T: 30–48cm. HS: 35–40cm. W: 4–10kg. ♂>♀.

Status: IUCN: Least Concern.

The Red Fox is the most widespread and abundant of all carnivores. The adult is red-brown with a bushy tail. The tail is often white-tipped, the ears usually black-tipped. The feet and legs are often darker than the body colour. Though most foxes conform to this colour pattern, there are exceptions. There are paler animals; the 'cross fox' (relatively abundant in Canada) is darker with much darker shoulders and back, these forming the cross of the name; the 'silver fox' is very dark, often black, with white-tipped guard hairs which give a silver sheen; and there is also a blue-grey form similar to the blue Arctic Fox. In the United States this morph is often called the 'bastard fox'.

Red Foxes breed across the Arctic, but confined to southerly latitudes, being absent from Greenland and high-latitude Arctic islands (i.e. Svalbard, Russian islands apart from the southern island of Novaya Zemlya, and Canada's northern islands). Also absent from Iceland.

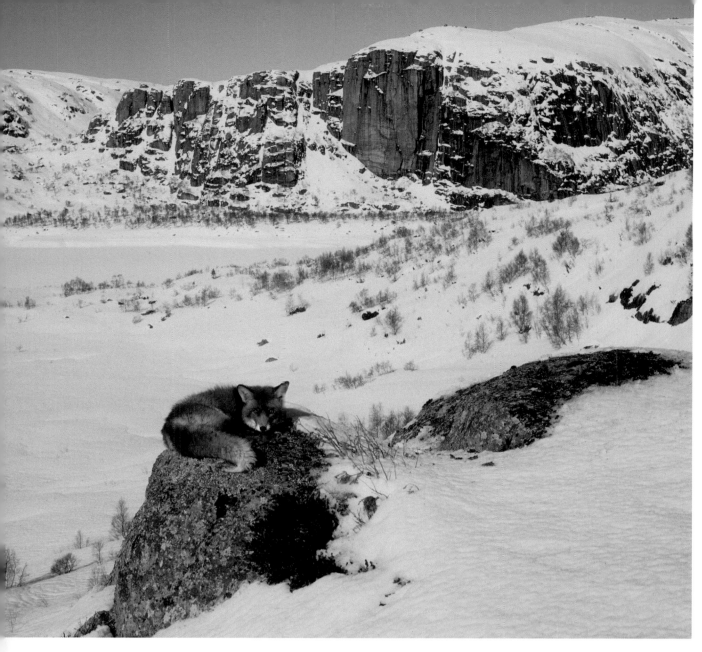

Left
Red Fox, Sirdal, Norway.

Below left
Red Fox, Churchill, Manitoba, Canada.

Below right
Red Fox, Aardal, Norway.

Unfriendly foxes

In areas where both Red and Arctic Foxes occur, the larger Red will drive the Arctic out. As the Red cannot thrive in areas of sparse prey, far-northern latitudes favour the Arctic Fox. The northern limit of the Arctic Fox is therefore defined by the availability of food (and of den sites), while the southern limit is defined by the northern limit of the Red Fox.

BEARS

The three northern species of bears – the Polar, Brown and Black Bears – are at least double the weight of the largest of their southern cousins, size and a low metabolic rate being adaptations for surviving the northern winter. The northern bears are large and powerful creatures, the Brown and Polar Bears being the largest terrestrial carnivores on Earth.

Both Brown and Black Bears exhibit periods of winter torpor that require the laying down of fat reserves. The Polar Bear does not have such periods (pregnant females do undergo winter torpor in the maternity den; males do not, though they will dig a den in which they rest during periods of bad weather), but it has retained the size of the Brown Bear from which it has relatively recently evolved. Exactly when the split occurred is still debated. It is assumed that a population of Brown Bears were isolated from conspecifics during an ice age and evolved to cater for the icy habitat they found themselves in. The split would have occurred during the last million years, and very probably within 250,000 years, but perhaps as recently as 100,000 years ago. The northern bears share a very similar dentition. Brown and Black Bears are omnivorous, and they have molars with broad, rounded cusps suitable for grinding plant material, and a diastema – a gap between the canines and the molars created by absent (or vestigial) premolars, which is used for stripping bark. Each of these adaptations for omnivory is a disadvantage for the wholly carnivorous Polar Bear.

Bears do not form long-lived bonds, mating occurring when a male bear encounters a female in mating condition. Male Polar Bears, which do not hold territories, attempt to keep a female away from other males while she is receptive. Male Brown and Black Bears do hold territories, and these usually overlap the territories of several females, all of which the male will mate with. However, females will also mate with other males they encounter while receptive. Ovulation in bears is stimulated by copulation, the fertilised egg developing to a blastocyst whose implantation is delayed. Delayed implantation evolved in Brown and Black Bears to allow the females to focus on laying down fat reserves in late summer and autumn, rather than cub-rearing. Courtship and mating take place late spring, the blastocyst being implanted during autumn. Birth occurs in the maternity den during the female's winter torpor. At birth the altricial cubs are very small. Mother bears lose up to 40% of their body weight during torpor (and up to 50% in some female Polar Bears).

Information on the dangers of bears is given in A Traveller's Guide to the Arctic below.

Polar Bear

Ursus maritimus

HB: ♂ 190–240cm, ♀ 170–200cm. T: 8–10cm. HS 120–150.
W: ♂ 350–650kg (exceptionally to 800kg) ♀ 150–300kg.
Status: IUCN: Vulnerable. CITES: Appendix II.

The symbol of the Arctic, not only for the traveller but also for the Inuit, who fear and admire the bear in equal measures. Polar Bears are cream or pale yellow, rather than white (though when seen against a dark background they certainly do look white). The fur comprises a thick underfur up to 5cm long with guard hairs that grow to 15cm. A layer of blubber 5–15cm thick lies beneath the skin. So good is the bear's insulation that they are more in danger of overheating than of hypothermia, particularly if they are running. In short bursts

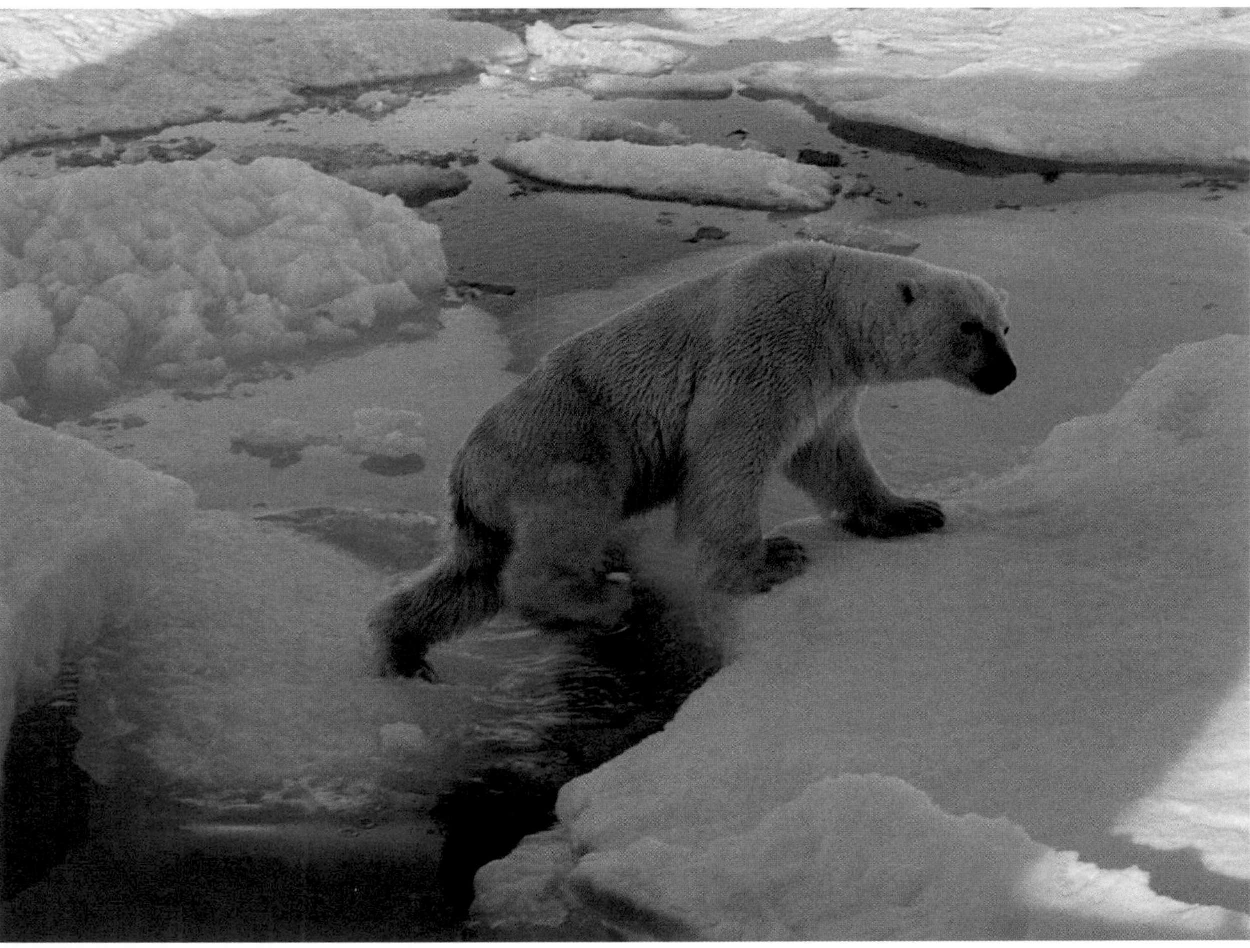

Polar Bear on summer sea ice, Kvitøya, Svalbard.

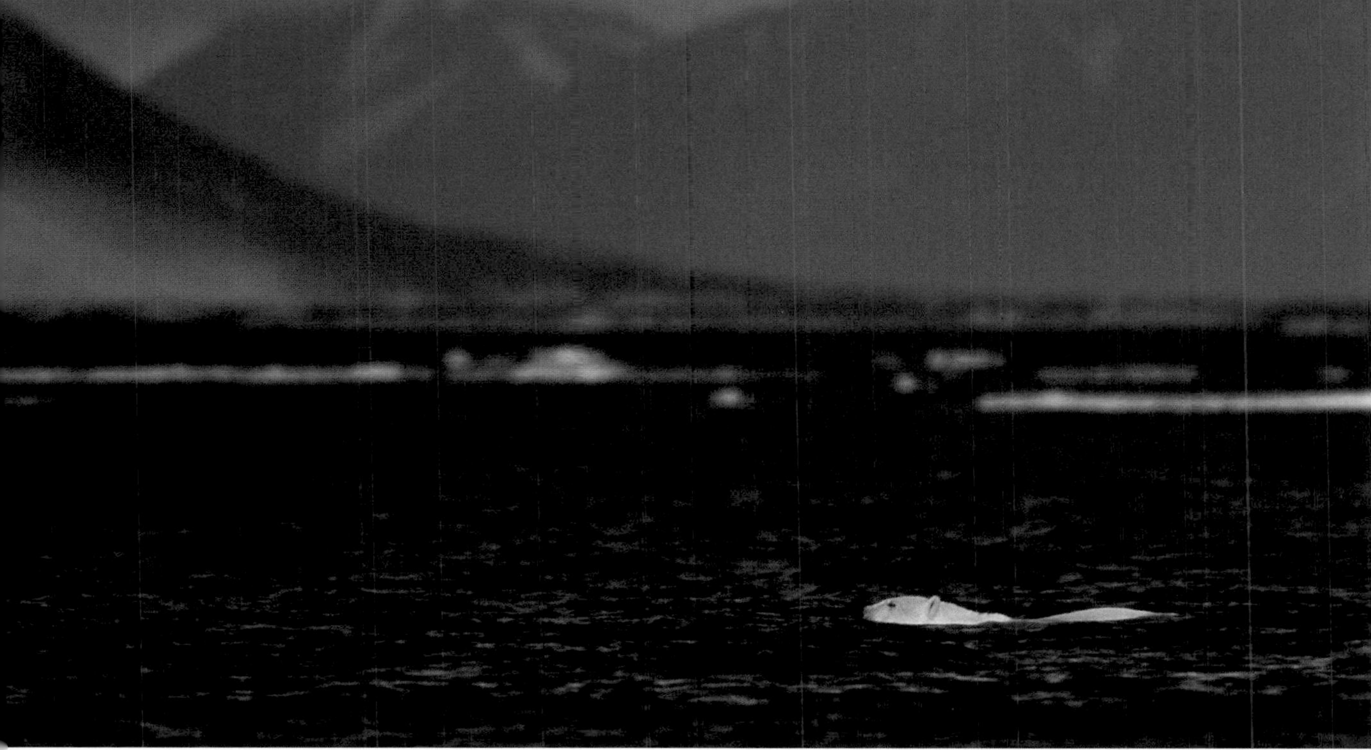

Above
Polar Bear on the sea ice of Agardhbukta, Spitsbergen, Svalbard.

Left
Swimming Polar Bear, Woodfjorden, Spitsbergen, Svalbard.

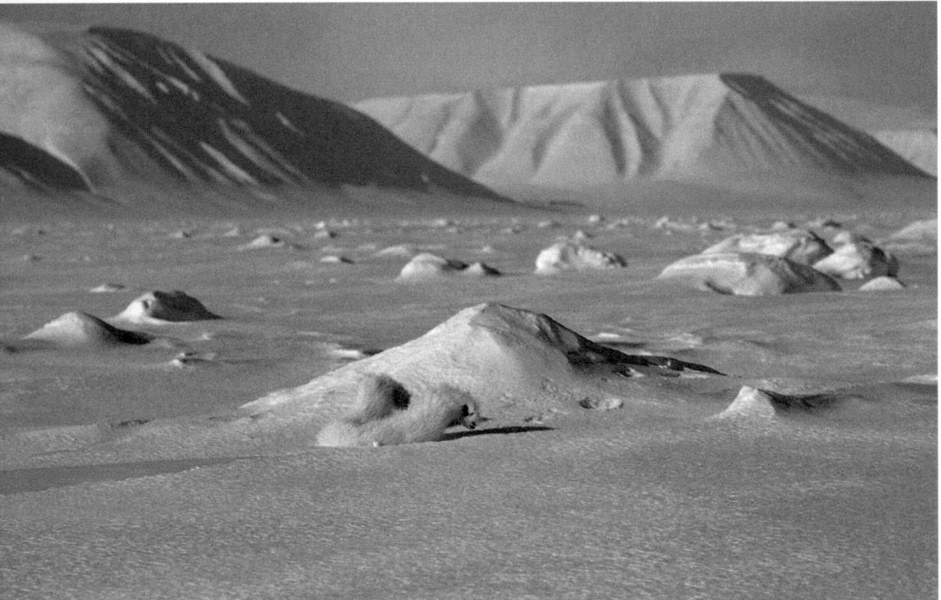

Polar Bear hunting on the sea-ice off Spitsbergen's east coast.

they can achieve 40km/h, but such activity rapidly causes overheating. Hot bears lie on their backs and expose the soles of the feet to cool down, an endearing posture. In warm weather the bears will excavate dens in the snow to keep cool. In water the bears travel at about 2–3kph and can cover great distances, though tales of bears up to 100km from shore almost certainly refer to individuals carried on an ice flow that subsequently melted.

Polar Bear hunting techniques

Polar Bears primarily hunt seals, chiefly the Ringed Seal. Female seals give birth to their pups in dens above the sea ice, the pups protected by a layer of compacted snow into which the female digs. When a bear detects a den it rises on its hind legs and crashes down through the den roof. If the bear is lucky it seizes the pup or blocks the escape hole into the ocean. If the bear is unlucky it fails to break through or misses the pup, which escapes. Bears that fail to break through immediately will often try again, but the chances of catching a pup are much reduced if more than one attempt is necessary. On average, a bear succeeds in catching a pup in about one in three attempts; if multiple attempts are needed to break through the roof this percentage falls rapidly. The technique is also used for hunting resting adult seals.

Bears also wait at breathing holes catching seals as they surface. They will also attack Belugas stranded in leads in the sea ice, clawing at a whale each time it surfaces until the animal becomes exhausted by blood loss and anxiety and can be hauled on to the ice. Polar Bears will also search among hauled-out walruses for pups. In the sea a walrus is a match for a bear, and may even inflict fatal damage with its tusks on land, but large walruses are not very mobile and the nimble bear can occasionally steal a new-born pup from an irate, but helpless, mother.

There are many stories of the cunning of bears; these tell of bears that excavate the breathing holes of seals to make capture easier, then shield the hole with their heads so the seal does not observe a change in light level, and of bears hunting with a paw over their noses (the only black mark on them). Though apparently easy to dismiss, there is historical evidence to support claims of such crafty prey-capture techniques. Clements Markham, a midshipman on the British ship *Assistance*, one of the four ships of Horatio Austin's Franklin search expedition of 1850–51, reported in a letter to his father that he watched a Polar Bear 'swimming across a lane of water [and] pushing a large piece of ice before him. Landing on a floe he advanced stealthily toward a couple of seals basking in the Sun at some little distance, still holding the ice in front of him to hide his black muzzle.' And there is a credible story of a bear stalking a seal in water by swimming towards it when the seal surfaced, then floating, motionless when the seal submerged. Seal eyes are at their best underwater so this strategy allowed the seal to believe the bear was a piece of floating ice. The strategy was apparently successful.

An adult Polar Bear has a characteristic 'roman' nose and lacks the shoulder muscle hump of a Brown Bear. The nose and lips are black. The ears are small, but the animal has large feet to aid walking on snow. The forepaws are also used as paddles by the swimming bear; the back legs are not used in water and trail behind the animal.

Polar Bears are found throughout the Arctic and have been seen as far south as Iceland, mainland Scandinavia and even Japan's northern island, Hokkaido. Female bears regularly den in James Bay (at the same latitude as London). These bears, forced to live on land when the sea ice retreats, may eat berries and plants while waiting for the sea ice to reform, though many actually fast for many months. The sea ice of western Hudson Bay forms first at Cape Churchill, explaining why the bears (and bear watchers) congregate there. When the sea ice forms, the bears disappear.

Female Polar Bear and twin cubs, Storfjorden, Spitsbergen, Svalbard.

Polar Bear on sea ice illuminated by the midnight Sun, Kapp Dufferin, Spitsbergen, Svalbard.

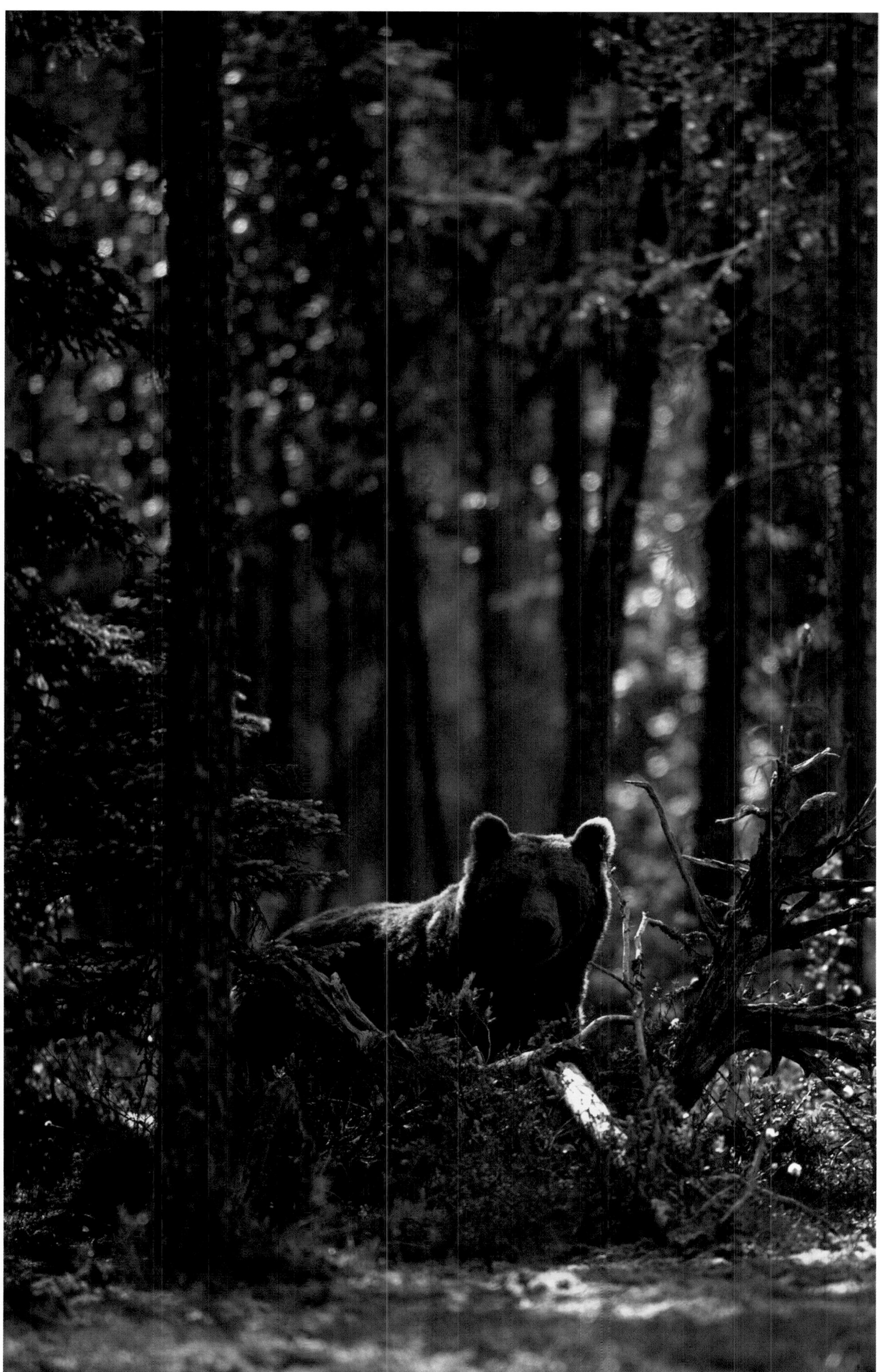

Left
Brown Bear in the 'no-man's-land between Finland and Russia.

Opposite page

Above
Newly emerged from the maternity den, these Polar Bear twins are having a lesson in seal catching on the sea ice of Storfjorden, Svalbard.

Below
Despite being primarily ice dwellers, Polar Bears are often seen on land. Leifdefjorden, northern Svalbard.

'Grizzly' Bear, Denali National Park.

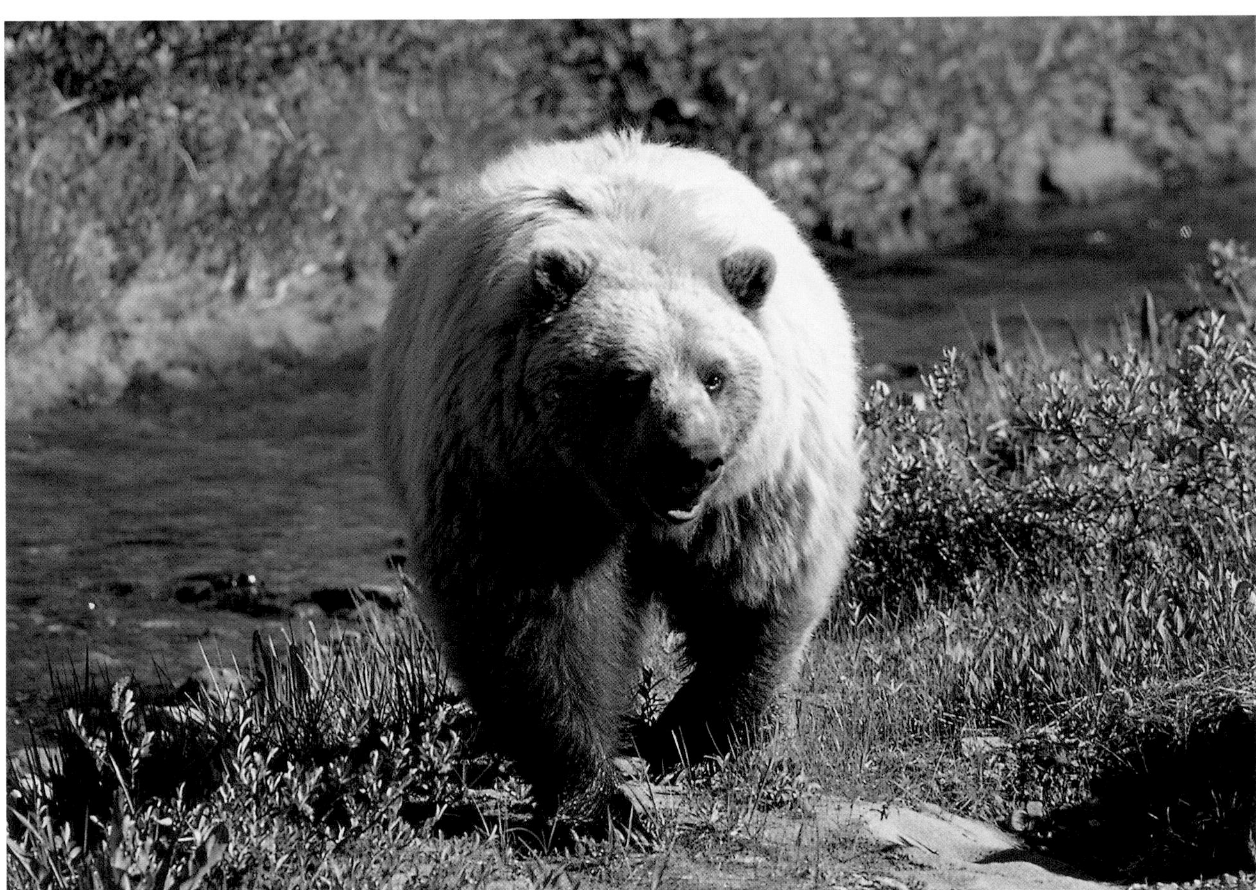

Brown Bear

Ursus arctos

HB: 1.7–2.8m. T: 6–21cm. HS 90–150cm. W: ♂ 150–400kg, ♀ 80–200kg.

Status: CITES: Appendix II.

Arguably the largest bear, though the largest male Polar Bears may be bigger. Weights in excess of 1,000kg have been claimed for Kodiak Brown Bears (which exceeds the largest-known Polar Bear weight). Similar weights may also be achieved by the bears of Kamchatka, which, like those of Kodiak, feed on spawning salmon and therefore put on huge fat reserves before winter torpor.

Brown Bears are uniformly dark brown, though some individuals are paler (and may even be very pale or grey-brown), while others may be almost black. Some bears have paler tips to the guard hairs, giving them a 'grizzled' appearance (hence the name Grizzly Bear). However, some Grizzlies may be so pale overall that this is barely discernible. The muscle-hump at the shoulders is prominent in many individuals. In general Brown Bears have a concave head profile, i.e. a 'dish' face. The bears are omnivorous, feeding chiefly on plant material but taking mammals opportunistically (they will sometimes excavate rodent burrows) and will occasionally chase down sick animals as large as Elk, or young animals, and some feed extensively on spawning salmon.

Brown Bears breed throughout the Arctic, but they are absent from Greenland and all Arctic islands (with the possible exception of Banks Island). The majority of the population is in Russia.

On a southern Kamchatka beach a Brown Bear searches for clams in the early morning mist, ignored by a flock of Slaty-backed Gulls.

Fish-eating Brown Bears

Although Alaskan Brown Bears, which famously feed on the McNeil River (where permits to photograph them are so sought-after that an annual lottery is organised to decide on the lucky few) and in the Katmai National Park, have achieved world-renown for both their fishing antics and their size, the bears of Kamchatka, which also feed on spawning fish, are also much larger than bears that do not benefit from this annual food bonanza. This has led to a 'bragging rights' competition as to which country has the biggest bears. From personal experience there seems little to choose between the larger individuals on each side of the ocean.

Above left
Woken early by the photographer, this Kamchatka Brown Bear roars its annoyance.

Above right
Fishing Brown Bear, McNeil River, Alaska.

Left
Black Bear, northern Ontario.

Wintering bears

In winter both Brown and Black Bears enter a state of torpor, a strategy forced on them by a lack of winter food. In each case the heart rate reduces (from 40–70 beats/minute to *c.*10 beats/minute in the case of the Brown Bear), though body temperature is maintained just a few degrees below normal; this means that the bears can swiftly rouse themselves if danger threatens, with this particularly important for females with cubs. The bears are able to survive for up to six months not only without eating or drinking, but also without urinating or defecating, an ability not shared by any other mammal.

Black Bear

Ursus americanus

HB: 1.4–2m. T: 8–14cm. HS: 60–90cm. W: ♂ 60–150kg, ♀ 40–80kg, exceptionally ♂ to 400kg, ♀ to 230kg

Status: CITES: Appendix II.

Adult bears have a range of pelage colours. Black is, not surprisingly, the usual colour, but the Kermode Bear of west central British Columbia (chiefly found on offshore islands), is white, the Glacier Bear of Glacier Bay, Prince William Sound is blue-grey and the Cinnamon Bear of Alaska varies from pale cinnamon to dark brown.

Black Bears breed in the forests of Alaska and Canada, rarely being seen above the treeline.

Black Bear numbers

Black Bears are the most numerous of the bears, with some estimates suggesting that there are more Black Bears than the combined populations of all the other species put together. The population is apparently stable despite an annual mortality due to hunting of more than 30,000 animals. One study suggested that if a bear reaches the age of two, it stands a 90% chance of dying as a result of being shot, trapped or being struck by a vehicle. Human activity therefore represents the greatest risk of mortality to an individual bear, a chastening statistic.

MUSTELIDS

The *Mustelidae* are perhaps the most diverse of the carnivore families, varying in size from the (Least) Weasel to the Sea Otter (the latter being more than 2,000 times heavier than the former). However, all share common features. The body is long and slender, the legs short, the shape ideal for pursuing prey in burrows (and seen even in mustelids that do not adopt this hunting technique – the Wolverine, for example, which is too large to do so). This shape, ideal for hunting small rodents, has the disadvantage of a large surface area-to-volume ratio, which is not optimal for reducing heat loss. As a consequence, the metabolic rate of these mammals is high and they must hunt frequently, despite the high energy value of their diet. Some of the smaller female mustelids, when nursing young, must consume in excess of 60% of their body weight daily. One other feature common to the group is the shape of the head, which is flattened and wedge-shaped, another adaptation for hunting in burrows.

Most mustelids are sexually dimorphic. This reaches an extreme in the Weasel, where the male is sometimes twice the weight of the female. This may be a response to prey availability, the two sizes meaning that males take larger prey and so do not compete with potential mates – but while this might be true of southern mustelids, the prey of most northern species is limited to the same range of rodents. An alternative theory suggests that females are smaller so that their energy needs are reduced, requiring them to catch fewer prey when they are lactating. Males could also be larger to increase the likelihood of their holding territories and competing for females.

In general mustelids kill their prey with a bite to the base of the skull, crushing the brain, or to the neck, severing the spinal cord.

(Least) Weasel

Mustela nivalis

HB: ♂ 18–21cm, ♀ 16–18cm. T: ♂ 2.5–4cm, ♀ 2–3cm. W: ♂ 40–55g, ♀ 30–45g.

Adult is chestnut brown above, white below, the delineation usually very distinct. The feet are white, the tail chestnut, lacking the black tip of the Stoat. In winter the animals are entirely white.

Black Bear, Chapleau, Ontario, Canada. Black Bears are frequent visitors to dumps near human settlements, and often require tagging and monitoring in case they become a nuisance. As the Earth warms and people spread north, interactions with northern bears will become more common, and inevitably the bears will lose out.

Above left
Stoat, Sirdal, Norway.

Above right
Stoat (Short-tailed Weasel), Kodiak Island, Alaska.

Formidable hunters

Size for size, the smaller mustelids are perhaps the most effective and formidable of all the carnivores, with the Weasel and Stoat the champion hunters. It is possible that the absence of a significant Weasel population might actually be the initial cause of a 'lemming year'. The absence of normal predation means a rise in the number of first-litter young reaching sexual maturity, which in turn drives up the population sharply.

Weasels breed throughout the Arctic, but they are absent from Greenland, Iceland and the Arctic islands of Canada and Russia.

Stoat (Short-tailed Weasel)

Mustela erminea

HB: ♂ 16–30cm, ♀ 13–25cm. T: 7–10cm. W: ♂ 70–170g, ♀ 30–90g.

Adult is chestnut above, cream or pale yellow below, with strong delineation between the two. The feet are chestnut, the tail chestnut with a distinct black tip. The black tip is retained when the rest of the fur turns white in winter. The North American name, Short-tailed Weasel, relates to the length of the tail relative to the Long-tailed Weasel *Mustela frenata* of the southern Canada and the USA.

The Stoat breeds throughout the Arctic, wherever rodents are found. This includes Greenland, but not Iceland or Svalbard. Breeds on Canada's Arctic islands as far north as Ellesmere. Not observed to date on Russia's Arctic islands, but they probably breed on islands with rodents, though in general Palearctic Stoats are boreal. Nearctic Stoats are the most northerly mustelids.

Ermine gowns

In Europe the winter Stoat, known as the ermine, was highly prized for its fur. In Britain ermine skins were used to create the upper sections of cloaks worn by members of the House of Lords, the tail-tips providing the black spots in the otherwise milk-white cloaks.

Below left and right
Stoats (Short-tailed Weasels) on Victoria Island, Canada. The animal to the left has normal coloration. The one to the right is not in winter pelage, but is albino. Despite their reputation for ferocity, stoats are prey to large birds of prey and other carnivores, and this conspicuous albino animal will need to stay alert to survive.

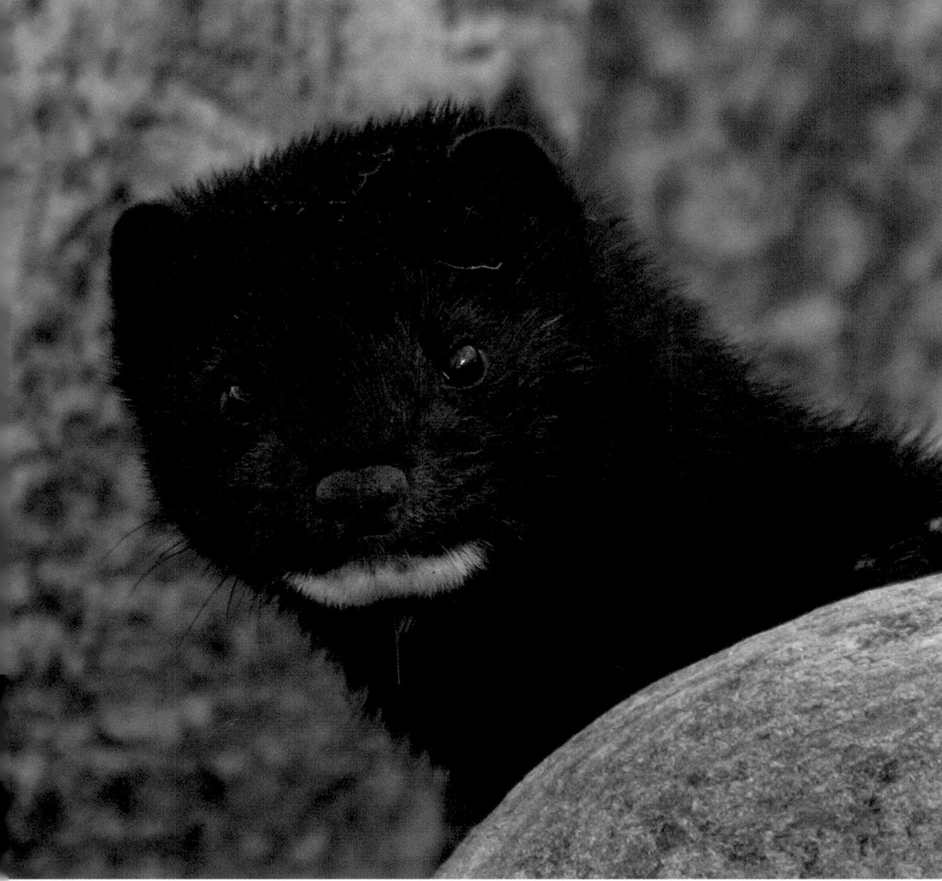

American Mink, Randaberg, Norway. The species has become established after escaping from fur farms and is now found wild throughout Scandinavia.

American Mink

Mustela vison

HB: 32–45cm. T: 13–23cm. W: 0.6–1.2kg. ♂>♀.

Adult has luxurious, lustrous dark brownish black fur, with a white patch on the lower lip. Feet and tail coloured as body fur. In Europe escapes from fur farms (which now breed over much of the continent) may be exotically coloured (which include cream and blue), but populations seem to be reverting to the natural colour.

American Mink breed throughout the Arctic, but are absent from Greenland and all Arctic islands (apart from Iceland, where a population has established from escapes). Originally found in the Nearctic only, Palearctic animals are localised but spreading, and now occur at sites throughout Scandinavia and Russia.

European Mink

Mustela lutreola

HB: 30–40cm. T: 12–20cm. W: 500–800g. ♂>♀.

Status: IUCN: Endangered.

Adult almost identical to American Mink, but has a white upper lip in addition to the lower-lip patch; also marginally smaller. Interestingly, despite the morphological similarities, DNA analysis shows that the two species are not closely related.

European Mink once bred in Scandinavia and western Europe, but are now extinct except in Russia, where they breed around the southern shores of the White Sea and eastwards to the Ob River.

American Marten

Martes americana

HB: 30–45cm. T: 18–23cm. W: 500–1200g. ♂>♀.

Adults vary from buff to very dark brown. Feet and bushy tail are as body fur, though legs, feet and tail are usually darker in paler animals.

American Martens are arboreal (in all forms of forest) and nocturnal. They may therefore be observed only to the treeline. They breed across North America.

Pine Marten

Martes martes

HB: 35–55cm. T: 17–25cm. W: 500–2200g. ♂>♀.

Adult is chocolate brown with a cream to yellow-buff throat patch (or bib). Pine Marten and Sable are the Old World equivalent of the American Marten, inhabiting conifer or mixed forests (rare in deciduous forests). As with the Nearctic species, the Pine Marten is chiefly nocturnal.

Pine Martens breed to the treeine in Scandinavia and western Russia, to the Ob River.

Wolverine, Karelia, Finland.

Wolverine, Karelia, Finland.

SABLE

Martes zibellina

HB: 35–55cm. T: 12–18cm. W: 0.9–2kg. ♂>♀.

Adults vary from golden-brown to almost black, but mainly dark brown. There are usually paler patches on the cheeks and nose, and a paler bib.

Sable replace Pine Marten as the boreal marten in eastern Russia. Formerly more widespread, but the population was severely reduced by trapping. Still relatively abundant in Kamchatka.

The glutton

The Wolverine is the largest Palearctic mustelid (in the Nearctic the Sea Otter is, in general, larger). In Europe the animal is often called the glutton (this being the basis of the species' scientific name) because of its reputation for greed. It is known to take bait from traps set by fur trappers, and to eat trapped animals, these habits hardly endearing the species to people. It also has a reputation for being a cruel killer. The Sámi claim that if a satiated Wolverine catches a Reindeer it will gouge out its eyes so that the deer cannot move. The Wolverine will then, it is said, return when it is hungry to kill and feed on the still-fresh animal. In the absence of significant competition from Wolves this strategy might just work, but historically Wolves and Wolverines have shared ranges. More importantly, Wolverines invariably dismember large prey and cache sections in well-separated places. The Sámi's tale is black propaganda against an occasional Reindeer predator.

WOLVERINE

Gulo gulo

HB: 75–100cm. T: 12–15cm. HS: 40–45cm. W: 16–30kg. ♂>♀.

Status: IUCN: Vulnerable.

Adult is dark brown, with yellow-brown/golden-brown stripes from behind the front leg across the lower flank to the rear, and across the base of the tail. There are similar patches between the eyes and the small ears. Wolverines are heavy animals with short legs, large paws and bushy tails.

The Wolverine breeds throughout the Arctic, but it is absent from Greenland, Iceland, Svalbard, Russia's Arctic islands and some Canadian Arctic islands.

(EURASIAN RIVER) OTTER

Lutra lutra

HB: 60–90cm. T: 35–45cm. HS: 30cm. W: 7–17kg. ♂>♀.

Status: IUCN: Near Threatened. CITES: Appendix I.

Adult is dark brown above, paler (even cream) below, the two colours not well delineated. On the face the pale colour extends to the lower ear. The tail is long, thick at the base and tapering to the tip, and uniformly dark brown. All the feet are fully webbed. The broad muzzle has many stiff hairs that are tactile and help locate prey in murky waters.

The Otter breeds in northern Scandinavia and across Russia to southern Chukotka and Kamchatka, but it is rarely found north of the Arctic boundary as defined in this book.

American River Otter (Northern River Otter)

Lontra canadensis

HB: 65–75cm. T: 30–50cm. HS: 30cm. W: 5–14kg. ♂>♀.
Status: IUCN: Least Concern. CITES: Appendix II.
Adult is almost identical to the Eurasian River Otter, being rich dark brown above, pale brown or cream below, with a silvery sheen on the breast.

More Arctic in range than its Palearctic cousin, breeding throughout Alaska (though rare in the far north and absent from the Aleutian and Bering Sea islands), the Yukon, North West Territories, around Hudson Bay and throughout Quebec and Labrador. However, the species is rarely found as far north as the coast.

Sea Otter

Enhydra lutris

HB: 1.1–1.5m. T: 25–45cm. W: 15–45kg. ♂>♀.
Status: IUCN: Endangered. CITES: Appendix II (apart from race *nereis,* which is Appendix I).
Adults vary in colour due to variation in the underfur and guard hairs; underfur can be light or dark brown, while the guard hairs can be silver, brown or even black. Overall the animal can therefore appear as pale as buff, or very dark, and the colour may also vary across the pelage. The tail is long and flat, an adaptation for swimming. The paws differ markedly from those of other otters. The rear paws are flippers, similar to those of seals, with full inter-toe webbing. The front paws are similar to those of other otters, but the digits are enclosed in a mitten-like structure, presumably an adaptation for the cold of the marine environment. The animals are clumsy on land, and they spend most of their time in water. Despite the mittens on the front paws, Sea Otters are remarkably dextrous in handling prey.

Sea Otters are Arctic-fringe animals, but few travellers heading north will ignore the possibility of seeing one. They are, without doubt, one of Earth's most cuddlesome animals, with perhaps only Polar Bear cubs coming close in terms of cuteness. Apart from having appealing faces, they also have winning habits. They attach themselves to kelp so they can sleep without floating away, and use their chests as dinner tables as they eat abalone and other marine invertebrates. Shellfish are cracked open by beating them against a stone placed on the chest. Sea Otters will also use a stone to dislodge abalones from the sea floor. Mother Sea Otters nurse their young while floating on their backs.

Sea Otters breed on the coast of North America from California to the western tip of the Aleutians, and from the Commander Islands along the Kamchatka coast to the Kuril Islands and Hokkaido.

The Sea Otter's teeth belie its cuddly appearance. This animal has a wound on its hind flipper, probably the result of a fight over a potential mate. Resurrection Bay, Alaska.

SKUNKS

The *Mephitidae*, the skunks and stink-badgers, are closely related to the mustelids (within which they are often classified and from which they have recently been split, on molecular evidence). The family derives its name from the Latin *mephitis* (foul smelling) and it is the smell for which the skunks are famous. The chemical responsible for the smell is stored in two glands close to the anus, the animal turning its back on a potential predator, raising its tail, and emitting a spray of pungent liquid, which is not only highly offensive but can cause temporary blindness if it hits the eyes. One member of the family may be seen near the Arctic boundary.

Striped Skunk

Mephitis mephitis

HB: 35–50cm. T: 17–30cm. W: 2.7–6.0kg. ♂>♀.
Adult is black apart from a narrow white stripe on the forehead, and a broader white stripe from the nape that divides in two, the two stripes reaching the base of the tail. However, some animals have minimal striping, appearing almost entirely black, while others have very broad stripes and appear almost white.

Striped Skunks are sub-Arctic, but occasionally reach the shores of James Bay and adjacent shores of Hudson Bay.

CATS

The *Felidae* or cats are the most carnivorous of the Carnivora. They are superbly adapted for the role, having exceptional eyesight, hearing and smell, phenomenal agility and (in all bar one) sheathed claws, the sheath maintaining the claws in good condition by avoiding wear. Although primarily warm-climate predators, some cats do live in cold conditions. The Siberian Tiger *Panthera tigris altaica* inhabits southern Siberia, as does the critically endangered Amur Leopard *Panthera pardus amurensis*, while the Snow Leopard *Panthera uncia* lives high among the snows of the Himalayas. However, no cats are truly Arctic. The Old and New World lynxes are primarily boreal hunters, but they may be seen beyond the treeline. Lynxes take rodents, hares, young deer and birds.

Eurasian Lynx

Lynx lynx

HB: 80–130cm. T: 11–25cm. HS: 60–75cm. W: 18–25kg.
Status: IUCN: Near Threatened. CITES: Appendix II.
Adult is stocky with a yellow-brown upper pelage, pale or

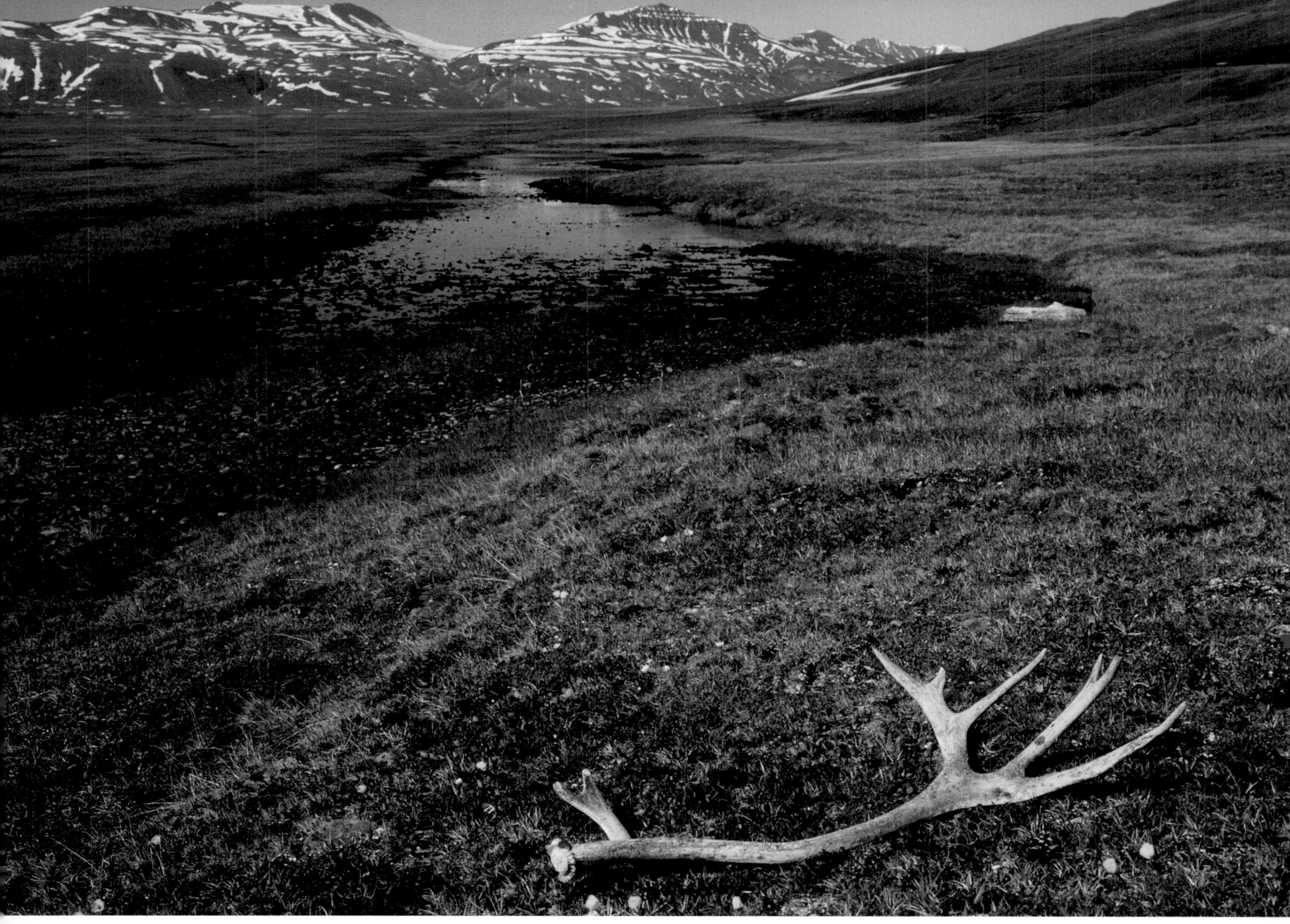

> **Reindeer antlers**
>
> Uniquely among deer, both male and female Reindeer grow antlers. The reason lies in the need to excavate holes in the snow to reach winter browse. The larger males might allow females to dig holes, then evict them to acquire the food for themselves. Antlers allow the female to prevent such piracy. To support this, females maintain their antlers for longer than the males, usually throughout the winter. Furthermore, females of woodland-dwelling Reindeer, which feed on lichens growing on tree trunks, often do not grow antlers – there is always another tree to browse. As with other deer, the energetic cost of producing antlers is considerable, and Reindeer often eat their shed antlers to regain the minerals within.
>
> Since female Reindeer not only possess antlers but maintain them through the winter, Santa's Reindeer is much more likely to be Rachel than Rudolf. The photograph above is of an antler from an extinct dwarf Reindeer at Badlanddalen, north-east Greenland.

cream below. There are usually dark spots and blotches on the body and the fronts of the long legs. The face is streaked black. The tail is short and black-tipped.

The Eurasian Lynx breeds in central Scandinavia (where it is rare) and across Russia to Kamchatka, though only to north coast near the White Sea and the Lena delta. In Kamchatka the animals take Snow Sheep.

Canadian Lynx

Lynx canadensis

HB: 65–110cm. T: 5–13cm. HS: 50–65cm. W: 8–17kg.
Status: IUCN: Least Concern. CITES: Appendix II.
Adult is as Eurasian Lynx but are overall grey or grey-brown, with denser dark flecking on the upper parts.

Canadian Lynx breed in Alaska (but not on the Yukon–Kuskokwin delta or the southern Alaska Peninsula, and rare in the north), the Yukon, North West Territories, Quebec and Labrador, but not to the northern coast.

UNGULATES

The large terrestrial herbivores of the Arctic are artiodactyls, or even-toed ungulates, hoofed animals of the families *Cervidae* and *Bovidae* (the other ungulate group, the perissodactyls or odd-toed ungulates, has no Arctic representatives). The *Cervidae* or deer are distinguished from other artiodactyls by the antlers that are grown by males (and females in Reindeer). In general, antlers are grown and shed annually. They are horn-like extensions that grow out from the frontal bone. The antlers grow within a sensitive, blood vessel-rich covering called velvet. Ultimately the velvet is shed, often hanging in shreds from the antlers for several days until it is finally rubbed free by the deer. In southern deer species the antlers are

Above and right
Feral Reindeer herd, Suldal, Norway.

rubbed against trees, staining them (and damaging the tree), while northern species have to be content with rubbing against the ground, which also stains the bone below. Antlers are used during the rut, the annual mating ritual when males compete to establish and maintain harems of females, mating each time a female becomes receptive. Although many competitions involve merely the showing of the antlers to a rival, accompanied by a bellowing that indicates the fitness of the male (the lower the bellow, the bigger and more worthy the male), occasionally males will lock antlers and engage in battle. Battles are usually trials of strength, the male forced backwards accepting defeat and retreating; antlers are fearsome weapons and could inflict considerable damage, so the males are keen to avoid real conflict. That antlers are a good guide to mating fitness has been confirmed by studies that show that females whose partners had impressive sets produced young that were stronger and matured faster. At the end of the rut bone-dissolving cells invade the base of the antlers, and they are then shed.

Information on the dangers posed by Moose and Musk Oxen is given in A Traveller's Guide to the Arctic below.

Reindeer (Caribou)

Rangifer tarandus

HB: 1.7–2.2m. T: 10–20cm. HS: 80–120cm. W: 60–150kg. ♂>♀.

Adult is dark brown or grey-brown, but paler on the underparts, rump and feet and usually darker on the muzzle and forehead. The tail is surprisingly short, leaving the deer defenceless against mosquitoes and parasitic flies. In winter Reindeer moult to a paler pelage. Reindeer have the widest feet of any deer and also have well-developed dew claws, both features being adaptations for walking on snow. The hooves are also sharp-edged to aid walking on ice. As the Reindeer walks, a tendon stretches across a bony nodule, causing a characteristic click.

There are several Reindeer subspecies. Tundra animals are the best known, but in both North America and Eurasia there are Reindeer that forage in forests – the Woodland Caribou and Forest Reindeer. Three subspecies also breed on islands, one on Svalbard, one on the southern island of Novaya Zemlya, and the third on some northern Canadian islands. In the case of the last two, interbreeding with mainland animals has occurred. This has meant that the pure-bred Novaya Zemlya subspecies has been lost, while the pure-bred Canadian island form (known as the Peary Caribou) now probably exists only on the Queen Elizabeth Islands. The Svalbard Reindeer, though, remains pure-bred. All three island forms are smaller than mainland animals, with shorter legs.

The annual migration

Reindeer use traditional calving grounds, some herds of Caribou travelling more than 5,000km annually between these and winter feeding grounds. The migrations are in part a search for new browse, but also an escape from the predators that feed on the big herds, Wolves and Brown Bears rarely following the Caribou on to the tundra. (This is not entirely true as there are tundra bears and tundra wolves, but there are far fewer of them.)

On migration north the females forge ahead of the males, which feed on the richer southern tundra to put on weight for the rut. The females' progress is so urgent – the animals may travel more than 100km each day (though 25–65km is more usual, maintaining a steady pace of about 7kph) – that if they give birth early they may abandon a calf that cannot keep up. Reindeer are good swimmers and they will cross rivers; the Bathurst Caribou herd crosses Bathurst Inlet twice each year, a swim of 10km.

Origin of the name

The Reindeer of the Palearctic and the Caribou of the Nearctic are the same species. The North American name derives from *xalibu*, which means 'pawer' in Mi'kmaq (Nova Scotian native American), a reference to the animal's pawing search for winter browse.

They are also more solitary, forming small herds or, often, being seen alone. These Reindeer are almost white in winter.

Reindeer were domesticated in Eurasia and truly wild animals are now found only in Russia (including the southern island of Novaya Zemlya and Wrangel Island), though there are feral herds in parts of Scandinavia. There are also feral Reindeer on Iceland. Caribou were never domesticated in North America and huge herds still cross the tundra on annual migrations. Caribou breed throughout Alaska, mainland Canada and the Arctic islands.

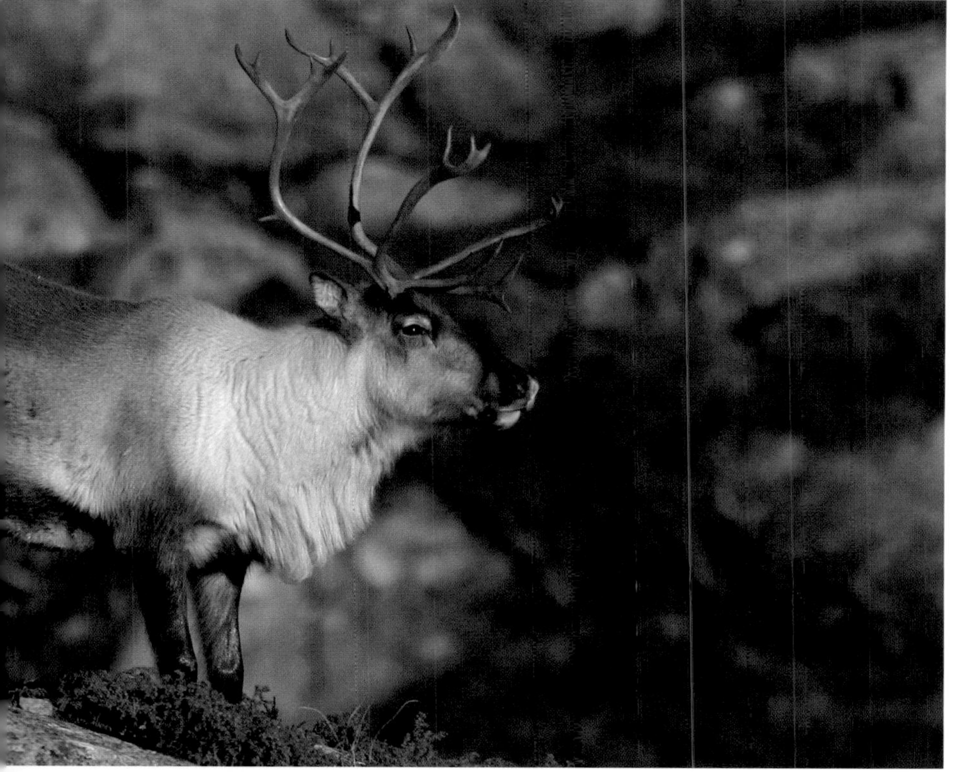

Elk (Moose)

Alces alces

HB: 2.0–2.9m. T: 7–10cm. HS: 1.5–2.2m. W: 300–800kg. ♂>♀.

The world's largest deer, and apart from extreme specimens of the bears, the largest terrestrial Arctic mammal. Adult is dark brown or dark grey-brown, the underparts paler, the legs pale grey-white or grey-brown. Elk have very long legs and a tail which, as with the Reindeer, is short and of little value in combating mosquitoes. The snout is bulbous and a large pendant 'bell' hangs from the throat. The function of this bell is unknown, but bulls spatter the bell with urine-soaked mud during the rut. Male Elk have enormous antlers, which are usually palmate, though regular 'deer-like' antlers have been seen. In some large males the antlers can weigh 30kg and have a spread of 2m.

Elk breed throughout the Arctic, though they are absent from Greenland, Iceland and all the Arctic islands. In Russia Elk do not breed east of the

Caribou, Seward Peninsula, Alaska.

Svalbard Reindeer.
The animal to the right was photographed at Forlandsundet, Spitsbergen, Svalbard, the animals below at Engelsbukta, also on Spitsbergen.

Ob River. Although essentially a boreal species, Elk are also found on tundra.

> **Elk or Moose?**
> The different names of this animal cause much more confusion than the Reindeer/Caribou pairing. The North American name, Moose, derives from an Algonquin name meaning 'twigeater', while the European name is from the Germanic *elch*. The confusion arises because in North America the name Elk is given to another animal – *Cervus canadensis*, also known as the Wapiti, and very similar to the European Red Deer *Cervus elaphus*.

Musk Ox

Ovibos moschatus

HB: 1.8–2.5cm. T: 10–12cm. HS: 90–160cm. W: 220–400kg (♂ exceptionally to 600kg). ♂>♀.

Although they belong to the same family (*Bovidae*) as cattle, Musk Oxen are not true oxen; they are more closely related to the goats and sheep. Adult unmistakeable, with its long straggling hair (individual hairs can be 70cm long), often long enough to cover the short legs. The pelage is dark brown or dark grey-brown, but with a paler saddle. The muzzle and legs are also paler. The fine underfur is claimed by many to provide the finest wool in the world. Known by the Inuit word *qiviut*, it is highly prized for the manufacture of (very expensive) small items of clothing, chiefly scarves. The upturned horns arise from each end of a central boss across the top of the head. The structure is formidable and is a significant fraction of the animal's total weight. The hooves are broad, with a sharp outer rim and a softer inner one, giving the Musk Ox surprising agility on rock.

Bull Elk photographed in the light of early morning, Vanern, Sweden.

Musk Oxen breed in western and northern Alaska (though these are introduced animals originally released near Fairbanks, then on Nunivak Island in 1935 as the native stock was eliminated by hunting – to provide meat for whalers – in the 1860s), on the northern rim of mainland Canada west of Hudson Bay, and on western and northern Canadian Arctic islands. Absent from Baffin Island, but a small herd breeds near

Female Elk, Vanern, Sweden.

The Moose of North America are now considered to be four subspecies of the Eurasian Elk. The largest animals are the sub-species which breeds in Alaska (*A. a. gigas*).

Above left
A female and twin calves on the Seward Peninsula.

Above right
A calf in the Denali National Park, Alaska.

Right
The calf's mother was fitted with a radio collar as part of a research programme. The curious 'bell' on the throat is clearly seen.

Ungava Bay in Quebec. Also breeds in north-east and north Greenland, and has been re-introduced to north-west and western Greenland. Absent from Iceland. Was introduced to Svalbard, where it almost certainly never occurred naturally, but this population is now extinct. Has been introduced to Scandinavia and (re-introduced) to Russia, but populations are small.

Dall's Sheep (White Sheep, Thin-horn Sheep)

Ovis dalli

HB: 1.3–1.8m. T: 7–11cm. HS: 90–105cm. W: 50–110kg. ♂>♀.
Adult is white (though Stone's Sheep, a subspecies from southern Yukon, is grey-brown). The hooves are black, the tail very short. The horns curve back from the forehead, and are then strongly down-curved with forward-pointing tips. The ram's horns are up to 100cm long; those of ewes are smaller and straighter, and up to 25cm in length.

Dall's Sheep breed in upland areas of Alaska and Yukon, but rarely to the north coast.

Snow Sheep

Ovis nivicola

HB: 1.6–1.8m. T: 7–12cm. HS: 80–100cm. W: 70–100kg (exceptionally to 140kg). ♂>♀.
Adults vary in colour. They are usually brown with paler underparts and rump patch. The rump patch is often white and may spread on to the lower back. The forelegs are usually darker. The horns are similar in size and form to those of Dall's Sheep.

Snow Sheep breed in upland areas of eastern Siberia, including Chukotka and Kamchatka.

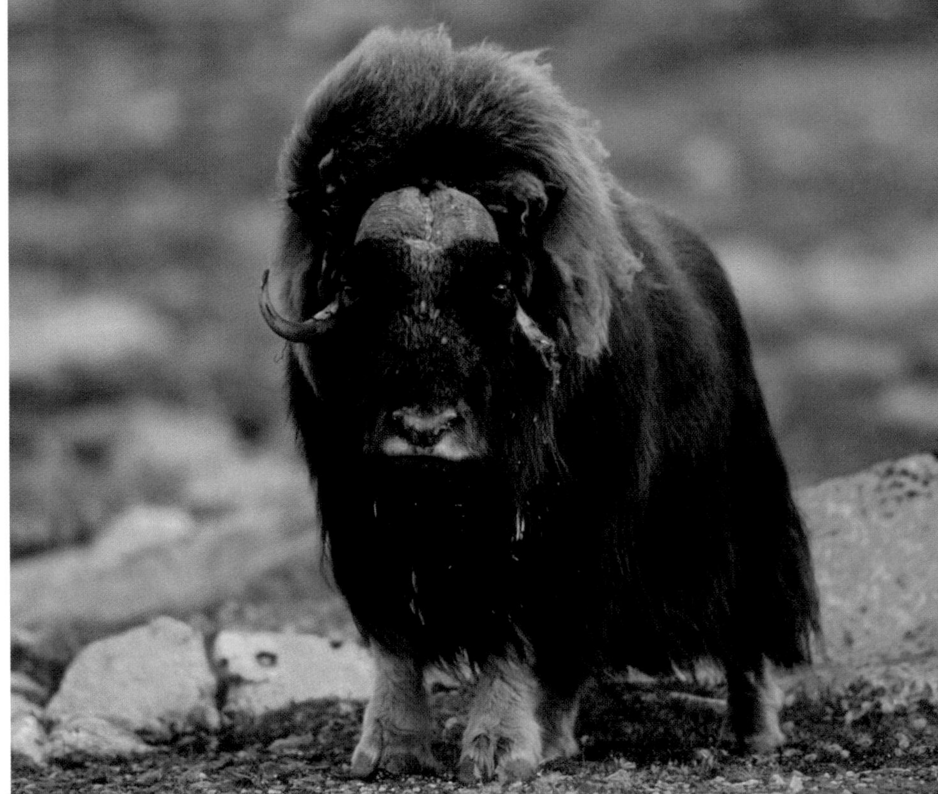

Bull Musk Ox, Kapp Petersens, north-east Greenland.

A defence against Wolves

When attacked by Wolves, Musk Oxen form a defensive circle with the calves at the centre. Each animal faces outwards, thus presenting the pack with a ring of massive horns and head bosses, a blow from which would inflict significant, perhaps fatal, injury to an individual Wolf. As long as the oxen maintain the circle they are almost invulnerable. Stand-offs lasting several hours have been observed, though usually the Wolves give up and leave if attempts to break the circle fail. The Wolves make occasional forays forward, seeking to make the herd break up and run. Even if the Musk Oxen do make a run for it, they can foil the Wolves so long as they remain a cohesive unit. But sometimes the Wolves run into the herd, biting at flanks and seeking out a young or weak animal. Once an individual has been isolated the pack concentrates on it: the outcome is then a foregone conclusion.

The circle is a good adaptation to Wolf predation, but is useless against a man with a rifle, and the Musk Oxen of north-east Greenland were almost hunted to extinction in the 1930s by Norwegian fur-trappers, who shot them to feed themselves and their dogs. A similar slaughter in the Canadian Arctic led to the government protecting the species in 1917, and was the primary reason for the creation of the Thelon Game Sanctuary in 1927.

The photograph above of a herd taking up its defensive position was taken near the Hood River in the Barren Lands of Nunavut, Canada.

RODENTS

With a species list that comprises more than 40% of all mammals, the rodents are one of the most successful and widespread of all the mammalian orders. They are also one of the most numerous, a consequence of their prodigious ability to breed. Female rodents can often breed when only six weeks old, have a gestation time of only *c.*20 days, and are often sexually receptive within days of giving birth. Studies on mice have shown that a single breeding pair can yield a population in excess of 500 within six months.

Rodents have an essential ecological role – they are pivotal in supporting many populations of predatory mammals and birds, for example. Several mycorrhizal fungi (the most famous of which are the truffles) are spread only by being consumed and then excreted by rodents. As the fungi are necessary for the growth of plants, the rodents play an important role in the spread and establishment of plants; the recolonisation of land uncovered by the retreating ice of the last Ice Age was hastened by the spread of mycorrhizal fungi.

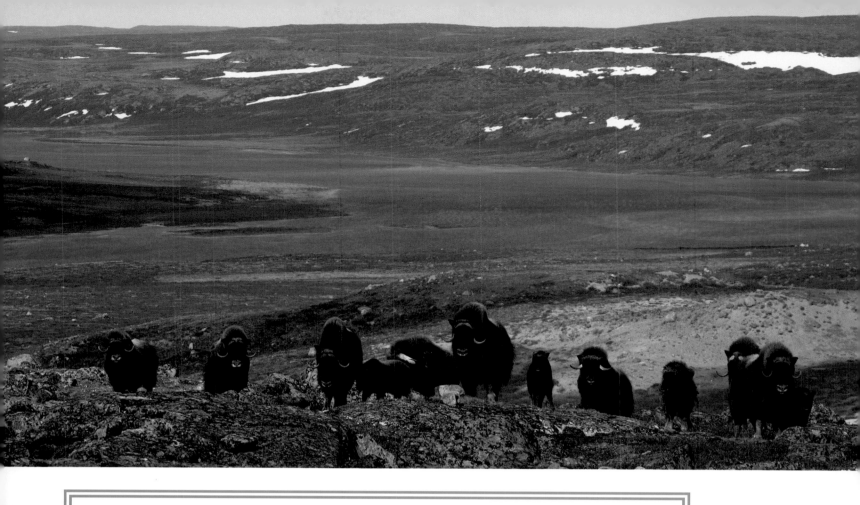

Snow Sheep, Kamchatka, Russia.

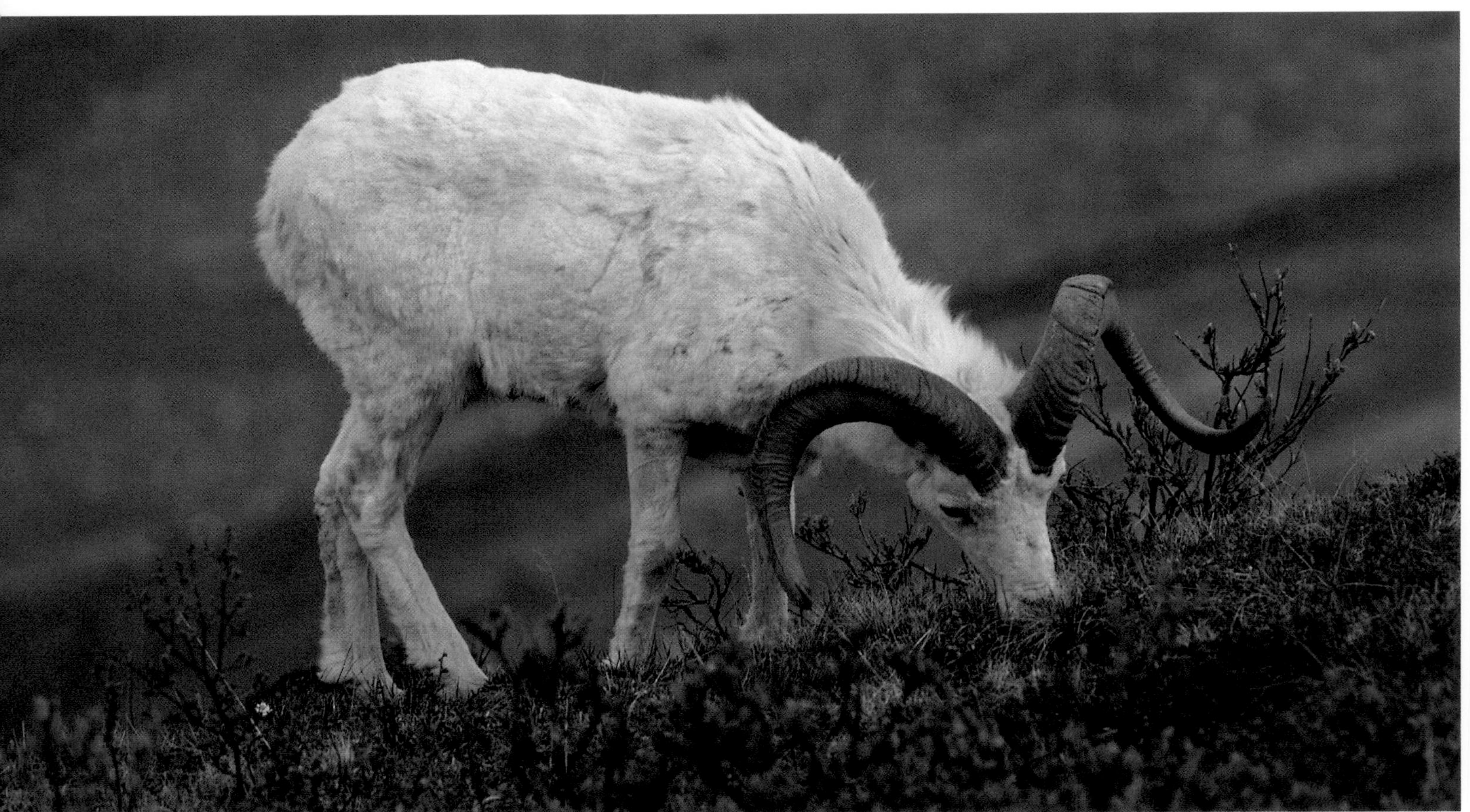

Dall's Ram, Denali National Park, Alaska.

SQUIRRELS

Squirrels are arboreal rodents and, as such, cannot be classified as true Arctic dwellers. Nevertheless, several species are found as far north as the treeline and may therefore be seen by Arctic travellers.

EURASIAN RED SQUIRREL

Sciuris vulgaris

HB: 18–25cm. T: 14–20cm. W: 250–350g.

Status: IUCN: Near Threatened.

Adult is red-brown overall, but paler on the underparts. In winter the pelage is darker. The tail is bushy. There are usually ear tufts, these being more prominent in winter.

The Eurasian Red Squirrel breeds to the treeline in Scandinavia and across Russia to Kamchatka.

AMERICAN RED SQUIRREL (SPRUCE SQUIRREL)

Tamiasciuris hudsonicus

HB: 15–20cm. T: 10–15cm. W: 140–250g.

Adult is red-brown above (usually darker and less 'warm' than the Eurasian Red Squirrel), paler below. There is sometimes a black band separating the upper and lower parts. In winter the pelage is brighter. The tail is bushy. In winter the ear tufts are more prominent.

The American Red Squirrel breeds to the treeline across North America.

NORTHERN FLYING SQUIRREL

Glaucomys sabrinus

HB: 12–18cm. T: 12–15cm. W: 75–140g.

Adult is light to dark brown above, cream below; has large, dark eyes (the species is nocturnal). There is a membrane between the front and hind legs, which allows it to glide between trees. The broad tail is also flattened to aid gliding. There is a cartilaginous bar from the wrist that gives the squirrel a certain amount of steering control in the glide.

The Northern Flying Squirrel breeds to the treeline across North America, but it is rarer in the west.

GROUND SQUIRRELS AND MARMOTS

ARCTIC GROUND SQUIRREL (LONG-TAILED SOUSLIK, PARKA SQUIRREL)

Citellus parryi

HB: 25–35cm. T: 7.5–15cm. W: 530–850g. ♂>♀.

Adult is tawny brown with buff and white flecking. The head is darker, the forehead and face usually red-brown. The tail is

Rodere – to gnaw

Rodents vary greatly in size (the smallest weigh just a few grams, while the Capybara *Hydrochoreus hydrochaeris* can weigh 70kg) and form, but they do have features in common, one of which is that in both the upper and lower jaws there is a pair of incisors that grow continuously. These teeth require the animal to gnaw in order to maintain incisor length – the word rodent derives from the Latin *rodere*, to gnaw. If the animal were to stop gnawing, the teeth of the lower jaw would eventually grow into the brain, while those of the upper jaw would grow through the lower lip, though in either case death through starvation would happen first. Feeding generally provides all the gnawing needed, but rodents will sometimes gnaw other materials to help keep their incisors a constant length (as people sometimes discover to their cost, if rodents gnaw at electricity cables).

Far left
American Red Squirrel, Great Slave Lake, NWT, Canada.

Left
Red Squirrel, Øvre Pasvik National Park, Norway.

short (the occasional name Long-tailed Souslik deriving from the fact that it is longer than in some other ground squirrels and sousliks). Though primarily vegetarian, the animals have been seen feeding on a Caribou carcass and males will kill and eat young they have not fathered. A true Arctic dweller, the squirrels form colonies of up to 50 individuals living in underground burrows, with numerous entrances to offer some protection against predation (virtually all Arctic terrestrial and avian predators take Arctic Ground Squirrels). The squirrels hibernate in the burrows in a nest of vegetation, laying down a store of seeds prior to sleeping so that they can feed as soon as they wake.

Arctic Ground Squirrels breed in Chukotka and Kamchatka, in northern Alaska and northern Canada to the eastern shores of Hudson Bay. Absent from Canada's Arctic islands.

Alaska Marmot (Brooks Range Marmot)

Marmota broweri

HB: 40–50cm. T: 13–18cm. W: 2.5–4kg. ♂>♀.

Adult is grey with silvery guard hairs, which give a frosted appearance. The head, back, rump and hind legs are often darker than the upper body.

Alaska Marmot is the most northerly of all marmots, breeding in the Brooks Range, Alaska, particularly on the northern slopes. There are unconfirmed reports of breeding to the northern coast.

Hoary Marmot

Marmota caligata

HB: 50–65cm. T: 17–25cm. W: 5–6kg. ♂>♀.

Adult is similar to Alaska Marmot but larger, and may be brown or grey-brown. Hoary Marmots breed in southern Alaska and Yukon; occurs in the Denali National Park.

Woodchuck (Groundhog)

Marmota monax

HB: 25–45cm. T: 10–15cm. W: 2–4kg. ♂>♀.

Adult is grey-brown, with a frosted appearance as in the other larger marmots. Primarily sub-Arctic, but breeds as far north as the southern shores of Hudson Bay.

Black-capped Marmot

Marmota camtschatica

HB: 50–55cm. T: 10–15cm. W: 3–5kg. ♂>♀.

The only marmot in the northern Palearctic. Adult has brown upperparts, with a distinctive black or dark brown cap. The cap actually covers both crown and nape, and extends below the eye.

The Black-capped Marmot is rare, with a curiously patchy distribution that includes the mountains and tundra of Baikalia, the Upper Yana and Kolyma rivers, northern Kamchatka and parts of central and northern Chukotka. Essentially an upland animal, found at altitudes to 1,900m. Black-capped Marmots excavate extensive burrow systems that may be up to 100m long and go into the permafrost.

BEAVERS

Although the beaver is a sub-Arctic animal – its lifestyle means it cannot thrive beyond the treeline – it is likely to be seen by Arctic travellers close to the northern limits of the forest, for instance near the Mackenzie delta, north of the Arctic Circle. The most distinctive feature of the beaver is the long, flattened and scaly tail, which acts as a paddle and also as a fifth leg, allowing the animal to stand on a tripod of two hind legs and tail when gnawing trees. The tail also aids walking on the hind legs when material is being carried (in the forelegs) to the top of a beaver's dam. Other adaptations include the closure of the beaver's ears and nose when it dives, while membrane covers

Arctic Ground Squirrel, Barren Lands of Nunavut, Canada.

Arctic Ground Squirrel, Barren Lands of Nunavut, Canada.

the eyes; also, the lips close behind the incisors so the animal can manipulate branches to build its dam without ingesting water.

The dam is essential to beaver life. Beavers are social, living in families of up to 12, though 5–6 is the more usual number. The family holds a territory that includes not only a lake or section of river, but the ground to the sides from which the animals harvest trees, mud and rocks to construct a dam, the dam usually placed at a narrowing of the river. Sometimes the animals excavate small streams within their territories, as they can move more easily in water than on land; they have even been known to deliberately divert streams to produce usable channels for bringing in dam material.

Dams can be up to 4m high, 6m thick at the base, and they can be 100m long, though they are usually smaller. Trees up to about 1.2m in diameter have been seen in dams, but such huge logs are not hauled in by the beaver, being felled close to the dam site. Although beavers do considerable damage to local trees, the species the animals prefer – aspen and willow – readily grow again from the stump; beavers can be said to practise coppicing.

The dam is not watertight, with water flowing through and over it (making it less susceptible to destruction if the river volume increases), but it is sufficiently resistant to flow that water backs up behind it to form a pond. In this, or at the edge of a lake if the beavers do not need to build a dam, the beavers build a lodge, a conical structure of branches and mud, with an underwater entrance to above-water living quarters. In the pond the animals cache fresh branches for eating during the winter (beavers are herbivorous and do not create ponds in which to fish). Ultimately the pond behind the dam silts up.

True hibernators

Marmots are the largest of all true hibernators. For Alaska Marmots hibernation begins in September, with the animals remaining in their burrows until early June, having spent almost nine months underground. Black-capped Marmots may spend even longer in their burrows: indeed, so long is the underground period of this species (altitude adds to latitude to create an environment that is harsh almost throughout the year) that they breed and may even given birth before they emerge for the brief summer. For all marmots except the Woodchuck, whose range is the most southerly of the group, the summer is so short that the young do not mature sufficiently to breed at one year and begin breeding only when they are two. For the Black-capped Marmot the short summer does not allow sufficient resources for females to breed annually, so instead breeding every two years is the norm.

The beavers then abandon the site and it reverts to 'beaver meadow', which itself reverts to forest, or becomes pure meadowland. It is sometimes suggested that much of the meadowland of North America derives from beaver meadow.

American Beaver

Castor canadensi

HB: 75–90cm. T: 28–38cm. HS: 30–60cm. W: 14–35kg. Adult is dark brown overall, with some animals almost black. The blunt muzzle is usually paler. The tail is dark grey-brown or black.

American Beavers breed to the treeline across North America. Has also been introduced into lakes in Finland.

Eurasian Beaver

Castor fiber

HB: 75–90cm. T: 28–38cm. HS: 30–60cm. W: 12–38kg.
Status: IUCN: Near Threatened.
Adult paler and more red-brown than American Beaver, though some animals may also be dark brown. Apart from colour the two species are indistinguishable, and so darker animals may be readily confused.

Eurasian Beavers breed to the treeline in Scandinavia and Russia (extremely scarce in central and eastern Russia), but the decimation of the species – in the early years of the 20th century it is estimated that the entire population throughout the range numbered no more than 1,000 animals – means that the present distribution is very patchy.

Hoary Marmot emerging from its den among boulders of the Denali National Park, Alaska.

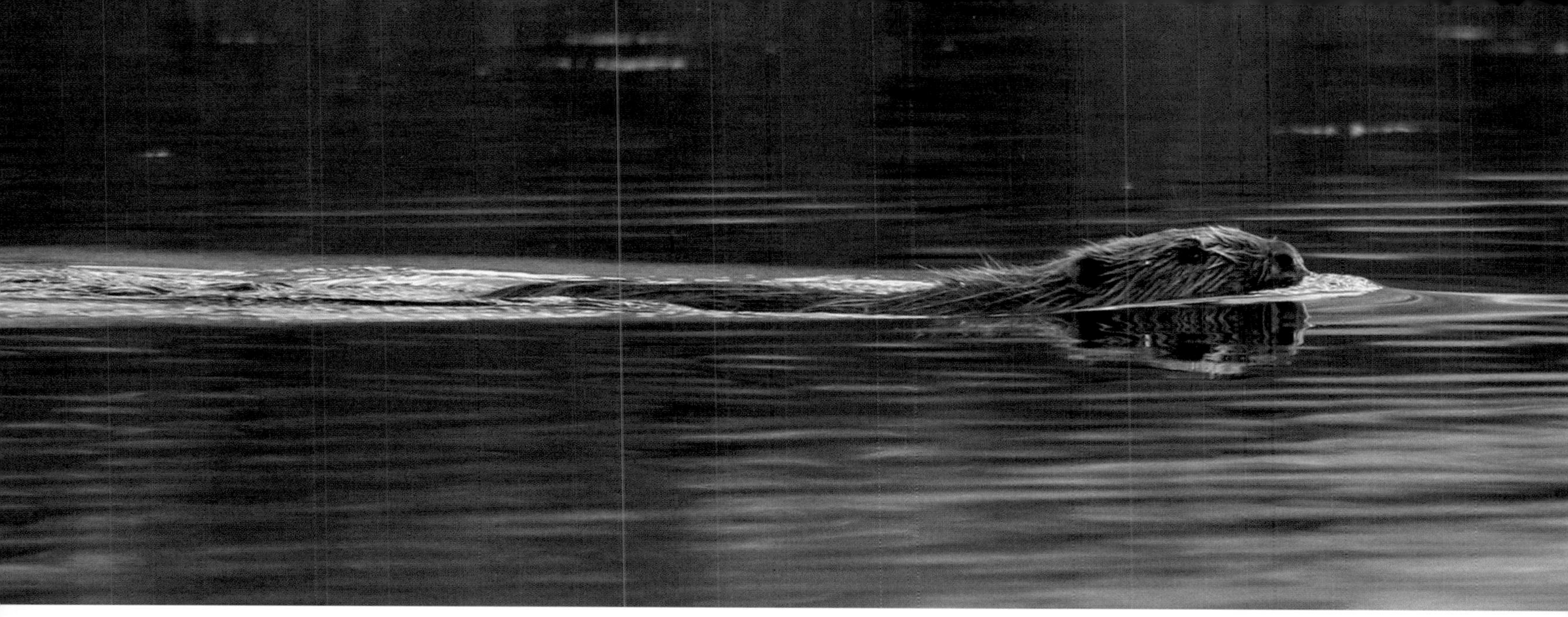

Eurasian Beaver, Sirdal, Norway.

MICROTINES

Lemmings and voles make up the largest fraction of the *Microtinae* rodent subfamily, and they include the most northerly of all rodent species. Most microtines, and all *Microtus* rodents, have, in addition to the incisors that characterise rodents, continuously growing molars, which aid the grinding of tough vegetation. Too small to be able to hibernate without starving, microtines are active throughout the winter, using a series of burrows beneath the snow to forage. The snow blanket offers excellent insulation against the Arctic winter, and also some protection against predation. However, some northern owls are able to detect rodents aurally beneath a significant layer of snow, mustelids can follow them in their burrows, and Arctic Foxes also pounce through the snow to reach them; the life of a microtine is one of constant threat from starvation and predation. Many Arctic predator populations are 'locked' into microtine populations, so that the regular sharp increases in rodent populations are mirrored by increases in predator numbers. For the Arctic traveller this can be a benefit; microtines are hard to spot, but become much more visible during 'lemming years', while the predators that are often the most sought-after species become more abundant.

There are many northern microtines, all with the same basic characteristics of being small, stocky and brown. Differentiating between them can therefore be difficult, particularly if a view of them consists only of a glimpse of a disappearing animal. In the section below, the basic details of colouring only are given, together with range – this is often more useful in deciding what it was that you almost just saw.

Beavers and the Arctic

Although not true Arctic dwellers, both the European and North American Beavers have aided the mapping and settlement of the area. The animals were hunted for their pelts and as food – beavers are large and so provide a good return in meat for the effort of trapping – and for castoreum, a secretion of the preputial gland that contains salicin (the basis of aspirin); this has been used as a medicine since at least the time of Hippocrates.

In North America, beaver pelts were the basis of the wealth of the Hudson's Bay Company, whose officers helped explore and map Canada and occasionally offered assistance (sometimes life-saving assistance) to British Royal Navy expeditions searching for the North West Passage. It is sometimes claimed that had Prince Albert, the Consort of Britain's Queen Victoria, not worn a silk top hat and, at a stroke, made beaver hats yesterday's fashion item, the North American Beaver might have been hunted to extinction. That is probably unlikely, but the change in fashion did make beaver trapping uneconomic.

LEMMINGS

Norway Lemming

Lemmus lemmus

HB: 7–16cm. T: 1.0–2.0cm. W: 60–130g.

Adult is a beautiful animal, exquisitely coloured. Golden brown above, paler below, the upperparts marked in black, with black crown and forehead, saddle and stripes on the flanks. The feet are silvery-white.

Norway Lemmings breed in northern Fennoscandia, but essentially a sub-Arctic species, breeding in central Norway and Sweden.

Siberian Brown Lemming

Lemmus sibiricus

HB: 11–14cm. T: 1.5–2.5cm. W: 60–120g.

Adult similar to Norway Lemming but a more subdued yellow-brown, with a thick black stripe on the head and back.

Siberian Brown Lemmings breed on the northern coast of Russia from the White Sea to the Kolyma (including the Taimyr Peninsula), on Novaya Zemlya, the New Siberian Islands and on Wrangel Island.

North American Brown Lemming

Lemmus trimucronatus

HB: 11–14cm. T: 2–3cm. W: 70–115g.

Adult very similar to Siberian Brown Lemming (with which it was once considered conspecific). The pelage is tawny with buff and darker brown flecking, paler on the flanks and paler again on the underparts. The head and neck are often grey-brown rather than tawny, and older animals show a distinctive rusty patch on the lower back.

North American Brown Lemmings breed in western and northern Alaska and across northern Canada to the western shore of Hudson Bay, on southern Canadian Arctic islands from Banks to Baffin, and on islands in the Bering Sea.

Wood Lemming

Myopus schisticolor

HB: 8–11.5cm. T: 1–2cm. W: 20–45g.

Status: IUCN: Near Threatened.

Adult is uniformly dark grey, with paler underparts. Develops a rusty patch on the lower back, but this is much more indistinct than in the brown lemmings.

Wood Lemmings breed in southern Scandinavia, but more northerly in Russia, though only to the north coast near the White Sea and the Lena and Kolyma deltas. Breeds throughout Kamchatka, but largely absent from Chukotka.

Northern Bog Lemming

Synaptomys borealis

HB: 10–12cm. T: 1.5–2.5cm. W: 25–35g.

Adult is mouse-like (apart from the tail). Grey-brown above, with occasional patches of grey and of red-brown, and grey below. The tail is bi-coloured, as in many vole species.

Northern Bog Lemmings breed in southern and central Alaska and across central Canada to southern Hudson Bay; more northerly on the bay's eastern shore.

COLLARED LEMMINGS

Collared lemmings, true Arctic animals, belong to the genus *Dicrostonyx*, the name derived from the Greek for 'forked claw', a reference to the growth of a double claw in winter to aid digging in the snow; the pad between the third and fourth toes hardens and enlarges, fusing with the claws. Most species have a 'collar'. If the collar is paler than the upper body it may be visible as a complete band, but often it merges with the colour of the upper body and so is visible only as a chest-band.

Suicidal lemmings

In one of his modern fables, James Thurber has a man meeting a talking lemming. At the end of their conversation the man asks if he can ask one personal question. The lemming says 'yes' as he also wants to ask one. The man's question is 'Why do lemmings occasionally commit mass suicide?' which surprises the lemming as his question is why it is that humans do not.

In reality the rodents do not commit mass suicide either, but the myth is so powerful that it is still frequently heard – a story too good to be untrue. The myth involves the Norway Lemming, because although similar population surges occur in other microtines, mass migrations in these are much less spectacular. The causes of population surges are not well understood, though most authorities favour either climate (an early spring with an abundance of food resulting in early mating and more litters) or a lack of predation. Whatever the cause, the population increases rapidly. The trapping of individuals during lemming years has shown that the majority of migrating animals are immature. Norway Lemmings are very intolerant of their fellows and it is assumed that aggression from older animals forces younger ones out. The topography of Norway, with its high ridges separating narrow valleys, concentrates migrating animals. Conflicts result and the population becomes increasingly panicky, something that is a feature of the mass movements. When a stream, river or lake is reached, pressure from following animals causes the leaders to start swimming. If the lake is large, or if it is the sea, the lemmings, with no concept of lake size or of an ocean, swim regardless, behaviour seen as suicidal by human observers who know that the animals will drown before reaching the far side.

Arctic Collared Lemming

Dicrostonyx torquatus

HB: 12–15cm. T: 1–2cm. W: 50–75g, up to 110g in winter.

Adults are variable, usually red-brown on the back (but grey-brown towards the lower back and on the head) with a dark dorsal stripe from the head to the tail. Some are grey-brown overall. The underparts are paler, often pale buff or grey-buff. The feet are pale grey or pale-greyish buff. The collar is pale grey or grey-buff. The tail is as the rump at the base, but with a whiter tip. In winter these lemmings turn white.

Arctic Collared Lemmings breed from the eastern shores of the White Sea to Chukotka and eastern Kamchatka, on the southern island of Novaya Zemlya and throughout Severnaya Zemlya and the New Siberian Islands.

Wrangel Island Lemming (Vinogradov's Lemming)

Dicrostonyx vinogradovi

HB: 14–19cm. T: 1.5–2.5cm.

W: 60–90g (heavier in winter).

Status: IUCN: Critical.

Adult is pale grey with grey-cream patches, but with chestnut ears. The underparts are usually washed yellow. The collar is paler, but it is often indistinct because of overall pale coloration. In general the dorsal stripe is absent, though it may be visible in younger animals.

Wrangel Island Lemmings breed only on Wrangel Island, where they are rare.

Norwegian Lemming, northern Norway.

The rare and elusive Wrangel Island Lemming.

NORTHERN COLLARED LEMMING (GREENLAND COLLARED LEMMING)

Dicrostonyx groenlandicus

HB: 10–16cm. T: 1–2cm. W: 35–55g (up to 110g in winter). Adult similar to Arctic Collared Lemming but greyer, with buff flanks and chest and pale grey head. Winter pelage is white.

Northern Collared Lemmings breed in north-east, north and north-west Greenland, the Aleutian and Bering Sea islands, western and northern Alaska and on the northern Canadian mainland east to Hudson Bay. Breeds on all Canada's Arctic islands to northern Ellesmere Island.

UNGAVA LEMMING (HUDSON BAY OR LABRADOR LEMMING)

Dicrostonyx hudsonicus

HB: 12–14cm. T: 2.0–2.5cm. W: 45–80g.

Adult is red-brown or, more usually, grey-brown above with a thin black dorsal stripe and red-brown patches close to the ears. The underparts are pale grey, often separated from the upperparts by a pale brown band. The collar is red-brown but indistinct. The winter pelage is white.

Ungava Lemmings breed on the Ungava Peninsula of northern Quebec and Labrador, and on islands of eastern Hudson Bay (such as Belcher and King George).

RICHARDSON'S COLLARED LEMMING

Dicrostonyx richardsoni

HB: 10.5–14cm. T: 1.0–1.5cm. W: 35–90g.

Adult is dark red-brown above, paler on the flanks and buff or buff-grey below. There is a dark dorsal stripe, this usually indistinct in adults. There are often pale red-brown cheek- and ear-patches. The collar is red-brown and so only visible on the chest.

Richardson's Collared Lemmings breed around the western shore of Hudson Bay.

VOLES

As with other rodents, differentiating voles is a job for experts. Voles differ from lemmings in having longer tails, which are invariably bi-coloured.

SOUTHERN RED-BACKED VOLE

Clethrionomys gapperi

HB: 8–13cm. T: 3–5cm. W: 20–40g.

Adult has red-brown back, grey flanks and cream underparts. The feet are grey, the tail brown above, grey below.

The Southern Red-backed Vole is a sub-Arctic species, but breeds to the southern shores of Hudson Bay and on the eastern side of the bay in central Quebec and Labrador.

GREY-SIDED VOLE

Clethrionomys rufocanus

HB: 11–13.5cm. T: 2.5–4cm. W: 15–50g.

Adult is grey above and on the flanks, with a broad chestnut band on the forehead, crown, nape and along the back to the base of the tail. The underparts and feet are pale grey. The tail is chestnut brown above, grey below.

Grey-sided Voles breed in northern Scandinavia and across Russia to Kamchatka, but only to the north coast on the Kola Peninsula and east to Baydaratskaya Bay.

RUDDY VOLE (NORTHERN VOLE, TUNDRA RED-BACKED VOLE)

Clethrionomys rutilus

HB: 8–11cm. T: 2.5–3.5cm. W: 15–40g.

Adult is distinctive; pale golden-brown above with a broad red-brown band from the forehead, across the crown, nape and back to the base of the tail. The underparts and feet are cream or pale buff. The tail is golden-brown above, cream below and has a small terminal tuft.

The Ruddy Vole breeds in northern Scandinavia, across Russia, throughout Alaska and northern Canada east to Hudson Bay. The Canadian range extends to the Boothia Peninsula, but does not include Arctic islands.

SINGING VOLE

Microtus miuris

HB: 10.5–13.0cm. T: 2.0–3.5cm. W: 25–55g.

Adults are variable, usually dark brown above, more tawny on flanks with grey-buff underparts. The crown often shows patches of grey, and there are usually pale tawny ear-spots. The tail is brown above, paler below.

Singing Voles breed in northern and southern Alaska, but absent from most of central Alaska, from the Alaska Peninsula and the Aleutian Islands. Also breeds in central Yukon.

INSULAR VOLE

Microtus abbreviatus

HB: 11–14.5cm. T: 2.5–3.0cm. W: 45–75g.

Status: IUCN: Data Deficient.

Adult almost identical to Singing Vole, having brown upperparts, yellow-brown flanks and pale buff underparts.

Insular Voles breed only on the islands of Hall and St Matthew in the Bering Sea.

FIELD VOLE

Microtus agrestis

HB: 8–13.5cm. T: 2.0–4.0cm. W: 45–75g.

Adult is red-brown or grey-brown above, with paler flanks and cream below. The feet are pale grey. The tail is relatively short for a vole.

The song of the Singing Vole

Adult Singing Voles occasionally sit in exposed places and 'sing' a high-pitched trilling 'song'. This may be an alarm call for young voles, as the singing usually takes place when litters have been weaned. Before winter arrives, Singing Voles make hay balls. These can be huge – up to 30 litres. They are placed above ground and provide winter sustenance.

A new species in the Arctic?

The Sibling Vole *Microtus rossiaemeridionalis*, which is dark brown above, paler on the flanks and grey below, with pale grey feet and a tail which, though darker above than below, appears all one colour, breeds in southern Scandinavia and south-west Russia. It is non-Arctic, but colonies have been found on Svalbard. It is assumed that these have been introduced from ships. Despite being a southern species the voles appear to have become established, surviving the Arctic winter better than other introduced rodents. It seems they counteract high winter mortality by increased fecundity, having up to four litters with the young breeding as early as one month after birth.

Field Voles breed in northern Scandinavia and on the southern Kola Peninsula, but more southerly across Russia to the Kolyma delta.

Narrow-headed Vole

Microtus gregalis

HB: 12–15cm. T: 3–5cm. W: 50–80g.

Adults are variable, light ochre to dark brown above with characteristic darker spotting and white tips to individual hairs, which give an overall silvery appearance. There is a dark stripe extending from the back of the head to the upper back. The underparts are pale grey or greyish brown. The tail is bi-coloured with a terminal tuft. The skull is narrow, particularly between the eyes (a diagnostic characteristic).

The Narrow-headed Vole has a patchy distribution across Russia, breeding close to the White Sea coast and east to the Ob delta, from Khatanga to the Kolyma delta. In the mountains of Kazakhstan and Kyrgizia the species breeds to 3,500m.

North Siberian Vole

Microtus hyperboreus

HB: 12–15cm. T: 3.5–5.5cm. W: 55–85g.

Adult is grey-brown above (often with a reddish wash), silver-grey below, this occasionally washed yellow. The vole has a long, bi-coloured tail.

The North Siberian Vole breeds in Russia from the Ob River to the western edge of Chukotka, but only to the north coast near the Lena and Kolyma deltas.

Tundra Vole (Root Vole)

Microtus oeconomus

HB: 8.5–16cm. T: 2.5–8cm. W: 25–65g.

Status: IUCN: Least Concern.

One of the larger northern voles. Adult is dark brown above with buff flecking, paler on the flanks and pale buff below. The feet are pale grey-brown. The long tail is grey-brown above, paler below. American animals tend to be longer and heavier, but with a shorter tail.

Tundra Voles breed in northern Scandinavia and across Russia to Kamchatka (to the north coast except on the Taimyr Peninsula), and to the north coast in Alaska and the Yukon.

Meadow Vole

Microtus pennsylvanicus

HB: 9–13cm. T: 3.5–6.5cm. W: 30–70g.

Adult is red or dark brown above and on the flanks, with pale grey-brown underparts. The feet are dark grey, the tail a uniform dark grey-brown.

Good housekeeping

The Latin name of the Tundra Vole means 'house keeper' (the Latin word is also the root of 'economic') and refers to the species' storage of seeds and rhizomes, which supplement its winter diet. In North America these stores were sought after by the Inuit who gathered them for their own use. For the poor voles this confiscation could lead to winter starvation.

The Meadow Vole breeds in central Alaska, but not to the west or north coasts, in northern Yukon, but then more southerly to the west coast of Hudson Bay, around the bay's southern shore and in southern Quebec and Labrador.

Taiga Vole (Yellow-cheeked Vole)

Microtus xanthognathus

HB: 15–18cm. T: 4–5.5cm. W: 110–170g.

Adult is dark brown or grey-brown above, paler below, and with a prominent yellow-brown cheek-patch. The feet are grey, the short tail dark grey above, paler below.

Taiga Voles breed in central Alaska, northern Yukon and the boreal belt to the south-western shore of Hudson Bay.

Lemming Vole

Alticola lemminus

HB: 12–13cm. T: 2–2.5cm. W: 20–45g.

Adult is grey-brown overall, including the tail, which ends with long bristles. The winter pelage is much lighter and may even be white in some.

The Lemming Vole breeds in a broad semi-circular belt from the Lena, curving towards the northern shore of the Sea of Okhotsk then north into Chukotka, reaching the Bering Sea as far north as Cape Dezhnev. There is a second belt that follows the western shore of the Sea of Okhotsk, then heads inland towards the northern tip of Lake Baikal.

Eurasian Northern Water Vole

Arvicola terrestris

HB: 16–24cm. T: 8–10cm. W: 200–300g.

Adult is dark brown, even black above, paler below. The feet are grey, the tail dark grey.

The Eurasian Northern Water Vole breeds in northern Scandinavia and across Russia to the Lena, though only to the north coast from the White Sea to Pecherskoya Bay.

Tundra Vole, St Lawrence Island, Alaska.

Muskrat

Ondatra zibethicus

HB: 24–40cm. T: 19–28cm. W: 600–1800g.

The largest microtine, and also one of the easiest to observe. The name derives from the odour of the scent glands, which is used to define territories. Adult is a rich red-brown above, becoming paler on the flanks and much paler on the underparts. The partially webbed feet are grey, as is the naked tail. The tail is laterally compressed (about three times as deep as it is wide) as an aid to swimming as the Muskrat is primarily aquatic. Though chiefly vegetarian, Muskrats also take molluscs.

The Muskrat breeds from western Alaska to Labrador, but not to the north coast. Because the animals were valued for their fur (called *musquash*), Muskrats were farmed in Europe and escapes have produced breeding populations in Scandinavia and across Russia.

Eastern Heather Vole

Phenacomys ungava

HB: 8–12cm. T: 2.5–4cm. W: 25–40g.

Adults are variable, but usually mid-brown above, paler below. The upperparts are often washed yellow, and white hair-tips give a grizzled appearance. The feet are pale grey, the tail grey-brown.

The Eastern Heather Vole breeds in Canada eastwards from British Columbia, north to the Great Slave Lake, around the southern and eastern shores of Hudson Bay and throughout Quebec and Labrador, including the Ungava Peninsula.

RATS AND MICE

Of the three primary rodent pests to mankind, the House Mouse *Mus musculus*, Brown Rat *Rattus norvegicus* and Black Rat *R. rattus*, the first two are found in association with people even in the Arctic. However, neither has ever become established independently from human habitation, with feral populations invariably dying out during their first Arctic winter.

PORCUPINES

It comes as a surprise to many that porcupines are rodents, so dissimilar are they in size and appearance to rats and mice. Palearctic porcupines are terrestrial animals, their quills grouped in clusters, while Nearctic species are arboreal and have single quills.

North American Porcupine

Erethizon dorsatum

HB: 50–100cm. T: 17–25cm. W: 8–18g. ♂>♀.

Adult is unmistakeable, whether curled up into a ball high in a tree or ponderously making its way through the forest. Black, but the quills and softer hairs may be white or tipped golden-brown, which gives the walking or climbing animal a pale grey or brownish wash.

The North American Porcupine breeds north to the tree-line across North America from central Alaska to Labrador, and even occasionally on the tundra if there is dwarf willow or dwarf alder. Though not, strictly, an Arctic species, the animals are found in the Arctic National Wildlife Preserve.

Muskrat, Yellowknife, Canada.

Northern mice

There are no Arctic mice or rats, though the Northern Birch Mouse *Sicista betulina* breeds along the shores of the White Sea, while the Deer Mouse *Peromyscus maniculatus* is found to the treeline in North America and so may be seen close to the southern shores of Hudson Bay, and in northern Quebec and Labrador; it is not found in Alaska. The Meadow Jumping Mouse *Zapus hudsonius* occurs in southern Alaska and to the southern shores of Hudson Bay.

LAGOMORPHS

Lagomorphs – rabbits, hares and pikas – differ from rodents in having a second pair of incisors known as peg teeth. While picas look very similar to rodents (the large ears, inconspicuous tail and very long whiskers of picas distinguish them from voles), hares and rabbits differ in body shape, having long back legs that allow them to run fast. Though the adaptation is the same in each group, the strategy for avoiding predators differs. While hares simply seek to outrun a predator, rabbits make short runs to their burrows or to available cover. These different escape strategies are reflected in the breeding biology of the two groups. Young rabbits are born underground and are altricial. By contrast, leverets are born above ground and are precocial. To avoid drawing unnecessary attention to the leverets, the female hare visits them only once each day. At that time the leverets, which spend the rest of the day in concealed places, congregate at their place of birth and are suckled for about five minutes. Because of the limited duration of nursing, hare milk has a very high fat and protein content and the leverets are weaned at three or four weeks.

As with shrews, lagomorphs practise refection, the redigestion of 'first-pass' faecal material, which is partially undigested. The 'second-pass' faecal material is in the familiar form of hard, black 'currants'.

Above
Arctic Hare in winter pelage, Barren Lands of North West Territories, Canada.

Opposite page
Arctic Hare, Churchill, Manitoba, Canada. It is spring and the hare is moulting from winter white to summer grey-brown.

Northern Pika

Ochotona hyperborea

TL: 18–25cm. W: 150–250g.

Adult is uniformly brown or dark brown, occasionally with darker patches on the sides of the neck and a darker wash to the lower back. There are white stripes around the periphery of the ears. The winter pelage is usually grey-brown or reddish-brown, the underparts paler.

The Northern Pika breeds in Russia from the Yenisey River to Chukotka and Kamchatka, north to the coast (and south into Mongolia).

Collared Pika

Ochotona collaris

TL: 18–20cm. W: 120–180g.

Adult is a uniform grey-brown, though usually with a reddish wash. There is usually a paler collar and the underparts are also often paler. The feet are grey.

Collared Pikas are much less Arctic than its Palearctic cousins, breeding in southern and central Alaska (including the Denali National Park) and southern Yukon.

Snowshoe Hare

Lepus americanus

HB: 30–45cm. Ear length: 9–10.5cm. W: 0.9–2.2kg. ♂>♀.

In summer adult is red-brown above, with pale grey-brown underparts, including the chin. The ears are relatively small for a hare, and black-tipped. The winter pelage is white apart from the black ear-tips. The hind feet are large (disproportionately so – hence the name, as the hare looks as if it were wearing snowshoes), an adaptation to allow the hare to move easily over soft snow. The hare is fast, with speeds of up to 40km/h claimed. In winter Snowshoe Hares occasionally burrow into the snow to escape bad weather.

Snowshoe Hare breeds across North America, but is rarely seen above the treeline.

Snowshoe Hare in summer pelage, Churchill, Manitoba, Canada.

The first pelage of Arctic Hare leverets reflect the colour changes of their parents.

Right
A young hare on Victoria Island, Canada, where adults are grey-brown in summer, but white in winter, is brown. In the photograph *below*, from Ellesmere Island, Canada, where adult hares are white at all times, the leveret is grey.

Opposite page
Arctic Hare in winter pelage, Barren Lands, North West Territories, Canada.

Arctic Hare

Lepus arcticus

HB: 40–60cm. Ear length: 7.5–10.5cm. W: 2.5–6.5kg.

In summer adults in the south of the hare's range are grey or grey-brown. In winter, and in the northern part of the range, they are white apart from the ear-tips and inner ear. Leverets are pale grey. Arctic Hares can reach speeds in excess of 60kph and can swim well.

The Arctic Hare breeds on the central and northern coasts of both east and west Greenland, but rare in the south. Also on Canada's northern mainland, and the Arctic islands to northern Ellesmere. The mainland population breeds as far south as Hudson Bay's southern shore. Absent from Alaska. In winter Arctic Hares occasionally burrow into the snow, excavating short tunnels to dens that offer shelter from the wind and intense cold.

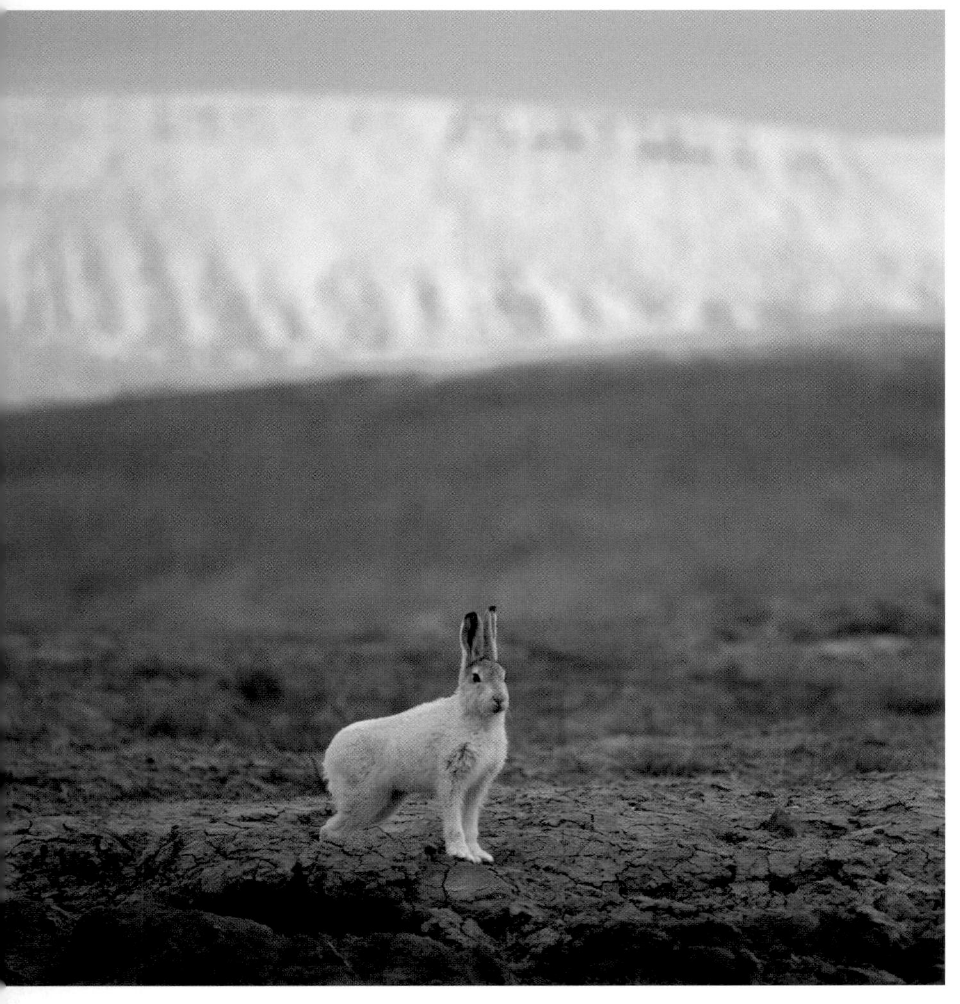

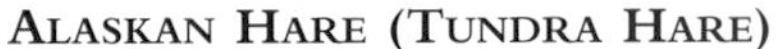

Alaskan Hare (Tundra Hare)

Lepus othus

HB: 50–60cm. Ear length: 7–11cm. W: 3.9–7.0kg.

The Alaskan equivalent of the Arctic Hare. Summer adult is red-brown above, paler below, with a darker crown. The ears are bi-coloured, the front half as the body, the rear half white. The ear-tips are dark brownish black, this colour maintained in winter. The winter pelage is white.

Alaskan Hares breed in south-western, western and northern Alaska. As with the Arctic Hare, this is a hare of the tundra rather than the forest.

Mountain Hare

Lepus timidus

HB: 45–60cm. Ear length: 7–10cm. W: 2.0–5.8kg. ♀>♂.

In summer adult is dark brown or grey-brown, paler below and with grey or white tail. The ears are black-tipped. The winter pelage is white, but not white to the body (as it is for the Arctic Hare), the underfur being slate-grey or blue-grey. This is occasionally visible, giving greyish blue patches on the flanks. Animals in northern Siberia are white at all times.

The Mountain Hare breeds in northern Scandinavia and across Russia to Kamchatka, to the northern coast, but absent from all Russia's Arctic islands.

Marine Mammals

Within the Arctic the summer sea temperature is ≤10°C, while in winter it is ≤5°C. The sea temperature below the sea ice is <0°C. As the solubility of gases in water increases with decreasing temperature, Arctic waters are oxygen-rich. They are also nutrient-rich, due to the huge inflow of the rivers of North America and Asian Russia. The combination makes the Arctic seas highly productive in summer, attracting not only seabirds but also marine mammals. While the pinnipeds that exploit this summer bounty remain in the Arctic year-long, moving with the ice edge, cetaceans travel to the area to feed in summer, then migrate to more productive waters during the winter.

The marine environment offers advantages to mammals in addition to a copious food supply. Freed from the major constraint imposed by gravity, marine mammals have fewer limits to size. Seals are restricted in size by the need to come ashore to give birth, but whales have overcome this restriction, and become massive as a result: Blue Whales are probably the largest animal ever to have lived on Earth. Giving birth in water would seem illogical for an air-breathing animal, but it has its advantages; female whales do not have to support the weight of their growing foetuses in the way that terrestrial mammals do, and so can carry larger young (within the obvious limitations of the birthing process) and these well-developed offspring are better able to seek air immediately, to contend with the problems of suckling underwater, and to survive the occasionally hostile environment into which they have been born.

The buoyancy of water means that the skeletons of marine mammals do not have to overcome gravity and so can be much less bulky. Honeycombed whale bones are remarkably light in comparison to those of heavy terrestrial mammals (such as elephants). The bones have a hard outer shell covering a sponge-like inner layer with numerous blood vessels and a marrow rich in oil; when whales were hunted, about 30% of the oil obtained from a carcass came from the bones. Though strong enough to act as anchors for the whale's huge muscles, some whale bones are so light that they float in water. Similarly, the bones of the larger seals are, despite the time the animal spends out of water, flimsy in comparison to terrestrial mammals. The practice of clubbing baby seals by fur hunters, a practice that causes outrage when photographs are published, is not carried out simply to prevent bullet holes reducing the value of the pelts (as reports often suggest) but because the cranial bones of seals are so thin that clubbing results in instantaneous death.

The marine environment also has disadvantages for mammals. Heat loss in water is significantly higher than in air so mammals must have excellent body insulation, a high metabolic rate, or both. As volume (and therefore mass) increases with the cube of diameter, but surface area only with the square, large animals have a proportionately smaller surface area from which to lose heat than small ones. The smallest marine mammal is many thousands of times larger than the smallest terrestrial mammal. As an insulator a layer of subcutaneous blubber is more efficient than fur, but as its insulating properties are, in part, dependent on thickness, good insulation requires a big body – another reason for marine mammals to be large. The smaller marine mammals are those that rely, at least partially, on fur for insulation. The blubber of pinnipeds and cetaceans is of variable thickness and lipid content, its distribution optimising streamlining and the insulation of vital organs. Marine mammals also employ counter-current heat exchangers to minimise heat loss. Cetaceans employ counter-current heat exchangers to cool the testes of the male, which are within the body cavity (for reasons of streamlining) and would therefore overheat if not cooled.

The other disadvantage of being a marine mammal is the breathing of air. Not only must the animals come to the surface to breathe – a procedure that might itself create problems for Arctic marine mammals because of the extent of ice cover – they must also store oxygen for relatively long periods if they are to feed successfully. The easy answer would appear to be large lungs – and large body size would appear to be just the thing to accommodate them. But storing a large supply of air has limitations. Large, air-filled lungs would act as buoyancy tanks making diving more difficult, and as pressure increases with depth the collapsing lungs would compress the air, with potentially lethal side effects. Water pressure increases by one atmosphere for each 10m of depth. At high concentrations oxygen is poisonous, while nitrogen is a narcotic. Bubbles of nitrogen and oxygen forming in the blood as the animal surfaced and the gases decompressed would also give rise to the bends, a problem that can be fatal to human sub-aqua divers. Marine mammals dive to prodigious depths – Sperm Whales are known to dive to 3,000m (and to stay submerged for more than two hours) – and must therefore overcome this problem. The muscles of marine mammals are rich in myoglobin, which 'stores' blood (in much the same way as haemoglobin) and releases it gradually during a dive. Marine mammal blood is also rich in haemoglobin, the oxygen storage potential of the two compounds reducing the need to store air when diving. Pinnipeds actually exhale before diving, effectively eliminating air storage and, therefore, the potential for the bends. But cetaceans inhale before diving. They possess networks of blood vessels known as a *rete mirabilia* (literally 'wonderful network'), in the chest cavity (and other areas), which, it is believed, may act as a sink for nitrogen as the animal surfaces. At the huge pressures of deep dives, the collapsing lungs of cetaceans also force air into the nasal passages, where nitrogen absorption into the bloodstream is not possible.

PINNIPEDS

The *Pinnipedia* (the name means 'wing-footed') are divided into two superfamilies, the *Phocoidea*, which contains only one family, the *Phocidae* (true seals), and the *Otarioidea*, which contains two families, the *Otariidae* (eared seals – fur seals and sea lions) and the *Odobenidae*, which contains just one species, the Walrus. Pinniped origins are shrouded in mystery. They are carnivores, relatives of the cats, dogs and bears. Some authorities consider the pinnipeds diphyletic, i.e. the two superfamilies represent two separate re-invasions of the sea, with an otter-like ancestor giving rise to the phocids and a bear-like ancestor the otarioids. However, molecular (DNA) research suggests that the group should actually be considered monophyletic.

Pinnipeds are extremely well adapted to the marine environment with spindle-shaped bodies, and limbs that have developed into flippers. However, there are significant differences between the two families. The phocids lack

Opposite page
A Fin Whale blows close to the coast of Jan Mayen in the North Atlantic.

external ears (which would enhance drag), and have hind flippers closely akin to the tail flukes of whales in shape that provide the power for swimming. The front flippers are short and are held close to the body during swimming, though they can function as fins to aid steering. Insulation is by blubber, ancestral fur having been reduced to a sparse scattering of coarse hairs. On land the hind flippers are useless for locomotion, the seal using its front flippers to haul itself along, with progress being an ungainly wriggle.

By contrast, the eared seals are able to rotate their hind flippers underneath their bodies. Using these and their long front flippers, the animals are then reasonably mobile and able to move surprisingly quickly. Travellers familiar with the slow-moving, essentially sedentary phocids are in for an unpleasant surprise if they stray too close to an eared seal. Not only does the animal accelerate and move quickly, it has an array of business-like teeth; being chased by an irate eared seal is somewhat akin to being pursued by a large dog, though thankfully the seal usually gives up more readily. Eared seals also differ in their insulation, relying, in part, on fur: the underfur of the fur seals is luxuriantly thick, a fact that led to their near-extinction due to overhunting. As a consequence of this different, and less effective, mode of insulation, fur seals and sea lions are chiefly animals of cool temperate waters. The Walrus, the sole member of the second otarioid family, is a true Arctic dweller: it has blubber insulation similar to the phocids though it shares the reversible hind flippers of the eared seals. Eared seals also differ in being gregarious, forming large, sometimes huge, colonies, whereas the phocids are more solitary.

One feature that all pinnipeds share is sensitive vibrissae, or whiskers. Studies have shown that these are sensitive to sound, which may be an advantage in avoiding predators. Studies with blindfolded seals have also shown that the seals are still able to catch fish, while studies in which the vibrissae have been removed indicate that the seals are then much less efficient at fishing. The suggestion is that the vibrissae can detect vibrations in the water such as those caused by the wake of a swimming fish. Vibrissae may also detect hydrodynamic changes caused by fixed features, and so help a seal to navigate in murky waters.

The smaller pinnipeds exhibit countershading, being darker above and paler below. The dorsal colour is also disrupted to break up the animal's outline when it hauls out. Ribbon and Harp Seals have striking patterns, which are more definite in males and which develop with age; these are likely to be related to courtship. Young seals are, in general, born with a covering of white fur (lanugo), a contrast to Antarctic seal pups, which are dark. The white fur is assumed to be camouflage against sea ice for animals born in the land of the Polar Bear, those pups that are not entirely white being pale or partially white, and having a disrupted pattern. The lanugo pelt of young seals is luxurious, compensating for the lack of blubber. The longer hairs of lanugo also trap air, adding extra insulation. Young seals also have brown fat which is metabolised as the first blubber layer is laid down.

Phocids moult their skin annually, but this is not equivalent to the moulting of fur-bearing mammals when losing or acquiring a winter pelt. For the seals such a change is unnecessary, the moult representing the replacement of potentially damaged skin.

TRUE SEALS

Phocids live in both fresh and saltwater, though species such as the fresh-water Baikal Seal *Pusa sibirica*, the inland (but salt water) Caspian Seal *Pusa caspica* and the Arctic-breeding marine Ringed Seal all evolved from the same ancestor. Apart from the monk seals, all phocids are polar or sub-polar, with all bar the two inland species of northern phocids being Arctic animals.

RINGED SEAL

Pusa hispida

TL: 1.3–1.7m. W: 45–110kg. ♂>♀.

The most numerous of all Arctic mammals, with a population estimated at around 6 million. Adult is dark grey or grey-brown above with a mosaic of pale grey rings (that give the seal its name). The rings are smaller or absent on the head. The underparts and flippers are silver, silver-brown or grey-brown. Ringed Seals can dive to 90m, though depths to 40m are more common, and they can stay submerged for 20 minutes, though 4–8 minutes is more usual.

Ringed Seal pups are born in a birthing chamber, which the female excavates above the sea ice, usually in a pressure ridge. It is estimated that predation by bears and Arctic Foxes accounts for around 50% of each year's pups.

Ringed Seals are found at the ice edge throughout the Arctic. The highest numbers are found in eastern Russia, the Bering Sea and the North American Arctic.

RIBBON SEAL

Phoca fasciata

TL: 1.5–1.7m. W: 70–85kg.

Adult male is dark brown or black with four distinct broad bands of pale grey and cream, one around the neck, two around the front flippers (these almost meeting on the breast) and a fourth around the lower abdomen. The flippers are as the body colour. Female has the same pattern, but the bands are much less distinct as the body colour is buff-brown.

The Ribbon Seal is found on pack ice far from land in the Bering Sea, southern Beaufort Sea and the Sea of Okhotsk.

Ringed Seal, Kongsfjorden, Spitsbergen, Svalbard.

Fresh-water Ringed Seals

Despite being marine mammals, Ringed Seals are actually found at three freshwater locations – Lake Ladoga in Russia and Lake Saimaa in Finland, both close to the Gulf of Finland, and Lake Nettilling on Baffin Island's west coast. Both Lake Ladoga and Lake Saimaa are connected to the sea, but there is no evidence to suggest that the seals travel along the connecting waterways. It is assumed that ancestral populations either migrated to the lakes, or have been isolated by landscape changes. The Lake Saimaa population contains only about 200 animals, so the seals must have arrived fairly recently, or be on the verge of extinction, as such a population is hardly sufficient to ensure genetic diversity and long-term survival. The populations at the other two sites are much higher.

Harbour Seal

Phoca vitulina

TL: 1.2–1.9m. W: 45–135kg. ♂>♀.

Adult is silvery-grey or, occasionally, buff with extensive dark grey, dark grey-brown or dark brown spotting dorsally, and on the crown and nape. There are usually fewer ventral spots. The hind flippers are dark grey or grey-brown, the front flippers paler.

Harbour Seals are found in coastal waters of southern Greenland, Iceland, northern Scandinavia and Svalbard (north to Prinz Karls Forland), but are absent from northern Russia. They are, however, found in the northern Pacific and southern Bering Sea from Kamchatka to southern Alaska, and in the waters of eastern Canada, including Hudson Bay, northern Quebec and Labrador, and southern Baffin Island.

Ribbon Seal, Bering Sea.

Harp Seal

Phoca groenlandica

TL: 1.7–1.9m. W: 115–140kg. ♂>♀.

Adult male is silver-grey with dark grey or black upper muzzle, crown and cheeks, and a black 'harp' on the back and flanks. The 'harp' is actually seen on the flanks, the two harps linked across the back so that the overall pattern is more saddle-shaped. Adult female is patterned as the male, but the head and back/flank patch are paler.

The Harp Seal is found from the Arctic islands of eastern Canada to the Laptev Sea.

Largha Seal

Phoca larga

TL: 1.4–1.7m. W: 80–110kg.

Adult is pale grey, grey-brown or mid-brown above, paler below with heavy, uniform dark brown and black spotting.

The Largha Seal is found in the North Pacific, the Sea of Okhotsk and the Bering Sea from Kamchatka to the coast of western Alaska, and from the Aleutians to the Chukchi and Beaufort Seas.

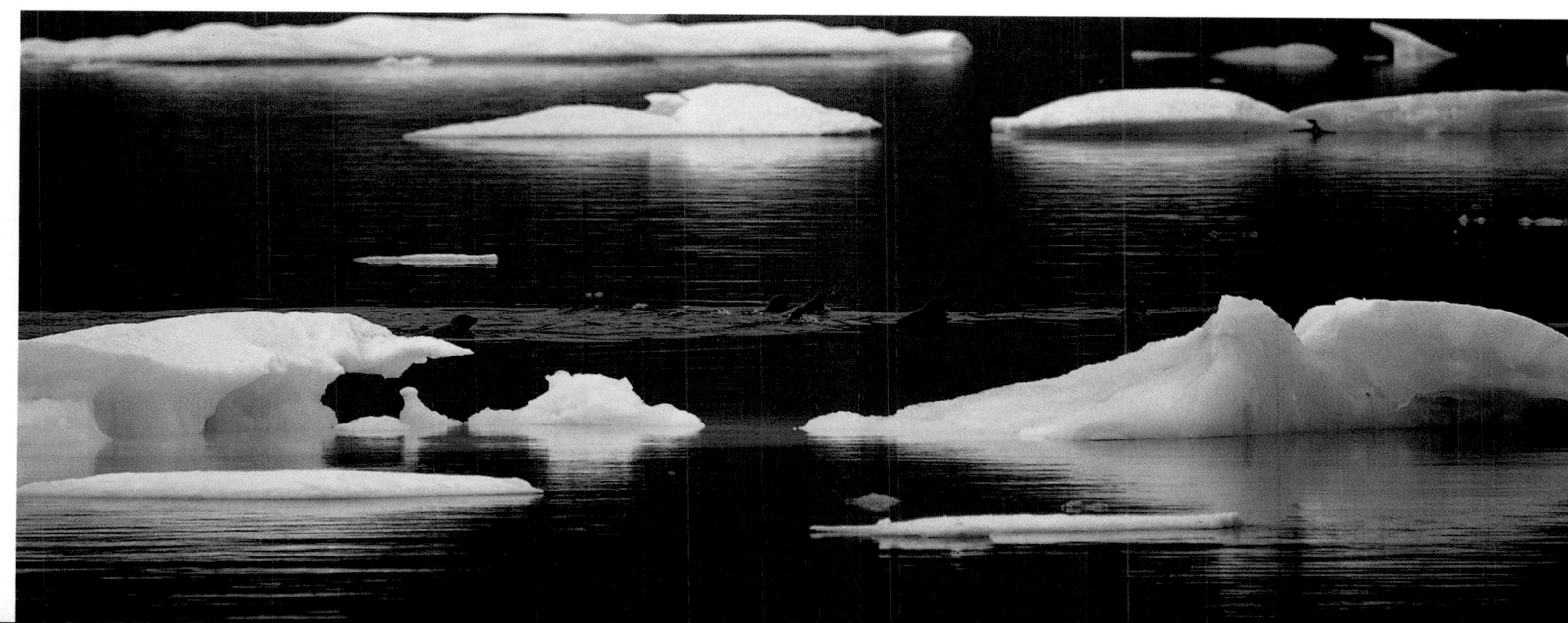

Harp Seals, north-east Greenland.

Largha Seal off southern Kamchatka's east coast. The name *largha* is that given to the seal by the Tungus people of the western Sea of Okhotsk. It was adopted because the North American name, Spotted Seal, though an accurate description, caused confusion with the Harbour Seal, which was occasionally called the Spotted Seal in Europe.

Grey Seal

Halichoerus grypus

TL: 2.1–3.3m. W: 125–300kg. ♂>♀.

Grey Seals are the largest of the northern phocids. They also exhibit the most striking sexual dimorphism, with the male up to three times larger than the female. The adult male is dark grey or grey-brown overall (though usually darker above than below) with light grey patches. Adult female is the reverse, being light grey with darker patches.

Sub-Arctic rather than Arctic, but found on the Labrador coast, the southern and western coasts of Iceland, and northern Scandinavia eastwards to the White Sea.

Bearded Seal

Erignathus barbatus

TL: 2.2–2.5m. W: 200–300kg. Unusually, females are slightly larger than males.

Adult is grey-brown or brown, darker above than below, and with some dark blotches. The head is small in comparison to the large, rotund body, making the seal look even fatter than it actually is. Unusually. females are slightly larger than males.

Harp Seal pups

The annual slaughter of the helpless, pure white, doe-eyed Harp Seal pups off Canada's eastern coast became a national and international issue in the 1980s. Today the seals are still hunted, less for their skins and more for their oil, which is rich in omega-3 fatty acids. The hunt is regulated, and carried out with less overt enthusiasm than previously. It is principally allowed as a concession to local fishermen who fear competition from an increasing seal population (though the cod fishery of the Newfoundland banks has declined as a consequence of human rather than seal predation). In 2007 the thinning of sea ice (as a consequence of global warming) caused many young seals to die, either by drowning or from hypothermia following a fall into the sea. The death toll was significant (with claims of up to 90%) and there was a (sadly ignored) call for the annual hunt to be abandoned.

Pups moult to a silver-grey pelage with dark grey spotting and blotching at about 4 weeks. In the language of sealers, pups are 'whitecoats', recently weaned pups 'beaters' (because their early attempts at swimming sees them beating at the water with their flippers), and spotted immatures 'bedlamers' (probably from the French *bête la mer*, beast of the sea, rather than a poor joke).

The seal has a profusion of long vibrissae that curl when dry, giving the moustached look that (more or less) explains the name.

The Bearded Seal is found throughout northern waters, and also in Hudson Bay and the Sea of Okhotsk.

Hooded Seal

Cystophora cristata

TL: 2.0–2.9m. W: 145–350kg. Significant sexual dimorphism, males being almost twice the weight of females (though only about 25% longer). Males with weights exceeding 400kg have been recorded.

The heaviest of the northern true seals, though not as long as the largest Grey Seals. Adult is silver-grey with extensive mottling of dark brown or black patches, these tending to be

Harbour Seals, Tracy Arm, Alaska.

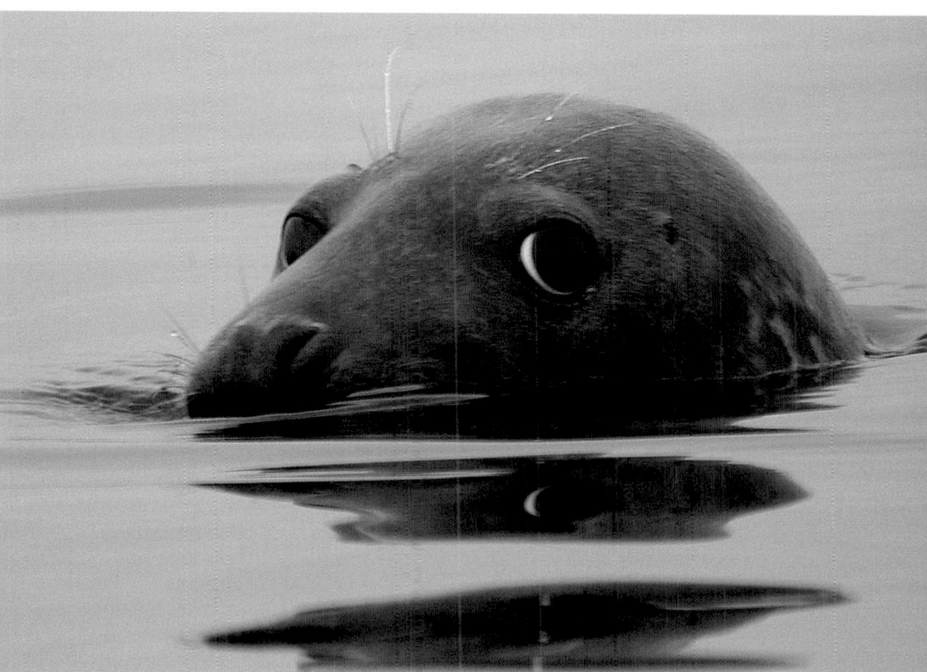

longer on the back and flanks. The hood of the name is an enlarged extension of the nasal cavity that forms a proboscis which, in males, hangs over the mouth, but is much less pronounced or absent in females. The hood can be inflated to form a large black cushion or blister that spreads from the forehead over the mouth. Males can also extrude and inflate the internasal septum membrane. This extrudes from one nostril, usually the left, as a red balloon. The inflation mechanisms of hood and balloon are dissimilar, the hood requiring closed nostrils, the balloon an open nostril. Consequently both hood and balloon cannot be inflated simultaneously. However a 'half-hood' and balloon can be inflated, the effect being grotesque. Although the hood and balloon are used in mating displays, they are also inflated if the seal is surprised by an observer (in anxiety or as a threat) and, occasionally, by resting seals, seemingly just for the fun of it. The hood develops in males from the age of 4 years.

The Hooded Seal is found on the eastern seaboard of North America from Newfoundland to Lancaster Sound, but

Above left
Harbour Seal.

Above right and below
Grey Seals.

All the photographs were taken at Kjorholmane, Norway.

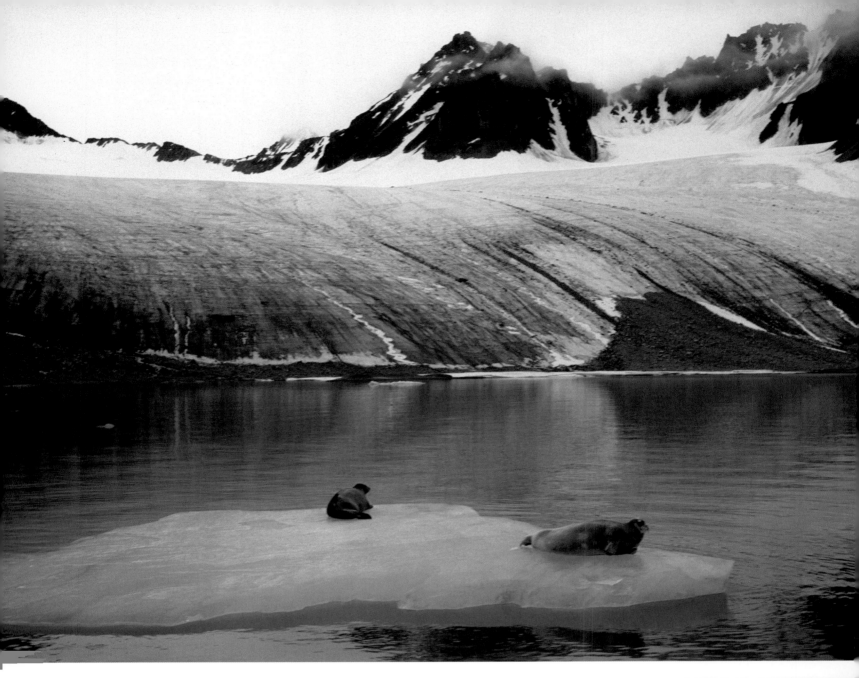

Above
Bearded Seals, Magdalenefjorden, Spitsbergen, Svalbard. The glacier behind the seals is Gullybreen.

Right
Hooded Seal on the pack-ice between Svalbard and north-east Greenland.

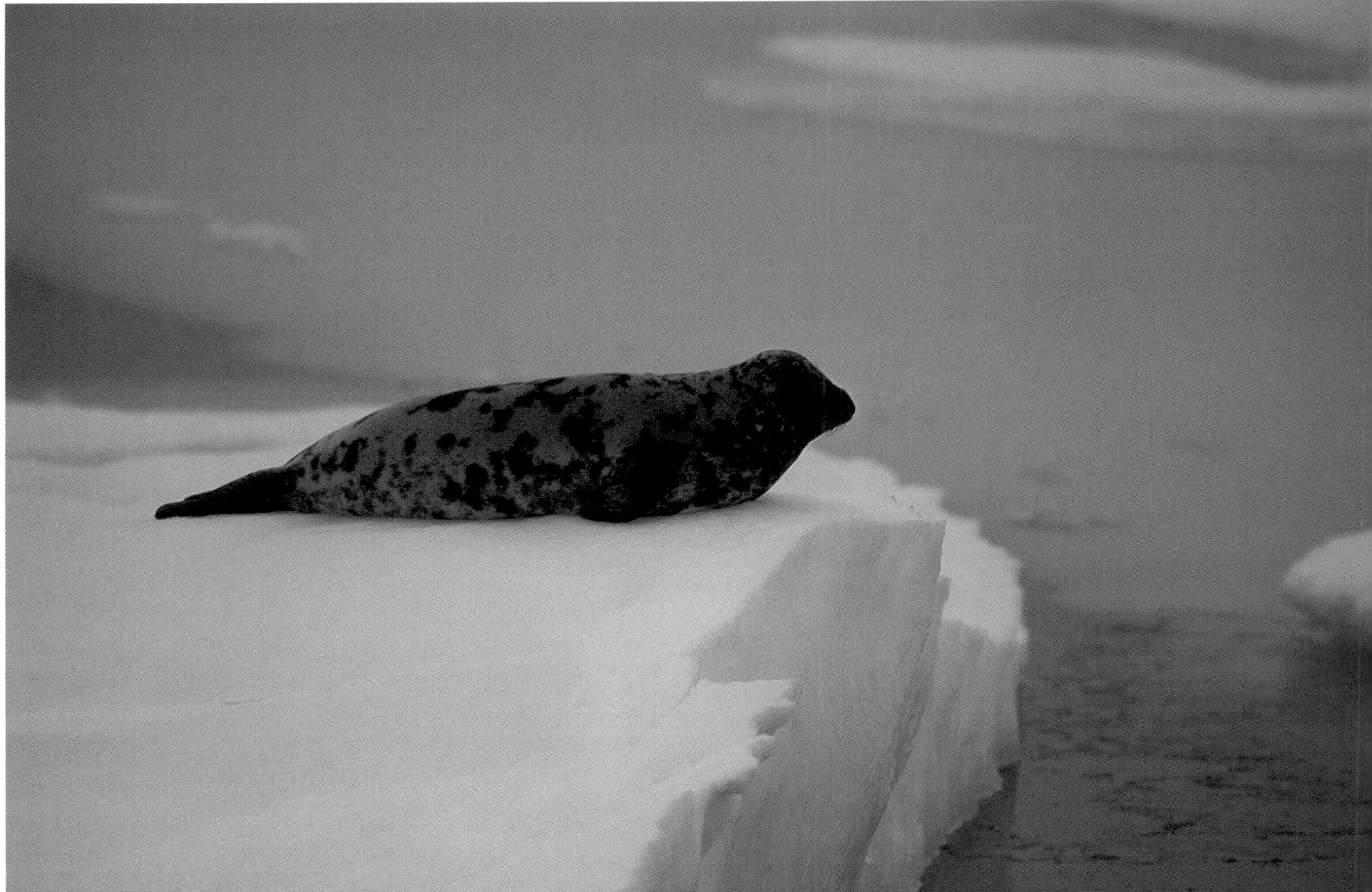

rarely west of Labrador's Cape Chidley or north into Smith Sound. Also found in the north-western Atlantic around Iceland's north coast, Jan Mayen, Svalbard and Bear Island, but rarely as far east as Franz Josef Land.

EARED SEALS

As noted above, most eared seals occur in cool temperate waters, but one sea lion and one fur seal are found at the edge of the Arctic boundary.

Steller's Sea Lion

Eumetopias jubatus

TL: 2.0–2.9m. W: 145–350kg. There is significant sexual dimorphism, with males almost twice the weight of females (though only about 25% longer). Recorded male weights have exceeded 400kg.

Status: IUCN: Endangered.

Adults vary from buff to red-brown, and are usually darker above than below. The flippers are dark grey or black. The male Steller's Sea Lion develops a thickened, muscular neck over which grows a mane of coarse hair.

Steller's Sea Lions occur in the western Sea of Okhotsk and across the southern edge of the Bering Sea from Kamchatka through the Commander Islands to the Aleutians and southern Alaska. Also found on the Kuril Islands and along the eastern seaboard of North America as far south as California.

Northern Fur Seal

Callorhinus ursinus

TL: 1.2–2.1m. W: ♂ 130–270kg, ♀ 30–50kg. Extreme sexual dimorphism, with males being up to 5 times heavier than females and *c.*70% longer.

Status: IUCN: Vulnerable.

Adult male is rich dark brown, with the female being grey-brown above, pale chestnut-grey below. Male becomes darker with age and develops thickened necks and shoulders, and a mane of coarse hair. The hind flippers are very long, the largest of any member of the Otariidae.

Declining populations

Occasionally called the Northern Sea Lion, the more usual name remembers Georg Wilhelm Steller, the naturalist on Bering's expedition, who first described the species. Unlike other eared seals, Steller's Sea Lion, the largest of the eared seals and the most northerly sea lion, does have a layer of blubber, relying less on its fur for thermoregulation. Concerns have been expressed in recent years over the health of the population as numbers on the Russian side of the Bering Sea have reduced by up to 90% over the last 40 years or so. A reduction of 80% has also been seen on the American side of the sea with one projection seeing the animal extinct within 50 years if present trends continue. The reason for the decline is not well understood, but it may be related to increased fishing in the Bering Sea. In British Columbia the population has been culled in response to pleas from fishermen, so the animal is rare away from Russia and Alaska.

Beautiful coats

The luxurious pelt of the Northern Fur Seal is reflected in the scientific name, which derives from *kallos rhinos*, beautiful skin. It was for its pelt that the species was ruthlessly exploited in the 19th century when the original population on the Pribilof Islands was reduced from c.3million to c.300,000). The underfur of the seal has around 55,000 hairs/cm²; only Sea Otters have a denser fur. So dense is the fur that water does not reach the skin even if the seal scratches itself under water. When hunting was regulated the population increased, but then cropped dramatically in the 20 years from the late 1960s to the late 1980s, possibly due to an increase of commercial fishing. Harvesting, which had continued, was also blamed, and was banned in 1988. Unfortunately the population is still declining, though slowly.

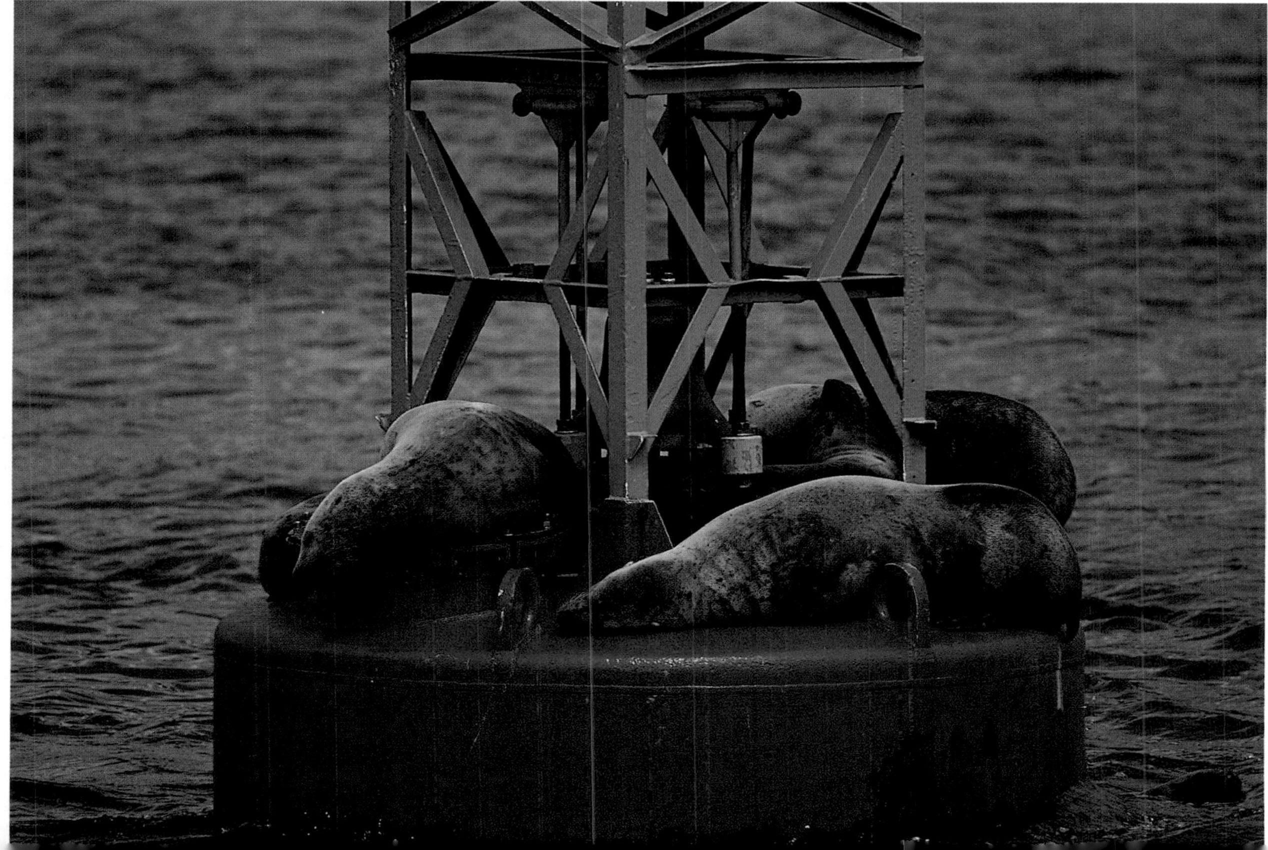

Steller's Sea Lions using a buoy in the Lynn Canal, Alaska as a resting place.

Above
While waiting for the females to come ashore to give birth and then to be ready to mate again, male Northern Fur Seals are very belligerent. St Paul Island, Pribilofs, Alaska.

The Northern Fur Seal is found in the Sea of Okhotsk and across the Pacific from Japan to the Californian coast, but chiefly in the southern Bering Sea. The primary breeding grounds are on the Pribilof and Commander Islands, where some 90% of the animals breed.

WALRUS

Odobenus rosmarus

TL: 2.3–3.6m. W: 700–2,000kg. Extreme sexual dimorphism with males being *c.*50% heavier and *c.*20% longer than females. Status: CITES: Appendix III (Canada).

Walruses split from the eared seals about 20 million years ago. The fossil record suggests that walruses were once the dominant pinniped group, but gradually they declined, leaving just a single form today. Walruses are the largest of all Arctic pinnipeds, and second in size only to the elephant seals in world terms.

The skin colour of adults varies with blood flow. In the water, or recently emerged, walruses can be very pale light grey or grey-brown. But when hauled out blood is pumped to the skin to aid cooling, and the animal becomes pink. Walrus skin is very thick (particularly around the neck, where it can be up to 4cm deep) and tough, and was used by the Inuit to cover summer and winter houses because of its durability. Walrus blubber can be up to 15cm thick, though on average it is only half that thickness. The upper canine teeth are massively extended to form protruding tusks. The species

Tooth-walker

The Walrus uses its tusks to make or maintain holes in the ice, and to help it haul out of the water, the latter task giving the animal its scientific name – Odobenus from *odontes baino* – tooth-walker. The second part of the name derives from *ros maris* – sea rose, a reference to the colour of the animal and its maritime habitat. The common name is from the Scandinavian *hvalross* – whale horse.

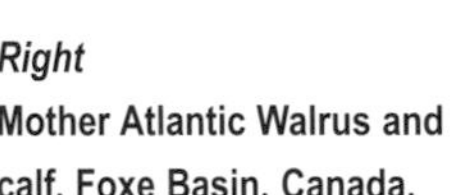

Right
Mother Atlantic Walrus and calf, Foxe Basin, Canada.

Opposite page

Above
Atlantic Walrus, Fosterbukta, Hold-with-Hope, north-east Greenland.

Below
Pacific Walrus, Chukotka, Russia.

exhibits extreme sexual dimorphism, with males being *c*.50% heavier and 20% longer than females. Atlantic and Pacific Walrus are different subspecies and differ in the length and shape of their tusks. Male Atlantic tusks are *c*.75cm, with those of the females to *c*.60cm. Pacific Walrus tusks are longer, those of males to 100cm, females to *c*.75cm, and they are also curved rather than straight (though there are exceptions). In general female tusks are circular in cross-section (whereas male tusks are elliptical) and more slender.

The Walrus is found in north-west and north-east Greenland, Svalbard, Franz Josef Land, Novaya Zemlya, north-east Siberia, Wrangel Island, the west coast of Alaska, Baffin Island and the islands to the north of Hudson Bay, particularly near Igloolik.

Mollusc suckers

Walrus feed by standing on their heads and feeling for prey in the sediment with their highly sensitive vibrissae. The chief food is molluscs, the meat being extracted from the shell by suction. Walrus have a formidable ability to suck, the Inuit telling of animals coming up beneath swimming ducks and sucking them under. Walrus also eat young seals, and the Inuit maintain they also occasionally kill Beluga. Adult Walrus have no enemies apart from humans. Polar Bears occasionally invade Walrus colonies, seeking to take a young animal. On land the Walrus is ponderous and no match for an agile bear, though bears ensure they stay well clear of adults as the tusks can inflict savage, potentially fatal, wounds. In water the tables are very definitely turned, the bears staying far away.

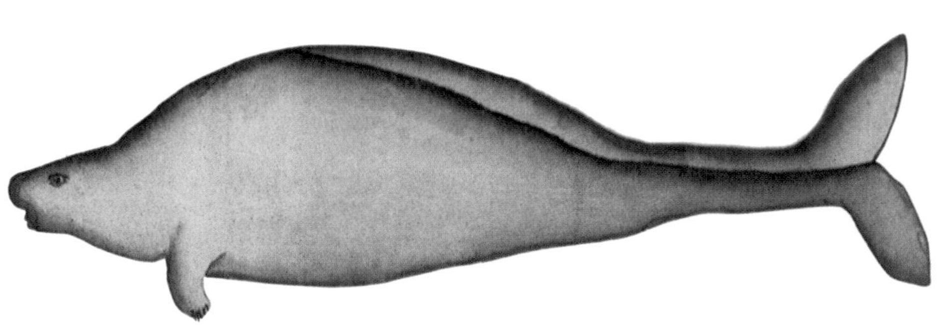

Steller's Sea Cow

In 1741–42, Bering's ship *St Peter* arrived at the Commander Islands while attempting to return to Kamchatka. It was a fateful landing for several of the crew, including Bering himself, who died of scurvy. It was fateful, too, for a huge manatee, a creature up to 8m long and weighing 6 tonnes, which was actually the only cold-water member of the sea-cow order *Sirenia*. The animal was described by the expedition's naturalist, Georg Wilhelm Steller, and was named after him – Steller's Sea Cow *Hydrodamalis gigas*. The sea cow was a strange animal, with a small head and flippers but a huge body. It grazed the kelp forests that surrounded what is now called Bering Island. It was docile, slow and provided an abundance of good quality eating. This proved a deadly combination. By 1768 no animals could be found on either Bering or Copper islands (the only two of the Commander Islands on which it had been observed) and it is assumed to have been hunted to extinction by hungry fur collectors. There have been occasional suggestions that the animals might have remained on other, more isolated, islands, and that they might still do so, but given the lack of unexplored islands in the southern Bering Sea there is no question that this gentle creature is now long-extinct.

The Walrus's only enemy is the Polar Bear. In the water a Walrus is more than a match for a bear, the latter risking fatal injuires if foolish enough to attack. On land fit adult Walruses are also in little danger; they may be slow moving, but their hide is very thick and any bear attempting to bite through will need time – time in which the Walrus can turn its tusks on to the attacker. Sick and calf Walrus are a different matter however, and there are many instances of Polar Bears roaming through Walrus colonies seeking out an isolated calf. If the bear can grip the calf and haul it away before the mother attacks then the bear may be successful.

In the photograph *above*, from Wrangel Island, Russia, a bear is making a tentative foray into a Pacific Walrus colony. The photograph below, from Manning Island, Foxe Basin, Canada, shows all that remained of a Walrus calf after a successful bear kill.

CETACEANS

Although Aristotle recognised that whales breathed air as early as the 4th century BC, it was not until the work of Linnaeus in the 18th century that they were formally identified as mammals (though earlier works, such as that of Konrad Gesner in the mid-16th century, had successfully illustrated many of the northern whales). The adaptations of the cetacean body for its marine environment took many more years to unravel, and even today aspects of the animals' physiology and lifestyle are still not completely understood.

The whale shape mirrors that of the pinnipeds in being streamlined for energy-efficient locomotion. The head merges with the body, there being no discernible neck and shoulders; this means that the head cannot move independently of the body (the Beluga is an exception in this regard, having unfused cervical vertebrae that allow the head to turn and nod). The hind limbs are vestigial and within the body so that they do not interfere with the streamlining, the power for swimming being provided by a large tail comprising twin flukes. The tail is powered by huge back muscles and moves vertically, the flukes staying parallel to the water surface; whales therefore differ in this respect from fish, the tails of which move from side-to-side. The front limbs have become flippers that are primarily used for steering, and many species have evolved a dorsal fin to aid stability. Unlike the hull of a ship, the whale's body is not rigid and so can move in response to water pressure. The skin also exudes a polymer that may assist the shedding of the outer layer of skin (the Beluga is again an exception to the cetacean norm in undergoing an annual moult rather than continuously shedding the outer skin), or may assist in overcoming turbulence; turbulence causes frictional losses (drag), the whale using much less energy for a given speed if drag is minimised.

The flippers and dorsal fin are the only protuberances on the body, the male penis being within the body cavity except during mating, and the teats of the female being set within slits close to the genital opening. Body hair is minimised, insulation being provided entirely by layers of subcutaneous blubber. In the case of the Bowhead, a true Arctic dweller, the blubber can be 50cm thick.

Whales are considered monophyletic, and to have evolved from a common ancestor in the Eocene, with two branches emerging in the Oligocene to form the two modern-day suborders, the toothed and baleen whales. Although the two groups have many common features, they differ markedly in feeding methods and, consequently, in the structure of the head. Toothed whales feed primarily on fish and squid. In general their jaws are extended into a beak-like snout (this being most pronounced in the beaked whales, the Sperm Whale being the major exception to the pattern). The jaws have an array of teeth for grasping prey (or tearing at it in the case of the Orca). The forehead is rounded, forming a 'melon' within which is a wax-like substance that is the basis of an echolocation system. This is used to find prey in the deep, dark waters in which the whales tend to feed. The melon of the Sperm Whale, the deepest diver, is huge. The head of this species accounts for 25–30% of the animal's total length. The wax it houses – spermaceti oil –was highly prized by early whalers. However, it is worth noting that the exact function of the spermaceti is still debated. While it is likely that the oil acts as a sonic lens to aid echolocation, it may also have a role in buoyancy regulation.

The structure of the head is very different in the baleen whales. The bones of the cranium and jaws have been extended and widened. The upper bones form the rostrum, from which the baleen plates hang. Although often called whalebone, baleen plates are not bone. Neither are they modified teeth. Rather, they are keratinous (hair-like) plates emerging from the jaw bone. The plates are smooth, but the inner edges abrade to form 'bristles', the bristles of individual plates overlapping to form a sieve that captures food as the whale swims forward. Food is obtained when the tongue is pressed against the baleen, with engulfed water being squeezed out through the sieves and the trapped prey items then being swallowed. Although this action is common in the baleen whales, they have different strategies for engulfing. Some swim slowly forward and allow their sieves to extract food continuously, while others take huge gulps of water. Sievers include the Right and Bowhead Whales; they have huge heads to allow space for large baleen plates. Gulpers include the Blue and Humpback Whales; they have pleats or furrows of skin on the lower jaw, which allows the mouth to expand so as to engulf vast quantities of water at each gulp. These furrows give this group of whales their common name, *rorqual*, though the original meaning of this is disputed. It could be from the Scandinavian for pleated, or from 'red throat', a reference to the colour

Sounding Sperm Whale, Lofoten Islands, Norway.

change of the skin when it is expanded, exposing the blood vessels. One species, the Sei Whale, feeds with a combination of sieving and gulping, while the Grey Whale differs in sieving bottom sediments. Some gulpers also employ lunge-feeding, rising from beneath a concentrated prey source. This is used by Humpback Whales, which occasionally hunt collectively, driving a shoal of fish into a tight ball and then lunging through them. Despite the fact that gulpers tend to seek out prey-rich areas, there is no indication that they use sophisticated echolocation systems. Baleen whales do emit sounds, but these are usually at low frequencies and so would not be much use for echolocation (as the 'visible' target cannot be smaller than the wavelength of the emitted sound). Instead, the sound emitted by baleen whales is primarily for communication, with low-frequency sounds travelling huge distances underwater. The 'song' of the Humpback Whale, an evocative, ethereal noise, has become a famous example of these sounds.

Toothed and baleen whales also differ in the number of nostrils present. In toothed whales the two nasal passages combine to form a single, crescent-shaped blowhole. In some species it seems that only one passage is used for breathing, the second being part of the echolocation system. In baleen whales the two nasal passages form a blowhole of two parallel slits. When the whale exhales, water trapped in folds around the blowhole is also expelled, forming the characteristic 'blow'. This effect is much more pronounced in the baleen whales where the blowhole is set deep in folds of skin: indeed, the blow pattern is a useful guide to species. In the smaller toothed whales the blow may be minimal – and may even appear absent – and is a much less useful identification feature. The statistics of whale breathing are amazing. For example, a Fin Whale exhales and inhales about 1,500 litres of air in just two seconds. That is several thousand times the volume a human exchanges. Some of the smaller dolphins, with lung sizes more comparable to those of humans, can exhale and inhale in a tenth of a second. Whales also extract more oxygen from a volume of air than humans, 10–12% against about 4%.

Whale passengers

Cetaceans, particularly the slow-moving baleen whales, are often infested with external parasites, one group of which are commonly called whale lice. These are actually cyamid amphipods *Cyamus* spp., woodlouse–like creatures about 2cm across that inhabit folds in the skin where water flow is minimal. The heads of right whales have prominent areas of callosities, patches of hard, roughened skin of unknown function. These areas are the favourite haunt of the cyamids, which feed on the outer layer of the skin. Many baleen whales also carry barnacles: acorn barnacles *Coronula* spp. and *Cryptolepas* spp., *stalked barnacles* Conchoderma spp, and the so–called pseudo–stalked barnacles *Xenobalanus* spp and Tubicinella spp. These may be seen on fins and tails. Grey and Humpback Whales seem particularly popular with barnacles: one estimate suggested that a Humpback could accumulate up to 500kg of barnacles while feeding during the polar summer, many of these dropping off when the whale migrates to warmer waters. In addition, Baleen whales carry a thin film of diatoms, also accumulated during the polar summer. Examination of diatom species has provided information on the feeding grounds and migration routes of some whales. In general, none of these passengers does any serious harm to the whale.

Intelligent whales?

While it is true that the brains of cetaceans are large – the 9kg brain of a Sperm Whale is the heaviest of any animal (compare the 1.5kg human brain) – the ratio of brain weight to body weight is more important than brain weight alone when comparing relative intelligence. On that basis, the Sperm Whale looks much less impressive, the brain/body ratio being 0.02%, compared to 2% for a human. However, the ratio for the Sperm Whale is actually low for a toothed whale (though larger than for most baleen whales). For the Bottlenose Dolphin the ratio is around 1.0% (close to that of chimpanzees *Pan* spp.), which implies a greater level of intelligence, and it is certainly true that studies on captive dolphins show that in terms of their response to spoken commands they exceed all non-primates.

They use a greater percentage of their lung capacity, exchanging about 90% of the volume each breath, compared to 10–15% in humans.

Cetacean eyes are relatively small, sight being much less useful in water. However, some whales 'spy hop', raising their heads out of the water, apparently to view the local area. Small eyes, acting as pinhole cameras, allow a greater depth of focus and may assist the whales – which for the most part stay close to shore – to locate land features. The larger rorquals do not do this, perhaps for biomechanical reasons, or alternatively it is possible that their low-frequency sounds are of use as coarse echolocation systems to help them identify underwater topography. However, the right whales do spy hop, as does the Minke.

Spy hopping is just one of many distinctive whale behaviours. Others include lob-tailing, the waving of the tail flukes and subsequent slapping of the water surface with them, fin-waving, which may also involve water slapping, and breaching. These are all forms of communication, though they are more common in some species than in others. Humpback Whales are famous for breaching, but it comes as a surprise to discover that the huge, slow Bowhead and Northern Right whales also do it.

Cetaceans mate and give birth in water, and whale calves suckle underwater. Mating occurs both horizontally and vertically in different species. Calves are born tail-first, as might be expected, and they are quickly ushered to the surface by their mothers to take their first breath. However, head-first births have occasionally been observed. The problem of suckling underwater has been overcome by the female having contractile muscles in the mammary glands, which enable her to squirt milk into her calf's mouth, allowing the transfer of large quantities of milk in a short time to help the calf avoid spending protracted periods feeding underwater. Whale gestation is, as would be expected, long, and the period between births is also long, this hindering the recovery of populations that were overhunted in the past. While northern toothed whales usually give birth in northern waters, many of the baleen whales migrate long distances to breeding grounds. The reasons for this are not clear; various suggestions have been made, but there is no consensus, particularly as any theory has to explain why Fin Whales, for example, do not migrate.

The range limitations of terrestrial mammals and, to a lesser extent, birds, are not applicable to cetaceans. Essentially southerly species may therefore been seen in Arctic waters if the weather and food resources allow. In the descriptions that follow a pragmatic approach has therefore been adopted, and some species that may occasionally be seen in northern waters have been excluded; such sightings are akin to the sightings of vagrant birds.

TOOTHED WHALES

Species of the suborder Odontoceti, the toothed whales, make up the majority of cetaceans. Most are surface feeders and show similar countershading to that of pinnipeds.

Orca (Killer Whale)

Orcinus orca

TL: ♂ 6–9m, ♀ 4–6.5m. W: ♂ 4–6.5 tonnes, ♀ 3–4 tonnes. ♂ dorsal fin 1–2m high.

Status: CITES: Appendix II.

The Orca is the largest member of the dolphin family. Adult is black above, white below, with a pale grey saddle behind the prominent dorsal fin. The male dorsal fin is tall and triangular, in females it is short and falcate (sickle-shaped). The tail flukes form a shallow V. Orcas can swim at up to 60kph, but usually swim at 5–10kph. They are social animals, occasionally forming large pods.

The Orca is found to the ice edge in both the North Atlantic and North Pacific. Also found in all Earth's oceans.

White-beaked Dolphin

Lagenorhynchus albirostris

TL: 2.2–2.8m. W: 160–240kg (exceptionally to 350kg). ♂>♀.

Status: CITES: Appendix II.

Adults highly variable, but back is black to the falcate dorsal fin (taller in the male than the female), then pale grey or white to the black tail stock. The flanks are striped in shades of grey with a black patch forward of, and below, the dorsal fin. The ventral side is white. The tail is notched, the flukes having concave trailing edges.

White-beaked Dolphins are found in the North Atlantic. It is the most northerly of the smaller dolphins, reaching the southern shores of Svalbard and the Barents Sea, though more southerly in the colder western Atlantic where it is rarely seen north of Labrador or south-west Greenland. Despite the northerly range the animals are poor ice travellers and many die after becoming entrapped in the pack ice.

Long-finned Pilot Whale

Globicephala melas

TL: 4.0–7m. W: 1.5–3.5 tonnes. ♂>♀.

Status: CITES: Appendix II.

The second largest dolphin after the Orca. Adult is dark grey or black with paler patches on the throat and belly, behind the dorsal fin, and paler banding on the head. Occasionally the patch behind the dorsal fin is part of a larger saddle. Has a noticeably bulbous head (hence the scientific name, which translates as 'globe headed, black'). The short dorsal fin is falcate with a long base, and is located relatively far forward on the body. The tail is notched, the flukes having a straight or slightly concave trailing edge.

Orca pod, Lofoten Islands, Norway.

Harbour Porpoise, Kjorholmane, Norway.

Above
Beluga pods are invariably attended by gulls looking to pick up fish scraps.

Right
A grey, immature Beluga.

Both photographs from Churchill, Manitoba, Canada.

Long-finned Pilot Whales are found in the North Atlantic, as far north as Iceland and southern Greenland.

Bottlenose Dolphin

Tursiops truncatus

TL: 2.1–3.9m. W: 150–500kg. ♂>♀.

Status: IUCN: Data Deficient. CITES: Appendix II.

Adult is dark grey above, paler on the flanks and paler again below. The prominent beak (the bottlenose of the name) is set below a rounded forehead. The dorsal fin, set mid-body, is falcate. The tail is notched, the flukes having a concave trailing edge and distinctly upturned tips.

The Bottlenose Dolphin is found in all the world's oceans, but primarily a species of temperate and tropical waters. Occasionally seen as far north as Iceland and southern Greenland.

Atlantic White-sided Dolphin

Lagenorhynchus acutus

TL: 1.5–3.0m. W: 170–230kg. ♂>♀.

Status: CITES: Appendix II.

Arguably the most colourful of the cetaceans. Adult has a dark grey back and dorsal fin, the colour strongly delineated from the flanks, which are pale grey with a white patch on the mid-body and a yellow or yellow-brown patch towards the tail. The underside is white with a dark greyish black patch on the belly. The beak is less prominent than in the Bottlenose Dolphin, the forehead also less rounded. The mid-body dorsal fin is tall with a pointed tip and a falcate trailing edge. The tail is notched, the flukes having a straight or shallowly concave trailing edge and upturned tips.

Atlantic White-sided Dolphins are found in the north Atlantic as far north as Svalbard in the west, and around Iceland, but only to southern Greenland in the east.

Pacific White-sided Dolphin

Lagenorhynchus obliquidens

TL: 2.2–2.6m. W: 150–220kg. ♂>♀.

Status: CITES: Appendix II.

Less colourful than its Atlantic cousin, but with a complex and strongly delineated pattern of black, grey and white. In general the back is black, the flanks black with pale grey or white stripes and larger pale patches at the head and tail. The underside is white. Both the dorsal fin and flippers are bi-coloured. The beak is hardly noticable, and there is no rounded forehead, the head being very sleek.

Pacific White-sided Dolphins occur in the north Pacific and southern Bering Sea.

Harbour Porpoise (Common Porpoise)

Phocoena phocoena

TL: 1.3–1.9m. W: 50–65kg (exceptionally to 95kg). ♀>♂.

Status: IUCN: Vulnerable. CITES: Appendix II.

Now rare and considered vulnerable, as tends to feed inshore, close to the seabed, and may consequently be trapped in gill-nets. Such deaths are apparently an important factor in limiting the population as they mainly involve young and female animals. Adults are dark grey or black above, diffusing into pale grey on the flanks and paler grey or white below. The dorsal fin is short and triangular, with a concave trailing edge. The tail flukes have a distinct notch.

Harbour Porpoises occur in the north Atlantic around Iceland, northern Scandinavia and east to Novaya Zemlya, around southern Greenland and off the Labrador coast, and in the north Pacific from southern Kamchatka across the Aleutians to south-west and southern Alaska.

Left
Orca
The upper painting is of the male, the lower of the female.

Left
Two colour variations of Dall's Porpoise.

Right
Two colour variations of White-beaked Dolphin.

The animals are painted to the same scale as the Orca above.

Dall's Porpoise

Phocoenoides dalli

TL: 1.9–2.4m. W: 170–210kg. ♂>♀.

Status: CITES: Appendix II.

Adult is black, with large white patches on the flanks stretching from just in front of the dorsal fin almost to the tail stock, and continuous ventrally. There are also variable white patches on the dorsal fin, and on the trailing edges of both flippers and flukes. Adult male has a dorsal hump forward of the dorsal fin. The dorsal fin is triangular with a hooked top. The flukes are notched.

Dall's Porpoise is found in the Sea of Okhotsk and from Kamchatka to Alaska, though does not extend far north into the Bering Sea.

Beluga

Delphinapterus leucas

TL: 3.0–5.0m. W: 500–1,500kg. ♂>♀.

Status: IUCN: Vulnerable. CITES: Appendix II.

One of the species in the family Monodontidae, both of which are true Arctic dwellers. Adult is entirely creamy-white (the name derives from the Russian 'white'). There is no dorsal fin, but a small triangular ridge is visible in many individuals. The head is broad with a distinctive 'melon' that becomes larger with age. Calf is uniformly grey, becoming white only at about 6 years old. Beluga swims at 5–15kph.

Beluga are rare in the Greenland Sea (and perhaps absent altogether). Occurs near Svalbard and east from there along the Russian Arctic coast to the Chukchi Sea. Also found in the Bering Sea and the Arctic waters of North America to eastern Greenland, and in Hudson Bay.

The Beluga and Polar Bear capital

The annual congregation of Polar Bears at Churchill, Manitoba at the south-western corner of Hudson Bay has led the town to christen itself the 'Polar Bear Capital of the World'. What is less well known is that Churchill also styles itself the 'Beluga Capital of the World' for the summer congregation of whales in the Churchill River. Unusually for a cetacean, Beluga moult annually, choosing river mouths where the warmth and low salinity of the mixed fresh and sea waters aid the process, and shallow water allows the animals to rub the old skin free on the river bed.

Narwhal
The upper painting shows a female, the lower a male.

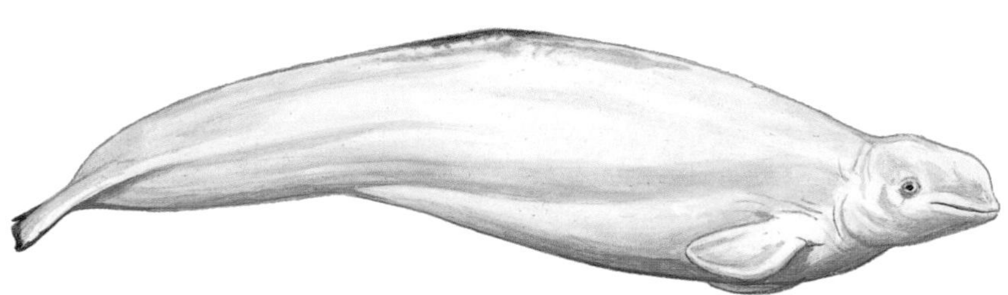

Beluga.
The animal is shown at the same scale as the Narwhals above.

NARWHAL

Monodon monoceros

TL: 3.5–5.5m (excluding tusk). W: 800–1,600kg. ♂>♀.
Status: IUCN: Data deficient. CITES: Appendix II.
Adult is mottled blue-grey or dark grey and white, the mottling usually more extensive on the upperparts. There is no dorsal fin, and the dorsal ridge is marked only by a dark line. Calf is uniformly mid-grey, becoming darker and more mottled as it matures. Older adults become paler, some being almost white. The flukes are convex in the male, less so, or even straight, in the female. Narwhal swims at 5–15kph. Narwhal skin (*muktuq*) is considered a great delicacy by the Inuit and is eaten as soon as a hunted animal is landed. It tastes, vaguely, of hazelnut.

The Narwhal is a true Arctic dweller. Rare from west Greenland to the New Siberian Islands, more common in the Canadian Arctic, from Banks Island to east Greenland.

A Narwhal sounds at the floe edge, Baffin Bay, Canada.

BAIRD'S BEAKED WHALE

Berardius bairdii

TL: 11–13m. W: 9–11 tonnes. ♀>♂.
Status: CITES: Appendix I.
Adult is dark grey or grey-brown with numerous white ventral patches. The lower jaw is longer than the upper and the two anterior teeth of the four in the jaw are visible when the mouth is closed. The dorsal fin is small with a straight or falcate trailing edge. The flukes are not notched and have a shallow concave trailing edge.

Baird's Beaked Whale is found north of a line from Japan to Baja California, as far north as the Sea of Okhotsk and the Pribilof Islands.

STEJNEGER'S BEAKED WHALE

Mesoplodon stejnegeri

Status: IUCN: Data Deficient. CITES: Appendix II.
TL: 4-6m, W: *c.*1.2tonnes. ♀>♂.
Known from a single skull found on Bering Island and described in 1885, and a dead whale washed ashore in Katchemak Bay, Alaska in 1977, but virtually unseen until 1994 when a group of four stranded on Adak Island in the Aleutians. Almost nothing is known of the whales' life or

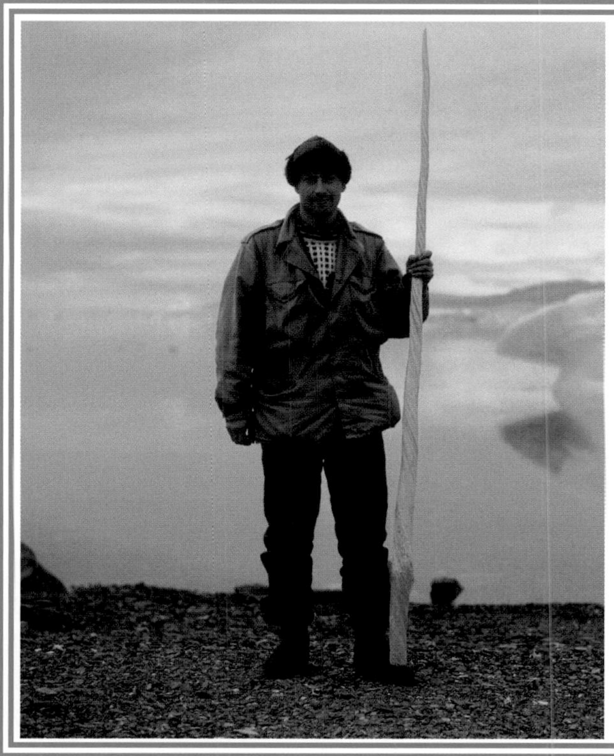

The Unicorn of the sea

Narwhal have only two teeth, both in the upper jaw. In males the left tooth pushes through the lip to form a tusk. In some males the right tooth also erupts, though these double-tusked narwhals are very rare. The tusk begins to grow when the animal is 2–3 years old (occasionally at one year) and grows continuously. Very old males may have tusks of 3m weighing 10kg. In females the teeth often do not erupt during the entire life of the animal, though tusked females have been seen. The Narwhal's tusk is claimed to be the source of tales of the Unicorn. This cannot be conclusively proved, but it does appear that the true source of the tusks was suppressed to promote the Unicorn legend (and hence the price of the tusks). Despite occasional nonsense written on the subject, the tusk is not used to skewer fish. The tusk is a secondary sexual characteristic. It is sometimes used as a weapon; scarred males and broken tusks are seen. The tusks are also sometimes laid across the back of another animal in what appears to be a gentle, tactile gesture.

The whale's curious name is from the Scandinavian *nár hvalr*, corpse whale, because the skin colour looks like that of a dead man.

In the photograph, taken at Qannaq, north-west Greenland, photographer Per Michelsen self-consciously holds a 2.2m tusk from a Narwhal killed by local hunters.

reproductive biology. Male is dark grey overall, female is paler ventrally. The whale has two tusk-like teeth in the lower jaw, set about 20cm back from the beak tip and protruding well above the upper jaw. The dorsal fin is small and triangular, with a falcate trailing edge. The flukes are not notched, with the trailing edge straight but upturned at the extremities.

Stejneger's Beaked Whales appear to be confined to a curved band of the north Pacific from Japan to the Aleutians and northern California, and in the Bering Sea north to southern Chukotka, but much more southerly on the North American side.

Northern Bottlenose Whale

Hyperoodon ampullatus

TL: 7.0–9.5m. W: 5.8–7.5 tonnes. ♂>♀.

Status: CITES: Appendix I.

Adults vary from dark brown through grey-brown to greenish brown, usually paler ventrally with cream or cream-buff blotches. The melon is very prominent and cream from the crown to the forehead. The dorsal fin is small and triangular, with a falcate trailing edge. The flukes are not notched, with the trailing edge straight or shallowly concave with sharply upturned tips.

The Northern Bottlenose Whale is found in the north Atlantic to the ice edge. Rare in the Barents Sea and Hudson Strait.

Sperm Whale

Physeter macrocephalus

TL: ♂ 11.0–18.5m, ♀ 8.0–13.0m. W: ♂ 11–70 tonnes, ♀ 2–24 tonnes. Exhibits the most extreme sexual dimorphism of any cetacean, with males weighing up to three times more than the female.

Status: IUCN: Vulnerable. CITES: Appendix I.

The largest toothed whale, with a legendary place in both the history of whaling, because of the ferocity of some whales towards their pursuers, and in literature as a result of Herman Melville's classic novel *Moby Dick*. Adult is dark grey, with occasional white patches. Surfacing whales often appear more grey-brown. Moby Dick was, of course, white, and white

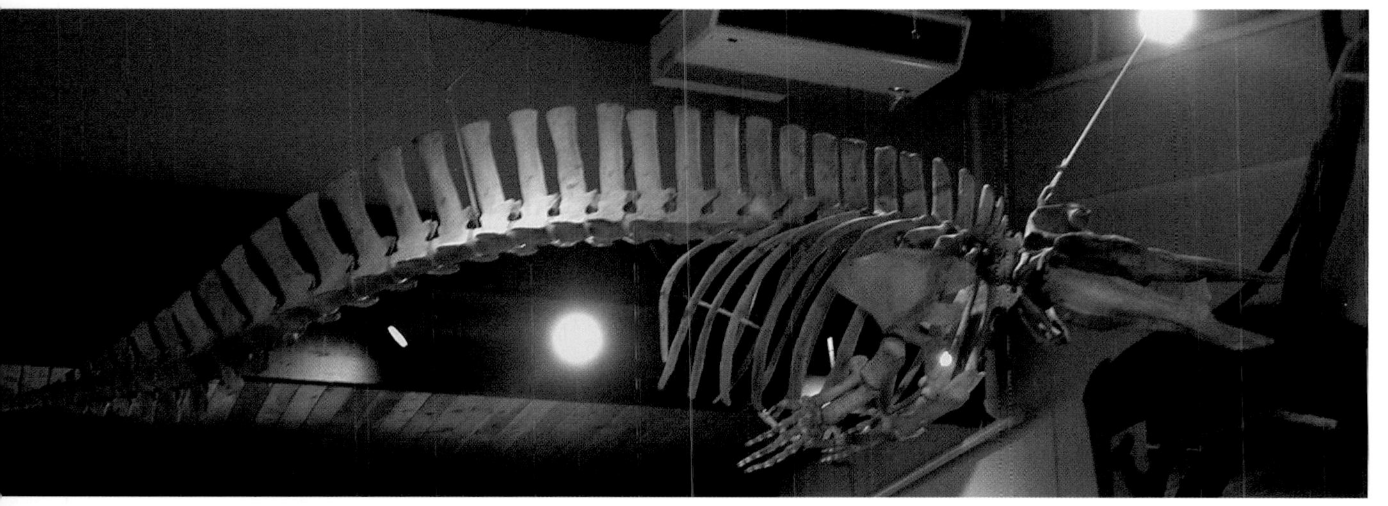

Probably the best view most traveller's will ever have of a Stejneger's Beaked Whale. This is the skeleton of the 1977 whale, now displayed in the Pratt Museum, Homer, Alaska.

Ambergris

The Sperm Whale's main food is squid – it feeds on the Giant Squid *Architeuthis* spp., another creature of legend. The squids' horny beaks are indigestible and irritate the stomachs of the whale. To ease the irritation the whale secretes a resinous substance that coats the beaks. Coagulated masses of this material, normally excreted, were occasionally vomited out by harpooned whales. The masses floated and were collected. Known as ambergris, the masses were highly prized for their use in the perfume industry. It would be interesting to observe the faces of users when they discovered that one ingredient of their expensive perfume could be termed 'whale faeces'.

Sperm Whales are known, these being truly white rather than cases of albinism. The lower jaw is long and narrow, and holds 18–25 conical teeth in each half. These teeth grow to around 25cm and fit into sockets in the upper jaw when the mouth is closed. The upper jaw has no teeth or just a few rudimentary ones. The dorsal fin is small, thick and rounded, and behind it there is a series of bumps along the dorsal ridge towards the tail stock. The flukes are notched, with a straight trailing edge. Sperm Whales usually swim at 4–6kph, but can reach 25km/h.

The Sperm Whale is found in all oceans, north and south, to the ice edge. However, it is rare in the far north.

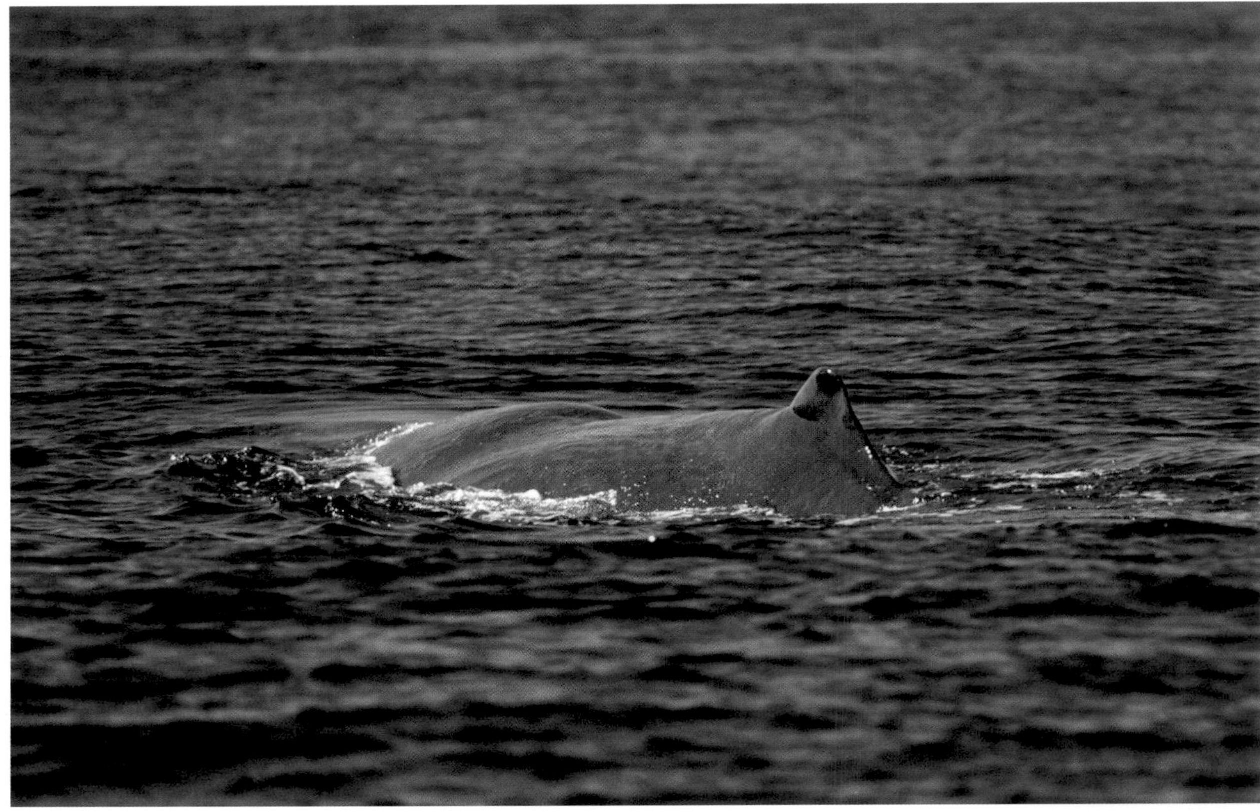

Right
Sperm Whale, Lofoten Islands, Norway.

Below
Minke Whales under the midnight Sun in waters off southern Svalbard.

BALEEN WHALES

The huge baleen plates of the second, smaller suborder of cetaceans is the basis of their scientific name – the *Mysticeti*, or 'moustached whales'. The *Mysticeti* represent only about 10% of all whale species, though in Arctic waters this rises to about 50% of species, the baleen whales trawling the rich polar waters for plankton and other prey. The *Mysticeti* comprises three families, the *Balaenopteridae* or rorquals, the *Eschrichtidae*, which contains one species, the Grey Whale, and the *Balaenidae* or right whales.

Blue Whale

Balaenoptera musculus

TL: 22–31m. W: 60–140 tonnes. ♀>♂.

Status: IUCN: Endangered. CITES: Appendix I.

The largest animal ever known – larger than any dinosaur. Adult is long and narrow. It is blue-grey with occasional white blotching. The dorsal fin is small and falcate, and set far back on the body. The tail is notched, the fluke trailing edge slightly concave. Blue Whales feed at 2–5kph, cruise at 5–30kph and can reach speeds of up to 50kph.

The Blue Whale is found in all oceans. It has been seen in the Bering Sea, in Baffin Bay, and in the Barents Sea.

Fin Whale

Balaenoptera physalus

TL: 18–24m. W: 45–70 tonnes. ♀>♂.

Status: IUCN: Endangered. CITES: Appendix I.

The second largest whale. Adult is long and narrow; slate-grey above, paler (even white) below, with a curious (and not understood) colour asymmetry between the two sides of the lower jaw. The dorsal fin is small and falcate, and set far back on the body. There is a well-defined dorsal ridge from the fin to the tail stock (hence the whalers' name, 'Razorback'). The tail is notched, with the fluke trailing edge shallowly convex but upturned at the tips. Fin Whales feed and cruise at similar speeds to Blue Whales, but may be faster in short bursts.

The Fin Whale is found in all oceans. It has a similar distribution to the Blue Whale, but tends to be more southerly.

Sei Whale

Balaenoptera borealis

TL: 12–16m. W: 8.5–15.5 tonnes. Females are significantly larger than males, up to 40% by weight, though only *c.*5% by length.

Status: IUCN: Endangered. CITES: Appendix I.

The name is pronounced 'sigh' rather than 'say' and derives from the Norwegian for pollock, which was believed to be a principal prey of the species. Adult is mid-grey or dark grey above, paler (occasionally cream-white) below. The falcate dorsal fin is larger than those of either the Blue or Fin Whales and is closer to the head than in those species. The flukes are notched, the trailing edge straight with upturned tips. Swimming speeds are similar to those of Blue and Fin Whales, though it is thought that the Sei is the fastest of the great whales.

The Sei Whale is found in all oceans. Tends to be more southerly than either Blue or Fin Whales, rarely being seen north of Jan Mayen, Labrador, south-east Greenland or the Aleutians.

Giants of the ocean

Blue Whales of the Southern Ocean are larger than their northern cousins, with extreme lengths to 33m and weights up to 190 tonnes, though the real giants that were encountered during the early days of rorqual hunting do not seem to have re–occurred, even though the species is now fully protected. Overhunting has drastically reduced the population of Blue Whales, though numbers are now slowly recovering. The current population is estimated at about 11,000 animals, about 15% of the pre-hunting population.

Interestingly, the second part of the species' scientific name means 'little mouse' which, given the whale's size, could be evidence of humour on the part of Linnaeus, or (and perhaps more likely) a mistranslation of 'muscle'.

Minke Whale

Balaenoptera acutorostrata

TL: 8–10.5m. W: 8–10 tonnes. ♀>♂.

Status: CITES: Appendix I (apart from West Greenland population, which is Appendix II).

The smallest of the Arctic baleen whales. Adult has a flattened head with a pointed snout, so from above the head forms a sharp V-shape. Dark grey above, this diffusing into white patches on the flanks and ventral body. The flank patches are mottled grey. The dorsal fin is tall and falcate, and set far back on the body. The flukes are notched, with the trailing edge shallowly concave. Minke swim at similar speeds to the other great whales.

Minke Whales are seen in the north Atlantic as far north as Davis Strait, though more southerly in the western Atlantic, occasionally reaching Svalbard and the Barents Sea. In the north Pacific they are found throughout the Bering Sea and into the Chukchi Sea.

Humpback Whale

Megaptera novaeangliae

TL: 11–18m. W: 25–45 tonnes. ♀>♂.

Status: IUCN: Vulnerable. CITES: Appendix I.

Adult is uniformly dark grey or black with variable white patches on the underside. The front sections of the upper and lower jaws have a variety of knoblike protuberances, each of which encloses a stiff hair that is probably a sensory aid for detecting prey or water current movements. The falcate dorsal fin is small and mounted on a hump, usually more easily visible in front of the fin. It is this hump, which is prominent when the whale arches its back before diving, that gives the species its common name. The pectoral fins are very long (up to 5m, often 30% of the whale's total length) and have a distinctive black-and-white pattern (above and below) and a knobbly leading edge. These patterns are highly individual and can be used to identify particular whales. This is also true of the flukes, which are also patterned with black and white. The tail shape is unique to individuals, though the often ragged trailing edge tends to be concave. The whales are slow swimmers, usually travelling at 2–6kph, but are capable of bursts to 30kph.

The Humpback Whale is found in all the world's oceans. Seen in the Atlantic as far north as Svalbard, but rarely east of the Barents Sea. In the Pacific occurs in the Bering Sea.

The larger Arctic cetaceans, painted to scale.

Right above
Male Sprem Whale

Right below
Female Sperm Whale

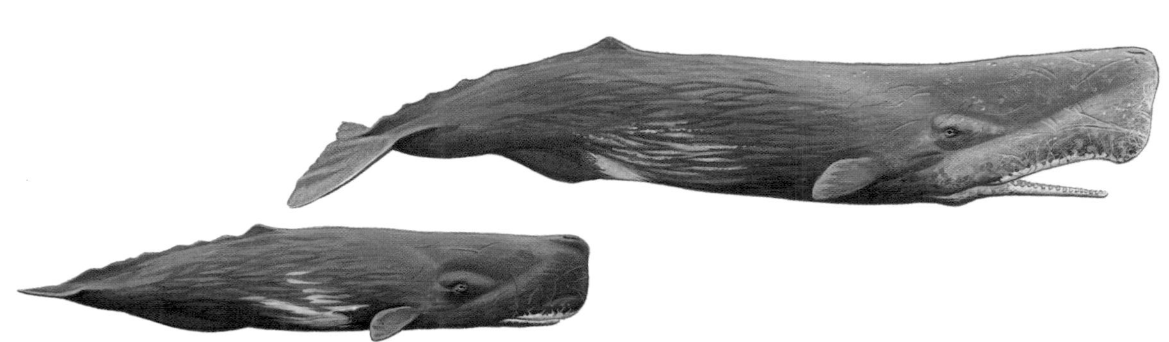

Blue Whale

Fin Whale, showing the curious asymmetry between the two sides

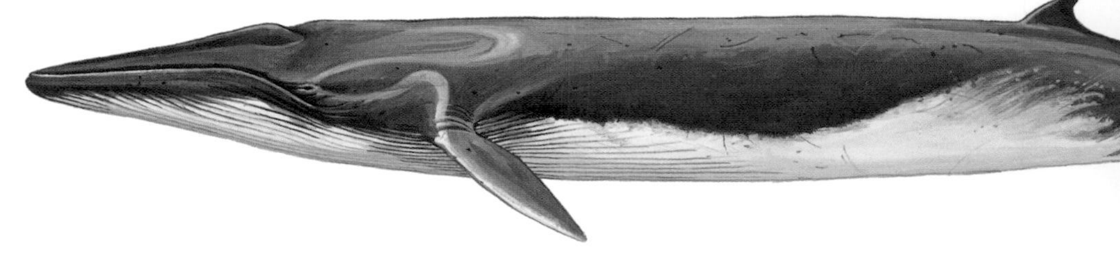

Right above
Atlantic Humpback Whale

Right below
Pacific Humpback Whale

Grey Whale

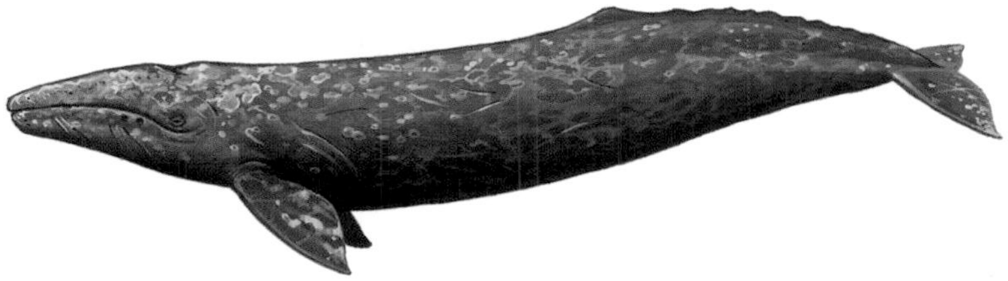

Sei Whale

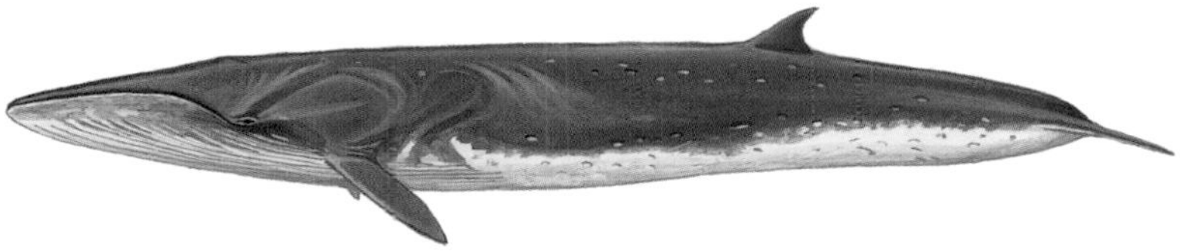

Minke Whale

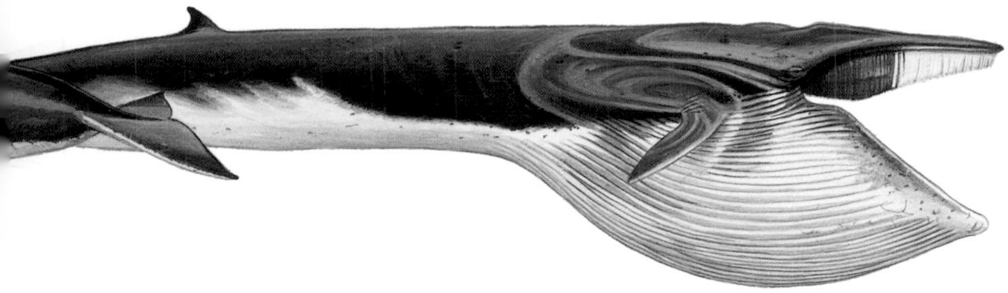

Left
Bowhead

Below left
Pacific Northern Right Whale

Below right
Atlantic Northern Right Whale

Humpbacks in the Lynn Canal, Alaska.

Above
A breaching whale. There was actually a double breach, the splash of the first whale just visible in the top right of the photograph.

Below
The hump which gives the species its name can be seen in front of the dorsal fin of the two larger whales.

GREY WHALE

Eschrichtius robustus

TL: 11–15m. W: 16–35 tonnes. ♀>♂.

Status: IUCN: Overall Low Risk, though the population of the North-west Pacific and Sea of Okhotsk is Critically Endangered. CITES: Appendix I.

The Grey Whale is the only representative of its family; once thought to be basal to other baleen whales, but DNA analysis has suggested a more recent evolution. The Grey Whale possesses characteristics of both the rorquals and the right whales. Adults are mottled dark grey, light grey and white, and invariably have barnacle clusters on the head and forward part of the back. There is no dorsal fin, merely a small, triangular dorsal hump, from which a series of small bumps runs along the dorsal ridge to the tail stock. The tail is notched, the flukes broad, with straight (though ragged) trailing edges and upturned tips. Grey Whales cruise at 7–10km/h. Because of their feeding method, ploughing through bottom sediments, the whales stir up clouds of silt and food particles, so feeding whales are often noticeable because of the accompanying flocks of gulls and other seabirds.

The Grey Whale is found in the North Pacific, as far north as the Chukchi and Beaufort seas, and in the Sea of Okhotsk. There was formerly an Atlantic population, the animals feeding off Iceland and Greenland and migrating as far south as the Bay of Biscay, but this population became extinct in the 18th century, probably as a result of overhunting by Basque whalers.

RIGHT WHALES

Right whales acquired their name from the early whalers – these were the right (i.e. correct) whales to kill: they were slow and so could be easily overhauled by a rowed boat; they were passive, and so did not turn every killing into a battle in which the whalers were at equal risk to the whale; they floated when dead, making them easier to transport to ships or shore; and they yielded huge amounts of baleen and oil. The mass of blubber, which yielded the oil, explains the reason dead whales floated. As a result of this combination, the three species of large right whales (two Arctic and one Antarctic species – the Southern Right Whale was once thought to be conspecific with the Northern Right, but is now considered a

Migrating whales

Grey Whales have one of the longest migrations of any mammal, moving between the Bering Sea and the lagoons of Baja California and the Gulf of California and back each year, a distance of 12,000km or more. The whales move continuously on migration, day and night, and apparently without sleeping. Mating and birth take place in the same lagoons, implying a 12-month gestation. The single calf (5m long and weighing 650–700kg) accompanies its mother on the long migration north. On this journey the calves are vulnerable to Orca attack, the Orcas attempting to isolate the calf from its mother, then drowning it by lying on its back. Often the Orcas will eat only the tongue. Calves that survive the migration are weaned at 6–7 months and are independent before undertaking the long migration south. Until recently the Grey Whale migration was considered the longest by any mammal, but in early 2007 a Humpback Whale travelling from the Antarctic Peninsula to waters off Costa Rica and Panama was found to have swum over 8,000km, implying a round trip in excess of 16,000km.

separate species) were hunted almost to extinction. Despite full protection (though the Bowhead is still hunted by native peoples in both Alaska and Siberia) the populations do not appear to be recovering, possibly due to inbreeding.

There are some key anatomical differences between right whales and rorquals. The right whales have an arched nostrum, which results in a bow-shaped mouth rather than the straight mouth of the rorquals – their baleen plates are consequently much longer. Right whales have no throat pleats, and so feed by skimming rather than gulping. Also, there is no dorsal fin.

A rare photograph of a Bowhead calf. The calf was asleep or resting at the floe edge in Foxe Basin, Canada. The white lower jaw and flipper can be clearly seen. After a short period of observation, hydrophones picked up the call of the mother whale and the calf submerged and disappeared.

Northern Right Whale

Eubalaena glacialis

TL: 15–18m. W: 50–90 tonnes. ♀>♂.

Status: IUCN: Endangered. CITES: Appendix I.

One of the world's rarest cetaceans. Reliable population figures are difficult to calculate, but the Atlantic population probably contains no more than 300–400 animals, while the Pacific population may number as few as 100. There appears to have been no increase in population since the species was protected.

The adult is large and rotund; black with variable ventral white patches. The head has a number of callosities (usually white, but occasionally yellow or pink), which are also seen in foetal whales; their function is unknown. The whale's blubber is up to 60cm thick and contributes 40% of the total weight. The tail is deeply notched, the flukes having a concave trailing edge. The whale rarely exceeds 10kph.

The Northern Right Whale is found in the Atlantic between Iceland and Norway (though extremely rare in this area), and between Labrador and Maine. In the Pacific the whale occurs from Japan to Kamchatka and in the Sea of Okhotsk, and, rarely, near the Aleutians and southern Alaska.

The age of Bowheads

Some Bowheads taken by native hunters in recent years have been found to have ancient harpoon heads embedded in them. These heads have been dated to well over 100 years old. This discovery encouraged scientists to investigate other methods for determining the life expectancy of Bowheads. One determination, analysing the ratio of two stereoscopic isomers of aspartic acid, a constituent of the lens protein of the Bowhead's eye, indicates ages of up to 200 years. That means that the whales rival the Giant Tortoises *Geochelone* spp. as the longest-lived animals.

Bowhead Whale

Balaena mysticetus

TL: 15–18.5m. W: 60–80 tonnes. ♀>♂.

Status: CITES: Appendix I.

Originally known as the Greenland Right Whale, this is the most Arctic of all whales. The massive head makes up 35–40% of total length and bears the huge bow-shaped mouth. The adult is black with a white lower lip, marked by black spots. The back is often marked with white, these marks thought to be scarring acquired when the whales break through the sea ice to breathe. Bowheads can break through ice of considerable thickness, up to 60cm thick. There is a prominent triangular bump in front of the blowholes, and a depression behind them. The tail is deeply notched, with the flukes having a shallow concave trailing edge. Bowheads swim slowly, at about 6kph.

17. Antarctic Wildlife

As we have already seen, Antarctica is, in general, colder than the Arctic. It is also surrounded by a wide, and often hostile, sea. These two facts have limited the wildlife that can be found there. The sea has prevented the immigration of terrestrial mammals, while the climate has ensured that any land-based creatures which existed on the landmass before it moved to the South Pole would have died out long ago.

Scientists usually divide Antarctica (the southern polar region as a whole that is, rather than just the continent itself) into three. Continental Antarctica comprises the landmass apart from the Antarctic Peninsula. Maritime Antarctica covers the Peninsula and the island groups which surround the continent – the South Sandwich, South Orkneys and South Shetlands, together with Bouvet Island. The final region, the sub-Antarctic islands, comprises Marion and Prince Edward islands, the Crozet islands, Kerguelen Island, Heard and McDonald islands, Macquarie Island, and South Georgia. From a point of view of wildlife, the main difference between the three is the increasing paucity of plants and terrestrial invertebrates as the observer moves south. On the sub-Antarctic islands there are over 50 flowering plants: just two grow in Maritime Antarctica, and none at all on the continent. The same story is repeated for ferns (and related plants), with 16 recorded on the sub-Antarctic islands, but none in either of the other two regions. On Continental Antarctica around 30 species of moss, and over 100 species of lichens have been identified to date, but these figures rise to about 100 mosses and 150 lichens in Maritime Antarctica, and over 400 mosses and 300 lichens on the islands. It is the same with the terrestrial invertebrates. Although some mites, springtails, crustaceans, nematode worms, rotifers and tardigrades (water bears) have been identified on the continent, there are no flies or molluscs, and even the invertebrate families which have been identified have few members. By contrast the waters of the Southern Ocean are very rich, with an abundance of both species and biomass. As a consequence those species which have found a home in the southern polar region – the birds and seals – exploit the resources of the sea rather than attempting to make a living on the land.

The sub-Antarctic islands vary from low-lying, unglaciated, to (relatively) high altitude and completely glaciated. The vegetation varies accordingly, with ground-hugging plants, tussock grasses and large herbs to 2m, and a wide variety of mosses and lichens.

Maritime Antarctica includes the only two vascular plants to have become established on the continent, each found only on the west side of the Antarctic Peninsula. The two are the grass *Deschampsia antarctica*, and the pearlwort (small, cushion-like plants) *Colobanthus quitensis*.

On Continental Antarctica plant life is restricted to areas free of ice and snow, these including the mountains which break through the ice-shroud that covers most of the continent, but being chiefly confined to coastal areas. In some of these breeding animals have added nutrients, aiding the establishment of plant life, but such areas are also favoured by humans for Antarctic bases, their presence having occasionally led to the areas being contaminated. Pollution has added to one surprising problem faced by plants in these coastal areas – in a land of snow and ice they suffer from a lack of water. In terms of precipitation, Antarctica is a desert. Mosses and lichens are prone to desiccation because they cannot control water loss as effectively as vascular plants, and continental species have evolved to accept routine periods of desiccation by reducing metabolism to a minimum, returning to 'normal' levels only when rehydration occurs. Away from such ice- and snow-free areas, life is restricted to algae which can grow on snow and ice, feeding on entrapped dust, etc. These algae occasionally bloom, colouring the snow in shades of green or red.

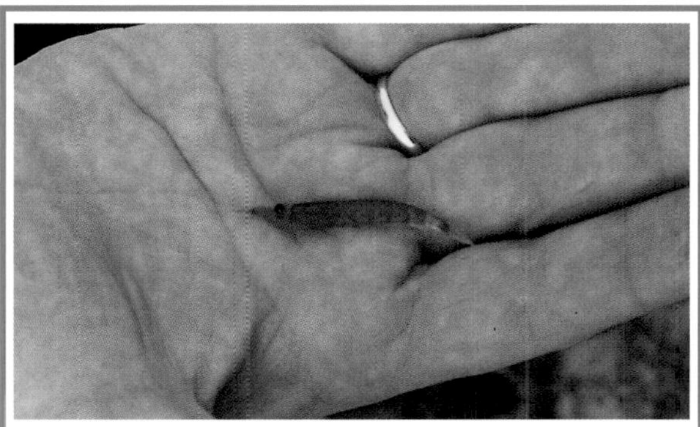

Antarctic krill

Despite the importance of krill to Antarctic birds and mammals, the crustacean was actually poorly understood until very recent times. Even now aspects of its biology are unknown. What is known is that krill lives up to ten years (though probably on average about five years), and is probably only sexually mature at three years old. Krill breed early in the Antarctic spring, females laying one or more masses of eggs, each numbering around 10,000. The number of times a female will lay depends on the availability of food. The tiny eggs, each about 0.5mm across, sink to depths of about 1,000m. Amazingly the animals that hatch do not feed at first, going through several larval stages before rising towards the surface. There they begin to feed. At one year they have grown to about 25mm – about half adult size. Then, and when they are adults, the krill form swarms with densities which can approach 30,000 animals per cubic metre. It is in such swarms that whales feed, the vast numbers of krill, and the fact that they are essentially packets of concentrated protein explaining why rorquals can survive on a diet of such small prey items. One vast swarm of krill studied near Elephant Island was estimated to have weighed about 2 million tonnes. Though this figure amounts to only about 0.5% of the estimated annual animal matter yield of the Southern Ocean (of about 360 million tonnes) it arose from just 400km² of sea.

Krill grow by moulting their exoskeleton (shell), but growth is restricted to the Antarctic summer when they can feed on phytoplankton. During the winter krill go without food – sometimes for several months – consuming muscle as they have little in the way of fat reserves. As a result they shrink, growing again when spring allows the phytoplankton to photosynthesise.

Because of the high protein content of krill, and because of a perceived surplus as a consequence of the decrease in whale populations due to hunting, the crustacean was considered to be a potentially valuable food stuff. But there are disadvantages to the harvest: the exoskeleton has to be removed as it is high in fluorides which would foul the meat, and the animal decomposes quickly when out of the water so processing has to be carried out at sea. Though krill is fished, reality has not yet matched up to the apparent potential.

Opposite page
Gentoo Penguin feeding chick, Carcass Island, west Falklands. The adult feeds by regurgitation, a process which presumably requires care as penguin bills are sharp.

The Southern Ocean

As with the Arctic seas, the Southern Ocean has food chains built on micro-organisms and the higher life forms which feed on them. Of benthic species, the most abundant are starfish, sponges, sea urchins and a variety of worms. Of particular importance to Antarctic food webs is krill, the generic name given to a group of around 85 crustaceans which flourish in southern waters. Of these the most well known is Antarctic Krill *Euphausia superba*, a 5–6cm shrimp-like crustacean which has occasionally been claimed to be the most abundant species on Earth (although recent research has suggested that the importance of krill in the food chain may have been over-emphasised, other crustaceans forming the bulk of the biomass in some study areas).

The waters surrounding the continent are usefully divided into three regions: an outer ring of permanently open sea, an inner ring of seasonally open sea (which is covered by sea ice each winter), and a coastal and continental shelf area which is ice-covered for a much longer period each year and may be covered by fast ice. Antarctic Krill is commonest in seasonal open water, the most abundant species in coastal waters being *Euphausia crystallorophias*, a smaller crustacean from the same family.

The zooplankton are taken by fish. Most Antarctic fish species are deep-water or bottom-feeding forms, pelagic, shoaling fish being notably absent. The most numerous fish are the Notothenioidei, which, in general, have long bodies, large heads and a dorsal fin split into a short first section and a longer second section. Fish of this sub-order constitute about two-thirds of all Antarctic species. The Antarctic cods, icefish, dragonfish and robberfish are among the best known, and represent four of the five families of the sub-order, all members of which are confined, or nearly so, to Antarctic waters. Most of these species mature slowly and produce few, but large, eggs. Arctic cod produce millions of eggs, while Antarctic cod produce only a few hundred. The eggs are usually laid in defensible nests and guarded by the parent fish. Once hatched, the fry are also guarded. Parental care is very unusual among fish, but is the norm in Antarctic species: it is not confined to fish as southern molluscs and crustaceans also exhibit similar care. Losses of fish fry do, of course, occur, and consequently the population is slow to recover if stocks are depleted. This has raised concerns regarding overfishing, the stocks of some species already showing signs of a significant reduction in numbers.

Fish are preyed upon not only by sea mammals and birds, but also by squid, which are now recognised as one of the most important components of Antarctic food chains. Squid in general, and southern species in particular, are poorly understood, the depths at which they normally occur and the difficulty of acquiring live specimens from those depths acting against a thorough knowledge. It is known that around 70 species live in Antarctic waters, about 50% of these being endemic. Some estimates suggest that the biomass of squid may be as high as 25% of the total biomass of the Southern Ocean. Squid, particularly the giant forms, are associated with

The curious icefish

Most Antarctic fish have a reduced red blood cell count (and hence haemoglobin content) in their blood compared to that of temperate fish, often only 50% or less. But the icefishes have gone a stage further, being the only vertebrates on Earth to have dispensed with haemoglobin altogether. Haemoglobin carries oxygen around the body as the gas is only poorly soluble in blood. But Antarctica's waters are so rich in oxygen, and the metabolic rate of local fish, including the icefish, so low that the protein is not required. Icefish have two or three times the blood volume of other fish, blood making up some 10% of their body weight. The blood circulates more quickly as the heart is larger and beats faster, and the fish's blood vessels have larger diameters. Icefish can also absorb oxygen directly through their skin which has no scales, the blood vessels lying very close to the surface. Not having to produce haemoglobin means the fish can use the energy saved on other adaptations: icefish are efficient predators suggesting that their evolutionary quirk has done them no harm. Lacking haemoglobin, icefish are deathly pale.

the Sperm Whale, but they also form significant fractions of the diet of seals, albatrosses and other toothed whales.

ANTARCTIC BIRDS

The Southern Ocean, being continuous around Antarctica, favours oceanic birds, while the lack of terrestrial predators has also allowed diving birds to dispense with flight, converting their wings to efficient paddles. Antarctic birds are therefore the albatrosses, shear-waters and petrels with their long, stiffened wings, the more delicate surface feeders (prions and storm petrels), and the penguins. In the absence of raptors, skuas and the giant petrels have become the principal avian predators.

ALBATROSSES, PETRELS AND SKUAS

Of the albatrosses, the most famous is the Wandering Albatross. It is the largest of the 'great' albatrosses, a group of seven birds which are today seen as comprising two groups of subspecies, the Wandering and Royal albatrosses. The 'true' Wandering Albatross (*Diomedea exulans* or the nominate of the *exulans* group if that taxonomy is followed) has a wingspan of up to 3.5m and a lifestyle which sees it spend extended periods (perhaps several years) at sea once it has hatched. Wandering Albatrosses are not sexually mature until they are 3–5 years old, and do not breed until they are 12–13 years old. Immature birds visit breeding sites to form pairs as they approach the time of first breeding. Pair bonds are life-long, the birds breeding only every second year as young Wanderers take almost twelve months to fledge. A single egg is laid: after incubation and a period of guarding the vulnerable chick, the chick is abandoned, being visited only for short feeding sessions during the remaining time it spends at the nest. All the great albatrosses follow a similar breeding pattern. The birds are also similar in appearance, being white, with black tips and trailing edges on the wings. The massive, wickedly hook-tipped bill is pink. The various subspecies are usually said to be distinguished by the degree of black on the over-wing, but this is not always a useful indicator as the birds tend to become paler with age. Birds of the Wandering subspecies may be seen above the waters around Antarctica, though none breed on the continent: nominate Wanderers breed on South Georgia, and other southern islands. Royal subspecies are seen in a broad arc from the southern tip of South America across to Tasmania. The Southern Royal Albatross (nominate *Diomedea epomophora*) breeds on Auckland and Chatham islands.

The medium-sized and smaller albatrosses follow the same general pattern as the larger species, though in gener-al they have grey heads, and bills which are yellow (or pinkish-yellow) or yellow and black. The lifestyle, diet and breeding biology of the various species (about ten species are recog-nised, depending on the detailed taxonomy) is similar to that of the larger albatrosses. About 50% of the total population of all the species are the Black-browed Albatross *Thalassarche melanophrys* which breeds on the Falkland Islands, and many of the islands of Maritime Antarctica. The Sooty Albatross *Phoebetria fusca* and Light-mantled Sooty Albatross *Phoebetria palpebrata* are highly distinctive albatrosses, with beautiful sooty-brown plumage. They also breed on islands of Maritime Antarctica.

Many of the southern albatrosses are vulnerable. Several are endangered, some critically so. Threats to species which nest on inhabited islands are loss of breeding sites and predation from introduced animals, while at sea the birds are victims of long-line fishing, taking bait (and hook), and then drowning.

Of the larger petrels, both the Southern *Macronectes giganteus* and Northern *Macronectes halli* Giant Petrels are scavengers and predators. They are large birds (up to 100cm in length with wingspans up to 2m) and take adult birds as well as feeding on the corpses of seals and whales. The Southern Giant Petrel breeds on the continent, though the Northern species is restricted to Maritime Antarctic islands. Other large petrels include two of the most beautiful of southern birds, the Pintado or Cape Petrel *Daption capensis* and the pure-white Snow Petrel *Pagadromo nivea*. Three other groups of petrels are

Top
Pintado Petrel, Coronation Island, South Orkneys.

Above
Incubating Snow Petrel. The bird has nested deep underground within a boulder field of Coronation Island, South Orkneys.

Wandering Albatross above the Southern Ocean.

Light-mantled Sooty Albatross, South Georgia.

The amazing diving-petrels

Three of the world's four species of diving-petrels are found in southern waters (the fourth, the Peruvian Diving-petrel *Pelecanoides garnotii* being found above waters off Peru and Chile). These relatively tiny, fragile-looking birds offer one of the most amazing sights of the Southern Ocean as they fly straight into steep waves, emerging from the far side despite the observer assuming they must be crushed. The diving-petrels are the southern equivalent of the northern auks, sharing a similar wing structure. The three southern diving-petrels (the Common *Pelecanoides urinatrix*, the South Georgian *P. georgicus*, and the Magellan *P. magellani*) and the Peruvian are very similar in size and appearance (length: 18–25cm, wingspan: 30–40cm, dark grey-brown above, white below), only the white half-collar of the Magellan distinguishing birds which are not in the hand. The birds breed in burrows, laying a single egg. Though the southern species have stable populations, the Peruvian Diving-petrel is an endangered species.

also found in southern waters. Gadfly petrels of the genus *Pterodroma* have short, black bills, while species of the genus *Procellaria* have longer, thinner, usually yellow, bills. The latter are usually lumped together with the southern shearwaters. The third group are the prions of the genus *Pachyptila*, a group of small petrels with blue-grey upperparts and white underparts which are almost impossible to tell apart when viewed above the ocean. A further difficulty is that the birds usually feed at night, when their diet of crustaceans, cephalopods and small fish rise to the surface (other southern species also take advantage of this fact), so that daytime observation is limited. The Blue Petrel *Halobaena caerulea*, the only species within its genus, is very similar to the prions in both appearance and habits. Antarctica has five species of Storm-petrels, each similar in appearance and habits to the two darker Arctic species, as well as diving-petrels (see Box).

The South Polar Skua *Catharacta maccormicki* breeds on islands close to the continent, and on the continent itself. As with some northern skuas, the species has two colour morphs, a dark phase in which the bird is chocolate brown overall apart from white bases to the flight feathers, and a pale phase which has a cream head and underparts. Intermediate forms also occur. Despite its scientific name, the Brown Skua *Catharacta antarctica* has a more northerly distribution, though it does nest

Black-browed Albatrosses engaged in ritual bill clacking to reinforce the pair bond, New Island, west Falklands.

on the outer Antarctic Peninsula. Subspecies of the Brown Skua are also found on the Falklands and Tristan da Cunha. South Polar Skuas are principally fish and krill feeders, though they do occasionally take the eggs and chicks of breeding species. The Brown Skua is much more predatory, taking eggs and chicks where it can (and in areas where they overlap taking these at the expense of the South Polar Skua with which it successfully competes) and scavenging on the corpses and afterbirth of seals. The Pale-faced Sheathbill *Chionis alba* is also a predator on eggs and small chicks. It breeds on the Peninsula and southern islands of Maritime Antarctica.

PENGUINS

All penguins share structural and plumage similarities. They have streamlined bodies, while the wings have evolved to short, powerful flippers. The legs are short and, together with the short tail, are used as rudders, the wings providing the motor for swimming. When on land, penguins stand upright and walk with a comical, waddling gait, though they occasionally fall on to their bellies to toboggan. Tobogganing is usually downhill, but also occasionally on flat ice, the wings being used as paddles. When standing, penguins occasionally use the stiff tail as a third leg, leaning backwards on to it. Penguins have efficient counter-current heat exchange systems as well as a layer of subcutaneous fat and three layers of feathers which provide both insulation and waterproofing. They are counter-shaded, dark (usually black) above, white below, with differing forms of head patterning and crests. The birds dive for fish, crustaceans and squid. Penguins breed colonially. Emperor and King penguins lay a single egg, the remaining species laying two, though occasionally only one chick is raised.

The penguins of Antarctica are:

Emperor Penguin *Aptenodytes forsteri*. The largest penguin, up to 1.3m tall and weighing up to 40kg. They have a half-collar which is white and orange-yellow. Emperors breed on the continent, enduring the coldest temperatures witnessed by any bird. The males hold the single egg on their feet to avoid its chilling on the ice, and huddle together for warmth while the females forage at sea. When the females return the egg is exchanged and the males leave to feed. In some colonies the over-ice walk to the sea can be 150km.

King Penguin *Aptenodytes patagonicus*. L: 0.8–1.0m. W: 10–18kg. Kings have a beautiful orange-yellow half-collar. They breed on islands of Maritime Antarctica.

Gentoo Penguin *Pygoscelis papua*. L: 70–90cm. W: 4–9kg. Gentoos have a distinctive white patch from the eye towards the crown. They breed on islands of Maritime Antarctica.

Adélie Penguin *Pygoscelis adeliae*. L: *c*.70cm. W: 4–8kg. Adélies are the least ornamented of the penguins, having only a white eye ring. They breed on the continent, and on islands of Maritime Antarctica.

Chinstrap Penguin *Pygoscelis antarctica*. L: 65–75cm. W: 3–5kg. Chinstraps are

Top
Emperor Penguins, Weddell Sea.

Middle
King Penguin, Gold Harbour, South Georgia.

Bottom
Chinstrap Penguins, Cooper's Bay, South Georgia. A male is bringing his mate a stone for her nest. Adjacent females habitually steal stones from neighbours so that stones regularly appear to migrate across the colony. Ultimately the females lose interest in stones and unpaired males, still driven to collect, accumulate impressively large (but rather sad) piles.

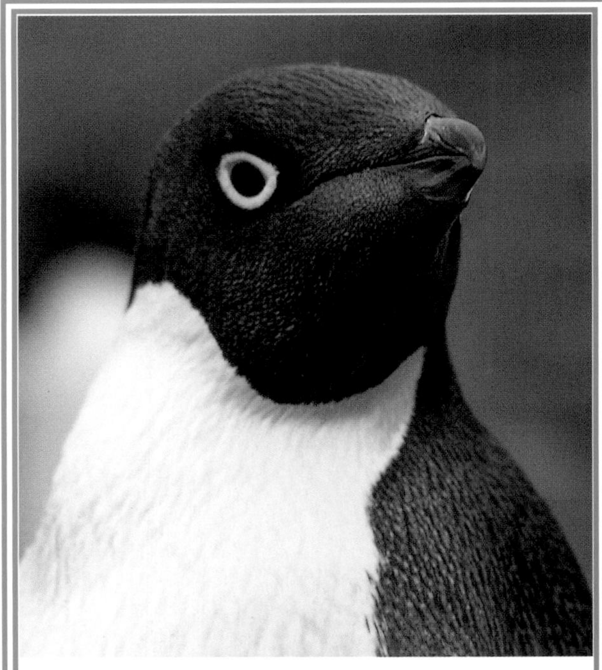

The Adélie Penguin

The Frenchman Jules-Sébastien-César Dumont d'Urville has two claims to fame. The first is that he was the man who brought the Venus de Milo to Paris from the Greek island for which it is named. The second is that he was the leader of a French expedition to Antarctica in 1837 on which the Adélie Penguin was first identified. It was the expedition's naturalist that made the identification, but Dumont d'Urville named the bird for his wife.

named for the thin black 'chinstrap' that extends across the throat and to the black crown. They breed on those islands of Maritime Antarctica close to South America.

Rockhopper Penguin *Eudyptes chrysocome*. L: 45–55cm. W: 2–4kg. Rockhoppers have distinctive yellow 'eyebrows' and crests. There are two sub-species, one breeding on the Falklands and islands off the tip of South America, the other on islands off New Zealand, including Macquarie.

Macaroni Penguin *Eudypte chrysolophus*. L: *c*.70cm. W: 3–6kg. Macaronis have yellow crests similar to those of Rockhoppers, but with 'bushier' eyebrows. They breed on islands in Maritime Antarctica in an arc from South America to Heard Island.

Royal Penguin *Eudyptes schlegeli*. L: 65–75cm. W: 3–8kg. Royals are very similar to Macaronis. They are rare, breeding only on Macquarie Island.

OTHER BIRDS

Other birds which might be seen by Antarctic travellers include several species of cormorant and shag, which breed on Maritime Antarctic islands. Kelp Gulls *Larus dominicanus* and Antarctic Terns *Sterna vittata* breed on the same islands. Travellers may also see the Arctic Tern which migrates south to enjoy two summers each year. There is also a wide variety of birds on the Falklands, and on the sub-Antarctic islands of New Zealand.

Below left
A mud-mound nest is hardly ideal for staying clean on a rain-soaked day. Macaroni Penguins, Cooper's Bay, South Georgia.

Below right
Rockhopper Penguin, New Island, west Falklands. The bird's brood patch can be clearly seen.

Above left
Magellanic Penguin, Carcass Island, west Falklands.

Above right
Imperial Cormorant *Phalacrocorax atriceps albiventer*, New Island, west Falklands.

> **Other southern penguins**
> Travellers starting out from South America, Australia and New Zealand might also see the following penguins close to their starting point or on islands visited as they travel south:
> **Magellanic** *Spheniscus magellanicus* on the southern coasts of South America and the Falkland Islands.
> **Snares** *Eudyptes robustus* on Snares Island.
> **Fiordland** *Eudyptes pachyrhynchus* on South Island, New Zealand and nearby islands.
> **Erect-crested** *Eudyptes sclateri* on Bounty and Antipodes islands near New Zealand.
> **Yellow-eyed** *Megadyptes antipodes* on Auckland and Campbell islands.
> **Little** *Eudyptes minor* on New Zealand, Stewart and Chatham islands, Tasmania and the nearby coast of Australia.
> **White-flippered** *Eudyptes albosignata* on the east coast of South Island, New Zealand.

ANTARCTIC MAMMALS

PINNIPEDS

Antarctica has true seals and eared seals, but no equivalent of the Walrus. Four of the five true seals breed on the continent, the fifth, the Southern Elephant Seal being found in continental waters and breeding on islands of Maritime Antarctica. Of the eared seals none breed on the continent or, indeed, on islands close to it, but they may be seen by southern travellers as the ships which transport them to the continent usually stop at islands with breeding colonies.

Crabeater Seal *Lobodon carcinophaga*. L: 2.0–2.6m. W: 180–400kg. ♀>♂. Adults are slim, brown above, paler below, with darker patches close to the tail. Most are heavily scarred from Leopard Seal or Orca attacks. The seals are not colonial, often being seen singly or in pairs. They breed around the continent, but primarily on the Antarctic Peninsula and near the Ross Sea.

Weddell Seal *Leptonychotes weddellii*. L: 2.5–3.0m. W: 400–600kg. ♀>♂. Adults are more rotund than the Crabeater. They are blue-grey, blotched and streaked paler. Unlike the smaller Crabeater, Weddell Seals catch fish, and have been known to take penguins. They breed all around the continent.

Ross Seal *Ommatophoca rossii*. The smallest southern true seal, L: *c.*2m, W: *c.*180kg. ♀>♂. Ross Seals are also the rarest of the southern species and are poorly studied as their home amongst the pack ice is difficult to access. Adults are dark grey or grey-brown above, paler below and are distinctive because of the lack of a defined neck and the dark stripes on both the throat and the back of the head. They feed on krill, fish and squid. Ross Seals breed all around the continent, but chiefly in the Ross and Weddell seas.

Leopard Seal *Hydrurga leptonyx*. The top predator of Antarctica. L: 2.8–3.3m. W: 320–370kg. Females are larger than males, and have been recorded to 4.5m and 600kg. They are highly distinctive in appearance, with long sinuous necks and slim bodies which give them a reptilean look, a comparison enhanced when the neck is drawn back so that the animal can strike forward, rather in the manner of a snake. Adults are blue-grey above, much paler, sometimes cream below, and are marked with darker spots and blotches. Though Leopard Seals eat penguins and other seals – chiefly pups – they also take fish and feed on krill, the latter being an important part of their diet. Leopard Seals breed all around the continent.

Southern Elephant Seal *Mirounga leonina*. By far the largest southern true seals. ♂ L: 4.5–6.5m, W: up to 3.5t. ♀ L: 2.5–4m, W: 350–800kg. Adults are brown, usually paler ventrally, but the colour is variable with locality as they

> **The most numerous seal**
> Estimates of Crabeater Seal numbers vary from as low as 10 million to as high as 75 million. The latter figure, estimated in the 1980s, is now discounted, most scientists considering that the likely population is *c.*15 million animals. That makes the Crabeater the most numerous seal on Earth, with more than double the population of the Arctic Ringed Seal. Crabeaters eat krill, swimming through the water with their mouths open – in the manner of some baleen whales – the teeth of the upper and lower jaws fitting together to form an effective sieve.

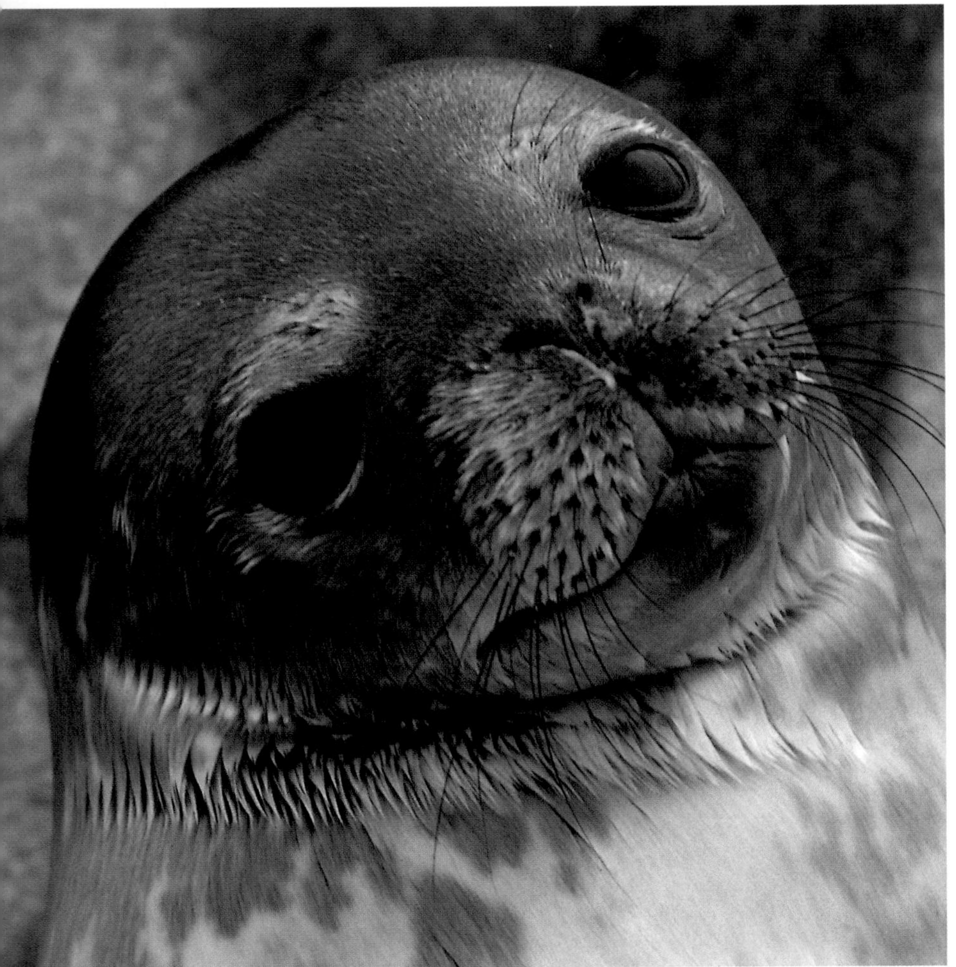

Top
Crabeater Seal, Cuverville Island.

Above
Weddell Seal, Pleneau Island.

become stained by soil and sand. Males have an inflatable proboscis – this giving the species its name – which acts as a resonating chamber for mating roars. Males establish mating harems, size and roar usually deterring rivals, though fights do occur, males rearing up and striking at the rival's head and neck. Blubber thickness usually prevents serious injury, but males are often scarred and in some fights one or both animals will become heavily bloodied. The seals come ashore annually to moult. Moulting takes 2–3 weeks and during that time the animal fasts. Southern Elephant Seals are found in continental waters, but breed on Maritime Antarctic islands, not on the continent itself.

EARED SEALS: SOUTHERN FUR SEALS

In common with the Southern Elephant Seals, and their northern counterparts, male southern fur seals attempt to form and maintain a harem of females. Usually the male will lay claim to a section of beach and all the females on it, behaviour which has led to the males being termed 'beachmasters'.

Antarctic Fur Seal *Arctocephalus gazella*. The most southerly of the eared seals. ♂ L: *c.*1.9m, W: 145kg. ♀ L: *c.*1.2m, W: *c.*35kg. Adult males are overall dark brown or grey-brown and much larger than the paler, grey-brown females. Antarctic Fur Seals are found in an arc of the Southern Ocean from the South Shetland islands to Heard and McDonald islands, breeding on those, and the islands between.

Subantarctic Fur Seal *Arctocephalus tropicalis*. ♂ L: *c.*1.8m, W: *c.*150kg. ♀ L: *c.*1.4m, W: *c.*35kg. Males are red-brown or olive-brown dorsally, diffusing to paler ventral parts, these most noticeable on the throat and chest of the resting seal. Found in an arc of the sea to the south of South Africa, from Tristan da Cunha and the Gough islands to Amsterdam and St Paul islands, breeding on those and several islands between.

South American Fur Seal *Arctocephalus australis*. ♂ L: *c.*1.9m, W: *c.*160kg. ♀ L: *c.*1.4m, W: *c.*50kg. Males are dark brown or grey-brown with a prominent paler mane. Breed on the southern mainland (Argentina and Chile) and on the Falkland Islands.

South African Fur Seal *Arctocepahlus pusillus*. ♂ L: *c.*2.2m, W: *c.*300kg. ♀ L: *c.*1.7m, W: *c.*120kg (the heaviest of all southern females, though 80kg is more usually). Males are dark brown overall, females being paler. Breed on the coasts of South Africa and Namibia.

Australian Fur Seal *Arctocepahlus doriferus* which breeds on Tasmania and the nearby coast of Australia is very similar to the South African Fur Seal, but somewhat more sea lion-like, and some authorities consider they are sub-species of the same animal, the South African animal being nominate, the Australian being *A. p. doriferus*.

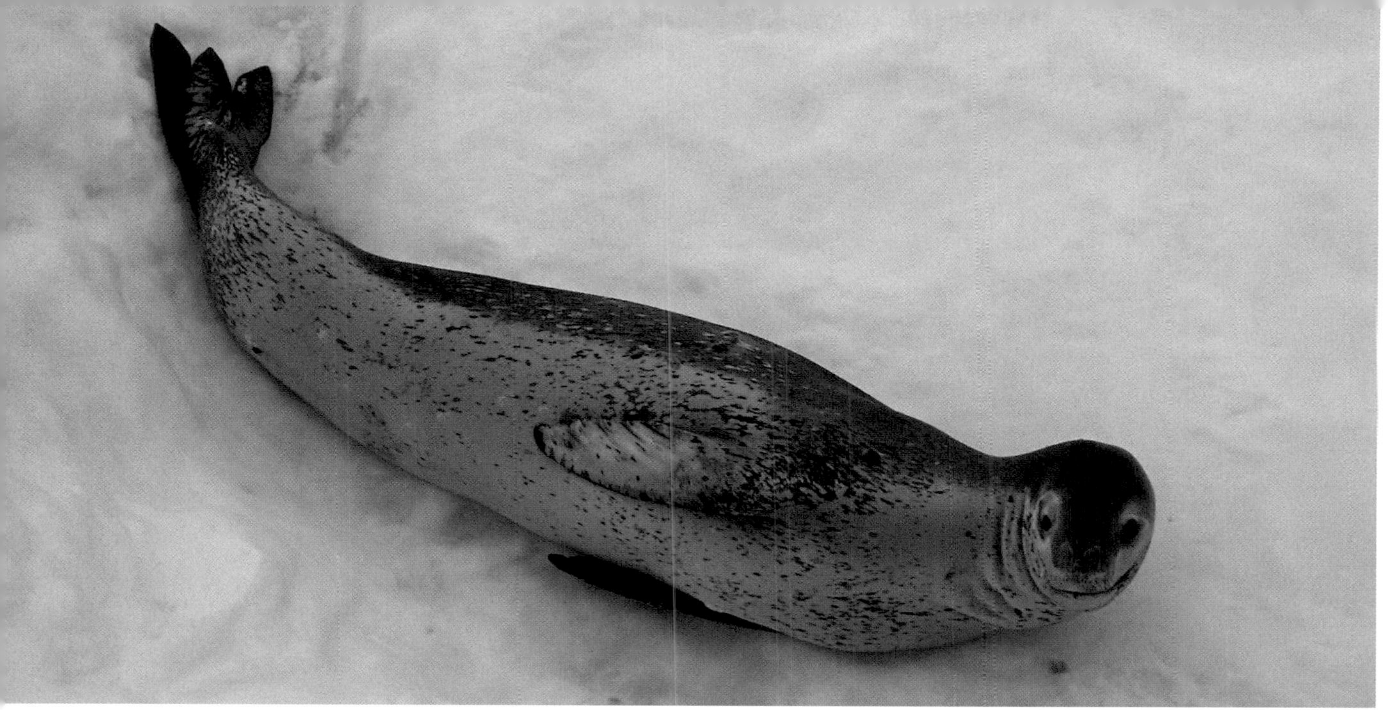

Leopard Seals prey on penguins, sometimes taking up a position close to a colony so they can grab the birds as they leave or return from fishing trips. The presence of Leopard Seals is the reason penguins are often reluctant to enter the water, each bird waiting for another to make the first (and therefore potentially most dangerous) move. When they catch a penguin the seal will thrash the bird repeatedly on the water surface to skin it. The photograph above was taken on the pack ice of French Passage, close to the Antarctic Peninsula.

New Zealand Fur Seal *Arctocepahlus forsteri*. ♂ L: 2.0–2.5m, W: 180–200kg. ♀ L: *c*.1.7m, W: *c*.40kg. Males are dark brown, often with a reddish tinge. Breed on New Zealand and islands to the south as far as Macquarie.

SEA LIONS

New Zealand Sea Lion *Phocarctos hookeri*. Also known as Hooker's Sea Lion, this is the most southerly of the three 'Antarctic' species. ♂ L: 2.5–3.5m, W: 320–450kg. ♀ L: 1.6–2.0m, W: 90–200kg. Males are overall dark brown with a

Female Southern Elephant Seals, Stromness, South Georgia.

CETACEANS

The problem of defining polar whales is even more difficult in the Southern Ocean than in the northern hemisphere as there are no land masses to impede the whale's travel. Again a pragmatic approach has been taken, listing those whales which are regularly seen in southern waters, but also mentioning species which might be seen closer to the ports of departure of ship-borne travellers.

TOOTHED WHALES

Members of the dolphin family which are seen regularly in the Southern Ocean are the Orca and the Long-finned Pilot Whale. The Bottlenose Dolphin is seen around the southern coasts of Australia and New Zealand. Other ocean dolphins which are regularly seen are:

Commerson's Dolphin *Cephalorhyncus commersonii*. L: 1.2–1.7m. W: 35–85kg. ♀>♂. Adults are highly distinctive, with black heads, flippers, dorsal fin and a black back from the dorsal fin to, and including, the tail. The remaining animal is white. The dorsal fin is rounded with a concave trailing edge. Found in the waters between Cape Horn and the Antarctic Peninsula, and around Kerguelen Island.

Above
Male Southern Elephant Seals have surprisingly long and flexible necks so that the unwary photographer, moving in for a superior head shot, can get a very unpleasant shock. The author makes no apology for the soft focus of this shot taken at Gold Harbour, South Georgia.

heavy mane on the neck and shoulders. They have a short, rounded muzzle, and do indeed look like lions. Females are much paler. Though primarily feeding on fish, squid and crustaceans, the animals will take penguins and the pups of fur and Southern Elephant seals. Breed on Snares, Auckland and Campbell islands.

South American Sea Lion (*Otaria flavescens*). ♂ L: 2.0–2.8m, W: *c.*350kg. ♀ L: *c.*2.0m, W: *c.*140kg. Males are dark brown overall, with a dog-like muzzle resembling that of fur seals. The manes of old males are large and very shaggy. Males are longer than the New Zealand Sea Lion, but are less heavily built. Females are paler. Found on the southern coasts of the continent (Argentina and Chile) and on the Falkland Islands.

Australian Sea Lion (*Neophoca cinerea*). The least numerous and least studied of the three sea lions, and will only be seen by Antarctic travellers who start from Australia and spend time exploring there first. ♂ L: 2.0–2.5m, W: *c.*300kg. ♀ L: *c.*1.75m, W: *c.*110kg. Breed on the southern Australian coast. Caution is advised as these animals can be very aggressive.

Right
A Beachmaster Antarctic Fur Seal roars out a challenge to all-comers at Stromness, South Georgia.

Other Dolphins and Porpoises

Dolphin and Porpoise species found close to departure points are

Black (or Chilean) Dolphin *Cephalorhyncus eutropia*. Found off the coast of Chile and the waters off Tierra del Fuego.

Hector's Dolphin *Cephalorhyncus hectori*. Coasts of New Zealand's South Island and the west coast of North Island.

Short-beaked Common Dolphin *Delphinus delphis*. Coasts of New Zealand and Tasmania.

Long-beaked Common Dolphin *Delphinus capensis*. Southern coast of South Africa.

Dusky Dolphin *Lagenorynchus obscurus*. Southern coasts of South America, South Africa, Australia and New Zealand and around many sub-Antarctic islands.

Peale's Dolphin *Lagenorynchus australis*. Southern South America and the Falkland Islands.

Risso's Dolphin *Grampus griseus*. Southern coasts of South America, South Africa, Australia and New Zealand

Spectacled Porpoise *Phocoena dioptrica*. Across the Southern Ocean at the latitude of Cape Horn-southern New Zealand, usually around the sub-Antarctic islands.

Burmeister's Porpoise *Phocoena spinipinnis*. Southern coasts of South America.

Other Beaked Whales

Beaked Whales found close to departure points are:

Cuvier's Beaked Whale *Ziphius cavirostris*. Found off the southern coasts of South America, South Africa, Australia and New Zealand. Occasionally found further south.

Shepherd's Beaked Whale *Tasmacetus shepherdii*. Rare and poorly studied. Has been seen off southern coasts of South America and New Zealand and several sub-Antarctic islands.

Hector's Beaked Whale *Mesoplodon hectori*. Coasts of south-eastern South America, Tasmania and New Zealand.

True's Beaked Whale *Mesoplodon mirus*. Coast of southern South Africa and south-central Australia.

Gray's Beaked Whale *Mesoplodon grayi*. In a broad band across the Southern Ocean including most sub-Antarctic islands.

Andrews' Beaked Whale *Mesoplodon bowdoini*. Coasts of southern Australia and New Zealand, and occasionally seen off sub-Antarctic islands.

Gingko-toothed Beaked Whale *Mesoplodon ginkgodens*. New Zealand's South Island.

Strap-toothed Whale *Mesoplodon layardii*. In a broad band across the Southern Ocean including most sub-Antarctic islands.

Blainville's Beaked Whale *Mesoplodon densirostris*. Southern coasts of South Africa, Australia and New Zealand.

HOURGLASS DOLPHIN *Lagenorynchus cruciger*. L: 1.4–2.0m. W: 70–90kg.
Adults are black dorsally, white ventrally, the hourglass of the name being a white shape on the otherwise black flanks, reaching to the black beak and to the tail. The dorsal fin is flattened at the top, with a strongly concave trailing edge. Found across the Southern Ocean to the continent.

SOUTHERN RIGHT WHALE DOLPHIN *Lissodelphis peronii*. L: 1.8–2.9m. W: 80–120kg. ♂>♀. Adults are black dorsally, white ventrally, but the white extends to the flanks towards the tail. The melon and beak are also white. There is no dorsal fin. Found across the Southern Ocean, but rarely as far south as the tip of the Antarctic Peninsula.

GREAT SPERM WHALES are found all around the continent.

PYGMY SPERM *Kogia breviceps* and **DWARF SPERM** *Kogia sima* Whales are found off the southern coasts of South Africa and Australia, and in waters off New Zealand.

Of the beaked whales, none are found at both ends of the Earth. Species seen regularly in southern waters are:

ARNOUX'S BEAKED WHALE *Berardius arnuxii*. L: 7.8–10m. W: 7–10t. ♀>♂. Adults are dark grey dorsally, with extensive white scarring, paler ventrally. The dorsal fin is small and rounded. Found to the continent, particularly near the Ross Sea and the Antarctic Peninsula.

SOUTHERN BOTTLENOSE WHALE *Hyperoodon planifrons*. L: 6.5–7.5m. W: 7–8t. ♀>♂. Adults are light tan or grey-buff dorsally, paler ventrally. The melon is paler and very prominent. Falcate dorsal fin placed towards the tail. Found close to the continent.

Baleen Whale species found in both southern and northern waters are the Blue, Fin, Sei and Humpback. Two further species may be seen:

ANTARCTIC MINKE WHALE (*Balaenoptera bonaerensis*). L: 7–11m. W: 5–9t. ♀>♂. Adults are virtually identical to the northern Minke, but in general paler. Found throughout the Southern Ocean as far as the continent.

DWARF MINKE WHALE *Balaenoptera acutorostrata ?*. L: to 7.5m. W: to 6t. Poorly studied. Considered a sub-species of the northern Minke Whale, though the taxonomy is still debated. Adults are as the northern Minke, but often have a paler saddle between the head and dorsal fin. Found throughout the Southern Ocean, but rarely as far south as the continent.

In addition, **Bryde's Whale** *Balaenoptera bonaerensis* may be seen off the southern coasts of South Africa, Australia and New Zealand.

There is one Antarctic right whale, the **Southern Right Whale** *Eubalaena australis* which is identical to the Northern Right Whale, but has been proved to be a separate species by DNA analysis. As with the Northern Right, the whale was relentlessly hunted, though its numbers are now recovering. A further species, the **Pygmy Right Whale** *Caperea marginata* also occurs. This poorly studied whale has features of both the right whales and the rorquals. Its range is as poorly known as its biology, but it seems to be found throughout the Southern Ocean as far south as the sub-Antarctic islands.

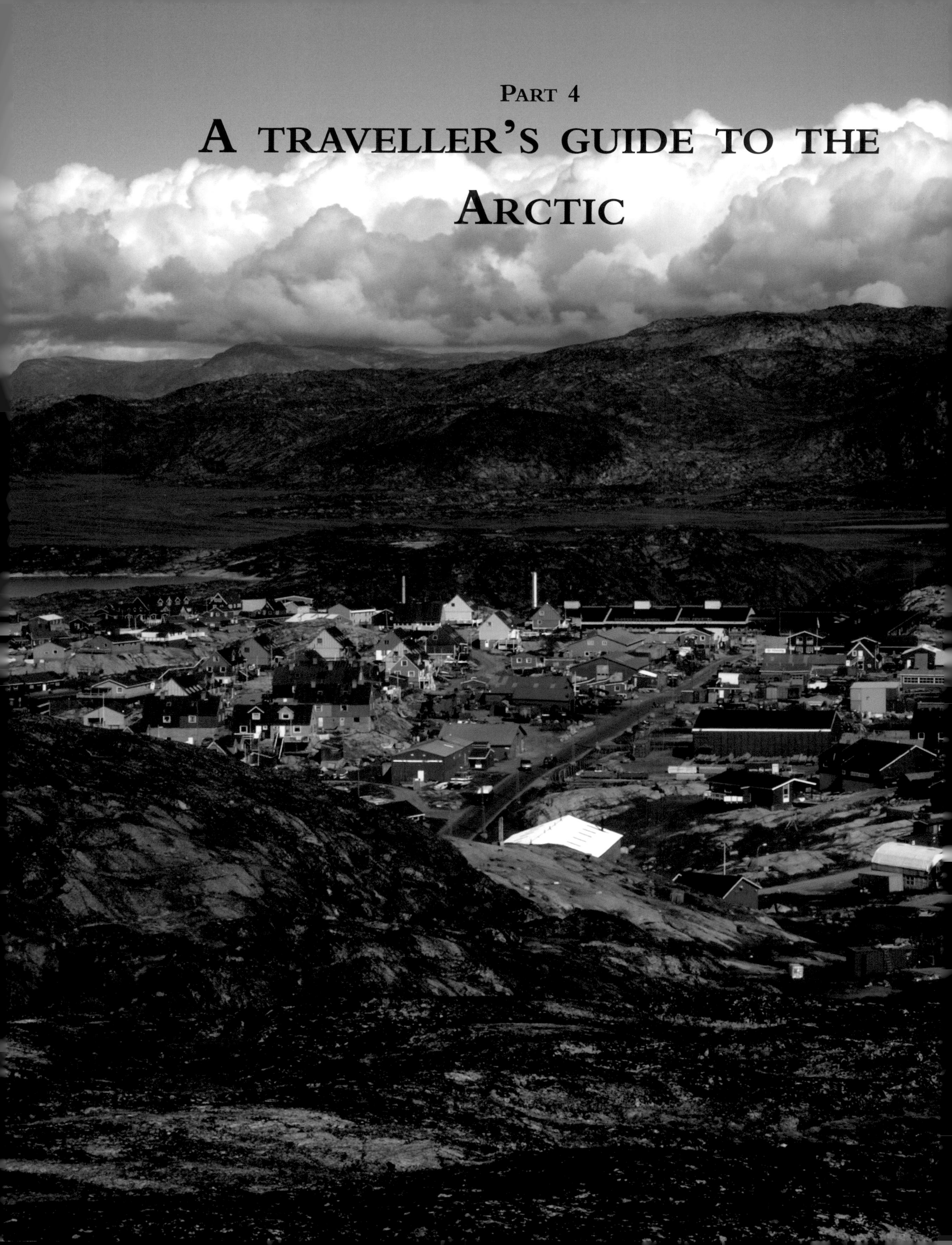

PART 4

A TRAVELLER'S GUIDE TO THE ARCTIC

A Traveller's Guide to the Arctic

Arctic travel is one of the growth industries of international tourism. In a sense that is sad as there is an underlying pessimism about much of it – visit now, a last chance to see the Arctic's wonders. A case could also be made that tourism itself represents a threat to the area. Yet in that threat lies the hope that those who visit will return home entranced and willing to make efforts to ensure the region's survival, celebrating its beauty and so encouraging others to do likewise.

It is with that hope that this section explores the options available for travellers. The fact that tourism is on the rise means that options are also increasing, so as with all guides this one will be out of date on a timescale as likely measured in months as years. With that in mind only brief details are given, exploring the geology, geography, human history and wildlife of the countries and areas that constitute the Arctic rim, together with details of the National Parks or other reserves within which the best of the scenery and wildlife may be seen. Equally brief details are given on the current position as regards travel to countries or areas. The guide starts in Iceland and moves east around the globe, finishing in Greenland.

Tourism – a problem or a solution?

The final decade of the 20th century and the first years of the 21st have seen a massive increase in Arctic tourism. Tourists heading north now very substantially outnumber those heading to Antarctica. Using cruise ships – some of them ex-Russian research ships, including icebreakers – it is possible to visit Svalbard (by far the most popular destination), Russia's Arctic islands, the Canadian Arctic and the North Pole itself, the trips adding history to scenery. The traditions of Reindeer-herding peoples can be sampled by organised visits to sites across Eurasia. By joining wildlife tours it is possible to visit remote areas of Alaska, Canada, Greenland and Russia. Visits to Iceland's marvellous volcanic scenery are straightforward, and those to Kamchatka's equivalent are becoming easier.

Sensitive tourism is, of course, an important factor in alerting people to the beauty of the area and the need to preserve it, and in encouraging governments to protect and sustain the Arctic environment. But questions must be asked: do the majority of the visitors see more than this year's picture-postcard tourist venue? Do governments care about sustaining more than their country's GDP and their own election prospects? Tourism brings cash to Arctic economies. The Inuit hope behind the establishment of Nunavut was that by controlling the region's resources, the difficult path between tradition and modernity could be more easily trodden. But too often, money derived from tourism heads south with the homeward-bound visitors. Perception of Arctic peoples is also a problem. Those tourists seeking culture rather than wildlife come to see folk dressed in skins performing ancient dances and rituals, or to be taken on trips that reconstruct their preconceptions of the Arctic way of life. That can lead to native peoples becoming little more than extras in an Arctic theme park, and does nothing to aid their absorption into the modern world; few visitors come north to see native shop-keepers or business managers.

The effect on wildlife should also not be understated. Research on penguins in Antarctica has shown that the arrival of visitors at breeding colonies often stresses the birds, even if the close approach that is allowed appears to suggest otherwise. Birds will alter their route to the sea to avoid contact – birds on nests sit tight, but that is more a strategy for chick survival than a lack of concern – and continue to follow the new route for a period after the visitors depart; such a route change places an extra burden on the birds. Presumably the arrival of humans at Arctic bird breeding sites is equally stressful.

The stress is not limited to the wildlife and native peoples. It is an irony that this brief review of Arctic destinations should be followed by one noting that it now seems almost certain that global warming has an anthropogenic source, that one of the main contributors to greenhouse gases is air travel, and that air travel is increasing. It would be an even bigger irony if Arctic travel increased as people rushed to see the area before it disappeared, and in doing so hastened the disappearance.

Goðafoss, northern Iceland.

ICELAND

Iceland lies between 63.5°N and 66.5°N, just below the Arctic Circle, which passes through the island of Grimsey off the northern coast; Icelanders tell a poor joke about how the only one of their number interested in crossing the Circle is the vicar of Grimsey, since it passes through the middle of his bed. Iceland lies halfway between New York and Moscow, the closest significant landmass being Greenland, 290km to the west. The island is about 300km from north to south and 500km from east to west, and covers 103,000km^2. The climate is variable, the island's position in mid-Atlantic keeping temperatures mild, but producing high precipitation and high winds.

History

The population maintains some interesting links with its Norse ancestry. Patronymic names are still the norm, sons adding *son*, and daughters *dóttir* to their father's first name. A nuclear family of husband, wife, son and daughter will therefore have four different surnames. The Icelandic language is close to Old Norse and cannot be understood by Norwegians, Swedes or Danes (who can understand each other, the three Scandinavian languages being, in essence, dialects of a single tongue).

Norse settlers began to arrive in Iceland from around 870 AD. By 930 it was considered that the island was fully settled and a parliament (the *Althing* – General Assembly) was set up to administer the 39 'chieftaincies' that it comprised. The assembly was at Þingvellir (pronounced Thingvellir) near Reykjavik (a name which means 'smoky bay' as the new arrivals were greeted by the sight of smoke – actually steam – rising from the land backing the natural harbour). Þingvellir is the world's oldest site of parliament. Icelanders are proud of this fact (though in reality the Althing had little to do with democracy as it is now understood, as only the island chiefs gathered, their discussions dealing with relationships between them rather than the societies they controlled) and the site is on the itinerary of almost all tours; it forms one point of the 'Golden Triangle', the others being Strokkur, as the sole remaining active geyser at Geysir is called, and the beautiful Gullfoss waterfall (the Golden Triangle is occasionally called the Golden Circle, a much less geometrically accurate name).

Þingvellir from the top of the mid-Atlantic Ridge outcrop. The site of the *Althing* is behind the church.

Icelandic weather

Iceland's weather is not only variable, but also often variable on a very short timescale. This has led to many island guides informing visitors that if they do not like the weather they need only wait five minutes and it will change for the better. Of course, the reverse also holds, so that if the weather is good, in a few minutes it will be poor.

During the years following the establishment of Þingvellir the famed Icelandic sagas were written, and Icelandic seafarers reached Greenland and North America. But warfare broke out between the chieftains and in 1262 the island came under Norwegian rule. In 1380 Norway, and therefore Iceland, became part of the Kingdom of Denmark. Home rule was granted in 1904, and sovereignty in 1918, though the island was still part of the Danish kingdom. Only in 1944 did Iceland achieve full independence, this being declared in a ceremony at Þingvellir on 17 June of that year.

Volcanic scenery

In addition to the historic and scenic delights of the Golden Triangle – Þingvellir is fascinating geologically as well as historically – there is much to delight the visitor. Volcanic activity, with its attendant lava flows, has created a magnificent landscape, with textbook examples of cinder cones, explosion craters, fissure eruptions, spatter cones and shield volcanoes.

Mývatn.

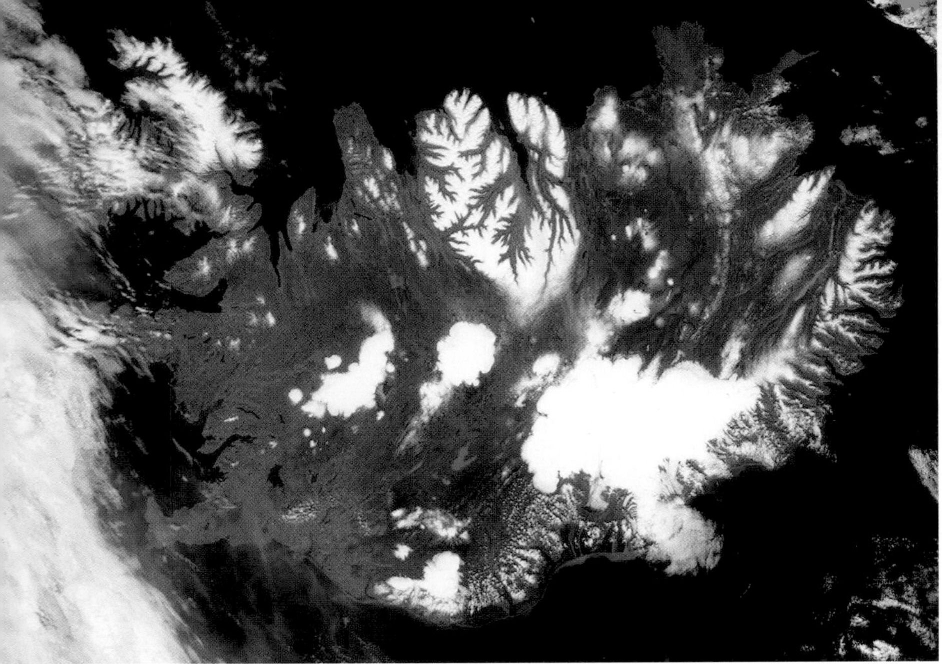

Iceland from space in summer (*left*) and winter (*right*).

The resultant lavas offer superb examples of ropy and scoria lavas. There are also classic volcanic features, such as the bubbling mud pits of Krisuvik and Hveragerði, the thermal springs that feed the Blue Lagoon close to the international airport of Keflavik, the basaltic columns behind the Svartifoss waterfall in the Skaftafell National Park, and, of course, the Strokkur geyser at Geysir. The distortions of the landscape have also created some of the finest waterfalls in Europe, not only Gullfoss, but the 'pony-tail' fall of Seljalandsfoss, and Skógafoss, all in the south of the island, and the northern falls of Dettifoss and Goðafoss. The moss-blanketed lava flows and craters of Lakigígar (the remains of the eruptions of Laki in 1783–85 that led to the 'haze of hunger) in south Iceland are spectacular, as is the coloured landscape of Landmannalaugar. Iceland also has a number of glacial ice caps, one of which, Vatnajökull, is by far Europe's biggest glacier.

Off Iceland's southern coast lie Vestmannaeyjar, the Westmann Islands, where, as previously noted, recent volcanic activities have created a new island (Surtsey) and new land (from the lava flows of Eldfell).

National Parks

Iceland has four National Parks: Þingvellir, set up to protect the site of the first parliament and the nearby volcanic features; Snæfellsjökull around the volcano and glacier; Jökulsárgljúfur, around Dettifoss, Europe's largest waterfall in terms of volume flow; and Skaftafell on the southern side of Vatnajökull. All the parks protect the natural environment rather than wildlife areas

Landmannalaugar.

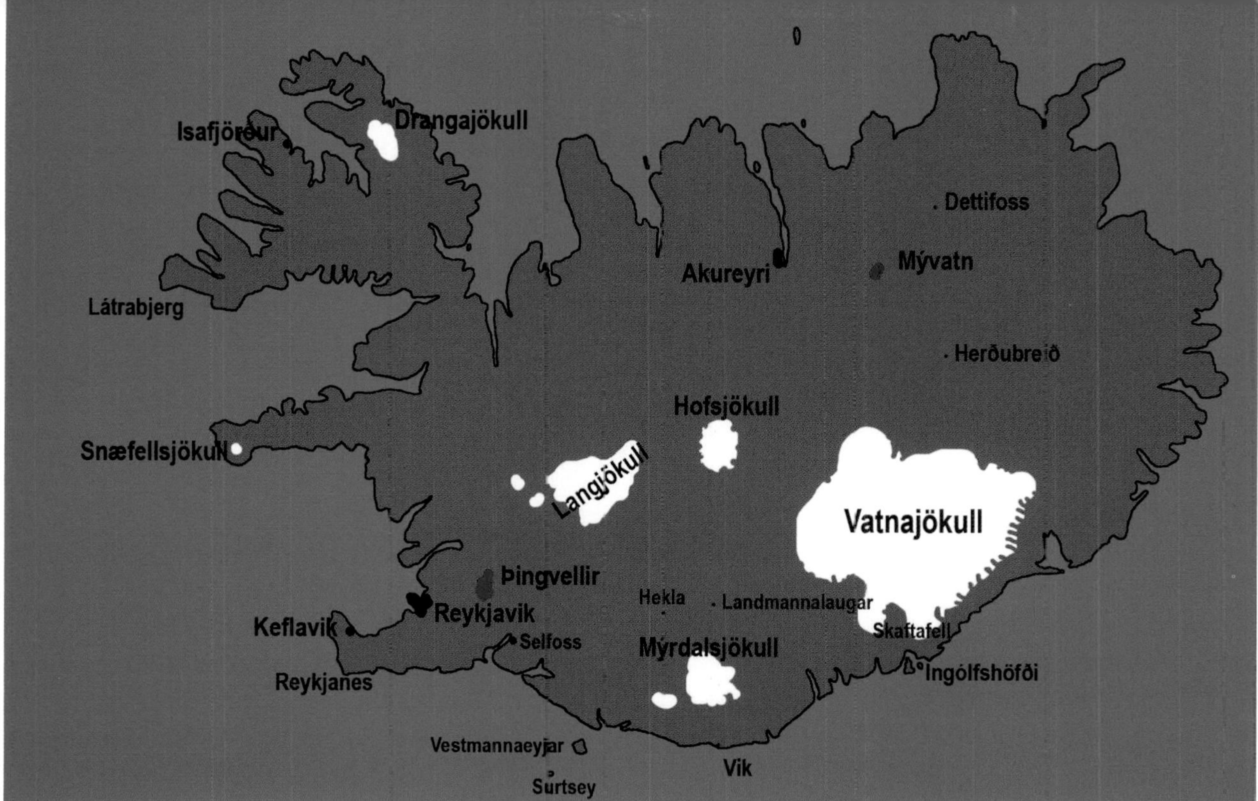

(though, of course, they encompass wilderness areas where wildlife finds a home). Iceland also has other protected areas, covering particular geological features, recreational areas, and wildlife habitats.

Wildlife

Iceland has only one indigenous terrestrial mammal, the Arctic Fox. Foxes populated the island during the retreat of the ice. They were ruthlessly hunted following the Norse occupation because of their perceived threat to sheep farming. Whether the fox was eradicated is not known – though it is unlikely. It is therefore probable that there has always been a fox population. This population has no doubt been augmented by escapes from fur farms, though the extent of such escapes and their effect on the wild population is debatable. In 1957 the Icelandic government enacted a law giving state aid to fox extermination programmes. This law was not repealed until 1994, though even after that date hunting of foxes was state-aided in areas where the species was considered a threat to sheep and eider farmers. Today, foxes may be observed in almost all areas of the country, but they are limited in number and elusive. Only in the Hornstrandir Nature Reserve is the fox truly welcome.

American Mink have also become established as a result of escapes from fur farms. Brown and Black Rats, House and Wood Mice have been accidentally introduced; Reindeer have been deliberately introduced, though numbers remain low.

Grey and Harbour Seals live in the waters around the island. Many species of whales are found close to the island, and whale-watching trips have increased substantially to cater for visitors' enthusiasm for seeing these magnificent creatures. The recent decision by the Icelanders to resume commercial

Icelandic forests

What do you do if you are lost in an Icelandic forest? The answer is – stand up. This stems from the fact that native forests are restricted to occasional stands of birch covering less than 1% of the island, and often consisting of windswept, stunted trees. The extent of forest cover when the Norse arrived on the island is debated, but there undoubtedly were forested areas (almost exclusively birch and willow). These were slashed and burned to provide land for agriculture and sheep-rearing. Sheep grazed seedlings, and the wind and cold of the Little Ice Age eroded exposed land. The result was the near-elimination of Iceland's forests, the degradation of much of the non-forest vegetation, and a significant increase in the area of 'desert'. Today an attempt is underway to restore the pre-Norse landscape, but there is much to do.

Alftafjorður, north-west Iceland.

whaling, and in particular the televised haul-out of a harpooned Fin Whale, has caused a major debate on the island; tour operators have seen a sharp reduction in whale-watch visitors and fear that the economic benefits of hunting will be vastly outweighed by losses in tourist income.

Iceland's main wildlife interest is its avifauna. Iceland is the only place in Europe where Barrow's Goldeneye and Harlequin Duck breed; Mývatn/Laxá is a known breeding area (though in 2007 I saw pairs of Harlequin Ducks in the Ranga river and the outflow river from Skógafoss, both in southern Iceland, suggesting an expansion of the duck's range). Barrow's Goldeneye is usually a tree-hole nesting species, but they use natural holes in the lava surrounding the lake as an alternative. The Harlequin Duck breeding colony on the River Laxá is believed to be the largest in the world. The island also has a small population of grey-morph Gyrfalcons, and is regularly visited by migrating Greenlandic white Gyrs. Three nature reserves are of great interest to the bird enthusiast:

Hornstrandir At the north-eastern tip of Iceland, reached by ship from Isafjörður. The reserve has more than 250 species of flowering plant and the sea cliffs of Hornbjarg, Hælavíkurbjarg and Ritur are important seabird breeding sites.

Fjallabak To the north of Vik (and Mýrdalsjökull). As well as including the exquisite scenery of Landmannalaugar, the reserve is important for both plants and birds. The reserve is traversed by roads.

Herðubreið To the south-east of Mývatn. A truly rugged section of interior Iceland. Wonderful country and important for both plants and birds.

Other worthwhile bird sites include:

Látrabjerg Sea cliffs at the western tip of Iceland's north-western landmass. This is one of the largest seabird nesting areas in the North Atlantic, and is particularly good for auks (though Little Auk does not breed there). Inland there are divers and waders. If a Snowy Owl visits Iceland it is likely to turn up close to Isafjördur, from where most visitors reach Látrabjerg.

Mývatn/River Laxá Harlequin Duck and Barrow's Goldeneye as well as divers, grebes, swans, geese and waders.

South Iceland One of the world's largest colonies of Great Skua occurs close to the Skaftafell National Park, as well as breeding Arctic Skua, the Arctic Terns that the skuas pirate, and a large number of geese. Offshore is the prominent island of Ingólfshöfði, which has a large Atlantic Puffin colony, as well as Northern Fulmar and other delights. The island is reached by an exciting walk through the sea at low tide, and is excellent both for its bird colonies and the black sands that surround it.

Reykjanes Peninsula South-west of Reykjavik. The sea cliffs here are excellent for seabirds, including a huge Northern Gannet colony on the offshore island of Eldey. The peninsula is also good for migrating waders. The lake in downtown Reykjavik has ducks and swans.

Travel

Iceland has a population approaching 300,000, about 40% of whom live in Reykjavik. Many of the rest live in the towns and farms set out around the island's coastal belt, and much of the interior is empty. This has aided the setting up of many National Parks, though these primarily protect the unique landscape rather than the wildlife. Travel to the island is straightforward, with scheduled flights from many of Europe's capital cities and an increasing number of cities in North America. Internal flights are good and have the advantage, when the weather is fine, of offering a view of inland Iceland, which is still difficult to access, particularly in winter. Outside the main towns Icelandic roads are gravel; care must be taken. The road system is mainly restricted to the coastal plain, with inland Iceland being road-free and difficult to access, though 4x4 vehicles, occasionally with large tyres, can make excursions. Car hire is expensive but readily available. Buses travel the coastal road, circling the island. A complete circuit takes several days and the buses, though regular, are not frequent, so careful planning is required if they are to be used. All main towns and cities have hotels and there are many good camp sites. Wilderness camping is allowed, except in the National Parks and protected areas. For the wildlife observer Iceland has the distinct advantage of being mosquito free, though it does have other irritants. Mývatn – midge lake – is named after the midges that swarm there. These are usually non-biting – some females do bite – but frequently irritating. On the River Laxá, which exits the lake, the black fly *Simulium vittatum* swarms, and the females of this species do bite.

Skógafoss.

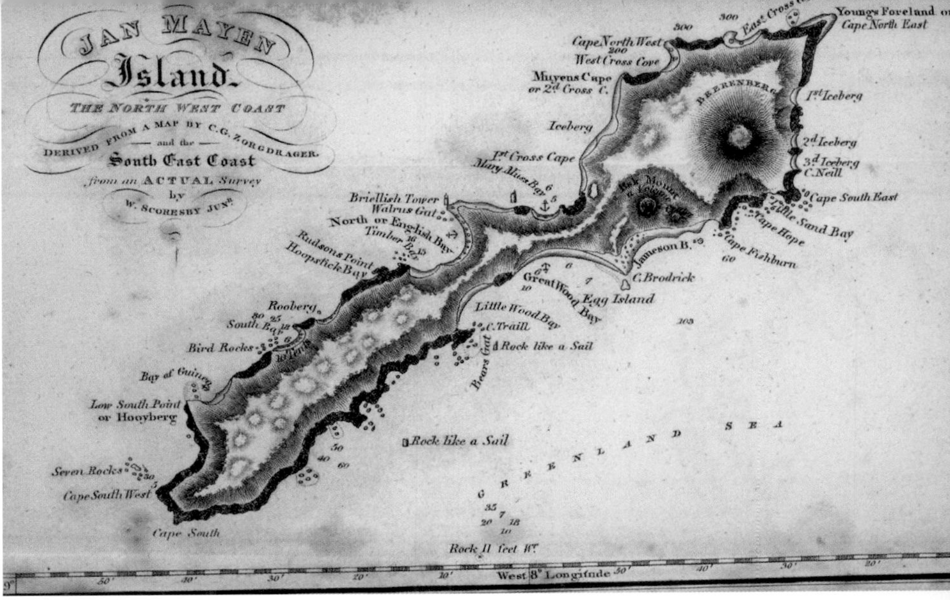

Map of Jan Mayen from William Scoresby's *An Account of the Arctic Regions....* published in 1820.

JAN MAYEN

Jan Mayen lies at 71°N, 8°30'W, about 600km north-west of Iceland. It is a spoon-shaped island, about 55km long and about 20km wide at its widest point, narrowing to around 2.5km, and covering an area of 375km^2. The climate is kept relatively mild by the ocean. The island is often cloud- or mist-shrouded because of the high relative humidity, with some years seeing as few as five clear days. Jan Mayen is also frequently windswept.

History

As noted previously, Beerenberg may have been seen by Abbot Brendon in the 9th century. It may also have been seen by Norse travellers, the sagas referring to a sighting of Svalbard (cold edge or cold coast). This might refer to Svalbard itself, to Greenland's icy eastern coast or to Jan Mayen. The island was almost certainly seen and named (Hudson's Touches) by Henry Hudson in 1607 (though there is ambiguity about exactly what Hudson saw). The name derives from Jan Jacobsz May van Schellinkhout, a Dutch whaling captain who landed on the island in 1614. The Dutch had a whaling station there until about 1650. It was a summer station, whales being hunted in local waters and hauled ashore for processing. An attempt to overwinter on the island in 1633–34, to prevent the plundering of shore stations by other whaling nations, which was common at the time, ended in disaster, with all seven men left as guards dying of scurvy.

When whaling ended the island was abandoned for two centuries, though possibly with occasional visits. In the First International Polar Year (1882–83) it was the base for the Austro-Hungarian expedition; later it was visited by fur trappers, who exterminated the Arctic Fox population. In 1922 the Norwegians set up a meteorological station, claiming formal sovereignty (which they retain) in 1929.

Volcanic activity

Beerenberg, a 2,277m volcano, dominates the 'spoon' section of the island. An eruption was witnessed by William Scoresby Jr, an English whaling captain, in 1818, but Beerenberg was then thought to have become extinct. In September 1970 it erupted again, adding 4km^2 to the island's surface area. There was another significant eruption in 1985. Beerenberg has active fumaroles at almost all times. Eggøya (Egg Island), off Jan Mayen's south coast, steams sufficiently to prevent ice from forming locally during the winter.

Habitats and wildlife

The island is composed of volcanic lavas accreted over the half-million or so years the island has been above water, with the beaches being especially eye-catching as the sand is black. They are also are littered with the bleached trunks of trees that have arrived after a long journey by ice and water current from the rivers of Siberia. The sombre colours of the island's lavas – from black to red-brown – are a complete contrast to the vivid green of mosses and liverworts. The colonisation of what would be assumed to be a sterile landscape – bare rock and thin, acidic soil – is astounding. The island flora also includes about 70 flowering plants, these including members of the saxifrages. One other flowering plant is Scurvy Grass *Cochlearia officinalis*, probably introduced by 17th century whalers. It grows in abundance near the bird cliffs, taking advantage of the guano. There are also many varieties of lichen.

Jan Mayen was famed for its blue Arctic Foxes, but with their extinction the only terrestrial mammal is the occasional Polar Bear. These are becoming less frequent visitors as the winter ice edge moves north. Northern Fulmars occupy the island throughout the year, these being joined by various waders, auks, skuas and gulls that breed there. Great Northern Diver and Snow Bunting also breed regularly.

Travel

In 1960 a LORAN (radar) station was added for both civilian and military trans-Atlantic aircraft. Both stations are still in operation. The stations are permanently manned and provisioned by air, but the few flights each year are always full so that visitors must either use the cruise ships which occasionally call during return trips from north-east Greenland, or make their own voyages. Permission for the latter should be obtained prior to the trip.

Because of Jan Mayen's position and the height of Beerenberg, the top of the volcano is usually shrouded in cloud, appearing only a handful of times each year. From the ice cap summit, tidewater glaciers flow down to calve icebergs into the north Atlantic.

SCANDINAVIA

The presence of the North Atlantic Drift eases the Arctic northward in Scandinavia, particularly in Norway. As a consequence, agriculture is possible north of the Arctic Circle and cities flourish at latitudes that make such habitation unthinkable further east in Eurasia and in North America. In winter, however, the region becomes much more Arctic, the combination of the long northern night, high snowfall and the rugged terrain (of much of northern Sweden in particular) combining to provide a polar experience.

Autumn in Finland's Urho Kekkonen National Park. The hills in the distance are in Russia.

History

Though the Sámi are the true Arctic dwellers of the region, the history of the Scandinavian countries has been defined by southern peoples, the Norse and the Finns, whose ancestors occupied the south of the countries, but who eventually dominated the whole area. Norway and Sweden, together with Denmark, share a common history that has, on occasions, included Finland. At various times Swedes and Danes have united for mutual benefit, or fought wars of imperial ambition. Sweden has invaded and controlled Norway and Finland, but ultimately lost the latter to the Russians. Finally, in the 17th century, Sweden and Denmark became kingdoms independent of each other, though it was only in 1905 that Norway gained its independence from Sweden. Finland became independent from Sweden in the early 19th century during the period of European unrest associated with the Napoleonic Wars, with the Russians invading and making the country a Grand Duchy of their empire. Finland gained its independence during the Russian Revolution, but the Soviets invaded both Finland and the Baltic states during the winter of 1939–40. Though the Finns fought the Soviets to a standstill, Finland was forced to relinquish its corridor to the Barents Sea.

Sámi settlements

In northern Scandinavia transport options are as good as would be expected of European countries. The capitals of the three nations are linked by air to all other European capitals and North America, as are an increasing number of other Scandinavian cities. Within Norway, Sweden and Finland there

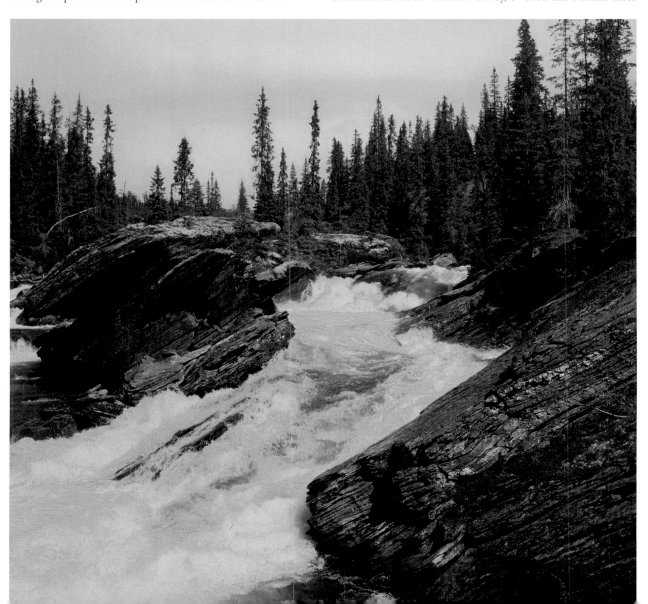

Børgefjell National Park, Norway.

Above right
Scandinavia from space.

Opposite page

Above
Dog-sledging in Norway's Øvre Dividal National Park.

Below
Norway's Anderdalen National Park.

Right
The Polar Cathedral, Tromsø.

are excellent air services to the northern cities and towns, and road links are equally good, the major highways being kept open throughout the winter. For travellers wishing to enjoy Sámi culture there are numerous possibilities, these including visits to, and stays with, reindeer herders, as well as numerous museums and cultural centres. The 'capitals' of the Sámi sections of the three countries – Kautokeino in Norway, Jokkmokk in Sweden and Rovaniemi in Finland – are excellent starting points for Sámi-based visits, though only Kautokeino has resisted (so far) the advance of 'European' culture. That the Norwegian town has maintained a decidedly non-European feel is surprising in view of its being surrounded by distinctly European cities such as Tromsø, Hammerfest and Kirkenes. In Finland, though Rovaniemi is the recognised 'capital' of the northern country and has, at the Arctic Circle which lies just 8km north of town, the 'official' home of Father Christmas (a fact that North Pole, Alaska, a town close to Fairbanks, would dispute), Inari, a much smaller town about 320km north, is a much more authentic Sámi settlement. It has, in Siida, one of the best Sámi museums in Scandinavia (*siida* is the Sámi name for a local community, a group of families occupying a defined area of land; within the *siida* the Sámi acted as a collective with tasks shared out among the group). There are several fine Sámi museums in Norway, with the one at Alta on a site that encompasses some of the best of Scandinavian Palaeolithic rock art.

Wildlife

Northern Scandinavia has small and endangered populations of Wolves and Brown Bears, and also other large mammals such as Elk, Lynx and Wolverine, as well as numerous smaller animals. It also has excellent birdlife. For the Arctic traveller, the highlights of the region are its National Parks and wilderness areas; the major sites are discussed briefly below, with selected other sites also listed. The delights or otherwise of the northern towns are left for personal exploration, though special mention must be made of Tromsø where travellers to Svalbard may choose to overnight. With the Polar Cathedral

(the embodiment of 1960s architecture and reached by a walk over a bridge which is impressive both architecturally and for its views), its museums, which cover various Arctic themes, Polaria, which also deals with the Arctic and includes a 180° cinema, an excellent waterfront (the German battleship *Tirpitz* was sunk in the fjord, with another museum covering the story), and a fine array of shops and restaurants, Tromsø is a great place to spend time.

In the following list, the nearest large town with an airport is noted. All the larger parks have excellent visitor centres with maps that detail walks which explore the landscape. Though many of these are multi-day excursions, there will also be day and half-day walks. It will be noted that several of the Parks are contiguous. This is very important as they create corridors across the landscape; studies have shown that there is greater genetic diversity in populations with access to such corridors compared to those isolated in parks.

National Parks: Finland

Lemmenjoki National Park and **Øvre Anarjokka National Park**, Norway. Inari, Finland. Vast area of birch scrub, lakes, bogs and hills. This area represents the best option for travellers hoping for a view of Eurasian Lynx, Brown Bear, Wolf and Wolverine. Inaccessible by road.
Oulanka National Park. Kuusamo. Old-growth forest, lakes and bogs extending to the Russian border. The lakes are important waterfowl sites.
Pallas-Ouastunturi National Park. Enontekiö. Important alpine plant area of high, rounded hills, Also valley lakes, bogs and forests.
Pyhätunturi National Park. Kemijarvi. Small area of forest, bog and fell field.
Riisittunturi National Park. Kuusamo. Small but superb area of bogs and fell fields, with some of the most beautiful views in Finland.
Urho Kekkonen National Park. Ivalo. Birch, pine and spruce forest, and upland tundra extending to the Russian border. Important for both boreal and tundra birds. Inaccessible by road.
Finland also has many northern Nature Reserves, mostly in areas of bog, lakes and old forest. These were set up to protect important botanical and bird breeding sites. One of the more interesting is Käsivarsi Fjelds near Kilpisjärvi, which has some of Finland's highest land and a botanically important area of limestone outcrops. The area is also important for tundra breeding birds

National Parks: Norway

Anderdalen National Park. Tromsø. Pine and birch forest on the island of Senja.
Børgefjell National Park, Norway. Mo i Rana. Although it lies some 100km south of the Arctic Circle, this vast park is a true 'Arctic' wilderness. Accessible only on foot and without either marked trails or huts, it is home to Brown Bear, Wolf,

Above left
The author on the *Trerikroset*, the Three Countries Stone, where Finland, Norway and Sweden meet.

Above
On the way to the Trerikroset. The photographer is in Finland, the author is in Sweden, while Norway lies beyond the bushes to his left.

Opposite page above
Lake Pierikjaure and the eastern Sarek national park from close to the summit of Vuoinestjåkkå which, at 1952m. is one of the highest peak's in the Park.

Opposite page below
Láddjuvággi, a valley leading towards Kebnekaise, Sweden's highest mountain which stands between the Abisko National Park, to the north, and the Stora Sjöfallet National Park, to the south.

Left
As interesting a place to reach as the Trerikroset is this spot on the Barents Sea coast where a few metres of beach and a river mouth separate Norway and Russia. Here the border markers for the two countries can be seen.

Øvre Pasvik National Park, north Norway.

Lynx, Wolverine and Reindeer and is one of the best areas in Scandinavia for Arctic Fox and Snowy Owl.

Øvre Anarjokka National Park. See Lemmenjoki National Park (Finland).

Øvre Dividal National Park. Tromsø. High fell-field, lakes and heaths.

Øvre Pasvik National Park, contiguous with **Pasvik Zapovednik**, Russia. Kirkenes, Norway. Pine forest with lakes and bogs.

Rago National Park, Norway, **Padjelanta**, **Sarek** and **Stora Sjöfallet National Parks**, Sweden. Bodø, Norway and Gallivare, Sweden. Vast area of magnificent country, one of the finest wilderness areas in Europe. A mix of high, rugged peaks and forested valleys. Inaccessible by road. Traversed in Sweden by the 500km Kungsleden (King's Way), arguably the finest and most remote European long-distance trail for walkers and skiers.

Saltfjellet National Park. Mo i Rana. Centred on Scandinavia's largest glacier (Svartisen – 'The Black Glacier'). Important for Wolverine and Eurasian Lynx.

Stabbursdalen National Park. Lakselv. The world's most northerly Scots Pine forest, intermixed with birch. Inaccessible by road.

Varangerhalvøya National Park. Lakselv, Kirkenes. Norway's newest National Park, created in December 2006. Important wader and waterfowl migration site, as well as having breeding seabird and raptors.

Norway also has a large number of Nature Reserves in the north set up to protect seabird colonies, waterfowl and wader migration sites, and raptor breeding sites.

National Parks: Sweden

Abisko National Park. Kiruna. High mountains, gorges and forest. Very important botanically.

Muddus National Park. Gallivare. Old growth forest and bogs.

Padjelanta National Park. See Rago NP, Norway.

Pieljekaise National Park. Arjeplog. High peaks, and valleys with birch forest and bogs.

Sarek National Park. See Rago NP, Norway.

Stora Sjöfallet National Park. See Rago NP, Norway.

Vadvetjåkka National Park. Narvik (Norway). Limestone country, with bogs and fell fields.

Sweden has a number of northern Nature Reserves set up to protect bird breeding sites and sites of botanical importance. Several are centred on lakes that are important waterfowl migration and breeding sites, e.g. Lake Laidure, near Kvikkjokk, which is a staging post for Whooper Swans.

A site that will delight the traveller is the 'tri-point', the place where Norway, Sweden and Finland meet. There is another such site, where Norway, Finland and Russia meet, close to the southern tip of the Øvre Pasvik National Park, but that is much less accessible. And as I am writing about 'tourist' sites, I must mention Nordkapp. As the 'official' northernmost point of Europe (though not of Eurasia, since large chunks of Russia lie to the north, culminating in Cape Chelyuskin, which is about 750km further north) this is on the itinerary of many visitors to northern Norway. Over-commercialised and rather mundane, it has little to recommend it. The true northernmost point of Europe, at Knivskjelodden (47" of latitude – about 1.5km – further north) is quieter and much more pleasant, but requires a 20km round-trip walk to enjoy.

Traveller's must use ships to reach Jan Mayen and Bear Island, these often leaving from Norwegian ports. Ships also occasionally travel from Norway to Svalbard. Although not as notorious as the Southern Ocean, the north Atlantic can be rough, as this photograph indicates. It was taken on the return from Jan Mayen to Norway when the author, photographer Per Michelsen and a few interested colleagues hired an old sealer for an Arctic voyage. Sealers have no keel - ideal for avoiding entrapment in pack ice, but allowing astonishing angles of list when the wind gets to Force 8.

BEAR ISLAND

Bear Island lies at 74°30'N between the northern coast of Norway and Svalbard. It is roughly triangular (base at the northern end, apex to the south, the main axis aligned roughly north–south) and measures around 20km north to south, 15km east to west at the triangle's base, and covers 178km^2. Bear Island's mean July temperature is +5°, while the mean January temperature is -7°C. Geologically the island is part of the Svalbard archipelago, the main rocks being Permian, Carboniferous and Devonian, with some Precambrian at the south-eastern tip. It is low-lying, so before the era of GPS sailors could easily pass it, especially when the island was covered with cloud. An alternative name, Island of Mists, reflects the prevalence of cloud cover. Standing where relatively warm and humid continental air masses meet cold Arctic waters this is no surprise; in July mist shrouds the island for at least 25% of the time.

History

Although it is possible that Viking sailors saw the island, particularly if they sailed far enough north to see Svalbard, the first known sighting was by Willem Barents on 10 June 1596. Two days later Barents' men met a swimming Polar Bear, killing it with muskets, knives and axes, an event that gave the island its name. In 1604 the Englishman Stephen Bennett saw 1,000 Walruses on a Bear Island beach, and killed 50 for their tusks, the first exploitation of the marine mammals of the Barents Sea. Hunting did not last long: within 15–20 years the number of Walruses had decreased to the point where visiting the island was uneconomic, and the hunt moved north to Svalbard. The population recovered so that in 1818 numbers were such that an English expedition reputedly killed 900 animals in seven hours; further exploitation reduced numbers significantly and the population has never recovered. Whales were also hunted from the island in the 17th century, and a Norwegian whaling station was active at Kvalrossbukta on the eastern side from 1905–08. At much the same time a coal mine operated at the northern end of the island. A Norwegian meteorological station was set up in 1923, and Bear Island formally became Norwegian territory with the signing of the Svalbard Treaty in 1925. The meteorological station still functions.

Wildlife

The relatively shallow waters around the island are among the most productive in the Barents Sea, which, together with the steep cliffs, makes it an important nesting site for seabirds. The main species are Common and Brünnich's Guillemots, Little Auks, Razorbills, Black-legged Kittiwakes, Northern Fulmars and Glaucous Gulls. It is estimated that more than 1,000,000 seabirds are present during the breeding period. However, a long-term decrease in the numbers of guillemots has been identified, almost certainly as a consequence of consistent overfishing of the waters close to the island. A further threat comes from the northern advance of the oil industry, following the opening of the Barents Sea for exploration. At the time of writing discussions are being held on the possibility of opening more northerly areas to the drillers.

As well as being important for seabirds, Bear Island also plays an important role as a staging post for the Svalbard populations of Barnacle, Brent and Pink-footed Geese on their autumn migration. Other birds include the Great Northern Diver, the most remote Palearctic outpost of this essentially Nearctic species. About 10 pairs of Grey Phalaropes also nest on the island.

Of mammals, only the Arctic Fox is resident, though most of the seals of the Barents Sea occur in relatively small numbers. The same is true of cetaceans. Polar Bears are occasionally seen if drift ice reaches the island.

Bear Island is now a Nature Reserve and though access is not actually restricted there is no possibility of aircraft landing, and sea journeys must be privately organised (although Arctic cruise ships, usually on their way to or from Svalbard, occasionally call by).

SVALBARD

Bear Island

Bear Island is of interest both to scientists, who can study the rich geology, and birds who populate the steep cliffs. The photograph below is of the southern end of the island. Off-shore is the Sylen rock needle

It was pointed peaks such as these at Hornsund which promoted the Dutch to call the largest island of the Svalbard archipelago 'Spitsbergen' – pointed mountains.

SVALBARD

Svalbard is the name given to the archipelago of islands lying between 74°N and 81°N to the north of Scandinavia. The archipelago includes Spitsbergen, the most widely known of the islands, and the name frequently used to cover the whole island group. Spitsbergen is the largest island, accounting for 38,000km², about 60% of the total land area (of some 61,000km²) of the archipelago. Other islands include Nordaustlandet, north-east of Spitsbergen (the second largest of the group at 14,500km², 24% of the total land area). Off Spitsbergen's east coast are Edgeøya and Barentsøya, to the north-east of which is Kong Karls Land, itself an archipelago of three small islands and a collection of islets. Off Spitsbergen's west coast is Prins Karls Forland, while off the northern coast are smaller islands, including Moffen and Amsterdamøya, the latter famous for its whaling station during the early years of Svalbard whaling. Finally, off Nordaustlandet's north-eastern coast is Kvitøya (White Island) where the Andrée balloon expedition team died. The archipelago is heavily glaciated, with about 60% of the land area covered in ice.

History

The discovery of Svalbard is shrouded in uncertainty. The Norse sagas indicate that 'Svalbard' was reached in 1194 during Viking explorations of the northern Atlantic. But it is by no means clear that the Svalbard of the sagas was today's Svalbard rather than Jan Mayen or, more likely, the north-east coast of Greenland. For political reasons the Norwegians claim the Norse were describing the archipelago, countering Russian claims that the Pomores were visiting Svalbard to hunt sea mammals as early as the 15th century. The evidence for this is not conclusive, being based on oral tradition backed by some documentation. Oral tradition claims that the Starostin family were hunting on Svalbard 'before the founding of the Solovetsk monastery' (i.e. before 1425). Danish letters suggest that the Russian Tsar had also included 'Greenland' in his realm at about the same time, but again exactly what was meant by 'Greenland' is open to dispute.

The 'official' discovery is credited to the Dutch in 1596. The expedition was commanded by Jacob van Heermskerk and Jan Cornelius Riip, but is much more famous for the inclusion of Willem Barents. The Dutch gave their discovery the prosaic name 'The New Land' on their charts, but their vernacular name, Spitsbergen, was adopted for the largest island. For those visiting the island the peaks at Hornsund, Haitanna, and especially the peak of Bautaen ('monolith') are the true pointed mountains.

Whoever the discoverer of the archipelago was, it is clear that Svalbard was not continuously inhabited before modern times. Whaling stations were set up and manned during the summer months, most famously by the Dutch at Smeerenburg on Amsterdamøya, but when whale stocks had been so depleted that the fishery was no longer economic these were abandoned. A 'hotel' was built beside Adventfjorden in 1898 to accommodate tourists keen to experience the Arctic, and coal was first mined commercially nearby in 1899, these two ventures setting the scene for later development. The American John Munroe Longyear came in 1901 as a tourist, but realised the potential of the area, bought a local mining company and began the town which now bears his name –

Longyear's Town or Longyearbyen, at 78°N. Coal was later mined by the Norwegians, at Longyearbyen, Sveagruva and Ny Ålesund, and by the Russians at Barentsburg and Pyramiden, the Russians (at that time the Soviets) taking advantage of the Svalbard Treaty to occupy a strategically important Arctic island. Today mining is carried out only at Longyearbyen and Barentsburg, though it is likely that mining will restart at Sveagruva in the near future.

The Svalbard Treaty was signed in 1920 as an adjunct to the Paris Peace Conference. The Treaty gave sovereignty of the archipelago to Norway, but gave equal rights of access and residence, and commercial exploitation of the islands (by fishing and mining) to both the initial and subsequent signatories. The fact that sovereignty was granted by Treaty explains Norwegian nervousness over Svalbard's discovery. Article Nine of the Treaty declares that the archipelago must not be used for 'warlike purposes' but there is little doubt that the strategic importance of the islands, positioned close to any route their navy might have chosen to take from its European ports, explains the Soviet presence and the continuing Norwegian and Russian presence. Coal mining on Svalbard is hardly economic, though the islands are a superb research base, being far to the north yet comfortably accessible in summer.

During the early stages of the 1939–45 war the Norwegians continued mining on Svalbard at first, despite concerns by the Allies that the coal was powering the German war effort, Germany having occupied Norway in 1940. Mining ceased in 1941. Svalbard was at first seen as strategically unimportant, but that position changed dramatically when Germany attacked Russia. The Germans occupied Svalbard, but retreated when Allied forces (including Free Norwegian soldiers, i.e. men who had left Norway after the occupation and were determined to regain it from German control) landed. The Germans later shelled the Allied positions from a naval force which included *Tirpitz* and *Scharnhorst*, as well as mounting a bombing raid on Sveagruva. German troops occupied the archipelago again, though Allied forces remained and there were sporadic fire fights between the groups, involving casualties on both sides. After the war, there was considerable pressure from the Soviets to enforce joint Norwegian-Soviet sovereignty, particularly after Norway joined NATO, but the situation remains today as it has been since 1920.

A drawing from Sir William Martin Conway's book *The First Crossing of Spitsbergen*, published in 1897, which recorded the journey and survey work of his expedition of 1896 which explored a considerable portion of the island.

Tourism

Tourism has gradually increased in importance, aided by regular scheduled flights from Oslo via Tromsø. The accessibility of the archipelago has resulted in the recent (early 2007) decision to use it as the site of the 'Doomsday Vault', a collection of

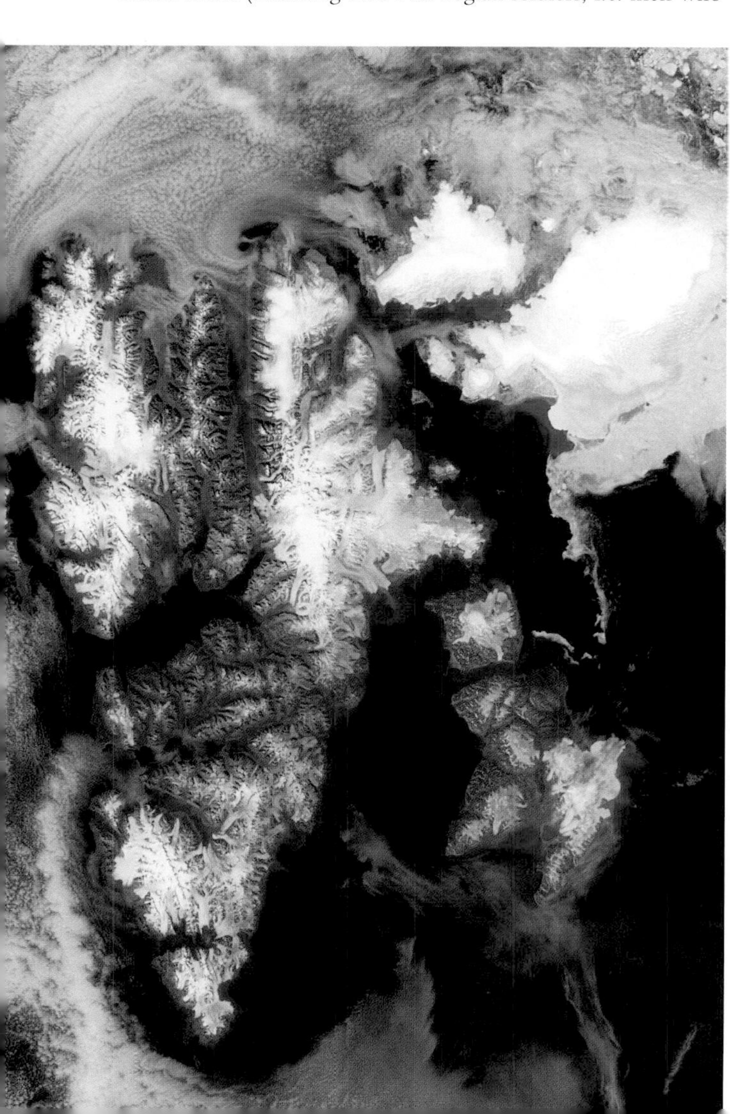

Above
The remains of the 400-year old Dutch whaling station of Smeerenburg on the island of Amsterdamøya at the north-western tip of Spitsbergen.

around 3,000,000 seeds representing biodiversity in agricultural plant life. The idea of the repository is to save strains in case climate change or plant diseases create challenges that strains no longer grown commercially can address. The repository is planned to be sited 120m deep within a Spitsbergen mountain and, it is hoped, will be open in early 2008.

Accessibility has also resulted in increased tourism, visitor numbers having accelerated significantly in recent years. The camp site close to Longyearbyen airport and the guesthouse in town have now been superseded by accommodation that includes a 5-star hotel serving haute cuisine. This change has been accompanied by the growth in shops selling standard tourist trinkets (as well as equipment for those who arrive ill-prepared for the Arctic). An increase in population – fuelled by the increase in tourist numbers, but also because of the opening of a research college (an outpost of the Norwegian university system) – also required a supermarket. The changes are not to everyone's taste, particularly as they have been accompanied by a massive increase in tourist-related businesses. Where once a handful of snow scooters took the genuinely interested in search of views and wildlife, now squadrons take thrill-seekers on day trips. The impact on the landscape and wildlife of Svalbard has, thankfully, been minimal so far. The ruts of wheeled vehicles take decades to disappear and so they are banned, meaning that summer travel must be made by ship or on foot. Ships usually explore the west coast of Spitsbergen, returning from a point at about 80°N, or circumnavigate the island. Other islands of the archipelago are rarely visited, many being off-limits due to their importance as Polar Bear denning sites, while some (such as Kvitøya) are usually too difficult to reach because of sea ice. The increase in the number of ships has caused problems, with tourists ransacking historic sites for souvenirs, but that seems to be under better control now. One advantage of the use of ships is that landings can, in principle, be carefully controlled in terms of the sites visited.

Such policing was not possible in winter when anyone with a snow scooter, a sledge loaded with supplies, good navigational skills and a modicum of nerve could go more or less anywhere. One problem of this unrestricted access was occasional examples of irresponsible behaviour. As a consequence, regulations have now been introduced on winter travel. In particular, travel on Spitsbergen's east coast – an important Polar Bear denning area – has been restricted. A map is available showing visitors where unescorted snow scooter travel and escorted group travel is allowed, and where all snow scooter travel is forbidden. In general, travel close to

Opposite page
Moonlight over a winter landscape. Aghardbukta, east Spitsbergen.

Right
The important bird breeding cliffs of Alkafjellet overlooking Hinlopen Stretet which separates Spitsbergen and Nordaustlandet.

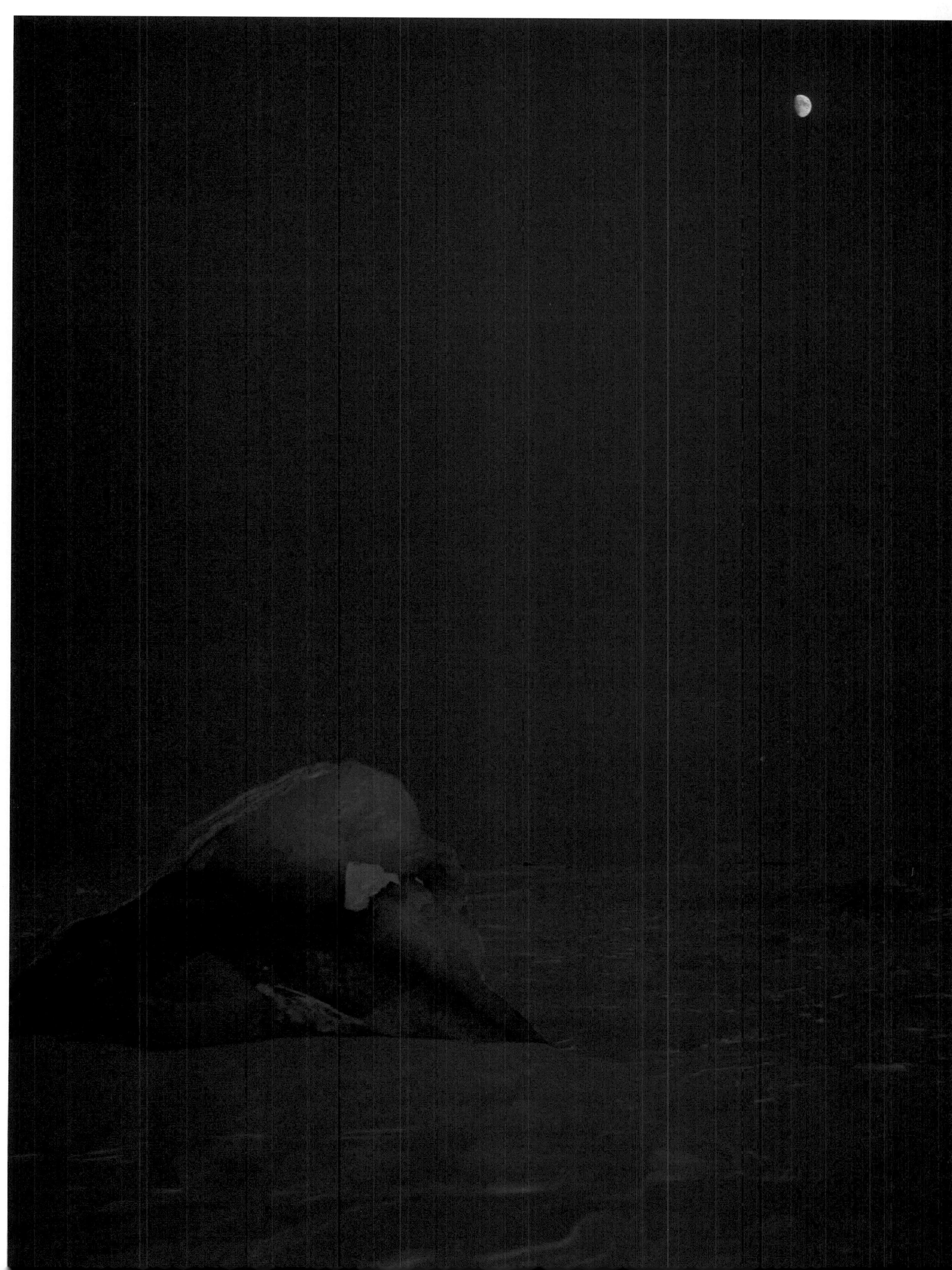

As well as magnificent scenery and wildlife, Svalbard also has important historical sites. These are the remains of Adolf Erik Nordenskiöld's observatory at Kapp Thordsen, Isfjorden, Spitsbergen. Nordenskiöld, who led the expedition which made the first transit of the North-East Passage, was a scientist as well as an explorer and led an expedition to Kapp Thordsen in 1872–3.

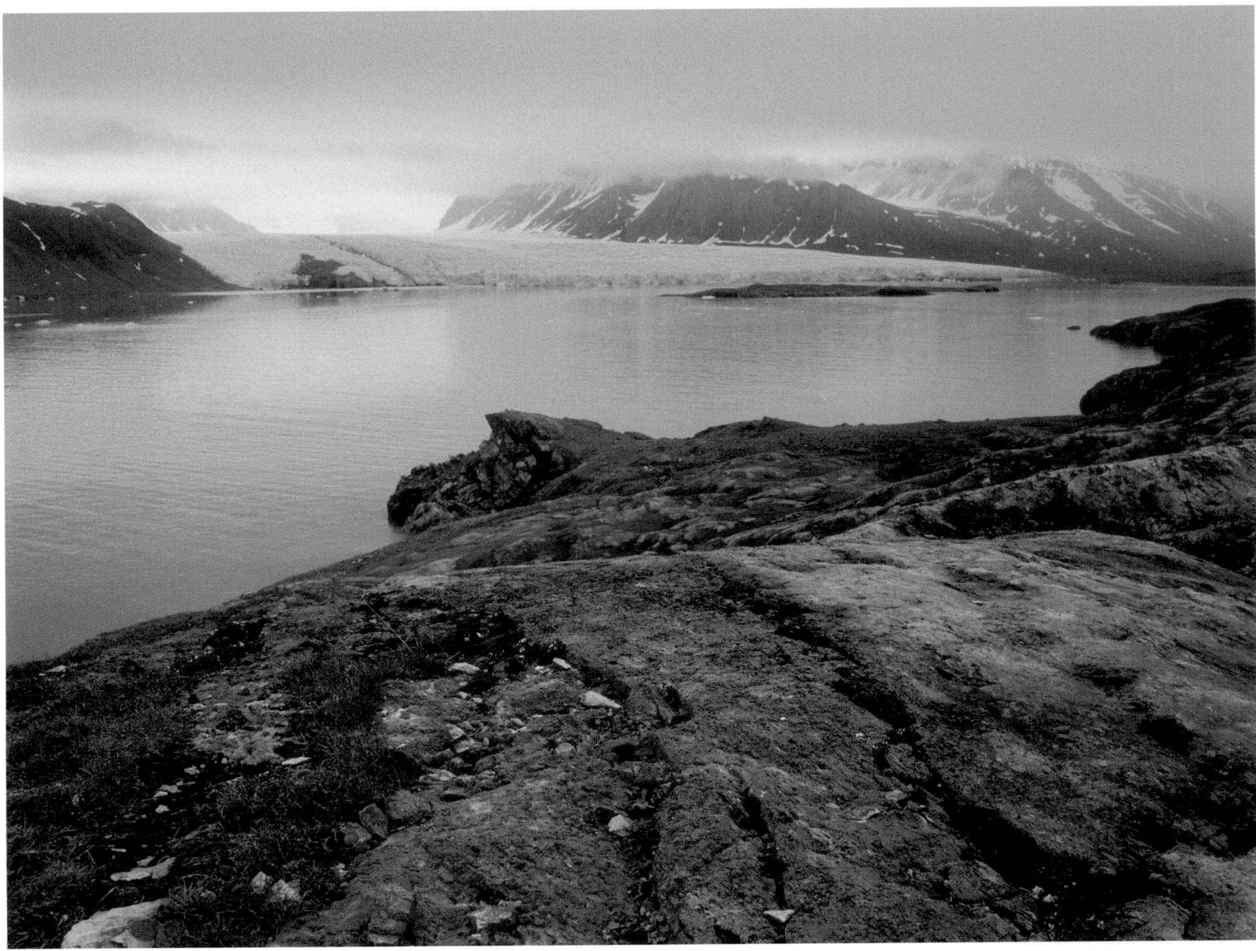

Lichen-encrusted rocks at the edge of Kongsfjorden, Spitsbergen, Svalbard.

Midnight, Kongsfjorden, Spitsbergen.

Longyearbyen and Ny Ålesund is permitted, as is travel from Longyearbyen to Barentsburg and Pyramiden. Travel on Spitsbergen's east coast, near Agardh Bay, and north from there to Wichebukta, is restricted to escorted groups.

Winter ethics

In winter, out of sight of authority, some visitors still fail to realise that chasing a Svalbard Reindeer on a snow scooter means that the fun of a few minutes is exchanged for a life-threatening run for the animal; so precarious are the winter survival prospects of the Reindeer that the energy lost in such a chase could mean the difference between life and death. There have even been folk who have chased Polar Bears on scooters. The bear is less likely to have its life threatened through energetic loss, but it might die of heat exhaustion; so efficient is the bear's insulating layers of fur and blubber that even an increase from its normal walking speed of 4kph to 7kph can raise its body temperature from 37°C to 39°C in a relatively short time. Bears can reach 40kph, but only in short bursts, these followed by long periods of cooling. A chased bear, having no time to cool, can have its body temperature raised to dangerous levels.

National Parks

To further protect Svalbard's magnificent wilderness, several National Parks have been set up. These cover north-west Spitsbergen from Krossfjorden to Woodfjorden; the north side of Isfjord; the head of Isfjord; the land south of Van Keulenfjorden; the land south of Barentsburg; 'Nordenskiöld Land', on the north side of Bellsund; 'Sassen-Bünsow Land' at the eastern end of Isfjorden; and Forlandet (Prins Karls Forland). In addition there are 6 Nature Reserves covering important plant or bird breeding areas, Polar Bear denning areas, and a number of smaller bird reserves that cover specific breeding sites. Permission to enter these parks must be sought in advance.

The regulations and restrictions must be seen in the context of the need to preserve a fragile, High Arctic land. Because of them Svalbard will hopefully remain a largely unsullied wilderness, and despite the limitations on travel people can still enjoy stunning landscapes and magnificent wildlife. As well as Polar Bears and Svalbard Reindeer, the traveller is likely to see Arctic Fox. Walrus, Bearded, Ringed and Harbour Seals are almost invariably seen, though Harp and Hooded Seals are more elusive. Of the birds, travellers to Ny Ålesund should see Barnacle Geese, while trips by ship visit cliffs where huge numbers of seabirds nest. Ivory and Ross's Gulls are rare, but are often seen.

Part of Nordaustlandet comprises Carboniferous-Permian sedimentary deposits which are rich in marine fossils.

A WARNING ON BEARS

Bears are very powerful and surprisingly quick over short distances. Polar Bears accelerate extremely quickly and maintain their footing on ice. Apart from adult Walrus there is nothing except humans that can threaten Polar Bears, and in many parts of their range the bears are protected (on Svalbard, for example) in those areas the bears are consequently not afraid of humans. This combination can cause serious problems. When the sea ice retreats in summer some Svalbard bears, usually those which have just begun to fend for themselves (i.e. those in their third year, usually males), are left behind on southern islands. Unable to find food and marooned too far from the ice to be able to swim to it, these bears grow hungry and very aggressive. If they see a traveller they may well decide to attack.

Even in less hostile circumstances potentially dangerous situations may arise. Polar Bears are naturally inquisitive and well-fed bears may approach a traveller simply to satisfy their curiosity. Such encounters, while wonderful for the observer, are potentially hazardous as the bear may suddenly become aggressive for no apparent reason. A strange or sudden movement may startle it and be seen as an aggressive move on the observer's part; the bear may attack, quickly and without warning, and the observer would be unlikely to survive such an attack.

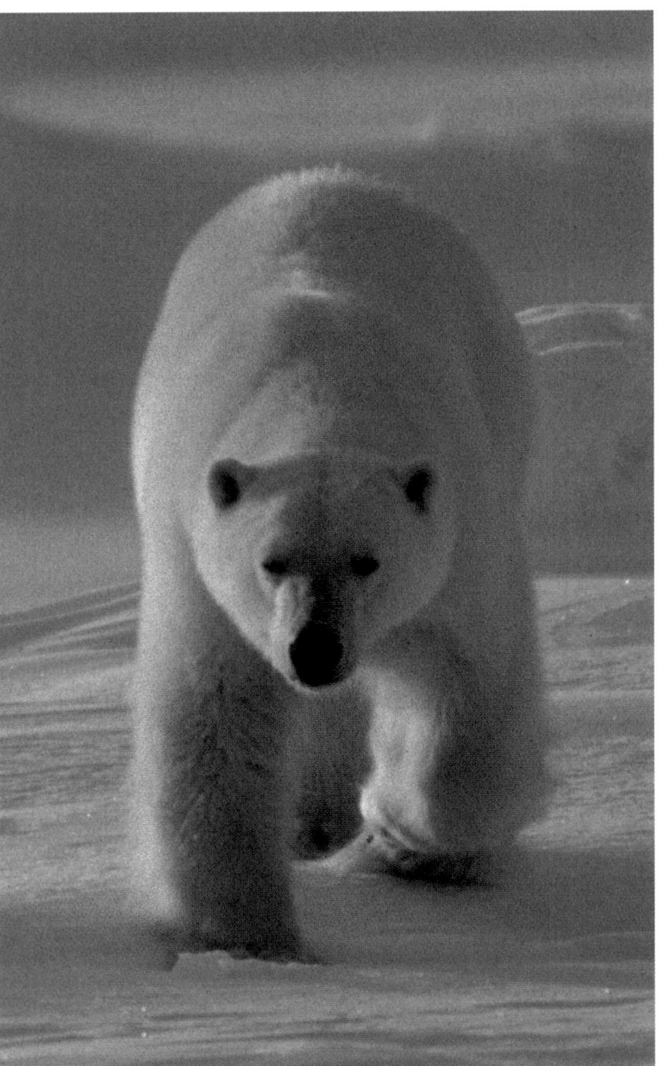

You should not approach bears closely and, if a bear approaches you, retreat. Remember that the bear can run faster than you can manage in ideal conditions – and the bear can do it on ice. An aggressive bear may blow hard from its nose, it may open and snap its mouth, it may lower its head or move it from side to side. But it may do none of these things before attacking.

An attack will be direct and swift. If you appear to be in danger retreat slowly. Do not make sudden movements. Take off an article of clothing such as a glove or hat and drop it on the floor. The bear will be curious and will knock the article about a few times before abandoning it; that may be all the time you need to reach safety. If you are camping in bear territory use trip wires around the camp to warn of a bear's approach and keep food and cooking well away from the tent. Camping high above the sea ice is a good idea, but bears have been seen in surprising places so do not be lulled into a false sense of security. Never feed a bear; not only may that lead to a dangerous situation for you, but it may endanger the next human the bear encounters. Never place yourself between a female bear and her cubs.

Brown Bears can also be aggressive, if an observer comes between a mother and her cubs, for example. Brown Bears are unpredictable, with attacks on people often being blamed on thundery weather, perfumes or even menstruating women (though the latter is now generally dismissed by bear researchers). In practice the likely cause is encroachment on territory, surprising the bear. To avoid attacks signal your presence by making a noise – the bear will probably move away before contact occurs. If contact does occur, it will almost certainly help to lower your head, avoiding eye contact, and to move slowly away; upright humans look like upright bears, an aggressive posture, while animals running speedily away are invariably prey, from the bear's point of view, and so may be pursued as an instinctive reaction. An aggressive bear will snap its teeth, salivate such that it appears to be frothing at the mouth, lay its ears back and growl or 'woof' (the latter are rapid exhalations, associated with deep breaths that allow the bear to 'taste' who you are). If an attack occurs, the standard wisdom is to assume a foetal position and stay motionless. However, as always with such advice, those who do not survive bear attacks are not available to offer advice on what did not work. This advice has resulted in some individuals surviving attacks, but it is questionable.

It is often written that Brown Bears do not climb trees and so, if available, a tree offers escape. However, this is not strictly true and may have contributed to the deaths of some unfortunate individuals. Brown Bears have straighter claws than Black Bears and so are less adept at tree-climbing, and they are also much heavier, restricting how far they can climb, but if sufficiently incensed they can manage 3m up a tree surprisingly quickly and there are documented tales of bears hauling people down from 5m and killing them. Brown Bears are also excellent swimmers.

Black Bears are, in general, more cautious and less aggressive than Brown Bears, but that should not be seen as an invitation to move closer. As for Brown Bears, make a noise to advertise your presence, and retreat slowly and with eyes lowered if contact is made. Startled Black Bears usually climb trees to escape potential danger. If that happens use the time offered you to retreat. Staying around might offer the chance of a good photograph, but if the bear decides to climb down you may not have too much time to admire the shot. One interesting statistic regarding Black Bears is that US authorities claim that people are about 90,000 times more likely to be murdered than to be killed by a Black Bear. I find this statistic rather less comforting than it was intended to be.

Bear sprays, which can confuse the bear and so offer a few vital seconds, can be purchased in most areas where bears live. The spray will, of course, irritate the bear and so leaving the bear quickly afterwards is essential. Flash-bangs are also widely available (but remember it is illegal to carry them on aircraft). These are excellent as the noise and flash will frighten the bear and give you time to escape.

ELK AND MUSK OXEN WARNING

Both Elk and Musk Oxen are dangerous. Female Elk with calves are particularly dangerous and will lash out with their front legs. The hooves are sharp, and as the animal weighs 500kg or more they can cause severe injury or death. Moose are also very quick, reaching speeds of 55kph, and have famously swum past canoes in which two terrified men were paddling furiously. It is far better not to be attacked, but if you are, a quick tree-climb offers the best escape route.

The Moose photographed to the right was inadvertently cornered in a blind snow 'alley' one Alaskan spring, forcing the author into a rapid retreat. Had climbing vertical snow banks been an Olympic sport, the author would have been a medal contender.

Musk Oxen are usually nervous and suspicious of a close approach. If the traveller persists in moving closer the Musk Oxen – particularly a lone animal or a female with a calf – will attack. The head and horns of the ox are formidable weapons, and a struck victim will also be trampled. If you are attacked turn and run as the ox will rarely pursue, especially if this means leaving the herd. One fact worth remembering is that being short-legged and very heavy-headed, Musk Oxen do not like running downhill. So if you are approaching, try to advance uphill and, if a charge occurs, turn and run downhill.

The photograph below is of an old bull Musk Ox on Alaska's North Slope.

RUSSIA

The Russian Arctic extends from its border with Finland in the west to the Bering Sea in the east, just a few kilometres from Alaska. Yet for much of this vast distance the mainland does not lie in the Arctic as defined here, the deep cold of the Siberian winter being moderated by warm summers. As a consequence, in general only a narrow section of the mainland is truly Arctic, though all of the country's northern islands are. Siberia is a wonderful land but it has had a bad press, the sad history of exploitation of its native peoples and animals having given way to exploitation of the landscape itself, when it was used as a repository for criminals and dissidents. Today, exploitation of the area's mineral wealth is threatening the landscape again, but now in a very real sense.

Despite *perestroika,* travel within Russia is still difficult, the invitations and permits required for journeys making genuinely independent travel difficult. Things are slowly improving, and some Russian tour companies (as opposed to western tour companies making trips to Russia) are now offering excellent trips to interesting places. Purpose-built trips are also possible as these new companies shake off the rigidity that characterised Intourist (the only Soviet tourist agency, and still the official Russian tourist agency). The better Russian Arctic destinations, the islands, still require a visitor to join an organised cruise as there are no airports, and use of helicopters from the mainland is prohibitively expensive even if it is available, which it may not be due to lack of machines or local bureaucracy. There are nuisances that can try the patience of the traveller, delays without explanation and changes likewise, and occasionally the bureaucracy can be exceedingly trying. I once spent an uncomfortable 12 hours at the entrance to Petropavlosk Bay, Kamchatka *en route* from Starichkov Island, with limited food, water and shelter on a nowhere nearly big enough boat when the bay was arbitrarily closed by the naval base commander. Internal flights in planes and helicopters are yet to reach western standards of either aircraft or comfort, and it is sometimes necessary just to count the hours to the destination and to tell oneself that the pilot does not want to crash and die either.

Because of the ever-changing nature of Russian travel only brief notes are given here.

For a map of Russia, see p117.

Kola Peninsula

Murmansk, the largest city on the Kola Peninsula (its population of 400,000 probably exceeds the sum of all other dwellers north of the Arctic Circle), is the headquarters of Russia's northern fleet and a base for nuclear submarines as well as surface vessels. Radioactive material has contaminated certain areas of the peninsula, but this has been localised. There are four nuclear reactors at the power station of Polyarnye Zori near the city.

The peninsula is composed of some of the Earth's oldest rocks, the base being Precambrian of the East European Platform, with an intrusion of the Lapland Granulite Belt crossing the border from Finland. The so-called 'grey gneiss' of Kola is 3.5 billion years old. There are rich deposits of copper and nickel, which have led to the construction of ore smelters,

Unlike the Trerikroset, where Finland, Norway and Sweden meet, the stone marking the meeting point of Finland, Norway and Russia is out-of-bounds to the traveller except for one day of the year when restrictions are lifted and skiers and walkers from the three countries meet - with the military keeping a watchful eye.

Murmansk, the largest city of northern Eurasia and the gateway to the west Russian Arctic.

the air pollution from these creating a dead zone of trees for many miles downwind. However, Kola remains heavily forested, particularly to the south, where the forest forms part of the northern taiga. To the north of this are areas of forest tundra and tundra with palsa mire in the permafrost region bordering on the Arctic Ocean. At the centre of the peninsula is the small (1,300km^2) Khibin Mountain range, which rises to 1,191m at Mount Fersman.

The peninsula is among the easier places to reach in all of northern Russia, as the infrastructure is reasonable. Transport is also available from Kirkenes, Norway to Murmansk, though the journey is depressing. Nikel is a centre for metal smelting (chiefly – and, given the name, no surprise – of nickel), with furnace emissions having poisoned local land. The combination of that and the architecture promote a gloomy atmosphere. The architecture of most Russian cities is similar. The heart of many older cities is often beautiful, though usually neglected. Surrounding it are dilapidated high-rise blocks whose style can be kindly described as utilitarian. The communist leadership persuaded the people to accept these shoddily designed and constructed dwellings, on the grounds that in just a few years they would be replaced by immaculate homes funded by the fabulous riches the system would undoubtedly generate. The new homes never materialised. Western travellers may occasionally smile at the shameless nature of leaders who made such claims, but history suggests that communist politicos do not have a monopoly on being economical with the truth.

Zapovedniks

Kola has three Zapovedniks, or Nature Preserves:
Kandalakshskiy, an inlet of the White Sea close to Monchegorsk. Here a combination of coastal grassland, bogs and salt marshes supports more than 500 species of plant, and is a breeding ground for over 200 species of bird. The reserve also covers two remote sites on the northern coast of the peninsula.
Laplandskiy, on the inland side of Monchegorsk has the peninsula's highest hills, as well as forest, bog and tundra, and is an important bird breeding area.
Pasvik is contiguous with Norway's Øvre Pasvik National Park.

Yamal

It is possible to fly to Nar'yan-Mar from both Moscow and Arkhangelsk and to travel along the Pechora River to the Arctic Ocean, or to visit local Nenet herders. The area is a centre for the Russian oil industry, which will probably mean that other opportunities will become available in future. Further east, Vorkuta can be reached by train from Moscow, but apart from city tours there is currently little in the way of travel potential. East again, Salekhard on the Ob River can be reached by plane. Boats ply the river, making cruises of several days duration both north towards the ocean and south. It is also possible to organise a trip to the Nenet Reindeer herders on the Yamal Peninsula, a truly wild area of tundra. Yamal is rich in natural gas deposits which are now being exploited. Exploitation will improve the infrastructure, but inevitably at a cost to the environment. The Yamal Peninsula, and the nearby Gydan Peninsula, are breeding areas for Red-breasted Geese.

Taimyr Peninsula

The Taimyr Peninsula is part of the Siberian Platform, a relatively high, dissected platform covering over 400,000km^2 with a complex geology. Averaging about 500m above sea level, the peninsula rises to 1,146m in the Byrranga Mountains, which form an elevated, essentially east-west ridge in the northern plateau. The Byrrangas are heavily glaciated, with 96 glaciers covering an area of over 30km^2 with ice. At the peninsula's northern tip is Cape Chelyuskin, the most northerly point of mainland Eurasia. The cape is named after Semen Chelyuskin, who mapped the area in 1742 as part of the Great Northern Expedition. Between the cape and Severnaya Zemlya is the Vilkitskiy Strait, an area of extremely heavy sea ice.

Taimyr is apparently mineral rich. The exploitation of copper and nickel deposits (as sulphide ores) near Noril'sk, in the southern peninsula, has created areas of considerable ecological damage. These are not confined to a downwind plume, but extend over a distance of 50–100km in all directions. The peninsula also overlays huge gas deposits (estimated at more than 4 billion cubic metres), the extraction of which will inevitably cause both mechanical damage and air pollution and affect both the indigenous population and wildlife.

To the south the peninsula is bordered by the Putorana Plateau, a high plain (to 1,700m) of volcanic rocks. The plateau is an area of polar desert, with the slopes as it falls away passing through alpine tundra to forest tundra, and it is renowned for its wildlife, including wild sheep. The plateau is a Zapovednik.

Wildlife

Taimyr is underlain with permafrost, in places over 500m thick, and shows the typical southward progression from barren to more hospitable southern tundras and forest tundra,

Above
Vast expanses of tundra, with numerous lakes and meandering streams characterise northern Russia close to the deltas of the great Arctic rivers.

Right
In their more southerly reaches the great rivers flow through the taiga; the Sinyaya, a tributary of the Lena.

Below
The Chukchi Peninsula from space.

where dwarf birch and dwarf willow blend into the larches of the northern taiga. The southern tundras of Taimyr are notable for the richness of their flora, and even the northern peninsula is surprisingly rich: at Cape Chelyuskin over 130 species of lichen, more than 70 species of moss, and 59 flowering plants have been identified. As well as tundra and taiga, Taimyr has both the uplands of Byrranga, and a number of lakes and large areas of mire, which provide habitats for some of Russia's rarer northern birds, including the Red-breasted Goose. The Taimyr tundra is also the habitat of the largest remaining Eurasian population of wild Reindeer, with more than 800,000 animals.

Travel

Both Noril'sk and Khatanga can be reached by air. From Noril'sk trips are now possible to the Putorana Plateau. In principle arrangements can also be made for helicopter flights northward to the peninsula. At present such arrangements are *ad hoc*, though it is likely that in the near future they will become more standardised. From Noril'sk it is possible to fly to Dudinka on the Yenisey River. Boats ply the river, but at the time of writing passages on these are forbidden to foreign travellers. This, too, is soon likely to change. There are two Zapovedniks on the peninsula, the Great Arctic, a vast (more than 4 million hectare) reserve covering four separate areas on the coast, and the Taimyrskiy, which encompasses the huge lake of Ozero Taimyr.

Eastern River Deltas

East of the Taimyr Peninsula is a flat coastal area of river deltas, those of the Anabar, Lena, Yana, Indigirka and Kolyma rivers. The area is underlain by permafrost, the ice content of the ground being among the highest both in Russia and in the northern hemisphere, with values in excess of 60% by volume. The habitats are the usual progression from tundra through forest tundra to northern taiga, but the low-lying deltas are especially notable for sedge meadows and mosses. The deltas are extremely important, particularly for endemic species and as a habitat for waterfowl and waders; the Siberian White Crane is among the rarest and most endangered of Arctic breeding species. However, the deltas are also among the most remote areas in Russia and are extremely difficult to reach. Bird tours are available to the Lena delta (which is a Nature Preserve – the Ust Lenskiy Zapovednik: the reserve has recently been extended to include the New Siberian Islands), these starting from Yakutsk. Boats also travel along the river from Yakutsk towards (but not reaching) the Laptev Sea.

Chukotka

Chukotka is a continuation of the low-lying deltaic landscapes to the west, though here the geology is complicated by the Pacific Fold Belt and Mesozoic lava intrusions. The area is partially glaciated and supports a vegetation that is notable for

Mosses and wild flowers on Franz Josef Land.

being primarily of species adapted to wet or poorly drained soils, and for sharing much of its vegetation with nearby Alaska, a consequence of the relatively recent existence of Beringia. Chukotka includes the most easterly point of Eurasia, at Cape Dezhnev. Chukotka's poorly drained landscape is ideal for wildfowl and waders; for example, Chukotka is the main breeding ground of the Spoon-billed Sandpiper, one of the Arctic's more exotic bird species.

Recently, Chukotka has been in the news in Britain because of the purchase of Chelsea Football Club by Roman Abramovich, billionaire and Governor of the province. Abramovich's entrepreneurial spirit seems to have rubbed off on some locals, and it is now possible to fly to Anadyr and to stay in well-placed huts close to the breeding sites of Bering Sea birds. At Bilibino, a town to the east of the Kolyma delta, there are four small EGP-6 nuclear reactors that provide power and heating for the town, which is the local administrative centre. Chukotka is quickly developing a tourist infrastructure, perhaps aided by the distance from Moscow and its bureaucrats. Flights are available from Moscow to Anadyr, with internal flights – regular, but infrequent – to many of the local villages. It is also possible to reach Providenya, a bleak, largely uninhabited town rather like the deserted towns with tumbleweed blowing down the main street that were popular in 1950s cowboy movies; at the height of the Cold War Providenya had a population of about 40,000. Trips can be organised from Providenya to the bird cliffs of the Bering Sea, to such interesting places as Cape Dezhnev and Uelen. From Anadyr it is also possible to organise a trip to the Spoon-billed Sandpiper breeding grounds. From Pevek there are occasional helicopter flights to Wrangel Island.

Arctic islands

The Arctic islands of Russia are some of the most historically and scenically interesting of any High Arctic destination, but they are difficult to access and have almost no infrastructure to assist the traveller. Recently, travel companies have been visiting the western islands and even prospecting the possibility of an annual transit of the North-East Passage. Wrangel Island was until recently routinely on the itinerary of a leading American company, though restrictions on landing sites limited the advantages of a visit. At the present time the visits have ceased.

Franz Josef Land

The archipelago of Franz Josef Land lies between 80°N and 82°N, from 45°E to 65°E and comprises almost 200 islands with a total area of 37,000km^2. The majority of the islands are small, only George Island (2,740km^2), Wilczeck Land (2,055km^2), Graham Bell Island (1710km^2) and Alexandra Land (1050km^2) exceeding 1,000km^2. The island furthest to the west, Victoria Island, is only 60km east of Svalbard's Kvitøya. About 85% of the land area of the archipelago is ice-covered, with many of the glaciers calving into the surrounding seas. The largest icebergs of the northern hemisphere are calved from Franz Josef glaciers. The main climatic problem the traveller faces in the archipelago is not temperature, as might be expected, but an abundance of low cloud, which tends to cover the island throughout spring and early summer.

Wildlife

Having been off-limits for some years, cruise ships are now visiting Franz Josef Land again. Though not ideal for the wildlife observer, such trips do offer a way of seeing a unique landscape, astonishing for its mosses and lichens, though the flowering plants are more limited, with only one-third of the number found on Svalbard (*c*.60 compared to *c*.170). Polar Bear and Arctic Fox are the only terrestrial mammals present. Marine mammals include Ringed, Harp and Bearded Seals and Walrus, while cetaceans include the true Arctic whales – Beluga, Narwhal and Bowhead – as well as Minke Whales and Orcas, and, more rarely, other north Atlantic species. The bird life is excellent, breeding species including Red-throated Diver, Ivory Gull and many other seabirds.

Novaya Zemlya

Novaya Zemlya consists of two islands, separated by the strait of Matochkin Shar, lying midway between the Kola and Taimyr Peninsulas. Structurally, the islands derive from the Hercynian fold of the Palaeozoic era, a fold that continues on the mainland as the Urals, traditionally the mountains that separate Europe and Asia. An extension of this tradition would see Novaya Zemlya separating the European Barents Sea from Asia's Kara Sea.

Geologically the two islands are similar, but geographically the two are very different. The northern island has an almost

Northern Novaya Zemlya, the tip of the Yamal Peninsula and the western edge of the Taimyr Peninsula from space.

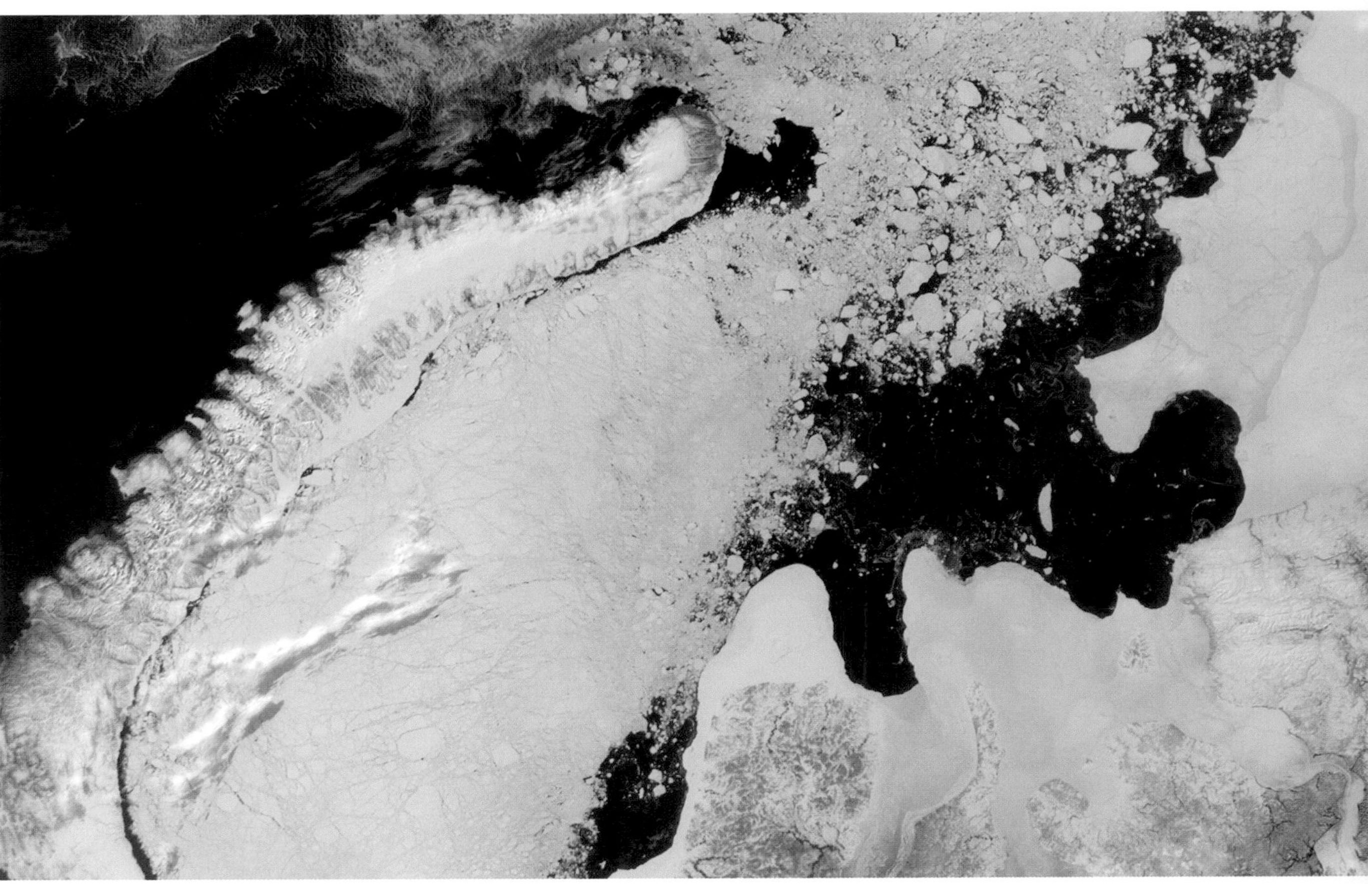

complete ice cap from which 60 glaciers derive, some reaching the sea, while the southern island has little permanent ice. The southern island was visited by Pomores from the mainland in search of sea mammals by as early as the 16th century, and probably much earlier; the island of Vaygach between the southern Novaya Zemlya island and the mainland was a sacred site to the indigenous people of the mainland (it was here that Jackson recorded his ritual site – see Native Peoples of the Arctic p109), and settlement was forbidden. In 1955 the Soviets exploded a nuclear bomb beneath the sea of Chernaya Bay. The sediments of the bay still have high levels of Caesium and Plutonium, and although these are presently stable they will, inevitably, reach the food chain. The test was the first of 132 nuclear weapon tests at three Novaya Zemlya sites between 1955 and 1990 (94% of all Soviet tests). In addition to weapons testing, highly radioactive material is believed to have been dumped illegally in the Barents and Kara seas to each side of the islands. Radioactive debris from the nuclear ice breaker *Lenin* was also dumped here.

As with Franz Josef Land, Novaya Zemlya is often covered by low cloud in spring and early summer.

Inostrantseva Bay, Novaya Zemlya.

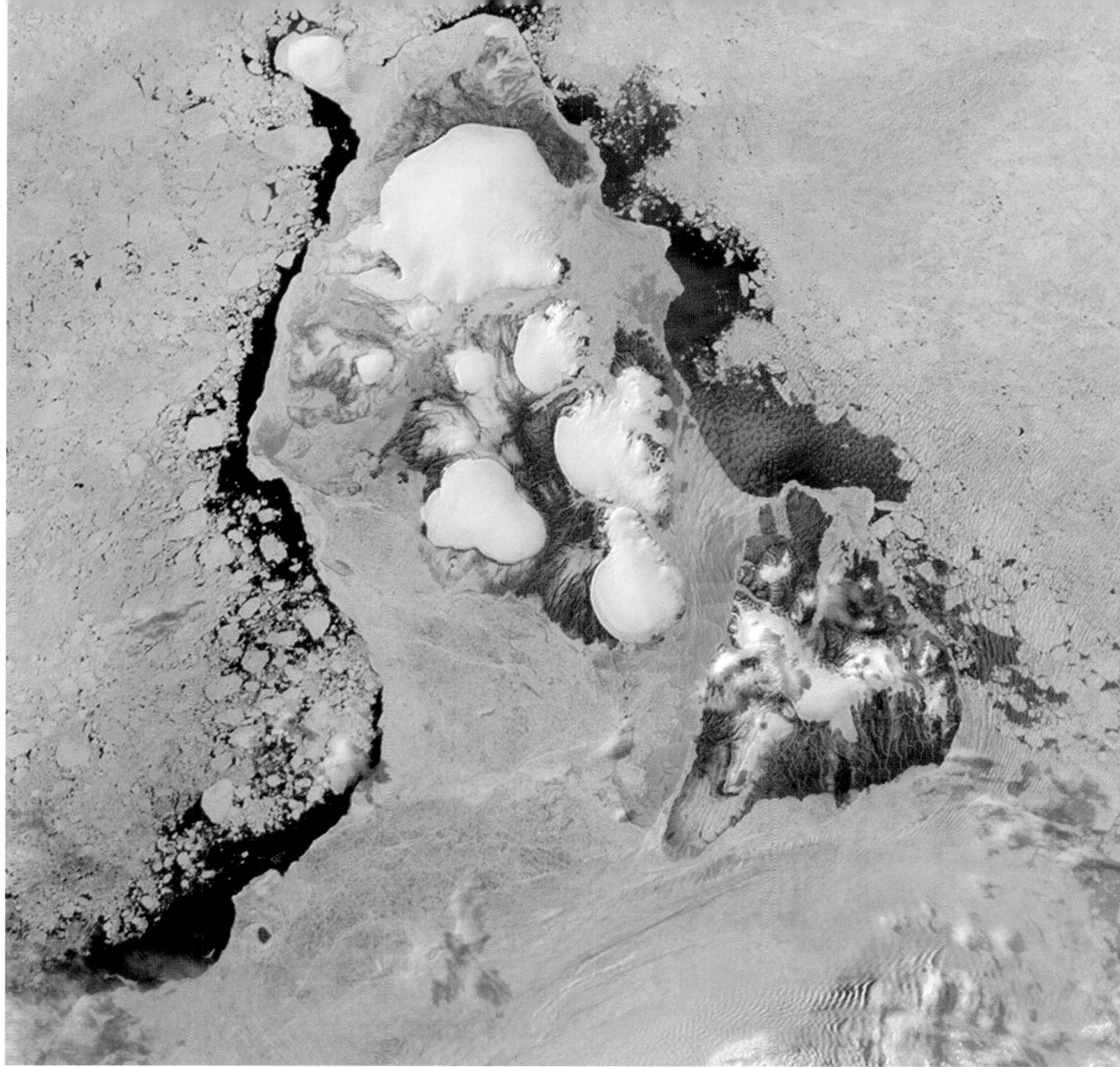

Severnaya Zemlya from space.

Wildlife

The northern island is a polar desert with a limited fauna, while the southern island has many more bird species, a breeding list similar to that of the nearby mainland. Polar Bears, Arctic Fox and Arctic Collared Lemming breed here, and there are also wild Reindeer on the southern island. Breeding sea mammals include Ringed and Bearded Seals and, perhaps, Harp Seals, together with Walrus.

A population of about 450 Nenet occupies Kolguyev Island, which lies close to the mainland south-west of Novaya Zemlya's southern tip. It is an important wildfowl breeding area, the absence of rodents meaning that the Arctic Fox population is small and the wildfowl populations large. It is estimated that more than 400,000 Greater White-fronted and Bean Geese nest annually, together with a further 12,000 Barnacle Geese and 6,000 Bewick's Swans. However, the discovery of oil and gas reserves in the 1980s has led to the drilling of many wells and significant environmental damage.

Severnaya Zemlya

Geologically, the archipelago of Severnaya Zemlya is an outlier of the Taimyr Peninsula. It is heavily glaciated, some 50% of the land area of 37,000km^2 being ice-covered; it has been calculated that the volume of ice on Franz Josef Land, Novaya Zemlya and Severnaya Zemlya represent 99% of Russia's total. In the Laptev Sea on the eastern edge of the archipelago lies an important polynya (the Eastern Severnaya Zemlya Polynya). Away from the ice the archipelago is a polar desert; just 17 flowering plants have been identified, compared with the 59 at Cape Chelyuskin just across the Vilkitskiy Strait. Officially the archipelago was discovered during the 1910–15 expedition of the Russian ice-breakers *Taymyr* and *Vaygach*, but there is good evidence that it had been seen, mistily and in the far distance, as early as 1810.

Wildlife

The terrestrial mammals of the archipelago are Polar Bear, Arctic Fox, Reindeer (which are wild here) and Arctic Collared Lemming. Sea mammals include Ringed and Bearded Seals and Walrus, with Beluga and Narwhal, other cetaceans being very rare. The lemmings are the prey of Snowy Owls, which occasionally breed on the islands. For the birder the main interest lies in the breeding colonies of Ivory Gulls. The colonies number up to 1,000 pairs on the islands of Domashniy, Golomyanny and Sredniy. Few other species breed, only Purple Sandpiper, Black-legged Kittiwake, Little Auk, Black Guillemot and Snow Bunting having been confirmed though other breeding species are suspected.

New Siberian Islands

The archipelago of Novosibirskie Ostrova, the New Siberian Islands, is the least visited and least studied of Russia's Arctic islands. It lies at a latitude of 73°N–76°N, midway between the Lena and Kolyma deltas off the north-eastern Siberian coast, and includes the smaller group of the De Long Islands.

Part of the rugged coastline of Kotel'nyy, the largest of the New Siberian Islands.

The vegetation is typical of the nearby mainland tundra, the proximity of the mainland meaning that many (about 65%) of the bird species found there are also seen in the archipelago, particularly on the most southerly island, Bolshaya Lyakhovskiy (the island is named after Ivan Lyakhov, who discovered it in 1770).

Wildlife

Reindeer still inhabit the island of Bolshaya Lyakhovskiy. They make an annual migration to the mainland for winter forage, a journey over the sea ice during which many animals may die. Endemic subspecies of the Siberian Brown Lemming and Arctic Collared Lemming are resident. The island also has large numbers of Polar Bears and an Arctic Fox population. The islands are a breeding ground for Laptev Sea Walrus, which are a possible third subspecies of this huge pinniped. As with Severnaya Zemlya, there is a very limited list of breeding birds.

Wrangel Island

Having escaped glaciation during the last Ice Age (when it acted as a refuge), and having formed part of Beringia, Wrangel Island has one of the most extensive and interesting floras of any of Russia's Arctic islands. More than 380 plants have been identified to date including a number of endemics. The island remains largely ice-free (though it is snow-covered for 8 months each year), but despite this Wrangel is a cold place in winter, with a mean January temperature of -30°C, and a cool place in summer, with a mean July temperature of +3°C. Wrangel is also very windy, particularly in winter, the prevailing winds piling the sea ice against both Wrangel and nearby Herald Island, the lee shores therefore tending to have areas of open water or areas with many leads. These are excellent for seals and, consequently, for Polar Bears; Wrangel is an important bear denning site. The island is relatively flat, rising to only just over 1,000m, and has extensive, shallow lakes on the northern flatlands that are excellent for waders and wildfowl. To protect this environment, the entire island is a Zapovednik.

The island is uninhabited, but excavations have revealed the existence of a Palaeo-Eskimo culture. Dated to *c*.3,000BP, the site represents the earliest Arctic settlement so far discovered in north-east Asia. The peoples of the site (which lies in Krasin Bay) hunted sea mammals, but they may also have been at least partly responsible for the extinction of Dwarf Mammoths, which are known to have inhabited Wrangel until *c*.4,000BP, up to 6,000 years after Mammoth disappeared from the rest of Siberia.

Wildlife

In addition to the Polar Bear, Arctic Foxes are common and there are herds of Reindeer and Musk Oxen. Neither Reindeer nor Musk Oxen are native, both having been introduced (Reindeer in the 1950s, Musk Oxen as recently as 1975). Wrangel is also home to the endemic Wrangel Island Lemming, and the Siberian Brown Lemming. Of sea mammals the most important is the Walrus, Wrangel being an important breeding area for the Pacific subspecies. It is estimated that about 50% of the population of this subspecies live around the island. Ringed and Bearded Seals also breed here. Of cetaceans, only the Bowhead Whale comes this way. Breeding birds include Snow Geese (the island and the nearby mainland are the only Palearctic breeding grounds for this Nearctic species), Baird's Sandpiper (another primarily Nearctic species), a number of other waders, Pelagic Cormorant (at the northern limit of its range), Ivory, Ross's and Sabine's Gulls, and Horned Puffin. Wrangel is also famous as a breeding site for Snowy Owl. Close to Cape Waring, at Wrangel's eastern tip, is Herald Island, a forbidding, craggy island, an excellent breeding site for seabirds.

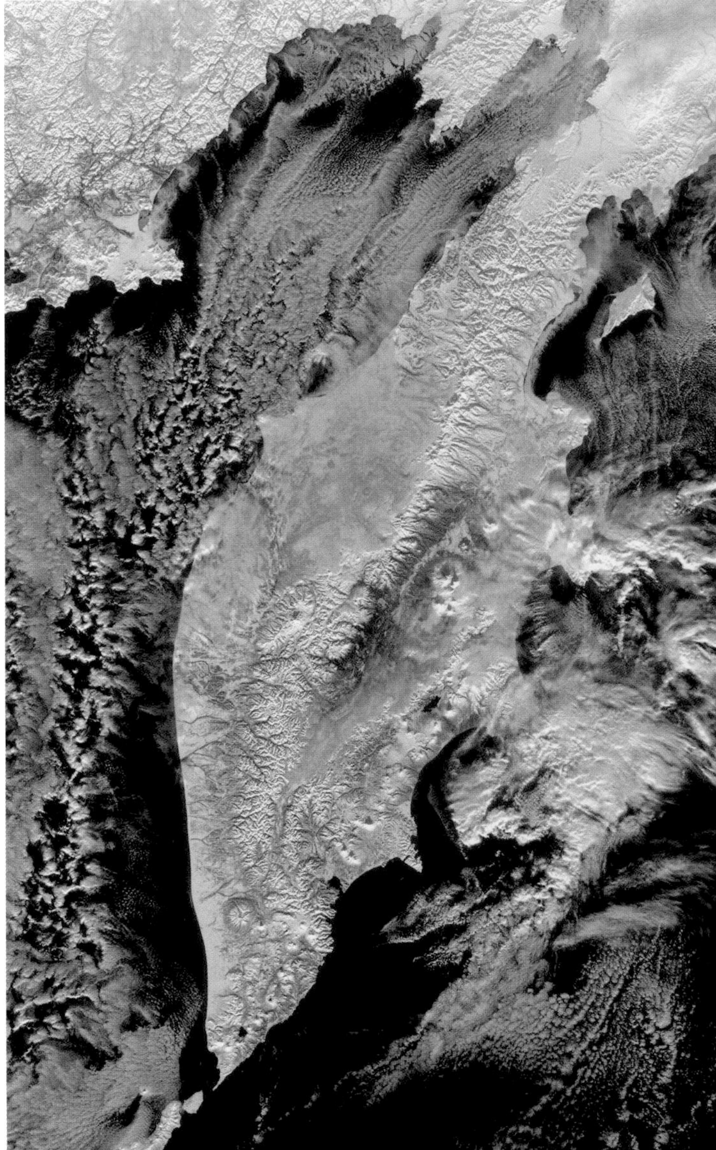

The Kamchatka Peninsula from space. The volcanic spine of the peninsula can be seen clearly.

Kamchatka

Geologically the peninsula is Mesozoic, its outline finally formed only in the Pleistocene. Gold and coal are mined in the north of the peninsula, while recently diamonds have begun to be mined in the south. Because of its size – it is 1,200km long, stretching from 51°N to 61°N – and the effect of the two latitudinal spines of extinct and active volcanoes, the peninsula is divided into five distinct longitudinal regions as well as having a pronounced climatic change between the southern tip and the northern peninsula, where it merges into Chukotka. From the west the five longitudinal zones are the western lowlands, the first longitudinal ridge (the Median or Sredinny Ridge), the central valley, the second (or eastern) ridge and the Eastern Volcanic Plateau. Each of these regions offers a different habitat for wildlife. The isolation and variation in habitat on the peninsula would be expected to produce a wealth of endemic species, but such is not the case, in part due to the effect of regular volcanic eruptions, and also due to the hostile climate. Though Kamchatka is borderline in terms of being an Arctic area as defined in this book, winter is very cold.

The peninsula is environmentally threatened as a consequence of the limited resources of the Russian state and the vast area, which is difficult to police. These two problems combine to allow poaching, in particular, to result in the over-exploitation of species. The peninsula's Brown Bears, renowned for their size, are now threatened by hunters. Petropavlosk is also one of the headquarters of the Russian Pacific Fleet, in particular its nuclear submarines, and it is known that radioactive leakage from waste disposal sites has occurred. In 1996 Kamchatka became a UNESCO World Heritage Site for its combination of scenery and geology, native peoples and wildlife.

Habitats and wildlife

As a consequence of the volcanism and the harsh winter climate only some 900 species of vascular plant have been identified, fewer (by *c.*10%) than the expected figure when considering latitude and general topography. Overall, the peninsula has tundra to the north, then a more complex mix of alpine tundra, volcanic landscape and forest to the south, much of the forest being shrubby forms such as Stone Pine *Pinus pumila* and Kamchatka Alder *Alnus kamtschatica*. Areas of the peninsula have now been designated as Zapodvedniks. Of these, the best scenery is without doubt in the Kronotsky Nature Preserve, which covers the Valley of the Geysers and the Uzon Caldera. In June 2007 a huge mudslide engulfed around 60% of the valley causing fears that it would be lost for ever, but it many of the geysers have become active again and there are hopes that, in time, the landscape will recover. Within the Preserve is one of the mysteries of botany, the Graceful Fir *Picea gracilis* which grows nowhere on Earth except one small area of Kronotsky. Native peoples considered the fir grove a sacred site. Other parks include the Koryakskiy at the northern end of the peninsula; the Yukno-Kamchatsky Preserve at the peninsula's southern tip, which includes lakes into which salmon swim for spawning, the runs accompanied by Steller's Sea Eagles and Brown Bears; the Nalychevo Nature Park, which covers the volcanoes close to Petropavlosk; the Bystrinsky Nature Park near the villages of Esso and Anavgai, which includes not only fine scenery and wildlife (the latter including Snow Sheep, Sable, Wolf and many bird species) but also covers the traditional pasture of the Reindeer-herding Eveni people; and the Klyuchevsky Nature Park, the newest park, to the east of the Bystrinsky.

For the wildlife observer, assuming that the significant (but usually not insurmountable – at a price) problems of access can be overcome, the wildlife highlights are undoubtedly the Brown Bears, Snow Sheep and Black-capped Marmot (the latter two essentially confined to the peninsula), Largha Seal, Steller's Sea Eagles, which are virtually confined to the southern peninsula, Black-billed Capercaillie, Far Eastern Curlew, Slaty-backed Gull, Spectacled Guillemot, Brown Dipper, Siberian Rubythroat, and Middendorf's Grasshopper Warbler, many of which are very rare or localised elsewhere.

Petropavlosk harbour in winter. The city is a long flight from Moscow, but in summer it can also be reached from Anchorage on a flight which crosses the International Date Line. The flight requires the traveller to think hard about which day the plane will land.

Zhupanovsky Volcano rises above the morning mist in this photograph from the Zhupanova River.

Travel

Kamchatka's volcanism offers the potential for geothermal energy as development and tourism grow. Visitors can reach Petropavlosk with flights from Moscow (crossing nine time zones in a nine-hour flight, which allows the interesting experience of return flights occasionally landing a few minutes before they took off, relatively speaking, and, if a connecting flight to western Europe is made, of allowing the traveller to experience a 36-hour day), Vladivostok and, during the summer months, Anchorage.

Commander Islands

East of central Kamchatka lie the two Komandorskiye Ostrova, the Commander Islands, named after Vitus Bering, commander of the Second Kamchatka Expedition of 1741–42 The larger of the islands is Bering Island, on which he died of scurvy when the return voyage to Petropavlosk was halted by winter. Bering's grave site is marked with an impressive memorial. The smaller island is Mednyy (Copper). Geologically, the Commander Islands form part of the 'Ring of Fire' chain, a continuation of the Aleutian Islands.

Visiting the islands is in one sense straightforward, flights being available from Petropavlosk, but the island weather is highly variable, with heavy rain, high winds and low cloud being frequent, so visitors may find themselves unable to reach Bering Island or unable to leave. A great deal of flexibility is therefore required, as is a willingness to suffer long delays.

Wildlife

In exchange for probable delays, the observer is offered a remarkably long list of birds, though the list of mammal species is much shorter and essentially confined to sea mammals, including Northern Fur Seal. It was on Bering Island that Georg Steller saw and described his sea cow. Breeding birds include many Bering Sea auks, including the Whiskered Auklet, plus Red-legged Kittiwakes, Red-faced Cormorants, Leach's and Fork-tailed Storm-petrels, and several smaller birds including Pechora and Red-throated Pipits, and a subspecies of either Arctic or Asian Rosy-finch (debate continues as to which species the Commander Island birds are related). The islands are now protected as a Zapovednik.

Bering Island, the largest of the Commander Islands.

ALASKA

With an area of more than 1,500,000km^2 Alaska represents about 16% of the total area of the United States. The landscape is dominated by the effect of the Pacific Plate subducting beneath the North American Plate, the movement having created the arc of volcanoes that forms the Alaska Peninsula and the Aleutian Islands, the upthrusting creating mountain ranges. Three mountain ranges cross the state: the Coastal Range in the south-east, a range whose arc continues as the Alaska Range north of Anchorage, which includes Mount McKinley, the highest North American peak, and the Brooks Range to the north. North of the Brooks Range is the North Slope; in this area are the oldest exposed rocks in the state. During the Ice Age the Brooks Range was covered by an ice cap, with ice-free land to the north and south, the whole of southern Alaska being beneath the Cordilleran ice sheet, an adjunct of the great Laurentide ice sheet, which covered much of North America.

Low sea levels during the ice ages led to the creation of Beringia. This meant people could move from Asia to North America, these being the ancestors of the Aleuts and Inuit who still occupy areas of the state. It is those early dwellers that named the region, though the exact derivation is not as clear-cut as is often claimed. The Athapaskans of the south-eastern state called the land to the west Alayeska (meaning Great Land to the West), and this is often quoted as the source of the name, but the name Unalaska, an island in the Aleutians, is said to derive from the Aleut *Agunalaksh* which refers to the way in which the sea crashed against the local land, appearing 'to break its back' in its effort to barge past. This name would seem to have an equally good claim as the derivation of Alaska.

Recent history

European peoples have only lived in Alaska for around 250 years. This period has seen occupation by the Russians and a sale to the United States. The Russians, particularly during the time when Alexander Baranov was manager of the Russian American Company, occupied many sites in southern Alaska, with distinctive Russian churches still being a feature of the area. Though the Russians principally settled the south of the state, they did explore much of the coastline; in 1816 Otto von Kotzebue reached a native Alaskan settlement in the north-west. The Russians were less active inland, though they did establish the Kolmakovski Redoubt on the Kuskokwim River, Nulato on the Yukon River, and Chitina on the Copper River.

Following the sale of Alaska to the United States there was an influx of people from the continental states, folk brought first by the prospect of gold, later by the oil industry and, in some cases, by a love of the wilderness, so that Alaskans of non-native heritage now dominate the population.

The sale of Alaska

The US purchase of Alaska – for $7.2 million, a price that, famously, worked out at 2 cents per acre – was not seen, at the time, as the bargain it is now considered. The Russians wanted the United States to have Alaska as they feared British ownership, Britain at the time being the predominant European power; if Canada expanded west to the Bering Sea, Russia would be 'surrounded' by Britain. The United States also feared British expansion to its north, but despite that the enthusiasm of William Seward, Secretary of State in 1867, for the purchase was not shared by most Americans, or by the press, and resulted in his ridicule. Alaska was Seward's Folly or Seward's Ice Box. After the purchase Congress, which had been reluctantly convinced, lost interest and the state remained a lawless place for two decades until the discovery of gold.

Travel

For the Arctic traveller, Alaska is the easiest destination for independent travel as car hire is readily available in many of the more interesting destinations – Anchorage, Barrow, Cold Bay, Nome. Quad bikes can be hired on St Lawrence Island, visitors to Pribilof are offered an out-and-back transfer service (and on St Paul one of the best auk-watching sites is within walking distance of the only available accommodation), while boat trips from Dutch Harbour help search out the elusive Whiskered Auklet. Bus transport is readily available in the Denali National Park. Some magnificent country can only be reached by aircraft and walking, but in general the species of interest can be observed in the most accessible areas.

Alaska's extraordinary scenic beauty, and the state's importance for Arctic and sub-Arctic animals, has led to the creation of a number of National Parks, Preserves and National Wildlife Refuges: many of these will be mentioned in the sections below. Details of all the refuges, together with access information, are available as a leaflet from the US Fish and Wildlife Service, US Department of the Interior. The leaflet is usually available from tourist outlets in the main towns.

The north

The most readily accessible northern destination is Barrow, which is reached by regular scheduled flights and where accommodation, restaurants and vehicle hire are available. From one restaurant I was once able to combine enjoyment of a meal with the photography of a Snowy Owl perched on the tundra, with sea ice forming a background. Excursions from the town will allow the traveller to stand at Point Barrow, where the Chukchi Sea meets the Beaufort Sea. The tundra around Barrow is often wet; it is the breeding ground of both Steller's and Spectacled Eiders, as well as other wildfowl and a fine collection of northern waders. Breeding birds from Russia are also seen frequently, these including Curlew Sandpiper, Sharp-tailed Sandpiper, Red-necked Stint and Grey-tailed Tattler. The autumn 'invasion' of Ross's Gulls, once such a feature of Barrow, has declined significantly in recent years, the gulls now rarely being seen in large numbers and, indeed, becoming increasingly rare as the ice moves further north.

To the west of Barrow, between the townships of Wainwright and Point Lay, and reachable only by chartered aircraft, are Icy Cape, a viewpoint for migrating birds and cetaceans, and Kasegaluk Lagoon, a premier site for wildfowl and waders. Permission is required to visit the area. Permission is also required for the Teshekpuk Lake area to the east of Barrow, another excellent spot for wildfowl and waders.

The west

Alaska's west coast is difficult to access except on the southern Seward Peninsula, where regular scheduled flights to Nome

Alaskan gold and oil

Gold was first discovered in south-east Alaska, near Juneau, but in 1898 it was also discovered at Nome, the 'Three Lucky Swedes', Jon Brynteson, Eric Lindblom and Jafet Lindeberg finding gold at Anvil Creek near the Snake River. The gold rush that followed brought miners, and entrepreneurs who sold articles and services to the miners, as well as finding numerous other ways of relieving them of their cash. By 1900 Nome was Alaska's biggest town. One of the town's more famous inhabitants was the legendary gambler and lawman Wyatt Earp. In its wake the gold rush brought a sense of statehood to Alaskans, but it was not until 1959 that it became the 49th state of the Union.

The discovery of oil at Prudhoe Bay in 1968 brought phenomenal wealth to the newly created state, the oil being transferred by a 1,250km pipeline to Valdez, an ice-free port on the southern coast. There were fears that the pipeline would disrupt the migration of Caribou. These fears have proved largely unfounded, though the *Exxon Valdez* disaster of 1989 showed that fears of the effect of an oil spillage were justified. Oil drilling in the Arctic National Wildlife Refuge (ANWR) has been the cause of fierce debate in recent years, a decision in early 2005 to go ahead with the project causing consternation in environmental circles as the area is much more sensitive than Prudhoe Bay.

Environmentalists fear not only oil drilling, but also the principle. There is such a limited amount of oil in ANWR that it is barely worth pursuing, the environmentalists believing that its exploitation will represent the thin end of a wedge: if permission is granted to drill here, there is no reason to deny drilling anywhere. Since the 2005 vote there has been a decline in President George W. Bush's popularity and the decision to drill has not been endorsed. However, there has not, as yet, been a formal decision not to drill.

The photographs are (*above*) an old gold dredger at Nome, and (*below*) an aerial view of the southern section of ANWR.

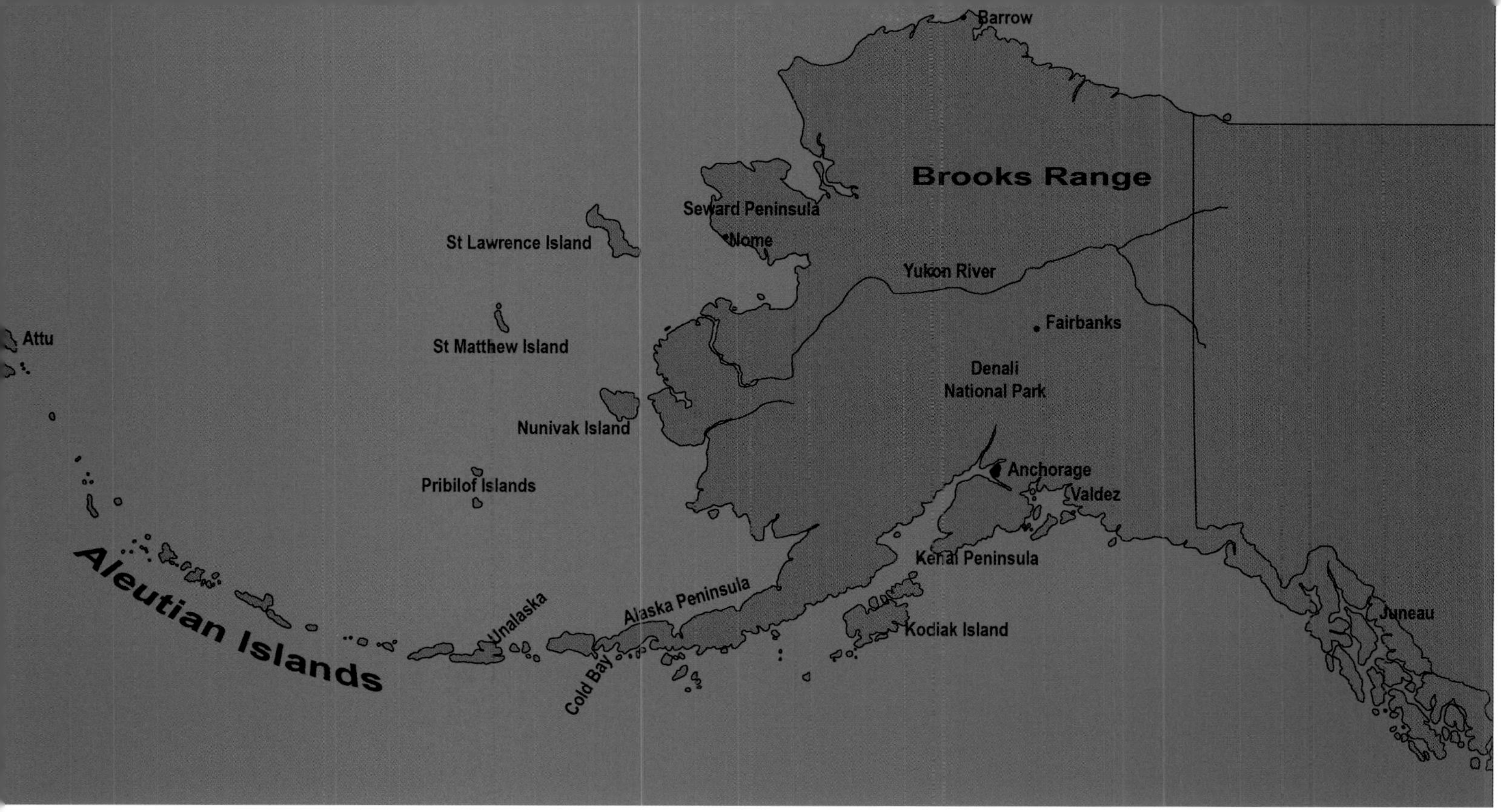

Barrow
Brooks Range
Seward Peninsula
Nome
St Lawrence Island
Yukon River
Fairbanks
Attu
St Matthew Island
Denali
National Park
Nunivak Island
Pribilof Islands
Anchorage
Valdez
Kenai Peninsula
Aleutian Islands
Unalaska
Alaska Peninsula
Kodiak Island
Juneau
Cold Bay

In this view of north-west Alaska from space, the Bering Strait, Russia's Chukchi Peninsula can be seen, together with the Diomede Islands, St Lawrence Island and the Seward Peninsula.

and vehicle hire there allow exploration of three roads (to Council, Taylor and Teller). Each year this access persuades many birdwatchers to come, searching for Bristle-thighed Curlew and Bluethroat, which breed in the area, and other rare North American species. Aleutian Terns nest beside the Nome–Council road. New World sparrows and warblers are also relatively common. For relaxation the traveller can view the wooden archway that is the end of the Iditarod dog-sledge race, the site of Wyatt Earp's saloon, and the bust of Roald Amundsen, which commemorates the arrival of the airship *Norge* at Teller after it had overflown the North Pole in 1926

To the north of Nome, on the north side of the Seward Peninsula, the Bering Land Bridge National Preserve is excellent for breeding and migrating birds, and sea and terrestrial mammals. The Preserve has a mix of habitats, including wet and dry tundra, forest tundra and numerous lakes. The coastal region includes a number of salt lagoons important for wildfowl. The Preserve can be reached by chartered aircraft from Nome and Kotzebue, a town on the Baldwin Peninsula across Kotzebue Sound from the Preserve. To the south of Nome across Norton Sound is the Yukon Delta National Wildlife Refuge, which includes the deltas of both the Yukon and

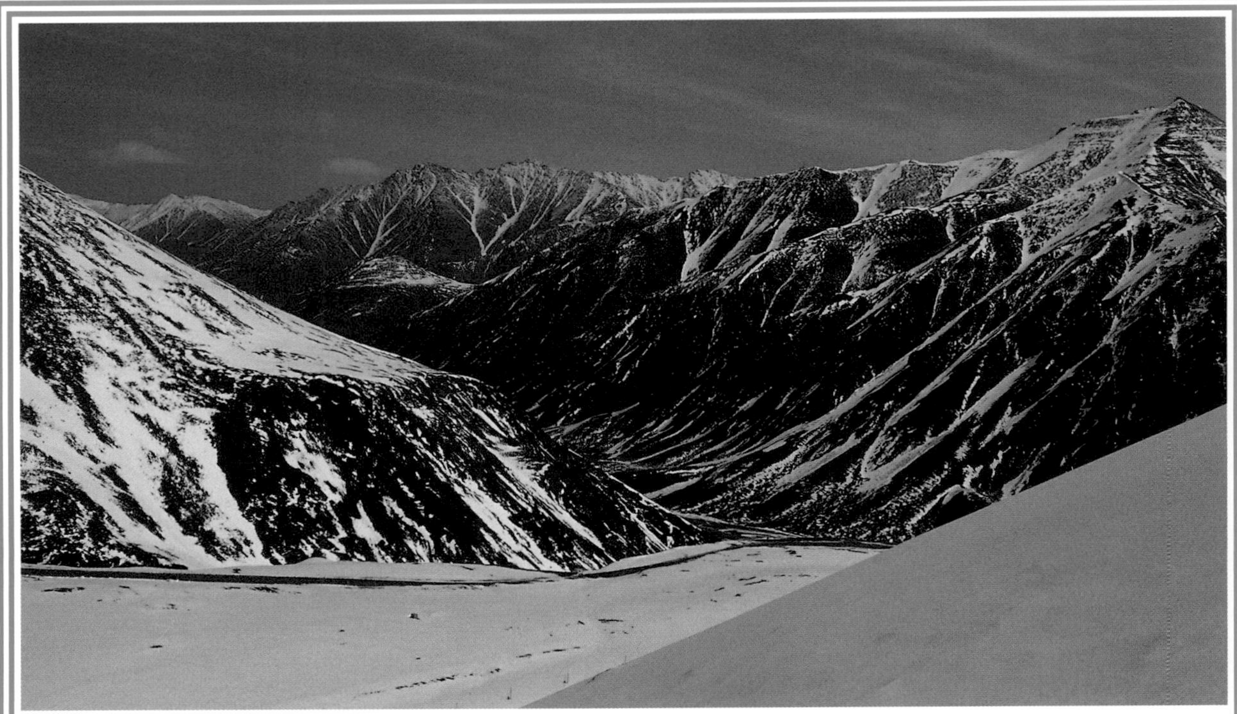

The Dalton Highway

The Dalton Highway links Fairbanks to Prudhoe Bay. It is the haul road for the oil industry. Formerly closed to visitors the road is now open as far as Deadhorse, a township close to the oil complex. Visitors wishing to view the complex itself are required to join an organised tour as security concerns mean that casual visitors are not allowed. The Dalton Highway is gravel and suffers from winter degradation so that sections may be potholed or under repair. There are limited facilities along the way, and none between Coldfoot and Deadhorse, so travellers must be self-sufficient in case problems arise.

The journey crosses the Arctic Circle, cutting through the Brooks Range at Atigun Pass, and edges the Gates of the Arctic National Park to the west and the Arctic National Wildlife Refuge to the east, though in each case a long walk or a chartered aircraft is required for access. The Refuge is an important denning area for Polar Bears, and home to the Porcupine Caribou herd. Both the National Park and the Refuge are excellent for mammals and birds, and for their scenery, as are the Noatak National Preserve, to the west of the Gates Park (and contiguous with it), and the Kobuk Valley National Park to the south. South of the Brooks Range, and normally accessed by air charter from Bettles, is the Kanuti National Wildlife Refuge, a vast area of wetlands and forest important for its waterfowl and wader populations, as well as for Moose, Wolf and Brown Bear.

The photograph above is of the view south from the top of the Atigun Pass, the highest point on the Highway.

The Gates of the Arctic National Park. The photograph was taken where the Noatak River leaves the Park.

Kuskokwim rivers. Offshore is Nunivak Island, which is a separate refuge. Regular flights reach St Mary's, on the Yukon River, Bethel, on the Kuskokwim, and Mekoryuk on Nunivak Island, but to reach deep into the Preserves the traveller will need to charter flights or walk. Birdwatchers visit in spring and autumn in the hope of catching sight of McKay's Bunting.

Further south is the Togiak National Wildlife Refuge, and the adjacent, coastal, Cape Newenham Wildlife Refuge, with upland tundra as well as excellent coastal sites. The closest town is Dillingham (reached by regular scheduled flights), which is also the starting point for trips to the Walrus Islands State Game Sanctuary. Most travellers visit Round Island, a famous haul-out for the Pacific subspecies of Walrus, and a nesting area for Pacific auks. Access to the island is controlled, so permission must be sought. Travellers must also be entirely self-sufficient and willing to experience unplanned extensions of their trip, both before leaving for the island and once on it, as bad weather frequently makes landings impossible.

The Iditarod dog-sledge race

The Iditarod Trail had its origins in the need to service gold-mining communities (one of which was Iditarod itself). Post and supplies were moved by dog sledge during the long (up to eight-month) snow-bound months of the northern winter, gold being taken out the same way. In January 1925 diphtheria broke out in Nome and the local doctor, Dr Curtis Welch, had limited supplies of serum. He placed the town in quarantine and sent an urgent request for assistance. Aircraft had only recently begun to be operated in Alaska, and there was no experience of winter flying and landing, so teams of dogs rushed the serum from Seward to Nome. The lead dog of the last team, Balto, became a hero and legend of the north, and a statue of him stands in New York's Central Park (the statue was unveiled in December 1925 by Balto himself, aided by his owner, Gunnar Kaasen, driver of the final leg of the journey). In the late 1960s the historian Dorothy Page and a local man, Joe Redington, decided to revive long-distance dog-sledging, partly in commemoration of the serum run, but also as a memorial of the role played by dog teams in the history of Alaska. The first official Iditarod race was held in 1973. The race is now annual, starting in Anchorage and finishing 1,680km later in Nome. One interesting aspect of the race has been the number of women who have won it, the prevalence of female victors at one stage leading to the phrase *Alaska: where men are men and women win the Iditarod* adorning many a T-shirt and becoming the state's unofficial slogan.

The south

Southern Alaska has so many possibilities for the independent traveller that to mention them all is beyond the scope of this book (plus it lies outside the Arctic as defined in this book). Nevertheless, few travellers to Alaska, having landed in Anchorage, will decline the plethora of opportunities for eating and sleeping offered by the state's largest city (though not its capital, that being Juneau in south-east Alaska), and the chances of wildlife viewing offered by the extensive local road system.

Moose are often seen in Kincaid Park, and at Potter Marsh, which lies beside the road heading east for Seward. Potter Marsh is also a good bird site. Further along the Seward road look out for Dall's Sheep on the cliffs close to Beluga Point (on one occasion I saw Dall's Sheep actually on the road). Beluga Point, overlooking Turnagain Arm, is a good lookout for the whales of the name. Close to Girdwood and the Portage/Whittier turn, evidence of the 1964 earthquake can still be seen. Whittier, now reached by a tunnel, was built during the 1939–45 war as a military base following the Japanese attack on the Aleutians. It was made to be inaccessible, and could only be reached by sea and rail before the tunnel was blasted. From the town boat trips are available to Prince William Sound, where there are Sea Otters and Pacific auks.

At Seward boat trips can be made to Resurrection Bay, where there is a Steller's Sea Lion colony. These trips usually encounter Sea Otters (which may also be seen in Seward harbour), and pass below Pacific auk colonies. Homer, reached by turning off the Seward road, is well known for its winter congregations of Bald Eagles. Homer Spit is good for waders and wildfowl, these including Black Turnstone, the three scoters and Harlequin Duck. Between Seward and Homer lies the Kenai Fjords National Park, which has breeding colonies of Marbled and Kittlitz's Auklets, Pigeon Guillemot, other Pacific auks and sea mammals. South of the Kenai Peninsula, Kodiak Island, reached by regular scheduled flights from Anchorage, is famous for its Brown Bears, often claimed to be the largest on Earth.

South-west across Cook Inlet from Anchorage is the Katmai National Park and, to its north, the McNeil River State Game Sanctuary, each famous for the annual Brown Bear feasts on spawning salmon. At McNeil visitor numbers are restricted to those lucky enough to have their name drawn from a lottery; it costs money to apply for one of the places

The Seward Peninsula north of Nome.

Western Alaska from space.

Looking east over the Iliuk Arm of Naknek Lake, Katmai National Park and Preserve.

Tikchik Mountain in the Wood-Tikchik State Park. The park is to the north of Dillingham.

and 90% of those who apply are unlucky. As well as bears the Katmai Park also has Beaver and Wolf.

On the Alaskan Peninsula a flight on a clear day offers stunning views of the peninsula's volcanic backbone, though the best volcano scenery is actually further on, on Unimak Island. At Cold Bay accommodation and vehicle hire are possible. The scenery here is excellent, though frequently mist-shrouded, the main wildlife interest being within the Izembek National Wildlife Refuge. Named after Karl von Izembek, the surgeon on the *Seniavine*, Feodor Lutka's ship during his exploratory trip of 1826–29, the refuge was set up to protect a lagoon that includes more than 18,000ha of eelgrass, over 50% of the world's total acreage of the plant. Each year the eelgrass attracts some 200,000 geese. More than 95% of the world population of the Black Brant stop here to feed before their flight south. Other wildfowl also visit, and some Emperor Geese and Steller's Eider spend the winter on the lagoon. The area is also good for Pigeon Guillemot, waders and songbirds, the latter including Golden-crowned Sparrow.

South-east Alaska

Though Anchorage is Alaska's largest city it is not the state capital, that being Juneau in the detached, south-eastern part of the state. Close to Juneau, travellers can get a close-up view of the Mendenhall Glacier, watch for breaching or bubble-netting Humpback Whales in the Lynn Canal, fly to Admiralty Island to see Brown Bears – the island has the highest density of bears on Earth – or walk in the temperate rainforest that links the mountains behind the city to the sea.

Denali National Park

Though not a part of the Arctic as defined here, there are few travellers who will visit Alaska and not drive north from Anchorage to see Mount McKinley or to visit Denali National Park. At 6,194m McKinley is the highest mountain in North America. The Athabaskan name for the mountain, Denali – Great One – has now been given to the park that surrounds it, the mountain having been given the name of William McKinley (25th President of the United States, who was assassinated in 1901).

In clear weather there is a magnificent view of McKinley from the road heading north, towards the park, from Anchorage. Though much lower than the Himalayan peaks, McKinley rises almost 5,500m from the surrounding plateau (compared to the 3,350m that Everest rises above its base), a true giant. The view from the Eielson Visitor Centre site

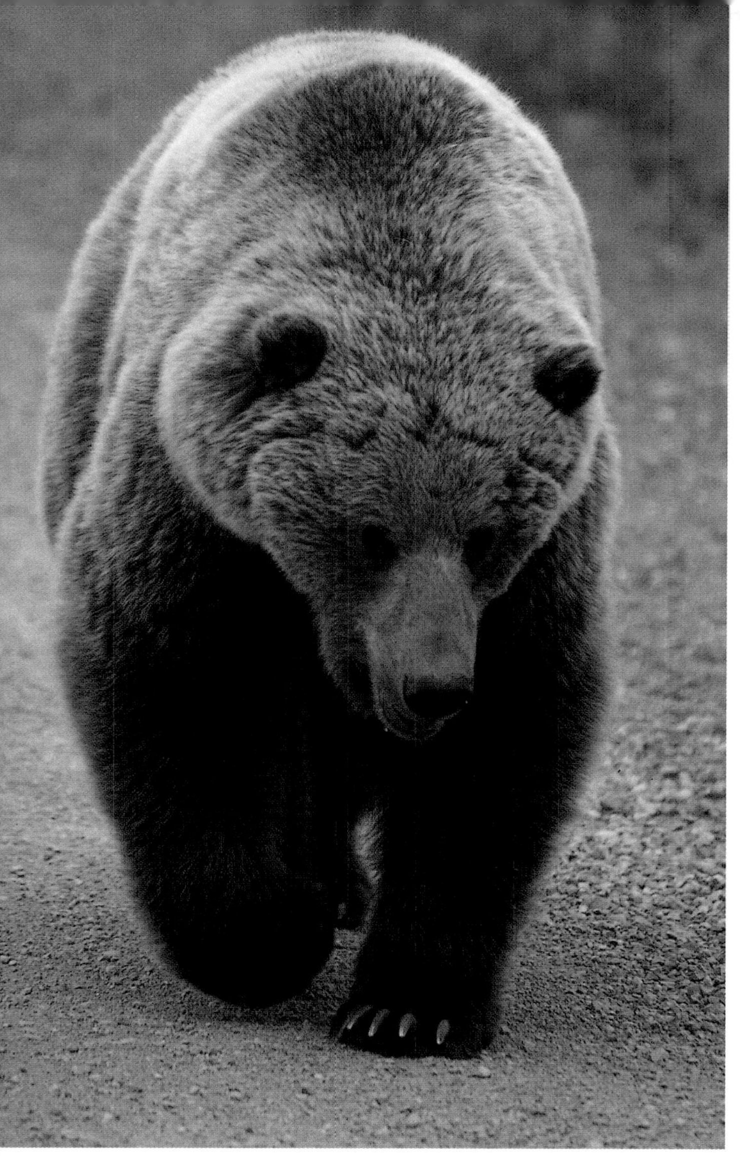

The ascent of Mount McKinley

The peak was first climbed in 1913 by a team led by Hudson Stuck (comprising Walter Harper, Harry Karstens, Robert Tatum and Stuck himself), though that ascent was preceded by the claim of a first ascent by Frederick Cook in 1906, which was later disputed. The debate over whether Cook's ascent was actually fraudulent has raged ever since; his companion on the climb later testified that they had not reached the summit, but this change of story is itself viewed with suspicion as he appears to have been paid for the disclaimer. Cook's story was not aided by his later disputed claim to have reached the North Pole and by the fact that his 'summit' photograph was clearly taken on a different mountain. Nevertheless Cook has an admirable, irrefutable claim as an explorer and there are still some who are minded to believe both his claims, though they are in the minority.

After Cook's claim another summit claim was made in 1910 by four 'sourdoughs', the somewhat disparaging name given to local gold panners. The four announced that they had summitted wearing their ordinary clothes, eating bacon, beans and Caribou meat along the way, and had planted a 4½m spruce trunk at the top as a flagpole, hanging a 2m x 4m US flag from it. The team comprised Welshman Tom Lloyd, the leader, Pete Anderson, Charlie McGonagall and Billy Taylor, though only Anderson and Taylor actually made it to the summit. The whole thing seemed so unlikely – especially as the men claimed to have climbed the last 2,400m to the top and descend again in 18 hours, a rate better than the vast majority of modern climbers can achieve – that it was dismissed by many, but on the true first ascent Stuck's team claimed to have seen the spruce pole on the mountain's North Summit. This claim is also viewed with suspicion by many, but if true the irony is that although the sourdoughs really had climbed to the top, they had reached the lower summit. Stuck's team went on to scale the higher South Summit.

Left
One of Denali's bears using a park road as an easy way to get around. Most visitors to the park see a bear, though not always in such exciting circumstances.

Opposite page above
The twin summits of McKinley. It was taken from the site where, at the time of shooting, the new Eielson Visitor Centre is being constructed.

Opposite page below
The north side of McKinley at sunset, taken from Wonder Lake.

(being rebuilt at the time of writing) on the road to Wonder Lake, where the two summits can be seen, is equally impressive. The Denali National Park was set up to protect the exquisite scenery around the peak, and local mammals and birds. A total of 37 mammal species, including Brown (Grizzly) Bear, Wolf, Beaver and Hoary Marmot, and more than 130 bird species have been identified in the park, the latter including Gyrfalcons.

The Aleutian Islands

The Aleutian Islands, together with the US sector of the Bering Sea, the Chukchi Sea (again the US sector), the sea around the Alaska Peninsula, the Gulf of Alaska, and a limited amount of 'mainland' shoreline form the Alaska Maritime National Wildlife Refuge, within which it is estimated that 40 million seabirds breed.

The Aleutian chain of islands lies immediately north of the Aleutian Trench, where the Pacific Plate subducts beneath the North American Plate. A cross-section of the Earth's crust at Adak Island would show the Pacific Plate at a depth of 5,000m diving down into the trench, to a depth of 7,500m, the North American Plate then rising to 1,100m on the island, giving a total height difference from the trench bed to Adak's highest point of 8,600m. Though the whole Aleutian chain is essentially volcanic, the most spectacular peaks are Shishaldin and Isanotski on Unimak Island, the former being a near perfect volcanic cone.

Travel to the Aleutians is not straightforward, particularly for the wildlife observer, as many of the best sites are either off-limits or very difficult to reach. Buldir Island, for instance, is closed to all except research workers, and even they have difficulty in landing. There are regular flights to Dutch Harbour where accommodation and vehicle hire is possible. Bald Eagles and Ravens abound here, but other birdlife is more elusive, though the Aleutian subspecies of Green-winged Teal can usually be found, as can the Grey-crowned Rosy-finch. However, most enthusiasts come for a sight of the Whiskered Auklet. For this a boat trip is required as the birds breed on uninhabited Uniaga Island to the west, and feed on the Chelan Banks. Unalaska was the first permanent Russian settlement in Alaska: the Church of the Holy Ascension, begun in 1825 and enlarged in 1894, is now the oldest Russian church in the state.

Below
Because of the chain's position, the weather on the Aleutians is often cloudy, but the views and interest are still maintained, Unalaska.

War in the Aleutians

Attu and Kiska Island, to the east, were occupied by the Japanese in June 1942, the only part of the United States to have been invaded and occupied during the war (though the Pacific island of Guam and the Philippines, both at the time US territories, were also occupied). Prior to the invasion, Dutch Harbour, the only place on the islands where there was a US military base, was attacked by aircraft from two carriers and by two heavy cruisers. On two successive days, 3–4 June, the town was attacked, but the Americans had spotted the Japanese fleet as it neared the island and were able to inflict sufficient damage for the Japanese to turn away. Then on 7 June 1,200 Japanese troops took Attu and Kiska.

The retaking of Attu in May 1943 involved heavy fighting over a 19-day period (11–29 May). The Americans landed 11,000 troops to battle with a Japanese force that by then numbered 2,600. Realising that defeat was certain, the Japanese commander ordered his men to fight to the death. Wounded soldiers were ordered to commit suicide, those physically unable to do so being given lethal injections. The Americans took only 28 prisoners. American losses were 549 dead and 1,148 wounded; as a percentage of fatalities of those taking part, Attu was second only to Iwo Jima in terms of losses for US forces. After Attu had been taken, the Americans launched an attack on Kiska. It had been defended by 5,000 Japanese, and fearing another bloody conflict the Americans sent in 35,000 American and Canadian troops, after several weeks of continuous bombing. To the relief of everyone, when the force landed on 14 August they discovered that the Japanese had removed all their men by sea during a period of heavy fog at the end of July.

The photograph above shows an old gun emplacement at Fort Abercrombie State Historical Park, Kodiak Island.

Until recently flights were also available to Attu as part of commercial bird tours. Attu is an interesting destination as the island, the most westerly of the Aleutians, lies close to Kamchatka; Asian birds are frequently seen there. However, these flights have now ceased, though whether this is temporary or permanent remains to be seen.

Another option for the traveller is the Alaska Marine Highway ferry, which operates from Kodiak to Dutch Harbour. It is intermittent, but it does have the advantage of stopping at some of the remote villages along the way and, if the weather is clear, of offering spectacular views of volcanoes.

Native fox populations once existed only on the islands as far west as Unimak, to which they were able to cross over winter sea ice; the island group from the Unimak Pass to the Samalga Pass is known as the Fox Islands because Bering noted the sizeable fox population during his first visit. However, both Red and Arctic Foxes were introduced to other islands to boost trapping income, the initial introductions being made by the Russians, who transported Arctic Foxes from the Commander Islands (where their numbers had caused such a headache for Bering's expedition). Only Bogoslof, Buldir and Chagulak escaped introductions, the former because they were so inaccessible, the latter because it was too rugged. The foxes had a devastating effect on the local bird populations, which had evolved in a terrestrial predator-free world and were not only responsible for a general decline in bird numbers but for driving the Aleutian subspecies of Lesser Canada Goose to the edge of extinction. Thankfully, the existence of fox-free islands

Autumn on the Kenai Peninsula.

Summer on the Kenai Peninsula. Pools such as this are a favourite haunt of Moose.

and the recent eradication of foxes on others has allowed the goose to increase in numbers. However, despite these eradications Buldir Island, with less than 1% of the land area of the Aleutians, has 70% of the total breeding population of the chain's birds, a total of over 3,500,000 birds from more than 30 species, including 12 auks plus Red-legged Kittiwakes.

Foxes are just one of several environmental threats with which Aleutian wildlife is, or has been, faced. In the 1960s the USA transferred its nuclear weapon testing from the Nevada Desert to Amchitka Island: in 1971 the last of a total of three tests was carried out.

The Pribilofs and other Bering Sea islands

North of the Aleutian chain lie the Pribilof Islands, St Paul and St George. The islands are reached by scheduled flight from Anchorage, which requires good visibility for landing, and good bladder control for passengers. On each of the islands there is a hostel that will accommodate visitors on a full-board basis (meals being taken at the local fish plant). Seasonal guides transport visitors around the island to the best wildlife viewing sites and also offer information. It is possible to be dropped at one place and collected from another a few hours later. The islands are excellent for Pacific auks and seabirds, the latter including Red-legged Kittiwakes, and for the occasional Asian rarity. St Paul is the primary breeding ground of the Northern Fur Seal, with vast colonies of seals occupying a few beaches during the breeding period. Arctic Foxes patrol the beaches at this time looking for afterbirths and stillborn or unattended cubs.

North of the Pribilofs are Matthew and Hall islands, on which McKay's Buntings breed. Each island is difficult to access and requires specific permission. St Lawrence Island, further to the north, is easier to reach, with regular scheduled flights linking Nome to Savoonga and Gambell. Of the two, Gambell is the more usual destination as it is renowned for its birdlife, particularly migrants. As Chukotka is only some 80km away and clearly visible, Asian species are frequent visitors to Gambell (the border between the United States and Russia, which crosses the Bering Sea between Gambell and Chukotka, is also the International Date Line, so that when standing on the beach looking across the 80km of sea it is tomorrow over there). Mammal watching at Gambell is poor to non-existent, as the local native population still hunt extensively (they have an annual Bowhead quota) and visitors are not allowed to travel outside a very restricted area to seek out more likely places. Transport in the form of quad bikes, to ease the burden of walking across the unremitting Gambell shingle, is readily available in the village. Hostel accommodation is also available, but meals are limited and most visitors prepare their own using a communal microwave. Food can be bought at the village shop.

Above
Kodiak Island, southern Alaska.

Right
Moose Pass, Kenai Peninsula, southern Alaska.

Above
Bylot Island across Pond Inlet, Canada.

Left
Victoria Island across Coronation Gulf, Canada.

CANADA

Canada is the second largest country on Earth, and its northern islands represent a large fraction of the land area of the Arctic. Because of the vagaries of the world's climate, the 'Arctic' also extends much further south into mainland Canada than it does into mainland Russia; the combined area of the Yukon and North West Territories together with Nunavut represents 40% of Canada. As a consequence, to attempt a realistic overview of the country is beyond the scope of this book. Below only brief notes on the area's National Parks and major wildlife sites are given.

For a map of Canada, see p146.

General travel

Travel to the Canadian Arctic usually involves charter flights and, consequently, a good deal of preparation, but more recently Russian ice-breaker cruises have been venturing into the area, offering trips through the North-West Passage – both the southern (approximately following the line of Amundsen's transit) and northern (via Melville Sound and McClure Strait) routes, and around Baffin Island.

In general the Canadian Arctic has escaped the major pollution threats seen in Russia and Alaska, though there are concerns at the extent of logging in the boreal belt at the Arctic fringe. The creation of Nunavut will hopefully ensure that exploitation of the north is well managed, but work will be required to escape an arising problem that the entrepreneurial skills needed to exploit the tourist potential of the area, with its heady mix of scenery, wildlife, history and native peoples, is coming from southerners, and that the tourist money is heading south rather than staying in the area. It is to be hoped that the Inuit gain some real, rather than apparent, control over the future of Nunavut instead of becoming attractions in a theme park territory.

YUKON

Bordering Alaska to the west, though separated from south-eastern Alaska by a sliver of British Columbia, Yukon stretches north from the St Elias Mountains (which include Mount Logan, Canada's highest peak) to the shores of the Arctic Ocean. At Yukon's Snag Weather Station the lowest temperature recorded to date in North America, -62.8°C, was registered, but the same station has also recorded a summer high of 31.7°C.

In the south of Yukon Territory, Whitehorse can be reached by air, as can Dawson City, close to the centre of the Territory, though the drive between the two towns through the Dawson Range is stunning. North of Dawson the traveller can drive the Dempster Highway to Inuvik in neighbouring North West Territories, from where a plane may be chartered to visit the two northern Yukon National Parks. Flights also link Dawson and Inuvik via Old Crow.

National Parks

In the north of mainland Yukon are two National Parks. The Ivvavik National Park extends from the British Mountains to the Arctic Ocean, including a section of coastline. Ivvavik escaped the glaciation of the last Ice Age and formed part of the Beringia Refuge, and consequently has an interesting flora. The park is the calving ground of the 125,000-strong Porcupine Caribou herd (the park's name means 'nursery' in the language of the local Gwich'in people), and has Brown Bear, Wolf and Dall's Sheep, and is a major migration stop-over for northern geese, with more than 100,000 Snow Geese gathering here to feed in the autumn.

To the south is the Vuntut National Park, which shares a border, and the British Mountains, with the Ivvavik. The park comprises a vast wetland plain with about 20,000 shallow lakes, ringed by mountains. It has populations of Brown Bear, Moose and Muskrat, and is an important breeding ground for waterfowl and waders. The park is also on the migration route of the Porcupine Caribou. To the west the two parks extend to the Alaska–Canada border and are contiguous with the Arctic National Wildlife Refuge.

The Klondike Gold Rush

In August 1896 George Carmack, a porter who had married a native American called Kate, Kate's brother, a man with the unlikely name of Skookum Jim, and another native, one with the equally unlikely name of Tagish Charlie, discovered gold at Rabbit Creek (later renamed Bonanza Creek), an inflow to the Klondike River. Exactly how the first gold was discovered has become the subject of myth; each of the men claimed to have seen the first nugget, and Kate Carmack also claimed to have found it while she was doing George's washing. However the discovery was made, it ignited the Klondike Gold Rush. Estimates vary, but it is likely that 40,000 hopeful men made their way to the Yukon, most arriving by sea at Skagway in south-eastern Alaska and fighting their way along the Chilkoot Trail. In winter the trail, which included a steep, icy path to a bitterly cold, windswept pass, represented a nightmare journey, but a necessity for the men (who had to transport their supplies and equipment as well as themselves) as there was no other route. Later, when the wealth of the Klondike strike became apparent, Dawson City grew up at the confluence of the Yukon and Klondike rivers (and close to where Bonanza Creek joined the Klondike) and stern wheelers plied the Yukon, taking the gold out and bringing miners, and those who profited hugely from them, in.

To get at the gold-bearing gravels the miners first had to thaw the permafrost, something they accomplished initially with wood fires, though later steam was used. The extracted pay gravel was then stored until the spring thaw brought an abundance of water for sluicing.

The photograph above is of Dawson City.

The Dempster Highway links Dawson City (though it actually starts from the Klondike Highway a short distance to the east) and Inuvik. As with the Dalton Highway it is gravel and so needs care to drive, but it is more plentifully supplied with accommodation and food stops. It does, however, involve two ferry crossings (of the Peel and Mackenzie rivers). The ferries are free, but operate only during the summer months. In winter there are ice roads on the frozen rivers, but crossings are not possible during freeze-up and break-up. The Dempster is much shorter than the Dalton (it is only 270km to Inuvik), but it passes through equally impressive scenery.

Across Workboat Passage from the Ivvavik Park is Herschel Island. Herschel – named by John Franklin for the British father-and-son astronomers – is the only island on Yukon's coast and is used by Caribou as a calving ground. Bowhead Whales and Beluga swim close to the island as they migrate, and waterfowl migrating to and from their northern breeding grounds stop here to 'refuel'. As a consequence the island attracted Inuit hunters, and excavations have revealed the presence of Thule people dating back at least 1,000 years. Over 100 early Inuit graves have been found. Later the island was a base station for the American whaling fleet, the fleet wintering here after hunting whales to the east. Charter flights to Herschel are available, chiefly from Inuvik, travellers being able to observe not only migrating birds and cetaceans in season but a good number of breeding species as well; Herschel is noted for its population of Rough-legged Buzzards. Caribou, Brown Bear and Arctic Fox are also likely to be seen, particularly the latter as the island has a thriving population.

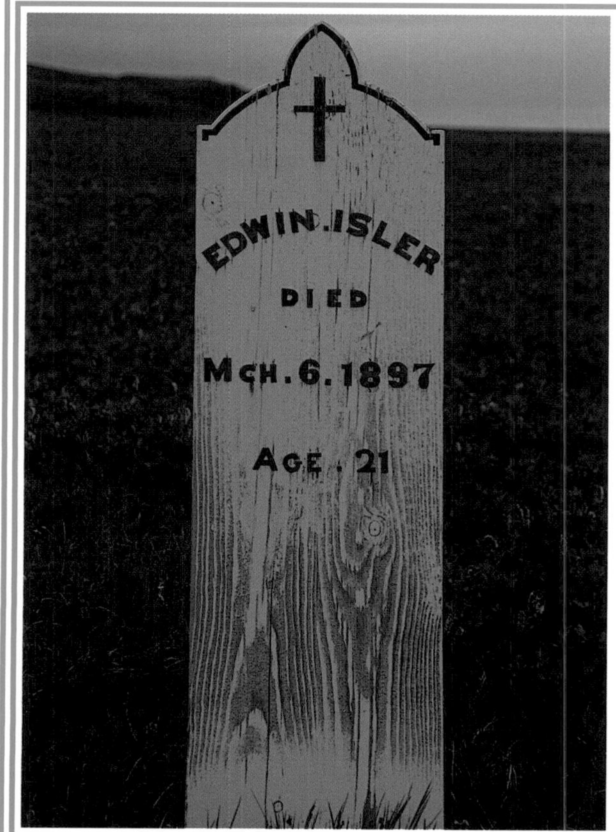

Herschel Island whalers

Herschel Island's whaler graveyard holds the remains of 24 whaling fleet men. Five of these died on 6 March 1897 when a baseball match under a blue sky, with the temperature at around 20°C, turned into a nightmare in seconds when a sudden storm and white-out enveloped the island, dropping the temperature to -20°C and visibility to zero. The five were found frozen to death the next morning, a reminder of the way in which an apparently benign Arctic can quickly turn hostile.

Dreadful though the tragedy was, it pales in the face of the devastation of the local Inuit population from diseases – chiefly syphilis and measles – brought by the whalers. It is estimated that around 90% of the Inuit of the island and local mainland died during the last decades of the 19th century. This, and tales of the debauchery of the whalers, brought the Royal Canadian Mounted Police to the island in 1903 (there are also RCMP graves on Herschel), though the problems only ceased when the whale population had been hunted to the point where whaling was no longer economic, and a flu epidemic forced the last whalers to leave.

Eight years after the baseball tragedy Roald Amundsen landed at Herschel having completed the first transit of the North-West Passage. Amundsen left his ship, *Gjøa*, here, travelling overland to Eagle City to announce his success.

The Mackenzie delta.

NORTH WEST TERRITORIES

Until 1 April 1999 North West Territories included all of Arctic Canada other than northern Yukon and the mainland east of Hudson Bay. At that time the creation of Nunavut split the old territory, though the rump decided to retain the name. The new North West Territories extends from the Yukon eastwards to include Paulutuk and the coast beyond as far as Clinton Point, then follows a series of curious northerly and easterly straight lines, with the occasional deviation to include (or exclude) certain areas, taking in a part of Victoria Island, the whole of Banks Island and parts of the Parry and Queen Elizabeth islands.

Inuvik is the most accessible town in the northern part of the territory, reached by scheduled flights, by road along the Dempster Highway, or on board the *Norweta* which journeys once a year along the Mackenzie River from Yellowknife to Inuvik and back. The *Norweta* takes 10 days downriver, 12 days upriver. West of Inuvik is the Mackenzie delta, one of the world's largest. The delta covers around 10,000km^2, the channels being alluvial and mobile. Underlying the delta is an area of permafrost that supports many shallow lakes in summer, so that the whole area is an ideal habitat for waterfowl and waders. The delta is, of course, difficult to access except by specialised craft, and travellers could easily become confused and lost in the shifting channels, but tours are available from Inuvik. If the Eskimo Curlew has escaped extinction (a somewhat forlorn hope), the delta is where the birds breed.

Sanctuaries and parks

Scheduled flights from Inuvik reach Tuktoyaktuk (also reached by a winter ice road), the pingo capital of the world, which lies within a Caribou grazing area, and Sachs Harbour on Banks Island. It may also be possible to visit the Anderson River Delta Bird Sanctuary to the east of Inuvik. This sanctuary, together with the bird sanctuaries on Kendall Island (north of the Mackenzie delta) and those on Banks Island, were set up to protect the tidal flats, which are important to breeding and migrating waterfowl and waders. A further bird sanctuary at Cape Parry, on the mainland, east of the Anderson delta, protects the major fraction of the western Arctic's population of Brünnich's Guillemot. East of Cape Parry the Tuktut Nogiat National Park protects the calving grounds of the Bluenose Caribou herd and some impressive canyon scenery. Other wildlife includes Brown Bear and Wolf. One final site on the itinerary of the Amundsen Route North-West Passage cruises is Franklin Bay, on the western side of Parry Peninsula (of which Cape Parry forms the northern extremity). Here are the Smoking Hills, cliffs of bituminous shale that ignited (probably as a result of a lightning strike) several thousand years ago and have been smouldering away ever since.

The only settlement on Banks Island grew up in the early 1950s around a

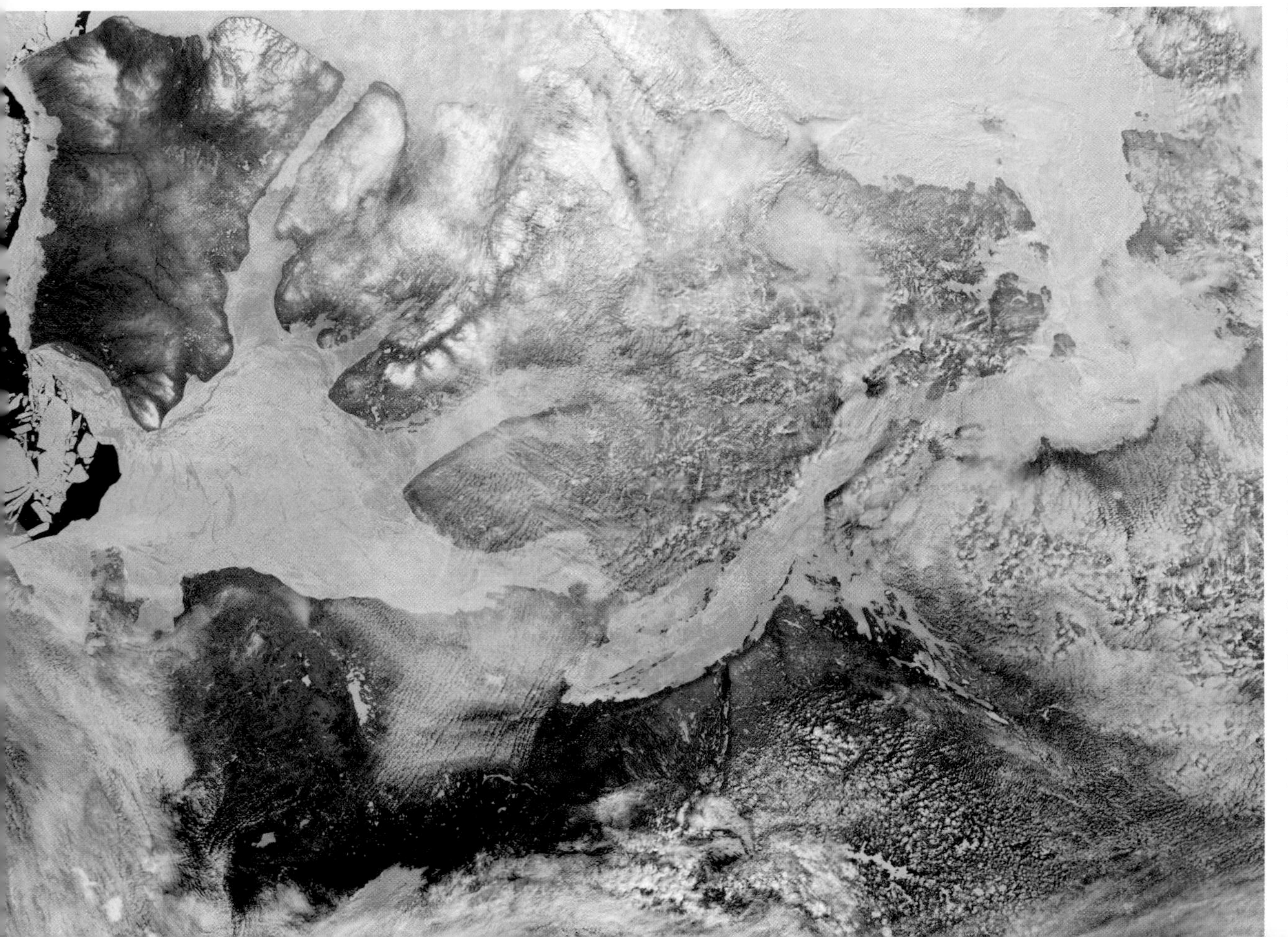

The western Canadian Arctic from space. To the left is Banks Island, with Victoria Island in the centre. To the right is the western section of King William Island. The Barren Lands lie on the mainland.

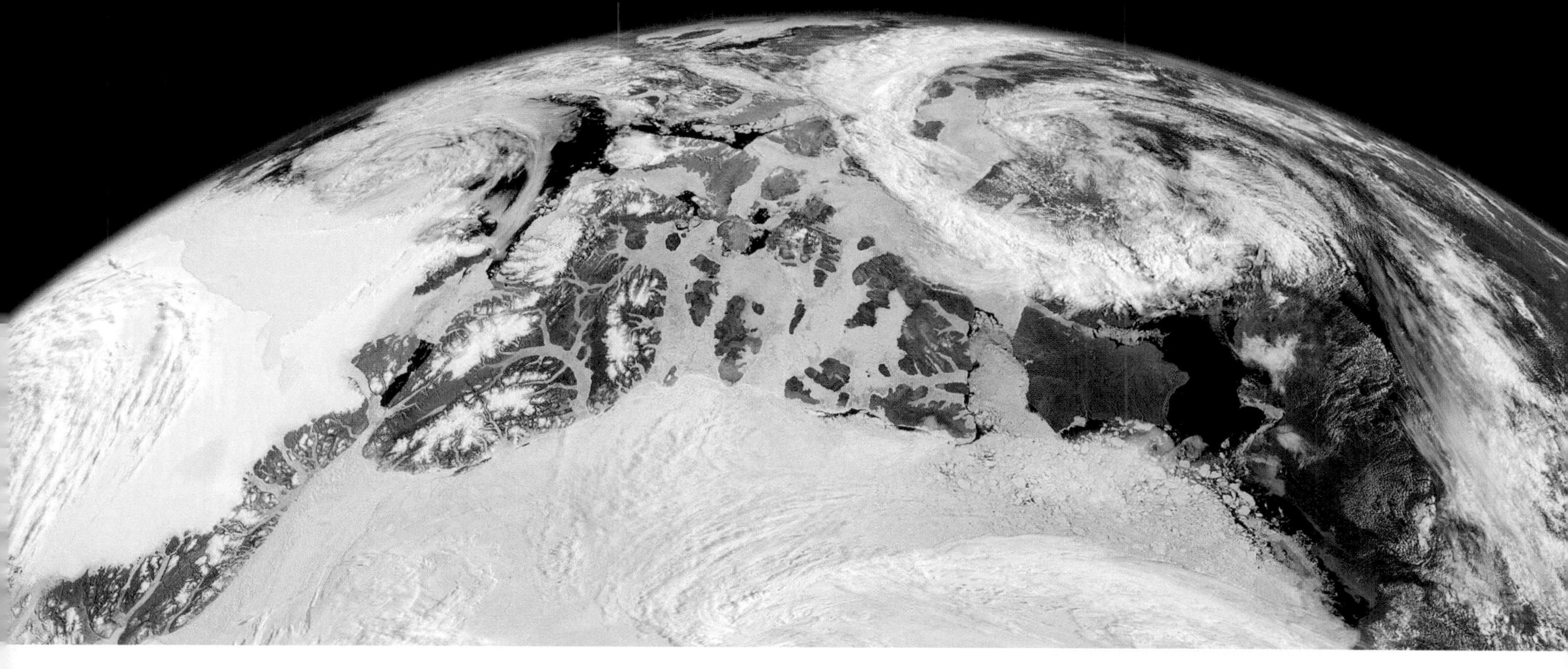

RCMP post at a sheltered bay named after the *Mary Sachs*, a ship of the 1913 Canadian Arctic Expedition. Prior to that settlement there had been only a handful of western visitors. It had been spotted from the north, from the winter quarters on Melville Island of Parry's first expedition, by Frederick Beechey, but not until the 1850 McClure expedition was a landing made. From Sachs Harbour, which is reached by scheduled flights from Inuvik, visitors can explore a huge (63,000km^2), essentially flat land (the highest point is barely 800m above sea level and lies close to the cliffs of Nelson Head, at the southern end of the island). For most visitors travel from the town is limited to local tours, though these usually include sightings of Musk Oxen and a good selection of birds. Charter flights can be arranged (though the starting point for these will often be the mainland towns). In addition to a bird sanctuary covering a vast area of the western island, there is a National Park in the north; the Aulavik National Park encompasses the valley of the Thomson River and Castel Bay, and was set up to protect one of the largest concentrations of Musk Oxen in the Arctic, as well as many species of waterfowl and waders.

As well as the National Parks, North West Territories also has a number of Territorial Parks, set up primarily to protect sites of historical importance. One such park covers the pingos of Tuktoyaktuk.

Nunavut

Nunavut came into being on 1 April 1999, the result of negotiations between representatives of the Inuit community and the Canadian government, aimed at giving back to the native people control of a land that they had occupied for several thousand years. Just as Inuit means simply 'the people', the name Nunavut was chosen because in Inuktitut it means 'our land'. The new territory includes the majority of the original

Northern Arctic Canada from space. To the left is Greenland, then Ellesmere and Axel Heiberg islands. Next come the Parry Islands. The large island to the right is Banks, with the Canadian mainland to the right of it. Beneath the swirl of cloud right of centre is Victoria Island.

The Sylvia Grinnell Provincial Park, Iqaluit, on Baffin Island, protects the superb scenery to the south of the town.

It is spring, but this area of the Barren Lands, on the northern Canadian mainland, is still ice-covered.

North West Territories, and covers a corridor of mainland Canada from Clinton Point to Hudson Bay, the western edge of Hudson Bay south to the 60th parallel, islands in Hudson Bay and James Bay, and Canada's Arctic islands apart from sections of the western islands, which remained in the residual North West Territories. Nunavut also includes Akpatok Island in Ungava Bay, but none of the native villages of northern Quebec. Nunavut therefore includes the major Arctic islands of Baffin and Ellesmere, as well as a large fraction of Victoria Island. As a consequence, it also includes many sites important to the history of the search for the North-West Passage, such as Beechey Island with its graves of three of the crewmen of Franklin's final expedition, King William Island where many of Franklin's expedition died, and Gjoa Haven where Amundsen overwintered during the first transit of the Passage At the northern end of Ellesmere Island is Ward Hunt Island, close to the main Arctic ice shelves and the starting point for many recent expeditions to the North Pole.

Although in general the ambient temperature decreases as the visitor moves north (in any season), on the west central coast of Ellesmere Island and the adjacent east coast of Axel Heiberg, stable high pressure systems mean that summers can include long periods of warm sunshine. This has led to the area being occasionally termed the 'Arctic Riviera'. That

Pond Inlet, which separates Baffin and Bylot islands. Bylot can be seen in the background.

description is obviously tongue-in-cheek, but temperatures in excess of 20°C are not uncommon and the flowering plants in the area are exceptional.

Geography

Geologically almost all of Nunavut lies on the Canadian Shield. Across the Shield there is evidence of the abrasive nature of ice, the rocks having been planed smooth by the glaciation of the last Ice Age. But nowhere is this more obvious than on Baffin Island, where the fjords of the eastern shore have been gouged out of the underlying Shield by glaciers. Also on eastern Baffin are the spectacular Precambrian granite peaks in the Auyuittuq National Park. The peaks here, and the mountains on both Ellesmere (where Mount Barbeau can be found, at 2,616m Nunavut's highest peak) and Axel Heiberg islands are exceptions to a general rule of a relatively flat land. Both Ellesmere and Axel Heiberg are heavily iced, the extent of the ice on Ellesmere (over 80,000km^2) being the second largest area of ice after the vast Greenland inland ice cap.

Wildlife reserves

Heading east from North West Territories the first town in Nunavut is Kugluktuk, formerly Coppermine, which is set on the Coppermine River. To the east, beyond Bathurst Inlet – crossed annually by the Bathurst Caribou herd – is the Queen Maud Migratory Bird Sanctuary, the most important breeding site of Ross's Goose. It is estimated that at least 90% of the world population of this goose nests within the 63,000km^2 reserve. The breeding grounds of Ross's Goose were discovered only in the 1940s. As well as Ross's there are Snow Geese, several other species of geese, divers, ducks and many wader species. The reserve is also a calving ground for the Bathurst Caribou herd.

South of the Queen Maud reserve is the Thelon Wildlife Sanctuary (shared with North West Territories), established in 1927 to preserve a remnant Musk Ox population. To the east is Southampton Island in the northern part of Hudson Bay (with two bird sanctuaries, again important principally for migratory and breeding waterfowl), the Harry Gibbons Sanctuary near Bay of God's Mercy in the south-west (Brant, Snow and Canada Geese, with some Ross's), and the East Bay Sanctuary (Snow Geese and Brant, other waterfowl) at the northern end of the Bell Peninsula east of Coral Harbour. There are scheduled flights to Coral Harbour, but travel on the island can be difficult, requiring a co-operative local and a quad bike or snow scooter. To the east of Southampton Island, Nunavut's newest National Park, Ukkusiksalik, encompasses Wager Bay, a habitat for Nunavut's largest concentration of Peregrine Falcons. At the other end of Hudson Bay (or, rather, in James Bay) there are bird sanctuaries on Akimiski Island and the nearby Hannah and Boatswain bays.

The huge rock faces of the Auyuittuq National Park on Baffin Island attract climbers from across the world. This is Mount Thor.

On southern Baffin Island, at Cape Dorset, at the southern tip of Foxe Peninsula, there is another bird sanctuary. The village of Cape Dorset itself is renowned as one of the premier places for Inuit carvers, much of the carved soapstone, bone and antler seen in Nunavut's shops having been made in this community. South-east of the Foxe Peninsula on the evocatively named Meta Incognita ('Almost Unknown') Peninsula, the Katannilik Territorial Park has Caribou and Wolves, and a bird

The Quttinirpaaq National Park on Ellesmere Island includes Lake Hazen, the most northerly High Arctic lake.

Ukkusiksalik, near Wager Bay, is Nunavut's newest National Park.

population that includes waterfowl, waders, grouse and Gyrfalcons. The park can be reached relatively easily from nearby Kimmirut (which is itself reached by scheduled air services from Iqaluit). A more important site lies north-west of Iqaluit, on the coastal plain south of the Koudjuak River. There in 1927, Canadian biologist Dewey Soper first located the breeding ground of blue-morph Snow Goose. The bird sanctuary named in his honour has the largest breeding colony of Snow Geese in the world. There are also other waterfowl and waders, and Caribou in the adjacent Bowman Wildlife Sanctuary to the south. On the east coast across from the Dewey Soper Reserve is the Auyuittuq National Park, with its imposing granite peaks.

At the northern end of Baffin Island the Sirmilik National Park covers two areas of the island and Bylot Island, making up one of Nunavut's largest and most biodiverse parks. Thirty species of bird breed in the park, these including colonies of Snow Geese, auks and seabirds. Bylot Island also has white-morph Gyrfalcons, while Cape Hay, on the northern island, is an excellent viewpoint for cetaceans migrating into Lancaster Sound. Access to the park is via the townships of Pond Inlet and Arctic Bay. To the east, the Prince Leopold Migratory Bird Sanctuary covers both the island of the name and the north-eastern tip of neighbouring Somerset Island, where more than 300,000 pairs of auks and seabirds breed.

Further north, the Polar Bear Pass National Wildlife Area on Bathurst Island is named after the pass that the bears use during spring and autumn traverses of the island. But despite the name, the reserve was set up to protect an important wetland area, a breeding habitat for Snow Geese and Thayer's Gulls, as well as other waterfowl, seabirds and waders. North again, the Quttinirpaaq National Park encompasses a vast area of Ellesmere Island, taking in fjords of the northern and eastern coast (the latter separated by just a few kilometres of the Robeson Channel from northern Greenland), and Lake Hazen, the largest High Arctic lake. The park, the whole of which lies north of the 80th parallel, is a habitat for Peary Reindeer and white Wolves, a large population of Arctic Hares, and more than 20 species of High Arctic breeding birds. Cruises using Russian ice-breakers often travel to

Churchill, Manitoba, has a wonderful mix of tundra and shrubs, as well as being at the treeline, and is renowned for its Polar Bears, Beluga and birdlife at different times of the year.

Hudson and James Bay from space. Cape Churchill is beneath the cloud swirl at the west edge of Hudson Bay.

Tanquary Fjord at the park's southern rim, making a thrilling passage between Ellesmere and Axel Heiberg. This is not only a scenically superb trip, but also one steeped in history as it follows, in part, the second polar journey of the *Fram*.

Though this brief overview of Nunavut's parks and reserves highlights the most important wildlife and some of the best scenery in the province, there is a vast area of the High Arctic outside them that is also worth investigating. Igloolik, a tiny island close to the entrance to the Fury and Hecla Strait, is reached by scheduled flights from Iqaluit and is renowned as a place to view Bowhead Whales, and also for Walrus. The bird life includes Sabine's Gulls. Pond Inlet – at the northern end of Baffin Island and a gateway for the Sirmilik National Park – is excellent for trips to the floe edge in Baffin Bay to view Narwhal. Resolute on Cornwallis Island can be reached by scheduled flights. Though not itself an especially interesting place for wildlife, charter flights from the town can be made to Cunningham Inlet on northern Somerset Island, where Beluga congregate to moult, and to Ellesmere Island. Cambridge Bay, at the southern end of Victoria Island, is reached by scheduled flights from Yellowknife, and is excellent for Musk Ox, Sabine's Gull and other wildlife, as well as a view of the sunken, rotting hulk of Amundsen's *Maud*. The Hudson Bay townships of Rankin Inlet, Repulse Bay and, as already mentioned, Coral Harbour are also excellent centres for exploration, while history beckons at Gjoa Haven on King William Island

Manitoba

Manitoba includes the south-western tip of Hudson Bay, where the town of Churchill is one of the best and most easily accessible wildlife destinations in the Canadian Arctic. There are scheduled flights from Winnipeg to the town, while rail enthusiasts can take a journey that makes a more leisurely exploration of northern Manitoba. In spring and early summer several thousand Beluga congregate in the Churchill River to moult, while during the autumn Polar Bears, which have been marooned on the southern shore of Hudson Bay, mass to await the winter freeze. Churchill is also famous for its remarkable birdlife. From the town a series of roads head off into habitat that varies from shoreline to tundra (some dry, but mostly wet) and boreal forest. The numbers of species that might be seen is staggering, and the area is renowned for rarities such as Ross's Gull, which has bred spasmodically over recent years.

Close to Churchill, the Wapusk National Park has recently been set up to protect the bears of this part of southern Hudson Bay. The park encompasses a coastal strip from west of Cape Churchill to the Nelson River, and includes one of

the most important bear-denning sites in the world. Access to the park is controlled, but there are tour operators in Churchill that offer tours.

As well as the wildlife opportunities, the town of Churchill is also interesting historically. Across the river mouth from Cape Merry is Prince of Wales Fort, built by the Hudson's Bay Company in the 18th century. Further down river on the western side is Sloop Cove, the natural dry dock where the Company's ships were repaired.

Accommodation and transport are available in Churchill, but both usually require an early booking because of the town's popularity. The same is also true for the tundra buggies, which take visitors to the best Polar Bear viewing sites.

Ontario

Ontario includes a section of the southern shore of Hudson Bay and half the shoreline of James Bay. James Bay is home to the world's most southerly population of Polar Bears, these coming ashore when the sea ice melts to await its autumnal

refreezing. Female bears also den on the shores of James Bay. James Bay can be reached by train from Toronto via Cochrane (the train being called – and this will come as a surprise to no one – the Polar Bear Express), which reaches Moosonee. From there trips into, or flights over, James Bay can be made: Beluga often congregate in southern James Bay. From Moosonee a short boat trip, often by freighter canoe, reaches the historically interesting Moose Factory, a Hudson's Bay Company establishment.

Quebec and Labrador

On the eastern side of Hudson Bay lies the final section of the mainland Canadian Arctic. That part of Quebec lying above the 55th parallel is known as Nunavik. Nunavik covers Inuit coastal villages scattered along the Hudson Strait and Hudson Bay shores of the Ungava Peninsula. The largest community is Kuujjuaq at the southern edge of Ungava Bay. Kuujjuaq, and many of the larger Nunavik settlements, are reached by scheduled flights from Montreal or Quebec City. Nunavik is essentially a land of low-lying, flat tundra, bordered on the east by the Torngat Mountains, which extend into Labrador; the mountains reach 1,676m.

At the centre of the Ungava Peninsula is Pingualuit, a 3.5km-wide lake, which formed in the crater of a meteor that struck the Earth some 1.5 million years ago. The lake is more than 250m deep and is claimed to have the purest water in the world. To the north of the lake the Ragland Mine is a deep underground nickel and copper mine. The deposit of metal ore is anticipated to last at least 20 years at the current level of production and has led to fears over run-off and air-borne contamination of the area, particularly because of its proximity to Pingualuit; there are plans to make Pingualuit into a provincial park. Nunavik's tundra is the habitat of huge Caribou herds. The George River herd is the largest of all North American herds, with more than 700,000 animals. Two other herds, the Leaf River and the much smaller Torngat Mountain herd, raise the total number of animals in Nunavik to at least one million.

The land between the Torngat Mountains and the sea is home to the Sikumiut Inuit (their name meaning 'people of the sea ice'), whose ancestors hunted on the ice of the Labrador Sea, and Caribou on the inland tundra. Agreement has been reached in principle between representatives of the Sikumiut and the Canadian Government to create an equivalent to Nunavut and Nunavik in northern Labrador. When the boundaries of the new territory have been finalised it is hoped that a National Park will be created to protect the Torngat Mountains.

As in Nunavik, travel within the area occupied by the Sikumiut is limited, but scheduled flights reach Nain and there is also a coastal ferry to the town. Flights to Labrador are occasionally weatherbound, particularly on the last stretch from Goose Bay to Nain, so travellers must be patient and flexible. Wildlife viewing in the area includes pinnipeds and cetaceans of the Labrador coast as well as Caribou, other mammals and birds in the interior.

Above
Nachvak Fjord, Torngat Mountains.

Opposite page

Above left
Saglek Fjord, Torngat Mountains.

Above right
Northern Quebec and Labrador from space. The two mainland provinces are separated by Hudson Strait from southern Baffin Island. The large bite out of the mainland is Ungava Bay.

Below
Pingualuit, Ungava Peninsula.

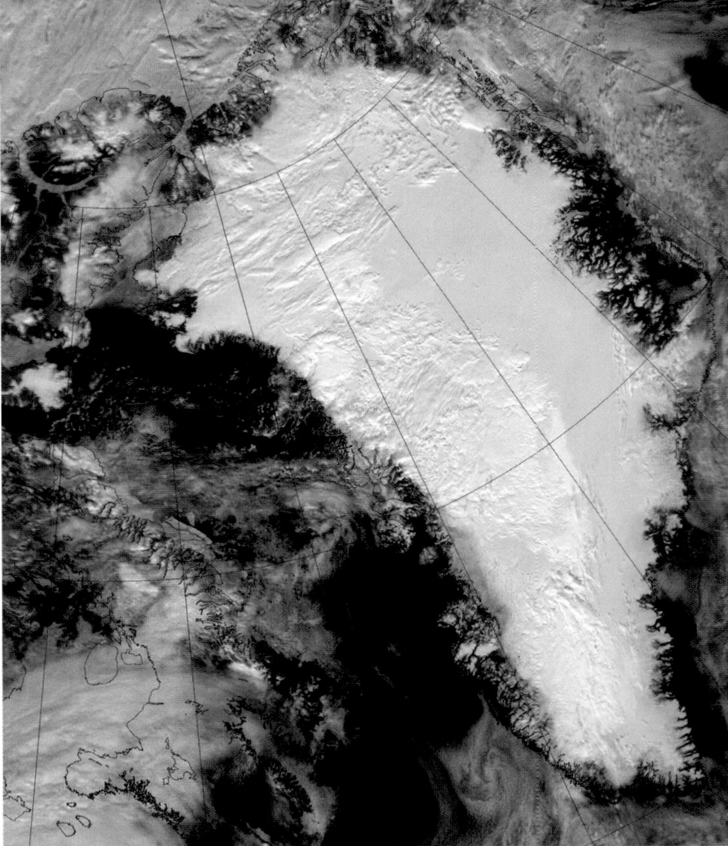
Greenland from space.

GREENLAND

Greenland extends from just below the 60th parallel, at Kap Farvel – Cape Farwell – north to Cape Morris K. Jesup (and on to Oodaaq Island). Greenland measures 2,670km between the two capes.

For a map of Greenland, see p177.

Geography

The Inland Ice, as the Greenlandic ice sheet is commonly called, covers about 80% of the island. It is up to 3km thick and is the second largest ice sheet on Earth after that covering Antarctica. Below the ice, and exposed on much of the western shore, is the Greenland Shield, of Precambrian rocks, similar to the Canadian Shield to the west and of similar age. On the north and west coasts the coastal strip is an exposed section of the Mesozoic-Cenozoic fold belt. In the Disko Bay area, and also both south and north of Scoresbysund, there are intrusions of Tertiary volcanic rocks. In southern Greenland, at the head of Tasermiut Fjord, there are granite peaks with huge, sheer walls that bear comparison with those of Baffin's Auyuittuq National Park. The east coast is more mountainous than the west; this is where Greenland's highest mountains are found. North again, beyond Scoresbysund – the world's longest and widest fjord – lie the Staunings Alps. These areas attract climbers and other adventurers. Ever since Nansen first crossed the ice in 1887 the ice cap, and Greenland in general, has been a magnet for those wishing to test themselves against nature. The entire length of the island has been traversed by (unsupported) pulk-hauling skiers, and a team of two has also kayaked and dog-sledged around the island's entire perimeter.

Greenland statistics

The largest Arctic island, Greenland has a surface area of 2,167,000km² including the off-shore islands. For comparison, the next largest Arctic island is Baffin, with an area of 476,070km². Greenland also has the highest Arctic mountains (if Mount McKinley and the other Denali peaks are assumed to be non-Arctic). The highest peak is Gunnbjörn Fjeld at 3,700m (at 68°54'N, 29°48'W). Mount Forel, 3,360m, at 67°00'N, 37°00'W is the only other Arctic mountain rising to more than 3,000m.

Recent history

Greenland became a Danish colony at the time of Hans Egede's fruitless search for surviving Norse settlers During the 1939–45 war the island saw several skirmishes between Allied soldiers (Danes, Norwegians and Americans) and Germans, the latter seeking to set up weather stations on the east coast. In 1953 Greenland became part of the Kingdom of Denmark, essentially a 'county' of Denmark. In 1972, when Denmark voted to become part of the European Economic Community (EEC, the forerunner of the European Union) Greenland voted heavily against, fearing, correctly, that entry would mean Greenland's waters becoming a common resource for member countries. The Danish vote came at a time when the Danish people, tolerant, liberal and progressive, were becoming increasingly concerned over the colonial overtones inherent in Denmark's sovereignty over Greenland. This concern, coupled with the arrival of EEC trawlers in Greenlandic waters and, more importantly, the discovery that the Faroe

Kulusuk, east Greenland.

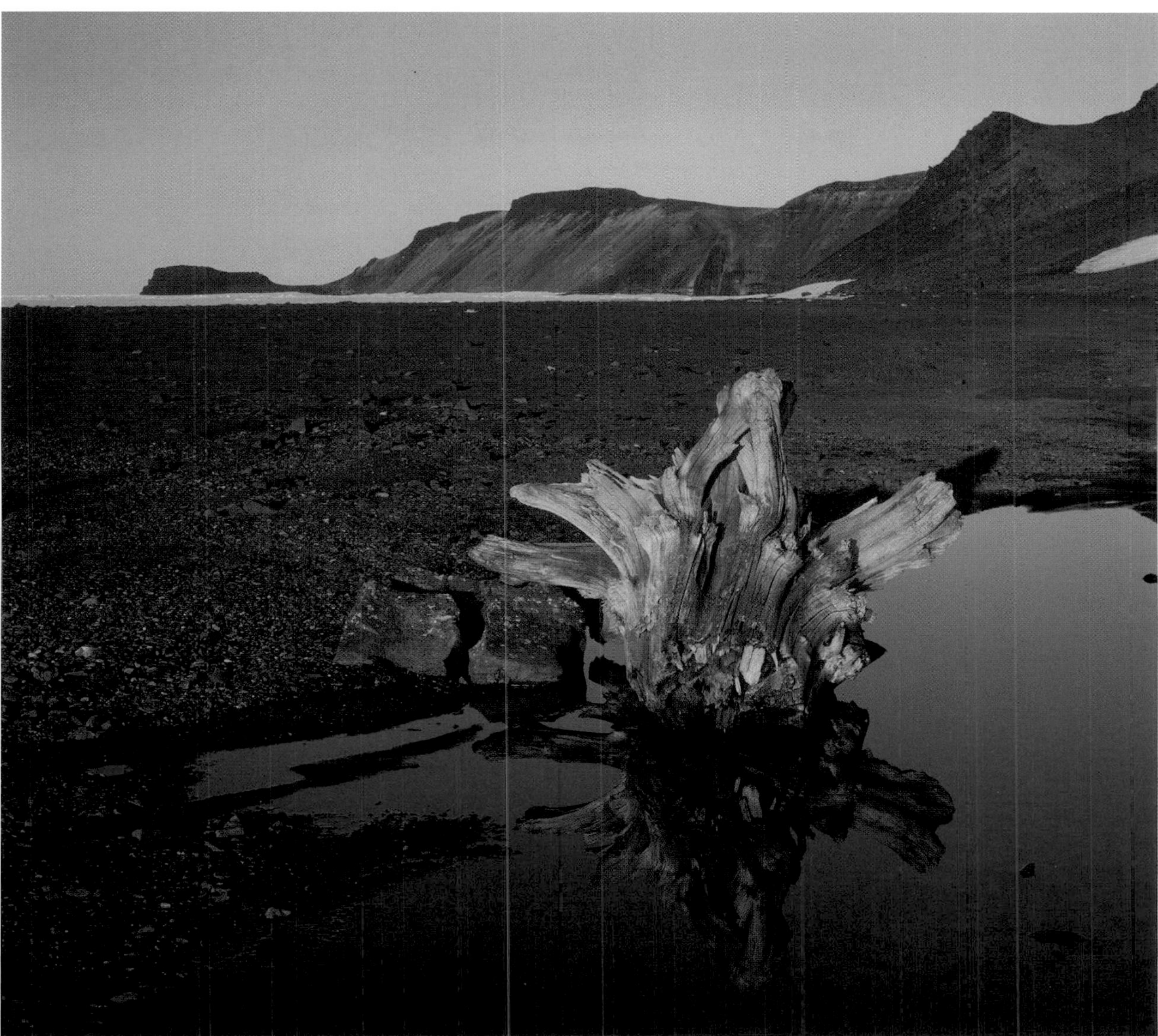

Siberian drift wood at Kapp Broer Ruys, north-east Greenland.

Islands, a Danish dependency, was not part of the Community led, ultimately. to Greenland being granted Home Rule in 1979. Following Home Rule, Greenland voted, in 1983, to withdraw from the Community. The transfer of power from Denmark to Greenland was much greater than in Nunavut, Denmark retaining control over foreign and defence issues, but all other aspects of government now resting with a legislature in Nuuk.

Greenlanders call their country Kalaallit Nunaat, the Land of the Kalaallit, the latter the name given to ethnic Greenlanders, a people of Inuit descent, though the country also has both Danish and mixed-origin inhabitants. The total population is about 60,000. Among them there is, at present, a groundswell in favour of full independence from Denmark, but this desire is tempered with the knowledge that without Danish subsidies Greenland would have difficulty fending off bankruptcy.

For the traveller, Greenland offers an odd mix of almost pure Inuit culture and modern western ways. In the north-west the 'Polar Eskimo' culture encountered by John Ross continues almost untouched, while further south the profitable shrimp fishery has bought modernity. On the east coast Greenlanders still hunt Polar Bear from dog-sledges, but use the income from selling the skins to North America to buy the latest electronic gizmos. Modern weapons and medicines (aiding a rise in population: since 1945 the population of Ilulissat has risen from a few hundred to several thousand) have led to a worrying destruction of island wildlife, particularly on the more heavily populated west coast. Yet the island remains in large part a magnificent, and truly Arctic, wilderness, one to be savoured.

Earth's northernmost land

Oodaaq Island, off Greenland's northern coast, is a 28m x 14m area of quartz and slate gravel 1m high at 83°40.5'N, 30°39.5'W, just 700km from the North Pole. Often covered with ice and so easily missed, it has proved an elusive target for those seeking the kudos of treading upon it. Though usually recognised as the most northerly piece of real estate on the planet, other gravel bars have been spotted to the north of Oodaaq, the status of these being disputed as it is possible that such, usually smaller, bars are transient features of the continental shelf. Bars have been spotted as far north as 83°42'N. If sea ice coverage continues to diminish it may be that one of these bars, or one as yet unseen, may usurp Oodaaq's record. However, if sea levels rise then Oodaaq may disappear.

Wildlife

Because of the latitudinal range of the island, the vegetation varies, being polar desert in the north but with birch and willow growing to around 3m in southern areas. The south is

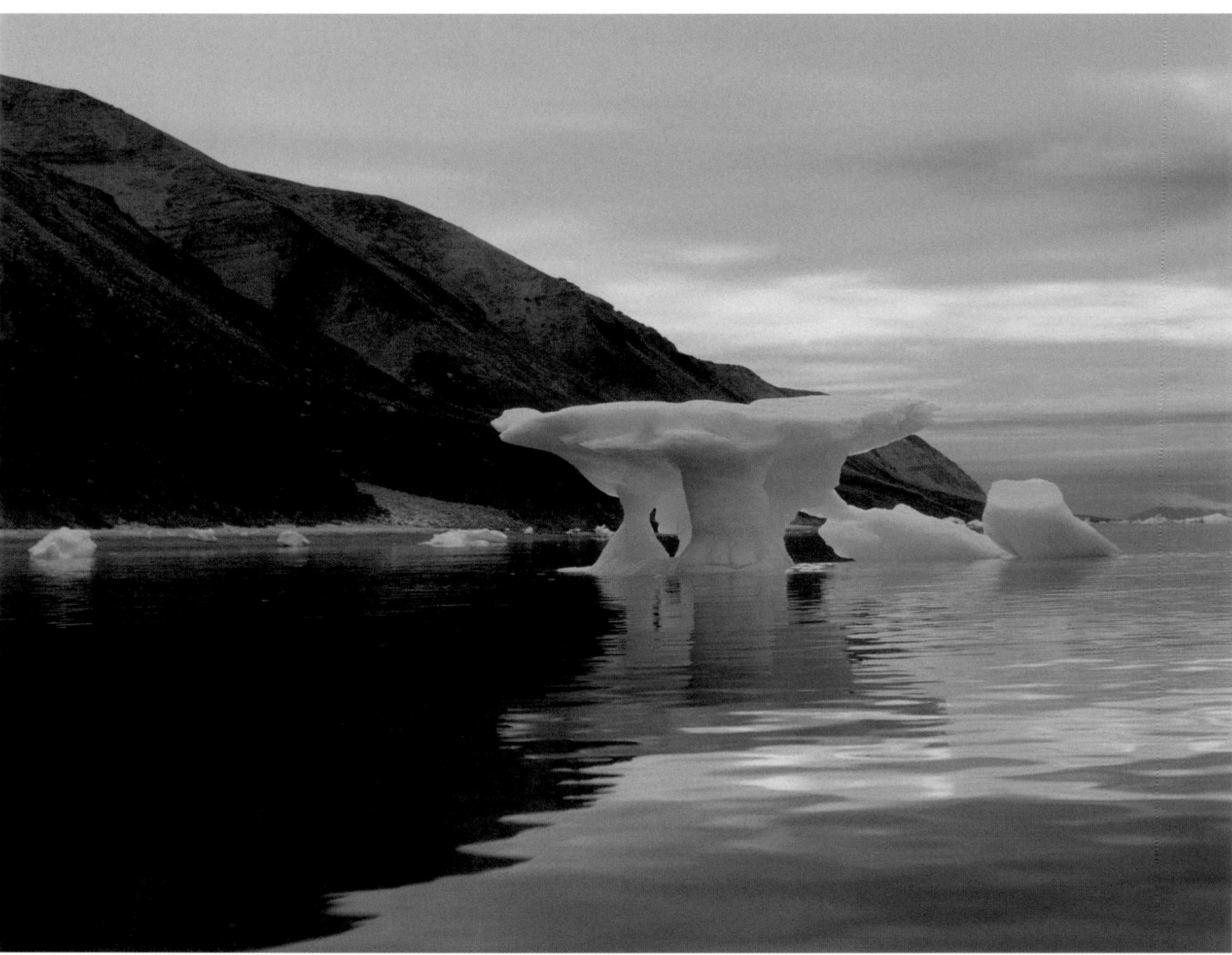

Sculpted iceberg, Inglefield Bredning, north-west Greenland.

also home to a range of vascular and flowering plants, with more than 500 species identified to date. One of the most impressive is the widespread Broad-leaved Willowherb *Chamaenerion latifolium*, Greenland's National Flower. In the north Musk Ox feed on the plants, the oxen hunted by a remnant population of High Arctic wolves, while Polar Bear and pinnipeds (Bearded, Harbour, Harp, Hooded and Ringed Seals) are seen. Further south, hunting has reduced numbers and it is the scenery that is of major interest, together with the historical Norse sites. As would be expected, the birdlife varies with latitude. In the south Great Cormorants breed, while in the north there are 'true' Arctic species – Barnacle Goose, King Eider, Red Knot, white-morph Gyrfalcon, Snowy Owl, and Iceland, Thayer's, Sabine's, Ivory and Ross's Gulls (though all these gulls are rare).

Travel

With such a vast area, no in-depth consideration is possible and only brief details are given. Outside the villages and townships there are no roads (and few tracks) so walking is the only way to explore. In winter snow scooters can be used, though hire options are limited and expensive. In winter the wildlife is also much scarcer. Getting around within the country requires air or sea travel. For the more experienced and determined traveller charter flights are an option. These are available from Iceland for the east coast, and Canada for the west. However, such flights are difficult to arrange, as Greenland is a foreign country to the pilots of both Canada and Iceland and so international regulations apply, and may limit the willingness of some operators. If chartering is not an option, Greenland's main towns are still worth visiting as the scenery close to them is excellent, though wildlife may be in short supply.

On the west coast, Narsarsuaq and Kangerlussuaq are reached by scheduled flights from Copenhagen. Narsarsuaq has very limited facilities, but is one of the few places where the Inland Ice can be visited in a (long) day's walk. The walk passes the site of a now-demolished US military hospital, whose activities remain a secret and which is the subject of (usually lurid) rumours. Was it for horribly mutilated victims of the Korean War deemed too dreadfully injured to be allowed home for fear of adversely affecting public morale? Or was it something even more horrendous? The walk also goes through the Valley of Flowers, a less disturbing place. From Narsarsuaq boats cross to Brattahlíð.

Narsarsuaq is a good starting place for an exploration of the south-west townships, these being reached by the helicopters of Air Greenland. At Qaqortoq a half-day trip can be made to the Norse church at Hvalsø, the most complete structure of the period in Greenland, while at Nanortalik boat trips can be made along Tasermiut to see the vast rock walls of Ketil and other peaks. These sheer walls have become popular with rock climbers in recent years.

Kangerlussuaq (the Danish name of the town, Søndre Strømfjord is still often seen) has slightly better facilities than Narsarsuaq. Visitors can join a trip to the inland ice (rather too far for a day's walk) with a good chance of spotting Musk Ox. Flights from the town reach Ilulissat, from where the iceberg-choked fjord fed by the Jakobshavn Glacier is a short walk away. Ilulissat can also be used as a base for boat trips around Disko Bay. Northward flights continue to

Above
Rugged, but beautiful, landscape between Kulusuk and Ammassalik, east Greenland.

Left
Autumn colours at Revet, north-east Greenland.

Descending Klosterdalen towards Tasermiut Fjord, southern Greenland. The sheer faces here attract many rock climbers. The most famous of the local peaks is Ketil, the right-hand peak in this photograph.

Uummannaq, with its excellent seabird cliffs, and Qannaq. Qannaq, in north-west Greenland, is the most culturally unspoilt part of Greenland. Descendants of Robert Peary, the result of his liaison with a local woman, still live in the town. Flights south from Kangerlussuaq reach Nuuk. Nuuk, Greenland's capital, is cosmopolitan, perhaps the most extreme example of the cultural mix that envelops the country as a whole. From Nuuk local flights visit outlying townships, one of which, Maniitsoq, is among the most picturesque towns on the island.

There are far fewer townships on the east coast, a more rugged and inhospitable land. Kulusuk is reached by scheduled flights from Reykjavik (and also has cross-ice flights to and from Kangerlussuaq). Kulusuk is a beautifully positioned and very picturesque town, and has onward flights to Ammassalik, one of the few places from which walking tours can be made. Further north Constable Point can also be reached from Reykjavik. The airport here is a remnant of a failed oil search, a helicopter shuttle operating to Ittoqqortoormiit. Created in the 1920s by Denmark to bolster their claim for Greenlandic sovereignty, this used to be a desolate, desperate place, but things have improved in recent years. Cruise ships visiting Scoresbysund (Kangertittivaq in the local language) now dock, and as visitors to both the fjord and the North-East National Park have increased, opportunities for locals have improved. Scoresbysund is the longest fjord on Earth, at more than

Landscape on the north-western edge of Scoresbysund. east Greenland.

300km, and also the widest. It is actually a complex of fjords with several huge side branches, the whole complex covering 13,400km^2. The power of glacial ice can be clearly seen here; not only has the terrestrial landscape been gouged from mountains almost 2,000m high, but the fjord water is up to 1,500m deep, so intense was the carving.

Reserves and protected areas

Greenland's North-East National Park is, at 700,000 km^2, the largest national park in the world. This vast area is both visually magnificent and an important wildlife reserve, with Polar Bear, Musk Ox, Wolf, Arctic Hare and Northern Collared Lemming, and all the North Atlantic pinnipeds, including Walrus. Breeding waterfowl include Barnacle Geese and Gyrfalcons. In the past the Danish authorities have restricted entrance to the park, but there has been some relaxation in recent years and cruise ships now visit regularly, either crossing the Denmark Strait from Iceland or sailing along the ice edge from Longyearbyen and then heading south along the coast. Charter flights from Akureyri in Iceland also land expeditions. Such expeditions must seek permission by December of the year prior to their intended visit.

Although the North-East Park is Greenland's only National Park, there are other protected areas including Melville Bay (Qimusseriarsuaq), Paradise Valley (Arnangarnup Qoorua) near Maniitsoq, and the Qingua Valley near Nonortalik.

An aerial view of Dusenfjorden, north-east Greenland.

Part 5

A Vulnerable ecosystem

The 'Boneyard' at Gambell, St Lawrence Island, Alaska. The yard is actually a centuries-old midden into which the remains of hunted sea mammals were thrown. The inhabitants of Gambell, who still hunt sea mammals, now excavate the yard. It is a treasure trove of old harpoon heads, carvings and other finds. These are sold to mainland collectors to supplement the villagers' meagre incomes.

A Vulnerable Ecosystem

Earth's ecosystems are finely balanced. Changes to a habitat or a change to the number or diversity of species, by the introduction of an 'alien' organism or the elimination of an existing one, can have profound effects. The Arctic is no exception to this rule, though it is a special case for several reasons. Firstly, the Arctic ecosystem is young, having developed only since the retreat of the ice at the end of the last Ice Age; such systems may be especially unstable. Secondly, the Arctic is an unforgiving and hostile environment, one in which climatic effects can be sudden and devastating, and recovery times can be lengthy. The Snow Goose population of Wrangel Island represents a good example. During the late 1960s and early 1970s a series of late springs prevented the birds from raising chicks; the population crashed by over 90% and was only at about 50% of the original level by 2000. In more southerly latitudes a late spring means that birds may raise just one clutch rather than two. If the following spring is early the population can soon recover. In the Arctic a late spring means no clutch, and even if the spring is early two clutches are very rare. The habitat itself is also slow to recover. In southerly latitudes a ploughed field will be seeded, the crop will ripen and be harvested and by the following spring the field will look much the same again. In the Arctic, soil denuded of its plant life may stay barren for years.

Because Arctic species are continuously stressed by their environment, any additional stresses imposed by external, man-made changes can cause major, and rapid, disruption. Here we explore the threats to the Arctic and its species, beginning with a history of the direct exploitation of Arctic animals, continuing with the exploitation of mineral resources and the subtle effects of pollution on the Arctic ecosystem, and a final discussion on the effect that climate change is having and will have on the Arctic.

The Exploitation of Arctic Animals

Although the native peoples of the Eurasian mainland exploited the terrestrial animals of the Arctic, hunting Reindeer for food and clothing and other species primarily for food, only the Pomores of the White Sea area and the Bering Sea Yuppiat ventured into the High Arctic. The Pomores certainly hunted seals, walrus and bears and also possessed Arctic survival skills as advanced as those of the Inuit; in 1743 four Pomores were accidentally marooned on Edgeøya (off Spitsbergen's eastern shore). In 1749 three of them were found in good health. They had lived by hunting, warding off scurvy by drinking blood. Only the man who had baulked at drinking blood had died – of scurvy.

Alaskan Yuppiat also hunted in the Bering Sea. But despite the skills of these peoples, it is the Inuit of Canada and north-western Greenland who are the true Arctic dwellers, and it is instructive to understand the way in which they used the High Arctic fauna in order to survive. The Inuit used the skins of Walrus for tents. Walrus hide also made a strong rope, so strong that when the British navy met Inuit for the first time they were amazed to discover that the ropes of these supposedly inferior people, made by braiding strips of smoked Walrus hide, were stronger than their own. Sealskin was used as clothing because it was water-repellent. Caribou skin was a good all-purpose clothing material. Polar Bear skins were warm, as were those of the Arctic Fox. Interestingly, the use of Polar Bear fur was more or less confined to Greenland Inuit; in Canada seal and Caribou were sufficiently abundant to provide an easier alternative. Qiviut, the fine underwool of the Musk Ox, is one of the lightest and warmest wools known. The wool is usually claimed to be superior to cashmere, but as it is extremely expensive it is used only in the manufacture of small

In Chukotka, across a narrow stretch of sea from St Lawrence Island, Siberian Yuppiat, who share a common ancestry with the Gambell villagers, also still hunt sea mammals. The man in the front of the boat has a rifle, the harpoon being used only to secure a dead Walrus before it sinks.

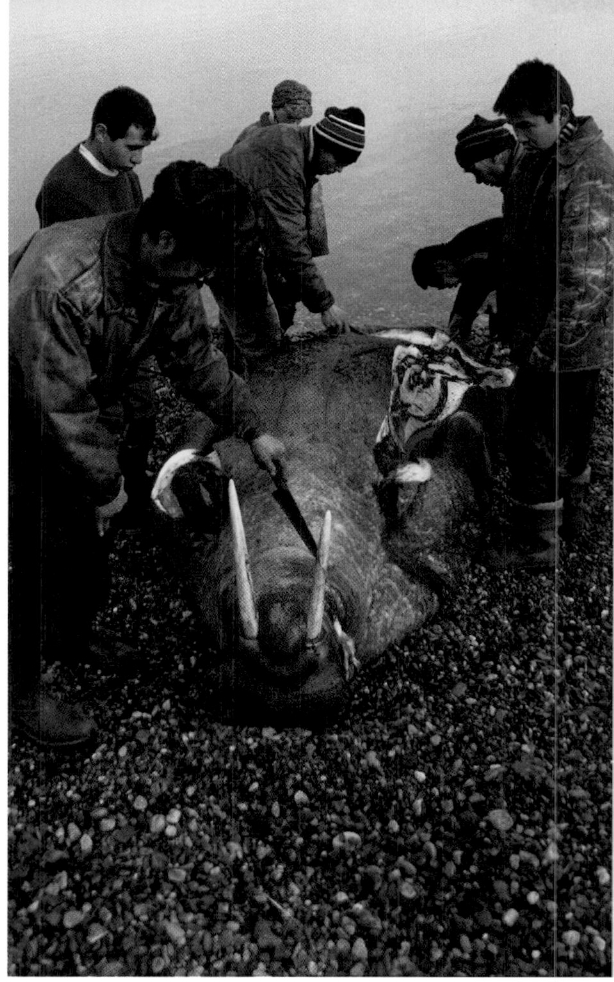

accessories such as scarves. The longer guard hairs of the Musk Ox's coat were made into caps that were claimed to be an effective mosquito deterrent. Personal observation suggests that Musk Ox caps are no better than any other protection against this most relentless Arctic predator. The Inuit also used the skins of birds to produce warm undergarments. Several of the mummies discovered at Qilakitsoq in west Greenland wore inner parkas made of bird skin, the skins including those of auks and divers. As the Greenland Inuit had no access to Caribou, the use of birds to supplement the skins of seal and Polar Bear was essential.

The Inuit ate the meat of all these and other animals. Occasionally they ate meat raw – lending support to the idea that the word 'eskimo' derives from 'raw meat eater' – but the meat of the Polar Bear was always cooked as it often contains parasites. Polar Bear fat is a good source of Vitamin A, but the liver was avoided (and not even fed to dogs) as the concentration of Vitamin A in the organ is lethal. Arctic Char are a good source of Vitamin B, while the soft bones of the fish are rich in calcium. The blubber of most Arctic animals is a rich source of omega-3 fatty acids. The skin of Beluga and, especially, of Narwhal are rich in Vitamin C. Another Inuit delicacy that would likely be passed on by the modern Arctic traveller is the stomach lining of the Caribou. Bowhead Whales provided meat and blubber, the latter prized as a cooking and lighting oil as it does not leave the sooty black residue of seal oil. The baleen of the Bowhead was used for the frame of kayaks. The uses other parts of prey species were put to reflect the understanding the native peoples acquired both for the prey and for their own environment. For example, the Inuit realised that the temperature at which the fats in a Caribou's leg went solid reduced as distance from the body increased, so they chose fats from the lower leg for greasing bow strings and other tasks that required work at very low temperatures.

The achievements of the other Arctic peoples should not, however, be ignored. The skills of the Asian Arctic peoples were legendary among the Russians who had to deal, and occasionally fight, with them. The Koryaks had sledges of wood bound together with strips of animal skin that could bend almost double and carry more than 100 times their own weight without breaking. Not only were they good for trade, but as the Russians discovered to their cost, the sledges could be used as war chariots, one man guiding the dogs while another let fly with a bow and arrow. The bows were made of strips of birch and cedar, the plies held together with vegetable glues and cords of nettles. They were incredibly strong, and the arrows, tipped with bone or rock crystal barbs, were lethal at great distances. The archers also devised a method of killing ducks that was remarkable, firing their arrows so close to the water's surface that the flight feathers dabbled the surface. Mother ducks, fooled into believing that the dabbling was the struggling of a swimming duckling, would move towards the disturbance – and into the path of the arrow.

Left
A dead walrus hauled ashore in Chukotka. The walrus was captured in the hunt illustrated on p578. It will now be cut up according to strict rules which define the amount of meat to be given to the successful marksman, the rest of the boat's crew, and the remaining villagers.

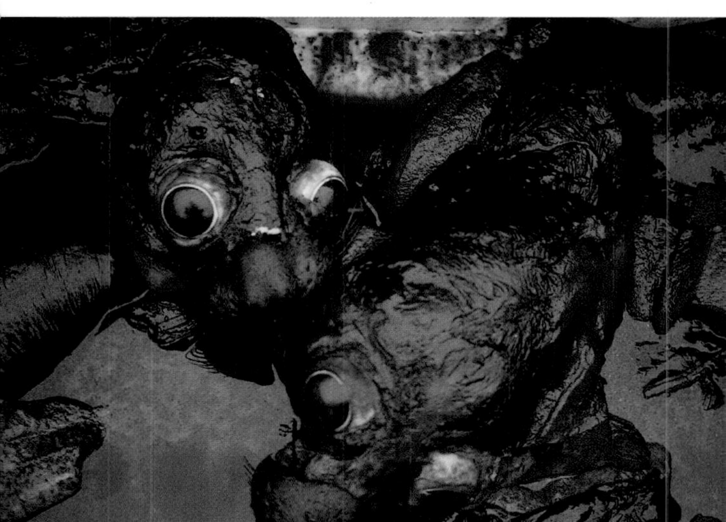

Below left
The Arctic is occasionally no place for the squeamish as this discarded group of heads from skinned seals indicates. But is it really so much worse than would be seen (but is more carefully hidden) at a slaughterhouse?

Below right
A Nenet sledge. All over the Arctic sledges were made entirely of wood and thongs so they could be readily repaired if broken. Such a sledge is superb on snow and ice, but equally good in summer when it slides on the top of the permafrost. Wheels, by contrast, dig into the surface or become bogged down in the active layer.

The village dump at Gambell, St Lawrence Island, Alaska. This is the modern equivalent of the 'Boneyard' illustrated on p578. It is relatively easy to persuade ships and planes to carry high-price consumer goods to out-of-the-way northern settlements, but almost impossible to get them to remove scrap. So quad bikes, snow scooters, TV sets, etc. come in – and stay. The dump therefore grows annually. One advantage it does offer is acting as a makeshift hardware store. With spare parts hard to come by, the locals forage, extracting likely looking bits which can be turned into spares. The ingenuity occasionally shown is impressive.

Fur trapping

Writing in 551AD, the Roman Jordanes noted that his countrymen were wearing furs that they had obtained from the *Suehans* (Swedes), who had themselves acquired the furs from the *Screrefennae* (presumably the Sámi). Other references point to a well-established fur trade from Fennoscandia in place since antiquity. It is probable that the Sámi were not only trading furs, but supplying them as tribute to the Norsemen of southern Scandinavia, who traded them to the countries of early medieval Europe. Furs were valuable not only because work and travel meant being out in the elements, and heating systems were much less efficient than today, but because of their status. Fur was the clothing of preference of royalty. Although there were fur-bearing animals throughout Europe, it was to northern Scandinavia and Russia that the crowned heads and aristocracy of Europe looked; the English Muscovy Company, set up after the first attempts to locate a North-East Passage, traded the skins of Sable and other northern animals. But trapping reduced animal numbers in Russia to such an extent that the country was in danger of economic ruin. It was at this point that the cossack Yermak crossed the Urals and 'discovered' Siberia. Here was a country that seemed limitless, and had within it fur-bearing animals whose numbers were apparently equally limitless.

Using boats to navigate Siberia's rivers, groups of *promyshlenniki* (hunters and trappers) explored the country, moving eastwards to conquer more land for the Tsar, who taxed the hunters and extracted tribute (*yasak*) from the native tribes encountered on the eastward push. The tributes were high, up to 20 Sables per person at first, though this figure had fallen to three within a century, such was the destruction of animal populations. In addition to yasak, the Russians also insisted on *pominki*, a 'voluntary' gift of furs to the Tsar. The number of animals slaughtered is difficult to estimate as the official figures for pelts collected as yasak and for those taxed cannot include the vast numbers smuggled past unknowing or bribed officials; the corruption and other abuses by officials far to the east of central government gave rise to the still-heard Russian comment 'God is high above and the Tsar a long way off', to express the unfairness of a life without checks and balances. Official estimates suggest 60,000 pelts annually, but these ignore the contraband, and seem much too low. Such accurate figures as are known suggest killing on a far more massive scale; in 1595 when the Holy Roman Emperor Rudolf II demanded soldiers from Tsar Boris Gudanov to help a crusade against the Turks, Gudanov feared repercussions on his valuable trade with Constantinople if he complied. He therefore declined, but sent a consignment of furs by way of

Fox and wolf pelts hanging outside a trapper's hut in north-east Greenland. It is believed the photograph dates from about 1928.

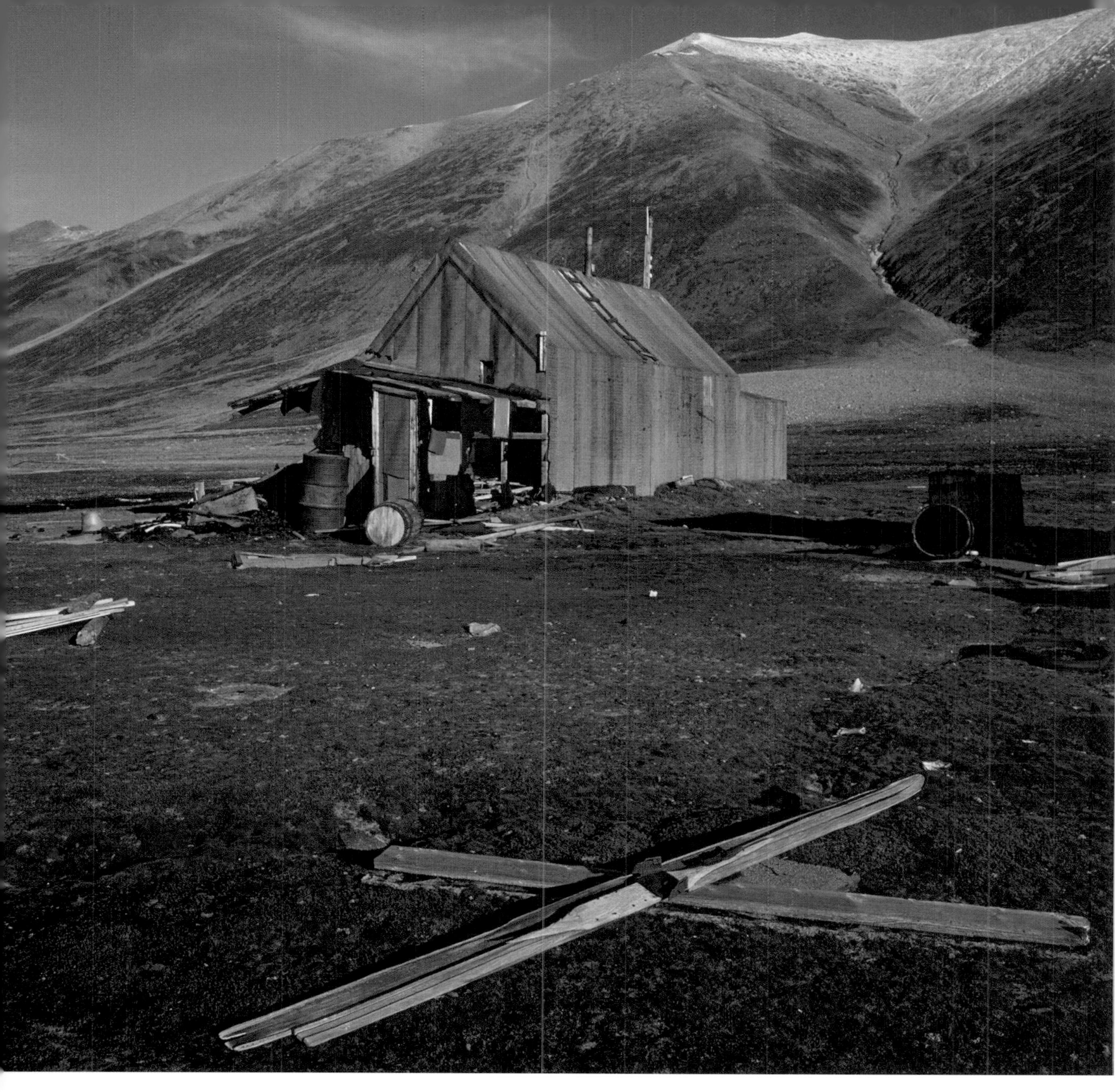

Fur trapper's hut at Antarctichavn, north-east Greenland. The beautiful locations and the isolation of such sites suggest a romantic lifestyle, but trapping was a hard and dangerous life, without even considering the brutal nature of the capture and dispatch of the animals.

compensation. The consignment comprised the pelts of 3,000 beaver and 40,360 Sable, with 20,760 other martens, 337,235 squirrels and 1,000 Wolves. The furs filled 20 rooms of the Emperor's palace, with numerous wagons parked outside still loaded with the less-valuable squirrel furs. When the consignment was valued in Prague, the merchants there declined to put a price on 120 Sable pelts, so rare and beautiful were the colours and quality. The 400,000 furs the consignment included are very unlikely to have represented the accumulation of seven years – even a gift to an Emperor would not go that far.

Sable was the chief prey of the trappers, the animals sought in winter (as were all the fur-bearers) when their pelts were at their thickest. Immense ingenuity went into the trapping methods as any damage to the pelt reduced its value. So good at their job were the trappers that within just a few years a location could become devoid of animals. When the Russians reached the Yenisey they were amazed to discover that Sable were so numerous that the local people used pelts as comfort padding on skis; within 30 years there were so few Sable left that trapping in the area ceased. Production of furs was such that supply exceeded demand in Europe, the position being exacerbated by the rising trade in North America.

The Russian trade (and economy) was saved by an increase in trade with China that underwrote further Russian expansion, to the Kamchatka Peninsula by the early 18th century, and into Chukotka by the mid-18th century. The expansion was not without its problems, the Chukchis and Koryaks being particularly aggressive in their response to Russian incursions and Moscow's demands for yasak. This belligerence was, in part, responsible for Bering's expeditions and the mapping carried out by the Great Northern Expedition that, it was hoped, would lead to the discovery of yet more sources of furs in less hostile areas.

Trapping on the Commander and Pribilof Islands

When Bering's ship struggled to what are now called the Commander Islands, his men found vast numbers of Arctic Foxes and Sea Otters. They killed and ate the otters (though the meat was disagreeable and they quickly found the sea cows to be much more palatable) and noted the luxuriousness of the animal's pelt. When they finally journeyed back to Kamchatka in a ship they had built from the remains of the *St Peter*, each man had a stock of pelts that he hoped to sell. The new ship was barely seaworthy and to keep her afloat the men had to jettison all surplus cargo, including their pelts. But one man secreted his pelts and, after successfully reaching Petropavlosk, sold them at an unimaginable profit. The deal caused a rush of hunters to sail east. The first ship returned with 1,600 otter pelts, together with around 2,000 fur seal pelts and 2,000 Arctic Fox furs. It is estimated that over the next 20 years 70,000 otters and 1,250,000 seals were taken, as well as huge numbers of foxes. This has to be seen in the context of the total fur trade: at around this time it is estimated that some 350,000 pelts were being taken out of Siberia annually, so the capture in Kamchatka and the Commander and Aleutian islands was now a large fraction of the total trade. Clearly the rest of Siberia had been largely hunted out.

Then, in 1768, Gerassim Pribilof spotted the islands that now bear his name; he sailed home with 40,000 Northern Fur Seal pelts and 2,000 Sea Otter pelts, as well as over seven tons of Walrus ivory. Russia's new fur trade with China was driven mainly by desire for Sea Otter pelts; within a few years the Pribilof Sea Otters had been exterminated. As noted before, this destruction of the fur-bearing animals was accompanied by the elimination of other species: Steller's Sea Cow and the Spectacled Cormorant were hunted to extinction by the fur trappers.

The killing of Sea Otters and fur seals continued when America purchased Alaska, but by now rifles had become commonplace, and in the rush to acquire pelts less care seems to have been taken in ensuring an undamaged skin. Otters were shot at sea, with many dying and sinking before they could be retrieved. Others were injured, escaping to die later. The losses could not be sustained, and by the early years of the 20th century a hunter might return from a season with only 20 pelts. Estimates of the original population of Sea Otters vary from 100,000 to 200,000 animals; by 1925 the take had shrunk to zero and it was widely assumed the animal had been hunted to extinction. Then, in 1931, a remnant colony was discovered. With full protection numbers increased spectacularly so that today's Arctic traveller can again enjoy the sight of this most beautiful and remarkable animal.

Although Sea Otters were quickly exterminated on the Pribilofs, the population of Northern Fur Seals was such that hunting went on for much longer. However, by the late 19th century numbers had reduced to the point where fears were being expressed for the health of the species. It is estimated that by the purchase date of 1867 the Russians had taken almost 2.5 million seals. The Americans probably took another million by the early 20th century. By then returns for hunters were diminishing markedly. The seals were hunted both on land and at sea and the leading pelagic sealing nations – Canada and Britain – resented the suggestion that pelagic hunting should be limited, a call led by the United States, whose land-based sealing industry would have been unaffected by any limit. Negotiations took place between interested

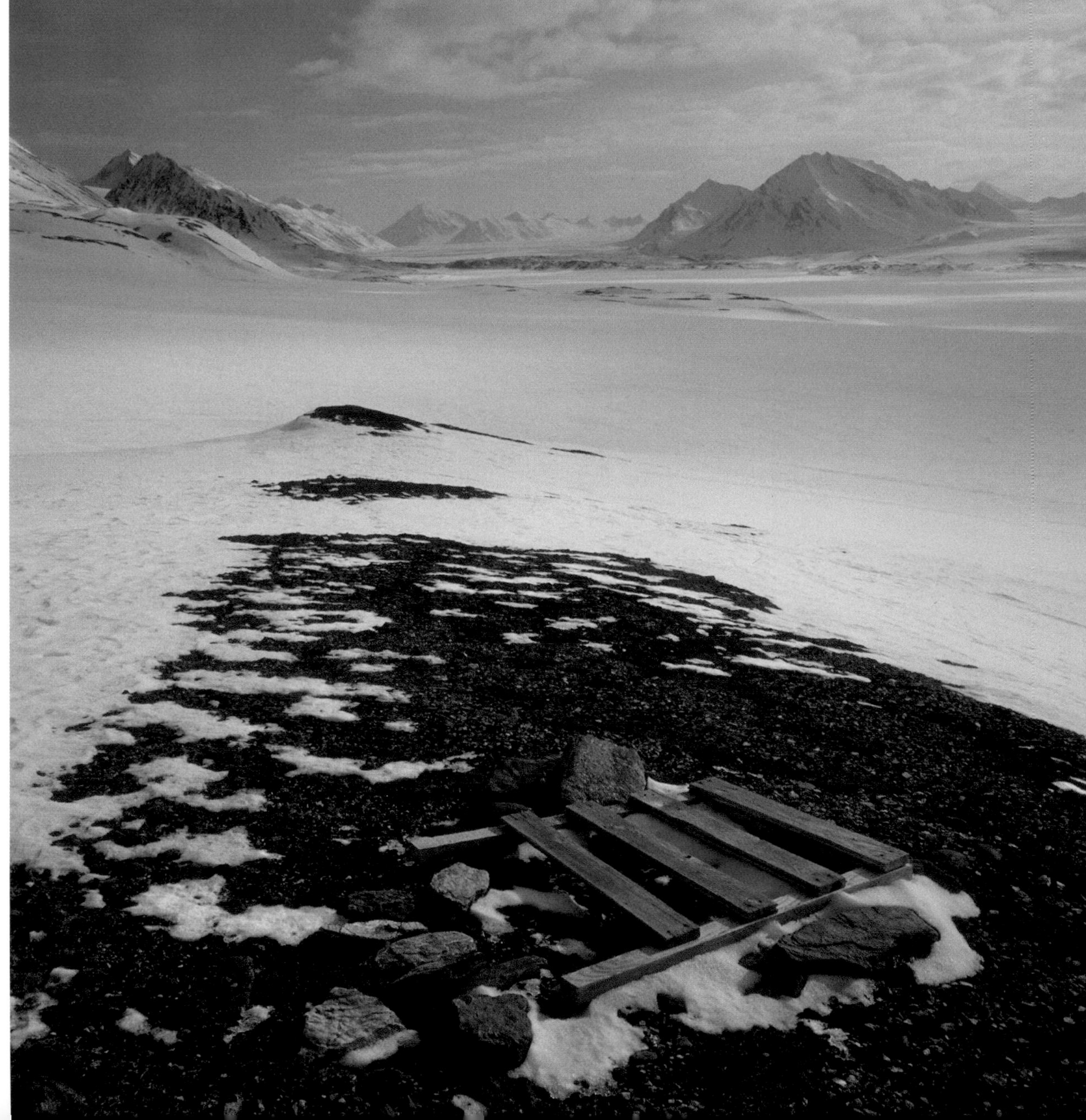

Old Arctic Fox trap, Spitsbergen, Svalbard

Old leg-hold traps, Victoria Island, Canada.

parties, but these became so heated and irrational that one man suggested, apparently without irony, that the ideal solution would be the hasty extinction of the species to avoid further conflict. Ultimately a grudging agreement was reached and the seal population increased again. Today, however, the population is once more in decline, having fallen by 30% in the last 30 years.

Trapping in Siberia

In Siberia, the invention of the snow mobile and the use of leg-hold traps made trapping easier, and the creation of the USSR pushed fur hunting to new extremes. As the communist regime maintained a monopoly on currency exchange and the rouble rate was artificially frozen, the government was continuously short of the valuable exportable commodities required to maintain the trade balance. Such commodities included precious metals, oil and furs (so-called 'soft gold'). By 1980 it is estimated that there was one Arctic Fox trap for every 10km^2 of tundra, with corresponding numbers of traps for other animals, particularly Sable. The Arctic Fox kill exceeded 100,000 animals in many years during the 1970s and 80s, representing as much as 60% of the total population. The fecundity of the fox could sustain such losses in years when the birth rate was high because of high prey density, but not in poor prey years and not surprisingly the trade eventually caused a significant fall in fox numbers. Added to the sheer destruction of the species was the effect on an individual animal. The leg trap causes terrible suffering as the animal rarely dies quickly; many bite through their own lower leg in order to escape (as a consequence of this cruelty the European Union (EU) banned the import of fur caught using leg-hold traps in 1991). Leg-hold traps can also kill other species such as Gyrfalcons and Snowy Owls attempting to take the bait or which, occasionally, perched on the traps and were captured. One estimate, based on capture records, gave a figure of one Gyrfalcon killed for every 50 traps, a mortality highly significant in terms of the overall number of falcons. In Russia an attempt to reduce the death rate of Arctic birds has led to the re-introduction of the *pasti*, the traditional log-fall trap that at least has the advantage of killing the animal quickly. One other effect of trapping has already been mentioned – the deliberate introduction of foxes on to all but a handful of Aleutian Islands and the effect of that on indigenous bird populations.

Trapping in North America

Though the capture rate in North America, in terms of sheer numbers, never matched that of Siberia, the continent's fur trade also had a significant effect on fur-bearing animals. The beginnings of commercial trapping can be dated to the French

It is often claimed that the idea of a fox (or other animal) caught in a leg-hold trap gnawing its foot off to escape is a myth. Here is the proof that it is not. The sprung leg-hold, still attached to a Caribou head which was the bait, grasps the paw and lower limb of an Arctic Fox. The fox would not have survived long with a severed foot and would have died a painful death. Victoria Island, Canada.

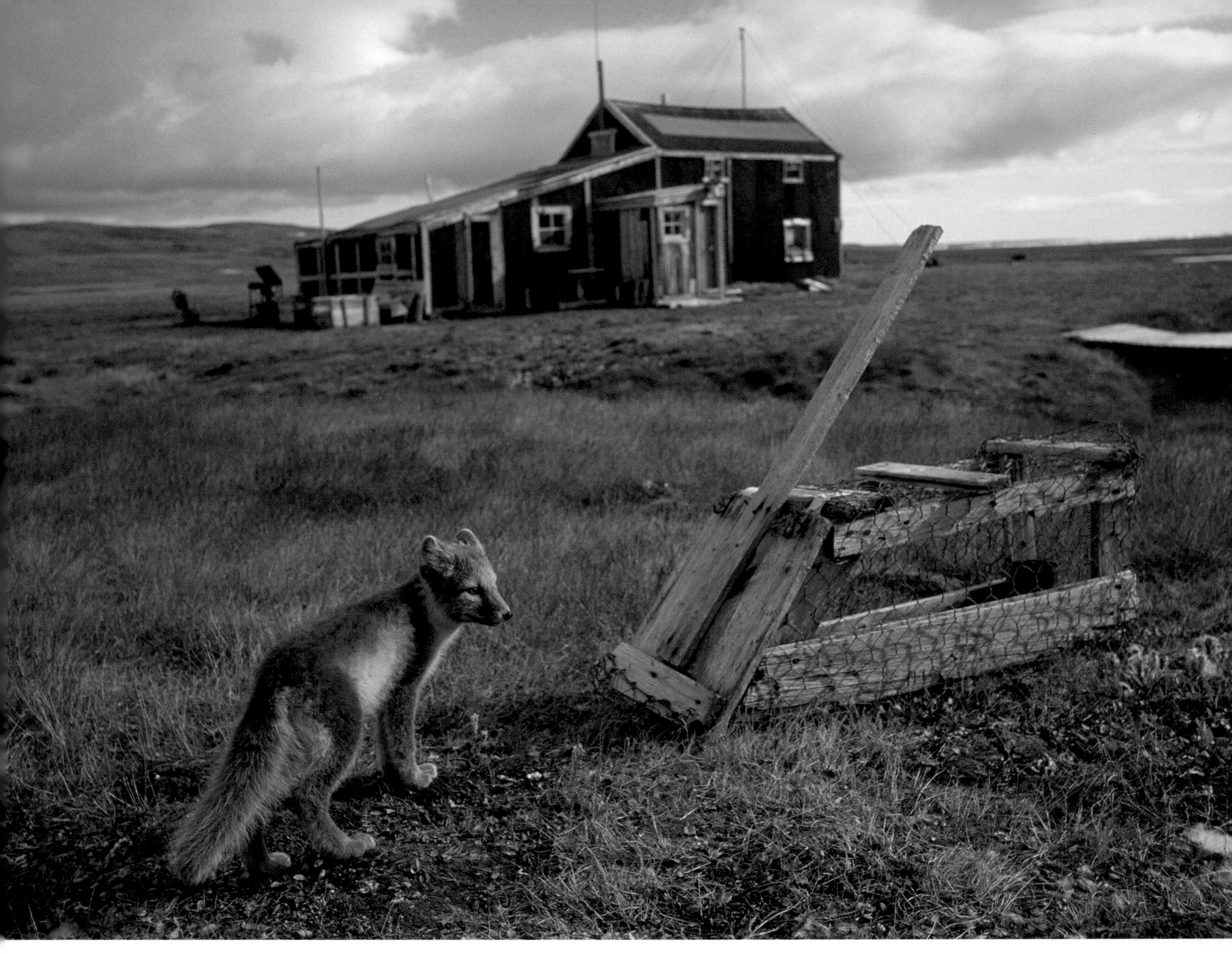

Without realising its significance, a young and curious Arctic Fox examines an old fox trap outside the trapper's hut at Myggbukta, north-east Greenland.

trade in North American beaver in the early 17th century. Beaver fur was waterproof, easily shaped and very durable, ideal material for hats, the Canadian animals being a lucky replacement for the European species that had been almost hunted to extinction to satisfy the trade. For half a century the French controlled the Canadian beaver trade. Then, in 1666, the restored English king, Charles II, was visited by two French trappers who enquired whether the king was interested in making himself (and them, of course) rich. Indeed he was, and an expedition was sent to Hudson Bay to see if the Frenchmen's tales were accurate. When the ship, the *Nonsuch*, returned loaded with furs the king granted his nephew Prince Rupert, son of the exiled King of Bohemia, jurisdiction over the fur-trapping lands. A group of merchants was assembled, the combination of the Prince and these merchants being termed the Governor and Company of Adventurers of England Trading into Hudson's Bay, a title soon shortened to the Hudson's Bay Company. The Company was granted 'sole trade … of all those Seas Streightes Bayes Rivers Lakes Creekes and Soundes … that lye within the entrance of … Hudson's Streightes'.

In his monarchical way, King Charles had dismissed both the claims of the native peoples and the French to the land he had given away. The French were eventually ousted by force (though it is not a good idea to suggest as much in modern French-speaking Quebec), while the Huron, Cree and other native tribes were just ignored. The Hudson's Bay Company established a series of forts, each in charge of a 'factor' (manager or governor) around the southern shores of Hudson Bay. The factor's task was to trade with the local native people who did most (if not all) of the trapping, Company employees rarely venturing out to explore the local area. The history of fur trapping in Canada is largely the history of the Hudson's Bay Company. Indeed, it could be said that the early history of Canada is largely the history of the Company as it was given jurisdiction over the country by the crown. The Company's factors occasionally used this authority to act as rulers rather than traders, the initials HBC being eventually said to mean 'Here Before Canada', reflecting the view outsiders took of the Company's methods. The Company was also charged with exploring and mapping Canada, which it did, though occasionally without the enthusiasm some back in Britain wished. It was, after all, not in the Company's interest that too many knew everything there was to know about the country, or to have a trade route running along their northern border. The Company traded guns, ammunition and other useful products of 'civilised' Europe for the furs of beaver and other Canadian animals. The Company motto was *Pro pelle cutem*, which translates roughly as 'a skin for its equivalent'. When the native hunters became a little more astute in their dealings with the Company, the factors were more inclined to suggest the motto meant 'we skin you before you skin us', though the native trappers preferred 'we risk our skins for your pelts'. Later still, when alcohol increasingly became the trading tool of choice, the motto was said to mean 'a skin for a skinful'.

Because the Hudson's Bay Company trade was better controlled than its equivalents in Siberia, and was also less open to corruption, the take of fur-bearing animals is better quantified in North America. In the century that began in 1769 the Company exported to London almost 5 million beaver furs, together with 1.5 million mink, 1.25 million marten, over one million lynx, almost 900,000 fox, almost 500,000 Wolf, 288,000 bear and 275,000 badger.

The economic crash of the 1930s, the 1939–45 war and then the development of central heating reduced the need for furs in the west, while fur farming (for instance of mink) and the import of nutria (the fur of the coypu) reduced the need for wild capture. Also, in the later years of the 20th century, a change of attitude led, both in the fashion industry and in the general public, to a significant reduction in the appeal and use of fur. While this led to a reduction in the slaughter of animals in Siberia, there was still a market within Russia itself, with the Russians not fully embracing the ethical issues of the west and fur still being the traditional way of combating winter's frightening cold. Trapping continues there, and to the surprise of many still continues in North America where the Alaskan trade is around 1,500 foxes annually (though much higher numbers are occasionally quoted), with numbers for the Canadian trade significantly higher.

Hopefully the very recent enthusiasm of the fashion industry for fur-trimmed accessories will be short-lived and will not lead to a revival of fur as a major fashion item. With modern, lightweight and warm materials now cheaply available there really is no need to wear fur. And has been said many times, the fur always looks better on the original wearer.

Whaling

Although the number of animals killed in the fur trade far exceeds the number of whales slaughtered during the era of 'industrial' whaling, the effect of whaling on populations of individual species has been much more dramatic. It is assumed from the existence of Stone Age rock carvings of whales that Neolithic folk knew of them, though it is not clear if their knowledge was from animals washed up or stranded on beaches, or whether they hunted whales, using boats to drive them close to shore for killing. That technique, still used in the Faroes today, was certainly in use in 9th century Norway. The construction of Whale Alley on Yttygran Island, which dates from a later, though still early, period, indicates that the ancestors of today's Inuit were also hunting whales many centuries ago. By the 16th century Basque fishermen, who had hunted whales in the Bay of Biscay and were already fishing cod near Newfoundland, began to hunt whales in that area. From written accounts and archaeological evidence it seems they killed around 450 whales annually, rendering them to oil at shore bases on both Newfoundland and Labrador. The Basques were clearly efficient whalers, because by the late 16th century the number of whales taken each season had reduced to such an extent that whale oil – the primary reason for taking the animals – had become an expensive luxury in Europe. The whale the Basques took was chiefly the species now called the Northern Right Whale, though the Basques also killed another, which they called the Greenland Right (now known as the Bowhead).

At about the same time that whale oil was becoming scarce Barents discovered Bear Island and Svalbard. In 1604, just a few years after Barents' journey, the Muscovy Company captain Stephen Bennet, in the *Speed*, reached Bear Island and its huge herd of Walrus. He killed 15 of them. The following year he killed many more, obtaining a great deal of oil and ivory. In 1606 his crew had become so good at killing Walrus that the quantity of both oil and ivory had doubled.

Then in 1607 Henry Hudson made his attempt to reach Cathay by sailing north over the Pole, and discovered the vast numbers of whales in Svalbard's sheltered bays; it is estimated that there were at least 25,000 Bowheads in Svalbard waters when Hudson made his voyage. Two years after Hudson's return Jonas Poole was dispatched to check the accuracy of his account; Poole not only did so, but also found large numbers of whales in the waters off Bear Island. The Muscovy Company immediately outfitted a ship to start whaling. They employed Basque whalers whose techniques had already proved efficient (and adopted some of their words as well – harpoon, for instance, is a Basque word). The expedition was a success, so a further one was mounted in 1611. This found that in some bays the whales were so densely packed that they often collided with the ship and its anchor cable. In 1612 there were two ships, in 1613 seven British and seven Dutch,

Mast of an old wooden whaling ship at Amsterdamøya, an island off Spitsbergen's north-western coast. The island was a major Dutch whaling station and is littered with remains from the period.

Debris from an old whaling station on Bear Island.

and in 1614 twice as many as the slaughter grew in pace. Relations between the two nations were not always cordial, with skirmishes occurring, these sometimes developing into battles with cannons fired on both sides leaving ships badly damaged, and resulting in the two governments having to agree terms over the division of the whale fishery. In the division the Dutch gained the most advantageous area.

The whaling involved large ships that transported men to the region. From the ships rowing boats were launched to kill the whale. A successful boat towed its kill to a shore station where the blubber was rendered and poured into barrels that were loaded back on to the ship. Some of the shore stations became seasonally permanent, the most famous being the Dutch Smeerenburg (Blubber Town), whose remains can still be seen on Amsterdamøya, off Spitsbergen's north-western shore. It is still common to see in the literature descriptions of Smeerenberg stating that it had a church, a bakery, a gambling hall, a dance hall and a brothel, serving a population of up to 10,000. So convincing were the descriptions that even Nansen repeated them. But the archaeological evidence does not support this delightful view of an Arctic Klondike town, suggesting a population of 200 at most, housed in barrack-like rooms, and an absence of clergy and women.

The Danes, French and Germans all sent ships to Svalbard to join in the killing, though it was the British and Dutch who made up the bulk of the fleet, and soon whale numbers were badly depleted. By the 1640s the catch barely covered the costs of the voyage; Smeerenberg was abandoned in the late 17th century, perhaps as early as the 1650s. The Dutch also had a whaling station on Jan Mayen, whales passing close to the island on their annual migration north. There, as on Svalbard, the station had to be manned annually. Setting them up each year was time-consuming and expensive as they had to be largely dismantled at the end of the season to avoid their being plundered when the whaling crew left. Attempts were made to overwinter, but these almost invariably ended in disaster; on Jan Mayen the seven men left in 1633 were found dead of scurvy in June 1634, and a similar fate befell a Smeerenberg party in 1634–35, though, ironically, eight English whalers survived an accidental wintering in 1630–31.

A pile of Beluga bones on a beach of Bellsund, Spitsbergen, Svalbard. Whalers were indiscriminate when it came to species, the oil from one whale being as good as that from another. Beluga might not be a large whale, but they form very large pods.

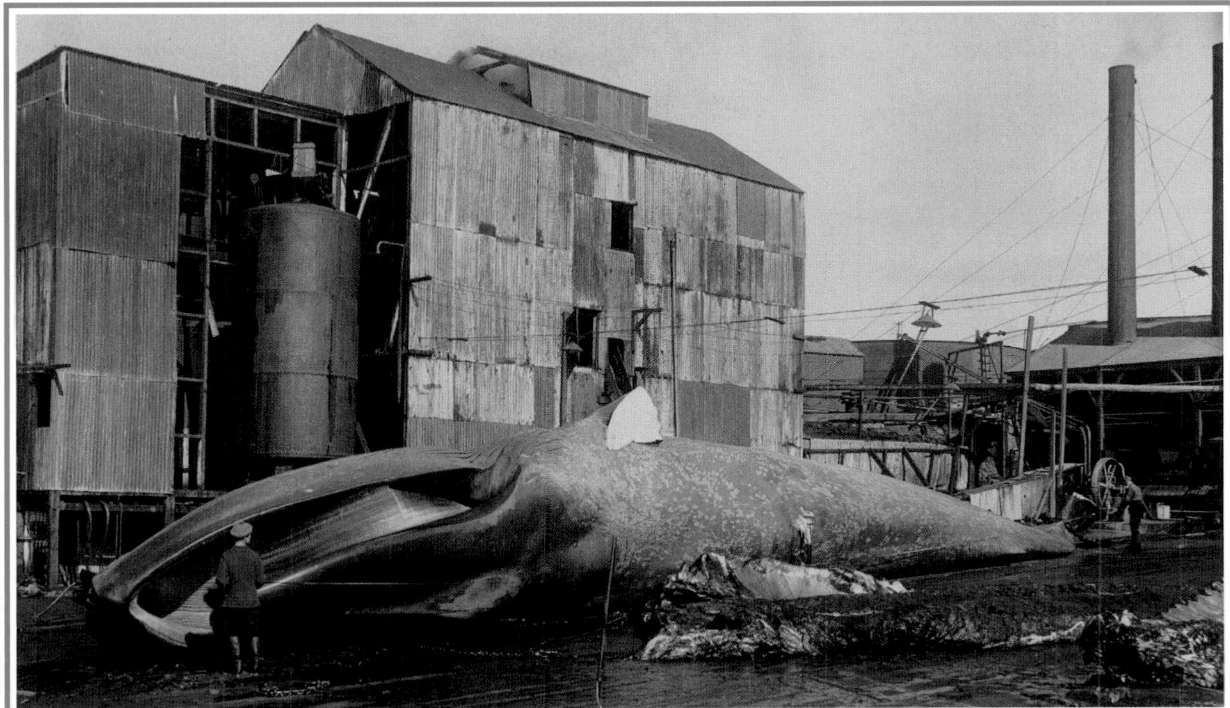

Whaling in Antarctica

The boom time of Antarctic whaling was the 20th century, with much of the industry concentrated on South Georgia. Whaling began here in 1904 when the Norwegians built a shore-based station at Grytviken, the first of six such stations on the island, and the longest to operate, closing only in 1965. During the period of station operations, 1904–1965, the whalers of South Georgia took almost 90,000 Fin Whales, over 40,000 Blues, about 27,000 Humpbacks, some 15,000 Sei and almost 4,000 Sperms. These figures are in addition to the catches of Southern Right Whales that had brought the species to the edge of extinction in the first phase of Antarctic whaling, just as it had for its northern cousin.

But if the catches registered for South Georgia seem high, they are dwarfed by those of Antarctica as a whole. In 1937–38, the catch – the highest in any Antarctic season – was 46,000 whales, and figures around 40 000 were caught annually for ten or so years on each side of this peak. It is estimated that overall at least 350,000 Blue Whales were killed over the period of hunting, about 90% of these in Antarctica. Fin Whales were killed in even greater numbers, perhaps 420,000 animals in total. The populations of the other great whales, Sei and Humpback, were also dramatically reduced, with some estimates putting the reduction of Humpbacks at 95%. Fortunately the populations of Humpback, Fin and Sei Whales show definite signs of recovery (the Humpback population is now thought to be about 35% of the pre-whaling figure), but that of the Blue Whale appears to be static, with some authorities concerned that the species may never recover and may even now be on a slow road to extinction.

The photograph above shows a Blue Whale being measured at a South Georgia whaling station, probably in the 1920s.

When whale numbers fell the Dutch also abandoned Jan Mayen. Whaling continued but the operation had changed. No longer were the whales conveniently found in bays close to shore. The remaining animals were further out, and at the ice edge. Shore stations were therefore useless, the rowing boats hauling their kill back to a mother ship with the whale being processed when it was tied alongside, chunks of blubber being hauled on deck. The requirement for the whaling ships to go further into the ice and to remain there meant an increase in catch, but a very great increase in danger, with significant losses in ships and men. Soon, the whales close to the ice edges near Svalbard and eastern Greenland were also exhausted, and the British and Dutch set out to explore Davis Strait. There Bowheads were still abundant. The west Atlantic hunting lasted longer than it had around Svalbard because the season was shorter and conditions were far more dangerous, so ship losses were much higher; in 1830 19 of the 91 British ships were lost, a further 12 being seriously damaged, and 21 more failing to kill a single whale. Further losses in subsequent years put an end to British whaling in the area.

Bowheads were also found in the Pacific, where they had sustained Yuppiat populations in both Siberia and Alaska for centuries. In 1845 a Danish whaler had found Bowheads in the Sea of Okhotsk; within 20 years an estimated population of 18,000 whales in the sea had been almost eliminated. Yet despite the killing in the Sea of Okhotsk, and the fact that the Americans were already hunting Sperm Whales in both the Atlantic and Pacific, the Bowheads of the Bering Sea were initially left in peace. They had been 'discovered' in 1848 when Thomas Roys took the *Superior* north towards the Bering Strait. Roys was acting on a hunch; in 1844 he had been injured during the harpooning of a Northern Right Whale and during treatment in Petropavlosk, on the Kamchatka Peninsula, he spoke with a Russian who told him about the curious whales he had seen towards the Strait. Roys later spoke to a Danish whaler who had also seen an odd-looking whale in the Bering Sea. Roys' hunch was that these were Bowheads, and he was proved right, his voyage resulting in the killing of 11 whales. But the whales of the Sea of Okhotsk were easier prey – the ice went early and so voyages were less dangerous, and robbed of the ice in which they could hide, the whales were also easier to catch.

But Roys' discovery was not forgotten. In 1858, while experimenting with a rocket-propelled harpoon, Roys is said

Fin Whale landed in Iceland in 2006. The landing was televised, but also drew a large crowd.

to have noticed, after the noise of the explosion had died away, that there was a finger lying on the deck. The captain recognised the ring on the finger – it was his own, and, when he checked further, he discovered that his left hand had been blown off: Roys was clearly the sort of man it was difficult to forget. American whalers, following Roys' lead, and concerned by the reduction in Bowhead kills in the Sea of Okhotsk, headed towards the Bering Strait. The Americans also began hunting Grey Whales near Baja California.

After the Americans had killed the Bowheads of the northern Bering Sea they discovered, as the Europeans had in the Atlantic, that pushing further north in pursuit of the remaining whales was a dangerous business. The ice-filled Beaufort and Chukchi seas were unforgiving and many ships and men were lost. The losses, and the development of a petroleum industry that offered a cheap alternative to whale oil, meant an end to whaling. But the relief for the whales was only temporary. Fashion decreed that hooped skirts and corsets should be worn and baleen – called whalebone by an industry that preferred a catchy name to a correct one – was needed for the stiffeners. Steamships also allowed the whalers to push through ice that would have imprisoned and sunk sailing ships. The ships allowed greater penetration into the Arctic, the Americans setting up a shore station near Alaska's Point Barrow, past which the Bowheads migrated, then following them even further east and setting up a station on Herschel Island. Because of the distance to Herschel the crews overwintered on the island. Herschel was finally abandoned early in the 20th century.

It is difficult to be exact about the number of Bowheads killed by the whalers, as in many cases a struck whale would escape, only to die later. Various figures have been suggested, but the most likely seems to be 120,000–150,000 in the whale's eastern range (the Atlantic and Hudson Bay), with 20,000 in the Sea of Okhotsk and at least the same number in the Bering Sea. The effect on the species was disastrous. When whaling ceased the Atlantic population was numbered in the hundreds, though Pacific numbers were higher. Today it is estimated that the Atlantic Bowhead population is still no more than 500–600 animals (perhaps 450 on the western side, no more than 100 on the east). In the Pacific the number of whales is thought to be around 6,000–8,000. For the Northern Right Whale the numbers are even more depressing, the present population being estimated as no more than 400 animals in the Atlantic and perhaps only 100 in the Pacific; the population is also failing to recover. The Bowhead population may be recovering slowly, though some experts doubt this. Inbreeding and consequent depressed breeding fitness as a result of the loss of genetic diversity act against recovery.

Another consideration is the 'Allee effect', named for W. C. Allee whose studies of fish indicated that for some species that habitually schooled, as the population level declined individuals suffered increased stress as a consequence of the absence of group members. The stress reduced lifetimes and

Gambell, St Lawrence Island, Alaska. The Yuppiat of the village are still granted an annual quota of Bowheads.

fecundity rates. Given the vastness of the oceans and the enormous reduction in the right whale populations it is possible that such stresses may also be affecting the whales. These effects are even more pronounced in the Northern Right Whale, and some experts believe that this species is actually doomed to extinction.

But it is not just a question of numbers. Death by harpooning was usually agonising and drawn-out. Some whales towed row boats for days before dying. There are stories of the men in the boats being covered in gore as the whale spouted blood, and one appalling tale of a Bowhead diving so fast that it crashed into the seabed, burying itself almost 3m into the sediment and breaking its neck in the process.

For the whales of the waters of the Arctic fringe, the pursuit was equally relentless. The Sperm Whale was the main target at first, to its size being added the fact that the species provided ambergris (a material that to the perfume industry was, literally, worth its weight in gold) and spermaceti oil. Sperm whale hunting had, as its capital, the ports of New England, particularly Nantucket, where the Quakers, a singularly rapacious and whale-bloodthirsty lot despite being Christian pacifists, made a great deal of money from the trade. The infamous 'Nantucket sleigh ride' was named for the occasionally lengthy tow a whale gave to the row boat that had harpooned it. The whale hero of Herman Melville's *Moby Dick* is pursued by a captain from New Bedford, a port near Nantucket. The whale is thought to have been based on Mocha Dick, a white Sperm Whale that wrecked two boats, killing two men, from a Bristol whaler operating close to the Falkland Islands in May 1841.

For the rorquals, coveted because of their huge size, the technique of using rowed boats that had been so deadly against the right whales was useless as the whales can reach speeds of 20 knots. But that situation changed in the 1860s with the introduction of steamships and the invention of the explosive harpoon gun by the Norwegian Sven Foyn. The slaughter of rorquals was greatest in southern waters, but the great whales of the Arctic fringe were also hunted mercilessly.

Finally, with many species on the edge of extinction, the slaughter of these magnificent creatures was halted by the

The remains of a hunted Bowhead Whale litter the beach at Gambell, St Lawrence Island, Alaska.

The Siberian Yuppiat also have a quota of Bowheads. For Yuppiat on both sides of the Bering Strait the hunting is a tradition centuries old, though their ancestors did not have the luxury of a giant tractor to haul a killed whale on to the beach.
In the lower photograph, chunks of blubber are being cut off the whale and hauled up the beach. They will be allocated to villagers according to traditional rules on the make-up and outcome of hunting trips.

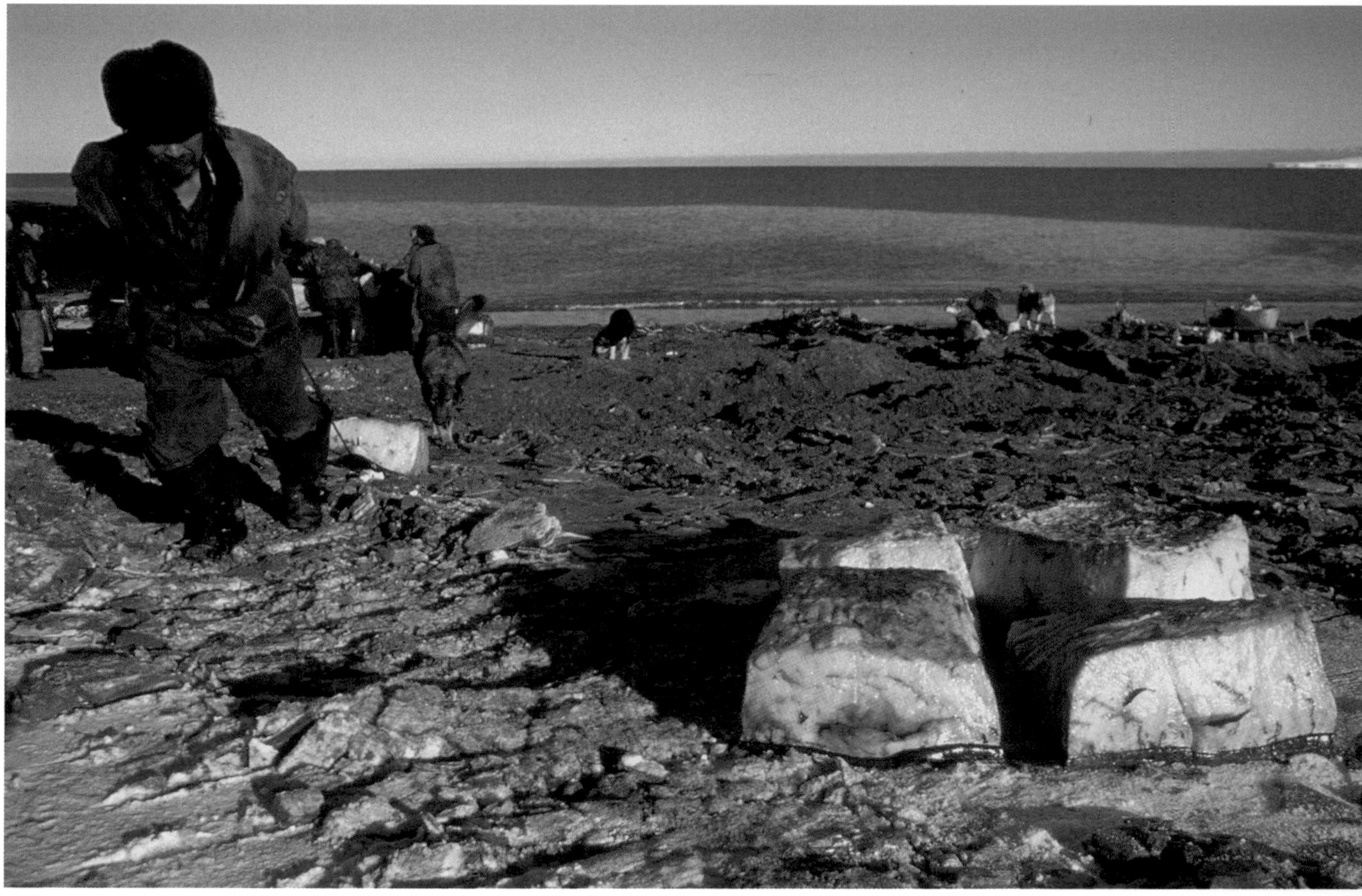

Native Arctic whale hunting

Before the advent of commercial whaling it is thought that the Inuit of the eastern Arctic took perhaps ten Bowhead annually, while the take in the Bering Sea was higher, perhaps 15–20 animals on both the Siberian and Alaskan sides. European whalers in the Atlantic reduced the Bowhead take by native folk effectively to zero by the early 19th century. In the Bering Sea, commercial whaling had a curious effect, actually increasing the take initially as native people acquired new technology that made their kills easier and less dangerous, but eventually also reducing the take to zero. By the 1970s there was no native whaling for Bowheads on either side of the sea, though the hunting of Grey Whales on the Russian side continued.

The development of the Prudhoe Bay oil fields pumped money into the local economy, allowing people to buy boats and modern equipment, and they began whaling again. But the native peoples had lost their basic skills and many more whales were struck and escaped to die elsewhere than were landed. However, these kills contravened the zero quota agreed by the IWC for the Bowhead and caused concern among environmentalists.

When the IWC asked the US government to intervene to stop native hunting the Yuppiat were outraged, considering the Bowhead hunt to be part of their heritage and pointing out that it was the southerners who had reduced the stock to dangerous levels. They also disputed the IWC figure for the Bowhead population and set up the Alaska Eskimo Whaling Commission, which used hydrophones to listen for whales, claiming that this was a better method of assessing numbers than visual counts.

The study gave a population estimate of 6,000, four times the IWC's estimate. As a consequence the IWC agreed a quota of 280 landed whales for the five-year period 1998–2002 and, subsequently, a quota of 255 for the five years to 2007. In the late 1990s the Yuppiat killing efficiency rose to over 75% so the number of whales struck and not landed decreased substantially. The quota for 2008–12 was increased to 280, with a limit of 67 whales in any one year and an allowance of 15 unstruck whales to be carried forward. For the same 5-year period the quota of Grey Whales is 620, with a maximum of 140 in any one year. Quotas are also allocated for the same period to native Greenlanders; these included annual figures of 2 Bowheads and 19 Fin Whales, as well as several hundred Minke Whales.

International Whaling Commission (IWC) in 1986, though Japan objected and continued to hunt, largely for 'scientific' purposes. Iceland and Norway have also hunted, though their take has been considerably smaller. About 2,000 whales have been killed each year; after the 'science' has been conducted on them the carcasses are sold to processing plants. Japan also takes numbers of smaller whales (for instance Baird's Beaked Whale) which are not included in the IWC moratorium.

Iceland left the IWC in 1992, but rejoined in 2002 stating its intention to return to commercial whaling in 2006 as it believed the moratorium was not consistent with the assessment of whale numbers. Norway has also reserved its position on the moratorium. Both countries have announced their intention to resume commercial whaling and in 2006 Iceland took 7 Fin Whales (an endangered species). The landing of one whale was televised apparently as a means of whipping up local support for the resumption. However, the pictures added to international disquiet and in some European countries environmentalists asked people to boycott Icelandic goods and not to travel to the island in protest. The latter request resulted in an anguished appeal from a spokesman for island tourism, though figures suggest that tourism to the island has, in fact, increased.

Iceland, Japan and Norway claim that stocks of some species are sufficient to allow harvesting without endangering populations, but opponents point out that population numbers are disputed, the method of calculation, using aerial photographs of the ocean and counting the number of whales seen not allowing for the known behaviour of the animals which tend to form groups. Opponents also point out that one justification for a resumption of whaling, that the whales take a huge volume of fish and so endanger commercial fisheries, is not supported by scientific studies.

The economics of commercial whaling are also dubious. There is, for instance, no market for the meat of the Fin Whales landed in Iceland and the hope that it might be exported to Japan has come to nothing as whale meat consumption there is apparently falling (despite official figures to the contrary) and there is an embargo on the import of meat from other countries. The Icelandic whales are therefore in cold storage. There is also a curiosity regarding the Icelandic Minke Whale catch, landed whale weights having decreased by over 50% in the last few years, the suggestion being that as there is a very limited market for the meat, only the better cuts are brought home, the rest of the whale being thrown overboard. The same thing appears to be happening in Norway, while there is considerable evidence that the Japanese whaling industry is in financial crisis as consumption does not match catch.

In all three whaling nations the position seems to have become entrenched more because of nationalism, a simmering resentment at being told what to do, than pure commercialism. The problem is exacerbated because the opponents of whaling are equally entrenched. Whales have become a totem, both for environmentalists and the general public, particularly with the latter as whale watching has become big business and has resulted in considerable sympathy for the animals. Whaling is also undoubtedly cruel, adding to public sympathy.

In June 2006 the IWC passed a resolution (by a majority of 1, with 1 abstention) which effectively opposed the 1986 ban on commercial (as opposed to 'scientific') whaling, largely as a result of many small, non-whaling countries (some land-locked, some tiny Pacific and Caribbean islands) voting with the Japanese. The fact that these countries had received Japanese aid packages and had joined the IWC as a result of Japanese pressure was stated to be a coincidence. Having gained effective control of the IWC, Japan declared its intention to increase its Antarctic and Pacific whale catch, doubling the number of Minke Whales taken, and adding Humpback and Fin Whales (they later bowed to international pressure and decided not to hunt Humpbacks). Though the 2007 IWC annual meeting passed a resolution asking Japan to refrain, conservationists fear that the future for whales will not be as peaceful as many had hoped.

Fishing

The northern native peoples have always taken fish as a supplement to their diet of terrestrial or marine mammals. The civilisations of northern Europe commercialised fishing, taking cod and herring in the seas off Norway and European Russia, as well as seas further south. The cod fisheries of the Canadian Grand Banks became accessible when ocean-going vessels became available. Over time, as both vessels and fishing equipment became more efficient, and people realised the potential of the sea for food and profit, catches increased. By the second half of the 20th century the apparently limitless fish stocks of the Barents Sea and northern Norwegian Sea were showing clear signs of overfishing. The normal migration patterns of herring in the north-east Atlantic were also disrupted, and the stock collapsed dramatically. The fishing fleets of Norway and Russia therefore transferred their attention to capelin and, predictably, stocks of that species also collapsed within a few years. Conservation measures have seen fishing activity reduced, though there is evidence that illicit fishing is being carried out and that the Barents cod stocks are being seriously depleted.

Elsewhere a similar story has unfolded. Cod fishing in the north Atlantic increased to the point where by the 1970s the Icelandic economy was based almost exclusively on the fish. Iceland extended its coastal limit to 200 miles (320km) in 1977 and fought 'cod wars', particularly with Great Britain, to confirm this limit, this being viewed as illegal by other nations. The limit has allowed cod fishing to continue in Icelandic waters (though the stocks of the fish elsewhere, such as in the North Sea, are now at dangerously low levels). Icelandic fisherman have, however, overfished local herring, and now pursue capelin, as well as pelagic fish. Icelandic and foreign fishermen have also fished the waters off eastern Greenland, catching Greenland halibut and cod, and some capelin. On the west Atlantic coast cod and halibut have also been fished, and shrimp fishing has been a major industry for many years. Stock reductions have again given cause for concern, but in general have not reached the worryingly low levels of those of the north-east Atlantic.

Off eastern Canada the history of the cod fishery centred on the Grand Banks deserves a book of its own, the story being one of astonishing riches, greed and incompetence. The fishery not only saw the virtual extinction of the cod, but also played a very large part in the actual extinction of the Great Auk. Fishing for Greenland halibut and shrimp continues.

Fishing in the Bering Sea has come under intense scrutiny in recent years because of its potential (some would say probable) involvement in the decline in the number of Sea Otters and pinnipeds. Historically, fishing for salmon species, herring and halibut have been important. Visitors to south-western Alaska need only read the menu of any local restaurant to recognise that salmon and halibut are a source of local pride; sport fishing for both fish provides an important tourist revenue. Salmon fishing is also important on the Russian side of the sea, and for Japanese trawlers. In the 1970s and 1980s the fishing of Walleye Pollock increased dramatically, with annual catches of up to 20 million tonnes eventually being recorded. However,

Above and right
Salmon fishing on the Zhupanova River, southern Kamchatka, Russia. When carried on at this level, fishing was sustainable, but now here, as elsewhere, the catching is on an industrial scale, with vast nets and mechanised net-hauling, bringing with it concerns that catches may be too high and the stock diminishing.

catches then dropped sharply, probably due to a combination of overfishing and a rise in water temperature, though experts are divided on which of these was the more significant. The populations of both Sea Otters and Steller's Sea Lion declined dramatically. One likely scenario sees warming water pushing temperature-sensitive organisms at the bottom of the food chain north, and crustaceans dying as they are unable to respond fast enough. Young fish also die from lack of food, and with fishing reducing adult fish numbers, populations decline dramatically. Next the sea lion population slumps because of a lack of fish. Now, perhaps, Orcas, deprived of the mainstays of their diet – fish and sea lions – take otters instead. The otters are the main predators of the sea urchins that graze on kelp. The subsequent increase in urchin numbers then causes the kelp forests around the Aleutians to thin or disappear. Many authorities believe that the ecology of the southern Bering Sea has been irreparably altered; as this sea is one of the wonders of the sub-Arctic, the loss of this ecosystem, which supports, among other things, millions of seabirds, would be a tragedy.

Two other effects of fishing cannot be ignored. Bycatch is the name given to the accidental taking of sea mammals and birds caught in, and killed by, fishing tackle. Birds and mammals can be entangled in nets and drowned, and birds may also take bait from long-line fishing and so become hooked. The latter is considered to be a real threat to albatross species in the North Pacific, particularly the endangered Short-tailed Albatross. The other effect is damage to the seabed by trawl nets. In shallow waters with soft seabeds it is likely that storms cause more disruption to sediments than trawling, and that benthic creatures have adapted to occasional disturbance. In deeper waters where the effects of storms are negligible, disturbance from the dragging trawl nets will have more impact. This impact increases on harder seabeds, with considerable damage being caused to corals and to rocky environments.

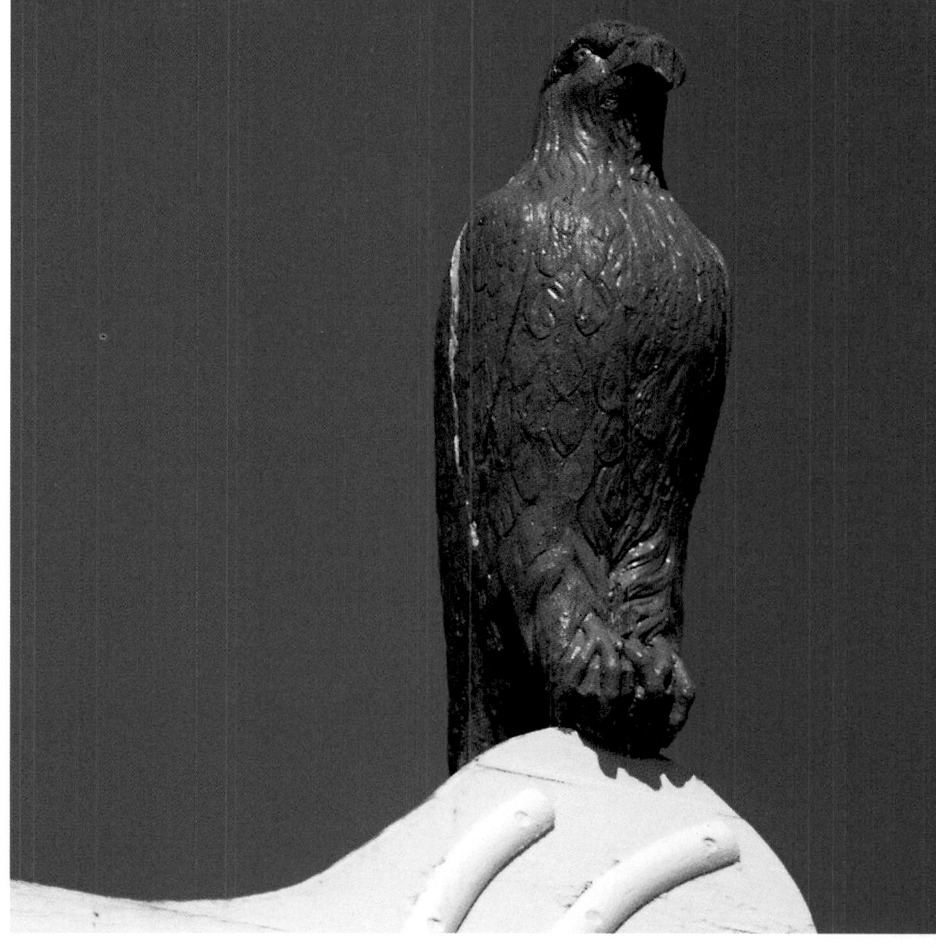

A carved Gyrfalcon on the roof of the *Falkhus* (Falcon House) in Reykjavik, Iceland. The house was originally built for white Gyrfalcons captured after flying in from Greenland to overwinter. The birds were prized gifts from the Danish crown to other royal heads of Europe and the house was far better than those of the average Icelander. White Gyrs are still highly prized, and the frequent target of poachers.

Poaching

Gyrfalcons, particularly the white morph of the species, are in great demand by falconers and there have been occasions when birds have been illegally trapped, then drugged and smuggled away. Such incidents have happened in North America, though the greater financial standing of protection agencies on the continent has reduced the trade. In Russia agencies have much less spending power and a vast area to police, and from the poaching incidents known to have occurred there seems to be a consistent trade. Such poaching can have a significant impact on the wild population in more accessible areas, as the density of the falcons is never high. As roads are built to service increased industrial activity, access to sensitive areas improves and the poacher's task is made easier.

Illegal hunting is also a problem. There seems to be a constant stream of hunters with a desire to take bear and other rare Arctic species, though this is incomprehensible to the majority of travellers since there is little kudos, given the killing range of a gun and the lack of competition involved. In Kamchatka, where the Brown Bears are renowned for their size, illegal hunting is now considered a threat to a species that was once relatively abundant. Again the lack of resources of Russian agencies does not help curb the trade.

The easy access of firearms has often meant that hunt kills have risen, occasionally beyond the needs of the hunter, endangering stock levels. This litter of dead Common Eiders, some from which the wings have been removed, but others where the entire bird has been abandoned, is an indication of the problem.

The Exploitation of Arctic Minerals

Oil

It is known that the Inuit of northern Alaska used the oil that seeped to the surface near Cape Simpson as fuel, compressing oil-soaked earth into bricks that could be burnt. Explorations in the 20th century indicated that large areas of the Arctic had sedimentary basins that were likely to be oil-bearing, these including northern Alaska, the Mackenzie delta and Beaufort Sea, the northern Canadian Arctic islands, off-shore western Greenland, and Yamal, Yakutia and Sakhalin Island in Russia.

Drilling operations and pipelines beneath the northern seas are in danger from moving ice, which occasionally gouges trenches in the seabed, and, perhaps, from sub-sea pingos. Added to these difficulties, and those of access and working, are the possibility of native land claims, as in most of the areas of production there is an indigenous population. In July 2007 Shell were forced to halt exploratory drilling in the Beaufort Sea when native Alaskans brought a court case based on the dangers the activity presented to Polar Bears and whales.

Oil production in the Arctic has unique environmental problems because of the long recovery times of the landscape in the event of damage. Although improving technology has reduced the footprint of the drill head (the drive to do so was as much to do with economics as environmental concerns), oil fields still do considerable, if localised, damage to the environment. Wheeled vehicles create ruts that deepen and widen, construction causes changes in local hydrology (the construction of a 7km section of road near Prudhoe Bay caused the subsequent flooding of more than 130ha of surrounding land), while oil production releases hydrocarbons and other pollutants, including heavy metals, into the environment. Oil spills in the sea, such as the *Exxon Valdez* disaster, have a devastating effect on all levels of the marine ecosystem. Oil also persists for longer in the Arctic than in more southerly areas, since the oil may become trapped under sea ice. On land, spillages tend to be more localised, but surface water can spread the oil. Oil does considerable damage to Arctic plants which, being shallow-rooted, cannot avoid the pollutants. Terrestrial birds and mammals are in less obvious danger than their marine counterparts, but nonetheless can become oiled, with similarly fatal consequences. In 1994 a spillage occurred in the Usinsk region of Russia's Komi Republic. Exact data are difficult to obtain. The most likely figure for the amount of oil lost is about 100,000 tonnes, though some estimates double this. Although the immediate effects of the spill are likely to have been less severe in terms of wildlife deaths, the longer-term effects on the local ecosystem are likely to be significant over the spill area of some 60km^2.

Prudhoe Bay, oil from which was spilled in the *Exxon Valdez* incident, is the most famous of the Arctic's oil fields, and is probably the best-studied in terms of its effect on local wildlife. The bay's oils derive from the Kingak shale, laid down during the Jurassic period. The bay lies in the 'North Slope' area – sometimes defined as all the land between the Brooks Range and the northern coast, from the western coast to the Yukon border, but usually taken to mean only the rectangle of land between the mountains, the north coast and the Colville and Canning rivers. The potential importance of the North Slope was recognised as early as the 1920s, and in 1923 the National Petroleum Reserve, Alaska (NPRA), to the west of the bay, was designated as an area within which oil production could proceed, but only in the case of a national emergency. Exactly what constitutes an emergency, particularly given the lead time of extraction, is a moot point. To the south and east of Prudhoe Bay lies the Arctic National Wildlife Reserve. Oil was discovered at Prudhoe Bay in 1968. In 1977 oil from the bay's wells was first loaded on to tankers at Valdez on Alaska's

Prudhoe Bay well-heads seen from Deadhorse.

The *Exxon Valdez*

On 24 March 1989 the tanker *Exxon Valdez* left the Valdez oil terminal, loaded with 1.3 million barrels of oil. To avoid floating ice Captain Joseph Hazlewood took the tanker out of the normal navigation lane. Hazlewood then left the bridge, placing a Third Mate in charge of the ship. *Exxon Valdez* moved off the coastguard's radar and at 12.04 went ashore on Bligh Reef, about 250,000 barrels being released into Prince William Sound. The disaster was then exacerbated by the lack of emergency preparedness, which meant that little effort was made to control the spread of the oil for many hours, by which time a storm had dispersed the oil slick. Ultimately the oil contaminated 2,500km of shoreline. At least 2,000 Sea Otters were killed (a more exact number has never been established, but figures as high as 5,000 have been suggested; the current best estimate is 2,800). Over 200 Harbour Seals and 20 Orca are also known to have died, while the total number of dead birds exceeded 250,000. The effect on lower trophic levels of the marine ecosystem are difficult to assess, but it is thought that the combination of oil and chemical residues from the spill and the clean-up, which made their way into the food chain, would have been considerable. The use of high-pressure hoses to clean up areas of contaminated beach also caused environmental damage, destroying organisms at the sea margin. The populations of some species, such as Harbour Seals and Harlequin Ducks, have not recovered and it is feared they never will. After the disaster Captain Hazlewood was found to have a blood alcohol level above that allowable for control of a ship but had apparently consumed two beers between the ship grounding and his test. He was sentenced to 1,000 hours of community service for a Class B misdemeanour. The Exxon Corporation were fined $1 billion for a violation of various Acts, with a further $5 billion in punitive damages.

In early 2007 a study of Prince William Sound and the Gulf of Alaska found that the oil was still a threat to wildlife as its decay was much slower than had been anticipated. Exxon, which has funded several hundred studies that indicate no significant long-term effects from the release, suggested that the study told us nothing that had not been anticipated. The study was released the day before Exxon Mobil revealed that its 2006 profit had been $39.5 billion dollars, the largest annual profit ever posted by a US company. Exxon Mobil are still engaged in appealing against the level of damages awarded following the *Exxon Valdez* incident.

Visitors who drive the Dalton Highway to Prudhoe Bay are, for security reasons, only allowed to visit the oil fields as part of an organised tour. The tour starts with a video that covers the economic benefits and engineering aspects of the field and pipeline. The measures taken by the companies working the oil field to protect the environment are explained, but there is no mention of the *Exxon Valdez*.

southern coast. The entire North Slope oil field covers an area of almost 9,000ha, huge, but representing only around 0.1% of the North Slope (defined as the area between the outflows of the two rivers). The fields produce 20–25% of all US oil production, and provide 85% of the Alaska State budget in taxes and royalties.

There is also oil exploitation at the Arctic fringe, particularly from non-conventional oil sources, the interest in these mounting as production from conventional oil sources is believed to be nearing its peak. Canadian tar (or oil) sands, close to the Athabasca river in Alberta, are estimated to hold 175 billion barrels (cf. Saudi Arabia quoted reserves of about 264 billion barrels) with another 135 billion barrels available once the technology to extract them has improved. In terms of global warming, the extraction of the oil is doubly disastrous as the removal of each barrel creates 3-4 times the CO_2 production of conventional oil as up to 30% of the available energy is used in the extraction and refining. The extraction process is also extremely destructive of the environment.

Well-heads, Prudhoe Bay, seen from the shore of the Beaufort Sea.

Effects on wildlife

On the North Slope 180 species of breeding birds have been identified, with a further 60 species having been noted. The total number of birds is estimated at 10 million. There are also 15 terrestrial mammals, while six species of marine mammals are regularly seen offshore. Studies of these animals and North Slope vegetation have revealed both costs and benefits. In summer the Dalton Highway (the 'haul road' beside the pipeline) is very dusty; the dust has killed roadside vegetation, though the effect reduces relatively quickly with distance from the road. For bird populations the effect has been essentially neutral. Road and site construction work has, of course, reduced nest site availability. However, there appears to have been no instance in which a habitat made unavailable does not exist elsewhere, so that the effect is short-term only. Nests have even been discovered on the pipeline structures.

For Caribou the oil field and pipeline have also been basically neutral. Some sections of the elevated pipeline were

The Trans-Alaska pipeline

Construction of the pipeline that links the oil fields of Prudhoe Bay and the oil tanker terminal at Valdez involved about 70,000 workers over a period of nine years and cost $8,000,000,000. The pipeline is 1,250km long, the pipe itself having an outside diameter of 1.22m and a wall thickness of 1.3cm. About 52% of this pipeline is above ground, to prevent thawing of sensitive areas of permafrost. In general, buried sections are in rock or dry gravel, though even there it is well insulated from the substrate. Where burial was essential in permafrost areas, circulating refrigerated brine chills the pipeline. The pipeline does not form a continuous straight line, the zig-zag pattern allowing for thermal expansion and contraction of the pipeline during the change from mid-winter to mid-summer. Although the pipe is insulated, the construction allows for thermal effects between extremes of -55°C (with the pipe assumed empty in winter) to +63°C (with the pipe assumed to be filled with oil at near-extraction temperature). In areas of potential seismic activity the pipeline sits on Teflon sliders, and is also designed to allow a movement of 60cm.

Oil reaches the well-head at a temperature of about 70°C. It enters the pipeline at about 45°C. The oil flows at 6–7kph, taking 8–9 days to reach Valdez, by which time its temperature has fallen to about 18°C. At any given time, when in operation, the pipeline holds about 9 million barrels of oil. Pumping is provided by five pump stations along the pipeline. The average daily throughput is about 1 million barrels, the maximum being 2,145,297 barrels on 14 January 1988. The pipeline is protected by four independent leak detection systems (which sounds excellent, but the systems do not protect the oil fields and feeder systems, as the loss of a considerable amount of oil when a BP pipe failed due to corrosion in 2006 showed).

The Valdez oil terminal has 18 storage tanks, each capable of holding 500,000 barrels. The terminal has one floating and three fixed loading bays, which have filled almost 20,000 tankers since the pipeline was commissioned.

The photograph above was taken immediately north of the Yukon Bridge.

constructed less than 1.5m above the ground, making it difficult for the animals to pass beneath; newer sections have greater ground clearance. Brown Bears that scavenge on the oil field dumps show lower cub mortality than those whose diets are not supplemented in this way. The reason appears to be less to do with the condition of the mother as a result of enhanced food intake (though heavier mother bears tend to have healthier cubs) and more to do with the relatively sedentary life of these animals. Cubs of peripatetic mothers may be drowned crossing rivers, injured in falls or become separated, and are more likely to meet predators. A similar effect has been seen in Arctic Foxes, which also scavenge at the dumps; scavenging foxes tend to have larger litters and higher survival rates. However, there is a downside for the prey of these larger, healthier bears: their numbers are not enhanced by scavenging, and the bears kill more of them. Arctic Ground Squirrels and some nesting birds have shown population decreases in areas where bears and foxes hold territories that include the dumps. While these studies are encouraging to a degree, the fact remains that poorly considered oil and gas pipelines can and do interfere with local animals. A railway built to service a Taimyr gas field, and the pipeline running beside it, affected local Reindeer, which declined to cross the lines and so were isolated from their traditional calving grounds. Though the problem was ultimately solved by creating a fenced migration corridor, the initial impact was severe.

The Arctic National Wildlife Refuge, Alaska. Conservationists fear that oil exploration in the refuge will irreparably damage its fragile ecosystem.

Gas

Natural gas is a by-product of oil production. In the case of the Prudhoe Bay fields, oil extraction results in about 1,000,000,000m³ of gas being brought to the surface each day. The gas is used to power the oil production process, or it is pumped back into the oil reservoir. However, gas can be the primary reason for drilling, particularly as its value as a fuel has become increasingly important in recent years. The potential for much greater quantities of gas production on the North Slope has led to the proposal of a second pipeline running beside the oil line, then beside the Alaska Highway and eventually to the rest of the continental United States. Although the gas could be liquefied for tanker transport, liquefaction and regassing is energy-intensive, consuming a significant fraction of the energy content of the gas, so compressor-driven pipelines are preferred. An alternative suggestion is the so-called 'over-the-top' route east to the Mackenzie delta, where the Canadians are set to exploit gas reserves. The gas would then be taken south in the proposed Mackenzie pipeline running through Norman Wells and Fort Simpson. Delta gas is already used to power Inuvik and other communities along the northern section of the river.

Russia has vast reserves of natural gas. The combined oil and gas reserves in Russia's West Siberia Basin make it one of the largest reserves in the world, and comfortably the world's largest natural gas field. Russian gas production is centred on Novyi Urengoi (about 500km east of Salekhard and 60km south of the Arctic Circle in the Yamal-Nenets Autonomous Okrug). The city is the home of Gazprom, the world's largest gas company. Gazprom controls more than 90% of Russian gas production and about 25% of world production. Russia already has a 150,000km national grid of gas pipes moving Arctic gas, and exports gas to neighbouring countries of the former USSR (in recent times Russia has appeared to use the gas as a political weapon, while suggesting purely economic motives), and increasingly to western Europe. Gas also exists beneath the Barents Sea. The sea is divided between Norway and Russia, but almost all the reserves seem to lie on the Russian side (though Norway has its own reserves under the Norwegian Sea). There is a plan to build a pipeline from the Barents drill sites through Finland and beneath the Baltic Sea to Germany.

As with oil production, gas extraction results in environmental damage. The drill sites and pipelines have their own footprints, but other damage occurs as a result of site construction; at the Bovanenkovo Gas Field on Russia's Yamal Peninsula the quarrying of sand for construction work destroyed over 1,200km² of tundra.

Hydrates

As well as gas in its 'natural' state, gas also exists as hydrates, gas molecules encased in ice, the gas usually being methane. Gas hydrates are found in ocean or inland sea or lake sediments, at depths greater than about 300m where sediment temperatures are below freezing, and in the Arctic either within or below the permafrost. Gas hydrates are at low temperature and high pressure. In the Arctic, hydrates are generally concentrated where there are oil and gas reserves, though there are also hydrates beneath the Bering Sea and in permafrost areas of China.

Hydrates represent an enormous energy source, some estimates suggesting that they may exceed natural gas reserves by a factor of ten in energy terms. At present hydrates are only being commercially exploited in Russia. But as well as offering significant energy, hydrate extraction brings sizeable problems. One is that methane is itself a greenhouse gas and so drilling for hydrates, or even near hydrate concentrations, may cause temperature rises and pressure decreases, and so release the gas before it can be captured (though some experts doubt that sufficiently high temperatures could be reached). There is some evidence that seafloor landslides might result when gas trapped in hydrate form is released; it has been suggested that large-scale release of methane as a result of landslides may have been the reason why the earth warmed abruptly at the end of the last Ice Age. The theory suggests that reduced ocean depth resulted in the depressurisation of hydrate concentrations, followed by the release of methane and a 'greenhouse' effect. Drilling could itself precipitate landslides and a potentially massive methane release. Of course whether we should continue to burn gas (and oil) is another matter.

Mining

Mining within the Arctic is not a new concept. The Klondike and Alaskan Gold Rushes saw men exploiting previously pristine wilderness areas, and gold is still extensively worked in the Dawson City area. Although Nome is no longer the gold town it was, gold is also mined in Alaska, close to Fairbanks, while in recent years other potential sites have been identified, though none has yet been exploited. In Canada, in addition to the Yukon mines, there are mines in Nunavut and again other possible sites have been identified. In Russia gold mining in the Far East accounts for almost three-quarters of the country's total gold output, the richest mines being in Yakutia, with other mines active near Magadan and Krasnoyarsk, and in Chukotka. Recently gold has been worked near Nanortalik in southern Greenland, a place where graphite was mined early in the 20th century. The deposits appear promising, but at present only limited effort has been put into exploiting them. Diamond mining has also begun at Garnet Lake near Kangerlussuak and as the ice retreats from the coast many companies have expressed an interest in exploring the mineral resources in the uncovered coastal rocks. Some in Greenland have welcomed the prospect of increased exploitation as it would aid the country to become fully independent of Denmark by reducing the need for subsidies. However, others are concerned that a country with such a small population would be unable to resist pressure from huge multi-nationals and that full independence would be disastrous.

Gold mining at Dawson City.

Historically, cryolite was mined in Greenland, particularly at Ivittuut. Cryolite, also known as Greenland Spar as deposits of the mineral were known only from there, was critical to the production of aluminium during the first decades of the 20th century; the mineral acted as a flux, reducing the melting temperature of bauxite and making the otherwise uneconomic electrolysis process viable. During the 1939–45 war the United States essentially annexed Ivittuut for the war effort, but in the post-war period a synthetic alternative was developed. Cryolite production slowed during the 1960s as this new source came on stream, and ceased altogether in 1987. During the period of cryolite production it is estimated that almost 4 million tonnes of the mineral was extracted.

The mining of coal has a long history on Svalbard. Norwegian coal mining on the archipelago began in earnest in 1905, though there had been some mining earlier, and the Soviets began production in 1932. Mining continues on the island: indeed, the Norwegians are likely to mine again at Sveagruva, where mining ceased some years ago. Coal is also mined at places on the north coast of Russia, and there are known reserves of bituminous and sub-bituminous coal in Alaska. Mining was carried out in Alaska, chiefly to power military bases, but production largely ceased (it continues at Healy) some years ago, when gas became a more economic fuel.

Iron ore has been mined in the Swedish Arctic for many years, the country's iron reserves being the foundation of the highly successful Volvo and Saab companies. Iron is still mined near Kiruna, Gällivare and Malmberget. In recent decades valuable sources of rarer metals have been discovered in the Arctic and the exploitation of these has raised environmental concern. At Maarmorilik, near Uummannaq in Greenland, where marble was successfully quarried for many years until 1972, zinc and lead were mined until 1990. When mining ceased there was little attempt to clean up the site, as a consequence of which the heavy metals have run off and are now polluting the local fjord. Much better has been the position at Nanisivik, in northern Baffin Island, where a mine exploiting deposits of cadmium, lead, silver and zinc that closed in 2002 is being cleaned up. Mining for lead and zinc continues on Cornwallis Island.

Elsewhere, serious contamination has resulted from the mining of heavy metals on the western Kola Peninsula and close to Noril'sk. With a population of about 250,000,

Noril'sk is the largest city in the Arctic. The mines there were originally a gulag; today the area is the largest producer of non-ferrous metals in Russia, the smelting of nickel, copper and cobalt, and smaller quantities of other rare metals (including platinum and gold), being fired by gas from local gas fields. But production has not come without significant pollution problems; noxious gases from the furnaces and heavy metals have contaminated local Reindeer grazing areas and poisoned local waters – emissions from Noril'sk have been detected in Alaska and northern Canada. A similar problem exists on the western Kola Peninsula, where the plume from the smelters at Nikel has created a large dead footprint downwind. At Monchegorsk, about 120km south of Murmansk, there is an even bigger smelting complex where nickel, copper and other heavy metals are produced. Some estimates suggest that 50% of all heavy-metal contamination detected in the Arctic comes from the metal smelters of northern Russia; anthropogenic heavy-metal pollution far outweighs that from natural sources such as volcanoes and forest fires. In an ironic twist, much of the nickel produced at Nikel is used in the manufacture of catalytic converters, to reduce pollution from motor vehicles.

While it is easy to categorise the environmental damage at Noril'sk and Nikel as the product of a system of government that considers such issues unimportant in comparison to competitive industrialisation – an argument that applies equally to the economies of emergent Asian countries – damage is not confined to such nations. The Red Dog Mine near Kotzebue in northern Alaska is the world's largest zinc mine currently in operation, the output of which represents a significant fraction of global production of the metal. Mining began here in 1980, the mills powered by local natural gas and oil. A haul road

Coal mining on Spitsbergen.

Above
An old Norwegian mine above Longyearbyen.

Left
The Russian town of Barentsburg.

Norwegian coal mining at Ny Ålesund, Spitsbergen involved the construction of the world's most northerly railway.

connects the mine to a purpose-built port from which the milled ore is transported to smelters around the world. Studies of the heavy-metal pollution close to the haul road showed high levels of contamination as a consequence of spillages, and infringements of regulations on the contamination of local water.

Nickel and copper are mined at the Raglan Mine in Nunavik, Quebec. The mine is believed to lie on one of the largest nickel deposits in the world. If permission for the mine's extension (Raglan South) is allowed following an environmental impact assessment, total production is expected to reach over 80,000 tonnes of nickel concentrate and 35,000 tonnes of copper concentrate annually, together with much smaller quantities of platinum and palladium. There were considerable environmental concerns when the mine opened, and further fears regarding the extension; the site is close to the Pingualuit crater lake, which is planned to be the centrepiece of a provincial park. Pingualuit holds extremely pure water and it was feared that run-off from Raglan, which lies to the north, might contaminate it. Raglan South is even closer, and one of the selling points for the project by the mine company is that an extension of the mine complex road system – the mine will include four open-pit excavations spread over a large area – will be able to take tourists to Pingualuit.

Mining and smelting activities also result in the emission of sulphur dioxide and nitrogen compounds, which have caused acid-rain damage to trees downwind of the plumes. Arctic waters are especially vulnerable to acid precipitation, as the acid burden may be contained in snow. Snow melt then results in acid pulses to local aquatic vegetation; such pulses are far more damaging than the year-averaged acidic concentration might imply.

Though heavy metals – antimony, cadmium, mercury,selenium and vanadium as well as those already mentioned – are a particular problem because of their toxic nature when released into soils and water, other forms of mining may affect the fragile Arctic ecology, as no mine can be entirely self-contained and all must therefore have some environmental impact. Deposits of copper, silver and molybdenum have been discovered in southern Alaska, while diamonds are currently mined in Yakutia and Kamchatka, and exploration has indicated untapped resources in other parts of the Russian north. The Ekati diamond mine in Canada's North West Territories began production in 1998 (a second mine operates at nearby Diavik), and there are indications of viable deposits in Finland. The North West Territories mines are at the centre of the range of the Bathurst Caribou herd, one of North America's largest. Eventually, Canada may become the world's largest producer of diamonds, with further deposits anticipated elsewhere in North West Territories, and in Ontario and Quebec on the western coast of Hudson Bay.

While the ecological footprint of many current Arctic mines remains reassuringly small, the ability to overcome the

Old lead mine on Bear Island.

problems of mining in permafrost areas is improving and the costs of transportation are falling, so mining is likely to become more significant in the Arctic. This will not only increase the total area of mines, but the roads constructed to service them will further fragment the ranges of species, particularly the larger and migratory species such as Reindeer. Such fragmentation could lead to a reduction in genetic diversity within populations.

Pollution in the Arctic

Chemical Pollutants

The Arctic is vulnerable to pollution besides that associated with metal mining and smelting and drilling for fossil fuels. These pollutants are carried north by ocean currents, rivers and atmospheric currents; warm air and warm water flow from the tropics to the Arctic, and in doing so these currents collect chemicals from the industrialised northern hemisphere, so the Arctic can in some ways be considered a litmus test for the planet's health. Arctic rivers carry run-off from the oil, gas and mining industries to the Arctic Ocean. As the rivers flow from more temperate regions they also carry pesticides and other agricultural chemicals, the run-off of southern farmlands. Although the huge flows of these rivers dilute the pollutants, the seasonal flow resulting from annual freezing and thawing also tends to concentrate them.

Of the transport mechanisms, atmospheric currents are the fastest, carrying pollutants north in days or weeks, and of the pollutants carried perhaps the most important are the persistent organic pollutants, the organochlorides. The story of DDT and its disastrous effect on wildlife, particularly birds where breeding failed as a result of egg-shell thinning, is well known. However, although DDT was banned in North America and Europe in the 1970s, it is still used to combat malaria-transmitting insects, and significant stocks are held worldwide; DDT is still making its way to the Arctic. More significant at present are the PCBs (polychlorinated biphenyls), of which there are some 200 variants. PCBs do not easily dissolve in water, but dissolve readily in lipids – fats and oils such as blubber and mammalian milk (including that of native people). The adaptations of Arctic wildlife and its peoples to their environment therefore make them especially vulnerable to

Trucks loaded with iron ore trundle out of the mine at Kiruna, Sweden on their way to the Norwegian port of Narvik.

The Russian town of Nikel. Emissions from the smelters here have devastated plant life downwind.

Noril'sk, Russia is usually the number one candidate for the unenviable record of world's most polluted town.

these pollutants. This is particularly true for animals that rely on fat reserves to survive the winter. This absorption transfers the PCBs to the animal's internal organs, the new spring's blubber growth taking up yet more chemicals. The Arctic's climate also makes it more susceptible to PCB pollution. The lack of photodegradation of the chemicals during the long Arctic winter allows survival rates higher than in southerly regions, while low temperatures inhibit the natural biodegradation of the compounds. Pollutant particles also attach readily to snowflakes, which have a large surface area relative to rain drops, and so are easily brought to the ground or ocean surface.

Low levels of PCB contamination in humans cause skin problems such as acne, as well as stomach, thyroid and liver damage. Higher levels can cause severe liver and immune system problems, and reductions in reproductive capacity. Similar effects must occur in contaminated Arctic animals. Because of their propensity for dissolution in fat and oil, the PCBs concentrate in seal blubber. Consequently Polar Bears show very high concentrations, as they are at the top of the food chain. In relative terms, assuming the concentration in sea water is 1, the concentration in Arctic zooplankton in the worst affected areas would be 12,000, in fish 200,000–500,000, in seal blubber 500,000–1,500,000, and in Polar Bears, Beluga and Narwhal, up to 30,000,000. Such huge differences arise because of the ratio of predators to prey: it has been calculated that before it is full grown a Polar Bear will eat around 2.5 tonnes of Ringed Seal flesh. Similar scale differences are seen in birds, with predatory birds (such as Glaucous Gulls) exhibiting concentrations of 5–10 times those of ducks and auks. Although the chemicals are not linked to birth defects in humans, this does not seem to be the case in bears, where there is a direct correlation between maternal organochloride concentration and increased birth rate of hermaphrodite cubs.

Because traditional food still forms a significant fraction of their diet, Inuit also show elevated PCB levels, this being particularly worrying in nursing mothers. The startling conclusion of one study was that some of the tested Inuit had

Rusting fuel drum trapped in the sea ice at the southern coast of Southampton Island, Canada.

Peregrine Falcon in the Barren Lands of Nunavut, Canada. The falcons suffered a dramatic population loss as a result of the use of DDT. Despite bans in North America and Europe, the chemical is still in use and finding its way to the Arctic.

such high concentrations of PCBs that their bodies would be classified as hazardous waste if they had to be disposed of as 'non-human' material. Recent studies also indicate that the ratio of girls to boys born to northern mothers has fallen from just under 1, consistent with the world ,wide average, to 2:1. In some northern communities, only girls are being born. Pollutants such as PCBs and flame-retardants which mimic the human hormones are believed to be the cause.

And, of course, if it is bad for the Inuit it is worse for Polar Bears, which also have other pressures and no access to medical facilities. Production and use of PCBs is now limited or banned by international convention, but although that is good news, history suggests caution; a succession of compounds has been synthesised, used, found to be toxic, banned and, soon, replaced by other compounds, so that the cycle begins again. Severe doubts are already being expressed about replacements such as polybrominated diphenyl ethers (PDBEs), and in the years to come similar fears will doubtless be raised about the next generation of organic compounds.

One further effect of persistent organic (and other chemical) pollutants is the creation of a blanket above the Arctic. As noted above, photochemical effects are minimised by the Arctic winter, and although snow is effective in bringing pollutants to ground, the Arctic is a relatively low precipitation area. Arctic travellers will notice the brown haze across the horizon present when the Sun returns after the long winter night. This is a combination of dust from the south (and from natural sources, such as volcanoes) and from the winter's build-up of chemicals. The haze alters the transmission properties of the atmosphere, and hence the energy balance of the earth. The overall effect is not, at present, well understood, and it may be limited in duration as the chemicals are reduced by photodegradation.

One final aspect of pollution must also be mentioned. The beaches of Svalbard and other Arctic coasts are now littered with plastic detritus and the remnants of fishing gear, as are the beaches of the rest of the world. That means the seas that lap Arctic beaches carry a burden of man-made discarded rubbish. As elsewhere this pollution can kill local wildlife, with animals swallowing the plastic or becoming entangled in discarded nylon fishing line and trawl nets. The entanglement of plastics in the baleen plates of whales and the subsequent inability of the whale to seal its mouth have been implicated in whale deaths.

Ozone Depletion

Ozone (O_3), a molecule of oxygen with three atoms compared to the more usual two, is present in the upper atmosphere, where it is formed by the interaction of free oxygen atoms with molecules of 'standard' oxygen. The free oxygen is produced by the interaction of ultraviolet (UV) radiation with oxygen molecules high in the atmosphere, the free atoms combining with other oxygen molecules at lower altitudes. About 90% of ozone is found within the stratosphere, at an altitude of 15–30km. Ozone is poisonous, and is therefore a hazard at sea level (where it is produced when the gases from petrol engines are broken down by sunlight), but in the upper atmosphere acts as a protective shield to life on earth by absorbing UV, particularly UV-B (that part of the UV spectrum with wavelengths in the range 290–320nm), which can cause cellular damage.

Despite there being only three molecules of ozone to every 10 million molecules of oxygen in the atmosphere, ozone's role as a shield is crucial, so there was immediate concern when some 30 years ago it was noticed that the ozone layer above Antarctica was thinning, and that a hole was appearing in the ozone cover. Similar, but reduced, thinning was then discovered above the Arctic. In the 1980s data from balloon flights above Antarctica showed that the thinning was due largely to the presence of chlorine, which was destroying the ozone molecules (chemicals other than chlorine, such as bromine, are also involved, but chlorine is by far the most important). The amount of chlorine required to have a significant effect was beyond that which could arise from natural sources, and it was soon established that the source was compounds such as chlorofluorocarbons (CFCs), used as coolants in refrigerators, in aerosol spray cans and other industrial products. When these compounds are broken down by UV radiation they release free chlorine atoms that react with ozone molecules, stripping off a single oxygen atom to form chlorine monoxide (ClO). This reacts with another free oxygen atom to form an oxygen molecule (O_2), with the chlorine atom being released to destroy another ozone molecule. It is estimated that a single chlorine atom can destroy up to 100,000 ozone molecules before it is absorbed by nitrogen compounds, bringing an end to the trail of destruction. The understanding of the reaction, particularly the importance of tiny ice crystals, won Professor Gerhardt Ertl of the Fritz-Huber Institute in Berlin the 2007 Nobel Prize for Chemistry.

The hole in the ozone layer is seasonal. It starts to form when the Pole emerges from the long polar night, and reaches a maximum during the polar summer. In Antarctica the size of the ozone hole increases until mid-October, at which point it stabilises, ozone rising from lower in the atmosphere to replace that which has been destroyed. At its maximum, the southern hole represents a reduction of about 70% in ozone concentration, the hole covering an area of some 30,000,000km^2 and including southern Chile, with reductions in cover over New Zealand and Australia. In the Arctic the extent and amount of the reduction in cover is lower, as the temperature of the Arctic is about 10°C higher than in Antarctica. However, during the very cold Arctic winter of 2003-04 near-record low ozone levels were reported over both the central Arctic and northern Europe and Canada.

As with global warming, the initial reaction of those with a vested interest in CFC production was that more research was needed and that the effects of reduced ozone levels had been exaggerated. (One American government official claimed that as people did not habitually stand in the Sun there was no problem, and in any case they could buy a hat and sunglasses.) However, in response to growing concern, in 1985 20 nations signed the Vienna Convention for the Protection of the Ozone Layer and accepted the need to control anthropogenic activities that caused the release of ozone-depleting chemicals. In 1987 these measures were incorporated into the Montreal Protocol on Substances that Deplete the Ozone Layer. Signatories of the Protocol now number more than 150, an encouraging international response. The Protocol called for the phasing out of CFCs and other chemicals linked to ozone depletion. At first the good intentions were rewarded with encouraging data on ozone recovery, but there have since been new findings sounding a note of caution. The increase in concentration of greenhouse gases has been found to be responsible for a cooling of the stratosphere and a consequent increase in the rate of ozone-depleting reactions. There has also been evidence that the initial recovery in ozone concentration seen in the late 1990s resulted from an increase in solar activity (which led to an increase in free oxygen atoms in the upper atmosphere), not from the reduction in CFCs. If that is correct then full recovery may take much longer than originally thought, particularly as CFCs are also now thought to persist in the atmosphere for much longer than was once believed, perhaps for a century or more. Allowing for both effects, the original estimate of full recovery of the ozone layer by around 2030 may prove optimistic.

False colour image of the Earth showing the extent of the ozone hole over the Arctic during the winter of 1999/2000. Following international protocols it was hoped that such large holes would not be seen in future years, but the hole increased in size during the winter of 2003/4. Measurements during the Antarctic winter of 2007 suggest that the hole there is not shrinking as anticipated.

Nuclear Weapons

In 1955, having forcibly removed the native population, the Soviets exploded a nuclear weapon beneath the sea of Chernaya Bay, on the western side of the southern island of Novaya Zemlya; the sediments of the bay still have high levels of caesium and plutonium. Between 1955 and 1990 the Soviet Union conducted a total of 132 nuclear tests, mainly at three land sites on Novaya Zemlya. These included 87 atmospheric tests (one of which was the largest bomb ever exploded, a 58-megaton hydrogen bomb on 23 October 1961). These tests resulted in the uncontained spread of radioactive material. In 28 of 42 underground explosions the resulting radioactive material was not completely contained (the remaining tests were underwater). At the test sites radiation levels remain high, but officially the rest of the islands are 'only marginally above background'. In addition to the weapons testing, as many as 11,000 containers of highly radioactive material are thought to have been dumped in the Barents and Kara seas, to each side of the islands. Radioactive debris in the seas apparently includes reactor units from the Soviet nuclear icebreaker *Lenin*. Unconfirmed reports suggest that the *Lenin* had two nuclear accidents in the mid-1960s (1965 and 1967 are the suggested years). In one (or perhaps both), the reactor cores melted down. Lives (maybe as many as 30) were lost, and on at least one occasion it was decided to dump the crippled core into the Kara Sea. Today the decommissioned *Lenin* is a museum ship in Murmansk fjord.

In April 1989 the Soviet nuclear submarine *Komsomolets* sank, about 120km south-west of Bear Island. A fire had forced the submarine to the surface, but despite efforts to contain the incident the vessel eventually sank. Only one of a skeleton crew of five survived the sinking. No attempt has been made to salvage the boat, its reactor power system or the two nuclear-tipped torpedoes it is rumoured it was carrying. Monitoring expeditions have detected increased levels of radioactive materials (Sr90, Cs137 and Co60) in benthic animals, but not at dangerous levels. There has been no indication, as yet, of massive increases in plutonium or nuclear fuel-related isotopes. More recently, the Russian nuclear submarine *Kursk* suffered a catastrophic explosion (in the bow torpedo compartment, away from the reactor) and sank in the Barents Sea. The attempt to rescue survivors trapped in horrific conditions involved several nations, but failed; all 118 men on board died. The bow of the submarine was cut free and blown up *in situ*; the rest of the boat, including the intact reactor, was salvaged. Aged, redundant nuclear submarines have also been left to decay in bays along the northern Kola coast.

Nuclear submarine activity in the area is due to Murmansk, an ice-free harbour, being the principal port for the Soviet Atlantic navy. There are storage facilities for spent nuclear fuel at nearby sites on the Kola Peninsula. Petropavlosk, in southern Kamchatka, is one of the headquarters of the Russian Pacific Fleet, in particular its nuclear submarines, and it is known that radioactive leakage from waste disposal sites has

Radioactive statistics

In all there have been more than 2,000 nuclear weapon tests, around half of these performed by the United States. On average since its first bomb test, the United States has exploded a nuclear device about every 20 days. For comparison, the approximate rates for the other nuclear powers are: Soviet Union once per 25 days; France once per 65 days; China once per 230 days; and the UK once per year. It is estimated that the atmospheric testing of nuclear weapons and the leakage of radioactivity from underground tests has resulted in the release of around 4.2 tonnes of plutonium into the atmosphere and a further 3.8 tonnes into the ground. There have been no atmospheric explosions since 1980.

The total release of radiation is about $2.5x10^{20}$Bq (one Bq – Becquerel – is equivalent to one atomic disintegration per second: it replaces the older unit, the Curie – Ci – which represented $3.7x10^{10}$ disintegrations per second. 10^{20} is a 1 followed by 20 zeroes, i.e. one hundred million million million.) For comparison, the Chernobyl accident, by far the worst accident in a civil nuclear reactor, released about $2x10^{18}$Bq, about half of which comprised inert noble gases. The most recent sampling of the Kara Sea suggests that the sea's radioactive burden from weapons testing fall-out and dumped nuclear material amounts to a total of more than $3x10^{15}$Bq. Some of the radioactive material in both the Barents and Kara seas originated at the UK's Sellafield nuclear fuel reprocessing plant; levels of Cs137 in Minke Whales, for example, show a direct correlation with releases from the plant.

The birth of Greenpeace

The US nuclear weapon testing on Amchitka was carried out to a background of strong local protest. The 1964 earthquake was fresh in the minds of local people and they feared that the explosions might precipitate a further shock. Massed protests for the two early tests were contained by the authorities, but the groundswell of feeling led one group of protesters to acquire a ship in 1971 with the intention of sailing to Amchitka. A combination of bad weather and the US coastguard stopped them, but despite the failure of their mission the protest spawned a worldwide environmental movement. Although the reasons for its choice of name are lost in history, the protest group called themselves Greenpeace.

occurred. It is thought that more than one Soviet nuclear submarine lies at the bottom of the sea off the Norwegian coast, but as with all things military, and certainly all things both nuclear and military, facts, as opposed to rumour, are sometimes hard to come by.

It appears that the previous use of Novaya Zemlya for weapons testing resulted (and perhaps still results) in an official view that nuclear dumping is acceptable. Any continuation of the practice would not only turn this otherwise pristine Arctic habitat into a nuclear dump site, but accentuate the view that the Arctic is little better than a wasteland.

US bomb testing chiefly took place in the Nevada desert, but three tests were carried out on Amchitka Island in the Aleutians (in 1965, 1969 and 1971). The use of Amchitka seems, in part, to have been the result of the failure of Project Chariot, the plan to use one or more nuclear devices to excavate a harbour at Ogotoruk Creek, near Cape Thompson, about 200km south-east of Kotzebue. The project was abandoned in the face of protests from environmentalists, local people and many scientists. However, as part of the planning for the explosion, trace radioactive material (Cs137 and Sr85) was placed in locations around the site. The position of this material was not on the public record and came to light only in 1992, five years after use of the site had been granted to a local man, as a result of an independent search of declassified documents. The material was then removed.

During the 1939–45 war the United States created 17 military sites on Greenland. After the war the US continued to consider Greenland strategically important. Several stations of the Distant Early Warning (DEW) system were established on the island (and at other sites across North America); most have been abandoned, but they leave a legacy of spilled oil and toxic waste that has been implicated in higher cancer rates of villagers close to some sites. In 1951 the Americans built an air base at Thule, the construction of which required the forced resettlement of local Inuit to Qannaq, 140km to the north. In later years the building of a radar system at Thule as part of the US National Missile Defence system caused problems with the Danish government, but a much bigger problem occurred in January 1968 when a B52 bomber crashed on to the sea ice about 12km west of the base. A clean-up operation followed, though it was not immediately announced that the plane had been carrying nuclear weapons. It is claimed that the cancer rate in those involved in the clean-up was higher than normal, and the Danish government later paid compensation to workers who exhibited health problems. Eventually it was admitted that the plane had been carrying four hydrogen bombs, and there had been an escape of plutonium into the environment. The nuclear fusion of a hydrogen bomb is triggered by a fission explosion: in the case of the Thule bombs the fission explosion would have been plutonium-based. Secrecy over the four bombs has been maintained. The fusion elements of the device present minimal risk to the environment, but that is not the case with the plutonium. The Americans admit that not all the plutonium was recovered, with an amount variously stated to be 0.5–1.8kg having gone missing. However, there are credible, but unconfirmed, reports that one bomb, with its fission trigger, was not recovered and had probably reached the sea bed. The plutonium loss could then be up to 12kg. Workers at the base claim that the clean-up involved the scooping up of contaminated ice and snow into barrels, which were then stored at the base, but that ultimately the barrels rotted and the contaminated water they contained leaked into the ground.

The carriage of nuclear weapons to Thule and their storage there contravened the agreement between the US and Denmark that Greenland would remain a nuclear-free zone. This led to strained relations and a concerted effort by the local Inuit to have the base closed. Nevertheless, the base lease was renewed in 2004. An environmental study was carried out, but the report – apparently running to 4,000 pages – has never been published and remains secret. Inuit hunters claim to have seen Musk Ox and seals with physical and internal deformities, but these are unconfirmed.

Only Russia has confirmed nuclear submarines stationed in an Arctic port, though it is known that US submarines routinely travel beneath the ice – the US has, of course, enjoyed the PR results of having their vessels surface at the

The US Thule airbase, north-west Greenland.

North Pole. Travel beneath the sea ice has its advantages, with airborne radar being much less useful as a detection tool. It is likely that nuclear submarines of many nations habitually ply the Arctic Ocean. Russia also has nuclear ice-breakers on the surface. The Soviet Union and, after its break up, Russia, have maintained a continuous interest in travelling the northern sea route from the Atlantic to the Bering Sea, and extremely powerful nuclear ice breakers have been built to allow this. Today the ice-breakers are regularly used to take paying passengers to the North Pole.

Nuclear power

Russia has four nuclear reactors at the Polyarnye power station, near the city of Polyarnye Zori close to Murmansk. The reactors are VVER-type, not the RBMK design involved in the accident at Chernobyl. However, the two older reactors at the site are considered by western nuclear experts to be as dangerous as the Chernobyl type. The reactors provide power to local heavy industry at Monchegorsk, Kirovsk and other local towns, and also export energy to towns in Karelia and Finland. There are also four reactors at Bilibino in Chukotka, built to

Norwegian border guards keeping an eye on Russia – see caption for photograph on opposite page.

Although there has been a decline in overt military activity in the Bering Sea the border between Norway and Russia near the Øvre Pasvik National Park is still closely watched. In the photograph on the opposite page Norwegian border guards peer into Russia, while the photograph on this page shows a Russian watch tower, from which vantage point the Russians survey Norway. Behind the tower the town of Nikel is just discernible through the haze and smoke.

power local gold and tin mines. The Bilibino reactors should be decommissioned in 2007, when they will be replaced by three new reactors. The Russian plants are the world's only nuclear power stations built on permafrost. Russia has recently announced a plan to build a floating nuclear power station in the White Sea to power the city of Severodvinsk.

Russia has three nuclear fuel reprocessing plants, at Kranoyarsk, Mayak and Tomsk. The first discharges into the Yenisey River, the latter two into the Ob. Both Finland and Sweden also have nuclear power stations, though these are situated in the south of each country.

Mention must also be made of two other incidents of radioactive waste hitting the Arctic. In January 1978 a nuclear-powered Soviet satellite, *Cosmos 954*, fell back to earth. It burned up in the atmosphere but spread a trail of radioactive material across 124,000km^2 of Canada's North West Territories (centred on the Great Slave Lake). The best estimate is that the clean-up that followed (partially paid for by the Soviet government, in a break from its usual behaviour) gathered only around 1% of the radioactive material involved. Then in 1986, Reactor 4 at the Chernobyl power station in the Ukraine exploded after a major reactor fault. The ejected radioactive material contaminated large areas of the northern hemisphere. In Scandinavia the Sámi suffered a double problem as they were advised not to eat the meat of the Reindeer herds, but they could not sell it either as it was banned from public consumption. It is estimated that 20,000 Reindeer were slaughtered and dumped.

Climate Change

As discussed earlier (see After the Ice), the ratio of two isotopes of oxygen, together with the distribution of plant life as indicated by the fossil record, enable a good estimate of the earth's climate over the last several million years to be established. As well as allowing the measurement of oxygen, ice cores also allow the variation of the concentration of other gases in the atmosphere to be measured, with bubbles of air trapped in the ice being analysed for gas composition. Ice cores from Antarctica have allowed the concentrations of carbon dioxide (CO_2) and methane (CH_4), two important greenhouse gases, to be studied over the last 400,000 years or so. As both these gases and oxygen can be sampled at the same time, the relationship of the earth's temperature and the concentration of greenhouse gases can also be inferred. Pushing the relationship back further in time is more complicated as other natural processes have to be considered, but the studies suggest a significant correlation between the concentration of greenhouse gases and the earth's temperature. Particularly significant is the fact that atmospheric CO_2 concentration during the Carboniferous/Permian ice age (some 300 million years ago) was almost the same as today's levels (when the earth is in a similarly cold phase); also, atmospheric concentrations of both CO_2 and methane correlate with earth's temperature over the last 400,000 years. These relationships suggest that the levels of greenhouse gases in the atmosphere and temperature are strongly correlated, and that an increase in gas levels will result in a rise in temperature. It is known that the concentration of CO_2 in the atmosphere has increased significantly since the Industrial Revolution, and there is considerable evidence that the earth's temperature is rising approximately in step. This has led most scientists to consider that global warming is related to human activities. There are still some who claim that the evidence for global warming is flawed, while others consider the link between warming and anthropogenic processes to be unproven, but as evidence mounts there are fewer in these camps. However, despite newspaper headlines that proclaim that the effect is real and the link proven, in the following section I attempt to separate evidence from supposition, and to present only 'best estimate' data for what the future holds for the Arctic.

Changes in CO_2 and Earth's temperature

The best estimate of the concentration of CO_2 in the atmosphere immediately prior to the Industrial Revolution is

0.028% by volume (280ppmv, or parts per million by volume). The present concentration (May 2008) is 387ppmv. Data released in early 2007 show that while the rate of rise had averaged 1.5ppmv/year between 1970 and 2000, the rate of increase had risen sharply in the early years of the new century, with an average of 2.1ppmv to 2007. The increase in 2006 was 2.6ppmv, the highest yet recorded (the increase in 2007, published in May 2008, was 2.14ppmv). Studies indicate that the sharp rise after 2000 was due to the general growth in the world economy, the use of coal in China, and a weakening of the ability of the Earth's natural CO_2 'sinks' (the oceans, forests and soil) to mop up the excess.

The concentration of methane has risen from about 0.8ppmv to almost 2ppmv over the same period. Although the concentration of methane is much lower than that of CO_2, methane is 23 times more effective as a greenhouse gas. Levels of other greenhouse gases have also increased and, as with methane, they are much more efficient greenhouse gases than CO_2. For example, CFC-12 (CCl_2F_2) is about 7,000 times more effective than CO_2. Its concentration is 700,000 times lower, which would seem to make it a negligible greenhouse gas, but there are many forms of CFCs, so when their individual contributions are added together the total effect is significant. The effect of other greenhouse gases can be included by adjusting the effective CO_2 rather in the way that a wind chill temperature is calculated. On that basis the present effective CO_2 concentration is about 460ppmv. The rise in concentration of atmospheric CO_2 is strongly correlated with the increase in the tonnage of fossil fuels used. Around 80% of the world's energy requirements are currently provided by fossil fuels in one form or another. Industry and agriculture are responsible for about 30% of CO_2 production (the manufacture of cement being responsible for about 5% of total emissions on its own: concrete is the second most used material on earth, after water, and its usage is increasing as the development in 'Third World' countries speeds ahead), with electricity and heat production adding a further 25% and transport another 15%. China is responsible for about 22% of the world's CO_2 emissions, having recently overtaken the US (about 20% of the total) as the major emitter. Russia, Japan and India are the next biggest emitters, with 4-6% each. Germany is responsible for 3%. The UK, together with a group of countries which includes Canada, South Korea and Italy is responsible for about 2%. However, though the US and China emit about the same proportion of CO_2, the population of the China is five times that of the US. An American produces about 20 tonnes of CO_2 annually, a Briton about 9.5 tonnes. By comparison, the annual emission of an Ethiopian is about 0.06 tonnes.

Since the start of the Industrial Revolution the average temperature of the earth has risen by 0.8°C, most of that change occurring in the last 25 years. The temperature in the Arctic has risen faster (for reasons that will be explored below), by an average of about 1°C, but by about 2°C in winter. In general, temperature rises for the Arctic are double those for the earth as a whole. The quoted values are averages: in some areas the temperature rises have been higher – in parts of Alaska for instance, winter temperatures have been up to 4°C warmer. On land these temperature rises have resulted in the shrinkage of glaciers (not only in the Arctic, but in all alpine areas; Mount Kenya's glaciers have shrunk by 75% in the last 100 years, while Alaska's Glacier National Park has lost 90% of its ice over the same period), while at sea the average summer coverage of Arctic sea ice reduced significantly during the last two decades of the 20th century.

Based on the most accurate computer models of the earth's climatic systems available, the average Arctic temperature will rise by 3–5°C by 2100 if the present production rate of greenhouse gases continues, with winter rises of up to 7°C. The temperature rise of the Arctic Ocean will be higher still, by up to 7°C overall and up to 10°C in winter. In general the models suggest the greatest temperature rise over the Russian Arctic and in eastern Canada.

Natural rises and falls in earth's temperature do occur – for example, during the years 1925-1945 there was a 10-year rise to a maximum of about 0.5°C in the Arctic (suggesting a lower average rise for the earth as a whole), followed by a 10-year decline – and the reasons are not always well understood. However, the current temperature rise is both very fast and shows no sign of slowing down, something that has convinced the majority of scientists that the cause is anthropogenic rather than Sun-based.

The greenhouse effect

As already noted, the Earth's atmosphere is essentially transparent to incident, short-wave solar radiation, but opaque to the long-wave radiation re-emitted from the Earth's surface. The long-wave raciation is absorbed by constituents of the atmosphere, its energy then being re-emitted and re-absorbed, causing a warming of the atmosphere. The incoming and outgoing radiations are balanced, and in the absence of an atmosphere the average temperature of the Earth would be about -20°C. In practice it is +15°C. The raising of the Earth's temperature appears analogous to that within a greenhouse, so the process has become known as the 'greenhouse effect' and the contributors to it 'greenhouse gases'. In practice greenhouses work chiefly by preventing convective heat losses rather than absorption and re-emission, but the analogy is not unreasonable.

The main atmospheric constituents responsible are water vapour, CO_2, methane, nitrous oxide (N_2O), ozone and chlorofluorocarbons (CFCs). Apart from the CFCs, the gases are produced by natural as well as anthropogenic processes; CO_2 from volcanoes and the metabolism of animals; methane from coal mines, by the decay of organic materials and the flatulence of ruminant mammals (which is no laughing matter when the number of domestic ruminants on Earth is considered – the main source of methane is actually the animal's mouth rather than its rear); and nitrous oxide from soil bacteria. But it is the man-made production that has caused the most alarm over recent years: N_2O as an anaesthetic and aerosol propellant; CH_4 release in oil and natural gas production; and CO_2 from the burning of fossil fuels. In 1896 the Swedish chemist Svante August Arrhenius recognised the effect of CO_2 on Earth's temperature and suggested that it might contribute to the starting or ending of ice ages: it is CO_2 that has become the 'shorthand' for all greenhouse gases

Temperature rises and feedback mechanisms in the Arctic

The average minimum Arctic sea-ice cover since 1979 (when accurate figures became available from satellite photography) was around 7,700,000km^2. In summer 2007, the coverage was 4,400,000km^2, a reduction of over 40%. Inevitably, as summer

A warming Arctic could mean the absence of summer sea ice within a couple of decades. Kongsfjorden, Spitsbergen, Svalbard.

ice coverage diminishes, winter coverage also reduces. The ice is also thinning, with thickness reductions of up to 40% observed over the last 40 years. Were the ice loss to continue at the most recently measured rate the Arctic Ocean would be ice-free by 2030. At the same time, the area of the Greenland ice sheet that experiences a degree of summer thaw increased by more than 15% during the last two decades of the 20th century, with the net annual loss of ice doubling in the decade to 2005.

Loss of sea ice is significant – possibly catastrophic – in itself, because of the loss of habitat for pinnipeds and Polar Bears. But it is also important as a feedback mechanism on the temperature of the region. The albedo from sea ice is high. That from the dark oceanic waters exposed by the loss of ice is very much lower. The water absorbs more energy from incident solar radiation, and the surface water then warms the atmosphere above it. As the water temperature is much lower than that of water in the tropics, there is much less evaporation in northern latitudes, so the heat absorbed by the atmosphere tends to stay there, raising ambient temperature further. Warmer water and air mean a subtle alteration to the pattern of oceanic and air currents, each of which tends to draw warmer water and air into the region. These positive feedbacks are reasons why temperatures are rising higher and faster in the Arctic than in more southerly latitudes.

Temperature rise also results in a loss of snow cover. Snow also has a high albedo, higher than that of the tundra below, so again energy from incident radiation is absorbed, warming the ground and, hence, the atmosphere. The northern hemisphere has a greater proportion of the earth's landmass than the southern hemisphere, and the Arctic Ocean is surrounded by land. Consequently loss of snow cover is another positive feed-back mechanism serving to raise Arctic temperatures.

As the earth warms, trees will also expand their range northward. Forests have even lower albedo than tundra, so again local energy absorption is higher. It is an irony that the idea of planting trees to offset carbon use (an idea that appeals to some in developed countries, where it is an expanding business) works only in the tropics where CO_2 absorption is higher (but where logging is intensive, negating the effect). That is not, of course, to say that planting trees is a bad thing. It is not: forests are an important part of the earth's biosphere and loss of them has diminished both wildlife habitat and recreational opportunities. But the 'feelgood' factor relative to climate change should not be overstated.

As snow cover reduces and air temperature rises, the active layer of the permafrost that underlies the Arctic tundra and boreal fringe deepens each summer, with the loss of snow causing both an increase in heat absorption (because of the reduction in albedo) and the removal of an insulating layer. Borehole data from northern Alaska indicate that the temperature of the permafrost has risen by 2–4°C over the last 80–100 years. The increase in active layer depth adds yet another positive feedback mechanism, though in this case it applies to the earth as a whole. Organic material trapped in the permafrost warms, leading to increased microbial activity, and increased CO_2 and methane release into the atmosphere. Though the magnitude of the release of these greenhouse gases as the permafrost thaws is debated, some estimates suggest that the upper (and therefore vulnerable) layer of the northern permafrost holds around 30% of all the carbon stored in the world's soils. In August 2005 Siberian scientists reported a record thaw in the West Siberian Bog, the world's largest peat bog. It is estimated that the bog holds 70,000 million tonnes of methane. In the same year a survey of permafrost areas indicated that at the present rate of loss, some 75% of the total permafrost will have thawed to a depth of 3m by 2050. Such changes in the active permafrost layer have the potential to affect local hydrology. Predicting actual effects is difficult as they depend on the distribution of water and on water chemistry, but concerns have been raised that lakes might shrink or disappear with a consequent loss of wildlife habitat. A continuing temperature rise might also result in the release of the methane in gas hydrates. Such a release could be catastrophic in terms of greenhouse gas concentration, but there is no consensus on whether such a release would occur based on current predictions of temperature rise.

Rain, snow and ice

Global warming will inevitably lead to increased evaporation from the earth's oceans and, consequently, an increase in both cloud cover and precipitation. Increased cloud cover in the Arctic will lead to warmer winters because of the back-reflection of infra-red radiation from the clouds and a reduced number of cloud-free skies, but would tend to reduce summer temperatures because of the albedo from the clouds, though this reduction is very unlikely to have a significant effect on the area's overall temperature rise. Current best estimates are that in the Arctic, precipitation will increase by 20% by 2100, with precipitation increasing faster in winter than summer. Much of the summer increase will fall as rain, but winter rainfall is also likely to increase as winter temperatures increase. Nothing clears lying snow faster than rain: the effect of increased rainfall will be to further reduce snow cover. Even if the enhanced precipitation falls as snow the news is not necessarily good, as the albedo of wet snow is much lower than that of dry snow. Either way, the consequence is yet another positive feedback mechanism to drive Arctic warming.

If the increased precipitation falls as snow on the upper reaches of glaciers, glacial thickness will increase. However, if it falls as rain, ice thickness will quickly reduce. The effect of winter rain can be devastating on wildlife. If rain is followed by hard and continuous frosts, the ground can disappear under a coating of ice as tough to penetrate as sheet metal. Already in Scandinavia there have been such incidents, Reindeer herds suffering as they were unable to break through the ice cover to reach forage. These incidents are thought to have been related to the North Atlantic Oscillation. When the NAO Index is high, the resulting warmer, wetter winters lead to high snowfall and freeze-thaw conditions that make life difficult for female deer: their condition deteriorates and calf mortality increases. With a warming climate such incidents may increase. Some experts attribute the fall in the population of Peary

The inhabitants of Fairbanks, Alaska are used to summer fires, usually caused by lightning strikes, but as the local climate has become warmer and drier, there are more, and bigger, fires. This one devastated a large area of forest south of the town.

Caribou in Canada from about 26,000 animals in the early 1960s to around just 1,000 by the end of the 20th century to warm, wet winters. Others are more cautious, though it is clear that at least some of the reduction has been due to autumn/winter rain: in both 1973-74 and 1995-96, both Peary Caribou and Musk Oxen died in large numbers on Bathurst Island as a consequence of frozen rain sheathing the ground. What is also undeniable is that an increase in winter rain and an increase in such incidents could seriously affect mainland North America's Caribou herds, and other foraging animals.

Storms and sea levels

Coupled with an increase in precipitation, it is predicted that the earth's climate will experience an increase in storminess. Indeed, such an increase is already being seen: 2005 saw one of the highest hurricane counts ever recorded, the number including Katrina, which devastated New Orleans (though it must be stressed that the link between hurricanes, and storms in general, and global warming has not been established, though it accords with the view of most climate scientists). Storms increase coastal erosion (as does permafrost melt), and as a large fraction of the earth's population lives in coastal areas this will be significant. Many of the Inuit population of North America and eastern Russia are coastal dwellers. A combination of the later freezing of the sea, and earlier thaw, and an increase in storminess is already having an effect. Shishmaref is a settlement of some 600 Inupiat on the island of Sarichef off Alaska's Seward Peninsula. The reduction in sea ice cover has meant that the traditional hunting of seals on the ice is becoming difficult, but the ice also protected the village from winter storms. Now the storms threaten the village and scour away the coastline. It is very likely that the villagers will soon need to be relocated, early victims of a changing climate.

To the effect of storms on coastal areas must be added a worldwide rise in sea levels. Currently, sea levels are rising by about 3mm/year. Computer models predict a rise of 20–80cm by 2100. Such a rise would have a significant impact on coastal areas, particularly in low-lying countries such as Bangladesh. In a recent British newspaper article by a global-warming sceptic, the point was made that if an ice cube was placed in a glass and it was then filled to the brim, the melting of the cube would not cause the glass to overflow. That is true, but as an analogy of the earth the exercise is deeply flawed. The density of water is temperature dependent. For a small volume of water over a limited temperature range the change is indeed small – but there is a vast amount of water in the world's oceans and so even a small temperature change can make a huge difference, with about 60% of predicted sea level rises on a warming earth resulting from the thermal expansion of water. Apart from density effects, the melting of sea ice does not contribute to sea level rise as the ice is already on the ocean (the ice cube analogy holding here), but the melting of land ice *will* cause sea levels to rise – and there is far more land ice than sea ice. It is estimated that the thaw area of the Greenland ice sheet has increased by over 15% since 1980. Were the sheet to melt completely, sea levels across the earth would rise by around 6m.

One other issue must be considered. Historically, the world's forests have been a 'sink' for CO_2, the rapid reduction in tree coverage, particularly in tropical rainforests, causing concerns about the 'excess' CO_2. At first these were, to an extent, alleviated by the thought that the oceans would act as a secondary 'sink', soaking up the CO_2. But it is now clear that there is a limit to this uptake. The oceans do absorb CO_2 (and methane) from the atmosphere and transfer it to deep waters. But increased rainfall reduces the density of the surface layer of water, creating a stratification that reduces the movement of absorbed gases to the deep ocean. Increasing winds across the earth (a consequence of global warming) also result in deep oceanic water, already rich in CO_2, being brought to the surface, reducing the ability of the oceans to absorb the excess. As the water temperature rises the solubility of both CO_2 and methane also decreases so that, eventually, the oceans could become a source rather than a sink of greenhouse gases.

The Future

The earth's temperature has been remarkably stable over the 10,000 years since the end of the last Ice Age, the stability likely to have been a significant factor in the development of civilisation. Increased temperatures will almost certainly mean increased instability, and while industrialised society may be able to overcome some aspects of this, it will create many problems. Ironically at a time of increased precipitation, water is likely to become scarce (for example, loss of the glaciers of

Reindeer use their hooves to scrape through lying snow to reach food. If it rains and then freezes, the iron-hard coating of ice can be impossible to break through.

A warmer Earth and a colder northern Europe?

The likely increase in precipitation in a warmer world will lead to enhanced flow in the rivers that drain northern Russia and northern North America into the Arctic Ocean. This influx of freshwater might influence the flow of the North Atlantic Drift, which keeps winters in northern Europe mild and wet.

The drift is a thermohaline current, i.e. salinity- and temperature-dependent. An increase in freshwater flow will reduce salinity, and the Earth's oceans are warming. Greenlandic ice cores suggest that at the end of the last Ice Age there was an abrupt cooling on the island of about 5°C, followed by an equally abrupt warming. Such rapid changes are the signature of natural systems that have more than one stable configuration, and the rapid change indicated by the ice cores could have been a switching off and on of the Drift.

In late 2005 measurements detected a 30% decrease in the bottom flow of the North Atlantic, i.e. a weakening of the Gulf Stream, and a 30% increase in the Azores Current, the latter suggesting a further reduction in the Drift. More alarming was the suggestion in 2004 data that the Drift apparently halted for a short period. Despite these data, expert opinion is divided on the likelihood of a permanent cessation of the Drift, with some believing that the probability is now less than 50% and that a 'point-of-no-return' may already have been passed, while others believe that the volume of freshwater required to completely turn off the Drift is more than that available from the increased flow in northern rivers and ice-cap thaw.

Both sides agree, however, that a slowing of the Drift (in terms of volume flow) is occurring, and that northern Europe will experience colder winters in the future as a result. It is ironic that at a time when Britain, for example, is experiencing warmer summers (2006 was the warmest year ever recorded), it might soon be experiencing winters with temperatures as low as those experienced by areas at the same latitude on the western side of the Atlantic.

the Himalayas will turn off the water to most of the inhabitants of the Indian subcontinent), while desertification, sea level rise and coastal erosion reduces agricultural land. Conflicts over water may result as nations lose the ability to feed and quench the thirst of their populations.

To consider the plight of the Arctic and its wildlife in the face of such global problems might seem indulgent. Yet the fact that the temperature rise in the Arctic is more rapid than across the rest of the earth means that the region acts as an indicator of what the future holds. In the Polar Bear, the Arctic also has one of earth's most iconic animals. The stress of environmental change will affect all Arctic species, but particularly the marine mammals for which sea ice is the habitat of choice. It will also affect the Inuit and other native northern dwellers, whose way of life depends on an increasingly scarce resource. But the loss of the Polar Bear would be the tragedy touching the soul of millions.

An ice-free ocean would almost certainly mean the extinction of the Polar Bear, but some populations of bear are already under threat and the species may perhaps become extinct in the wild even before the ice disappears. Male Polar Bears coming ashore in southern Hudson Bay, then moving to Churchill to await winter's freeze, may lose up to 30% of their body weight as they wait. Pregnant females giving birth in maternity dens around Hudson and James bays may lose 55%. As summer ice has thawed earlier and winter's freeze has happened later, the condition of the bears has declined over the past two decades, with a 15% reduction in average weight, and a reduction in the number of cubs reaching adulthood. There has also been a reduction in the number of cubs that become independent in their first year, a figure that was once around 40% in Hudson Bay, but which has dropped to around 5%. The recent decision to increase the quota of bears that could be hunted by Hudson Bay Inuit adds to the bears' problems. The increase followed the more frequent appearance of bears in summer near the bay's Inuit settlements. Rather than being interpreted as the effect of a prolonged ice-free period and a desperate search for food, the increase in bears near the settlements was seen as evidence of a population rise. The higher quota meant that a population already under pressure from changes to their environment now had to suffer increased hunting as well. Hopes were raised when the US Government agreed to add the bear to the list of endangered species, only for the decision to be delayed to allow the granting of oil and gas drilling licences for the Chukchi Sea. When a federal judge finally ordered the addition, in May 2008, the Government agreed, but stressed that the listing would not lead to any measures aimed at limiting global warming. In Svalbard, where the bears are not hunted, the toxic chemical burden of the bears is creating its own pressure.

The world does now seem to have woken to the threat presented by a warming world. There seems little doubt that the chief culprit is humanity, the huge human population and the desire of the poorest nations to acquire the lifestyle of the citizens of the richest resulting in industrialisation on a scale that inevitably leads to the output of further vast quantities of greenhouse gases. Yet doubts are still regularly expressed in the popular press. In general these are made by columnists with no scientific expertise – polemical, ill-considered articles that refer to information gleaned from sources which, when examined, are often based on reports that have subsequently been withdrawn as inaccurate, or that reference scientific articles which do not exist, or that contain information fundamentally at odds with the data ascribed to them. There are also frequent

Opposite page
The flow speed of Jakobshavn glacier in west Greenland has more than doubled in the last decade, with ice calving increasing accordingly (and, consequently, individual icebergs being smaller). The probable cause is the increase in surface meltwater on the Greenland ice sheet, the water percolating down to the base of the glacier where it acts as a lubricant.

Right
Surface water accumulating on Greenland's Inland Ice.

references to internet websites that dispense an unhelpful mix of pseudo-science (such as the ice cube in the glass of water: see above) and downright untruths (such as the suggestion that the majority of the world's glaciers are growing, when the opposite is overwhelmingly the case). Many of these websites emanate from organisations that are funded (often indirectly) by companies with a vested interest. They are akin to the organisations that sprang up to disseminate bogus information on the link between cigarette smoking and lung cancer some years ago. Information that threatens the profits of mega-rich businesses is invariably treated to the same insidious negative propaganda. Such lobbying power do these organisations wield that there is evidence that even at the highest levels of government, unhelpful information is suppressed or diluted.

In late 2006 the US government attempted to influence the report of the United Nations Intergovernmental Panel on Climate Change (UN IPCC). They wanted to change the conclusion that binding targets on greenhouse emissions were necessary to one suggesting that voluntary agreements were preferable. The US also wanted criticisms of the Kyoto Protocol (see below) included. Shortly after, in early 2007, the US exhorted the world's scientists to think of ways to reduce the solar flux to earth – mirrors in space, and an upper atmosphere seeded with reflective droplets that would imitate volcanic dust in shrouding the earth were mentioned. This seemed desperate, an attempt to carry on as usual in the hope that a technological fix would be found. The suggestions were too close to 'smoke and mirrors' for the analogy to be missed by many commentators. The jibe was easy, but as the suggestion came only days before the announcement that CO_2 levels were rising faster than had been predicted – so global warming was accelerating and might already have passed a point of no return – any laughter was soon seen as hollow.

In early 2007 the US Congress heard that the administration of George W. Bush had pressured scientists into 'watering down' references to global warming in reports, and had even advised that the phrases 'global warming' and 'climate change' were not to be used. The effect of this was to make the case for climate change less certain and to cast doubt on its anthropogenic cause. Some scientists had also been banned from giving interviews or talks, occasionally with threats of severe consequences if they disobeyed. Around the same time, it was discovered that as part of the International Polar Year (IPY) in 2007–08, BP and Norway's Statoil were part-financing a survey headed by the US Geological Survey to look for oil- and gas-bearing strata under the Arctic Ocean. As IPY was intended to look at the effects of global warming on the Arctic and Antarctic, this apparent conflict of interest has caused considerable disquiet among scientists.

The Antarctic ice sheet and sea level rise

As melting of the Greenland ice sheet would have such a devastating effect on Earth's sea level it might be assumed that the Antarctic ice sheet represents an even bigger threat, with the rise following its melting being closer to 80m. A specific concern is the West Antarctic ice sheet which covers land which is below sea level. Melting of this and the Greenland ice sheet would raise world sea levels by 10–12m. However, it is widely believed that Antarctica does not represent a corresponding threat as the predicted increase in precipitation as a result of global warming would fall as snow on the Antarctic plateau, where altitude enhances the extreme cold of the southern continent. The increase in snow depth on the plateau outweighs the loss of ice sheet at the coast, so that overall the effect on sea level is negative, though small, the contribution being about -2% in the best computer models. On Greenland the position is very different as thawing at the ice sheet margin outweighs the effect of enhanced snowfall at the centre. Overall, the contribution of melting of the Greenland ice sheet to the predicted sea level rise by 2100 is about 30%. As noted above, thermal expansion contributes a further 60%. The remaining rise (about 10%) derives from a combination of melting Arctic ice caps and thawing glaciers around the world.

A warming Arctic: benefits and threats

The reduction of sea-ice coverage will allow easier shipping in Arctic seas. It may allow both the North-West and North-East Passages to become available to conventional ships, as opposed to the ice-breakers and ice-strengthened ships that currently ply these waters. Lack of sea ice may also allow easier exploitation of the oil and gas reserves below the seas of the northern continental shelf. Each of these, which many view as benefits, will bring with them the threat of increased pollution. There may also be sovereignty problems as land previously thought too difficult to exploit becomes valuable: the recent decision of the Russians to plant a flag on the North Pole seabed has raised both national anxieties about ownership of the Arctic and renewed interest in the potential mineral wealth of the area.

Reduced sea-ice cover may allow the opening of northern fisheries, while increased Arctic temperatures may allow the northward expansion of agriculture. Each is a benefit to an overpopulated, hungry world, but the farming of former tundra will result in a reduction of habitat for northern wildlife, while increased fishing will apply further pressure to an already over-exploited resource. The northern expansion of forests will increase the uptake of carbon dioxide, but will not compensate for either the reduction in albedo in the north or the frightening loss of tropical rainforests.

The Kyoto Protocol

The Kyoto Protocol (the Kyoto Protocol to the United Nations Framework Convention on Climate Change, to give it its full title) was an attempt to persuade world governments of the importance of global warming. The plan was for industrialised nations to reduce their aggregate emission of CO_2 by 5.2% (from 1990 levels) by 2012, with individual countries assigned specific targets. The US signed, but did not ratify, Kyoto: indeed, lobbyists for the US oil industry attempted to persuade European business and political leaders to abandon their support for the Protocol. The situation improved in December 2005 when, at Montreal, the signatories of Kyoto discussed an extension beyond 2012 and the US was persuaded, apparently by the shock of the negative world reaction after their negotiators had initially walked out, to agree to future negotiations – though not to binding commitments. Shortly after the meeting it was announced that US emissions of greenhouse gases were at their highest-ever level, had doubled since 1990, and that not only was the level of emissions increasing, but the rate of increase was also rising.

In June 2007 the G8 group of industrialised nations (Canada, France, Germany, Italy, Japan, Russia, the United

The northern movement of vegetation and species

As Earth's temperature rises, southern species of plants and animals will expand their ranges northward. The effect of forests invading the tundra has already been mentioned as a positive feedback mechanism in the Arctic, but all northward range expansions will impact Arctic ecology. Shrinkage of the tundra is a reduction in habitat for both Arctic residents and the migrant birds that breed there. The living space of true Arctic dwellers will also be squeezed as southern species head north: for example, as already noted, the northern limit of the Arctic Fox's distribution is defined by food and den sites, while the southern limit is defined by the northern limit of the Red Fox, which outcompetes its smaller cousin where the two overlap. Ultimately the Arctic Fox might be left with nowhere to go. For terrestrial animals pushed northward by competitors better suited to the changing habitat, the Arctic Ocean represents a final border. The same is true for trees. White Spruce is the most widespread boreal species in North America and is a valuable timber tree. But it is sensitive to temperature. As temperature increases the tree's growth rate decreases. If the temperature rises high enough the tree dies. As the ocean limits its northward spread, the tree's range – expanding northwards, but shrinking to the south – may eventually decrease dramatically.

More immediately devastating is the effect on breeding seabirds of the movement of fish. Northern species of fish are moving further north as sea temperatures increase, the fish heading for cooler waters in pursuit of prey species also seeking a cooler environment. In the Bering Sea the increase of El Niño activity (coupled ocean-atmosphere warming events in the Pacific Ocean) has contributed to already rising sea temperatures. Many fish species can respond quickly to such changes (though some use traditional spawning grounds and so may starve when traditional prey abundance is reduced: this can be a real threat to populations already at risk due to overfishing). But birds cannot respond as fast as zooplankton and fish. Breeding areas are in relatively short supply and consequently have been used for millennia. The birds are 'programmed' to return to these traditional breeding grounds. If the fish depart the birds will need to fly further to find enough food to feed their chicks. Fewer chicks are then raised and the species becomes endangered. Reductions in the number of chicks raised and in breeding populations are already being seen. In Britain, seabirds dying of starvation have been seen in recent years, along with reductions in breeding populations. One reason is the northern movement and overfishing of sandeels, but there has also been an explosion in the number of pipefish (*Syngnathidae*; relatives of the seahorses), a formerly southern group. Pipefish are longer than sandeels and are unsuitable food for chicks, with instances of birds being unable to either swallow or regurgitate the fish, and choking to death.

The photograph above is of Atlantic Puffins on Runde Island, Norway. Puffins are one of the species at risk from a northern migration of their traditional food species.

Kingdom and the United States which together represent about two-thirds of the world's economy) met in Germany. Anticipating a United Nations meeting to be held in Bali in December 2007 with the aim of agreeing a successor to the Kyoto Protocol, it was hoped that the G8 group would agree both to halving their greenhouse gas emissions by 2050 and, more importantly, to going to Bali with a proposal to try to limit the earth's temperature rise to 2°C. But shortly before the G8 meeting President George W. Bush announced that the US intended to set up a meeting of the 15 countries that represented the overwhelming majority of CO_2 emitters, in order to create a new global framework for curbing greenhouse gas emissions. The US initiative would run in parallel to the UN attempts. The US position was that there was no point in any agreement that did not include China and India, the two fastest-growing economies, and that to be bound by an agreement that excluded them would hand over an unacceptable economic advantage. Diplomacy required the other G8 leaders to welcome the initiative, noting that it meant the US was finally acknowledging the climate crisis, but many experts were much less enthusiastic, fearing that the US was merely avoiding the compulsory emission caps or temperature targets that were a likely outcome of the UN meeting, and injecting a delay into negotiations. In the event,

The IPCC Report

In February 2007 the UN Intergovernmental Panel on Climate Change (IPCC) issued a follow-up to its 2001 report, in which the panel had cited computer models that indicated a maximum average temperature rise across the Earth of 5.8°C by the end of the century. The 2007 report increased this maximum to 6.4°C, largely because of greater recognition of the influence of the positive feedback mechanisms outlined in this chapter. The 2007 report also stated that there was a 90% probability that the observed increase in temperature arose due to anthropogenic greenhouse gas emissions. For its contribution to the debate on climate change the IPCC was jointly awarded the 2007 Nobel peace prize with ex-US Vice President Al Gore, who had been communicating the same message.

The IPCC report was a sobering read, yet on the same day it was made public – and endorsed by the American scientists on the panel – it was revealed that the American Enterprise Institute (AEI), an organisation funded by ExxonMobil, was offering scientists $10,000 to write essays that criticised the report or disputed its conclusions. Responding to this news, ExxonMobil said that the AEI was one of several organisations they aided financially, but that they did not specify policy issues and so were not responsible for AEI's activities.

the G8 called for a 'substantial reduction' in greenhouse emissions and the US agreed to 'seriously consider' the 50% cut which had been originally proposed. Environmentalists were unimpressed by either declaration and pointed out that in the face of rapidly rising levels of CO_2, the time for talking was long past. In particular they considered that the Bush initiative would allow the US to ignore any attempt by the G8 to create meaningful targets, on the grounds that these issues would be discussed at the Bush meeting at some (as yet unspecified) date in the future. This lack of enthusiasm was echoed by other world leaders, notably the Brazilian President, who declined to become involved in the Bush meetings on the grounds that the UN was the correct forum.

Shortly after the US announcement China, which had previously stated it was in favour of mandatory cuts (provided all nations were involved), declared that it would not agree to any target for its own greenhouse gas emissions, as to do so would be detrimental to its development. The Chinese stated that there might be a time in the future for a binding target, but that time was not now. They also pointed out that it was unfair to compare the US with China, as the latter had a much larger population and the intention was to raise that population from poverty, just as the developed world had done for its own populations. Not surprisngly, the Bali conference in December 2007 produced little in the way of real progress, despite the general air of self-congratulation of the delegates. 2008 began with the publication of data which showed that the CO_2 emissions from shipping had been under-estimated, adding yet another area of concern to an issue already overburdened with problems. 2008 seemed to offer little except more pessimism and the likelihood that the first decade of the new millenium would yield little cheer for a beleagured Actic.

With the leading emitters apparently refusing to contemplate targets for emission cuts, it is perhaps not surprising that most governments are ambivalent about targets. In the UK, the government talks of cutting emissions while at the same time pursuing a transport policy that includes major road-building schemes and increased airport capacity. When the then British Prime Minister Tony Blair was asked what he was intending to do about the proliferation of low-cost airlines in the UK, he replied that political reality meant that the subject was difficult to tackle. Political reality translates as there being a probable loss of votes in limiting it. Commercial reality is also apparent in newspapers throughout the developed world which carry gloomy articles on climate change but have advertisements for cheap air travel or expensive motor cars on the same pages.

Alternative energy sources and carbon trading

To the discouraging story of greenhouse gas emissions has to be added the even more worrying news that most scientists now believe that the Kyoto targets were set a long way below what is actually required, pointing out that a cut of closer to 90% by the developed nations of the western world is required to avoid a world climate catastrophe. If energy production alone is considered (and as already noted, electricity and heat generation are not solely responsible for greenhouse gas emissions), such reductions are feasible, but the possible solutions are expensive and bring their own problems. Nuclear power increases the chances of nuclear weapon proliferation, as

Renewable energy: good and bad

Global warming, and the implications of fossil fuel burning, has led to calls for investment in renewable energy sources. These are clearly preferable, but they are not cost-free. The increased use of biofuels has led to the loss of vast areas of rainforest (an undisputed absorber of CO_2) and an increase in food prices as agricultural land is turned over to profitable biofuel production (President Hugo Chavez of Venezuela has stated that increased land usage for biofuels is effectively taking food from the poor to fill the fuel tanks of the rich). In Norway a large wind farm on the island of Smøla resulted in the deaths of nine White-tailed Eagles during a seven-week period in the summer of 2005. Most of the birds killed (both there and at wind farms elsewhere) were adults. Smøla once had a thriving population of eagles – but no more. At present Norway is planning further wind farms, generating enough power to provide around 50% of the country's energy needs. But they will all be at coastal sites, and further significant losses of eagles and other birds are likely. One proposed wind farm is on the islands of Solvaer, which has the world's densest population of Eagle Owls.

Hydropower also has its problems. Reservoir construction in northern Scandinavia (for both power production and water supplies) has occasionally caused traditional Reindeer migration routes to be flooded, with animals drowning as they attempted to cross newly formed lakes. The James Bay project in Canada involved the construction of a number of dams on the La Grande River on the bay's eastern shore, and the alteration of local watersheds to provide enhanced river flow. The local Cree and Inuit people were not consulted before the work began. The scheme resulted in the flooding of more than 10,000km^2 of local forest, and with the watershed alteration involved an area of over 350,000km^2 in total – almost 20% of Quebec's land area. The flooding resulted in the release of large amounts of methyl mercury into the water, which poisoned the fish that were a mainstay of local communities.

Iceland: clean energy v the environment

As this book is going to press power will be generated for the first time from the 690MW Kárahnjúkar hydro-electric power station to the north-east of Iceland's Vatnajökull glacial ice cap. The station will harness the flow of the glacial rivers Jokulsá a Dal and Jokulsá í Fljotsdal and feed it 50km by two 220kV transmission lines to power an under-construction Alcoa aluminium smelter at the head of Reyðarfjörður. The idea of using renewable energy to create a metal which the world requires would seem a good one, but the scheme has raised disquieting issues.

Alcoa has a licence from the Icelandic government to emit 12kg of sulphur dioxide per manufactured tonne of aluminium, far in excess of the World Bank 'limit' for such smelters. It means, in essence, that Alcoa are using not only Icelandic electricity, but a large portion of the 10% increase in permitted emissions that Iceland negotiated under the Kyoto Protocol (an allowance granted because of the island's 'green' power, limited population and limited industrialisation). More pertinently, water for the power station is held in a reservoir formed behind three dams, the main one of which is gigantic (190m high and 770m wide) and out of keeping with the local environment. The reservoir will cover 57km^2 of pristine wilderness including part of the Dimmugljúfur (Dark Canyon), a natural wonder which is 7km long and up to 200m deep. A further 730 km^2 of wilderness will be disturbed by the diversion of streams and related works, with 90 km^2 more being disturbed by road works. The affected area is an important breeding ground for Pink-footed Geese, Great Skuas and many other Arctic species (some very rare in Iceland). The trapping of sediment formerly washed to Heradsfloi, where it formed a bar, will allow coastal erosion and endanger the local seal population. The trapped sediment will eventually block the power station water intake and power production will cease: estimates of how long that might take vary, with most experts considering 80 years the likely figure, though figures as low as 50 years have been quoted. The effect of the massive weight of the water and dams has raised concerns among geologists as the area is volcanically active, while surges in the glaciers which feed the inflow rivers mean that icebergs will occasionally be calved into the reservoir: the effect of these on the dams has not, apparently, been considered.

Environmentalists also worry about the way in which the project has been handled by the government, with accusations of independent reports being suppressed and critics being silenced by dubious means. It would seem that the government has been determined to push through a programme aimed at industrialising a country with a middle-class population that is unsure it wishes to travel that road. The suggestion that the project will create jobs hardly merits much consideration. There is limited unemployment in Iceland and many fear that there will be few local takers for dirty, risky jobs at odds with the way Icelanders wish to work so that most of the jobs will be filled by imported workers, chiefly from eastern Europe.

The photograph to the right shows what has been lost.

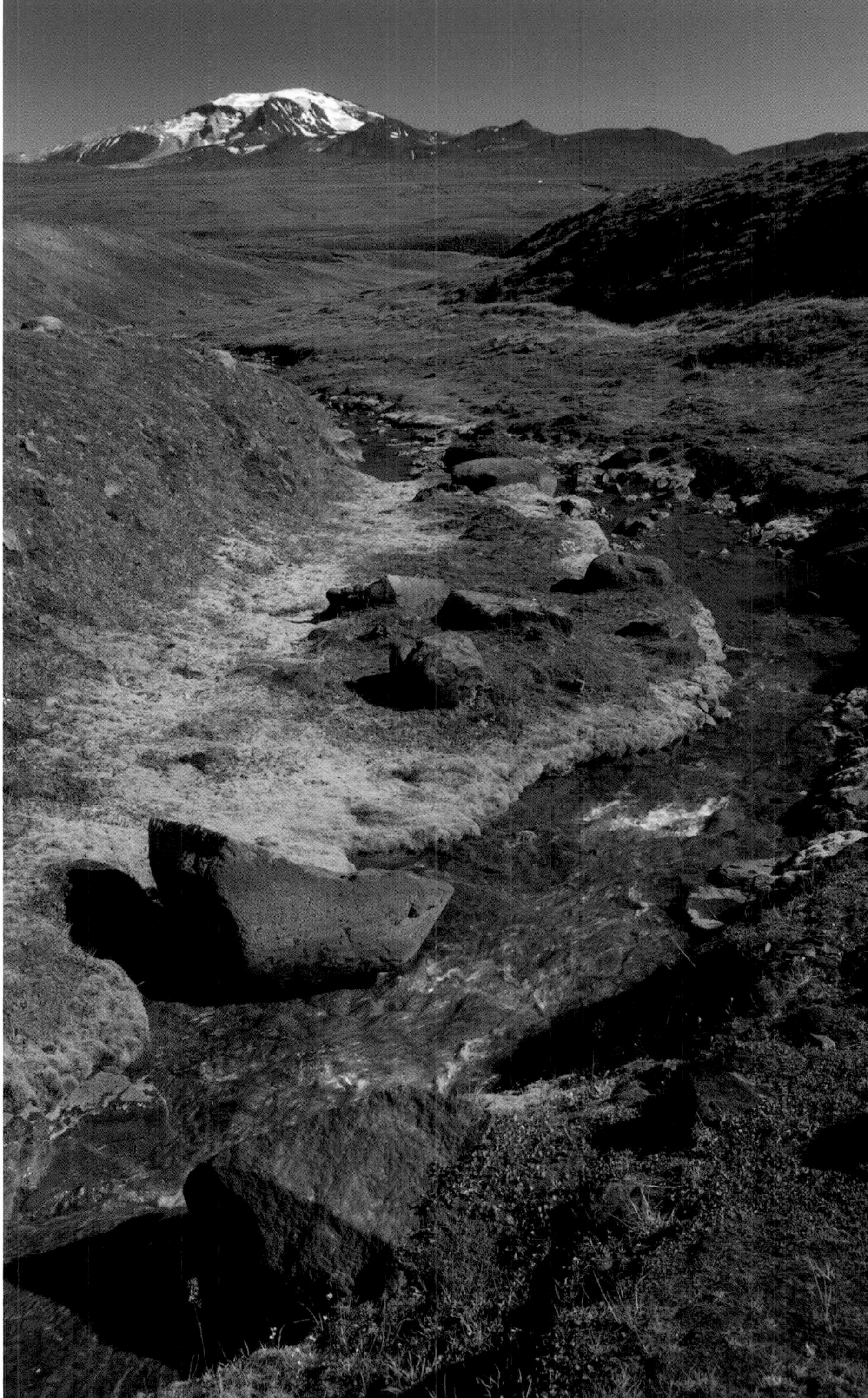

well as the risks of nuclear accidents and the problems of waste disposal. Uranium mining and power station construction are also accompanied by CO_2 emission (though this still makes nuclear power a considerably lower carbon emitter than either gas or coal for electricity production, by factors of 20 and 50 respectively). The recent decision by the Finnish government to build a third nuclear reactor at the Olkiluoto power station on the west coast – the first nuclear station to be constructed in Europe since Chernobyl – has received much press coverage, because hidden subsidies by both the Finnish and French governments (a French company is building the plant) have been seized upon as evidence that nuclear power is not cost-effective. That argument seems to entirely miss the point: fossil-fuel power production is cheaper than all the alternatives, but it might ultimately cost the earth.

Renewable energy sources – solar power, wind, wave and tidal power – have their proponents; if the world's deserts could be covered with solar panels and the electricity generated somehow shipped everywhere it was required, the world's energy problems could be solved at a stroke. But that solution would require co-operation between the earth's nations on an epic, unheard-of level. In most countries renewable energy usage is limited by erratic availability. In the UK, for example, most power is consumed in winter when sunshine is in limited supply, and even though there is abundant wind and a surrounding sea, almost all the current fossil-fuel power stations would need to be retained to cater for days when the wind does not blow and the sea is calm, and for occasions when demand suddenly increases. Nevertheless, the UK is reasonably well placed for alternative power production and it was disappointing to learn in 2008 that the country would miss the 20% target for energy from renewable sources that the EU had set for 2020 and was seeking loopholes in the legislation to avoid compliance. Equally disappointing was the news that government ministers were being advised that 'statistical interpretations of the target' were required to make the position look less gloomy. The idea of using sleight-of-hand rather than trying harder, while at the same time pushing ahead with energy-intensive transport schemes, infuriated environmentalists.

Realisation that CO_2 emissions are rising relentlessly has resulted in the search for methods to minimise releases. One such has been the suggestion of carbon capture on the emission stacks of coal-fired power stations. Capture has been used to justify the UK's decision to build new coal-burning power stations, despite the technology having yet to be proven. There is also a search for alternatives to cuts, with discussions on carbon taxing and carbon trading. The latter are favoured by industry because, it would seem, the first permits issued within the EU were overly generous. The cynic would say that carbon trading looks remarkably similar to the sale of indulgences in medieval Europe, that idea involving the wealthy rich paying someone to say prayers for the relief of their sins while they busied themselves as before. There has also been a rise in 'carbon offsetting' in which, for instance, travellers can buy emission permits to offset the effect of flights. As the permits are easy to obtain, the perceived offset is largely illusory. The permits are also open to fraud; they are cheap to buy and can be sold expensively, or many times over, and the companies selling them are unregulated. A British Airways scheme offering passengers the chance to buy offsets also floundered as it was at odds with the company's commercial interest, which sought to detach flying and climate change. Air travel is a particular problem because of its rapid expansion and its impact on the environment. Air transport produces less CO_2 per passenger mile than cars and superficially appears to be a more efficient transport method. But the distances aircraft travel are so vast that total gas emission can dwarf that from the cars of individual passengers. Aircraft also emit hot, damp exhaust gases into cold air, the condensation trails often accompanying high-flying planes being a contributor to the greenhouse effect. A further difficulty is that the 'open skies' treaty being negotiated between the US and the EU has, at draft stage, a US-driven clause that effectively boycotts any attempt to limit air traffic on the grounds of environmental damage. The US followed this up by threatening to take legal action against the EU if it attempted to include continental flights rather than EU-only flights in its carbon-trading plan, as the inclusion of flights from the US would result in economic hardship for US airlines and airports. Such an exclusion would reduce the impact of the proposal by about 80%.

Opposite page
Extinct in the wild within the lifetime of the reader?

Conclusions

A warming earth threatens the Arctic. But its threat to all species on the planet, including humans, is even more profound. Yet governments settle for saying much and doing little. One leading environmentalist has suggested that this approach is actually favoured by politicians, as they believe it represents the public's attitude to the problem – talk about it, worry about it, but carry on as before in the hope that it will go away or will not happen in our lifetime. The EU's original target of a limiting the earth's temperature rise to 2°C requires a greenhouse gas limit of 550ppmv CO_2 equivalent. Many leading climate scientists consider 550ppmv to be much too high a target figure, yet the UK government has muddied the waters by declaring its own target as 550ppmv CO_2, carefully avoiding pointing out that this is actually about 670ppmv CO_2 equivalent which would create a much higher temperature rise and much greater chaos. The government also omits the emissions from aviation, shipping and several other important sources from the published figures.

Politicians often exhort the people they govern to learn the lessons of history. Yet of these, only one appears absolute – that the privileged only give up their privileges under duress. The potential loss of their position of pre-eminence is the factor that stops the United States government and its corporations from accepting the reality of global warming, and their role in its causes.

Motor cars and air travel are good examples of individual behaviour, and individual privilege, being in conflict with societal good. Altruism is not a notable behaviour pattern in any species and humans are no exception. Individuals are often willing to tolerate short-term pain for gain in the longer term. But in this case the pain is now, the gain is for future generations, an equation that has never been a vote winner. So lip-service is paid, but progress is hard to identify.

In *Collapse*, his authoritative book on the survival and failure of civilisations, Jared Diamond wondered what was actually going through the minds of the population of Easter Island as they felled the last tree and so doomed themselves to a collapsing civilisation. Was it 'jobs not trees', was it a Micawberesque faith (spurious as it turned out) that something would turn up, or was it the apparently sensible, though ultimately foolish, idea that what was needed was more research and that fears of a lack of trees represented scaremongering? Although he did not mention it, Diamond could have added that one island tribe dared not stop because another might not, leading to a power imbalance that would have spelt doom for the leader who chose the cautious approach. The situation is analogous to present-day earth, where western countries decline to initiate meaningful reductions in greenhouse gas emissions as it would harm their economies, while developing countries decline to do so as they seek western lifestyles. Everyone waits for the other guy to make the first move. And the last tree falls.

We may have a few years yet to avert total disaster, but even if decisive action was taken tomorrow and greenhouse gases did not rise above their present concentrations, it is probable that the earth's temperature will rise by at least 0.6°C over the next 30 years. Such a rise might not, of itself, threaten the existence of human life, but it will bring Polar Bears to the very edge of extinction, and imperil all that is celebrated in this book.